United States

HARCOURT BRACE SOCIAL STUDIES

Teacher's Edition
Volume 2

HARCOURT BRACE & COMPANY
Orlando Atlanta Austin Boston San Francisco Chicago Dallas
New York Toronto London

Visit The Learning Site at http://www.hbschool.com

Acknowledgments

STUDENT ACTIVITY BOOK

For permission to reprint copyrighted material, grateful acknowledgment is made to the following sources:

Chelsea House Publishers, a division of Main Line Book Co.: From "If You Miss Me from the Back of the Bus" in *Songs of Protest and Civil Rights,* compiled by Jerry Silverman. Lyrics copyright © 1992 by Chelsea House Publishers, a division of Main Line Book Co.

Dutton Children's Books, a division of Penguin Putnam Inc.: From *Immigrant Kids* by Russell Freedman. Text copyright © 1980 by Russell Freedman.

HarperCollins Publishers: From *Frontier Living* by Edwin Tunis. Text copyright © 1961 by Edwin Tunis.

The McGraw-Hill Companies: From book #60660 *The Log of Christopher Columbus* by Robert H. Fuson. Text copyright 1987 by Robert H. Fuson. Original English language edition published by International Marine Publishing Company, Camden, ME.

Printed in the United States of America

ISBN 0-15-312109-2

7 8 9 10 030 2004 2003 2002 2001

Contents

United States

Tabbed Section

Harcourt Brace Social Studies

Components

For content updates and new ideas for teaching *Harcourt Brace Social Studies,* see the Harcourt Brace home page on the Internet. You can find it at http://www.hbschool.com

	K	1	2	3	4	5	6
Student Support Materials							
Pupil Editions		•	•	•	•	•	•
Literature Anthology Big Books	•						
Unit Big Books		•	•				
Activity Books	•	•	•	•	•	•	•
Social Studies Libraries	•	•	•	•	•	•	•
Teacher Support Materials							
Teacher's Editions	•	•	•	•	•	•	•
Activity Book, Teacher's Editions				•	•	•	•
Assessment Programs		•	•	•	•	•	•
Write-On Charts	•	•	•	•			
Vocabulary Picture Cards		•	•				
Take-Home Review Books		•	•				
Big Book Libraries		•	•				
Daily Geography	•	•	•	•	•	•	•
Overhead Transparencies		•	•	•	•	•	•
Unit Posters	•	•	•	•	•	•	•
Desk Maps		•	•	•	•	•	•
Text on Tape Audiocassettes	•	•	•	•	•	•	•
Music Audiocassettes	•	•	•	•	•	•	•
The Map Book				•	•	•	•
Atlases	•	•	•	•	•	•	•
Game Time!		•	•	•	•	•	•
Reading Support and Test Preparation		•	•	•	•	•	•
Reading Rainbow Videotape Series	•	•	•	•			
Video Experiences: Social Studies				•	•	•	•
Making Social Studies Relevant Videos					•	•	•
Technology							
The Amazing Writing Machine and Resource Packages		•	•	•	•	•	•
Graph Links		•	•	•	•	•	•
Looking Ahead: Earning, Spending, Saving						•	•
Imagination Express	•	•	•	•	•	•	•
Destination Neighborhood	•	•	•	•	•		
Destination Castle							•
Destination Ocean			•		•	•	•
Destination Rain Forest				•	•		•
Destination Time Trip		•	•	•	•	•	
Destination Pyramids							•
TimeLiner				•	•	•	•
TimeLiner Data Disks						•	•
Decisions, Decisions						•	•
Revolutionary Wars						•	•
Immigration						•	•
Colonization						•	•
Building a Nation						•	•
Feudalism							•
Ancient Empires							•
Choices, Choices	•	•	•	•			
Taking Responsibility	•	•	•				
On the Playground	•	•	•				
Kids and the Environment	•	•	•	•			
Geography Search						•	•
National Inspirer					•	•	
MapSkills					•	•	•
Neighborhood MapMachine	•	•	•	•			
Trudy's Time and Place House	•	•	•				

United States

HARCOURT BRACE SOCIAL STUDIES

Series Authors

Dr. Richard G. Boehm

Claudia Hoone

Dr. Thomas M. McGowan

Dr. Mabel C. McKinney-Browning

Dr. Ofelia B. Miramontes

Dr. Priscilla H. Porter

Series Consultants

Dr. Alma Flor Ada

Dr. Phillip Bacon

Dr. W. Dorsey Hammond

Dr. Asa Grant Hilliard, III

HARCOURT BRACE & COMPANY

Orlando Atlanta Austin Boston San Francisco Chicago Dallas
New York Toronto London

Visit The Learning Site at http://www.hbschool.com

Series Authors

Dr. Richard G. Boehm
Professor and Jesse H. Jones Distinguished Chair in Geographic Education
Department of Geography and Planning
Southwest Texas State University
San Marcos, Texas

Claudia Hoone
Teacher
Ralph Waldo Emerson School #58
Indianapolis, Indiana

Dr. Thomas M. McGowan
Associate Professor
Division of Curriculum and Instruction
Arizona State University
Tempe, Arizona

Dr. Mabel C. McKinney-Browning
Director
Division for Public Education
American Bar Association
Chicago, Illinois

Dr. Ofelia B. Miramontes
Associate Professor of Education and Associate Vice Chancellor for Diversity
University of Colorado
Boulder, Colorado

Dr. Priscilla H. Porter
Co-Director
Center for History–Social Science Education
School of Education
California State University, Dominguez Hills
Carson, California

Series Consultants

Dr. Alma Flor Ada
Professor
School of Education
University of San Francisco
San Francisco, California

Dr. Phillip Bacon
Professor Emeritus of Geography and Anthropology
University of Houston
Houston, Texas

Dr. W. Dorsey Hammond
Professor of Education
Oakland University
Rochester, Michigan

Dr. Asa Grant Hilliard, III
Fuller E. Callaway Professor of Urban Education
Georgia State University
Atlanta, Georgia

Media, Literature, and Language Specialists

Dr. Joseph A. Braun, Jr.
Professor of Elementary Social Studies
Department of Curriculum and Instruction
Illinois State University
Normal, Illinois

Meredith McGowan
Youth Services Librarian
Tempe Public Library
Tempe, Arizona

Rebecca Valbuena
Language Development Specialist
Stanton Elementary School
Glendora, California

Grade-Level Consultants and Reviewers

Eunice Anderson
Teacher
Sobey Elementary School
Flint, Michigan

Dr. Ira Berlin
Professor
Department of History
University of Maryland at College Park
College Park, Maryland

Dr. Eugene H. Berwanger
Professor
Department of History
Colorado State University
Fort Collins, Colorado

Dr. Glen Blankenship
Program Director
Georgia Council on Economic Education
Atlanta, Georgia

Gloriela Chiappelli
Director of Bilingual Education
Compton Unified School District
Compton, California

Dr. John Henrik Clarke
Professor Emeritus
Department of Africana & Puerto Rican Studies
Hunter College
New York, New York

Dr. Donald L. Fixico
Professor
Department of History
Western Michigan University
Kalamazoo, Michigan

Kathryn M. Glaser
Staff Development Trainer
Edison Township School District
Edison, New Jersey

Maria B. Gregory
Teacher
Heards Ferry Elementary School
Atlanta, Georgia

Dr. Lois Harrison-Jones
Former Superintendent of Boston, Massachusetts, Public Schools and Richmond, Virginia, Public Schools

Dr. Donald Hata
Professor of History
California State University, Dominguez Hills
Dominguez Hills, California

Dr. Don Holder
Coordinator of Curriculum
Selma Unified School District
Selma, California

Cathy M. Johnson
Supervisor
Office of Social Studies
Detroit Public Schools
Detroit, Michigan

Timothy L. Mateer
Principal
East Petersburg Elementary School
East Petersburg, Pennsylvania

Marie A. McDermott
Teacher
Kingsbury School
Waterbury, Connecticut

Adell Miles
Teacher
Escatawpa Elementary School
Moss Point, Mississippi

Dr. Howard H. Moon, Jr.
Coordinator of Language Arts/Social Studies
Kenosha Public Schools
Kenosha, Wisconsin

Richard Nichols
(Santa Clara Pueblo Tewa)
Vice President
ORBIS Associates
Washington, D.C.

Dr. Estelle Owens
Chairman of the Social Studies Division and Professor of History
Wayland Baptist University
Plainview, Texas

Larita Primrose
Curriculum Support Teacher
Oak Knoll Elementary School
East Point, Georgia

Albert Reyes
Title One Coordinator
Hammel Street School
Los Angeles, California

Dr. L. Anita Richardson
American Bar Association
Chicago, Illinois

Dr. Linda Kerrigan Salvucci
Associate Professor
Department of History
Trinity University
San Antonio, Texas

Karen R. Santos
Teacher
George G. White Middle School
Hillsdale, New Jersey

Dr. Stephen L. Schechter
Director of Council for Citizenship Education
Russell Sage College
Troy, New York

Carolyn Smith
Teacher
Farragut Intermediate School
Knoxville, Tennessee

Dr. Judith B. Smith
Supervisor of Humanities
Baltimore City Public Schools
Baltimore, Maryland

Dr. Mary Jane Turner
Senior Education Advisor
Close Up Foundation
Alexandria, Virginia

Jeannie E. Ward
Teacher
Millwood Elementary School
Sumter, South Carolina

Acknowledgments and other credits appear in the back of this book.

Printed in the United States of America

ISBN 0-15-312101-7

7 8 9 10 048 2004 2003 2002 2001

Contents

iii

An Olmec statue

Dora Pino

iv

Unit 2 Explorations and Encounters 104

CHAPTER 3

Amerigo Vespucci

The Age of Exploration 110

CHAPTER 4

Motecuhzoma

Encounters in the Americas 134

v

Unit 3 Our Colonial Heritage 166

CHAPTER 5

Junípero Serra

CHAPTER 6

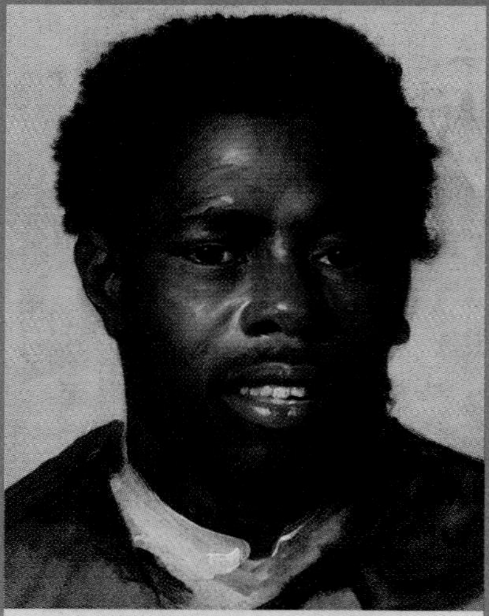
A British colonist

Unit 4 The American Revolution 218

John Adams

Mercy Otis Warren

Unit 5 The New Nation 278

CHAPTER 9

Abigail Adams

CHAPTER 10

George Washington

viii

Mary Prosser

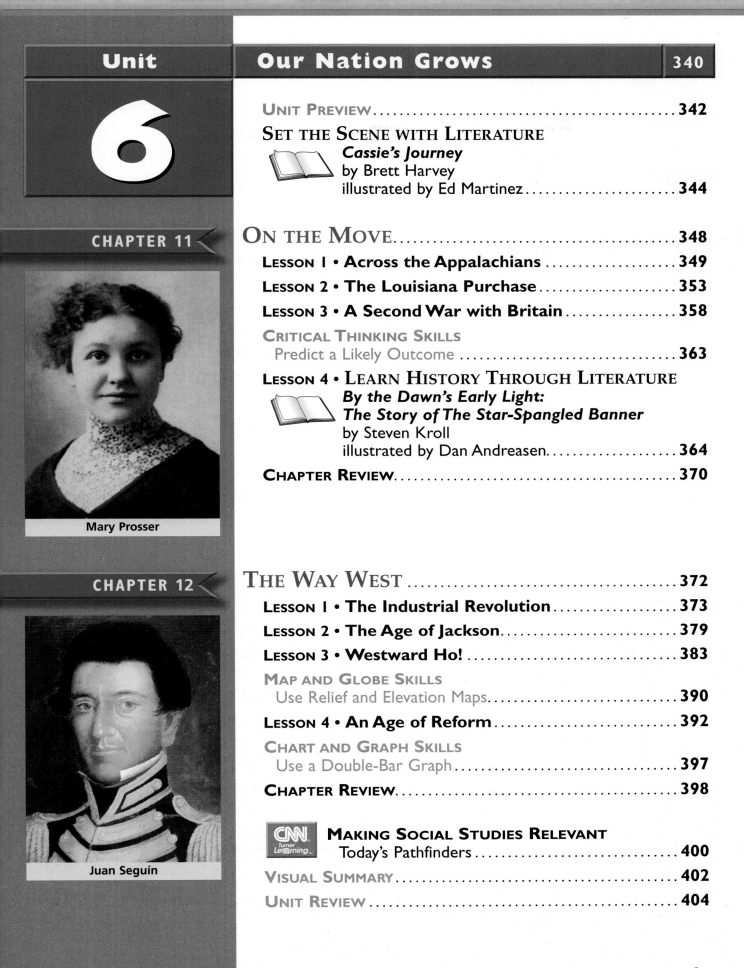

Juan Seguín

Unit 7 War Divides the Nation 406

CHAPTER 13

Frederick Douglass

CHAPTER 14

Edwin Jennison

Unit 8 — Invention and Change 476

CHAPTER 15

An Asian woman

INDUSTRY AND IMMIGRATION 482

CHAPTER 16

A cowhand

THE LAST FRONTIER 512

xi

Unit 9

Becoming a World Power 540

CHAPTER 17

Theodore Roosevelt

CHAPTER 18

Zora Neale Hurston

xii

Unit 10 The Americas Today 604

Martin Luther King, Jr.

CHAPTER 19 THE COLD WAR YEARS 610

Cinthya Guzman

CHAPTER 20 THE WESTERN HEMISPHERE TODAY 642

xiii

For Your Reference R1

The Lincoln Memorial, Washington, D.C.

F.Y.I.

Literature, Primary Sources, and Documents

Building Basic Study Skills

Map and Globe Skills

Chart and Graph Skills

Reading and Research Skills

Building Citizenship

Critical Thinking Skills

F.Y.I.

Participation Skills

Comparing Viewpoints

Features

Biographies

Counterpoints

Making Social Studies Relevant

Maps

xvi

Time Lines

Charts, Graphs, Diagrams, and Tables

xviii

Atlas

Contents

THE WORLD: POLITICAL

Define the Purpose

Ask a volunteer to read aloud the title of the map of the world on pages A2–A3. Have students speculate on what is meant by a political map. Guide them to understand that political maps show the variety of sizes of the countries of the world. A political map is a way that people have divided places on the Earth for the purpose of governing them. Tell students that this political map shows political borders between countries. Other political maps may include capitals and other cities, major bodies of water, and continents.

Understanding the Map

Point out the map key on page A2. Tell students that a map key explains what the symbols on a map stand for. In this map key a gray line is the symbol for a national border.

Point out the inset maps on pages A2–A3. Explain that inset maps make it possible to show places in greater detail or to show places that are beyond the area shown on the main map.

Geography

Place Point out that this political map shows only countries, which are the largest political units in each continent.

Q. **What country in North America has the largest area?** Canada

Atlas

The World: Political

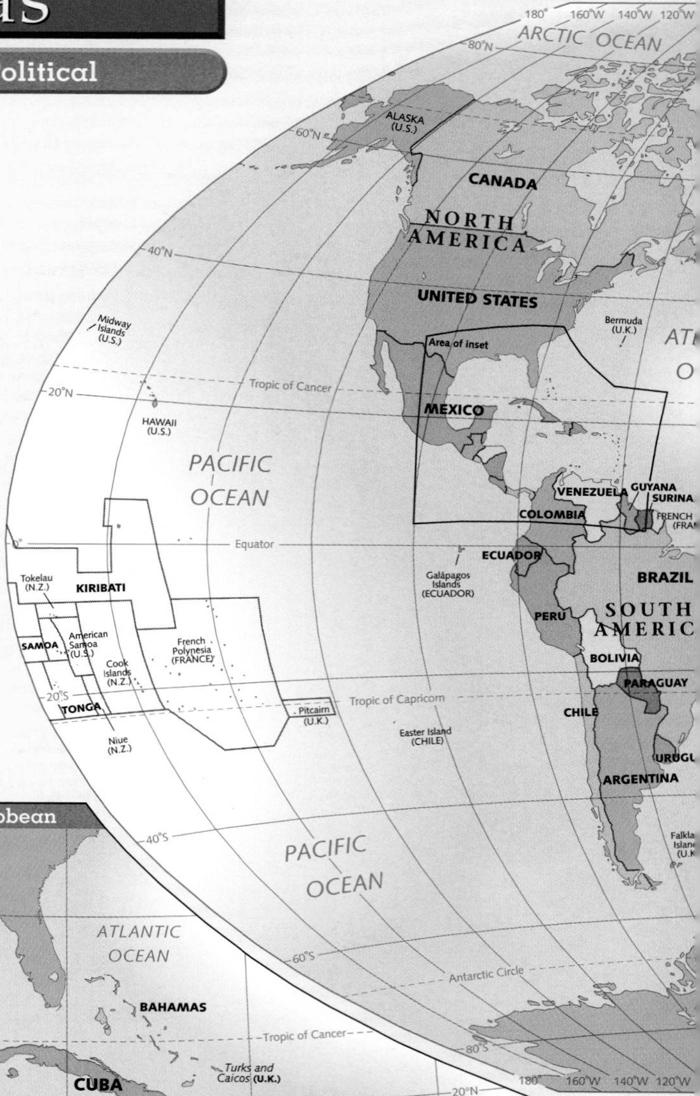

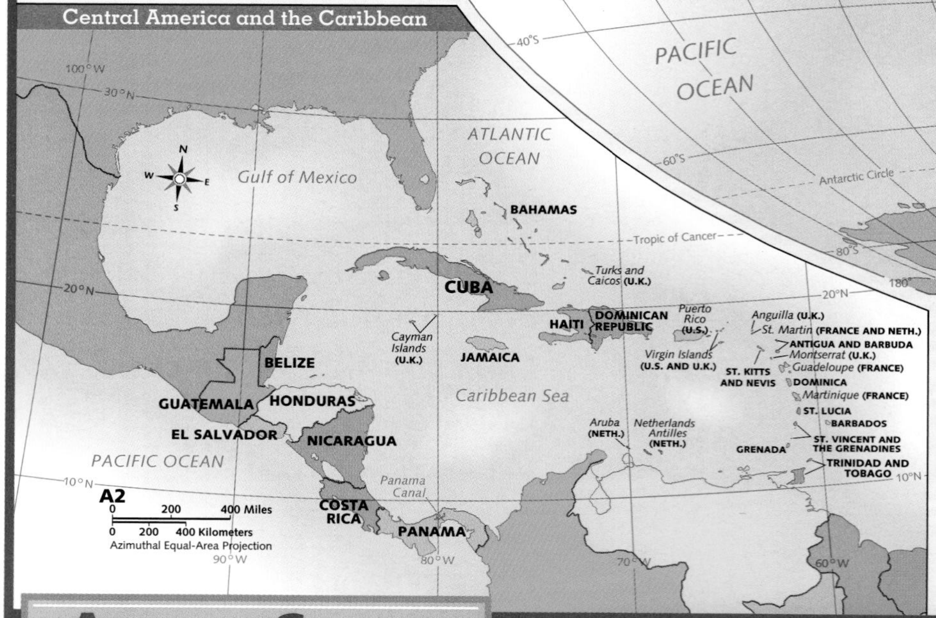

ACTIVITY CHOICES

Meet Individual Needs

ADVANCED LEARNERS Have students use library or Internet resources to research what changes in borders and names occurred in the former Soviet Union after the fall of communism in 1990. Encourage students to make a chart that shows the changes. Students may also want to locate political maps of the area before 1990 and after 1990 and compare them.

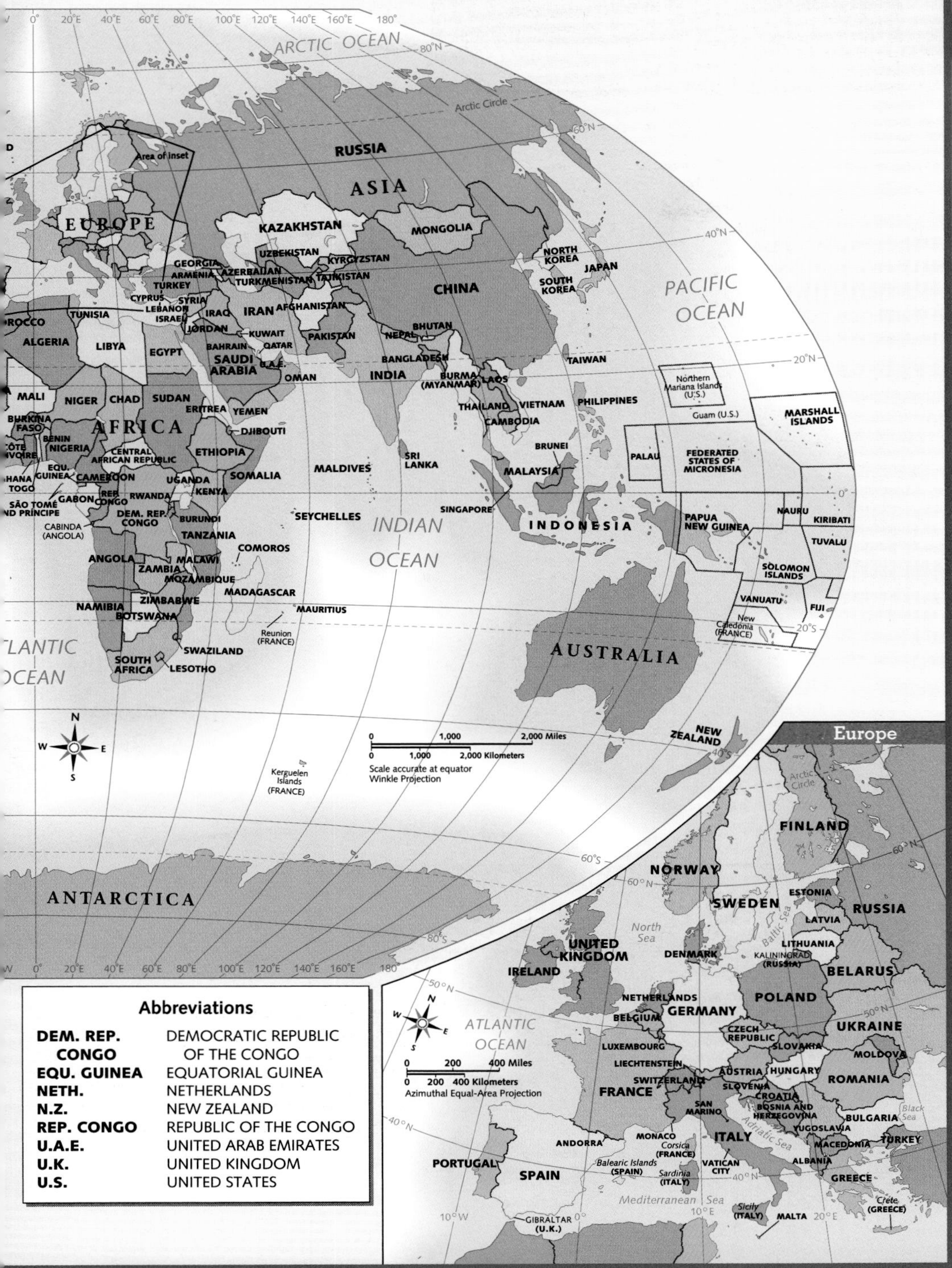

Geography

Location Review latitude and longitude with students. Then ask them to point out the equator and prime meridian and name some countries that lie along these imaginary lines.

Q. **Using latitude and longitude, describe the location of the United States.** The United States (including Alaska and Hawaii) lies between about 180°W and 60°W longitude and about 70°N and 20°N latitude.

Have students use the compass rose to describe the location of countries in relation to each other.

Geography

Regions Review with students what regions are, and ask them to identify different kinds of regions. These include physical and cultural regions. Tell students that a political region is an area that has a common government and is surrounded by a political boundary. Identify political regions on the map of the world. Explain that each country in the world is a political region.

Q. **What continents have more than 20 political regions?** Europe, Asia, Africa

Background

POLAND Throughout history, borders between nations have changed. At one time, around 1500, Poland, for example, was the largest nation in Europe. However, in 1772 it became part of Austria, Russia, and Prussia. After World War I, it became independent, and its borders again changed. Finally, after World War II in 1945, Poland's borders were changed one more time.

Extend and Enrich

MAKE A TABLE

COOPERATIVE LEARNING

Divide the class into seven groups—for Central America and the Caribbean, South America, Europe, Africa north of the equator, Africa south of the equator, Asia west of 80°E, Asia east of 80°E. Then have students use reference materials to research the governments or political systems of the area. Students should present the data in a table.

THE WORLD: PHYSICAL

Define the Purpose

Direct students' attention to the title of the map on pages A4–A5. Explain that a physical map focuses on what the surface of the Earth looks like. It shows locations of physical features such as landforms and bodies of water.

Understanding the Map

Point out to students that this map shows the names of the continents rather than individual countries. However, it does show in red the national borders. Explain that almost all maps provide more than just one kind of information. Some physical maps may include political boundaries and label political units such as countries, states, and cities.

Q. **Why is it helpful to have the national borders shown on a physical map?** so people can see the physical features of a country

Geography

Location Review cardinal and intermediate directions with students. Then have them describe the locations of the continents and oceans in relation to each other. For example: North America is to the northwest of South America and is bordered on the east by the Atlantic Ocean, on the west by the Pacific Ocean, and on the North by the Arctic Ocean. Students can use the compass rose as necessary.

Atlas

The World: Physical

Northern Polar Region

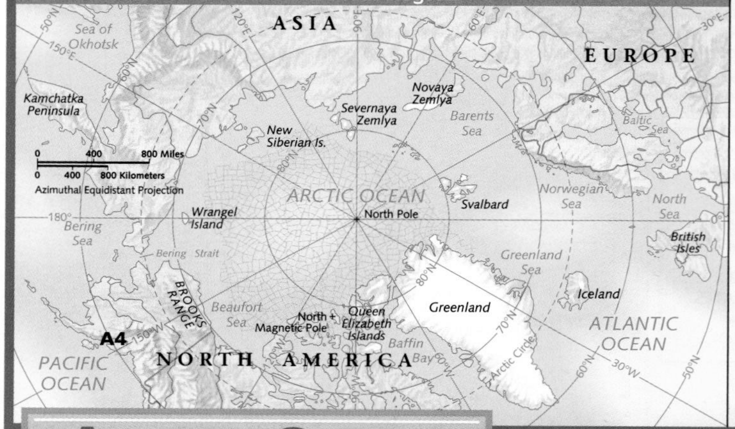

ACTIVITY CHOICES

Meet Individual Needs

ENGLISH LANGUAGE LEARNERS Have students work in groups to create a glossary of physical features. Ask students to make a list of features, define each one, and provide an example found on the map on pages A4–A5.

Meet Individual Needs

ADVANCED LEARNERS Invite students to find information to answer this question: *How do internal and external forces change the physical makeup of the Earth?* Suggest students research information about plate tectonics, earthquakes, volcanoes, weathering, and erosion. Students can present their answers to the class.

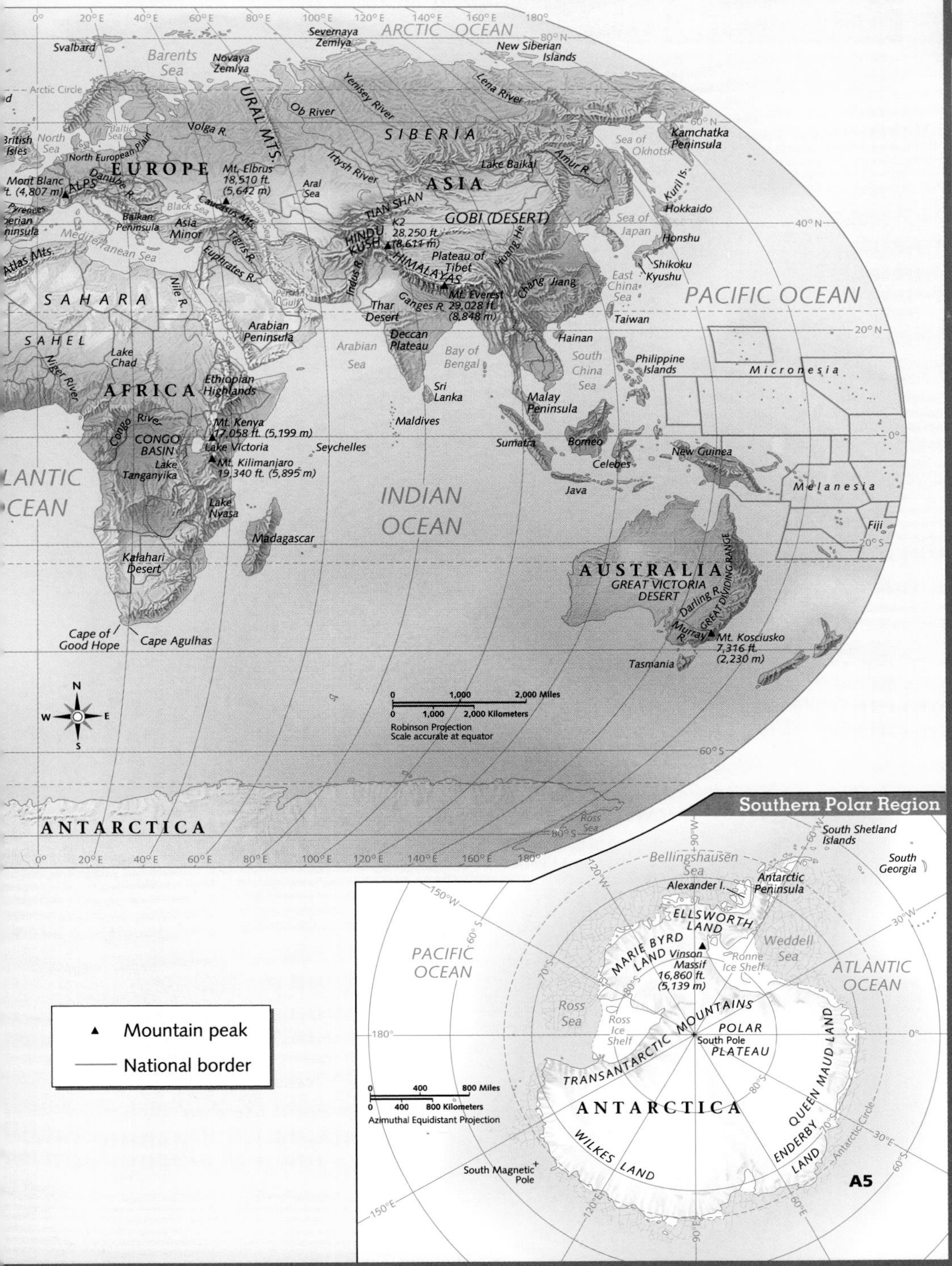

Understanding the Map

Explain to students that different colors are used to show the elevation, or the height, of the land. Point out the use of triangles to symbolize mountains.

Q. **What is the highest mountain in the world?** Mt. Everest, in Asia
What is its elevation? 29,028 feet (8,848 m)

Encourage students to identify the highest mountain on each continent and give its elevation.

Geography

Regions Discuss with the class what a physical region is. Have students recall that features of physical regions include climate, soils, vegetation, and the shape of the land. Point out that the physical map on pages A4–A5 shows only some features of physical regions.

Geography

Movement Discuss how physical features affect the movement of people, goods, and ideas.

Q. **What physical feature brings people of southern Europe, western Asia, and northern Africa together?** the Mediterranean Sea

Background

PHYSICAL GEOGRAPHERS People who study the land and discover how people's actions change it are called *physical geographers*. These geographers may study landforms and water forms, weather, climates, soils, vegetation, and other features that affect the natural environment.

Because there are so many ways to harm the environment, physical geographers work to solve such problems as those related to air and water pollution, fuel and water shortages, and damage caused by natural disasters.

Extend and Enrich

COOPERATIVE LEARNING

LEARN ABOUT CONTINENTS Divide the class into seven groups, one for each continent. Ask each group to study the map on pages A4–A5 and make a list of the landforms and bodies of water found on or near its assigned continent. Then have each group member research information about one of the landforms or bodies of water. Group members can then compile their information in a book titled *Landforms and Bodies of Water.*

TECHNOLOGY

Use MAPSKILLS to complete this activity.

WESTERN HEMISPHERE
Political

Define the Purpose

Tell students that this is a political map of the Western Hemisphere. Explain that the equator divides the Earth into the Northern and Southern Hemispheres and that the prime meridian divides the Earth into the Eastern and Western Hemispheres.

Understanding the Map

Have students look at the symbols in the map key. Point out the symbol that is used to indicate the location of a nation's capital.

Q. What is the national capital of the United States? Washington, D.C.

Which national capital is on the border of Uruguay and Argentina? Buenos Aires

Geography

Movement Point out to students that many cities on this map are located on or near a coast.

Atlas

Western Hemisphere: Political

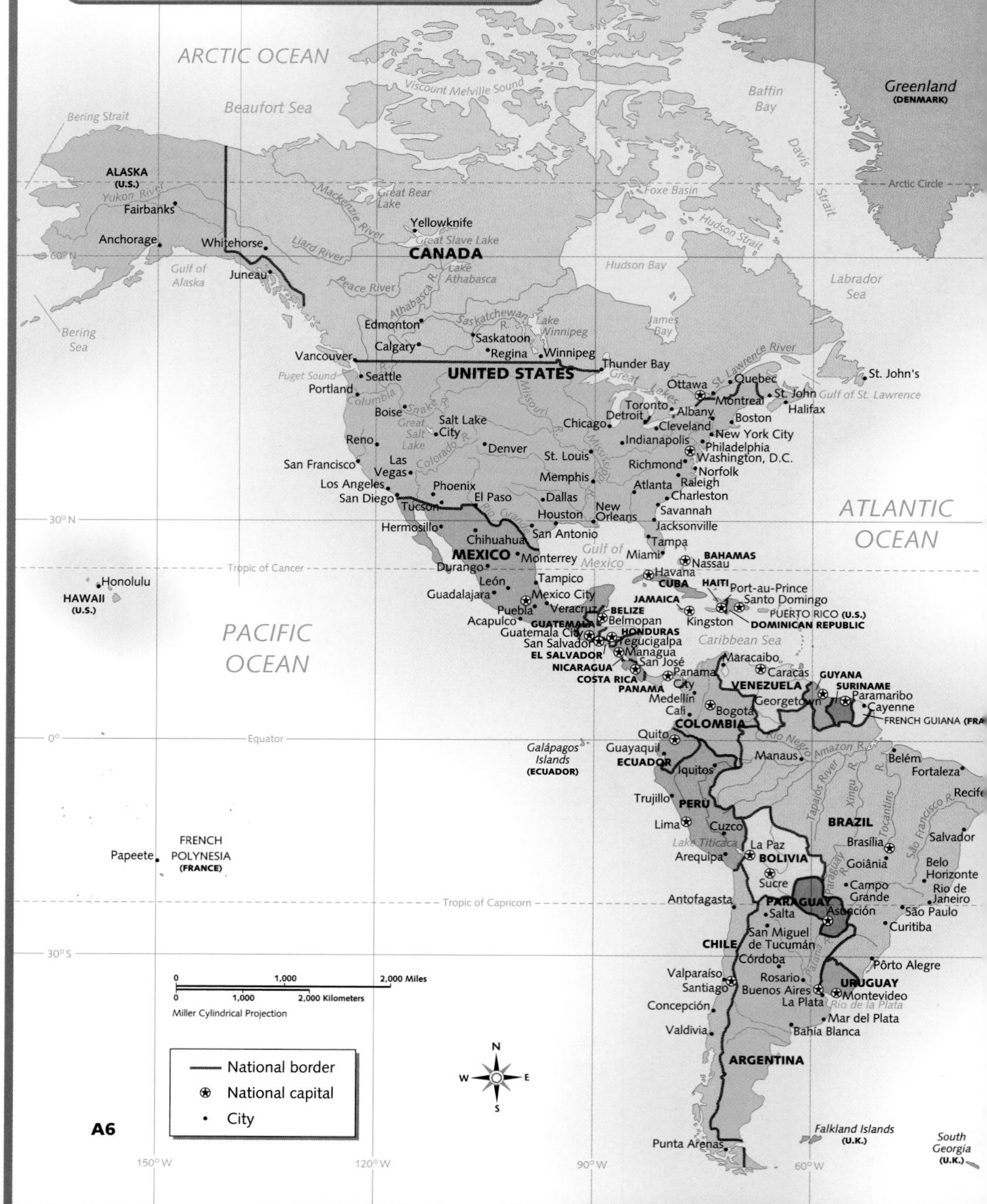

ACTIVITY CHOICES

Background

COMPACT NATIONS AND FRAGMENTED NATIONS Political geographers classify nations by their shapes or forms. Two classifications they use are compact nations and fragmented nations. A *compact nation* is one whose land areas are not separated by bodies of water or other countries. The shape of a compact nation is usually rectangular or round. Uruguay is one compact nation in the Western Hemisphere. A *fragmented nation* is one whose land areas are geographically separated from each other. The United States is a fragmented nation because Alaska and Hawaii are separated from the rest of the United States.

Extend and Enrich

COOPERATIVE LEARNING

MAKE A POLITICAL MAP Divide the class into small groups. Ask the members of each group to make a political map of their state. Groups should include county or local borders as well as state borders. Display the maps and have students discuss them.

TECHNOLOGY

Use MAPSKILLS to complete this activity.

Atlas

Western Hemisphere: Physical

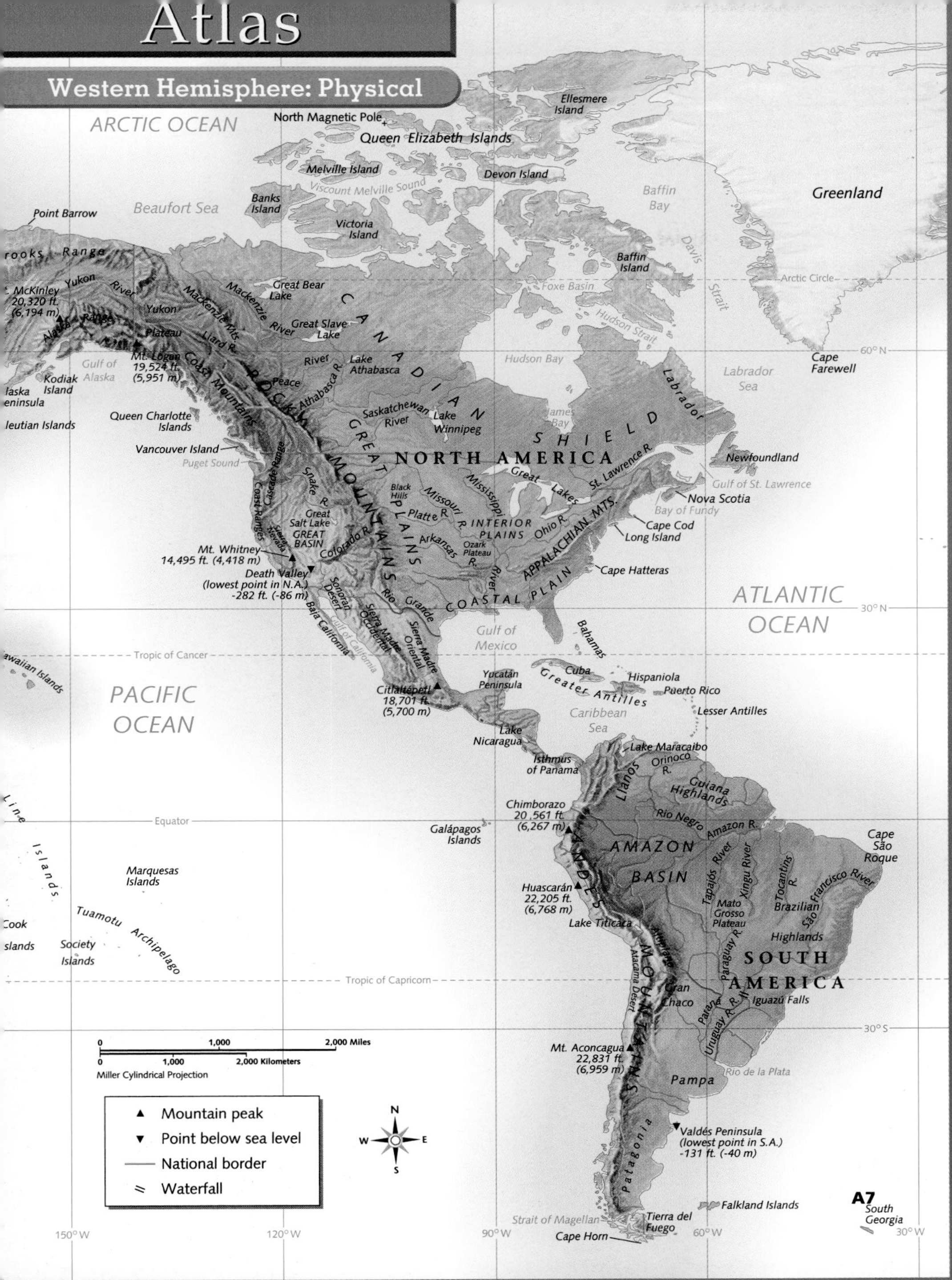

WESTERN HEMISPHERE

Physical

Define the Purpose

Have students identify the kind of map that is shown on page A7. Then review the features that are often illustrated on physical maps.

Understanding the Map

Point out the symbols in the map key. Ask students to identify the symbols that are used to show mountain peaks and points below sea level.

Q. **What is the lowest point in North America?** Death Valley

What is the highest point in North America? Mt. McKinley

Geography

Location Have students use latitude and longitude to determine the location of specific physical features.

Meet Individual Needs

ENGLISH LANGUAGE LEARNERS Have students make vocabulary cards for the following words that describe physical features: *altiplano, archipelago, highland, llano, pampa, point, range, shield, sierra, sound.* Students can illustrate each feature and write a sentence about it. Then have students share their cards with the rest of the class.

Extend and Enrich

COOPERATIVE LEARNING

MAKE A PHYSICAL MAP Divide the class into small groups. Ask the members of each group to make a physical map of their state. Groups should create their own symbols to show the physical features. Display the maps and have students discuss them.

TECHNOLOGY

Use MAPSKILLS to complete this activity.

UNITED STATES: OVERVIEW

Define the Purpose

Ask students to look at the map on pages A8–A9. Have a volunteer tell what the map shows. Then ask students to name major bodies of water.

Understanding the Map

This map of the United States shows the state borders, the national borders, and the major bodies of water that border the United States. Point out that the postal abbreviations for all of the states are also shown.

Q. **What might you use this map for?** to identify where states, bodies of water, and neighboring countries are located

Geography

Location Direct students' attention to Washington, D.C. Then explain that the nation's capital is not a part of any one state.

Atlas

United States: Overview

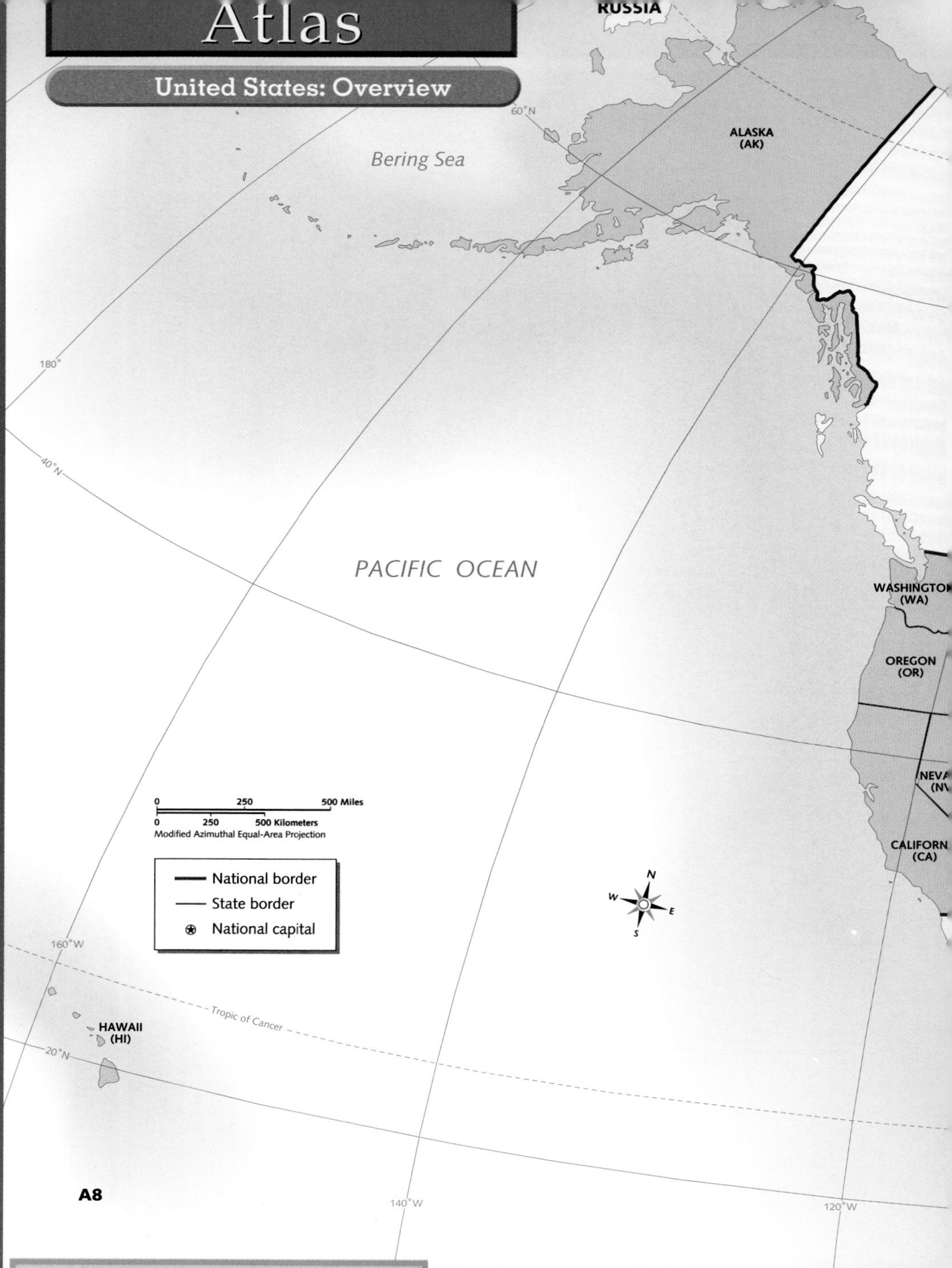

ACTIVITY CHOICES

Background

BOUNDARY FACTS The boundaries for states have not always been the same. They have been changed by charters, treaties, purchases, and acts of Congress. Except for Hawaii and Alaska, each state touches the border of at least one other state.

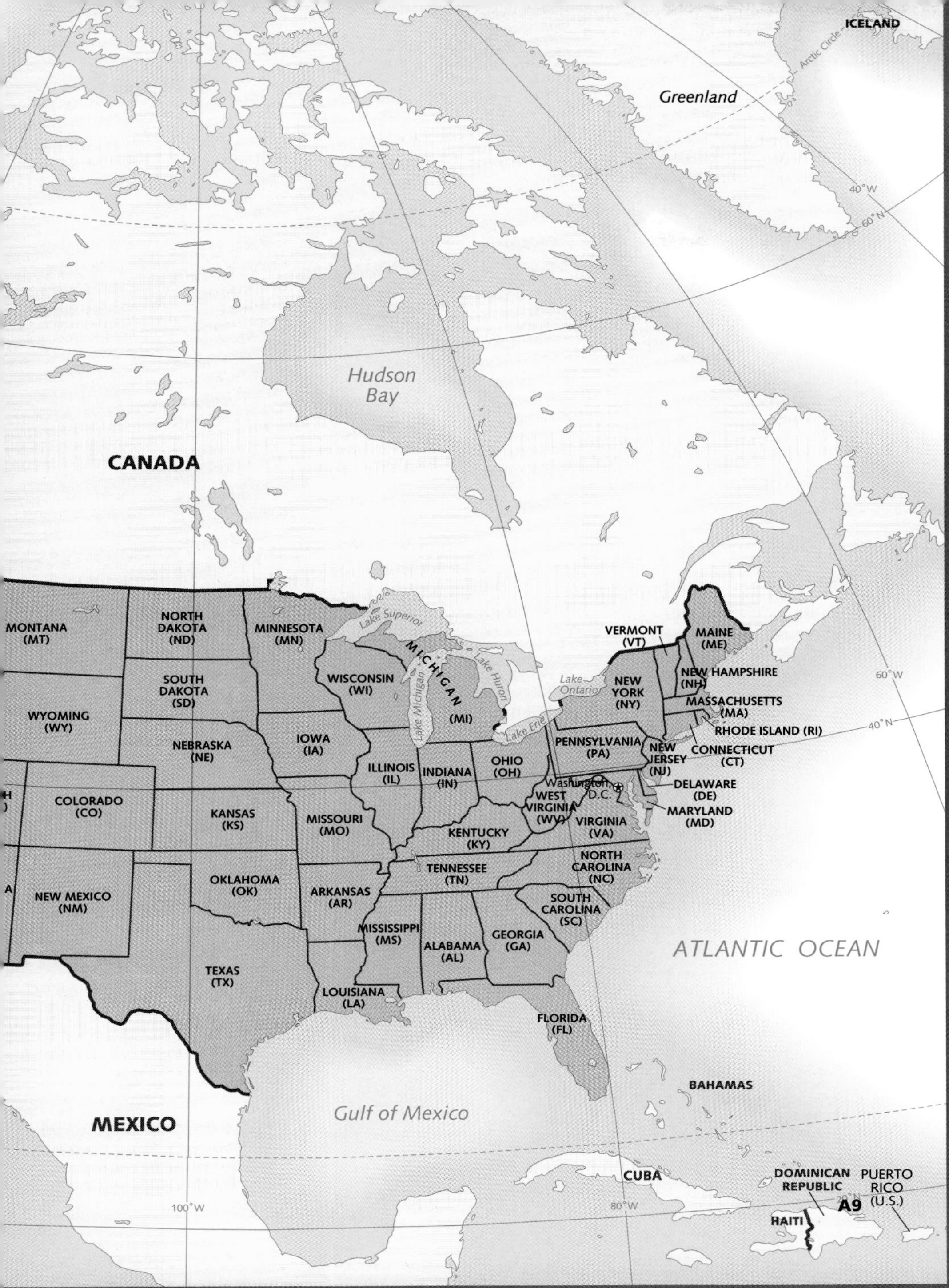

Understanding the Map

Tell students that the map scale on page A8 helps people find the real distances between places on a map. Ask students what units of measurement are shown on this map scale. miles and kilometers

Geography

Place Discuss with students how borders for countries and states are decided. Point out that people determine borders. Mention that some national and state borders, however, follow the paths of physical features, such as rivers and lakes. Have students look at the state borders on the map and speculate on which might follow a physical feature.

Q. **What physical feature forms a part of the border around New York?** Lake Ontario and Lake Erie

Meet Individual Needs

ENGLISH LANGUAGE LEARNERS Use the map on pages A8–A9 to help students learn the names of the 50 states. Direct students to list the states alphabetically. Then, as you name each state, have them point to it on the map.

Extend and Enrich

COOPERATIVE LEARNING

MAKE STATE FACT CARDS Divide the class into ten small groups. Assign each group five states, alphabetically. Have groups create fact cards for their states. For each state students should include the state's name, postal abbreviation, location, and states or countries that border it. Groups can also do research in an encyclopedia or almanac to find out when each state became part of the United States. Students can add to their fact cards after studying the maps on pages A14–A15.

TECHNOLOGY

Use MAPSKILLS to complete this activity.

UNITED STATES: POLITICAL

Define the Purpose

Ask a volunteer to read the map title on page A10 and tell the purpose of a political map. Point out the political units (states, countries) shown on the map.

Understanding the Map

Have students look at the map key. Ask them to focus on the items in the map key that may be unfamiliar to them. Explain that the United States is divided not only into political units, or states, but also into geographic regions. Each region has a different number of states and features that make it different from other regions. Then have students tell the difference between the state capital symbol and the national capital symbol.

Ask a volunteer to name each geographic region. Students can locate each region on their maps.

Q. **Which region is the smallest?** the Northeast

In which region do you live? Students should correctly identify the region they live in.

Geography

Regions Review that a geographic region is an area with features that make it different from other places. Discuss the regions of the United States. Have students name features of each region. Make a chart on the board to record their responses.

Q. **What things do you think the states in a region might have in common?** Answers will vary but may include the following: climate, physical features, vegetation or plant life, ways of life, economic activities.

Atlas

United States: Political

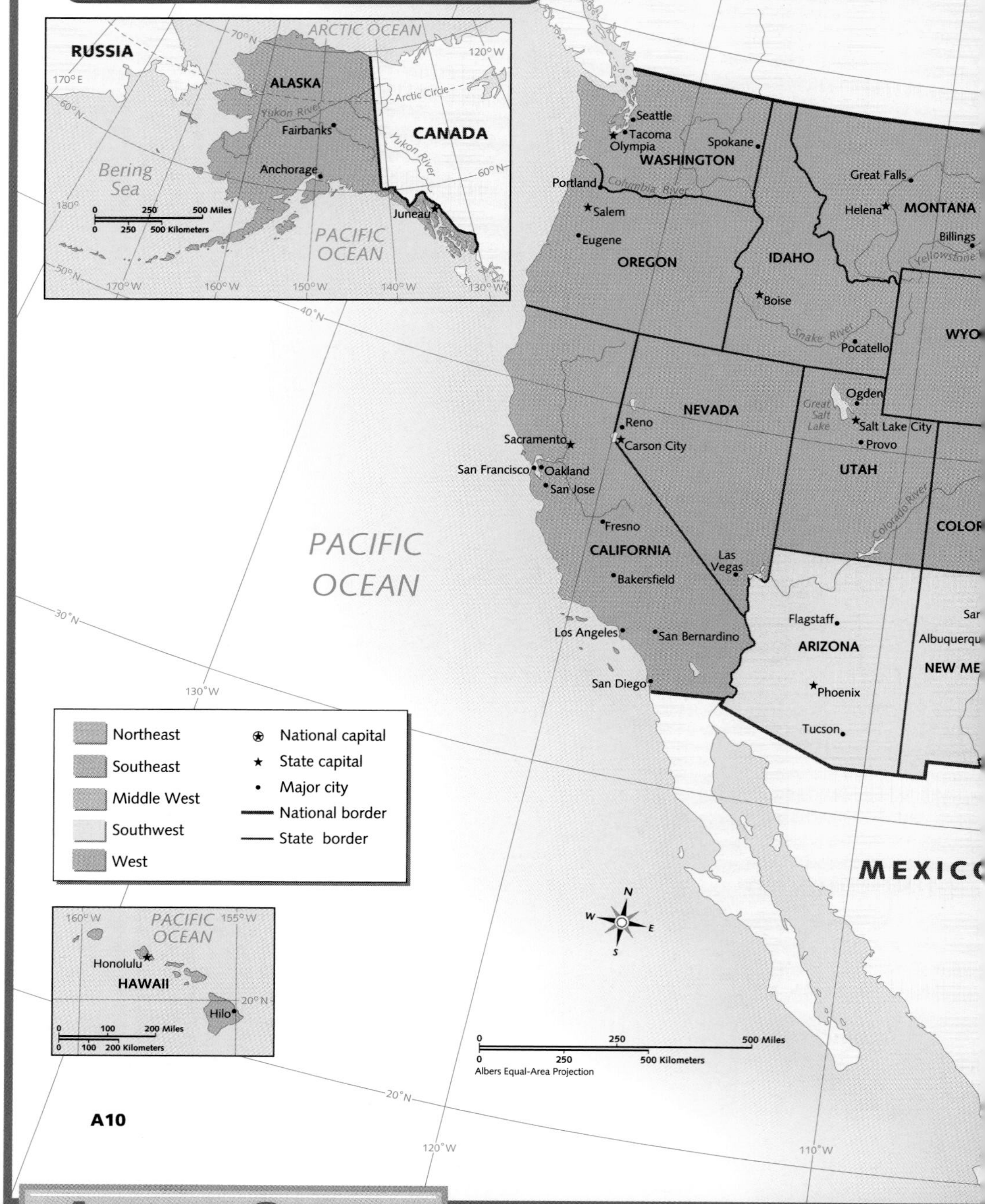

ACTIVITY CHOICES

Background

NORTHEAST AND WEST REGIONS While the Northeast region of the United States is the smallest in size, it is the most densely populated. In fact, the Northeast region has four of the largest metropolitan areas in the country— Philadelphia, New York City, Boston, and Washington, D.C. In addition, the Northeast cities between Washington, D.C., and Boston, Massachusetts, form a *megalopolis*. This is a term used to describe several cities that have grown together and form an urban area. More than 60 percent of the country's industry, finance, and commercial production takes place in this megalopolis.

The West region has grown rapidly. More than 14 percent of the country's population lives in some of the states in this region. The cities of Los Angeles and San Francisco/Oakland, in California, are two of the largest metropolitan areas in the country.

Geography

Place Have students find the symbols for major cities on the map. Ask what they think is meant by the term *major city*. Guide them to determine that major cities are those with large populations.

Q. **Which state do you think has a larger population, California or Nevada?** California

Why do you think so? because more cities are shown in California than in Nevada

Geography

Location Ask students to look at the map and notice the locations of the state capitals.

Q. **Why do you think Washington, D.C., is not in the middle of the country?** The location for the national capital was chosen before the United States was as big as it is today, and at the time its location was chosen, Washington, D.C., was in the middle of the country.

Meet Individual Needs

ADVANCED LEARNERS Ask students to work in groups to create a *Regions of the United States* chart. In the chart, students should include the following information: name of region, states in region, population, land area, main industries, and products. Students may use library or Internet resources to gather information. Invite students to share their charts with the rest of the class.

Extend and Enrich

MAKE A POSTER Have students choose a state capital. Then ask them to look through newspapers and magazines to find photographs, paintings, diagrams, or maps and use these illustrations to make a poster about the capital. They can also include the city's population, size, and location. Suggest students use library or Internet resources as necessary.

UNITED STATES: PHYSICAL

Define the Purpose

Recall with students the purpose of a physical map. Tell students that a physical map focuses on the landforms of a place.

Understanding the Map

Refer students to the map key. Point out that the colors represent different kinds of terrain, vegetation, or plant life. Ask a volunteer to describe each type of vegetation. Then have students identify each type on the map. Remind students that shading is used to show relief, or differences in the heights of an area of land.

Q. **What do you think is the difference between tundra and arid land?** Tundra is flat land without trees that is frozen for much of the year. Arid land is dry.

Geography

Location Have students describe the relative locations of major physical features of the United States.

Q. **How would you describe the location of the Mojave Desert?** Answers will vary but may include the following: The Mojave Desert lies on the border of California and Nevada, not far from Death Valley and Lake Mead. It is in the western part of the country.

Atlas

United States: Physical

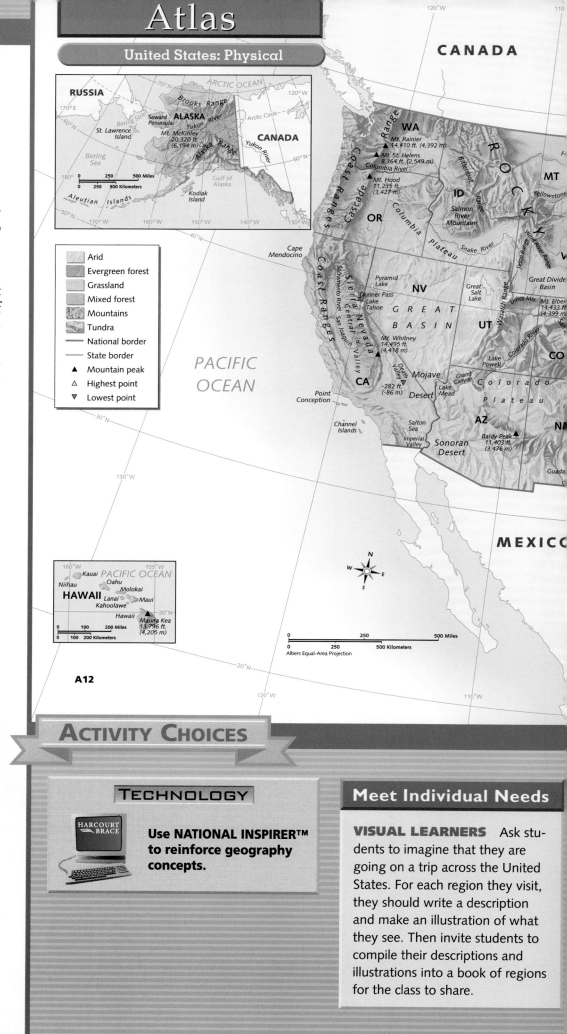

ACTIVITY CHOICES

TECHNOLOGY

Use NATIONAL INSPIRER™ to reinforce geography concepts.

Meet Individual Needs

VISUAL LEARNERS Ask students to imagine that they are going on a trip across the United States. For each region they visit, they should write a description and make an illustration of what they see. Then invite students to compile their descriptions and illustrations into a book of regions for the class to share.

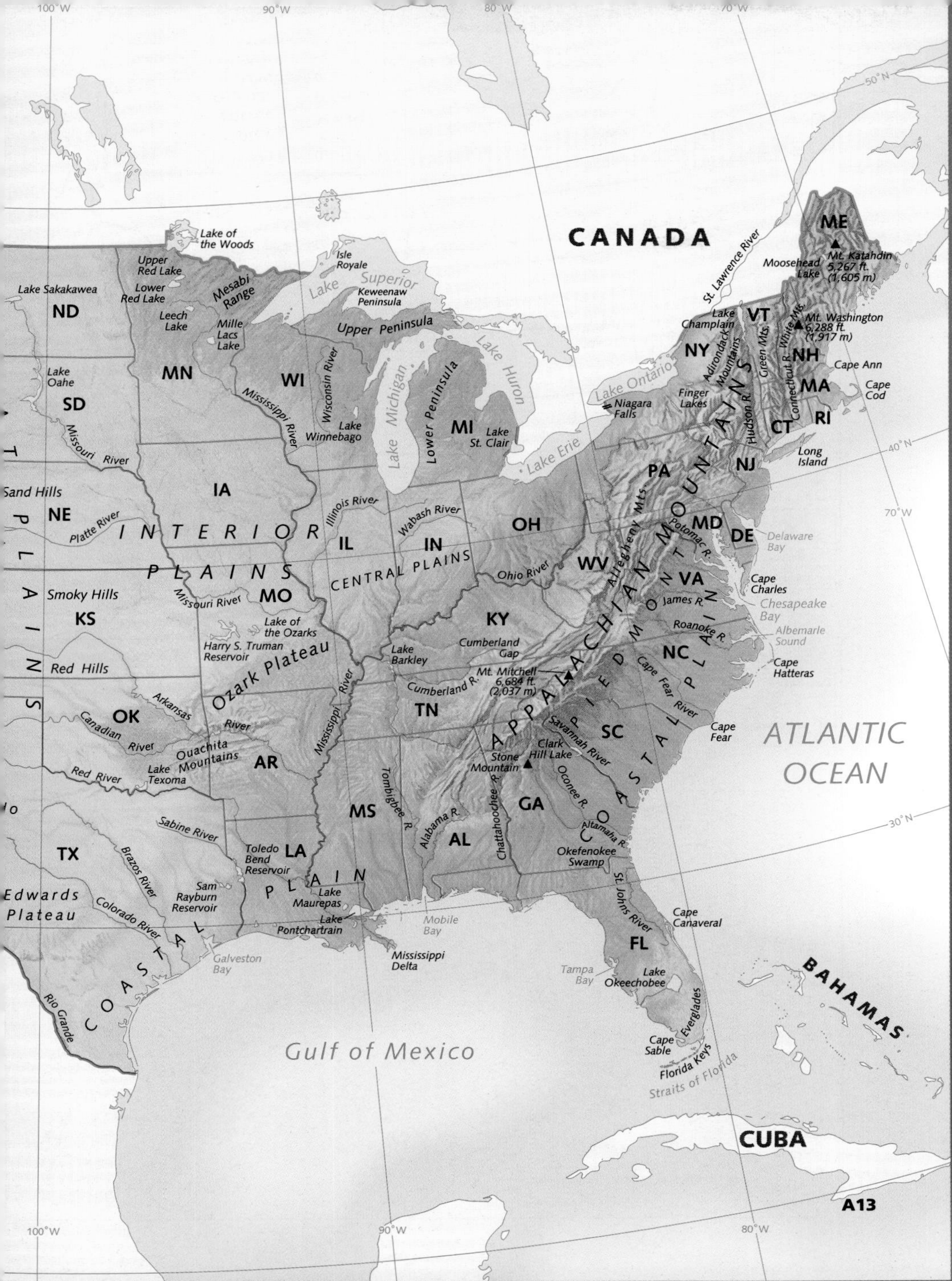

Geography

Place Have students look at the physical features shown on the map. Then have students compare and contrast landforms and bodies of water in different parts of the country.

Q. **How is the land in northern Alaska different from the land in northern Maine?** Northern Alaska is tundra; northern Maine has mountains.

What landforms or bodies of water are near where you live? Students should identify appropriate landforms or bodies of water.

Geography

Human-Environment Interactions Ask students to think about a landform or body of water in their state that poses a challenge. For example, are there rivers that flood, mountains that have avalanches, or desert areas? Have students tell how these physical features affect their lives.

Background

LANDFORMS AND WATER FORMS Mauna Kea in Hawaii is an ocean-based mountain. It is almost a mile taller than Mt. Everest. That's because the base of the mountain is on the ocean floor, and that makes it about 33,476 feet (10,203 m) tall.

Sandstone cliffs on the Colorado Plateau were once sand dunes. When lime, sand, and mud buried the sand dunes, the grains of sand became rock. Then erosion brought the rocks to the surface, and they were shaped into cliffs.

Lava beds in California were formed quickly when hot lava came out of volcanoes and flowed over the land. The top layer cooled and then hardened. But the lower layer kept flowing and drained away. Then lava tubes were left, which eventually became lava tube caves.

Extend and Enrich

COOPERATIVE LEARNING

WRITE AND PRESENT A TRAVELOGUE Divide the class into small groups, and assign each group a region of the United States. The groups should use library or Internet resources to research information about the landforms or bodies of water in their regions. Then the groups should write travelogues to present to the class. After the presentations, allow time for the class to ask questions.

UNITED STATES

Population Density

Define the Purpose

Direct students' attention to the population density map on the top of page A14. Then explain that population density refers to the number of people who live in 1 square mile or 1 square kilometer of land.

Understanding the Map

Point out that the map key explains the colors that stand for different population densities.

Q. **Is the United States more populated in the western or eastern part of the country?** eastern

Land Use and Resources

Define the Purpose

Explain that this map shows the ways the United States uses its land and its resources.

Understanding the Map

Point out the map key and have students note the symbols.

Q. **How does the map show land use?** through colors

How does it show resources? with symbols

Geography

Location Ask students to examine the land use and resources map and identify how the land is used in different parts of the country. Then have them identify how the land is used in their state.

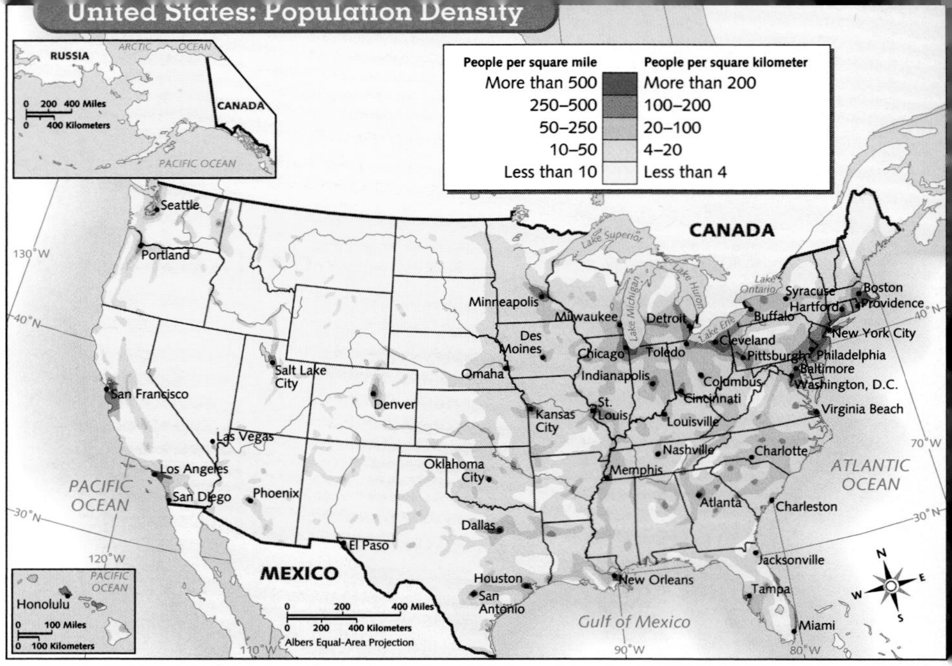

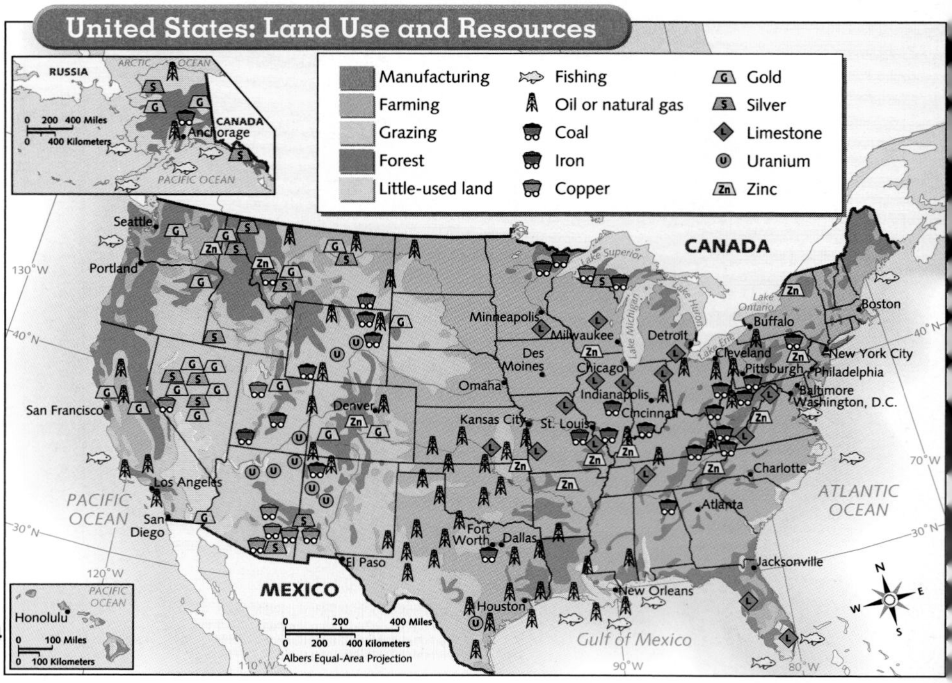

A14

ACTIVITY CHOICES

Extend and Enrich

MAKE A CHART Have students refer to the land use and resources map to make charts of the land use and resources in their state. Then ask volunteers to share their charts with the class.

United States: Climate

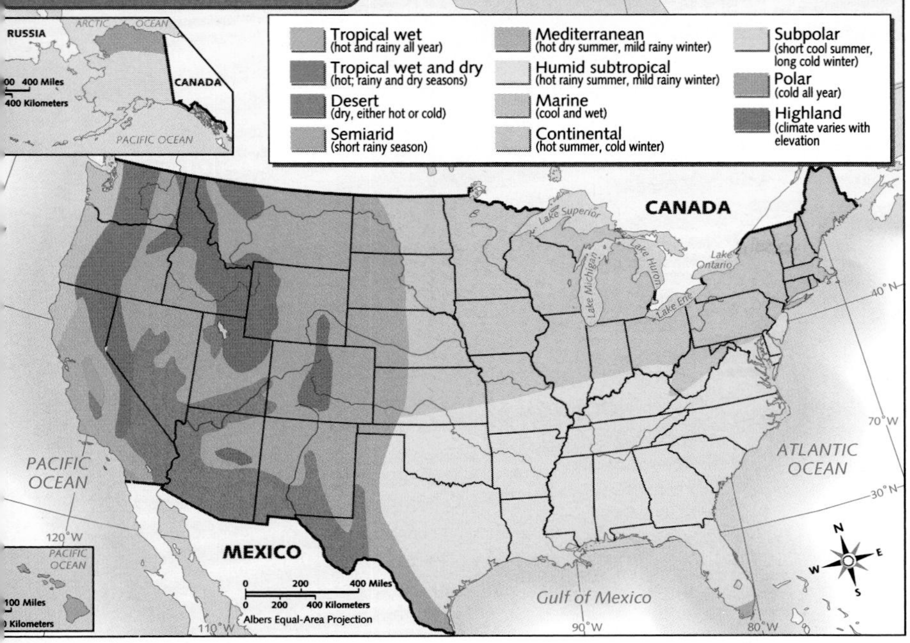

United States: Vegetation

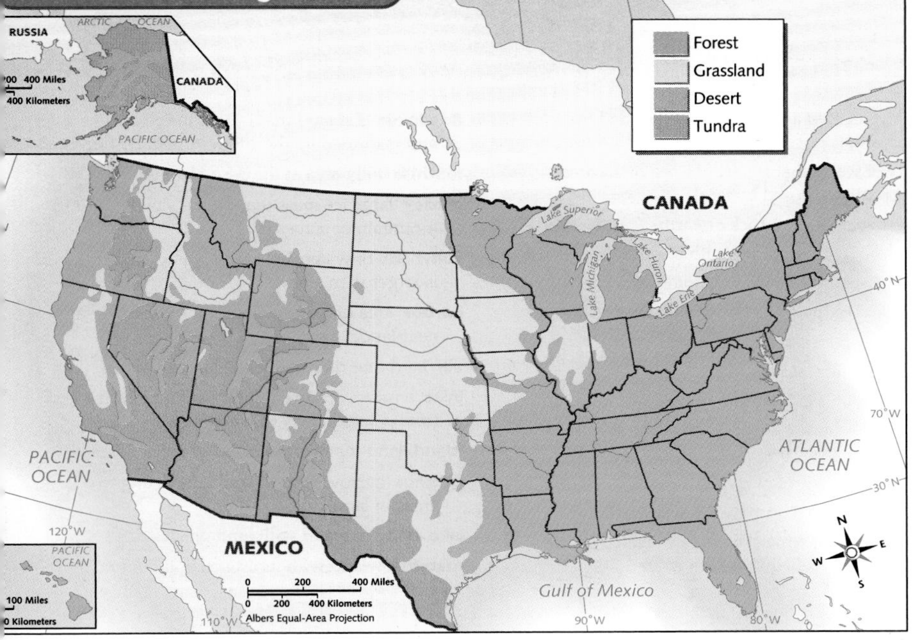

A15

Meet Individual Needs

ENGLISH LANGUAGE LEARNERS Have students look through newspapers and magazines to find illustrations of the types of vegetation shown on the map titled *Vegetation.* Then ask students to make a collage showing the different types of vegetation in the United States. Students may also write captions for the collages.

Extend and Enrich

MAKE A CHART Have students make four-column charts that show the four kinds of vegetation illustrated on the map. For each kind of vegetation, students should include the states where that vegetation exists as well as the general characteristics of the vegetation. Students can use reference materials as necessary.

United States

Climate

Define the Purpose

Point out that the map at the top of page A15 shows the average weather conditions of the United States over a long period of time.

Understanding the Map

Refer students to the map key, and have them note the colors used to show the various climates.

Geography

Place Discuss the type of climate in your state.

Q. **What climate is shown for the area where you live?** Students should correctly identify the type of climate.

Vegetation

Define the Purpose

Ask volunteers to explain what is illustrated on the map on the bottom of this page. Then discuss the different types of vegetation that exist in the United States.

Understanding the Map

Point out the use of color in the map key to show vegetation.

Q. **What color does the map use to show an area where there are a lot of forests?** green

Geography

Location Have students identify major areas for each type of vegetation.

Q. **What type of vegetation is found in the Southeast region of the United States?** forest

GEOGRAPHY TERMS

Define the Purpose

Tell students that the diagram on pages A16–A17 illustrates geography terms for landforms and bodies of water. Point out the glossary at the bottom of the pages. Encourage students to use the diagram and the glossary as they read the textbook.

Visual Analysis

Learn from Diagrams Ask students to identify the large landforms and large bodies of water labeled in the diagram.

Q. **To what landform do the labels timberline, peak, mountain, mountain pass, volcano, and slope relate?** mountain range

What parts of an ocean are shown? channel, harbor, sea, strait, gulf, bay, inlet

Atlas

Geography Terms

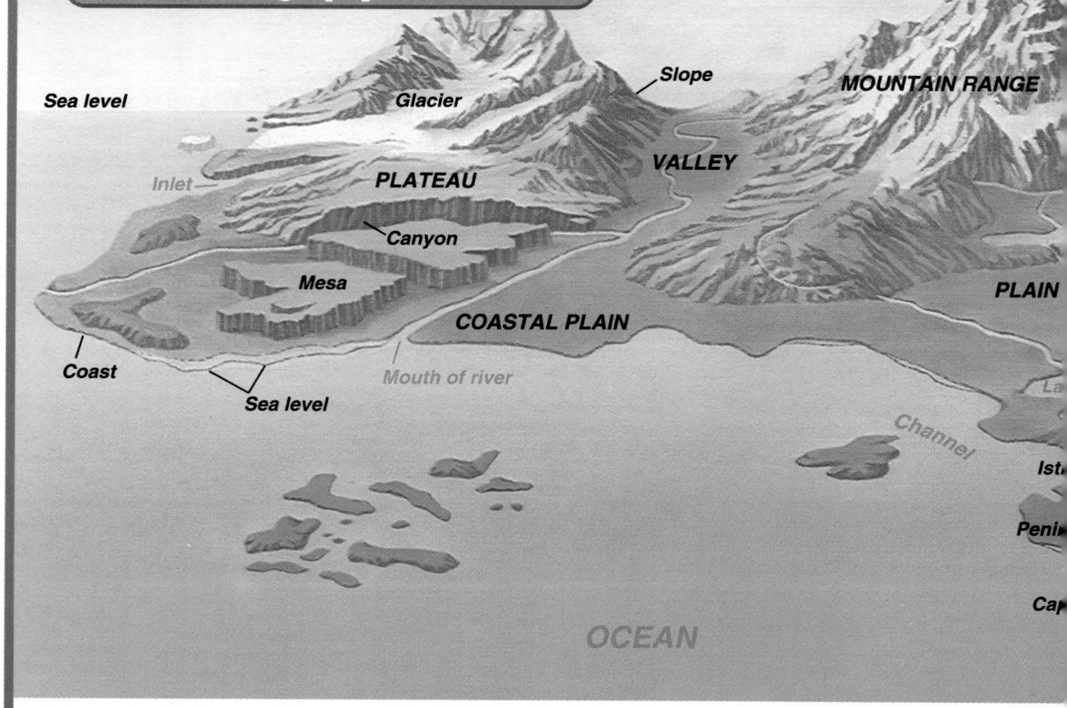

basin bowl-shaped area of land surrounded by higher land

bay body of water that is part of a sea or an ocean and is partly enclosed by land

bluff high, steep face of rock or earth

canyon deep, narrow valley with steep sides

cape point of land that extends into water

channel deepest part of a body of water

cliff high, steep face of rock or earth

coast land along a sea or ocean

coastal plain area of flat land along a sea or ocean

delta triangle-shaped area of land at the mouth of a river

desert dry land with few plants

dune hill of sand piled up by the wind

fall line area along which rivers form waterfalls or rapids as the rivers drop to lower land

floodplain flat land that is near the edges of a river and is formed by the silt deposited by floods

foothills hilly area at the base of a mountain

glacier large ice mass that moves slowly down a mountain or across land

gulf body of water that is partly enclosed by land but is larger than a bay

harbor area of water where ships can dock safely near land

hill land that rises above the land around it

inlet a narrow strip of water leading into the land from a larger body of water

island land that has water on all sides

isthmus narrow strip of land connecting two larger areas of land

lake body of water with land on all sides

marsh lowland with moist soil and tall grasses

A16

ACTIVITY CHOICES

Meet Individual Needs

ENGLISH LANGUAGE LEARNERS Ask students to select five of the landforms or bodies of water shown in the diagram. Have them draw an imaginary place and include these landforms or bodies of water. Students should label each landform or body of water.

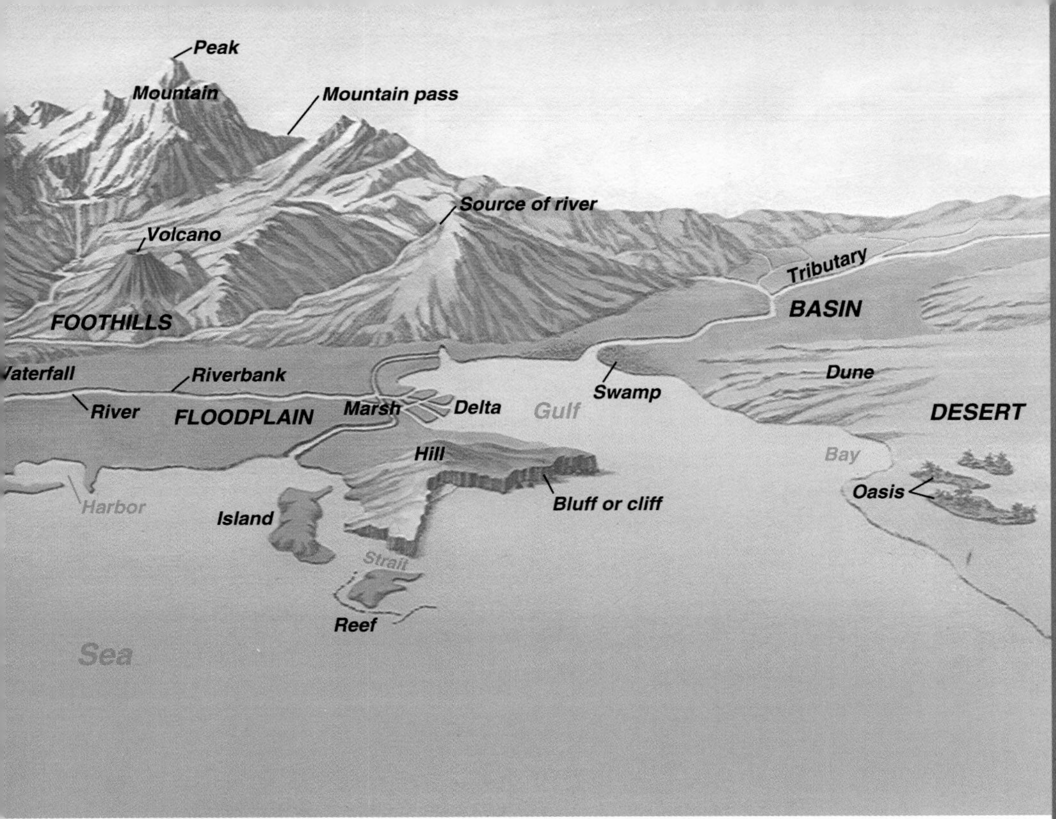

mesa flat-topped mountain with steep sides
mountain highest kind of land
mountain pass gap between mountains
mountain range row of mountains
mouth of river place where a river empties into another body of water
oasis area of water and fertile land in a desert
ocean body of salt water larger than a sea
peak top of a mountain
peninsula land that is almost completely surrounded by water
plain flat land
plateau area of high, flat land with steep sides
reef ridge of sand, rock, or coral that lies at or near the surface of a sea or ocean
river large stream of water that flows across the land
riverbank land along a river
sea body of salt water smaller than an ocean
sea level the level that is even with the surface of an ocean or sea
slope side of a hill or mountain
source of river place where a river begins
strait narrow channel of water connecting two larger bodies of water
swamp area of low, wet land with trees
timberline line on a mountain above which it is too cold for trees to grow
tributary stream or river that empties into a larger river
valley low land between hills or mountains
volcano opening in the Earth, often raised, through which lava, rock, ashes, and gases are forced out
waterfall steep drop from a high place to a lower place in a stream or river

A17

Understanding the Diagram

Direct students' attention to the terms and their definitions at the bottom of pages A16–A17. Ask volunteers to read the terms and the definitions. Then have students use the glossary to identify additional distinguishing characteristics of physical features included in the diagram.

Q. **Which features are defined in part by the kinds of plants that grow on them?** marsh, swamp, timberline

Which features are defined in part by their elevation, or height above sea level? bluff, cliff, hill, mesa, mountain, plateau

Which features may be close to, or at, sea level? coast, coastal plain, delta, marsh, mouth of river, swamp, valley, inlet

Meet Individual Needs

TACTILE LEARNERS Have students make a diorama to show the landforms and bodies of water shown on the diagram. Ask students to plan the layout before starting to construct the diorama. Then have students make labels for each physical feature shown in the diorama.

Extend and Enrich

WRITE A POEM Ask students to write poems about the geography of the place where they live. Poems can be about the land, bodies of water, weather, or plants and animals that live there. Ask students to share their poems with the class.

TECHNOLOGY

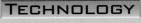

Use THE AMAZING WRITING MACHINE™ to complete this activity.

Unit 6

pages 340–405

Our Nation Grows

The major objectives in this unit are organized around the following themes:

UNIT THEMES

- ▶ CONFLICT & COOPERATION
- ▶ CONTINUITY & CHANGE
- ▶ INDIVIDUALISM & INTERDEPENDENCE
- ▶ INTERACTION WITHIN DIFFERENT ENVIRONMENTS

Preview Unit Content

Unit 6 tells the story of how the United States achieved what many believed to be its manifest destiny—to stretch from the Atlantic to the Pacific. In the course of studying this unit, students will learn about the westward movement, the Louisiana Purchase, and the battles with Britain and Mexico that won even more land for the nation. Students will also learn how the Industrial Revolution changed the way Americans lived and how reformers worked to make life better for all Americans.

You may wish to begin the unit with the Unit 6 Visual Summary Poster and activity. The illustration that appears on the poster also appears on pages 402–403 in the Pupil Book to help students summarize the unit.

UNIT POSTER

Use the UNIT 6 VISUAL SUMMARY POSTER to preview the unit.

1 The Industrial Revolution brought great changes to the United States. The nation's first factory was built in 1790.

4 In 1811 work began on the National Road. It became the main land route between the East and the West.

6 By the mid-1800s, the nation had gained Texas, the Oregon Country, and other western lands. At the Alamo in 1836, Texans had fought for independence from Mexico.

2 In 1803 the Louisiana Purchase doubled the nation's size. Lewis and Clark explored the new territory with help from Sacagawea.

3 In the early 1800s, steamboats made travel by river much faster.

5 The first locomotive in the nation was built in 1830. Railroads grew quickly after that.

7 The Indian Removal Act of 1830 forced American Indians to leave their homes and make difficult journeys to the West.

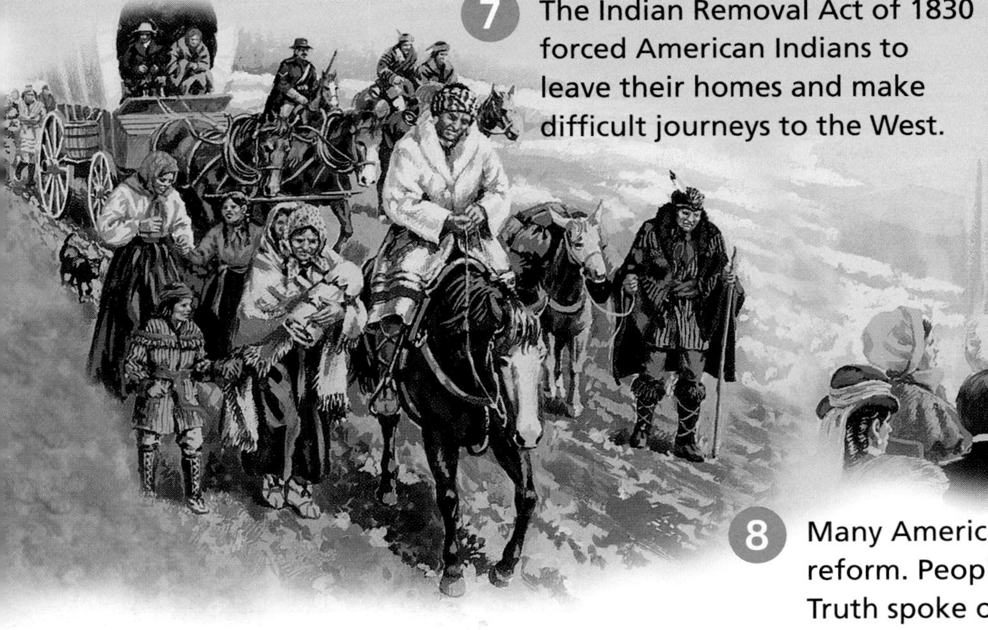

8 Many Americans saw the need for reform. People such as Sojourner Truth spoke out against slavery.

Unit 6 Planning Chart

	CONTENT AND SKILLS	RESOURCES INCLUDING ▶ TECHNOLOGY
UNIT INTRODUCTION **Our Nation Grows** pp. 340–347	Unit Opener and Unit Preview Set the Scene with Literature **Cassie's Journey** by Brett Harvey illustrated by Ed Martinez	Unit 6 Visual Summary Poster Unit 6 Home Letter Unit 6 Text on Tape Audiocassette Video Experiences: Social Studies ▶ TIMELINER
CHAPTER 11 **On the Move** pp. 348–371	LESSON 1: Across the Appalachians LESSON 2: The Louisiana Purchase LESSON 3: A Second War with Britain **SKILL:** Predict a Likely Outcome LESSON 4: Learn History Through Literature **By the Dawn's Early Light: The Story of the Star-Spangled Banner** by Steven Kroll illustrated by Dan Andreason Chapter Review	Activity Book, pp. 66–71 Music Audiocassette Transparencies 29–30 Chapter 11 Test, pp. 95–98 ▶ THE AMAZING WRITING MACHINE ▶ TIMELINER ▶ INTERNET
CHAPTER 12 **The Way West** pp. 372–399	LESSON 1: The Industrial Revolution LESSON 2: The Age of Jackson LESSON 3: Westward Ho! **SKILL:** Use Relief and Elevation Maps LESSON 4: An Age of Reform **SKILL:** Use a Double-Bar Graph Chapter Review	Activity Book, pp. 72–79 Desk Maps Transparencies 31–33 Chapter 12 Test, pp. 99–102 ▶ THE AMAZING WRITING MACHINE ▶ GRAPH LINKS ▶ DECISIONS, DECISIONS ▶ THE ALAMO ▶ NATIONAL INSPIRER ▶ TIMELINER ▶ MAPSKILLS ▶ INTERNET
UNIT WRAP-UP pp. 400–405	Making Social Studies Relevant Visual Summary Unit Review	Making Social Studies Relevant Video Unit 6 Visual Summary Poster Game Time! Unit 6 Test, Standard Test, pp. 103–107 Performance Tasks, pp. 108–109 ▶ IMAGINATION EXPRESS ▶ THE AMAZING WRITING MACHINE ▶ TIMELINER ▶ INTERNET

4 WEEKS

TIME MANAGEMENT

WEEK 1	WEEK 2	WEEK 3	WEEK 4
Unit Introduction / Chapter 11	Chapter 11	Chapter 12	Chapter 12 / Unit Wrap-Up

See pages 348A and 372A for Chapter Planning Charts with details by lesson.

Multimedia Resource Center

Books

Easy

Adler, David A. *A Picture Book of Sojourner Truth.* Holiday House, 1994. The life of well-known abolitionist Sojourner Truth is chronicled in this book.

Kroll, Steven. *By the Dawn's Early Light: The Story of The Star-Spangled Banner.* Scholastic, 1994. This book tells the tale of the inspiration behind the writing of our national anthem.

McCully, Emily Arnold. *The Bobbin Girl.* Dial, 1996. A young girl who works in a textile factory faces a difficult decision about workers' rights.

Average

Blumberg, Rhoda. *The Incredible Journey of Lewis and Clark.* William Morrow, 1987. Meriwether Lewis and William Clark's odyssey of scientific discovery helped unlock the mystery of the land west of the Mississippi River in 1804.

Connell, Kate. *They Shall Be Heard: Susan B. Anthony and Elizabeth Cady Stanton.* Steck-Vaughn, 1993. These two women became good friends during their struggle for women's rights.

Greenwood, Barbara. *A Pioneer Sampler: The Daily Life of a Pioneer Family in 1840.* Houghton Mifflin, 1995. Readers will participate in pioneer activities as they learn about daily life on the frontier.

Harvey, Brett. *Cassie's Journey: Going West in the 1860s.* Holiday House, 1988. In a tale filled with danger and adventure, Cassie narrates the story of her family's westward move from Illinois to California.

Lourie, Peter. *Erie Canal: Canoeing America's Great Waterway.* Boyds Mills Press, 1997. The author takes readers on a historical canoe tour of the Erie Canal.

Challenging

Blumberg, Rhoda. *Full Steam Ahead: The Race to Build a Transcontinental Railroad.* National Geographic Society, 1996. This text, combined with historic photographs, tells the tale of the building of the transcontinental railroad.

Greenberg, Judith E. and Helen Carey McKeever. *A Pioneer Woman's Memoir.* Franklin Watts, 1995. In a compilation of journal entries and additional documentation, read about one pioneer woman's journey west on the Oregon Trail.

Lawlor, Laurie. *Daniel Boone.* Albert Whitman & Company, 1989. Trace the life of legendary woodsman, hunter, and pioneer from his Pennsylvania childhood to his exploration of the Kentucky frontier.

LIBRARY

See the SOCIAL STUDIES LIBRARY for additional resources.

Computer Software

CD-ROM

Expanding Our Nation. Clearvue/eav, 1996, URL *http://www.clearvue.com,* (800) 253-2788. Windows/Macintosh dual format. The cultural and territorial development of the nation is tracked as the journeys of those who traveled to Mississippi and beyond are chronicled.

Wild West Encyclopedia. Entrex Software, 1997, URL *http://www.entrex.org,* (800) 667-0007. Windows/Macintosh dual format. Topics include "Claiming Texas," "Expansion West," "The Gold Rush," and "War on the Plains." An index of Native American leaders and groups is available, as well as a geographic index of western regions, plants, and animals.

Video

Videotape

America's Westward Expansion. Knowledge Unlimited, 1996, URL *http://www.knowledgeunlimited.com,* (800) 356-2303. The progression from 13 coastal colonies to 48 continental states is examined. Coverage spans the settlement of the Northwest Territories until the Civil War.

The Lewis and Clark Expedition. United Learning, 1992, URL *http://www.unitedlearning.com,* (800) 424-0362. The combination of reenactments, visuals, and quotes from the journals of Lewis and Clark offers insight into the Lewis and Clark expedition.

FREE & INEXPENSIVE MATERIALS

History Game

For a resource titled "Great Women Biographic Card Game: Foremothers," which features photos and facts about women in history, request item #9458 and send $8.95 plus $3.00 shipping and handling to:

The National Women's Hall of Fame
76 Fall Street
P.O. Box 335
Seneca Falls, NY 13148
http://www.greatwomen.org

Booklet

For a free copy of a biography of Meriwether Lewis, write to:

Natchez Trace Parkway Superintendent
2680 Natchez Trace Parkway
Tupelo, MS 38801

Note: one copy per school.

TECHNOLOGY

Visit the Internet at **http://www.hbschool.com** for additional resources.

Note that information, while correct at time of publication, is subject to change.

Linking Social Studies

BULLETIN BOARD IDEA

Make a Pioneer Poster To help students appreciate the many different people who explored and built the United States, have them outline the contributions of famous pioneers. Divide the class into small groups, and hand out posterboard to each group. Assign each group three to four names of pioneers mentioned in this unit. Have students in each group draw the outlines of a set of footprints (a right and a left foot) for each pioneer assigned to the group. Have students write the words *WHO* and *WHEN* on one footprint and *WHAT* on the other and fill in the appropriate information on each set of footprints for each pioneer assigned to the group. After students have completed the footprints, have them put an outline map of the United States on the bulletin board. In bold letters across the top of the board, write the title *Leading Our Country Through History*. Have each group paste the footprints on the map in the area of the country in which the pioneer had the greatest effect. As students put up each set of footprints, have them tell about the pioneer's place in history.

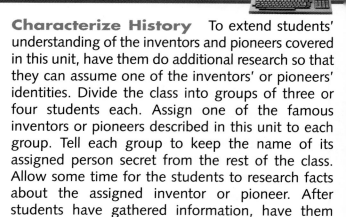

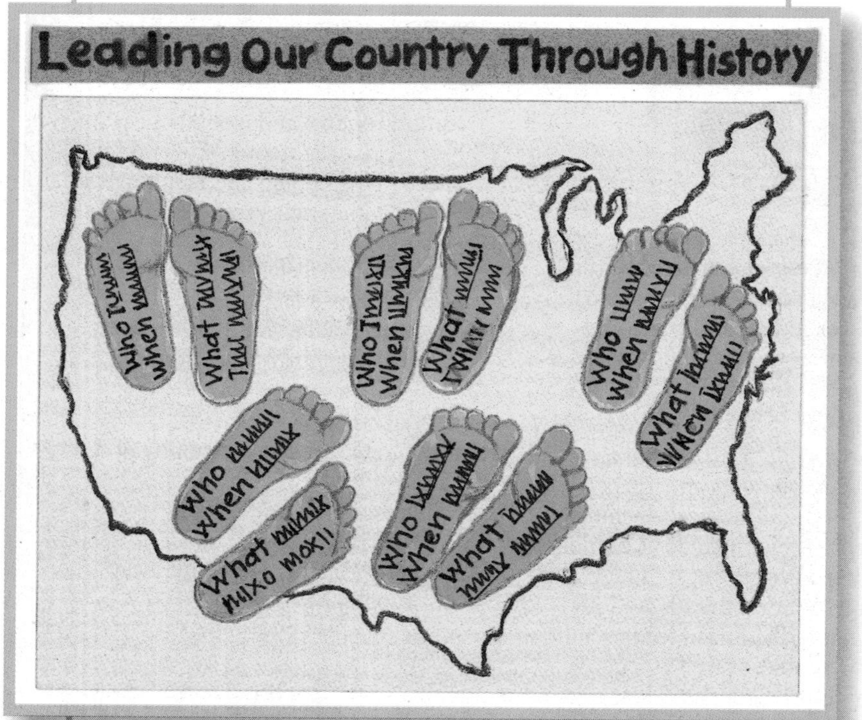

LANGUAGE ARTS

Characterize History To extend students' understanding of the inventors and pioneers covered in this unit, have them do additional research so that they can assume one of the inventors' or pioneers' identities. Divide the class into groups of three or four students each. Assign one of the famous inventors or pioneers described in this unit to each group. Tell each group to keep the name of its assigned person secret from the rest of the class. Allow some time for the students to research facts about the assigned inventor or pioneer. After students have gathered information, have them discuss their findings with their groups and make lists of the information they have found.

Then have the class play "Twenty Questions." Have each group, in turn, sit in front of the class while the other groups ask questions to try to find out the name of the person assigned to that group. Any student in the group can answer the question, but the answer should be discussed among the group members first.

TECHNOLOGY

Visit the Internet at
http://www.hbschool.com
for additional resources.

Smithsonian Institution®

Harcourt Brace Social Studies helps to bring the Smithsonian Institution to your classroom. Visit the Internet site at *http://www.si.edu/harcourt/socialstudies* for a directory of virtual tours, on-line exhibits, and pictures of primary sources from the Smithsonian Institution.

Across the Curriculum

MATHEMATICS

Calculate Time and Distance

To enhance students' understanding of the challenges pioneers faced, have students calculate time and distance traveled on trails west.

Divide the class into five groups. Assign one of the following trails to each group: Oregon Trail, Mormon Trail, California Trail, Old Spanish Trail, and the Santa Fe Trail. Have students in each group use the map on page 390 to measure the total distance of the assigned trail. Then have each group figure the time traveled in total hours for the assigned trail, using the following methods of transportation and rates of speed: by foot, 3 miles per hour; by horseback, 6 miles per hour; and by horse-drawn carriage, 9 miles per hour.

ART

Market an Invention To help students relate to the difficulties of marketing an invention, have them propose a new invention and devise a way to market it.

Divide the class into small groups, and provide colored paper, old magazines, and plain white paper. Have each group brainstorm an invention that could change people's lives, name it, and design a brochure to market it.

Have students write copy describing the invention, illustrate the brochures with their own drawings or cutouts from the magazines, and paste up the copy and the illustrations in the appropriate place on the colored paper. Display the brochures on a bulletin board called *Students of Invention*.

SCIENCE

Research Discoveries: Then and Now

Divide the class into small groups, and hand out posterboard to each group. Have each group research an invention that still exists today but that has changed from its original form (for example, the phonograph to the CD player). Have each group draw two diagrams on the posterboard, one illustrating the original invention and the other illustrating the invention today. Label the original invention *THEN* and today's invention *NOW*. Post the completed posters around the classroom.

HOW TO INTEGRATE YOUR DAY

Use these topics to help you integrate social studies into your daily planning.

READING THEMES

- Pioneers
- Life Stories
- Technology
- Dare to Dream
- Time
- Measurement

INTEGRATED LANGUAGE ARTS

- Characterize History, p. 340E
- Write a Poem, p. 350
- Write a Letter, p. 354
- Write to Persuade, pp. 359, 394
- Write to Explain, p. 374
- Write a Journal Entry, p. 386

ART

- Market an Invention, p. 340F
- Make a Display, p. 342
- Illustrate the Story, p. 345

MATHEMATICS

- Calculate Time and Distance, p. 340F
- Make a Line Graph, p. 375
- Calculate Costs, p. 376
- Interpret Graphs, p. 380
- Calculate Averages, p. 387

WORLD LANGUAGES

- Study Cherokee Place-Names, p. 350
- Research Spanish Place-Names, p. 384

SCIENCE

- Research Discoveries: Then and Now, p. 340F
- Collect Data, p. 356
- Research Cotton Manufacturers, p. 375
- Report on Steam Engines, p. 377
- Understand Technology, p. 401

READING

- Read a Biography, pp. 361, 384
- Read Diaries and Other Accounts, p. 390

MUSIC

- Sing the National Anthem, p. 366

Unit 6

Assessment Options

The **Assessment Program** allows all learners many opportunities to show what they know and can do. It also provides ongoing information about each student's understanding of social studies.

Portfolio Assessment

- *Lesson Reviews* (**Pupil Book,** at end of lessons)
- *Chapter Reviews* (**Pupil Book,** at end of chapters)
- *Chapter Tests* (**Assessment Program,** pp. 95–102)
- *Unit Review* (**Pupil Book,** pp. 404–405)
- *Unit Assessment* (**Assessment Program:** *Standard Test,* pp. 103–107, *Individual Performance Task,* p. 108, *Group Performance Task,* p. 109)

Student Self-Evaluation

- *Individual End-of-Project Summary* (**Assessment Program,** p. 6)
- *Group End-of-Project Checklist* (**Assessment Program,** p. 7)
- *Individual End-of-Unit Checklist* (**Assessment Program,** p. 8)

Informal Assessment

- REVIEW *Questions* (**Pupil Book,** throughout lessons)
- *Think and Apply* (**Pupil Book,** at end of skill lessons)
- *Visual Summary* (**Pupil Book,** pp. 402–403)
- *Social Studies Skills Checklist* (**Assessment Program,** pp. 4–5)

Performance Assessment

- *Show What You Know* (**Pupil Book,** at end of Lesson Reviews)
- *Cooperative Learning Workshop* (**Pupil Book,** at end of Unit Review)
- *Scoring Rubric for Individual Projects* (**Assessment Program,** p. 9)
- *Scoring Rubric for Group Projects* (**Assessment Program,** p. 10)
- *Scoring Rubric for Presentations* (**Assessment Program,** p. 11)

Portfolio Assessment

Student-selected items may include:

- *Link to Language Arts—Write a Journal Entry* (**Teacher's Edition,** p. 386)
- *Practice and Apply* (**Activity Book,** p. 77)
- *Home Involvement* (**Teacher's Edition,** p. 341)
- *A Guide to My Social Studies Portfolio* (**Assessment Program,** p. 12)

Teacher-selected items may include:

- *Unit Assessment* (**Assessment Program,** pp. 103–109)
- *Individual End-of-Unit Checklist* (**Assessment Program,** p. 8)
- *Social Studies Portfolio Summary* (**Assessment Program,** p. 13)
- *Portfolio Family Response* (**Assessment Program,** p. 14)

Objectives

Chapter 11

- Explain how Daniel Boone was able to reach Kentucky. (p. 349)
- Summarize the effects of Daniel Boone's determination to settle Kentucky. (p. 349)
- Analyze the cooperation of pioneers in overcoming problems they faced. (p. 349)
- Explain how President Jefferson was able to buy Louisiana. (p. 353)
- Analyze the accomplishments of the Lewis and Clark expedition. (p. 353)
- Evaluate the importance of Zebulon Pike's expedition. (p. 353)
- Describe Tecumseh's plan for the Indian tribes. (p. 358)
- Explore the actions that led to the Battle of Tippecanoe. (p. 358)
- Summarize the events that led to the War of 1812. (p. 358)
- Evaluate the American victory over the British on Lake Erie. (p. 358)
- Describe the British attack on Washington, D.C., and the American victory at New Orleans. (p. 358)
- Describe the United States after the War of 1812. (p. 358)
- Identify a method of predicting likely outcomes. (p. 363)
- Practice making predictions about historical trends. (p. 363)
- Compare and contrast the British and American efforts in the conflict over Fort McHenry. (p. 364)
- Analyze the defense the Americans put up during the conflict. (p. 364)
- Explain how Francis Scott Key came to write the words to "The Star-Spangled Banner," our national anthem. (p. 364)

Chapter 12

- Identify the technology Slater brought to the United States. (p. 373)
- Evaluate the advantages of using mass production. (p. 373)
- Describe how factory work had changed by the 1840s. (p. 373)
- Analyze the advantages brought about by the Erie Canal. (p. 373)
- Explain why the National Road was built. (p. 373)
- Investigate improvements in long-distance transportation. (p. 373)
- Explain how a change in voting practices helped Andrew Jackson become President. (p. 379)
- Analyze how sectionalism threatened the interdependence between the different regions of the United States. (p. 379)
- Evaluate the government's actions in removing the Cherokees from their native lands. (p. 379)
- Describe the conflict between American settlers in Texas and the Mexican government. (p. 383)
- Summarize how Texas became an independent republic. (p. 383)
- Analyze why people settled the Oregon Country. (p. 383)
- Explore the role of cooperation in the settlement of Utah by the Mormons. (p. 383)
- Summarize the results of the conflict with Mexico. (p. 383)
- Describe the California gold rush. (p. 383)
- Interpret and compare map symbols on relief and elevation maps. (p. 390)
- Trace the route of the Oregon Trail. (p. 390)
- Analyze Horace Mann's efforts to improve the nation's schools. (p. 392)
- Evaluate the work of the abolitionists. (p. 392)
- Describe the movement to secure greater rights for women. (p. 392)
- Interpret information in a double-bar graph. (p. 397)
- Analyze population trends in the 1800s. (p. 397)

STANDARD TEST

NAME ______________________ DATE ____________

Unit 6 Test

Part One: Test Your Understanding *(4 points each)*

DIRECTIONS: ***Circle the letter of the best answer.***

1. Who led American settlers across the Appalachian Mountains into Kentucky?
A. Meriwether Lewis **B.** Zebulon Pike
C. William Clark **(D.)** Daniel Boone

2. Which of the following doubled the size of the United States?
A. the Monroe Doctrine **(B.)** the Louisiana Purchase
C. the War of 1812 **D.** the Erie Canal

3. Which of the following people was responsible for American traders' carrying out an economic invasion of New Mexico?
(A.) Zebulon Pike **B.** Stephen F. Austin
C. Brigham Young **D.** Sam Houston

4. As a result of the War of 1812,
A. France established new colonies in North America.
(B.) a wave of nationalism swept the United States.
C. Spain was added to the United States.
D. the Americans defeated the British at the Battle of Washington, D.C.

5. The term *mass production* refers to
A. hiring many people to work in factories.
B. transporting goods, products, and people by water.
C. making parts by hand.
(D.) producing large amounts of goods at one time.

6. When the Erie Canal was finished, traders could transport goods by water from New York City to
(A.) the Great Lakes. **B.** the Hudson River.
C. the Mississippi River. **D.** the Ohio River valley.

7. Horace Mann was a leader in the movement for
A. women's rights. **B.** manifest destiny.
(C.) public schools. **D.** mass production.

(continued)

UNIT 6 TEST Assessment Program 103

STANDARD TEST

NAME ______________________ DATE __________

DIRECTIONS: ***Match the description on the left with the correct name on the right. Write the correct letter in the space provided.***

8. <u>C</u> the name for the pass through the Appalachian Mountains into Kentucky

9. <u>E</u> the person who brought the plans for a spinning machine to the United States

10. <u>G</u> the Shoshone woman who acted as a translator for the Lewis and Clark expedition

11. <u>F</u> the abolitionist speaker who was a runaway slave

12. <u>A</u> the person who invented the first steam-powered boat

13. <u>D</u> the person who established a colony of Americans in Texas

14. <u>B</u> the American President who ignored the Supreme Court's ruling about the protection of the Cherokees

A. Robert Fulton
B. Andrew Jackson
C. Cumberland Gap
D. Stephen F. Austin
E. Samuel Slater
F. Frederick Douglass
G. Sacagawea

(continued)

STANDARD TEST

NAME ______________________ DATE __________

Part Two: Test Your Skills *(20 points)*

DIRECTIONS: ***Use the information in the maps below to answer the questions.***

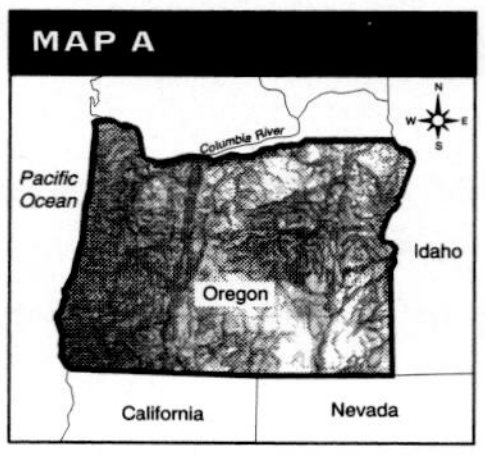

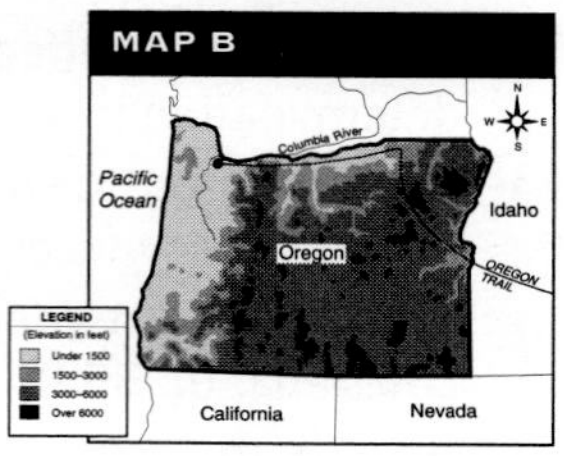

15. What physical feature did the people using the Oregon Trail want to avoid?
They wanted to stay away from mountains.

16. Across what type of land did the people using the Oregon Trail hope to travel?
They wanted to travel across flat land.

17. What is the highest elevation crossed by the Oregon Trail in Oregon? What is the lowest elevation? The highest elevation is between 3,000 and 6,000 feet. The lowest elevation is less than 1,500 feet.

18. Why did the Oregon Trail not go straight across Oregon to the Pacific Ocean?
There are two mountain ranges people would have to go over if the trail went directly across Oregon.

(continued)

STANDARD TEST

NAME ______________________ DATE __________

Part Three: Apply What You Have Learned

DIRECTIONS: ***Complete each of the following activities.***

19. ***Label the Map*** *(14 points)*
Use the map below to locate each of the items that follow. Show the location of each item by writing its letter on the map.

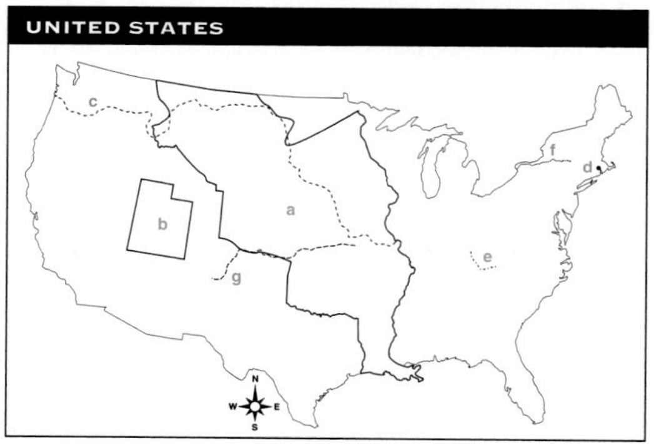

a. the area purchased from France by Thomas Jefferson in 1803
b. the place where Brigham Young and the Mormons settled
c. the path taken by Lewis and Clark
d. the location of Samuel Slater's textile mill
e. the Wilderness Road
f. the Erie Canal
g. the Santa Fe Trail

(continued)

STANDARD TEST

NAME ______________________ DATE __________

21. ***Essay*** *(10 points)*
In the early 1800s, there were several conflicts between the United States and Britain that led to the War of 1812. Write a paragraph describing one of those conflicts.

Possible response: One conflict between the United States and Britain concerned the Indian attacks that occurred after the Battle of Tippecanoe. Many people blamed the attacks on Britain, claiming that the British were giving guns to the Indians and talking against American settlers. Another conflict concerned the British practice of impressment. The British took American sailors off their ships and put them to work on British ships to stop Americans from trading with the French and other Europeans. The British practice of stopping American ships angered many Americans, who called on the U.S. government to declare war on Britain.

PERFORMANCE TASK

NAME ______________________ DATE __________

Individual Performance Task

Life on the Road

During the nineteenth century many people moved west from where they were living in the United States to start all over in a new place with new opportunities. In this activity you will create a diary for a person who moved west with his or her family.

Step 1 Select one of the following events as the basis for your diary:
- traveling with Daniel Boone to Kentucky
- traveling with Marcus and Narcissa Whitman to the Oregon Country
- traveling with Brigham Young to Utah

Step 2 Use a blank outline map of the United States to draw the route taken by the group you have chosen.

Step 3 Use your textbook and library resources to research the actions of your group.

Step 4 Write at least five diary entries for different events on different days and locations of the journey. Mention who is with you, the geography of the area you are passing through (landforms, vegetation, climate, and wildlife), and some of the events and activities of your daily life. You should be as creative as you can but remain historically accurate.

Step 5 Make a cover for your diary, and share the diary with your classmates.

108 Assessment Program UNIT 6

PERFORMANCE TASK

NAME ______________________ DATE __________

Group Performance Task

Traveling West

A mobile is a piece of sculpture that hangs balanced in midair. Air currents cause the mobile to move. In this task your group will make a mobile that shows the paths taken by certain groups of settlers as they moved west.

Step 1 You will work in a group of at least five students.

Step 2 Your group should select one of the following:
- Daniel Boone and settlers going through the Cumberland Gap into Kentucky
- Brigham Young and the Mormons going to Utah
- the forty-niners heading for the California gold mines
- travelers along the Erie Canal
- Lewis and Clark exploring the lands of the Louisiana Purchase
- Marcus and Narcissa Whitman going to the Oregon Country
- travelers along the National Road
- Stephen F. Austin going to Texas to set up a colony

Step 3 Make a map showing the route of the group of settlers chosen. Draw a picture that shows some event or location connected with that group. Each member of your group should show a different scene.

Step 4 Paste your map and picture on both sides of a single sheet of construction paper.

Step 5 Use a coat hanger and string to create a mobile. Properly balance each person's artwork so that the mobile will move when it is hit by an air current. Hang the mobiles where others in the school can see them.

UNIT 6 Assessment Program 109

Rubrics

SCORING RUBRICS The scoring rubrics for evaluating individual projects, group projects, and students' presentations may be found in the **Assessment Program,** pages 9–11.

CRITERIA The criteria listed below may be used when looking for evidence of the students' understanding of social studies content and ability to think critically.

Individual Task

Life on the Road

- Use appropriate reference materials to reconstruct the route taken by Daniel Boone, Marcus and Narcissa Whitman, or Brigham Young.
- Demonstrate an understanding of the geography and living conditions experienced by settlers traveling west in the early 1800s.

Group Task

Traveling West

- Use appropriate reference materials to create maps of the routes taken by selected early settlers.
- Create a historically accurate picture or graphic representation of a location or an event that is associated with one of the selected early settlers.

REMINDER

You may wish to preview the performance assessment activities in the COOPERATIVE LEARNING WORKSHOP on page 405. Students may complete these activities during the course of the unit.

Introduce the Unit

Personal Response

Discuss with students what they already know about the westward movement. Ask them to consider what might motivate them to move to a different region from the one they are living in today. Also ask them to infer what might have happened to American Indians as European settlers continued to move west. Use this discussion as an opportunity to identify misconceptions or conflicting understandings.

Link Prior Learning

Use the titles on the bar across the top of pages 340–341 to review the chronology of earlier units. Then discuss the illustration.

Q. **What does the picture tell you about the unit you will be studying?** It will concern the expansion of the United States and the movement of people westward.

Our Nation Grows

Activity Choices

Background

THE LARGE PICTURE
The large picture shows a painting by Albert Bierstadt titled *Emigrants Crossing the Plains,* completed in 1867. Bierstadt was born in Solingen, Germany, in 1830. His parents immigrated to the United States when he was a baby. Between the ages of 23 and 27, Bierstadt studied painting in Germany. When he saw the magnificence of the American West in 1858, he began making sketches of it. Later he used his sketches to create panoramic paintings of the western mountains.

AUDIO

Use the UNIT 6 TEXT ON TAPE AUDIOCASSETTE for a reading of this unit.

HOME LETTER

Use the UNIT 6 HOME LETTER. See Teacher's Edition pp. HL11–12.

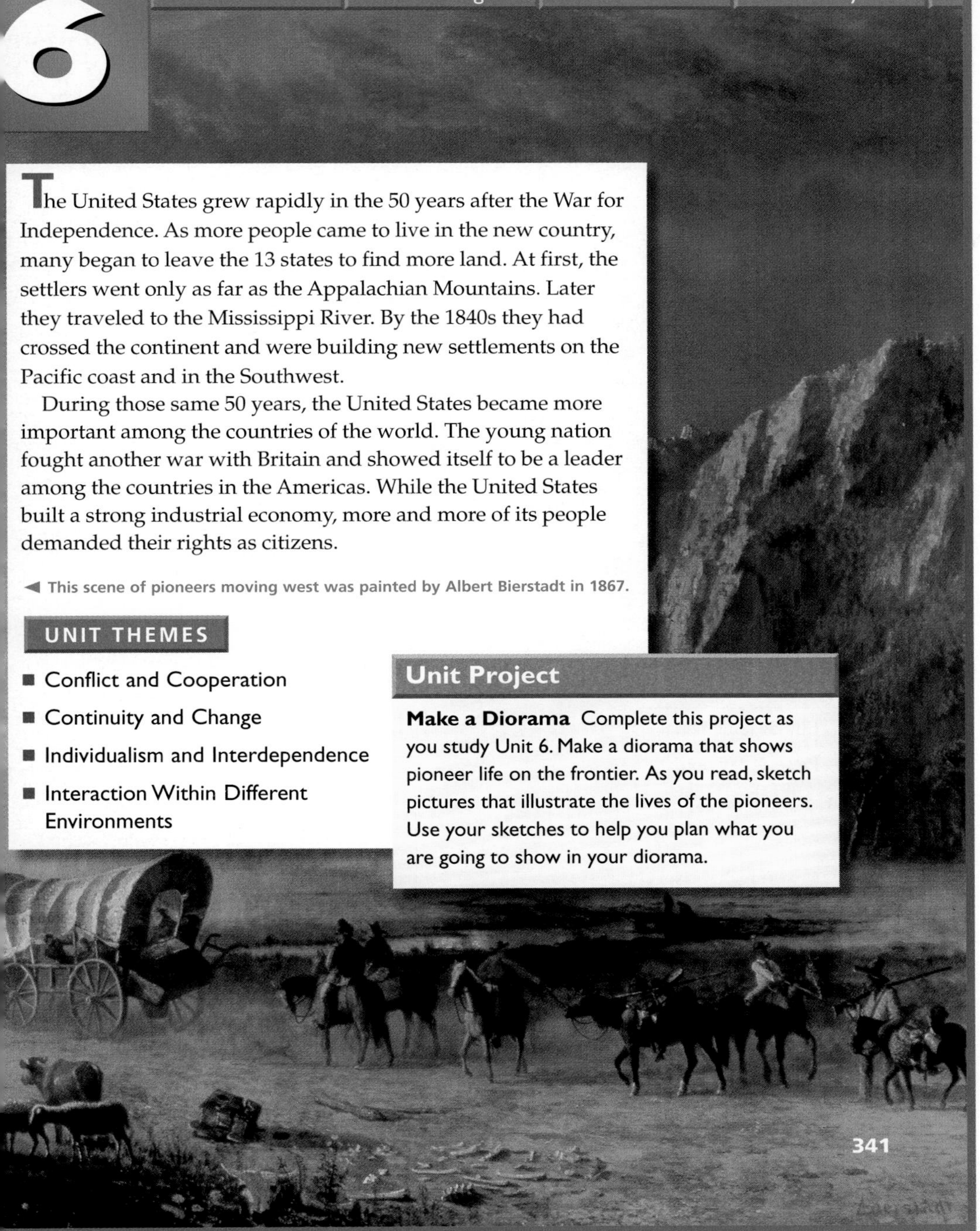

The United States grew rapidly in the 50 years after the War for Independence. As more people came to live in the new country, many began to leave the 13 states to find more land. At first, the settlers went only as far as the Appalachian Mountains. Later they traveled to the Mississippi River. By the 1840s they had crossed the continent and were building new settlements on the Pacific coast and in the Southwest.

During those same 50 years, the United States became more important among the countries of the world. The young nation fought another war with Britain and showed itself to be a leader among the countries in the Americas. While the United States built a strong industrial economy, more and more of its people demanded their rights as citizens.

◀ This scene of pioneers moving west was painted by Albert Bierstadt in 1867.

UNIT THEMES

- Conflict and Cooperation
- Continuity and Change
- Individualism and Interdependence
- Interaction Within Different Environments

Unit Project

Make a Diorama Complete this project as you study Unit 6. Make a diorama that shows pioneer life on the frontier. As you read, sketch pictures that illustrate the lives of the pioneers. Use your sketches to help you plan what you are going to show in your diorama.

Home Involvement

Ask students to look into their own family histories to discover whether they are descendants of early settlers who moved westward to claim new areas of what is today the United States. Some students may discover that their ancestors were Indians. Other students may discover that their ancestors came to the United States from Europe. Have volunteers share family histories related to the events in this unit.

Options for Reading

Read Aloud Read each lesson aloud as students follow along in their books. Strategies for guiding students through working with text and visuals are provided with each lesson.

Read Together Have pairs or small groups of students read the lesson by taking turns reading each page or paragraph aloud. Encourage students to use the new vocabulary words as they discuss what they read.

Read Alone Strong readers may wish to read the lessons independently before you read or discuss each lesson with the class.

Read the Introduction

Ask students to read the unit introduction on page 341.

Q. **How did the United States change in the years after the War for Independence?** The population grew, many people headed to new lands in the West, and the United States became a more important country in the world.

In what ways do you think people lived better lives after the war? For most people the country was more democratic, and the growth of industry provided goods they had never had before.

Unit Themes

Discuss with students the Unit Themes. Throughout the study of this unit, ask for volunteers to identify the events, maps, illustrations, and pictures that represent each of these themes.

Unit Project Start-Up

Before students begin their Unit Projects, ask them to look over the Unit Preview on pages 342–343. Challenge them to imagine what life must have been like on the frontier. Suggest that they try to put themselves in the role of a pioneer and speculate on the kinds of adventures pioneers experienced. As the unit progresses, have students complete their dioramas.

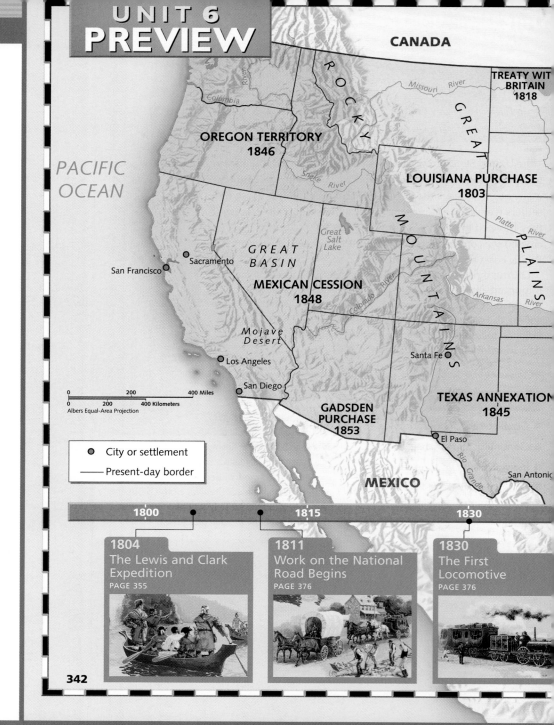

PREVIEW THE UNIT

Link Prior Learning

Have students discuss what they have learned in previous units about the United States and its newly formed government. Then ask students to tell what they know about the westward expansion and growth of the United States.

Understanding the Map

This map shows the United States and the land west of the original 13 states from 1783 to 1853. Ask students to identify the cities and settlements shown on the map, as well as landforms such as mountains and bodies of water. Help students distinguish between the different landforms.

Q. **Where are the Great Lakes located?** on the border of Canada and the United States

What landform is at the western edge of the Great Plains? the Rocky Mountains

1800 — 1815 — 1830

1804 The Lewis and Clark Expedition
PAGE 355

1811 Work on the National Road Begins
PAGE 376

1830 The First Locomotive
PAGE 376

342

ACTIVITY CHOICES

VIDEO

VIDEO EXPERIENCES: SOCIAL STUDIES *How Blue Jeans Became a Business*
See the video guide for additional enrichment material.

TECHNOLOGY

Use TIMELINER™ DATA DISKS to construct a time line of events in this unit.

Link to Art

MAKE A DISPLAY Have students find pictures of parts of the country that illustrate its different landforms. Students should describe their pictures and then display them on a bulletin board. Students can write captions for their pictures.

Meet Individual Needs

ENGLISH LANGUAGE LEARNERS Have students work in pairs and use the map of the United States on pages 342–343. One partner should call out names on the map. The other partner should point to the location on the map and describe it. Partners can switch roles.

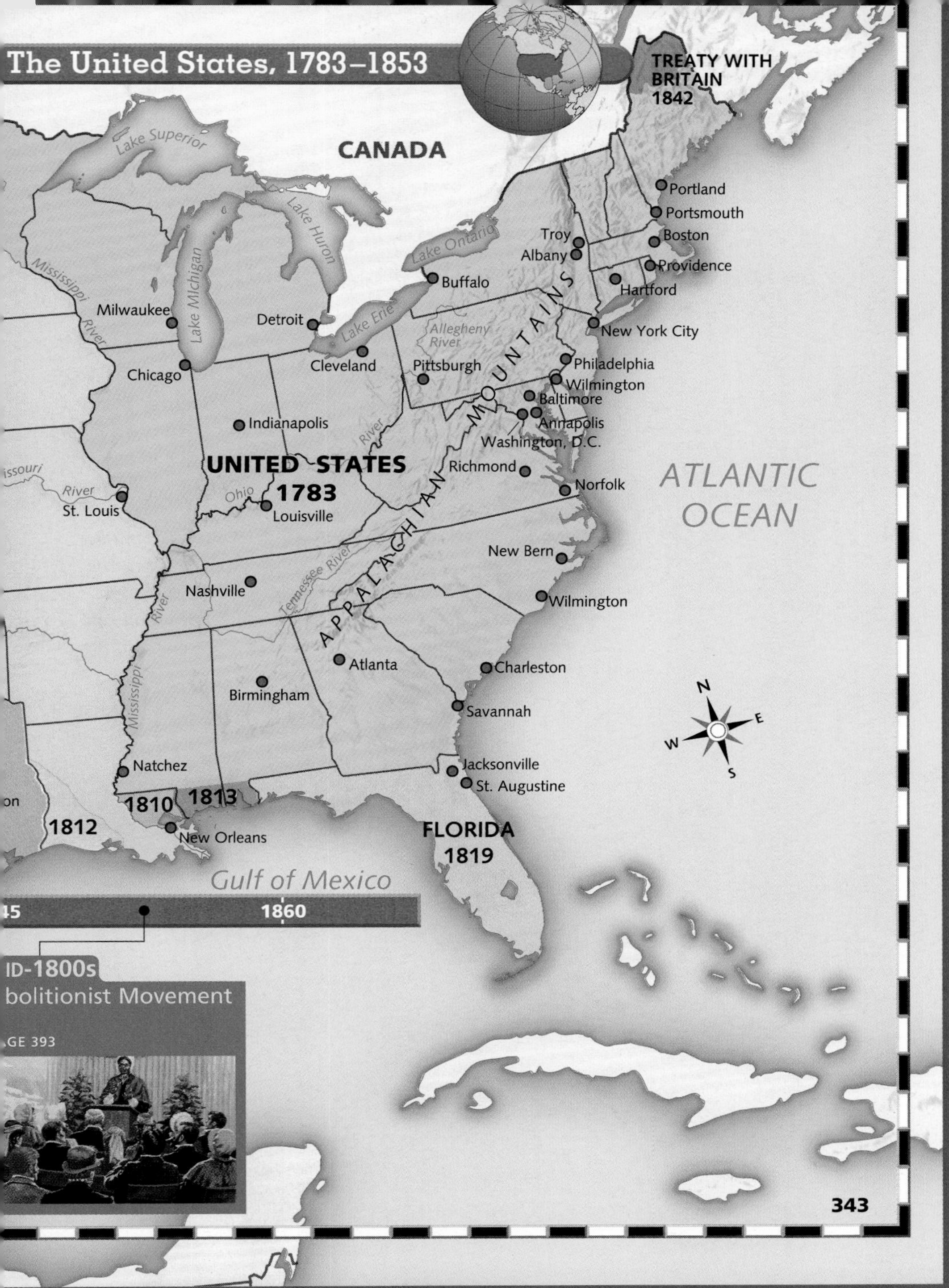

Understanding the Time Line

Explain to students that the time line shows people, places, and events related to the westward movement and expansion of the United States. Explain that in this unit students will learn about how the United States grew.

Q. **What can you tell about each event by looking at the time line?** Explorers traveled to unknown lands and helped the United States grow. People began work on the National Road. The first locomotive was built. People spoke out against issues they believed were wrong.

How many years does the time line cover? 60 years

Look Ahead to the Unit

Students may wish to preview the chapters, lessons, and illustrations in the unit to get a sense of the 75-year period immediately following the War for Independence.

Challenge students to predict what they will learn about in the unit. Record their predictions. As the unit progresses, refer to the predictions and have students revise them as needed.

Meet Individual Needs

ADVANCED LEARNERS
Interested students can select one of the rivers shown on the map and find information about it, such as length, uses, source, location of mouth, and any other information. Students selecting different rivers can then combine their information to create a river chart to share with the class.

Background

THE TIME LINE In May of 1804 the Corps of Discovery, led by Lewis and Clark, set out to explore the Louisiana Purchase.

In 1811 work on the National Road began. The road stretched from Maryland to Pennsylvania and on to present-day West Virginia.

Peter Cooper built the first locomotive in 1830 for the Baltimore and Ohio Railroad.

Abolitionists worked to end slavery during the mid-1800s.

These events are also shown in the Visual Summary on pages 402–403 in the Pupil Book.

UNIT POSTER

Use the UNIT 6 VISUAL SUMMARY POSTER to preview the unit.

Set the Scene with Literature

Prereading Strategies

Personal Response

Ask volunteers to share with the class experiences they may have had that made them happy or sad or a little of both. Explain that they will read about the experiences and feelings a young pioneer girl had when she moved to the West with her family.

Set the Purpose

The selection from *Cassie's Journey: Going West in the 1860s* by Brett Harvey tells the story of a family moving west in a wagon train in the 1860s. As students read pages 344–347, ask them to think about the hardships Cassie and her family experience while traveling in their covered wagon and tell why they think the selection ends on a positive note.

Read & Respond

Auditory Learning

Read to Set the Scene Read the introduction aloud or have a volunteer do so. Ask the class to listen for the places people who settled the West came from. Then have students predict what the story will be about.

Understanding the Story

Select a volunteer to read the first paragraph aloud, stressing that the student should read with expression to show Cassie's feelings. Tell students to picture the scene in their minds. Discuss Cassie's feelings, and have students express how they would feel if they were traveling on a wagon train.

Q. **Why do you think the mother is drilling the children in multiplication?** to take their minds off the ride; to give them something else to think about

Set the Scene with Literature

CASSIE'S JOURNEY

by Brett Harvey
illustrated by Ed Martinez

The people who settled the West came from many different places. Most came from the first 13 states, but some came from as far away as Europe and Asia. Almost everyone had read about the American West in newspapers, magazines, books, or letters. Many had heard about it in songs.

The West promised a new life to people like Cassie and her family, whom you will meet in this story. But getting to the West to enjoy its benefits was not easy. People traveling in wagon trains faced long, hard journeys. Sometimes food ran out, or water or firewood could not be found. People moving to the West faced these problems and more.

344

Activity Choices

Background

THE LITERATURE SELECTION *Cassie's Journey: Going West in the 1860s* by Brett Harvey is based on the diaries of female pioneers. The book describes Cassie's feelings about leaving her home in Illinois, her experiences on the journey, and the friend she found.

THE AUTHOR Brett Harvey is a native New Yorker who has written several books about pioneers. She became interested in this subject through her grandmother, who wrote about her childhood journey to the Dakotas. Harvey comes from a family of book people. Her grandmother, whom she never met, became a children's book illustrator, and her mother was a cookbook writer.

It's been raining for two days and everything is wet, wet, wet—our clothes, our bedding, even our food. Last night the rain was so heavy and the wind was blowing so hard that we couldn't make a fire. We had cold coffee and soggy bread for supper. This morning Mama cooked our breakfast under an umbrella. Today it's raining in sheets of gray so we have to stay in the wagon with the flaps tied down tight. I hate riding in the wagon—its swaying motion and the screeching noise of the wheels make me feel seasick. Mama is drilling us in our multiplication tables. I wonder if we'll ever be dry again.

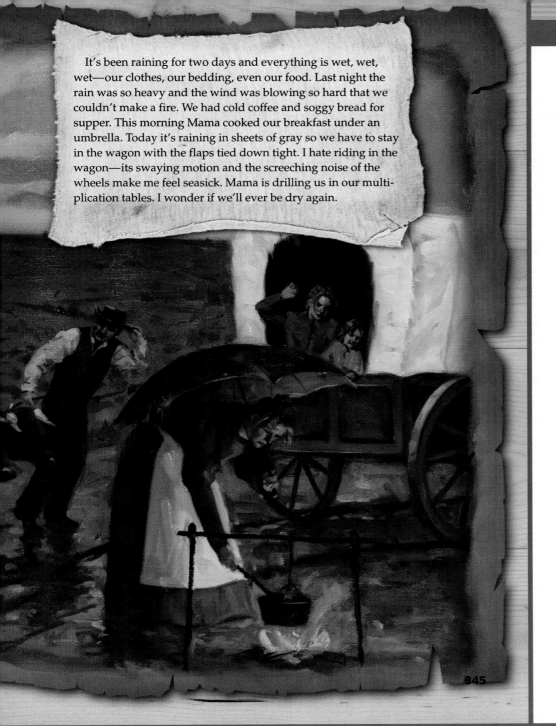

Auditory Learning

Read Dramatically You may wish to have different student volunteers read each paragraph of the story to the class. Remind students to read with expression as appropriate to the lines they are reading.

Understanding the Story

Discuss the change that has occurred from wet to dry. Help students focus on the change of climates and landforms as Cassie and her family travel farther west. Then discuss water pollution, and explore why it is necessary for the health of the environment and for the needs of people to keep rivers and lakes clean.

Geography

Location Have students look at a map of North America and identify the path of the Platte River.

Q. **In which present-day states is the Platte River located?** Nebraska, Iowa, and Missouri

Meet Individual Needs

ENGLISH LANGUAGE LEARNERS Have students add unfamiliar words or phrases to their vocabulary notebooks. Suggest students include synonyms and definitions of the words or phrases. Have them write each word or phrase in a sentence that will help them remember the meaning.

Link to Art

ILLUSTRATE THE STORY Invite students to work in groups of five. Challenge each student to choose one paragraph from the story and to draw an illustration of what is described. Then combine students' illustrations to show the entire story. Each group can share its illustrations with other groups and explain which event is shown.

Understanding the Story

Cassie describes the graves they see along the way. Make sure students understand the hardships and dangers these travelers had to face.

Kinesthetic Learning

Trace a Route Have volunteers use a large wall map to trace with their finger possible routes that Cassie's family might have taken to the West. Although the specific destination is not mentioned in the selection, tell students to assume it is Oregon. Have them use the geographic features mentioned in the selection (such as the Platte River) as a guide in plotting their routes.

Economics

Interdependence and Income Ask students to describe Cassie's first encounter with the Indians. Then discuss the idea of interdependence. Remind students that when people cannot provide for all their own needs, they often trade goods and services with others.

Q. **Why did the settlers trade with the Indians?** to get food and moccasins

Now we are dry as dust and hard as bones and all we think about is water. We are following along the Platte River, and sometimes I want to throw myself in and drink it all up. But the Platte has a bad taste, and Mama warned us not to drink it because people are getting sick and dying from the water. Papa says Platte means "flat," and that the Platte is "too thin to plow, too thick to drink, and too muddy to bathe in." We still have plenty of water in our rain barrel, but Papa says it has to last us a long time. We can only have two cups a day. Even the wheels of our wagon will dry out if we don't take them off every night and soak them in the river. There are mosquitoes, too—so many they even got in the bread dough and turned it gray. Plato and I wouldn't eat it at first, but then we got so hungry we had to.

On this trip we see many, many graves—some of them are no more than wooden crosses with signs on them stuck in the dirt. Alice and I have been counting and so far, we've seen thirty-one.

ACTIVITY CHOICES

Meet Individual Needs

ADVANCED LEARNERS Have interested students find out more about Oregon as it was during the 1860s. Suggest that they use library and Internet resources to find information. Ask them to describe the area and the people who moved and settled there and to give examples of the hardships these people may have faced.

We always read the signs and think about the people who died. Especially the children. One said "Here lies Eliza Harris. Born July 7 1840, died July 1 1843 from falling out of her family's wagon." Another sign said "Here lize our onlee son, John Hanna, bit by a snake at 7 years of age." There are so many dangers on this journey. It makes me shiver to think of all the narrow escapes we've already had, and we're not yet near the end of our journey.

Today we saw our first Indians! We're camped on the Sweetwater River at South Pass [in Wyoming] now—it's called that because the easiest place to pass through the Rocky Mountains is in the south. When the Indians first came into camp at sunset, we were all frightened because they looked so strange. They wore soft animal skins with beads and feathers sewn onto them. But they let us know they didn't mean to hurt us, only to trade with us. We gave them calico cloth and bread in return for moccasins and buffalo meat. I hate buffalo meat because it's too chewy.

Today when I was riding up with Papa, we came 'round a mountain and suddenly, spread out far below us, was a soft green valley, like a velvety carpet with little hills under it. Papa says that's where we're going. We still have to go down the other side of these terrible mountains, and Papa says we have yet another river to cross. But now I can close my eyes and see a picture of that green valley, and imagine Aunt Rose and her family waiting for us in a little house with windows and doors that sits still on the ground and doesn't go anywhere.

Now I know we're going to get there!

Geography

Location Have students look at a map and identify the river and mountains Cassie and her family still need to cross to reach their destination. While the selection doesn't tell this information, students can assume it is the Columbia River and the Cascade Range.

Q. **Why do mountains and rivers pose a threat to travelers?** They are hard to cross, and they slow travelers down.

Summarize the Literature

Stress to students that cooperation was essential for families like Cassie's if they were to survive the long, dangerous journey to the West. Families had to ration food and water to make them last, as well as battle the elements and the difficult terrain. Conflict with the Indians through whose lands they passed was always a possibility. Despite these problems, Cassie's family always kept its goal in sight.

Link Literature

There is a variety of literature available related to the westward movement and the rise of industry. All students in the class should enjoy reading *Cassie's Journey: Going West in the 1860s.* The following are other selections that can be used during the course of this unit with students of differing reading abilities. In addition to these titles, you may wish to suggest some of the books listed in the Multimedia Resource Center on page 340D of this Teacher's Edition.

EASY
The Bobbin Girl **by Emily Arnold McCully. Dial, 1996.**

AVERAGE
They Shall Be Heard: Susan B. Anthony and Elizabeth Cady Stanton **by Kate Connell. Steck-Vaughn, 1993.**

CHALLENGING
A Pioneer Woman's Memoir **by Judith E. Greenberg and Helen Carey McKeever. Franklin Watts, 1995.**

CHAPTER 11

Planning Chart

	THEMES • Strands	VOCABULARY	MEET INDIVIDUAL NEEDS	RESOURCES INCLUDING ▶ TECHNOLOGY
LESSON 1 **Across the Appalachians** pp. 349–352	**INDIVIDUALISM & INTERDEPENDENCE** • Culture • Geography • History	pioneer	Advanced Learners, p. 351 Extend and Enrich, p. 351 Reteach the Main Idea, p. 352	Activity Book, p. 66 ▶ THE AMAZING WRITING MACHINE
LESSON 2 **The Louisiana Purchase** pp. 353–357	**INTERACTION WITHIN DIFFERENT ENVIRONMENTS** • Geography • Economics • Culture • History	purchase pathfinder	Advanced Learners, p. 355 Extend and Enrich, p. 356 Reteach the Main Idea, p. 357	Activity Book, p. 67 ▶ THE AMAZING WRITING MACHINE
LESSON 3 **A Second War with Britain** pp. 358–362	**CONFLICT & COOPERATION** • Geography • History • Civics and Government	impressment nationalism annex doctrine	Extend and Enrich, p. 361 Reteach the Main Idea, p. 362	Activity Book, p. 68 ▶ THE AMAZING WRITING MACHINE
SKILL **Predict a Likely Outcome** p. 363	**BUILDING CITIZENSHIP** • Critical Thinking Skills	prediction	Reteach the Skill, p. 363	Activity Book, p. 69 Transparency 29
LESSON 4 **Learn History Through Literature** **By the Dawn's Early Light: The Story of The Star-Spangled Banner** by Steven Kroll illustrated by Dan Andreasen pp. 364–369	**CONFLICT & COOPERATION** • Geography • Culture • History • Civics and Government		Auditory Learners, p. 366 English Language Learners, p. 367 Extend and Enrich, p. 368 Reteach the Main Idea, p. 369	Activity Book, p. 70 Music Audiocassette
CHAPTER REVIEW pp. 370–371				Activity Book, p. 71 Transparency 30 Assessment Program Chapter 11 Test, pp. 95–98 ▶ THE AMAZING WRITING MACHINE ▶ TIMELINER ▶ INTERNET

7 DAYS

TIME MANAGEMENT

DAY 1	DAY 2	DAY 3	DAY 4	DAY 5	DAY 6	DAY 7
Lesson 1	Lesson 2	Lesson 3	Skill	Lesson 4	Chapter Review	Chapter Test

Activity Book

LESSON 1
Identify Historical Figures

NAME ________________________ DATE ____________

BLAZING A TRAIL WEST

Identify Historical Figures

DIRECTIONS: On the blanks provided, write the word or name that best completes each sentence. Some letters in your answers will have numbers under them. Write these letters in the appropriate boxes below, and you will find the name of Daniel Boone's wife.

1. After the Revolutionary War, the land between the Appalachian Mountains and the Mississippi River was called the American F R O N T I E R (1).
2. Settlers west of the Appalachians were called P I O N E E R S (12).
3. Daniel Boone came to love the woods and hunting after his family moved to the Y A D K I N (10) V A L L E Y (11) of North Carolina.
4. A man named J O H N F I N L E Y (4) told Boone stories about land far to the west over the Appalachian Mountains.
5. After the French and Indian War, Boone set out to find an Indian trail called the W A R R I O R ' S (9) P A T H.
6. Boone told about the rich land and buffalo in K E N T U C K Y (6).
7. Both the C H E R O K E E S (5, 2) and Shawnees lived in settlements throughout Kentucky.
8. Boone cleared a path through the Cumberland Gap that came to be known as the W I L D E R N E S S R O A D (7).
9. Boone built a fort in this wilderness and named the new pioneer settlement B O O N E S B O R O U G H (8, 3).

R	E	B	E	C	C	A		B	R	Y	A	N
1	2	3	4	5	6	7		8	9	10	11	12

Use after reading Chapter 11, Lesson 1, pages 349–352.

LESSON 2
Identify Historical Figures

NAME ________________________ DATE ____________

Follow their Footsteps

Identify Historical Figures

DIRECTIONS: Each of the footprints below contains a paragraph that could have been written by one of the people involved with the Lewis and Clark expedition. Write the name of that person in the space provided.

One of my greatest accomplishments was the Louisiana Purchase. I asked the members of the Corps of Discovery to learn all they could about this unexplored land.
Thomas Jefferson

As chief of the Shoshones, I welcomed the members of the Corps of Discovery. I was especially happy to see my sister. To help Lewis and Clark make their way over the Rockies, I gave them horses.
Chief Cameahwait

I was William Clark's slave. My skills in hunting and fishing made a valuable contribution to this exciting and informative expedition.
York

The leader of the expedition was my good friend. He chose me to go on the expedition because of my skills in mapmaking. We called our group of explorers the Corps of Discovery.
William Clark

I was a Shoshone. The members of the expedition asked me to go with them to translate when they reached my tribe's lands. I agreed to go.
Sacagawea

After working as an army officer in the wilderness of the Northwest Territory, I led the expedition to explore the lands of the Louisiana Purchase. I kept a journal of our experiences.
Meriwether Lewis

Use after reading Chapter 11, Lesson 2, pages 353–357.

LESSON 3
Understand Cause and Effect

NAME ________________________ DATE ____________

The Growth of NATIONALISM

Understand Cause and Effect

DIRECTIONS: Complete the following chart. Fill in either the cause or the effect.
Accept all reasonable answers. Use the following completed chart as a guide.

CAUSES	EFFECTS
Harrison sends 1,000 soldiers to Prophetstown, the Shawnee headquarters. Tenskwatawa orders the Indians to attack first.	The Americans and the Indians fight in the Battle of Tippecanoe.
Many people in the Northwest Territory blame Britain for Indian attacks. People in the South are angry about impressment of American sailors and stopping of trade. War Hawks are eager for more land.	War fever pushes Congress to declare war on Britain in 1812.
American Captain Oliver Hazard Perry defeats the British in a battle on Lake Erie on September 10, 1813.	British control on the Great Lakes is weakened. Harrison moves soldiers into Canada.
The War of 1812 ends.	A wave of nationalism sweeps the country.
President Monroe wants to stop the growth of Spanish, French, and British colonies in the Americas.	President Monroe announces the Monroe Doctrine.

Use after reading Chapter 11, Lesson 3, pages 358–362.

SKILL PRACTICE
Apply Critical Thinking Skills

NAME ________________________ DATE ____________

HOW TO PREDICT A LIKELY OUTCOME

Apply Critical Thinking Skills

DIRECTIONS: The following flow chart lists the steps for predicting likely outcomes. Choose a class event, such as a test, that you expect to happen soon. Copy the flow chart onto another sheet of paper and use the steps to predict the outcome of the event.

Accept all reasonable predictions that students can substantiate.

- THINK ABOUT WHAT YOU KNOW.
- MAKE A PREDICTION.
- READ OR GATHER MORE INFORMATION.
- ASK YOURSELF SOME QUESTIONS:
  Does the new information support my prediction?
  Do I need to change my prediction?
- DECIDE IF YOUR PREDICTION SEEMS CORRECT.
- GO THROUGH THE STEPS AGAIN, IF NECESSARY.

Use after reading Chapter 11, Skill Lesson, page 363.

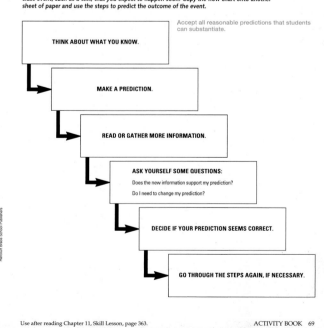

LESSON 4
Understand Patriotic Symbols

NAME ____________________ DATE __________

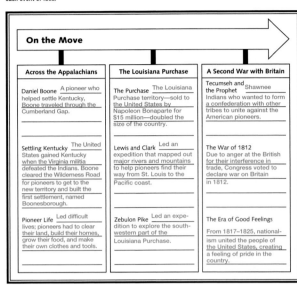

The Flag *was still there*

After the British attack on Fort McHenry, Francis Scott Key peered through the early dawn and saw that the American flag still flew over the fort. He wrote the words to "The Star-Spangled Banner," our national anthem, to honor this national symbol.

Understand Patriotic Symbols

DIRECTIONS: Read the statements below. Decide which statements tell how to respect and care for the flag and which statements give general information about the flag. Then place an X in the appropriate column.

THE FLAG	RESPECT/ CARE	GENERAL INFORMATION
1. The present flag has 64 separate elements.		X
2. The flag has the exact shades of blue and red, which are numbers 70075 and 70180 in the *Standard Color Card of America.*		X
3. The flag is to be flown at half-mast as a mark of respect after the death of a major official.	X	
4. The present flag dates back to July 4, 1960, when the fiftieth star was added for Hawaii.		X
5. The flag is taken down in bad weather.	X	
6. The flag is never to be allowed to touch anything beneath it, such as the ground, the floor, or water.	X	
7. The United States flag is called the "Stars and Stripes."		X
8. The flag that Key wrote about had 15 stars and 15 stripes.		X
9. Congress passed a law in 1818 requiring that the flag have 13 stripes to represent the original 13 colonies.		X
10. The flag is to be displayed during school days in or near every school.	X	

 Use after reading Chapter 11, Lesson 4, pages 364–369.

CHAPTER 11 REVIEW
Connect Main Ideas

NAME ____________________ DATE __________

ON THE MOVE

Connect Main Ideas

DIRECTIONS: Use this organizer to show how the chapter's main ideas are connected. Write one or two sentences to tell about each person or pair of people or to summarize each event or idea.

On the Move

Across the Appalachians	The Louisiana Purchase	A Second War with Britain
Daniel Boone: A pioneer who helped settle Kentucky, Boone traveled through the Cumberland Gap.	The Purchase: The Louisiana Purchase territory—sold to the United States by Napoleon Bonaparte for $15 million—doubled the size of the country.	Tecumseh and the Prophet: Shawnee Indians who wanted to form a confederation with other tribes to unite against the American pioneers.
Settling Kentucky: The United States gained Kentucky when the Virginia militia defeated the Indians. Boone cleared the Wilderness Road for pioneers to get to the new territory and built the first settlement, named Boonesborough.	Lewis and Clark: Led an expedition that mapped out major rivers and mountains to help pioneers find their way from St. Louis to the Pacific coast.	The War of 1812: Due to anger at the British for their interference in trade, Congress voted to declare war on Britain in 1812.
Pioneer Life: Led difficult lives; pioneers had to clear their land, build their homes, grow their food, and make their own clothes and tools.	Zebulon Pike: Led an expedition to explore the southwestern part of the Louisiana Purchase.	The Era of Good Feelings: From 1817–1825, nationalism united the people of the United States, creating a feeling of pride in the country.

Use after reading Chapter 11, pages 348–371.

COMMUNITY RESOURCES

Ideas for using community resources, including speakers and field trips

Historical Societies:

____

____

____

____

____

Museums:

____

____

____

____

____

Experts on Westward Expansion:

____

____

____

____

____

Historic Sites:

____

____

____

____

____

Chapter 11 Assessment

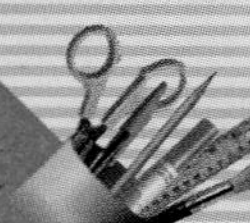

For ongoing **PERFORMANCE ASSESSMENT,** see Show What You Know, pp. 352, 357, 362.

CONTENT

NAME ______________________ DATE __________

Chapter Test 11

Part One: Test Your Understanding (4 points each)

DIRECTIONS: ***Circle the letter of the best answer.***

1. To make his way over the mountains into Kentucky, Daniel Boone first tried to find the
- **A.** Mississippi River.
- **B.** Louisiana Purchase.
- **C.** Warrior's Path.
- **D.** Northwest Passage.

2. When Daniel Boone first went to Kentucky, he found many
- **A.** wild horses.
- **B.** trading settlements.
- **C.** canals.
- **D.** buffalo.

3. What did Daniel Boone do to help settle the West?
- **A.** He helped make the Wilderness Road.
- **B.** He explored the Mississippi River.
- **C.** He traded goods with people in New Orleans.
- **D.** He signed a peace treaty with the Cherokees and the Shawnees.

4. One of the first things that pioneer families had to do when they moved to the western frontier was to
- **A.** build adobe houses.
- **B.** build missions.
- **C.** clear thick forests.
- **D.** set up a government.

5. To stop the United States frontier from moving farther west, Spain
- **A.** declared war on Tennessee.
- **B.** closed the port of New Orleans to western farmers.
- **C.** ordered the Indian tribes to stop trading with Americans.
- **D.** sent Spanish settlers into Kentucky.

6. How did the Louisiana Purchase change the United States?
- **A.** It cut the size of the United States in half.
- **B.** It outlawed slavery in all states east of Louisiana.
- **C.** It doubled the size of the country.
- **D.** It increased the number of states in the country to 14.

7. Which of the following people served as a guide for the Lewis and Clark expedition?
- **A.** Sacagawea
- **B.** Tecumseh
- **C.** the Prophet
- **D.** Cameahwait

(continued)

CHAPTER 11 TEST — Assessment Program 95

CONTENT

NAME ______________________ DATE __________

8. The Lewis and Clark expedition helped later pioneers by
- **A.** building the National Highway.
- **B.** mapping passes through the Rockies.
- **C.** finding a route to the Atlantic Ocean.
- **D.** clearing the Cumberland Gap.

9. Who wanted to form a strong confederation of Indians in Kentucky and Tennessee?
- **A.** Andrew Jackson
- **B.** William Henry Harrison
- **C.** Tecumseh
- **D.** Sequoyah

10. One result of the Battle of Tippecanoe was that
- **A.** the Americans and the Indians signed a peace treaty.
- **B.** the Indians agreed to leave the Northwest Territory.
- **C.** the Americans agreed to pay the Indians for the cost of the war.
- **D.** the Americans destroyed Prophetstown.

11. Which of the following groups of Americans did not want the United States to go to war with Britain in 1812?
- **A.** western farmers
- **B.** southern planters
- **C.** War Hawks
- **D.** northern merchants

12. Which of the following was a turning point in the War of 1812?
- **A.** the battle on Lake Erie
- **B.** the impressment of American sailors
- **C.** the formation of the War Hawks
- **D.** the Battle of New Orleans

13. After the War of 1812, during the Era of Good Feelings, the United States government
- **A.** was stronger in its dealings with foreign nations.
- **B.** sent people to explore land gained from France.
- **C.** was too weak to stop European countries from expanding their American empires.
- **D.** lost land to Spain and Britain.

14. Who wrote a poem about American bravery as the British bombed Fort McHenry in Baltimore Harbor?
- **A.** James Monroe
- **B.** Francis Scott Key
- **C.** Meriwether Lewis
- **D.** Zebulon Pike

(continued)

96 Assessment Program — CHAPTER 11 TEST

SKILLS

NAME ______________________ DATE __________

Part Two: Test Your Skills (18 points)

DIRECTIONS: ***In this chapter you read about the Louisiana Purchase. President Thomas Jefferson spent $15 million to gain more than 800,000 square miles of land for the United States. You also learned about the Lewis and Clark expedition through the unexplored lands. Think about the history of the United States up to that time. Then make three predictions about what you think will happen to the lands that were part of the Louisiana Purchase.***

THE LOUISIANA PURCHASE

PREDICTIONS ABOUT THE LANDS OF THE LOUISIANA PURCHASE	
15. Prediction 1	Possible responses: Settlers will begin moving into the Louisiana Purchase territory or to the Pacific coast, and more states will soon be added to the United States. Valuable resources or fertile farmlands will be found in the Louisiana Purchase territory or on the Pacific coast, and
16. Prediction 2	people will need to travel throughout the new territory. A road or trail will be built across the Louisiana Purchase territory to take people to the Pacific coast. A transcontinental railroad will be built to link the Atlantic coast with the Pacific coast.
17. Prediction 3	

(continued)

CHAPTER 11 TEST — Assessment Program 97

APPLICATION/WRITING

NAME ______________________ DATE __________

Part Three: Apply What You Have Learned

DIRECTIONS: ***Complete each of the following activities.***

18. ***National Heroes*** *(16 points)*
Many people helped develop the United States in the early 1800s. Four of them are listed below. Because of their actions, these people are known as national heroes. In the space provided, briefly explain what each person did to become a national hero. Possible responses:

HERO	WHAT THE PERSON DID
Daniel Boone	He proved it was possible to travel west through the Cumberland Gap into Kentucky. He supervised the construction of the Wilderness Road, led settlers into Kentucky, and built the first settlement in Kentucky at Boonesborough.
Andrew Jackson	He defended the city of New Orleans from British attack during the War of 1812.
Francis Scott Key	He wrote a poem when he saw that the American flag was still flying after an all-night bombing of Fort McHenry during the War of 1812. His poem became our national anthem.
Zebulon Pike	He led an expedition into the southwestern part of the Louisiana Purchase territory. He went to Santa Fe in Spanish New Mexico. His actions led to the development of the Santa Fe Trail and the settlement of the Southwest.

19. ***Essay*** *(10 points)*
One result of the War of 1812 was the growth of nationalism in the United States. Write one paragraph explaining what nationalism is and how it is shown by Americans today.

Possible response:
Nationalism is a patriotic feeling for one's own country. Displaying the American flag, celebrating national holidays, honoring military heroes, and singing the national anthem are all examples of how Americans show their feelings of nationalism today.

98 Assessment Program — CHAPTER 11 TEST

INTRODUCE THE CHAPTER

This chapter examines the territorial growth of the United States in the years following the American Revolution. It deals first with the expansion beyond the Appalachians up to the Mississippi and then with the Louisiana Purchase and the expeditions of Lewis and Clark and Zebulon Pike. The chapter also explores the War of 1812.

Link Prior Learning

Have students share what they already know about what was regarded as the West at the time of the American Revolution, particularly the Northwest Territory. Explain that the concept of the West kept changing as people moved farther and farther in that direction.

Visual Analysis

Interpret Portraits Explain to students that this photograph shows Mary Prosser, a pioneer woman. Ask students to speculate on how women contributed to pioneer life in the early 1800s.

Auditory Learning

Interpret Poems Have a volunteer read the poem aloud. Explain that in the poem Elizabeth Coatsworth mentions specific images such as cutting down the forest and growing apple trees to describe the ways in which pioneers changed the frontier.

Q. **Although no pioneers are mentioned in the poem, what do you think they accomplished?** They cut the forest down and, with the help of oxen, made it level. They also planted apple trees and brought cows to graze on the land.

"PRIMARY SOURCE"

Source: *Away Goes Sally*. Elizabeth Coatsworth. Macmillan Publishing Company, 1934.

CHAPTER 11

ON THE MOVE

"The ax has
cut the
forest down,
The laboring
ox has
smoothed
all clear,
Apples now
grow where
pine trees stood,
And slow cows
graze instead
of deer."

From the poem "The Wilderness Is Tamed" by Elizabeth Coatsworth

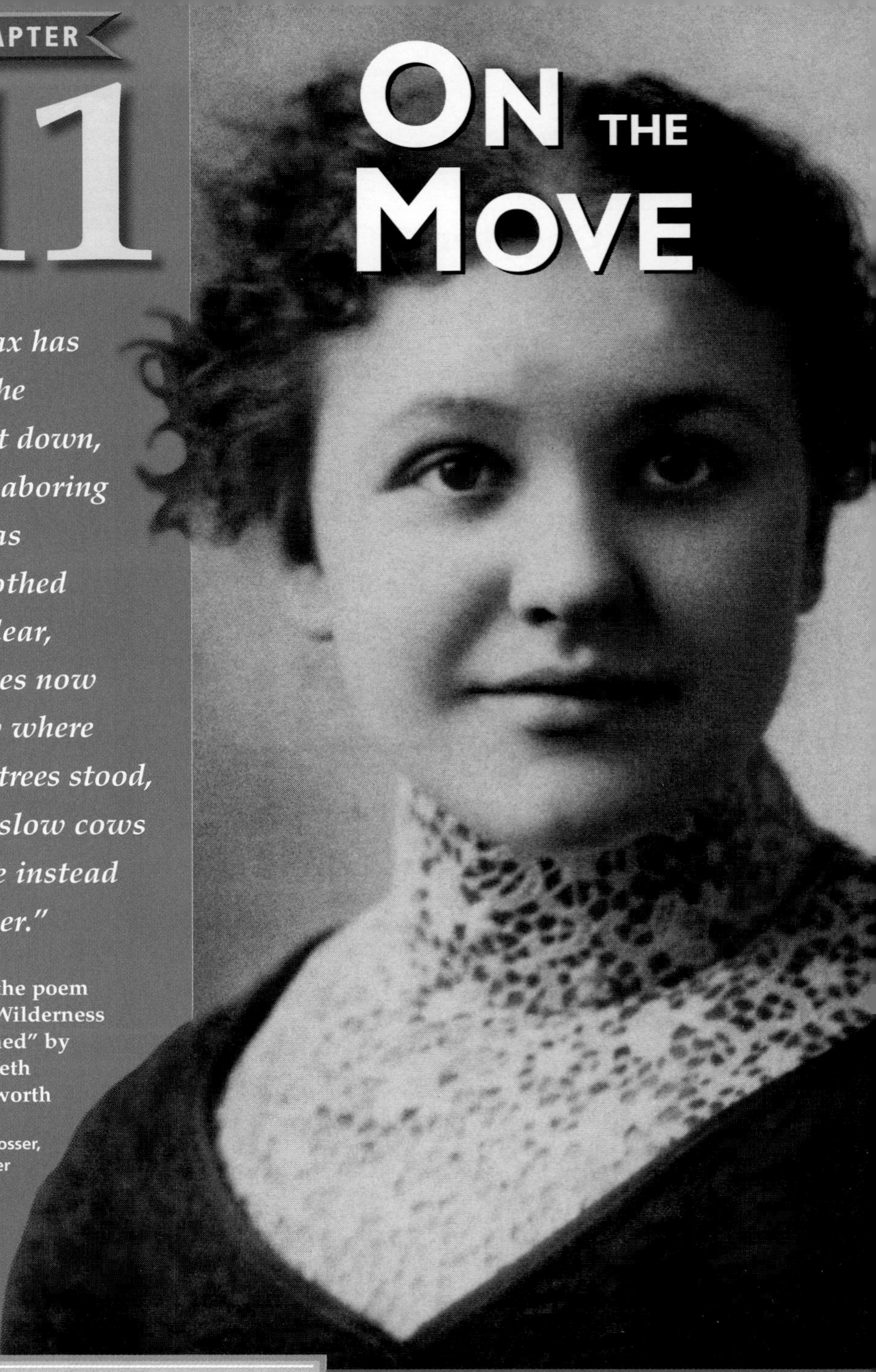

Mary Prosser, a pioneer woman

348

ACTIVITY CHOICES

Background

ELIZABETH COATSWORTH Coatsworth was an American poet who wrote more than 70 books for children. She was one of a number of female writers who wrote about brave pioneers and their accomplishments. Willa Cather was another female writer who dealt with this subject in books such as *O Pioneers!* and *My Ántonia*. Although these books were written for adults, you may wish to read aloud the sections that reinforce the theme of the excerpt from Coatsworth's poem.

Across the Appalachians

LESSON 1

FOCUS What problems might a person face in moving to a new place today?

Main Idea As you read, look for some of the problems the early settlers faced when they crossed the Appalachian Mountains.

Vocabulary
pioneer

In 1783 the Treaty of Paris, which ended the War for Independence, set the Mississippi River as the new nation's western border. When people talked about the West in those days, they meant all of the land between the Appalachian Mountains and the Mississippi River. This was the American frontier.

Daniel Boone

Even before the Treaty of Paris, American pioneers were pushing the frontier west. A **pioneer** is a person who first settles a new place. Daniel Boone was one of the earliest and best-known American pioneers to cross the Appalachians.

Boone was born in Pennsylvania. He was 16 years old when his family moved to the Yadkin Valley of North Carolina. Boone came to love living in the woods and hunting.

During the French and Indian War, Boone served in the army. There he met John Finley, a fur trader. Boone later remembered the stories Finley told about a wonderful land west of the Appalachian Mountains. There, Finley said, green forests and meadows stretched for miles.

After the war Boone tried to find this land, now known as Kentucky. But he could not find a way over the mountains. He looked for the Warrior's Path, an Indian trail Finley had described that crossed the mountains, but he could not find it.

Soon after Boone returned home, a peddler, or seller, came to the door of the Boone house in North Carolina. The peddler was John Finley! With Finley's help, Boone again tried to find Kentucky. This time he found the Warrior's Path and followed it across the Appalachian Mountains through what was called the Cumberland Gap. Boone later told a friend what he had seen on the other side.

> "Thousands of Buffalo roamed the Kentucky hills and the land looked as if it never would become poor."

Pioneer leader Daniel Boone was dedicated to exploring and settling the American frontier.

Reading Support

ANTICIPATION GUIDE Before students read the lesson, ask them to predict whether each of the following statements is true or false. Students may correct their predictions as they read.

1. Daniel Boone found the Cumberland Gap by accident. false
2. Stories about Daniel Boone's adventures in Kentucky made people want to settle there. true
3. The Indians welcomed pioneer settlements in Kentucky. false
4. The trip over the mountains and through the Cumberland Gap was slow and difficult. true
5. It was easy for settlers to clear the wilderness of the frontier. false

Objectives

1. Explain how Daniel Boone was able to reach Kentucky.
2. Summarize the effects of Daniel Boone's determination to settle Kentucky.
3. Analyze the cooperation of pioneers in overcoming problems they faced.

Vocabulary

pioneer (p. 349)

1. ACCESS

The Focus Question

Have students volunteer experiences they have had moving to new places. Ask them to discuss some of the problems involved in relocating.

The Main Idea

In this lesson students focus on the early explorations of Daniel Boone. After students have read the lesson, have them discuss how difficult it was for settlers to reach Kentucky when that area lay beyond almost impassable mountains. Discuss with students the spirit of cooperation that guided the pioneers who settled there.

2. BUILD

Daniel Boone

Key Content Summary

Daniel Boone sought to find the land now known as Kentucky, which lay west of the Appalachian Mountains. He succeeded, but only with the help and cooperation of his friend John Finley. Stories of Boone's adventures and the richness of Kentucky led many others to want to settle there.

Culture

Human Relationships Boone's relationship with the Indians was typical of those of most pioneers. He was well aware that he was trespassing on Indian territory in his explorations and that the Indians might resist. But he saw no reason to quit because of that. Have students discuss and analyze Boone's relationship with the Indians.

Settling Kentucky

Key Content Summary

After a brief conflict with the Indians, Virginia's leaders forced the Indians to sign a treaty giving up their lands in Kentucky. Thousands of settlers poured through the Cumberland Gap on Daniel Boone's Wilderness Road, and by 1800 Kentucky and Tennessee had become states.

Visual Analysis

Learn from Maps Have students examine the map of the Wilderness Road. Lead students to infer the difficulties of traveling through this region. Then have students answer the question in the caption. the Wilderness Road

Geography

Human-Environment Interactions

Invite a student to read aloud the quotation and explain what it means. Remind students that at one time buffalo were plentiful. Discuss the role that the hunters played in the eventual disappearance of the buffalo.

Both the Cherokees and Shawnees lived in settlements throughout Kentucky. Several times the Shawnees captured Boone during his visits there. Each time they let him go with a warning not to come back. But Boone did not listen. He returned again and again to Kentucky to explore and to hunt. Stories of Boone's adventures and Kentucky's rich land soon spread, making people want to settle there.

REVIEW ***What did Daniel Boone find when he reached Kentucky?*** buffalo and rich land

Settling Kentucky

As word spread about Kentucky, several families tried to make their way over the mountains. But the Cherokees and Shawnees did not want to give up their land. They fought the pioneers, who had to turn back. Finally, in 1774, the Virginia militia fought a battle with the Indians and won. Virginia leaders made Indian leaders sign a treaty giving up their lands in Kentucky.

As soon as the treaty was signed, a land developer hired Daniel Boone to clear a road to Kentucky. In March 1775 Boone led a group through the Cumberland Gap. Cutting down trees and bushes to make way for wagons, the workers cleared a path through the wilderness. This path came to be known as the Wilderness Road.

Once in Kentucky, Boone built a fort and named it Boonesborough. He then returned to North Carolina to lead a group of settlers to Kentucky. In August he set out with his family and some neighbors for the new land. It was a slow, hard trip over the mountains. Getting a cow to walk 300 miles (483 km) was not easy. Sometimes wild animals scared the horses so much, they ran off in all directions. The Cherokees and Shawnees made surprise attacks, hoping to scare off the pioneers. But

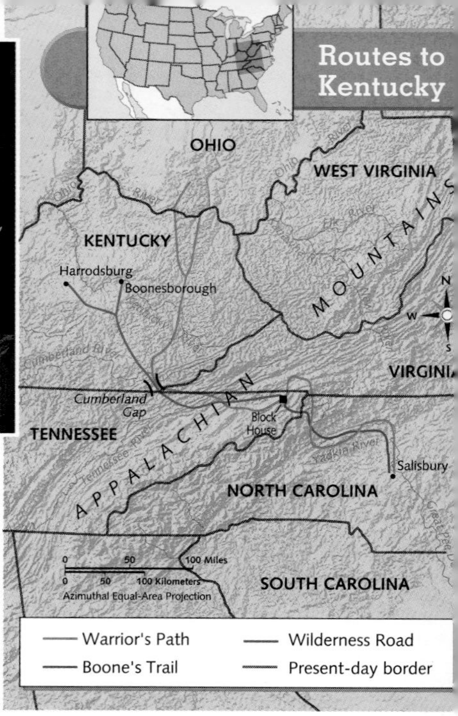

Human-Environment Interactions This map shows the different routes people used to travel to Kentucky. In the painting by George Caleb Bingham (above left) Daniel Boone leads pioneers through the Cumberland Gap.
■ *What route did Boone follow through the Appalachian Mountains?*

ACTIVITY CHOICES

Link to Language Arts

WRITE A POEM Tell students to imagine that they are among the group of settlers who traveled with Daniel Boone over the mountains into Kentucky. Have students write a poem that describes their experiences on the journey, including the hardships they faced. Tell students that their poems should also express the emotions they felt in leaving their homes for new lives on the frontier. Have volunteers share their poems with the class.

TECHNOLOGY

Use THE AMAZING WRITING MACHINE™ to complete this writing activity.

Link to World Languages

STUDY CHEROKEE PLACE-NAMES The people who settled in Kentucky and Tennessee adopted Indian words to name their new homes. *Kentucky* is a Cherokee word meaning "meadowland." Tennessee's name comes from the word *Tanasi,* which was the name of a Cherokee village.

the settlers pushed on to Boonesborough, joining others at Kentucky's first pioneer settlement.

Over the next few years, thousands of pioneers took the Wilderness Road to the rich valleys beyond the Appalachian Mountains. Many more settlements were built in Kentucky and in Tennessee to the south. By 1800, American and European settlers had moved as far west as the Mississippi River. Kentucky and Tennessee had become states. Farmers in these states shipped their crops and animals on flatboats down the Mississippi River to the port of New Orleans, then controlled by Spain. From New Orleans the goods went by ship to markets on the east coast of the United States.

REVIEW ***How did Daniel Boone help settle the West?*** by clearing the Wilderness Road and leading settlers to Kentucky

Pioneer Life

Life on the western frontier was hard for pioneer families like the Boones. After they bought their land from a land developer, they had to clear thick forest in order to build their homes and farms. Most pioneers had little food to last until their first crops were ready. One pioneer told how poor his family was when they first settled in Kentucky.

> “My Wife and I had neither spoon, dish, knife, or any thing to do with when we began life.”

Pioneer families had to become self-sufficient very quickly, or they did not survive on the frontier. They built their own homes, grew their own food, and made their own clothes and tools. They bartered with the

HISTORY

Log Cabins

Most pioneers in Kentucky lived in log cabins because such homes were quick and easy to build. First, a number of straight trees, all about the same size around, were chosen. Then, the trees were cut down and trimmed to the right length. The logs were pulled by horses or dragged by hand to where the cabin was to be built. Notches were cut at the ends so that the logs would fit together. Next, the logs were lifted into place. The spaces between the logs were "chinked," or filled with mud, clay, or moss. Finally, a roof and a fireplace were added. Following this plan, two people could build a log cabin in about two weeks.

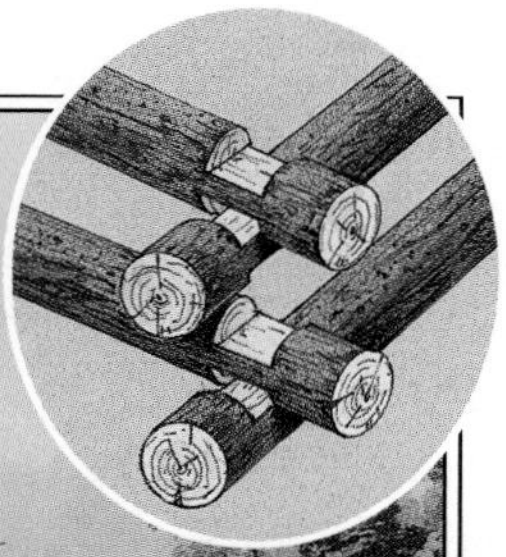

History

Patterns and Relationships The movement of settlers into Kentucky disrupted the lives of the Indians already living there. Ask students to speculate on how this settlement affected the everyday lives of the Indians.

Geography

Movement Select a student to trace a route, on a classroom wall map or in an atlas, from Kentucky and Tennessee to the Mississippi River. Then have the student follow the river to New Orleans and on to the East Coast. Challenge students to infer why farmers west of the Appalachians had to ship their crops and animals down the Mississippi to reach markets on the East Coast.

Pioneer Life

Key Content Summary

The pioneers brought change to the frontier, clearing the land and growing crops. Through cooperative effort, they often built a high log fence around a cluster of homes to protect themselves.

Culture

Interdependence Have students summarize ways in which life on the frontier forced settlers to be interdependent.

“PRIMARY SOURCE”

Source: *The Trans-Appalachian Frontier: People, Societies, and Institutions 1775–1850.* Malcolm J. Rohrbough. Oxford University Press, 1978.

Meet Individual Needs

ADVANCED LEARNERS Ask students to use library references to research the shipment of goods down the Mississippi. They should try to find the answers to the following questions: What goods were made or grown for trade? How long did it take for a shipment to get from a chosen point to New Orleans? Who operated the flatboats? What happened to the flatboats after they reached New Orleans? Have students share their findings with the class.

Extend and Enrich

COOPERATIVE LEARNING

CREATE A BULLETIN BOARD DISPLAY Divide the class into six small groups. Explain that each group is to research one of the following aspects of life on the frontier: food, clothing, housing, education, occupations, and medicine. Have group members illustrate their topic and then label and write a brief explanation for their illustrations. All the groups should work together to create the final bulletin board display.

Visual Analysis

Learn from Maps Have students study the map and answer the question in the caption. west of the Appalachian Mountains, including the Ohio River Valley and the Mississippi delta area

3. CLOSE

Have students consider again the Focus question on page 349.

What problems might a person face in moving to a new place today?

Have students use what they have learned in this lesson to compare the problems faced by pioneers with the problems faced by people who move to a new place today.

LESSON 1 REVIEW—Answers

Check Understanding

1. because of stories about Boone's adventures and Kentucky's rich land
2. crossing rough terrain, wild animals scaring the horses, conflict with Indians

Think Critically

3. The Wilderness Road provided a path across the Appalachians so that settlers could reach the rich lands of Kentucky and Tennessee.
4. Some students might say that the pioneers should have been more tolerant of the Indians' ways and even invited the Indians to become part of their settlements. Others might point out that the settlers were trespassing on Indian land, and the two groups were too different for them to live peacefully together.

Show What You Know

Performance Assessment You may also ask students to write descriptions of the items they chose and explain what problems the items will help the pioneers overcome.

What to Look For In evaluating the posters, look for student understanding of the main idea of the lesson—the problems and challenges the pioneers faced settling the wilderness.

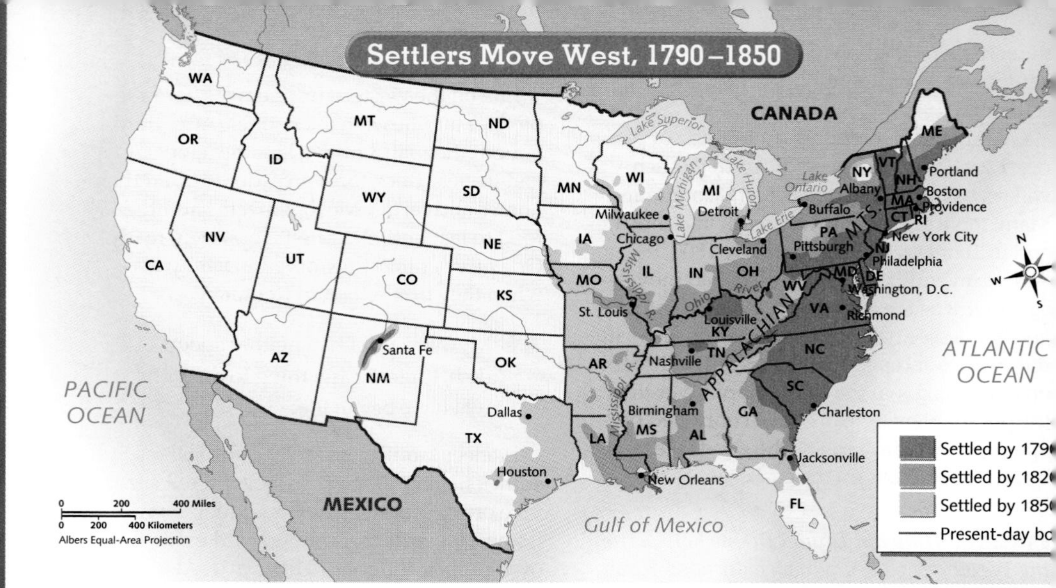

Regions This map shows the westward settlement of American pioneers at different times.
■ *What areas did pioneers settle from 1790 to 1820?*

Indian peoples, who traded furs, tobacco, cotton, and corn for cloth and other useful goods.

As pioneers continued moving onto Indian lands, many banded together in forts to protect themselves. In some settlements they built their log houses close together with a high log fence all around.

REVIEW ***How did pioneer families become self-sufficient?*** they built their homes, grew their food, made their clothes and tools, and traded with the Indians

LESSON 1 REVIEW

Check Understanding

1. **Remember the Facts** Why did pioneers push west into the frontier?
2. **Recall the Main Idea** What problems did the early settlers face when they crossed the Appalachian Mountains?

Think Critically

3. **Cause and Effect** How did Daniel Boone's Wilderness Road help the settlement of Kentucky and the West?
4. **Think More About It** Do you think the Indians and the pioneers could have lived peacefully together in the American West? Explain your answer.

Show What You Know

Poster Activity It is 1775, and you own a general store in North Carolina. Create a poster with pictures of some of the supplies you think a pioneer would need to take west. Display your poster in the classroom.

ACTIVITY CHOICES

ACTIVITY BOOK

Reinforce & Extend

Use ACTIVITY BOOK, p. 66.

Reteach the Main Idea

COOPERATIVE LEARNING

MAKE A LIST Divide the class into small groups, and challenge each group to use the textbook as a resource to list the problems faced by western pioneers and the solutions the pioneers found for those problems. Let the group members share and discuss their lists with each other and with other groups.

The Louisiana Purchase

LESSON 2

FOCUS
What might people today learn from the examples set by people in the past?

Main Idea As you read, look for things that American pioneers learned from the explorers who traveled west before them.

Vocabulary
purchase
pathfinder

In time some of the pioneers who had settled between the Appalachians and the Mississippi began to look beyond the mighty river. Spain and France claimed these rich lands, although it was mostly Indian peoples who lived there. In one of the largest land sales in history, the United States bought part of this region from France in 1803. The way was now open for settlers to move even farther west.

The Incredible Purchase

Shortly before noon on March 4, 1801, Thomas Jefferson walked through the muddy streets of Washington, D.C., to the Capitol building. The writer of the Declaration of Independence was about to become the third President of the young nation. His simple clothes seemed right for the new capital, which was only half built.

After he took the President's oath of office, Jefferson spoke of his hopes for the country. He called the United States "a rising nation, spread over a wide and fruitful land." He knew, however, that the country faced a big problem. Spain had closed the port of New Orleans to western farmers, hoping to stop the United States frontier from moving farther west.

Spain had taken over all of Louisiana, including New Orleans, after France lost the French and Indian War. The French had given this huge area to Spain to keep the British from getting control of it. In 1802 President Jefferson learned that Spain had secretly given Louisiana back to France. Now, Jefferson thought, was the time to act.

Jefferson had two representatives ask the French leader, Napoleon Bonaparte (nuh•POH•lee•uhn BOH•nuh•part), to sell part of Louisiana, including New Orleans, to the United States. Jefferson was willing to offer

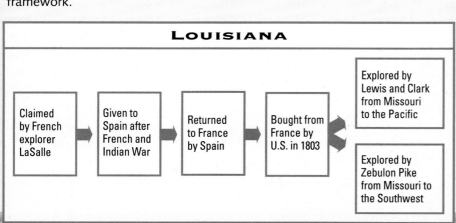

Thomas Jefferson became the third President of the United States.

353

Reading Support

IDENTIFY A SEQUENCE Provide students with the following visual framework.

LOUISIANA

Claimed by French explorer LaSalle → Given to Spain after French and Indian War → Returned to France by Spain → Bought from France by U.S. in 1803 → Explored by Lewis and Clark from Missouri to the Pacific / Explored by Zebulon Pike from Missouri to the Southwest

Objectives

1. Explain how President Jefferson was able to buy Louisiana.
2. Analyze the accomplishments of the Lewis and Clark expedition.
3. Evaluate the importance of Zebulon Pike's expedition.

Vocabulary

purchase (p. 354) pathfinder (p. 355)

1. ACCESS

The Focus Question

Ask students to volunteer the names of individuals from the past whom they admire. Have students summarize what they have learned from the work of these historical heroes and how their qualities might be valuable for a person living in today's world.

The Main Idea

In this lesson students learn about how President Thomas Jefferson was able to purchase Louisiana for the United States and about the explorers who mapped the new territory. After students have read the lesson, have them analyze what American pioneers learned from individual explorers who traveled west before them.

2. BUILD

The Incredible Purchase

Key Content Summary

Through independent action, Spain and France kept the United States from expanding past the Mississippi River. Then, in 1803, Napoleon Bonaparte needed money to pay for two wars, and President Thomas Jefferson was able to purchase Louisiana from France.

Geography

Regions Ask students to analyze the options left to farmers for shipping their produce east after the port of New Orleans closed. Discuss the problems associated with these options. Ask students to evaluate the advantages and disadvantages of the Louisiana Purchase.

Economics

Markets and Prices The Louisiana Purchase was a great bargain for the United States. Have students use the figures in the textbook to calculate the approximate price per square mile paid for Louisiana. approximately $18.75 per square mile

Visual Analysis

Learn from Maps Refer students to the map of the Louisiana Purchase. Discuss with students the geographic features of the territory.

Q. **What natural boundary of the Louisiana Purchase might slow the progress of pioneers wishing to settle on the shores of the Pacific Ocean?** the Rocky Mountains

Have students answer the question in the caption. the many rivers

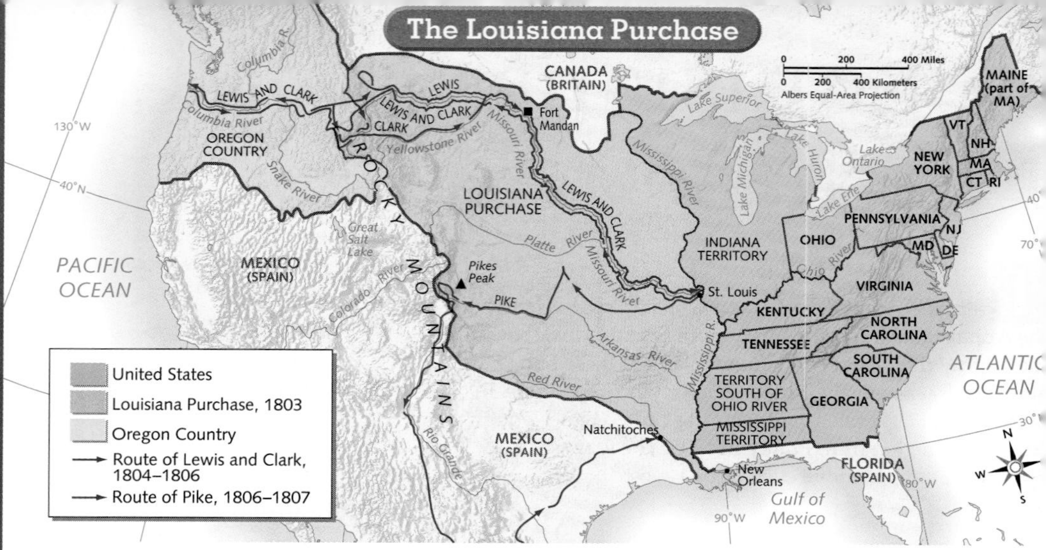

MAP THEME **Place** The huge territory of the Louisiana Purchase was later divided among 15 states.

■ *What natural features of the territory made it easier to explore?*

$10 million. But Bonaparte had other problems on his mind. France was preparing for war with Britain. And people in the French colony of St. Domingue (SEN daw•MENG) in the Caribbean had rebelled against France. Needing money to pay for two wars, Bonaparte offered to sell *all* of Louisiana to the United States. To the surprise of the Americans, the price was $15 million—for more than 800,000 square miles (2,071,840 sq km)!

On April 30, 1803, the United States agreed to **purchase**, or to buy, the huge territory, reaching from the Mississippi River west to the Rocky Mountains and from New Orleans north to Canada. The territory became known as the Louisiana Purchase. With it the United States doubled in size and became one of the largest countries in the world.

REVIEW ***How did the Louisiana Purchase change the United States?*** It doubled the size of the country.

354 • Unit 6

BIOGRAPHY

Toussaint-Louverture 1743–1803

In 1791 Pierre Dominique Toussaint-Louverture (TOO•san LOO•ver•tur) helped lead a slave revolt in St. Domingue. Peace returned only after France agreed to end slavery in its colonies. An experienced soldier, Toussaint held several military positions on the island and soon became its most important leader. In 1802 the French tried to take back St. Domingue, and Toussaint was arrested. He died in prison, but the French could not defeat the rebels. On January 1, 1804, St. Domingue became the independent country of Haiti.

ACTIVITY CHOICES

Link to Language Arts

WRITE A LETTER Tell students to imagine that they are living in the United States of 1803. Ask them to write a letter to their local newspaper either supporting or criticizing President Jefferson for buying Louisiana.

TECHNOLOGY

Use the AMAZING WRITING MACHINE™ to complete this writing activity.

Background

PRESIDENT JEFFERSON Before he agreed to the purchase of Louisiana, Jefferson was concerned that the Constitution did not specifically give the federal government the right to acquire foreign territory. He considered asking for a constitutional amendment giving him the right, but then he justified the purchase on the grounds that it was part of the President's implied powers to protect the nation.

Multicultural Link

Jefferson and other government leaders envisioned that much of the land from the Louisiana Purchase would be used to provide a home for Indian tribes being expelled from the East. However, as the country grew the government could not protect these lands from being settled by pioneers. The lands finally set aside as the Indian Territory are in what is today the state of Oklahoma.

The Lewis and Clark Expedition

Few people in the United States knew much about the lands of the Louisiana Purchase. It was an area that Americans had never explored. President Jefferson asked Meriwether Lewis to lead an expedition to learn all he could about the new land. Lewis was to be a **pathfinder**, someone who finds a way through an unknown region.

Lewis had been an army officer in the wilderness of the Northwest Territory. He chose William Clark, a good friend, to help him lead the expedition. Clark was an excellent cartographer. Lewis and Clark put together a group of about 30 men, most of them frontier soldiers. One member of the group was York, William Clark's African slave. York contributed to the mission through his skill in hunting and fishing.

The leaders called their group the Corps of Discovery. On a spring morning in May 1804, the group left St. Louis and traveled up the Missouri River. The pathfinders spent the summer and fall pushing deep into the Louisiana Purchase. When they reached present-day North Dakota, they built a winter camp near a Mandan village.

While there, Lewis and Clark hired a French fur trader to translate some Indian languages for them. The fur trader was married to a Shoshone (shoh•SHOH•nee) woman who was named Sacagawea (sak•uh•juh•WEE•uh). Sacagawea agreed to serve as a translator when the Corps of Discovery reached the land of the Shoshones.

In the spring of 1805, the Lewis and Clark expedition again moved up the Missouri River by boat. But they would need horses in order to cross the Rocky Mountains. They put their hope in Sacagawea and the Shoshones.

This picture shows Sacagawea (below) using sign language to communicate with the Chinooks during the Lewis and Clark expedition. This page from William Clark's journal (right) shows a drawing he made during the journey.

The Lewis and Clark Expedition

Key Content Summary

President Jefferson asked Meriwether Lewis to lead an expedition to explore the lands of the Louisiana Purchase. Lewis chose William Clark to help him lead the expedition. For more than two years these adventurous individuals mapped the region from the Mississippi River to the Pacific Coast and described the plants, animals, and people there. Later pioneers depended on this information in their travels west.

Geography

MAP THEME

Regions Remind students that the Louisiana Purchase included the region from the Mississippi River to the Rocky Mountains, yet Lewis and Clark explored all the way to the Pacific Coast. Have students hypothesize as to why Lewis and Clark explored so far beyond the western boundary of the Louisiana Purchase.

Culture

Interdependence Review with students some of the skills and experiences of various members of the Lewis and Clark expedition. Have students discuss how these skills and experiences contributed to the success of the expedition.

Background

THE TRIP HOME When Lewis and Clark reached tidewater on the Columbia River, they met coastal Indians. Discovering that the Indians' speech was laced with expressions learned from English-speaking sailors, Lewis and Clark learned that trading vessels from New England often visited the Columbia. Lewis and Clark hoped that such a vessel might arrive to take them and their company home in relative comfort. However, no ship arrived for several months, so the expedition returned as it had come. Lewis took the water route across Montana, while Clark went overland to the Yellowstone River and floated down to its junction with the Missouri River. There he met up with Lewis. The expedition reached St. Louis on September 23,1806, to the cheers of the city's people.

Meet Individual Needs

ADVANCED LEARNERS Ask students to research the life of York, the African who was a member of the Lewis and Clark expedition. They will be interested to learn of his relationship with Indians and of his later career. Have students share what they have learned with the class.

History

Origins, Spread, and Influence Ask students to speculate on the reasons for Jefferson's interest in accurate records of the geography, climate, people, plants, and animals in the lands of the Louisiana Purchase.

"PRIMARY SOURCE"

Source: *Lewis & Clark: The Journey of the Corps of Discovery.* Dayton Duncan. Alfred A. Knopf, 1997.

Journey to the Southwest

Key Content Summary

Zebulon Pike led an expedition to explore the southwestern part of the Louisiana Purchase, which led to his capture by Spanish soldiers. When American traders learned about the need of the Spanish in the Southwest for manufactured goods, they headed there, creating an economic interdependence between the United States and the Spanish settlements.

Geography

Movement Have the students examine the map on page 354, which shows the region Pike explored, and explain the similarities and differences between the expedition of Zebulon Pike and that of Lewis and Clark.

"If we do not find them or some other nation who have horses, I fear the successful issue of our voyage will be very doubtful," Lewis wrote in his journal.

At last the expedition reached the lands of the Shoshones. Sacagawea's brother, Cameahwait (kah•MEE•ah•wayt), was now the chief. He gave the expedition horses, and the pathfinders continued their journey over the Rockies.

BIOGRAPHY

Sacagawea 1786?–1812?

Sacagawea, whose name in Shoshone means "Bird Woman," helped the members of the Lewis and Clark expedition survive. With her help the pathfinders completed their journey to the Pacific Ocean and back. In 1809 Clark brought Sacagawea, her husband, and her young son to St. Louis, where they settled on a farm. Little more is known about Sacagawea. One story says that she died on the Missouri River as early as 1812. Other stories say she died and was buried on the Wind River Reservation in Wyoming in 1884.

Once over the mountains, they built more boats. They went down the Snake River to the Columbia River and on to the Pacific Ocean. In November 1805, after traveling for more than a year and more than 3,000 miles (4,828 km), Clark wrote in his journal,

> "Great joy in camp. We are in view of the . . . great Pacific Octean which we have been so long anxious to see, and the roreing or noise made by the waves brakeing on the rockey shores (as I may suppose) may be heard distinctly."

The Corps of Discovery returned to St. Louis in September 1806. Lewis and Clark brought back seeds, plants, and even living animals. Among these were many birds. Lewis and Clark were able to report much about the land and its people. The expedition also brought back maps showing the major rivers and mountains. Clark had carefully mapped important passes through the Rockies. In later years these maps helped pioneers on their way to the Pacific coast.

REVIEW ***What did Lewis and Clark learn from their expedition?*** the geography of the region and the ways of its people

Pikes Peak (below) was named after Zebulon Pike, who tried to climb to the top but failed.

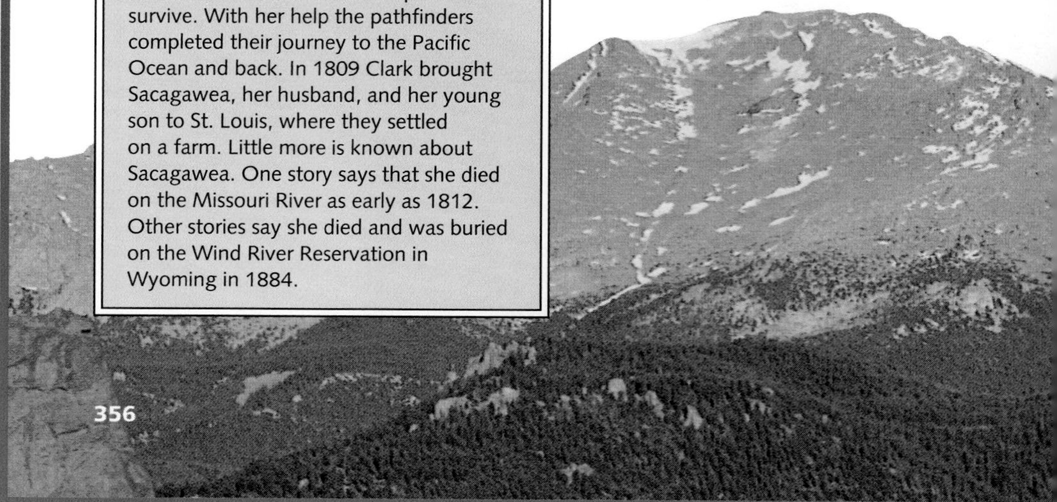

356

ACTIVITY CHOICES

Link to Science

COLLECT DATA Divide the class into groups, and take them on a hike near the school or in a local park. Ask the groups to imagine that they are on the Lewis and Clark expedition. Have one member of each group keep a journal, and ask the other members to provide scientific data to the journal writer about the plants, animals, weather, and other things observed during the hike. Some students in each group may want to assist the journal writer by drawing diagrams of plants and animals. At the end of the hike, have groups share and discuss what they learned from the experience.

Extend and Enrich

MAKE A POSTER Divide the class into small groups. Have each group select a state from the region that was once part of the Louisiana Purchase. Ask each group to make a poster with an outline of the state. On the outline individual group members should supply and label such information as the route taken by the early explorers and the resources and major physical features of the state. Students should complete the map by drawing at least three specimens of plants or animals that an early explorer might have brought back to President Jefferson. Completed posters might be displayed in the classroom.

Journey to the Southwest

Zebulon Pike became a general in the War of 1812 and was killed in battle.

A few weeks before Lewis and Clark returned to St. Louis, another expedition set out from Missouri to explore the southwestern part of the Louisiana Purchase. A small group of pathfinders led by Captain Zebulon Pike followed the Arkansas River through the middle part of the new lands.

By the winter of 1806, Pike had reached a great prairie in present-day Kansas. He saw with wonder that the prairie was covered with thousands of buffalo.

As the expedition traveled farther west, Pike saw what he described as a "blue mountain" in the distance. Today that blue mountain is called Pikes Peak, for the explorer. It is part of the Rocky Mountain range.

Pike's expedition followed the mountains south. The explorers built a small fort beside what Pike thought was the Red River. It was really the northern part of the Rio Grande. The expedition had wandered out of the Louisiana Purchase and onto Spanish land!

Spanish soldiers soon arrived and took Pike and the other explorers to Santa Fe, the capital of the Spanish colony of New Mexico. The explorers were put in jail for being on Spanish land. In Santa Fe the Spanish governor asked Pike if the United States was getting ready to invade the Spanish lands. Pike said no, but in fact the expedition did lead to an "invasion" of another kind.

When he was set free several months later, Pike described the route to the Spanish lands. He reported that the people of Santa Fe needed manufactured goods. Soon American traders were heading for New Mexico as part of a great economic invasion.

REVIEW ***How did Pike help start an economic invasion of the West?*** After Pike reported that Santa Fe needed manufactured goods, more traders headed West.

LESSON 2 REVIEW

Check Understanding

1. **Remember the Facts** What were the boundaries of the Louisiana Purchase?
2. **Recall the Main Idea** What did American pioneers learn from those who traveled west before them?

Think Critically

3. **Think More About It** Why do you think President Jefferson thought it was important for Lewis and Clark to explore the Louisiana Purchase?
4. **Explore Viewpoints** Why did the Spanish fear Pike's entry into their lands? What might Pike have thought of their viewpoint?

Show What You Know

Simulation Activity Imagine that you are planning an expedition into an unknown land. List the things you hope to learn during your travels. Share your list with a classmate.

357

Reteach the Main Idea

MAKE A CHART Divide the class into small groups. Challenge each group to use the textbook as a resource to make a chart of what the Lewis and Clark and the Pike expeditions learned that was of use to the pioneers who followed them. Ask the group members to share and discuss their charts with each other and with the other groups.

COOPERATIVE LEARNING

ACTIVITY BOOK

Reinforce & Extend

Use ACTIVITY BOOK, p. 67.

History

Origins, Spread, and Influence Ask students to review what they learned earlier about the Spanish in the Southwest. They should remember that this was largely a Spanish-speaking region that had a very different culture from that of the United States. Have students infer the Spanish governor's reason for asking whether the United States was planning to invade the Southwest.

3. CLOSE

Have students consider again the Focus question on page 353.

What might people today learn from the examples set by people in the past?

Have students evaluate the explorers' courage, persistence, and thoroughness. Discuss what people today might learn from the examples set by Lewis, Clark, Pike, and other historical figures in this lesson.

LESSON 2 REVIEW—Answers

Check Understanding

1. the Mississippi River, the Rocky Mountains, Canada, and New Orleans
2. Pioneers learned about the terrain, plants, animals, and people.

Think Critically

3. No one in the United States had ever explored the new land. Jefferson wanted maps made of the land, and he wanted to know what the physical features of the land were like. He probably also wanted to know about the Indian tribes living there. All this information would help the government with the settlement and statehood process.
4. They feared that the United States might want to take over the Southwest. Pike might have thought that indeed the Spanish were right. Accept other reasonable responses.

Show What You Know

Performance Assessment Consider having several students write their lists on the board, with each student adding items to what previous students have written, thus making a master list.

What to Look For Check for evidence that the students understand the importance of learning about the Louisiana Purchase.

Objectives

1. Describe Tecumseh's plan for the Indian tribes.
2. Explore the actions that led to the Battle of Tippecanoe.
3. Summarize the events that led to the War of 1812.
4. Evaluate the American victories over the British on Lake Erie.
5. Describe the British attack on Washington, D.C., and the American victory at New Orleans.
6. Describe the United States after the War of 1812.

Vocabulary

impressment (p. 360)
nationalism (p. 362)
annex (p. 362)
doctrine (p. 362)

1. ACCESS

The Focus Question

Have students discuss times when they felt pride in the accomplishments of a team or organization to which they belonged. Explain that Americans often have the same sense of pride in their country, especially at times of conflict with other nations.

The Main Idea

In this lesson students explore the War of 1812. After students have read the lesson, have them analyze how the Americans cooperated to defeat the British and developed a sense of unity within their country.

2. BUILD

Tecumseh and the Prophet

Key Content Summary

Conflict erupted when Tecumseh and his brother, Tenskwatawa, tried to unite the Indians against American settlement of Indian land. When some tribes agreed to sell land, Tecumseh denied their right to do so.

LESSON 3

FOCUS What do you think makes people feel proud of their country?

Main Idea Read to learn how the War of 1812 helped make Americans proud of their country.

Vocabulary
impressment
nationalism
annex
doctrine

A Second War with Britain

The exciting stories of pathfinders such as Meriwether Lewis, William Clark, and Zebulon Pike made many people want to move to the West. But American Indians still fought with American pioneers, trying to turn them back. In the Northwest Territory, the British helped the Indians by selling them guns. Before long, trouble in the Northwest Territory helped push the United States into a second war with Britain.

Tecumseh and the Prophet

As more and more pioneers moved to the Northwest Territory, many Indians grew angry that so much of their land was being lost. The leader of these Indians was a Shawnee named Tecumseh (tuh•KUHM•suh). Tecumseh dreamed of forming a strong Indian confederation. He went from one tribe to another with his brother, Tenskwatawa (ten•SKWAHT•uh•wah), whom people called the Prophet, talking about his plan. Tecumseh called on the tribes to stop fighting one another and to unite against the Americans settling their land.

Prophetstown was the Shawnee town where Tecumseh had his headquarters. It was just below the mouth of the Tippecanoe River, near where Lafayette, Indiana, is today.

In 1809, by signing the Treaty of Fort Wayne, a group of Indian tribes agreed to sell 3 million acres of land to the United States government. Upon hearing the news, Tecumseh cried, "Sell a country! Why not sell the air, the clouds, and the great sea?"

Tecumseh said that no one tribe had the right to sell land. He warned the Americans that the Indians would fight if they were made to give up any more of their land. The Indians led by Tecumseh were eager for battle, but Tecumseh would not let them fight unless they were attacked first.

The Prophet was a well-known religious leader of the Shawnee people.

358

ACTIVITY CHOICES

Reading Support

USE CONTEXT CLUES Have students skim the lesson and use context clues to create a series of flash cards relating to important terms, people, and events discussed in the lesson. Students should write each term, name, or event on the front of an index card and write a definition or an explanation on the back of the card. You may wish to have students pair off to review the information on their flash cards or keep their flash cards for later review.

Smithsonian Institution®

Go to the Internet site at *http://www.si.edu/harcourt/socialstudies* to examine a portrait of Tenskwatawa in Native Americans at the National Portrait Gallery.

The Shawnee chief Tecumseh (left) wanted the United States to stop forcing Indians from their homelands. A computer drawing (above) shows what Prophetstown may have looked like before it was attacked.

In 1811 Tecumseh decided to talk with the Creeks and other Indian tribes living in Kentucky and Tennessee about his plan for a confederation. Before he left, he told the Prophet to keep the peace until he returned.

REVIEW ***What plan did Tecumseh have for the Indian tribes?*** to form a confederation to stop American settlement in the West

Battle of Tippecanoe

William Henry Harrison was governor of the Indiana Territory in 1811. Knowing that Tecumseh was away from Prophetstown, Harrison sent 1,000 soldiers to the Shawnee town. They camped nearby on the night of November 6, 1811. The Prophet feared that the soldiers would soon attack, so he ordered the Indians to attack first. The morning of November 7, the terrible Battle of Tippecanoe took place.

Neither side clearly won the battle. The Americans destroyed Prophetstown, but the Indians went through the Northwest Territory, attacking settlers.

Many people blamed the Indian attacks on Britain. They said the British were giving guns to the Indians and talking against American settlers. People in the Northwest Territory thought the answer was simple—take over Canada and drive the British out of North America.

REVIEW ***What were the results of the Battle of Tippecanoe?***

War Fever

People in the South, too, were angry with Britain. To stop Americans from trading with the French and other Europeans, the British stopped American ships at sea. They even

Americans destroyed Prophetstown, and Indians went through the Northwest Territory, attacking settlers.

Auditory Learning

Interpret Primary Sources Ask a volunteer to read Tecumseh's quotation on page 358. Have students explain why Tecumseh felt that people cannot buy and sell land.

Battle of Tippecanoe

Key Content Summary

Although many Indians died in the Battle of Tippecanoe, the Indians prolonged the conflict by attacking settlers throughout the Northwest Territory. Many Americans believed the Indians had been armed by the British.

Geography

Place Refer students to the map on page 288, and have them locate the Northwest Territory—the area that by 1803 included the state of Ohio and the Indiana Territory. Have students draw conclusions about why the Northwest Territory was important to both the American settlers and the British.

War Fever

Key Content Summary

When British ships began the impressment of American sailors, War Hawks in the West and South called for war against Britain. Northern merchants did not want open conflict, which would end trade with Britain. In spite of this opposition, Congress declared war on Britain in 1812.

Background

WILLIAM HENRY HARRISON As governor of the Northwest Territory, Harrison did much to encourage American settlement there, having concluded many treaties with the Indians. Although the Battle of Tippecanoe was not a clear-cut American victory, Harrison's use of the 1840 presidential campaign slogan "Tippecanoe and Tyler [the vice presidential candidate] too" brought him many votes. Harrison won the election but died after only one month in office.

Link to Language Arts

WRITE TO PERSUADE Ask students to imagine that they are settlers in the Northwest Territory. Have them prepare an advertisement for a local newspaper, in which they try to persuade fellow settlers that the British are to blame for Indian attacks on settlements.

TECHNOLOGY

Use THE AMAZING WRITING MACHINE™ RESOURCE PACKAGE to complete this writing activity.

History

Patterns and Relationships Ask students to infer why the British would risk war with the United States by impressing American sailors.

Visual Analysis

Learn from Time Lines Have students answer the question in the caption. It was slow—soldiers did not know that a peace treaty had been signed before the battle occurred.

The War of 1812

Key Content Summary

Oliver Hazard Perry led his naval vessels in a victory over the British on Lake Erie. General William Henry Harrison then went on to defeat the weakened British forces at the Battle of the Thames. Tecumseh died in the battle, as did his plan for an Indian confederation, making the Northwest Territory now safe from attacks by Indians.

Visual Analysis

Learn from Maps Have students answer the question in the caption. 6

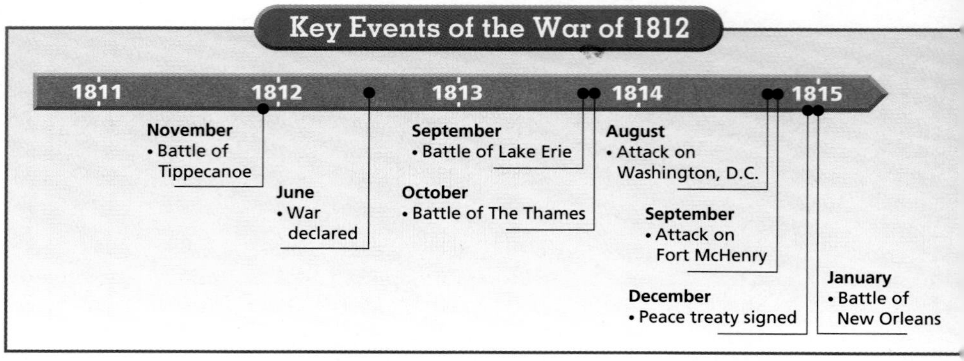

LEARNING FROM TIME LINES This time line shows the key events of the War of 1812.

■ *What do the last two dates on the time line tell you about communication in the early 1800s?*

took sailors off American ships and put them to work on British ships. Taking workers this way is called **impressment**.

People in the West and the South called on the United States government to declare war on Britain. Those who spoke up the most were known as War Hawks. The War Hawks blamed the British in Canada for encouraging the Indians to fight against settlers in the West. They blamed the British government for stopping trade in the South. Eager for more land, the War Hawks even hoped to take Canada from Britain.

Not everyone wanted war, however. Northern merchants had made a lot of money trading with the British. They did not want a war that would end their trade. Yet the desire for war was so great all over the rest of the country that Congress voted to declare war on Britain in 1812. It seemed as if a "war fever" had swept the nation.

REVIEW ***Which regions of the United States wanted war with Britain?*** the West and the South

Regions Both sides won major battles during the War of 1812.

■ *How many battles were fought near the Great Lakes?*

The War of 1812

As the fighting began, Britain had the strongest navy in the world. Yet the small United States Navy, with only 16 ships, won an important battle on Lake Erie that became

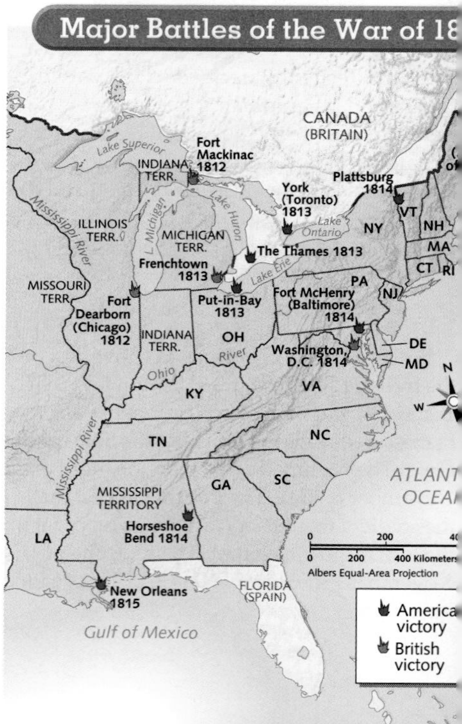

ACTIVITY CHOICES

Background

IMPRESSMENT The British had long used impressment as a way of keeping their merchant sailors from deserting. Pay in the British merchant navy was very low, so many sailors deserted their ships when they reached American ports and signed up on American vessels, where pay was better. The British claimed they had the right to stop American ships and search for British sailors, whom they would force back onto their ships. That was the excuse they used when they took American sailors.

Simulation Activity

COOPERATIVE LEARNING

ROLE-PLAY Select several students to enact a scene in which a British captain boards an American vessel and demands the return of British sailors. In addition to the British captain, the cast of characters should include the American captain and several American and British sailors.

a turning point in the war. Ships commanded by American Captain Oliver Hazard Perry defeated the British on September 10, 1813. After the battle, Perry sent a message to General William Henry Harrison saying, "We have met the enemy and they are ours."

With British control weakened on the Great Lakes, General Harrison was able to lead American soldiers across Lake Erie into Canada. At the Battle of The Thames (TEMZ) on October 5, 1813, the American forces led by Harrison defeated the British and their Indian allies. Among the dead was Tecumseh, who was fighting on the British side.

Tecumseh's plan for a strong Indian confederation died with him. From that time on, settlers in the Northwest Territory were free from attacks by Indians.

REVIEW ***What was a turning point in the War of 1812?*** the battle on Lake Erie

During the war the British burned several buildings in Washington, D.C.—the White House, the Capitol, the Treasury, and some private homes. Dolley Madison (above left) was able to save just a few things from the White House before she was forced to flee from British troops.

British Raids

In August 1814, British troops marched on Washington, D.C.—a city of only 8,000 people. As the cracking of rifles and the booming of cannons filled the air, President James Madison rode to the battle 7 miles (11.3 km) away. First Lady Dolley Madison stayed behind, racing through the White House to save what she could from the British soldiers. She narrowly escaped. When the British arrived, they set fire to the White House, the Capitol, and other buildings.

With Washington in flames, the British sailed up Chesapeake Bay to Baltimore. But Baltimore was protected by Fort McHenry. Although British ships bombed the fort for hours, the Americans refused to surrender.

Unable to defeat the American forces at Baltimore, the British sailed south to New Orleans. But American soldiers under General Andrew Jackson were waiting for them.

The British laid siege to New Orleans for ten days. Fierce fighting from Jackson's soldiers finally made the British leave the city. Americans would later learn that the Battle of New Orleans had not been necessary. On December 24, 1814—two weeks before the battle—the British and Americans had signed a peace treaty in Europe. Word that the war was over had not reached New Orleans in time.

REVIEW ***What were the results of British attacks on American cities?*** The British burned Washington. The Americans successfully defended Baltimore and New Orleans.

History

People and Events Across Time and Place Have students evaluate the importance of Perry's victory over the larger British fleet. Ask them to explain why Americans would be so proud of Perry's victory that his message, "We have met the enemy and they are ours," would become a kind of slogan in later wars.

British Raids

Key Content Summary

In 1814 the British marched on Washington, D.C., and set fire to the White House, tried to capture Fort McHenry in the Chesapeake Bay, and laid siege to New Orleans.

History

Patterns and Relationships Remind students that in 1814 Washington, D.C., was still a very small city and that President Madison was only the third President to occupy the mansion.

Q. **Why do you think the British set fire to the White House?** to destroy a strong symbol of American government

Link to Reading

READ A BIOGRAPHY Select students to read biographies of Tecumseh, Oliver Hazard Perry, William Henry Harrison, James Madison, Dolley Madison, Andrew Jackson, and James Monroe. Have students prepare oral reports and illustrations to present to the class. You may want to assign a team of two students for each biography.

Extend and Enrich

COOPERATIVE LEARNING

MAKE A SPEECH Divide the class into small groups. Tell each group that they will work together to write and edit a speech that might have been given by one of these people: Tecumseh, a War Hawk, President Madison, or President Monroe. Ask students to divide the work. Each group will select a member to deliver the speech in front of the class. The group as a whole will help the orator rehearse the speech. After the speeches are presented, have students discuss what they learned from the experience.

The Era of Good Feelings

Key Content Summary

After the War of 1812 a newly nationalistic United States dealt strongly with other countries. Monroe set a new border between the United States and British Canada, convinced Spain to give up claims in Florida, and established the Monroe Doctrine.

Civics and Government

Civic Values Ask students to recall how most Americans at the time of the American Revolution valued state loyalty more than national loyalty.

3. CLOSE

Have students consider again the Focus question on page 358.

What do you think makes people feel proud of their country?

Have students discuss reasons Americans felt proud of the United States in the early 1800s and reasons the students feel proud of the United States today.

LESSON 3 REVIEW—Answers

Check Understanding

1. Tecumseh hoped to unite them against the Americans settling on Indian lands.
2. By standing up to Britain, the United States had proved itself equal to the great European nation.

Think Critically

3. Northern merchants did not want a war that would interfere with their trade with Britain. The South and the West urged war. The South accused the British of stopping trade there. The West wanted British land.
4. Choices will vary, depending on events at the time this lesson is studied. Make sure students provide substantial reasons for identifying an individual as a national hero.

Show What You Know

Performance Assessment Display students' pictures while the creators of the pictures read their reports aloud.

What to Look For Look for evidence that the students understand how important naval action was in the war.

Birth of the Monroe Doctrine, a painting by Clyde DeLand, shows President Monroe (standing) discussing his doctrine with members of his Cabinet.

The Era of Good Feelings

After the War of 1812, Americans were proud that the United States had proved itself equal to a great European nation. A wave of **nationalism**, or pride in the country, swept the land. People began to feel for the first time that they were Americans, not Ohioans, Virginians, or New Yorkers. For this reason the years from 1817 to 1825 have been called the Era of Good Feelings.

National pride could be seen in the government's strong dealings with other countries. President James Monroe set a new border between the United States and British Canada. He also convinced Spain to give up claims in West Florida, which had been **annexed**, or added on, earlier, and to give East Florida to the United States.

President Monroe knew that if the United States wanted to keep growing, it had to stop the growth of the Spanish, French, and British colonies in the Americas. So on December 2, 1823, the President announced a **doctrine**, or government plan of action, that came to be called the Monroe Doctrine. The Monroe Doctrine declared that the United States was willing to go to war to stop European countries from expanding their American empires.

REVIEW ***How did the War of 1812 affect the United States and its people?*** The war helped Americans feel proud of their country.

LESSON 3 REVIEW

Check Understanding

1. **Remember the Facts** What did Tecumseh hope to accomplish by talking to other Indian tribes in the Northwest Territory?
2. **Recall the Main Idea** How did the War of 1812 help make Americans proud of their country?

Think Critically

3. **Explore Viewpoints** Why did people from the North, the South, and the West feel differently about going to war with Britain?
4. **Past to Present** Many Americans who took part in the War of 1812 became national heroes. Who are some heroes of today? What actions helped them become known as heroes?

Show What You Know

Research Activity Use the Internet or encyclopedias to find out more about the navy's battles in the War of 1812. Write a report about one battle. Draw a picture to illustrate your report. Present your findings to the class.

ACTIVITY CHOICES

ACTIVITY BOOK

Reinforce & Extend

Use ACTIVITY BOOK, p. 68.

Reteach the Main Idea

COOPERATIVE LEARNING

MAKE A LIST Divide the class into groups of four or five students each. Give each group a sheet of paper. Explain that the group members are to take turns listing the ways in which the War of 1812 helped Americans cooperate to defeat the British and feel proud of their country. When a suitable period of time has elapsed, ask a representative from each group to share the group's list with the class. Create a class list of their ideas.

Skills

Predict a Likely Outcome

1. Why Learn This Skill?

People often make **predictions**. This means that they look at the way things are and decide what they think will most likely happen next. When people make predictions, they are not guessing about what will happen in the future. They are using information and past experiences to predict a probable, or likely, outcome.

2. Understand the Process

You have read about the War of 1812. The British lost the Battle of The Thames. The Indian leader Tecumseh died during the battle, and Indian attacks on settlers in the Northwest Territory soon ended.

You can use this information to predict what probably happened next in the westward movement of settlers after the War of 1812. Follow these steps:

1. Think about what you already know about the loss of Indian lands as settlers moved west during the early years of the United States. Look for patterns in the events that took place.
2. Review the new information you learned about Tecumseh and the War of 1812.
3. Make a prediction about the westward movement of settlers following the war.
4. As you read or gather more information, ask yourself whether you still think your prediction is correct.
5. If necessary, go through the steps again to form a new prediction.

After going through these steps, you should have been able to predict that pioneers would continue to move west, building settlements on Indian lands.

3. Think and Apply

BUILDING CITIZENSHIP

In 1823 the Monroe Doctrine was announced. Follow the steps listed above to predict how the Monroe Doctrine would affect the growth of the United States. As you read the next chapter, see whether the new information you learn supports your prediction.

This painting, by German American artist Emanuel G. Leutze, shows one person's view of the westward movement of settlers.

Reteach the Skill

PREDICT AN OUTCOME

COOPERATIVE LEARNING

Have students work together in small groups to select topics of which they have some prior knowledge, such as school sports or other outside activities. Have the groups work through the steps outlined in Understand the Process to predict some likely outcome related to their topics. If necessary, allow them time to gather additional information from persons outside the classroom. Display the predictions and evaluate them later for accuracy. If they prove not to be correct, have volunteers explain why.

ACTIVITY BOOK

Practice & Apply

Use ACTIVITY BOOK, p. 69.

TRANSPARENCY

Use TRANSPARENCY 29.

MODEL & APPLY SKILLS

Objectives

1. Identify a method of predicting likely outcomes.
2. Practice making predictions about historical trends.

Vocabulary

prediction (p. 363)

1. ACCESS

List some significant classroom events that might point to future outcomes. Have students predict these outcomes and explain the reasoning that led to their predictions. Ask students to make other predictions based on their personal knowledge. Have them share these examples.

2. BUILD

Have students make predictions about the western movement of settlers after the War of 1812, using the steps in Understand the Process. Have them base their predictions on what they know about the War of 1812, as well as on what they know about the loss of Indian lands in colonial times and the early years of the nation. Encourage students to look for patterns in the earlier events. Have them share the reasoning that led to their predictions.

3. CLOSE

Have students use the steps for making predictions to complete the activity described in Think and Apply. After they have shared their predictions with partners, have the students make a class list of their predictions. Display the list and refer to it as students study the next chapter. At that time, have them evaluate and, if necessary, revise their predictions.

Objectives

1. Compare and contrast the British and American efforts in the conflict over Fort McHenry.
2. Analyze the defense the Americans put up during the conflict.
3. Explain how Francis Scott Key came to write the words to "The Star-Spangled Banner," our national anthem.

1. ACCESS

Discuss with students the many ways they might record an exciting event, such as videotaping it. Have students compare present-day technology for recording events with what was available in the 1800s. Lead students to draw conclusions about the ways in which a poem can make a vivid record of an event. Mention that Francis Scott Key's "The Star-Spangled Banner" made the attack on Fort McHenry vivid for future generations.

The Main Idea

In this lesson students read an account of the writing of the words of "The Star-Spangled Banner," our national anthem. After students have read the literature selection, discuss with them the events that led Francis Scott Key to write the poem and the qualities they believe a national anthem should have.

LESSON
4
LEARN HISTORY through Literature
By the Dawn's Early Light
The Story of The Star-Spangled Banner
by Steven Kroll
Illustrated by Dan Andreasen
364 • Unit 6

ACTIVITY CHOICES

Reading Support

PREVIEW AND READ THE LESSON Provide students with the following visual framework.

"THE STAR-SPANGLED BANNER"

"The Star-Spangled Banner"	Key pleads with British for release of Dr. Beanes.
	British detain Key and his two friends.
	Key sees bombardment of Fort McHenry.
	The Army and militia defend Fort McHenry.
	Key writes poem about the flag, which is still flying over the fort.
	The poem is printed and distributed in Baltimore the next day.
	The poem is set to music and becomes the national anthem.

While the British prepared to attack Baltimore during the War of 1812, an American doctor named William Beanes was held prisoner on the warship H.M.S. Tonnant. *With the permission of President Madison, Beanes's friend, Francis Scott Key, along with Colonel John S. Skinner, went to the ship to ask that Beanes be set free. Key explained to the British commanders that Beanes had cared for many wounded British soldiers during the Battle of Bladensburg. Major General Sir Robert Ross agreed to free Beanes, but said the three men would not be set free until after the British had attacked Fort McHenry.*

Read now about the frightening days early in September 1814 when the British fleet approached Baltimore. Key and Skinner have just been taken to see Dr. Beanes and have told him what is happening. As you read, think about how Francis Scott Key chose to describe his experiences.

2. BUILD

Key Content Summary

While the British bombard Fort McHenry in Baltimore, Francis Scott Key and two friends watch the action from a small vessel. Key is so inspired by the successful defense of the fort that he writes a poem, "The Star-Spangled Banner," which becomes the lyrics for our national anthem.

Auditory Learning

Express Ideas Orally Select one or two students to read aloud the introduction to the selection. Ask students to describe the circumstances under which Key was able to observe the British attack on Fort McHenry.

Visual Analysis

Learn from Pictures Have students examine the pictures on pages 364–365. Then ask them to describe which event is being shown.

Background

THE LITERATURE SELECTION *By the Dawn's Early Light: The Story of The Star-Spangled Banner* recounts the incident that inspired Francis Scott Key's poem. The author describes the efforts of Key, a Washington lawyer, to free his friend Dr. William Beanes from incarceration by the British. With President Madison's permission, Key boards a British ship to negotiate. Forced to remain in British custody by the impending attack on Baltimore, Key is inspired by the American victory to record his impression of the event in a poem. The book includes a photograph of the original manuscript of the poem as well as the entire text of the national anthem.

THE AUTHOR Steven Kroll was born on August 11, 1941, in New York City. A Harvard graduate, Kroll has had a long career in the literary world, beginning as an associate editor with the *Transatlantic Review* in London, England. Other children's books written by Kroll include *Is Milton Missing?* (a Junior Literary Guild selection), *Fat Magic, Monster Birthday*, and *Are You Pirates?*

Understanding the Story

Have students discuss the reasons Baltimore was defended both by the regular army and by a citizen militia. Ask students to speculate on the effectiveness of the trenches and ramparts built by the Baltimore citizens.

Q. **How had United States troops tried to slow the progress of the British fleet?** They had sunk small ships and barges in the northern channel of the river and stationed gunboats behind the sunken hulls.

Geography

Place Have students use a wall map or an atlas to locate Baltimore, the Patapsco River, and Fort McHenry. Discuss why Fort McHenry was in a good location to defend the city.

Understanding the Story

As students read pages 366–367, have them look for the words and phrases that describe what happened from dawn, through the day, and into the night of Tuesday, September 13. Make a class list of the descriptive words and phrases, and have students discuss the importance of words for creating pictures in the reader's mind when he or she reads a story.

Q. **How do you think Key, Skinner, and Beanes felt as they listened to and watched the bombardment?** concerned, scared, overwhelmed by the noise

"And we must sit and watch while our country is attacked?" Beanes exclaimed.

"I'm afraid so," Colonel Skinner replied.

The three Americans were put up on the frigate *Surprise*, and for three days the British fleet crept up Chesapeake Bay.

Meanwhile, Baltimore was getting ready. Though inexperienced, the militia was on call. The city was ringed by trenches and ramparts[1] built by citizens. At star-shaped Fort McHenry, out on Whetstone Point overlooking the Patapsco River, a thousand troops were under the command of Major George Armistead. They had thrown up barriers outside the moat, placed sandbags around the powder magazine,[2] and sunk many small ships and barges in the north channel of the river to slow enemy progress. They had also stationed a half-dozen small gunboats between the sunken hulls and the city.

There was a bold, new flag flying over the fort. Forty-two by thirty feet, fifteen stars and fifteen stripes, it was the work of Mary Pickersgill and her daughter, Caroline.

On Saturday, September 10th, the British fleet anchored off North Point at the mouth of the Patapsco River. Francis, Colonel Skinner, and Dr. Beanes were hustled from the *Surprise* back to their own small boat. Admiral Cochrane had decided to take personal command of the bombardment. He wanted the smaller, faster frigate as his flagship.

Sunday morning, Baltimore's church bells called the militia to arms. Monday, boats filled with British soldiers in scarlet uniforms began leaving for shore. Francis watched grimly. Things did not look good for the Americans.

With the troops underway on land, the fleet began moving upriver. As the ships came within view of Fort McHenry, the Stars and Stripes were waving overhead.

Later that afternoon, word came from shore. The Americans had retreated to positions outside the city. General Ross had been killed.

[1]**rampart:** protective barrier
[2]**powder magazine:** storage area for gunpowder

ACTIVITY CHOICES

AUDIO

Use the UNIT 6 MUSIC AUDIOCASSETTE to hear "The Star-Spangled Banner."

Link to Music

SING THE NATIONAL ANTHEM
Ask the music teacher to teach students to sing the national anthem. Alternatively, you might wish to have students sing the anthem with a recording.

Meet Individual Needs

AUDITORY LEARNERS Have students use dictionaries as necessary to discuss the meanings of the footnoted words in the lesson. Then ask students to discuss the pronunciation of each word, and remind them to refer to the footnotes as necessary when they read the lesson.

A silence seemed to fall over the fleet, but preparations continued. Francis, Dr. Beanes, and Colonel Skinner spent a restless night as sixteen smaller British ships moved into the shallower water closer to the fort.

At dawn the bombardment began. The noise was so great and the smell of burning powder so strong that the three hostages were forced to take refuge in their cabin. When the response from the fort seemed to die away for a moment, it became clear that the Americans' thirty-six-pound shells were not reaching the ships. But then the heavy shelling and rocketing began again and went on hour after hour.

At dusk Francis crawled out onto the deck. "Can you see the flag?" Dr. Beanes called after him.

Francis squinted through the smoke and the din and the glow of the setting sun. "The flag is flying," he replied.

Soon after, it began to rain.

Thunder and lightning joined the booming of the guns. Very late that night, Francis struggled out on deck again. Though he could not know it, at that moment the British were trying to land a thousand men at Ferry Branch. An American sentry discovered them and Fort McHenry began to fire. As the barges fled, every available American gun pursued them.

The rainy night sky was suddenly lit up, and in that moment Francis could see the flag again. It was soaked now and drooping from its staff, but it was there, still there.

By dawn the rain had stopped and the fight was over. Peering through the clouds, Francis, Dr. Beanes, and Colonel Skinner strained to see what flag was flying over the fort. Had the British triumphed in the night? But no, there it was, unfurling in the breeze, the Stars and Stripes!

All his life, Francis had written poetry. He reached into his pocket and found an old letter. With the tune to the song, "To Anacreon[3] in Heaven" in mind, he scribbled *O say can you see* and then *by the dawn's early light.*

He wrote a few more lines, crossed out a few, but there wasn't much time.

[3]**Anacreon:** a Greek poet

Culture

Symbols Discuss with students the significance of the American flag to Key and his two companions.

Q. **What do you think Key would have seen if the fort had been taken by the British?** the British flag

History

People and Events Across Time and Place Have students compare and contrast the attack on Fort McHenry with modern artillery bombardments. Discuss the fact that Key and Skinner were able to talk to the British commander and obtain Dr. Beanes's release. Have students provide examples of similar present-day negotiations.

Background

THE NATIONAL ANTHEM For many years after it was written, "The Star-Spangled Banner" was sung by Americans as the national anthem. However, it did not become the official national anthem until 1916, when President Woodrow Wilson issued an executive order to that effect. His order was confirmed by Congress in 1931.

Meet Individual Needs

ENGLISH LANGUAGE LEARNERS The words to "The Star-Spangled Banner" can be difficult to understand. Have English language learners work with advanced learners. The English language learner should read the lines aloud, one at a time. After each line, the advanced learner should explain what the line means. Students should continue through the entire song. Then have pairs perform the song for the class, either by singing it or by reading it expressively as a poem.

Understanding the Story

As students read page 368, have them look for examples of the reactions to the American victory over the British.

Q. **Why do you think Judge Nicholson was in such a hurry to get Key's poem printed and handed out?** There was so much excitement over the American victory that Judge Nicholson probably realized that the people of Maryland would appreciate the poem at that momentous time.

Civics and Government

Patriotic Identity Ask students to describe their personal responses to the playing of the national anthem at such events as the Olympics. Lead students to draw conclusions about the value of having a national anthem. Discuss whether hearing the anthem might affect the listener's willingness to cooperate with other citizens in civic activities.

Already redcoats were leaving for the ships. The fleet was abandoning the assault!

The sails of the little cartel boat[4] were returned to the members of its American crew. By afternoon, Francis, Dr. Beanes, and Colonel Skinner were back in Baltimore.

Cheering crowds were everywhere. The three men went straight to the Indian Queen Hotel on Baltimore Street, rested and had supper, but later that night, Francis finished the four stanzas[5] of his poem.

The next day he went to visit his brother-in-law, Judge Joseph Nicholson, who had been at Fort McHenry. Judge Nicholson loved the new poem. "Let's get it printed," he insisted.

The judge rushed over to the *Baltimore American*, but the printers weren't back from defending the fort. A young apprentice, Samuel Sands, agreed to set the verses in type and run off the handbills. Because Francis hadn't thought of a title, Judge Nicholson came up with "The Defense of Fort McHenry," but it wasn't long before everyone was singing what had come to be known as "The Star-Spangled Banner."

[4]**cartel boat:** cargo boat
[5]**stanza:** section of a poem

Activity Choices

Smithsonian Institution®

Go to the Internet site at *http://www.si.edu/harcourt/socialstudies* to explore the history of "The Star-Spangled Banner" on the Timeline at the National Museum of American History.

Extend and Enrich

COOPERATIVE LEARNING

MAKE A MURAL Divide the class into groups of four to six students each. Provide each group with crayons or markers and a large sheet of butcher paper about 6 feet in length. Instruct groups to create a series of connected drawings on the butcher paper depicting the battle of Fort McHenry. Each member of the group will be responsible for completing an individual panel in the group's mural. You might want to display the completed murals in the classroom or in the hallway.

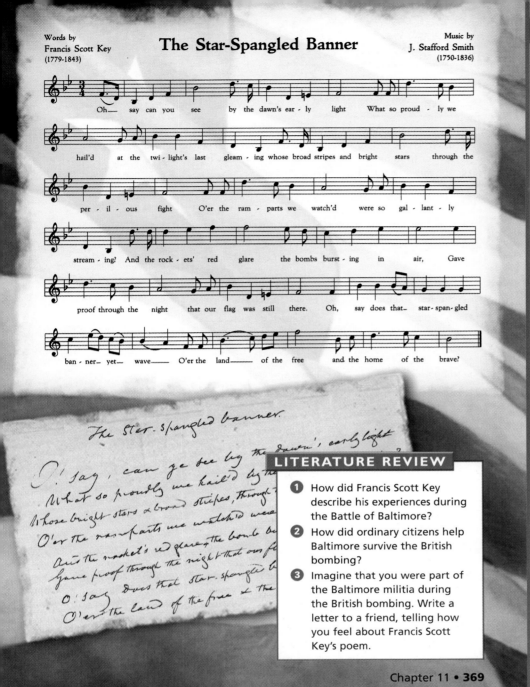

Words by
Francis Scott Key
(1779-1843)
The Star-Spangled Banner
Music by
J. Stafford Smith
(1750-1836)
Oh— say can you see by the dawn's ear - ly light What so proud - ly we
hail'd at the twi - light's last gleam - ing whose broad stripes and bright stars through the
per - il - ous fight O'er the ram - parts we watch'd were so gal - lant - ly
stream - ing? And the rock - ets' red glare the bombs burst - ing in air, Gave
proof through the night that our flag was still there. Oh, say does that— star - span - gled
ban - ner- yet— wave— O'er the land— of the free and the home of the brave?

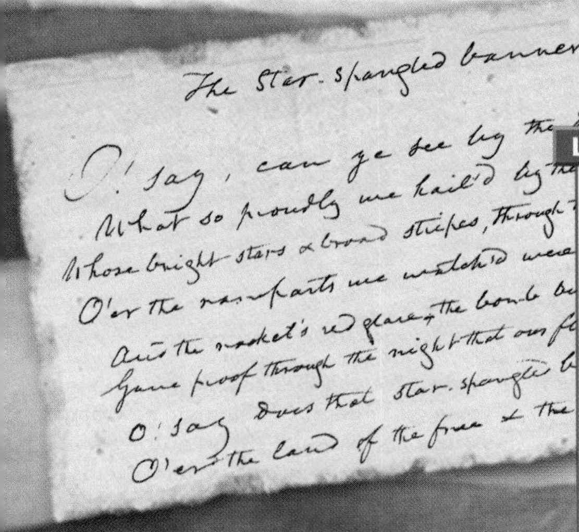
The Star-spangled banner.

LITERATURE REVIEW

1. How did Francis Scott Key describe his experiences during the Battle of Baltimore?
2. How did ordinary citizens help Baltimore survive the British bombing?
3. Imagine that you were part of the Baltimore militia during the British bombing. Write a letter to a friend, telling how you feel about Francis Scott Key's poem.

Auditory Learning

Read Dramatically Have students volunteer to read aloud the first stanza of "The Star-Spangled Banner." Remind them to concentrate on the words and their meanings so that they do not slip into the rhythm of the music as they read the poem.

3. CLOSE

Ask students the following question to focus on our national anthem.

Why is "The Star-Spangled Banner" our national anthem today?

Have students think about what they have learned about "The Star-Spangled Banner." Ask them to speculate on why it continues to be our national anthem today.

LITERATURE REVIEW—Answers

1. by writing a poem
2. They built trenches and ramparts.
3. The letter should express pride in the fact that the poem reflected the courage of the defenders of Fort McHenry.

Reteach the Main Idea

COOPERATIVE LEARNING

WRITE A VERSE Divide the class into groups of four to six students. Explain to students that their task is to work together to write and perform a new verse for the national anthem. The new verse is to reflect events of the twentieth century just as the original verses reflect events of the nineteenth century. Tell students they may include references to wars if they wish, but that the verse might also celebrate scientific and cultural achievements. Tell students to work as a group to write the verse, edit it, and make a final draft. Allow students time to rehearse their verses. Then have each group sing its verse for the class.

ACTIVITY BOOK

Reinforce & Extend

Use ACTIVITY BOOK, p. 70.

CHAPTER 11
REVIEW

Time Line
Ask students to share what they recall about each event shown on the time line.

Connect Main Ideas
Use the organizer to review the main ideas of the chapter. Have students use their textbooks to complete or check their work. Allow time for them to compare and discuss their responses with those of their classmates.

ACTIVITY BOOK

Summarize the Chapter

A copy of the graphic organizer appears on ACTIVITY BOOK, p. 71.

TRANSPARENCY

A copy of the graphic organizer appears on TRANSPARENCY 30.

Write More About It
Express an Opinion
Students' opinions will vary but should reflect an understanding of the importance of the Louisiana Purchase and its impact on the United States.

Write a Newspaper Article
Students' newspaper articles should include the answers to journalism's basic questions: *who*, *what*, *when*, *where*, and *why*. The articles should also reflect an understanding of the events that occurred at Fort McHenry and include information pertaining to Francis Scott Key.

TECHNOLOGY

Use THE AMAZING WRITING MACHINE™ to complete the writing activities.

TECHNOLOGY

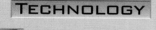

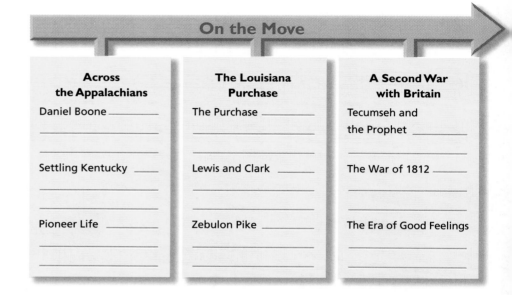

Use TIMELINER™ DATA DISKS to discuss and summarize the chapter.

CHAPTER 11
REVIEW

1775 | 1785

1775
- Daniel Boone settles Kentucky

CONNECT MAIN IDEAS

Use this organizer to show how the chapter's main ideas are connected. Write one or two sentences to tell about each person or pair of people or to summarize each event or idea. A copy of the organizer appears on page 71 of the Activity Book.

Possible answers to this graphic organizer are provided on page 348C of this Teacher's Edition.

On the Move

Across the Appalachians	The Louisiana Purchase	A Second War with Britain
Daniel Boone ______	The Purchase ______	Tecumseh and the Prophet ______
Settling Kentucky ______	Lewis and Clark ______	The War of 1812 ______
Pioneer Life ______	Zebulon Pike ______	The Era of Good Feelings ______

WRITE MORE ABOUT IT

Express an Opinion Suppose that President Jefferson has asked for your opinion on whether or not the United States should purchase the Louisiana Territory. Write what you would tell him.

Write a Newspaper Article Imagine that you are a writer for a Baltimore newspaper. Write a headline and a short article about Francis Scott Key and the exciting events at Fort McHenry.

370 • Chapter 11

Use Vocabulary
1. pioneers (p. 349)
2. purchase (p. 354)
3. pathfinders (p. 355)
4. impressment (p. 360)
5. nationalism (p. 362)
6. annex (p. 362)

Check Understanding
7. the path taken by Daniel Boone and other settlers through the Appalachian Mountains into Kentucky (p. 350)
8. to protect themselves from attacks by Indians (p. 352)
9. Spain hoped to stop the United State from moving its frontier farther west (p. 353)
10. They explored the northwestern portion of the land obtained in th Louisiana Purchase, reaching th Pacific Ocean. Sacagawea served as translator. (pp. 355–356)
11. They said the British were giving gun to the Indians and talking agains American settlers. (p. 359)
12. Northern merchants had made a lo of money trading with the British They did not want a war that woul end their trade. (p. 360)

1805 1815 1825

1801
• Thomas Jefferson becomes the third President

1804
• Lewis and Clark expedition begins

1812
• The War of 1812 begins

1823
• The Monroe Doctrine is announced

Use Vocabulary

Use the terms from the list to complete the paragraphs that follow. Use each term once.

annex	**pathfinders**
impressment	**pioneers**
nationalism	**purchase**

When the American Revolution ended, __1__ settled the western frontier. Then, in 1803, the United States decided to __2__ land west of the Mississippi River. __3__ soon found ways through this unknown region.

The United States found itself at war with Britain. Americans were upset over the __4__ of sailors. Although neither side was clearly the winner, a wave of __5__ swept the land. The United States decided to __6__ Spanish West Florida.

Check Understanding

7 What was the Wilderness Road?

8 Why did pioneers often band together in forts?

9 What did Spain hope to do by closing the port of New Orleans to western farmers?

10 What did Lewis and Clark accomplish? How did Sacagawea help them?

11 Why did many Americans blame the British for Indian attacks on settlers?

12 Why were many northern merchants against the idea of declaring war on Britain?

13 What was the Era of Good Feelings?

14 Who was Francis Scott Key?

Think Critically

15 **Think More About It** What do you think Tecumseh meant when he said that no one tribe had the right to sell land?

16 **Personally Speaking** Why do you think so many pioneers chose to risk their lives to settle in Kentucky and Tennessee? Would you have made the same choice? Explain.

17 **Explore Viewpoints** How do you think Americans viewed the Monroe Doctrine? How do you think Europeans viewed the Monroe Doctrine?

Apply Skills

Predict a Likely Outcome Think about the events that usually take place in school on each day of the week. Predict the events that are likely to take place next week. What steps might you follow to make these predictions?

Read More About It

A Pioneer Sampler: The Daily Life of a Pioneer Family in 1840 by Barbara Greenwood. Houghton Mifflin. This book tells about daily pioneer life and contains many activities for readers to enjoy.

Visit the Internet at **http://www.hbschool.com** for additional resources.

CHAPTER 11 REVIEW

Apply Skills

Predict a Likely Outcome Students' lists should include events that really do occur regularly in your school. Have students explain the steps they follow to make predictions.

Read More About It

Additional books are listed in the Multimedia Resource Center on page 340D of this Teacher's Edition.

Unit Project Check-Up

Check to make sure that students have started their sketches. Also make sure students have reference materials having to do with pioneers. Some illustrations of pioneers that students may have begun sketching include pictures that show relations with the Indians, clearing the land, building log cabins and forts, growing food, making clothes, and making tools.

ASSESSMENT PROGRAM

Use CHAPTER 11 TEST, pp. 95–98.

3 The Era of Good Feelings was the period of time following the War of 1812 when a wave of nationalism swept over the United States. (p. 362)

4 Key is the author of the poem "The Star-Spangled Banner," which later became our national anthem. (pp. 365–369)

hink Critically

5 Tecumseh believed that the land, like the water and the air, was there for everyone to share. He believed that no one could own something that had been here for thousands of years and that would be here long after we are all gone.

16 Some students may like the idea of exploring new frontiers, while others may cite the many dangers faced by the pioneers as good reasons not to cross the Appalachians.

17 Some students may think that Americans supported the Monroe Doctrine because it would allow the United States to grow and to control most of the continent's rich land. Others may think that Americans believed that the doctrine made unfair claims to land. Students may think Europeans did not like the Monroe Doctrine because it put limits on the Europeans' ability to colonize.

Planning Chart

	THEMES • Strands	VOCABULARY	MEET INDIVIDUAL NEEDS	RESOURCES INCLUDING ▶ TECHNOLOGY
LESSON 1 **The Industrial Revolution** pp. 373–378	**CONTINUITY & CHANGE** • History • Economics • Geography	Industrial Revolution textile mill mass production interchangeable part transport canal locomotive	Visual Learners, p. 374 Extend and Enrich, p. 377 Reteach the Main Idea, p. 378	Activity Book, p. 72 ▶ THE AMAZING WRITING MACHINE ▶ GRAPH LINKS ▶ DECISIONS, DECISIONS
LESSON 2 **The Age of Jackson** pp. 379–382	**INDIVIDUALISM & INTERDEPENDENCE** • Geography • Civics and Government • History • Culture	sectionalism states' rights secede ruling	Extend and Enrich, p. 381 Reteach the Main Idea, p. 382	Activity Book, p. 73
LESSON 3 **Westward Ho!** pp. 383–389	**INTERACTION WITHIN DIFFERENT ENVIRONMENTS** • Culture • History • Geography	Manifest Destiny dictator forty-niner	Visual Learners, p. 385 Extend and Enrich, p. 388 Reteach the Main Idea, p. 389	Activity Book, p. 74 ▶ THE ALAMO ▶ THE AMAZING WRITING MACHINE ▶ NATIONAL INSPIRER ▶ TIMELINER
SKILL **Use Relief and Elevation Maps** pp. 390–391	**BASIC STUDY SKILLS** • Map and Globe Skills	relief elevation	Tactile Learners, p. 390 Reteach the Skill, p. 391	Activity Book, p. 75 Transparency 31 Desk Maps ▶ MAPSKILLS
LESSON 4 **An Age of Reform** pp. 392–396	**CONTINUITY & CHANGE** • Culture • Civics and Government • History	reform public school abolish abolitionist equality suffrage	English Language Learners, p. 395 Extend and Enrich, p. 395 Reteach the Main Idea, p. 396	Activity Book, p. 76 ▶ THE AMAZING WRITING MACHINE
SKILL **Use a Double-Bar Graph** p. 397	**BASIC STUDY SKILLS** • Chart and Graph Skills		Reteach the Skill, p. 397	Activity Book, pp. 77–78 Transparency 32 ▶ GRAPH LINKS
CHAPTER REVIEW pp. 398–399				Activity Book, p. 79 Transparency 33 Assessment Program Chapter 12 Test, pp. 99–102 ▶ THE AMAZING WRITING MACHINE ▶ TIMELINER ▶ INTERNET

8 DAYS

TIME MANAGEMENT

DAY 1	DAY 2	DAY 3	DAY 4	DAY 5	DAY 6	DAY 7	DAY 8
Lesson 1	Lesson 2	Lesson 3	Skill	Lesson 4	Skill	Chapter Review	Chapter Test

Activity Book

LESSON 1
Link Past Technology to the Present

NAME ______________________ DATE ____________

Inventors and their Inventions

Link Past Technology to the Present

DIRECTIONS: Complete the following chart about inventions of the Industrial Revolution by filling in the missing information.

INVENTOR	INVENTION	IMPORTANCE OF INVENTION	WHAT YOUR LIFE WOULD BE LIKE WITHOUT THE INVENTION
Unknown	spinning machine	made large textile mills possible; helped bring the Industrial Revolution to the United States	Answers in this column should reflect students' understanding of uses of these inventions.
Eli Whitney	interchangeable parts	mass production	
Francis Cabot Lowell	one-factory system	spinning, dyeing, and weaving could be done under one roof	
Robert Fulton	steamboat, the *Clermont*	sped up travel and trade over water	
Peter Cooper	locomotive, the *Tom Thumb*	sped up travel and trade over land	

 Use after reading Chapter 12, Lesson 1, pages 373–378.

LESSON 2
Sequence Events

NAME ______________________ DATE ____________

The Trail of Tears

Sequence Events

DIRECTIONS: Read the following events leading up to the Trail of Tears. Then identify the year in which each event took place. You may wish to review the information in your textbook before you begin.

1829 Gold is discovered on Cherokee lands; settlers pour in to stake their claims.

1832 Chief Justice John Marshall gives the Court's ruling that the United States should protect the Cherokees and their lands in Georgia, but President Jackson ignores the ruling.

(1830) Congress passes the Indian Removal Act, forcing all Indians living east of the Mississippi to move to the Indian Territory.

1791 The United States government agrees to accept the independence of the Cherokee nation.

1829 Andrew Jackson becomes the seventh President of the United States.

[1838] A large group of Cherokees begin the journey that has come to be known as the Trail of Tears; more than 4,000 Cherokees die.

DIRECTIONS: Use the information above to complete the following activities.

1. Circle the date of the event that marks the beginning of forced relocation of native peoples from the East to the West.
2. Underline an economic reason why the Cherokees were forced from their lands.
3. Draw a box around the year that marks the beginning of the Trail of Tears.
4. On a separate sheet of paper, draw a horizontal time line using the dates and events listed above. Start your time line at 1790 and end it at 1840. Make one inch represent a ten-year period.
   Accept all time lines with the following characteristics: all dates and events listed in the correct order, starts at 1790 with ten-year increments every inch up to 1840, and measures 5" in length.

Use after reading Chapter 12, Lesson 2, pages 379–382.

LESSON 3
Arrange Information in Order

NAME ______________________ DATE ____________

THE Oregon Trail

Arrange Information in Order

DIRECTIONS: Read the following sentences about a trip on the Oregon Trail. Then place the sentences in the proper order by numbering them from 1 to 6, with 1 being the earliest event and 6 being the latest event.

2 A steamboat carries our family up the river from St. Louis to Independence, Missouri.

6 The wagons in our group finally arrive in Willamette Valley. Oregon at last!

4 At nightfall the wagons in our group circle for camp.

3 In Independence we load our possessions onto a wagon and hear the cry, "Wagons roll!"

1 We leave our home in the East and board a train headed for St. Louis, Missouri.

5 In the morning we eat breakfast, and then continue our journey by wagon to Oregon.

DIRECTIONS: Study the list of supplies below. Then complete the activities that follow.

One box of sardines	*$16*	1
One pound of hard bread	*$ 2*	4
One pound of butter	*$ 6*	2
One-half pound of cheese	*$ 3*	3
Total	$27	

1. Number the items from most expensive to least expensive in the spaces provided. Start numbering with *1* as the most expensive.
2. Write the total cost of the supplies in the space provided.
3. Imagine that you can spend only $25. Put a line through the item or items that you would have to take off your list. Answers will vary, although many students may put a line through *"one pound of hard bread,"* which costs $2.

 Use after reading Chapter 12, Lesson 3, pages 383–389.

SKILL PRACTICE
Apply Map and Globe Skills

NAME ______________________ DATE ____________

HOW TO USE RELIEF and Elevation Maps

Apply Map and Globe Skills

DIRECTIONS: Study the map of the Oregon Trail. Then answer the questions that follow.

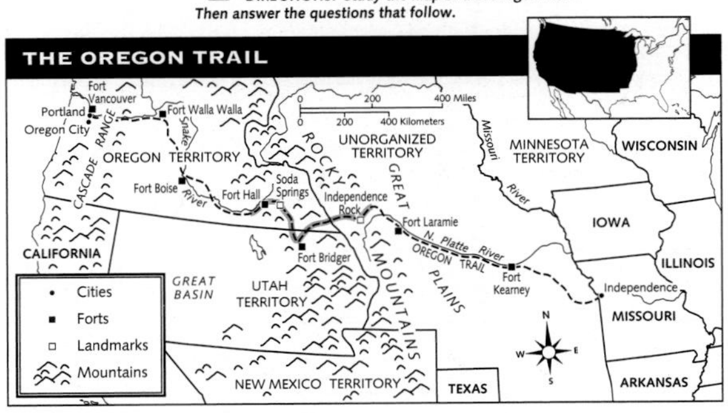

1. Write in the correct sequence the names of the physical features you would pass through if you traveled the Oregon Trail from Independence, Missouri, to Fort Vancouver.
   Great Plains, N. Platte River, Rocky Mountains, Snake River, Cascade Range
2. Trace over the part of the Oregon Trail that passes through the Rocky Mountains.
   Through which forts does this part of the trail pass? Fort Bridger and Fort Hall
3. Which river did the Oregon Trail follow just west of the Rocky Mountains?
   Snake River
4. On a separate sheet of paper, describe the trip along the Oregon Trail from Independence to Portland. Include in your description the forts and landmarks along the way and the changes in the geography. Answers may vary but should include descriptions of forts and landmarks as well as of plains and mountainous areas.

Use after reading Chapter 12, Skill Lesson, pages 390–391.

LESSON 4
Compare Primary Sources

NAME ______________________________ DATE ____________

Seneca Falls

Compare Primary Sources

DIRECTIONS: Read the following opening lines of the Declaration of Sentiments by Elizabeth Cady Stanton. Complete the activities that follow by comparing these lines with the opening lines of the Declaration of Independence, which can be found on page R19 in your textbook.

Declaration of Sentiments

When, in the course of human events, it becomes necessary for one portion of the family of man to assume among the people of the earth a position different from that which they have hitherto occupied, but one to which the laws of nature and of nature's God entitle them, a decent respect to the opinions of mankind requires that they should declare the causes that impel them to such a course.

We hold these truths to be self-evident: that all men and women are created equal; that they are endowed by their Creator with certain inalienable rights; that among these are life, liberty, and the pursuit of happiness. . . .

1. Underline the words in the Declaration of Sentiments that are different from the words in the Declaration of Independence.
2. Why do you think the author of this document did not change the word "mankind"?
   Accept answers that discuss the historical usage of the word *mankind*, which was used at that time to refer to both men and women.
3. Write the phrase from the Declaration of Independence that was completely left out of the Declaration of Sentiments. (Don't include words used as substitutes.)
   to dissolve the political bands which have connected them with another
4. Why do you think the author would model the Declaration of Sentiments after the Declaration of Independence?
   Accept answers that refer to the Declaration of Independence, which expresses the rights of the people, as a document Americans respect.

 Use after reading Chapter 12, Lesson 4, pages 392–396.

SKILL PRACTICE
Apply Chart and Graph Skills

NAME ______________________________ DATE ____________

HOW TO USE A Double-Bar Graph

Apply Chart and Graph Skills

DIRECTIONS: Use the facts at the right to make a double-bar graph in the space below. Create a key and title for your graph. Then answer the questions on the next page.

POPULATION GROWTH 1790–1860 (IN THOUSANDS)

YEAR	AFRICAN	WHITE
1790	757	3,172
1800	1,002	4,306
1810	1,378	5,862
1820	1,772	7,867
1830	2,329	10,537
1840	2,874	14,196
1850	3,639	19,553
1860	4,442	26,923

KEY
- African
- White

Population Growth, 1790–1860
(TITLE)

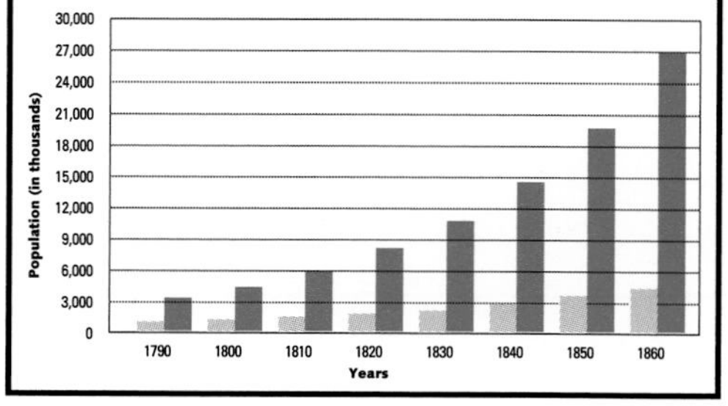

(continued)

Use after reading Chapter 12, Skill Lesson, page 397.

SKILL PRACTICE
Apply Chart and Graph Skills

NAME ______________________________ DATE ____________

1. What interval is used on the bar graph to show the increase in population?
   Accept either 3,000 or 3,000,000.
2. What interval is used to show the passage of time? 10 years
3. How many years does this bar graph cover? 70 years
4. During which ten-year period did the white population grow the least?
   1790–1800
5. During which ten-year period was there the least growth in the African population?
   1790–1800
6. Compare the growth of the African population with that of the white population. List two generalizations you can make using the data.
   Answers include: white population grew more but also started with a larger population; both African and white populations grew steadily, but white population grew faster; white population was always larger than African population regardless of growth.
7. Compare the table on page 77 with the double-bar graph you created. Which of the two makes it easier for you to understand the information? Why?
   Accept all answers that students can defend.

 Use after reading Chapter 12, Skill Lesson, page 397.

CHAPTER 12 REVIEW
Connect Main Ideas

NAME ______________________________ DATE ____________

THE WAY WEST

Connect Main Ideas

DIRECTIONS: Use this organizer to show how the chapter's main ideas are connected. Write three details to support each main idea.

The Industrial Revolution
New technology changed life in the United States in the 1800s.
1. Textile technology was brought to the United States in 1790.
2. Manufacturing became more efficient when spinning, dyeing, and weaving were done under one roof.
3. Advances in transportation, such as the Erie Canal, National Road, and railroads, spurred the Industrial Revolution.

The Age of Jackson
Problems divided the American people in the early 1800s.
1. Sectionalism led to long debates over states' rights versus the Union.
2. South Carolina threatened to secede because of tariffs.
3. President Jackson forced Cherokees to move to the Indian Territory.

The Way West

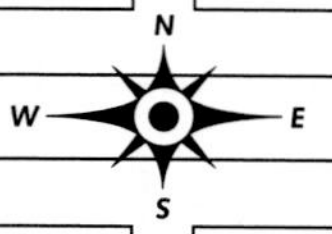

Westward Ho!
The United States expanded its territory in the 1800s.
1. A treaty was signed with Britain to establish the United States–Canadian border and acquire Oregon, Washington, Idaho, Wyoming, and western Montana.
2. President James K. Polk wanted to see the United States reach the Pacific Ocean.
3. In the Treaty of Guadalupe Hidalgo, the United States purchased California and other lands in the Southwest.

An Age of Reform
People in the 1800s worked to make American society better.
1. Educational reforms improved public schools.
2. Abolitionists worked to end slavery.
3. Reformers worked to gain rights for women, including the right to vote.

Use after reading Chapter 12, pages 372–399.

Chapter 12 Assessment

For ongoing **PERFORMANCE ASSESSMENT,** see Show What You Know, pp. 378, 382, 389, 396.

CONTENT

NAME ______________________ DATE ____________

Chapter Test 12

Part One: Test Your Understanding (4 points each)

DIRECTIONS: *Use a name from the box below to complete each of the sentences that follow.*

Frederick Douglass	Robert Fulton
Francis Cabot Lowell	Horace Mann
Samuel Slater	Harriet Beecher Stowe

1. A British factory worker named ___Samuel Slater___ brought the plans for a spinning machine to the United States.

2. ___Francis Cabot Lowell___ built a textile mill in which spinning, dyeing, and weaving all took place in the same factory.

3. ___Robert Fulton___ built a steamboat that he called the *Clermont*.

4. ___Horace Mann___ believed schools should be supported by taxes and should be free and open to all children.

5. ___Harriet Beecher Stowe___ wrote *Uncle Tom's Cabin*, which turned many people against slavery.

6. A runaway slave named ___Frederick Douglass___ told many people about his escape from slavery.

DIRECTIONS: *Circle the letter of the best answer.*

7. One thing that helped Andrew Jackson become President in 1828 was the fact that
- **A.** only people who could read and write were allowed to vote.
- **B.** married women could vote if they promised to vote the same way as their husbands.
- **(C.)** white men no longer had to own property to vote.
- **D.** free Africans were allowed to vote for the first time.

(continued)

CONTENT

NAME ______________________ DATE ____________

8. Who was responsible for forcing the Cherokees off their land and onto the Trail of Tears?
- **A.** John Calhoun
- **B.** James Monroe
- **C.** John Marshall
- **(D.)** Andrew Jackson

9. Which of the following statements best describes the idea of Manifest Destiny?
- **A.** All American citizens should have the right to vote.
- **B.** All American women should have the right to own property.
- **(C.)** The United States should stretch from the Atlantic Ocean to the Pacific Ocean.
- **D.** All Native Americans should live in the land west of the Mississippi River.

10. In order to practice their religion where no one would bother them, the Mormons settled in what is now
- **A.** Texas.
- **(B.)** Utah.
- **C.** Oregon.
- **D.** Kansas.

11. The United States purchased California and much more land in the West after it won a war with
- **A.** Spain.
- **B.** France.
- **C.** Britain.
- **(D.)** Mexico.

12. Forty-niners were people who
- **A.** wanted to end slavery.
- **B.** traveled on the Oregon Trail.
- **(C.)** went to California to search for gold.
- **D.** supported the idea of states' rights.

13. Abolitionists worked to
- **(A.)** put an end to slavery.
- **B.** persuade people to use tax money to support schools.
- **C.** start a war with Mexico.
- **D.** give women the vote.

14. Which of these people was a former slave who traveled across the United States speaking out against slavery?
- **(A.)** Sojourner Truth
- **B.** William Lloyd Garrison
- **C.** Harriet Beecher Stowe
- **D.** Horace Mann

(continued)

SKILLS

NAME ______________________ DATE ____________

Part Two: Test Your Skills (20 points)

DIRECTIONS: *Use the information in the double-bar graph to answer the questions.*

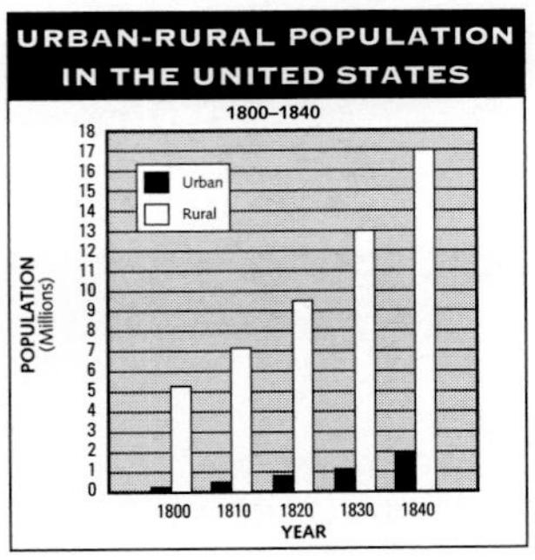

15. Between 1800 and 1840, did more people live in urban areas, such as New York City, or in rural areas? ___in rural areas___

16. About how many people lived in rural areas in 1810? ___about 7 million people___

17. In which year on the graph did the population in urban areas first pass one million? ___in 1830___

18. To the closest million, what was the **total** (urban and rural) population of the United States in 1840? ___19 million people___

19. The population in both areas grew a lot in the 40 years shown on the graph, but which population grew at the faster rate? ___the urban population___

(continued)

APPLICATION/WRITING

NAME ______________________ DATE ____________

Part Three: Apply What You Have Learned

DIRECTIONS: *Complete each of the following activities.*

20. ***The Industrial Revolution*** (8 points)
The Industrial Revolution brought many changes to the United States. In the boxes below, list two changes in transportation and two changes in manufacturing brought about by the Industrial Revolution.

CHANGES IN TRANSPORTATION	CHANGES IN MANUFACTURING
Possible responses: new roadways, such as the National Road; the steamboat; the locomotive	Possible responses: mass production; interchangeable parts; Lowell's factory system

21. ***Abolitionists Spread Their Message*** (6 points)
Abolitionists used speakers, newspapers, and books to tell Americans about slavery. In the chart below, give one example of each method.

METHODS	EXAMPLES
Speakers	Possible responses: Frederick Douglass or Sojourner Truth
Newspapers	*Freedom's Journal* or *The Liberator*
Books	*Uncle Tom's Cabin*

22. ***Essay*** (10 points)
President Andrew Jackson and Vice President John C. Calhoun disagreed on the issues of sectionalism and states' rights. Write one paragraph explaining how the two leaders differed in their views.

Possible response: The views of the President and the Vice President on sectionalism and states' rights were very different. President Jackson supported national unity and was opposed to sectionalism. Vice President Calhoun, on the other hand, believed strongly in sectionalism and the idea that states have final authority over the national government.

Introduce the Chapter

This chapter discusses the great internal changes that took place in the United States following the War of 1812. As the Industrial Revolution got under way, factories, with their mass production methods, sprang up, and canals and roads were built for long-distance travel. Meanwhile, sectional conflicts intensified, and Indians were removed from their native lands. The country continued to add new territory in the Far West, and reformers were becoming more outspoken.

Link Prior Learning

Explain to students that in this chapter they will learn about dramatic changes that took place in the United States following the War of 1812. Have students use what they learned in Chapter 11 to predict what some of those changes might be. Compile their predictions, and have students compare them to the events they read about in the chapter.

Visual Analysis

Interpret Pictures As students examine the picture of Juan Seguín, point out that he was involved in the fight for Texas independence. Have students speculate about what the artist of this portrait wanted people to know about Seguín. Then share with the class the background information about Seguín.

Auditory Learning

Interpret Primary Sources Have a volunteer read the quotation by William Travis aloud.

Q. **What can you conclude about Travis from the quotation?** He was strongly committed to Texas independence and was willing to die for it.

“PRIMARY SOURCE”

Source: *Susanna of the Alamo: A True Story.* John Jakes. Harcourt Brace Jovanovich, Publishers, 1986.

CHAPTER

12 The Way West

“I am determined to sustain myself as long as possible & die like a soldier who never forgets what is due to his own honor & that of his country— victory or death.”

The words of William Travis, describing the determination of those fighting for Texas independence

Juan Seguín, fighter for Texas independence

372

Activity Choices

Background

JUAN SEGUÍN Captain Juan Seguín supported the Texas movement for independence. He commanded a scouting company for the Texas army, under the leadership of Sam Houston. When San Antonio, Seguín's birthplace, was threatened by the Mexican army, Seguín recruited Tejanos who volunteered to join the fight to save San Antonio. *Tejano* refers to Mexicans living in Texas.

WILLIAM TRAVIS Colonel William B. Travis commanded the Texans at the Alamo. He felt strongly that the future of Texas depended upon his success at the Alamo. His courage and determination helped inspire the small group of volunteers to fight Santa Anna to the death. Although the Alamo was a defeat for the Texas army, the effort was an inspiration in later battles for independence.

The Industrial Revolution

LESSON 1

FOCUS How might a new technology change a person's life today?

Main Idea As you read, look for ways new technology changed life in the United States in the 1800s.

Vocabulary
Industrial Revolution
textile mill
mass production
interchangeable part
transport
canal
locomotive

Before the War of 1812, the economy of the United States had been growing. This growth increased after the war. New inventions changed the way goods were made. People began using machines instead of hand tools. New transportation routes were built. This **Industrial Revolution** brought great changes in the ways people lived, worked, and traveled.

Industry Comes to the United States

In a factory in Britain, a young worker named Samuel Slater carefully studied the new spinning machine until he could remember exactly how each iron gear and wooden spool worked. This invention made large textile mills possible. **Textile mills** are factories where fibers such as cotton and wool are woven into cloth, or textiles. In 1789 Britain was the only country in the world that had this technology.

The British kept new inventions, such as those in the British textile mills, closely guarded secrets. Anyone caught leaving Britain with machine designs was put in jail. Samuel Slater was about to break British law.

Slater took his knowledge to the United States. Remembering each part he had studied, he made a spinning machine for a business person named Moses Brown. In 1790 Brown and Slater built a textile mill at Pawtucket, Rhode Island. It was America's first factory. Samuel Slater had brought the Industrial Revolution to the United States.

REVIEW ***What technology did Samuel Slater bring to the United States?*** Britain's new spinning machine

Born in Britain, Samuel Slater came to the United States in 1789.

Reading Support

PREVIEW AND READ THE LESSON Provide students with the following visual framework.

A Changing Nation	
Part of the Economy	**Changes**
Industry	Machines are introduced to replace human labor. Factories are built. People go to work in the factories.
Transportation	Erie Canal is built from Lake Erie to the Hudson River. National Road is built joining East and West. Steamboats and railroads carry goods and people.

Objectives

1. Identify the technology Samuel Slater brought to the United States.
2. Evaluate the advantages of using mass production.
3. Describe how factory work had changed by the 1840s.
4. Analyze the advantages brought about by the Erie Canal.
5. Explain why the National Road was built.
6. Investigate improvements in long-distance transportation.

Vocabulary

Industrial Revolution (p. 373)
textile mill (p. 373)
mass production (p. 374)
interchangeable part (p. 374)
transport (p. 375)
canal (p. 375)
locomotive (p. 378)

1. ACCESS

The Focus Question

Have students consult older relatives or friends about major changes that have taken place in communication, transportation, entertainment, and other fields in the past ten or twenty years.

The Main Idea

In this lesson students explore the technology that changed life in the early 1800s. After students have read the lesson, have them analyze the impact of the new technology.

2. BUILD

Industry Comes to the United States

Key Content Summary

Samuel Slater came to the United States from Britain with plans for a spinning machine. Soon after, Slater and Moses Brown built the first textile mill in the United States, thus launching the Industrial Revolution in this country.

History

Origins, Spread, and Influence Emphasize how important the building of Slater's and Brown's textile mill was to the history of the United States. Have students speculate on Britain's reasons for keeping the designs of the machines in its textile mills secret.

Mass Production Starts

Key Content Summary
An important change introduced by the Industrial Revolution was the development of machines that produced interchangeable parts. This led to the introduction of mass production, which made it possible for workers to produce large quantities of goods.

Economics

Productivity and Economic Growth Make sure students understand the great economic change brought about by mass production. Ask students to speculate on how mass production could affect the prices of goods and the size of markets.

The Lowell System

Key Content Summary
Francis Cabot Lowell started a textile mill in which all the steps in the manufacture of cotton, from raw cotton to finished cloth, were performed in the same factory. This changed the way textiles were produced.

Samuel Slater built America's first textile mill (above). The machines in the mill, such as this wooden spinning machine (right), ran on waterpower and made yarn quickly at low cost.

Mass Production

Another idea changed American manufacturing forever. An inventor named Eli Whitney thought of a new way of manufacturing that could produce large amounts of goods at one time. His idea came to be called **mass production**.

Before this time, one craftworker made each product from start to finish. Muskets, for example, were made by hand, one at a time. Because each craftworker had his or her own way of making parts and putting them together, no two muskets were exactly the same. To repair a broken musket, a craftworker had to make a new part to fit it.

Whitney thought of a way workers could make more muskets. He built machines that made identical copies of each part. Such **interchangeable parts** could be used to make or repair any musket. Whitney also made machines to put the parts together quickly.

Mass production made it possible to use untrained workers in factories. No longer were craftworkers needed to make most products. Anyone could put together machine-made parts. Using interchangeable parts, factory workers could manufacture more goods much more quickly than craftworkers could.

REVIEW ***How did the idea of mass production change manufacturing?*** More goods could be produced more quickly.

The Lowell System

From 1810 to 1812 Francis Cabot Lowell of Massachusetts visited textile mills and factories in Britain. As Samuel Slater had done earlier, Lowell studied the way the machines worked. He took care to remember the way the separate spinning, dyeing, and weaving mills were planned.

When Lowell returned to the United States, he started his own textile mill at Waltham, Massachusetts. He put spinning, dyeing, and weaving together under one roof. This was a change from having a different factory for each step. In Lowell's textile mill, raw cotton went into the factory and finished cloth came out. Nothing like that had ever been done

Activity Choices

Meet Individual Needs

VISUAL LEARNERS Have students conduct library or Internet research to locate a diagram of an early spinning machine. Ask students to speculate about how difficult it was for Samuel Slater to memorize all the working parts of the machine and how long it might have taken him to do so. Then have students discuss why Slater was willing to risk imprisonment to bring the spinning machine to the United States.

Link to Language Arts

WRITE TO EXPLAIN Ask each student to write a paragraph explaining whether he or she would rather be a craftworker, who spent the day making a complete product, or a mass production worker, who produced copies of only one part of a product all day long.

TECHNOLOGY

Use THE AMAZING WRITING MACHINE™ to complete this writing activity.

Background

ELI WHITNEY Although Whitney became famous for his invention of the cotton gin in 1793, he did not profit from his invention. His use of interchangeable parts in the production of muskets did prove profitable. Contracts from the national government and several states made Whitney a wealthy man. After his death, his company was run by his son and then his grandson.

before. Other manufacturers began following Lowell's lead as they built factories.

Young women and children came to work in Lowell's textile mills. When a girl named Harriet Hanson was ten years old, she began work as a "doffer." From five o'clock in the morning until seven in the evening, Harriet changed spools of thread on the spinning machines. She "wanted to earn money like the other little girls."

The hours were long, but Harriet did not think the work was hard. She had time to read, sew, and sometimes play. She enjoyed living in a boardinghouse where meals and rooms were provided for mill workers.

Lowell took care to set up good living conditions for his workers. Other manufacturers did not show the same care. As the demand for many manufactured goods grew, more factories—and more factory workers—were needed. Many workers, both young and old, soon were working long hours in dangerous conditions.

By the 1840s thousands of immigrants were coming to the United States each year to take jobs in the new factories. The populations of manufacturing cities like New York, Boston, Philadelphia, and Baltimore grew quickly. Almost half of the immigrants were from Ireland. Others came from Germany, Poland, and other parts of northern and central Europe.

REVIEW ***Why were immigrants coming to the United States in the 1840s?*** to take jobs in the new factories

The Erie Canal

The new factories turned out many products. But factory owners had a problem. How could they **transport**, or carry, their products from the factories to their customers, many of whom lived in the West? The people in the West, too, needed to transport their farm products to the cities in the East.

To help solve this problem, the New York legislature voted in 1817 to build a **canal**, or human-made waterway. The Erie Canal would link Buffalo on Lake Erie with Troy on the Hudson River. It would be 363 miles (584 km) long—the longest canal in the world.

Most of the Erie Canal was dug by hand by some 3,000 Irish immigrants. The workers were paid 80 cents a day and were given meals and housing. These wages were three times what the immigrants could earn in Ireland. The high wages acted like a magnet to attract thousands of Europeans to the United States.

Bells rang to tell Lowell's workers (right) when it was mealtime and when it was time to start work. The picture (below) shows a young girl packing cotton into containers.

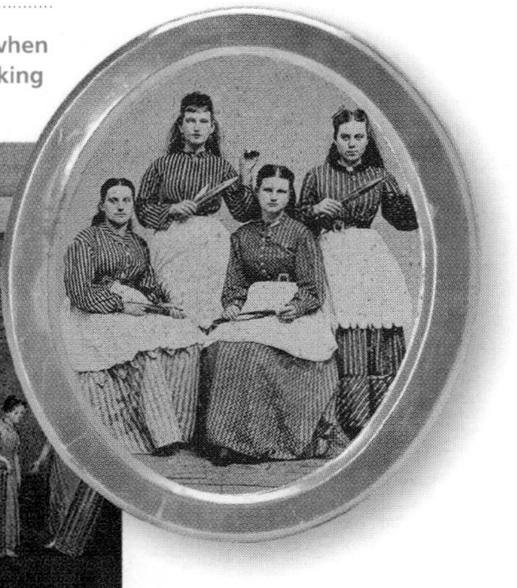

Economics

Productivity and Economic Growth Discuss with students why a textile mill owner would want to use the Lowell system. Explain that the basic idea of the system has continued to be used in this century. Have students analyze the relationship of the Lowell system to mass production.

Economics

Economic Institutions Discuss with students in what ways working conditions in most textile mills were poor. Elicit such ideas as long working hours, poor safety conditions, and low pay. Have students draw conclusions about why so many people wanted to work in factories in spite of the poor working conditions.

Q. **How many hours did ten-year-old Harriet Hanson work each day?** 14 hours

On average, how many hours do people work each day today? 8 hours

The Erie Canal

Key Content Summary

In 1825 the Erie Canal, which linked Buffalo on Lake Erie with Troy on the Hudson River, was opened. The canal, built mainly by Irish immigrants, became a major transportation route and made New York City the leading trade city in the United States.

Link to Mathematics

MAKE A LINE GRAPH Supply students with the following immigration statistics. Provide students with graph paper, and have them make line graphs using the statistics. Students should position the years on the horizontal axis and the number of immigrants on the vertical axis. Have students calculate the percentage increase in immigration from 1820 to 1845 and discuss the reasons for the increase.

YEAR	IMMIGRANTS
1820	8,385
1825	10,199
1830	23,322
1835	45,374
1840	84,066
1845	114,371

Link to Resources

RESEARCH COTTON MANUFACTURERS Ask selected students to research the steps involved in the manufacture of cotton cloth and to draw a flow chart showing how the steps would be carried out in Lowell's factory.

TECHNOLOGY

Use GRAPH LINKS to complete this graphing activity.

Geography

Movement Have students examine the map of major canals on page 377. Ask them to draw conclusions about why the Erie Canal was built so that it ended at the Hudson River.

Visual Analysis

Learn from Diagrams Have students examine the diagram of a canal lock. Then ask students to trace with their fingers the path a boat follows as it travels through the canal lock. As students trace the route, ask them to explain each step illustrated in the canal lock diagram. Then ask students to answer the question in the caption. They were pulled.

The National Road

Key Content Summary

In the 1700s major roads in the United States were mostly dirt paths full of tree stumps and holes. Things began to change in 1811 when work began on the National Road. The road stretched from the Atlantic Coast west to Vandalia, Illinois, and became the main land route linking the East and West.

When the Erie Canal was finished in 1825, it opened a transportation route to the heart of the young nation. The opening of this route helped make New York City the leading trade city in the United States.

REVIEW ***Why was the Erie Canal built?*** to help transport products between the eastern and western United States

The National Road

During the early years of the nation, Americans lacked a good system of roads. Most roads were just dirt paths that were full of tree stumps and holes. The roads turned into rivers of mud when it rained.

Just before Ohio became a state in 1803, Congress voted to build a road from the Atlantic coast to Ohio. The road would be used to transport goods and help settlers travel to the new state. This route became known as the National Road.

Work on the National Road began on November 20, 1811. The road was built using the best technology of the day. It was wide and level, and it was paved with stones and tar. It was opened for traffic in 1818, when it stretched from Maryland to what would become West Virginia. It was then built through Ohio and Indiana and was finished in Vandalia, Illinois, in 1841. The National Road became the land route that linked the East with the West.

REVIEW ***Why was the National Road built?*** to improve transportation between the East and the West

Steamboats and Railroads

At about the same time that the National Road and the Erie Canal were being built, Americans were inventing new forms of travel. Steamboats took the place of flat-bottom barges as the main form of river

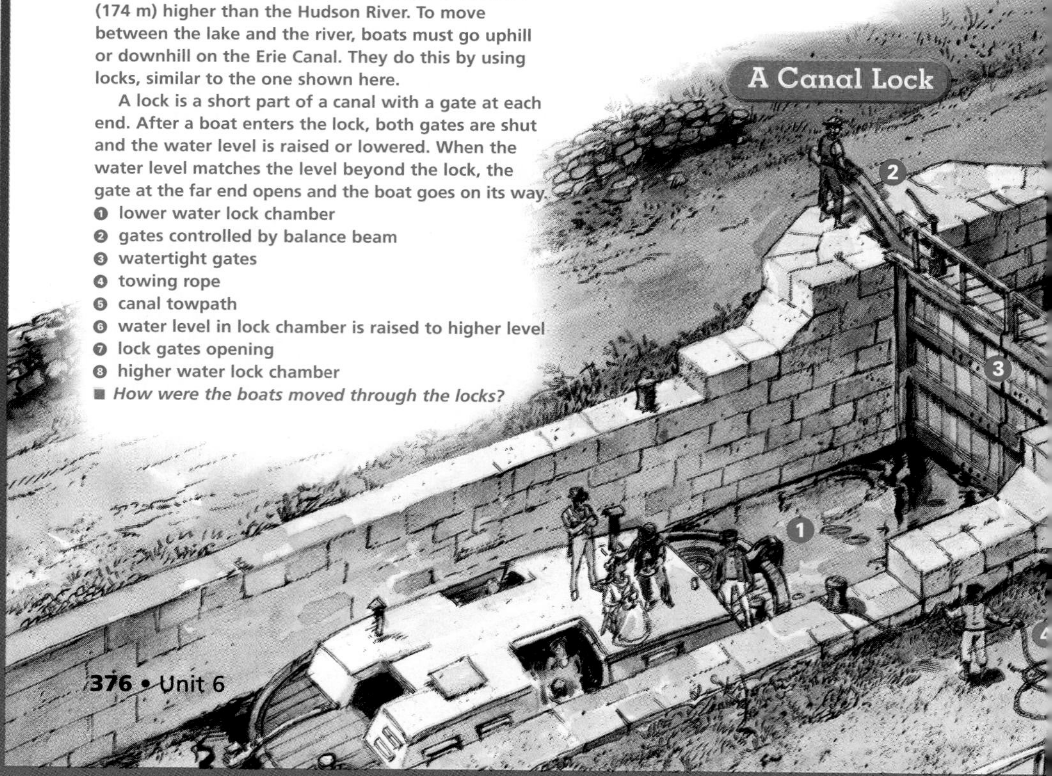

LEARNING FROM DIAGRAMS Lake Erie is 572 feet (174 m) higher than the Hudson River. To move between the lake and the river, boats must go uphill or downhill on the Erie Canal. They do this by using locks, similar to the one shown here.

A lock is a short part of a canal with a gate at each end. After a boat enters the lock, both gates are shut and the water level is raised or lowered. When the water level matches the level beyond the lock, the gate at the far end opens and the boat goes on its way.

1. lower water lock chamber
2. gates controlled by balance beam
3. watertight gates
4. towing rope
5. canal towpath
6. water level in lock chamber is raised to higher level
7. lock gates opening
8. higher water lock chamber

■ *How were the boats moved through the locks?*

ACTIVITY CHOICES

TECHNOLOGY

Use DECISIONS, DECISIONS™: IMMIGRATION for a simulation about immigration.

Link to Mathematics

CALCULATE COSTS Have students use their mathematics skills to answer the following questions: If the 3,000 Irish workers were paid 80 cents a day, what was the total daily labor cost to the canal builders? If the canal was built in 8 years, or about 2,900 days, what was the total cost of labor? daily labor cost: $2,400; total labor cost: $6,960,000

Background

THE NATIONAL ROAD After the road was extended to St. Louis, it served as the main overland link between East and West for well over a hundred years. Eventually becoming U.S. 40, it was supplanted only when the interstate highway system of the 1960s and 1970s was established.

Movement These maps show major transportation links that had been built in the United States by 1850.

Why do you think few links had been built west of the Mississippi River?

ransportation. Railroads changed the way people and goods moved on land.

In 1807 Robert Fulton amazed watchers vhen his steamboat, the *Clermont*, chugged ıp the Hudson River. The steamboat was ɔowered by a steam engine, which had been ınvented in Britain in the 1700s. In 1811 the *Vew Orleans* made the first steamboat voyage rom Pittsburgh to New Orleans. By the 1820s great paddle-wheel steamboats could be seen ɔn most large rivers and lakes in the United States. Trips that once took months by flatɔoat now took only a few days.

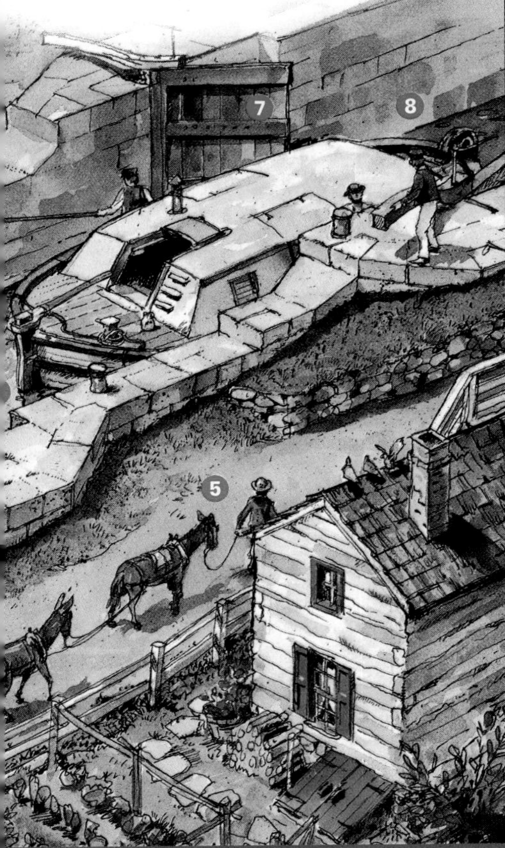

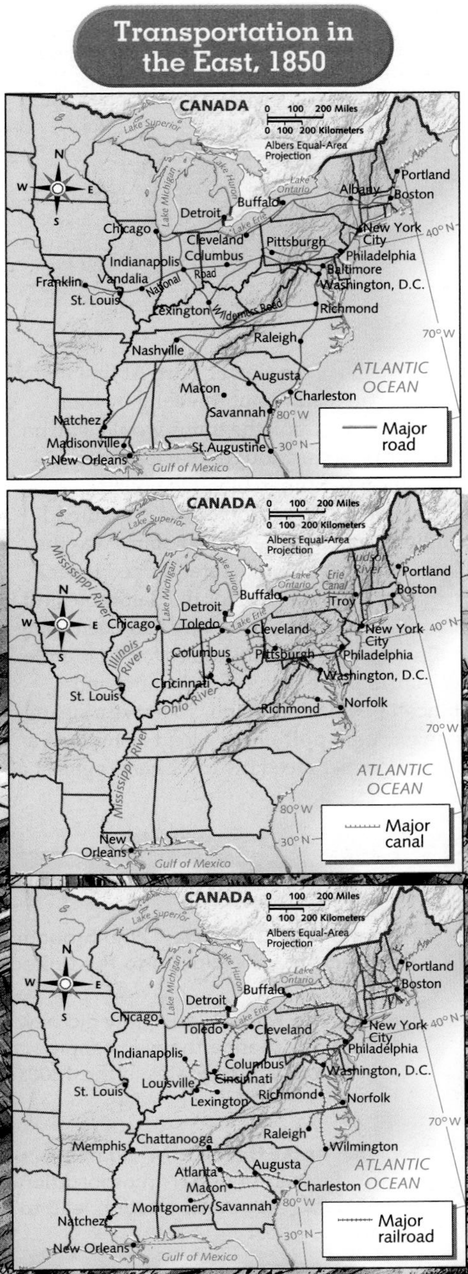

Geography

Movement Have students discuss the ways road travel might have improved because of the existence of the National Road.

Q. **How do you think the West changed because of the National Road?** The road probably opened the way for much faster settlement of the West and faster economic growth.

Visual Analysis

Learn from Maps Have students answer the question in the caption. Most of the population lived to the east of the river.

Steamboats and Railroads

Key Content Summary

Beginning in 1807, steamboats replaced flatboats as the main form of water transportation. Starting somewhat later, railroads rapidly changed overland transport. Railroads brought goods to all regions of the United States, hastening the growth of manufacturing.

Economics

Productivity and Economic Growth Discuss with students the economic connection between manufacturing and transportation. Have them speculate on why the growth of steamboat transportation and railroads resulted in the growth of manufacturing.

Link to Science

REPORT ON STEAM ENGINES

Ask volunteers to research and prepare oral reports explaining how steam engines worked in the early locomotives and steamboats. Make sure students make diagrams to use as aids in their presentations.

TECHNOLOGY

Use THE AMAZING WRITING MACHINE™ to complete this writing activity.

Extend and Enrich

COOPERATIVE LEARNING

WRITE A NEWSPAPER FRONT PAGE Arrange the class in small groups. Explain that each group will create the front page of a newspaper that covers one of the following events: the opening of Slater's and Brown's factory, the opening of the Erie Canal, the completion of the National Road, Fulton's voyage on the *Clermont*, or the race between the *Tom Thumb* and a horse. Each group will have to research the topic, write the front page stories, type the stories, and create a newspaper page. Suggest to students that they divide the tasks among themselves. Have each group read its front page to the other groups. Provide an area in the classroom for display of the finished newspaper pages, and have students discuss the experience.

Geography

Movement Have students discuss the changes brought about by the railroads in terms of the movement of people and goods.

Q. **How did railroads affect the time it took to travel between cities?**
They shortened travel time and made the trips easier for the general population.

3. CLOSE

Have students consider again the Focus question on page 373.

How might a new technology change a person's life today?

Ask students to review what they have learned about the Industrial Revolution in this lesson and to explore ways in which recent technology has affected their lives and the lives of the adults they know.

LESSON 1 REVIEW—Answers

Check Understanding

1. Samuel Slater
2. They could buy cheaper, mass-produced goods, work in factories, and travel faster on steamboats and railroads.

Think Critically

3. More factories meant more goods that had to be transported to market, which made it profitable for people to find new and better means of transportation. With better transportation, manufacturers had larger markets, and to satisfy them, they produced more goods.
4. airplanes, railroads, highways, and water routes for ships

Show What You Know

Performance Assessment Consider asking students to read other students' letters as though they were the recipients of the letters. Ask the readers to explain whether or not the letters persuaded them to join their friends in factory work.

What to Look For In evaluating the letters, look for evidence that the writers have understood the nature of early factory work.

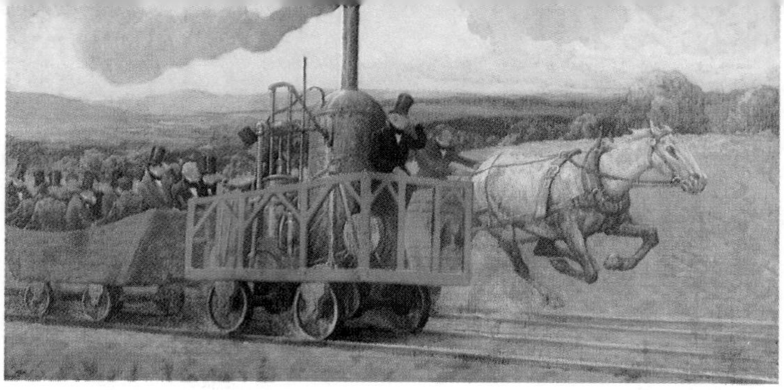

The *Tom Thumb* was made famous in a race with a horse. The locomotive was small, but powerful for its day. The first locomotives went about 10 miles (16.1 km) per hour.

Railroads had a slower start. At first many people had fears about traveling by train. Some did not think the trains would stay on the tracks. Some thought that fast speeds would cause human blood to boil!

One of the first **locomotives**, or railroad engines, made in the United States was the *Tom Thumb.* A manufacturer named Peter Cooper built it in 1830 for the Baltimore and Ohio Railroad. The company had been using railroad cars pulled by horses for its 13-mile (21-km) service between Baltimore and Ellicott's Mills, Maryland. To prove a steam engine could pull a heavy load faster than a horse, Cooper raced his *Tom Thumb* against a railroad car pulled by a horse. The locomotive broke down before the finish line and lost the race. Even so, it was clear that the steam locomotive had better pulling power than a horse.

The number of railroads grew quickly after 1830. By 1850 about 9,000 miles (14,484 km) of track had been laid, mostly near the Atlantic coast. Railroads made it easier to move raw materials and manufactured goods to all regions of the country. As the railroads grew, so did manufacturing in the United States.

REVIEW ***What inventions improved transportation in the early 1800s?***
steamboats and locomotives

LESSON 1 REVIEW

Check Understanding

1. **Remember the Facts** Who brought the Industrial Revolution to the United States?
2. **Recall the Main Idea** How did new technology change the way people lived in the United States in the 1800s?

Think Critically

3. **Cause and Effect** How did more factories lead to better transportation? How did better transportation lead to more factories?
4. **Past to Present** What kinds of transportation connect the regions of the United States today?

Show What You Know

Writing Activity Imagine that you work at a Lowell textile mill or another early factory. Write a letter to a friend, telling what you like and do not like about working in the factory. Share your letter with a classmate.

378 • Unit 6

ACTIVITY CHOICES

ACTIVITY BOOK

Reinforce & Extend

Use ACTIVITY BOOK, p. 72.

Reteach the Main Idea

COOPERATIVE LEARNING

MAKE A LIST Divide the class into small groups. Challenge each group to use the textbook as a resource to list the ways in which technology changed life in the United States in the 1800s. Have the group members share and discuss their lists with each other and with other groups in the class.

The Age of Jackson

On July 4, 1826, the United States was 50 years old. Americans everywhere celebrated with parades, speeches, and parties. Many hoped that the two old patriots John Adams and Thomas Jefferson would live to see the celebration. Both men did live to greet that Fourth of July, but they both died before sunset. In Philadelphia the Liberty Bell tolled at their passing. The deep sound of the bell marked the end of an age that had brought the American people independence and a new nation. But as the old age ended, a new age dawned with new leaders and new challenges for the United States.

LESSON 2

FOCUS
What problems might divide people living in a country today?

Main Idea Read to learn about the problems that divided the American people in the early 1800s.

Vocabulary
sectionalism
states' rights
secede
ruling

"Old Hickory"

On March 4, 1829, Andrew Jackson took the oath of office as the seventh President of the United States. The Union he was to lead had grown from the original 13 states to 24 states. Vermont, Maine, Kentucky, and Tennessee had become states. The states of Ohio, Illinois, and Indiana had been carved from the Northwest Territory. The states of Louisiana and Missouri had been formed from the Louisiana Purchase territory. Alabama became a state after the Creeks were forced off their land. The state of Mississippi and the Territory of Florida had been created from land once claimed by Spain.

The Presidents before Jackson had all been property owners from either Massachusetts or Virginia. They also had all been well educated. Jackson had a different background. He had been born on the frontier of South Carolina to a poor family living in a log cabin. Tough and stubborn, he taught himself law and became a judge. As a soldier he earned the nickname Old Hickory, hickory being a very hard wood. "He's tough," said his soldiers. "Tough as hickory." As a general he had become a hero during the War of 1812.

The election that made Jackson President was the first in which all white American men could vote.

President Andrew Jackson

Reading Support

ANTICIPATION GUIDE Before students read the lesson, ask them to predict which of the following statements most likely refers to southerners, northerners, or westerners. Students may correct their predictions as they read.

1. We oppose the tariff on imports. southerners
2. We want a President who will understand frontier life. westerners
3. States' rights are more important than the national government. southerners
4. The tariffs will help us sell more goods in the United States. northerners

Objectives

1. Explain how a change in voting practices helped Andrew Jackson become President.
2. Analyze how sectionalism threatened the interdependence between the different regions of the United States.
3. Evaluate the government's actions in removing the Cherokees from their native lands.

Vocabulary

sectionalism (p. 380)
states' rights (p. 380)
secede (p. 380)
ruling (p. 382)

1. ACCESS

The Focus Question
Discuss how, even though the United States is one country, each region has distinct characteristics that make it different from all the others. Have students speculate on what concerns might cause people in different parts of the country to react differently.

The Main Idea
In this lesson students learn how strong sectional feelings in different parts of the United States, particularly the North and the South, resulted in political conflicts. After they have read the lesson, ask students to think about how the regional differences might have affected individuals living in the regions.

2. BUILD

"Old Hickory"

Key Content Summary
President Andrew Jackson was different from his predecessors in office. Like many westerners of his time, Jackson was an individualist. He was elected with the support of voters in the new western states.

Geography

Location Have students use a classroom wall map of the United States to locate all of the 24 states that comprised the nation when Jackson became President. Have students deduce which states supported Jackson in the election of 1828.

Visual Analysis

Learn from Graphs Have students answer the question in the caption. about 58 percent

Regional Disagreements

Key Content Summary

Sectionalism arose when Congress set a high tariff on imports in 1828. Citing their individual states' rights, southern states protested. A second high tariff in 1832 prompted South Carolina to threaten secession, but the state backed down when Jackson warned the action would be treason.

Civics and Government

Political Institutions and Processes Remind students that states' rights was an important issue at the Constitutional Convention and in the process of ratifying the Constitution. Explain that the federal-versus-states question still arises in our own day from time to time.

Q. **Why do you think South Carolina objected so strongly to a high tariff on imports?** because the tariff hurt them economically and because Vice President Calhoun, a strong supporter of states' rights, was from South Carolina

"PRIMARY SOURCE"

Source: *John C. Calhoun and the Roots of War.* Teresa Celsi. Silver Burdett Press, 1991.

SOURCE: *Historical Statistics of the United States*

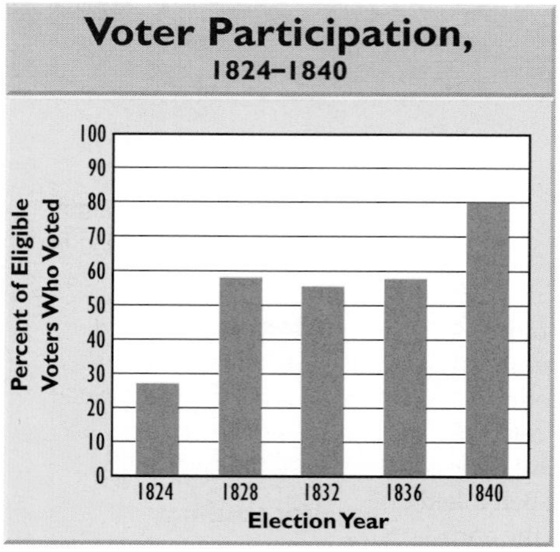

LEARNING FROM GRAPHS This graph shows the percent of eligible voters who voted between 1824 and 1840.

■ *About what percent of eligible voters voted in the election of 1828?*

Before that time, voting had been only for men who owned property. The change came about partly because of the new western states. There the vote was given to all white men, not just property owners. By the election of 1828, the eastern states were following this example. Many of the new voters chose Jackson because they felt he was a "common man," like them.

REVIEW ***What change in voting helped Andrew Jackson become President?***
Men did not have to own property to vote.

Regional Disagreements

As President, Jackson went right on being both tough and stubborn. He vetoed a bank bill that would have helped the rich factory owners in the North. Government should not help the rich get richer, he said. The government should instead "shower its favors alike on the high and the low, the rich and the poor."

Many of President Jackson's decisions were based on his background of living on the western frontier. People from the North and the South were more interested in helping their own section, or region, rather than the country as a whole. This regional loyalty is called **sectionalism**.

Sectionalism became a problem in 1828 when Congress set a high tariff on imports. The tariff was supposed to help northern factory owners sell their manufactured goods because it made European goods cost more. However, the tariff also raised the prices southerners had to pay for goods they could get only from Europe.

Jackson's Vice President, John C. Calhoun of South Carolina, was loyal to the South. He argued against the tariff. Calhoun believed in **states' rights**, or the idea that the states have final authority over the national government. No one knew how President Jackson felt about states' rights until he spoke at a dinner in honor of the late Thomas Jefferson. Jackson looked straight at Calhoun and said,

> "Our Union—It must be preserved [kept]."

Calhoun answered, "The Union—next to our liberty most dear." Calhoun also believed that the Union was important. But he still felt that the rights of individual states were more important than the Union. This was the beginning of a deep split between Jackson and Calhoun. Calhoun soon resigned as Jackson's Vice President.

The debate over states' rights went on. In 1832 Congress passed another tariff. South Carolina said it would **secede**, or leave the Union, because of it. President Jackson warned South Carolina's leaders that leaving the Union was treason. South Carolina's leaders backed down, but sectionalism only grew stronger in the years to come.

REVIEW ***What leader spoke out for states' rights? Who spoke against it?***
John C. Calhoun; Andrew Jackson

ACTIVITY CHOICES

Background

THE WHIG PARTY Jackson's opponents called themselves Whigs, after the antimonarchist Whigs of Britain. The American Whigs identified with the British who opposed the monarchy because the American Whigs thought that Jackson was behaving like a king rather than a democratically elected President.

Link to Mathematics

INTERPRET GRAPHS Have students calculate the increase in voter participation between 1824 and 1840 and speculate on the reasons for the increase. The percent of eligible voters who voted increased by approximately 53% between 1824 and 1840.

Indian Removal

Pathfinders had reported that the plains west of the Mississippi were of no use to the settlers. At that time people believed that soil was good only where trees grew. They began to think that the Indians should move west to those treeless lands. Jackson put the idea into action.

In 1830 Congress passed the Indian Removal Act. This act said that all Indians east of the Mississippi must leave their land and move west. Once this bill became a law, President Jackson ordered the Choctaws, Creeks, Seminoles, Chickasaws, Cherokees, and other tribes to live in the Indian Territory, which is today the state of Oklahoma.

Many tribes fought against removal. Among them were the Seminoles of Florida, led by Chief Osceola. Many runaway slaves helped the Seminoles in their fight. But, like other tribes, most of the Seminoles were either killed or forced to leave their homes.

The 15,000 Cherokees made up one of the richest tribes in the United States. They had many towns and villages throughout the Southeast. Many Cherokees owned small farms, and a few had large plantations where Africans were enslaved. The Cherokees had their own government, a republic with a constitution and elected leaders who met at their capital of New Echota (ih•KOHT•uh) in Georgia.

In 1791 the United States government had agreed to the independence of the Cherokee nation by signing a treaty. However, in 1828 lawmakers in Georgia said that Cherokee laws were no longer in effect. In 1829, when gold was discovered on Cherokee lands, settlers poured in to stake their claims.

The Cherokee nation, led by Chief John Ross, fought back in the United States courts, and their case went all the way to the United

GEOGRAPHY

New Echota, Georgia

By the 1830s, New Echota, the capital of the Cherokee republic, was a city like any other city in the United States. It had churches, businesses, and schools. It also had its own newspaper, the *Cherokee Phoenix*, which was printed in both English and Cherokee. Although spoken for hundreds of years, the Cherokee language was not written until 1821. In that year a Cherokee leader named Sequoyah (sih•KWOY•uh) created an alphabet and a writing system for it.

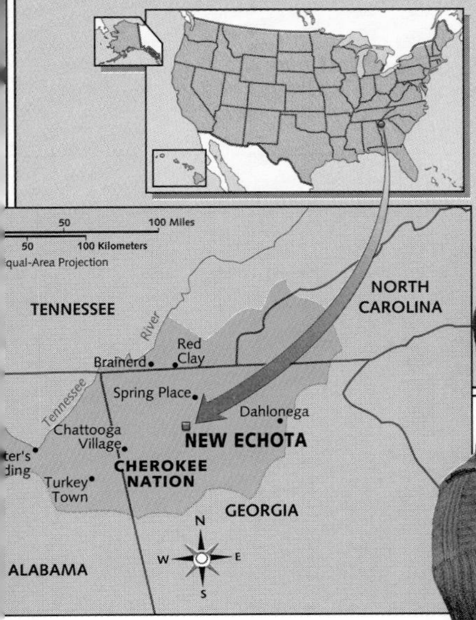

This picture of Sequoyah shows the Cherokee alphabet he invented.

Indian Removal

Key Content Summary

Defying a Supreme Court order, President Jackson ordered the army to force the Cherokees to leave their lands in the East and move to the Indian Territory. More than 4,000 Cherokees died on the journey, which came to be known as the Trail of Tears.

History

Turning Points Discuss with students the reasons the Cherokees were ordered to leave their lands east of the Mississippi. Ask students to draw conclusions about the role sectionalism played in Jackson's decision to force the Cherokees to move. Also have students speculate on why Jackson chose to ignore the Supreme Court decision.

Visual Analysis

Interpret Pictures Direct students' attention to the picture of Sequoyah on this page. Have students discuss Sequoyah's contribution to the Cherokee nation.

Q. **Which letters in the Cherokee alphabet are similar to those in the English alphabet?** Letters students might identify include R, D, G, U, F, A, B, P, M, W, T, Y, H, Z, J, E, N, C, K.

Smithsonian Institution®

Go to the Internet site at *http://www.si.edu/harcourt/socialstudies* to examine portraits of Chief Osceola and Sequoyah in Native Americans at the National Portrait Gallery.

Multicultural Link

Born the son of a Cherokee woman and a white trader in 1766, Sequoyah set out to do what had never been done before—devise a way of writing the Cherokee language and teach thousands of his fellow Cherokees to read and write it. In constructing his written language, he used many English letters and variations of them to represent the sounds of the Cherokee language. Sequoyah's writing system united the Cherokee people and made them leaders among Indian groups. The giant sequoia tree is named for him.

Extend and Enrich

COOPERATIVE LEARNING

RESEARCH INDIAN TRIBES Divide the class into small groups. Tell students that each group will select an Indian tribe of the Southeast to research. Groups may select from the following: Cherokees, Seminoles, Choctaws, Chickasaws, and Creeks. Tell each group to find information about their tribe's culture and history. Students should bring to class drawings or photographs of their tribes' artifacts. Have each group share its information with the class.

Culture

Philosophy and Ethics Discuss with students President Jackson's view that Indians should move to the lands west of the Mississippi River.

Visual Analysis

Learn from Pictures Have students answer the question in the caption. sadness, despair, resignation

3. CLOSE

Have students consider again the Focus question on page 379.

What problems might divide people living in a country today?

Have students reflect on what they have learned in this lesson about the sectional conflicts in the 1820s and 1830s. Then have students discuss possible reasons for differences between regions today and the dangers that might result if the different regions forget they are truly interdependent.

LESSON 2 REVIEW—Answers

Check Understanding

1. white male voters who did not own property
2. specifically, differences over the tariffs of 1828 and 1832; more generally, the different ways of life of people in the North, the South, and the West

Think Critically

3. The Cherokees would strongly oppose it since it would mean having to leave their lands, while Georgia settlers would favor it since it would allow them to farm the Cherokee land and mine the gold that had been found there.
4. Most people living on the frontier were more or less economically equal, and people had to work together for their mutual benefit and protection.

Show What You Know

Performance Assessment Consider using the students' slogans as the basis for television commercials for Jackson.

What to Look For In evaluating the students' material, look for evidence that they have understood Jackson's character and achievements as described in the lesson.

This painting, called *The Choctaw Removal,* was created by the Choctaw artist Valjean Hessing. The Choctaw were one of the many Indian tribes that were forced to leave their homes. What feelings does the artist show in the painting?

States Supreme Court. In 1832 the Chief Justice of the Supreme Court, John Marshall, gave the Court's **ruling**, or decision. He said that the United States should protect the Cherokees and their lands in Georgia. Yet, instead of supporting the court ruling, President Jackson ignored it.

By late 1838, soldiers had forced the last large group of Cherokees to leave their lands and travel more than 800 miles (1,287 km) to the Indian Territory. Their long, painful journey came to be called the Trail of Tears. It ended on March 26, 1839, after more than 4,000 Cherokees had died of cold, disease, and lack of food. John G. Burnett, a soldier who was there, said, "The trail was a trail of death."

REVIEW *What was the Trail of Tears?* the journey the Cherokees traveled to the Indian Territory

LESSON 2 REVIEW

Check Understanding

1. **Remember the Facts** What group of people helped Andrew Jackson win the election of 1828?
2. **Recall the Main Idea** What problems divided the American people in the early 1800s?

Think Critically

3. **Explore Viewpoints** How would the Cherokees have viewed the Indian Removal Act? How would Georgia's settlers have viewed it?
4. **Think More About It** How do you think life on the frontier encouraged the growth of democracy?

Show What You Know

Writing Activity Make a list of the qualities that helped Andrew Jackson get elected President. Then write phrases that he might have used as campaign slogans for his elections in 1828 and 1832. Copy your slogans onto large sheets of paper and display them in the classroom.

ACTIVITY CHOICES

ACTIVITY BOOK

Reinforce & Extend

Use ACTIVITY BOOK, p. 73.

Reteach the Main Idea

COOPERATIVE LEARNING

DEBATE THE ISSUES Divide the class into three groups. Have the groups use the textbook as a resource to discuss and debate the concerns Americans in different parts of the country had in the early 1800s. One group should represent the northern view, the second group should represent the southern view, and the third group should represent the western view.

Westward Ho!

LESSON 3

FOCUS How might a country today expand its territory?

Main Idea Read to learn how the United States expanded its territory in the 1800s.

Vocabulary
Manifest Destiny
dictator
forty-niner

In the early 1800s Americans began to move beyond their country's borders. With the rallying cry "Westward Ho!," they looked to the Spanish colony of Texas, the Oregon Country in the Pacific Northwest, and other western lands. The idea of the lands in the West being set aside for Indian peoples was soon forgotten. In 1845 the words *manifest destiny* were heard for the first time. The **Manifest Destiny** was the belief shared by many Americans that it was the certain future of the United States to stretch from the Atlantic Ocean to the Pacific Ocean.

Americans in Texas

Since the earliest years of European settlement, Spain had built missions and presidios all over Texas. Yet few settlers lived on this open borderland. In 1820 Moses Austin, a Missouri banker, asked Spanish leaders if he might start a colony of Americans in Texas. The Spanish agreed, but Austin died before he could carry out his plan.

Stephen F. Austin, Moses Austin's son, took up his father's work and started the colony. He chose land between the Brazos and Colorado rivers. In 1821 the first colonists began to settle there. That same year, Mexico won its independence from Spain. Texas now belonged to Mexico.

Austin and the American settlers worked hard, and they soon did well in raising cotton, corn, and cattle. Encouraged by their success, the Mexican government decided to let more people settle in Texas. At first the Mexican government left the Americans in Texas alone. But in time Mexico's leaders became worried about the growing number of Americans on their land.

In 1830 the Mexican government passed a law that said no more American settlers could come to Texas. The Mexican government also said that settlers already in Texas had to obey Mexico's laws and pay more taxes. These changes angered Texans.

Stephen F. Austin began a settlement in Texas. Present-day Austin, Texas, was named for him.

Reading Support

PREVIEW AND READ THE LESSON Provide students with the following visual framework.

THE NATION GAINS MORE LAND	
LAND ACQUIRED	HOW ACQUIRED
Texas	Republic of Texas becomes a state.
Oregon Territory	Treaty with Britain; territory becomes Oregon, Washington, Idaho, western Montana, and Wyoming.
Utah	Mormon Territory applies for statehood.
Southwest	Treaty ending war with Mexico gives U.S. territory that becomes California, Utah, Nevada, and parts of Arizona, New Mexico, Colorado, and Wyoming.
California	California applies for statehood after the gold rush.

Objectives

1. Describe the conflict between American settlers in Texas and the Mexican government.
2. Summarize how Texas became an independent republic.
3. Analyze why people settled the Oregon Country.
4. Explore the role of cooperation in the settlement of Utah by the Mormons.
5. Summarize the results of the conflict with Mexico.
6. Describe the California gold rush.

Vocabulary

Manifest Destiny (p. 383)
forty-niner (p. 389)
dictator (p. 384)

1. ACCESS

The Focus Question

Ask students to recall, from their own experience, instances when they wanted to acquire something very badly. Discuss why a country today might want to own more land.

The Main Idea

In this lesson students learn about the nation's drive to acquire land in the years between 1820 and 1850. After students have read the lesson, have them analyze why the United States wanted its lands to reach from the Atlantic Ocean to the Pacific Ocean.

2. BUILD

Americans in Texas

Key Content Summary

People from the United States first began settling in Texas with Stephen F. Austin in 1821. By 1834 the settlers were so numerous that the Mexican dictator, General Santa Anna, sought to bring them firmly under control, resulting in conflict between the settlers and the Mexican government.

Culture

Shared Humanity and Unique Identity Explore with students some differences between the settlers from the United States and the Mexicans. You might discuss, for example, language and food.

History

People and Events Across Time and Place Have students speculate on why Mexico changed its laws regarding American settlers. Also have them analyze why Santa Anna intensified the conflict between the settlers and the Mexican government.

The Texas Revolution

Key Content Summary

In 1836 Santa Anna's army attacked San Antonio, killing the defenders of the city who had taken shelter in the Alamo. During the conflict, Texas declared its independence. After defeating Mexico, Texas was an independent republic until 1845, when it became a state of the United States.

Then, in 1834, another change took place. General Antonio López de Santa Anna took over the Mexican government and made himself **dictator**, a leader who has total authority. When Santa Anna sent soldiers to Texas to enforce Mexican laws, fighting broke out.

REVIEW ***Why did Americans first come to Texas?*** to start a colony

The Texas Revolution

Working together, a force of Americans and Mexicans living in Texas attacked the town of San Antonio on December 5, 1835. After four days of fighting, Mexican troops were driven from the center of the town. They surrendered on December 11. The defeat angered General Santa Anna. He marched on San Antonio with thousands of soldiers, planning to take back the city.

Church bells rang out a warning as the huge Mexican army came close to the city in February 1836. Texas rebels in San Antonio took shelter behind the walls of the Alamo, an old Spanish mission church. Among them were American volunteers willing to help the Texas rebels in their fight for freedom. They included James Bowie, Davy Crockett, and William B. Travis, who served as commander. Juan Seguín and several other Texans also arrived to help. Some fighters were joined by their wives and children.

For 13 days the Mexican soldiers attacked the Alamo. The defenders fought to the end. Finally, on March 6, 1836, the Alamo fell. The force of about 189 Texans had been killed. Santa Anna spared the lives of the women and children.

During the attack at the Alamo, Texas leaders met. On March 2, 1836, they declared

At the Alamo fewer than 200 Texans faced more than 2,000 Mexican soldiers. In this painting Davy Crockett swings his rifle at the enemy after having run out of ammunition. The Alamo was one of the most well-known battles of the Texas revolution.

Activity Choices

Technology

Use THE ALAMO™ for a review of the Texas fight for independence.

Link to World Languages

RESEARCH SPANISH PLACE-NAMES Ask students to research how strong the influence of Spanish is on place-names in Texas. Have them develop lists of Spanish place-names and, where possible, give the English equivalent of these names.

Link to Reading

READ A BIOGRAPHY Assign students to read biographies of the key players in the Texas Revolution, such as David G. Burnet, General Antonio López de Santa Anna, Sam Houston, William B. Travis, James Bowie, Davy Crockett, and Juan Seguín. After students have read their biographies, have them prepare oral reports to present to the class. For their presentations they may want to dress up like the person and speak from the first-person perspective. You may wish to have the students prepare large time lines to use as visual aids with their presentations.

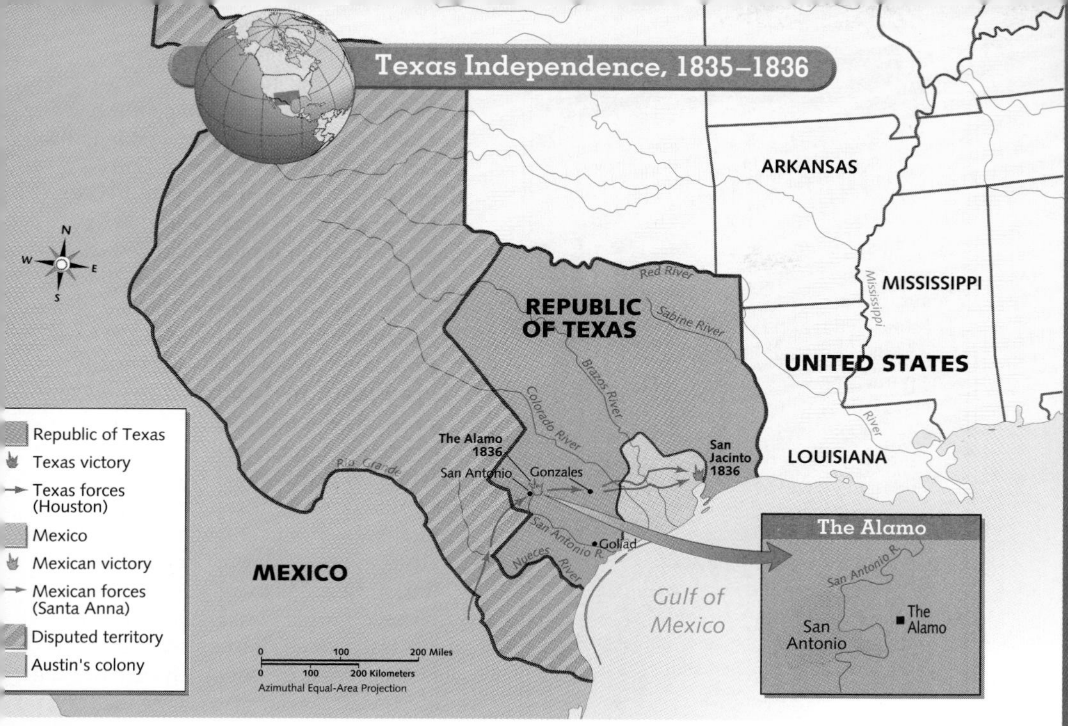

Place This map shows Austin's original colony and the battles for Texas independence fought with Mexico from 1835 to 1836.
■ *Which battle did the Texans win during their fight for independence?*

independence from Mexico and set up the Republic of Texas. They chose David G. Burnet as president and Sam Houston as commander of the army.

After the fall of the Alamo, Santa Anna moved quickly to end the Texas revolution. On March 27 he ordered more than 300 prisoners killed at Goliad. But other Texans fought on, yelling "Remember the Alamo!" and "Remember Goliad!"

On April 21 Houston's army took the Mexicans by surprise at the Battle of San Jacinto (juh•SINT•oh) and captured Santa Anna. Houston offered to let Santa Anna live in return for Texas's independence. Santa Anna agreed, and his army returned to Mexico. Texas remained an independent republic until it became a state of the United States in 1845. Sam Houston served twice as president of the republic and later as governor of the state of Texas.

The Texas flag, adopted in 1839, has a single white star and red, white, and blue bars. For this reason Texas was known as the Lone Star Republic. Today it is known as the Lone Star State.

REVIEW ***When did Texas become a republic?*** March 2, 1836

History

Turning Points Discuss the events that led to Texas independence. Have students conclude why the Alamo inspired other settlers to continue to fight for independence rather than give up.

Q. **What does the fight at the Alamo tell you about the Americans who settled Texas?** They were probably fiercely independent, determined, and certainly brave.

Geography

Human-Environment Interactions Have students study the map. Suggest that they trace the routes of Santa Anna and Sam Houston on the map. Have students draw conclusions about why Santa Anna wanted to keep that territory for Mexico.

Q. **Did the Republic of Texas include the same land area as the state of Texas does today?** no, only a portion of it

Visual Analysis

Learn from Maps Have students answer the question in the caption. San Jacinto

Background

SAM HOUSTON Born in Virginia, Houston moved to Tennessee with his family and spent much of his youth with the Cherokees, who adopted him. He fought under Andrew Jackson in the War of 1812. After serving as governor of Tennessee, he moved first to Oklahoma and then to Texas in 1833, when he was 40 years old. He became commander of the Texas military forces when Texas declared its independence from Mexico. His greatest military triumph was the Battle of San Jacinto, and his popularity that followed the battle led to his election as president of the republic. When Texas became a state, he represented it in the U.S. Senate and later was governor of the state. His staunch opposition to secession in 1861 led to his removal from the governorship. The city of Houston, Texas, was named for him.

Meet Individual Needs

VISUAL LEARNERS Have students conduct library research to locate pictures of historical landmarks in Texas related to Texas independence. Have students share these pictures or their own drawings of the historical landmarks with the class. Students should describe each landmark and explain its relationship to the fight for Texas independence.

The Oregon Country

Key Content Summary

The first pioneers from the United States who settled the Oregon Country went there to teach the Indians about Christianity. Thousands of others heard stories of the rich farmland in Oregon and followed the Oregon Trail to get there.

Culture

Shared Humanity and Unique Identity Have students compare and contrast the Whitmans' missionary goals with those of the Spanish. Ask them to conclude why some American settlers thought it was important to convert Indians to Christianity.

History

Origins, Spread, and Influence Discuss with students the British claims to the Oregon territory.

Q. **Why was President Polk eager to fix the boundary between the United States and British territory in Canada?** to protect the settlements in the Oregon territory from conflict with the British

BIOGRAPHY

John C. Frémont
1813–1890

In the early 1800s the United States government decided that maps of the West needed to be made. These maps would help traveling settlers decide which routes to take and where to settle. John C. Frémont, a surveyor, was chosen to lead the expedition. In 1842, 1843, and 1844 he explored much of the land between the Rocky Mountains and the Pacific Ocean. His detailed written accounts of the land, bodies of water, and climate helped thousands of Americans settle the West.

The Oregon Country

American pioneers continued to push west. In 1834, Christian missionaries journeyed to the Oregon Country. This region was made up of present-day Oregon, Washington, and Idaho, and parts of Montana and Wyoming. In 1836 Marcus and Narcissa Whitman and Henry and Eliza Spalding set up missions near the Walla Walla Valley. They hoped to teach Christianity to the Indians.

The missionaries' letters to people back East told of the green valleys, wooded hills, and fertile soil of the Oregon Country—a place many began to dream of. In 1842 the first large group of pioneers headed for Oregon. Thousands more followed. The route they took came to be called the Oregon Trail. The Oregon Trail led northwest more than 2,000 miles (3,219 km) from Independence, Missouri, to the Platte River. The pioneers then traveled across the Continental Divide, an imaginary line that runs north and south along the highest points of the Rocky Mountains. The trail then continued to the Snake and Columbia rivers and ended at the Willamette (wuh•LA•muht) Valley of Oregon.

The journey took as long as six months. What a hard trip it was! Fresh water was scarce, but sudden storms soaked the travelers. Wagons broke down. Rivers had to be crossed. Many people died along the way. Yet many reached Oregon, and the settlements there grew quickly.

To protect its settlements, the United States wanted a clear dividing line between its Oregon territory and nearby British land. In 1846 President James K. Polk signed a treaty with Britain fixing the 49th parallel of latitude as the boundary between the United States and the British territory in Canada. The treaty gave the United States the lands now known as Oregon, Washington, Idaho, western Montana, and Wyoming.

This quilt was signed by people traveling together in a wagon train.

REVIEW ***How did people in the East learn about the Oregon Country?*** from letters of missionaries

ACTIVITY CHOICES

Background

THE WHITMANS Marcus and Narcissa Whitman were dedicated Christian missionaries. Marcus also was a doctor. Narcissa Whitman and Eliza Spalding were the first white women to travel the Oregon Trail to the Oregon territory. The Whitmans set up a mission among the Cayuse Indians. In 1847 a group of settlers brought an epidemic of measles with them. Many Cayuse, including children, died from the disease. In retaliation the Cayuse killed the Whitmans and 12 others at the mission. News of the Indian attack helped speed passage of the bill making Oregon a U.S. territory.

Link to Language Arts

WRITE A JOURNAL ENTRY Tell students to imagine that they are about to travel across the country to Oregon in the 1840s. Have them write journal entries describing how they feel about the journey ahead and what they will miss most about their hometown.

TECHNOLOGY

Use THE AMAZING WRITING MACHINE™ to complete this writing activity.

The Mormons in Utah

In the 1840s the Mormons, or members of the Church of Jesus Christ of Latter-day Saints, joined the pioneers moving west. Under their first leader, Joseph Smith, the Mormons had settled in Nauvoo (naw•VOO), Illinois. But their beliefs caused problems with other settlers, and in 1844 an angry crowd killed Joseph Smith.

When Brigham Young became the new leader of the Mormons, he decided that they should move to a place where no one would bother them. In 1846 Young and the first group of Mormons to head west set out for the Rocky Mountains.

In July 1847 the Mormons reached the Great Salt Lake valley in the Great Basin. Young chose this harsh land to settle in because he thought that no other settlers would want it. He used words from the Bible to tell his followers, "We will make this desert blossom as the rose."

One of the first things the Mormons did was build irrigation canals. The canals brought water from the mountains to turn the dry land into farmland.

The Mormons did make the land blossom with crops of grain, fruit, and vegetables. The region grew rapidly, and soon it became the Utah Territory. Brigham Young became its first governor.

REVIEW ***Why did the Mormons move to present-day Utah?*** to find a place to live where no one would bother them

War with Mexico

The land the Mormons settled in the Great Basin belonged to Mexico. In 1848, only a few months later, that land became part of the United States.

James K. Polk was President then, and he wanted to see the United States reach to the Pacific Ocean. He thought that all the lands west of Texas should be part of the United States.

Mormon pioneers get ready to move out from what is today Omaha, Nebraska. They stayed there for the winter before completing their journey westward.

The Mormons in Utah

Key Content Summary

Mormons, disliked for their religious beliefs in Illinois, settled in the Great Salt Lake valley, in what was to become the Utah Territory under the leadership of Brigham Young. There they cooperated in an effort to build irrigation canals that helped turn the desert into fertile farmland.

Culture

Shared Humanity and Unique Identity Have students discuss other groups of people, both historical and contemporary, whose beliefs have made them the target of discrimination.

War with Mexico

Key Content Summary

President Polk's desire to extend the United States to the Pacific Ocean was an important element leading to the war with Mexico. After a year of conflict, the United States defeated Mexico. In the peace treaty ending the war, the United States acquired land that now makes up California, Utah, Nevada and parts of Arizona, New Mexico, Colorado, and Wyoming.

Smithsonian Institution®

Go to the Internet site at *http://www.si.edu/harcourt/socialstudies* to visit the exhibit "Moving West" in Binding the Nation at the National Postal Museum.

Link to Mathematics

CALCULATE AVERAGES Present students with the following information, and have them answer the question. In 1848 there were 2,000 Mormons living in Utah. Over the next 12 years, 38,000 more Mormons came to settle there. What was the average number of newcomers each year from 1849 to 1860? approximately 3,166

Background

THE MORMONS The Mormon settlement in Nauvoo, Illinois, maintained its own militia and its own laws. It attracted many settlers from abroad and by 1842 was the largest town in Illinois. The Mormons in Nauvoo prospered, but they deliberately isolated themselves from their neighbors in the town. The neighbors were envious of the Mormons' success and hostile to them because of their religious beliefs. After Joseph Smith's death, Brigham Young provided strong leadership, as evidenced by his election to the governorship of Utah. Utah was admitted as a state in 1896.

History

People and Events Across Time and Place Have students identify the reasons that made war with Mexico inevitable.

Q. **How do you think the American settlers felt about the American victory in the war with Mexico?** relieved and excited about acquiring new lands for the United States

Q. **How do you think the Mexicans felt about losing the war?** angry that they had land taken away from them

Geography

Regions Have students examine the map. Ask them to estimate the percentage of United States territory that was purchased from other countries. Suggest that they also estimate the percentage of territory acquired as a result of wars or treaties.

Visual Analysis

Learn from Maps Have students answer the question in the caption. 1846

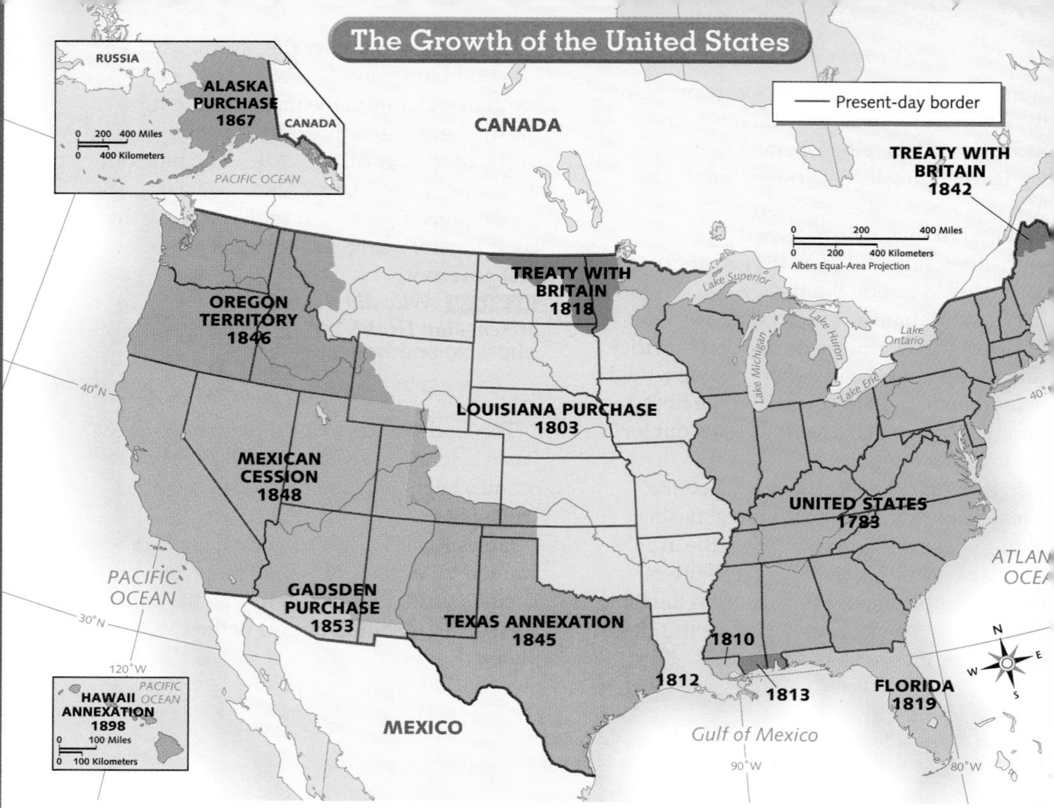

Regions By 1898 the United States had gained the land for what would become the present-day 50 states.
■ *When did the United States first gain land on the Pacific coast?*

In January 1846 President Polk sent American soldiers into lands in southern Texas that were disputed between the United States and Mexico. In April Mexican troops crossed the Rio Grande and attacked an American patrol. Polk then asked Congress to declare war on Mexico.

In 1847 the United States invaded Mexico by sea. American soldiers led by General Winfield Scott marched from Veracruz to Mexico City. After a year of fighting, the war was over. In 1848 Mexico and the United States signed the Treaty of Guadalupe Hidalgo (gwah•dah•LOO•pay ee•DAHL•goh). In the treaty, the United States agreed to pay $15 million for California and the land that now makes up Utah, Nevada, and parts of Arizona, New Mexico, Colorado, and Wyoming. Then in 1853, the United States purchased more land from Mexico in the Gadsden Purchase. This brought the part of the country between Canada and Mexico to its present size. This area, made up of 48 states, is known as the Continental United States.

REVIEW ***What did the United States agree to purchase in its treaty with Mexico?***
land that is now California, Utah, Nevada, and parts of Arizona, New Mexico, Colorado, and Wyoming

ACTIVITY CHOICES

TECHNOLOGY

Use NATIONAL INSPIRER™ to reinforce geography concepts.

Background

THE BATTLE OF CHAPULTEPEC
When United States forces stormed the castle of Chapultepec on a hill near Mexico City, the Mexicans put up a heroic defense, especially the "boy heroes" from a nearby military college who chose to die rather than surrender. The Battle of Chapultepec became a symbol of glory for Mexicans.

Extend and Enrich

COOPERATIVE LEARNING

BROADCAST THE NEWS
Divide the class into groups. Tell students that their groups will produce a television news broadcast about an event covered in this lesson, such as the Texas Revolution, the war with Mexico, the settlement of Utah, or the California gold rush. Suggest that different members of each group take the roles of newswriter, news anchor, and various interviewers. Provide classroom time for each group's broadcast.

The California Gold Rush

Just a few days before the treaty with Mexico was signed, gold was found in California. In January 1848 James Marshall and his workers were building a waterwheel for John Sutter's new sawmill near Sacramento. Something in the water glittered. Marshall picked it up. He held a shiny stone that was half the size of a pea. Then he and his workers saw another and another. The news soon reached the eastern states. Gold had been discovered!

Less than a year later, more than 80,000 gold seekers came to California. They were called **forty-niners** because they arrived in the year 1849. Most had made their way west on the Oregon Trail, cutting south across the Nevada desert to California. The easier but much more expensive way was to travel around Cape Horn, the tip of South America, by clipper ship. Clipper ships were the fastest ships to sail the oceans. For gold seekers in a hurry to reach California and willing to pay extra to get there fast, the journey around Cape Horn took from three to four months.

These forty-niners are trying to find gold among stones in a riverbed. Looking for gold was hard work, and the chances of finding any were slim.

The gold rush quickly filled California with new people. They came from Europe and Asia as well as from the United States. In 1850, only two years after Marshall's discovery at Sutter's Mill, California became a state.

REVIEW ***Why did thousands of people travel to California in 1849?*** to find gold

LESSON 3 REVIEW

Check Understanding

1. **Remember the Facts** Why did American settlers move west into Texas, Oregon, Utah, and California?
2. **Recall the Main Idea** How did the United States expand its territory in the 1800s?

Think Critically

3. **Personally Speaking** What qualities do you think a pioneer needed in order to settle on the frontier? Why would those qualities be important?
4. **Past to Present** Are there still pioneers and frontiers today? Explain your answer.

Show What You Know

Art Activity Make a picture map of the growth of the western United States. On your map, show the Alamo, the Whitman and Spalding missions, travelers on the Oregon Trail, Mormon settlers, and forty-niners. Share your map with family members.

Reteach the Main Idea

COOPERATIVE LEARNING

MAKE A TIME LINE Divide the class into small groups. Have each group make a time line of the events in the lesson that led to President Polk's push to acquire western lands all the way to the Pacific Ocean. When the time lines have been completed, have the groups share and discuss the events they selected. You may wish to make a class time line on the board.

ACTIVITY BOOK

Reinforce & Extend

Use ACTIVITY BOOK, p. 74.

TECHNOLOGY

Use TIMELINER™ to complete this activity.

The California Gold Rush

Key Content Summary

In 1848 gold was found in California, and thousands of people from the United States, Europe, and Asia rushed there to mine the precious ore. Some came over the Oregon Trail. Others took the longer route around Cape Horn. In 1850 California became a state.

3. CLOSE

Have students consider again the Focus question on page 383.

How might a country today expand its territory?

Have students use what they have learned in this lesson about the growth of the United States to identify the ways that countries today might expand their borders.

LESSON 3 REVIEW—Answers

Check Understanding

1. Settlers followed Stephen F. Austin to Texas and the Whitmans to Oregon to find new farmland; they followed Brigham Young to Utah in pursuit of religious freedom, and they went to California to find gold.
2. It expanded its territory by moving west beyond its borders. People moved into Texas, the Oregon Country, and other western lands, including present-day Utah and California. It also purchased land that makes up California, Utah, and Nevada and parts of Arizona, New Mexico, and Wyoming after defeating Mexico.

Think Critically

3. Courage, determination, strength, and optimism would be needed to help pioneers survive the difficulties facing them.
4. There are pioneers and frontiers today in space exploration, undersea exploration, and the sciences. There are many things that remain to be learned in these and many other fields.

Show What You Know

Performance Assessment Consider having selected students present their maps to the class.

What to Look For In evaluating the maps, look for evidence that students have understood the significance of the items they are identifying.

MODEL & APPLY SKILLS

Objectives

1. Interpret and compare map symbols on relief and elevation maps.
2. Trace the route of the Oregon Trail.

Vocabulary

relief (p. 390) elevation (p. 391)

1. ACCESS

Using a map of your state, select a site and have students describe routes they could take to get there. If possible, choose a site that is separated from your area by a mountain, lake, or other natural obstacle. Have students explain how that land feature affected the routes they chose.

Then have students imagine that they are pioneers traveling to the same site on foot or in wagons. Have them consider how their routes would change with no paved highways or large bridges. Point out how special maps can help us understand the difficulties faced by pioneers on their journeys.

Map and Globe Skills

Use Relief and Elevation Maps

1. Why Learn This Skill?

When we think of traveling long distances today, we think of going by airplane, car, or train. Early pioneers, however, had to travel long distances by walking or by riding in wagons. They had to cross steep mountains and wade across wide rivers.

Relief maps and elevation maps can help you better understand how difficult the journeys of the pioneers must have been. Both types of maps show how high or how low the land is.

2. Relief and Elevation

A relief map helps you picture the physical features of the land. **Relief** (rih•LEEF), or the differences in height of an area of land, is often shown by shading. Heavily shaded areas on a relief map show high relief, or sharp rises and drops in the land. Lightly shaded areas show low relief, where the land gently rises or falls. Areas with no shading show land that is mostly flat.

Look at the relief map showing trails to the West. You will see that there is heavy shading in the western lands—showing areas of high relief, such as the Rocky Mountains and the Cascade Range. In the eastern lands, there is little shading—showing land that has low relief, such as the Great Plains, which is mostly flat land.

Relief Map: Trails to the West

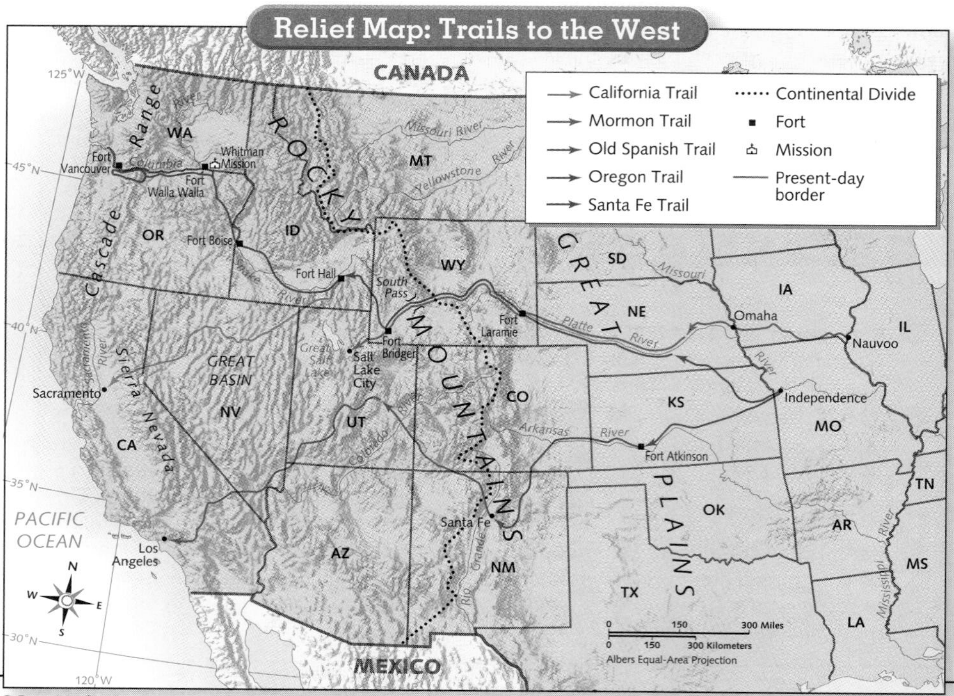

ACTIVITY CHOICES

Meet Individual Needs

TACTILE LEARNERS Have students work with partners to create their own land trails to the West. They can decide their own starting point in the East and a destination in the West. One student can draw a line map showing the trail and some physical features that affect it. The other student can write a description of how the trail crosses the western half of the country. Allow partners to share their work with the class.

DESK MAPS

Use DESK MAPS to complete this activity.

Link to Reading

READ DIARIES AND OTHER ACCOUNTS Ask students to read pioneer diaries or other early accounts of travel on the western trails. Have students relate their reading to the relief map in this lesson. Also ask them to consider how landforms affected the trips West.

TECHNOLOGY

Use MAPSKILLS to complete this activity.

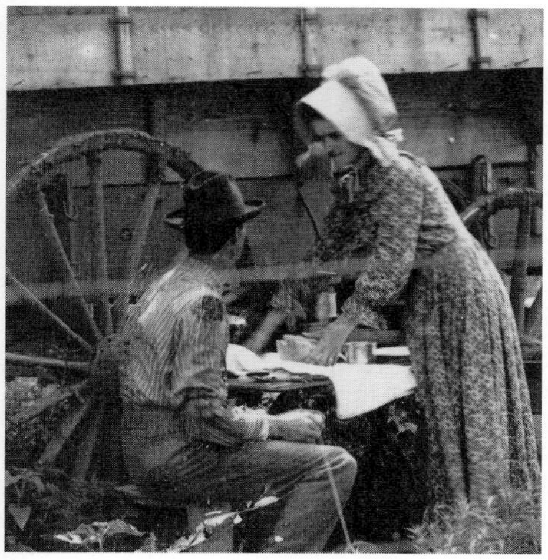

This picture was taken of pioneers traveling in Kansas. Using the relief map that shows trails to the West, how would you describe the land in Kansas?

A relief map, however, does not tell you the elevation (eh•luh•VAY•shuhn) of the land. **Elevation** is the height of the land. Land that is level with the surface of the ocean is said to be at sea level. Its elevation is zero. The elevation of all other land is measured from sea level, up or down, in feet or meters. To find the elevation of a place, you must look at an elevation map.

Most elevation maps use color to show elevation. Look at the elevation map showing the end of the Oregon Trail. The map key tells you which colors are used to show different elevations. Green is used for the lowest land shown on this map, which is between sea level and 655 feet (200 m). Purple is used for the highest land, which is above 13,120 feet (4,000 m).

3. Understand the Process

Use the questions that follow as a guide to help you learn how to use relief maps and elevation maps.

Elevation Map: The End of the Oregon Trail

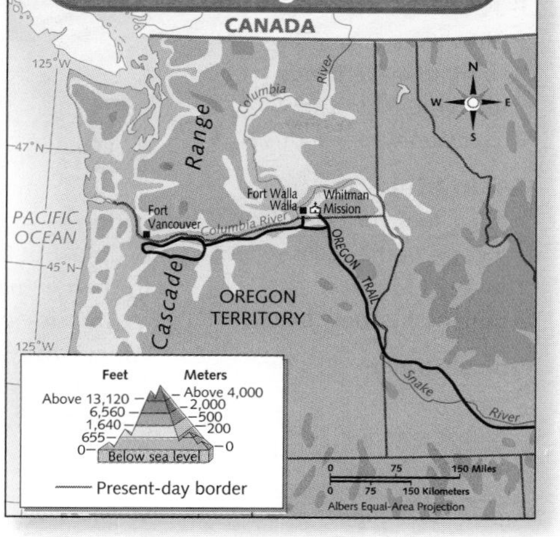

1. What is the difference between a relief map and an elevation map?
2. To find the elevation at Fort Walla Walla, should you use a relief map or an elevation map?
3. Will a relief map tell you whether western Oregon is flat or mountainous?
4. How high are the highest areas in Oregon?
5. Where are the lowest areas in Oregon?
6. What is the elevation of the land at Fort Vancouver?

4. Think and Apply

MAP SKILLS

Imagine that you are a pioneer on the Oregon Trail. On the relief map, use your finger to trace the route of the trail from Independence to Fort Vancouver. Describe the landforms you pass along the way. Once you reach Oregon, use the elevation map to describe in greater detail the final days of your journey.

2. BUILD

Have students note the definition of the term *relief*. Point out that relief is often indicated on maps by shading. Have students find areas of high relief, low relief, and no relief on the relief map showing trails to the West.

Direct students to the definition of the term *elevation*. Point out that color is used to indicate elevation on most elevation maps. Have students find four different elevation categories on the map showing the end of the Oregon Trail. Make sure students understand the difference between relief and elevation.

Have students answer the questions in Understand the Process.

1. A relief map shows the physical features of an area—that is, whether it is mountainous, hilly, or flat. An elevation map shows the land's height in relation to sea level.
2. an elevation map
3. Yes. Relief maps show mountains and flat areas by shading or lack of shading.
4. The highest areas are in the Cascade Range in western Oregon, with heights of 1,640 to 6,560 feet (500 to 2,000 m) above sea level.
5. The lowest areas are along the Pacific Coast and along major rivers.
6. The elevation of Fort Vancouver is in the 0–655 feet (0–200 meter) range.

3. CLOSE

Have students complete the Think and Apply activity, either individually or in small groups. Have them think about the difficulties each landform might have presented to the pioneers and how it might have influenced the route taken. As students work, look for an understanding of how to use relief and elevation maps. Emphasize how these maps can provide information about the nature of pioneer journeys and other historical events.

Reteach the Skill

COOPERATIVE LEARNING

TRACE A TRAIL Have students work together in small groups, with each group concentrating on either the Mormon, California, Old Spanish, or Santa Fe Trail. Tell them to select one member of the group to act as a guide to lead them along the trail and another member to monitor the relief map. Have all group members use their fingers to trace the trail. The guide can periodically stop the progress along the trail to ask for an explanation of how physical features are affecting the journey.

ACTIVITY BOOK

Practice & Apply

Use ACTIVITY BOOK, p. 75.

TRANSPARENCY

Use TRANSPARENCY 31.

Objectives

1. Analyze Horace Mann's efforts to improve the nation's schools.
2. Evaluate the work of the abolitionists.
3. Describe the movement to secure greater rights for women.

Vocabulary

reform (p. 392)
public school (p. 392)
abolish (p. 393)
abolitionist (p. 393)
equality (p. 393)
suffrage (p. 395)

1. ACCESS

The Focus Question

Ask students how they, their friends, or adults they know have worked to make their communities better. Discuss the many things that people can do to improve life in their school, community, or nation.

The Main Idea

In this lesson students explore three areas of life in the United States in the first half of the 1800s that became the focus of reform—education, slavery, and the position of women. After students have read the lesson, lead them in a discussion of these issues and what effect the effort toward reform had on the nation's later history.

2. BUILD

Better Schools

Key Content Summary

Horace Mann did much to change and improve the public schools. He pressed for laws requiring children to attend school and for special schools to train teachers.

Visual Analysis

Learn from Documents Have students answer the question in the caption. Many books continue to list words and show examples of how they can be used in sentences.

LESSON 4

FOCUS
How do people today work to make things better in their school, community, or country?

Main Idea As you read, look for ways people in the 1800s worked to make American society better.

Vocabulary
reform
public school
abolish
abolitionist
equality
suffrage

An Age of Reform

The fast growth of the United States in the first half of the 1800s made many Americans hopeful. They saw how the nation's growth in manufacturing and in size helped many people. But they also saw the need to **reform**, or change for the better, many parts of American life.

America's growth caused some problems, too. So many Americans were concerned about these problems that the 1830s through the 1850s became an age of reform. During this time many Americans worked to improve life for others.

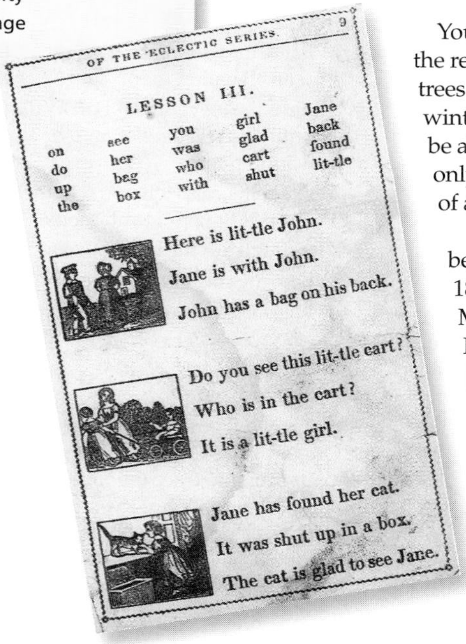
OF THE ECLECTIC SERIES. 9

LESSON III.

on	see	you	girl	Jane
do	her	was	glad	back
up	beg	who	cart	found
the	box	with	shut	lit-tle

Here is lit-tle John.
Jane is with John.
John has a bag on his back.

Do you see this lit-tle cart?
Who is in the cart?
It is a lit-tle girl.

Jane has found her cat.
It was shut up in a box.
The cat is glad to see Jane.

This spelling book was used in some schools during the early 1800s. How is this similar to spelling books used today?

Better Schools

Young Horace Mann was excited to see the red leaves falling from the oak and maple trees in Massachusetts. He knew that when winter put an end to farm work, he would be able to go to school. Horace's school had only one room and one teacher for children of all ages. And there were very few books.

When Horace Mann grew up, he became a reformer in education. In 1837 Mann was made secretary of the Massachusetts Board of Education. He worked to improve the state's **public schools**, the schools paid for by taxes and open to all children.

Horace Mann wanted more specific laws requiring children to go to school. He called for special schools to train teachers. In Mann's day most teachers worked only

ACTIVITY CHOICES

Reading Support

IDENTIFY RELATED WORDS Have students scan the lesson to find the meaning of each vocabulary word. Ask them to explain how the vocabulary words relate to each other. Use the terms *abolish* and *abolitionist* to discuss how endings can change a word's meaning. Ask students to discuss the differences between the words *reform* and *reformer* and *suffrage* and *suffragist.*

part-time. They were often students of law or of religion. Mann wanted full-time, well-trained teachers. He also wanted new schools built. Before this time most public-school classes were held in stores or in people's homes.

By 1850 many of Horace Mann's ideas were being used in the North and the West. Most white children received an elementary school education and sometimes a high-school education. Free African children, however, had to go to separate schools. In the South, most boys who were white went to private schools. Girls had few chances for education. Enslaved children had none.

REVIEW ***What reforms in education did Horace Mann try to bring about?*** laws requiring children to go to school, special schools to train teachers, and new schools

The Fight Against Slavery

While Horace Mann worked to improve education during the age of reform, other reformers worked to **abolish**, or end, slavery. Since the early days of the country's history, some Americans had been deeply troubled by slavery. Soon they started working together to help enslaved people gain their freedom. Among the first to speak out were members of a religious group called the Quakers. In 1775 the Quakers formed the first group to work against slavery—an antislavery society.

Abolitionists (a•buh•LIH•shuhn•ists), or people who wanted to abolish slavery, worked to end slavery in different ways. Some abolitionists used the written word to spread their message. In 1827 Samuel Cornish and John Russwurm started a newspaper that called for **equality**, or the same rights, for all Americans. The newspaper, *Freedom's Journal*, was the first to be owned and written by Africans in the United States. "Too long," Cornish and Russwurm wrote, "have others spoken for us."

A few years later another abolitionist, William Lloyd Garrison, founded a newspaper called *The Liberator*. In it he called for a complete end to slavery at once.

> "On this subject I do not wish to think, or speak, or write with moderation. I will not retreat a single inch—AND I WILL BE HEARD."

In 1852 a novel by abolitionist Harriet Beecher Stowe turned many people against slavery. The book, called *Uncle Tom's Cabin*, told the heartbreaking story of slaves being mistreated by a cruel slave owner. The book

Millions of people around the world read about the cruel conditions of slavery in the novel *Uncle Tom's Cabin*.

Culture

Social Organizations and Institutions Have students compare and contrast Horace Mann's school with their school today.

Civics and Government

Civic Values and Democratic Principles Explore with students why education is important in a democracy like the United States. Ask students to speculate on how Horace Mann's reforms affected nineteenth-century students.

The Fight Against Slavery

Key Content Summary

In the 1800s the abolitionist movement intensified. William Lloyd Garrison and Harriet Beecher Stowe were among white Americans who tried to change Americans' views on slavery. Frederick Douglass and Sojourner Truth were Africans who traveled the country speaking out against slavery.

PRIMARY SOURCE

William Lloyd Garrison wrote this in an article in the first issue of *The Liberator*.

Source: *Frederick Douglass*. Sharman Apt Russell. Chelsea House Publishers, 1988.

Background

HORACE MANN Although Mann received only a sparse elementary education, he was able to enter Brown University as a sophomore and graduate with honors. He became a lawyer and served as the first secretary of education in Massachusetts. Over a 12-year period Mann aroused the nation's interest in education, leading to major improvements in the public schools. He later served as the first president of Antioch College in Yellow Springs, Ohio.

Community Involvement

Select a small group of students to contact the historical society in the community and request as much information as possible about the community's first school. Ask students to prepare a report for the class, with visuals to accompany their presentation. If the original schoolhouse is still in the community, arrange for a class visit.

Auditory Learning

Interpret Primary Sources Ask a volunteer to read aloud the quotation by William Lloyd Garrison on page 393. Then have students demonstrate that they understand Garrison's stand toward slavery by restating the quotation in their own words.

Q. **Why do you think Garrison named his newspaper *The Liberator?*** because he wanted it to stand for freedom

Culture

Thought and Expression Have students identify the ways abolitionists spread their antislavery message. Discuss the ways people or groups try to bring about change today.

Q. **In your opinion, how effective was the work of the abolitionists?** Students' viewpoints may vary. Some students may think the abolitionists found very effective ways to spread their message about slavery. Other students may think the abolitionists did not do enough.

History

People and Events Across Time and Place Discuss with students the fact that Frederick Douglass was a runaway slave. Ask students to speculate on the risks Douglass took by admitting his runaway status publicly.

The Webb family (above) were abolitionists who read the novel *Uncle Tom's Cabin* to audiences in the North. Large crowds came to hear Sojourner Truth (right). She spoke against slavery and in favor of women's rights.

quickly became a best-seller and was made into a play.

While some abolitionists were writing, other abolitionists were giving speeches. One of the speakers was Frederick Douglass, a runaway slave. William Lloyd Garrison had asked him to speak at an abolitionist meeting. Douglass slowly rose and walked up to the stage. He shared from the heart how it felt to be free. Douglass also told his listeners the story of his daring escape from slavery.

When Douglass finished speaking, everyone cheered. Before long, he had become the leading abolitionist speaker. His speeches made many people agree that slavery had to be stopped.

Like Douglass, Sojourner Truth traveled the country speaking out against slavery. Sojourner Truth was a former slave named Isabella. She believed that God had called he to "travel up and down the land" to preach. She decided to change her name to Sojourner which means "traveler." She chose Truth as a last name.

Sojourner Truth believed that slavery coul be ended peacefully. Frederick Douglass argued in his speeches that only rebellion would end it.

In the end, Douglass was proved right. Th nation that grew large and strong in the 1800 would soon be divided by civil war.

REVIEW ***How did abolitionists work to end slavery?*** through antislavery societies, newspapers, books, and speeches

394 • Unit 6

Activity Choices

Background

HARRIET BEECHER STOWE The daughter of a New England minister, Stowe saw for herself the mistreatment of enslaved people when she traveled in Kentucky. While there she helped slaves escape to Ohio. *Uncle Tom's Cabin* was first published in a magazine and then as a two-volume book. In one year it sold more than 300,000 copies and was translated into many European languages. In addition to her interest in the abolitionist movement, Stowe was active in the fight for women's suffrage.

Link to Language Arts

WRITE TO PERSUADE Ask students to imagine that they work for William Lloyd Garrison on his newspaper, *The Liberator.* Have students write an editorial to persuade other young people to join the fight against slavery.

Technology

Use THE AMAZING WRITING MACHINE™ RESOURCE PACKAGE to complete this writing activity.

Multicultural Link

Discuss with students why many women, such as Sojourner Truth and Harriet Beecher Stowe, were active in both the antislavery and the women's rights movements. Point out that while some abolitionists, such as William Lloyd Garrison, also supported the women's rights movement, many abolitionists actually opposed it.

Rights for Women

In 1840 Elizabeth Cady Stanton and Lucretia Mott went to a convention of abolitionists in London, Britain. However, they were not allowed to speak because they were women. Stanton and Mott were so angry that they decided to hold their own convention—for women's rights.

The first women's rights convention met on July 19 and 20, 1848, at Seneca Falls, New York. Those who attended the convention wanted women to have the same political, social, and economic rights as men. They wrote a statement saying that women should have "all the rights and privileges which belong to them as citizens of the United States." The statement called for women to be able to own property, to keep the wages that they earned, and to be given **suffrage**, or the right to vote.

The reformers began to get some support. In 1850 Susan B. Anthony of New York worked for women teachers to have the same pay as men teachers and for women to have the same property rights as men. She later became a leader of the women's suffrage movement.

GEOGRAPHY

Seneca Falls, New York

Seneca Falls is a small town in the middle of New York State, between Rochester and Syracuse. Seneca Falls was the home of Elizabeth Cady Stanton. With Lucretia Mott, Stanton planned the first women's rights convention in the summer of 1848. Those attending the Seneca Falls Convention called for women to work together to win their rights as citizens. Today Seneca Falls has a Women's Hall of Fame.

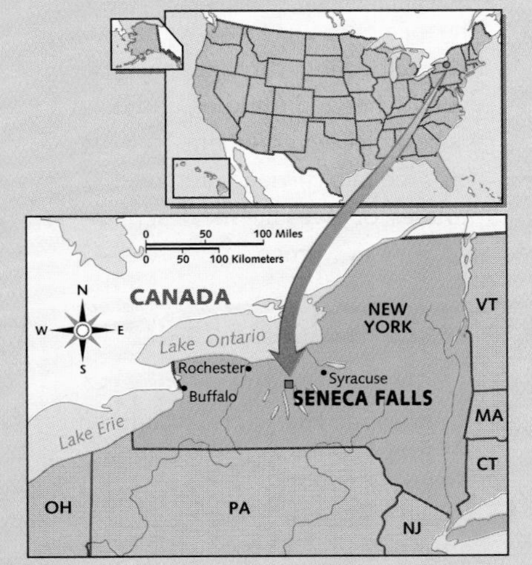

Elizabeth Cady Stanton (left) spoke at the first women's rights convention and wrote a document called the Declaration of Sentiments. The document describes women's rights by using words from the Declaration of Independence. But Stanton added some words, as in "all men *and women* are created equal."

Rights for Women

Key Content Summary

Elizabeth Cady Stanton, Lucretia Mott, Susan B. Anthony, and Sojourner Truth were among many nineteenth-century women who worked for women's rights. They demanded the same political, social, and economic rights as men. However, women continued to be denied equal rights for many years after the struggle for women's rights began.

History

Origins, Spread, and Influence Discuss the reasons it took so long for women to begin to secure the same rights as men. Ask students to compare and contrast the fight for women's rights with the fight to abolish slavery.

Visual Analysis

Interpret Pictures Have students examine the picture of the speaker at the Seneca Falls Convention.

Meet Individual Needs

ENGLISH LANGUAGE LEARNERS As students read the lesson, have them fill in a chart such as the following:

	Better Schools	The Fight Against Slavery	Rights for Women
Who?			
Where?			
When?			
What Happened First?			
What Happened Next?			

Extend and Enrich

READ AND ROLE-PLAY Have each student choose a reform leader from the chapter or other reform leaders of the time, such as Dorothea Dix, Thomas Gallaudet, Mary Lyon, or Louisa May Alcott. After students have read about their reform leaders, have them role-play one or several aspects of the reform leaders' lives for the class. You may wish to videotape the performances.

"PRIMARY SOURCE"

Source: *The 19th Century and Abolition.* Modern Curriculum Press, 1994.

3. CLOSE

Have students consider again the Focus question on page 392.

How do people today work to make things better in their school, community, or country?

Ask students to analyze what they have learned in this lesson about the reform movements of the first half of the 1800s and to consider why such movements are still important today.

LESSON 4 REVIEW—Answers

Check Understanding

1. the educational system, slavery, and the rights of women
2. They worked to change laws, wrote articles and books, and spoke at public meetings.

Think Critically

3. Schools might still be in stores or homes and teachers might still be untrained.
4. Many white northerners had probably never heard about slavery directly from someone who had been a slave. In addition, Douglass's personal story was interesting and emotional in appeal.

Show What You Know

Performance Assessment Consider having students read their letters aloud as though they were addressing the school board. Other students can act as members of the board and interrogate the letter writers about their arguments.

What to Look For In evaluating the students' letters, look for evidence of their understanding of the theme of the lesson.

BIOGRAPHY

Susan Brownell Anthony 1820–1906

For most of her life, Susan B. Anthony worked to get women the right to vote. She was once arrested and fined $100 for breaking the law by voting in an election for President. Anthony also started a weekly newspaper and wrote books to spread her message. Susan B. Anthony died 14 years before the Nineteenth Amendment to the Constitution became law. From 1979 to 1981, the United States government honored her work for women's rights by minting one-dollar coins with her picture on them. Susan B. Anthony was the first woman to have her picture on a coin in the United States.

Sojourner Truth used her speaking skills to help. In 1851 Truth was at a women's rights convention in Ohio. When a man said, "Women are weak," she answered,

> "The man over there says women need to be helped into carriages and lifted over ditches and puddles, and have the best place everywhere. Nobody helps me into carriages and over puddles, or gives me the best place—and ain't I a woman?"

Women won a few rights during this time. A few states gave women control of the money they earned and of the property they owned. Some places, like Wyoming Territory allowed women to vote. Wyoming Territory was the first place in the United States and in the world to grant women the right to vote. However, it would not be until 1920 that the Nineteenth Amendment gave all women in the United States this right.

REVIEW ***What reforms did Elizabeth Cady Stanton and others work for?*** suffrage and all other rights of citizens

LESSON 4 REVIEW

Check Understanding

1. **Remember the Facts** What did reformers want to change about American society?
2. **Recall the Main Idea** How did reformers in the 1800s work to improve American society?

Think Critically

3. **Cause and Effect** How might public schools today be different if Horace Mann had not worked to reform education in the early 1800s?
4. **Personally Speaking** Why do you think so many people wanted to hear Frederick Douglass tell his story?

Show What You Know

Writing Activity Imagine that you are a reformer in the 1800s. Write a letter in which you try to persuade a member of the school board to make a change in the public schools. Be sure to give the reason the change is needed. Collect the letters in a binder for classroom display.

ACTIVITY CHOICES

ACTIVITY BOOK

Reinforce & Extend

Use ACTIVITY BOOK, p. 76.

Reteach the Main Idea

MAKE A CONCEPT MAP (COOPERATIVE LEARNING) Divide the class into groups. Give each group a large sheet of butcher paper. In the center of the paper, have students write the word *Reformers.* In three circles around the word, have students write the words *education, slavery,* and *women's rights.* Direct students to complete the web by writing in the names of famous reformers in each area and the efforts they made to change society. Groups should display their completed concept maps in the classroom.

Chart and Graph Skills

Skills

Use a Double-Bar Graph

. Why Learn This Skill?

People often make comparisons and look at ow things have changed over time. Some par-nts mark their children's heights on a wall to eep a record of how much the children have rown each year. If records are kept for two hildren, the parents can compare how much ach has grown over the years and how much ach has grown compared with the other. A ood way to compare such information is by naking a double-bar graph. A double-bar raph allows you to compare information uickly and to see changes over time.

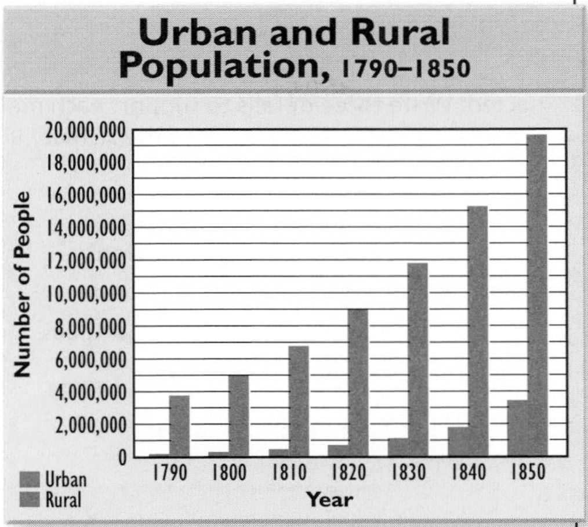

SOURCE: *Historical Statistics of the United States*

. Understand the Process

Between 1790 and 1850 both the urban and ural populations of the United States grew at a teady pace. The double-bar graph on this page hows the differences in urban and rural popu-ations for these years. It also shows how urban nd rural populations have changed over time.

1. Look at the words and numbers along the top, bottom, and left-hand side of the graph. Years are listed along the bottom, and numbers of people are listed along the left-hand side.
2. Notice that the information on this graph is shown only for every tenth year from 1790 to 1850.
3. Notice how different colors—blue and red—are used to show the urban population and the rural population.
4. Read the graph by running your finger up to the top of each bar and then left to the population number. If the top of the bar is between numbered lines, estimate the population by selecting a number between those two numbers.
5. Compare the heights of the blue bars with one another. Then compare the heights with the red bars. How did the urban population change over time? How did the rural population change over time?
6. Now compare the heights of the blue bar and the red bar for each year shown. This allows you to compare urban growth with rural growth over time. How does the double-bar graph help you understand how the population of the United States grew between 1790 and 1850?

3. Think and Apply

Make a double-bar graph of your test scores in social studies and in another subject. Label the bottom of your graph by grading periods. Along the left-hand side of your graph, list possible test scores. For example, you could mark 0 percent on the bottom and go up in 10-percent units, reaching 100 percent at the top. Each period, make a bar to represent your test scores in each subject. Remember to use a different color for each subject.

Reteach the Skill

COOPERATIVE LEARNING

GRAPH YOUR SCHOOL POPULATION Have students work in small groups to construct a double-bar graph showing how the population of boys and girls in your school has changed over time. List the data the groups need on the board. One student in each group can create the grid. Some students can cut the bars from colored construction paper while others adjust and paste these on the grids. Then have students analyze the information.

TRANSPARENCY

Use TRANSPARENCY 32.

ACTIVITY BOOK

Practice & Apply

Use ACTIVITY BOOK, pp. 77–78.

TECHNOLOGY

Use GRAPH LINKS to complete this graphing activity.

Objectives

1. Interpret information in a double-bar graph.
2. Analyze population trends in the 1800s.

1. ACCESS

Use the example from Why Learn This Skill? to introduce the double-bar graph. Illustrate the example on the board by using growth records for two fictional siblings. Emphasize the graph's usefulness in comparing two sets of changes over time. Relate the double-bar graph to previous learning about graphs in other curriculum areas, such as mathematics.

2. BUILD

Work through the steps shown in Understand the Process. Make sure students understand that urban and rural growth are represented by different colored bars. Have students practice interpreting a double-bar graph by answering the questions in steps 5 and 6.

5. Both the urban and the rural populations grew during this time period.
6. The graph shows that the U. S. population was largely rural during this time period. Both the urban and the rural populations grew, the rural population was consistently larger.

3. CLOSE

Provide students with ruled graph paper for use in the Think and Apply activity. Caution them to label lines rather than spaces as they indicate percentages along the left side and weeks along the bottom of the graph. As students work, look for an understanding of the form and function of a double-bar graph. Emphasize the usefulness of the graph for comparing two sets of data over time.

CHAPTER 12 REVIEW

Time Line

Ask students to share what they recall about each event shown on the time line.

Connect Main Ideas

Use the organizer to review the main ideas of the chapter. Have students use their textbooks to complete or check their work. Allow time for them to discuss and compare their responses.

ACTIVITY BOOK

Summarize the Chapter

A copy of the graphic organizer appears on ACTIVITY BOOK, p. 79.

TRANSPARENCY

A copy of the graphic organizer appears on TRANSPARENCY 33.

Write More About It

Write a Conversation

Students may wish to depict a factory owner who is in favor of Whitney's ideas or one who is skeptical of them. In the conversation, Whitney and the factory owner should speak of the changes that will be brought about by the use of interchangeable parts and mass production.

Write a Letter

Letters could mention whether the writer was cheering for the locomotive or for the horse and how he or she felt about the outcome of the race.

TECHNOLOGY

Use THE AMAZING WRITING MACHINE™ to complete the writing activities.

TECHNOLOGY

Use TIMELINER™ DATA DISKS to complete the time line activities.

CHAPTER 12 REVIEW

1820 — 1830

1829
• Andrew Jackson becomes the President of the United States

1830
• Steam locomotives

CONNECT MAIN IDEAS

Use this organizer to show how the chapter's main ideas are connected. Write three details to support each main idea. A copy of the organizer appears on page 79 of the Activity Book.

Possible answers to this graphic organizer are provided on page 372C of this Teacher's Edition.

The Industrial Revolution
New technology changed life in the United States in the 1800s.
1. ______
2. ______
3. ______

The Age of Jackson
Problems divided the American people in the early 1800s.
1. ______
2. ______
3. ______

The Way West (N, W, E, S)

Westward Ho!
The United States expanded its territory in the 1800s.
1. ______
2. ______
3. ______

An Age of Reform
People in the 1800s worked to make American society better.
1. ______
2. ______
3. ______

WRITE MORE ABOUT IT

Write a Conversation Write a conversation that could have taken place between Eli Whitney and a factory owner. Whitney and the factory owner should discuss how mass production will affect Americans.

Write a Letter Imagine that you witnessed the race between the *Tom Thumb* locomotive and the railroad car pulled by a horse. Write a letter to a friend describing the excitement of the event.

398 • Chapter 12

Use Vocabulary

1. transport (p. 375)
2. secede (p. 380)
3. Manifest Destiny (p. 383)
4. equality (p. 393)

Check Understanding

5. Lowell's factory had spinning, dyeing, and weaving all done under one roof. (p. 374)
6. It ran from Maryland to Illinois and was the land route linking East and West. (p. 376)
7. Because a tariff on imports th helped northern factory owners rai the prices of goods that southerne could get only from Europe. (p. 380
8. The Trail of Tears was the name give to the long, deadly journey taken the Cherokees when U.S. soldie forced them to leave their home Georgia. (p. 382)
9. the Mormons, who wanted to mo to a place where no one would both them (p. 387)
10. California, Utah, and Nevada ar parts of Arizona, New Mexico, Co orado, and Wyoming (p. 388)

1840	1850	1860
1838 • Cherokees are forced from their land	**1848** • Gold is found in California	**1853** • Continental United States is formed

USE VOCABULARY

Write a term from this list to complete each of the sentences that follow.

equality **secede**
Manifest Destiny **transport**

1. Factories needed to ____ their products to their customers.
2. South Carolina threatened to ____ in 1832 because Congress passed another tariff.
3. In 1845 the term ____ was first used to describe the idea that the United States would one day stretch from the Atlantic Ocean to the Pacific Ocean.
4. Some reformers called for ____, or the same rights, for all Americans.

CHECK UNDERSTANDING

5. How was Francis Cabot Lowell's textile mill different from earlier ones?
6. How was the National Road important to the country's growth?
7. Why did sectionalism become a problem in 1828?
8. What was the Trail of Tears?
9. What group settled the Utah Territory? Why did they go there?
10. What lands did the United States purchase after the war with Mexico?
11. Who were Frederick Douglass and Sojourner Truth? How did they spread their messages?
12. Why was the first women's rights convention held?

THINK CRITICALLY

13. **Explore Viewpoints** How did Vice President Calhoun's view of states' rights differ from the one held by President Jackson?
14. **Cause and Effect** What effect did the California gold rush have on the growth of the United States?

APPLY SKILLS

Use Relief and Elevation Maps Use the maps on pages 390 and 391 to answer these questions.

15. What is the elevation of the land at the Whitman Mission?
16. How would you describe the land near Fort Laramie?

Use a Double-Bar Graph Make a double-bar graph showing the high and low temperatures over the next five days. Each day, make bars for the high and low temperatures. Use different colors for the two temperatures.

READ MORE ABOUT IT

Erie Canal: Canoeing America's Great Waterway by Peter Lourie. Boyds Mills Press. Enjoy a historical canoe tour of the Erie Canal.

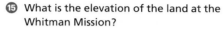

Visit the Internet at **http://www.hbschool.com** for additional resources.

CHAPTER 12 REVIEW

Apply Skills

Use Relief and Elevation Maps

15. between 655 and 1,640 feet (200–500 meters)
16. plains to the east, mountains to the west

Use a Double-Bar Graph

Make sure students understand that there should be enough space on their graphs so each day has room for two bars.

Read More About It

Additional books are listed in the Multimedia Resource Center on page 340D of this Teacher's Edition.

Unit Project Check-Up

Students should be finishing their dioramas. Their sketches should be completed and they should be able to discuss what they have included in the diorama.

ASSESSMENT PROGRAM

Use CHAPTER 12 TEST, pp. 99–102.

11. They were Africans who had been slaves and were abolitionists. They spread their message by traveling around the country and giving speeches. (p. 394)
12. It was held because women wanted to have the same political, social, and economic rights as men. (p. 395)

Think Critically

13. Vice President Calhoun believed states' rights were more important than federal laws. President Jackson, on the other hand, thought the federal Union was more important than states' rights.
14. The California gold rush of 1849 brought so many people to California that by 1850 California became a state.

Making Social Studies Relevant

See the Link

Personal Response

Ask students to share what they know about the atmosphere in space and the environment of the ocean. Then have students discuss where they might find information on these topics.

The Main Idea

Ask students to read the selection to learn about frontiers that are currently being explored.

Q. **What do you think people can learn from exploring space and the ocean?** People can learn about other climates, planets, moons, the sun, galaxies, plants, tides, and sea life.

Understand the Link

History

People and Events Across Time and Place On March 22, 1995, Valery Polyakov, a cosmonaut from the former Soviet Union, returned to Earth after a record 438 days in space. Polyakov lived on the Russian space station *Mir*.

Visual Analysis

Interpret Pictures Have students examine the pictures on pages 400–401. Point out that the special suit people use to explore the deep ocean waters is called a *Jim-suit*.

MAKING Social Studies RELEVANT

TODAY'S PATHFINDERS

Two hundred years ago much of North America was still unknown to people living in the United States. It lay beyond the frontier—the edge of settled regions. Today most places on the continent have been explored, and those that can be lived in have been settled. People today are exploring new kinds of frontiers.

Two of today's new frontiers are space and the deep ocean. Instead of traveling by horse or by wagon, present-day pathfinders explore in special vehicles that can travel great distances above the Earth or deep within the ocean waters. Instead of clothes made from animal furs to protect them from cold weather, today's explorers wear special suits to protect them from the harsh environments of space or the ocean floor.

Like those of the past, today's pathfinders are leading the way for others who will follow. Space stations and underwater laboratories already have been built where pathfinders can live and work for a period of time. Their success may lead to the building of permanent settlements in the future. One day people may live their whole lives in space or in the ocean waters.

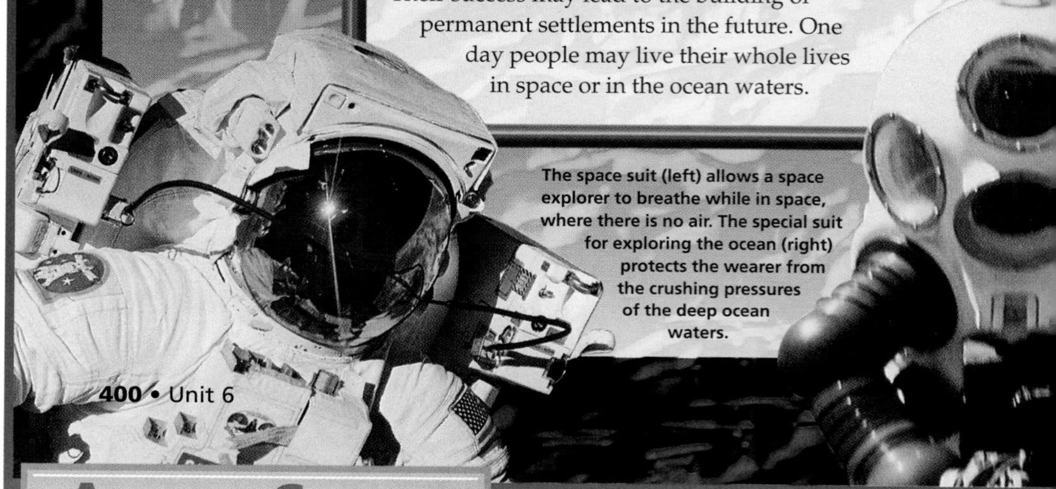

The space suit (left) allows a space explorer to breathe while in space, where there is no air. The special suit for exploring the ocean (right) protects the wearer from the crushing pressures of the deep ocean waters.

400 • Unit 6

Activity Choices

Background

THE SPACE SHUTTLE The space shuttle is a reusable spacecraft designed to go into orbit around the Earth. It carries people and cargo, and it lands back on Earth. The first shuttle was launched on April 12, 1981.

THE NAUTILE This submersible is capable of diving to depths of 20,000 feet (6,000 m). It carries three people and dives about 100 feet (30.5 m) per minute.

VIDEO

CNN Turner Learning

Check your media center or classroom video library for the Making Social Studies Relevant videotape of this feature.

Technology

Use IMAGINATION EXPRESS™: DESTINATION OCEAN to explore ocean environments.

he *Deepstar 4000* (bottom left) was one of the irst vehicles used to explore the depths of the ocean. The *Nautile* (below) was used to explore the unken ship *Titanic* that lies 12,300 feet (3,750 m) below the ocean's surface. Space explorers (bottom ight) perform tasks outside the space shuttle far above the Earth.

Think and Apply

BUILDING CITIZENSHIP

Think about ways the work of present-day pathfinders could change the way people live. Create a poster that shows what life might be like in the future because of the exploration taking place today. Share your poster with classmates.

HARCOURT BRACE — Visit the Internet at **http://www.hbschool.com** for additional resources.

CNN Turner Le@rning — Check your media center or classroom video library for the Making Social Studies Relevant videotape of this feature.

Geography

Location Explain to the class that the ocean covers more than 70 percent of the Earth's surface. The scientists who study the ocean are called oceanographers. Oceanographers work to discover answers to questions such as how the sea affects the atmosphere and how the sea floor was shaped.

Complete the Link

Summarize

People today continue to explore unknown frontiers. People use specially designed vehicles and protective suits that allow them to explore space and the ocean.

Think and Apply

Prior to creating the posters, have students work together to brainstorm a list of ways new information about space or the ocean could change the way people live their lives. Once posters are complete, have students write captions that help explain what life may be like in the future.

Meet Individual Needs

ENGLISH LANGUAGE LEARNERS
Discuss with students the pictures on pages 400–401. Ask students what information the illustrations provide.

Link to Science

UNDERSTAND TECHNOLOGY
Ask for student volunteers to locate and bring to class photographs of Earth taken from space. Have the class compare the photographs with maps of the corresponding regions, and ask students to discuss similarities and differences between the photographs and the maps.

Visual Summary

Take a Look

Remind students that a visual summary is a way to represent the main events in a story. Point out that this visual summary reviews some of the main events students read about in Unit 6.

Visual Analysis

Interpret Pictures Divide the class into small groups of three or four students each. Ask each group to identify the images shown and explain what each image tells about the expansion period of United States history. Have them discuss how the changes during that period of history still affect us today. Then have the groups share their descriptions and ideas.

Summarize the Main Ideas

Have students read aloud the summary statements on pages 402–403. Lead a class discussion about each scene, and ask students to offer supporting details for each main idea illustrated. You may wish to have students summarize the main ideas in a time-line format.

UNIT 6
REVIEW

Visual Summary

Summarize the Main Ideas
Study the pictures and captions to help you review the events you read about in Unit 6.

Create a Visual Summary
Choose a topic that is discussed in this unit. Then create your own visual summary about that topic. Draw simple pictures, and label each one. Remember to add a title.

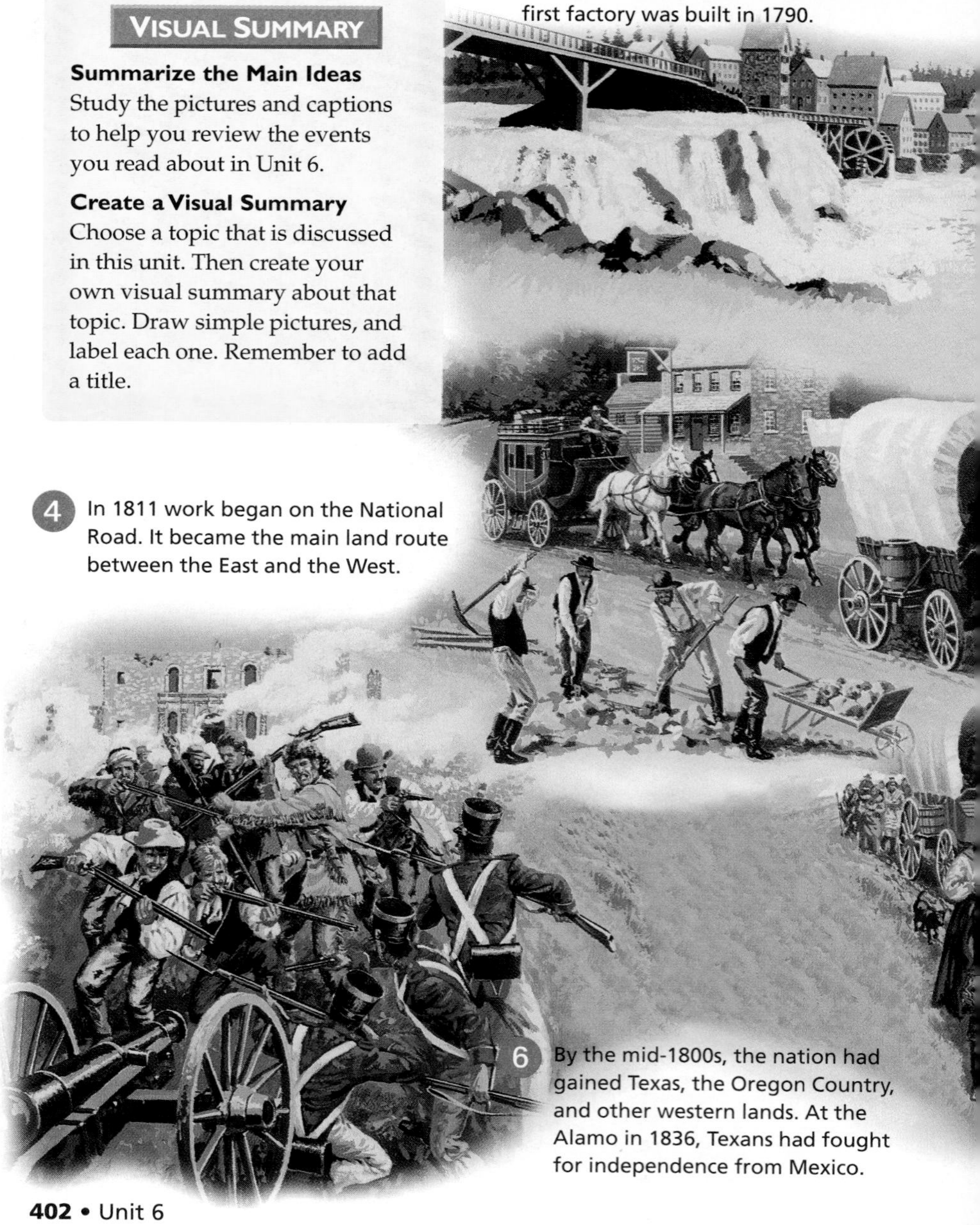

1 The Industrial Revolution brought great changes to the United States. The nation's first factory was built in 1790.

4 In 1811 work began on the National Road. It became the main land route between the East and the West.

6 By the mid-1800s, the nation had gained Texas, the Oregon Country, and other western lands. At the Alamo in 1836, Texans had fought for independence from Mexico.

402 • Unit 6

Activity Choices

UNIT POSTER

Use the UNIT 6 VISUAL SUMMARY POSTER to summarize the unit.

Meet Individual Needs

ENGLISH LANGUAGE LEARNERS Provide key words to help students identify supporting details for each main idea illustrated. You may wish to ask beginning language learners to point to the area on the visual summary that relates to the events as they are being discussed.

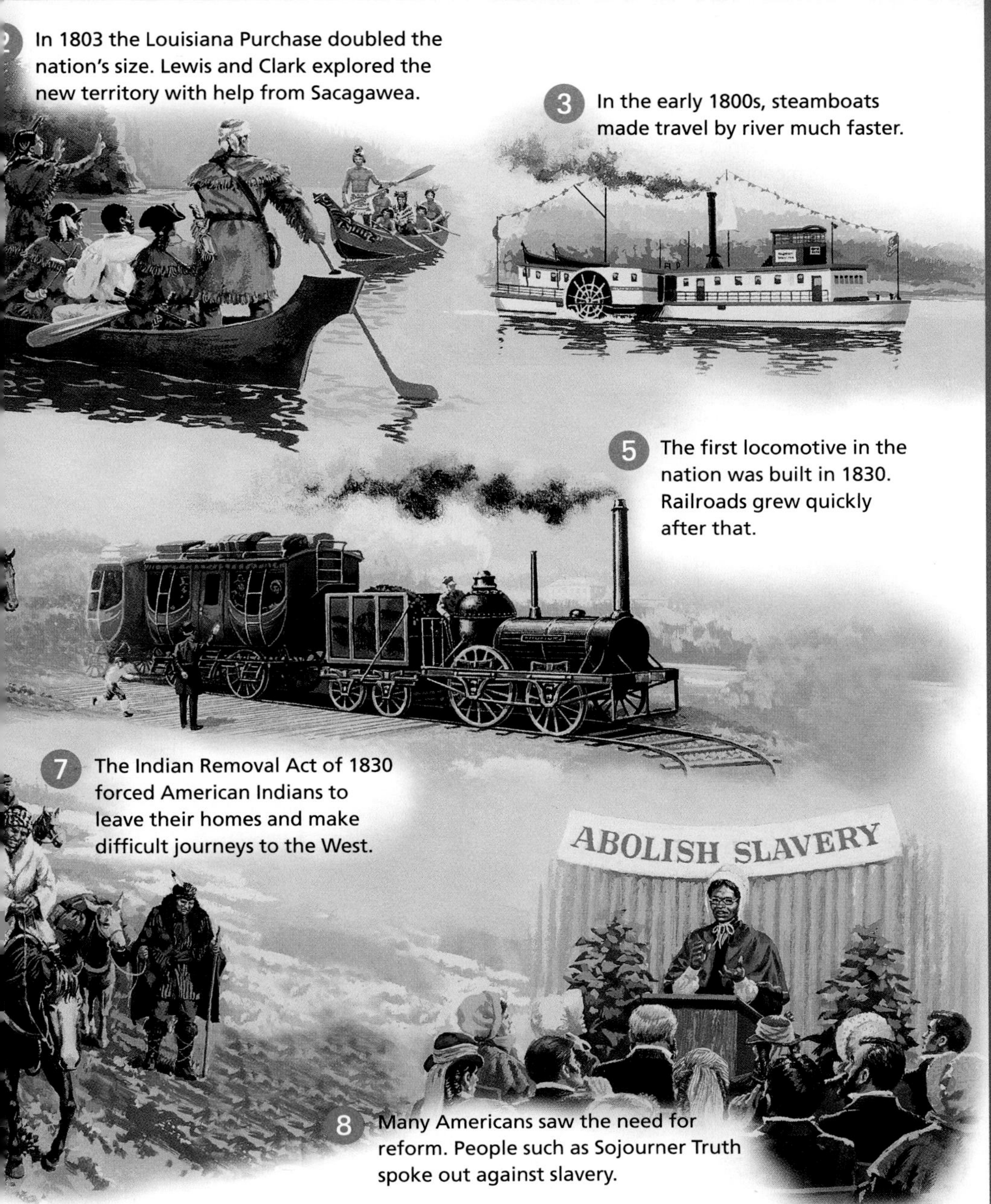

2 In 1803 the Louisiana Purchase doubled the nation's size. Lewis and Clark explored the new territory with help from Sacagawea.

3 In the early 1800s, steamboats made travel by river much faster.

5 The first locomotive in the nation was built in 1830. Railroads grew quickly after that.

7 The Indian Removal Act of 1830 forced American Indians to leave their homes and make difficult journeys to the West.

8 Many Americans saw the need for reform. People such as Sojourner Truth spoke out against slavery.

Sharing the Activity

Provide time for students to complete the Make Your Own Visual Summary activity on page 402. Before students begin their visual summary illustrations, make sure that each topic in the visual summary will be illustrated by at least one student in the class. When students have completed their visual summaries, have them share and explain their illustration choices to the class. You may wish to display the illustrations.

Summarize the Unit

Have students use the illustrations in the unit and in the visual summary to create a chain story about the unit. The first student in the chain will start the story. The next student will continue the story where the first student stopped. Continue the process until each student in the class has had a chance to tell part of the story.

TECHNOLOGY

Use THE AMAZING WRITING MACHINE™ to complete the writing activities.

TECHNOLOGY

Use TIMELINER™ DATA DISKS to discuss and summarize the unit.

Extend and Enrich

WRITE AND PRESENT A SPEECH Pair students and have each pair select one or more persons from the time period represented in the unit, such as Meriwether Lewis, William Clark, and Sacagawea; John Stevens and Peter Cooper; John Fitch and Robert Fulton; Daniel Boone; Andrew Jackson; James Monroe; Samuel Slater and Eli Whitney; Marcus and Narcissa Whitman; Sam Houston; or James Marshall. Ask students to prepare speeches explaining how their person or persons made an important contribution to the expansion of the United States between 1775 and 1850. After students have presented their speeches, discuss the role individualism, interdependence, conflict, and cooperation played in the expansion of the United States.

Use Vocabulary

1. When a person buys something, he or she *purchases* it. (p. 354)
2. United States *doctrine* after 1823 opposed the expansion of European colonies in the Americas. (p. 362)
3. Prior to the *Industrial Revolution*, most goods were made by hand. (p. 373)
4. The cloth for my shirt was woven at a *textile mill*. (p. 373)
5. Before the *canal* linking the Great Lakes region to eastern New York was completed, the only way to transport goods between those places was by land. (p. 375)
6. If I had been alive in 1849, I would have gone to California and looked for gold with the other *forty-niners*. (p. 389)
7. Horace Mann wanted to *reform* public schools by requiring teachers to be better educated. (p. 392)
8. In the 1850s *abolitionists* traveled around the country and gave speeches against slavery. (p. 393)

Check Understanding

9. It was the route Daniel Boone traveled through the mountains into Kentucky that was later cleared to make the Wilderness Road. Many people traveled on the Wilderness Road to get to the frontier. (p. 350)
10. by buying the territory known as the Louisiana Purchase (p. 354)
11. to learn about the land acquired in the Louisiana Purchase (p. 355)
12. Mass production is a way to produce large numbers of goods at one time using interchangeable parts. It was first put into practice by Eli Whitney. (p. 374)
13. to transport goods between eastern New York and cities in the West (p. 375)
14. All American Indians east of the Mississippi were forced to move west. (p. 381)
15. green valleys, wooded hills, and fertile soil (p. 386)

Think Critically

16. Computers and communication technology are changing the way Americans today live and work. People are able to communicate much faster over greater distances.

UNIT 6 REVIEW

Use Vocabulary

Use each term in a sentence that will help explain its meaning.

1. purchase
2. doctrine
3. Industrial Revolution
4. textile mill
5. canal
6. forty-niners
7. reform
8. abolitionist

Check Understanding

9. How was the Cumberland Gap important to Daniel Boone, the development of the Wilderness Road, and the settlement of the American frontier?
10. How did Thomas Jefferson help double the size of the United States?
11. What was the purpose of the Lewis and Clark expedition?
12. What is mass production? Who first put this idea for producing goods into practice?
13. Why was the Erie Canal built?
14. What was the result of the Indian Removal Act of 1830?
15. What physical features first attracted pioneers to the Oregon Country?

Think Critically

16. **Past to Present** Technology changed life for Americans in the 1800s. How does technology change life for Americans today?
17. **Personally Speaking** If you had been alive in 1849, would you have gone to California in search of gold? Explain your answer.
18. **Think More About It** What do you think helped make Frederick Douglass such an effective abolitionist speaker?

Apply Skills

Use Relief and Elevation Maps Use the map below to answer the questions.

19. Where did the Trail of Tears lead to?
20. Which part of the Trail of Tears passed through mountains? How do you know?
21. What is the elevation of the land near Murfreesboro? near Springfield?

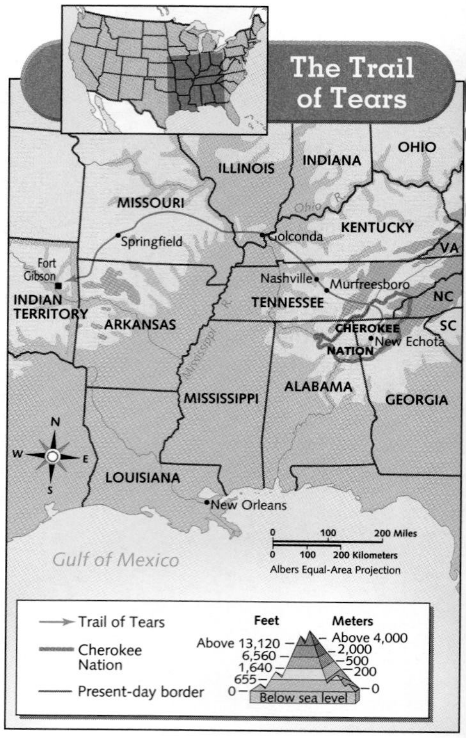

17. Some students may relate to the forty-niners who wanted to improve their economic situations and strike it rich. Other students may think that the trip was too long and that the chances of finding gold were too slight.
18. Frederick Douglass was a runaway slave and could draw upon firsthand experiences dealing with mistreatment and indignity.

Apply Skills

Use Relief and Elevation Maps

19. Fort Gibson
20. the first part in Tennessee; becaus[e] the map key shows an area there tha[t] is over 1,640 feet (over 500 m)
21. 655 to 1,640 feet (200 to 500 m); th[e] same

ASSESSMENT PROGRAM

Use UNIT 6 TEST,
Standard Test, pp. 103–107.
Performance Tasks, pp. 108–109.

REMEMBER
- Share your ideas.
- Cooperate with others to plan your work.
- Take responsibility for your work.
- Help one another.
- Show your group's work to the class.
- Discuss what you learned by working together.

ACTIVITY
Write and Perform a Scene for a Play

Work with members of a group to write a scene for a play about a typical workday at an early textile mill. The scene should tell something about the workers and the working conditions at the mill. Decide who the characters in the scene will be, and write dialogue for them. Then choose roles, practice the scene, and perform it for your class.

ACTIVITY
Draw a Map

Work together to draw a map showing how the United States grew in the first half of the 1800s. Maps in your textbook and in atlases can help you. First, draw an outline map of the country, and label major landforms and bodies of water. Then, color the boundaries of the United States in 1783, following the American Revolution. Use different colors to show the Louisiana Purchase, Florida, Texas, the Oregon Country, and the land that the United States purchased following its war with Mexico. Add a map key to your map.

ACTIVITY
Make a Time Line

Work in a group to draw a time line on a large sheet of paper. Show the years from 1770 to 1850, using ten-year periods. Then label the time line with events from this unit. Draw pictures to illustrate the events.

Unit Project Wrap-Up

Make a Diorama Finish the Unit Project from page 341. Then work in groups to discuss the scenes shown in each diorama. Discuss how important it was for the pioneers to cooperate with each other if they were to survive. Work together to write descriptions for each scene shown. Be sure to include examples of how pioneers helped one another. Share your dioramas and descriptions with the class.

UNIT 6 REVIEW

MAKE A TIME LINE

Performance Assessment Advise students to first make a list of events and to agree upon what pictures will illustrate each event. Then have them check their lists to make sure the events are in chronological order. Remind them to leave plenty of room on their time lines so that the pictures will fit.

What to Look For Check students' time lines for accuracy in listing events in chronological order.

Unit Project Wrap-Up

Performance Assessment Students should discuss the scenes they depicted and explain the importance of cooperation among the pioneers. Display the dioramas in the classroom.

What to Look For Scenes should show aspects of self-sufficiency among the pioneers and an understanding of how important cooperation is to groups of people trying to settle a foreign wilderness.

GAME TIME!

Use GAME TIME! to reinforce content.

Cooperative Learning Workshop

WRITE AND PERFORM A SCENE FOR A PLAY

Performance Assessment Help students find information in their textbooks or in the library that will help them with selecting scenes and writing dialogue.

What to Look For Look for an understanding of the difficult working conditions in a mill and of the changes brought about by the Industrial Revolution.

DRAW A MAP

Performance Assessment Provide students with drawing materials and drawing paper. Also provide them with reference materials for use in researching how the United States grew in the first half of the 1800s. Display the students' maps in the classroom.

What to Look For Look for correct placement of boundaries, landforms, and bodies of water. Make sure that students correlate their map keys to their maps and that the various territories acquired are marked and placed properly.

Unit 7

pages 406–475

WAR DIVIDES THE NATION

The major objectives in this unit are organized around the following themes:

UNIT THEMES

- CONFLICT & COOPERATION
- CONTINUITY & CHANGE
- INDIVIDUALISM & INTERDEPENDENCE

Preview Unit Content

Unit 7 tells the story of the Civil War, its many causes, and its complex aftermath. In the course of studying this unit, students will discover how economic differences divided Americans in the North and the South, how slavery became the flash point for the conflict between the two regions, how Abraham Lincoln led the country during this serious challenge to the Union, and how slavery in the United States finally came to an end as a result of the Civil War.

You may wish to begin the unit with the Unit 7 Visual Summary Poster and activity. The illustration that appears on the poster also appears on pages 472–473 in the Pupil Book to help students summarize the unit.

UNIT POSTER

Use the UNIT 7 VISUAL SUMMARY POSTER to preview the unit.

1 As slavery continued in the South, more and more enslaved people tried to escape by running away.

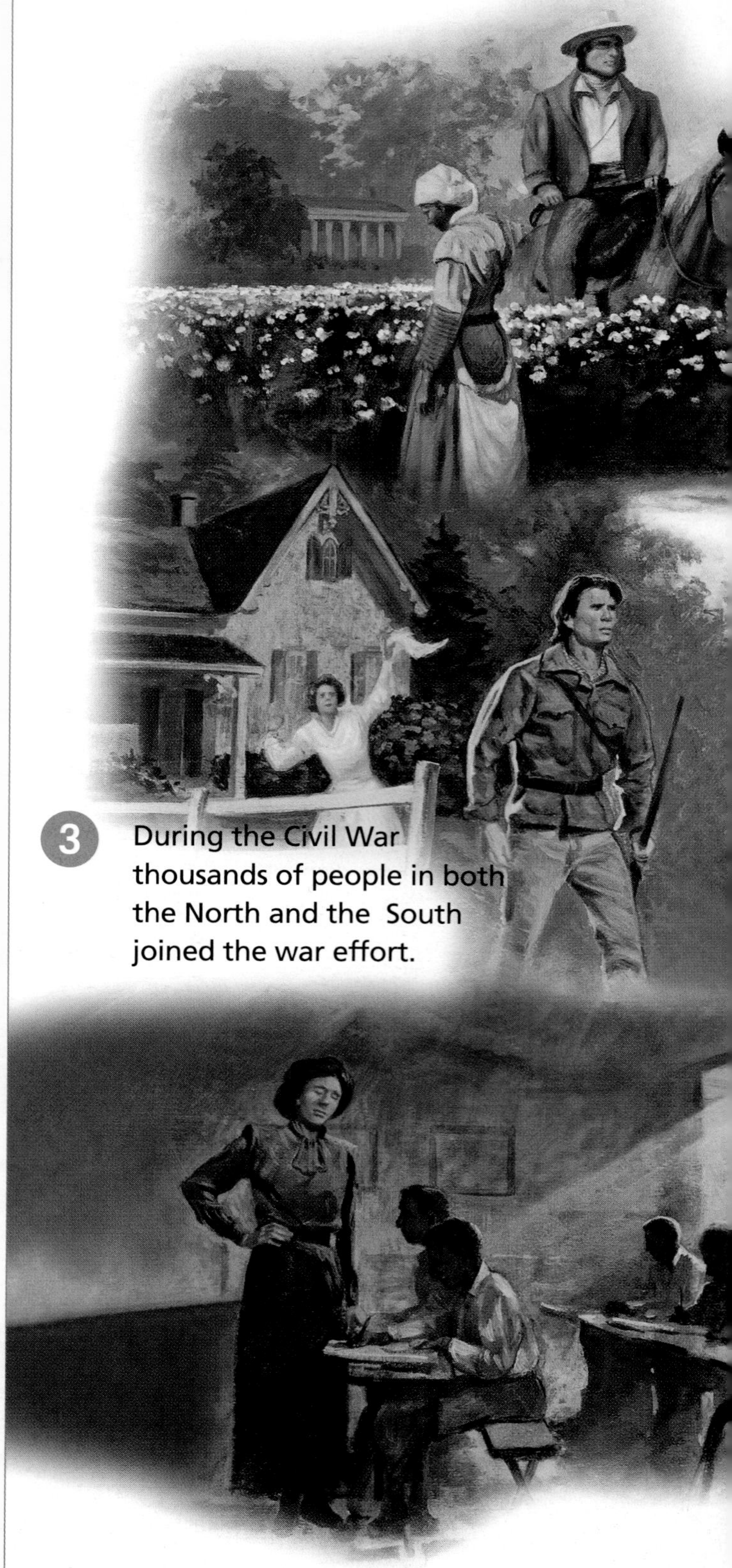

3 During the Civil War thousands of people in both the North and the South joined the war effort.

6 During Reconstruction the Freedmen's Bureau opened schools for former slaves.

2 After Abraham Lincoln was elected President in 1860, Southern states seceded from the Union.

4 The war dragged on for four long years, destroying property and lives on both sides.

5 Robert E. Lee surrendered his Confederate forces to Union General Ulysses S. Grant at Appomattox Courthouse in 1865.

7 After the war, life was difficult for former slaves, even though they were now free. Many tried to build new lives as sharecroppers.

Unit 7 Planning Chart

	CONTENT AND SKILLS	RESOURCES INCLUDING ▶ TECHNOLOGY
UNIT INTRODUCTION **War Divides the Nation** pp. 406–413	Unit Opener and Unit Preview Set the Scene with Literature **Stonewall** by Jean Fritz	Unit 7 Visual Summary Poster Unit 7 Home Letter Unit 7 Text on Tape Audiocassette Video Experiences: Social Studies ▶ TIMELINER ▶ THE AMAZING WRITING MACHINE
CHAPTER 13 **Background to the Conflict** pp. 414–439	LESSON 1: Differences Divide North and South **SKILL:** Use Graphs to Identify Trends LESSON 2: Africans in Slavery and Freedom LESSON 3: Facing a National Problem LESSON 4: A Time for Hard Decisions **SKILL:** Make a Thoughtful Decision Counterpoints: Union or Secession? Chapter Review	Activity Book, pp. 80–86 Transparencies 34–36 Assessment Program Chapter 13 Test, pp. 111–114 ▶ GRAPH LINKS ▶ THE AMAZING WRITING MACHINE ▶ TIMELINER ▶ INTERNET
CHAPTER 14 **Civil War and Reconstruction** pp. 440–469	LESSON 1: The Fighting Begins LESSON 2: Learn History Through Literature **The Signature That Changed America** by Harold Holzer LESSON 3: The Long Road to a Union Victory **SKILL:** Compare Maps with Different Scales LESSON 4: Life After the War Chapter Review	Activity Book, pp. 87–92 Music Audiocassette Transparencies 37–38 Assessment Program Chapter 14 Test, pp. 115–118 ▶ IMAGINATION EXPRESS ▶ THE AMAZING WRITING MACHINE ▶ MAPSKILLS ▶ TIMELINER ▶ INTERNET
UNIT WRAP-UP pp. 470–475	Making Social Studies Relevant Visual Summary Unit Review	Making Social Studies Relevant Video Unit 7 Visual Summary Poster Game Time! Assessment Program Unit 7 Test, Standard Test, pp. 119–123 Performance Tasks, pp. 124–125 ▶ THE AMAZING WRITING MACHINE ▶ TIMELINER ▶ INTERNET

4 WEEKS — TIME MANAGEMENT

WEEK 1		WEEK 2	WEEK 3		WEEK 4
Unit Introduction	Chapter 13		Chapter 14		Unit Wrap-Up

See pages 414A and 440A for Chapter Planning Charts with details by lesson.

Multimedia Resource Center

Books

Easy

Harness, Cheryl. *Abe Lincoln Goes to Washington: 1837-1865.* National Geographic Society, 1997. A biography of Abraham Lincoln that shows that he was a caring husband, devoted father, and strong President.

Loeper, John J. *Going to School in 1876.* Macmillan, 1984. Students can read to learn about school in 1876.

Average

Archer, Jules. *A House Divided: The Lives of Ulysses S. Grant and Robert E. Lee.* Scholastic, 1995. This dual biography shows the differences in the military careers and personal lives of Ulysses S. Grant and Robert E. Lee.

Beatty, Patricia. *Who Comes with Cannons?* William Morrow, 1992. Twelve-year-old Truth becomes involved with the Underground Railroad when she stays with her aunt and uncle.

Connell, Kate. *Tales from the Underground Railroad.* Steck-Vaughn, 1993. Read about the network of people who comprised the Underground Railroad and helped many African Americans escape slavery.

Fritz, Jean. *Stonewall.* Putnam & Grosset, 1979. A biography about one of the South's greatest war heroes, Confederate general "Stonewall" Jackson.

Meltzer, Milton. *Lincoln In His Own Words.* Harcourt Brace, 1993. Abraham Lincoln's thoughts, life, and actions are examined through his own words.

Challenging

Cohn, Amy L. *From Sea to Shining Sea: A Treasury of American Folklore and Folk Songs.* Scholastic, 1993. A collection of American folktales, folk songs, essays, and poems that trace the multicultural history of this country.

Reeder, Carolyn. *Across the Lines.* Simon & Schuster, 1997. Edward, the son of a Southern plantation owner, and Simon, a slave and lifelong friend of his, learn to understand the meaning of courage and freedom during the Civil War.

Reeder, Carolyn. *Shades of Gray.* Macmillan, 1989. After the Civil War comes to an end, a young Confederate boy must come to terms with the notion that all people suffer needlessly from war.

Computer Software

CD-ROM

The Civil War: America's Epic Struggle. MultiEducator, 1997, URL *http://www.multied.com*, (800) 866-6434. Windows/Macintosh dual format. This two CD-ROM set includes over 3,000 photographs, paintings, and drawings that offer an overview of the Civil War, a chronology, and a review of the major battles. A biographical section is devoted to approximately 400 Union and Confederate generals.

The Civil War. National Geographic Society, Educational Services, 1997, URL *http://www.nationalgeographic.com*, (800) 368-2728. Windows/Macintosh dual format. Trace the conflict between the North and South, beginning with the Missouri Compromise of 1820 and culminating with Lee's surrender at Appomattox.

Video

Videotape

The Civil War. Thomas S. Klise Company, 1993, URL *http://www.klise.com*, (800) 937-0092. An in-depth look at the battles, the economic conditions, and the leaders of the Civil War is presented as the causes of the Civil War are explored.

Reuniting the State: Reconstuction After the Civil War. Thomas S. Klise Company, 1993, URL *http://www.klise.com*, (800) 937-0092. This video discusses Lincoln's assassination and Johnson's presidency as it examines the political aspects of Reconstruction. The impact of reunification of the states and the end of slavery is explored.

FREE & INEXPENSIVE MATERIALS

Brochure

For a free copy of a brochure titled *Lincoln Birthplace*, which explains the history of Sinking Springs Farm, write to:

Abraham Lincoln Birthplace
National Historic Site
2995 Lincoln Farm Road
Hodgenville, KY 43748

Activity

For free profiles of Sojourner Truth, Harriet Tubman, Frederick Douglass, and other important nineteenth-century African Americans, each of which is followed by an activity, visit the Internet at: *http://www.brightmoments.com/blackhistory*

LIBRARY

See the SOCIAL STUDIES LIBRARY for additional resources.

TECHNOLOGY

HARCOURT BRACE

Visit the Internet at **http://www.hbschool.com** for additional resources.

Note that information, while correct at time of publication, is subject to change.

Linking Social Studies

BULLETIN BOARD IDEA

Create a Bulletin Board To illustrate how the Civil War divided the nation, have students create a three-part bulletin board display. Divide the class into small groups. Randomly assign to each group the states that were part of the United States in 1860. Have each group draw an outline of each of the assigned states on a sheet of 8½-in. × 11-in. posterboard and cut out the outlined shape. Have students write the name of the state and the date it became a state on the cutout. Divide the bulletin board into three parts by drawing two thick, jagged lines across the board, about six inches above and below the center. Title the bulletin board *The Civil War*. Write between the jagged lines in bold letters *Border States*. Title the top part of the board *Northern States* and the bottom part *Southern States*. Call out the names of the states at random and have a student from the group with that state paste the cutout on the appropriate section of the bulletin board.

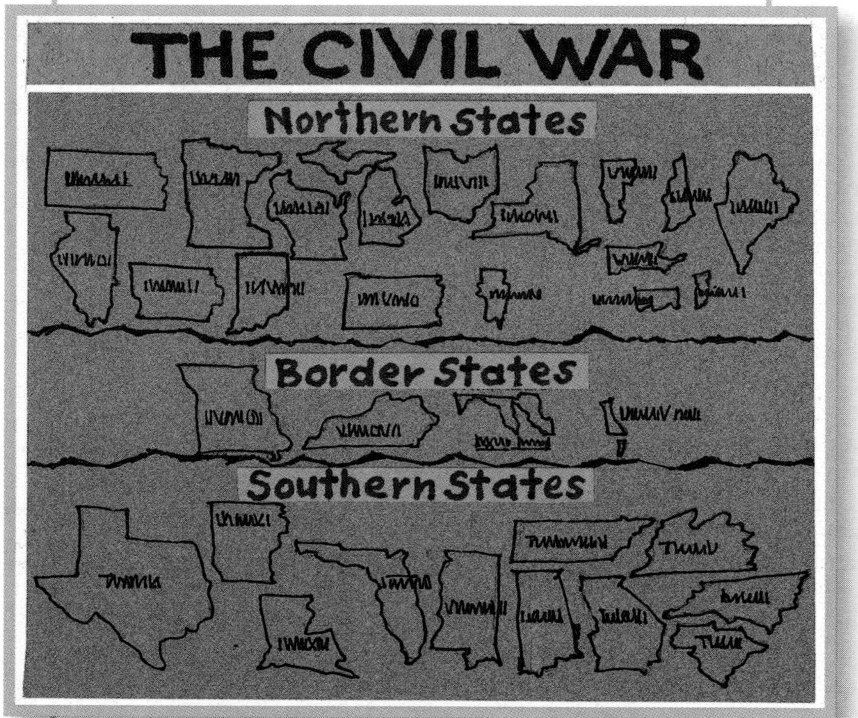

ART

Illustrate Freedoms To encourage students to express their thoughts on freedom, have them create a poster-size collage. Divide the class into small groups. Provide each group with a set of markers, old magazines, decoupage glue, and posterboard. Have students in each group discuss which freedoms in the United States are most important to them. Then have each group, by unanimous vote, choose one freedom to portray on the poster. Next, have each group create a title for the poster that expresses that freedom and use the markers to write the title in bold letters on the posterboard. Have each group tear out from the old magazines pictures that symbolize that freedom and use the decoupage glue to make a collage on the posterboard. Have each group discuss the completed poster with the class, explain why that freedom is so important, and explain what each picture has to do with that freedom. After each group has discussed the poster, display the posters in the classroom.

TECHNOLOGY

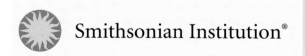

Visit the Internet at **http://www.hbschool.com** for additional resources.

Smithsonian Institution®

Harcourt Brace Social Studies helps to bring the Smithsonian Institution to your classroom. Visit the Internet site at *http://www.si.edu/harcourt/socialstudies* for a directory of virtual tours, on-line exhibits, and pictures of primary sources from the Smithsonian Institution.

Across the Curriculum

MUSIC

Interpret Symbolism in Spirituals For students to appreciate what spirituals meant to enslaved people, play some notable pre–Civil War spirituals to the class. Discuss with the class the significance these spirituals had for slaves during this time period. Explain that many of the songs used symbolism to express feelings about slavery and the desire for freedom. For example, in the song "Michael, Row the Boat Ashore," the river Jordan stood for freedom and stepping into its chilly waters meant throwing the plantation owner's dogs off the escaped slave's trail. Divide the class into small groups. Assign each group a spiritual, or have each group choose a spiritual to research. Have students in each group write out the words to the spiritual. Then discuss the symbolism used in the song and explain what the symbolism means. Have each group share the song and the explanations with the class. If possible, play each group's spiritual to the class before discussing the words and symbolism.

SCIENCE

Make a Weather Vane To help students understand how Americans predicted the weather without advanced technology, have students make a weather vane. Discuss with students the important clues, such as wind direction, used to predict the weather. Divide the class into small groups. Provide each group with the following materials: a wire hanger, a sheet of aluminum foil, tape, a pint-size plastic tub filled with sand and covered with a plastic lid, scissors, and a marker. Have students straighten the hook of the hanger, cover one-half of the hanger with the foil, and tape the foil in place over the hanger. Then poke a hole in the center of the lid of the plastic container, using the straight end of the hanger, and push the hanger down into the sand so it touches the bottom of the container but turns freely. Use a compass to find north. Have students use the marker to label north, south, east, and west on the containers. Place the completed weather vanes in an open area outside where they can catch the wind. (The open end of the weather vane will point in the direction from which the wind is coming.) Explain this rule of thumb for the weather: a wind from the west is best; a wind from the east is least.

HOW TO INTEGRATE YOUR DAY

Use these topics to help you integrate social studies into your daily planning.

READING THEMES

- American Ideals
- Courage
- Citizenship
- Conflict/Resolution
- People

INTEGRATED LANGUAGE ARTS

Make a Chart, p. 408
Write a Description, p. 413
Write a Report, p. 423
Write to Persuade, p. 429
Write a Diary Entry, p. 432
Write a Dialogue, p. 443
Write a Viewpoint, p. 449
Write to Explain, p. 455
Write a How-to Paragraph, p. 460
Write a Personal Narrative, p. 464

SCIENCE

Make a Weather Vane, p. 406F
Research Communications Technology, p. 457

MATHEMATICS

Make a Circle Graph, p. 416

ART

Illustrate Freedoms, p. 406E
Research Photographs, p. 453
Draw a Political Cartoon, p. 465

HEALTH AND PHYSICAL EDUCATION

Report on Diseases, p. 422

MUSIC

Interpret Symbolism in Spirituals, p. 406F
Sing Songs, p. 422
Write a Song, p. 447
Sing Civil War Songs, p. 454

READING

Distinguish Fact from Fiction, p. 406
Read the Constitution, p. 466

Unit 7

Assessment Options

The **Assessment Program** allows all learners many opportunities to show what they know and can do. It also provides ongoing information about each student's understanding of social studies.

Formal Assessment

- *Lesson Reviews* (**Pupil Book,** at end of lessons)
- *Chapter Reviews* (**Pupil Book,** at end of chapters)
- *Chapter Tests* (**Assessment Program,** pp. 111–118)
- *Unit Review* (**Pupil Book,** pp. 474–475)
- *Unit Assessment* (**Assessment Program:** *Standard Test*, pp. 119–123 *Individual Performance Task*, p. 124 *Group Performance Task*, p. 125)

Student Self-Evaluation

- *Individual End-of-Project Summary* (**Assessment Program,** p. 6)
- *Group End-of-Project Checklist* (**Assessment Program,** p. 7)
- *Individual End-of-Unit Checklist* (**Assessment Program,** p. 8)

Informal Assessment

- REVIEW *Questions* (**Pupil Book,** throughout lessons)
- *Think and Apply* (**Pupil Book,** at end of skill lessons)
- *Visual Summary* (**Pupil Book,** pp. 472–473)
- *Social Studies Skills Checklist* (**Assessment Program,** pp. 4–5)

Performance Assessment

- *Show What You Know* (**Pupil Book,** at end of Lesson Reviews)
- *Cooperative Learning Workshop* (**Pupil Book,** at end of Unit Review)
- *Scoring Rubric for Individual Projects* (**Assessment Program,** p. 9)
- *Scoring Rubric for Group Projects* (**Assessment Program,** p. 10)
- *Scoring Rubric for Presentations* (**Assessment Program,** p. 11)

Portfolio Assessment

Student-selected items may include:

- *Link to Language Arts—Write a How-to Paragraph* (**Teacher's Edition,** p. 460)
- *Practice and Apply* (**Activity Book,** p. 81)
- *Home Involvement* (**Teacher's Edition,** p. 456)
- *A Guide to My Social Studies Portfolio* (**Assessment Program,** p. 12)

Teacher-selected items may include:

- *Unit Assessment* (**Assessment Program,** pp. 119–125)
- *Individual End-of-Unit Checklist* (**Assessment Program,** p. 8)
- *Social Studies Portfolio Summary* (**Assessment Program,** p. 13)
- *Portfolio Family Response* (**Assessment Program,** p. 14)

Objectives

Chapter 13

- Describe the key differences between the North and the South. (p. 415)
- Analyze why slaves became an important human resource for the South. (p. 415)
- Determine the impact of the cotton gin. (p. 415)
- Compare conflicting attitudes that led to increased tension as people moved west. (p. 415)
- Recognize a trend on a line or bar graph. (p. 420)
- Analyze trends to describe the connection between cotton production and the growth of slavery. (p. 420)
- Summarize the way enslaved Africans were treated and how they helped one another. (p. 421)
- Analyze the resistance to slavery by enslaved people. (p. 421)
- Evaluate the effectiveness of the Underground Railroad. (p. 421)
- Summarize the advantages and disadvantages in the lives of free Africans. (p. 421)
- Analyze Henry Clay's attempts to resolve conflicts over the spread of slavery. (p. 426)
- Evaluate the impact of the Kansas-Nebraska Act and the Dred Scott decision on the debate over the spread of slavery. (p. 426)
- Explain the cause-and-effect relationship that brought about the new Republican party and Abraham Lincoln's Senate race. (p. 426)
- Compare and contrast the views of Abraham Lincoln with those of Stephen Douglas concerning the spread of slavery. (p. 426)
- Compare and contrast the diverse views of Americans on the spread of slavery, and analyze the effect of these views on the election of 1860 and events that followed it. (p. 431)
- Evaluate the choices facing the leaders of the Union and the Confederacy in 1861, and discuss the consequences of the leaders' decisions. (p. 431)
- Analyze how Lincoln and Davis came to their decisions concerning Fort Sumter. (p. 435)
- Analyze a personal decision. (p. 435)
- Recognize that not all Southerners supported secession. (p. 436)
- Identify contrasting viewpoints held by Southerners on the issue of secession. (p. 436)

Chapter 14

- Summarize the choices one had to make in deciding which side to support in the Civil War. (p. 441)
- Analyze the dilemma Robert E. Lee faced. (p. 441)
- Draw conclusions about why the battle of Bull Run was a shock to the Union, and evaluate the battle plans of the North and South. (p. 441)
- Describe Lincoln's views on writing an order to free the slaves. (p. 441)
- Analyze the reasons Lincoln decided to write an order to free the slaves. (p. 446)
- Summarize the Emancipation Proclamation. (p. 446)
- Describe the nation's reaction to the freeing of slaves in the Confederate states. (p. 446)
- Evaluate the role of Africans in fighting for the Union. (p. 452)
- Determine the importance of Grant's victories. (p. 452)
- Summarize the key points of Lincoln's Gettysburg Address. (p. 452)
- Evaluate Sherman's March to the Sea. (p. 452)
- Analyze the reasons Lee surrendered. (p. 452)
- Describe the assassination of President Lincoln. (p. 452)
- Identify appropriate uses of maps with large and small scales. (p. 460)
- Practice comparing distances on maps with different scales. (p. 460)
- Describe how free Africans rebuilt their lives. (p. 462)
- Analyze the purpose of the Freedmen's Bureau. (p. 462)
- Explain the system of sharecropping and its effect on the lives of former slaves. (p. 462)
- Summarize Johnson's ideas for Reconstruction, and evaluate the impact of the black codes. (p. 462)
- Analyze how Congress's plans better protected the rights of African Americans. (p. 462)
- Evaluate the successes and failures of Reconstruction. (p. 462)

STANDARD TEST

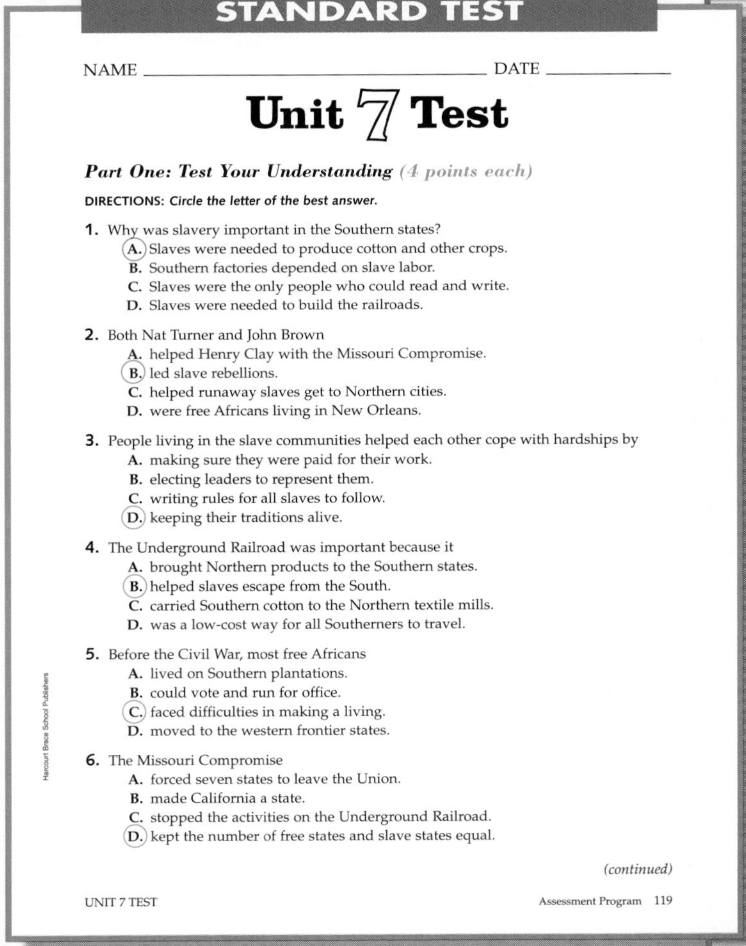
NAME ______________________ DATE __________

Unit 7 Test

Part One: Test Your Understanding *(4 points each)*

DIRECTIONS: *Circle the letter of the best answer.*

1. Why was slavery important in the Southern states?
   A. Slaves were needed to produce cotton and other crops.
   B. Southern factories depended on slave labor.
   C. Slaves were the only people who could read and write.
   D. Slaves were needed to build the railroads.

2. Both Nat Turner and John Brown
   A. helped Henry Clay with the Missouri Compromise.
   B. led slave rebellions.
   C. helped runaway slaves get to Northern cities.
   D. were free Africans living in New Orleans.

3. People living in the slave communities helped each other cope with hardships by
   A. making sure they were paid for their work.
   B. electing leaders to represent them.
   C. writing rules for all slaves to follow.
   D. keeping their traditions alive.

4. The Underground Railroad was important because it
   A. brought Northern products to the Southern states.
   B. helped slaves escape from the South.
   C. carried Southern cotton to the Northern textile mills.
   D. was a low-cost way for all Southerners to travel.

5. Before the Civil War, most free Africans
   A. lived on Southern plantations.
   B. could vote and run for office.
   C. faced difficulties in making a living.
   D. moved to the western frontier states.

6. The Missouri Compromise
   A. forced seven states to leave the Union.
   B. made California a state.
   C. stopped the activities on the Underground Railroad.
   D. kept the number of free states and slave states equal.

(continued)

UNIT 7 TEST Assessment Program 119

STANDARD TEST

NAME ______________________ DATE ____________

7. The Missouri Compromise and the Compromise of 1850
   - (A.) tried to settle the question of slavery in the western states.
   - B. limited the production of cotton.
   - C. were both written by Stephen Douglas.
   - D. allowed runaway slaves to live in the free states.

8. The Kansas-Nebraska Act led to
   - A. the decision to allow two more free states to join the Union.
   - B. the decision to allow Dred Scott to become a United States citizen.
   - C. passage of the Compromise of 1850.
   - (D.) violence between people who supported slavery and those who opposed it.

9. Which of the following statements best describes Abraham Lincoln's view on slavery before he became President?
   - A. He wanted to end slavery in the South.
   - B. He believed the framers of the Constitution wanted slavery to continue.
   - (C.) He was against the spread of slavery to new states.
   - D. He wanted to send runaway slaves back to Southern states.

10. Why was the battle at Fort Sumter important?
    - A. It showed how strong the Union army was.
    - B. It demonstrated the importance of sea power.
    - C. It was caused by the assassination of President Lincoln.
    - (D.) It marked the start of the Civil War.

11. Those states that remained in the Union after the Civil War started and that still allowed slavery were called
    - A. slave states.
    - B. rebel states.
    - C. Confederate states.
    - (D.) border states.

12. The First Battle of Bull Run was important because it demonstrated that the South
    - A. had very poor military leaders.
    - B. could only win battles fought on its own territory.
    - (C.) was more powerful than the North had expected.
    - D. had difficulty getting enough soldiers for its army.

13. Which of the following statements about African American soldiers in the Civil War is correct?
    - A. Fewer than 1,000 Africans served in the Union army.
    - (B.) Africans bravely served and died in many battles.
    - C. Many Africans served in the Confederate army.
    - D. The Emancipation Proclamation prevented Africans from serving in the army.

(continued)

STANDARD TEST

NAME ______________________ DATE ____________

14. The Confederacy was cut into two parts after the Union victory at the Battle of
    - A. Gettysburg.
    - B. Manassas Junction.
    - (C.) Vicksburg.
    - D. Savannah.

15. After the Civil War, the Freedmen's Bureau was established to
    - A. return plantations to their former owners.
    - B. give African Americans the right to vote.
    - C. encourage African Americans to move North.
    - (D.) build schools and educate former slaves.

16. Many members of Congress wanted to change President Johnson's plan for Reconstruction because
    - A. they wanted to be more fair to the Southern states than Johnson had been.
    - B. they agreed with the black codes.
    - C. Johnson had been impeached.
    - (D.) former slaves in some Southern states were being treated harshly.

(continued)

STANDARD TEST

NAME ______________________ DATE ____________

Part Two: Test Your Skills (20 points)

DIRECTIONS: *Use the maps below to answer the questions that follow.*

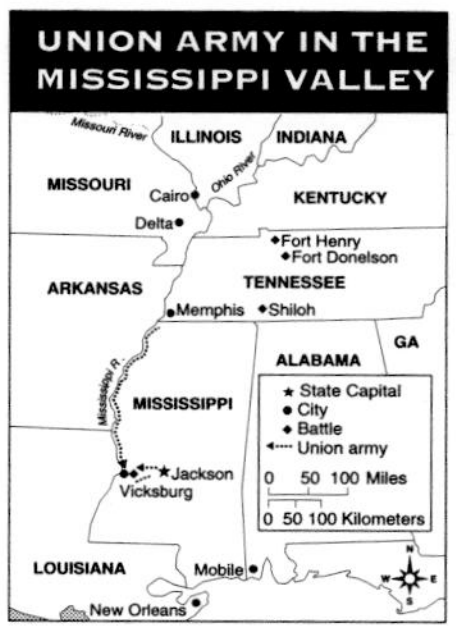

Map 1

Map 2

17. What is the distance between Memphis and Vicksburg on Map 1?
    about 200 miles

18. What is the distance between Vicksburg and Jackson on Map 1? about 50 miles on Map 2? about 50 miles

19. Which cities on Map 2 did the Union army probably pass through during the siege of Vicksburg?
    Jackson, Greenville

20. Which map would you use if you wanted to visit Vicksburg? Explain.
    Possible response: Map 2, because it shows the area in more detail

(continued)

STANDARD TEST

NAME ______________________ DATE ____________

Part Three: Apply What You Have Learned

DIRECTIONS: *Complete each of the following activities.*

21. ***Protesting Slavery*** (6 points)
    Describe three methods used by enslaved people to protest slavery.
    Possible responses:
    - a. They secretly damaged the plantation by breaking tools, leaving gates open, letting boats drift away, and hiding household goods.
    - b. They acted as if they did not understand what they had been told and said that they would try to do better.
    - c. They participated in rebellions.

22. ***Essay*** (10 points)
    Imagine that you are the son or daughter of a conductor on the Underground Railroad. Write a letter to your closest friend, describing your family's experiences while taking part in the work of the Underground Railroad.
    Accept all reasonable responses.

PERFORMANCE TASK

NAME ______________________ DATE __________

Individual Performance Task

Gettysburg Time Capsule

A *time capsule* is a sealed container that holds articles and/or written documents that are representative of a specific time period and place. A time capsule is buried and preserved by people in one time period for people in a future age.

On November 19, 1863, President Abraham Lincoln went to Gettysburg, Pennsylvania, to dedicate the national cemetery for the soldiers who had died during the Battle of Gettysburg. A special memorial was built to honor the individuals who had fought so bravely in the battle. A time capsule was buried near that memorial. Your task is to imagine that you are in charge of the time capsule. As the person in charge, you must do two things:

- Select six items that will go into the time capsule.
- Explain why you have chosen each item.

These items should be representative of the time period of the Civil War. They should be items that would help someone in today's world better understand the events of the Civil War and the men and women who were alive at that time. Your teacher will tell you what resources you may use to decide what you would put into the time capsule.

Time-Capsule Items	Reasons for Including Them
______	______________________
______	______________________
______	______________________
______	______________________
______	______________________
______	______________________

PERFORMANCE TASK

NAME ______________________ DATE __________

Group Performance Task

You Are There

Radio stations often have news and current-events programs in which a reporter speaks with two or three different people to get their reactions and opinions about a specific individual or event. In this task the class will be divided into groups of four or five students. Each group will create a script of a radio news interview that might have taken place at the end of the Civil War.

One member of each group will act as the radio news reporter, and the other members will act as different people who were living at the end of the Civil War. Together, group members will create a set of written questions for the reporter to ask and a set of written answers to the questions. Then you will present your material to the class as if it were a live radio broadcast. Be sure that your script is representative of the people and the time period immediately following the war.

The people who might be included in your group are:

- a former slave
- a Northern soldier
- an African who served in the Union army
- a Southern soldier
- Clara Barton
- President Andrew Johnson
- General Ulysses S. Grant
- General Robert E. Lee
- Harriet Tubman

The questions that the radio reporter might ask are:

- What are your feelings and emotions at the end of the war?
- What political events during the war were important to you?
- What financial problems do you have today?
- What happened to your family during the war?
- How has the war changed your community?
- What do you think the future will bring for the country?

Rubrics

SCORING RUBRICS The scoring rubrics for evaluating individual projects, group projects, and students' presentations may be found in the **Assessment Program,** pages 9–11.

CRITERIA The criteria listed below may be used when looking for evidence of the students' understanding of social studies content and ability to think critically.

Individual Task

Gettysburg Time Capsule

- Identify items that help explain events and people of the Civil War.
- Group items to show relationships or tell a story.
- Justify the items selected.

Group Task

You Are There

- Select characters that offer different perspectives on the Civil War.
- Generate questions that elicit significant facts and opinions about the Civil War from the characters selected.
- Create answers to the questions that reflect the perspective of the character and are historically accurate.

REMINDER

You may wish to preview the performance assessment activities in the COOPERATIVE LEARNING WORKSHOP on page 475. Students may complete these activities during the course of the unit.

Unit 1	Unit 2	Unit 3	Unit 4	Unit 5
The Ancient Americas	Explorations and Encounters	Our Colonial Heritage	The American Revolution	The New Nation

INTRODUCE THE UNIT

Personal Response

Have students discuss what they already know about the conflict over slavery. Also review the regional differences that existed between the North and the South from colonial times to the mid-1800s. Allow students the opportunity to share what they may already know about the Civil War. If they express conflicting understandings or misconceptions, identify those understandings and have students look for clarification as they read the unit.

Link Prior Learning

Use the titles on the bar across the top of pages 406–407 to review the chronology of earlier units. Then discuss the illustration.

Q. **What does the picture tell you about the unit you will be studying?** a war will occur

WAR DIVIDES THE NATION

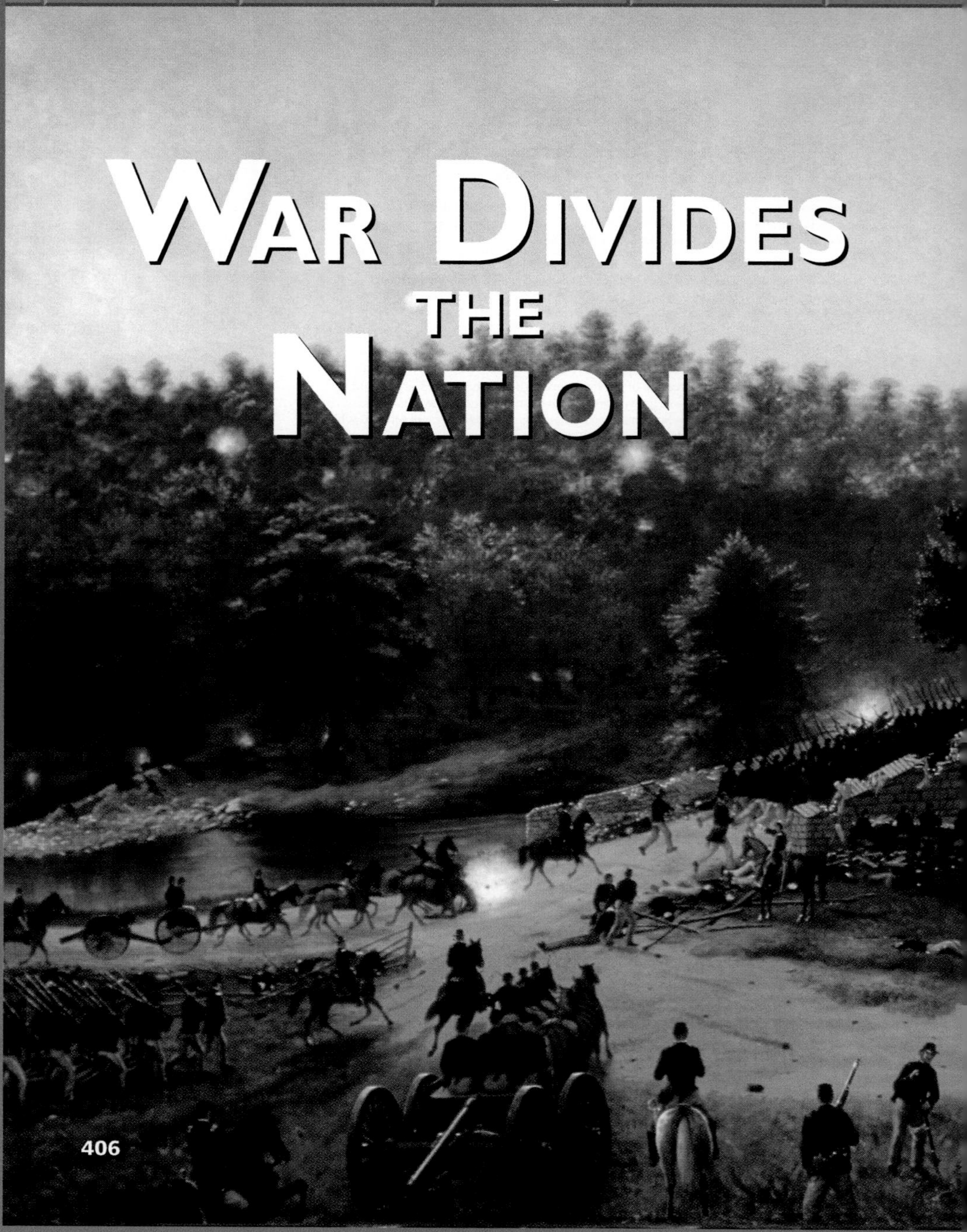

406

ACTIVITY CHOICES

Background

THE LARGE PICTURE During the Antietam battle, Union General Ambrose E. Burnside and his troops tried to cross the lower bridge over Antietam Creek. For hours, about 500 Confederate soldiers prevented the Union soldiers from crossing. Finally, the Union army made it across and forced the Confederates back to Sharpsburg. Today this bridge is known as "Burnside Bridge."

Link to Reading

DISTINGUISH FACT FROM FICTION Help students separate fact from fiction in history by pointing out two common misconceptions. FICTION: The war was fought entirely over slavery. FACT: Slavery was just one of many complex issues that divided the North and the South. FICTION: All Southerners fought for the South, and all Northerners fought for the North. FACT: Thousands of Northerners fought for the South, and thousands of Southerners fought for the North.

HOME LETTER

Use UNIT 7 HOME LETTER. See Teacher's Edition pp. HL13–14.

Unit 7

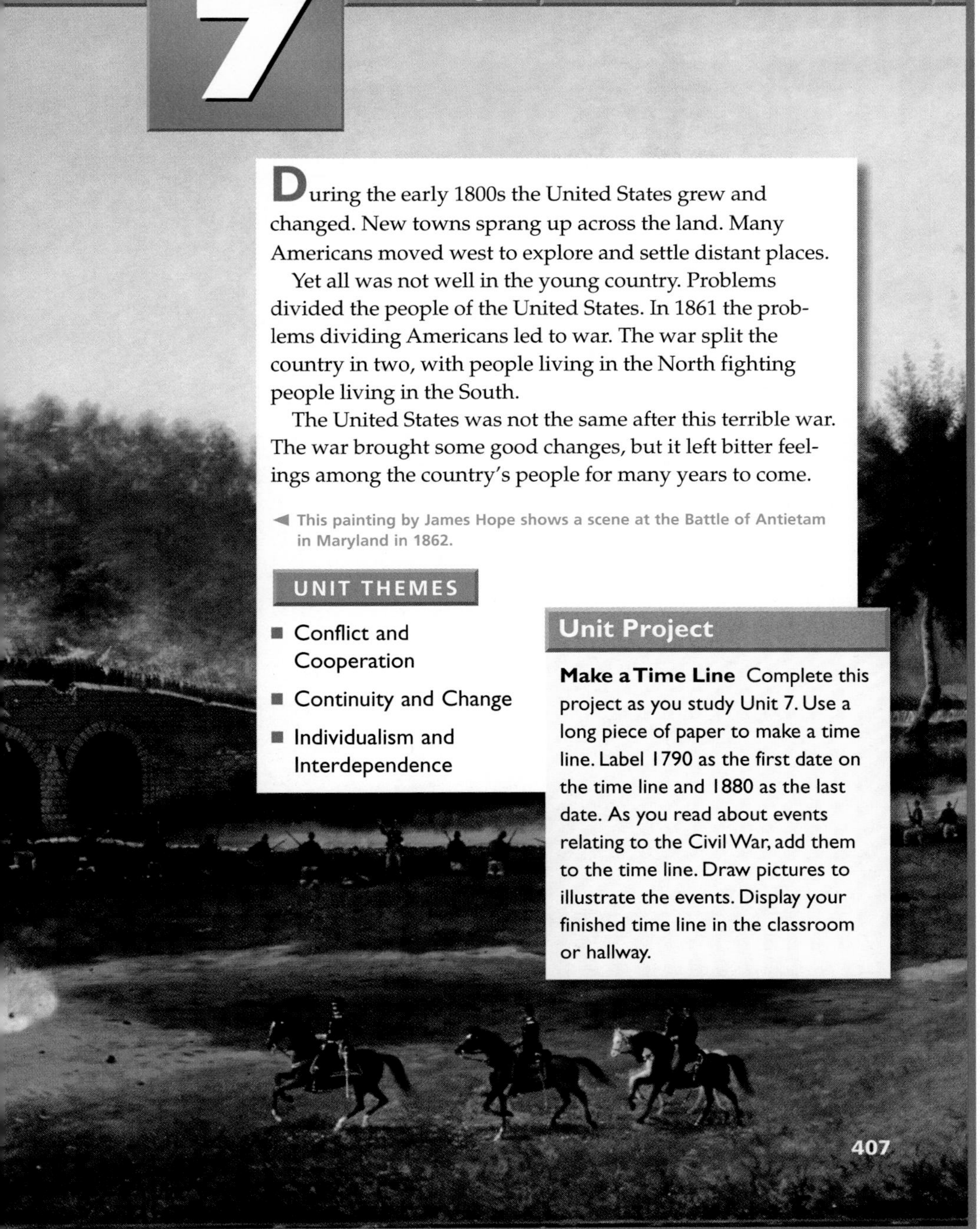

During the early 1800s the United States grew and changed. New towns sprang up across the land. Many Americans moved west to explore and settle distant places.

Yet all was not well in the young country. Problems divided the people of the United States. In 1861 the problems dividing Americans led to war. The war split the country in two, with people living in the North fighting people living in the South.

The United States was not the same after this terrible war. The war brought some good changes, but it left bitter feelings among the country's people for many years to come.

◄ This painting by James Hope shows a scene at the Battle of Antietam in Maryland in 1862.

UNIT THEMES

- Conflict and Cooperation
- Continuity and Change
- Individualism and Interdependence

Unit Project

Make a Time Line Complete this project as you study Unit 7. Use a long piece of paper to make a time line. Label 1790 as the first date on the time line and 1880 as the last date. As you read about events relating to the Civil War, add them to the time line. Draw pictures to illustrate the events. Display your finished time line in the classroom or hallway.

407

AUDIO

Use the UNIT 7 TEXT ON TAPE AUDIOCASSETTE for a reading of this unit.

Home Involvement

Encourage students to view the evening news with their families and to discuss current events, particularly those dealing with regional conflicts. Also encourage them to visit local libraries and museums to learn more about the Civil War era. If Civil War reenactments are conducted nearby, you may wish to suggest that they visit those as well.

Options for Reading

Read Aloud Read each lesson aloud as students follow along in their books. Strategies for guiding students through working with text and visuals are provided with each lesson.

Read Together Have pairs or small groups of students read the lesson by taking turns reading each page or paragraph aloud. Encourage students to use the new vocabulary words as they discuss what they read.

Read Alone Strong readers may wish to read the lessons independently before you read or discuss each lesson with the class.

Read the Introduction

Have students read the unit introduction on page 407.

Q. **How did the United States change in the early 1800s?** New towns sprang up; many Americans moved west to explore and settle distant places.

What do you think were some of the problems that divided Americans and eventually led to the Civil War? slavery; rivalry over land; different ways of viewing issues between the North and the South

Unit Themes

Discuss with students the Unit Themes. Throughout the study of this unit, ask for volunteers to identify the events, maps, illustrations, and pictures that represent each of these themes.

Unit Project Start-Up

Before students begin their Unit Projects, ask them to look over the Unit Preview on pages 408–409. Challenge students to speculate on some of the historical, biographical, and cultural information that may be shown in their time lines. As the unit progresses, have students add to their time lines.

PREVIEW THE UNIT

Link Prior Learning

Have students discuss what they already know about the differences between the northern part of the United States and the southern part of the United States. Then ask them to discuss what they know about the Civil War.

Understanding the Map

This map shows the United States in 1861. Ask students to identify the states that remained in the Union, those that joined the Confederacy, and border states.

Q. **Why might border states have more people with conflicting views about issues concerning both the North and the South?** because of their location between the Northern and Southern states

UNIT 7 PREVIEW

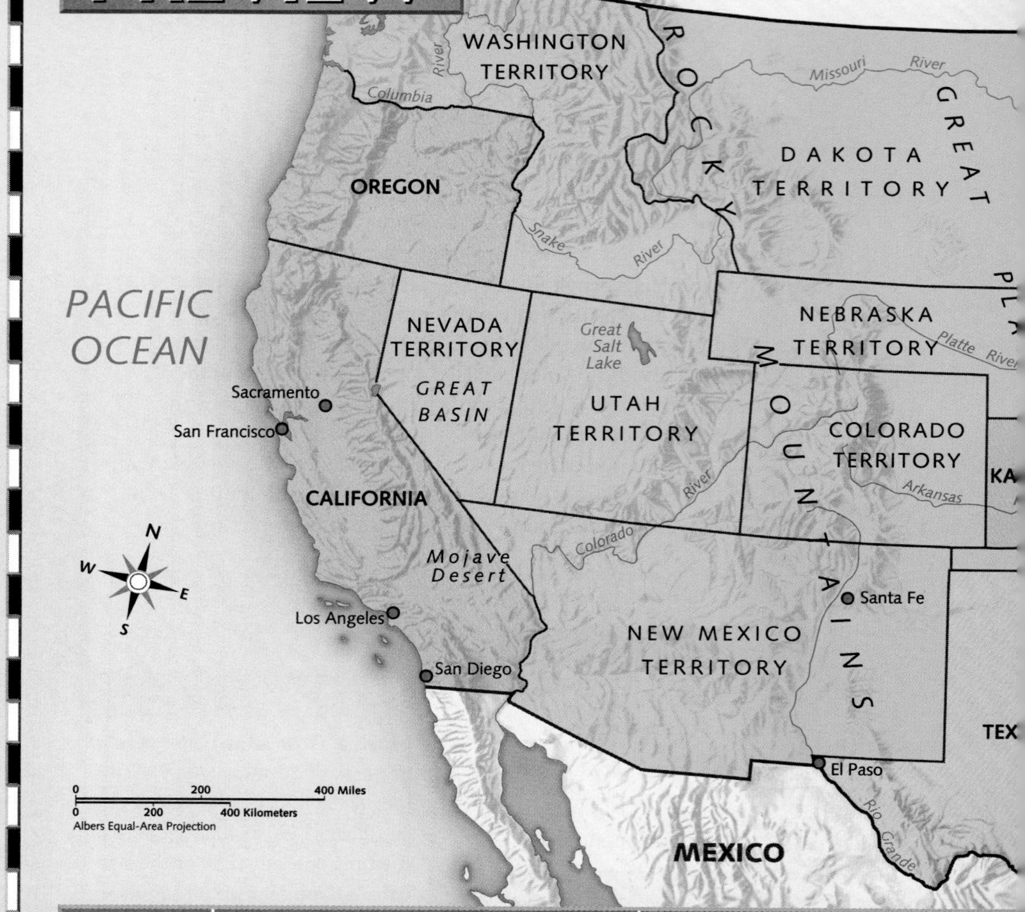

1860 — 1862

1860
Lincoln Is Elected President
PAGE 431

1861
Civil War Begins
PAGE 432

408

ACTIVITY CHOICES

VIDEO

VIDEO EXPERIENCES: SOCIAL STUDIES
Secret Train to Freedom
See the video guide for additional enrichment material.

Link to Language Arts

MAKE A CHART Create a three-column chart on the board. Have students brainstorm what they already know about the Civil War, and record their comments in the first column, titled *What We Know*. Next, ask students to provide questions related to what they want to find out about the Civil War, and record them in the second column, titled *What We Want to Know*. After students have read the unit, have them fill in the third column, titled *What We Learned*.

Meet Individual Needs

ENGLISH LANGUAGE LEARNERS
Have each student work with a partner to answer the following questions about the unit: *Who? What? Where? When?* and *Why?* As partners read the unit, they can fill in a diagram similar to the following one to show their responses.

WHO?	WHAT?	WHERE?	WHEN?	WHY?

The Nation Divided, 1861

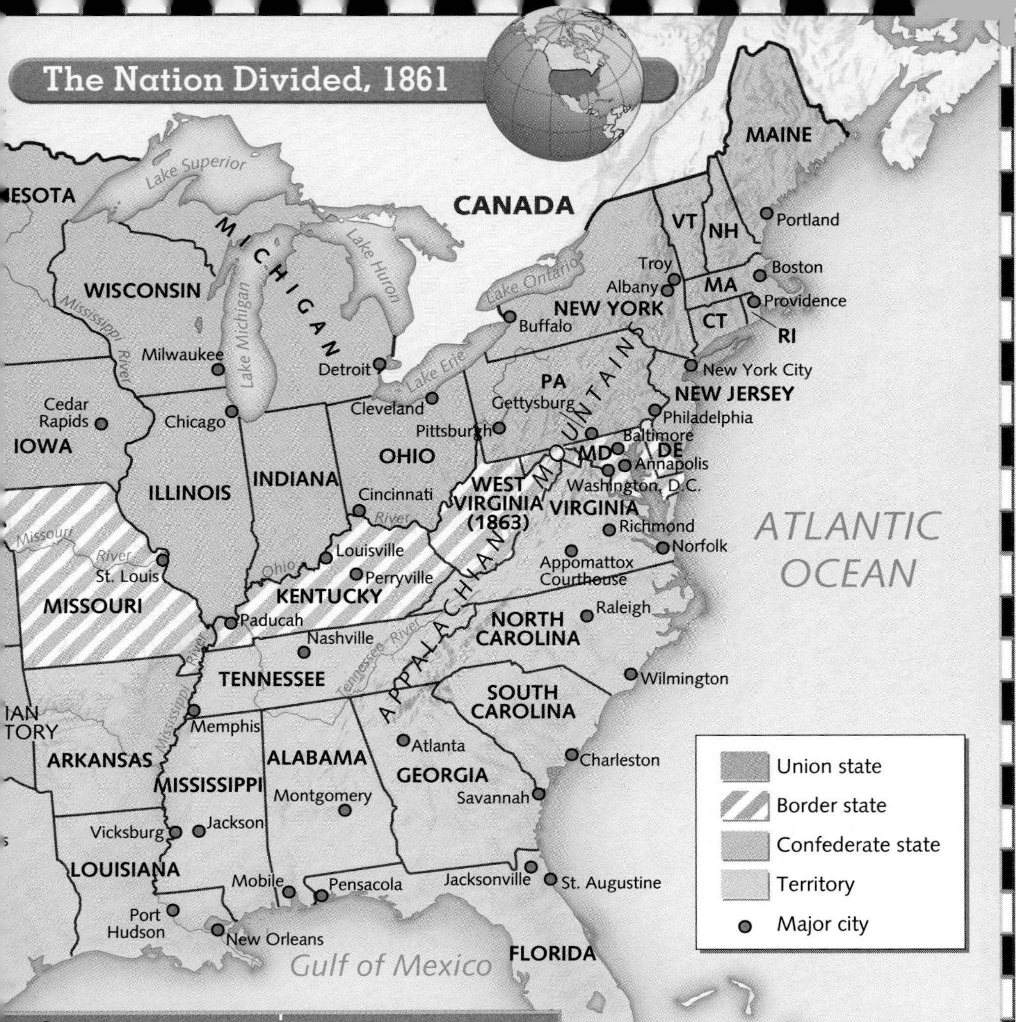

1866

Surrenders

58

1865
Freedmen's Bureau

PAGE 464

409

Understanding the Time Line

Explain to students that the time line includes people, places, and events leading up to the Civil War, during it, and shortly after it. Explain that in this unit students will learn that compromises between the North and the South did not solve their differences and that actions taken by both sides eventually tore the United States apart and led to the Civil War.

Q. **What can you tell about each event by looking at the time line?** Abraham Lincoln was elected President. In 1861 fighting broke out between the North and the South. In 1865, the Confederacy surrendered to the Union, and the Freedmen's Bureau was organized.

Look Ahead to the Unit

Students may wish to preview the chapters, lessons, and illustrations in the unit to become familiar with the many faces and voices of the Civil War and Reconstruction eras in American history.

Challenge students to predict what they will learn about in the unit. Record their predictions. As the unit progresses, refer to the predictions and have students revise them as needed.

TECHNOLOGY

Use TIMELINER DATA DISKS™ to construct a time line of events in this unit.

Background

THE TIME LINE In 1860 Abraham Lincoln was elected President of the United States. By the time of his inauguration, seven states had already seceded from the Union.

In 1861 the Confederate attack on Fort Sumter started the Civil War.

In 1865 Robert E. Lee surrendered to Ulysses S. Grant.

During Reconstruction in 1865 Congress set up an organization called the Freedmen's Bureau to help former slaves.

These events are also shown in the Visual Summary on pages 472–473 in the Pupil Book.

UNIT POSTER

Use the UNIT 7 VISUAL SUMMARY POSTER to preview the unit.

Set the Scene with Literature

Prereading Strategies

Personal Response

Ask volunteers to share with the class experiences they may have had doing something for the very first time. Have students compare what they expected to happen with what actually did happen. Explain that not every soldier who fought in the Civil War knew what to expect when marching into battle for the very first time.

Set the Purpose

The selection from *Stonewall* by Jean Fritz tells a powerful story about the first major battle of the Civil War, which took place in the small Virginia town of Manassas Junction. As students read pages 410–413, encourage them to think about how war affects the individuals involved. After students have read the selection, direct a class conversation about the story.

Read & Respond

Auditory Learning

Read Dramatically Have students imagine that they are television journalists about to present a "special report" on the first battle of the Civil War to the American public. Then assign sections of the selection to be read aloud by student "journalists." Have the students read their sections in a professional yet dramatic manner.

Understanding the Story

Challenge students to picture in their minds the beginning of the battle as Jean Fritz describes it.

Q. **Why does the author's description seem more like the start of a parade than a battle?** No one seemed frightened of what was about to take place.

Set the Scene with Literature

STONEWALL

by Jean Fritz

Confederate General Thomas Jackson earned the name "Stonewall" during the Civil War.

In towns and cities across the country, thousands of excited young men signed up to join the army. It was 1861, and the country was at war. Northerners and Southerners alike signed up, but not to fight on the same side. They signed up to fight each other.

Most people said that it would be a quick and easy war. It would be over, they said, after only one or two battles. Most people also said that their side would win.

Read now about the war's first major battle, which took place near the small Virginia town of Manassas Junction, not far from Washington, D.C. Imagine Northern soldiers, called Yankees, lining up for the first time against Southern soldiers, called Confederates or Rebels, as crowds looked on.

410 • Unit 7

Activity Choices

Background

THE LITERATURE SELECTION The complete book *Stonewall* is a biography of General Thomas "Stonewall" Jackson, a military leader who grew up as a poor orphan. The book traces the development of Jackson's character and his rise to national prominence during the Civil War.

THE AUTHOR Jean Fritz is an award-winning author who writes historical fiction for young people. Some of her other books include *Where Do You Think You're Going, Christopher Columbus?* about European exploration; *Can't You Make Them Behave, King George?* about the American Revolution; and *Shhh! We're Writing the Constitution*, about the United States Constitution.

This building, known as the "Stone House," was used as a hospital by Confederate and Union soldiers during the Battle of Bull Run.

As the participants gathered at Manassas, excitement mounted. At last! This was it! The war was starting! Victory was in the air as if nothing else could possibly exist. The Confederates, obviously outnumbered, were lined up in a defensive position beside a small stream known as Bull Run, but if they worried, they didn't show it. Hadn't they always believed that one rebel could beat five Yankees? As for the Yankees, they straggled down to Manassas, stopping to pick blackberries—in no hurry, for hadn't they been told that the Rebs would run once they saw how bold the Yanks were? Even the civilians in Washington, high-ranking officials and their wives, were so sure of a Union victory that they planned to picnic on the outskirts of Manassas on the Big Day. They would drink champagne and toast the army and cry "Bravo! Bravo!" What could be nicer?

Although there had been several days of initial skirmishing, the Big Day turned out to be Sunday, July 21st. A beautiful sunny day—perfect for a picnic. Carriages were drawn up on a hill overlooking Bull Run; ladies rustled under parasols; gentlemen adjusted field glasses; couriers galloped up with the latest news. Good news, all of it. Yankee advances. Confederate confusion. So it went for the first six hours.

Yet not all the Confederates had been heard from. The Army of the Shenandoah that was supposed to be held in the hills by the Union watchdog forces had eluded their enemy on July 18th and had left for Manassas. At first they'd been slow. The men didn't know where they were going or why and saw no reason to rush just because their officers told them to. Finally General Thomas Jackson, whose brigade led the march, stopped them and read an official statement. "Our gallant army under General Beauregard is now attacked by overwhelming numbers," Jackson read. He asked the troops if they would not "step out like men and make a forced march to save the country."

A battle! The men yelled their approval—a special rebel yell. . . . It was a fierce sound that a Yankee soldier once said sent a corkscrew sensation down the spine. Woh-who-ey. The yell rose to a pitch on the *who* and held there, trembling and drawn out, then fell with a thud on the *ey*. The men quickened their pace. Woh-who-ey. For eighteen hours they marched until at last, having waded waist deep through the green Shenandoah River, they dropped, exhausted. They marched and they rode a train for a few hours, and then they marched again. But they were there now. The question was: Were they in time?

Geography

Location Have students turn to the map on page 457 in their textbook. Explain that the town of Manassas Junction is less than 30 miles from Washington, D.C. Help students to comprehend this distance by using familiar locations as reference points.

Q. **How does this distance help explain the presence of spectators at this first battle?** The short distance made it possible for spectators to reach the battle site in a few hours.

Multicultural Link

At the beginning of the war, many Africans tried to join the Union army, but regulations prohibited their enlistment. By July 1862, however, with no end to the war in sight and the number of white volunteers dwindling, Congress approved legislation allowing Africans to enlist. Yet it was not until the following year, after Lincoln had issued the Emancipation Proclamation, that large numbers of Africans joined the Union army. From then on, Africans fought in almost every battle of the war, including Cold Harbor, in which seven African units participated.

Background

FIGHTING IN THE CIVIL WAR During Civil War battles, as many as 25 percent of the soldiers were killed, wounded, or captured. This grim reality led soldiers to devise the first "dog tags"—pieces of paper or cloth with names and addresses that soldiers pinned to their uniforms before battle for possible identification later.

Visual Analysis

Interpret Photographs Point out that many of the soldiers who fought at Bull Run were young men and boys.

Q. **What clues in the photographs support the idea that many Civil War soldiers may not have been experienced fighters?** young faces and new uniforms

Understanding the Story

It was in this battle that General Thomas Jackson received his now-famous nickname.

Q. **How did the general get his nickname, "Stonewall"?** Soldiers started to call him "Stonewall" after General Bee described him as "standing like a stone wall."

What does this nickname tell you about General Jackson? The general held firm and would not be moved or frightened in battle.

By noon on the 21st it was clear that Beauregard had positioned the major part of his army in the wrong place. While the enemy was concentrating its forces on the left, the Confederates were wasting their time on the right. In the general scramble to change positions, Jackson and his brigade found themselves in the thick of the activity. Union men were in the distance but steadily advancing; the Confederates were retreating. As one officer passed Jackson, he shook his head. "The day is going against us," he said.

"If you think so, sir," Jackson replied, "don't say anything about it."

Jackson did not plunge forward to meet the enemy, as his men might have expected. Looking over the field, he saw a plateau which he recognized as the best possible position for making a stand. Here he placed his men and artillery and when the enemy fire closed in, Jackson stood before his brigade, his blue eyes blazing, the old battle fever upon him. Walking back and forth, indifferent to bullets, he was lifted out of himself, possessed with a power he'd known only once before, in Mexico. He understood exactly how to get the most out of every man and every gun and he *willed* victory into the day. "The fight," as one officer put it, "was just then hot enough to make [Jackson] feel well." Shot in the hand as he held it up, Jackson wrapped a handkerchief around the wound and went on as if nothing had happened.

In another part of the field, General Bee, a West Point classmate of Jackson's, was desperately trying to stop a retreat. "Look yonder!" he cried to his men. "There's Jackson standing like a stone wall."

General Bee was killed almost as soon as he'd finished speaking, but retreating Confederates did see how well Jackson's line was holding and gradually they began to rally around it. The last reinforcements from Shenandoah army, which had just arrived, were rushed to the scene. And the tide of the battle began to turn.

Men were supposed to be at least 18 years old to join the army, but some boys much younger—like the two shown here—still signed up. Most boys were not allowed to fight. Instead they tended horses, drove wagons, or served as drummer boys.

Activity Choices

Link Literature

For advanced readers, you may wish to assign the complete book *Stonewall*. The following are other selections that can be used during the course of this unit with students of differing reading abilities. In addition to these titles, you may wish to suggest some of the books listed in the Multimedia Resource Center on page 406D of this Teacher's Edition.

Easy
Abe Lincoln Goes to Washington: 1837–1865 **by Cheryl Harness. National Geographic Society, 1997.**

Average
Tales from the Underground Railroad **by Kate Connell. Steck-Vaughn, 1993.**

Challenging
Across the Lines **by Carolyn Reeder. Simon & Schuster, 1997.**

What started out for many as an exciting adventure ended in fear, injury, and death at the Battle of Bull Run (above). One Union soldier, staggering from the battlefield, told an onlooker, "I've had enough fighting to last my lifetime." During the battle, Private A. P. Hubbard's pocket-sized Bible (right) saved his life, protecting him from a bullet that ripped the book apart.

When the center of the Union line was in plain sight, General Beauregard ordered a charge. Jackson relayed the order.

"Reserve your fire till they come within fifty yards," he shouted, "then fire and give them the bayonet. And when you charge, yell like furies."

The orders were carried out precisely.

Woh-who-ey!

Woh-who-ey!

Suddenly the entire Union army was falling back, then turning around and hurrying off the field. A huge, confused mob mixed with panic-stricken picnickers headed pell-mell back to Washington.

The battle was over and with it some of the innocent glory was gone. For the fields were strewn with bodies—young men who only the day before had been laughing and making jokes. Two thousand Confederates killed or wounded; three thousand Union men. Stopped right in the midst of doing something. In the middle of a sentence perhaps, in mid-step, in the act of raising a rifle, at the beginning of a smile. Struck down, blown apart as if they weren't *people*. As if they weren't *young*. How could inexperienced men have imagined what death would be like on a battlefield?

In one day soldiers on both sides became veterans, but of course the victors felt better than the losers. If they could win a battle, southerners said, they could win a war.

Understanding the Story

Point out how appropriately expressions such as *yell like furies*, which means "to yell wildly, with anger," and the word *pell-mell*, which means "in a confused or disorderly way," describe the battle scene.

Have students consider how the cooperation of General Thomas Jackson's soldiers brought victory to the Confederates at Manassas Junction.

Visual Analysis

Interpret Photographs Have students examine the picture of the Bible that saved Private A. P. Hubbard's life in the battle.

Q. **What does this photograph tell you about the fierceness of the battle?** Bullets flew fiercely; the fighting was intense.

What does this photograph tell you about A. P. Hubbard's attitudes or beliefs? Hubbard was probably a religious man.

Summarize the Literature

By the end of this battle, soldiers and civilians alike had learned what fighting a war would mean. Although this dramatic scene is about one isolated battle, it represents what happens when two opposing sides come into bitter conflict.

Link to Language Arts

WRITE A DESCRIPTION Ask students to think of themselves as young Civil War soldiers or civilian spectators who survived the day of fighting at the Battle of Bull Run. Now it is evening. They are exhausted, hungry, dirty, and shocked by their experience, but they are anxious to tell someone about the battle. Have students write a descriptive paragraph that describes their day as either a soldier or a civilian spectator.

Technology

Use THE AMAZING WRITING MACHINE™ to complete this writing activity.

Home Involvement

Have students share with adult family members the story of the Battle of Bull Run. Then have students invite their family members to share with them some of their own experiences during times of war.

CHAPTER 13

Planning Chart

	THEMES • Strands	VOCABULARY	MEET INDIVIDUAL NEEDS	RESOURCES INCLUDING ▶ TECHNOLOGY
LESSON 1 **Differences Divide North and South** pp. 415–419	CONFLICT & COOPERATION • Geography • Culture • History • Economics	cotton gin	Tactile Learners, p. 417 Advanced Learners, p. 418 Extend and Enrich, p. 418 Reteach, p. 419	Activity Book, p. 80 ▶ GRAPH LINKS
SKILL **Use Graphs to Identify Trends** p. 420	BASIC STUDY SKILLS • Chart and Graph Skills	trend	Reteach the Skill, p. 420	Activity Book, p. 81 Transparency 34 ▶ GRAPH LINKS
LESSON 2 **Africans in Slavery and Freedom** pp. 421–425	INDIVIDUALISM & INTERDEPENDENCE • Civics/Government • Culture • History	slave code overseer spiritual resist Underground Railroad	Tactile Learners, p. 424 Extend and Enrich, p. 424 Reteach, p. 425	Activity Book, p. 82 ▶ THE AMAZING WRITING MACHINE
LESSON 3 **Facing a National Problem** pp. 426–430	CONTINUITY & CHANGE • Civics/Government • History	free state slave state	Auditory Learners, p. 427 English Language Learners, p. 428 Extend and Enrich, p. 429 Reteach, p. 430	Activity Book, p. 83 ▶ THE AMAZING WRITING MACHINE ▶ TIMELINER
LESSON 4 **A Time for Hard Decisions** pp. 431–434	INDIVIDUALISM & INTERDEPENDENCE • Civics/Government • History	Confederacy	Advanced Learners, p. 433 Extend and Enrich, p. 433 Reteach, p. 434	Activity Book, p. 84 ▶ THE AMAZING WRITING MACHINE
SKILL **Make a Thoughtful Decision** p. 435	BUILDING CITIZENSHIP • Critical Thinking Skills		Reteach the Skill, p. 435	Activity Book, p. 85 Transparency 35
COUNTERPOINTS **Union or Secession?** pp. 436–437	BUILDING CITIZENSHIP • Participation Skills • Critical Thinking Skills		Reteach, p. 437	
CHAPTER REVIEW pp. 438–439				Activity Book, p. 86 Transparency 36 Assessment Program Chapter 13 Test, pp. 111–114 ▶ THE AMAZING WRITING MACHINE ▶ TIMELINER ▶ INTERNET

9 DAYS

TIME MANAGEMENT

DAY 1	DAY 2	DAY 3	DAY 4	DAY 5	DAY 6	DAY 7	DAY 8	DAY 9
Lesson 1	Skill	Lesson 2	Lesson 3	Lesson 4	Skill	Counterpoints	Chapter Review	Chapter Test

Activity Book

LESSON 1
Analyze Information in a Table

NAME _____ DATE _____

A TALE OF TWO REGIONS
1860

Analyze Information in a Table

DIRECTIONS: The table below compares the North with the South in 1860. Use the information in your textbook to complete the table. Then answer the questions that follow to show that you understand how the two regions differed.

TWO WAYS OF LIFE: 1860		
	NORTH	SOUTH
Total Number of People	More than 19 million	About 11 million
Number of Enslaved People	– 0 –	Nearly 4 million
Number of Factories	119,500	20,850
Number of Factory Workers	1,300,000	110,000
Annual Value of Factory Products	$1,730,000,000	$156,000,000
Miles of Railroad Track	21,500	8,500
Value of Exports	$175,000,000	$226,000,000
Money in Banks	$345,900,000	$76,000,000

1. List three details from the table that support the idea that there was more manufacturing in the North than in the South.

The North had more factories than the South.

The North had more factory workers than the South.

The annual value of factory products was greater in the North than in the South.

2. List one detail from the table that supports the idea that the South relied on trade with other countries more than the North did. The value of exports from the South was greater than the value of exports from the North.

3. Which region had more miles of railroad track? the North
How might having more miles of railroad track affect that region's economy?
Responses will vary but should reflect an understanding that having more miles of railroad track might lead to increased profits from trade.

Use after reading Chapter 13, Lesson 1, pages 415–419.

SKILL PRACTICE
Apply Chart and Graph Skills

NAME _____ DATE _____

HOW TO USE Graphs To Identify Trends

In the early 1800s most people in both the North and the South lived and worked on farms. Today, farming continues to be an important economic activity throughout much of the United States. However, the number of farms has changed greatly over time.

Year	Number of Farms
1850	1,500,000
1880	4,000,000
1920	6,500,000
1980	2,400,000
1992	2,100,000

Apply Chart and Graph Skills

DIRECTIONS: Use the facts at the right to make a line graph in the space below. Add a title to your graph. Then answer the questions that follow.

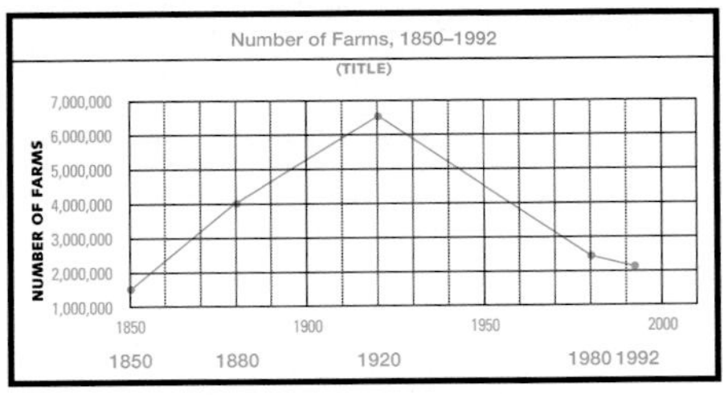

1. What was the trend between 1850 and 1920? The number of farms increased.

2. What was the trend between 1920 and 1992? The number of farms decreased.

3. How would you explain the trends? Possible responses: increases in population from 1850 to 1920 led to an increase in the number of farms; technology has made farms more productive, so fewer farms are needed today; modern machinery allows larger farms, reducing the total number of farms; fewer people choose to live on farms today.

Use after reading Chapter 13, Skill Lesson, page 420.

LESSON 2
Gather Information from Reference Books

NAME _____ DATE _____

THE LIFE AND TIMES OF A SLAVE

Gather Information from Reference Books

DIRECTIONS: Read the passage from Frederick Douglass's autobiography, The Life and Times of Frederick Douglass.

My first experience of life, as I now remember it, began in the family of my grandmother and grandfather, Betsey and Isaac Bailey. . . .

. . . Whether because she [Grandmother Betsey] was too old for field service, or because she had so faithfully done the duties of her station in early life, I know not, but she enjoyed the special right of living in a cabin separate from the other cabins, having given her only the charge of the young children and the burden of her support. . . The practice of separating mothers from their children and hiring them out at distances too great to allow their meeting, except after long periods of time, was a marked feature of the cruelty and hardness of the slave system. . . .

My grandmother's five daughters were hired out . . . and my only recollections of my own mother are of a few hasty visits made in the night on foot, after the daily tasks were over, and when she had to return in time to answer the driver's call to the field in the early morning. These little glimpses of my mother under such conditions and against such odds, meager as they were, are permanently stamped upon my memory. She was tall and had dark, glossy skin with regular features, and amongst the slaves was remarkably sedate and dignified.

DIRECTIONS: Use the passage above and other available resources to answer the following questions about Frederick Douglass on a separate sheet of paper. For each question, tell whether you used only the passage to find the answer or whether you needed to use an encyclopedia, a dictionary, or some other reference book.

1. When was Frederick Douglass born, and when did he die?
born: 1817; died: 1895; encyclopedia, dictionary, or some other reference book
2. In what state did Douglass live as a slave?
Maryland; encyclopedia, dictionary, or some other reference book
3. Who raised Douglass as a boy?
his grandparents; passage
4. How did Douglass describe his mother?
tall, with dark, glossy skin and regular features; sedate and dignified; passage

Use after reading Chapter 13, Lesson 2, pages 421–425.

LESSON 3
Expand Thinking About an Issue

NAME _____ DATE _____

"BLEEDING KANSAS"

Kansas and Nebraska were organized as territories. → People in these territories were given an opportunity to decide whether or not they wanted to allow slavery. → People for and against slavery moved to Kansas to vote on the issue. → Bitter fighting broke out between people for and those against slavery. → Kansas was admitted as a free state.

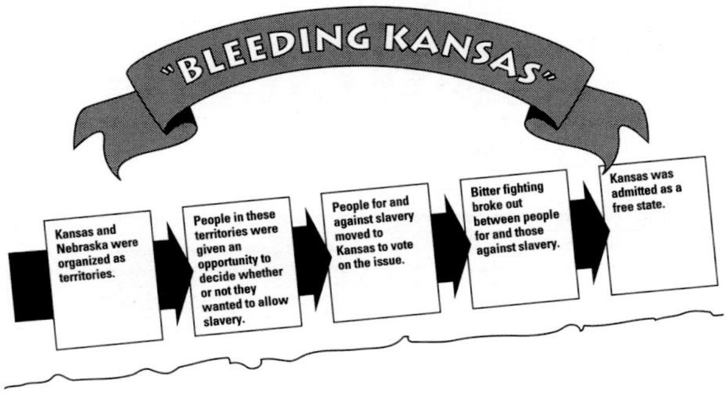

Expand Thinking About an Issue

DIRECTIONS: Use the flow chart above and the information in your textbook to answer the questions below.

1. How did the Kansas–Nebraska Act deal with the spread of slavery?
It allowed people in the Kansas and Nebraska territories to vote on whether or not they wanted slavery.

2. How do you think people in the North reacted to the Kansas–Nebraska Act?
They probably opposed it because it could allow slavery in two more territories.

3. How do you think people in the South viewed the Kansas–Nebraska Act?
They probably supported it because it could allow slavery in two more territories.

4. What were the major effects of the Kansas–Nebraska Act in Kansas?
More people moved there; fighting broke out between those for and those against slavery.

5. Why did Southern states begin to talk more about secession after Kansas became a state?
Because the North had more people, Southerners may possibly have come to believe they could not win future elections.

6. Do you think the Kansas–Nebraska Act was a good law? Why or why not?
Accept any reasonable answer that students can defend.

Use after reading Chapter 13, Lesson 3, pages 426–430.

LESSON 4
Recognize Point of View

NAME ______________________ DATE __________

WHY DID SOUTH CAROLINA SECEDE?

Recognize Point of View

DIRECTIONS: Read the following paragraph from the South Carolina Secession Ordinance of December 20, 1860.

SOUTH CAROLINA SECESSION ORDINANCE
December 20, 1860

An agreement between the states set up a government with specific purposes and powers. We feel that the reasons for which this government was begun have been defeated. The government itself has destroyed them by the action of the Northern, nonslaveholding states. **(1)** Those states have assumed the right to decide the properness of our domestic practices (that is, slavery). **(2)** They have denied our rights of property recognized by the Constitution. They have denounced as sinful the practice of slavery. **(3)** They have permitted the organization of abolitionist groups, whose goal is to disturb the peace of and to take away the property of the citizens of our states. **(4)** Those groups have encouraged and helped thousands of our slaves to leave their homes; and the slaves who remain have been incited by special agents, books, and pictures into insurrection.

DIRECTIONS: *For each numbered sentence in the South Carolina Secession Ordinance, state in your own words a South Carolina complaint from a Southern point of view. Then write a response that tells the Northern point of view. Use your textbook if you need more information.*

	Southern Complaint	Northern Response
1.	Northern states are trying to end slavery.	
2.	They are trying to take away property.	Accept any reasonable responses
3.	They have allowed abolitionist groups.	that students can defend.
4.	They encourage slaves to run away.	

 Use after reading Chapter 13, Lesson 4, pages 431–434.

SKILL PRACTICE
Apply Critical Thinking Skills

NAME ______________________ DATE __________

HOW TO MAKE A THOUGHTFUL DECISION

Apply Critical Thinking Skills

DIRECTIONS: Think about a decision you made recently at school, or think about a decision that someone made during the Civil War. Then use the organizer below to record and analyze that decision. Fill in as many possible actions and consequences as you can.

THE GOAL

Students' responses should demonstrate an ability to analyze decisions.

POSSIBLE ACTIONS	POSSIBLE CONSEQUENCES
1.	1.
2.	2.
3.	3.
4.	4.

THE CHOICE	REASONS FOR THE CHOICE

THE RESULT

Use after reading Chapter 13, Skill Lesson, page 435.

CHAPTER 13 REVIEW
Connect Main Ideas

NAME ______________________ DATE __________

Background to the CONFLICT

Connect Main Ideas

DIRECTIONS: *Use this organizer to show how the chapter's main ideas are connected. Write three details to support each main idea.*

Differences Divide North and South
People in the North and the South disagreed during the middle 1800s.
1. The North had more people living in cities and more factories, while the South depended upon farming as a way of life.
2. As demand for cotton increased, Southern plantation owners used more slaves to help raise and harvest their crops.
3. Bad feelings over the growth of the North and the question of the spread of slavery to the frontier led to fierce arguments.

Africans in Slavery and Freedom
Enslaved people protested against being held in slavery.
1. Some slaves secretly damaged the plantations they worked on.
2. Some slaves attacked people in rebellions. Some slaves used the Underground Railroad to reach freedom in the North.
3.

Background to the Conflict

Facing a National Problem
Northerners and Southerners tried to settle disagreements during the 1800s.
1. The Missouri Compromise balanced free and slave states and created an imaginary line between
2. them. The Kansas-Nebraska Act allowed people living in those territories to decide whether or not to allow
3. slavery. The Compromise of 1850 allowed people in New Mexico and Utah to decide whether or not to allow slavery and punished people who helped slaves escape.

A Time for Hard Decisions
Americans had to make important decisions in 1860 and 1861.
1. After Abraham Lincoln was elected President of the United States, South Carolina seceded from the Union.
2. Other states joined South Carolina to create the new country called the Confederate States of America.
3. After President Lincoln decided to send supply ships to Fort Sumter, Jefferson Davis decided to attack the fort—leading to the Civil War.

 Use after reading Chapter 13, pages 414–439.

COMMUNITY RESOURCES

Ideas for using community resources, including speakers and field trips

Historical Societies and Civil War Experts:

____

____

____

____

____

Museums and Historic Sites:

____

____

____

____

____

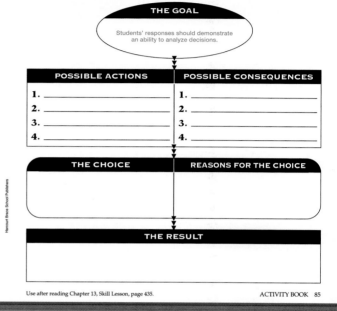

Chapter 13 Assessment

For ongoing **PERFORMANCE ASSESSMENT,** see Show What You Know, pp. 419, 425, 430, 434.

CONTENT

NAME ______________________ DATE ____________

Chapter Test 13

Part One: Test Your Understanding *(4 points each)*

DIRECTIONS: ***Circle the letter of the best answer.***

1. The biggest farms in the South were located
- **A.** near salt marshes.
- **B.** along the Coastal Plain.
- **C.** far from the Mississippi River.
- **D.** near many factories.

2. Most of the people who lived in the South lived
- **A.** on small farms.
- **B.** in the cities.
- **C.** on plantations.
- **D.** along the sea coast.

3. In the early 1800s, life in the North changed more than life in the South because
- **A.** slavery became more important.
- **B.** the number of factories and cities increased.
- **C.** plantations became more popular.
- **D.** farmers raised more crops.

4. The invention of the cotton gin by Eli Whitney
- **A.** caused most of the textile mills in the North to close down.
- **B.** increased the need for slaves.
- **C.** decreased the need for cotton.
- **D.** made people move away from plantations.

5. The most serious disagreement between the North and the South concerned
- **A.** how much money farmers in the South should be paid for their crops.
- **B.** whether slavery should be allowed to spread to the frontier.
- **C.** how best to deal with the Indian peoples living in the North.
- **D.** whether to pay Eli Whitney for the invention of the cotton gin.

6. Slaves helped each other deal with their daily hardships by
- **A.** electing leaders to represent them.
- **B.** demanding that plantation owners pay them more money.
- **C.** keeping their traditions alive.
- **D.** writing letters of protest to the President.

(continued)

CONTENT

NAME ______________________ DATE ____________

7. Who helped runaway slaves escape on the Underground Railroad?
- **A.** Dred Scott
- **B.** Nat Turner
- **C.** Jefferson Davis
- **D.** Harriet Tubman

8. Who persuaded Congress to agree to the Missouri Compromise?
- **A.** Henry Clay
- **B.** Abraham Lincoln
- **C.** Stephen Douglas
- **D.** Frederick Douglass

9. The Compromise of 1850
- **A.** encouraged western states to allow slavery.
- **B.** kept the number of free and slave states equal.
- **C.** required people to return runaway slaves to the South.
- **D.** limited the production of cotton.

10. The Kansas-Nebraska Act
- **A.** outlawed slavery in both Kansas and Nebraska.
- **B.** led to fighting in Kansas between people for and against slavery.
- **C.** gave the vote to slaves living in these two places.
- **D.** offered public education to slaves living in Kansas and Nebraska.

11. In the case of Dred Scott, the Supreme Court ruled that
- **A.** Scott was property and should not be given his freedom.
- **B.** slavery should be outlawed in the United States.
- **C.** slaves should have the same rights as other American citizens.
- **D.** Congress had the right to outlaw slavery in the Wisconsin Territory.

12. Abraham Lincoln joined the Republican party in order to
- **A.** make sure each state could decide the slavery question for itself.
- **B.** run for the U.S. House of Representatives.
- **C.** fight against the spread of slavery.
- **D.** work with Stephen Douglas.

13. Shortly after Lincoln was elected President in 1860, a group of Southern states
- **A.** withdrew from the Union and formed their own country.
- **B.** agreed to abolish slavery in the next five years.
- **C.** made plans to stop the spread of slavery to the new states.
- **D.** passed laws to protect the rights of slaves.

14. The president of the Confederacy was
- **A.** Jefferson Davis.
- **B.** James Forten.
- **C.** Roger B. Taney.
- **D.** Eli Whitney.

(continued)

SKILLS

NAME ______________________ DATE ____________

Part Two: Test Your Skills *(16 points)*

DIRECTIONS: ***Use the graph below to answer the questions that follow.***

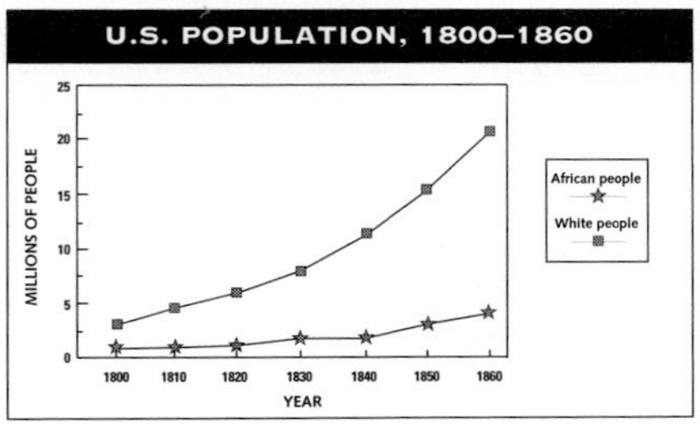

15. Approximately how many African people were living in the United States in 1860?

almost 3 million African people

16. In which decade did the population of white people increase the most?

the 1850s

17. Based on this graph, what was the **total** population of white people and African people in the United States in 1860?

about 25 million people

18. What conclusions can you draw from this graph?

Possible responses: There were more than six times as many white people as African people in the United States in 1860; the population of white people in the United States grew much faster than the population of African people during the 1800s.

(continued)

APPLICATION/WRITING

NAME ______________________ DATE ____________

Part Three: Apply What You Have Learned

DIRECTIONS: ***Complete each of the following activities.***

19. ***The Slave Codes*** *(6 points)*
Most states in the South in 1860 had slave codes, laws that shaped the day-to-day lives of enslaved people. List three ways that the lives of slaves were shaped by these slave codes.

Possible responses: Slaves were not allowed to leave their owner's land. Slaves were not allowed to meet in groups. Slaves were not allowed to buy goods. Slaves were not allowed to sell goods. Slaves were not allowed to learn to read and write.

20. ***What Do They Have in Common?*** *(12 points)*
Listed below are famous people who lived during the 1800s. Form four pairs of people and explain why you grouped them.

General Beauregard	John Brown	Henry Clay
Jefferson Davis	Stephen Douglas	Abraham Lincoln
Harriet Tubman	Nat Turner	Eli Whitney

Possible responses.

Pairs of People	Reason for Placing Them Together
Brown and Turner	Both took action to oppose slavery.
Lincoln and Douglas	Both ran for public office.
Davis and Beauregard	Both were Confederates.
Tubman and Lincoln	Both wanted slavery to end.

21. ***Essay*** *(10 points)*
Stephen Douglas and Abraham Lincoln had very different ideas about how the question of slavery should be settled. Write a paragraph explaining how the two men differed in their viewpoints concerning slavery.

Possible response: Stephen Douglas thought that each new state should decide the slavery question for itself. He believed that was what the country's founders had intended and what the Kansas-Nebraska Act allowed. Abraham Lincoln, on the other hand, believed that the framers of the Constitution intended and expected slavery to end. He argued that slavery should not be allowed to spread to the West.

INTRODUCE THE CHAPTER

This chapter examines conflicting ways of life that developed in the North and in the South. It looks at the lives of both enslaved and free Africans and the growing crisis caused by the spread of slavery. The chapter also focuses on Abraham Lincoln's rise to national prominence and the creation of the Confederate States of America.

Link Prior Learning

Have students share what they already know about slavery. You may wish to review the discussions of slavery found in Units 2, 3, and 6. This review will help students grasp the conflict of viewpoints on slavery that intensified in the early to mid-1800s.

Visual Analysis

Interpret Photographs Explain that this photograph shows Frederick Douglass, a leading spokesperson for Africans in the 1800s. After fleeing slavery, Douglass devoted his life to ending slavery and securing rights for Africans.

Q. **What do you think this photograph shows about Frederick Douglass?** He was strong, determined, and serious.

Auditory Learning

Interpret Primary Sources Have a volunteer read aloud the quotation. Tell students that this was a favorite line used by Douglass in speeches as he traveled the country, speaking out against slavery.

Q. **What does this quotation tell you about how Frederick Douglass gained his freedom?** Douglass gained his freedom by running away.

What clues does the quotation give you about how slave owners viewed their slaves? They viewed slaves as property, as something that could be stolen from them.

"PRIMARY SOURCE"

Source: *The Civil War: An Illustrated History.* Geoffrey C. Ward. Alfred A. Knopf, 1990.

CHAPTER 13

BACKGROUND TO THE CONFLICT

"I appear this evening as a thief and robber. I stole this head, these limbs, this body from my master, and ran off with them."

Frederick Douglass, a runaway slave and abolitionist, about 1842

This photograph of Frederick Douglass was taken in 1856.

ACTIVITY CHOICES

Background

FREDERICK DOUGLASS When Frederick Douglass (1817–1895) was eight years old, he was sent to Baltimore, Maryland, to work for one of his owner's relatives. It was there, helped by his new master's wife, that Douglass began to educate himself. In 1838 Douglass fled north to New Bedford, Massachusetts. His speaking abilities so impressed members of the Massachusetts Antislavery Society that they hired him to lecture about his experiences as a slave. Douglass later founded the *North Star,* an antislavery newspaper.

Differences Divide North and South

LESSON 1

FOCUS
What might cause people living in different regions to disagree today?

Main Idea As you read, look for the reasons that caused people in the North and the South to disagree during the middle 1800s.

Vocabulary
cotton gin

Differences among Americans help make the nation ;trong. Sometimes, however, differences come between people. n the mid-1800s differences became disagreements between \mericans living in two regions—the North and the South. These disagreements threatened to tear the country apart.

Regional Differences

Many of the differences between the North and the South leveloped over time, as people in each region found different vays of making a living. In the mid-1800s most Americans ;till lived and worked on farms. For many people, however, ife was changing.

In the North, factories seemed to be springing up every-vhere, making all kinds of goods. Many people were moving rom their farms to towns and cities, where they hoped to vork in the factories. People even came from other countries o find jobs.

Life in the South was not changing as quickly. Factories vere being built and cities were growing, yet farming emained the most common way to earn a living. The biggest arms were plantations along the Coastal Plain and near the Mississippi River. Planters there raised acres and acres of cash rops, such as cotton, rice, tobacco, and sugarcane, to sell at narket.

Wealthy plantation owners were among the South's eaders. Many white Southerners copied the ways of hese planters and dreamed about owning their own plantations someday. Yet few ever did. Most lived on small farms, where they raised cattle, cut lumber, and grew only enough food to feed their families.

Cotton was an important cash crop in the South. Many Southerners depended on cotton to make a living.

Objectives

1. Describe the key differences between the North and the South.
2. Analyze why slaves became an important human resource for the South.
3. Determine the impact of the cotton gin.
4. Compare conflicting attitudes that led to increased tension as people moved west.

Vocabulary

cotton gin (p. 417)

1. ACCESS

The Focus Question

Discuss differences that might cause people living in different regions to disagree. Consider examples of present-day conflicts in the United States and throughout the world. Point out that regional differences often build slowly over time.

The Main Idea

In this lesson students explore the causes of regional differences between the North and the South that led to the Civil War. After students have read the lesson, lead them in a conversation that builds an understanding of those differences, particularly their causes and later effects.

2. BUILD

Regional Differences

Key Content Summary

During the mid-1800s most Americans, both in the North and in the South, lived and worked on farms. While the South continued to concentrate on farming, the North was developing an economy based on trade and manufacturing.

Reading Support

PREVIEW AND READ THE LESSON Provide students with the following visual framework.

DIFFERENCES DIVIDE NORTH AND SOUTH

	NORTH	SOUTH
ECONOMY	Many people moved to towns and cities to work in factories.	Farming remained the most important industry.
POPULATION	More people lived in the North than in the South.	Fewer people lived in the South than in the North.
SLAVERY	The North ended slavery and was against its spread to the West.	The South allowed slavery and was for its spread to the West.

Geography

Regions Have students discuss the elements that define a region—common features, such as climate, resources, language, and traditions.

Q. **What distinguished the North from the South?** different population sizes, different economies, and the fact that the South allowed slavery and the North did not

Visual Analysis

Interpret Pictures Have students look at the pictures for clues that support the idea that the North and the South had been developing different ways of life.

The Slave Economy

Key Content Summary

Because some Northerners thought slavery was wrong and because others did not find it profitable, slavery did not last in the North. In Southern states, where plantations depended on slave labor, slavery continued.

Culture

Social Organizations and Institutions Explain that the white population in the South was divided into social and economic groups, determined in part by the number of slaves owned. Although those who owned 20 or more slaves and had the largest pieces of land were few in number, they often held the most important positions in Southern society.

Many people in the North were moving to cities to find work. This painting (top) shows a busy street scene in New York City. In the South farming continued to be the center of life. This scene (below) shows a cotton plantation along the Mississippi River.

Partly because of the differences in work opportunities between the two regions, many more people lived in the North than in the South. By 1860 the population of the North had grown to more than 19 million. Only 11 million people lived in the South. Of those 11 million people, nearly 4 million were Africans held as slaves.

REVIEW ***How was the North different from the South?*** The North had more factories, and more people were moving to cities. In the South farming was the most common way to earn a living.

The Slave Economy

Slavery had been a part of American life since colonial days. In many places, however, slavery did not last. Some people thought that slavery was wrong. Others could not make money using enslaved workers. The cost of feeding, clothing, and housing slaves was too great.

Yet slavery continued in the South, where owners had come to depend on the work of

Activity Choices

Background

THE CIVIL WAR ERA When discussing the Civil War Era, it is customary for textbooks to capitalize the first letter of the terms *Northern, Southern, Northerner,* and *Southerner.* This is done to indicate that the terms refer to political units rather than to geographical areas.

Link to Mathematics

MAKE A CIRCLE GRAPH Have students make a circle graph showing population differences between the North and the South in 1860. Students can use these statistics: the North had 19 million people (roughly 63%) and the South had 11 million people (roughly 37%) in a total national population of 30 million (100%).

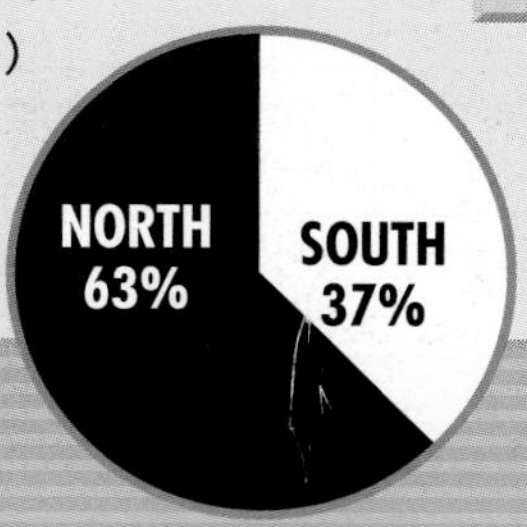

Technology

Use GRAPH LINKS to complete this graphing activity.

SOURCE: *Compendium of the Eighth Census, 1860*

Southern Slaveholders, 1860

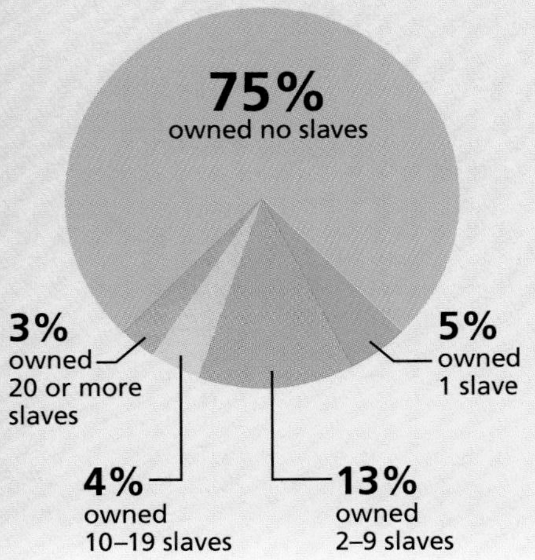

LEARNING FROM GRAPHS Most Northerners once thought that all Southerners owned slaves. Look at the circle graph to tell if this is true.
- *What percent of Southerners owned no slaves at all in 1860? What percent did own slaves?*

enslaved people. Slaves were made to work as miners, carpenters, factory workers, and house servants. Most, however, were taken to large plantations. There they worked in the fields, raising acres of cash crops for the planters to sell at market.

Not every white Southerner owned slaves. In fact, most did not. By 1860 only one white Southern family in four owned slaves. Many of these families lived on small farms with one or two slaves. Only a few wealthy slaveholders lived on large plantations with many slaves. These planters together owned more than half of the population of slaves in the South.

REVIEW *Why was slavery important in the Southern states?* Owners had come to depend on the work of enslaved people.

"King Cotton"

In the early years of settlement in the South, few planters grew cotton—the plant from which soft, cool cotton cloth is made. Cotton was in great demand. But before it could be sold, workers had to separate the small seeds from the white cotton fibers. This was a slow, tiring job that took too many people too much time. Inventor Eli Whitney changed this.

In 1793 Whitney invented a machine called the cotton gin, or engine. The **cotton gin** removed the seeds from the cotton fibers much faster than workers could. This one change in technology led to many other changes.

BIOGRAPHY

Eli Whitney
1765–1825

Eli Whitney taught school and studied law. He also liked to fix things. While visiting a friend's Georgia plantation, he learned how difficult it was to remove the seeds from cotton. Whitney invented a machine that could take care of the problem. Soon so many people wanted cotton gins that he could not make enough to keep up with the demand. Other people began to make and sell copies of his invention. Whitney had to pay lawyers to stop others from copying his work. This used up most of the money he made from inventing the cotton gin.

Visual Analysis

Learn from Graphs Remind students that circle graphs show the parts that make up a whole. Have students answer the question in the caption. 75%; 25%

Q. **What percentage of slaveholders owned 20 or more slaves?** 3%

"King Cotton"

Key Content Summary

The invention of the cotton gin changed the way cotton was processed, making it easier to remove the seeds from the fibers. Instead of eliminating the need for slaves, the new technology increased the demand for slave labor to grow more cotton.

History

Innovation Have students discuss the impact of Eli Whitney's invention of the cotton gin.

Q. **In what ways did Eli Whitney contribute to change?** His invention changed the way people processed cotton and changed the way people worked.
What other technology did Whitney invent that changed the way people worked? interchangeable parts

Background

THE COTTON GIN Simple cotton gins were first developed in India during ancient times. Some forms of these machines were even used in the American colonies. Eli Whitney is credited with inventing a faster, more economical machine.

Although Whitney is credited with the invention, a woman named Catherine Littlefield Greene helped make the cotton gin a reality. Whitney's cotton gin had a flaw in it that he was unable to overcome. Greene corrected the flaw by installing a brush in the cotton gin. Not only did Greene participate in the invention of the cotton gin, she also sold her entire estate to help Whitney take legal action to win all patent rights.

Meet Individual Needs

TACTILE LEARNERS If possible, have students handle some raw cotton so they can see how hard it is to remove the seeds. Before the cotton gin, workers had to pull the seeds out one at a time. (Note: Packets of raw cotton often are available in novelty shops, in craft stores, and from science supply companies that cater to schools.)

Economics

Interdependence and Income Point out that Southern cotton was sold to textile mills in Britain and France as well as to mills in the North.

***Q.* How might this interdependence have affected the attitudes of people in Britain and France toward Southerners and slavery?** Responses will vary but may include acceptance or indifference by mill owners and workers alike.

Visual Analysis

Learn from Diagrams Have students answer the question in the caption. the cotton gin, steamboat, and spinning machines

North and South Disagree

Key Content Summary

As the South's economy continued to rely on agriculture, its people came to depend more and more on Northern manufactured goods, causing friction between people in the two regions. Changing attitudes toward states' rights and slavery caused more serious disagreements.

"PRIMARY SOURCE"

Source: *Economic Aspects of Southern Sectionalism, 1840–1861*. Robert Royal Russel. Arno Press, 1973.

LEARNING FROM DIAGRAMS Turning raw cotton into cloth was a long process that led from farms and plantations to textile mills. The steps shown here are ❶ harvesting the cotton on the plantation; ❷ removing the seeds and cleaning the cotton with the cotton gin; ❸ shipping the cleaned cotton; and ❹ spinning the fibers into threads at the textile mill.

■ *What inventions helped speed up the process of turning raw cotton into cloth?*

With Whitney's cotton gin, cotton could be cleaned and prepared for market in less time. Planters could then sell more cotton and make more money. They sold the cotton to textile mills in the North and in Europe.

Worldwide demand for cotton made both Southern planters and Northern textile-mill owners rich. It also created a demand for more enslaved workers. Planters needed slaves to plant the seeds, weed the fields, pick the cotton, and run the cotton gins. "Cotton is King," said Senator James Henry Hammond of South Carolina, "and the African must be a slave, or there's an end of all things, and soon."

REVIEW ***How did the cotton gin help speed up cotton production?*** It could remove the seeds from the cotton fibers much faster than workers could.

North and South Disagree

By the mid-1800s some Southerners did not like the way growth was booming in the North. As a writer for one Alabama newspaper described it,

> "The North fattens and grows rich upon the South. We depend upon it for our entire supplies. . . . The slaveholder dresses in Northern goods, rides in a Northern saddle. . . . His land is cleared with a Northern axe, and a Yankee clock sits upon his mantel-piece. . . ."

Activity Choices

Meet Individual Needs

COOPERATIVE LEARNING

ADVANCED LEARNERS After discussing the changes brought about by the invention of the cotton gin, have students work in groups to identify another invention and to list the changes it has brought about in people's lives. As the groups present their findings, have students examine the trade-offs regarding each invention and discuss whether or not they think the inventions have had positive effects.

Extend and Enrich

COOPERATIVE LEARNING

REPORT ON COTTON Divide the class into groups, and assign each group one of the following topics: Products Made from Cotton, How Cotton Is Grown, Kinds of Cotton, Bringing Cotton to Market, Making Cotton into Cloth, and Cotton-Growing Regions of the World (including their amount of production). Have the groups use library or Internet resources to prepare oral presentations. After the groups have completed their presentations, have the class compare the importance of cotton today with its importance in 1860.

Bad feelings over growth were not the worst of the troubles between the North and the South. Far worse was the disagreement over states' rights and slavery. Northerners and Southerners had argued since colonial days about whether states should allow slavery. The argument flared up again with the rapid settlement of the western frontier.

Over the years pioneers and soldiers had pushed many of the Indian peoples off their lands. This made it possible for more settlers to move west. The settlers took with them their own ways of life. For settlers from the North, this meant a way of life without slaves. For some settlers from the South, however, this meant taking their enslaved workers with them.

It was not long before the question of the spread of slavery to the frontier became one of the most argued issues in the country. Most white Northerners thought that slavery should go no farther than where it already was—in the South. Most white Southerners believed that slave owners had the right to take their slaves wherever they wanted, including to the West.

The disagreement over slavery led to fierce arguments. Even so, the number of people held as slaves in the South continued to grow. So did the number of enslaved people who were taken west.

REVIEW ***Why did the settlement of the western frontier bring about new arguments over slavery?*** because people disagreed about whether slavery should be allowed on the frontier

LESSON 1 REVIEW

Check Understanding

1. **Remember the Facts** In what ways were the North and the South different?
2. **Recall the Main Idea** What caused people living in the North and the South to disagree during the middle 1800s?

Think Critically

3. **Think More About It** How did the differences between the North and the South affect the ways of life in the two regions?
4. **Cause and Effect** How did the invention of the cotton gin affect Northern textile-mill owners?

Show What You Know

Art Activity Think about how the cotton gin changed life in the 1800s. Create an advertisement for the people of that time that explains how the cotton gin affects those who make and buy cotton and cotton products. Then present your advertisement to the class.

Reteach the Main Idea

MAKE A LIST COOPERATIVE LEARNING Divide the class into small groups, and challenge each group to use the textbook as a resource to list some of the ways that the North and the South were different in the 1800s. Let the group members share and discuss their lists with each other and with other groups.

ACTIVITY BOOK

Reinforce & Extend

Use ACTIVITY BOOK, p. 80.

Geography

MAP THEME

Movement Point out that when people move from one place to another, they take with them their own ways of life.

Q. **Why might settlers from the South want to take their enslaved workers west with them?** They had always had enslaved workers; they would need them if they were to build plantations.

3. CLOSE

Have students consider again the Focus question on page 415.

What might cause people living in different regions to disagree today?

Have students use what they have learned about regional differences in the 1800s to suggest factors that might cause people living in different regions to disagree today.

LESSON 1 REVIEW—Answers

Check Understanding

1. In the North more people were moving to towns and cities to work in factories, while in the South farming remained most important; the North had more people; Northern states ended slavery and opposed its spread west, while Southern states continued to allow it.
2. Southerners resented the North's rapid growth, wealth, and influence; Northerners disapproved of the South's slave economy and the spread of slavery to the West.

Think Critically

3. In the North life was changing quickly from a farm economy to a factory-based economy. In the South farming continued to be the primary income producer.
4. Both planters and mill owners profited from the increased efficiency of the cotton gin.

Show What You Know

Performance Assessment Consider presenting the finished advertisements as video commercials. Have students explain the benefits of this new product.

What to Look For In evaluating the advertisements, look for evidence that students fulfill one of the lesson objectives—to determine the impact of the cotton gin.

MODEL & APPLY SKILLS

Objectives

1. Recognize a trend on a line or bar graph.
2. Analyze trends to describe the connection between cotton production and the growth of slavery.

Vocabulary

trend (p. 420)

1. ACCESS

Ask students to imagine that a restaurant wants to change its menu. To decide which foods to keep and which to eliminate, the manager will keep track of the numbers of each meal sold. He or she will then graph the results to see if there is a trend that indicates the most popular and least popular meals.

Make sure students understand the word *trend*. Point out that both line graphs and bar graphs are useful for identifying trends.

2. BUILD

Have students respond to the questions in Understand the Process.

1. About 100,000 bales of cotton in 1800; about 700,000 bales in 1830; almost 4 million bales in 1860. Have students identify the trend: cotton production increased.
2. Almost 1 million people in 1800; about 2 million people in 1830; almost 4 million people in 1860. The trend is an increase in the number of enslaved workers.

3. CLOSE

Have students link the information in the two graphs by completing the Think and Apply activity. Student responses should indicate that as cotton production increased, the number of enslaved workers increased.

TRANSPARENCY

Use TRANSPARENCY 34.

Skills

Chart and Graph Skills

Use Graphs to Identify Trends

1. Why Learn This Skill?

Some graphs show information that can help you see patterns of change over time. These patterns are called **trends**. A graph showing the number of people living in the United States since 1800 would show that the number has gone up steadily over the years. The trend, then, has been for the population of the United States to increase.

Graphs can show trends that go upward, go downward, or hold steady. Some graphs show trends that change. For example, a graph could show a downward trend for a time and then an upward trend.

2. Understand the Process

Follow the numbered steps to identify the trends shown by the two graphs on this page. The first is a line graph that shows the amount of cotton produced in the United States from 1800 to 1860. The second is a bar graph that shows the number of people enslaved in the United States from 1800 to 1860.

1. Look at the line graph. About how much cotton was produced in 1800? About how much cotton was produced in 1830? About how much cotton was produced in 1860? You can see that the amount of cotton produced from 1800 to 1860 went up. The trend, then, was for cotton production to go up during this period of time.
2. Look at the bar graph. About how many people were enslaved in 1800? About how many people were enslaved in 1830? About how many people were enslaved in 1860? What trend does the bar graph show?

3. Think and Apply

Think about the trends that are shown in these graphs. Write a paragraph that describes what the trends tell you about the connection between cotton production and slavery between 1800 and 1860. Share your paragraph with a classmate.

Cotton Production, 1800–1860

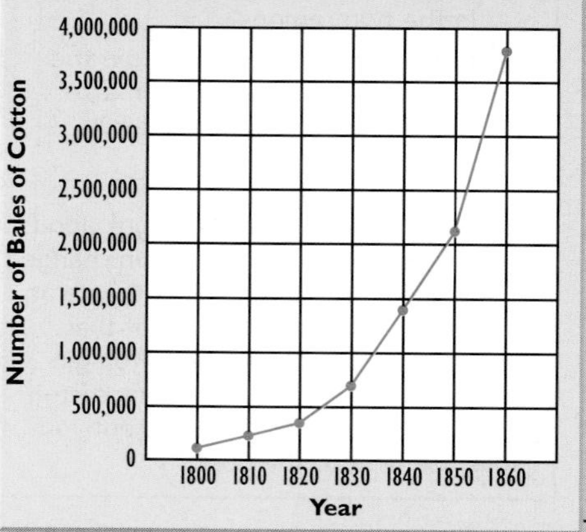

Slavery, 1800–1860

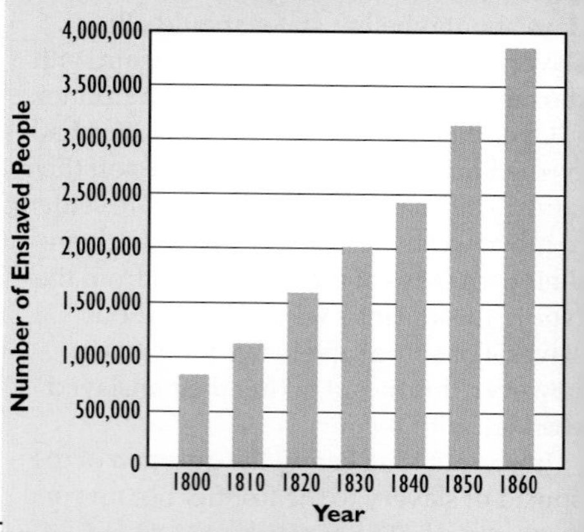

SOURCE: *Historical Statistics of the United States*

ACTIVITY CHOICES

ACTIVITY BOOK

Practice & Apply

Use ACTIVITY BOOK, p. 81.

Reteach the Skill

COOPERATIVE LEARNING

USE GRAPHS TO IDENTIFY TRENDS Have students work together to create a bar graph and a line graph to illustrate a trend of their choice. Have them use a current newspaper or magazine to identify trends. Students may also consult the school librarian for help in finding historical statistics or almanacs.

TECHNOLOGY

Use GRAPH LINKS to complete this graphing activity.

Africans in Slavery and Freedom

LESSON 2

FOCUS In what ways do people today protest against unfair treatment?

Main Idea As you read, look for ways enslaved people protested against being held in slavery.

Vocabulary
- slave code
- overseer
- spiritual
- resist
- Underground Railroad

In 1800 there were nearly 900,000 slaves in the United States. By 1860 there were nearly 4 million. Some Africans—both in the North and in the South—were free. In fact, by 1860 nearly 500,000 free Africans were living in the United States. Yet they did not have the rights of full citizenship. Despite the hardships, most Africans found ways to survive. Some also found ways to fight back.

Life Under Slavery

Most Southern states had laws that shaped the day-to-day lives of enslaved people. These laws were called **slave codes**. Under these codes slaves were not allowed to leave their owners' land, to meet in groups, or to buy or sell goods. Most were not allowed to learn to read and write. They were treated as property, and few were given any special privileges.

Some slave owners hired people called **overseers** to watch the slaves as they worked and to punish them if they fell behind. Slave owners broke up families by selling husbands without their wives, and children without their parents. They punished enslaved people harshly for disobeying.

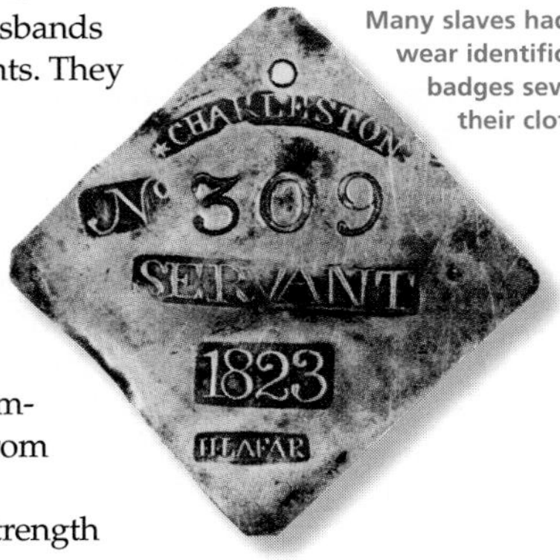

Many slaves had to wear identification badges sewn to their clothing.

"No day ever dawns for the slave, nor is it looked for," one African of the time wrote. "For the slave it is all night—all night, forever."

To help themselves survive, many enslaved people formed close-knit communities. Families, friends, and neighbors helped one another, giving comfort and support. They talked of what they remembered about Africa or what they had heard about it from others. They tried to keep their traditions alive.

Religious beliefs gave many enslaved people the strength they needed to handle the hardships of life under slavery.

Reading Support

DEVELOP THE LESSON VOCABULARY Before students read the lesson, write the lesson vocabulary terms on the board. Have volunteers use each vocabulary term in a sentence. Then have students write one paragraph explaining how each vocabulary term relates to slavery. After students have read the lesson, have them revise their paragraphs as needed to reflect their newly acquired knowledge.

Objectives

1. Summarize the way enslaved Africans were treated and how they helped one another.
2. Analyze the resistance to slavery by enslaved people.
3. Evaluate the effectiveness of the Underground Railroad.
4. Summarize the advantages and disadvantages in the lives of free Africans.

Vocabulary

slave code (p. 421)
overseer (p. 421)
spiritual (p. 422)
resist (p. 422)
Underground Railroad (p. 424)

1. ACCESS

The Focus Question

Help students understand that people who have strong feelings about an injustice sometimes protest through individual or group action. Have students evaluate the methods and effectiveness of different forms of protest.

The Main Idea

In this lesson students discover that many enslaved Africans found ways to protest slavery. After students have read the lesson, have them discuss the risks enslaved Africans took, individually and as a group, to protest or change their situation.

2. BUILD

Life Under Slavery

Key Content Summary

The day-to-day lives of enslaved Africans were tightly controlled by the slave codes. Many slaves suffered physical and emotional punishment. Enslaved Africans formed close-knit communities to support one another.

Civics and Government

Rights and Responsibilities of Citizens Discuss with students why the lawmakers who wrote the slave codes had to define slaves as property. Point out that if slaves had been considered citizens of the United States, their rights to freedom and human dignity would have been protected.

Culture

Shared Humanity and Unique Identity Discuss the ways that enslaved Africans preserved their cultural identity and created new traditions despite the hardships they faced.

Q. **Why do you think it was important for enslaved Africans to preserve their cultural identity?** They were in a strange land, often separated from their families. They wanted to hold on to as much of their identity as possible.

"PRIMARY SOURCE"

Source: *To Be a Slave.* Julius Lester. Scholastic, Inc., 1968.

Fighting Back

Key Content Summary

Many slaves took individual action to resist slavery. A few slaves, such as Nat Turner and some followers of John Brown, led violent rebellions against slave owners.

Enslaved people were sold, usually one at a time, at auctions. Families were often separated because relatives could be bought by different slave owners.

Some slaves expressed their beliefs by singing spirituals. **Spirituals** (SPIR•ih•chuh•wuhlz) are religious songs based on Bible stories. One spiritual told the deepest feelings of those who were enslaved.

> "If I had my way,
> If I had my way,
> If I had my way,
> I'd tear this building down."

REVIEW ***How did people in slave communities help one another?***

They gave comfort and support. They talked about what they remembered from Africa. They kept traditions alive.

Fighting Back

Most enslaved Africans did whatever they could to **resist**, or act against, slavery. Some resisted in quiet ways, secretly damaging the plantation. They broke tools, making the damage look like an accident. They left gates open so that farm animals could escape. They let boats drift away. They hid household goods.

Such actions were dangerous, and slaves had to be careful to escape punishment. Some acted as if they did not understand what they had been told. They said they were sorry and would try to do better. "Got one mind for the boss to see," one slave song went. "Got another mind for what I know is me."

Other slaves chose a more violent way to resist—they rebelled. One rebellion took place in Southampton County, Virginia, on a hot August night in 1831. An enslaved African named Nat Turner led an attack that killed 57 people, among them Turner's owner and the owner's family. Slave owners trying to end the rebellion killed more than 100 slaves. Turner and the other leaders were caught, put on trial, and hanged.

Despite the dangers, the rebellions went on. On the night of October 16, 1859, a white abolitionist named John Brown and a group of followers seized a government storehouse in Harpers Ferry, in what is now West Virginia. The storehouse was filled with

Activity Choices

Link to Health

REPORT ON DISEASES Slaves working on plantations were especially vulnerable to certain ailments, such as those caused by poisonous snake bites, parasites, and mosquitoes. Enslaved people were also vulnerable to diseases caused by nutritional deficiencies, such as pellagra and beriberi. Select individual students to prepare oral reports on these ailments and share their findings with the class. Also have students discuss what foods can be eaten to prevent the various nutrition-related diseases.

Link to Music

SING SONGS Ask a resource person, such as the school music teacher or a musician in the community, to discuss the history and characteristics of the spiritual with the class. Have the resource person teach students to sing some of the more popular spirituals sung by slaves, such as "Swing Low, Sweet Chariot," "Deep River," and "Go Down Moses."

guns. Brown planned to give the guns to slaves so they could fight for their freedom. Like Turner, Brown was caught, put on trial, and hanged.

Such rebellions frightened many white Southerners. As one visitor to the South reported, "I have known times here when not a single planter had a calm night's rest. They never lie down to sleep without . . . loaded pistols at their sides."

REVIEW ***In what ways did enslaved people resist slavery?*** They damaged the plantation. They rebelled.

Running Away

Over the years, thousands of slaves chose another way to resist slavery. They tried to gain their freedom by running away.

Some slaves ran away alone. Others tried to escape with their families or friends. Some planned their escape carefully, slowly gathering what they would need. Others saw a sudden chance and decided quickly—they ran.

Once away from their owners' land, runaways had to find safe places to hide. Many were helped along the way by other slaves. Some were taken in by Indian peoples. Other slaves hid in forests, swamps, or mountains—sometimes for years. One former slave from Virginia remembered,

> "Father got beat up so much that after a while he ran away and lived in the woods. Mama used to send John, my oldest brother, out to the woods with food for Father. . . . Father wasn't the only one hiding in the woods. There was his cousin, Gabriel, that was hiding and a man named Charlie."

Some runaways stayed in hiding, but others went on with their journey until they

Slave owners often sent out posters (above) offering rewards for the return of runaway slaves. This painting by Eastman Johnson (left) shows one family's escape. The painting is called *A Ride for Liberty—The Fugitive Slaves.*

Culture

Thought and Expression Ask students how they would feel if they could not express their anger or hurt feelings after being mistreated by their friends. Help them understand that slaves suffered punishment if they expressed their anger over being enslaved. Discuss the nonverbal actions Africans used to express their feelings about slavery.

Running Away

Key Content Summary

Sometimes individual slaves took great risks to run away from terrible treatment. The runaways hid in the forests, swamps, and mountains, often using the Underground Railroad. They traveled to freedom in the Northern states, Canada, Mexico, and the Caribbean.

History

Patterns and Relationships Have students analyze the cause-and-effect relationships among the following: slavery, the desire for freedom, and becoming a runaway. Then ask students to compare running away with other forms of resistance used by slaves.

"PRIMARY SOURCE"

Source: *To Be a Slave.* Julius Lester. Scholastic, Inc., 1968.

Background

NAT TURNER Nat Turner was a leader among the slaves on the plantation where he lived. He was also a religious preacher who saw visions and claimed that God had sent him a signal—a February 1831 solar eclipse—to plan the uprising. When Turner started the uprising, he had just six slaves with him. By the end of the uprising, more than 60 supporters had joined them. Turner escaped arrest for two months. During that time many white Southerners became fearful, and because of that fear, the slave codes were made harsher and were more strictly enforced.

Link to Language Arts

WRITE A REPORT Have students research and write reports on individual runaway slaves and those who helped them, such as Frederick Douglass, Harriet Tubman, William and Ellen Craft, David Ruggles, Robert Purvis, Henry Highland Garnet, Henry "Box" Brown, William Still, Josiah Henson, Levi Coffin, Laura Haviland, Allan Pinkerton, and Thomas Garrett. *The Underground Railroad* by Sharon Cosner (Franklin Watts, 1991) and *African Americans' Voices of Triumph: Perseverance* by the Editors of Time-Life Books (1993) are excellent sources.

TECHNOLOGY

Use THE AMAZING WRITING MACHINE™ to complete this writing activity.

Culture

Shared Humanity and Unique Identity Help students understand that the desire for freedom created a unique interdependent network between runaways and those who helped them. Point out that both black and white abolitionists were among the conductors of the Underground Railroad.

Q. **Why do you think Harriet Tubman and the other conductors took such serious risks to help runaways?** They felt so strongly about the injustice of slavery that for them the risks were worth taking.

Visual Analysis

Learn from Maps Direct students' attention to the map of the Underground Railroad. Have them speculate on the difficulties the runaway slaves must have faced. Discuss the landforms such as mountains and rivers that would have helped or hindered the slaves in their journey. Then have students answer the caption question. the Mississippi River, the Ohio River, and the Missouri River

Culture

Shared Humanity and Unique Identity Have students discuss some of the hardships to which free Africans were subjected. Ask students to describe how they would feel if they were in constant danger of losing their freedom.

reached free land in the Northern states or in Canada or Mexico. They traveled for weeks or months, some guided only by the North Star. Others found helping hands to lead the way—the brave men and women of the Underground Railroad.

The Underground Railroad was not under the ground, and it was not a real railroad. The **Underground Railroad** was a system of escape routes leading to freedom. Most routes led from the South to the Northern states and to Canada. Some led to Mexico and to the Caribbean.

Members of the Underground Railroad were called conductors. Working at night, conductors led runaways from one hiding place to the next along the routes. These hiding places—barns, attics, secret rooms—were called stations. There the runaways could rest and eat, preparing for the next night's journey to the next station on the route.

Most conductors of the Underground Railroad were either free Africans or white Northerners who opposed slavery. Harriet Tubman, who had escaped from slavery herself, was one of the best-known conductors of the Underground Railroad. During the 1850s Tubman returned to the South 20 times and guided about 300 people to freedom. She proudly claimed, "I never lost a single passenger."

REVIEW ***How did the Underground Railroad help slaves escape?*** Members led runaways from one hiding place to the next along escape routes.

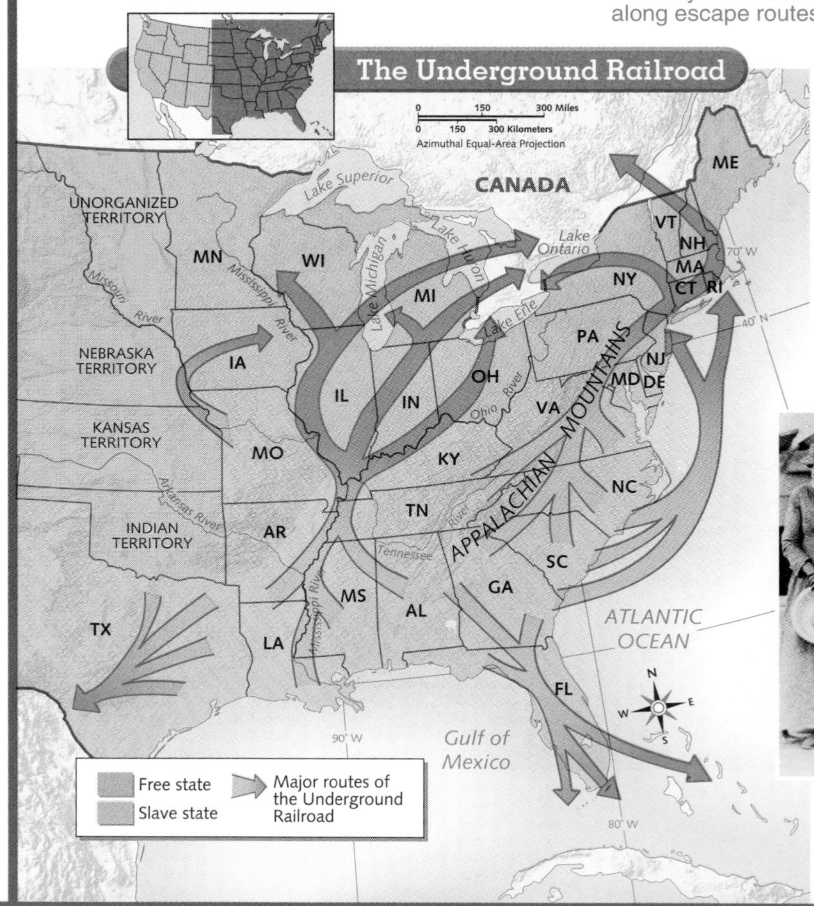

MAP THEME **Movement** This map of the Underground Railroad shows the major routes leading to free land. Harriet Tubman (below) used the routes to help this group of Africans escape from slavery.

■ *Which rivers may have been used as water routes to free land?*

Activity Choices

Meet Individual Needs

TACTILE LEARNERS Have students look at the map of the Underground Railroad routes. Have students trace some of the routes taken by runaways traveling both north and south.

Extend and Enrich

COOPERATIVE LEARNING

MAKE A DISPLAY Divide the class into groups. Assign each group a topic, such as Nonverbal Slave Resistance, Nat Turner's Rebellion, John Brown's Rebellion, Wanted Poster for Runaway Slaves, The Underground Railroad, Harriet Tubman, Frederick Douglass, Support in the Slave Community, James Forten, Thomy Lafon, William C. Nell, and Sarah Mapps Douglass. Have members of each group create illustrations and write an informational paragraph about their topic. Combine the illustrations and paragraphs on a wall or bulletin-board display, and have students discuss the importance of each item.

Technology

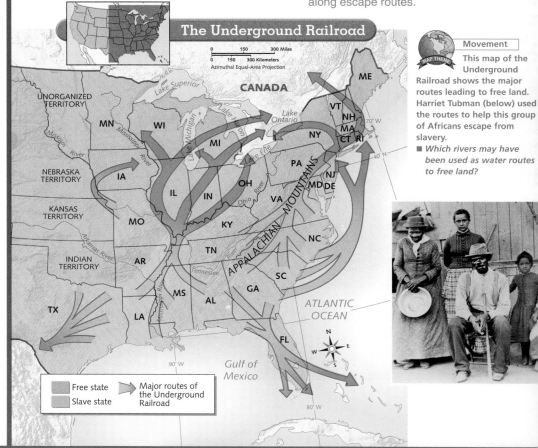

Use THE AMAZING WRITING MACHINE™ RESOURCE PACKAGE to complete the writing activity.

Free Africans

Not all Africans of the time were enslaved. By 1860 nearly half a million free Africans lived in the United States. A few were members of families that had been free since colonial times, or at least since the American Revolution. Some were former slaves who had been freed by their owners. Others had bought their freedom or had become free by running away.

Many free Africans lived in cities, where they had a better chance of finding a job. They worked in many different professions. Some were carpenters, tailors, blacksmiths, and shopkeepers. Others became ministers, doctors, nurses, and teachers.

Some free Africans became quite wealthy. Jehu Jones, for example, owned and ran one of South Carolina's best hotels. James Forten ran a busy sail factory in Philadelphia, where many ships were built. Thomy Lafon made a fortune from his businesses in New Orleans.

For most Africans, however, life was hard no matter where they lived. They were unwelcome in many places and often were treated unfairly. State laws in both the North and the South gave them little freedom. Most were not allowed to vote or to meet in groups. They could not attend certain schools or hold certain jobs. Some free Africans were wrongly accused of being runaways. Others were taken and sold into slavery. The danger of losing the little freedom they had was very real.

SOURCE: *Historical Statistics of the United States*

Africans in the United States, 1800–1860

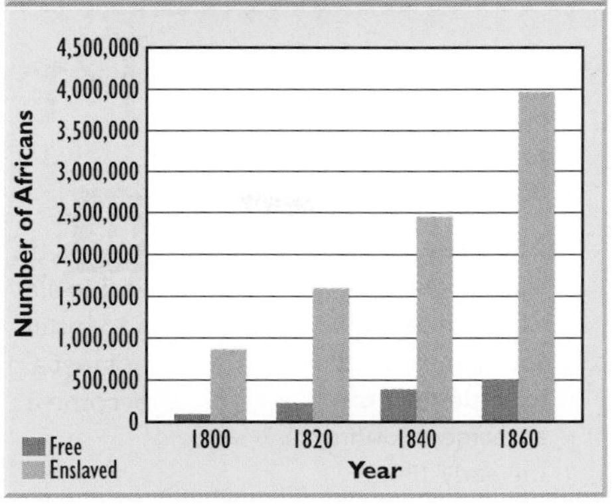

LEARNING FROM GRAPHS This graph shows the numbers of free and enslaved Africans in the United States from 1800 to 1860.

■ *What trends does the graph show?*

REVIEW *What was life like for most free Africans in the early 1800s?*

Life was hard. They were unwelcome in many places. They were treated unfairly. They had little freedom.

LESSON 2 REVIEW

Check Understanding

1. **Remember the Facts** What was the Underground Railroad?
2. **Recall the Main Idea** In what ways did enslaved people protest against being held in slavery?

Think Critically

3. **Personally Speaking** Why do you think many enslaved people were willing to risk their lives to resist being held as slaves? Explain your answer.
4. **Past to Present** In what ways do people today protest if they are denied freedom?

Show What You Know

Poster Activity Think about some symbols of freedom. Look through old magazines and newspapers for pictures that express the meaning of freedom. Cut out the pictures, and use them to create a poster that shows the idea of freedom. Add your poster to a class display titled *Freedom*.

Free Africans

Key Content Summary

Some Africans—former slaves and members of free families—were free. While free Africans had some economic opportunities, they were denied many rights.

Visual Analysis

Learn from Graphs Have students answer the question in the caption. The number of both free and enslaved Africans increased over time; the number of enslaved Africans increased dramatically, while the number of free Africans reached only 500,000.

3. CLOSE

Have students consider again the Focus question on page 421.

In what ways do people today protest against unfair treatment?

Have students use what they have learned in this lesson to compare the ways enslaved Africans protested against unfair treatment with the ways people today protest against such treatment.

LESSON 2 REVIEW—Answers

Check Understanding

1. a series of escape routes and hiding stations that took enslaved Africans from the South to places of freedom
2. They secretly damaged tools, fences, and other property on the plantation; openly rebelled; ran away from slavery; and helped other runaways.

Think Critically

3. The desire for freedom was so strong, and in some cases their treatment was so terrible, that it was worth the risk.
4. People today protest with boycotts, sit-ins, marches, demonstrations, speeches, writings, and sometimes violence.

Show What You Know

Performance Assessment Before students look for pictures, brainstorm some examples of freedom symbols, such as the American flag, peoples of many cultures working together, voting, or going to school.

What to Look For The pictures on students' posters should reflect an understanding of the rights and responsibilities of freedom.

Reteach the Main Idea

MAKE ILLUSTRATIONS (COOPERATIVE LEARNING) Divide the class into four or five groups. Have each group use the textbook as a resource to draw illustrations of the ways enslaved Africans protested being held in slavery. Have students share their illustrations and evaluate the effectiveness of the different forms of protest.

ACTIVITY BOOK

Reinforce & Extend

Use ACTIVITY BOOK, p. 82.

Objectives

1. Analyze Henry Clay's attempts to resolve conflicts over the spread of slavery.
2. Evaluate the impact of the Kansas-Nebraska Act and the Dred Scott decision on the debate over the spread of slavery.
3. Explain the cause-and-effect relationship that brought about the new Republican party and Abraham Lincoln's Senate race.
4. Compare and contrast the views of Abraham Lincoln with those of Stephen Douglas concerning the spread of slavery.

Vocabulary

free state (p. 426) slave state (p. 426)

1. ACCESS

The Focus Question

Ask students to volunteer examples of how people, such as family members, friends, or neighbors, settle disagreements. Have students focus on examples that illustrate compromise.

The Main Idea

In this lesson students analyze the causes and effects of the political conflicts between the North and the South, particularly over the spread of slavery to the West. After students have read the lesson, have them discuss the attempts by political and judicial leaders to settle those conflicts.

2. BUILD

New Compromises

Key Content Summary

Fearing the results of the explosive conflict in Congress over the spread of slavery to the West, Henry Clay took a leadership role in seeking cooperation on the issue. The results of his efforts were the Missouri Compromise and the Compromise of 1850.

LESSON 3

FOCUS
In what ways do people today try to settle disagreements?

Main Idea Read to learn about the ways Northerners and Southerners tried to settle their disagreements during the early 1800s.

Vocabulary
free state
slave state

Facing a National Problem

As time passed, more and more Northerners wanted an end to slavery, while more and more slave owners grew angr and bitter. Americans began to understand that slavery was not just a problem between the people of two regions. It had become a problem for the whole country.

New Compromises

One leader who worked hard to help settle the differences dividing the country was Henry Clay of Kentucky. As a member of Congress, Clay often found himself in the middle of heated arguments about slavery.

The worst arguments broke out over the spread of slavery to the West. Each time groups of settlers asked to join the Union as a new state, the same question arose. Would the nev state be a free state or a slave state? A **free state** did not allow slavery. A **slave state** did.

For a time there were as many free states as slave states. This kept a balance between the North and the South. Then, in 1819, settlers in the Missouri Territory, a part of the Louisiana Purchase, asked to join the Union as a slave state. If this happened, slave states would outnumber free states.

The Missouri question became a heated debate that dragged on for months. Henry Clay worked day and night to help solve the problem. Clay himself owned slaves. But he did not want to see the question of slaver tear the country apart. Finally, in 1820, he persuaded Congress to agree to a compromise—the Missouri Compromise.

Under this plan Missouri would be allowed to join the Union as a slave state. Maine would join as a free state. This would keep the balance between free states and slave states. Then an imaginary line would be drawn through the rest of the lands gained in the Louisiana Purchase. Slavery would be allowed south of the line. Places north of the line would be free.

Henry Clay became known as the Great Compromiser because of his work to help settle the differences between the North and the South.

ACTIVITY CHOICES

Reading Support

COMPARE AND CONTRAST Provide students with the following visual framework and ask them to complete the chart.

FACING A NATIONAL PROBLEM

Missouri Compromise	Compromise of 1850	Kansas-Nebraska Act	Dred Scott Decision
• Admitted Missouri as a slave state • Admitted Maine as a free state • Divided Louisiana Purchase lands into slave and free areas	• Admitted California as a free state • Voters in the lands won from Mexico to make decisions about slavery • Fugitive Slave Law included	• Voters in Kansas and Nebraska to decide whether or not to allow slavery • Led to fighting in Kansas over slavery	• Denied Dred Scott his freedom • Declared Missouri Compromise unconstitutional

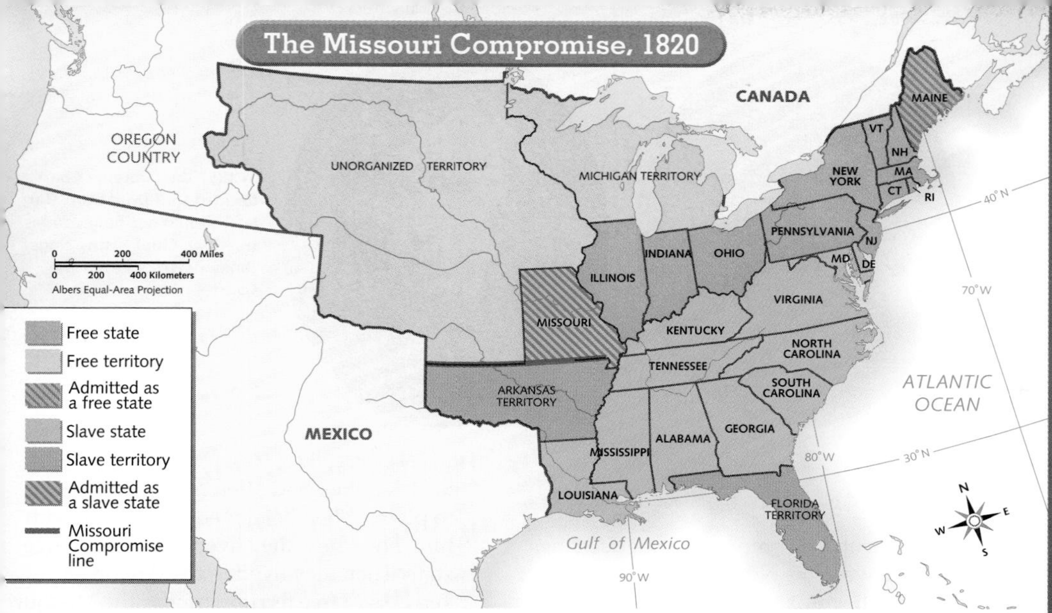

MAP THEME **Regions** The Missouri Compromise line divided lands that could join the Union as free states from lands that could join as slave states.

■ *Which two states were admitted to the Union as part of the compromise? Were they admitted as free states or as slave states?*

The Missouri Compromise kept the peace for nearly 30 years. During this time six new states joined the Union, but the number of free states and slave states remained equal.

Then, in 1848, the United States gained new lands after winning the war with Mexico. Settlers in California, a part of these new lands, soon asked to join the Union as a free state.

Henry Clay once again found himself in the middle of an argument in Congress over slavery. Once again he worked toward a compromise. This plan became known as the Compromise of 1850.

Under this compromise California joined the Union as a free state. The rest of the lands won from Mexico were divided into two territories—New Mexico and Utah. The people there would decide for their territory whether or not to allow slavery.

The Compromise of 1850 also had a new law dealing with runaway slaves. Under the Fugitive Slave Law, anyone caught helping slaves to escape would be punished. People who found runaway slaves—even runaways who had reached the North—had to return them to the South.

Henry Clay, who became known as the Great Compromiser, died in 1852. He never gave up hope that the country would find a peaceful way to settle its differences. On a marker by his grave in Lexington, Kentucky, are the words *I know no North—no South—no East—no West.*

REVIEW ***What two compromises on the spread of slavery did Congress reach?*** the Missouri Compromise and the Compromise of 1850

Civics and Government

Political Institutions and Processes Point out that it was important to maintain a balance between the number of free states and slave states because each new state brought with it new votes in Congress. If a new free state joined the Union, votes in Congress could tip against slavery. If a new slave state joined the Union, votes could tip in favor of slavery.

Q. **How did the Missouri Compromise temporarily quiet the concerns in Congress?** The number of free states and slave states stayed the same.

Civics and Government

Purposes and Types of Government Make sure students understand that by admitting California as a free state, there would be more free state votes than slave state votes in Congress. Discuss the causes of the new conflicts that led to the Compromise of 1850.

Visual Analysis

Learn from Maps Have students answer the question in the caption. Missouri and Maine; Missouri was a slave state and Maine was a free state.

Background

HENRY CLAY Born in Virginia, Henry Clay grew up under the guidance of his father, a Baptist minister. Clay had little chance for formal schooling, but he learned on his own and studied law as a young man. During his 42-year tenure in Congress representing Kentucky, Clay first served in the House of Representatives and then in the Senate. He proposed the "American System," which called for a strong national defense, a national system of roads and canals, and the protection of American industry through tariffs on imported goods. The North wanted the tariffs; the South did not. Henry Clay ran for President five times, but he never won.

Meet Individual Needs

AUDITORY LEARNERS Tell students to imagine that they are members of Congress who are considering the request by the Missouri Territory to become a state. Ask several volunteers to serve as members of Congress from free states, and ask other volunteers to serve as members of Congress from slave states. Then have the two groups debate whether Missouri should be admitted as a free state or as a slave state. Discuss with the class how the Missouri Compromise settled the issue.

Hopes for Peace Fade

Key Content Summary

The Kansas-Nebraska Act and the Dred Scott decision rekindled the bitter conflict over the expansion of slavery into new territories. The Supreme Court's decision in the Scott case challenged the constitutionality of the Missouri Compromise.

Civics and Government

Political Processes Remind students that the Supreme Court can review the constitutionality of laws. Ask students to explain the Court's decision to deny Dred Scott his freedom and declare the Missouri Compromise unconstitutional. Make sure they understand that defining slaves as property was the key to the Court's decision.

Q. **Which groups of people in the United States were probably most upset by the Court's decision?** enslaved and free Africans; abolitionists; Northerners

In 1857 the Supreme Court decided that Dred Scott (far left) should not be given his freedom. Chief Justice Roger Taney (left) spoke for the Court.

Hopes for Peace Fade

Even with the compromises, bad feelings grew between the North and the South. In 1854 harsh words turned to violence.

The problem began when Congress passed the Kansas-Nebraska Act. This new law changed the rules of the Missouri Compromise. Under the compromise, slavery would not have been allowed in the territories of Kansas and Nebraska. Under the Kansas-Nebraska Act, people living in those lands were now given the chance to decide for themselves whether to allow slavery. They would decide by voting.

Kansas quickly became the center of attention. People for and against slavery rushed into the territory, hoping to help decide the vote. It was not long before fighting broke out between the two sides. More than 200 people were killed in the dispute that came to be known as Bleeding Kansas.

While fighting went on in Kansas, those against slavery suffered another defeat. In 1857 the Supreme Court decided the case of an enslaved African named Dred Scott. Scott had asked the Court for his freedom. The Court said no.

Scott argued that he should be free because he had once lived on free land. Scott's owner had often moved from place to place. When he moved, Scott went with him. For a time they lived in Illinois, a free state. Then they lived in the Wisconsin Territory, a free territory under the Missouri Compromise.

After Scott's owner died, Scott took his case to court. The case moved from judge to judge until it landed in the Supreme Court. There Scott lost his fight for freedom. Chief Justice Roger B. Taney (TAW•nee) said that Scott had "none of the rights and privileges" of American citizens. He was a slave, Taney said. Living on free land did not change that.

Taney had more to say. He declared that Congress had no right to outlaw slavery in the Wisconsin Territory to begin with. The Constitution protects people's right to own property. Slaves, he said, were property. He believed that the Missouri Compromise was keeping people in some places from owning property. This, he said, went against the Constitution.

Many people had hoped that the Dred Scott decision would settle the battle over slavery once and for all. Instead, it made the problem worse.

REVIEW ***Why did the Supreme Court deny freedom to Dred Scott?*** The Court said that slaves were property and had none of the rights and privileges of citizens.

Activity Choices

Background

ROGER B. TANEY Roger B. Taney was born to a wealthy slave-owning family in Maryland. He studied law and became Maryland's attorney general in 1827. By 1835 he was chief justice of the United States Supreme Court. Before the Dred Scott case, Taney had ruled that any slave who voluntarily returned to a slave state after living in a free state would be treated as a slave. During the Dred Scott case, five of the nine justices were Southerners. Taney hoped that the Court's decision would end the agitation by abolitionists.

Meet Individual Needs

ENGLISH LANGUAGE LEARNERS Have students fill in a cause-and-effect chart for the events in this lesson. You may wish to provide students with the causes and have them fill in the effects.

Causes	Effects
New states join the Union	Arguments broke out over slavery
Keeping number of free and slave states equal	Missouri Compromise
California wants to join Union	Compromise of 1850
The Court rules enslaved people are property	People are angry and violence occurs

Abraham Lincoln Works for Change

The Kansas-Nebraska Act and the Dred cott decision caused violence and anger that aught the attention of Americans across the ountry. Soon new leaders began to speak out.)ne of these leaders was Abraham Lincoln.

Abraham Lincoln had grown up on the rontier in Kentucky and Indiana. Like other ioneers, he had had a hard life. He worked o many hours on the family farm that he ften could not go to school. But he borrowed ooks and read all he could.

When Lincoln was a young man, he noved with his family to Illinois. There he eld several jobs before serving in the state egislature. He studied law, and in time he ecame a lawyer. In the late 1840s he served term in Congress. During these years the natter of the spread of slavery to the West ecame an important question.

Lincoln was against the spread of slavery. Ie did not think the government had the ight to end all slavery in the country. But e hoped that if slavery were not allowed to pread, it would one day die out.

Lincoln joined a new political party that vas formed to fight the spread of slavery. 'his party was called the Republican party. Ie even thought about running again for government office. The Kansas-Nebraska Act and the Dred Scott decision helped him make up his mind. In 1858 Lincoln entered a race for the United States Senate. He ran against Stephen A. Douglas, who had written the Kansas-Nebraska Act.

REVIEW ***Why did Abraham Lincoln join the Republican party?*** to fight against the spread of slavery

his ticket was to a fair held in 1858 where money vas raised to fight slavery.

The Lincoln-Douglas Debates

Few people could have been more different from each other than Lincoln and Douglas. Abraham Lincoln was a tall, thin man from the frontier. His thick, black hair looked uncombed. He wore plain, dark clothes that were a bit rumpled. He was not well known around the country. In fact, few people outside of Illinois had heard of him.

Stephen Douglas was heavy and a full foot shorter than Lincoln. He was well educated and wore fine clothes—a ruffled shirt, tailored suit, and polished boots. He was already serving in the Senate, and many Americans across the country knew of him. People called him the Little Giant.

In one way, though, Lincoln and Douglas were very much alike. They were both powerful public speakers. In the summer of 1858, the two men traveled around Illinois and debated questions that were important to voters. Huge crowds turned out to listen. Everyone wanted to hear Lincoln and Douglas debate about whether slavery should be allowed in the West.

Stephen Douglas argued that each new state should decide the slavery question for itself. That was what the country's founders had allowed, he said, and that was what the new Kansas-Nebraska Act allowed.

Abraham Lincoln disagreed. He said that "the framers of the Constitution intended and expected" slavery to end. The problem, he pointed out, was more than a question of

Abraham Lincoln Works for Change

Key Content Summary

The conflict over the expansion of slavery into western territories led to the formation of the Republican party and drew Abraham Lincoln into running again for government office. Lincoln, a self-taught lawyer, sought to take the United States Senate seat from Stephen Douglas.

History

People and Events Across Time and Place Ask students to brainstorm words that describe Abraham Lincoln, and write the words on the board. Have them decide what qualities might have made Lincoln a good leader in the United States Senate.

The Lincoln-Douglas Debates

Key Content Summary

The conflict over the spread of slavery became the focus of the debates between Lincoln and Douglas in the Illinois race for the U.S. Senate seat. Douglas thought the decision about slavery should be made by the states, while Lincoln thought slavery should not be allowed to spread because it was wrong.

Link to Language Arts

WRITE TO PERSUADE When Lincoln accepted the nomination to become a candidate for Illinois senator, his acceptance speech contained these famous words: "A house divided against itself cannot stand. . . . I believe this government cannot endure permanently half slave and half free." Ask each student to write a speech to persuade voters that slavery should end. Have them use Lincoln's words as either the beginning or the ending of the speech.

TECHNOLOGY

Use THE AMAZING WRITING MACHINE™ RESOURCE PACKAGE to complete this writing activity.

Extend and Enrich

COOPERATIVE LEARNING

MAKE A TIME LINE Have students work together to plan a time line that provides dates and illustrations for the years 1819–1858. Have students include important dates and events from the lesson and research other important dates and events in the lives of Clay, Lincoln, and Douglas during that same time period.

TECHNOLOGY

Use TIMELINER™ to complete this activity.

Auditory Learning

Interpret Primary Sources Ask a volunteer to read aloud Lincoln's quotation. Have students restate the quotation in their own words.

> **"PRIMARY SOURCE"**
>
> Source: *Created Equal? The Complete Lincoln-Douglas Debates of 1858*. Paul M. Angle, ed. The University of Chicago Press, 1958.

3. CLOSE

Have students consider again the Focus question on page 426.

In what ways do people today try to settle disagreements?

Have students list and evaluate the different ways Americans tried to settle their disagreements over the expansion of slavery in the 1800s. Have them compare their lists with the ways people try to settle political and social disagreements today.

LESSON 3 REVIEW—Answers

Check Understanding

1. the Kansas-Nebraska Act and the Dred Scott decision
2. legislative compromise in the Missouri Compromise and the Compromise of 1850

Think Critically

3. The Kansas-Nebraska Act permitted the people of Kansas and Nebraska to vote on whether they wanted slavery or not, even though the Missouri Compromise would not have allowed slavery in these territories. The Dred Scott decision declared the Missouri Compromise unconstitutional.
4. Students' responses will vary.

Show What You Know

Performance Assessment Consider setting up the interviews in a way that is similar to those on television news programs, with introductions by an anchorperson.

What to Look For In evaluating the students' questions and answers, look for an understanding of the important issues as they relate to each individual being interviewed.

Stephen Douglas and Abraham Lincoln held seven debates in 1858. This painting shows Lincoln (standing) and Douglas (to Lincoln's right) debating in Charleston, Illinois.

what each state wanted. It was a question of right and wrong. Slavery should not spread to the West, he said, because slavery was wrong. Lincoln said,

> "That is the real issue. That is the issue that will continue in this country when these poor tongues of Judge Douglas and myself shall be silent. It is the eternal struggle between these two principles—right and wrong—throughout the world."

Stephen Douglas won the race for the Senate. But people around the country now knew who Abraham Lincoln was.

REVIEW *How did Lincoln's views differ from those of Douglas?*

LESSON 3 REVIEW

Check Understanding

1. **Remember the Facts** What events led Abraham Lincoln to speak out against slavery?
2. **Recall the Main Idea** In what ways did the Northerners and the Southerners try to settle their disagreements during the early 1800s?

Think Critically

3. **Think More About It** How was the Missouri Compromise changed by the Kansas-Nebraska Act and the Dred Scott decision?
4. **Past to Present** Do you think it is still important for leaders today to hold debates before elections? Explain your answer.

Show What You Know

Simulation Activity Imagine that you have been asked to interview Henry Clay, Dred Scott, Stephen Douglas, or Abraham Lincoln. Write the questions you would ask and the answers the person might give. With a classmate, practice role-playing your interview. Present your interview to the class.

Douglas thought each new state should decide the slavery question fo itself. Lincoln thought slavery was wrong and that it should not spread.

ACTIVITY CHOICES

ACTIVITY BOOK

Reinforce & Extend

Use ACTIVITY BOOK, p. 83.

Reteach the Main Idea

COOPERATIVE LEARNING

DEBATE THE ISSUES Divide the class into five groups, and assign each group one of these topics: The Missouri Compromise, The Compromise of 1850, The Kansas-Nebraska Act, The Dred Scott Case, The Lincoln-Douglas Debates. Have each group prepare and present a five-minute debate that provides both sides of the issue(s). Ask each group to summarize how the disagreements over its particular issue(s) were settled. Then ask students to discuss what they learned about settling disagreements.

A Time for Hard Decisions

LESSON 4

FOCUS
When must people today make difficult decisions in their lives?

Main Idea Read to learn about the difficult decisions Americans had to make in 1860 and 1861.

Vocabulary
Confederacy

In 1860 Americans prepared to choose a new President. ney listened to speeches. They read newspapers. They atched parades. They also worried. Anger and bitterness ere driving the North and the South farther apart than ever. ould a new President hold the country together?

The Election of 1860

The question of the spread of slavery to the West seemed to all that people talked about during the election of 1860. ephen Douglas ran as a member of the Democratic party. e argued that western settlers should decide for themselves hether to allow slavery. However, many Democrats in the uth backed another leader—John Breckinridge of entucky. Breckinridge thought that the government ould allow slavery everywhere in the West.

Abraham Lincoln ran as a member of the Republican party. e spoke out strongly against the spread of slavery. He omised not to stop slavery in the South, where it was ready practiced. But he said that he hoped it would one ay end there, too.

Many white Southerners worried about what would appen if Lincoln became President. They thought that e problem was far greater than the question of slavery. ey believed that their whole way of life was being tacked. Some said that their states would secede om the Union if Lincoln was elected.

On election day, November 6, 1860, Lincoln won e Presidency. Southern leaders did not wait long fore carrying out their threat. On December 20, uth Carolina's leaders declared that

> " . . . the United States of America is hereby dissolved. "

With these words South Carolina seceded from the nion. The state refused to have a President who was against avery.

A supporter of Stephen Douglas wore this campaign button during the election of 1860.

Reading Support

ANTICIPATION GUIDE Before students read the lesson, ask them which of the following statements they might associate with the North and which they might associate with the South. Students may correct their guesses as they read.

1. We will secede if Lincoln is elected President. South
2. We must preserve the Union. North
3. We have joined the Confederacy. South
4. We must fight to defend Fort Sumter. North
5. We will take over Fort Sumter. South

Objectives

1. Compare and contrast the diverse views of Americans on the spread of slavery, and analyze the effect of these views on the election of 1860 and events that followed it.
2. Evaluate the choices facing the leaders of the Union and the Confederacy in 1861, and discuss the consequences of the leaders' decisions.

Vocabulary

Confederacy (p. 432)

1. ACCESS

The Focus Question

Discuss circumstances in which people must make difficult decisions. Lead students to realize that decisions that affect many people or cause conflict are often the most difficult decisions to make.

The Main Idea

In this lesson students learn about the difficult decisions facing Americans just before the outbreak of the Civil War. After students have read the lesson, discuss the issues of 1860 and 1861 concerning slavery and states' rights.

2. BUILD

The Election of 1860

Key Content Summary

As the election of 1860 approached, candidates took conflicting positions on the spread of slavery. Fearing they would lose their whole way of life after the election of President Lincoln, seven Southern states seceded from the Union.

"PRIMARY SOURCE"

Source: *Encyclopedia of American History.* Richard B. Morris and Jeffrey B. Morris, eds. HarperCollins, 1996.

Civics and Government

Political Processes Write the names *Breckinridge*, *Douglas*, and *Lincoln* on the board. As students explain the political position of each candidate, write the information under each name. Discuss the differences among the candidates' viewpoints, and ask students to speculate on which states would vote for which candidate.

Visual Analysis

Learn from Pictures Ask students to examine the campaign poster on this page.

Q. **How would a campaign poster for a presidential election today differ from the one shown here?** The candidates would probably be smiling. The words would be larger. Overall, the poster would be more lively.

Fort Sumter

Key Content Summary

President Lincoln's goal of keeping Fort Sumter under Union control conflicted with Jefferson Davis's goal of establishing Confederate control of the fort. Although both leaders carefully considered their choices and the possible outcomes, their final decisions resulted in war.

There were six other states—Mississippi, Florida, Alabama, Georgia, Louisiana, and Texas—that soon followed South Carolina's example.

Together these seven states formed a new country. They called the new country the Confederate States of America, or the **Confederacy** (kuhn•FEH•duh•ruh•see). They elected a Mississippi senator, Jefferson Davis, as president. The United States was now split in two.

REVIEW ***What did seven Southern states decide to do after Lincoln was elected President?*** secede from the Union

This poster (above) urged people to vote for Lincoln and his running mate, Hannibal Hamlin. The gold ax (right) was a campaign pin worn by Lincoln's supporters. The "WIDE AWAKE" on the handle meant that his supporters were "wide awake" to dangers that might affect the Union.

Fort Sumter

Abraham Lincoln had little time to celebrate winning the election. He wanted to save the Union—to keep the country together. Yet seven states had said that they were no longer part of the Union. What would he do about those states?

Some people told Lincoln to let the seven states go. Others said that he should give in on the slavery question and hope that the Southern states would return. Still others fe that Lincoln should use the army to end the revolt.

Lincoln thought a great deal about his choices. He hoped to prevent a war. "We are not enemies, but friends," Lincoln told Southerners after taking the oath of office as President of the United States on March 4, 1861. "We must not be enemies." The very next day, however, Lincoln received an important message. When he read it, he knew that time was running out. The message was from Major Robert Anderson. Anderson was the commander of Fort Sumter.

When the Southern states seceded, they had taken over post offices, forts, and other federal government property. Fort Sumter, which was located on an island off the coast of South Carolina, near Charleston, was one of the few forts in the Confederate States of America that remained in Union hands. The message from Major Anderson said that supplies at the fort were almost gone. If new supplies were not sent soon, Anderson would have to surrender the fort to the Confederacy.

Lincoln knew that he had an important decision to make. His goal was to keep Fort Sumter under Union control. But several problems stood in the way. The most important problem was that the fort was running out of supplies.

Lincoln thought very carefully about his choices. Each one had its own possible

Activity Choices

Background

DOUGLAS AND BRECKINRIDGE A senator from Illinois, Stephen Douglas was nominated for President by the Northern wing of the Democratic party. When the Civil War broke out, Douglas gave his support to Lincoln. However, he saw only the beginning of the war. While on a speaking engagement to build support for the Union cause in June 1861, Douglas was stricken with typhoid and died. When he was nominated as the Southern Democratic candidate for President, John Breckinridge was Vice President of the United States under James Buchanan. Although a strong Southern sympathizer, Breckinridge worked to stop the Southern states from seceding and to prevent civil war. After the war had begun, however, he went over to the Confederacy, becoming a general and fighting in several major battles.

Link to Language Arts

WRITE A DIARY ENTRY To enhance students' understanding of Lincoln's and Davis's decision-making processes, have each student compose a diary entry that might have been written by each leader. In each entry students should list the leader's goal, the choices available to him, and the consequences of each choice. Volunteers may read their entries to the class.

Technology

Use THE AMAZING WRITING MACHINE™ to complete this writing activity.

nsequences. He could send supplies to the rt. If he did, the Southerners might attack. e could send troops to the fort. If he did, e Southerners would surely attack. He uld choose to do nothing at all. By doing othing, he would really be giving the fort the Confederacy because Major Anderson ould have to surrender.

Finally, President Lincoln made the choice thought was the best. He decided that he ould send supply ships to the fort. Then he aited to see how the Southerners would act.

Now Confederate president Jefferson avis had to make a decision. His goal as to take control of Fort Sumter for the onfederate states. His problem was that nion troops held the fort. President Lincoln

GEOGRAPHY

Fort Sumter

Fort Sumter was one of several forts built to protect American coastlines following the War of 1812. Building the fort was a long, difficult job. Workers first had to build the island on which the fort would stand. Then they built the fort itself, with walls 5 to 10 feet (1.5–3 m) thick and nearly 40 feet (12 m) high. Today Fort Sumter is part of the national park system.

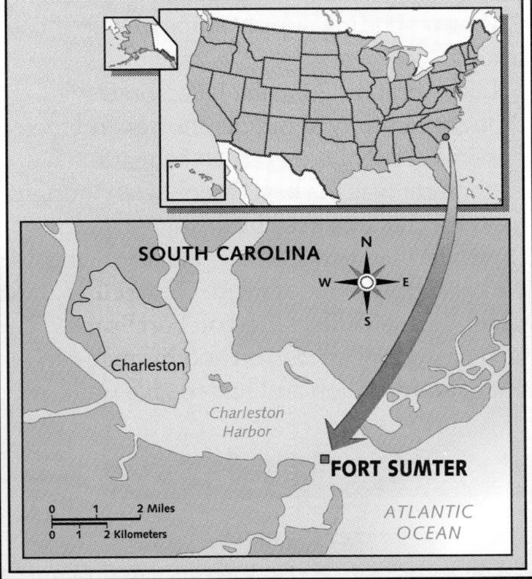

is scene shows the Confederate attack on Fort mter.

433

History

Turning Points Have students analyze why seven Southern states decided they should form the Confederate States of America with their own president. Discuss the difficult decisions Lincoln faced as he started his presidency. Make sure students understand that the conflict was not just over slavery, but also over states' rights.

Civics and Government

Purposes of Government Lincoln and Davis had opposing goals that created tension and finally led to conflict. Have students discuss whether there were any alternatives to war.

Q. **Why do you think Lincoln chose to send supply ships first?** He wanted to prevent fighting and thought sending supplies was a precautionary action.

Why do you think Davis chose to attack the fort? He believed that it was the most effective way of achieving his goal.

Visual Analysis

Interpret Pictures Direct students' attention to the maps of Fort Sumter. Have students discuss why Fort Sumter was a strategic location for the Southern states. Make sure students note in particular the location of Charleston, an important Southern port city.

Smithsonian Institution®

Go to the Internet site at *http://www.si.edu/harcourt/socialstudies* to examine the exhibit "A Nation Divided" in Binding the Nation at the National Postal Museum.

Meet Individual Needs

ADVANCED LEARNERS
Have students conduct library research and prepare an oral presentation, with illustrations, about Jefferson Davis and the establishment of the Confederate States of America. Make sure they include the Confederacy's capital city, its form of government, and some of the other key Confederate leaders.

Extend and Enrich

COOPERATIVE LEARNING

INVESTIGATE AND DEBATE To make students aware that Lincoln's decision to send supplies to Fort Sumter was opposed by most of his Cabinet, divide the class into groups, and challenge them to investigate what members of Lincoln's Cabinet thought should be done instead. Have students use library resources and note in particular the views of William H. Seward, Lincoln's secretary of state. After the groups are comfortable with the different viewpoints, select students to debate Lincoln's decision to send supplies to the fort.

Visual Analysis

Learn from Time Lines Have students answer the questions in the caption. South Carolina; Arkansas, Tennessee, and North Carolina

3. CLOSE

Have students consider again the Focus question on page 431.

When must people today make difficult decisions in their lives?

Encourage students to reflect on what they have learned in this lesson about the choices facing the leaders of the Union and the Confederacy, the decisions they finally made, and the impact of their decisions.

LESSON 4 REVIEW—Answers

Check Understanding

1. the election of Abraham Lincoln to the presidency
2. They decided who to vote for as the new President; some states decided to secede; Lincoln and Davis had to decide what to do about Fort Sumter.

Think Critically

3. Accept all responses that students can reasonably defend; for example, yes, because the Union troops needed help and sending supplies was a nonviolent method of supporting the fort.
4. It was a fort under Union control in Confederate territory.

Show What You Know

Performance Assessment Interested students might create an entire front page of a newspaper, choosing to write from the viewpoint of the North or the South.

What to Look For In evaluating students' headlines, look for evidence that they understand the lesson objectives to evaluate the choices facing the leaders of the Union and the Confederacy in 1861 and to discuss the consequences of the leaders' decisions.

The Union Breaks Apart

November 1860	December 1860	January 1861	February 1861	March 1861	April 1861	May 186
Lincoln is elected President	South Carolina secedes	Mississippi, Florida, Alabama, Georgia, and Louisiana secede	Texas secedes	Lincoln is inaugurated President	Southern troops attack Fort Sumter Virginia secedes	Arkansas Tennesse and Nort Carolina secede

LEARNING FROM TIME LINES This time line shows when each of 11 Southern states seceded from the Union.

■ *Which state was the first to secede from the Union? Which states were the last to secede?*

was now sending supply ships to help those troops.

Like Abraham Lincoln, Jefferson Davis thought carefully about his choices and their possible consequences. Then he made what he thought was the best choice, even though he knew that one possible result was war. Davis decided to attack the fort before the Union supply ships arrived. On April 12, 1861, Confederate soldiers fired on Fort Sumter. The next day Major Anderson and his men ran out of ammunition and had to give up.

Davis had met his goal. Lincoln had not. Lincoln quickly called for Americans to join an army to stop the rebellion. Fearing that Northern armies would march into the South, the states of Virginia, Arkansas, Tennessee, and North Carolina joined the seven states already in the Confederacy. No the country was even more divided. The Civil War had begun.

REVIEW ***What did Davis decide to do when Lincoln said he would send supplies to Fort Sumter?*** attack the fort before the supply ships arrived

LESSON 4 REVIEW

Check Understanding

1. **Remember the Facts** What event led South Carolina's leaders to secede from the Union?
2. **Recall the Main Idea** What difficult decisions did Americans make in 1860 and 1861?

Think Critically

3. **Personally Speaking** Do you think Abraham Lincoln made the right decision when he decided to send supplies to Fort Sumter? Explain your answer.
4. **Think More About It** Why do you think Fort Sumter was important to both Abraham Lincoln and Jefferson Davis?

Show What You Know

Writing Activity Write two headlines that could have appeared in newspapers following the attack on Fort Sumter. The first should be a headline for a newspaper in the North. The second should be a headline for a newspaper in the South. Present the headlines to your classmates.

ACTIVITY CHOICES

ACTIVITY BOOK

Reinforce & Extend

Use ACTIVITY BOOK, p. 84.

Reteach the Main Idea

COOPERATIVE LEARNING

MAKE A CHART On the board, draw a two-column chart with the lesson section heads as column headings: *The Election of 1860* and *Fort Sumter*. Divide the class into small groups, and instruct them to copy the chart and work together with other group members to identify and list difficult decisions Americans made in relation to the two events. Each student in the group should complete a chart. When groups have finished, students may use their charts to participate in a class discussion of the main idea of the lesson.

Critical Thinking Skills

Skills

Make a Thoughtful Decision

. Why Learn This Skill?

Did you have to make a decision today? Did ɔu have to decide whether to go somewhere ith your friends? Did you have to decide how settle a disagreement with someone?

You make many decisions every day. Some ecisions are easy. Other decisions are more ifficult. The difficult ones may require more ought because your choices may have lasting ɔnsequences.

. Remember What You Have Read

You have read about the difficult decisions braham Lincoln and Jefferson Davis had to ake as supplies ran out at Fort Sumter in ɔuth Carolina. The ways in which these aders came to their decisions show how a oughtful decision can be made. Think again ɔout what happened.

- What goal did each leader have?
- What steps did each leader follow in making a decision?
- What choice did each leader make?
- What were the consequences of Lincoln's choice? of Davis's choice?

3. Understand the Process

You can use similar steps to help make a thoughtful decision.

- Identify your goal.
- Think about problems that may keep you from reaching your goal.
- Identify the actions that you could take to reach your goal.
- Think about the possible consequences of each action.
- List your choices for action. Begin with those that might have the best results, and end with those that might have the worst results.
- Make the choice that seems best.
- Put your choice into action.
- Think about whether your choice helped you reach your goal.

4. Think and Apply

BUILDING CITIZENSHIP

Think about a decision you made at school. What steps did you follow? What choice did you make? What were the consequences? Do you think you made a thoughtful decision? Explain your answers.

Abraham Lincoln (far left)
Jefferson Davis (left)

eteach the Skill

COOPERATIVE LEARNING

MAKE A CLASSROOM DECISION Have the class use the steps in Understand the Process to arrive at a decision that needs to be ıade concerning some classroom procedure. For exam- le, limited resources in the classroom or library may ften pose a problem for students. The goal in this case for all students to have the benefit of these resources. hoices may include working in groups or rotating ssignments so that students do not need the same esource at the same time. Have the class work through ıe steps until they arrive at a decision. Then have them onsider carefully whether their decision will help reach ıe desired goal.

ACTIVITY BOOK

Practice & Apply

Use ACTIVITY BOOK, p. 85.

TRANSPARENCY

Use TRANSPARENCY 35.

MODEL & APPLY SKILLS

Objectives

1. Analyze how Lincoln and Davis came to their decisions concerning Fort Sumter.
2. Analyze a personal decision.

1. ACCESS

Brainstorm with the class all the decisions they have made today, starting with what to have for breakfast and what to wear to school. Point out that decision making is an important skill we all use.

2. BUILD

Review the events that occurred at Fort Sumter as the Civil War began. Have the students answer the questions in Remember What You Have Read.

1. Lincoln wanted to save the Union. Davis wanted to take over the fort and strengthen the Confederacy.
2. Each leader thought carefully about his choices and their consequences.
3. Lincoln shipped supplies to help his troops. Davis attacked the fort before the Union's supplies arrived.
4. Lincoln lost control of the fort. Davis won the fort for the Confederacy. The Civil War was started.

Work through the steps in Understand the Process with the students, using Lincoln's and Davis's decision making as examples. Have students speculate on what might have happened if Lincoln or Davis had acted differently.

3. CLOSE

Have students complete the Think and Apply activity individually. Have volunteers share their experiences with the class, noting which of the steps in Understand the Process they used. Look for an understanding of the fact that thoughtful decision making is a process.

COUNTERPOINTS

Objectives

1. Recognize that not all Southerners supported secession.
2. Identify contrasting viewpoints held by Southerners on the issue of secession.

1. ACCESS

Ask students whether they have ever disagreed with someone over an issue or idea that seemed important. Have them relate how they expressed their views. Remind students that in 1860 Americans were speaking and writing about many different issues.

2. BUILD

Identify the Issue and the Speakers

Have students read pages 436–437, and lead a class conversation to build understanding. Ask students to determine who is speaking and what issue they are discussing.

Q. **What issue is being discussed?** whether or not the Southern states should secede from the Union in 1860

Which two people are taking a stand on this issue? Edmund Ruffin and Sam Houston

Which state did each person represent? Ruffin represented Virginia, and Houston represented Texas.

Comparing Viewpoints

Union or Secession?

The Union flag as it looked in 1861

An early Confederate flag

At the news of Abraham Lincoln's election as President, Americans in both the North and the South got ready for what some called the Revolution of 1860. Some hoped that the South would not carry out its threat to secede. Lincoln himself said, "The people of the South have too much sense to attempt the ruin of the government." But he and others did not understand how badly many Southerners wanted their independence.

Not all Southerners agreed about seceding, though. Some were against it. Others thought that the South should first give Lincoln a chance. They would be willing to secede only if nothing else worked. Still others wanted to secede right away.

Two Southerners who made their feelings clear were Edmund Ruffin of Virginia and Sam Houston, the governor of Texas. The words of the two men show how they felt about secession, or seceding from the Union.

436 • Unit 7

ACTIVITY CHOICES

Background

EDMUND RUFFIN Edmund Ruffin (1794–1865) was a noted Virginia planter. He not only supported secession, but also favored the spread of slavery to the western territories. For his support of secession, South Carolina forces gave Ruffin the honor of firing the first shot on Fort Sumter in Charleston Harbor, where the Civil War started in 1861. Ruffin was so upset when the South lost the war that he committed suicide.

SAM HOUSTON Sam Houston (1793–1863) played a leading role in the fight for Texas's independence and later served as president of the Republic of Texas. After Texas joined the Union, he was elected to the U.S. Senate. In 1859 Houston ran for governor on a platform built on opposition to secession. He won the election and refused to let Texas secede from the Union. By 1861, however, enough Texans favored secession that they removed Houston from office.

Edmund Ruffin

“I will be out of Virginia before Lincoln’s inauguration, and so . . . avoid being, as a Virginian, under his government even for an hour. I, at least, will become a citizen of the seceded Confederate States, and will not again reside in my native state, nor enter it except to make visits to my children, until Virginia shall also secede. . . . This result . . . cannot be delayed long.

The bloodshed of South Carolinians defending their soil and their rights, or maintaining the possession of their harbor . . . will stir doubly fast the sluggish blood of the more backward Southern States into secession.”

Sam Houston

“Let me tell you what is coming. . . . Your fathers and husbands, your sons and brothers, will be herded at the point of the bayonet. . . . You may, after the sacrifice of countless millions of treasure and hundreds of thousands of lives, as a bare possibility, win Southern independence. . . . But I doubt it. I tell you that, while I believe with you in the doctrine of States’ Rights, the North is determined to preserve this Union. They are not a fiery, impulsive people as you are, for they live in colder climates. But when they begin to move in a given direction . . . they move with the steady momentum and perseverance of a mighty avalanche.”

Compare Viewpoints

1. What viewpoint about seceding did Ruffin hold? How do you know?
2. What viewpoint about seceding did Houston hold? How do you know?
3. What other viewpoints might Southerners have held on the matter of secession? Governor Thomas H. Hicks of Maryland said, “The only safety of Maryland lies in preserving a neutral position between our brethren of the North and of the South.” What view did the governor hold?

Think and Apply

BUILDING CITIZENSHIP

You have read that three Southerners—Ruffin, Houston, and Hicks—each had a different view about secession. At what other times in history have people from the same region held different views about something?

Compare Viewpoints

Use the Compare Viewpoints questions to guide a discussion of Ruffin’s and Houston’s statements.

1. Ruffin supported secession. You know this because of what he said. He would not live under Lincoln’s government.
2. Houston opposed secession. You know this because of what he said. The cost of Southern independence would be “the sacrifice of countless millions of treasure and hundreds of thousands of lives.”
3. A third person who took a stand on the issue of secession was Governor Thomas H. Hicks of Maryland, who was also a Southerner. Hicks believed that his state should stay out of the conflict and remain neutral, that is, not take a stand.

Explore with students the differences and commonalities among speakers.

Q. **How were the three men different?** Each held a differing position on the issue of secession.

What did each person have in common with the others? Each person represented a Southern state.

3. CLOSE

Have students summarize the three contrasting viewpoints held by Southerners on the issue of secession. Some Southerners supported secession, some opposed secession, and some remained neutral. Then use the Think and Apply activity to have students identify other times in history when people from the same area or region held contrasting viewpoints about an issue.

Background

THE ISSUE Underlying the issue of secession was the question of states’ rights. Does a state have the right to secede from the Union? Southerners such as Ruffin believed each state had that right. Many of those who opposed secession believed that a strong Union was more important than the individual states. At this time you may want to refer students to Unit 5 and review some of the rights and powers of the states as defined by the Constitution.

Reteach

SUMMARIZE THE VIEWPOINTS If students have difficulty identifying the three contrasting viewpoints held by Southerners on the issue of secession, pair them with students who have mastered this understanding. Then have the students work together to summarize each statement in their own words.

CHAPTER 13
REVIEW

Time Line
Ask students to share what they recall about each event shown on the time line.

Connect Main Ideas
Use the organizer to review the main ideas of the chapter. Have students use their textbooks to complete or check their work. Allow time for them to discuss and compare their responses.

ACTIVITY BOOK

Summarize the Chapter

A copy of the graphic organizer appears on ACTIVITY BOOK, p. 86.

TRANSPARENCY

A copy of the graphic organizer appears on TRANSPARENCY 36.

Write More About It

Write Your Opinion
Students' personal views will differ as to whether compromise is always a good way to settle differences.

Compare Viewpoints
Students should explain in their paragraphs that Stephen Douglas wanted each state or territory to decide for itself whether slavery would be allowed within its borders. Lincoln wanted to keep slavery from spreading because then it might be ended. In the beginning, Lincoln did not want to abolish slavery in the Southern states.

TECHNOLOGY

Use THE AMAZING WRITING MACHINE™ to complete the writing activities.

TECHNOLOGY

Use TIMELINER™ DATA DISKS to discuss and summarize the chapter.

CHAPTER 13
REVIEW

1820 | 1830

1820
• The Missouri Compromise

1831
• Nat Turner's rebellion

CONNECT MAIN IDEAS

Use this organizer to show how the chapter's main ideas are connected. Write three details to support each main idea. A copy of the organizer appears on page 86 of the Activity Book.

Possible answers to this graphic organizer are provided on page 414C of this Teacher's Edition.

Differences Divide North and South
People in the North and the South disagreed during the middle 1800s.
1. ______
2. ______
3. ______

Africans in Slavery and Freedom
Enslaved people protested against being held in slavery.
1. ______
2. ______
3. ______

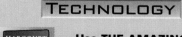

Facing a National Problem
Northerners and Southerners tried to settle disagreements during the 1800s.
1. ______
2. ______
3. ______

A Time for Hard Decisions
Americans had to make important decisions in 1860 and 1861.
1. ______
2. ______
3. ______

WRITE MORE ABOUT IT

Write Your Opinion Tell whether or not you think agreeing to a compromise is always a good way to settle differences. Explain your answer.

Compare Viewpoints Write a paragraph that compares Stephen Douglas's and Abraham Lincoln's points of view on how the slavery question should be settled.

438 • Chapter 13

Use Vocabulary

1. *Overseers* were hired by slave owners to watch the slaves as they worked and to punish them if they fell behind. (p. 421) *Slave codes* were laws that shaped the day-to-day lives of enslaved people. (p. 421) *Overseers* enforced *slave codes.*
2. Slaves found the strength they needed to handle the miseries of slavery by *resisting* (p. 422) in different ways and by singing *spirituals.* (p. 422)
3. A *free state* did not allow slavery. (p. 426) A *slave state* did allow slavery. (p. 426) Each time groups of settlers asked to join the Union as a new state, the same question arose: Would th new state be a *free state* or a *slave stat*

Check Understanding

4. Many people were moving fro farms to towns and cities, where the hoped to work in the factories th were springing up. (p. 415)
5. Southern planters felt they neede slaves to plant cotton seeds, wee fields, pick cotton, and run cotto gins, in order to meet the worldwi demand for cotton. (p. 418)
6. Cotton could be cleaned and pr pared for market in less time. Plante could then sell more cotton and mak more money. (p. 418)

1850 1860 1870

1850
- The Compromise of 1850

1861
- Confederate soldiers attack Fort Sumter

CHAPTER 13 REVIEW

USE VOCABULARY

For each pair of terms, write a sentence or two that explains how the terms are related.

1. slave code, overseer
2. resist, spiritual
3. free state, slave state

CHECK UNDERSTANDING

4. How was life in the North changing in the middle 1800s?
5. Why did Southern planters feel they needed enslaved workers?
6. How did the invention of the cotton gin affect cotton production?
7. How did the settlement of the West add to the argument over slavery?
8. What kinds of laws affected the everyday lives of slaves?
9. What role did religion play in the lives of many enslaved people?
10. Why was the North Star important to some runaway slaves?
11. How did the Compromise of 1850 help satisfy the demands of slaveholders?
12. Why did the Kansas-Nebraska Act lead to fighting?
13. What major decisions led to the start of the Civil War?

THINK CRITICALLY

14. **Personally Speaking** What kind of person do you think a conductor on the Underground Railroad needed to be?
15. **Cause and Effect** Why did compromises fail to settle disagreements over the issue of slavery?
16. **Explore Viewpoints** How do you think Henry Clay would have felt about the Dred Scott decision?
17. **Think More About It** How did the Lincoln-Douglas debates affect Lincoln's political career?

APPLY SKILLS

Use Graphs to Identify Trends Look in newspapers or magazines for a bar graph or a line graph that shows a trend. Cut out the graph and tape it to a sheet of paper. Below the graph, identify the trend shown. How does the trend change over time?

Make a Thoughtful Decision Imagine that a friend has asked you to allow your home to be used as a station on the Underground Railroad. What steps might you follow to come to a decision?

READ MORE ABOUT IT

Lincoln: In His Own Words by Milton Meltzer. Harcourt Brace. In this book, read about Lincoln's life, thoughts, and actions through his own words.

Visit the Internet at **http://www.hbschool.com** for additional resources.

7. Northerners felt slavery should not be allowed in the West; however, Southerners believed slave owners had the right to take their slaves wherever they wanted. (p. 419)
8. laws that prohibited them from leaving their owner's land, from meeting in groups, from buying or selling goods, and from learning to read and write (p. 421)
9. Religious beliefs gave many enslaved people the strength they needed to handle the hardships of life under slavery. (pp. 421–422)
10. It guided them to the North. (p. 424)
11. It included the Fugitive Slave Law, which said anyone caught helping slaves to escape would be punished. (p. 427)
12. People on both sides of the slavery issue rushed into the territories, hoping to help decide the vote. (p. 428)
13. Lincoln's decision to send supplies to Fort Sumter; the attack on Fort Sumter by the Confederacy (pp. 433–434)

Think Critically

14. Conductors needed to be brave, smart, concerned about other people, tough, able to survive in the wilderness, and quick thinkers who could handle emergency situations.
15. Compromises did not address the root cause of the disagreements, which was that some people did not believe slavery should exist at all and other people believed it should be legal. Accept all answers that students can defend.
16. Students' responses may include that Clay would probably have been unhappy with the decision because it went against the Missouri Compromise.
17. The debates made Lincoln known outside his home state of Illinois and thus helped him get elected President.

Apply Skills

Use Graphs to Identify Trends
Students will have chosen different graphs. Make sure each student's interpretation is appropriate for the graph chosen.

Make a Thoughtful Decision
Steps listed by the students should include weighing the pros and cons, listing the possible consequences of being a station on the Underground Railroad, talking to other people who live in the house, and then making a decision. Accept all logical answers.

Read More About It

Additional books are listed in the Multimedia Resource Center on page 406D of this Teacher's Edition.

Unit Project Check-Up

Check to be sure that students have labeled their time lines with the dates from 1790 to 1880. The following events may be added to their time lines: invention of the cotton gin, seizing of Harpers Ferry, the Underground Railroad, the Missouri Compromise, the Compromise of 1850, the Kansas-Nebraska Act, the Dred Scott decision, the Lincoln-Douglas debates, the election of 1860, and the Confederate attack on Fort Sumter. Encourage students to illustrate some of the events.

ASSESSMENT PROGRAM

Use CHAPTER 13 TEST, pp. 111–114.

CHAPTER 14

Planning Chart

	THEMES • Strands	VOCABULARY	MEET INDIVIDUAL NEEDS	RESOURCES INCLUDING ▶ TECHNOLOGY
LESSON 1 **The Fighting Begins** pp. 441–445	**CONFLICT & COOPERATION** • Geography • History • Economics	border state Emancipation Proclamation	Advanced Learners, p. 442 Kinesthetic Learners, p. 443 Extend and Enrich, p. 444 Reteach the Main Idea, p. 445	Activity Book, p. 87 ▶ THE AMAZING WRITING MACHINE ▶ MAPSKILLS
LESSON 2 **Learn History Through Literature** **The Signature That Changed America** by Harold Holzer pp. 446–451	**INDIVIDUALISM & INTERDEPENDENCE** • History • Civics and Government		Advanced Learners, p. 448 Extend and Enrich, p. 450 Reteach the Main Idea, p. 451	Activity Book, p. 88 ▶ THE AMAZING WRITING MACHINE
LESSON 3 **The Long Road to a Union Victory** pp. 452–459	**CONFLICT & COOPERATION** • Civics and Government • Geography • History • Economics	Gettysburg Address assassination	Auditory Learners, p. 457 Extend and Enrich, p. 458 Reteach the Main Idea, p. 459	Activity Book, p. 89 Music Audiocassette ▶ THE AMAZING WRITING MACHINE
SKILL **Compare Maps with Different Scales** pp. 460–461	**BASIC STUDY SKILLS** • Map and Globe Skills		Tactile Learners, p. 460 Reteach the Skill, p. 461	Activity Book, p. 90 Transparency 37 ▶ MAPSKILLS ▶ THE AMAZING WRITING MACHINE
LESSON 4 **Life After the War** pp. 462–467	**INDIVIDUALISM & INTERDEPENDENCE** • Culture • Economics • History • Civics and Government	sharecropping Reconstruction scalawag carpetbagger segregation	English Language Learners, p. 463 Advanced Learners, p. 464 Extend and Enrich, p. 466 Reteach the Main Idea, p. 467	Activity Book, p. 91 ▶ THE AMAZING WRITING MACHINE
CHAPTER REVIEW pp. 468–469				Activity Book, p. 92 Transparency 38 Assessment Program Chapter 14 Test, pp. 115–118 ▶ THE AMAZING WRITING MACHINE ▶ TIMELINER ▶ INTERNET

7 DAYS

TIME MANAGEMENT

DAY 1	DAY 2	DAY 3	DAY 4	DAY 5	DAY 6	DAY 7
Lesson 1	Lesson 2	Lesson 3	Skill	Lesson 4	Chapter Review	Chapter Test

Activity Book

LESSON 1
Link Music to History

NAME ____________________ DATE ____________

THE BONNIE BLUE FLAG

When South Carolina joined the Confederacy, its flag changed, but Harry Macarthy's song, "The Bonnie Blue Flag," which was about South Carolina's first flag, quickly became the Confederacy's national anthem.

Link Music to History

DIRECTIONS: Read the words to the song. Then answer the questions that follow.

Verse One
1. We are a band of brothers, and native to the soil,
2. Fighting for the property we gained by honest toil;
3. And when our rights were threatened, the cry rose near and far:
4. Hurrah! for the bonnie blue flag that bears a single star.

Verse Two
1. As long as the Union was faithful to her trust,
2. Like friends and like brothers, kind were we and just;
3. But now, when Northern treachery attempts our rights to mar,
4. We hoist, on high, the bonnie blue flag that bears a single star.

Last Verse
1. Then here's to our Confederacy—strong we are and brave,
2. Like patriots of old, we'll fight, our heritage to save;
3. And rather than submit to shame, to die we would prefer—
4. So cheer for the bonnie blue flag that bears a single star.

Chorus
1. Hurrah! hurrah! for Southern rights! hurrah!
2. Hurrah! for the bonnie blue flag that bears a single star.

1. Write the phrase that is repeated in line 4 of each verse.
the bonnie blue flag that bears a single star

2. Which line in Verse One describes how the Confederate soldiers felt about one another? Describe that feeling. Line 1; they felt as if they were brothers.

3. Each verse has one line that states a reason that the Confederacy was fighting. List each line number and give the reason.

Verse One	Line Number: 2	Reason: property
Verse Two	Line Number: 3	Reason: rights
Last Verse	Line Number: 2	Reason: heritage

LESSON 2
Interpret Primary Source Documents

NAME ____________________ DATE ____________

THE Emancipation Proclamation

Interpret Primary Source Documents

DIRECTIONS: The passage below from the Emancipation Proclamation contains words in boldface type. Use context clues to define those words. Match each word in the list with its definition, and write the correct letter in the blank. Then, on a separate sheet of paper, answer the questions that follow.

And **by virtue of** the power and for the purpose **aforesaid,** I do order and declare that all persons held as slaves within said **designated** States and parts of States are, and **henceforward** shall be, free; and that the Executive Government of the United States, including the military and naval authorities thereof, will recognize and maintain the freedom of said persons.

And I hereby enjoin upon the people so declared to be free to **abstain** from all violence, unless in necessary self-defense; and I recommend to them that, in all cases when allowed, they labor faithfully for reasonable wages.

And I further declare and make known that such persons of **suitable** condition will be received into the armed service of the United States to **garrison** forts, positions, stations, and other places, and to **man** vessels of all sorts in said service.

C	by virtue of	**A.**	pointed out; shown
E	aforesaid	**B.**	from this time on
A	designated	**C.**	because of; on the grounds of
B	henceforward	**D.**	right; proper
H	abstain	**E.**	spoken of before; mentioned previously
D	suitable	**F.**	to station troops in a fort or town
F	garrison	**G.**	to take an assigned place for work or defense
G	man	**H.**	to keep oneself back; to choose not to do

1. What is the most important message in the first paragraph?
the freeing of slaves in designated states

2. What did President Lincoln recommend to former slaves in the second paragraph?
that they not take part in violence and that they work for pay

3. In the last paragraph, what did President Lincoln declare about the armed services?
that the armed services would accept former slaves fit for duty for various positions

LESSON 3
Apply Information from a Chart

NAME ____________________ DATE ____________

★ CIVIL WAR ★ HORSES

Apply Information from a Chart

DIRECTIONS: Study the chart below. Then complete the activities that follow.

CIVIL WAR GENERALS' HORSES

HORSE'S NAME	RIDER'S NAME	ARMY	DESCRIPTION	FURTHERMORE
Don Juan	George Armstrong Custer ★	Union	Bay stallion	Custer had more horses (7) killed under him than any other Union leader.
Butler	Wade Hampton ★	Confederate	Bay stallion	One of Hampton's officers gave him the horse as a gift.
Sam	William Tecumseh Sherman ★	Union	Half-breed bay stallion	The horse was so steady under gunfire that Sherman could write orders while riding.
Lexington	William Tecumseh Sherman	Union	Kentucky thoroughbred	Sherman rode Lexington during his final review of his army.
Traveller	Robert E. Lee	Confederate	Iron gray gelding	Traveller was called the greatest warhorse of all time, except for Alexander the Great's horse.
Old Spot	Judson Kilpatrick	Union	Arabian	The horse outlived its master.

1. Underline the name of the general who had seven horses killed under him.

2. Put a star next to the name of each general who rode a bay stallion.

3. Put a box around the name of the horse that outlived its master.

4. a) Imagine you are a Civil War general. Explain why it is important to choose a good horse.
Accept all reasonable answers that show an understanding of the role horses played in battle.

b) Which of the horses on the chart would you have chosen? Explain your answer.
Answers should substantiate the choice, using information in the chart.

SKILL PRACTICE
Apply Map and Globe Skills

NAME ____________________ DATE ____________

HOW TO COMPARE MAPS with DIFFERENT SCALES

FINAL CIVIL WAR CAMPAIGNS

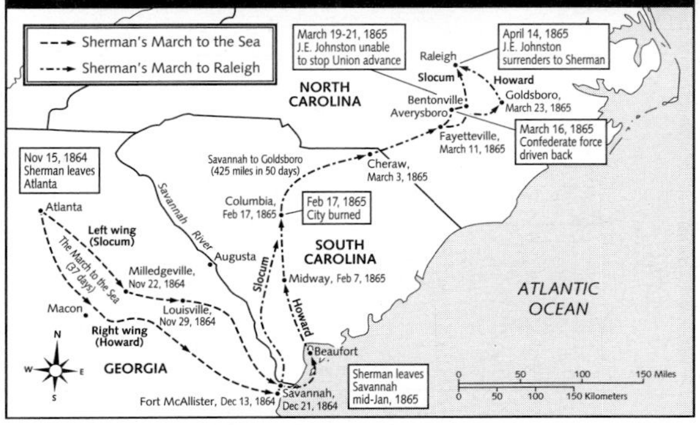

Apply Map and Globe Skills

DIRECTIONS: Compare the map above with the map in your textbook on page 457. For each of the following statements, decide which map is more useful. Write A in the answer blank if the map above is better and B if the textbook map is better.

B **1.** Show the most miles per inch.

A **2.** Determine the distance between Cheraw and Fayetteville.

A **3.** Determine how many miles Sherman traveled on his March to the Sea.

B **4.** Identify the extent of the Union blockade.

A **5.** Measure the distance from Atlanta, Georgia, to Macon, Georgia.

B **6.** Identify battles that took place in Mississippi and Virginia.

A **7.** Determine the number of miles traveled by Sherman's army between February 17, 1865, and March 11, 1865.

LESSON 4
Interpret Visuals and Point of View

NAME ______________________ DATE __________

IT'S IN THE BAG!

Interpret Visuals and Point of View

***DIRECTIONS:** Study the illustrations and the captions below. Then on a separate sheet of paper, answer the questions that follow.*

After the Civil War inexpensive suitcases called carpetbags (above) were made from carpeting.

THE MAN WITH THE (CARPET) BAGS
Cartoonist Thomas Nast helped shape the U.S. public's view of Reconstruction. This 1872 cartoon shows a former Union general.

1. Circle the name of the Union general in Nast's cartoon.
2. Underline the direction in which the general is heading.
3. Compare the bags in the cartoon with the one in the illustration next to the cartoon. What similarities and differences do you notice? Answers should describe similarities and differences in shape, size, texture, handle, design, and so on.
4. Look at the illustration on the left. How do you think this type of bag got its name? It was made out of carpeting.
5. How do you think Nast viewed the type of person in this cartoon? List the features of this cartoon that support your answer. Nast probably did not think highly of the carpetbaggers. Accept any features of the cartoon that students can support.
6. Nast said about this cartoon, "The bag in front of him, filled with others' faults, he always sees. The one behind him, filled with his own faults, he never sees." Explain what you think Nast meant. Answers should point out that the character is trying to fix someone else's faults (the South's) without fixing his own (the North's) first.

Use after reading Chapter 14, Lesson 4, pages 462–467. ACTIVITY BOOK 91

CHAPTER 14 REVIEW
Connect Main Ideas

NAME ______________________ DATE __________

Civil War and Reconstruction

Connect Main Ideas

***DIRECTIONS:** Use this organizer to show how the chapter's main ideas are connected. Write a sentence or two telling how each event or idea affected the lives of Americans during the Civil War and Reconstruction.*

Civil War and Reconstruction

Choosing Sides
Most Northerners supported the Union, wanting to help maintain the government. Most Southerners supported the Confederacy, wanting to win their independence. Others had a difficult choice to make, especially those people who lived in border states or Indian nations.

Emancipation Proclamation
President Lincoln signed an order to free slaves in states that had seceded.

Union Victories
Union victories such as the battles of Vicksburg and Gettysburg as well as General Sherman's March to the Sea forced General Lee to surrender his ragged troops in April 1865.

Rebuilding America
President Johnson pardoned most Confederates who promised loyalty to the United States and said that the Confederate states must abolish slavery.

Congress wanted a plan that was tougher on white Southerners than President Johnson's plan.

92 ACTIVITY BOOK Use after reading Chapter 14, pages 440–469.

COMMUNITY RESOURCES

Ideas for using community resources, including speakers and field trips

Historical Societies:

____

____

____

____

____

Historians:

____

____

____

____

____

Museums:

____

____

____

____

____

Historic Sites:

____

____

____

____

____

Chapter 14 Assessment

For ongoing **PERFORMANCE ASSESSMENT,** see Show What You Know, pp. 445, 459, 467.

CONTENT

NAME ______________________________ DATE ____________

Chapter Test 14

Part One: Test Your Understanding *(4 points each)*

DIRECTIONS: ***Circle the letter of the best answer.***

1. What new state was formed out of a slave state by people who were against slavery and wanted to remain in the Union?
- **A.** Alabama
- **B.** Kansas
- **C.** Nebraska
- **(D.)** West Virginia

2. An early Northern plan for fighting the war was based on
- **A.** invading the border states.
- **B.** having Indian allies capture the Confederate capital.
- **(C.)** cutting off Southern trade by setting up a blockade.
- **D.** invading Georgia and Alabama by sea.

3. The Confederate states
- **A.** hoped to keep the war only in the South.
- **(B.)** hoped that Britain and France would help them fight the war.
- **C.** had more people, factories, and railroads than the Northern states.
- **D.** welcomed all women who wanted to become soldiers.

4. Which of the following happened when President Abraham Lincoln signed the Emancipation Proclamation?
- **A.** Great Britain and France were allowed to buy Southern cotton.
- **B.** Most of the border states switched sides and joined the Confederacy.
- **(C.)** The Union fought against both the Confederacy and slavery.
- **D.** All of the slaves in the United States were freed.

5. General Grant's victory in the siege of Vicksburg was important because
- **A.** it was the first battle won by the Union army.
- **B.** it strengthened the Confederate army.
- **(C.)** it gave the Union control of the Mississippi River.
- **D.** it caused the South to surrender and end the Civil War.

6. In the Gettysburg Address, President Abraham Lincoln
- **A.** issued the Emancipation Proclamation and freed the slaves.
- **(B.)** honored the soldiers who had died fighting for liberty and equality.
- **C.** named General Ulysses S. Grant to lead the Union army.
- **D.** created the Freedmen's Bureau to help Africans in the South.

(continued)

CONTENT

NAME ______________________________ DATE ____________

7. "The soldiers did not have enough food. Many of them were nearly starving. Their clothes were dirty and torn." This statement best describes
- **(A.)** Confederate troops just before General Lee surrendered.
- **B.** Union troops at the end of the siege of Vicksburg.
- **C.** Confederate troops after they captured Savannah, Georgia.
- **D.** Union troops at the Battle of Gettysburg.

8. Which of these events happened **last**?
- **(A.)** President Lincoln was assassinated.
- **B.** General Lee surrendered to General Grant at Appomattox.
- **C.** The Civil War ended.
- **D.** General Sherman destroyed the city of Atlanta.

9. Slavery in the United States was ended forever by the passage of the
- **A.** First Amendment.
- **B.** Fourteenth Amendment.
- **C.** Freedmen's Bureau.
- **(D.)** Thirteenth Amendment.

10. The most important work of the Freedmen's Bureau was
- **A.** helping former slaves find their family members.
- **B.** helping former slaves find jobs in Northern factories.
- **(C.)** educating the newly freed slaves.
- **D.** making loans to the newly freed slaves so that they could buy plantations.

11. The black codes were laws that
- **(A.)** limited the freedom of African Americans.
- **B.** gave African Americans their own land to farm.
- **C.** made African Americans citizens of the United States.
- **D.** allowed African Americans to travel freely throughout the United States.

DIRECTIONS: ***Match the person on the left with the description on the right. Write the correct letter in the space provided.***

12. __C__ Clara Barton — **A.** led Union soldiers through Georgia on the March to the Sea

13. __A__ William T. Sherman — **B.** became President after the assassination of Abraham Lincoln

14. __B__ Andrew Johnson — **C.** helped sick and wounded Union soldiers during the Civil War

(continued)

SKILLS

NAME ______________________________ DATE ____________

Part Two: Test Your Skills *(24 points)*

DIRECTIONS: ***You learned about the problems and the difficult decisions Abraham Lincoln and Jefferson Davis had to make as supplies ran out at Fort Sumter. The first chart shows how Lincoln might have made his decision. Imagine you are Jefferson Davis. Use what you have learned about making decisions and about Fort Sumter to complete the second chart.***

PROBLEM: FORT SUMTER MIGHT SURRENDER TO THE SOUTH.	
Possible Solutions:	**Consequence of Each Solution:**
Send supplies to the fort.	Southerners might attack the fort.
Send troops to the fort.	Southerners would surely attack the fort.
Do nothing at all.	After a while, the fort would surrender to the South.
Decision: Send supplies and wait to see what happens.	

PROBLEM: LINCOLN HAS ANNOUNCED THAT HE WILL SEND SUPPLY SHIPS TO FORT SUMTER.	
Possible Solutions:	**Consequence of Each Solution:**
15. Attack the fort **after** the supply ships arrive.	Possible response: The fort might repel the attack.
16. Attack the fort **before** the supply ships arrive.	Possible response: The South will win the fort, but the result could be war.
17. Do nothing at all.	Possible response: The fort will remain under Union control.
18. Decision: Possible response: Attack the fort before the supply ships arrive.	

(continued)

APPLICATION/WRITING

NAME ______________________________ DATE ____________

Part Three: Apply What You Have Learned

DIRECTIONS: ***Complete each of the following activities.***

19. ***Famous People*** *(10 points)*
Listed below are the names of famous people who played a role in the Civil War and Reconstruction. Form two groups of names that go together. A group must have at least two names in it. You may use a name in more than one group. After you form a group, write a brief explanation of why you formed that group. An example has been done for you.

Clara Barton	Ulysses S. Grant	Andrew Johnson
Robert E. Lee	Abraham Lincoln	William H. Seward
William T. Sherman	Sally Tomkins	Harriet Tubman

Example: Lee, Grant — Civil War generals

Possible responses:

Barton, Tomkins—both army nurses

Lincoln, Johnson—both United States Presidents

20. ***Essay*** *(10 points)*
Imagine that you are Robert E. Lee. Last night, April 18, 1861, President Lincoln asked you to take command of the Union army. Shortly after that, you learned that your home state of Virginia had seceded from the Union. You thought long and hard about whether you should accept Lincoln's offer. Write an entry for April 19, 1861, in your journal about your decision.

Possible response:
Last night President Lincoln asked me to head the Union army. This would be a great honor. But last night I also heard that my beloved Virginia has decided to secede from the Union. I am sure that Confederate leaders will also be asking me to serve in its army and to fight for Virginia. It is a difficult decision that I have to make. But I cannot fight against my friends and neighbors. I must turn down President Lincoln's request.

INTRODUCE THE CHAPTER

This chapter focuses on the years of the Civil War and the Reconstruction that followed. It compares and contrasts the strengths of the North with those of the South during the war and examines some of the major battles. It explains why President Lincoln finally decided to free the enslaved Africans in the Confederate states. The chapter also explores the effects of Reconstruction on the South.

Link Prior Learning

Have students share what they already know about the disagreements between the North and the South that led to armed conflict between former friends, neighbors, and even family members. Make sure students understand that the Civil War was the culmination of long-standing economic, political, and cultural differences between the two parts of the nation.

Visual Analysis

Interpret Photographs Have students examine the photograph and think about what this young soldier might be feeling.

Q. **About how old do you think this soldier is?** He is probably in his teens.

Auditory Learning

Interpret Primary Sources Have a volunteer read aloud Rhodes's statement as the other members of the class listen carefully.

“PRIMARY SOURCE”

Source: *The Civil War: An Illustrated History.* Geoffrey C. Ward. Alfred A. Knopf, 1990.

CHAPTER 14

CIVIL WAR AND RECONSTRUCTION

“I put in many hours of weary work and soon thought myself quite a soldier. . . . I was elected First Sergeant, much to my surprise. Just what a First Sergeant's duties might be, I had no idea.”

Elisha Rhodes,
Pawtucket,
Rhode Island, 1861

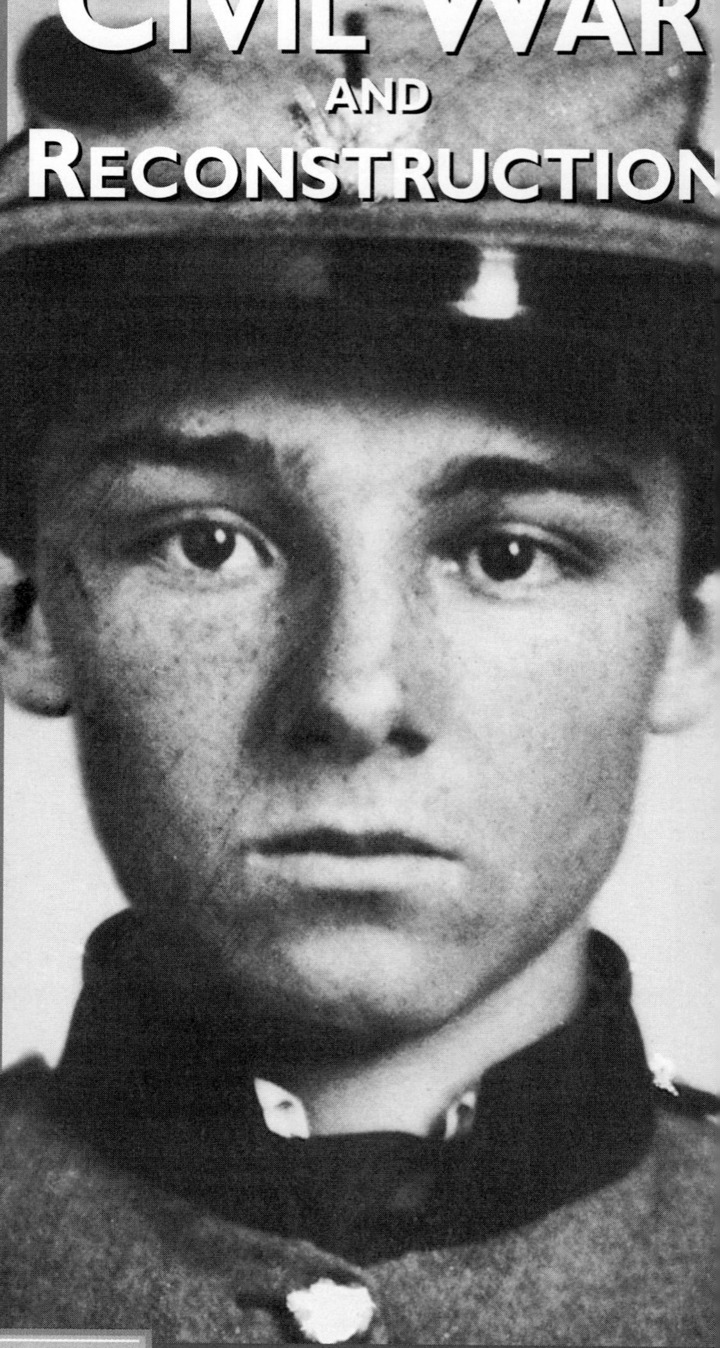

Confederate private Edwin Jennison, killed at the Seven Days' Battles in 1862

440

ACTIVITY CHOICES

Background

TRAINING SOLDIERS In the early days of the war, the training of Union soldiers was superficial and consisted mostly of marching and reading a manual of arms. Regiments learned to fight on the battlefield, not in training camps. Some regiments went into battle only three weeks after they had been organized.

Meet Individual Needs

VISUAL LEARNERS Have students use technology to make their own books about what life would be like in a town affected by the war in 1865.

TECHNOLOGY

Use IMAGINATION EXPRESS™: DESTINATION TIME TRIP to complete this activity.

The Fighting Begins

When Confederate soldiers fired on Fort Sumter, hopes or peace between the North and the South ended. Now Americans had to make some difficult decisions.

Taking Sides

In the weeks following the attack on Fort Sumter, many people thought that the war would be short and easy. For most, the choice of which side to support was clear.

Most Northerners supported the Union. They believed that t was wrong that the Southern states had broken away from he Union. They were willing to go to war to save their flag and all that it stood for. "If it is necessary that I should fall on the battlefield for my country," wrote a soldier from New England, "I am ready. . . . I am willing—perfectly willing—to lay down all my joys in this life, to help maintain this government."

Most white Southerners supported the Confederacy. They were willing to go to war to win their independence. Whether they owned slaves or not, many felt that the North was trying to change the South. They thought that the government was taking away their rights. The only way to get those rights back, they believed, was to secede.

The need to defend their land also led many Southerners to join the fight. One young soldier, caught early in the war by Union troops, told his captors, "I'm fighting because you're down here."

For some Americans, however, the choice between the Union and the Confederacy was not an easy one. People in Missouri, Kentucky, Maryland, and Delaware were torn between the two sides. These **border states** were between the North and South. Although they

LESSON **1**

FOCUS

Why is it sometimes difficult to choose sides in a disagreement?

Main Idea As you read, think about why it was difficult for many Americans to choose sides during the Civil War.

Vocabulary

border state

Emancipation Proclamation

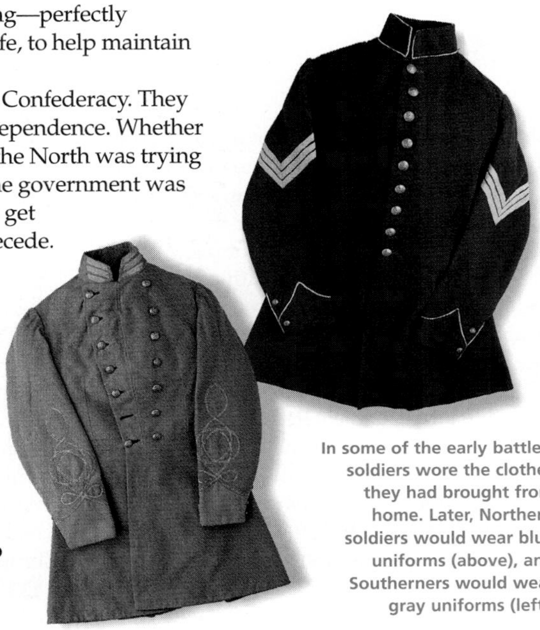

In some of the early battles, soldiers wore the clothes they had brought from home. Later, Northern soldiers would wear blue uniforms (above), and Southerners would wear gray uniforms (left).

Reading Support

ANTICIPATION GUIDE Create a three-column chart on the board. Have students brainstorm what they already know about the Civil War, and record their comments in the first column, titled *What We Know.* Next, ask students to provide questions related to what they want to find out about the Civil War and record them in the second column, titled *What We Want to Know.* After students have read the lesson, record their responses to the questions in the third column, titled *What We Learned.* Have students volunteer additional information for the third column.

Objectives

1. Summarize the choices one had to make in deciding which side to support in the Civil War.
2. Analyze the dilemma Robert E. Lee faced.
3. Draw conclusions about why the Battle of Bull Run was a shock to the Union, and evaluate the battle plans of the North and South.
4. Describe Lincoln's views on writing an order to free the slaves.

Vocabulary

border state (p. 441)

Emancipation Proclamation (p. 445)

1. ACCESS

The Focus Question

Have students recall times they might have had trouble deciding which side to take in a conflict, such as a conflict among friends. Also discuss examples from current events in which students may feel sympathy for both sides in a conflict.

The Main Idea

In this lesson students examine the early stages of the Civil War prior to President Lincoln's decision to issue the Emancipation Proclamation. After students have read the lesson, have them explore the difficult choice some people faced.

2. BUILD

Taking Sides

Key Content Summary

Although most Northerners and Southerners supported the cause of the region in which they lived, some people had conflicting feelings. These included people of the border states, Southerners living in areas where there were few slaves, and many in the Indian nations.

Visual Analysis

Learn from Maps Have students answer the question in the caption. Missouri, Kentucky, West Virginia, Maryland, and Delaware

Q. **Were there more states in the Union or in the Confederacy?** in the Union

Geography

Place Have students examine a physical map of Virginia and West Virginia in an atlas or on a classroom wall map of the United States.

Q. **Why do you think there were fewer slaves in western Virginia than in eastern Virginia?** Because of the mountainous terrain in western Virginia, people living there could not have the large plantations that people living in eastern Virginia had.

The Union and the Confederacy

Regions This map shows the division of the nation at the start of the Civil War.

■ *Which states were border states?*

allowed slavery, they had remained a part of the Union. When the time came for people in the border states to choose sides, some fought for the North. Others fought for the South.

Taking sides was also hard for people living in some parts of the South. In the mountains of eastern Tennessee and northern Alabama, there was very little slavery. Many people there sided with the North. In western Virginia, feelings for the Union were so strong that the people voted to break away from Virginia and form a new state. West Virginia joined the Union in 1863.

Taking sides was also hard for many in the Indian nations. By the time of the war, the Cherokee, Creek, Seminole, Choctaw, and Chickasaw peoples had been driven from their lands to the Indian Territory, which is today Oklahoma. When it came time to choose sides, most people in these five tribes had little reason to like either the North or the South. In the end the Choctaws and the Chickasaws fought for the South. The Creeks, Seminoles, and Cherokees were divided between the Union and the Confederacy.

The decisions people had to make in these early days of the war divided families and friends. When war finally came, four of Henry Clay's grandsons decided to join the Confederacy. Three others fought for the Union. Even President Lincoln's own family was divided. Mary Todd Lincoln, his wife, had been born in Kentucky. Four of her brothers fought for the South.

REVIEW ***Why was taking sides hard for people in the border states?*** The states allowed slavery, yet they had remained in the Union.

Activity Choices

Background

WEST VIRGINIA Even before the Civil War, western Virginians resented the plantation owners of the eastern part of the state. Western Virginians were discriminated against in taxation and representation in the state legislature. At one time, for example, owners of slaves, mostly eastern Virginians, were taxed at a lower rate than owners of cattle, which were a main asset of western Virginians. These resentments and Virginia's secession from the Union led to the creation of a new state.

Meet Individual Needs

ADVANCED LEARNERS Ask students to use library resources to prepare oral reports about families and neighbors who fought on opposite sides during the Civil War. Encourage students to find out why family members and neighbors were divided and what happened to them during the course of the war. Have students present their findings to the class.

He loved his country, yet he did not want to lead an army to fight his family and neighbors.

Lee Joins the Confederacy

On April 19, 1861—a week after the attack on Fort Sumter—Robert E. Lee paced his bedroom floor. It was nearly midnight. Lee was a United States Army colonel. The day before, President Lincoln had asked him to take command of a Union army. Just hours later Lee had learned that his home state of Virginia had seceded.

Lee loved his country. He was a graduate of the United States Military Academy at West Point, New York. He had fought in the war with Mexico and had served his country for 32 years. Yet Lee also loved Virginia. Could he lead an army that would fight his family and neighbors?

The next morning Lee told Mary, his wife, what he had decided. He turned down Lincoln's offer and quit the Union army. A few days later he took command of Virginia's troops. Lee knew he would be fighting old friends who were fighting for the Union. Even so, he decided to serve Virginia. "I cannot raise my hand against my birthplace, my home, my children," he said.

REVIEW ***Why was it difficult for Robert E. Lee to choose sides in the war?***

Battle Plans

Three months after the attack on Fort Sumter, two armies of eager young men prepared for the first major battle of the war. The battle took place at Bull Run, a stream near the town of Manassas Junction, Virginia.

After hours of fighting, the South won the battle. The defeat shocked the Union. Northerners had entered the war feeling very strong. The North had nearly twice as many people as the South. It had more factories to make weapons and supplies. It had more railroads to get those supplies to the troops.

But the South had proved more powerful than most Northerners had expected. Southerners fighting to defend their own land had a very strong will to win. Stories were already being told about the bravery of officers such as "Stonewall" Jackson.

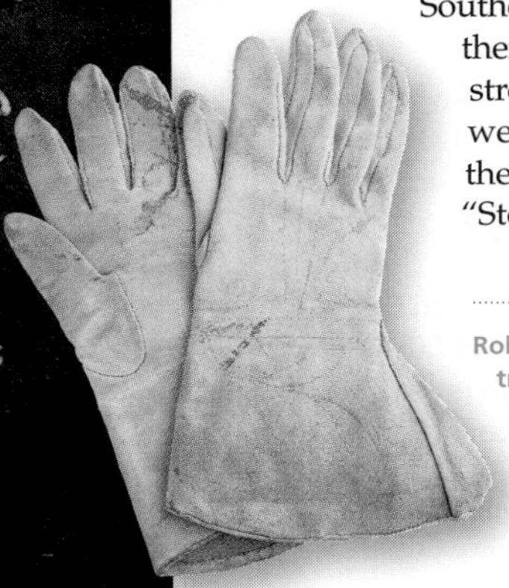

Robert E. Lee led the Confederate troops throughout the war. These gloves (left) protected Lee's hands when he was in battle.

Chapter 14 • **443**

Lee Joins the Confederacy

Key Content Summary

Robert E. Lee, an outstanding officer in the United States Army, experienced conflict between his love for the United States and his love for his native state of Virginia. Turning down President Lincoln's offer to serve as commander of the Union army, Lee finally decided to fight for the South.

History

Leaders and Achievers Have students note that Robert E. Lee was a highly regarded and experienced military leader. His fateful decision to fight for the South was one of the reasons the war lasted longer than Northerners thought it would. Have one-half of the class provide reasons they think Lee should have fought for the North and the other half provide reasons they think Lee should have fought for the South.

Battle Plans

Key Content Summary

The first major battle of the Civil War took place at Bull Run, near Manassas Junction, Virginia. Although soldiers on both sides were untrained, the South shocked the North by defeating them in the conflict.

Meet Individual Needs

KINESTHETIC LEARNERS To help students better understand the Northern and Southern battle plans and the advantages each region had over the other, have them bring in or make materials that are representative of each point in the lesson. Examples include small ships representing ports and railroad tracks representing train transportation. Have students organize the materials into North and South displays and explain the importance of the items to the class.

Link to Language Arts

WRITE A DIALOGUE Have students imagine the dialogue that might have taken place between Lee and Mary, his wife, when he told her of his decision to fight for the Confederacy. Remind them to use correct grammar, spelling, and punctuation when writing down what they imagine might have been said.

TECHNOLOGY

Use THE AMAZING WRITING MACHINE™ to complete this writing activity.

Geography

Location Have students turn to the map on page 457 to locate the site of the Battle of Bull Run, which has also been called the Battle of Manassas.

Q. **Why was that location important to both the North and the South?** It was close to Washington, D.C., the nation's capital.

Visual Analysis

Learn from Graphs Have students discuss the advantages each side had over its opposition. Then have them answer the question in the caption. the North

Q. **In which category is the percentage difference greatest?** factories

Economics

Interdependence and Income Explore the importance of Southern cotton to markets in France and Britain. Have students analyze why the South needed to continue to trade in order to fight the war.

The War and Slavery

Key Content Summary

By 1862 the North was discouraged by its limited success in the war. Some people thought that freeing the slaves in the Confederate states would help, but Lincoln feared emancipation would create conflict in the border states and even with some people in the North.

SOURCE: *Historical Statistics of the United States*

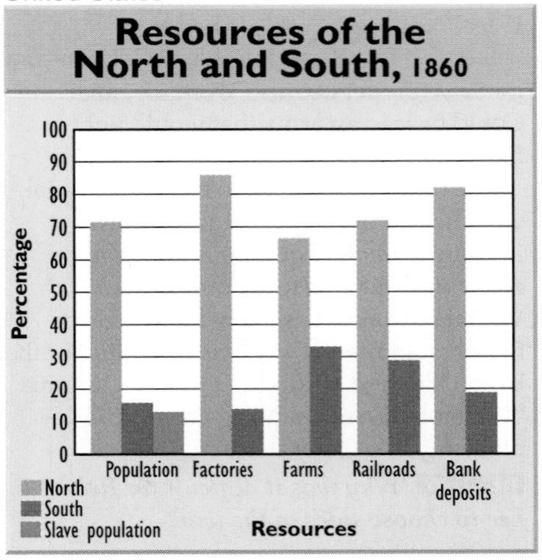

LEARNING FROM GRAPHS This graph compares the resources of the North and the South at the beginning of the Civil War.

■ *Which side had more resources?*

Lincoln quickly began to look for new officers of his own. He called for more soldiers. He also called for new battle plans.

An early Northern plan to win the war had to do with trade. The South depended on trade with the North and with other countries to buy such goods as cloth, shoes, and guns. The North hoped to cut off trade by setting up a blockade. Northern warships would stop trading ships from leaving or entering Southern ports. Without trade, the South would slowly become weaker.

Not everyone in the North liked the idea of a blockade. Some made fun of it, calling it the Anaconda (a•nuh•KAHN•duh) Plan. An anaconda is a large snake that squeezes its prey to death. Although this plan would slowly weaken the South, many people in the North wanted quicker action. They said the government should send the army to enter the South by force—to invade. "On to Richmond!" they cried. Richmond, Virginia, had become the capital of the Confederacy.

At first the most important fighting plan of the Confederate leaders was simply to protect their lands. Some Southerners compared their situation with the way things were for George Washington and the Patriots during the Revolutionary War. Southerners hoped to defend their homes against invaders and slowly wear down their enemy, just as the Patriots had worn down the British.

But many Southerners, just like many Northerners, were impatient. Cries of "On to Washington!" were soon answered with plans to invade the North.

Southerners also hoped that some countries in Europe would help them win the war. Britain and France depended on cotton to keep their textile mills running. Many thought that these countries would help the South as soon as their supplies of cotton ran low.

In both the North and the South, only men were allowed to join the army. Women, however, found many ways to help. They took over factory, business, and farm jobs that men left behind. They sent food to the troops, made bandages, and collected supplies. Many women, such as Clara Barton and Sally Tompkins, worked as nurses. A few served as spies, and some even dressed as men, joined the army, and fought in battles.

REVIEW ***What were the strengths of the North? of the South?***

The War and Slavery

As the fighting dragged on into 1862, Northern plans seemed to be working. The blockade brought trade to a halt, and supplies ran very low in the South. Plantations and shops were destroyed.

Even so, the North had not won yet. Thousands of Union soldiers were dying in battle.

444 • Unit 7

The North had more people, factories, and railroads. Southerners were fighting to protect their lands and hoped Britain and France would help them.

ACTIVITY CHOICES

Community Involvement

Clara Barton organized the Red Cross in the United States after the Civil War. Have students write a class letter to the local chapter of the American Red Cross, inviting a representative to speak to the class on how and why Clara Barton organized the American Red Cross and on the work of the Red Cross today.

TECHNOLOGY

HARCOURT BRACE

Use THE AMAZING WRITING MACHINE™ to complete this writing activity.

Extend and Enrich

COOPERATIVE LEARNING

PRESENT AN ORAL REPORT Divide the class into small groups. Have one group draw a large map of the United States, locate and label the states and capital cities as of 1861, and locate and label the major battles of the Civil War from 1861 to 1862. Have each of the other groups prepare oral reports on selected battles such as Shiloh, the battle between the *Monitor* and the *Merrimack*, Antietam, Fredericksburg, and the second Battle of Bull Run.

TECHNOLOGY

HARCOURT BRACE

Use MAPSKILLS to complete this activity.

BIOGRAPHY

Clara Barton 1821–1912

"While our soldiers stand and fight, I can stand and feed and nurse them." Clara Barton followed the fighting from battle to battle, caring for sick and wounded Union soldiers. Barton had always tried to help people in need. She taught school for a time and then worked as a government clerk. When the Civil War broke out, she wanted to help. Her work is still carried on by the American Red Cross. Barton founded the American branch of this world organization in 1881.

President Lincoln knew he had to find a way to push the North to victory.

To Lincoln, the purpose of the war was to keep the country together—to save the Union. Yet he knew that slavery was the issue that had divided the country. He realized that writing an order to free the slaves would greatly help the North. The loss of millions of enslaved workers would be a blow to the South. Freeing the slaves would also help in another way. It would turn the British, who needed cotton but were against slavery, toward the Union.

Abraham Lincoln held back on declaring an **Emancipation Proclamation**, an order freeing the slaves. He feared that such a step might turn people in the border states, as well as some states in the North, against the Union. Lincoln's waiting made the abolitionists angry. William Lloyd Garrison wrote that Lincoln was "nothing better than a wet rag."

As the war went on, Lincoln thought more and more about the question of slavery. Had the time come to write an Emancipation Proclamation? What would be the consequences if he made such a decision?

REVIEW *Why did Lincoln think that an Emancipation Proclamation would help the North?* The loss of enslaved workers would hurt the South and would turn the British away from the South.

LESSON 1 REVIEW

Check Understanding

1. **Remember the Facts** What were the battle plans of the North and the South?
2. **Recall the Main Idea** Why was it difficult for many Americans to choose sides during the Civil War?

Think Critically

3. **Explore Viewpoints** Why might a person in a border state have joined the Union army or the Confederate army?
4. **Past to Present** During the war many people told President Lincoln how they felt about slavery. How do government leaders learn about people's opinions today?

Show What You Know

Writing Activity Imagine that you are living in the South during the Civil War. Write a diary entry describing how the Union's blockade is changing your life.

Reteach the Main Idea

COOPERATIVE LEARNING

MAKE A CHART Divide the class into small groups. Challenge each group to use the textbook as a resource and to make a chart showing the reasons it was difficult for many people to choose sides during the Civil War. The chart could be titled *Taking Sides*, headed with columns *North* and *South*. Have the groups share and discuss their charts.

ACTIVITY BOOK

Reinforce & Extend

Use ACTIVITY BOOK, p. 87.

History

Leaders and Achievers Have students analyze why Lincoln held back on giving an order to free the slaves.

Q. **How did abolitionists react to Lincoln's indecision concerning an Emancipation Proclamation?** They became angry.

3. CLOSE

Have students consider again the Focus question on page 441.

Why is it sometimes difficult to choose sides in a disagreement?

Have students use what they have learned in this lesson to analyze why it is sometimes difficult for people to choose sides in a disagreement.

LESSON 1 REVIEW—Answers

Check Understanding

1. The North's plan was to blockade Southern trade and invade the South. The South's plan was to wear down the North, invade it, and get aid from Britain and France.
2. For some people there were conflicts between loyalty to country, loyalty to state, loyalty to family, and loyalty to ideals.

Think Critically

3. A person owning slaves might choose to fight for the South, while one not owning slaves might choose to fight for the North.
4. public opinion polls, letters to the editors of newspapers, demonstrations and marches by citizens, letters and telephone calls to government leaders

Show What You Know

Performance Assessment You may want to have students brainstorm a list of ways a blockade would affect them. Volunteers may read their diary entries to the class.

What to Look For In evaluating the diary entries, look for evidence that students understand how the blockade would affect their lives. They should mention a lack of supplies due to the blockade.

Objectives

1. Analyze the reasons Lincoln decided to write an order to free the slaves.
2. Summarize the Emancipation Proclamation.
3. Describe the nation's reaction to the freeing of slaves in the Confederate states.

1. ACCESS

Ask students to recall times in their own lives when they found it difficult to make a decision about something important to them. Then have students discuss how they finally made their decisions. Explain that political leaders also often have to make hard choices, such as declaring wars or raising taxes, that affect the lives of many people.

The Main Idea

This literature selection provides students with insight into President Lincoln's decision to free the slaves. After students have read the selection, have them analyze the different viewpoints regarding emancipation.

2. BUILD

Key Content Summary

President Lincoln hesitated to free the slaves when the war began because he believed many Americans were not ready for the change and because he did not want to alienate the border states. Over the course of 1862, Lincoln made the decision to emancipate the slaves in the Confederacy, hoping to preserve American democracy and the ideal of freedom in the United States.

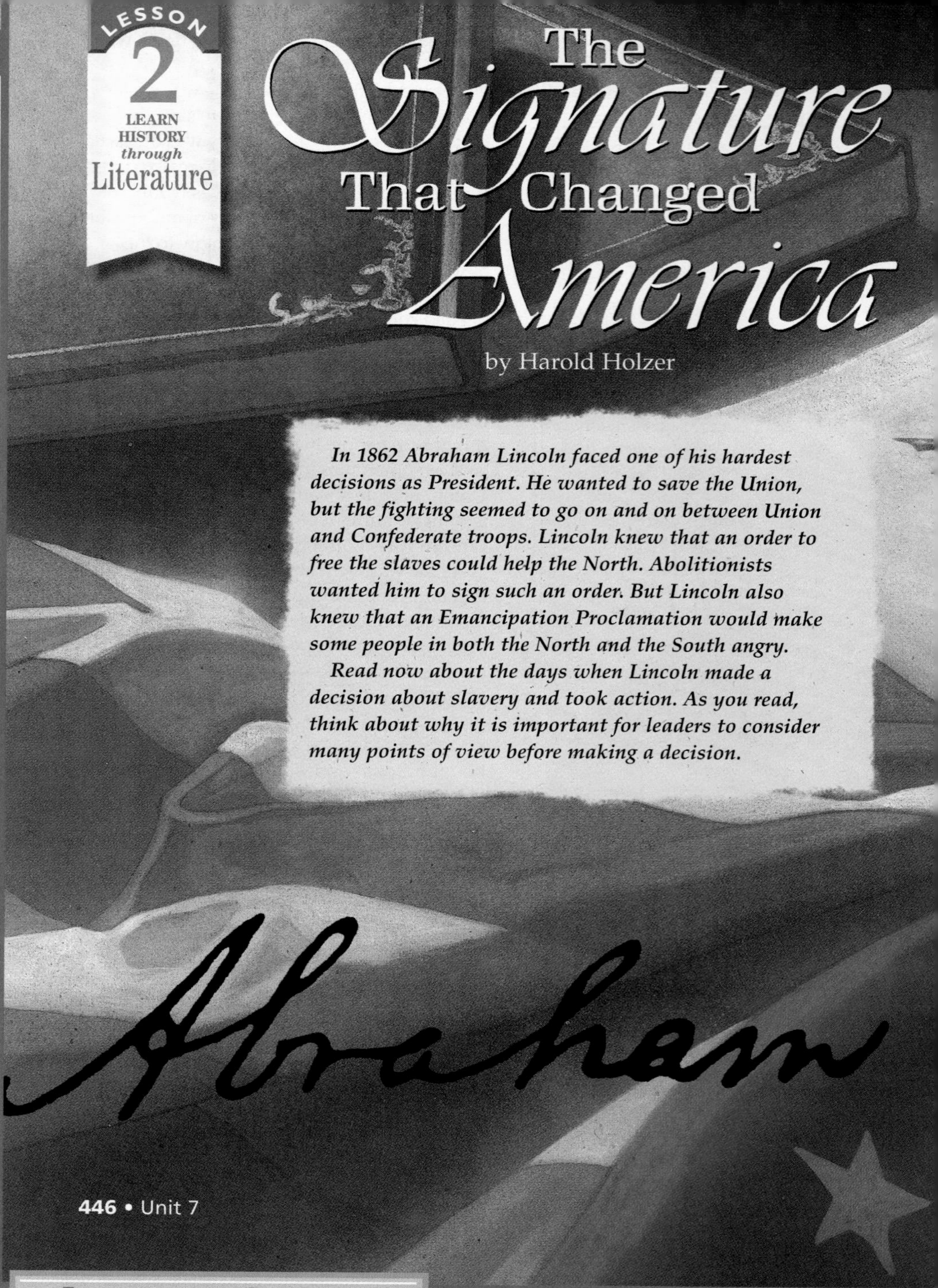
LESSON 2 LEARN HISTORY *through* Literature

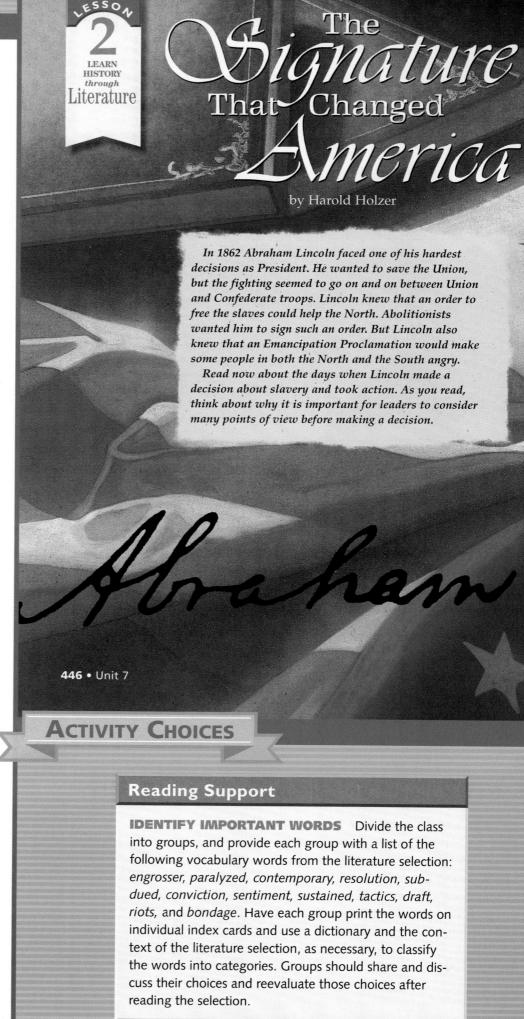

The Signature That Changed America

by Harold Holzer

In 1862 Abraham Lincoln faced one of his hardest decisions as President. He wanted to save the Union, but the fighting seemed to go on and on between Union and Confederate troops. Lincoln knew that an order to free the slaves could help the North. Abolitionists wanted him to sign such an order. But Lincoln also knew that an Emancipation Proclamation would make some people in both the North and the South angry.

Read now about the days when Lincoln made a decision about slavery and took action. As you read, think about why it is important for leaders to consider many points of view before making a decision.

446 • Unit 7

ACTIVITY CHOICES

Reading Support

IDENTIFY IMPORTANT WORDS Divide the class into groups, and provide each group with a list of the following vocabulary words from the literature selection: *engrosser, paralyzed, contemporary, resolution, subdued, conviction, sentiment, sustained, tactics, draft, riots,* and *bondage*. Have each group print the words on individual index cards and use a dictionary and the context of the literature selection, as necessary, to classify the words into categories. Groups should share and discuss their choices and reevaluate those choices after reading the selection.

It was January 1, 1863. The Civil War was still raging, but in Washington, D.C., this was a day of celebration. At the White House, President and Mrs. Abraham Lincoln welcomed the new year by hosting a party. For hours they greeted hundreds of visitors, just as Presidents and First Ladies had done for years.

But this was no ordinary New Year's Day at the White House. Today history would be made.

In mid-afternoon the President quietly left the party and walked upstairs to his office on the second floor. Waiting for him there were Secretary of State William H. Seward and members of Lincoln's staff. On a large table in the center of the room sat an official-looking document, written out in beautiful handwriting by a professional "engrosser." Lincoln sat down at the table, the document spread out before him. The moment was at hand. Now, at last, the President would sign the Emancipation Proclamation.

Abraham Lincoln took pen in hand, dipped it in ink, and then, unexpectedly, paused and put the pen down. To his surprise—and to everyone else's—Lincoln's hand was trembling.

It was not, Lincoln later said, "because of any uncertainty or hesitation on my part." As he put it, "I never in my life felt more certain that I am doing right than I do in signing this paper."

But greeting so many guests had taken a toll. "I have been shaking hands since 9 o'clock this morning, and my hand is almost paralyzed," Lincoln explained. "If my name ever goes into history it will be

Auditory Learning

Read Dramatically Have a volunteer read aloud the opening paragraphs in a dramatic way to set the scene for the literature. Prior to having students read the literature, have them brainstorm reasons it is important for leaders to consider many viewpoints before making decisions.

Understanding the Story

Select student volunteers to read aloud the first eight paragraphs. Encourage them to read dramatically about this event. Have students discuss the scene and analyze why Lincoln felt strongly that his hand must not tremble when he signed his name to the Emancipation Proclamation.

Q. **Why do you think Seward and the members of Lincoln's staff were quiet as Lincoln signed the Emancipation Proclamation?** They understood how significant the document would be in United States history, and they knew what the public reaction would be, especially in the South.

History

Connections Past to Present to Future Explain that a professional engrosser in the 1860s was trained to write in large, distinct letters, especially for legal documents, and that the original Emancipation Proclamation is preserved in the National Archives in Washington, D.C.

Background

THE LITERATURE SELECTION *The Signature That Changed America* was written especially for this textbook.

AUTHOR Harold Holzer is among the leading authorities on the politics and culture of the Lincoln years. He coauthored *The Lincoln Family Album, The Confederate Image*, and *The Lincoln Image*. He has also written more than 200 magazine articles, primarily about the Lincoln era. Twice he has won the Lincoln/Barondess Award of the Lincoln Round Table. Holzer lives in Rye, New York, and works as chief communications officer at the Metropolitan Museum of Art in New York City.

Link to Music

COOPERATIVE LEARNING

WRITE A SONG Divide the class into groups. Have the members of each group write a song that tells the story of the signing of the Emancipation Proclamation. After the groups have completed the project, have them perform their songs for the class. Students who play musical instruments may wish to provide accompaniment.

Understanding the Story

Have student volunteers read paragraphs nine through thirteen. Explain that many Presidents find it difficult to make major decisions, such as asking Congress to declare war, signing a treaty with a foreign nation, or choosing members of the Cabinet. Ask students to look for changes in Lincoln's attitude toward emancipation as they read this part of the selection. Have them analyze why it was difficult for Lincoln to write an order to free the slaves after he had become President despite the fact that he thought slavery was wrong.

Q. **Do you think Lincoln worried too much, or do you think his worries were justified?** Allow students to express and support their viewpoints.

History

Turning Points Have students draw conclusions about why some historians have likened the effects of the Emancipation Proclamation to those of the Declaration of Independence. Then have students decide whether they agree or disagree with this statement.

for this act, and my whole soul is in it. If my hand trembles when I sign the proclamation, all who examine the document hereafter will say, 'He hesitated.'"

After a few moments Lincoln again took pen in hand. The room was quiet except for the muffled sounds of laughter and music drifting upstairs from the party below. Slowly but firmly he wrote "Abraham Lincoln" at the bottom of the document that declared all slaves in the Confederacy "forever free."

With that, Lincoln glanced at his signature, looked up, smiled, and modestly said, "That will do."

What Lincoln's proclamation did—and did not do—has been debated ever since. Some argue that the Emancipation Proclamation did little. After all, it ordered slaves freed only in the states of the Confederacy—the states where Lincoln had no authority. But in the words of one contemporary, the document struck like a second Declaration of Independence. In truth, nothing so revolutionary had happened since the Revolutionary War itself. Perhaps that is why Lincoln worried so long before finally doing what some thought he should have done the moment he became President.

Lincoln had been against slavery all his life. Seeing slaves in chains for the first time in New Orleans, he vowed: "If I ever get a chance to hit this thing, I'll hit it hard." As a young legislator in Illinois, he had been one of the few lawmakers to sign a resolution against slavery. Years later he spoke angrily against the idea that slavery should be allowed to spread to the western territories.

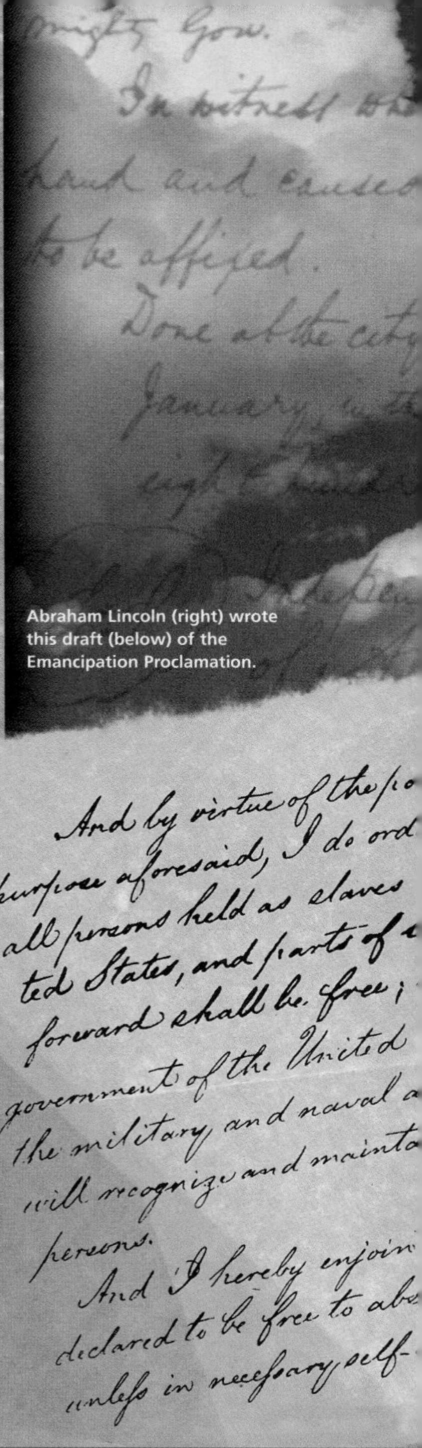

Abraham Lincoln (right) wrote this draft (below) of the Emancipation Proclamation.

Activity Choices

Smithsonian Institution®

Go to the Internet site at *http://www.si.edu/harcourt/socialstudies* to examine a portrait of Abraham Lincoln in the Hall of Presidents at the National Portrait Gallery.

Meet Individual Needs

ADVANCED LEARNERS Ask students to use library resources to explore the activities of the abolitionists during the Civil War. Have students write newspaper headlines and articles describing abolitionists' activities. Then have them share and discuss their articles with the class.

Background

EFFECTS OF THE EMANCIPATION PROCLAMATION The Emancipation Proclamation inspired many Africans to take advantage of the opportunity for freedom. More than 100,000 former slaves joined the Union army. Most Europeans, especially in Britain, supported freeing the slaves. The Emancipation Proclamation significantly reduced the likelihood that British leaders would aid the Confederacy. In addition, before the end of the war, border states voluntarily freed their slaves.

True, Lincoln did not then believe in equality for Africans living in the United States. He did not yet think they should be permitted to vote or sit on juries. But he differed with most citizens of the day by declaring, "In the right to eat the bread which his own hands earn," a black man "is my equal and . . . the equal of every living man."

When Lincoln was elected President in 1860, he promised to do nothing to interfere with slavery in the slave states. He still believed that slavery was wrong, but he felt that personal belief did not give him the right to act. After a year of war, however, Lincoln decided that the only way to put the Union back together was to fight not only against Confederate armies but also against slavery itself. "We must free the slaves," he confided, "or ourselves be subdued."

Then why did he not order slaves freed immediately? Lincoln believed that the country was simply not ready for it. "It is my conviction," he said, "that had the proclamation been issued even six months earlier than it was, public sentiment would not have sustained it." The President worried that if he acted against slavery too soon, he would lose support in the important border states, which he wanted so much to keep in the Union. Lincoln could not afford to lose the slave state of Maryland, for example. If Maryland seceded, then Washington, D.C., would become a capital city inside an enemy country! Lincoln worried, too, that Northern voters might turn against Republicans and elect a new Congress unwilling to continue the war. So he waited.

Not until July 1862 did Lincoln finally decide that he could safely act. "Things had

Civics and Government

Rights and Responsibilities of Citizens Discuss with students the meaning of Lincoln's statement, "In the right to eat the bread which his own hands earn," an African man "is my equal and . . . the equal of every living man." Point out that although Lincoln's beliefs shocked some Americans, others, especially abolitionists, agreed with Lincoln.

History

Evidence At this point, have students synthesize all they have learned about slavery and its effects on the development of the United States. Ask them to consider whether the country ever would have been unified had slavery continued. Relate the discussion to Lincoln's concern, "We must free the slaves or ourselves be subdued."

Link to Language Arts

WRITE A VIEWPOINT Ask students to express in writing their own viewpoints about the timing of Lincoln's decision to issue the Emancipation Proclamation. Have them explain whether they would have done the same thing had they been President Lincoln. Student volunteers may want to read aloud their ideas for discussion.

TECHNOLOGY

Use the AMAZING WRITING MACHINE™ to complete this writing activity.

Understanding the Story

Ask student volunteers to read aloud paragraphs fourteen through nineteen. Have students discuss how the Emancipation Proclamation might help the Union in the war effort. Then have them discuss the advantages and disadvantages of Seward's suggestion to hold back and wait for a victory.

Q. **Why do you think President Lincoln decided in July 1862 to issue a proclamation freeing Confederate slaves?** He felt that, since the war effort was going badly for the North, he must make a change and try to turn things around. He hoped that freeing the enslaved Africans in the South would help bring about that change.

History

Cause-and-Effect Relationships Point out the reaction to the Emancipation Proclamation discussed in paragraph seventeen. Have students analyze why, even in the North, there were people opposed to it.

Q. **How did the Emancipation Proclamation affect the congressional elections of 1862?** The Republican party suffered losses.

gone on from bad to worse," he said, "until I felt that we had reached the end of our rope . . . that we had about played our last card and must change our tactics, or lose the game."

On July 22, a blisteringly hot summer day, Lincoln called a meeting of the Cabinet and told the members he had an important decision to announce. He warned them that he would listen to no arguments. He had already made up his mind. Then he unfolded some papers and slowly read aloud his first draft of the proclamation. No one present dared speak against it, but Secretary of State Seward expressed a reasonable concern. With the war going so badly, wouldn't the announcement be taken by most Americans as "a cry for help—our last shriek on the retreat?" Seward wanted the President to postpone the proclamation until the Union could win a victory on the battlefield. Lincoln agreed.

Over the next two months, emancipation was the best-kept secret in America. Then, on September 17, 1862, Union troops finally gave Lincoln a victory. The North defeated the South at the Battle of Antietam in Maryland. Five days later Abraham Lincoln announced the Emancipation Proclamation.

Just as Lincoln had feared, the emancipation was immediately and bitterly attacked. Some newspapers warned that it would set off riots. Union soldiers began deserting in greater

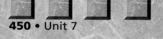

ACTIVITY CHOICES

Extend and Enrich

COOPERATIVE LEARNING

SUMMARIZE A DOCUMENT Divide the class into groups, and provide each group with a copy of the Emancipation Proclamation. Have a teacher-led oral reading of the document, and discuss vocabulary as necessary. Then ask each group to identify and summarize the key points of the document. Have the groups meet to compare their summaries. Compile the summaries into a master list for discussion.

braham Lincoln meets with members of his binet to discuss the Emancipation Proclamation ft). William H. Seward is sitting across from Lincoln. To celebrate the Emancipation Proclamation, the document was reprinted on this poster (below).

numbers than ever. That fall, Lincoln's Republican party suffered losses in elections for Congress.

But Lincoln did not back down. On January 1—with his trembling hand steadied—he signed the final proclamation. He even added his hope that former slaves would now join Union armies to fight for the freedom the emancipation promised. Everyone knew that, for all its good intentions, the Emancipation Proclamation would do nothing unless Union armies could win victories in Rebel states. That is exactly what happened. The Emancipation Proclamation freed 200,000 slaves as Union troops marched farther and farther into the Confederacy.

By the stroke of his pen, Lincoln had launched a second American Revolution. He not only had helped end the shame of human bondage in America but had guaranteed the survival of American democracy. As he put it, "By giving freedom to the slave, we assure freedom to the free."

LITERATURE REVIEW

1. Why was it important for Lincoln to think about all points of view before deciding to write the Emancipation Proclamation?
2. Why did some people think the Emancipation Proclamation did very little?
3. Lincoln said, "By giving freedom to the slave, we assure freedom to the free." Rewrite Lincoln's words in your own words to show classmates what you think he meant.

Civics and Government

Rights and Responsibilities of Citizens Ask students why they think some Americans believed democracy could not survive while slavery was condoned in the United States.

History

Leaders and Achievers Explain to students that although Lincoln believed slavery was wrong, he was more concerned about saving the Union. He was afraid that the Emancipation Proclamation might cause the border states to secede.

3. CLOSE

Ask students the following question to focus on the difficult decision that preceded writing the Emancipation Proclamation.

Why is it important for a leader to consider many viewpoints before making a decision?

Have students use what they learned about Lincoln's struggle in deciding to issue the Emancipation Proclamation to evaluate the importance of considering many viewpoints before making a decision, especially if one is in a leadership role.

LITERATURE REVIEW—Answers

1. He had to consider how the border states would react to freeing slaves, whether citizens in the Union were ready for this decision and would support it, and whether freeing the slaves would help the Union cause.
2. It freed the slaves only in the Confederacy where the Union had no authority, while it did not free the slaves in the Union.
3. Rewrites will vary but might read, "Everyone in the United States must be free. Giving freedom to slaves strengthens the freedom of the entire nation."

Reteach the Main Idea

ANALYZE A VIEWPOINT

COOPERATIVE LEARNING

Divide the class into groups representing the following viewpoints: Africans in the Northern states, Africans in the Southern states, Northern abolitionists, border state slave owners, border state citizens who did not own slaves, Northerners with concerns about freeing slaves, and Southern plantation owners. Have each group prepare a speech explaining its members' viewpoints about the Emancipation Proclamation. Ask a volunteer from each group to deliver the speech.

ACTIVITY BOOK

Reinforce & Extend

Use ACTIVITY BOOK, p. 88.

Objectives

1. Evaluate the role of Africans in fighting for the Union.
2. Determine the importance of Grant's victories.
3. Summarize the key points of Lincoln's Gettysburg Address.
4. Evaluate Sherman's March to the Sea.
5. Analyze the reasons Lee surrendered.
6. Describe the assassination of President Lincoln.

Vocabulary

Gettysburg Address (p. 455) assassination (p. 458)

1. ACCESS

The Focus Question

Discuss the reasons people who are in conflict might want to end the hostilities. Consider examples of present-day conflicts that have ended either because one side has proved to be stronger than the other or because both sides have become tired of fighting.

The Main Idea

In this lesson students explore the crucial conflicts in the last years of the Civil War that led to Lee's surrender. After students have read the lesson, have them analyze how cooperative Union efforts led to the defeat of the Confederacy.

2. BUILD

African Regiments

Key Content Summary

In 1862 Congress finally allowed Africans to enlist in the Union army. African soldiers, who often were given poor equipment and few supplies, formed 166 regiments and brought cooperation, determination, and valor to the Union army.

LESSON 3

FOCUS
What actions might help bring a difficult conflict to an end?

Main Idea As you read, think about the events that helped bring the Civil War to an end.

Vocabulary
Gettysburg Address
assassination

The Long Road to a Union Victory

The Emancipation Proclamation did not give enslaved people instant freedom. The order was only for the states tha had left the Union—not the four border states. And until Union troops were sent to the Confederate states to see that the Emancipation Proclamation was carried out, many peop there remained enslaved. Still, it gave new hope to Africans and new spirit to the North.

In the months that followed, the North seemed to be winning the war. Yet terrible battles lay ahead, and many more soldiers would die before the war's end.

African Regiments

Africans had fought to defend the United States since the Revolutionary War. Over the years, however, many had beer kept from joining the army. By the start of the Civil War, they were not allowed to serve in the army.

As the war went on, many Africans decided to form their own regiments to fight for the Union. While they trained, their leaders asked Congress to let them enlist. Finally, in 1862, witl no end to the war in sight and fewer white soldiers joining the army, Congress agreed. More than 186,000 Africans signed up. They formed 166 regiments of artillery, cavalry, infantry, an engineers.

At first African soldiers were not paid as much as white soldiers. They were given poo equipment, and they often ran out of supplies. To make things worse, Confederate soldiers said that they would enslave or kill any African soldiers they captured.

Even with the hardships and the dangers, African soldiers soon proved themselves in battle. They led raids behinc Confederate lines and served as spies and scouts. They fought in almost every battle,

Like many other Africans in the United States, this soldier, Andrew Scott, fought for the Union.

452 • Unit 7

ACTIVITY CHOICES

Reading Support

IDENTIFY A SEQUENCE Provide students with the following visual framework. Then ask them to write the events that occurred for each date in the framework.

THE LONG ROAD TO A UNION VICTORY	
DATE	EVENT
1862	Africans allowed to enlist in Union army
1863	Emancipation Proclamation; Confederate defeat at Vicksburg gives Union control over Mississippi River; Union victory at Gettysburg raises Northern morale
1864	Sherman begins his March to the Sea after occupying Atlanta
1865	Lee surrendered at Appomattox Courthouse, Virginia; Lincoln assassinated

frican troops played a key role in support of the Union. This photograph shows embers of an artillery unit completing cannon drills.

cing some of the worst fighting of the war. lore than 38,000 African soldiers lost their ves defending the Union.

EVIEW ***How did African regiments help e Union war effort?*** They led raids, served s spies and scouts, and fought in almost very battle.

Grant Leads the Union

Another boost for the North came when resident Lincoln finally found a general as ood as Confederate general Robert E. Lee. lis name was Ulysses S. Grant.

Like Lee, Grant had been educated at West oint and had fought in the war with Mexico. Vhen the Civil War began, Grant offered his ervices to the Union army. His quick deci- ons in battles soon led to Union victories. fter one battle, when the Confederates sked for the terms of surrender, Grant replied, "No terms except an unconditional and immediate surrender can be accepted." After that, Northerners liked to say that Grant's initials, *U. S.*, stood for *Unconditional Surrender*.

One of Grant's most important battles began in May 1863 at Vicksburg, Mississippi. After two attacks Grant decided to surround and lay siege to the city. For weeks Union guns pounded Vicksburg. Grant and his soldiers cut off all supplies to the city. The trapped Confederates, both soldiers and townspeople, soon ran out of food. They had to tear down houses for firewood and dig caves in hillsides for shelter. Finally, on the Fourth of July, the starving people of Vicksburg gave in.

Vicksburg proved to be a key victory. It gave the Union control of the Mississippi River. This, in turn, helped weaken the Confederacy by cutting it into two parts. As

Civics and Government

Rights and Responsibilities of Citizens Have students analyze why so many Africans were eager to fight for the Union, even though they had been denied the rights of citizens for many years and were given poor equipment and less pay than other soldiers.

Grant Leads the Union

Key Content Summary

General Ulysses S. Grant proved to be as capable a general as Robert E. Lee. He defeated the Confederate army at Vicksburg, giving the Union control of the Mississippi River and splitting the Confederacy into two parts. After Vicksburg, President Lincoln put Grant in command of all Union troops.

Geography

MAP THEME

Place Have students find Vicksburg, Mississippi, on the map on page 457 and explain why its location was strategically important in helping the Union army defeat the Confederate army.

Q. **Why was Union control of the Mississippi River important?** because the Mississippi River had been used by the South to move troops and supplies

Smithsonian Institution®

Go to the Internet site at *http://www.si.edu/harcourt/socialstudies* to examine "Mathew Brady's Gallery of Illustrious Americans" at the National Portrait Gallery.

Link to Art

RESEARCH PHOTOGRAPHS The Civil War was the first war to be photographed in detail. The most famous Civil War photographer was Mathew Brady. Have some student volunteers locate books in the school or local library that have examples of Mathew Brady's Civil War photographs. Ask students to select some of the photographs to present and explain to the class.

Background

AFRICAN REGIMENTS About 10 percent of the Union army consisted of Africans, although they comprised only 1 percent of the North's population. They were paid $7 per month compared with the $13 per month paid to white soldiers. In 1864 the government eliminated the pay differential. For the most part, Africans served in segregated units commanded by white officers. The movie *Glory* tells the story of one of the units.

History

Cause and Effect Discuss the reasons for Grant's siege of Vicksburg and the effects of the siege on the civilians in the city. Have students evaluate the effectiveness of Grant's strategy.

Visual Analysis

Interpret Photographs Have students study the photographs and read the caption.

***Q.* What other supplies might a Civil War soldier have carried?** a bedroll, a Bible, a canteen, pictures and letters from home

Gettysburg

Key Content Summary

The major conflict between the Union and Confederate armies at Gettysburg was won by the North and proved to be a turning point in the Civil War. President Lincoln, in his Gettysburg Address, emphasized the ideals of liberty and equality.

History

Turning Points Have students analyze the impact of the Union victories at Vicksburg and Gettysburg on the Confederate army.

Geography

Movement Have students locate Gettysburg, Pennsylvania, on the map on page 457. Discuss the movement of troops from the North and the South to the battlegrounds at Gettysburg.

one Union soldier wrote from Vicksburg, "This was the most glorious Fourth I ever spent." President Lincoln was overjoyed when he heard about the victory. Before long he gave Grant command of all Union troops.

REVIEW ***Why was Grant's victory at Vicksburg important?*** It cut the Confederacy into two parts.

"I can't spare this man," President Lincoln once said about Ulysses S. Grant (above). "He *fights*." Grant used this box (right) to carry his saddle and other field equipment.

Gettysburg

At about the same time that Grant won Vicksburg, other Union troops were facing the invading army of Robert E. Lee in the small town of Gettysburg, Pennsylvania. Th Battle of Gettysburg ended in one of the mos important Union victories of the war. But more than 3,000 Union soldiers and nearly 4,000 Confederates were killed. More than 20,000 on each side were wounded or reported missing.

The fate of the Fourteenth Tennessee Regiment tells the story. When the battle began, there were 365 men in the unit. Wher the battle ended, there were only 3.

On November 19, 1863, President Lincoln went to Gettysburg to dedicate a cemetery fo those who had died there. A crowd of nearly 6,000 people gathered for the ceremony.

Lincoln gave a short speech that day. In fact, he spoke for less than three minutes. A photographer who was there hoped to take a picture of the President as he gave his speech But by the time the photographer had set up his heavy camera, Lincoln had already sat down!

Activity Choices

Community Involvement

If your community has or is located near a Civil War battle site, plan a class trip to visit the site. Have students learn about the battle prior to the visit. If your community is not near a battle site, visit a local museum that houses Civil War artifacts. Another option is to invite a Civil War specialist to visit the class to share facts about the Civil War and display some artifacts.

Link to Music

SING CIVIL WAR SONGS The Civil War inspired songwriters to write music and lyrics expressing the emotions and events of the time. Ask the music teacher to teach students to sing Civil War songs, such as "Tenting Tonight" or "The Bonnie Blue Flag." Ask students to analyze the meanings of the words and phrases in the songs.

AUDIO

Use the UNIT 7 MUSIC AUDIOCASSETTE to hear the song "Battle Hymn of the Republic."

THE GETTYSBURG ADDRESS

Four score and seven years ago our fathers brought forth on this continent, a new nation, conceived in Liberty, and dedicated to the proposition that all men are created equal.

Now we are engaged in a great civil war, testing whether that nation, or any nation so conceived and so dedicated, can long endure. We are met on a great battlefield of that war. We have come to dedicate a portion of that field, as a final resting place for those who here gave their lives that that nation might live. It is altogether fitting and proper that we should do this.

But, in a larger sense, we can not dedicate—we can not consecrate—we can not hallow—this ground. The brave men, living and dead, who struggled here, have consecrated it, far above our poor power to add or detract. The world will little note, nor long remember what we say here, but it can never forget what they did here. It is for us the living, rather, to be dedicated here to the unfinished work which they who fought here have thus far so nobly advanced. It is rather for us to be here dedicated to the great task remaining before us—that from these honored dead we take increased devotion to that cause for which they gave the last full measure of devotion—that we here highly resolve that these dead shall not have died in vain—that this nation, under God, shall have a new birth of freedom—and that government of the people, by the people, for the people, shall not perish from the earth.

Lincoln's speech at Gettysburg was so hort that many people in the crowd were isappointed. Lincoln himself called it "a at failure." But people soon realized that nis short speech, later known as the **Gettysburg Address**, was one of the most nspiring ever given by an American eader.

In the Gettysburg Address, Lincoln spoke o the heart of the war-weary North. He poke of the ideals of liberty and equality on which the country had been founded. He honored the soldiers who had died defending those ideals. And he called on Americans to try even harder to win the struggle those soldiers had died for—to save the "government of the people, by the people, for the people" so that the Union would be preserved.

REVIEW ***What did President Lincoln ask Americans to do in his speech at Gettysburg?*** to try harder to save the Union

History

Connections Past to Present to Future Discuss with students the circumstances under which Lincoln gave his address at Gettysburg. Ask students to analyze why this speech, which Lincoln considered a failure, became one of his most famous speeches.

Auditory Learning

Interpret Primary Sources Ask student volunteers to read aloud different sections of the Gettysburg Address as President Lincoln might have delivered them. Help students use context clues to unlock the meaning of words, and be sure they understand what Lincoln meant when he asked Americans to "resolve that these dead shall not have died in vain."

"PRIMARY SOURCE"

Source: "Gettysburg Address."

Link to Language Arts

WRITE TO EXPLAIN Point out to students that the Gettysburg Address is carved into the walls of the Lincoln Memorial in Washington, D.C. Ask students to reread the Gettysburg Address and explain why this speech is so highly regarded in American history.

TECHNOLOGY

Use THE AMAZING WRITING MACHINE™ to complete this writing activity.

The March to the Sea

Key Content Summary

In 1864 General William T. Sherman led his army from Tennessee to Atlanta, Georgia, and then on to Savannah, destroying everything in his path that could help the South. The goal of Sherman's March to the Sea was to make the people so sick of war that they would surrender.

Geography

Movement Have students trace Sherman's March to the Sea on the map on page 457. Ask them to analyze why the railroad center in Atlanta and the port city of Savannah were important targets for the Union army.

History

Leaders and Achievers Have students note that Sherman was defeated at the first Battle of Bull Run. However, in 1863 he aided Grant in capturing Vicksburg. Ask students to compare and contrast the siege of Vicksburg with Sherman's March to the Sea.

This photograph shows a home that was damaged in Atlanta, Georgia, during the Union army's March to the Sea.

The March to the Sea

More Union victories followed those at Vicksburg and Gettysburg. Then came one of the worst times for the South—the invasion of Georgia.

In 1864 Union General William Tecumseh Sherman led his army south from Tennessee into Georgia. Through heavy fighting Sherman pushed to Atlanta, the railroad center of the South. As he took the city, much of it burned to the ground.

From Atlanta, Sherman's troops headed toward Savannah, on the Atlantic coast. Their march has become known as the March to the Sea. The goal of this march was to destroy everything that could help the South in the war. Sherman hoped that this would break the South's will to fight. "We cannot change the hearts of those people of the South," Sherman said, "but we can make war so terrible . . . make them so sick of war that generations would pass away before they would again appeal to it." Cutting a path of destruction 60 miles (97 km) wide and 300 miles (483 km) long, Union troops burned homes and stores, destroyed crops, wrecked bridges, and tore up railroad tracks.

On December 22, 1864, Savannah fell to Union troops. That night Sherman sent a message to President Lincoln. "I beg to present you as a Christmas gift the city of Savannah." Sherman then turned north and marched through South Carolina, destroying even more than he had in Georgia.

REVIEW ***What was the purpose of Sherman's March to the Sea?*** to destroy everything that could help the South in the war

ACTIVITY CHOICES

Background

SHERMAN'S VICTORIES Sherman's victories in the South had more than military significance. In September 1864 Lincoln faced a reelection battle in which he feared that the voters, who were tired of war, might reject him for a second term. Lincoln was buoyed by the message from Sherman that Atlanta had fallen. The people of the North also were elated by the victory and gave Lincoln a resounding victory at the polls. He received 212 electoral college votes to his opponent's 21.

Home Involvement

Have students share with their older family members the information concerning Sherman's March to the Sea. Tell students to discuss with their family members how their lives would have been affected if they had been living in Savannah in December 1864. Have students invite their family members to work with them to create a bulletin-board display of news articles about wars occurring in other parts of the world. Display the bulletin boards in class, and have students discuss how the lives of the people living in war-torn areas of the world are being affected by the war.

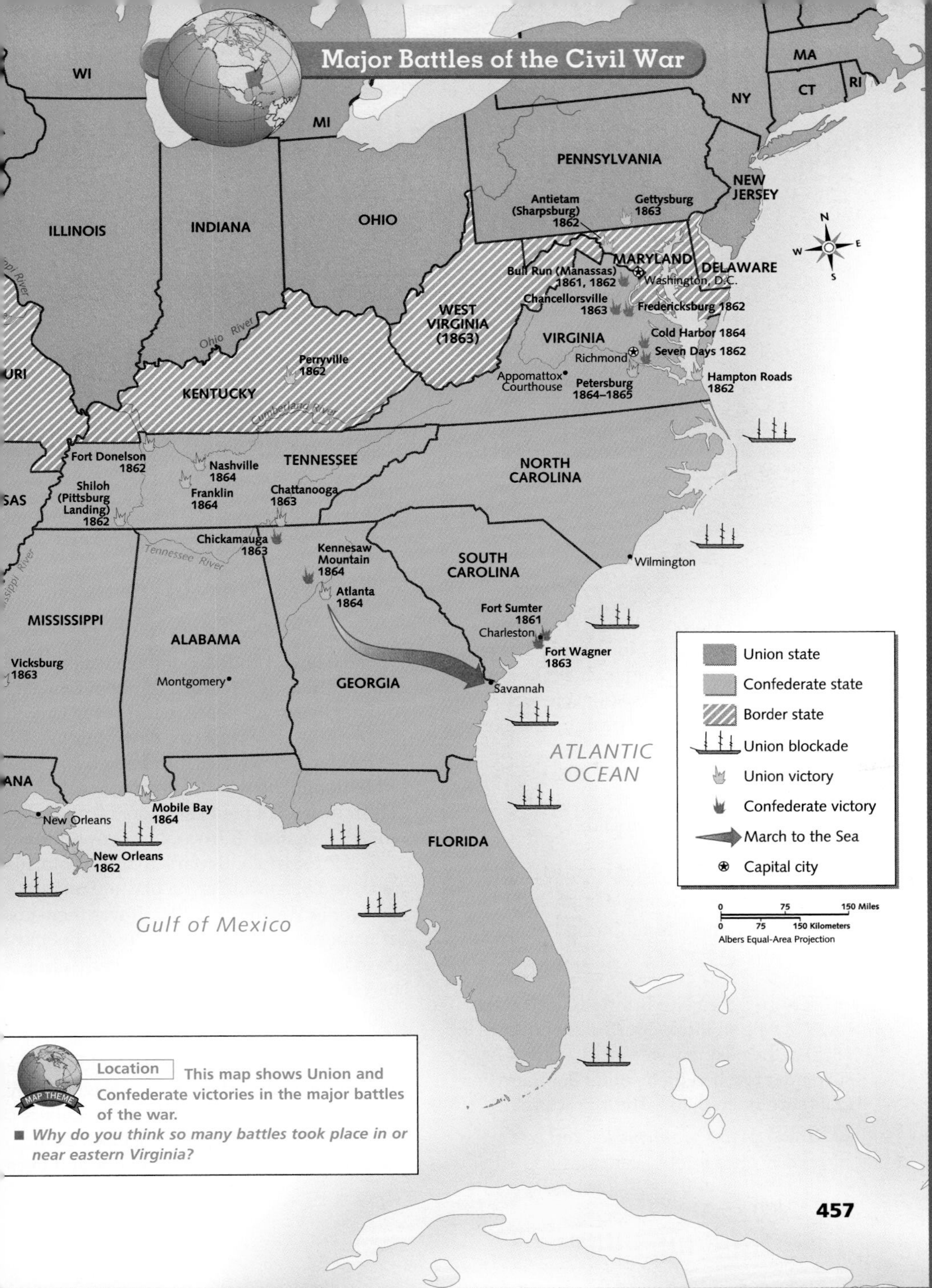

Location This map shows Union and Confederate victories in the major battles of the war.

■ *Why do you think so many battles took place in or near eastern Virginia?*

457

Visual Analysis

Learn from Maps Have students answer the question in the caption. The North wanted to capture the Confederate capital in Virginia. The South wanted to capture Washington, D.C.

***Q.* Why do you think the Union army blockaded Southern ports?**
to limit or cut off military and food supplies

Link to Science

RESEARCH COMMUNICATIONS TECHNOLOGY Telegraphs were used to transmit information and battle plans during the Civil War. Have some student volunteers use library resources to prepare reports describing how the telegraph works and how the telegraph was used during the Civil War. Have them present their reports to the class. Students may wish to create diagrams or other illustrations to accompany their reports.

Meet Individual Needs

AUDITORY LEARNERS Robert E. Lee was admired and respected by both Northerners and Southerners. Grant said of him, "There was not a man in the Confederacy whose influence with the whole people was as great as his." Ask students to use library resources to find other quotations that indicate why Robert E. Lee was such an influential and respected individual. Have students read these quotations to the class.

Lee Surrenders

Key Content Summary

Lee's starving troops were no match for Grant's strong, well-fed army. Lee had no choice but to surrender to Grant at Appomattox Courthouse in Virginia on April 9, 1865.

Economics

Interdependence and Income Have students relate the tattered and starving condition of Lee's troops to the Union strategy of cutting off the South from all trade routes.

"PRIMARY SOURCE"

Source: *R. E. Lee: A Biography.* Vol. IV. Douglas Southall Freeman. Charles Scribner's Sons, 1935.

One More Tragic Death

Key Content Summary

For John Wilkes Booth, the conflict between the North and the South was not over. Just five days after Lee's surrender, Booth assassinated President Lincoln at Ford's Theater in Washington, D.C. The whole nation went into mourning, wondering what would now happen to the country.

Robert E. Lee (seated at left) surrendered to Ulysses S. Grant (seated at right) at the home of Wilmer McLean in Appomattox Courthouse, Virginia.

Lee Surrenders

In April 1865 Grant's Union army met Lee's Confederate army in Virginia. Lee's troops were starving, and their clothes were in rags. Grant's soldiers, who were well armed and well fed, kept pushing the Confederate troops.

Finally, Lee and his troops were trapped. Lee could neither fight nor retreat. He decided to surrender. Lee said,

> "There is nothing left for me to do but to go and see General Grant, and I would rather die a thousand deaths."

Lee surrendered his army to Grant at the town of Appomattox Courthouse on April 9, 1865. In the next few weeks, as word of Lee's surrender reached them, other Southern generals surrendered, too. The war was over.

REVIEW ***What problems led to Lee's surrender?*** His troops were starving, their clothes were in rags, and they were trapped.

One More Tragic Death

The war had ended, but there was still another tragedy to come. Abraham Lincoln did not live to see peace return to the Union. On April 14, 1865, just five days after Lee's surrender, Lincoln was murdered by a man who thought he was helping the South. The murder of a political leader is called an **assassination** (uh•sa•suhn•AY•shuhn).

The President and Mary Todd Lincoln, his wife, had been watching a play at Ford's Theater in Washington, D.C. It was there that an actor named John Wilkes Booth shot the President and ran. Booth died later, during his escape.

Lincoln's assassination shocked both the North and the South. Northerners had lost the leader who had guided the Union to victory. Many gathered in the streets when they heard the news. Some cried openly. Others marched silently. People hung black cloth everywhere—on buildings, fences, and trees.

ACTIVITY CHOICES

Background

JOHN WILKES BOOTH This actor and fanatic supporter of the Southern cause entered the President's theater box a little after 10 P.M., fired one shot at the President, jumped to the stage (breaking his leg), and shouted, *"Sic semper tyrannis"* ("Thus always to tyrants"). Booth escaped, but two weeks later he was discovered by government forces in a barn in Virginia. The barn was set afire, and Booth was either shot by his pursuers or shot himself rather than surrender. It was later known that Booth's action was part of a conspiracy.

Background

CONFEDERATE HEROES DAY Explain to the class that in addition to Memorial Day, many Southern states also celebrate Confederate Heroes Day. This holiday is held in honor of the Confederate soldiers who fought for the South.

Extend and Enrich

ROLE-PLAY Have each student choose a well-known person from Civil War history to represent. Ask students to use library resources to research the person's role in the Civil War and prepare an oral presentation. The presentation should be in the form of a first-person account. Encourage students to use props. The class may ask questions of each Civil War character, and some students may be put in charge of videotaping the presentations.

HERITAGE

Memorial Day

On May 5, 1866, people in Waterloo, New York, honored those who died in the Civil War. The people closed businesses for the day and decorated soldiers' graves with flowers. This was the beginning of the holiday known as Memorial Day, or Decoration Day. On this day Americans remember those who gave their lives for their country. At the Arlington National Cemetery, a wreath is placed on the Tomb of the Unknowns. Three unknown American soldiers who were killed in war are buried there. Today most states observe Memorial Day on the last Monday in May.

The Tomb of the Unknowns at Arlington National Cemetery is guarded 24 hours a day, 365 days a year, by the United States Army.

Many Southerners were also saddened by he death of the President. Lincoln had said e would treat the South fairly in defeat. He ad promised to bring the country together gain "with malice toward none, with charity or all." What would happen now that the resident was dead?

Mary Chesnut feared the worst. When she learned of the assassination, Chesnut wrote in her diary, "Lincoln—old Abe Lincoln—killed . . . I know this foul murder will bring down worse miseries on us."

REVIEW ***Why was Lincoln's death a shock to both the North and the South?***

ESSON 3 REVIEW

Check Understanding

1. **Remember the Facts** What is the Gettysburg Address?
2. **Recall the Main Idea** What events helped bring the Civil War to an end?

Think Critically

3. **Think More About It** In what ways did individual Americans make a difference during the war?
4. **Past to Present** Why do you think people today still find meaning in the words of Abraham Lincoln's Gettysburg Address?
5. **Explore Viewpoints** If you had lived in the North during the Civil War, how might you have felt about General Sherman's March to the Sea? How might you have felt about it if you had lived in the South?

Show What You Know

Diorama Activity Make a diorama of one of the events described in this lesson. Your diorama should show either conflict or cooperation. Share your diorama with your classmates.

Northerners lost the leader who had guided them to victory. Southerners lost the leader who said he would treat the South fairly in defeat.

Reteach the Main Idea

WRITE A NEWSPAPER ARTICLE Divide the class into groups, and assign each group an event that helped bring the Civil War to an end. Ask each group to write headlines and one or more articles about its assigned event. Have a spokesperson in each group read the articles to the other groups. Through discussion of the article(s), make sure students understand the series of events that helped end the Civil War.

COOPERATIVE LEARNING

ACTIVITY BOOK

Reinforce & Extend

Use ACTIVITY BOOK, p. 89.

3. CLOSE

Have students consider again the Focus question on page 452.

What actions might help bring a difficult conflict to an end?

Have students use what they have learned in this lesson to identify actions that might be taken to end difficult conflicts.

LESSON 3 REVIEW—Answers

Check Understanding

1. the speech given by President Lincoln at the dedication of a cemetery after the tragic Battle of Gettysburg
2. major Union victories at Vicksburg and Gettysburg, and Sherman's March to the Sea, which economically crippled the South

Think Critically

3. Lincoln: held a strong belief in preserving the Union, which gave him the strength to continue the war and seek a victory despite major defeats; Grant: proved himself to be a strong and shrewd military leader; Sherman: set a goal that he knew would help break the South economically and pursued it; Lee: was a strong, shrewd, and well-respected military leader whose success surprised the North
4. Lincoln spoke of equality and liberty, which are the foundation of our nation and are still important to Americans today.
5. Northerners might have been distressed at the toll the march took on civilians or might have had no sympathy for the Southerners who were in the way of Sherman's advance. Southerners probably hated Sherman and the Union troops for the massive destruction of their lives and property.

Show What You Know

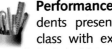

Performance Assessment Have students present their dioramas to the class with explanations of what they have included and how their scenes show either conflict or cooperation.

What to Look For In evaluating the dioramas and students' presentations, look for understanding of the chosen event and its relation to the theme of conflict and cooperation.

Objectives

1. Identify appropriate uses of maps with large and small scales.
2. Practice comparing distances on maps with different scales.

1. ACCESS

Talk with students about the value of choosing appropriate tools. For example, what would happen if someone tried to use a saw to drive a nail? Explain that the same principle applies to using maps. Different kinds of maps are made for various purposes. Have students suggest when they would use a map with many details and when they would use a map that shows only the major features of the area.

2. BUILD

Point out that both maps show the same area around Gettysburg, Pennsylvania. Tell students that Map A has the advantage of requiring less space, but that Map B is able to show more detail. Have students note that in addition to showing more of the landscape, such as the woods, Map B has enough space to show the positions of Union and Confederate troops.

Map and Globe Skills

Compare Maps with Different Scale

1. Why Learn This Skill?

A map scale compares a distance on a map to a distance in the real world. It helps you find the real distance between places. Map scales are different depending on how much area is shown. Knowing about different map scales can help you choose the best map for gathering the information you need.

2. Map Scales

Look at the map below and the map on page 461. They show the same area around Gettysburg, Pennsylvania, but with different scales. On Map A, Gettysburg looks smaller. For that reason the scale is said to be smaller. On Map B, Gettysburg appears larger, and the scale is said to be larger.

When the map scale is larger, more details can be shown. For example, note the details of the woods on Map B. Also note that Map B is a larger map. It takes a larger piece of paper to show a place on a map with a large scale than to show it on a map with a smaller scale. Although they have different scales, Maps A and B can both be used to measure the distance between the same two places.

3. Understand the Process

On July 2, 1863, the second day of the Battle of Gettysburg, the Union line stretched from Spangler's Spring north to Culp's Hill, on to Cemetery Hill, south along Cemetery Ridge to the hill called Little Round Top, and beyond. What was the real distance in miles between Cemetery Hill and Little Round Top? To find out, follow the steps below:

1. On Map A, use a ruler to measure the exac length of the scale, or use a pencil to mark off the length on a sheet of paper. How long is the line that stands for one mile?

Map A: Gettysburg, July 1–3, 1863

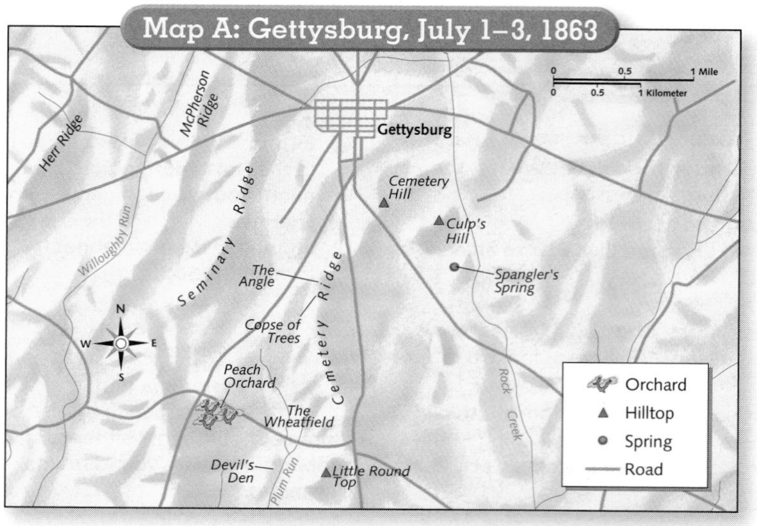

ACTIVITY CHOICES

TECHNOLOGY

Use MAPSKILLS to complete this activity.

Link to Language Arts

WRITE A HOW-TO PARAGRAPH Have students write paragraphs explaining how to use a map scale to compute distance on a map. Have them work in pairs or small groups to compare and refine their instructions.

TECHNOLOGY

Use THE AMAZING WRITING MACHINE™ RESOURCE PACKAGE to complete the writing activity.

Meet Individual Needs

TACTILE LEARNERS Use sidewalk chalk to draw a large map of the United States on a paved area of the school playground. Establish a map scale, and cut a length of wood to the measurement of the scale. A simple scale, such as 1 foot = 500 miles, will work best. Have students turn the length of wood end-over-end to measure the distance across the country.

2 Still using Map A, find Cemetery Hill and Little Round Top. Using the ruler or the sheet of paper you marked, measure the distance between these two hills. How many times can you fit the scale length end to end between the two hills? Multiply the number of scale lengths between the hills by the distance that the scale length represents. What is the real distance in miles between Cemetery Hill and Little Round Top?

3 Now go through the same steps for Map B. How long is the scale length that stands for one mile? Use that scale length to measure the distance between Cemetery Hill and Little Round Top on the map. What is the real distance in miles? Are the real distances you found on the two maps the same? You should see that even when map scales are different, the real distances shown on the maps are the same.

4 Now measure the distance between the Confederate line at the Peach Orchard and the Union line at Little Round Top. What is the real distance between the Confederate line and the Union line? Which map did you use to find the distance? Explain why you chose that map.

4. Think and Apply

Think about how you use maps when you travel. Find two road maps with different scales—perhaps a road map of your state and a road map of a large city within your state. Compare the real distances in miles between two places that are on both maps. How far apart are the two places? Are the distances the same on both maps? When would it be more helpful to use the state map, with the smaller scale? When would it be more helpful to use the city map, with the larger scale? Share your answers with a classmate.

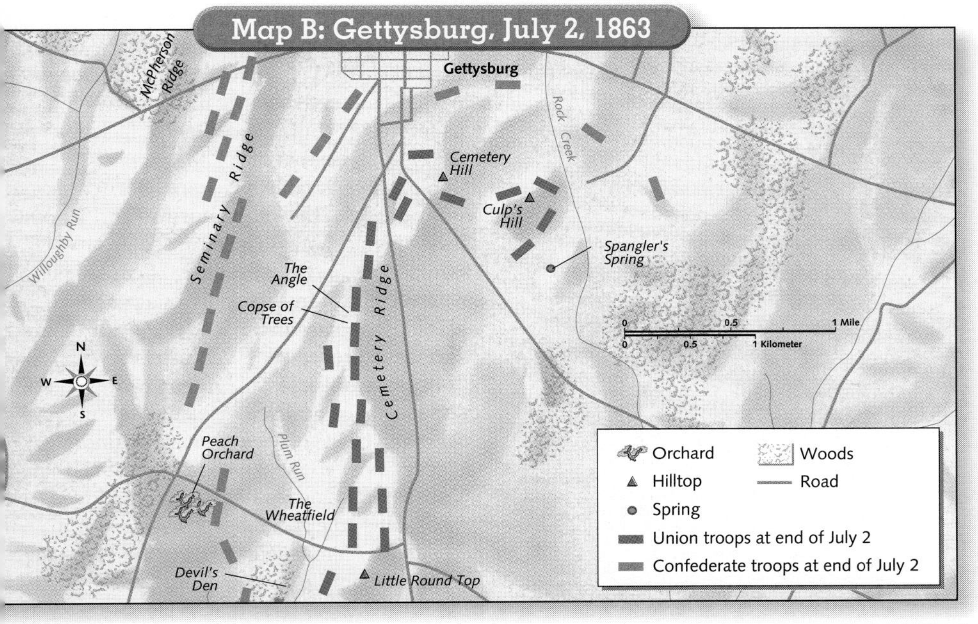

Have students locate the Union line on Map B. Also have them locate the various points on that line mentioned in Understand the Process and answer the questions in the section. Have students follow the steps to determine the distance between Cemetery Hill and Little Round Top.

1 about 1 inch stands for 1 mile.

2 about $2\frac{1}{2}$ times; about 2.5 miles

3 On Map B, 1.2 inches stand for 1 mile. yes

4 about 1 mile; Map B; because it shows the lines of the Union and Confederate troops

3. CLOSE

Have students apply map skills by completing the Think and Apply activity. To compare the distance between two places on two different maps, they should use a method similar to steps 1 and 2 in this lesson. First, have them measure the length of the map scale, and then have them determine the number of scale lengths between the two places. Finally, have them multiply the number of scale lengths by the distance the scale length represents. The distance indicated between the two places should be the same on both maps. The small-scale state map might be helpful when driving through the state. The large-scale city map would be useful for finding locations in a city. As students work, look for an understanding of how to use and compare different map scales.

Reteach the Skill

COOPERATIVE LEARNING

COMPARE DISTANCES ON ATLAS MAPS Have small groups of students use an atlas to determine the distance between two cities on maps with different scales. Have them use a map of the United States, for example, to determine the distance between San Antonio and Dallas, Texas, or between Los Angeles and San Francisco, California. Then have them make a similar determination using a state map from the atlas. Have the groups consider the following questions: Do the two maps indicate the same distance? When would it be more helpful to use one or the other of the maps?

ACTIVITY BOOK

Practice & Apply

Use ACTIVITY BOOK, p. 90.

TRANSPARENCY

Use TRANSPARENCY 37.

Objectives

1. Describe how free Africans rebuilt their lives.
2. Analyze the purpose of the Freedmen's Bureau.
3. Explain the system of sharecropping and its effect on the lives of former slaves.
4. Summarize Johnson's ideas for Reconstruction, and evaluate the impact of the black codes.
5. Analyze how Congress's plans better protected the rights of African Americans.
6. Evaluate the successes and failures of Reconstruction.

Vocabulary

sharecropping (p. 464)
Reconstruction (p. 465)
scalawag (p. 467)
carpetbagger (p. 467)
segregation (p. 467)

1. ACCESS

The Focus Question

Discuss changes that might have occurred recently in school rules or in local laws. Have students evaluate the impact of the changes.

The Main Idea

In this lesson students learn how new laws affected the lives of Americans after the Civil War. After students have read the lesson, have them analyze the impact of these new laws on the lives of Southerners.

2. BUILD

A Free People

Key Content Summary

After the Civil War ended, former slaves set about building new lives. They formed new communities and tried to find missing loved ones. However, their lives remained difficult, and many began to look for help from the United States government.

LESSON 4

FOCUS How can new laws affect the lives of citizens?

Main Idea Read to learn about how new laws affected the lives of Americans in the years following the Civil War.

Vocabulary
sharecropping
Reconstruction
scalawag
carpetbagger
segregation

Life After the War

When the Civil War finally ended, it was clear that peace had not come easily. More than 600,000 soldiers had died. Many others had returned home wounded. Much of the South was destroyed. And now the President was dead. As one Southerner remembered, "All the talk was of burning homes, houses knocked to pieces . . . famine, murder, desolation."

The years following the war were hard ones. However, the end of the war brought new hope to at least one group of people—the former slaves.

A Free People

With the Union victory, 4 million enslaved people were freed. Most slaves were already free by the time the Civil War ended in 1865. In December of that year, the Thirteenth Amendment to the Constitution ended slavery in the United States forever. "I felt like a bird out of a cage," one former slave remembered, looking back on the day he was set free. "I could hardly ask to feel any better than I did that day."

Free Africans quickly began to form new communities. They built churches and schools. They opened stores. They formed groups to help people find jobs and to take care of people who were sick. In 1866, only one year after the war ended, one African leader proudly said, "We have progressed a century in a year."

As soon as they could, many former slaves began to search for family members who had been sold and sent away under slavery. Newspapers were filled with advertisements asking for help in finding loved ones. This ad appeared in a newspaper in Nashville, Tennessee. "During the year 1849, Thomas Sample carried away from this city, as his slaves, our daughter, Polly, and son,

By making slavery against the law, the Thirteenth Amendment ended slavery in the United States forever.

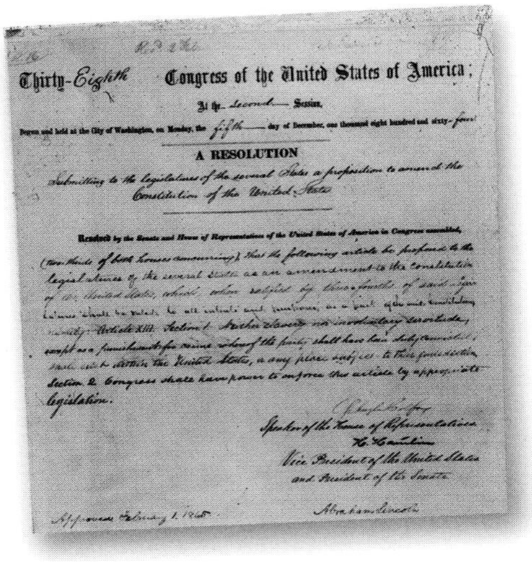
Thirty-Eighth Congress of the United States of America;
At the second Session,
A RESOLUTION

ACTIVITY CHOICES

Reading Support

PREVIEW AND READ THE LESSON Provide students with the following visual framework.

Reconstruction and New Laws	
Protecting Equal Rights	**Undermining Equal Rights**
Thirteenth Amendment Fourteenth Amendment Fifteenth Amendment New state constitutions (former Confederate states)	Black codes (former Confederate states) Segregation laws (former Confederate states)

In this painting a preacher visits a family of former slaves. Many African families had been split up because of slavery.

George. . . . We will give $100 each for them to any person who will assist them, or . . . get word to us of their whereabouts."

Many families never found their missing loved ones. But for those that did, it was a time of great joy. "I wish you could see this people as they step from slavery into freedom," one Union soldier wrote to his wife. "Families which had been for a long time broken up are united and oh! such happiness."

Former slaves worked hard to build new lives. Yet life remained difficult. Often it was hard just to find food, clothing, and shelter. Many began to look to the United States government for help.

REVIEW ***How did free Africans help one another after the war?*** They built churches and schools, opened stores, and formed groups to help people.

HERITAGE

Juneteenth

Abraham Lincoln signed the Emancipation Proclamation on January 1, 1863. But because Union troops did not control Texas at the time, the order had little effect there. On June 19, 1865, Union soldiers landed at Galveston, Texas. On that day Union General Gordon Granger read an order declaring that all slaves in Texas were free. Today people in Texas and across the country celebrate June 19, or Juneteenth, as a day of freedom. It is a holiday marked by picnics, parades, and family gatherings.

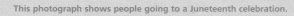

This photograph shows people going to a Juneteenth celebration.

Culture

Social Organizations and Institutions Explore with students the support systems Africans formed to help one another following the Civil War. Ask students to draw conclusions about the kinds of adjustments Africans had to make once they were free.

Auditory Learning

Read Dramatically Have a student volunteer read aloud the newspaper ad and another volunteer read aloud what the Union soldier wrote to his wife. Ask students to express their own viewpoints about the emotions involved in the reunification of broken families.

Meet Individual Needs

ENGLISH LANGUAGE LEARNERS Have students add the vocabulary words for this lesson to their vocabulary notebooks. Encourage them to illustrate those words that lend themselves to illustrations. Suggest that they include example sentences to show their understanding of each word's meaning.

Background

AFRICAN CHURCHES Before the Civil War, slaves worshipped in segregated sections of white churches. After the war, Africans set up many of their own churches. Churches were not only places of worship, but also places for social gatherings, political meetings, and schooling. African ministers were among the most respected leaders of the communities, with many of them holding political office.

The Freedmen's Bureau

Key Content Summary

The Freedmen's Bureau was set up by Congress in 1865 to help former slaves adapt to the changes in their lives. Although the bureau helped white Southerners rebuild their farms, its greatest contribution was in providing education for former slaves in the South.

Culture

Social Organizations and Institutions Have students draw conclusions about why the Freedmen's Bureau emphasized education in aiding former slaves.

Sharecropping

Key Content Summary

Although Africans were free, many continued to work on plantations. There was a change in the working relationship, however. In return for farming the land, many workers received a cabin, mules, tools, seed, and a share of the crop.

Economics

Economic Systems and Institutions Explore with students the nature of the sharecropping system. Emphasize the economic relationship between the sharecropper and the planter.

Many former slaves, like those shown outside of this Freedmen's Bureau school, were eager to learn to read and write.

The Freedmen's Bureau

In 1865 Congress set up an organization to help former slaves. This group was called the Bureau of Refugees, Freedmen, and Abandoned Lands—or the Freedmen's Bureau.

The Freedmen's Bureau gave food and other supplies to freed slaves. It also helped some white farmers rebuild their farms. The most important work of the Freedmen's Bureau, however, was education. Newly freed slaves were eager to learn to read and write. To help meet this need, the Freedmen's Bureau built more than 4,000 schools and hired thousands of teachers.

The Freedmen's Bureau also wanted to help former slaves earn a living by giving them land to farm. This plan, however, did not work out. The land was to have come from the plantations taken during the war. But the government decided to give the plantations back to their original owners. In the end, most former slaves were not given land. Without money to buy land of their own, they had to find work where they could.

REVIEW *What was the purpose of the Freedmen's Bureau?* to help former slaves

Sharecropping

In their search for jobs, some former slaves went back to work on plantations. Many planters welcomed them. Fields needed to be plowed, and crops needed to be planted. Now, however, planters had to pay Africans for their work.

In the days following the war, there was not much money. Instead of paying workers in cash, many landowners paid them in shares. Under this system, known as **sharecropping**, a landowner gave a worker a cabin, mules, tools, and seed. The worker then farmed the land. At harvesttime the landowner took part of the crops, plus enough to cover the cost of the worker's rent and supplies. What was left was the worker's share.

Sharecropping gave landowners the help they needed to work the fields. It also gave former slaves work for pay. Yet few people got ahead through sharecropping. When crops failed, both landowners and workers suffered. Even in good times, most workers' shares were very little, if anything at all.

REVIEW *Why did landowners pay workers in shares rather than in cash?* because there was not much money following the war

464 • Unit 7

ACTIVITY CHOICES

Meet Individual Needs

ADVANCED LEARNERS Have students use library resources to research the contributions of schools created by the Freedmen's Bureau, such as Howard University, Fisk University, Atlanta University, and the Hampton Institute. Ask students to share their findings with the class.

Link to Language Arts

WRITE A PERSONAL NARRATIVE
Remind students that by the time sharecroppers paid rent for the land, there was little money left for them to get ahead. Ask students to imagine that they are sharecroppers and to write how they feel about sharecropping compared with slavery, including their hope or lack of hope for the future.

TECHNOLOGY

Use THE AMAZING WRITING MACHINE™ RESOURCE PACKAGE to complete this writing activity.

As sharecroppers, former slaves were paid for their work. But sharecropping was a hard way to make a living, and it put many families in debt.

A New President

As Americans were getting used to their new lives after the war, government leaders began making plans for bringing the country back together. This time of rebuilding was called **Reconstruction**.

After Lincoln's death the Vice President, Andrew Johnson, became the new President. Johnson tried to carry out Lincoln's promise to be fair to the South in defeat. He pardoned most Confederates who promised loyalty to the United States. They were then given back the rights of citizenship and were allowed to vote. Their states held elections, and state governments went back to work.

Johnson also said that the Confederate states must abolish slavery. This requirement was met when the Thirteenth Amendment was passed late in 1865. Johnson then said that the last of the Confederate states could return to the Union.

Such easy terms, however, made some people angry. Many Northerners felt that the Confederates were not being punished at all. White Southerners were being elected to office and taking over state governments just as they always had. Yet no one talked about the rights of former slaves. What would happen to them?

It was not long before laws were passed in the South to limit the rights of former slaves. These laws were called black codes. The black codes differed from state to state. In most states Africans were not allowed to vote. In some they were not allowed to travel freely. They could not own certain kinds of property or work in certain businesses. They could be made to work in the fields without pay if they could not find another job.

Many, however, faced an even worse problem. Shortly after the war ended, secret groups formed in the South that tried to keep Africans from having their rights as free persons. Most of those who joined these groups were upset about their war losses and angry about the new rights of former slaves.

One such group was the Ku Klux Klan, or the KKK. Dressed in white robes and hoods, its members delivered nighttime messages of hate. Klan members broke into homes and attacked and killed Africans. They burned African schools and churches. They punished anyone who helped former slaves. It was a time of terror for many people.

REVIEW ***What did Andrew Johnson try to carry out when he became President?***
Lincoln's promise to be fair to the South in defeat

A New President

Key Content Summary

While changes had to be made in the South, President Andrew Johnson tried to be fair. Many Northerners, however, criticized his easy treatment of the South. When Southerners regained control of their state governments, they passed laws called black codes, which restricted some changes that had helped former slaves. Secret groups such as the Ku Klux Klan (KKK) formed to further restrict the rights of Africans.

History

Leaders Have students analyze President Johnson's ideas concerning how the South should be treated.

Q. **How did the Thirteenth Amendment help former slaves?** It abolished slavery in the United States.

Culture

Social Organizations and Institutions Compare and contrast conditions for Africans under the black codes with those under slavery. Have students draw conclusions about the intentions of the black codes.

Multicultural Link

Select student volunteers to research and prepare oral presentations on Blanche K. Bruce and Hiram Revels, two African Americans elected to the United States Senate during the period of Reconstruction.

Link to Art

COOPERATIVE LEARNING

DRAW A POLITICAL CARTOON Divide the class into small groups. Tell some of the groups that they are to represent the Northern viewpoint. Tell the other groups that they are to represent the Southern viewpoint. Ask each group to use an issue from the lesson to create a political cartoon. Have groups share and discuss their completed cartoons.

Background

RADICAL REPUBLICANS Johnson's opponents in Congress were known as Radical Republicans. The leading Radical Republican in the House of Representatives was Thaddeus Stevens of Pennsylvania. He believed the Southern states should be treated as "conquered provinces" and punished for their rebellion. Because Stevens firmly believed in equality for Africans, he initiated the Fourteenth Amendment and was a leading voice for the impeachment of Johnson.

Congress Takes Action

Key Content Summary

Displeased with the terms of Johnson's Reconstruction plan, Congress passed stricter requirements on the Southern states, including more protection and more opportunities for former slaves. Johnson objected to these changes, and Congress impeached him.

Civics and Government

Purposes and Types of Government Point out that Congress recognized the attempt by the Southern states to restrict the rights of African Americans as citizens. Discuss the rights that were being violated, and have students analyze the ways Congress's plan would remedy those violations.

Q. **How did the Fourteenth Amendment help former slaves?** It gave them United States citizenship and all the rights provided by citizenship.

Reconstruction Ends

Key Content Summary

White Southerners were angry with greedy Northerners and state governments under Reconstruction. They began to regain control of state governments and to pass laws limiting the rights of African Americans.

---

because of the way African Americans in some Southern states were being treated

Congress Takes Action

Many leaders of Congress were alarmed about the way former slaves in some Southern states were being treated. They believed that President Johnson's Reconstruction plan was not working. So they voted to change to a plan of their own—a plan that was much tougher on white Southerners.

First, Congress did away with the new state governments and put the Southern states under the army's rule. Union soldiers kept order, and army officers were made governors. Before each Southern state could reestablish its government, it had to write a new state constitution giving all men, both black and white, the right to vote. To return to the Union, a state also had to pass the Fourteenth Amendment. This amendment gave citizenship to all people born in the United States—including former slaves.

Johnson was very angry about this plan and about other laws that Congress passed to cut back his authority. Believing that these laws were unconstitutional, Johnson refused to carry them out. Then, in 1868, the House of Representatives voted to impeach the President, or charge him with a crime. He was put on trial in the Senate. There, in a very close vote, he was found not guilty. Although he stayed in office, Johnson was no longer a strong leader.

The Southern states began to write new state constitutions and pass the Fourteenth Amendment. State elections were held once again. For the first time, African Americans from the South were elected to Congress. They also served in state governments that took over the job of rebuilding the South.

REVIEW ***Why did Congress vote to change Johnson's Reconstruction plan?***

Reconstruction Ends

The new state governments made many important changes. They did away with the black codes. They approved the Fifteenth Amendment, which said that no citizen could be kept from voting because of race. They built hospitals and schools and repaired roads, bridges, and railroads.

Yet the work of the state governments did not make everyone happy. To pay for their Reconstruction projects, state leaders placed high taxes on land. These taxes hurt landowners, who were trying to get their farms and plantations working again. Some were forced to sell their land because they could not pay the taxes.

Many white Southerners soon grew angry with their state leaders. They did not like the fact that African Americans were voting and

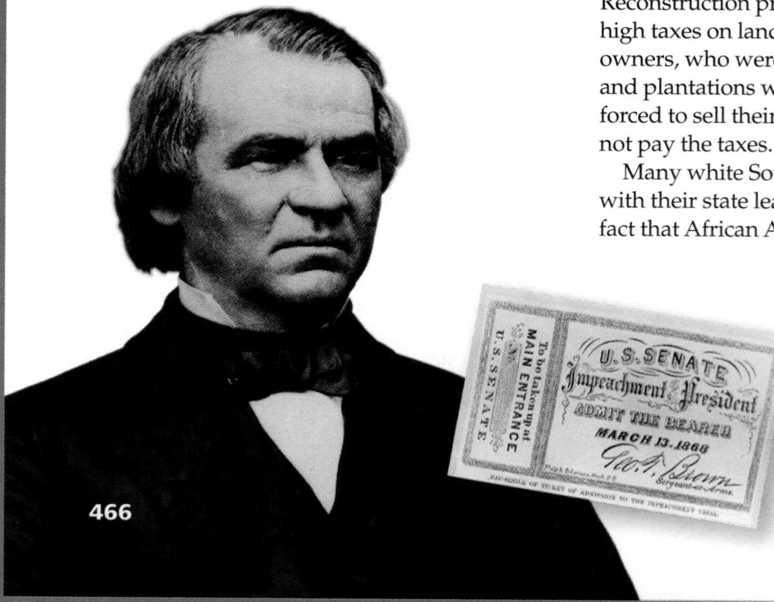

The disagreements between Congress and Andrew Johnson (far left) led to his impeachment. Johnson's trial in the Senate drew crowds of people, and tickets (left) were scarce.

466

Activity Choices

Link to Reading

READ THE CONSTITUTION Have students read the Thirteenth, Fourteenth, and Fifteenth amendments to the Constitution on pages R38–R39. Discuss the meaning of each section, and have students note that these were the most important changes in laws to come out of the Reconstruction years. Discuss why Congress felt the need to enact these laws. Also have students identify those persons still excluded from voting and discuss why this was so.

Background

AFRICAN AND AFRICAN AMERICAN In referring to people of African descent living in the United States, it is the style of this textbook to use the term *African American* after passage of the Fourteenth Amendment in 1868. Before passage of this amendment, the term *African* is used.

Extend and Enrich

COOPERATIVE LEARNING

MAKE A COLLAGE Divide the class into small groups, and assign each group a topic from the lesson, such as sharecropping, the Freedmen's Bureau, new amendments, or Radical Republicans. Have the groups use library resources to research their topics further and to create collages that show the negative and positive effects of their topics during the Reconstruction years. Have students discuss the displayed collages.

taking part in government. They did not like the white Southerners who supported the government. They called them **scalawags** (SKA•lih•wagz)—people who support something for their own gain. They also did not like being told what to do by Northerners. Under military rule Northern soldiers guarded their streets. Other Northerners went to the South to try to help with Reconstruction or to make a profit by buying land or opening businesses. White Southerners called them **carpetbaggers** because many of them arrived carrying their belongings in suitcases made of carpet pieces.

Some white Southerners tried again to take the authority away from their state leaders. One way they did this was to control the way people voted. Groups such as the Ku Klux Klan used violence to keep African Americans from voting or to make sure that they voted as they were told. Sometimes the votes of African Americans simply were not counted.

In time white Southerners once again took control of their state governments. New state laws were passed that made it very hard, if not impossible, for African Americans to vote. African Americans had to go to separate schools and churches and sit in separate railroad cars. Such laws led to the **segregation**, or separation, of black people and white people.

Reconstruction was over by 1877. In that year the last of the Union troops left the South. The rights and freedoms African Americans had just won were again taken away in the South.

The first African Americans to serve in the United States Congress were elected during Reconstruction.

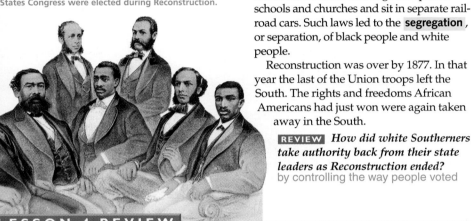

REVIEW *How did white Southerners take authority back from their state leaders as Reconstruction ended?* by controlling the way people voted

LESSON 4 REVIEW

Check Understanding

1. **Remember the Facts** In what ways did the government try to help former slaves?
2. **Recall the Main Idea** How did new laws affect the lives of Americans in the years following the Civil War?

Think Critically

3. **Think More About It** In what ways did life change for former slaves who became sharecroppers?
4. **Explore Viewpoints** Why do you think Lincoln wanted to be fair to the South in defeat?

Show What You Know

Writing Activity Imagine that you are a news reporter. Write an interview with a former slave, a Southern landowner, a Union soldier in the South, or a carpetbagger. Provide both questions and answers.

Chapter 14 • **467**

History

Patterns and Relationships Discuss with students the ways in which the conflicts between the North and South continued despite the end of the Civil War. Have students decide whether the Union achieved its goal of preserving a "government of the people, by the people, and for the people."

3. CLOSE

Have students consider again the Focus question on page 462.

How can new laws affect the lives of citizens?

Have students use what they have learned in this lesson to analyze how new laws can affect the lives of citizens.

LESSON 4 REVIEW—Answers

Check Understanding

1. by educating them, giving them food, giving them United States citizenship, and giving them the right to vote
2. At first, Southerners were pardoned and given back their rights; then the Thirteenth Amendment abolished slavery and the Southern states passed black codes that limited the rights of Africans, which led Congress to put Southern states under army rule until they wrote new state constitutions. The Fourteenth Amendment gave citizenship to all people born in the United States, and the Fifteenth Amendment protected voting rights. Eventually, new Southern state laws led to segregation.

Think Critically

3. They were free working people, but the sharecropping system put many of them deep into debt that they could never repay.
4. He wanted to reunite the country.

Show What You Know

Performance Assessment You may want to assign the different viewpoints to students and to have them work in pairs for the writing process as well as for the interviews.

What to Look For Hold the writers responsible for conveying viewpoints that they were able to infer from the lesson.

Reteach the Main Idea

COOPERATIVE LEARNING

MAKE A CHART Divide the class into groups, and ask each group to make a chart titled *How New Laws Affected the Lives of Americans After the Civil War.* The first section of the chart should show how national and state laws affected the lives of Africans. The second section should show how new national and state laws affected Southerners. The third section of the chart should show how new national and state laws affected Northerners. Have the groups discuss their completed charts.

ACTIVITY BOOK

Reinforce & Extend

Use ACTIVITY BOOK, p. 91.

Time Line

Ask students to share what they recall about each event shown on the time line.

Connect Main Ideas

Use the organizer to review the main ideas of the chapter. Have students use their textbooks to complete or check their work. Allow time for them to discuss and compare their responses.

ACTIVITY BOOK

Summarize the Chapter

A copy of the graphic organizer appears on ACTIVITY BOOK, p. 92.

TRANSPARENCY

A copy of the graphic organizer appears on TRANSPARENCY 38.

Write More About It

Write a Diary Entry
Although diary entries will vary, they should reflect the fact that border states allowed slavery but remained a part of the Union.

Write a News Story
News stories should explain that (a) the Emancipation Proclamation ordered the freeing of the slaves; (b) Lincoln issued it as a tool to put the Union back together; and (c) it gave hope to slaves and new spirit to the North.

TECHNOLOGY

Use THE AMAZING WRITING MACHINE™ to complete the writing activities.

TECHNOLOGY

Use TIMELINER™ DATA DISKS to discuss and summarize the chapter.

CHAPTER 14 REVIEW

1860 — 18

1863
- The Emancipation Proclamation is signed
- Abraham Lincoln delivers the Gettysburg Address

1865
- The Civil War ends
- Abraham Lincoln is assassinated

Connect Main Ideas

Use this organizer to show how the chapter's main ideas are connected. Write a sentence or two telling how each event or idea affected the lives of Americans during the Civil War and Reconstruction. A copy of the organizer appears on page 92 of the Activity Book.

Possible answers to th graphic organizer are provided on page 440 of this Teacher's Editio

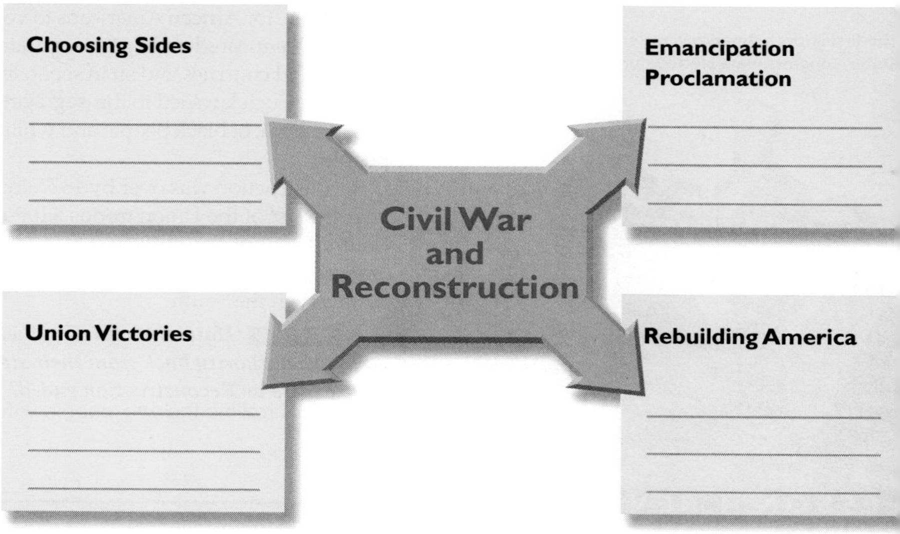

Write More About It

Write a Diary Entry Imagine that you are living in one of the border states at the beginning of the Civil War. Write a diary entry in which you tell why you think some members of your family have chosen to fight for the North while others have chosen to fight for the South.

Write a News Story Imagine that you are newspaper reporter covering the White Ho in 1863. Write an article for your newspape which you tell readers what the Emancipat Proclamation will do, why President Lincoln has decided to issue it, and how it will affe the war.

468 • Chapter 14

Use Vocabulary

1. *Border states* were those states between the North and the South. (p. 441)
2. The *Emancipation Proclamation* was a decree or an order that freed the slaves. (p. 445)
3. The *assassination* of Abraham Lincoln shocked both the North and the South; no one could believe that anyone would murder the President. (p. 458)
4. Under the system of *sharecropping* used after the war, workers gave landowners part of their crops in exchange for goods and the right to farm the land. (p. 464)
5. Northerners who came to help wit Reconstruction or to make money i the South were called *carpetbagger* (p. 467)
6. *Segregation* was the separation c black people and white people b state laws. (p. 467)

Check Understanding

7. because both Britain and Franc depended on cotton to keep their tex tile mills running (p. 444)
8. because Union troops finally gav Lincoln a victory (p. 450)
9. They led raids, served as spies an scouts, and fought in almost ever battle. (pp. 452–453)

1870 1875 1880

1868
- The House of Representatives votes to impeach President Johnson

1877
- Reconstruction ends

Use Vocabulary

Use each term in a complete sentence that will help explain its meaning.

1. border state
2. Emancipation Proclamation
3. assassination
4. sharecropping
5. carpetbagger
6. segregation

Check Understanding

7. Why did the Confederacy hope to receive help from Britain and France?
8. Why did Lincoln finally decide to issue the Emancipation Proclamation?
9. How did African soldiers help the North?
10. Why were some Southerners sad about Lincoln's death?
11. What was the purpose of the Freedmen's Bureau?
12. How did the black codes help bring about the end of President Johnson's Reconstruction plan?

Think Critically

13. **Personally Speaking** If you had been in Robert E. Lee's place, would you have made the decision to join the Confederacy? Why or why not?
14. **Explore Viewpoints** Mary Chesnut wrote, "I know this foul murder will bring down worse miseries on us." What do you think she meant? Explain your answer.
15. **Think More About It** The most important work of the Freedmen's Bureau was education. Why is education important to people in a free country?
16. **Past to Present** Government leaders raised taxes to pay for rebuilding the South. Today government leaders sometimes increase taxes to help pay for new projects. How can taxes both help and hurt people?

Apply Skills

Compare Maps with Different Scales The maps on pages 460 and 461 show the area around Gettysburg. You can visit this area today at the Gettysburg National Military Park in Pennsylvania. Use either map to answer the questions.

17. How far would you have to walk to go from the battle sites of Devil's Den to the Wheatfield?
18. Which map did you use to answer this question? Why did you choose that map?

Read More About It

A House Divided: The Lives of Ulysses S. Grant and Robert E. Lee by Jules Archer. Scholastic. This book tells about two well-known military leaders in the Civil War.

Visit the Internet at **http://www.hbschool.com** for additional resources.

Chapter 14 • **469**

CHAPTER 14 REVIEW

Lincoln had promised to treat the South fairly in defeat. (p. 459)

to help former slaves (p. 464)

Because former slaves were being treated harshly in the South, Congress voted and decided to change to a Reconstruction plan of its own. (p. 465)

hink Critically

Students' personal opinions will vary. Accept all thoughtful responses. Look for students to express conflict between loyalty to their country and loyalty to their families and friends.

14. Students should understand Mary Chesnut's fears about what would happen now that the South had lost the war and the man who had promised to be merciful was dead. Students may suggest that Reconstruction would have been longer lasting if Lincoln had lived.

15. Students' answers should reflect the understanding that in a free country the citizens make the decisions that run the country, and education helps people make wise choices.

16. Answers should indicate an awareness that higher taxes hurt people because people then have less money to spend. Higher taxes help people who benefit from the social programs paid for by the taxes.

Apply Skills

Compare Maps with Different Scales

17. about $\frac{1}{2}$ mile
18. Map B; the scale is larger and more details are shown

Read More About It

Additional books are listed in the Multimedia Resource Center on page 406D of this Teacher's Edition.

Unit Project Start-Up

Students should have begun their time lines with information from Chapter 13. For Chapter 14 the following events might be added to the time line: Congress allowing Africans to enlist in the Union army, Lincoln's delivery of the Gettysburg Address, Lee's surrender to Grant, the assassination of Lincoln, the end of the Civil War, and the passing of the Thirteenth, Fourteenth, and Fifteenth Amendments. Encourage students to illustrate some of the events.

ASSESSMENT PROGRAM

Use CHAPTER 14 TEST, pp. 115–118.

Making Social Studies Relevant

See the Link

Personal Response

To make sure students understand what is meant by civil rights, ask them what freedoms they think all Americans should have. Explain that while much progress has been made in the United States in ensuring civil rights for all, many people continue to work for justice for all Americans.

The Main Idea

Have students read the selection and analyze why ending slavery was only the first step in the process of ensuring the full rights of citizenship to African Americans.

Q. **What did African Americans do to help gain civil rights?** They organized the Civil Rights movement in the 1950s and 1960s.

Understand the Link

Civics and Government

Civic Values and Democratic Principles Refer students to the amendments to the Constitution, beginning on page R36, and have them identify the amendments they believe apply to civil rights.

Visual Analysis

Interpret Photographs Have students carefully observe the people in the photograph and read the signs the marchers are carrying. Ask them if they know why these marchers were promoting the NAACP (National Association for the Advancement of Colored People).

"PRIMARY SOURCE"

Source: *The World Book Encyclopedia*. World Book, Inc., 1997.

MAKING Social Studies RELEVANT

The Fight For FREEDOM Goes On

The Civil War changed forever the way most Americans thought about one another. People who had been friends had fought as enemies. People who had been enslaved were now free. Those who had been thought of as property were now citizens of the United States.

Yet the rights that African Americans had fought so long for were still kept out of reach. In the years following the Civil War, many African Americans were kept from voting and holding office. They were made to live their lives apart from other citizens, in separate neighborhoods and schools. It would be 100 years after the Civil War before African Americans would gain the full rights of United States citizenship.

In the 1950s and 1960s, Americans across the country began to take part in the Civil Rights movement. This was a movement to gain the rights promised to all people in the Constitution. One of the greatest leaders of the Civil Rights movement was Dr. Martin Luther King, Jr. In 1963 King gave a speech about his hopes for the future. He said that he dreamed of a time when all the unfair ways of the past would end. He dreamed of a day when "the sons of former slaves and the sons of former slave owners will be able to sit down together at the table of brotherhood." On that day, King said, all Americans will finally be able to sing together the words of an old spiritual,

> *"Free at last!*
> *Free at last!*
> *Thank God Almighty,*
> *We are free at last!"*

470 • Unit 7

Activity Choices

Background

THE LARGE PICTURE The National Association for the Advancement of Colored People continues its civil rights work today to end discrimination against African Americans and other minority groups. The work of the NAACP has ranged from working for people's rights in the areas of fair housing, military opportunities, voting and voter education, desegregation of public schools, job opportunities, and legal issues to reducing poverty and hunger and encouraging academic, scientific, and artistic excellence among African American students. The NAACP played a key role in the passage of the Civil Rights Act of 1957, the Civil Rights Act of 1964, and the Voting Rights Act of 1965. In the 1970s and 1980s it was a leader in strengthening the Voting Rights Act, increasing the power of the Equal Employment Opportunity Commission, and improving the Fair Housing Act of 1968.

Think and Apply

BUILDING CITIZENSHIP

Think about people today who are working for equal rights. Identify an individual or a group working to protect people's rights and freedoms. Gather information about the person or group, and prepare a report for the class.

HARCOURT BRACE — Visit the Internet at **http://www.hbschool.com** for additional resources.

CNN Turner Le@rning — Check your media center or classroom video library for the Making Social Studies Relevant videotape of this feature.

History

Leaders and Achievers Have students use the information provided about Dr. Martin Luther King, Jr., to conclude why he was considered one of the greatest leaders of the Civil Rights movement.

Complete the Link

Summarize

Although slavery was abolished after the Civil War, African Americans did not gain the full rights of citizenship. They could not vote in many places, they lived in segregated neighborhoods, and they attended separate schools. To change this situation, African Americans organized the Civil Rights movement in the 1950s and 1960s. An important leader of the Civil Rights movement was Dr. Martin Luther King, Jr., who hoped that the time would come when all Americans would join together in freedom and equality.

Think and Apply

In preparing the reports, students should identify the individual leader or group of leaders, describe the rights or freedoms being denied, identify the actions being taken to protect or restore those rights or freedoms, and analyze the success of the actions taken.

Meet Individual Needs

ENGLISH LANGUAGE LEARNERS Ask volunteers to share information about civil rights movements in their country of origin. Students may relate information from personal experience or from their country's history.

Technology

HARCOURT BRACE — Visit the Internet at **http://www.hbschool.com** for additional resources.

Video

CNN Turner Le@rning™

Check your media center or classroom video library for the Making Social Studies Relevant videotape of this feature.

Background

CIVIL RIGHTS LEGISLATION The first post–Civil War civil rights law was passed in 1866, over President Andrew Johnson's veto. It granted freed people citizenship and access to federal courts to secure their rights. Weak federal civil rights legislation was passed in 1957. The Civil Rights Act of 1964 and the Voting Rights Act of 1965 were the first major steps at the federal level in granting minorities and women their full civil rights.

Visual Summary

Take a Look

Remind students that a visual summary is a way to represent the main events in a story. Explain that this visual summary reviews some of the main events students read about in Unit 7.

Visual Analysis

Interpret Pictures Have individuals or pairs of students examine the visual summary and have the class discuss its images. Ask students to describe the various images shown and to suggest what each one might tell about the Civil War and Reconstruction.

Summarize the Main Ideas

Have students read the summary statements on pages 472–473. Lead a class conversation about each scene, and have students offer supporting details for each main idea illustrated. Also, you may wish to have students draw a flow chart showing the progression of other events presented in the unit in addition to those illustrated on the visual summary.

UNIT 7 REVIEW

Visual Summary

Summarize the Main Ideas
Study the pictures and captions to help you review the events you read about in Unit 7.

Dramatize the Story
Choose any of the people shown in this visual summary, and invent a conversation they might have with us today describing their experiences. Act out the conversation with a classmate.

1 As slavery continued in the South, more and more enslaved people tried to escape by running away.

3 During the Civil War thousands of people in both the North and the South joined the war effort.

6 During Reconstruction the Freedmen's Bureau opened schools for former slaves.

Activity Choices

Meet Individual Needs

ENGLISH LANGUAGE LEARNERS Provide key words to help students identify supporting details for each main idea. You may wish to ask beginning language learners to point to the area on the visual summary that relates to the events as they are being discussed.

UNIT POSTER

Use the UNIT 7 VISUAL SUMMARY POSTER to summarize the unit.

2 After Abraham Lincoln was elected President in 1860, Southern states seceded from the Union.
4 The war dragged on for four long years, destroying property and lives on both sides.
5 Robert E. Lee surrendered his Confederate forces to Union General Ulysses S. Grant in Appomattox Courthouse in 1865.
7 After the war, life was difficult for former slaves, even though they were now free. Many tried to build new lives as sharecroppers.
473

Sharing the Activity

Provide time for students to complete the Dramatize the Story activity on page 472. You may wish to have students write their dialogues on paper first and then have volunteers perform for the entire class. After each performance, have students discuss how the dialogue relates to the main idea illustrated in the visual summary.

SUMMARIZE THE UNIT

Pair students and have them use their textbooks and the visual summary as references to tell the unit's story to their partners, or have volunteers use the visual summary to tell the unit's story to the class.

TECHNOLOGY

Use TIMELINER™ DATA DISKS to discuss and summarize the unit.

TECHNOLOGY

Use THE AMAZING WRITING MACHINE™ to complete the writing activities.

Extend and Enrich

ILLUSTRATE A HISTORICAL EVENT Ask students to select other events from the unit that they would like to add to the visual summary. Have them draw pictures to illustrate the events, and then have them explain where the events should be placed on the visual summary. Have students share with the class their illustrations and information about the events they chose.

Use Vocabulary

1. spiritual; To take her mind off her suffering, she sang a *spiritual.* (p. 422)
2. Confederacy; The states that seceded from the Union formed a new country they called the *Confederacy*. (p. 432)
3. Gettysburg Address; Lincoln's *Gettysburg Address* focused on the ideals of liberty and equality. (p. 455)
4. Reconstruction; The time of rebuilding after the Civil War was called *Reconstruction*. (p. 465)

Check Understanding

5. Slaves worked as miners, carpenters, factory workers, house servants, and field workers. (p. 417)
6. It led them to free land. (p. 424)
7. Under the Missouri Compromise, Missouri would join the Union as a slave state and Maine would join as a free state; an imaginary line was drawn and states south of that line would join the Union as slave states, and those north of it as free states. Under the Kansas-Nebraska Act, Kansas and Nebraska would decide for themselves if they would allow slavery. (pp. 426, 428)
8. It gave hope to the slaves and new spirit to the North. (p. 452)
9. the way former slaves in some Southern states were being treated (p. 466)

Think Critically

10. At the time, people had very strong opinions about slavery and how the country should be run. Lincoln was against slavery, but the South's economy depended on it.
11. The world is very complicated, so the President needs to consider all sides of an issue before making a decision.

Apply Skills

Compare Maps with Different Scales

12. the map on page 474; the scale is larger and more details can be seen

UNIT 7 REVIEW

USE VOCABULARY

Write the term that correctly matches each definition. Then use each term in a complete sentence.

Confederacy	**Reconstruction**
Gettysburg Address	**spiritual**

1. a religious song based on a Bible story
2. the new country formed by the Southern states after they seceded from the Union
3. a famous speech given by Abraham Lincoln
4. a time of rebuilding

CHECK UNDERSTANDING

5. In what ways had the South come to depend on the work of enslaved people?
6. How did the Underground Railroad help enslaved Africans?
7. What was the Missouri Compromise? What was the Kansas-Nebraska Act?
8. How did the Emancipation Proclamation affect the war?
9. What problems led Congress to change President Andrew Johnson's Reconstruction plan?

THINK CRITICALLY

10. **Explore Viewpoints** Lincoln once was called "the miserable tool of traitors and rebels." Today he is thought of as a great leader. Why might someone at the time have been so critical of him?
11. **Past to Present** Why is it important for Presidents today to consider different viewpoints before making a decision?

APPLY SKILLS

Compare Maps with Different Scales The Battle of Gettysburg ended when Pickett's Charge—led by Confederate General George Pickett—was stopped at the Angle and the Copse of Trees. Use the map below and the maps on pages 460–461 to answer the questions.

12. Compare the map on this page to Map A on page 460. Which would more clearly show Pickett's Charge or other troop movements over small distances? Explain.

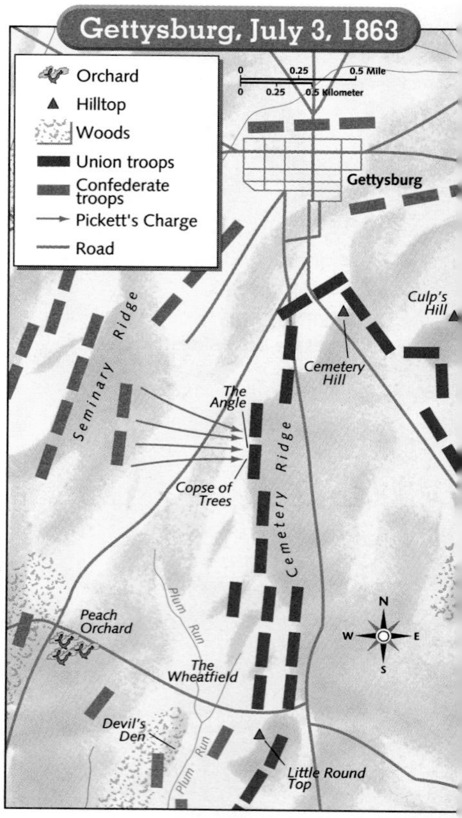

ASSESSMENT PROGRAM

Use UNIT 7 TEST,
Standard Test, pp. 119–123.
Performance Tasks, pp. 124–125.

REMEMBER
- Share your ideas.
- Cooperate with others to plan your work.
- Take responsibility for your work.
- Help one another.
- Show your group's work to the class.
- Discuss what you learned by working together.

ACTIVITY: Publish a Class Magazine

You and your classmates have decided to put together a magazine about the Civil War. First, plan your magazine by preparing a table of contents. Decide what articles and illustrations you would like to include. Give your magazine a title. Then form several small groups, with each group working on a different part of the magazine. Once all the groups have finished, put the parts together. Ask permission to display the magazine in the school library.

ACTIVITY: Draw a Map

Work together to draw a ıap of the United States at the ıme of the Civil War. Use dif- ɛrent colors for the states of ıe Union and the states of the onfederacy. Write the date n which each Southern state ɛceded. Draw diagonal lines n the border states. Label the ıpitals of the North and the ɔuth and the major battle tes. Use your map to tell your assmates about one event of ıe Civil War.

ACTIVITY: Honor Your Hero

Choose someone you admire from the Civil War as the subject of a poster for a display called *Heroes of the Civil War*. Work together to find or draw a picture of the person or a picture of a scene showing the person in action. Then add words or phrases around the picture that tell what made that person a hero. Present your poster to the class.

ɭnit Project Wrap-Up

ɭake a Time Line Work with a partner to finish ıe Unit Project that was described on page 407. rst, make a list of the major events of the Civil Var. Then exchange lists with your partner to make ure that you have included the most important vents on your time line. Write captions describing ıy illustrations that you have drawn for the time ne. Share your time lines with the class.

475

ooperative Learning Workshop

JBLISH A CLASS MAGAZINE

ɛrformance Assessment Have stu- ɛnts come up with ideas for a agazine cover design. They may wish illustrate the back cover as well. Stu- ɛnts could also create an illustrated le page, a table of contents, and any her material they feel is necessary to mplete the magazine.

Vhat to Look For The magazine ould contain clear and informative ustrations and articles that show stu- ɛnts did research and were careful in riting and editing.

DRAW A MAP

Performance Assessment Provide students with materials such as maps of the Civil War, atlases, large sheets of paper, and art materials. Then allow each group to decide which colors to use to represent the Union and the Confederacy. Have each group present its map and show one event of the Civil War to the rest of the class. Have students show one place on their maps where conflict occurred and one place where cooperation, either between states or between individuals, occurred.

What to Look For Look for each group to provide accurate information about the United States at the time of the Civil War and to have followed the directions given in the text for making the map.

HONOR YOUR HERO

Performance Assessment Pair up students who want to honor the same hero. Picture books of the Civil War, encyclopedias, and famous paintings of the time can help students find their heroes in action.

What to Look For Look for students to present the characteristics that distinguish the people they chose as heroes.

Unit Project Wrap-Up

Performance Assessment Have students finish their time lines. Link the activity to the theme of conflict and cooperation by discussing how the scenes students included on their time lines led to the Civil War and eventual freedom for enslaved Africans. Display the time lines on the classroom wall.

What to Look For Make sure that students include all the main events that led to the Civil War and freedom for enslaved Africans.

GAME TIME!

Use GAME TIME! to reinforce content.

Unit

8

pages 476–539

INVENTION AND CHANGE

The major objectives in this unit are organized around the following themes:

UNIT THEMES

- COMMONALITY & DIVERSITY
- CONFLICT & COOPERATION
- CONTINUITY & CHANGE
- INDIVIDUALISM & INTERDEPENDENCE

Preview Unit Content

Unit 8 describes the major changes that have taken place in the United States during the late 1800s and early 1900s. Students will learn how new inventions changed people's lives; how industry boomed; how cities grew; how Americans moved within the country while immigrants came from other lands; and how farmers and ranchers settled the Great Plains. Students also will learn about the problems Americans experienced during this time of change.

You may wish to begin the unit with the Unit 8 Visual Summary Poster and activity. The illustration that appears on the poster also appears on pages 536–537 in the Pupil Book to help students summarize the unit.

UNIT POSTER

Use the UNIT 8 VISUAL SUMMARY POSTER to preview the unit.

1 After the Civil War, American industry grew and changed. Asian immigrants worked on the transcontinental railroad, which linked the Atlantic and Pacific coasts.

3 During the late 1800s and early 1900s, millions of immigrants came to the United States hoping to find better lives.

6 Mining towns developed, as prospectors moved to the West in the hope of finding gc

2 Inventions helped industry grow. A new process allowed steel to be produced more cheaply. The inventions of the lightbulb and the telephone changed everyday life.

Offers of free and low-cost land brought many settlers to the Great Plains.

5 Ranchers on the Great Plains raised cattle. Cowhands worked hard, especially on cattle drives and roundups.

7 Indians on the Great Plains fought for their homelands against United States soldiers. But by 1890, most Indians in the United States had been forced onto reservations.

Unit

8 Planning Chart

	CONTENT AND SKILLS	RESOURCES INCLUDING ▶ TECHNOLOGY
UNIT INTRODUCTION **Invention and Change** pp. 476–481	Unit Opener and Unit Preview Set the Scene with Literature **The Story of Thomas Alva Edison** by Margaret Cousins	Unit 8 Visual Summary Poster Unit 8 Home Letter Unit 8 Text on Tape Audiocassette Video Experiences: Social Studies ▶ TIMELINER
CHAPTER 15 **Industry and Immigration** pp. 482–511	LESSON 1: Big Business and Industrial Cities **SKILL:** Use a Time Zone Map LESSON 2: Growing Pains LESSON 3: New Immigrants LESSON 4: Learn History Through Literature **The Great Migration: An American Story** by Jacob Lawrence LESSON 5: The Growth of Cities **SKILL:** Solve a Problem Chapter Review	Activity Book, pp. 93–101 Transparency 39 Transparency 40 Transparency 41 Assessment Program Chapter 15 Test, pp. 127–130 ▶ LOOKING AHEAD! EARNING, SPENDING, SAVING ▶ THE AMAZING WRITING MACHINE ▶ MAPSKILLS ▶ IMAGINATION EXPRESS ▶ TIMELINER ▶ INTERNET
CHAPTER 16 **The Last Frontier** pp. 512–533	LESSON 1: Farming the Great Plains **SKILL:** Understand a Climograph LESSON 2: The Cattle Kingdom LESSON 3: Mining in the West LESSON 4: Conflict in the West Chapter Review	Activity Book, pp. 102–107 Transparency 42 Transparency 43 Music Audiocassette Assessment Program Chapter 16 Test, pp. 131–134 ▶ GRAPH LINKS ▶ THE AMAZING WRITING MACHINE ▶ TIMELINER ▶ INTERNET
UNIT WRAP-UP pp. 534–539	Making Social Studies Relevant Visual Summary Unit Review	Making Social Studies Relevant Video Unit 8 Visual Summary Poster Game Time! Assessment Program Unit 8 Test, Standard Test, pp. 135–139 Performance Tasks, pp. 140–141 ▶ THE AMAZING WRITING MACHINE ▶ TIMELINER ▶ INTERNET

4 WEEKS

TIME MANAGEMENT

WEEK 1		WEEK 2	WEEK 3		WEEK 4
Unit Introduction	Chapter 15		Chapter 16		Unit Wrap-Up

See pages 482A and 512A for Chapter Planning Charts with details by lesson.

Multimedia Resource Center

Books

Easy

Lawrence, Jacob. *The Great Migration: An American Story.* HarperCollins, 1993. This story of the northern migration of African Americans is told through paintings.

MacLachlan, Patricia. *Skylark.* Harper Trophy®, 1994. In this sequel to the novel *Sarah Plain and Tall,* Sarah visits Maine to escape fires and drought that are plaguing the prairie.

Average

Cousins, Margaret. *The Story of Thomas Alva Edison.* Random House Children's Publishing, 1997. Highlights Edison's life and contributions.

Freedman, Russell. *Immigrant Kids.* Puffin Books, 1995. Describes the everyday lives of immigrant children during the late 1800s and early 1900s.

Hest, Amy. *When Jessie Came Across the Sea.* Candlewick, 1997. Jessie, a young orphan, immigrates to New York and after three years, has saved enough money to bring her Grandmother to the United States, too.

Ross, Lillian Hammer. *Sarah, Also Known as Hannah.* Albert Whitman & Company, 1994. The true story of Sarah, a girl who must assume her older sister's identity in order to immigrate to the United States from the Ukraine.

Warren, Andrea. *Pioneer Girl: Growing Up on the Prairie.* Morrow, 1998. Describes the life of a young Nebraska homesteader and her family.

Woodruff, Elvira. *The Orphan of Ellis Island.* Scholastic, 1997. On a school field trip to Ellis Island, an orphaned boy learns about family.

LIBRARY

See the SOCIAL STUDIES LIBRARY for additional resources.

Challenging

Cohn, Amy. *From Sea to Shining Sea: A Treasury of American Folklore and Folk Songs.* Scholastic, 1993. A collection of American folktales, folk songs, essays, and poems that trace the multicultural history of this country.

McKissack, Patricia. *Mary McLeod Bethune: A Great American Educator.* Childrens Press, 1985. The life and accomplishments of an educator who sought equality.

Computer Software

CD-ROM

Immigration. National Geographic Society, Educational Services, 1998, URL *http://www.nationalgeographic.com,* (800) 368-2728. Windows/Macintosh dual format. The diversity of the United States is introduced as the history of immigration is traced. Students explore the reasons for immigration and the challenges immigrants faced during the process of coming to and settling in America.

The Industrial Revolution in America. Queue, 1996, (800) 232-2224. Windows/Macintosh dual format. Period songs and original film footage introduce the impact of industrialization on the United States. The growth of cities, the revolution of transportation, and the rise of big business are documented. Carnegie, Morgan, and Rockefeller are featured, as is the movement toward unionization.

Video

Videotape

The Golden Door. Knowledge Unlimited, 1996, (800) 356-2303, URL *http://www.knowledgeunlimited.com.* Students explore immigration to the United States by examining the struggles of each wave of immigrants.

Industrialization and Urbanization. Schlessinger Media, 1996, URL *http://www.libraryvideo.com/sm/smhome.html,* (610) 645-4000. Archival films and interviews with historians detail the growth of railroads and the rise of industry. An introduction to the Homestead Act of 1862 and the development of mechanized farming is presented.

FREE & INEXPENSIVE MATERIALS

Activity

For a free activity about Alexander Graham Bell, a man famous for the invention of the telephone, visit the Internet at: *http://www.att.com/attlabs/brainspin/alexbell*

Lesson Plans

For a set of lesson plans titled *Carnegie Libraries: The Future Made Bright,* which examines how and why industrialist and philanthropist Andrew Carnegie chose libraries to be one of his greatest benefactions, write or phone:

Jackdaw Publications
P.O. Box 503
Armawalk, NY 10501
(800) 789-0022

For an order form and a list of 54 other classroom lesson plans, visit the National Register of Historic Places on the Internet at: *http://www.cr.nps.gov/nr/twhp/descrip.html*

TECHNOLOGY

HARCOURT BRACE

Visit the Internet at **http://www.hbschool.com** for additional resources.

Note that information, while correct at time of publication, is subject to change.

Linking Social Studies

BULLETIN BOARD IDEA

Illustrate Different Lifeways To help students visualize what it was like to live in the United States during the era covered in this unit, have them design a city/country bulletin board. Draw a line vertically down the center of the bulletin board. Title the bulletin board *Lifeways in the United States.* Label one side of the board *City* and the other side *Country*. Divide the class into two groups. Provide each group with colored paper and markers or colored pencils. Assign one group the city lifeway and the other group the country lifeway. Each group is to design a mural depicting the assigned lifeway, including illustrations of homes and workplaces, the different types of transportation used, and the style of clothing worn at that time. When each group has completed the mural, discuss with the class the differences and the similarities between the two ways of life.

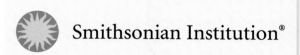

SCIENCE

Light a Bulb Thomas Edison's invention of the lightbulb caused quite a stir. To extend students' understanding of how the lightbulb works, have students light a bulb. Divide the class into small groups. Provide each group with the following materials: a flashlight bulb, two pieces of copper wire with the ends stripped, a D-cell battery, and masking tape. Ask each group to figure out how to connect all the materials to get the bulb to light. If one group is successful, have that group show the rest of the class how to do it. If no group is successful, then follow these steps: (1) Touch one end of the bare wire to the bottom, or negative end, of the battery and the other end of the bare wire to the base of the bulb. Use masking tape to hold the wires in place. (2) Using the other wire, touch one end to the top, or positive end, of the battery, holding it in place with masking tape. Touch the other end of the bare wire to the base of the bulb. (3) The bulb will light up. Brainstorm with the class what life would be like without the lightbulb. Discuss the importance of persistence by reviewing Edison's "failures" and how they led to his successes.

TECHNOLOGY

HARCOURT BRACE

Visit the Internet at **http://www.hbschool.com** for additional resources.

Smithsonian Institution®

Harcourt Brace Social Studies helps to bring the Smithsonian Institution to your classroom. Visit the Internet site at *http://www.si.edu/harcourt/socialstudies* for a directory of virtual tours, on-line exhibits, and pictures of primary sources from the Smithsonian Institution.

Across the Curriculum

LANGUAGE ARTS

Communicate by Morse Code To enrich students' understanding of the impact of technology on communication, have them focus on the telegraph. Divide the class into small groups and provide each group with a copy of the Morse code alphabet. Have each group write a sentence in Morse code and take turns sending it to the other groups by tapping out the code with a pencil on a desk. Have the other groups decode the message as it is tapped out. Continue until all groups have tapped out messages.

MUSIC

Sing About the West To help students capture the feeling of life on the range, have them work in groups to create their own illustrated songs about the West. Assign the following roles to group members: verse writer, chorus writer, background information writer, song illustrator, and music composer. Have students paste their completed songs, illustrations, background information, and music on construction paper. Have each group present the song sheet to the class and read or sing the song.

ART

Make Rope For students to gain hands-on experience working with an important and expensive commodity in the settlement of the West, have them make rope. Divide the class into groups of four to five students. Provide each group with a pencil and several lengths of string, yarn, or other cord cut at three times the desired length of rope. Have each group lay out the strands and knot both ends. Have one student hold one knotted end while another student slides the pencil through the other end just above the knot. Have the student with the pencil twist the strands, keeping them taut. Have students take turns twisting. When the strands are twisted tightly, have one student grab the center of the strands and have the students holding the ends of the strands walk toward each other but away from the student holding the center, keeping the rope taut. The strands should twist together, doubling in thickness. Have them remove the pencil. Groups should compare the ropes produced and discuss the process used.

HOW TO INTEGRATE YOUR DAY

Use these topics to help you integrate social studies into your daily planning.

READING THEMES

- Homes and Shelters
- Migration
- Technology
- Adventures

ART

Make Rope, p. 476F
Research Art of the West, p. 521
Research and Draw a Cattle Brand, p. 522

MATHEMATICS

Estimate Costs, p. 485
Convert Fahrenheit Temperatures to Celsius, p. 518

MUSIC

Sing About the West, p. 476F
Sing a Cowhand Song, p. 521

INTEGRATED LANGUAGE ARTS

Communicate by Morse Code, p. 476F
Write a Personal Narrative, p. 491
Write a Letter, p. 498
Write a Description, p. 503
Write to Explain, p. 530

READING

Prepare a Book Report, p. 478
Write a Book Report, p. 507
Read Aloud, p. 523
Write Book Reports, p. 535

HEALTH AND PHYSICAL EDUCATION

Report on Industry and Health, p. 492
Report on Immigrant Health, p. 497

SCIENCE

Light a Bulb, p. 476E
Research Wheat, p. 516
Build a Rain Gauge, p. 518

WORLD LANGUAGES

Understand Spanish, p. 516

Unit 8

Assessment Options

The **Assessment Program** allows all learners many opportunities to show what they know and can do. It also provides ongoing information about each student's understanding of social studies.

Formal Assessment

- *Lesson Reviews* (**Pupil Book,** at end of lessons)
- *Chapter Reviews* (**Pupil Book,** at end of chapters)
- *Chapter Tests* (**Assessment Program,** pp. 127–134)
- *Unit Review* (**Pupil Book,** pp. 538–539)
- *Unit Assessment* (**Assessment Program:** *Standard Test,* pp. 135–139 *Individual Performance Task,* p. 140 *Group Performance Task,* p. 141)

Student Self-Evaluation

- *Individual End-of-Project Summary* (**Assessment Program,** p. 6)
- *Group End-of-Project Checklist* (**Assessment Program,** p. 7)
- *Individual End-of-Unit Checklist* (**Assessment Program,** p. 8)

Informal Assessment

- **REVIEW** *Questions* (**Pupil Book,** throughout lessons)
- *Think and Apply* (**Pupil Book,** at end of skill lessons)
- *Visual Summary* (**Pupil Book,** pp. 536–537)
- *Social Studies Skills Checklist* (**Assessment Program,** pp. 4–5)

Performance Assessment

- *Show What You Know* (**Pupil Book,** at end of Lesson Reviews)
- *Cooperative Learning Workshop* (**Pupil Book,** at end of Unit Review)
- *Scoring Rubric for Individual Projects* (**Assessment Program,** p. 9)
- *Scoring Rubric for Group Projects* (**Assessment Program,** p. 10)
- *Scoring Rubric for Presentations* (**Assessment Program,** p. 11)

Portfolio Assessment

Student-selected items may include:

- *Link to Language Arts—Write a Letter* (**Teacher's Edition,** p. 498)
- *Practice and Apply* (**Activity Book,** pp. 94–95)
- *Home Involvement* (**Teacher's Edition,** p. 477)
- *A Guide to My Social Studies Portfolio* (**Assessment Program,** p. 12)

Teacher-selected items may include:

- *Unit Assessment* (**Assessment Program,** pp. 135–141)
- *Individual End-of-Unit Checklist* (**Assessment Program,** p. 8)
- *Social Studies Portfolio Summary* (**Assessment Program,** p. 13)
- *Portfolio Family Response* (**Assessment Program,** p. 14)

Objectives

Chapter 15

- ▶ Analyze the changes that railroad expansion made in the United States. (p. 483)
- ▶ Summarize the events that gave Andrew Carnegie a monopoly over the steel industry. (p. 483)
- ▶ Describe the way John D. Rockefeller gained a monopoly in the oil industry. (p. 483)
- ▶ Relate the rise of industry in the late 1800s to the growth of inland cities. (p. 483)
- ▶ Summarize the system of time zones. (p. 488)
- ▶ Analyze a time zone map. (p. 488)
- ▶ Summarize the problems of workers in factories. (p. 490)
- ▶ Analyze the actions workers took to improve working conditions. (p. 490)
- ▶ Explain the causes and effects of the Homestead Strike. (p. 490)
- ▶ Contrast workers' and owners' views about government's role in business. (p. 490)
- ▶ Explain why Americans wanted to stop Asian immigration. (p. 495)
- ▶ Summarize how barrios helped Mexican immigrants. (p. 495)
- ▶ Identify the areas of Europe from which many immigrants came after the 1890s. (p. 495)
- ▶ Describe how immigrants could become United States citizens. (p. 495)
- ▶ Identify the reasons African Americans left the South between 1916 and 1919. (p. 500)
- ▶ Analyze the conditions African Americans faced in the North. (p. 500)
- ▶ Evaluate the advantages and disadvantages of the northern migration for African Americans. (p. 500)
- ▶ Analyze the problems faced by people living in overcrowded cities. (p. 505)
- ▶ Describe how individuals improved conditions for the cities' poor. (p. 505)
- ▶ Identify inventions that helped cities change and grow. (p. 505)
- ▶ Identify steps for solving problems. (p. 509)
- ▶ Apply a problem-solving method. (p. 509)

Chapter 16

- ▶ Identify the factors that attracted settlers to the Great Plains. (p. 513)
- ▶ Summarize the life of farm families on the Great Plains. (p. 513)
- ▶ Describe the operation of bonanza farms on the Great Plains. (p. 513)
- ▶ Interpret climographs. (p. 518)
- ▶ Create a climograph. (p. 518)
- ▶ Explore the development of the cattle industry on the Great Plains. (p. 520)
- ▶ Analyze why open range lands were important to cattle ranchers. (p. 520)
- ▶ Describe the work of the cowhands. (p. 520)
- ▶ Identify the reasons for the decline of the Cattle Kingdom. (p. 520)
- ▶ Explain the difference between a mining boom and a mining bust. (p. 525)
- ▶ Analyze why mining communities needed Vigilance Committees. (p. 525)
- ▶ Identify the causes for the disappearance of the buffalo from the Great Plains. (p. 528)
- ▶ Analyze why the United States did not uphold its treaty with the Sioux. (p. 528)
- ▶ Summarize the tragedy of the Nez Perces. (p. 528)
- ▶ Analyze the conflict between the Apaches and the United States government. (p. 528)

STANDARD TEST

NAME ______________________ DATE __________

Unit 8 Test

Part One: Test Your Understanding *(4 points each)*

DIRECTIONS: ***Circle the letter of the best answer.***

1. Which of the following was the first kind of business to set up corporations?
   - A. bonanza farms
   - (B.) railroads
   - C. steel mills
   - D. refining

2. With the growth of industries such as steel and oil, new industrial cities developed
   - A. near good harbors.
   - B. in the West.
   - C. near the oceans.
   - (D.) inland.

3. To try to improve their working conditions, workers in the late 1800s sometimes
   - A. fought against the labor unions.
   - B. volunteered to be fired so that family members would be hired.
   - (C.) went on strike.
   - D. offered to work longer hours for less pay.

4. What were the two basic goals of the American Federation of Labor?
   - A. to end strikes and hire more children as workers
   - B. to get a five-day workweek and summer vacations
   - (C.) to get higher wages and a shorter workday
   - D. to do away with accident insurance and hire fewer children as workers

5. Many Americans wanted to stop the immigration of Asians because
   - (A.) they worried that Asian immigrants would take their jobs.
   - B. they did not want the Asian immigrants to create any more barrios in the Southwest.
   - C. the law required that Asian immigrants be paid more than other people.
   - D. the eastern part of the United States was becoming too crowded.

6. During the early 1900s, many African American families moved to the northern cities because
   - A. they wanted to get better land to farm.
   - B. they were forced to leave the southern states.
   - C. the climate in the North was better.
   - (D.) there were more jobs in the northern cities.

(continued)

UNIT 8 TEST   Assessment Program 135

STANDARD TEST

NAME ______________________ DATE __________

7. What was the purpose of a settlement house?
   A. to give cowhands a place to stay after the cattle drives
   (B.) to help immigrants learn American skills and customs
   C. to teach farmers about irrigation
   D. to improve the education of schoolteachers

8. Many settlers in the West bought land at low prices from the
   A. Indians. B. vaqueros.
   (C.) railroads. D. miners.

9. Most houses on the Great Plains were made with
   A. adobe. B. bricks.
   (C.) sod. D. logs.

10. It was important for ranchers to get their cattle to northern cities because
   A. people in the southern cities did not eat beef.
   B. all the cattle buyers in the country lived in the North.
   C. northern cities had more open range in which to raise cattle.
   (D.) they could earn a higher profit in the northern cities.

11. How did Joseph Glidden help to bring an end to the Cattle Kingdom?
   A. He made the first steel plow.
   B. He founded the first mining town.
   (C.) He invented barbed wire.
   D. He built the first transcontinental railroad.

12. When did mining towns experience the most rapid population growth?
   A. when windmills were invented
   B. when people moved away from the mines
   C. when the gold, silver, and copper mines closed
   (D.) when there was quick economic growth

13. The traditional way of life of the Plains Indians came to an end when
   A. the cattle drives began. B. the range wars ended.
   (C.) settlers killed off the buffalo. D. the mining boom started.

14. Geronimo and his people refused to stay on the reservation because
   A. they wanted to return to the Black Hills of South Dakota.
   (B.) there was not enough food on their reservation.
   C. there was no railroad on their reservation.
   D. they wanted to follow the buffalo on their migration.

(continued)

STANDARD TEST

NAME ______________________ DATE __________

Part Two: Test Your Skills (24 points)

DIRECTIONS: *Problem solving is an important skill. Homesteaders on the Great Plains faced many problems as they made a new life in this region. One of the problems they had to solve was that of getting water for their families and their animals. For each possible solution to the problem listed in the table below, give reasons as to why it is a good solution or why it is a bad solution.*

SOLVING A PROBLEM

Problem: Getting water to the farms on the Great Plains

Possible Solution	Results of Solution
15. Build pipelines to carry water from rivers to the farms.	Possible response: Building pipelines from rivers to the farms would be very expensive. In many parts of the Great Plains, there are not enough rivers to supply all the farms.
16. Build dams on streams to store water for the farms.	Possible response: Building dams would be very expensive. If dams were built across streams, there would not be enough water for any farms downstream from the dams.
17. Bring in water by wagons or by railroads to the farms.	Possible response: Bringing in water by wagons or by railroads would not be practical. Wagons could not carry enough water and railroad tracks would have to be laid to every farm.
18. Build windmills to pump water from the ground for the farms.	Possible response: Windmills could be used on the Great Plains because it is windy there and because there is enough water underground for the needs of many farms.

(continued)

STANDARD TEST

NAME ______________________ DATE __________

Part Three: Apply What You Have Learned

DIRECTIONS: *Complete each of the following activities.*

19. **Magic Square** (10 points)
From the statements below, select the best match for each name listed. Put the number of the name with the matching statement letter in the magic square. You can check your answers by adding across each row or down each column. You should get the same number each way. Record that number in the magic number space.

a = 2	b = 4	c = 9
d = 7	e = 3	f = 5
g = 6	h = 8	i = 1

1. Sitting Bull
2. Samuel Gompers
3. George Westinghouse
4. William Jenney
5. Henry Bessemer
6. Chief Joseph
7. Joseph McCoy
8. Jane Addams
9. James Oliver

Magic Number = 15

a. started the American Federation of Labor
b. built the first skyscraper
c. invented a steel plow that helped farmers on the Great Plains
d. built the stockyards at Abilene, Kansas, that started the cattle drives
e. invented the safety brake for trains
f. created a new, improved process for making steel
g. led the Nez Perces on an escape to Canada
h. started Hull House in Chicago to teach new skills to immigrants
i. led the Sioux at the Battle of Little Bighorn

(continued)

STANDARD TEST

NAME ______________________ DATE __________

20. **Essay** (10 points)
The government had different policies toward unions, immigrants, and Indians at the end of the nineteenth century. Choose one of these groups. Explain in one paragraph the government's policy toward that group.

Possible responses:

Unions—The government's policy toward unions was to support free enterprise and business. The government did not help the unions in their battles with factory owners.

Immigrants—The government passed laws to keep Chinese and Japanese immigrants out of the United States. The government also created naturalization, which allows immigrants to become citizens of the United States.

Indians—The government used force to take away land that belonged to the Indians. The government also used force to make Indians live on reservations.

PERFORMANCE TASK

NAME ______________________ DATE __________

Individual Performance Task

Have We Got a Deal for You!

Many businesses use a brochure to advertise to the public. In this task you are going to create a brochure that could have been used by one of the transcontinental railroads to get people to move into the areas along its path.

Step 1 Use library materials and your textbooks to find the paths of the first four transcontinental railroads (Northern Pacific, Union Pacific-Central Pacific, Santa Fe, and Southern Pacific). Select one of these railroads. Then select an area along the railroad that you will advertise in the brochure.

Step 2 Decide who will read the brochure. Will it be people immigrating to the United States? Will it be people who want to move from the East to the West? The information you give will depend on who your readers will be.

Step 3 Determine what information you will put in the brochure. You must include the name and address of the railroad company and a map of the area you are advertising. You should also tell in the brochure what is good about the area you are advertising. You might cover some of these topics and add others of your own.

- climate
- mineral resources
- religious freedom
- water resources
- crops
- political freedom
- lumber resources
- wild animals
- land prices
- soil
- plants

Step 4 Make a rough draft of the brochure. Put information on the front of the brochure that will make people want to open it and read further. Draw the map on the back of the brochure, along with the name and address of the railroad company. (You do not have to use a real address. Make up an address in the area you are advertising.) After you have made the rough draft, show it to a classmate and ask whether all the material is clear.

Step 5 Make a final copy. Present the brochure to the rest of the class.

PERFORMANCE TASK

NAME ______________________ DATE __________

Group Performance Task

Words of the Old West

A *lexicon* is a collection of words. In this task your small group will create a book called *A Lexicon of the Old West.*

Step 1 With your group, brainstorm words from *A* to *Z* that deal with the West as covered in this unit. The words should be about farmers, ranchers, cowhands, miners, and Indians during the last years of the nineteenth century. For example, an *A* word might be *Abilene* and a *B* word might be *Bonanza Farm.* The letter does not have to be the first letter of the word. For example, an *X* word could be *Sioux*. Try to come up with as many words for each letter as possible.

Step 2 Help your group choose one word for each letter of the alphabet. It should be one for which a picture could be drawn to show its meaning or importance.

Step 3 Divide the letters of the alphabet among the members of the group. Each person should be responsible for about the same number of letters. Each student will create a page for the lexicon for each of his or her words. There should be three parts to each page.

Part 1 At the top of the page will be the words *A is for Abilene, B is for Bonanza Farm,* and so on.

Part 2 In the center of the page will be a drawing that shows the meaning of the word. For example, under *A is for Abilene* could be a drawing of a railroad train, a stockyard, and cattle being loaded on the train.

Part 3 At the bottom of the page will be a two-sentence explanation of the importance of the word. For example, you could write "Joseph McCoy built the first stockyards in Abilene, Kansas, in 1867. This was the beginning of the Cattle Kingdom and cattle drives." Be sure your sentences fit with your drawing.

Step 4 One student from the group should make a cover sheet for the lexicon. Another student should make a Table of Contents. In the Table of Contents, there should be one line for each letter. It should state the name of the page, for example, *A is for Abilene*, the name of the student responsible for the page, and the page number. When the lexicon is finished, your group can display it for others to enjoy.

Rubrics

SCORING RUBRICS The scoring rubrics for evaluating individual projects, group projects, and students' presentations may be found in the **Assessment Program,** pages 9–11.

CRITICAL The criteria listed below may be used when looking for evidence of the students' understanding of social studies content and ability to think critically.

Individual Task

Have We Got a Deal for You!

- Identify the route of one of the first four transcontinental railroads.
- Select an audience that railroads during this time period were likely to target.
- Create a brochure containing historically accurate information about the selected railroad and one of its locations that convinces people to move to that location.

Group Task

Words of the Old West

- Select words or terms that were significant during the period of early westward expansion.
- Create graphic illustrations that symbolize the meanings of the selected words or terms.
- Write brief but accurate definitions of the selected words or terms.

REMINDER

You may wish to preview the performance assessment activities in the COOPERATIVE LEARNING WORKSHOP on page 539. Students may complete these activities during the course of the unit.

INTRODUCE THE UNIT

Personal Response

Challenge students to describe the conditions of different parts of the nation when Reconstruction ended in 1877. Remind students that although both sides suffered heavy losses during the Civil War, the North continued to grow as an industrial leader. Have students predict ways in which this industrial strength could increase and how it might benefit the country as a whole.

Link Prior Learning

Use the titles on the bar across the top of pages 476–477 to review the chronology of earlier units. Then have students look at the illustration.

Q. **What does the picture tell you about the unit you will be studying?** Cities grew as more and more people moved to locations where they could find jobs.

INVENTION AND CHANGE

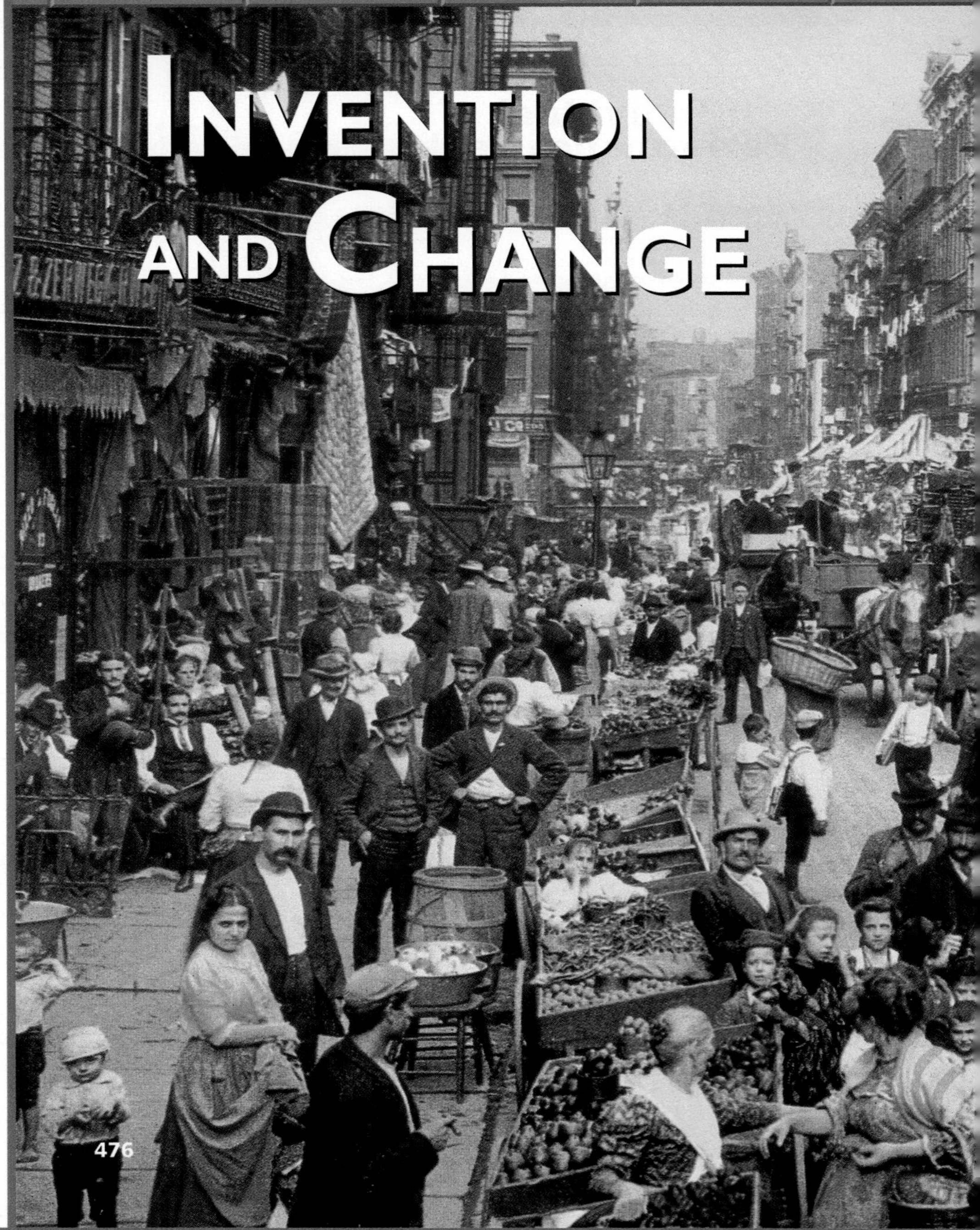

476

ACTIVITY CHOICES

Background

THE LARGE PICTURE This picture is a Photochrom print. The print is made by combining a photograph with a lithograph. William H. Jackson of the Detroit Publishing Company used this process to make postcards for immigrants to send to their families back home. This Photochrom print shows the market of Mulberry Street on Manhattan's Lower East Side. This area was home to thousands of immigrants.

HOME LETTER

Use the UNIT 8 HOME LETTER. See Teacher's Edition pp. HL 15–16.

AUDIO

Use the UNIT 8 TEXT ON TAPE AUDIOCASSETTE for a reading of this unit.

Unit 8

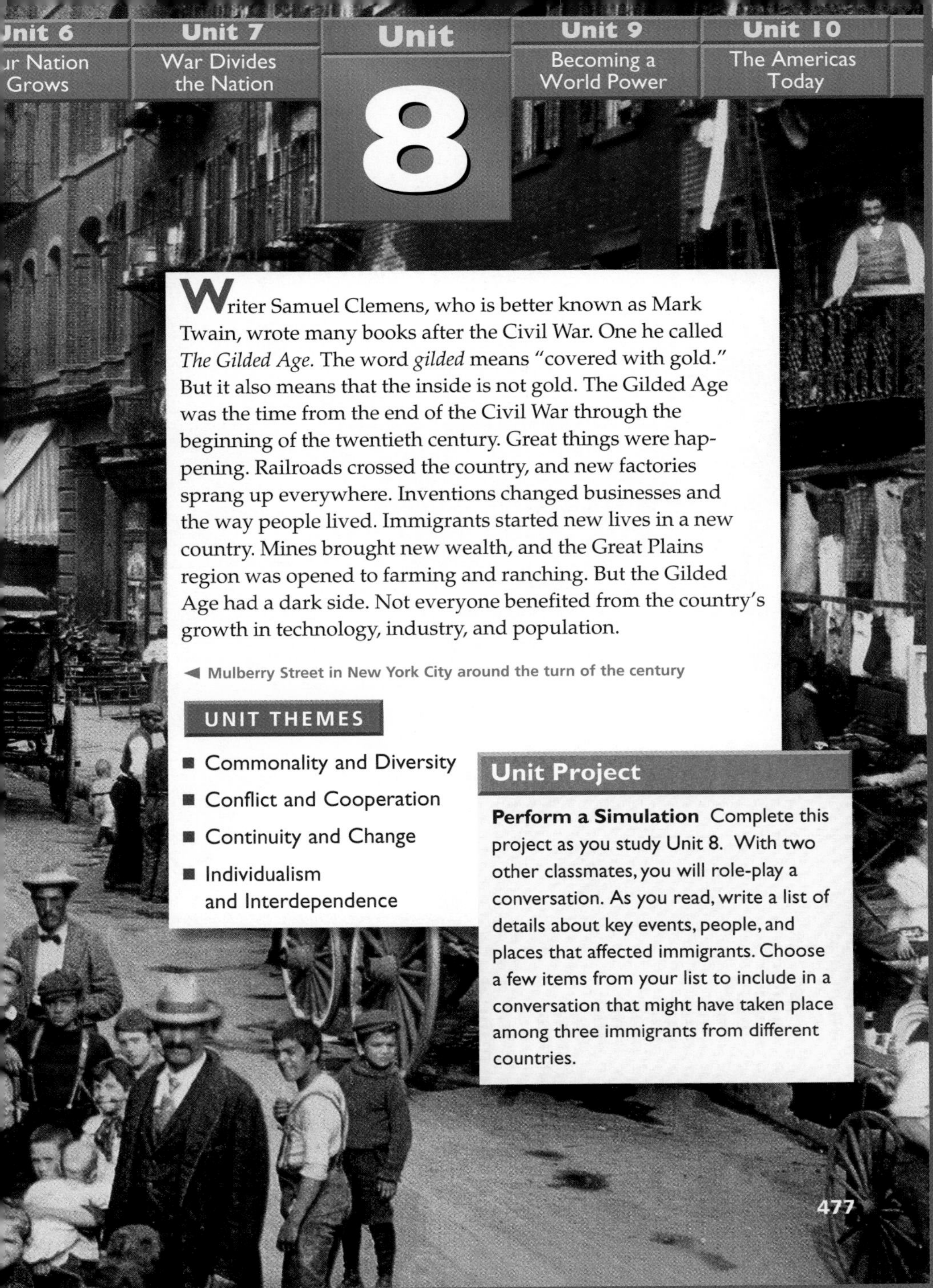

Writer Samuel Clemens, who is better known as Mark Twain, wrote many books after the Civil War. One he called *The Gilded Age.* The word *gilded* means "covered with gold." But it also means that the inside is not gold. The Gilded Age was the time from the end of the Civil War through the beginning of the twentieth century. Great things were happening. Railroads crossed the country, and new factories sprang up everywhere. Inventions changed businesses and the way people lived. Immigrants started new lives in a new country. Mines brought new wealth, and the Great Plains region was opened to farming and ranching. But the Gilded Age had a dark side. Not everyone benefited from the country's growth in technology, industry, and population.

◄ Mulberry Street in New York City around the turn of the century

UNIT THEMES

- Commonality and Diversity
- Conflict and Cooperation
- Continuity and Change
- Individualism and Interdependence

Unit Project

Perform a Simulation Complete this project as you study Unit 8. With two other classmates, you will role-play a conversation. As you read, write a list of details about key events, people, and places that affected immigrants. Choose a few items from your list to include in a conversation that might have taken place among three immigrants from different countries.

477

Options for Reading

Read Aloud Read each lesson aloud as students follow along in their books. Strategies for guiding students through working with text and visuals are provided with each lesson.

Read Together Have pairs or small groups of students read the lesson by taking turns reading each page or paragraph aloud. Encourage students to use the new vocabulary words as they discuss what they read.

Read Alone Strong readers may wish to read the lessons independently before you read or discuss each lesson with the class.

Read the Introduction

Ask students to read the unit introduction on page 477.

Q. **What changes took place in the United States after the Civil War?** Railroads crossed the nation, factories and cities sprang up, inventions changed businesses and ways of life, immigrants came to the United States, mines brought wealth, and the Plains were opened to farming and ranching.

Unit Themes

Discuss with students the Unit Themes. Throughout the study of this unit, ask for volunteers to identify the events, maps, illustrations, and pictures that represent each of these themes.

Unit Project Start-Up

Before students begin their Unit Projects, ask them to review the Unit Preview on pages 478–479. Challenge them to imagine what life must have been like for immigrants. Suggest they try to put themselves in the role of an immigrant and speculate on what experiences immigrants had. Encourage students to keep this in mind as they write their lists.

Home Involvement

Ask students to find out from adult family members whether they have ancestors who came to the United States during the late 1800s or early 1900s. Also have students discuss how their ancestors' lives might have been affected by the changes that were taking place in the country during that era. Have volunteers share with the class what they learn.

Multicultural Link

In the late 1800s immigrants from parts of the world that had been only sparsely represented in the American population, such as Russia, Italy, and China, began to pour into the country. In addition, many African Americans moved from the South into other regions. With the economy expanding in industry and farming, the newcomers found work, but many faced the same problems to which earlier immigrants had been subjected to.

PREVIEW THE UNIT

Link Prior Learning

Have students discuss what they already know about the settling of the West, the influx of immigrants to this country, and the battles Native Americans fought to stay in their homelands. Tell them that this is the era of cowhands and the "iron horse."

Understanding the Map

This map shows the land's natural resources and its physical features. Ask students to classify the natural resources listed in the key into categories of similar items.

Q. **In what regions of the country were beef cattle primarily raised? Dairy cattle?** the Middle West; the Northeast, Southwest, and West Coast

What cities were the most populated in 1870? Boston, New York, Newark, Philadelphia, Baltimore, Washington, D.C., New Orleans, Louisville, Cincinnati, St. Louis, Chicago, Buffalo, and San Francisco

UNIT 8 PREVIEW

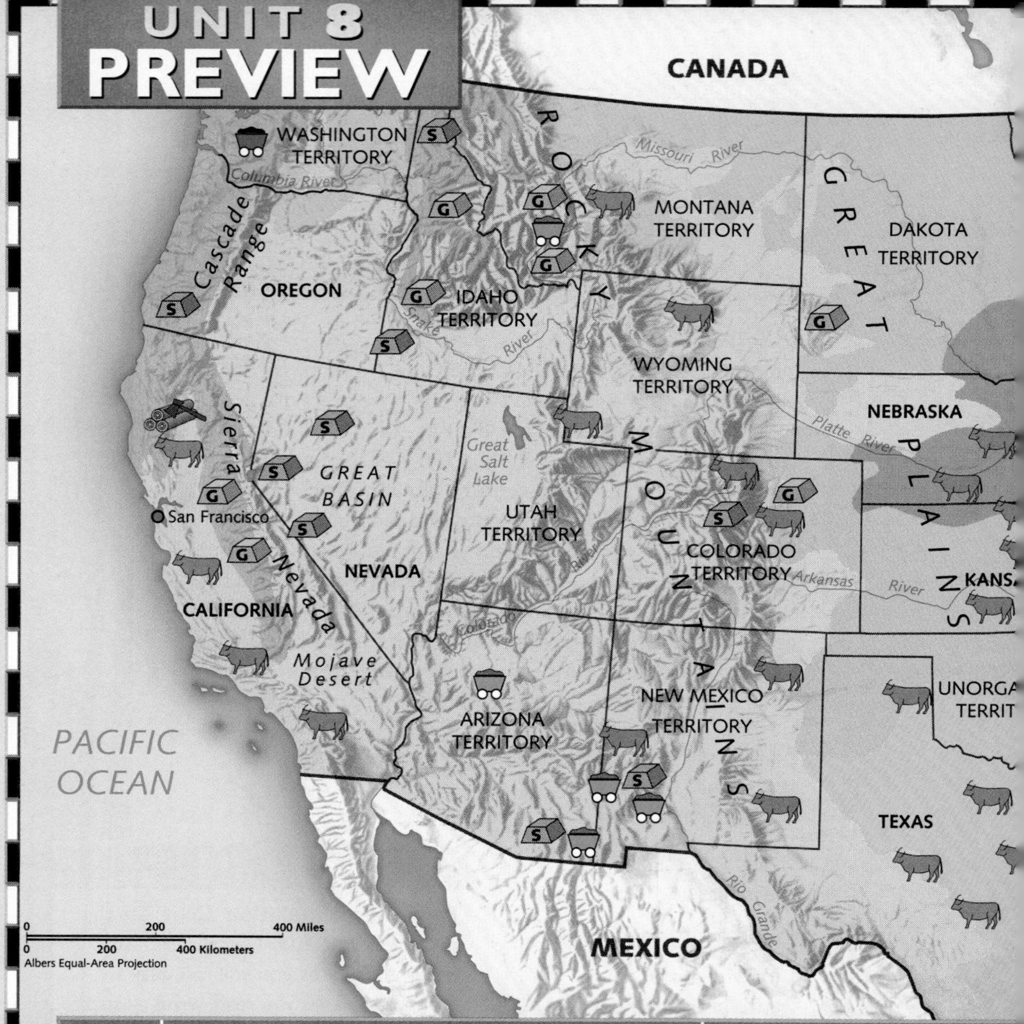

1840 1860

1850s Miners Rush to the West
PAGE 525

1862 Homestead Act Passed
PAGE 513

1869 Transcontinental Railroad Completed
PAGE 483

478

ACTIVITY CHOICES

VIDEO

VIDEO EXPERIENCES: SOCIAL STUDIES

See the video guide for additional enrichment material.

TECHNOLOGY

Use TIMELINER™ DATA DISKS to construct a time line of events in this unit.

Link to Reading

PREPARE A BOOK REPORT
Suggest that each student select and read a nonfiction book about an event shown on the time line. Students can use the information gathered to write a short book report that focuses on the changes that occurred in the United States or the significance of the event. Ask volunteers to share their book reports with the class.

Meet Individual Needs

COOPERATIVE LEARNING

ENGLISH LANGUAGE LEARNERS Have students work in small groups. Refer them to the time line. Ask them to write their own captions for the images on the time line. Students can share their captions with the class or other groups.

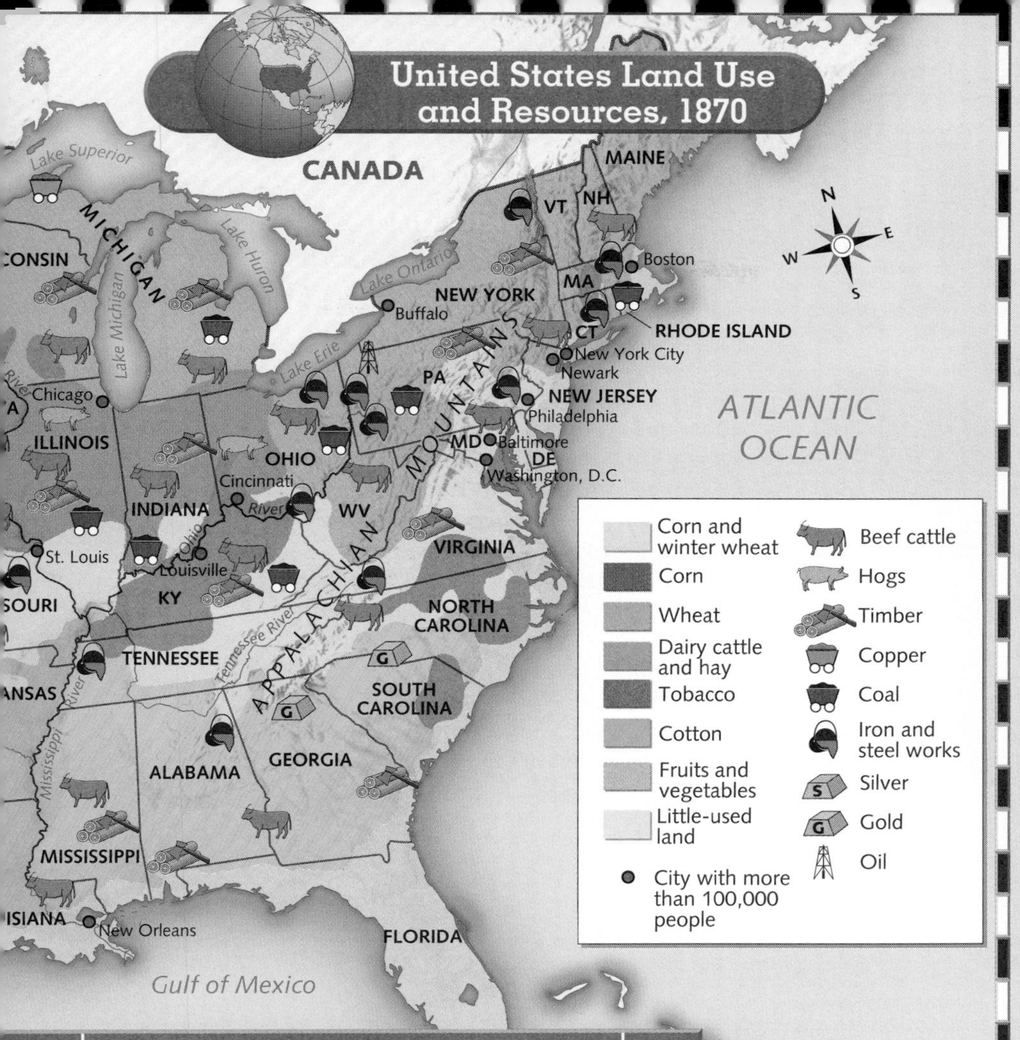

1880 | 1900

Late 1800s
New Immigrants Come to the United States
PAGE 495

Late 1800s
Plains Indians Fight for Their Homelands
PAGE 529

479

Understanding the Time Line

Explain to students that the scenes on these pages show events that took place in the second half of the 1800s and in the early 1900s.

***Q.* What can you tell about each event by looking at the scenes and the dates?** 1850s—people looked for gold in the West; 1862—settlers built homes on the Plains when the Homestead Act was passed; 1869—workers helped complete the Transcontinental Railroad; late 1800s—Plains Indians fought for their homelands; 1890s—immigrants from other countries came to the United States

Look Ahead to the Unit

To encourage synthesis of the information in the unit, have each student make a two-column chart with the first column labeled *Gold* and the second *Gilded.* Direct students to record developments in the nation's history that furthered progress under *Gold* and developments that reflect conflict and problems under *Gilded.* You may prefer to create a class chart on the wall on which students add entries while studying the unit.

Background

THE TIME LINE When gold was found near Sacramento, California, many people hurried to stake claims in the West.

The frenzy to move West heightened when Congress passed the Homestead Act, which gave 160 acres in the Great Plains to eager settlers.

The transcontinental railroad went across the continent, linking the Atlantic and Pacific coasts.

Native Americans lost their homelands and had to relocate.

By the end of the century, progress in the United States attracted immigrants from all over the world.

These events are also shown in the Visual Summary on pages 536–537 in the Pupil Book.

UNIT POSTER

Use the UNIT 8 VISUAL SUMMARY POSTER to preview the unit.

Set the Scene with Literature

Prereading Strategies

Personal Response

Ask students to think about a time when they did something that they were proud of. Were they excited to share their accomplishment with others? Tell students that in this literature selection they will read about Thomas Alva Edison and his invention of the electric lightbulb.

Set the Purpose

The selection from Margaret Cousins's biography of Thomas Alva Edison describes the first public demonstration of Edison's electric lightbulb. Tell students that Edison was responsible for many important inventions that are today a part of our everyday lives. Ask students to think about the need for the products Edison invented as they read pages 480–481. Ask them also to look for evidence of Edison's modesty about his invention of the electric lightbulb.

Read & Respond

Auditory Learning

Read Orally Read aloud to the class the introduction to the literature selection. Have students discuss the ways their lives would be different without the electric lightbulb. Also have them analyze why Edison was motivated to invent an electric bulb. Include in the discussion the dangers of candles and kerosene oil lanterns, used before the electric lightbulb.

Set the Scene with Literature

The Story of Thomas Alva Edison

by Margaret Cousins

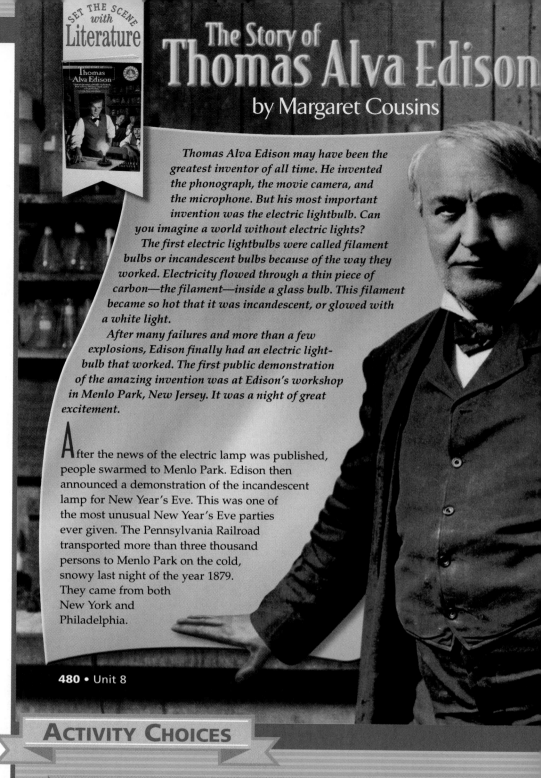

Thomas Alva Edison may have been the greatest inventor of all time. He invented the phonograph, the movie camera, and the microphone. But his most important invention was the electric lightbulb. Can you imagine a world without electric lights?

The first electric lightbulbs were called filament bulbs or incandescent bulbs because of the way they worked. Electricity flowed through a thin piece of carbon—the filament—inside a glass bulb. This filament became so hot that it was incandescent, or glowed with a white light.

After many failures and more than a few explosions, Edison finally had an electric lightbulb that worked. The first public demonstration of the amazing invention was at Edison's workshop in Menlo Park, New Jersey. It was a night of great excitement.

After the news of the electric lamp was published, people swarmed to Menlo Park. Edison then announced a demonstration of the incandescent lamp for New Year's Eve. This was one of the most unusual New Year's Eve parties ever given. The Pennsylvania Railroad transported more than three thousand persons to Menlo Park on the cold, snowy last night of the year 1879. They came from both New York and Philadelphia.

Activity Choices

Background

THE LITERATURE SELECTION *The Story of Thomas Alva Edison* describes the life of the inventor whose work is so much a part of our daily lives. The book presents Edison as a bright and curious young boy and introduces readers to his mother and father. The biography follows Edison's life to adulthood and describes how his experiences led to his interest in electricity and invention.

THE AUTHOR Margaret Cousins grew up in Dallas, Texas, and graduated from the University of Texas at Austin. She began her editorial career in New York City as a managing editor for *Good Housekeeping* and *McCall's* magazines. Cousins has written several books for children, including *Ben Franklin of Old Philadelphia*, *Uncle Edgar and the Reluctant Saint*, and *We Were There at the Battle of the Alamo.*

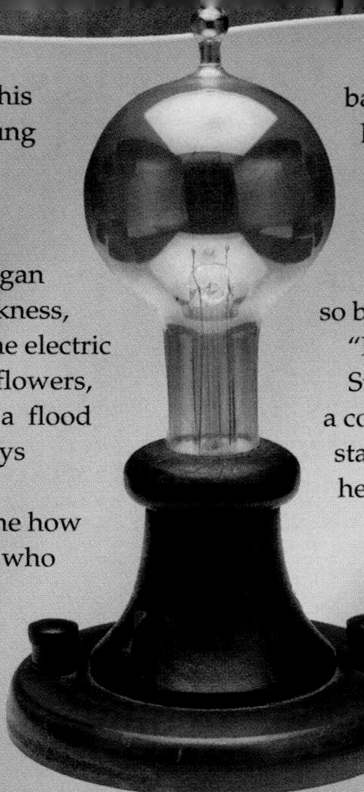

Edison had put some of his lamps along two wires strung between the leafless trees on the road leading from the railway station to his laboratory. As the trains began to pull in in the winter darkness, he pulled the switch and the electric lamps glowed like golden flowers, illuminating the road with a flood of light and casting long rays across the snow.

It is hard for us to imagine how exciting this was to people who had never seen an electric light. Many of them were sophisticated city people, dressed in their New Year's Eve party clothes; but they all gasped. It was the most beautiful sight they had ever seen. It was fairyland!

Edison stood in the power house, watching the dynamo turn steam power into the electric current to light the lamps. He was wearing an old gray shirt, a flannel coat full of acid holes and some chalk-stained, dusty trousers. A broad-brimmed black felt hat sat on the back of his head. Some people took him for a coal stoker[1], so he had a good chance to listen to what they were saying.

"It's a miracle!"

"Did you ever see anything so beautiful?"

"He's a wizard! A wizard!"

Suddenly there was a scream and a commotion. A young lady was standing near the generators with her hair down her back.

"I'm sorry," Edison said. "The generators magnetized her hairpins and pulled them all out of her hair!" He apologized to the lady and gave her a silk kerchief to put on her head. "Maybe this will help," he said, but she fled back to the train.

The success of the New Year's Eve demonstration at Menlo Park created excitement all over the world. Cables, letters, telegrams and gifts descended on Edison. He was no longer just a hero, but the "American Wizard."

Thomas Edison was not the only inventor making important discoveries in the years after the Civil War. Alexander Graham Bell invented the telephone in 1876, and a revolution in communication began. The first automobiles came into use, and transportation changed forever. This growth of technology sparked the growth of industry that marks the period of history in the United States from 1865 to 1920.

[1] **coal stoker:** person who shovels coal into a furnace

Understanding the Story

Challenge students to picture the scene outside Edison's laboratory when visitors came to witness the demonstration of Edison's incandescent lamp. Have students infer why thousands of people would want to descend upon Menlo Park, N.J., to see incandescent lightbulbs.

History

Innovation Explain that sometimes new inventions are regarded with suspicion.

Q. **What episode indicated that some people were suspicious and uncomfortable about Edison's inventions?** the reaction of the woman whose hairpins had been magnetized and pulled out of her hair by the generators

Summarize the Literature

Thomas Alva Edison's imagination, scientific knowledge, and determination led him to discover how to light the world with electricity. After demonstrating his invention on a cold, snowy New Year's Eve in 1879, Edison became famous all over the world. He changed the way people in many parts of the world would light their homes, streets, and businesses.

Link Literature

You may wish to assign the complete book *The Story of Thomas Alva Edison* to advanced readers. To the right are books that may be used in the course of this unit with students of varying reading abilities. In addition to these titles, you may wish to suggest some of the books listed in the Multimedia Resource Center on page 476D of this Teacher's Edition.

EASY
Skylark **by Patricia MacLachlan. Harper Trophy®, 1994.**

AVERAGE
Sarah, Also Known as Hannah **by Lillian Hammer Ross. Albert Whitman & Company, 1994.**

CHALLENGING
Mary McLeod Bethune: A Great American Educator **by Patricia McKissack. Childrens Press, 1985.**

Smithsonian Institution®

Go to the Internet site at *http://www.si.edu/harcourt/socialstudies* to visit the exhibit "Edison's Timeline of Invention" on the Timeline at the National Museum of American History.

CHAPTER 15

Planning Chart

	THEMES • Strands	VOCABULARY	MEET INDIVIDUAL NEEDS	RESOURCES INCLUDING ▶ TECHNOLOGY
LESSON 1 **Big Business and Industrial Cities** pp. 483–487	**CONTINUITY & CHANGE** • Geography • Economics • History	free enterprise transcontinental railroad capital resource corporation entrepreneur consolidate invest refinery stock monopoly hub	Auditory Learners, p. 484 Extend and Enrich, p. 486 Reteach the Main Idea, p. 487	Activity Book, p. 93 ▶ LOOKING AHEAD! EARNING, SPENDING, SAVING ▶ THE AMAZING WRITING MACHINE
SKILL **Use a Time Zone Map** pp. 488–489	**BASIC STUDY SKILLS** • Map and Globe Skills	time zone	Kinesthetic Learners, p. 488 Reteach the Skill, p. 489	Activity Book, pp. 94–95 Transparency 39 ▶ MAPSKILLS
LESSON 2 **Growing Pains** pp. 490–494	**CONFLICT & COOPERATION** • Economics • History • Civics/Government	human resource strike labor union federation regulate	Visual Learners, p. 492 Extend and Enrich, p. 493 Reteach the Main Idea, p. 494	Activity Book, p. 96 ▶ IMAGINATION EXPRESS
LESSON 3 **New Immigrants** pp. 495–499	**CONFLICT & COOPERATION** • Culture/History • Geography • Economics	prejudice barrio tenement naturalization	Extend and Enrich, p. 498 Reteach the Main Idea, p. 499	Activity Book, p. 97 ▶ THE AMAZING WRITING MACHINE
LESSON 4 **Learn History Through Literature** The Great Migration: An American Story by Jacob Lawrence pp. 500–504	**CONTINUITY & CHANGE** • Geography • Economics • Culture • Civics/Government		English Language Learners, p. 502 Extend and Enrich, p. 503 Reteach the Main Idea, p. 504	Activity Book, p. 98 ▶ THE AMAZING WRITING MACHINE
LESSON 5 **The Growth of Cities** pp. 505–508	**CONTINUITY & CHANGE** • History/Culture • Geography	settlement house skyscraper	Extend and Enrich, p. 507 Reteach the Main Idea, p. 508	Activity Book, p. 99
SKILL **Solve a Problem** p. 509	**BUILDING CITIZENSHIP** • Critical Thinking Skills		Reteach the Skill, p. 509	Activity Book, p. 100 Transparency 40
CHAPTER REVIEW pp. 510–511				Activity Book, p. 101 Transparency 41 Assessment Program Chapter 15 Test, pp. 127–130 ▶ THE AMAZING WRITING MACHINE ▶ TIMELINER ▶ INTERNET

9 DAYS

TIME MANAGEMENT

DAY 1	DAY 2	DAY 3	DAY 4	DAY 5	DAY 6	DAY 7	DAY 8	DAY 9
Lesson 1	Skill	Lesson 2	Lesson 3	Lesson 4	Lesson 5	Skill	Chapter Review	Chapter Test

Activity Book

LESSON 1
Categorize Information

NAME ______________________ DATE __________

Famous Entrepreneurs

Categorize Information

***DIRECTIONS:** Read the stories that follow, and use the information to fill in the chart. Use your textbook and library reference materials to fill in the information about Andrew Carnegie.*

Levi Strauss, a Jewish immigrant from Germany, left New York City for the West in 1850. He went west to sell canvas to settlers to use for sails and coverings for their wagons. When he arrived there, he found that settlers could not find pants strong enough to last. Strauss took his canvas material and made it into the first pair of jeans. His company became Levi Strauss & Co.

John Harvey Kellogg, of British ancestry, believed that a healthful diet would help people heal more quickly from illness. He was once sued by an elderly woman who broke her false teeth on a zwieback (hard bread) that he had recommended for her to eat. As a result of this incident, he started to think about producing a softer ready-to-eat food. One night he dreamed of how to make flaked foods. This dream resulted in his producing the first dry cereal, which today is known as Kellogg's Cornflakes.

Fannie Merritt Farmer was born in Boston of British descent. She suffered a childhood illness that left her with a limp. After doctors discouraged her from going to college, she entered cooking school in 1887. By 1891 she was running it! In those days, cooking ingredients were measured by "pinches and dabs." Farmer applied science to cooking. In her best-selling cookbook, she standardized measurements. You can thank her for the level teaspoon.

FAMOUS ENTREPRENEURS

ENTREPRENEUR	HERITAGE	COMPANY/PRODUCT	FUN FACT
Levi Strauss	German	Levi Strauss & Co./ jeans	Accept all answers students can verify.
John Harvey Kellogg	British	Kellogg's/cereals	
Fannie Merritt Farmer	British	cooking school; cookbook/food	
Andrew Carnegie	Scottish	Carnegie Steel/ steel	

SKILL PRACTICE
Apply Map and Globe Skills

NAME ______________________ DATE __________

***DIRECTIONS:** Study the time zone map on page 94. Complete the activities that follow.*

1. How many time zones are located in the United States? 6
2. In which time zone is your city located? Answers should state appropriate time zone.
3. In which time zones are these cities located?
   Chicago, Illinois central — St. Louis, Missouri central
   Cleveland, Ohio eastern — Atlanta, Georgia eastern
4. Andrew Carnegie produced his steel in Pittsburgh, Pennsylvania. If he transported it by railroad from Pittsburgh to the West Coast, through how many time zones would the steel travel? 4
5. John D. Rockefeller set up an oil refinery in Cleveland, Ohio. He later bought refineries in West Virginia. If he traveled from his refinery in Ohio to his refinery in West Virginia, through how many time zones would he travel? One; both states are in the same time zone.
6. The Union Pacific Railroad built west from Omaha, Nebraska. The Central Pacific Railroad built east from Sacramento, California.
   A. If it is 7:00 P.M. in Sacramento, what time is it in Omaha? 9:00 P.M.
   B. If it is 8:00 A.M. in Omaha, what time is it in Sacramento? 6:00 A.M.
7. The two railroads met at Promontory, Utah. If it is 10:00 A.M. in Promontory,
   A. What time is it in Omaha? 11:00 A.M.
   B. What time is it in Sacramento? 9:00 A.M.
8. If the Super Bowl aired on TV from New Orleans at 3:00 P.M., what time would sports fans in Hawaii have to turn on their television sets to see the game? 11:00 A.M.
9. Imagine you live in Denver, Colorado, and have a scheduled school lunch at noon.
   A. What time would it be in our nation's capital? 2:00 P.M.
   B. What do you think students in the nation's capital would be doing at that time? Accept all answers that students can support, such as attending their last class or getting ready to go home from school.

Page 94 of the Activity Book does not appear here but is included in the full-sized book.

LESSON 2
Understand Economics

NAME ______________________ DATE __________

ORGANIZING Resources

Understand Economics

***DIRECTIONS:** Three kinds of resources are needed to make a product: natural resources, or raw materials, such as minerals and ores; capital resources, such as money, tools, and equipment; and human resources, or workers. Conduct library research and complete the organizer below to show what resources are needed to make each product listed in the center box.*

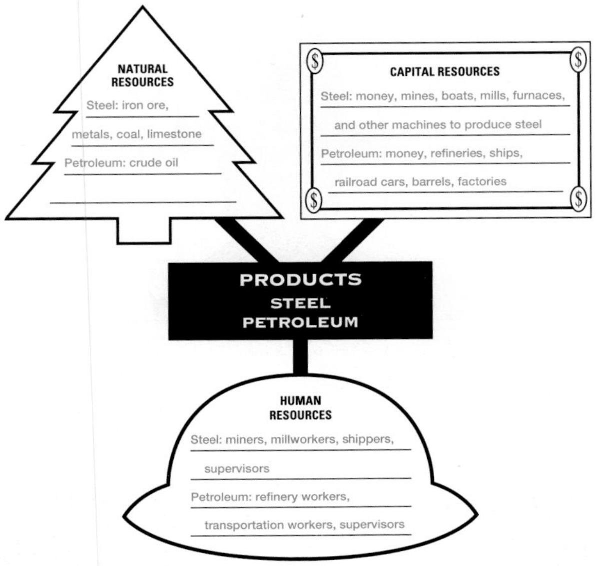

LESSON 3
Distinguish Fact from Opinion

NAME ______________________ DATE __________

Immigration

Distinguish Fact from Opinion

***DIRECTIONS:** Study the quotations below, which were made by immigrants who came to the United States at the beginning of the twentieth century. Then decide which of the following statements is fact and which is opinion. Write an F next to the statements of fact. Write an O next to the statements of opinion.*

"As far as Ellis Island was concerned, it was a nightmare. After all, none of us spoke English."
Nina Goodenov

"The examiner [at Ellis Island] sat bureaucratically . . . I was questioned as to the state of my finances and I produced the required twenty-five dollars."
Louis Adamic

"We lived there [Ellis Island] for three days . . . Because of the rigorous physical examination that we had to submit to, particularly of the eyes, there was this terrible anxiety that one of us might be rejected."
Angelo Pellegrini

"America is . . . the great Melting Pot where all the races of Europe are melting and re-forming."
Israel Zangwill

O **1.** Ellis Island was a nightmare.
F **2.** Immigrants were required to produce $25 to enter the United States.
F **3.** Immigrants had to take a physical examination.
O **4.** The examiner at Ellis Island was unfriendly.
O **5.** America is a great Melting Pot.
F **6.** Immigrants who were not in good physical health could be rejected from the United States.
F **7.** Some immigrants had to spend several days waiting on Ellis Island.
F **8.** Many immigrants could not speak English.

LESSON 4
Read a Table

NAME ______________________ DATE ____________

AN African American PORTRAIT

Read a Table

DIRECTIONS: *Study this table, which shows what percentage of the African American population lived in different regions of the United States during different time periods. Look for patterns. Then complete the activities that follow.*

AFRICAN AMERICANS IN THE UNITED STATES, BY REGION (in percentages)

YEAR	NORTHEAST	NORTH CENTRAL	SOUTH	WEST
1860	3.5	4.1	92.2	0.1
1870	3.7	5.6	90.6	0.1
1880	3.5	5.9	90.5	0.2
1890	3.6	5.8	90.3	0.4
1900	4.4	5.6	89.7	0.3
1910	4.9	5.5	89.0	0.5
1920	6.5	7.6	85.2	0.8
1930	9.6	10.6	78.7	1.0

1. In which region did the percentage of African Americans decrease steadily from 1860 to 1930? South

2. In which region did the percentage of African Americans increase the most from 1860 to 1930? What was the amount of percentage increase in this region?
North Central; 6.5 percent

3. During which ten-year period did the percentage of African Americans living in the South decrease the most? How much of a decrease was there during this period?
1920 to 1930; 6.5 percent

4. Migration was one reason that the percentage of African Americans in the South decreased during this time. Reread Jacob Lawrence's *The Great Migration: An American Story* in your textbook. Look for reasons that African Americans migrated. Copy the following headings onto a separate sheet of paper, and use information from the story to complete a chart showing reasons for African American migration.

FACTORS PUSHING AFRICAN AMERICANS OUT OF THE SOUTH	FACTORS PULLING AFRICAN AMERICANS TO OTHER REGIONS
floods ruined farms, boll weevils destroyed cotton crops, high cost of food, lack of justice in courts, harsh and unfair treatment by white landowners, segregation, limited opportunity for education	need for factory workers, workers were lent money to purchase railroad tickets, promise of better housing, encouraging letters from relatives living in the North

 Use after reading Chapter 15, Lesson 4, pages 500–504.

LESSON 5
Relate Past to Present

NAME ______________________ DATE ____________

School Days

Relate Past to Present

DIRECTIONS: *The following excerpt from Immigrant Kids by Russell Freedman describes a typical school day in New York City in the early 1900s. Read the excerpt. Then answer the questions that follow.*

When teacher called out in her sharp, penetrating voice, "Class!" everyone sat up straight as a ramrod, eyes front, hands clasped rigidly behind one's back. We strived painfully to please her. With a thin smile of approval on her face, her eyes roved over the stiff, rigid figures in front of her.

Beautiful script letters across the huge blackboard and a chart of the alphabet were the sole adornments of the classroom. Every day the current lesson from our speller was meticulously written out on the blackboard by the teacher. . . . We spent hours over our copybooks, all conveniently lined, as we laboriously sought to imitate this perfection.

We had to learn our lessons by heart, and we repeated them out loud until we memorized them. Playgrounds were nonexistent, toilets were in the yard, and gymnasiums were an unheard-of luxury.

1. Use context clues to define *penetrating.* Possible answers include "sharp," "piercing," and "deep."

2. Use context clues to describe your image of a ramrod. Accept all answers that describe something rigid or unyielding. Discuss with students the definition of *ramrod:* "a rod used for ramming down the charge in a gun that is loaded through the muzzle."

3. Compare the adornments, or decorations, in the classroom described with the ones in your classroom. Responses should describe both differences and similarities.

4. Describe differences between the way the teacher presented lessons in the early 1900s and the way your teacher presents lessons. Include descriptions of methods and materials.
Responses should address the use of the blackboard, copybooks, and memorization compared with computers, textbooks, and examples of higher-order thinking skills.

5. On a separate sheet of paper, write three paragraphs about your school, using the above three paragraphs as a guide. Describe the same things described in each paragraph, but use your school and class as the topic.
Responses should parallel description provided in each paragraph.

Use after reading Chapter 15, Lesson 5, pages 505–508.

SKILL PRACTICE
Apply Critical Thinking Skills

NAME ______________________ DATE ____________

HOW TO SOLVE A PROBLEM

Apply Critical Thinking Skills

DIRECTIONS: *Choose a problem in your school, such as one related to school lunches, bus schedules, or class size. Use the flow chart below to suggest a solution. You may copy the flow chart onto a separate sheet of paper if necessary.*
Responses should address a specific school problem.

Decide what the problem is. List the problem.

Think of possible solutions. List the solutions.

Think about the possible results of each solution. List the possible results of each solution.

Choose one solution. List this solution.

Think about how well your solution solves the problem. Explain how your solution solves the problem.

 Use after reading Chapter 15, Skill Lesson, page 509.

CHAPTER 15 REVIEW
Connect Main Ideas

NAME ______________________ DATE ____________

INDUSTRY AND IMMIGRATION

Connect Main Ideas

DIRECTIONS: *Use this organizer to show that you understand how the chapter's main ideas are connected. Complete the organizer by writing three examples to support each main idea.*

Industry and Immigration

New inventions changed life in the United States.
1. Air brake and telegraph improve rail transportation.
2. Investors make it possible for companies to expand, creating corporations and shareholders.
3. Consolidating companies leads to monopolies in oil and steel industries.

People worked to solve problems in the cities.
1. Disease, fire, and crime make city life dangerous.
2. Community centers teach new skills to people, improve living conditions, and abolish child labor.
3. Skyscrapers, elevators, and trolley cars improve growing cities.

People fought for better working conditions.
1. Labor unions and federations help improve working conditions and increase wages.
2. Workers go on strike.
3. People work to get laws passed that will regulate child labor.

Immigrants in the United States faced problems.
1. Immigrants face prejudice from people born in the United States.
2. Sixteen million European immigrants come to the United States.
3. Immigrants live together in tenements and earn very low wages.

African Americans shared problems with other newcomers to cities.
1. Families live in crowded, dirty quarters.
2. Northerners do not welcome migrants because they have to compete with them for housing and jobs.
3. Migrants experience segregation.

Use after reading Chapter 15, pages 482–511.

Chapter 15 Assessment

For ongoing **PERFORMANCE ASSESSMENT,** see Show What You Know, pp. 487, 494, 499, 508.

CONTENT

NAME ______________________ DATE __________

Chapter Test 15

***Part One: Test Your Understanding** (4 points each)*

***DIRECTIONS:** Match the description on the left with the correct word or name on the right. Write the correct letter in the space provided.*

1. __A__ economic system in which people are able to start and run their own businesses

2. __I__ money needed to run a business

3. __D__ business that sells shares of stock to investors

4. __M__ person who takes a chance by opening up a business

5. __C__ what made many inland cities important centers of industry

6. __L__ what workers did to get factory owners to listen to them

7. __O__ group of workers who take action to improve their working conditions

8. __H__ organization made up of many groups

9. __F__ a city neighborhood of Spanish-speaking people

10. __J__ what many people born in America feared they would lose to immigrants

11. __B__ entry place into the United States for most immigrants from Europe

A. free enterprise
B. Ellis Island
C. railroad
D. corporation
E. skyscrapers
F. barrio
G. trolley car
H. federation
I. capital resources
J. jobs
K. naturalization
L. strike
M. entrepreneur
N. settlement houses
O. labor union

(continued)

CONTENT

NAME ______________________ DATE __________

12. __K__ way for immigrants to become United States citizens

13. __N__ community centers in cities that helped immigrants learn skills

14. __E__ steel-framed buildings that helped cities grow upward

15. __G__ invention that helped make it possible for more people to move to suburbs

(continued)

SKILLS

NAME ______________________ DATE __________

***Part Two: Test Your Skills** (24 points)*

***DIRECTIONS:** Use the time zone map below to answer the questions that follow.*

WORLD TIME ZONES

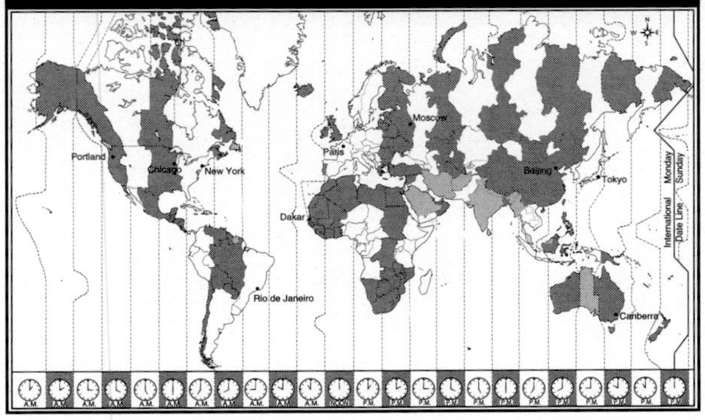

16. When it is 4:00 P.M. in Rio de Janeiro, what time is it in Chicago? __1:00 P.M.__

17. When it is 7:00 A.M. in New York, what time is it in Moscow? __2:00 P.M.__

18. When it is 10:00 A.M. in Tokyo, what time is it in Paris? __1:00 A.M.__

19. When it is 7:00 A.M. in Portland, what time is it in Beijing? __11:00 P.M.__

(continued)

APPLICATION/WRITING

NAME ______________________ DATE __________

Part Three: Apply What You Have Learned

***DIRECTIONS:** Complete each of the following activities.*

20. ***Becoming a Citizen*** *(6 points)*
Many immigrants felt that becoming United States citizens was very important. To become a citizen, an immigrant had to complete a series of steps. List these steps below.

a. Immigrants had to live in the United States for five years, pass a

b. test on the government and history of the United States, and take an

c. oath promising allegiance to the United States.

21. ***Essay*** *(10 points)*
At the end of the nineteenth century and the beginning of the twentieth century, factory workers and new immigrants living in American cities faced many problems. Choose one of these groups and explain in one paragraph the problems they faced living and working in the cities.

Possible responses:
Factory workers had to deal with low wages, unsafe working conditions, and many accidents. In addition, many adults were without jobs while children worked long hours under harsh conditions.

New immigrants in the cities faced many problems. Among these problems were poor housing, disease, no garbage collection, many fires, and crime.

INTRODUCE THE CHAPTER

This chapter describes the great changes that took place in the United States in the latter part of the nineteenth century and the early years of the twentieth century. It looks at the growth of big business in the steel and oil industries and the parallel growth of industrial cities. It also examines the changes in population patterns caused by the flood of European, Asian, and Mexican immigrants to the United States and the migration of African Americans from the South to the North.

Link Prior Learning

Have students recall the early stages of the Industrial Revolution and the idea of mass production. Ask them to summarize the changes in lifeways in the United States at that time. Explain that the process of change in industry continued, impacting daily life for many in the United States.

Visual Analysis

Interpret Pictures Ask students to imagine that they are getting off a ship with this Asian woman and are about to see the United States for the first time.

Q. **What do you think you and this woman would be talking about?**
Students' responses might include feelings of excitement about the new land, sorrow about being so far from home and loved ones, anxiety over where they would eat and sleep, and hope for a better future.

Auditory Learning

Interpret Primary Sources Ask a student to read aloud the quotation, and have the class analyze what the primary source is communicating.

"PRIMARY SOURCE"

Source: *Mountains of Gold: The Story of the Chinese in America.* Betty Lee Sung. Macmillan, 1967.

CHAPTER

15 INDUSTRY AND IMMIGRATION

"When we set foot on these shores, . . . we were bewildered and lost. We did not know where to turn for shelter or food. Fortunately, there were enough of us so that some set to putting up these houses while others looked for food."

The leader of an Asian miners' organization, addressing a group of newly arrived immigrants

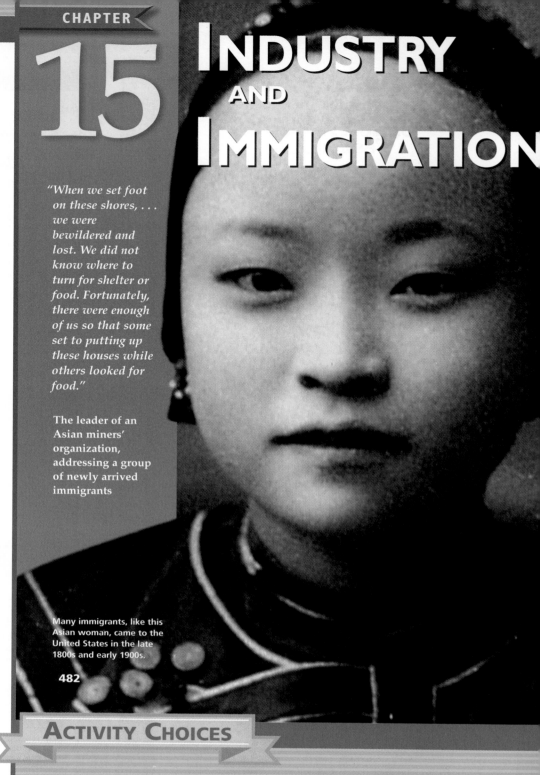

Many immigrants, like this Asian woman, came to the United States in the late 1800s and early 1900s.

482

ACTIVITY CHOICES

Background

JAPANESE IMMIGRATION
Because the Japanese government did not want its citizens to leave Japan for the United States, laws were passed forbidding emigration until 1868. Laborers were not allowed to emigrate until 1885. From 1885 to 1924 about 270,000 Japanese emigrated to the United States. Most Japanese immigrants did not intend to stay. They came to earn money so they could return to Japan in more financially secure positions. Some Japanese immigrants, however, settled permanently. They bought land for farming, introduced rice as a crop, and proved that potatoes could be grown commercially.

Big Business and Industrial Cities

LESSON 1

FOCUS
How have new inventions changed your life?

Main Idea Read to learn how new inventions changed life in the United States in the years after the Civil War.

Vocabulary
free enterprise
transcontinental railroad
capital resource
invest
stock
corporation
entrepreneur
consolidate
refinery
monopoly
hub

The Industrial Revolution came to the United States in he early 1800s. During this time, machines started to replace and tools, and factories began to replace craft shops. After he Civil War, even greater changes took place in American ndustry. Inventors developed new technologies, and busiess owners had more freedom to run their businesses in new vays. It was an important time for **free enterprise**—an ecoomic system in which people are able to start and run their wn businesses with little control by the government.

Railroads

When Abraham Lincoln ran for President in 1860, the Republican party promised to build a **transcontinental ailroad**. This was to be a railroad that went across the contiient, linking the Atlantic and Pacific coasts. When Lincoln vas elected, he kept his party's promise. In 1862 Congress gave two companies the right to build the railroad. The govrnment gave them land and lent them money. Railroads lready had been built from the Atlantic coast west to Nebraska. The Union Pacific built west from Omaha, Nebraska. The Central Pacific built east from Sacramento, California. On May 10, 1869, the two railroads met at Promontory, Utah.

The Union Pacific–Central Pacific was not the only railroad across the West for long. By the 1890s four more railroads had been built from midwestern cities to the Pacific coast. Railroads in the East added to their systems, too. In 1860 the United States had just over 30,000 miles (48,000 km) of track. By 1900 it had more than 193,000 miles (311,000 km) of track.

One reason for the growth of railroads was the development of new inventions that improved rail transportation. George Westinghouse's air brake made trains safer by stopping the locomotive and all the cars at the same time. Inventor Granville T. Woods improved the air brake and developed a telegraph system that let trains and stations communicate with one another.

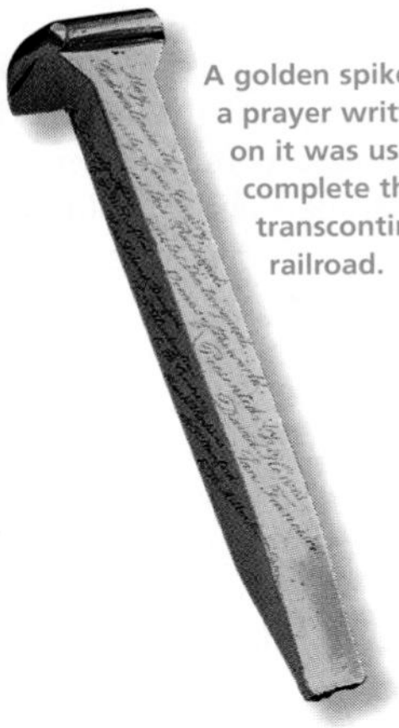

A golden spike with a prayer written on it was used to complete the first transcontinental railroad.

Reading Support

IDENTIFY RELATED WORDS Start the lesson by writing the words *transcontinental railroad* on the board or on chart paper. Have students brainstorm words or phrases that relate to the topic. Students may add to the web diagram during and after the reading. You may want to do a web diagram for several of the more challenging lesson vocabulary words.

Objectives

1. Analyze the changes that railroad expansion made in the United States.
2. Summarize the events that gave Andrew Carnegie a monopoly over the steel industry.
3. Describe the way John D. Rockefeller gained a monopoly in the oil industry.
4. Relate the rise of industry in the late 1800s to the growth of inland cities.

Vocabulary

free enterprise (p. 483)
transcontinental railroad (p. 483)
capital resource (p. 484)
invest (p. 484)
stock (p. 484)
corporation (p. 484)
entrepreneur (p. 484)
consolidate (p. 485)
refinery (p. 485)
monopoly (p. 486)
hub (p. 487)

1. ACCESS

The Focus Question

Ask students for examples of recent inventions that have changed their lives. Have students discuss how their lives today would be different if these technological advancements had never been made.

The Main Idea

Students will explore the changes brought about by inventions and by the rise of big business. After students have read the lesson, have them discuss why the changes might have had both advantages and disadvantages.

2. BUILD

Railroads

Key Content Summary

The completion of the transcontinental railroad in 1869 sparked a railroad boom in the United States. This boom helped turn the railroad industry into a big business.

Geography

Place Have students locate Omaha, Nebraska; Sacramento, California; and Promontory, Utah, on a classroom wall map or atlas. Tell students how the physical features of the land challenged those people who built the transcontinental railroad.

Economics

Productivity and Economic Growth Focus on the advantages provided by railroad transportation as compared with other early forms of travel.

Q. **How do you think the transcontinental railroad affected economic growth?** It improved transportation of goods, allowing goods to be shipped to new markets; it increased job opportunities in these new markets, in the railroad industry, and in businesses servicing the railroad.

The Steel Industry

Key Content Summary

The demand for steel increased as the railroads expanded. Andrew Carnegie learned a cheaper, easier way to process steel, and his steel mills dramatically changed the steel industry in the United States.

TECHNOLOGY

The Telegraph

By tapping out messages on the telegraph, people could communicate over long distances.

Just as railroad tracks carried people and goods across the country, the telegraph began carrying messages. An American inventor, Samuel F. B. Morse, experimented with sending electricity along iron wires during the 1830s. To send messages along the wires, Morse invented a code system in which dots and dashes stand for letters of the alphabet. The railroads quickly saw how useful Morse code and the telegraph would be, and telegraph lines were soon strung from pole to pole along railroad tracks. The telegraph helped railroads send messages ahead to warn of dangers and to tell people when trains were late. It also carried news to every part of the country in minutes. For the first time, news could travel faster than people.

As the railroads grew, their owners faced many problems. The railroad companies had to buy more locomotives, cars, and tracks. They had to pay the workers who laid and repaired the tracks, as well as the workers who ran the trains. To do all this, they needed **capital resources**, or money to run their businesses. Railroad owners, including Cornelius Vanderbilt and James J. Hill, received millions of dollars from the government, but they needed more. They got the money they needed from people who invested in the railroads. To **invest** is to buy shares of a business in the hope of earning a profit. These shares are called **stocks**.

As the railroads grew, many people bought stock in railroad companies. Buying stock let them own part of the railroad. When the railroad company made money, stock owners received part of the profit. Businesses that sell shares of stock to investors are called **corporations**.

Although people who bought stock were part owners of businesses, they did not run them. A board of directors ran each corporation. Managers took care of the day-to-day activities. Many railroad businesses became corporations in the late 1800s.

REVIEW ***Why did people invest money in railroads?*** to earn a profit

The Steel Industry

In the early part of the Industrial Revolution, iron was used to build bridges, buildings, and railroads. In fact, the early growth of railroads depended on iron tracks. As locomotives got bigger and heavier, however, iron tracks were no longer strong enough. Many lasted only about three years.

Steel tracks were harder and lasted longer, but steel cost a great deal to make. Steel is made from iron with small amounts of other metals added. Because of its cost, steel was used only for small items, such as knives and swords.

By the 1850s inventors in both Britain and the United States had developed ways to make steel more cheaply and easily. The British way was named after the British inventor Henry Bessemer, who came up with the new process of making steel. The Bessemer process melted iron ore and other metals together in a new kind of furnace. The higher heat of this "blast furnace" made the steel stronger.

During the 1860s an American entrepreneur (ahn•truh•pruh•NER) named Andrew Carnegie visited Britain and saw the Bessemer process for the first time. An **entrepreneur** is a person who sets up a new business, taking a chance on making or losing

ACTIVITY CHOICES

Multicultural Link

The construction of the first transcontinental railroad was accomplished in large part by the labor of two immigrant groups. The Central Pacific employed hundreds of Chinese immigrants, who worked under almost inhuman conditions for very little pay. With no safety regulations to protect them, many Chinese workers dynamited mountains or hung by ropes from steep cliffs, chipping away at the rock with hand tools. Workers on the Union Pacific were largely Irish immigrants, who also worked for low wages but did not have to cope with the same kind of difficult terrain the Chinese workers had to conquer. Working mainly with hand tools, the Irish crews sometimes laid as much as 10 miles of track in one day.

Meet Individual Needs

AUDITORY LEARNERS Have students conduct library research to find quotations by people speaking about the completion of the transcontinental railroad. Ask volunteers to read the quotations to the class, and have the class discuss whether people of the day saw the railroad as beneficial or harmful.

by buying coal and iron mines as well as ships to carry the resources to his steel mills

noney. After returning to the United States, Carnegie looked for investors to help him uild a small steel mill near Pittsburgh, Pennsylvania. By the early 1870s business vas good for Carnegie. With his profits he uilt more steel mills and made even larger rofits.

Carnegie bought mines to supply his steel nills with coal and iron. He then bought hips to carry these natural resources to his nills. With his mines and ships, he could nake more steel at a lower cost than other nills could. He could then afford to lower he price of his steel.

Other steel mills were not able to compete vith the low prices that Carnegie could offer. oon Carnegie bought these other mills and **consolidated**, or joined, their businesses with his. In 1899 he formed a large new corporation called the Carnegie Steel Company. This company became one of the largest steel businesses in the United States, and Andrew Carnegie became one of the richest people in the world.

REVIEW ***How was Carnegie able to make more steel for less money?***

The Oil Industry

Just as Andrew Carnegie did, John D. Rockefeller saw that he could become rich in business. Rockefeller was 24 years old in 1863 when he set up an oil refinery near Cleveland, Ohio. A **refinery** is a factory where crude, or raw, oil is made into usable products. The first products made by Rockefeller's refinery

LEARNING FROM GRAPHS Andrew Carnegie (left) helped the steel industry grow in the United States.
■ *Between which years did steel production increase the most?*

LEARNING FROM GRAPHS John D. Rockefeller (right) controlled most of the oil business in the United States.
■ *About how many barrels of oil were produced in 1890?*

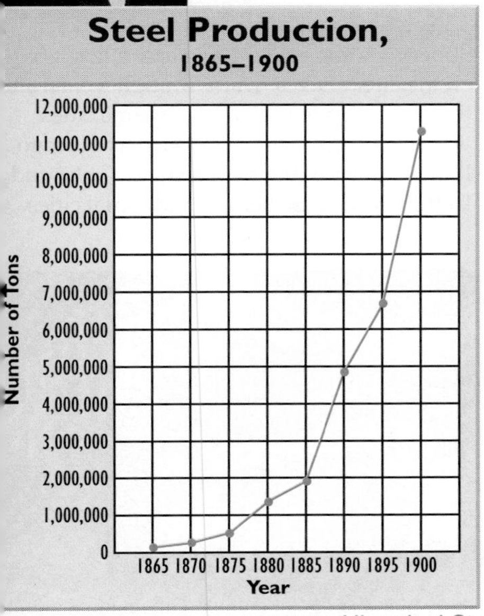

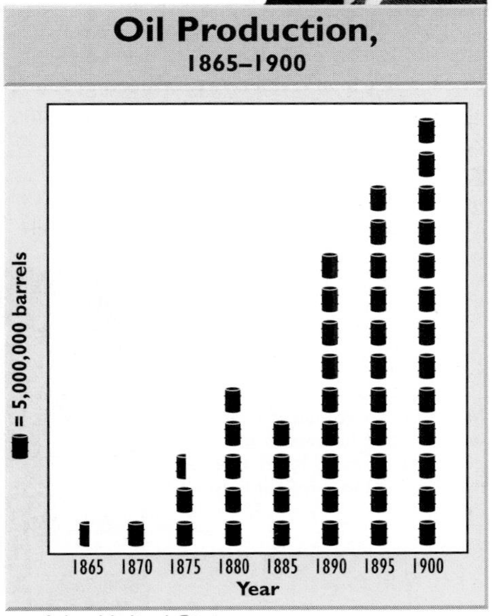

SOURCE: *Historical Statistics of the United States*

History

Leaders and Achievers Have students analyze how Henry Bessemer recognized a need for steel and contributed to major industrial changes in the United States.

Economics

Economic Institutions Ask students for examples of entrepreneurs in the local community and have the class speculate on why some entrepreneurs succeed while others fail. Then have students analyze the steps taken by Carnegie to build the steel business and speculate on the reasons for his success.

Visual Analysis

Learn from Graphs Direct students' attention to the graph on steel production and have them answer the question in the caption. between 1895 and 1900

The Oil Industry

Key Content Summary

An oil boom in Ohio, West Virginia, and Pennsylvania and new uses for oil brought more changes to American industry. John D. Rockefeller saw opportunity in the oil industry and by the late 1890s monopolized almost all of the nation's oil refining business.

Visual Analysis

Learn from Graphs Ask students to examine the graph on oil production and answer the caption question. about 45,000,000

TECHNOLOGY

Use LOOKING AHEAD! EARNING, SPENDING, SAVING to reinforce the idea of making responsible economic decisions.

Community Involvement

Invite a local businessperson or investment counselor to come to the class to discuss the concepts of corporations, stocks, capital resources, investments, and monopolies as they apply to the world today. Ask the resource person to present information in concrete terms, using visual aids such as diagrams, stock certificates, or sections of the stock market report.

Link to Mathematics

ESTIMATE COSTS Tell students to imagine that they are the owners of a steel mill in Birmingham, Alabama. Have them use a map of the United States to estimate how much it would cost to ship 20 tons of steel to New Orleans by railroad if they had to pay $.50 a ton per mile for the shipment. Tell them to assume that the rail line goes on a straight line between the two cities.

Economics

Monopoly Have students discuss how a monopoly affects trade and competition. Tell students why laws today protect against the formation of monopolies.

The New Industrial Cities

Key Content Summary

The need for certain natural resources brought railroad lines and new industries to areas far from the nation's major cities. These changes sparked the growth of new inland industrial cities such as Pittsburgh and Chicago.

were grease and kerosene for lamps. Electricity was not yet in use.

Many business people were building refineries because oil had been found in Ohio, Pennsylvania, and West Virginia. The Rockefeller refinery was one of 30 in the Cleveland area. Within a few years, Rockefeller had bought most of the other refineries. In 1870 he consolidated them into one business, which he called the Standard Oil Company.

Rather than let other companies make a profit from his business, Rockefeller did something similar to what Carnegie had done. He bought forests to get his own lumber. He bought a barrel factory to make his own barrels. He bought ships and rail-road cars to carry his products. Soon other companies could not match Rockefeller's low prices for oil products. Before long, Rockefeller had a **monopoly**, or almost complete control, of the oil business. By 1899 the Standard Oil Company controlled about 90 percent of the country's oil refining business.

After the invention of the gasoline engine, automobiles came into use, and Rockefeller's oil refineries produced gasoline and engine oil. Standard Oil's yearly profits zoomed to more than $45 million.

REVIEW ***How did Rockefeller get a monopoly in the oil business?*** He bought forests, a barrel factory, and ships and rail-roads to carry his products.

The New Industrial Cities

Before the Civil War the most important cities in the United States were those on good harbors near the oceans. But with the growth of railroads and industries such as steel and oil after the Civil War, new industrial cities developed inland, far from the coast. Some were built close to the resources needed by their mills and factories. Others depended on railroads to bring these materials from great distances.

The region west of the Appalachians and east of the Mississippi had many important resources. Because western Pennsylvania had iron ore, coal, and limestone—the resources needed for making iron and steel—places such as Pittsburgh were among the first iron and steel centers in the North. Birmingham, Alabama, in the South, was close to iron and coal deposits, and also became an iron and steel center.

Iron ore deposits also were found in the hills of the Mesabi Range near Lake Superior. The ore was taken by barge across Lake Superior and on to Chicago and other cities on the Great Lakes. Trains brought coal from the Appalachian region to the same cities. With these resources, cities such as Chicago, Illinois; Gary, Indiana; Cleveland, Ohio; and Detroit, Michigan, became industrial cities.

Most of the new industrial cities were far from harbors. They depended on trains to bring in raw materials and to carry out finished products.

Activity Choices

Background

CHICAGO No city better illustrates the impact of industry than Chicago. During the 1830s Chicago was a frontier town with a few hundred people. By 1910 it had become the nation's second-largest city, with a population of more than 2 million. In addition to being a rail center, Chicago was a busy industrial city, with factories that produced farm implements, railroad cars, steel, and many other products. It was also one of the nation's great meatpacking centers. In fact, the author Carl Sandburg called Chicago the "hog butcher for the world."

Extend and Enrich

COOPERATIVE LEARNING

RESEARCH AND REPORT Divide the class into several groups, and assign each group a topic to research. Members of the group should work together to write a report on the topic to share with the class. Topics might include John D. Rockefeller, Andrew Carnegie, George Westinghouse, Cornelius Vanderbilt, the telegraph, or the oil-refining or steel-making process. Have the groups share and discuss what they learned.

Technology

Use THE AMAZING WRITING MACHINE™ to complete this writing activity.

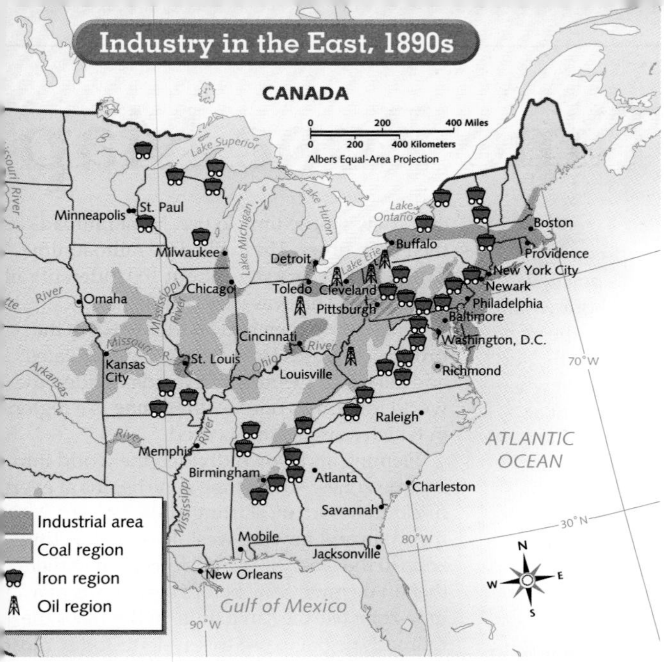

MAP THEME Human-Environment Interactions

This map shows industrial areas and resource regions in the eastern part of the United States in the 1890s.

■ *If you were going to build an oil refinery in 1890, where would you put it? Where would you build a steel mill?*

Because of the railroads, businesses that sed iron and steel to make their products uilt factories near iron and steel centers. ailroads brought in raw materials to the actories and carried out finished products to eliver to customers. Cities such as Chicago, Cleveland, and Pittsburgh, as well as Atlanta, Georgia, became railroad hubs. A **hub** is a city where many trains make stops on their way to different destinations.

REVIEW ***Why did inland cities become important in the late 1800s?*** They were close to the resources needed by their mills and factories.

ESSON 1 REVIEW

Check Understanding

1. **Remember the Facts** Who were the important business leaders in the steel and oil industries?
2. **Recall the Main Idea** How did new inventions change life in the United States in the years after the Civil War?

Think Critically

3. **Past to Present** What kinds of businesses do you think are the most important today?
4. **Explore Viewpoints** How do you think other oil refinery owners felt about Rockefeller's monopoly of the oil business?

Show What You Know

Table Activity Make a table comparing information about Andrew Carnegie and John D. Rockefeller. Be sure to include information about their businesses. Share your table with a classmate.

Reteach the Main Idea

WRITE AN OUTLINE Divide the class into small groups. Challenge each group to use the textbook as a resource and make an outline of the changes in industry brought about by new inventions in the United States after 1865. Ask the group members to share their outlines and discuss them with each other and with the other groups.

COOPERATIVE LEARNING

ACTIVITY BOOK

Reinforce & Extend

Use ACTIVITY BOOK, p. 93.

Visual Analysis

Learn from Maps Have students answer the questions in the caption. Ohio, Pennsylvania, or West Virginia; best choices would be Pittsburgh or Birmingham

3. CLOSE

Have students consider again the Focus question on page 483.

> **How have new inventions changed your life?**

Have students use what they have learned in this lesson to compare the changes brought about in their lives by new inventions with the changes brought about by new inventions in the railroad, steel, and oil industries in the nineteenth century.

LESSON 1 REVIEW—Answers

Check Understanding

1. Andrew Carnegie and John D. Rockefeller
2. A cheaper steel-making process and the need for steel railroad tracks caused the steel industry to boom, leading to the development of corporations. New oil discoveries and new uses for oil caused the oil-refining industry to expand. New industries and expanded railroads gave rise to new cities.

Think Critically

3. Student responses may include computers, automobiles, communications, and air travel.
4. angry and resentful because Rockefeller was forcing them out of business

Show What You Know

Performance Assessment Consider having selected students copy their tables on the board for discussion.

What to Look For Look for evidence that the students have understood the similarities in Rockefeller's and Carnegie's visions of opportunity and in their business practices.

Objectives

1. Summarize the system of time zones.
2. Analyze a time zone map.

Vocabulary

time zone (p. 488)

1. ACCESS

Pose some problems that could arise if there were no time zones. For example, suppose a person needs to be in a neighboring city promptly at noon in order to collect a prize. According to sun time, the sun is at its highest point at noon. Unfortunately the person forgets that noon occurs a little earlier in the neighboring city because it is located to the east. As a result, the person loses the prize because he or she has arrived too late.

Discuss the problems faced by the railroads because of time differences and how these problems led to the development of time zones. Make sure students understand the meaning of the term *time zone.* Have a volunteer find the prime meridian on a globe or world map and, moving east, determine approximately where time zone boundaries occur.

2. BUILD

Introduce the time zone map used in this skill. Have students identify the six U.S. time zones and some states located in each zone. Call attention to the clocks at the bottom of the map that indicate the time in each zone when it is seven o'clock in New York.

Work through the steps shown in Understand the Process. At each step, have students check the time on the appropriate clock on the map. As you locate the six states, you may want to have students identify other states in the same time zone. Make sure to identify the time zone in which your own state lies.

Map and Globe Skills

Use a Time Zone Map

1. Why Learn This Skill?

People have always used sun time, basing the time of day on the sun's position. According to sun time, noon is the hour when the sun reaches its highest position in the sky. By this rule, you know it is noon when the sun is directly overhead. But when it is noon where you are, the sun is not at its highest point at other places. Because of the Earth's rotation, the sun has not yet reached its highest point at places west of you. And the sun is past its highest point at places east of you. So according to sun time, these other places have different times.

Telling time by the sun was not a problem until people began to travel long distances. When railroads began to cross the United States and Canada, no one knew what time to use to follow train schedules. So a new time system was developed. Knowing how to use this system is just as important today as it was during the 1800s.

2. Time Zones

As the railroad industry grew, managers set schedules of times that trains would arrive at and depart from places along their routes. But setting schedules was difficult because of the many time differences from place to place. No one knew whose time to use. Most railroads s their own times. They called it "railroad time. By the 1880s there were about 100 different ra road times. This was very confusing.

Finally, two men had an idea to solve the problem. Charles Dowd of the United States and Sandford Fleming of Canada divided the world into time zones. A **time zone** is a regior in which a single time is used.

Fleming and Dowd divided the world into 24 time zones. A new time zone begins at ever fifteenth meridian, starting at the prime meridian and moving west. In each new time zone to the west, the time is one hour earlier than in the time zone before it. All parts of a time zone use the same time. In the 1880s the railroads began to use this system. Today mos of the countries in the world follow it.

The United States has six time zones. From east to west, they are the eastern, central, mountain, Pacific, Alaska, and Hawaii-Aleutian time zones.

3. Understand the Process

How can you figure out what time it is in different time zones? Following the steps in th examples below can help you.

1. Find Maryland on the map. It is in the eastern time zone.

An accurate pocket watch was important to the engineer on a train. Time zones solved the problem of how to set the watch.

ACTIVITY CHOICES

Meet Individual Needs

KINESTHETIC LEARNERS Have students use chalk to draw a large map of the United States on the playground. Add time zone lines and some major cities. Have students travel from one city to another on the map. As they cross each time zone, have them set a large clock or a watch to the time in the zone just entered. When they reach their destinations, have them note the time on the clock or watch and compare it to the time in the zone from which they began their trips.

TECHNOLOGY

Use MAPSKILLS to complete the activities.

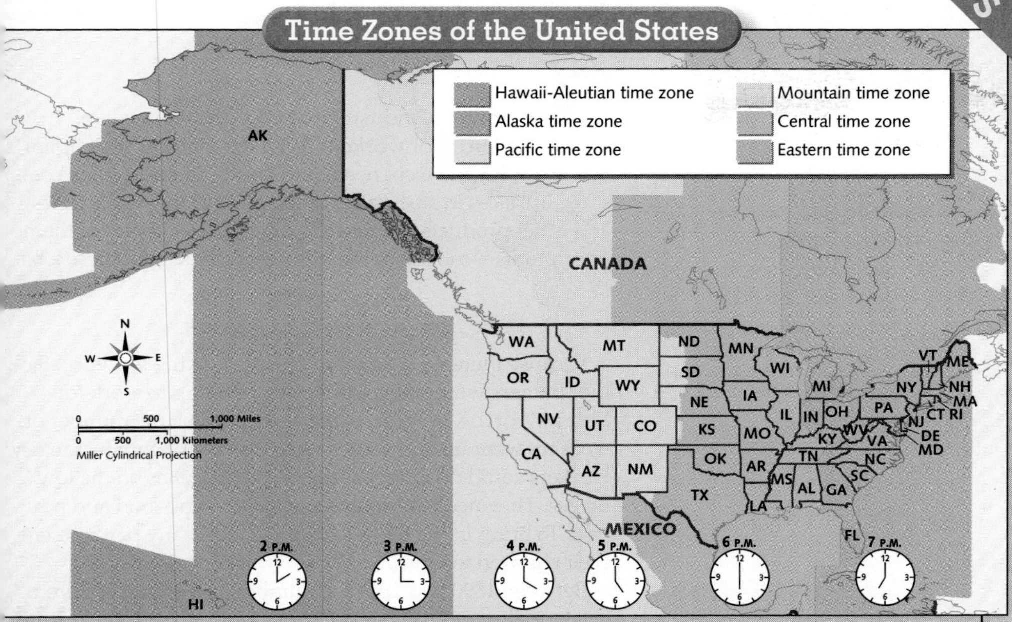

2. Now find Arkansas. It is in the central time zone, which is just west of the eastern time zone. The time in the central time zone is one hour earlier than in the eastern time zone. To find the time in Arkansas, subtract one hour from the time in Maryland.
3. Find Colorado on the map. It is in the mountain time zone. The time is two hours earlier in Colorado than in Maryland. To find the time in Colorado, subtract two hours from the time in Maryland.
4. Now look to the west on the map to find California. It is in the Pacific time zone. The time is three hours earlier in California than in Maryland. To find the time in California, subtract three hours from the time in Maryland.
5. Locate the largest part of Alaska, in the Alaska time zone. The time there is four hours earlier than in Maryland. To find the time in this part of Alaska, subtract four hours from the time in Maryland.
6. Find Hawaii on the map. It is in the Hawaii-Aleutian time zone. The time is five hours earlier in Hawaii than in Maryland. To find the time in Hawaii, subtract five hours from the time in Maryland.

4. Think and Apply

Use an almanac or atlas to find a world time zone map. Suppose it is 9:00 A.M. where you live. Find the time in each of these cities: London, England; Tokyo, Japan; and Cairo, Egypt. Help other students understand time zones by describing how you figured out the time for each of these cities. Then explain when it would be helpful to know the time in different places.

Have students describe experiences they have had with different time zones. Point out that bus and airline schedules are given in local time. A plane may arrive in Chicago, Illinois (central time zone), at an earlier hour than it left Toledo, Ohio (eastern time zone).

3. CLOSE

You may want to project an almanac map so all of the students may use it. Also consider having students work in groups. Before students begin, model an example using one faraway city. As students work, look for an understanding of how time is determined around the world. Have students add other cities to the map.

Home Involvement

Remind students of the language used to promote upcoming television programs: "9 o'clock eastern time, 8 o'clock central," for example. Suggest they choose a favorite television show and, with their families, figure out when that program might be seen in several time zones. Include the time zone for Hawaii and explain that many television viewers there watch delayed broadcasts.

Reteach the Skill

FIGURE TIME FOR AIRLINE OR BUS TRIPS
Furnish students with bus or plane schedules. Have them plan dream trips across at least two time zones. Then have them check departure and arrival times, which are given in local time on bus or plane schedules. Have students determine in what time zones departure and arrival terminals lie. Finally, have them use departure and arrival times in combination with time zone information to compute the actual amount of driving or flying time required for each trip.

ACTIVITY BOOK

Practice & Apply
Use ACTIVITY BOOK, pp. 94–95.

TRANSPARENCY

Use TRANSPARENCY 39.

Objectives

1. Summarize the problems of workers in factories.
2. Analyze the actions workers took to improve working conditions.
3. Explain the causes and effects of the Homestead Strike.
4. Contrast workers' and owners' views about government's role in business.

Vocabulary

human resource (p. 490)
strike (p. 491)
labor union (p. 491)
federation (p. 492)
regulate (p. 494)

1. ACCESS

The Focus Question

Have students discuss job situations in which working conditions might be unsafe or might demand more than is reasonable from employees. Discuss how workers sometimes cooperate in taking action to resolve conflicts with employers.

The Main Idea

In this lesson students explore the growing conflict between workers and owners in the new industries of the late 1800s and early 1900s. After students have read the lesson, have them summarize the conflicts and explain the ways workers cooperated to fight for better working conditions.

2. BUILD

Work in the Factories

Key Content Summary

In the late 1800s and early 1900s, the number of factory workers increased and the wages paid to them decreased. Many workers were children, and conditions were such that workers could be injured or even killed by the machines they used.

LESSON 2

FOCUS
How do people today improve their working conditions?

Main Idea Read to find out how people fought for better working conditions in the late 1800s and early 1900s.

Vocabulary
human resource
strike
labor union
federation
regulate

Growing Pains

The growth of industry caused a greater need for **human resources**, or workers, as well as natural and capital resources. People were needed to build railroads, mine coal, stoke furnaces in steel mills, refine oil, and make machines and other products. Thousands of workers—many of them immigrants—moved to the industrial cities to fill these jobs.

Work in the Factories

Because there were so many people looking for work, factory owners were able to hire people willing to work for little pay, or low wages. As the years passed, the number of workers went up and wages went down. Soon many factory workers could no longer support their families on the low wages. They needed more money just to buy food and pay rent. To bring in the money they needed, many parents sent their children to work.

Between 1890 and 1910 the number of working children between the ages of 10 and 15 went from 1.5 million to 2 million. By 1910, almost one-fifth of the workers in the United States were children.

Many children no longer had time for school. They worked in factories all day or, in some cases, all night. In 1906 John

This photo shows men and women working in a clothing shop in New York City. People often had to work long hours for little pay.

ACTIVITY CHOICES

Reading Support

PREVIEW AND READ THE LESSON Provide students with the following visual framework.

CONFLICTS BETWEEN WORKERS AND BUSINESS OWNERS

WORKERS' DEMANDS AND ACTIONS
higher pay, end of child labor, shorter workday, safe working conditions, accident insurance; form unions, strike

BUSINESS OWNERS' RESPONSES
resist demands, cut wages, hire private police during strikes, resist government regulation

Spargo, a reporter, described what he saw in one glassmaking factory.

> "The hours of labor for the 'night shift' were from 5:30 P.M. to 3:30 A.M. . . . Then began the work of . . . the 'carrying-in boys,' sometimes called 'carrier pigeons,' [who] took the red-hot bottles from the benches, three or four at a time. . . . The work of these 'carrying-in boys,' several of whom were less than twelve years old, was by far the hardest of all. They were kept on a slow run all the time from the benches to the annealing [finishing] oven . . . [the trip] was one hundred feet, and the boys made seventy-two trips per hour, making the distance traveled in eight hours nearly twenty-two miles. Over half of this distance the boys were carrying their hot loads to the oven. The pay of these boys varies from sixty cents to a dollar for eight hours' work."

Workers of all ages had another problem, too—machines that were unsafe. Hundreds of workers were killed each year in factory accidents, and thousands more were badly hurt.

REVIEW ***What problems did working children face?*** long workdays, low wages, unsafe working conditions

Owners Against Workers

Some workers complained about their working conditions. Others went on **strike**, or stopped work, as a way to get factory owners to listen to them. Few factory owners did. They just fired the people who complained and hired new workers. Plenty of people were still looking for jobs.

An employer saved money by hiring children because they could be paid much less than adults. The children shown in this photograph are working in a textile mill.

As conditions grew worse, some workers started to fight back. By themselves they could do little against the powerful factory owners. So they joined together to form labor unions. A **labor union** is a group of workers who take action to improve their working conditions.

One early labor union leader was Samuel Gompers. When Gompers was 13 years old, he went to work in a cigarmakers' shop. The cigarmakers often worked from sunrise until sunset. Most were paid only pennies an hour. Gompers joined a cigarmakers' union, and soon he was the union leader in his shop. In 1877 Gompers helped bring all of the cigarmakers' unions together to form one large union. Members of the union went on strike because they wanted a shorter workday and better wages. The strike failed. The people who owned the cigarmakers' shops also owned many of the apartment buildings where workers lived. They fired the striking workers and put them out of their apartments.

After this experience Gompers decided that cigarmakers needed the support of other workers to make the labor union stronger. So he asked other workers to join

Economics

Factors of Production Identify the kinds of costs a factory owner might face in setting up a factory. Have students conclude why a factory owner might pay low wages.

Economics

Economic Systems and Institutions Ask students to share what they know about the operation of factories today. Have a volunteer read aloud John Spargo's report. Ask students to express their views on the working conditions in the glassmaking factory, and have them consider whether those working conditions would be allowed today.

"PRIMARY SOURCE"

Source: *The Bitter Cry of the Children.* John Spargo. Quadrangle Books, 1968.

Owners Against Workers

Key Content Summary

To improve working conditions, Samuel Gompers organized workers of many trades into a cooperative organization called the American Federation of Labor. This organization asked for a shorter workday, higher wages, better working conditions, accident insurance, and an end to child labor.

Link to Language Arts

WRITE A PERSONAL NARRATIVE Tell students to imagine that they are children working in a factory in 1900. Have them write letters to their relatives or friends describing a typical workday, including the work they do, the hours they work, the lunch and dinner breaks, what their boss is like, and the working conditions. Have volunteers read their letters to the class.

TECHNOLOGY

Use IMAGINATION EXPRESS™: DESTINATION TIME TRIP to complete this activity.

Background

CHILD LABOR Children worked in factories almost from the beginning of the Industrial Revolution, but their numbers rose with the advance of the new industrial age. Of the 340,000 school-age children living in New Jersey in 1885, 90,000 had jobs. Most of them were full-time workers. Working children were perhaps even more vulnerable to injury than adult workers. In 1876 a Pennsylvania newspaper reported that in one week nearly one boy a day had been killed while working.

History

Patterns and Relationships Discuss with students the cause-and-effect relationship between working conditions and the formation of labor unions.

Q. **Why did Samuel Gompers and other workers believe that cooperative action rather than individual action would help improve working conditions?** By cooperating in a union, workers could present their demands as a group. If a strike were necessary, it would be more effective as a collective action.

Economics

Economic Institutions Have students consider why business leaders started to listen to the demands made by the AFL's representatives.

Visual Analysis

Learn from Graphs Have students answer the question in the caption. It rose by about 4,500,000 members.

Labor Unions and Strikes

Key Content Summary

Labor unions used the strike as their most effective weapon in the conflict with factory owners. Two of the most serious strikes of the late 1800s, one against the McCormick Harvesting Machine Company and the other against a steel mill, resulted in violence.

his union. He believed that only skilled workers should be in this group. If skilled workers went on strike, it would be hard to replace them. A strike might then have a better chance of success. Gompers and other leaders organized groups of carpenters, plumbers, and bricklayers to join with the cigarmakers in one large federation. A **federation** is an organization made up of many related groups.

In 1886 Samuel Gompers helped form the American Federation of Labor, or AFL. As the AFL got larger, business leaders began to listen to its representatives. The AFL asked for higher wages and a shorter workday. Workers sang,

> "Eight hours for work,
> eight hours for rest,
> eight hours for what we will."

The AFL also wanted better working conditions, accident insurance, and an end to child labor. The insurance would pay the wages and medical bills for workers who were hurt on the job.

REVIEW ***What were the goals of the American Federation of Labor?*** a shorter workday, better wages, better working conditions, accident insurance, an end to child labor

SOURCE: *Historical Statistics of the United States*

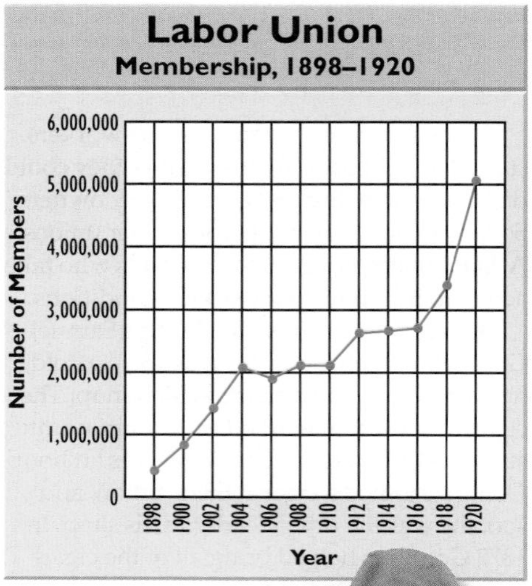

LEARNING FROM GRAPHS Samuel Gompers (right) helped form the American Federation of Labor. The graph (above) shows the number of workers who joined unions from 1898 to 1920.

- *How did union membership change during this time?*

Labor Unions and Strikes

Going on strike became the labor unions' most important way to be heard by the factory owners. Sometimes, however, strikes became violent. Violence did not help the unions. In fact, some labor unions lost their power as a result.

In 1886, workers belonging to a labor union known as the Knights of Labor went on strike against the McCormick Harvesting Machine Company. The union demanded higher wages and an eight-hour workday. During one protest meeting, strikers clashed with police at Haymarket Square in Chicago. When someone threw a bomb, seven police officers were killed and many other people were hurt. The police did not find out who threw the bomb, but people blamed the labor union. The Knights of Labor soon lost many of its members.

One of the most violent strikes during this time took place in 1892 at a Carnegie steel mill in Homestead, Pennsylvania, near Pittsburgh. While Andrew Carnegie was in Scotland, one of his managers, Henry Clay Frick, announced a pay cut. In June the workers went on strike. Frick fought back. He shut down the mill and hired private police

Activity Choices

Link to Health

REPORT ON INDUSTRY AND HEALTH Have students research the health consequences for workers in industries such as coal mining, textiles, and steel during the 1890s and early 1900s. Ask students to prepare and present television news reports on the working conditions and the related injuries and illnesses. Allow students time to express their views on whether they would strike over those working conditions.

Meet Individual Needs

VISUAL LEARNERS Have students sketch a progression of pictures that depict why labor unions arose in the United States. Have the students mount their pictures on cardboard to create a "storyboard" about the formation of unions. Ask volunteers to show their storyboards to the class and describe the progression of events.

One of the demands of these New York City clothing workers was an eight-hour workday. Many of the workers in this photograph were immigrants and carried signs in their own languages, including Italian, Yiddish, and Russian.

from the Pinkerton National Detective Agency to protect it.

When 300 Pinkertons, as Pinkerton agents were called, arrived in Homestead, they were met by hundreds of angry union workers. A fight broke out, and 7 Pinkertons and 9 strikers were killed. The governor of Pennsylvania sent in soldiers from the National Guard to keep order.

The Homestead strike went on for more than four months. Finally the union gave up. Frick won, but many people began to think that factory owners should listen to labor unions' demands.

REVIEW ***What caused the Homestead strike?*** A manager announced a pay cut.

Government and Business

Workers went on strike in the hope of making their lives and working conditions better. But pay was still low, and many children still had to work. More and more workers were hurt in accidents every year. Workers hoped that the government would help, but many government leaders took the side of the factory owners.

Government leaders believed that business people helped make the country's economy strong by producing goods and creating new jobs. The leaders felt that government should leave factory owners and

Visual Analysis

Interpret Photographs Draw students' attention to the picture of the striking workers and have them discuss why the workers carried signs during the strike.

Economics

Economic Institutions Have students conclude why strikes were helpful to labor unions, focusing on the economic effects of strikes on factory owners. Also have students speculate on why the Homestead strikers gave up after four months.

Civics and Government

Purposes of Government Review the fact that one of the purposes of government is to promote order and security. Have students keep that in mind and analyze why strikers sometimes resorted to violence and why the police became involved. Have students discuss alternatives to violence.

Government and Business

Key Content Summary

A new conflict arose when workers looked to the government for help. The workers wanted the government to abolish abusive working conditions, but government and business leaders believed that industries should not be regulated.

Community Involvement

Have the class compose a letter inviting a local union representative to talk to them about the history of unions in the community and about the role of unions today. Make sure students prepare a list of questions prior to the arrival of the guest speaker. Remind students about proper etiquette when the guest is in the classroom, and guide them in writing a thank-you letter after the visit.

Extend and Enrich

WRITE A SPEECH Select a few students to go to the library and borrow books containing some of the photographs of child labor taken during this era. Have them share the pictures with the class and talk about them. Then tell students to imagine that they are living during the late 1800s. Have each student write a speech to be given to Congress, convincing the members that laws are needed to protect children from unfair labor practices. After students share their speeches with the class, lead a discussion about the kinds of laws needed.

Economics

Economic Systems and Institutions Ask students to express their views on whether the government should have helped the workers or the business leaders in the late 1800s.

Q. **Why didn't government leaders help the workers?** They felt it was more important for industry to grow.

3. CLOSE

Have students consider again the Focus question on page 490.

How do people today improve their working conditions?

Have students use what they have learned in this lesson to compare and contrast methods used by workers in the late 1800s and early 1900s to improve working conditions with methods used by workers today.

LESSON 2 REVIEW—Answers

Check Understanding

1. Wages were low, hours were long, conditions in factories were poor and often dangerous.
2. They formed unions and went on strike to force owners to meet their demands.

Think Critically

3. Workers felt that the strike was the best way to bring about change. Business owners felt workers should not go on strike.
4. Most students probably would not have liked the job because of low wages and poor working conditions. Accept reasonable answers.

Show What You Know

Performance Assessment Consider asking students to imagine that they are members of a union and are choosing posters to be used in a union recruiting drive. Have them vote for the posters that should be used in the drive.

What to Look For Make sure students understand the substance of the workers' grievances against the factory owners.

HERITAGE

Labor Day

In New York City on September 5, 1882, Americans held the first Labor Day parade. Matthew Maguire, a machine worker, and Peter McGuire, a carpenter and a founder of an early labor union, came up with the idea of Labor Day. It is a day to honor working people and to recognize their importance to the United States. In 1894 Congress made Labor Day a legal holiday. Today the United States and Canada celebrate Labor Day on the first Monday in September. Many other countries also honor workers with labor celebrations.

A Labor Day parade in the early 1900s

their businesses alone. For industry to grow, they said, businesses had to be free to produce goods in the ways that were best for them.

Business leaders also felt that the government should leave their companies alone. They did not want government leaders telling them how to run their own businesses. They feared that the government would then **regulate** their businesses, or control them by law. Business owners wanted to be controlled by as few laws as possible.

REVIEW ***Why did the government choose to leave business owners alone?*** Government leaders believed it would help industry and the country's economy grow.

LESSON 2 REVIEW

Check Understanding

1. **Remember the Facts** What were conditions like for factory workers during the late 1800s and early 1900s?
2. **Recall the Main Idea** How did people fight for better working conditions in the late 1800s and early 1900s?

Think Critically

3. **Explore Viewpoints** How do you think workers in the late 1800s felt about going on strike? How do you think business owners felt about strikes?
4. **Personally Speaking** Suppose you had been one of the young workers in the glassmaking factory that the reporter John Spargo described. How do you think you might have felt about your job?

Show What You Know

Art Activity Think about the problems factory workers faced in the late 1800s. Draw a poster that a labor union might have used to get people to join. Display your poster in the classroom.

ACTIVITY CHOICES

ACTIVITY BOOK

Reinforce & Extend

Use ACTIVITY BOOK, p. 96.

Reteach the Main Idea

MAKE A DRAWING Have students review the lesson and select two examples of how people fought for better working conditions in the late 1800s and early 1900s. Provide them with materials for illustrating each of their selected examples. Canvass the class to make sure all examples provided in the lesson will be illustrated. Have students share and discuss their completed drawings and then display them in class.

New Immigrants

LESSON 3

FOCUS
What problems do immigrants to the United States face today?

Main Idea Read to learn about some of the problems that immigrants to the United States faced in the past.

Vocabulary
prejudice
barrio
tenement
naturalization

A bout three of every four workers in the Carnegie steel nills had been born outside the United States. Carnegie himelf had been born in Scotland. When he was 12 years old, he ıad moved to the United States with his father. Between 1860 ınd 1910, about 23 million immigrants arrived in the United ›tates. Those from Asia and Latin America settled mostly in he West and Southwest. Latin America is made up of all the ountries in the Americas south of the United States. Those rom Europe settled mostly in the cities in the East and in the ;rowing industrial cities of the Middle West. Immigrants from ıll over the world played an important part in the growth of ndustry and agriculture in the United States.

Asian Immigrants

Chinese people came to the United States in great numbers ıfter the California gold rush of 1849. By 1852 about 25,000 Chinese people had arrived in San Francisco and were vorking in the goldfields.

Like other immigrant groups, the Chinese faced prejuılice from some Americans. **Prejudice** is a negative feeling ›ome people have toward others because of their race or :ulture. The Chinese had to pay a tax to pan for gold hat no one else had to pay. Some Americans tried to 'orce the Chinese out of the goldfields.

As less and less gold was found in the gold'ields, the Chinese looked for other work. Because they wanted to stay in the United States, hey worked for low wages. Some Chinese mmigrants worked in mining and agriculture. Thousands worked for the Central Pacific Railroad to build the transcontinental railroad.

By the 1870s many Americans wanted to stop he Chinese from coming to the United States. They also vanted Chinese people who were already in the United States to go back to China. The Americans worried that the

Thousands of Asians entered the United States through Angel Island in San Francisco.

Reading Support

ANTICIPATION GUIDE Before students read the lesson, ask them to predict which statements are true and which are false. Students may correct their predictions as they read.

1. After about 75,000 Chinese immigrants were in the United States, Congress passed a law stopping immigration from China. true
2. Most Mexican immigrants moved to the Northeast. false
3. Between 1890 and 1920 the largest group of immigrants came from Europe. true
4. Immigrants found it easy to get good jobs, comfortable homes, and plenty of food in the United States. false
5. Immigrants who had come to the United States in the early and mid-1800s welcomed immigrants who came from 1890 to 1920. false
6. Immigrants had to pass a test before they could become United States citizens. true

Objectives

1. Explain why Americans wanted to stop Asian immigration.
2. Summarize how barrios helped Mexican immigrants.
3. Identify the areas of Europe from which many immigrants came after the 1890s.
4. Describe how immigrants could become United States citizens.

Vocabulary

prejudice (p. 495)
barrio (p. 497)
tenement (p. 498)
naturalization (p. 499)

1. ACCESS

The Focus Question

Ask volunteers to discuss how they felt when they joined a new club or group or moved to a new school. Have students speculate on the problems they might face moving to a new country where they know very few people and do not speak the language.

The Main Idea

In this lesson students discover that a wave of immigration swept over the United States in the late 1800s and early 1900s. After students have read the lesson, have them identify some of the conflicts between the Americans and the new immigrants and analyze the reasons for those conflicts.

2. BUILD

Asian Immigrants

Key Content Summary

The prejudice of Americans against Chinese immigrants led to conflicts between the two groups. Because of anti-Chinese feelings, Congress passed a law banning immigration from China. Other Asians, also subjected to prejudice, were discouraged from immigrating.

Culture

Shared Humanity and Unique Identity Have students discuss how the Chinese immigrants were treated by Americans and why the Americans treated them that way. Then have students speculate on how the Chinese probably felt about their treatment in the United States.

Latin American Immigrants

Key Content Summary

Many Latin American and Mexican immigrants came to the United States in the late 1800s. Mexican immigrants settled in barrios in the Southwest and in California. The Mexicans faced the same prejudice experienced by the Asians, and conflicts resulted.

History

Origins, Spread, and Influence Stress the point made in the textbook that many people of Mexican origin became Americans when the Southwest was ceded to the United States after the war with Mexico.

Q. **How was the Mexican immigrant experience eased by the fact that the Southwest originally was part of Mexico?** Immigrants could find people from their own culture in the United States, and they formed barrios.

Some Mexican American families had lived in the United States for many years. This photograph shows five generations of the Aguilar family in Texas in 1902.

immigrants would take their jobs. California and other western states passed laws that made life harder for the Chinese. Chinese people could not get state jobs, and they had to pay higher state taxes. State courts would not hear lawsuits brought by Chinese people. Finally, in 1882, Congress passed a law that stopped all immigration by Chinese people for ten years. By this time there were about 75,000 Chinese immigrants living in the United States.

Japanese and other Asian people were still allowed to come to the United States. Most found jobs in agriculture. Many bought small farms in California and in other parts of the Southwest. But in time they, too, met with prejudice. By the early 1900s many Americans were calling for a stop to all immigration from Asia. But instead of putting a stop to it, the United States government passed laws to limit the number of immigrants from Asia.

REVIEW ***Why did many Americans want to stop Asian immigration?*** They worried that Asian immigrants would take their jobs.

496 • Unit 8

Latin American Immigrants

During the late 1800s, immigrants from Latin America moved to many places in the United States to find work. By 1900 about 80,000 Mexican immigrants had settled in Texas, New Mexico, Arizona, and southern California. Some immigrants from Cuba came to the United States to find work in cigarmakers' shops. During the 1860s people from Chile and Peru settled in the western United States to mine for gold and silver. By 1900 more than 14,000 people from Central and South America had moved to the United States. Mexicans made up the largest group of immigrants that came from Latin America at this time.

Some Mexicans had lived in the southwestern part of the United States for years. Many lived in places that had been part of Mexico before the Treaty of Guadalupe Hidalgo, which ended the war between the United States and Mexico in 1848. By the late

Activity Choices

Background

CHINESE IMMIGRANTS In the first three years of the gold rush, more than 25,000 Chinese came to California. The first Chinese who arrived in California were warmly greeted because they helped supply much-needed labor in the mining camps. In the 1860s they made up 90 percent of the workforce on the Central Pacific line of the transcontinental railroad that crossed the Rocky Mountains. But when a depression hit in 1873, the Chinese were seen as a threat to American workers, and racial prejudice was directed toward the immigrants.

Multicultural Link

COOPERATIVE LEARNING

Divide the class into small groups, and ask each group to learn about and prepare items to share in a Southwest culture fiesta. For example, groups may want to prepare a Mexican dish, play library tapes of Mexican music, or draw pictures of Mexican art or architecture.

800s, newcomers from Mexico began to ettle in the United States.

Like most other new immigrants to the Jnited States, few Mexicans spoke English or new people in the United States. Imagine ow these immigrants must have felt when hey first met people from their homeland lready living in the United States. Just to be ble to talk with people in their own lanuage made them feel more at home.

Soon barrios sprang up in most cities in the outhwest. A **barrio** is a neighborhood of panish-speaking people. People in the barios helped one another. The immigrants who ad been in the Southwest longer helped the newcomers find homes and jobs. Many Mexican immigrants found jobs on farms. They spent up to 14 hours a day planting, weeding, and picking lettuce, tomatoes, and grapes. Others found factory jobs in the cities.

Like other immigrants, those from Mexico met with prejudice. Some people tried to make them go back to Mexico. In 1910 a writer for a Mexican newspaper wondered what made "our workingmen, so attached to the land, . . . abandon the country [Mexico], even at the risk of the Yankee contempt [lack of respect] with which they are treated on the other side of the Bravo [Rio Grande]."

REVIEW ***How did living in the barrios help immigrants from Mexico?*** People in the barrios helped one another find homes and jobs.

EARNING FROM GRAPHS The number of mmigrants to the United States is shown on this raph for four different periods of time. Many mmigrants, like this family (below right), came from urope.

When were there more immigrants from eastern Europe than from northwestern Europe?

Immigration to the United States, 1871–1910

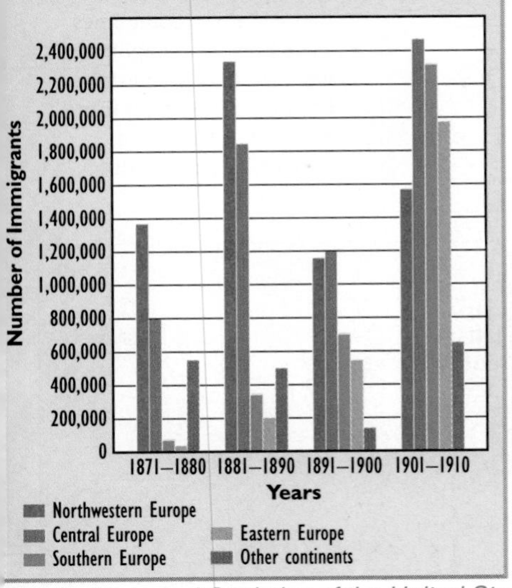

OURCE: *Historical Statistics of the United States*

European Immigrants

European immigrants were by far the largest group to come to the United States. Between 1890 and 1920, nearly 16 million immigrants arrived from countries in Europe.

Before 1890 most European immigrants had come from northern and western Europe. They had come from countries such as Britain, Ireland, Scotland, Germany, Norway, and Sweden. These were the immigrants who had helped build the Erie Canal and who had taken part in the great westward movement.

European Immigrants

Key Content Summary

Most immigrants who came to the United States between 1890 and 1920 were from Europe. With almost 16 million new immigrants settling in the United States, American citizens continued to have conflicting feelings about immigration.

Geography

Movement Have students use a large wall map or atlas of Europe to locate the countries of southern and eastern Europe mentioned in the textbook. Ask students to find the possible port cities and routes these immigrants might have used to reach the United States. Remind students that there was no air transportation.

Visual Analysis

Learn from Graphs Have students answer the question in the caption. 1901–1910

Link to Health

REPORT ON IMMIGRANT HEALTH Direct a small group of students to conduct library research to learn about the health problems some immigrants had that resulted in their being returned to their homeland. Also have students find out what health procedures officials conducted before they released people from the immigrant processing centers. Have students report their findings to the class.

Economics

Scarcity and Choice Lead a discussion about this massive European immigration from an economic perspective. Have students analyze immigrants' decisions to come to the United States in terms of wealth versus poverty, standard of living, and costs versus benefits.

Culture

Shared Humanity and Unique Identity Have students review the meaning of the term *prejudice*. Ask them to conclude why earlier immigrants, who themselves experienced prejudice, became prejudiced toward later immigrant groups.

Geography

Place Have students locate Angel Island and Ellis Island on the maps on this page.

Q. **Why do you think immigrants were processed on islands rather than on the mainland?** to keep large numbers of immigrants under control; to protect Americans from criminals or serious illnesses

Around 1890 a new period of immigration began. Some people still came from the countries of northern and western Europe, but now many came from countries in southern and eastern Europe. They came from Italy, Greece, Poland, Austria, Hungary, Armenia, and Russia. Many of these people were poor and unhappy in their homelands. Often they did not have enough to eat. They came to the United States hoping for a better life.

Most of the ships that brought European immigrants to the United States landed at Ellis Island in New York Bay. Many immigrants stayed in New York City. After a while some moved to the new industrial cities, where they hoped to find factory jobs. Many immigrants had lived on small farms in Europe, and they had hoped to buy land in the United States. But few had enough money to do that. Most lived with relatives or friends. Many lived crowded together in poorly built apartment houses called **tenements**. Wages were so low that everyone in the family, even young children, had to work just to earn enough money for food.

Like other immigrants, the Europeans often met with prejudice. Posters about jobs sometimes said things like "Irish need not apply." Some newcomers were even treated badly by immigrants who had arrived earlier. Immigrants who were already living and working in the United States worried that the new immigrants would take away their jobs.

REVIEW ***From what parts of Europe did many immigrants come before 1890?*** northern and western Europe

GEOGRAPHY

Angel Island and Ellis Island

In the late 1800s and early 1900s, Angel Island in San Francisco Bay and Ellis Island in New York Bay were the places where ships carrying immigrants landed in the United States. At the immigration stations on both islands, immigrants were checked for health problems. Anyone with a serious illness was sent back to his or her country. Immigrants also had to tell about themselves, their families, and their job skills. Sometimes the names of immigrants were changed by mistake because the workers filling out papers could not understand different languages.

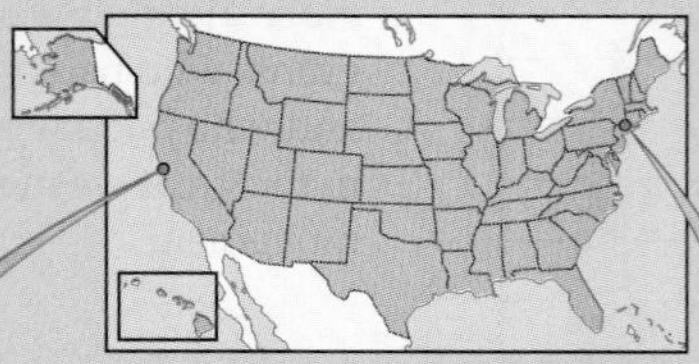

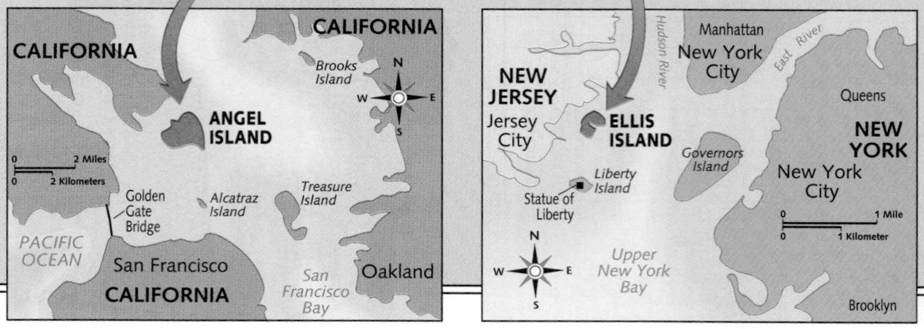

Activity Choices

Link to Language Arts

WRITE A LETTER Have the class write letters to city officials in New York City and San Francisco requesting information about Ellis Island and Angel Island and about the museums located there. Individual students may want to write letters to their grandparents to find out whether any of their ancestors came to the United States through Ellis Island or Angel Island. Students may share and discuss the information they gather.

Technology

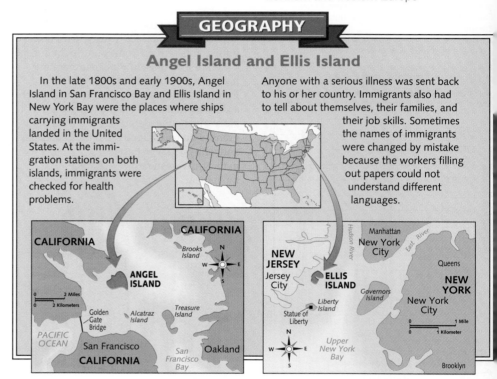

Use THE AMAZING WRITING MACHINE™ to complete this writing activity.

Extend and Enrich

COOPERATIVE LEARNING

REPORT ON AN IMMIGRANT GROUP Divide the class into small groups, and have each group choose an immigrant group that came to the United States between 1890 and 1920. Students should analyze a variety of sources and develop a report on the immigrant group, including information on why members of the group may have left their homeland, how many immigrated, where most of them settled, what jobs they found, the names of individuals in the group who made outstanding contributions, and how the group influenced the culture of the United States. Have groups share and discuss what they learned from the project.

Immigrant children came from many different cultures. This diversity is shown by these children who were living in Gary, Indiana.

Becoming a Citizen

No matter how hard their lives were, many mmigrants felt that becoming an American itizen was very important. Being a citizen neant taking part in the government, voting, nd serving on juries. To many immigrants, hese rights were something new.

Immigrants could become American citizens hrough a process called **naturalization**. They ad to live in the United States for five years nd then pass a test. The test asked questions bout the government and history of the Jnited States, such as *Who makes the laws in the United States?* and *Who was the first President?*

The questions on the test had to be nswered in English. Thousands of immigrants went to school after work so they ould learn English to take the test. Those who passed the test pledged allegiance, or oyalty, to the United States.

> "I pledge allegiance to the Flag of the United States of America, and to the Republic for which it stands, one Nation under God, indivisible, with liberty and justice for all."

REVIEW ***How did an immigrant become a citizen of the United States?*** He or she had to live in the United States for five years, pass a test, and then pledge allegiance to the United States.

LESSON 3 REVIEW

Check Understanding

1. **Remember the Facts** What were some of the reasons immigrants came to the United States?
2. **Recall the Main Idea** What were some of the problems that immigrants to the United States faced in the past?

Think Critically

3. **Personally Speaking** How might you feel if someone showed prejudice toward you?
4. **Think More About It** Why was becoming a United States citizen important to many immigrants?

Show What You Know

Writing Activity Imagine that it is the late 1800s and you are an immigrant who has just arrived in the United States. You are looking for a job. Use the information in this lesson to write a journal entry about what you might see and do. Share your writing with a classmate.

Becoming a Citizen

Key Content Summary

Becoming an American citizen was very important to many immigrants. As a result, millions of immigrants went through the naturalization process to become citizens.

"PRIMARY SOURCE"

Source: *United States Code Annotated: Title 36, Patriotic Societies and Observances.* West Publishing Company, 1988.

3. CLOSE

Have students consider again the Focus question on page 495.

What problems do immigrants to the United States face today?

Ask students to compare the problems of today's immigrants with those of earlier immigrants.

LESSON 3 REVIEW—Answers

Check Understanding

1. poverty in their homelands, chance for better jobs, gold, chance to own their own land
2. prejudice, low-paying jobs, poor housing, unfair taxes, physical abuse, pressure to leave

Think Critically

3. Students may say they would feel angry, resentful, or hurt.
4. It made them feel they were part of the United States—their adopted country. Students may add that immigrants valued the freedoms they had never had in their homeland.

Show What You Know

Performance Assessment Consider having students present their journal entries as part of a television newsmagazine program. Select volunteers to be the anchors.

What to Look For In evaluating the journal entries, look for evidence that students understand the problems faced by the early immigrants in the late 1800s.

Reteach the Main Idea

COOPERATIVE LEARNING

MAKE A CHART Divide the class into small groups. Challenge each group to use the textbook as a resource for making a chart identifying the major immigrant groups and listing the problems each group faced in the United States in the late 1800s and early 1900s. Have the groups share and discuss their completed charts.

ACTIVITY BOOK

Reinforce & Extend

Use ACTIVITY BOOK, p. 97.

Objectives

1. Identify the reasons African Americans left the South between 1916 and 1919.
2. Analyze the conditions African Americans faced in the North.
3. Evaluate the advantages and disadvantages of the northern migration for African Americans.

1. ACCESS

Have students think about their neighborhoods and estimate the number of families who have moved out of their neighborhoods in the past two years. Have students discuss the problems some people face when they move from one place to another.

The Main Idea

In this lesson students will read an account of the migration of thousands of African Americans from the South to the cities of the North during World War I. After students have read the selection, have them analyze the reasons for the migration and the problems African Americans shared with other newcomers to the cities during this time.

2. BUILD

Key Content Summary

From 1916 to 1919 African Americans seized an opportunity to change their lives. Factory jobs were available in northern cities because many people had gone to fight in World War I. Many African Americans moved North to improve their lives. But some things, such as segregation and prejudice, did not change.

LESSON 4 LEARN HISTORY *through* Literature

THE GREAT MIGRATION

AN AMERICAN STORY

story and paintings by Jacob Lawrence

Even as immigrants were moving to the United States from other countries, people within the United States were moving from place to place. This was true of many different groups of Americans, including African Americans.

After the Civil War, most African Americans in the South found jobs as workers on farms or as sharecroppers on plantations. Few moved into the cities. But between 1916 and 1919, many decided to move to the industrial cities in the North—to New York, Chicago, Detroit, Pittsburgh, Cleveland, and St. Louis. During these years workers were needed to take over the factory jobs of those who had left to fight in a war in Europe. The war would later be called World War I. When African Americans left their farms to become factory workers, their lives changed forever.

Jacob Lawrence's family took part in this great migration from the South. Read his story to learn more about the migration and about the problems African Americans shared with other newcomers to northern cities in the early 1900s.

500 • Unit 8

ACTIVITY CHOICES

Reading Support

ANTICIPATION GUIDE Before students read the lesson, ask them to predict which statements are true and which are false. Students may correct their predictions as they read.

1. Life for most African Americans had greatly improved in the South since the Civil War. false
2. World War I opened up factory jobs in northern cities. true
3. Southern landowners were glad to see African American farmers migrating to northern cities. false
4. African American migrants were jailed as soon as they exited the trains in northern cities. false
5. Life in the North was much easier for African Americans. false

Around the time I was born, many African-Americans from the South left home and traveled to cities in the North in search of a better life. My family was part of this great migration.

There was a shortage of workers in northern factories because many had left their jobs to fight in the First World War.

The factory owners had to find new workers to replace those who were marching off to war.

Northern industries offered southern blacks jobs as workers and lent them money, to be repaid later, for their railroad tickets. The northbound trains were packed with recruits.

Nature had ravaged the South. Floods ruined farms. The boll weevil destroyed cotton crops.

The war had doubled the cost of food, making life even harder for the poor.

Railroad stations were so crowded with migrants that guards were called in to keep order.

The flood of migrants northward left crops back home to dry and spoil.

Chapter 15 • 501

Auditory Learning

Have a volunteer read aloud the introduction to the literature selection on page 500 while the other students listen carefully. Ask students to summarize in a few sentences what they will learn about in the literature selection.

Q. **How was the African American experience similar to that of other immigrant groups?** African Americans moved to industrial cities to find factory jobs, hoping for a better life.

Understanding the Story

Have students identify the reasons African Americans were motivated to move North. Compare and contrast those reasons with the reasons immigrants had for coming to the United States.

Geography

Human–Environment Interactions Have students relate the boll weevil and the floods in the South to the migration of African Americans northward.

Economics

Productivity and Economic Growth Ask students to speculate on why northern industries were willing to pay for railroad tickets in order to convince African American workers to move to northern cities.

Q. **What effect did the northward migration of African Americans have on southern farms?** There were not enough workers to tend and harvest the crops. The crops dried and the harvest spoiled.

Background

THE LITERATURE SELECTION
The Great Migration: An American Story is beautifully illustrated throughout with Jacob Lawrence's narrative sequence of paintings. It took Lawrence one year to create the sixty panels in the sequence. The paintings, along with the words, give the reader a sense of the emotion, conflict, cooperation, and courage involved in the great migration.

THE AUTHOR Jacob Lawrence's family migrated north to New York City along with thousands of other African Americans in the early 1900s. Lawrence started painting in an after-school program. He furthered his art education at the Harlem Workshop and the American Artists School. Lawrence has done many paintings related to African American history, and he has won the National Medal of Arts, among other awards, for his work.

Understanding the Story

Point out that people usually do not make important changes in their lives, such as moving to a new place, without having good reasons.

Q. **How does the author indicate that life for African Americans in the South had not changed much by 1916?** Many African Americans were still poor farmworkers who were treated harshly and who suffered from injustice.

Culture

Human Relationships Have students consider whether as many African Americans would have migrated to the North if they had had better opportunities open to them in the South after the Civil War.

Economics

Scarcity and Choice Have students provide examples of other times in United States history when people's basic needs and wants motivated them to migrate.

Q. **What were the costs and benefits to African Americans who moved to northern cities?** costs: moving away from friends, family, and homes; benefits: a chance for better incomes, better housing, and more freedom

For African-Americans the South was barren in many ways. There was no justice for them in the courts, and their lives were often in danger.

Although slavery had long been abolished, white landowners treated the black tenant farmers harshly and unfairly.

And so the migration grew.

Segregation divided the South.

The black newspapers told of better housing and jobs in the North.

Families would arrive very early at railroad stations to make sure they could get on the northbound trains.

Early arrival was not easy, because African-Americans found on the streets could be arrested for no reason.

And the migrants kept coming.

In the South there was little opportunity for education, and children labored in the fields. These were more reasons for people to move north, leaving some communities deserted.

There was much excitement and discussion about the great migration.

Agents from northern factories flocked into southern counties and towns, looking for laborers.

Families often gathered to discuss whether to go north or to stay south. The promise of better housing in the North could not be ignored.

Activity Choices

Background

ESCAPE For African Americans in some southern states, leaving the plantations where they worked as sharecroppers was risky. In Georgia, for example, a state law banned sharecroppers from moving until they had paid all their debts. If they did try to move, sheriffs had the right to stop them and return them to their farms. This is why in some places sharecroppers had to slip away to the railroad stations in the dead of night.

Meet Individual Needs

ENGLISH LANGUAGE LEARNERS
Have students note that the selection contains many short paragraphs. Explain that although this makes the reading of individual paragraphs easier, students must be sure to relate each paragraph to the one that precedes it and the one that follows it in order to understand the flow of ideas.

The railroad stations were crowded with migrants.

Letters from relatives in the North and articles in the black press portrayed a better life outside the South.

Many migrants arrived in Chicago.

In Chicago and other cities they labored in the steel mills . . . and on the railroads.

And the migrants kept coming.

Southern landowners, stripped of cheap labor, tried to stop the migration by jailing the labor agents and the migrants. Sometimes the agents disguised themselves to avoid arrest, but the migrants were often taken from railroad stations and jailed until the trains departed.

Black and white southern leaders met to discuss ways to improve conditions to stop the flow of workers north.

Although life in the North was better, it was not ideal.

Many migrants moved to Pittsburgh, which was a great industrial center at the time.

Although they were promised better housing in the North, some families were forced to live in overcrowded and unhealthy quarters.

The migrants soon learned that segregation was not confined to the South.

Many northern workers were angry because they had to compete with the migrants for housing and jobs. There were riots.

Longtime African-American residents living in the North did not welcome the newcomers from the South and often treated them with disdain.

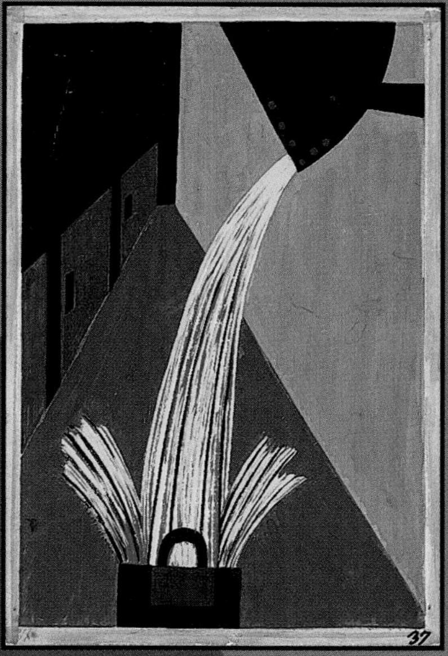

Understanding the Story

After students have read the paragraphs on this page, have them discuss the images Jacob Lawrence creates with his words. Have each student select a phrase and draw a picture to go with the words. Display the pictures on a bulletin board, and have the class observe and identify the pictures.

Geography

MAP THEME

Movement Have students use a map of the United States to find the distances between selected cities in the South and Pittsburgh and Chicago. Then ask them to compare these distances with the distances of journeys made by immigrants from Asia and Europe.

Civics and Government

Rights and Responsibilities of Citizens Point out the desperate measures taken by southern landowners to stop the northern migration of African Americans. Have students analyze these efforts in relation to the rights of United States citizens.

Link to Language Arts

WRITE A DESCRIPTION Ask students to imagine that they are reporters for an African American newspaper in Chicago. Have them write news articles about the arrival of a train from a southern city at a Chicago railroad station. Students should use the information supplied in the selection but supplement it with other details.

TECHNOLOGY

Use THE AMAZING WRITING MACHINE™ to complete this writing activity.

Extend and Enrich

COOPERATIVE LEARNING

CONDUCT A PANEL DISCUSSION Divide the class into four groups: northern factory owners, southern landowners, southern African Americans who wanted to stay in the South, and southern African Americans who wanted to migrate. Have each group conduct library research to gather additional information to support its views about the great migration, and then select a spokesperson to present the group's views in a panel discussion.

Understanding the Story

Explain to students that the realities of moving are often different from the hopes and dreams. Discuss the features of life in the North that disappointed the African American migrants, and have students draw conclusions about why those disappointments occurred.

Understanding the Story

Have students evaluate whether the African Americans who moved to the North improved their lives.

Q. **On balance, does the author believe the move to the North was beneficial?** Yes, because African American children were going to school and African Americans in the North were voting. Students may add some of their own insights.

3. CLOSE

Ask students the following question to focus on the movement of people from place to place.

What kinds of problems might people face today when moving from one area of the United States to another?

Have students share personal experiences related to moving or speculate on the kinds of problems people might face when moving from one area of the United States to another.

LITERATURE REVIEW—Answers

1. poverty, destruction of their farm, high cost of food, harsh treatment by landowners, the promise of jobs and better pay in the North
2. overcrowded and unhealthy living quarters, poor treatment
3. Letters should mention that life in the North meant earning more pay, living in crowded apartments, getting an education for their children, facing prejudice, and having the right to vote.

The migrants had to rely on each other. The storefront church was a welcoming place and the center of their lives, in joy and in sorrow.

Black professionals, such as doctors and lawyers, soon followed their patients and clients north. Female workers were among the last to leave.

Life in the North brought many challenges, but the migrants' lives had changed for the better. The children were able to go to school, and their parents gained the freedom to vote.

And the migrants kept coming.

Theirs is a story of African-American strength and courage. I share it now as my parents told it to me, because their struggles and triumphs ring true today. People all over the world are still on the move, trying to build better lives for themselves and for their families.

LITERATURE REVIEW

1. What events and problems caused Jacob Lawrence's family to move to the North?
2. What problems did African Americans share with other newcomers to northern cities in the early 1900s?
3. Imagine that you are an African American who has moved to the North during the time of World War I. Write a letter to Jacob Lawrence's family describing how life in the North is different from life in the South.

ACTIVITY CHOICES

ACTIVITY BOOK

Reinforce & Extend

Use ACTIVITY BOOK, p. 98.

Reteach the Main Idea

COOPERATIVE LEARNING

DESCRIBE A PAINTING Divide the class into groups. Assign each group one of the paintings that appear in this literature selection. Ask the members of each group to write a conversation that could have taken place among the people shown in the paintings. Have each group present its conversation to the class and explain what the painting illustrates in the story of the great migration.

LESSON 5

The Growth of Cities

FOCUS
What problems do people face in cities today?

Main Idea Read to learn about problems people faced as cities grew larger, and about how some people worked to solve them.

Vocabulary
settlement house
skyscraper

By the beginning of the twentieth century, cities in the nited States were growing fast. Some people thought they ere growing too fast. No one had expected such growth, and o one had planned for it. Millions of people were moving to merican cities from farms, and millions more were coming om other countries. There were just too many people in one lace. As cities grew, so did their problems.

City Problems

One problem was that of overcrowded tenements. When ne person in a tenement became ill, disease spread through ie tenement quickly. In one overcrowded Chicago tenement, iree out of every five children born in 1900 died before they ere three years old. A newspaper reporter named Jacob Riis EES) described the same kind of poor living conditions in ew York City tenements.

Riis saw that when someone died in a tenement, a ribbon ed into a bow was hung on the tenement door—black for an dult and white for a child. Riis wrote,

> “Listen! That short hacking cough, that tiny, helpless wail—what do they mean? They mean that the soiled bow of white you saw on the door downstairs will have another story to tell—Oh! a sadly familiar story—before the day is at an end. The child is dying with measles. With half a chance it might have lived; but it had none.”

Insects and rats in the garbage spread the germs of ill- ess. With so many people in the cities, garbage piled p. At this time there was no regular garbage collec- on. Even in the largest cities, garbage was eaten by igs in the streets.

The danger of fire became greater as new buildings vent up. Most were made partly of wood. Terrible ires burned down whole city blocks. The Great Chicago

Jacob Riis was a Danish immigrant whose photographs and newspaper articles helped improve living conditions in the cities.

505

Reading Support

PREVIEW AND READ THE LESSON Provide students with the following visual framework.

THE GROWTH OF U.S. CITIES

CITY PROBLEMS
overcrowded housing
unhealthy living conditions
poor sanitation
danger of fire
crime
disease

SOCIAL CHANGES
settlement houses

PHYSICAL CHANGES
skyscrapers
elevators
trolley cars
suburbs

Objectives

1. Analyze the problems faced by people living in overcrowded cities.
2. Describe how individuals improved conditions for the cities' poor.
3. Identify inventions that helped cities change and grow.

Vocabulary

settlement house (p. 506)
skyscraper (p. 507)

1. ACCESS

The Focus Question

Ask students to describe what they believe are the good and bad features of their city or nearby cities. List on chart paper some of the common problems faced by people living in cities today.

The Main Idea

Students will explore the growth of cities in the late 1800s, the problems people faced, and the individuals who helped solve the problems. After students have read the lesson, have them analyze the problems facing large cities and evaluate the solutions to those problems.

2. BUILD

City Problems

Key Content Summary

Disease, inadequate sanitation facilities, fire, and crime were among the serious problems facing the rapidly growing and changing cities of the late 1800s and early 1900s.

“PRIMARY SOURCE”

Source: *How the Other Half Lives: Studies Among the Tenements of New York.* Jacob A. Riis. Corner House Publishers, 1972.

History

Cause and Effect Have students analyze the cause-and-effect relationships that can arise from overcrowding in cities. You may want to draw a cause-and-effect chart on the board for students to complete.

Geography

Human–Environment Interactions Have students speculate on what can be done to improve overcrowded cities, both by individuals and by the government.

***Q.* Why do you think Jacob Riis reported on the poor living conditions in New York City tenements?** He wanted to make people aware of how serious the problems were.

Help for the Cities' Poor

Key Content Summary

Jane Addams pioneered the settlement-house movement in the United States. Settlement houses helped the poor and worked to improve the living conditions in tenements. By 1900 nearly 100 settlement houses had opened in the United States.

“PRIMARY SOURCE”

Source: *Twenty Years at Hull-House.* Jane Addams. Macmillan, 1973.

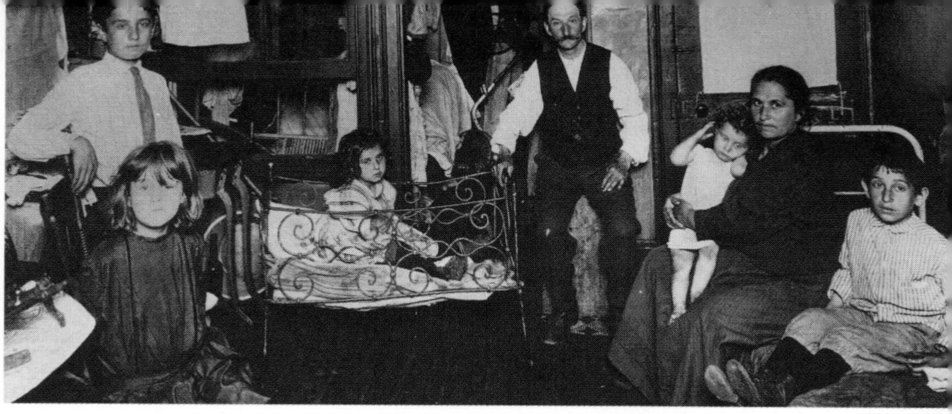

This photograph of a family living in a crowded tenement apartment was taken by Jessie Tarbox Beals, the first woman to work as a news photographer.

Fire of 1871 was one of the worst. It burned for 24 hours, killing at least 300 people and leaving more than 90,000 people homeless. Few cities at that time had full-time fire departments.

Crime was another problem in cities. Because of the crowds, it was hard for the police to find lawbreakers. Sometimes a gang would take over an entire city neighborhood, and even the police would be afraid to go into it.

REVIEW ***What problems faced many people who were living in cities?*** overcrowded tenements, garbage piling up, illness, fire, and crime

Help for the Cities' Poor

Some people who lived in cities tried to solve the problems they saw around them. Jane Addams was one of these people. Addams came from a wealthy family and had gone to college, something few women at that time were able to do. She worried about the growing problems of the tenements in Chicago.

While traveling in Britain, Addams had visited a place called Toynbee Hall. It was a **settlement house**, a community center where people could learn new skills. Addams took the idea back to Chicago.

> “It is hard to tell just when the very simple plan . . . began. . . . But I gradually became convinced that it would be a good thing to rent a house in a part of the city where many . . . needs are found.”

In 1889 Addams started Hull House in Chicago with Ellen Gates Starr. The workers in Hull House ran a kindergarten for childre[n] whose mothers worked. They taught classes in sewing, cooking, and the English languag[e]. Later they worked to improve living condition[s] in tenements and health and safety condition[s] in the mills and factories. They also tried to get laws passed to regulate child labor.

Hull House became a model for other com[-]munity centers. In 1890 African American teacher Janie Porter Barrett founded a settlement house in Hampton, Virginia. Three years later, Lillian Wald started the Henry Street Settlement in New York City. By 1900 almost 100 settlement houses had opened.

REVIEW ***Why were settlement houses important in the cities?*** They ran kindergartens for the children of working mothers and taught new skills and the English language to immigrants.

Activity Choices

Background

GARBAGE According to a 1905 study, people in the United States produced more trash than any other people in the world—almost twice as much per person as in British cities and almost three times as much as in German cities. A 1912 report stated that if the garbage of New York City was gathered in one place, it would be equal in volume to a cube an eighth of a mile long on each edge. This volume is more than three times that of the great pyramid of Giza.

Community Involvement

Have the class write a letter inviting a local doctor to compare and contrast community health issues from the late 1800s with those of today. In the letter students should describe the community health problems studied in the lesson and ask the doctor to elaborate on those problems. Students should also ask the doctor to discuss how a community protected itself against those problems in the past and how we protect ourselves today.

The Changing City

Even with their many problems, cities came to stand for all that was good in industrial America. Besides factories, stores, and tenements, cities had parks, theaters, and zoos that people could enjoy when they had free time. Cities also had schools, railroad stations, and tall office buildings.

Before this time buildings could not be taller than four or five stories because their walls were made only of bricks. The bricks on the bottom had to hold up the weight of all the bricks above them. In the 1880s an engineer named William Jenney found a way to build taller buildings. Jenney used steel frames to hold up a building the way a skeleton holds up a body. In 1885 Jenney finished building the ten-story Home Insurance Company Building in Chicago. It was the world's first tall steel-frame building, or **skyscraper**.

As buildings were made taller and taller—20 stories, then 50 stories, then 100 stories—fast, safe elevators were needed. The first electric elevator was put into a skyscraper in New York City in 1889.

As cities grew upward, they also grew outward. When the first cities were built in the United States, people walked to and from work. As people began moving away from the center of the city, transportation was needed to help them get to their jobs.

In 1865 most cities had streetcars pulled by horses. Horses could go only about 6 miles (9.7 km) an hour on flat ground, and each horse cost about $200—about the price of a car in today's money. In San Francisco the

A Skyscraper

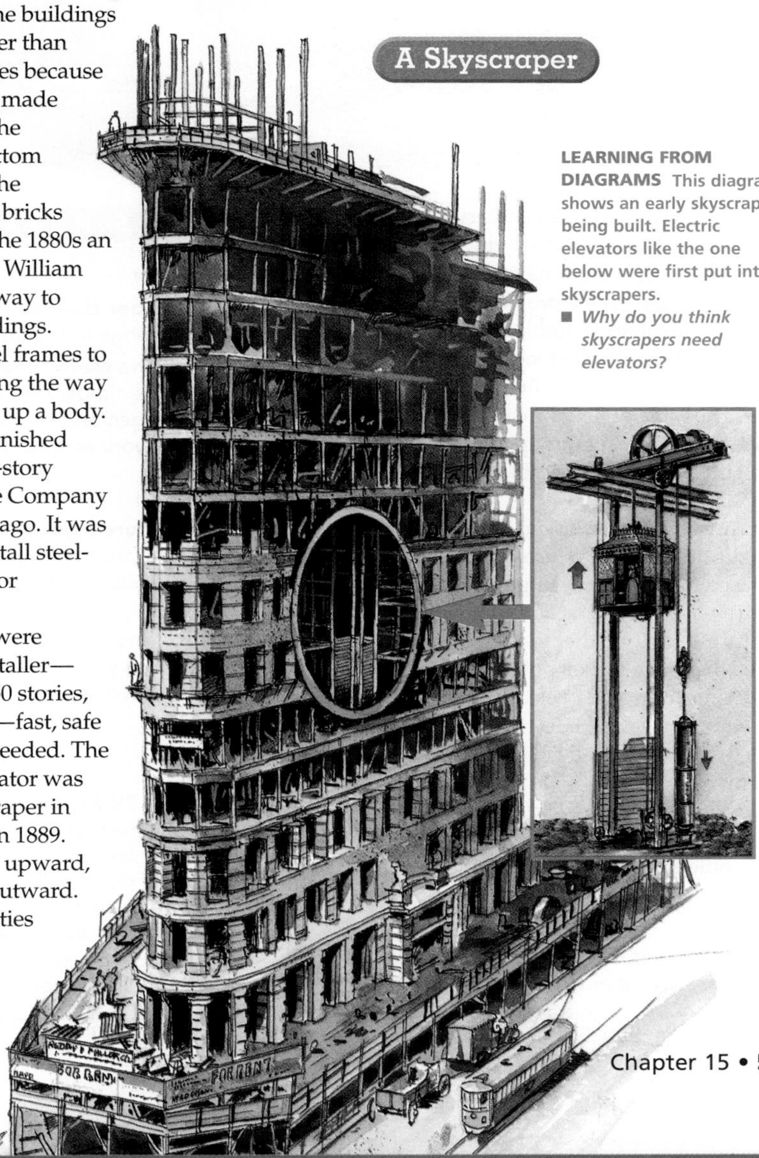

LEARNING FROM DIAGRAMS This diagram shows an early skyscraper being built. Electric elevators like the one below were first put into skyscrapers.

■ *Why do you think skyscrapers need elevators?*

Culture

Social Organizations and Institutions Have students explore the reasons institutions such as settlement houses were needed and compare and contrast them to similar institutions today.

The Changing City

Key Content Summary

To meet the needs of the growing cities, individuals invented new ways of constructing city buildings, new ways of moving people through tall buildings, and new ways of transporting people around the cities. These inventions brought changes in the size and appearance of cities and in the way of life of the cities' inhabitants.

Culture

Social Organizations and Institutions Have students identify all the exciting and positive characteristics of cities today and analyze how those characteristics make a city a community.

Visual Analysis

Learn from Diagrams Direct students' attention to the diagram of the skyscraper. Ask students who have been to the top of a skyscraper to share their experiences. Have students answer the question in the caption. Students' answers may include that elevators were necessary to save the time and effort needed to climb stairs.

Link to Reading

WRITE A BOOK REPORT Ask the school librarian to help students select books about events or famous people mentioned in the lesson. Have students read the books and then write book reports. Remind them that they are to set the purpose for the book report, use appropriate grammar and punctuation, and evaluate the book. Invite students to draw illustrations to include in their book reports.

Extend and Enrich

COOPERATIVE LEARNING

BUILD A MODEL Divide the class into groups, and have each group use library or Internet resources to aid them in building a model of a city. Assign each group one of the following cities and time periods: New York City in the early to mid-1800s; New York City circa 1910–1920; Chicago in the 1800s; Chicago in the early 1900s; San Francisco circa 1850–1860; San Francisco circa 1910–1920. You may want to have students concentrate on the central section of the city when making their models. Make sure each group draws a plan before building the model. Have students use the models as a basis for discussing changes in city life.

Geography

Movement Have students discuss the reasons that people were able to move to the suburbs.

***Q.* Why do you think people wanted to move away from the center of cities?** They wanted to get away from the noise, dirt, and crime in the cities; they also wanted more land.

3. CLOSE

Have students consider again the Focus question on page 505.

What problems do people face in cities today?

Ask students to compare and contrast the problems faced by people in cities today with the problems faced by city dwellers in the late 1800s.

LESSON 5 REVIEW—Answers

Check Understanding

1. Cities became more crowded and more dangerous. They also became more interesting, with zoos, schools, theaters, parks, railroad stations, and tall office buildings.
2. Many people lived in overcrowded tenements in which there were fire hazards, sanitation was poor, disease spread easily, and crime and gangs were rampant. Jane Addams and others tried to solve the health and educational problems by establishing settlement houses.

Think Critically

3. Like Gompers, Addams tried to help poor people lead better lives. Gompers focused on people's working conditions, while Addams aimed at improving their social conditions.
4. Steel frames and the elevator made it possible to build taller buildings so that more people could live and work in an area without taking up more land; the electric trolley car made it possible for people to live farther away from the inner city.

Show What You Know

Performance Assessment Consider selecting several script outlines to use for simulated classroom TV programs.

What to Look For Look for an understanding of the main idea of the lesson—the problems faced by city dwellers and their solutions to those problems.

Streetcars were an important form of transportation in many cities. This streetcar had open sides that made it easy to board.

horses had to pull the cars up very steep hills. This was hard for the horses and slow for the passengers. An inventor named Andrew S. Hallidie worked on the problem. In 1871 he invented the cable car. Cable cars ran on tracks and were attached to a steam-powered cable, or strong wire, that ran in a slot in the street. The cable pulled the cars at about 9 miles (14.5 km) an hour up and down steep hills. Fifteen cities put in cable cars. Chicago had 710 cable cars!

Then, in the late 1880s, inventor Frank Sprague built an electric streetcar that was first used in Richmond, Virginia. Sprague's streetcar also ran on tracks, but it was powered by electricity rather than by steam. A small wheel on a trolley pole on top of the car rode along an overhead electric wire. The new streetcar was called a trolley car. By 1890 more than 50 cities had trolley transportation systems.

As more tracks were laid, people moved farther and farther from the center of the city. They could ride trolley cars to work or shop in the city and live away from the inner city's problems.

REVIEW ***What inventions helped cities grow upward and outward during the late 1800s?*** skyscrapers, electric elevators, cable cars, and trolley cars

LESSON 5 REVIEW

Check Understanding

1. **Remember the Facts** How did cities change in the late 1800s?
2. **Recall the Main Idea** What problems did people face as cities grew larger, and how did some people work to solve them?

Think Critically

3. **Think More About It** In what ways do you think Jane Addams was like the labor union leader Samuel Gompers? How were they different?
4. **Cause and Effect** How did the inventions you read about in this lesson affect the way people lived in cities?

Show What You Know

TV Report Activity With several classmates, prepare an outline for a TV program on life in the cities in the late 1800s. Write down topics for your program. Then list ideas for interviews, pictures, maps, charts, and graphs. Present your outline to your classmates.

ACTIVITY CHOICES

ACTIVITY BOOK

Reinforce & Extend

Use ACTIVITY BOOK, p. 99.

Reteach

COOPERATIVE LEARNING

WRITE AN OUTLINE Divide the class into small groups, and tell each group to use the textbook as an aid in writing an outline of the lesson. The outlines should summarize the problems people faced as cities grew in the late 1800s and describe how people worked to solve the problems. Have the groups share, compare, and discuss their completed outlines.

Skills

Solve a Problem

. Why Learn This Skill?

People everywhere face problems at one ne or another. Many people face more than ne problem at the same time. Think about a oblem you have faced recently. How did you ow you had a problem? Were you able to lve it? Did you wish you could have found a etter way to solve the problem? Knowing how solve problems is a skill that you will use all our life.

. Remember What You Have Read

You have read about the many problems at made city life difficult in the late 1800s nd early 1900s. Overcrowding, disease, fire, nd crime were among the problems that eople faced. Jane Addams was one person ho tried to help. Think again about the probms Addams saw and the way she tried to lve them.

- What problems did Jane Addams see in Chicago?
- What solution did Addams learn about when she visited Toynbee Hall?
3. What did Addams decide was a good way to solve the problems in Chicago?
4. How did Addams carry out her solution?
5. How did Addams's solution help solve the problems of city life?

3. Understand the Process

You can use similar steps to help solve problems.

- Identify the problem.
- Think of possible solutions.
- Compare the solutions, and choose the best one.
- Plan how to carry out the solution.
- Try your solution, and think about how well it helps solve the problem.

4. Think and Apply

Identify a problem in your community or school. Write a plan for solving the problem. What steps did you follow? What solution did you choose? Do you think that your solution will help solve the problem? Explain your answer.

Jane Addams started Hull House (far left) to help Chicago's immigrants. Addams (left, with a child at Hull House) was one of the country's best-known reformers.

MODEL & APPLY SKILLS

Objectives

1. Identify steps for solving problems.
2. Apply a problem-solving method.

1. Access

Have volunteers answer the questions found in Why Learn This Skill? Encourage students to discuss both simple and complex problems they have faced.

2. Build

To help students understand how people solve problems, have them answer the questions listed under Remember What You Have Read.

1. poor conditions in tenements; child labor; bad health and safety conditions in factories
2. forming a community center to teach people new skills
3. to start a community house
4. started Hull House, where children and mothers received education; also worked for better living and economic conditions
5. Hull House became a model copied by other cities, helping them solve the same types of problems.

Point out that communities as well as individuals face problems. Choose a problem that interests your students and use it to model the steps in Understand the Process.

3. Close

Have students complete the activity in Think and Apply. Emphasize the importance of giving careful thought to the solution of problems.

Reteach the Skill

COOPERATIVE LEARNING

SOLVE A PROBLEM Have students work in small groups to consider a common problem of their own choosing. Have them use the steps in Understand the Process to choose a possible solution to the problem. Have each group report to the class, which may then discuss the problem and the solution chosen. Emphasize the value of collective effort as well as of a methodical approach. Consider whether some of the solutions could be implemented.

ACTIVITY BOOK

Practice & Apply

Use ACTIVITY BOOK, p. 100.

TRANSPARENCY

Use TRANSPARENCY 40.

CHAPTER 15 REVIEW

Time Line

Ask students to share what they recall about each event shown on the time line.

Connect Main Ideas

Use the organizer to review the main ideas of the chapter. Have students use their textbooks to complete the organizer and check their work. Allow time for them to discuss and compare their responses.

ACTIVITY BOOK

Summarize the Chapter

A copy of the graphic organizer appears on ACTIVITY BOOK, p. 101.

TRANSPARENCY

A copy of the graphic organizer appears on TRANSPARENCY 41.

Write More About It

Write a Magazine Article

Articles should describe workers doing hard labor, using dangerous machines, and enduring other poor working conditions. Students should point out that many of the workers are children or immigrants.

Write a Letter

Letter writers may mention that cities had electricity, streetcars, factories, and businesses; that conditions were crowded; and that city dwellers came from many cultural backgrounds. Accept all well-supported explanations.

TECHNOLOGY

HARCOURT BRACE

Use THE AMAZING WRITING MACHINE™ to complete the writing activities.

TECHNOLOGY

HARCOURT BRACE

Use TIMELINER™ DATA DISKS to discuss and summarize the chapter.

CHAPTER 15 REVIEW

1865 — 1875

1869
• Transcontinental railroad completed

1886
• Samuel Gompers helps form the AFL

CONNECT MAIN IDEAS

Use this graphic organizer to show how the chapter's main ideas are connected. Write three details to support each main idea. A copy of the organizer appears on page 101 of the Activity Book.

Possible answers to the graphic organizer appe[ar] on page 482C of this Teacher's Edition.

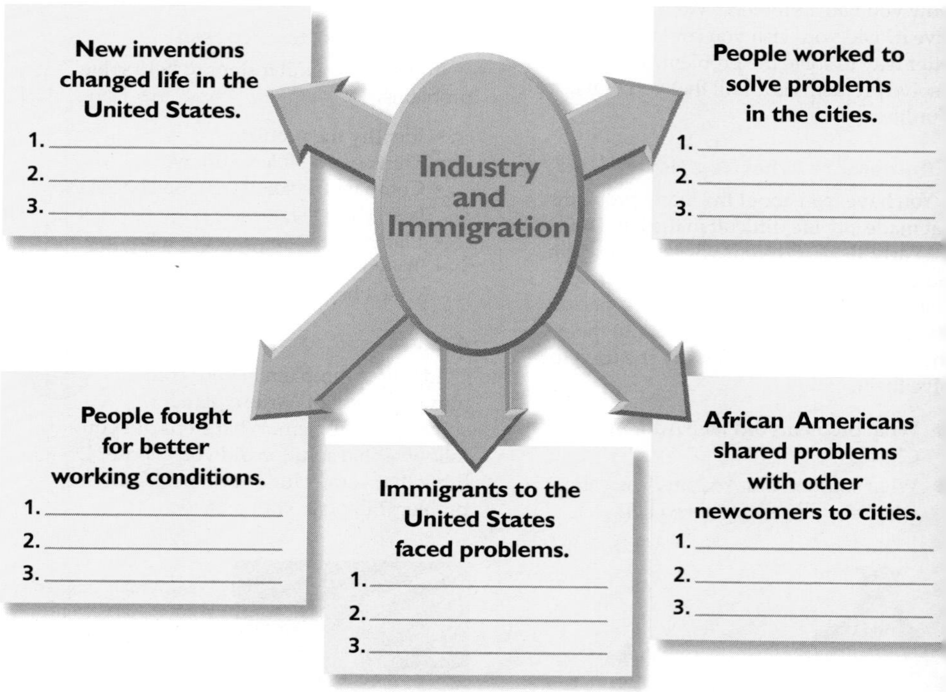
Industry and Immigration
New inventions changed life in the United States.
1. 2. 3.
People worked to solve problems in the cities.
1. 2. 3.
People fought for better working conditions.
1. 2. 3.
Immigrants to the United States faced problems.
1. 2. 3.
African Americans shared problems with other newcomers to cities.
1. 2. 3.

WRITE MORE ABOUT IT

Write a Magazine Article Imagine that you have been asked to write a magazine article about working conditions in the United States in the early 1900s. As part of your research, you visit several factories. Describe what you see there.

Write a Letter Imagine that it is the early 1900s and you and your family have just moved from a farm to a big city. Write a letter to a friend. Describe how your new life in the city is different from your old life on the farm.

Use Vocabulary

1. invest (p. 484)
2. corporation (p. 484)
3. labor union (p. 491)
4. prejudice (p. 495)

Check Understanding

5. a railroad that went across the con[ti]nent, linking the Atlantic and Paci[fic] coasts (p. 483)
6. They have to live in the United Sta[tes] for five years and then pass a te[st] (p. 499)
7. to find work in factories, for educ[a]tion opportunities, and to live a bett[er] life (pp. 500, 504)
8. They offered kindergarten classes f[or] children whose mothers worked; th[ey] gave classes in sewing, cooking a[nd] English; and they worked towa[rd] abolishing child labor. (p. 506)

1895 1905 1915 1925

Late 1800s
• Immigrants from Asia, Latin America, and Europe come to the United States

1916
• Many African Americans from the South begin moving to industrial cities in the North

Use Vocabulary

For each group of underlined words in the ntences, write the term from the list below at has the same meaning.

corporation	labor union
invest	prejudice

- Some people buy shares of a business in the hope of making money.
- People can own part of a business that sells shares of stock to investors.
- Workers sometimes form a group that tries to improve their working conditions.
- Immigrants sometimes face a negative feeling some people have toward others because of their race or culture.

Check Understanding

- What was the transcontinental railroad?
- What did immigrants have to do to become citizens of the United States?
- Why did many African Americans move to industrial cities in the North?
- How did settlement houses improve life for people in the cities?

Think Critically

- **Personally Speaking** How would your life be different if the electric lightbulb had not been invented?
- **Explore Viewpoints** How do you think workers' views of labor unions differed from the views held by the factory owners?

⑪ **Think More About It** Why do you think some factory owners in the early 1900s treated their workers badly?

⑫ **Cause and Effect** How did railroads affect the growth of cities?

Apply Skills

Use a Time Zone Map Use the time zone map on page 489 to answer these questions:

⑬ If it is 5:00 P.M. in Georgia, what time is it in California?

⑭ If it is 10:00 A.M. in Illinois, what time is it in Ohio?

⑮ If it is 3:00 A.M. in North Carolina, what time is it in Colorado?

Solve a Problem Identify a problem faced by a person you read about in this chapter. Use the steps listed on page 509 to write a plan that you think might help solve the problem.

Read More About It

Immigrant Kids by Russell Freedman. Puffin. Read about the everyday lives of immigrant children during the late 1800s and early 1900s.

Visit the Internet at **http://www.hbschool.com** for additional resources.

CHAPTER 15 REVIEW

Apply Skills

Use a Time Zone Map

⑬ 2:00 P.M.

⑭ 11:00 A.M.

⑮ 1:00 A.M.

Solve a Problem Look for the ability to follow the steps, to select a workable solution, and to plan how to best carry out the solution.

Read More About It

Additional books are listed in the Multimedia Resource Center on page 476D of this Teacher's Edition.

Unit Project Check-Up

Check to make sure that students have started their lists of details for their conversations. Some events that might be on their lists include the tenements and the naturalization process.

ASSESSMENT PROGRAM

Use CHAPTER 15 TEST, pp. 127–130.

Think Critically

Students should realize that they would have to use candlelight or lanterns to see in the dark.

Answers will vary. Students should understand that what the workers and the factory owners wanted from the businesses were different, and that these differences caused many workers to agree with the unions and many factory owners to resent or fear the unions.

⑪ Factory owners wanted to make a profit. Some were concerned only with making money, not with the welfare of their workers. Accept all answers that mention the conflict between higher profits and treating the workers well.

⑫ Students should realize that railroads permitted factories to be built far from ocean harbors. As a result, many inland cities became industrial centers. The jobs that new mills, factories, and other businesses created caused the growth of cities.

Planning Chart

	THEMES • Strands	VOCABULARY	MEET INDIVIDUAL NEEDS	RESOURCES INCLUDING ▶ TECHNOLOGY
LESSON 1 **Farming the Great Plains** pp. 513–517	**COMMONALITY & DIVERSITY** • Culture • Geography • Economics	homesteader bonanza farm	English Language Learners, p. 515 Tactile Learners, p. 515 Extend and Enrich, p. 516 Reteach the Main Idea, p. 517	Activity Book, p. 102
SKILL **Understand a Climograph** pp. 518–519	**BASIC STUDY SKILLS** • Chart and Graph Skills	climograph	Reteach the Skill, p. 519	Activity Book, p. 103 Transparency 42 ▶ GRAPH LINKS
LESSON 2 **The Cattle Kingdom** pp. 520–524	**INDIVIDUALISM & INTERDEPENDENCE** • Economics • Geography • History • Culture	long drive open range vaquero barbed wire range war	Extend and Enrich, p. 523 Reteach the Main Idea, p. 524	Activity Book, p. 104 Music Audiocassette
LESSON 3 **Mining in the West** pp. 525–527	**INDIVIDUALISM & INTERDEPENDENCE** • Geography • Economics • Culture • Civics and Government	prospector boom bust vigilance	Extend and Enrich, p. 526 Reteach the Main Idea, p. 527	Activity Book, p. 105 ▶ THE AMAZING WRITING MACHINE
LESSON 4 **Conflict in the West** pp. 528–531	**CONFLICT & COOPERATION** • Culture • Civics and Government • Geography • History	reservation	Advanced Learners, p. 529 Extend and Enrich, p. 530 Reteach the Main Idea, p. 531	Activity Book, p. 106
CHAPTER REVIEW pp. 532–533				Activity Book, p. 107 Transparency 43 Assessment Program Chapter 16 Test, pp. 131–134 ▶ THE AMAZING WRITING MACHINE ▶ TIMELINER ▶ INTERNET

7 DAYS

TIME MANAGEMENT

DAY 1	DAY 2	DAY 3	DAY 4	DAY 5	DAY 6	DAY 7
Lesson 1	Skill	Lesson 2	Lesson 3	Lesson 4	Chapter Review	Chapter Test

Activity Book

LESSON 1
Illustrate History

NAME ______________________ DATE ____________

Life in a Sod House

Illustrate History

***DIRECTIONS:** The following excerpt is from Frontier Living by Edwin Tunis. Read the excerpt. Then complete the activities that follow.*

A family couldn't live forever in its wagon and the Homestead Act required a house; but there wasn't enough wood for a house. The Mandan and the Pawnee Indians solved the problem with earth lodges and the white men did the same; they cut the sod into blocks and laid up walls with it as bricks are laid. . . . If they could find a bank, they dug the back of the house into it, building only the front and part of the side walls of sod. Poles for roof rafters came from a river bank and on them the builders spread brush, grass, and more sod. The floor was dirt. Canvas or leather made a door, and anything but glass covered a window. A ditch across the bank behind the dugout and down the slope on either side prevented a complete washout, but the roofs of dugouts and of four-walled "soddies," too, leaked so badly that people customarily hung small tents over their beds. Even in dry weather, dirt falling from the roof got over and into everything; women loathed [hated] the soddies. Dirt wasn't all that fell; there were also bugs and mice and sometimes a cow wandered onto a dugout roof and suddenly joined the family below.

1. Why did the homesteaders build sod houses?
There was not enough wood for a house, and the Homestead Act required they build a house.

2. List the steps homesteaders followed to build sod houses.
cut sod into blocks; laid up walls using sod like bricks; sometimes dug back into a bank; made roof rafters from poles and spread brush, grass, and more sod on them; made a door from canvas or leather

3. On a separate sheet of paper, describe what it was like to live in a sod house, and explain how you would feel if you had to live in such a house.
Responses should reflect students' interpretation of the description above, such as dirty, dark, crowded, damp, bug-filled, and should explain how students would feel living in a sod house.

4. Use the above description of life in a sod house to draw a diagram of a sod house. Make sure you label each part of the house.
Illustrations should reflect the description above and include labels for parts of the sod house.

 Use after reading Chapter 16, Lesson 1, pages 513–517.

SKILL PRACTICE
Apply Chart and Graph Skills

NAME ______________________ DATE ____________

HOW TO UNDERSTAND A Climograph

Apply Chart and Graph Skills

***DIRECTIONS:** Below is a table that provides average monthly temperature and precipitation data for Pittsburgh, Pennsylvania. Answer the questions that follow by comparing the data in this table with the climograph of Cheyenne, Wyoming, at the right.*

Temperature is given in degrees Fahrenheit. Precipitation is given in inches.

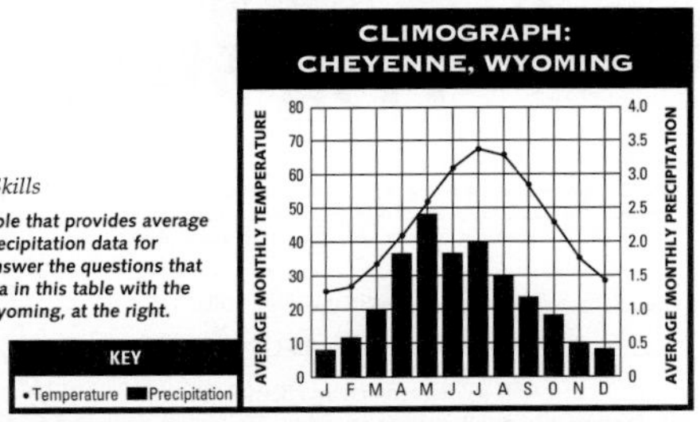

PITTSBURGH, PENNSYLVANIA

	Jan	Feb	Mar	April	May	June	July	Aug	Sept	Oct	Nov	Dec
Temperature	30	31	40	51	62	71	75	73	67	55	43	34
Precipitation	2.9	2.5	3.3	3.1	3.3	3.7	4.0	3.2	2.7	2.5	2.4	2.7

1. During which month does Cheyenne receive the most precipitation?
May ______ Pittsburgh? July

2. Which place is more likely to require irrigation for farming? Cheyenne
Why? It is very dry during parts of the year.

3. What is the average temperature for each place in December?
Cheyenne: 28°; Pittsburgh: 34°

4. Use the physical map in the atlas of your textbook to explain why one place is colder on average than the other. Accept justifiable answers such as that Cheyenne has a higher altitude and a more northerly location.

Use after reading Chapter 16, Skill Lesson, pages 518–519.

LESSON 2
Read a Table

NAME ______________________ DATE ____________

World Roundup

Read a Table

***DIRECTIONS:** Study the chart below, which describes cowhands from around the world. Then complete the activities that follow.*

NAME	LOCATION	CLOTHING	MISCELLANEOUS FACTS
cowhand X	United States	chaps, brimmed hat, spurs, cotton shirt, bandanna, boots, blue jeans, holster	most famous in world because of legendary role on the western frontier
gardian	France	flat-crowned, wide-brimmed black hat; brightly colored shirt; black velvet jacket; heavy cotton trousers	herded special black bulls raised just for bullfights; rode white horses
gaucho ★	Argentina and Uruguay	bloused trousers called *bombachas;* tall, small-brimmed hat; knotted scarf	word *gaucho* comes from South American Indian word for "outcast"
vaquero X	Mexico	wide-brimmed, felt sombrero or straw hat; cloak or plain, short jacket; flared woolen trousers or cotton pants	owned no land and often no horse; rode horses belonging to others; taught American cowhands their trade

1. Circle the name of the cowhand that is located in Europe.

2. Put a star next to the name of the cowhand that is located in South America.

3. Put an X next to the names of the cowhands that are located in North America.

4. Choose the cowhand from the chart that you find the most interesting. Use the information in the chart to draw a diagram of what you think your selected cowhand looks like. Be sure to label your diagram and include a caption describing why you think this cowhand is the most interesting.
Accept all diagrams with appropriate labels and captions.

 Use after reading Chapter 16, Lesson 2, pages 520–524.

LESSON 3
Describe a Method of Transportation

NAME ______________________ DATE ____________

THE STAGECOACH RIDE WEST

Describe a Method of Transportation

***DIRECTIONS:** Study the diagram of a stagecoach. Answer the questions. Then, on a separate sheet of paper, complete the writing assignment.*

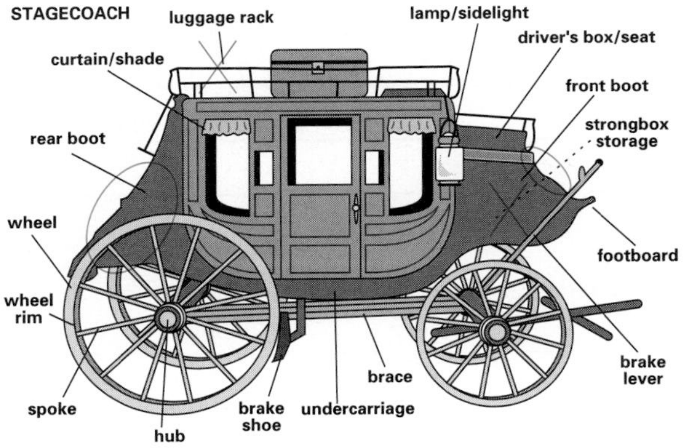

1. A boot is a trunk or baggage compartment. Circle the two boots on the stagecoach.

2. Put an X through two other places on the stagecoach made specifically for storage.

3. How do you think a stagecoach was powered? by horses

4. Stagecoach roads were extremely bumpy because of the drainage ditches that cut across them. When the roads ended, the ride continued on an even rougher trail. Study the physical map in the atlas in your textbook. Imagine that you are traveling by stagecoach from the Missouri River to the Rocky Mountains. The trip will take six days. Write a journal account of your trip describing the scenery and your feelings about the trip. Journal accounts should cover the six-day trip and include a description of both the geography and students' impressions.

Use after reading Chapter 16, Lesson 3, pages 525–527.

LESSON 4
Put Events in Sequence

NAME ______________________ DATE ____________

THE UNITED STATES & THE SIOUX

Put Events in Sequence

DIRECTIONS: Below is a listing of nine events discussed in the lesson. In the blanks to the left of each event, place a number from one to nine to indicate the order in which these events took place.

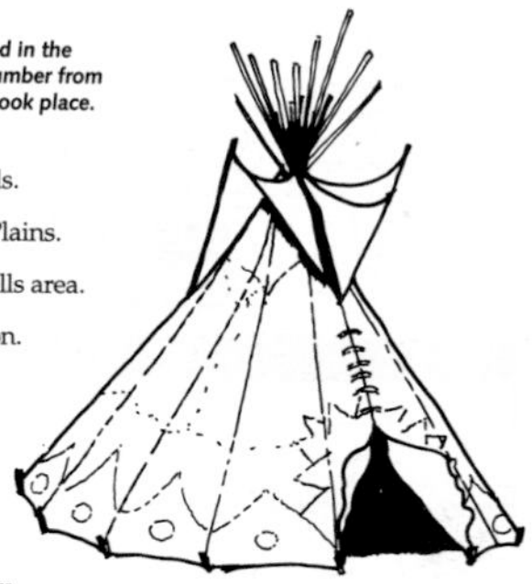

4 Gold discovered in the Black Hills.

2 Railroads built across the Great Plains.

6 U.S. soldiers march into Black Hills area.

8 Sioux returned to their reservation.

5 Sioux refuse United States offer to purchase Black Hills area.

1 Fifteen million buffalo roam the Great Plains.

3 Sioux reservation created in the Black Hills of the Dakota Territory.

7 George Custer and his troops killed at the Battle of Little Bighorn.

9 Fewer than one thousand buffalo roam the Great Plains.

DIRECTIONS: Listed below are five names. Circle the one name that does not belong, and explain why.

Geronimo Joseph Crazy Horse (Custer) Sitting Bull

because the other four were Native American chiefs

 Use after reading Chapter 16, Lesson 4, pages 528–531.

CHAPTER 16 REVIEW
Connect Main Ideas

NAME ______________________ DATE ____________

THE LAST FRONTIER

Connect Main Ideas

DIRECTIONS: Use this organizer to show that you understand how the chapter's main ideas are connected. Complete the organizer by writing two or three sentences that summarize the main idea of each lesson.

The Last Frontier

Farming the Great Plains
Homesteaders settled on the Great Plains in the late 1800s to farm the land. Although farming was difficult, the region would later become known as the "breadbasket" of the United States.

Conflict in the West
Settlement of the West and the killing of buffalo caused problems for the Plains Indians—Indians fought to keep their way of life but eventually were made to leave their lands and move to reservations.

The Cattle Kingdom
Cattle ranches covered the West, from Texas to Montana, in the 1800s. Ranchers supplied meat to other parts of the country by driving herds of cows to towns where they were loaded onto trains and then prepared for market.

Mining in the West
Prospectors roamed the West searching for minerals, such as gold, silver, or copper. Mining towns grew quickly and often were dangerous places to live because there was no law and little order.

Use after reading Chapter 16, pages 512–533.

COMMUNITY RESOURCES

Ideas for using community resources, including speakers and field trips

Historical Societies:

____

Community Members:

____

Historic Sites:

____

Museums:

____

Chapter 16 Assessment

For ongoing PERFORMANCE ASSESSMENT, see Show What You Know, pp. 517, 524, 527, 531.

CONTENT

NAME ______________________ DATE ____________

Chapter Test 16

Part One: Test Your Understanding *(4 points each)*

DIRECTIONS: *Circle the letter of the best answer.*

1. The purpose of the Homestead Act was to
- A. give companies money to build a railroad across the country.
- **B.** encourage people to settle on the Great Plains.
- C. open the first cattle trail to the railroads.
- D. end the battles between ranchers and farmers.

2. Railroad owners wanted more people to settle on the Great Plains because
- **A.** settlers would use the railroads for travel.
- B. they needed more people to build railroad tracks.
- C. they needed sharecroppers to farm the land owned by the railroads.
- D. settlers would grow cotton and ship it to the South.

3. Settlers on the Great Plains used sod to build their houses because
- A. sod houses were cleaner than other buildings.
- **B.** there were few trees that could be used for wood.
- C. houses made from wood were too cold in the winters on the Great Plains.
- D. the railroads paid people to live in sod houses.

4. The person who invented a stronger plow to help people cut through the thick sod was
- A. Joseph Glidden.
- B. Richard King.
- **C.** James Oliver.
- D. George Custer.

5. Which of the following caused some farmers to leave their farms on the Great Plains?
- A. railroads
- **B.** bad weather
- C. immigrants
- D. barbed wire

6. After Joseph McCoy opened his stockyards near some railroad tracks in Abilene, Kansas,
- A. many farmers moved to the Great Plains.
- B. the Indians started moving to the reservations.
- **C.** ranchers started moving herds of cattle to the "cow towns."
- D. the mining boom in the West ended.

(continued)

CONTENT

NAME ______________________ DATE ____________

7. What were long drives?
- A. transportation by railroad
- B. special areas of farmland on the Great Plains given to homesteaders
- C. the path of the buffalo migration on the Great Plains
- **D.** trips on which cowhands moved large numbers of cattle to the railroads

8. The range wars were caused by
- **A.** the use of barbed wire.
- B. the British.
- C. the steel plow.
- D. railroad owners.

9. What happened during a mining boom?
- A. Most people lost all of their money.
- B. People moved away from mining areas.
- C. Gold, silver, and copper mines were closed.
- **D.** There was quick economic growth.

10. Which of the following caused some mining towns to become ghost towns?
- A. The range wars destroyed all the buildings in the towns.
- **B.** The mines ran out of gold, silver, or copper.
- C. The railroads moved away.
- D. The vaqueros ordered everyone to leave the towns.

11. Law and order was maintained in the mining towns by
- A. the United States Army.
- B. county sheriffs.
- **C.** Vigilance Committees.
- D. the Union army.

12. The most important resource of the Plains Indians was
- **A.** the buffalo.
- B. wheat.
- C. the horse.
- D. corn.

13. Why did General George Custer take his soldiers to the Little Bighorn River in 1876?
- A. to open a new railroad through the Black Hills
- B. to protect cowhands on long drives across the Sioux reservation
- C. to help miners in a boom town
- **D.** to take back land the government had given to the Sioux

14. Why did U.S. Army soldiers chase the Nez Perces for more than 1,700 miles?
- A. because the Nez Perces were living on land that contained gold
- B. to punish them for defeating Custer and his soldiers
- **C.** because the Nez Perces were trying to escape to Canada
- D. to stop them from going to war with the Sioux

(continued)

SKILLS

NAME ______________________ DATE ____________

Part Two: Test Your Skills *(25 points)*

DIRECTIONS: *Use the climographs to answer the questions that follow.*

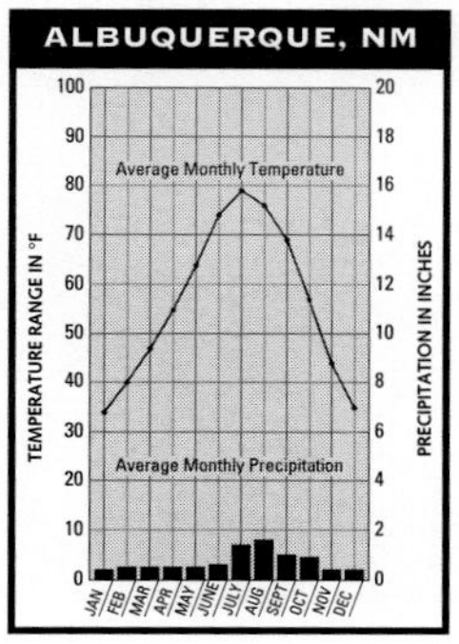

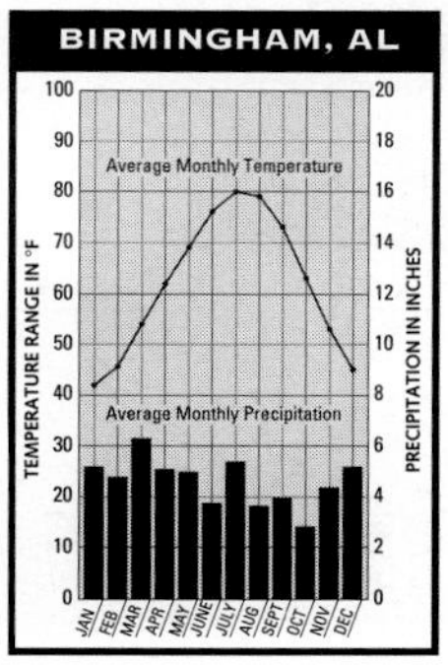

15. What is the wettest month in each city?
Albuquerque, August; Birmingham, March

16. What is the average temperature in each city in April?
Albuquerque, 55° F; Birmingham, 62° F

17. What is the coldest month in each city?
Albuquerque and Birmingham, January

18. What is the warmest month in each city?
Albuquerque and Birmingham, July

19. Which city receives more precipitation? Birmingham

(continued)

APPLICATION/WRITING

NAME ______________________ DATE ____________

Part Three: Apply What You Have Learned

DIRECTIONS: *Complete each of the following activities.*

20. ***Indian Reservations*** *(9 points)*
Indian reservations were created by the United States government as places where the Native American peoples could live. Describe how each of the groups below resisted living on reservations.

Sioux
Possible response: The Sioux fought back at the Battle of Little Bighorn.

Nez Perces
Possible response: The Nez Perces tried to relocate to Canada.

Apaches
Possible response: The Apaches attacked Arizona settlers and hid from the U.S. Army for five years.

21. ***Essay*** *(10 points)*
The western part of the United States was settled mainly by farmers and miners. Explain in one paragraph how farmers and miners were alike and how they were different.

Possible response:
Farmers and miners were alike in some ways. Both had to work hard and had to face the hardships of life in the West. Both usually had very little money. Farmers and miners also were different in some ways. Farmers usually lived and worked with their families, while miners usually lived near the mines and worked alone. Farmers stayed in one place, while miners often moved from place to place.

INTRODUCE THE CHAPTER

This chapter examines the changes that took place in the West in the late 1800s and early 1900s. It compares and contrasts the work of farmers, who turned the Great Plains into one of the world's great wheat-growing regions, and ranchers, who raised cattle there. It also looks at the growth and impact of the mining industry. Finally, the chapter explores how all these changes affected the lifeways of American Indians in the West.

Link Prior Learning

Have students recall what they already know about the West, why people wanted to settle there, and what happened to the American Indians as a result.

Visual Analysis

Interpret Photographs Ask students to observe the photograph of the cowhand and discuss what they know about the role of the cowhand in the West.

Q. **Why did cowhands wear broad-brimmed hats?** to keep the sun and wind out of their eyes and to catch rainwater to drink

Auditory Learning

Interpret Primary Sources Ask a student volunteer to read aloud Charles Goodnight's statement.

Q. **Who were the "solitary adventurers" and why were they "free and full of the zest of darers"?** The "solitary adventurers" were the cowhands and ranchers of the West. They were probably "free and full of the zest of darers" because they were out on the wide open plains, far from people, newspapers, and other signs of community life.

PRIMARY SOURCE

Source: *America Past and Present*. Robert A. Divine. Scott, Foresman and Company, 1984.

CHAPTER 16

THE LAST FRONTIER

"Most of the time we were solitary adventurers in a great land as fresh and new as a spring morning, and we were free and full of the zest of darers."

Charles Goodnight, Texas cattle driver and rancher

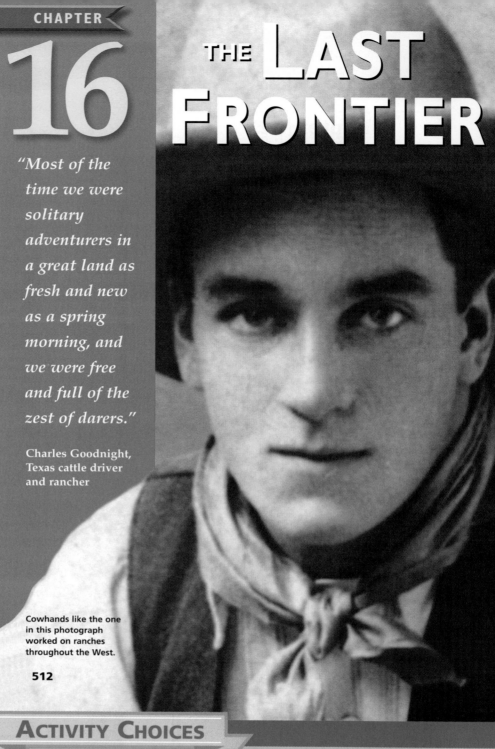

Cowhands like the one in this photograph worked on ranches throughout the West.

512

ACTIVITY CHOICES

Background

CHARLES GOODNIGHT Although Charles Goodnight was born in Macoupin County, Illinois, in 1836, he is remembered as a Texan. Goodnight was an adventurer who spent his early adulthood on the frontier, establishing ranches and cattle trails in New Mexico, Wyoming, and Colorado. In 1876 he started a cattle ranch in the Texas Panhandle; the ranch grew to encompass 1 million acres of rangeland. Goodnight bred Angus cattle and crossed them with buffalo to produce cattalo. He also organized a stock raiser's association to pacify the residents of the Panhandle who were not happy about cattle ranches.

Farming the Great Plains

LESSON 1

FOCUS
How do people today change their ways of life to suit their environments?

Main Idea As you read, look for changes farmers made in order to live on the Great Plains.

Vocabulary
homesteader
bonanza farm

The explorers of the early 1800s who crossed the Great Plains described the region as a desert. By the late 1800s, however, farmers were turning the plains into fields of wheat. The Great Plains would become the "breadbasket" of the United States and the greatest wheat-growing region in the world.

Settling the Plains

In 1862, while the Civil War was being fought in the East, Congress passed the Homestead Act. This law opened the Great Plains to settlers by giving 160 acres of land to any head of a family who was over 21 years of age and who would live on it for five years. Between 1862 and 1900 about 80 million acres of government land on the Great Plains was settled. The government lands were called homesteads, and the people who settled them were known as **homesteaders**.

Thousands of other settlers bought western land at low prices from the railroads. Over the years the government had given the railroads millions of acres of land on the Great Plains. Railroad owners used the land to build new railroad lines. But they also wanted people to settle the Plains because settlers would bring more business. Settlers would use the railroads for travel. Farmers would use the railroads to send their products to the cities in the Middle West and in the East.

The railroads placed advertisements for land sales in newspapers all over the United States and in other countries. Many Americans jumped at the chance to buy land in the West. Most wanted to start farms or ranches. Some planned to open businesses. More than 100,000 immigrants moved to the West from northern and western Europe.

This poster (below) advertised land for sale in northern Missouri. The price of the land was often less than $10 an acre. Farmers raised millions of tons of wheat (bottom) on the Great Plains.

Objectives

1. Identify the factors that attracted settlers to the Great Plains.
2. Summarize the life of farm families on the Great Plains.
3. Describe the operation of bonanza farms on the Great Plains.

Vocabulary

homesteader (p. 513) bonanza farm (p. 515)

1. ACCESS

The Focus Question

Ask students to consider how they might have to change their ways of life if they moved from a rural region to a city or vice versa, or from a mountainous region to a coastal or plains region. Help students to understand the relationship between environment and people's ways of life.

The Main Idea

In this lesson students learn about the farmers who moved to the Great Plains and turned this huge area into one of the world's great farming regions. After students have read the lesson, have them analyze how western farmers changed some of their ways to suit conditions on the Great Plains.

2. BUILD

Settling the Plains

Key Content Summary

Both the United States government and the railroads encouraged people to move to the Great Plains. Between 1862 and 1900, thousands of people from the United States and northern Europe settled the Great Plains.

Reading Support

ANTICIPATION GUIDE Before students read the lesson, ask them whether they agree (+) or disagree (−) with the following statements, and have them defend their decisions. After students have read the lesson, ask them whether they have changed any of their decisions. Have them defend any changes by referring to the lesson.

1. The Great Plains is a desert. (−)
2. The railroads profited from the settlement of the Great Plains. (+)
3. Families lived in log houses on the Great Plains. (−)
4. The soil of the Great Plains was soft and fine. (+)
5. Bonanza farms were more profitable than family farms. (+)

Culture

Shared Humanity and Unique Identity Explain that many politicians who pushed for the Homestead Act thought undeveloped land was worthless. Ask students to compare and contrast this view of the land with the view held by the Plains Indians.

Geography

Movement Direct students' attenention to the map showing the settlement of the United States between 1870 and 1890. Discuss the movement of farmers from the East to the Great Plains region, and have students suggest reasons farmers might decide to move from one region to another.

Visual Analysis

Learn from Maps Have students answer the question in the caption. The frontier moved west.

Life on the Family Farm

Key Content Summary

The environment of the Great Plains was dramatically different for farmers who had moved there from other regions. Farm families had to adapt to the shortage of wood, extreme weather changes, insect swarms, and prairie fires.

By 1890 there were 5 million people living on the Great Plains.

The best lands on the Great Plains were quickly taken. In the Oklahoma land rush of 1889, thousands of homesteaders raced one another to claim land. By 1890 most of the territories in the Great Plains had enough people to become states. North Dakota, South Dakota, and Montana joined the Union in 1889. Wyoming joined in 1890. Oklahoma followed in 1907.

REVIEW ***How did settlers get land on the Great Plains?*** by buying government land or land from the railroads

Life on the Family Farm

Living on the Great Plains was very different from living in most other places in the United States. Trees for building homes were scarce, but there was plenty of sod. Many settlers used sod to build their houses. Sod houses were cool in summer and warm in winter, but keeping them clean was a problem. Dirt often fell from the sod ceiling onto the furniture. Sometimes snakes did, too! Leaky roofs were common. "There was

MAP THEME **Movement** This map shows the areas of the United States that were settled by 1870 and by 1890.

■ *As settlers moved west, what happened to the frontier?*

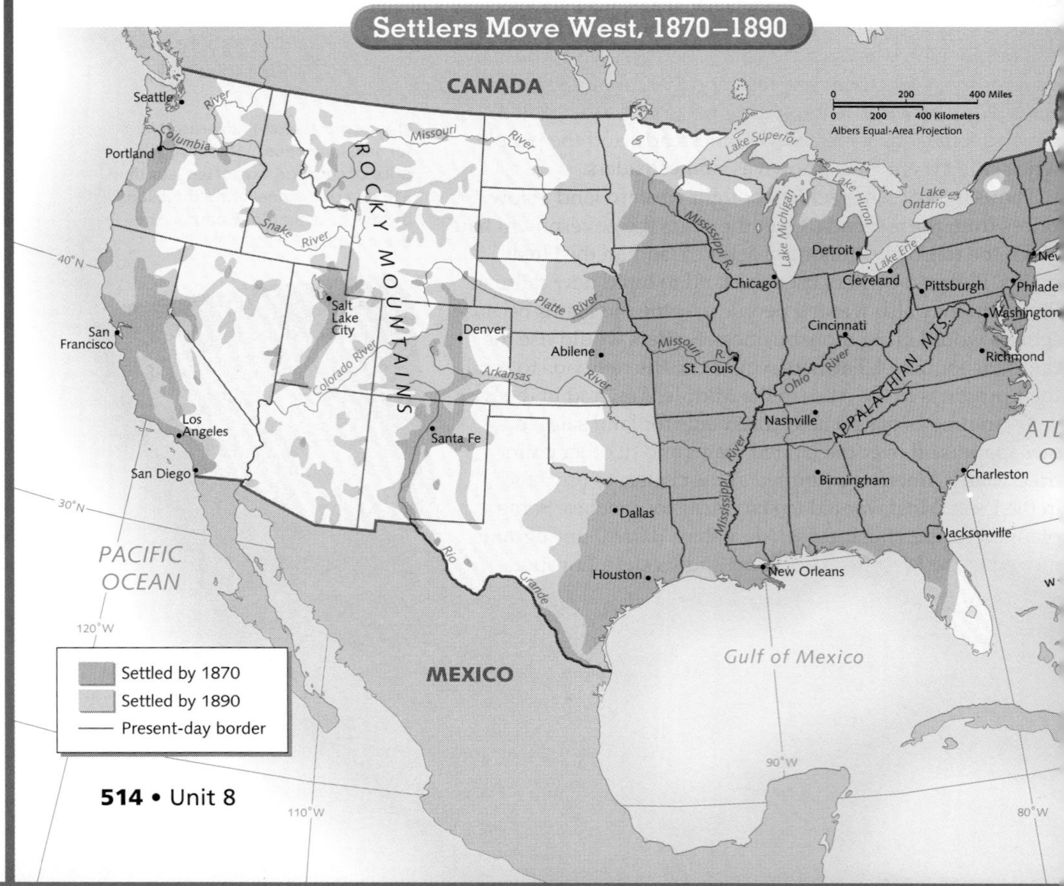

514 • Unit 8

ACTIVITY CHOICES

Multicultural Link

About 40,000 African Americans joined the march to the Great Plains, calling themselves the Exodusters, after the biblical Exodus of the Jews from Egypt. White southerners tried to block them from leaving, and many of them were turned back. Those who left settled mainly in Kansas. They tried to raise cotton, but this was not a good crop for the region. Eventually, most of the Exodusters left their farms and settled in cities such as Topeka and Kansas City.

Multicultural Link

After 1873 a group of Mennonite immigrants from Russia settled in Kansas and Oklahoma. A Mennonite named Bernhard Warkentin, from the Crimea in southern Russia, brought with him a variety of wheat called Turkey Red, never before grown in the United States. Turkey Red could be planted in the fall rather than in the spring, escaping many of the insects and diseases of spring wheat. With Turkey Red, wheat production expanded rapidly in Kansas and Oklahoma.

Smithsonian Institution®

Go to the Internet site at *http://www.si.edu/harcourt/socialstudies* to visit the exhibit "Mail by Rail" in Moving the Mail at the National Postal Museum.

Because few trees grew on the Great Plains, many families lived in houses made of sod. Windmills were used to pump water from wells dug in the ground.

running water in our sod house," joked one Kansas girl. "It ran through the roof."

Farm families on the Great Plains faced other problems. In summer, sun baked the soil into dust. In winter, snow and bitter temperatures froze the region. In years of drought nothing grew. When crops did grow, farmers worried about prairie fires and hailstorms. One settler on the Plains, Susan Orcutt, wrote that they would have had plenty to eat "if the hail hadn't cut our rye down and ruined our corn and potatoes."

Insects, too, were a problem on the Plains. Grasshoppers attacked in 1874. They came by the millions, turning the sky black and eating anything that was green. Adelheit Viets was wearing a white dress with green stripes the day the grasshoppers came. "The grasshoppers settled on me and ate up every bit of green stripe in the dress before anything could be done about it," she exaggerated.

Changes in technology helped many farm families survive tough times on the Great Plains. New models of windmills let farmers pump water from hundreds of feet below the ground. A stronger plow, invented by James Oliver of Indiana, helped homesteaders cut through the thick sod. And harvesting machines made farm work easier.

Sometimes the hardships became so great that some people left their farms. But most stayed. They built churches and schools, starting towns and cities all over the Great Plains.

REVIEW ***What hardships did the early Plains farmers face?*** dirty sod houses; crops ruined by bad weather, fires, and insects

"Bonanza Farms"

Using the new technology and the railroads, some companies started large farms on the Great Plains. People in the East invested money in these **bonanza farms**. A bonanza is something that brings a good profit or other reward.

The first bonanza farms on the Great Plains grew wheat in the Red River valley of present-day North Dakota and Minnesota. By 1890

Geography

Region After students have read this section about farm life on the Great Plains, ask them to describe the land, climate, and vegetation of the region.

Geography

Human–Environment Interactions Have students explain how the early settlers interacted with the Great Plains environment. Then have them compare and contrast the experiences of the settlers with the lifeways of the Mandan Indians, discussed in Chapter 2.

Q. **How did the challenges of the Great Plains environment lead people to find new ways of dealing with it?** They brought in new windmills to pump water from hundreds of feet below the ground. Stronger plows helped farmers cut through thick sod. Harvesting machines made farm work easier.

"Bonanza Farms"

Key Content Summary

Bonanza farms used the latest farm technology to produce tons of wheat, feeding people in the cities of the Middle West and the East. These farms, run like factories, earned large profits for their owners.

Meet Individual Needs

ENGLISH LANGUAGE LEARNERS Have students work in pairs to draw a picture that shows life on a family farm. Encourage students to show scenes that are described in the text. Then ask each pair to show and describe its picture to the class.

Meet Individual Needs

TACTILE LEARNERS Obtain permission from the school administration to have students cut sod squares from the ground or have students grow sod squares in the classroom, using heavy soil and grass seed. You may wish to have them make a miniature sod house.

Economics

Markets and Prices Have students analyze the economic advantages of bonanza farms over family farms.

Q. **Why were bonanza farms successful in selling large quantities of wheat to big cities?** Because they were able to keep their production costs low, they could sell their wheat at lower prices than could family farms.

Visual Analysis

Learn from Maps Have students study the map and relate weather and physical characteristics of the land to agriculture in various regions of the United States.

Have students answer the question in the caption. winter wheat, wheat, cotton, or corn

there were about 300 of these farms, each one spreading over thousands of acres.

Bonanza farms were run just like factories. Managers ran the farms. Farm workers had specialized jobs, and everything was done by machines. When the wheat crop was ripe, workers used 30-horse teams to pull harvesting machines across the fields. Tons of wheat from bonanza farms were sent by railroad to feed millions of people in the cities of the Middle West and the East.

Bonanza farms could raise crops cheaply, and their investors made very large profits. Managers bought seed and equipment in large amounts, so they paid lower prices. But in times of drought and when wheat prices were low, profits fell. When profits fell, many bonanza farms on the Great Plains went out of business. This left many managers and farm workers without jobs.

REVIEW ***How was a bonanza farm like a factory?*** A manager ran it, farm workers had specialized jobs, and everything was done by machines.

MAP THEME Regions This map shows the areas where American farm products were raised during the late 1800s.

■ *If you had lived on the Great Plains during this time, what crops would you probably have grown?*

Agriculture in the Late 1800s

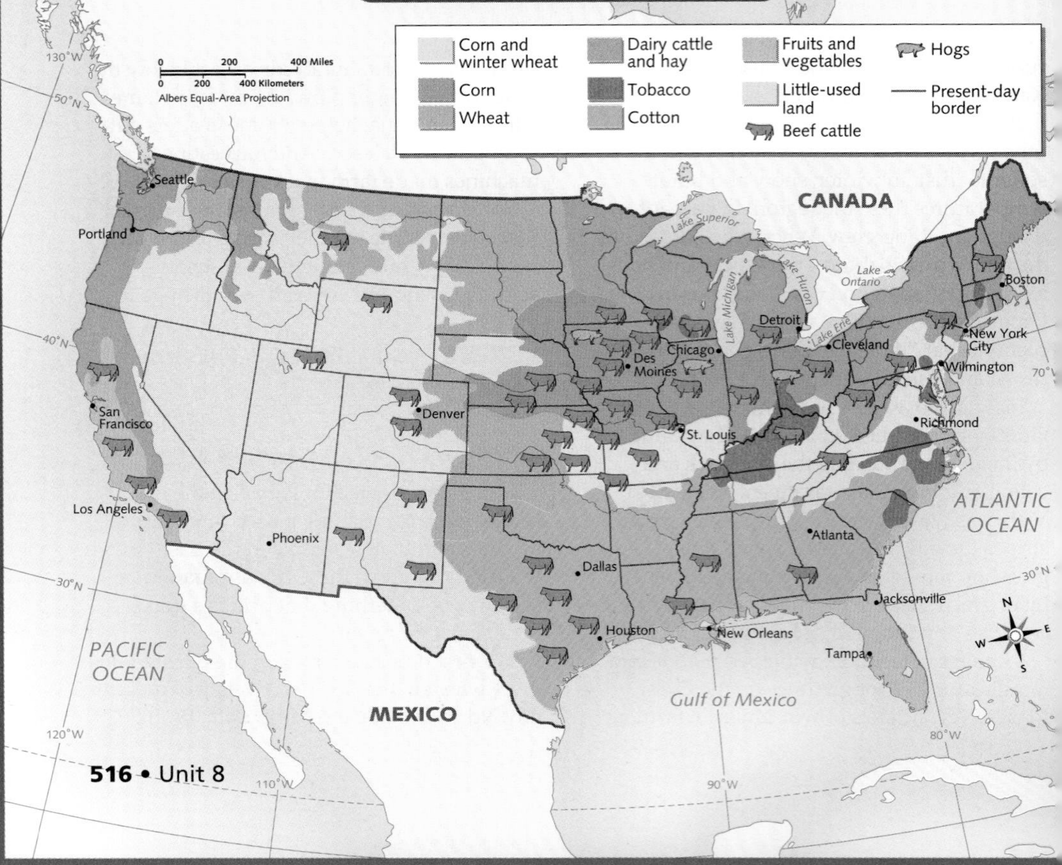

Activity Choices

Link to World Languages

UNDERSTAND SPANISH Ask volunteers to look up the meaning of the Spanish word *bonanza* ("fair weather at sea") and explain how it came to mean any venture that returned a high profit.

Link to Science

COOPERATIVE LEARNING

RESEARCH WHEAT Divide the class into several groups, and have each group prepare an oral report and illustrations on an aspect of wheat or wheat farming. Topics might include the wheat plant; uses of wheat; growing different kinds of wheat; insects and diseases that attack wheat; the sickle, scythe, cradle, and flail; Cyrus McCormick and the reaper; Sylvanus Locke and the self-binder; and John and Hiram Pitts and the threshing machine.

Extend and Enrich

COOPERATIVE LEARNING

RESEARCH AND READ ALOUD Divide the class into several groups. Ask each group to locate stories, diaries, or poems about farm life on the Great Plains in the mid- to late-1800s. The works of Willa Cather, Laura Ingalls Wilder, and Hamlin Garland are among possible choices. Students in each group should select a chapter, poem, or several diary entries to read aloud to the other groups. After all readings are completed, allow students time to discuss what life was like on the Great Plains.

In the late 1800s some farmers began to use combines (above). Combines are both reapers that cut the crops and threshers that separate the grain from the straw.

TECHNOLOGY

The Reaper

For hundreds of years, farmers harvested crops such as wheat by using a scythe (SYTH), a long, curved knife with a handle. Using a scythe was very hard work. In 1831 an inventor named Cyrus McCormick built a harvesting machine called a reaper. Farmers could cut as much wheat in one day with McCormick's reaper as they could cut in two weeks with a scythe. In 1847 McCormick started a reaper factory in Chicago. Many of the reapers used on farms on the Great Plains were built by the McCormick Harvesting Machine Company.

LESSON 1 REVIEW

Check Understanding

1. **Remember the Facts** What hardships did the homesteaders face?
2. **Recall the Main Idea** What changes did farmers have to make in order to live on the Great Plains?

Think Critically

3. **Think More About It** Why do you think people stayed on the Great Plains despite the hardships?
4. **Personally Speaking** How do you think you would have liked living on the Great Plains during this time? Explain your answer.

Show What You Know

Art Activity Draw a picture of a settlement on the Great Plains. Include a house and farm equipment. Share your picture with classmates or a family member.

Reteach the Main Idea

COOPERATIVE LEARNING

MAKE A CHART Divide the class into small groups. Challenge each group to use the textbook as a resource to make a chart comparing a farm family's life in the East with farm life on the Great Plains. The chart can be titled *How Farm Families Adapted to Life on the Great Plains.* The column titles can be *Eastern Farms* and *Western Farms.* Have the groups share and discuss their charts and make a class chart from the discussion.

ACTIVITY BOOK

Reinforce & Extend

Use ACTIVITY BOOK, p. 102.

3. CLOSE

Have students consider again the Focus question on page 513.

How do people today change their ways of life to suit their environments?

Have students use what they have learned about farmers on the Great Plains to compare and contrast the ways Great Plains farmers adapted to their environment with the ways people today adapt to their environments.

LESSON 1 REVIEW—Answers

Check Understanding

1. drought, wind, hail, hot summers, icy winters, fires, grasshoppers
2. They had to live in sod houses, plant wheat, develop bonanza farms, and use stronger plows and better windmills.

Think Critically

3. They may have had no choice financially; they had hope for the future.
4. Answers will reflect students' viewpoints. Some might note the challenge of coping with the environment and natural elements. Others might note that they would be unwilling to take the financial risks associated with farming on the Plains.

Show What You Know

Performance Assessment Display students' pictures and have them discuss what they learned.

What to Look For Look for evidence that students understand how the farmers adapted to life on the Great Plains.

Objectives

1. Interpret climographs.
2. Create a climograph.

Vocabulary

climograph (p. 518)

1. ACCESS

Focus on the hypothetical situation posed in Why Learn This Skill? Have students choose places to which they might like to move. What kind of weather would they expect to find there? What kinds of clothes would they take? Point out that they could find the answers on a climograph.

2. BUILD

Define the term *climograph* and introduce the graphs in this lesson. Have students locate the lines on the graphs that show average monthly temperature and the bars on the graphs that show average monthly precipitation. If necessary, review the term *precipitation*, pointing out that it includes both rain and snow. Have students locate the labels that indicate the months at the bottom of each graph.

Chart and Graph Skills

Understand a Climograph

1. Why Learn This Skill?

In the late 1800s, many Americans who moved from eastern cities to the Great Plains were surprised by much of what they found there. Nothing surprised them more than the constant wind and the extremes of temperature and precipitation. Suppose that you and your family were moving to another part of the country or another part of the world. You probably would want to know more about the climate before you moved there.

2. Understand the Process

One way to learn about the climate of a place is to study a climograph, or climate graph. A **climograph** shows the average monthly temperature and the average monthly precipitation for a place. Both temperature and precipitation information are shown on the same graph. The temperatures are shown as a line graph. The amounts of precipitation are shown as a bar graph. The months are listed along the bottom of a climograph, from January to December.

Study the climographs on page 519. Along the left-hand side of each climograph is a Fahrenheit scale for temperature. A point is shown on the climograph for the average temperature for each month. These points are connected with a red line. By studying the line, you can see which months are hotter and which are colder.

Along the right-hand side of each climograph is a scale for precipitation. The average monthly amounts of precipitation are shown in inches. By studying the heights of the green bars, you can see which months are usually dry and which are usually wet.

These two climographs show weather averages for Omaha, Nebraska, and Philadelphia, Pennsylvania. Omaha is on the Great Plains, and Philadelphia is near the Atlantic coast. By comparing the climographs, you can see the differences in temperature and precipitation between these two places. This might help you understand why many early settlers on the Great Plains were surprised by new climates. Use the climographs to answer the questions on page 519.

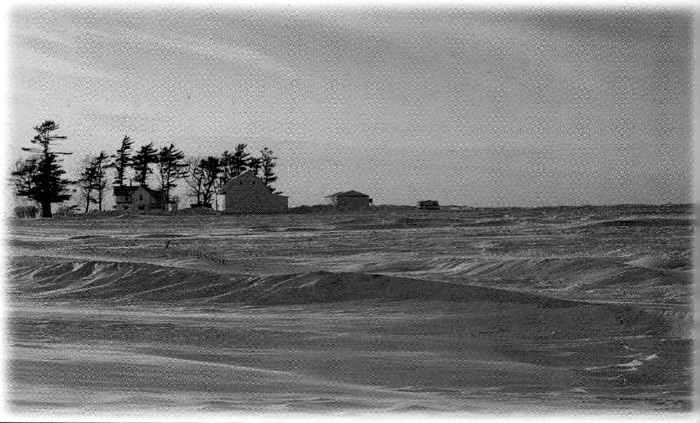

Many pioneers experienced blizzards in the northern part of the Great Plains. A blizzard is a dangerous snowstorm with winds of 35 miles (56 km) per hour or more.

ACTIVITY CHOICES

Link to Science

BUILD A RAIN GAUGE Have students design, or research a design, for a rain gauge. Have them build the rain gauge and use it to record rainfall for a month. Is the rainfall for the month higher or lower than the average shown on the climograph they created in Think and Apply? Students could also record daily high and low temperatures for a month, compute the average monthly temperature, and compare it to data from the climograph.

Link to Mathematics

CONVERT FAHRENHEIT TEMPERATURES TO CELSIUS Have students convert their own area's average monthly temperatures from Fahrenheit to Celsius, using the formula °C = $\frac{5}{9}$ (°F − 32).

TECHNOLOGY

Use GRAPH LINKS to complete this graphing activity.

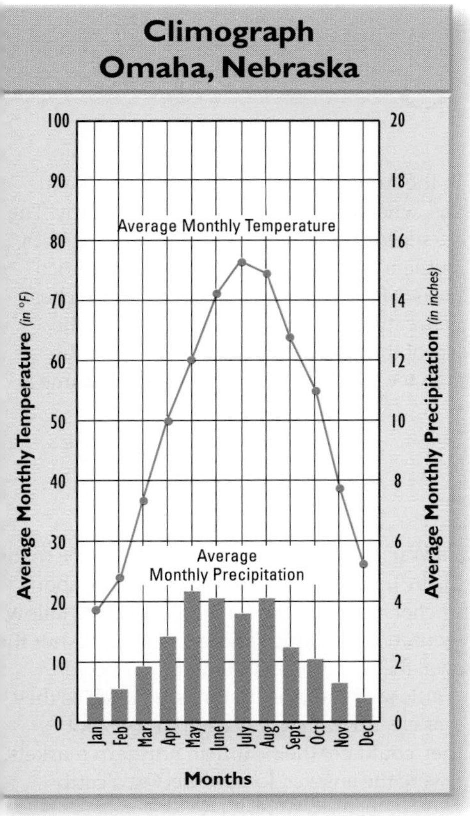

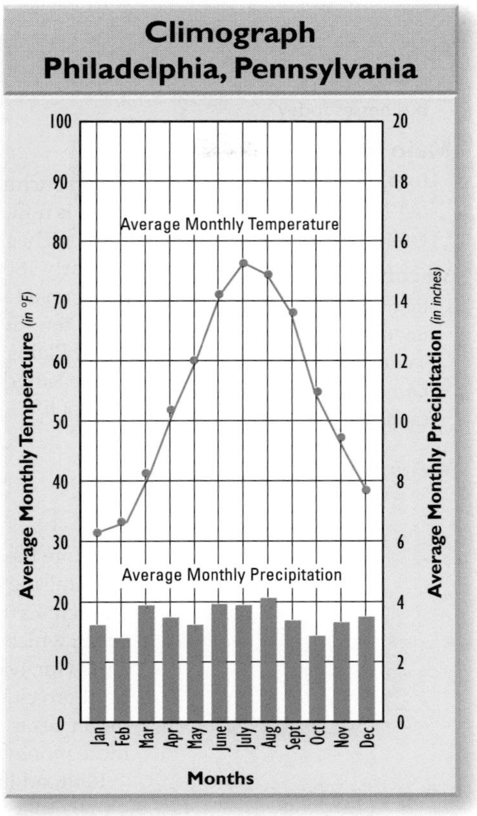

1. Which is the warmest month in each of the cities?
2. Which is the coldest month in each place?
3. What are the wettest months in each city?
4. What are the driest months in each city?
5. Which city receives more precipitation during the year?
6. What is the average temperature for each place in January?
7. How much precipitation falls during January in each place?

3. Think and Apply

Use an almanac or encyclopedia to create a climograph for your city or for a city close to where you live. Compare your climograph with the ones shown on this page. Which place shows the greatest changes in temperature and precipitation? Share your findings with a family member or friend. Then discuss the importance of this information. When might people need to know this information? What does it tell you about the place where you live?

Direct students' attention to the scale along the left side of each graph. Point out that these numbers indicate temperature on the Fahrenheit scale. Have students review their graph skills by finding the average temperature for Omaha, Nebraska, in the month of April (50°F). Tell students that the average monthly temperature is found by adding together the average temperatures for each day in the month and then dividing that figure by the number of days in the month.

Next, have students locate the precipitation scale along the right side of each graph. Have students practice by finding the average precipitation in Philadelphia for the month of June (almost 4 inches).

Then have students answer the questions in Understand the Process.

1. July
2. January
3. Omaha: May; Philadelphia: August
4. Omaha: December and January; Philadelphia: February and October
5. Philadelphia
6. Omaha: about 19°F; Philadelphia: about 31°F
7. Omaha: about 1 inch; Philadelphia: about 3 inches

3. CLOSE

Supply students with graph paper and have them complete the activity in Think and Apply. To help students understand the usefulness of the information they have gathered, have them consider how temperature and precipitation affect clothing needs, home construction, heating costs, outdoor activities, and vacations.

Reteach the Skill

COOPERATIVE LEARNING

COMPARE CITIES Have advanced learners prepare climographs for two cities that have dramatically different climates—perhaps Anchorage, Alaska, and Phoenix, Arizona. Have other students work in small groups to analyze the climographs. In what respect are the climates different? similar? Ask students when would be the best time to visit each place and why. Look for an understanding of how to read a climograph.

ACTIVITY BOOK

Practice & Apply

Use ACTIVITY BOOK, p. 103.

TRANSPARENCY

Use TRANSPARENCY 42.

Objectives

1. Explore the development of the cattle industry on the Great Plains.
2. Analyze why open range lands were important to cattle ranchers.
3. Describe the work of the cowhands.
4. Identify the reasons for the decline of the Cattle Kingdom.

Vocabulary

long drive (p. 521)
open range (p. 522)
vaquero (p. 522)
barbed wire (p. 523)
range war (p. 524)

1. ACCESS

The Focus Question

Ask students to think about how local businesses get started, including how much money is needed to start them, how they attract customers, and what the costs are before any profit is made. Have students speculate on the risks and benefits of starting a business.

The Main Idea

Students explore the efforts of cattle ranchers to develop cattle ranches on the Great Plains. They also explore the interdependence that developed among the ranchers, the railroads, and the eastern markets. After students have read the lesson, have them summarize how ranchers built the Cattle Kingdom.

2. BUILD

The Rise of the Cattle Industry

Key Content Summary

Individual cattle ranchers discovered that profits on cattle would be greater if they could get the cattle to northern cities. An interdependent system developed among ranchers, cow towns, and the railroads.

LESSON 2

FOCUS
How do people build businesses today?

Main Idea As you read, find out how ranchers built the Cattle Kingdom.

Vocabulary
long drive
open range
vaquero
barbed wire
range war

The Cattle Kingdom

Ranching in the American West began in the 1700s in what is now Texas, when that area was a Spanish colony. The first ranches were started with cattle brought from Spain. By the early 1800s, settlers from the United States and Mexico had moved to Texas. Many of these settlers started ranches. After the Civil War, cattle ranches spread throughout the Great Plains. Parts of the region came to be known as the Cattle Kingdom. In the Cattle Kingdom, ranching became a way of life.

The Rise of the Cattle Industry

Before the Civil War, there was not much money to be made from raising cattle in Texas. There, cattle sold for only about $4 each. Early ranchers raised cattle for leather and for tallow, or fat, which they used for making candles and soap. After the Civil War, however, there was a great demand for beef in northern cities. Cattle sold there for 10 times as much as they did in Texas. It was clear that ranchers could make a lot more money if they could get their cattle to northern markets.

Railroad lines were the answer. Joseph McCoy, a cattle trader, built large cattle pens called stockyards near some

Cowhands today continue to take care of cattle on ranches.

ACTIVITY CHOICES

Reading Support

IDENTIFY IMPORTANT WORDS Write the lesson vocabulary terms on the board, and have students skim the lesson to find the definition for each term. Then tell students to choose five additional terms from the lesson that are related to the Cattle Kingdom and to write a definition for each term. Have students use the ten terms and their definitions to construct a word-find puzzle. Students may write the definitions and the puzzle on one side of a sheet of paper and the solution to the puzzle on the other side. Students may exchange papers and solve the puzzles or keep them for later review.

railroad tracks in Abilene, Kansas. Then he sent word to ranchers in Texas that he would buy whole herds of cattle. In 1867 Texas ranchers started moving huge herds of cattle north to Abilene. Later, as the railroad was built farther west, other cities also became important "cow towns," or places where stockyards were located. These were Dodge City, Kansas; Ogallala, Nebraska; and Cheyenne, Wyoming.

A cattle drive was the best way to get cattle to the cow towns. On a cattle drive, ranch workers on horseback would drive the cattle, or make them move to another place. Between 1867 and 1890, Texas ranchers drove about 10 million head of cattle north. These trips were called **long drives**.

Each long drive took about three months. During the drive a trail boss managed a crew of 10 to 12 cowhands, who were all skilled ranch workers. During a long drive a crew could move as many as 3,000 cattle.

The long drives followed several trails. One of these was the Chisholm (CHIZ•uhm) Trail. It started in southern Texas and ran all the way to Abilene. When the herds reached Abilene, the cattle were loaded onto freight cars and sent to Chicago, where they were prepared for market. Their meat was then sent in refrigerated freight cars to northern markets. The invention of the refrigerated freight car also allowed farmers from as far away as California to send fruits and vegetables across the country without spoiling.

REVIEW ***What were the long drives?*** trips in which cowhands drove cattle north on trails to cow towns

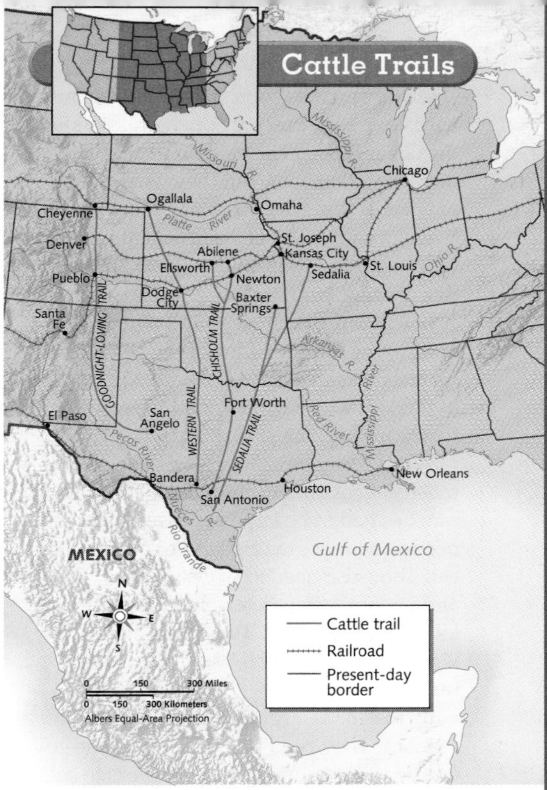

MAP THEME **Movement** This map shows four of the major cattle trails used during the 1880s.
■ *Why did the trails run north and south?*

Economics

Markets and Prices Explain that the price of an item may differ from one market to another, and have students speculate on why this happens. Ask them to calculate the difference between the price for cattle in Texas and the price for cattle in northern cities. Have students discuss the reasons that people in northern cities were willing to pay more for beef.

Visual Analysis

Learn from Maps Have students answer the question in the caption. to connect the cattle ranches to the cow towns along the railroad lines, which ran east and west

AUDIO

Use the UNIT 8 MUSIC AUDIO-CASSETTE to hear the song "Home on the Range."

Link to Art

RESEARCH ART OF THE WEST
Frederic Remington is probably the most famous artist of the American West, having drawn, painted, and sculpted more than 2,700 works of art. Assign student volunteers to locate examples of Remington's art in library books, select ten of their favorite examples, and share them with the class. Also have students provide a brief oral biography of Remington.

Link to Music

SING A COWHAND SONG Cowhands sang songs to help pass the long, lonely hours out on the range and to calm the cattle. Many of the songs were adaptations of English and Spanish folk songs. Ask the music teacher to teach students to sing "The Chisholm Trail," "The Lone Prairie," and "The Streets of Laredo." Have students discuss the insights into cowhand life provided by the lyrics.

The Open Range

Key Content Summary

Cattle ranchers needed a source of water for the cattle and thousands of acres of grazing land. A ranching boom took place because the government allowed ranchers to use public land on the Great Plains as free grazing land.

Geography
Human–Environment Interactions
Explain that cattle consumed a lot of grass and had to be moved from pasture to pasture so that the grass would have a chance to grow back.

Economics
Productivity and Economic Growth
Have students speculate on why investors would invest in large company-owned ranches in the 1880s. Discuss the similarities and differences between cash-crop plantations and large ranches.

Ranch Life

Key Content Summary

Cowhands were known as rugged individuals who had hard lives. In a roundup they guided the cattle to the stockyards. Most worked as cowhands for only a few years before settling in towns or on farms.

The Open Range

Cattle ranchers soon started letting their herds graze on the huge open grasslands of the Great Plains. The cattle ranchers did not own the grasslands, but they used millions of acres of this government land for their herds of cattle. The government allowed the ranchers to use this land as **open range**, or free grazing land.

Many of the early ranches were owned and run by families. One of the best-known ranches was started by Richard King in Texas in the 1850s. The King Ranch covered more than 1 million acres.

While few ranches were as large as King's, most still covered thousands of acres. The ranches had to be large because the cattle needed a lot of grazing land to get enough to eat. They also needed water. Rivers, lakes, and streams often determined the size and location of ranches. "Wherever there is any water, there is a ranch," said one cattle rancher.

By the 1880s large companies owned many ranches. They used land offered by the government and money from investors to set up huge ranches. About 20 companies invested $12 million in Wyoming ranches alone.

REVIEW ***Why were open range lands important to ranchers?*** They allowed ranchers to feed their cattle at no cost.

Ranch Life

Living on a ranch meant hard work for everyone. Women often cooked for all the cowhands and did other chores. Even children did adults' jobs, such as caring for the horses and herding cattle.

One of the most important events in ranch life was the roundup. Each spring and fall ranchers and hired cowhands rounded up the cattle and drove them from the open range to a stockyard. There they marked the cattle with a brand. A brand is a small piece of iron with a long handle. The piece of iron is heated and pressed against the animal's hide to leave a mark. Each rancher's brand had a special shape, so it was easy to tell from the brand who owned which cattle.

Cowhands learned many of their skills from Mexican **vaqueros** (bah•KAY•rohs), the first cowhands. About one-fourth of all early cowhands in the United States were Mexican.

BIOGRAPHY

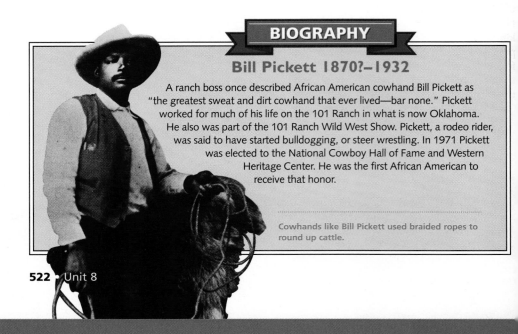

Bill Pickett 1870?–1932

A ranch boss once described African American cowhand Bill Pickett as "the greatest sweat and dirt cowhand that ever lived—bar none." Pickett worked for much of his life on the 101 Ranch in what is now Oklahoma. He also was part of the 101 Ranch Wild West Show. Pickett, a rodeo rider, was said to have started bulldogging, or steer wrestling. In 1971 Pickett was elected to the National Cowboy Hall of Fame and Western Heritage Center. He was the first African American to receive that honor.

Cowhands like Bill Pickett used braided ropes to round up cattle.

Activity Choices

Link to Art

RESEARCH AND DRAW A CATTLE BRAND Have volunteers use encyclopedias or other library reference materials to locate examples of ranch brands of the old West used for branding cattle. After the volunteers share pictures of the brands with the class, have each student design his or her own brand.

Multicultural Link

The cowhand traditions were established in the late 1700s and early 1800s when wealthy Spanish families sent their second sons to Spanish California. There the young men established ranches and taught their workers how to ride horses and rope cattle. These cowhands dressed in the Spanish style and used Spanish terms such as *chaparreras* ("chaps"), *la reata* ("lariat"), and *dar la vuelta* ("dally"), which means to stop an animal by wrapping a rope around its horns. As ranches spread, many young men, including African Americans, eagerly sought jobs as cowhands. African American cowhands often suffered less prejudice than African American workers in other occupations. One of the best-known African American cowhands was Bill Pickett. Another was Nat Love, who was also known as Deadwood Dick. Love, born a slave, worked as a cowhand for 20 years and was a rodeo champion.

This photograph shows mealtime in a cowhand camp.

Many familiar cowhand words, such as *lariat*, or rope, and *chaps*, or leather trousers, come from Spanish words. The word *rodeo* is the Spanish word for "roundup."

The cowhand has become a legend of the American West. People picture a rider wearing boots with pointed toes, wide-brimmed hat, and leather chaps. But real cowhands had hard lives. They made little money and sometimes worked under poor weather conditions. The long drives and the roundups also kept them away from their families for long periods of time. Most worked as cowhands for only a few years before they settled in towns or on farms. A popular song of this time ended with these words:

> "Good-by, old trail boss, I wish
> you no harm;
> I'm quittin' this business to go
> on the farm.
> I'll sell my old saddle and buy me
> a plow;
> And never, no never, will I rope
> another cow."

REVIEW ***What work did cowhands do?*** They rounded up the cattle, drove them from the open range to stockyards, and marked them with a brand.

End of the Cattle Kingdom

The cattle industry continued to grow throughout the late 1800s. At its peak, the Cattle Kingdom stretched all the way from Texas to Montana. But it was not long before a number of different problems began to affect cattle ranching.

It was difficult for farmers to grow crops in the same areas where cattle ranchers kept their herds. The cattle wandered into the farmers' fields and trampled or ate the crops. To keep the cattle out, farmers built fences. Some ranchers also built fences to keep cattle from wandering off the ranches.

In 1874 Joseph Glidden invented a new kind of wire that could be used to make fences. Glidden twisted two strands of steel wire together. Then he placed sharp points, or barbs, every few inches along the wire. This new kind of wire became known as **barbed wire**. A farmer or rancher could fence in fields by using wooden posts with this wire strung between them. A barbed-wire fence was easier and cheaper to build than one made of rock or wood.

History

Origins, Spread, and Influence Have students discuss the realities of cowhand life.

Q. How was the real life of a cowhand different from the way it is pictured in movies and on television? In real life cowhands were paid poorly and led hard lives, working in all kinds of weather.

End of the Cattle Kingdom

Key Content Summary

The invention of barbed wire, conflicts between farmers and ranchers, and new restrictions on the use of public lands contributed to the end of the Cattle Kingdom.

Geography

MAP THEME

Human–Environment Interactions Have students discuss the origins of the barbed-wire fence and assess the advantages and disadvantages of barbed wire.

Q. Who benefited more from barbed-wire fencing, ranchers or farmers? Most students will probably agree that farmers benefited more, since barbed wire protected their fields from cattle and restricted grazing lands, which hurt the ranchers.

Link to Reading

READ ALOUD Have volunteers read a story or poem with a western theme to the class. Possible choices include *Pecos Bill*, *The Log of a Cowboy* by Andy Adams, sections of Owen Wister's *The Virginian*, or poems by Joaquin Miller. Have students discuss whether the story or poem seems true to life.

Extend and Enrich

COOPERATIVE LEARNING

DRAW A WALL DISPLAY Divide the class into groups, and assign each group a topic related to ranching. Topics may include a cattle drive, the clothing and equipment of a cowhand, the daily routine and yearly cycle of cattle ranching, or the layout of a ranch. Challenge each group to research its topic and create a wall display. Upon completion, have groups share and discuss their portion of the wall displays.

Culture

Shared Humanity and Unique Identity Have students synthesize what they have learned about the farmers and ranchers of the Great Plains and decide why conflicts arose between these two groups.

3. CLOSE

Have students consider again the Focus question on page 520.

How do people build businesses today?

Have students use what they have learned in this lesson to compare the way ranchers built the Cattle Kingdom with the way people build businesses today.

LESSON 2 REVIEW—Answers

Check Understanding

1. by driving them to rail terminals, from which they were shipped to Chicago for slaughtering, and then on to markets in the East via refrigerated railroad cars
2. The demand for beef rose after the Civil War; ranches spread into the huge grasslands of the Great Plains; expanding railroad lines transported beef quickly; cow towns grew by railroad lines.

Think Critically

3. With thousands of head of cattle to manage over long distances through difficult country and often bad weather, cowhands had to work together to get the cattle safely to their destinations.
4. Refrigerated freight cars allowed people to ship meat to faraway markets. Barbed wire closed off the open range and water sources.

Show What You Know

Performance Assessment Have students use natural materials such as grass, sticks, and dirt. They might also want to use toy cowhand characters and plastic horses and cattle. Dioramas could be displayed on a table in the hall.

What to Look For Look for evidence that students have applied what they have learned in this lesson about cattle ranching.

Cowhands wore protective clothing such as these leather chaps (right). People began using barbed-wire fences (above) in the late 1800s. The use of barbed-wire fences led to fights between farmers and ranchers.

Not all farmers and ranchers on the Great Plains wanted fences built on open range land. Farmers did not like having the barbed-wire fences of large cattle ranches near their land. And ranchers did not like fences that kept their cattle from getting to water. Angry farmers and ranchers soon were cutting one another's barbed-wire fences. People even started shooting one another. These fights, called **range wars**, went on through the 1880s.

Finally the ranchers were told they had to move their cattle off government land or buy it. Later, farmers began raising cattle themselves. Before long, the days of the open range and the Cattle Kingdom were over.

REVIEW ***How did fences affect the Cattle Kingdom?*** They helped cause range wars between farmers and ranchers.

LESSON 2 REVIEW

Check Understanding

1. **Remember the Facts** How did ranchers in Texas get their cattle to markets in the North?
2. **Recall the Main Idea** How did ranchers build the Cattle Kingdom?

Think Critically

3. **Think More About It** Why was it important for cowhands to work together on the long drives?
4. **Cause and Effect** How did new inventions affect the Cattle Kingdom?

Show What You Know

Diorama Activity Think about the activities that would take place on a ranch. Use pictures, models, or computer visuals to make a diorama of a ranch scene. Display your diorama for the class.

ACTIVITY CHOICES

ACTIVITY BOOK

Reinforce & Extend

Use ACTIVITY BOOK, p. 104.

Reteach the Main Idea

MAKE A DIAGRAM Have students work individually to create diagrams that illustrate how ranchers built the Cattle Kingdom. You may want students to brainstorm ideas before they get started, but urge them to use their own creativity to visually represent the steps of the process. Have students share and discuss their completed diagrams.

Mining in the West

LESSON 3

FOCUS
How do individuals and groups play important roles in history?

Main Idea Read to learn how individual miners and mining companies helped settle the West.

Vocabulary
prospector
boom
bust
vigilance

While homesteaders farmed the Great Plains and cowhands worked on ranches, miners rushed to the West to get rich. After the California gold rush of 1849, there were other finds. Thousands hurried to the Colorado Territory after gold was found near Pikes Peak in 1858. Wagons with the words "Pikes Peak or Bust" painted on their sides crowded the western trails. In 1859 silver was found in the Virginia City area of present-day Nevada. Later, finds in what are now Arizona, Idaho, Montana, and Alaska started a mining boom in the West.

Mining Booms and Busts

Many of the early **prospectors**—people who searched for gold, silver, or other mineral resources—worked alone. They roamed the West, leading their packhorses loaded with gear and mining tools. With luck they might find $25 worth of gold or silver—a lot of money in those days—by scooping gravel in a stream.

In most places, the minerals above the ground were taken out in just a few years. The land was then said to have been "worked out." To get to the minerals below the ground, mines had to be dug. It became harder for prospectors working alone to find and dig out the minerals. Only large companies could afford to buy heavy equipment and to pay workers to dig mines deep underground.

Towns soon grew up around the mines. Some sprang up almost overnight. Miners at first made shelters out of whatever materials they could find, such as blankets, old shirts, and even potato sacks.

Some miners panned for gold. They used a pan to sift through gravel in a stream.

Objectives

1. Explain the difference between a mining boom and a mining bust.
2. Analyze why mining communities needed Vigilance Committees.

Vocabulary

prospector (p. 525) bust (p. 526)
boom (p. 526) vigilance (p. 527)

1. ACCESS

The Focus Question

Ask students whether they have ever taken risks to accomplish something important. Have them consider the risks individuals take today when they try to open new frontiers in space, achieve world peace, or do experiments for medical breakthroughs. Have students also identify groups today whose goals and actions may have historical significance.

The Main Idea

In this lesson students explore the mining boom and bust in the West after 1859. After students have read the lesson, have them consider how individual miners and mining companies helped settle the West.

2. BUILD

Mining Booms and Busts

Key Content Summary

The early prospectors who searched for gold, silver, and other precious minerals usually worked alone. When the minerals above ground ran out, however, the prospectors became dependent on big companies that mined the metals below ground. Towns were dependent on the success or failure of the mines.

Reading Support

PREVIEW AND READ THE LESSON Provide students with the following visual framework.

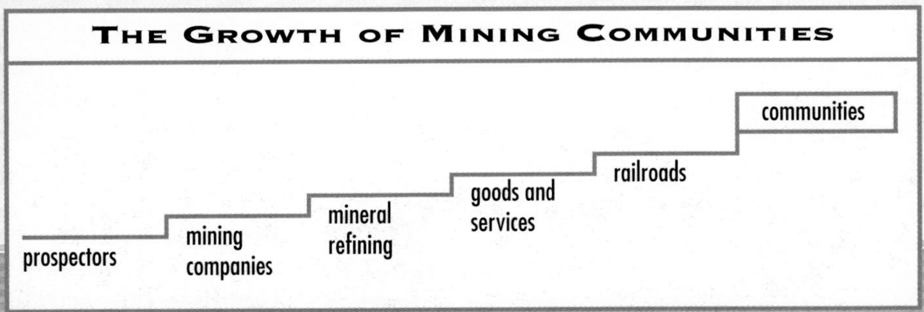

Geography

Human–Environment Interactions Have students discuss the interaction between prospectors and the environment and analyze the short-term and long-term environmental effects of the mining boom.

Economics

Productivity and Economic Growth Have students draw web diagrams that illustrate how a natural resource can lead to a primary economic activity in a region and how that primary economic activity can lead to other economic opportunities.

Life in Mining Communities

Key Content Summary

Mining camps and towns were dangerous places where fights often broke out among prospectors. Without a government, there was no law and order. Interdependent groups of people formed Vigilance Committees to help maintain law and order until governments could be formed.

Culture

Human Relationships Have students identify the conditions in mining camps that probably contributed to conflict.

Q. **Why do you think prospectors did not take their families with them?** because of the rough living conditions

As the towns grew, refineries were built to process the minerals. Stores and other businesses moved in as the mines and refineries hired more workers. Many of these workers came from cities in the East. Others were immigrants from Asia, Europe, and Latin America.

Some mining towns grew quickly. During the mining **boom**, or time of quick economic growth, towns such as Denver, Colorado, and Boise, Idaho, became centers of industry and transportation as well as mining. Other mining towns were just as quickly abandoned. During a **bust**, or time of quick economic decline, people left these towns as soon as all of the gold, silver, or other valuable minerals ran out. Some of these deserted towns, called ghost towns, can still be seen in the West today.

REVIEW ***What is the difference between a boom and a bust?*** A boom is a time of economic growth. A bust is a time of economic decline.

Life in Mining Communities

Mining towns usually started as mining camps made up of prospectors looking for minerals in the same place. Unlike farmers and ranchers, most prospectors did not take their families with them. Fights often broke out among prospectors, and mining camps were not safe places.

Mining brought many different groups of people to the West in the late 1800s. Prospectors from Mexico, the United States, Chile, and Peru each formed their own settlements. In other mining regions, the settlers were a mix of Americans born in the United States and immigrants from Europe and Asia.

Many Asian immigrants, like those in this photograph (left), came to the United States to work in mining towns. Prospectors weighed gold with a balance (above) to find out how much the gold was worth.

ACTIVITY CHOICES

Background

THE COMSTOCK LODE The richest deposit of silver and gold in the West was found in the Comstock Lode in western Nevada. Named for Henry Tompkins Paige Comstock, who laid claim to the lode, it yielded more than $300 million in gold and silver. This was the biggest strike up to that time. Virginia City became the "capital" of the lode, attracting thousands of would-be millionaires from all over the world. Wasteful mining methods and the devaluation of silver led to the decline of the lode in the 1870s.

Extend and Enrich

COOPERATIVE LEARNING

WRITE A REPORT Divide the class into groups. Assign each group a topic to research, such as Horace A. Tabor, Silver King; comparing gold and silver; different types of mining; the Homestake Gold Mine in South Dakota; and the Comstock Lode in Nevada. Tell the groups to research and write reports about their assigned topics, and to draw informative diagrams and illustrations. Have each group select a spokesperson to present its report to the other groups. Allow time for questions and answers.

TECHNOLOGY

Use THE AMAZING WRITING MACHINE™ to complete this writing activity.

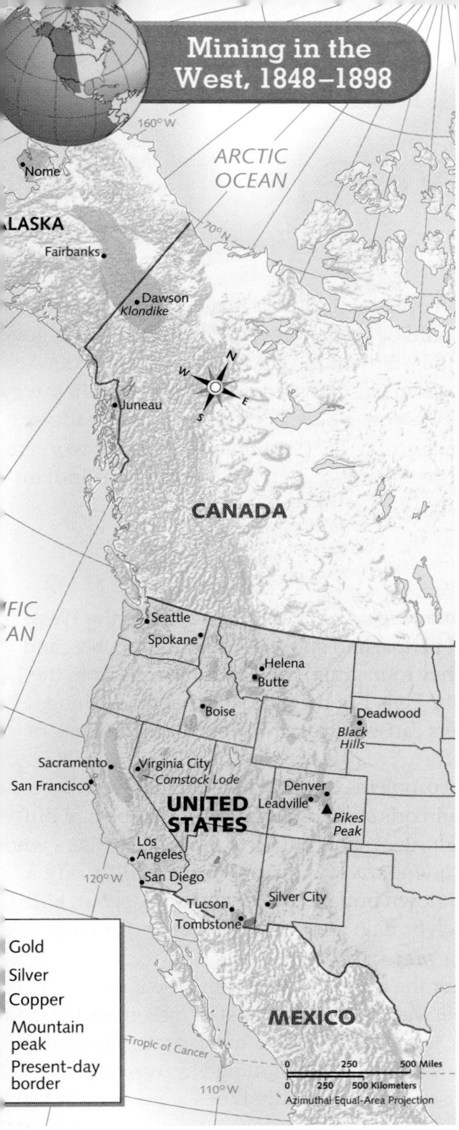

Place During the late 1800s, hundreds of thousands of people hoped to get rich by mining in the West. This map shows many of the places that had deposits of gold, silver, and copper.

■ *What mineral had the largest deposits? Where was it found?*

Irish and Chinese workers who came to work on the transcontinental railroad stayed to work in the mines when the railroad was completed.

As mining camps grew into towns, some families arrived. But there was no law and little order. The towns had no organized governments, and there were no sheriffs. "Street fights were frequent," one writer reported, "and . . . everyone was on his guard against a random shot."

In some mining communities, groups of people would form Vigilance Committees. **Vigilance** means watching over something or someone. Vigilance Committees watched over towns to maintain law and order. As more families arrived, many mining towns set up governments and started schools, hospitals, and churches.

REVIEW *What was a Vigilance Committee?*

LESSON 3 REVIEW

Check Understanding

1. **Remember the Facts** What cities of today started as mining communities?
2. **Recall the Main Idea** How did individual miners and mining companies help settle the West?

Think Critically

3. **Cause and Effect** What caused some mining communities to become ghost towns?
4. **Think More About It** Why do you think early mining communities were dangerous places to live?

Show What You Know

Brainstorming Activity Think about the problems in mining communities. Work with a partner to prepare a list of five laws you might make in starting a new government in a mining community.

a group that watched over a mining town to maintain law and order

Civics and Government

Purposes of Government Have students discuss why groups of people formed Vigilance Committees.

***Q.* How did mining camps prove that groups of people living in a community need some form of government?** There were frequent street fights, random shootings, and no guidelines for organizing the community.

Visual Analysis

Learn from Maps Have students answer the question in the caption. gold; Alaska

3. CLOSE

Have students consider again the Focus question on page 525.

How do individuals and groups play important roles in history?

Have students use what they have learned in this lesson about prospectors and mining companies to explain how individuals and groups both can play important roles in history.

LESSON 3 REVIEW—Answers

Check Understanding

1. Denver, Colorado, and Boise, Idaho
2. Individual miners and mining companies both brought economic activity to the region, which led to the establishment of permanent communities in the West.

Think Critically

3. economic decline due to the depletion of precious minerals
4. There were no governments to impose law and order; greed for gold and silver bred conflict.

Show What You Know

Performance Assessment Have students present their laws to the class, and record their suggestions on the board. Then hold a class referendum to select the five most important laws.

What to Look For Look for an understanding of the basic rules that allow a community to function peacefully.

Reteach the Main Idea

COOPERATIVE LEARNING

DRAW A DIAGRAM Divide the class into groups. Assign some groups to draw diagrams showing how individual miners helped settle the West. Assign other groups to draw diagrams showing how mining companies helped settle the West. Have students share and discuss their diagrams.

ACTIVITY BOOK

Reinforce & Extend

Use ACTIVITY BOOK, p. 105.

LESSON 4 PAGES 528–531

Objectives

1. Identify the causes for the disappearance of the buffalo from the Great Plains.
2. Analyze why the United States did not uphold its treaty with the Sioux.
3. Summarize the tragedy of the Nez Perces.
4. Analyze the conflict between the Apaches and the United States government.

Vocabulary

reservation (p. 529)

1. ACCESS

The Focus Question

Ask students to analyze why people in the United States celebrate holidays such as Presidents' Day, Memorial Day, Independence Day, and Thanksgiving. Have volunteers describe the traditions they consider special and conclude why it is important to preserve traditions.

The Main Idea

In this lesson students explore the growing conflict between the Indians of the Great Plains and the United States government. After students have read the lesson, have them analyze the reasons for the conflict and identify the changes that were forced on the Indians.

2. BUILD

Railroads and the Buffalo

Key Content Summary

As a result of railroads and the influx of settlers to the Great Plains, almost 15 million buffalo were killed between 1860 and 1880. The destruction of the buffalo changed forever the traditional way of life of the Plains Indians.

LESSON 4

FOCUS In what ways do people today work to keep their traditions?

Main Idea As you read, find out how Native Americans in the late 1800s worked to keep their ways of life.

Vocabulary
reservation

Conflict in the West

The native peoples of the Great Plains thought the western lands would be theirs forever. The United States government had promised them the lands in a treaty in 1830. At first miners and traders just crossed Indian lands on their way to California and Oregon. By 1862, however, homesteaders and ranchers were settling the Great Plains. Railroad workers arrived, too. The newcomers began killing the Plains Indians' most important resource—the buffalo.

Railroads and the Buffalo

The railroads made it easier for settlers to live in the West. Railroads carried people and supplies to farms, ranches, and mining towns. They took grain, beef, and minerals from the West to cities in the East. But the railroads that made things easy for the settlers caused great problems for the Indians of the Plains.

In this scene from the 1870s, railroad workers shoot at buffalo blocking the tracks.

The problems began when hunters working for the railroads started killing large numbers of buffalo. Hunters shot buffalo to feed the workers who were laying track. William "Buffalo Bill" Cody, a well-known buffalo hunter and army scout, killed enough buffalo to feed 1,000 workers for more than a year.

After the railroads were built, the killing continued. Many buffalo were shot by settlers for their hides, which were sold to make coats. The Plains Indians believed this hunting was wasteful because only the animals' hides were used. When they hunted, the Plains Indians used almost every part of the buffalo to meet their needs.

In the 1860s about 15 million buffalo lived on the Great Plains. Within 20 years, fewer than 1,000 were left. Without the buffalo for food, clothing, and shelter, the traditional way of life of the Plains Indians came to an end.

REVIEW ***Why did the buffalo disappear from the Plains?***
They were killed by hunters and settlers.

ACTIVITY CHOICES

Reading Support

USE CONTEXT CLUES Before students read the lesson, ask them which of the following statements would have been made by the American Indians and which would have been made by the United States government. Students may correct their answers as they read.

1. This is our land; we should not be asked to leave. American Indians
2. We will give you a reservation where you may preserve your traditional way of life. United States government
3. We must send in soldiers so that we can reclaim the land and mine the gold. United States government
4. "Once I moved about like the wind. Now I surrender to you and that is all." American Indians

Location This map shows the major battles fought during the struggle between Native Americans and the United States Army over land in the West.

- *Where was the Battle of the Little Bighorn? Where was the last major battle between Native Americans and the Army?*

Fighting Back

The Sioux (SOO) were a powerful tribe of he northern Plains. In the mid-1800s miners nd settlers began appearing on Sioux land. o protect these people, in 1865 the United tates Army began guarding a road that assed through Sioux land and led to the gold nines of Montana. For three years the Sioux, ed by Chief Red Cloud, fought miners and oldiers as they traveled through Indian lands.

Finally, in 1868, the United States govern-nent signed a treaty with the Sioux. In the reaty, the government leaders promised that he Indians would have a reservation west of he Missouri River in the Black Hills of the Dakota Territory. A **reservation** is an area of and set aside by the government as a home or Native Americans. In the treaty, the gov-rnment promised that this land would elong to the Sioux forever.

The treaty did not last long, however. In 1875 gold was discovered on the Great Sioux Reservation. Thousands of miners paid no attention to the treaty and went looking for gold in the Black Hills. The government tried to buy back the land from the Sioux, but the Sioux would not sell it. In 1876 United States soldiers marched in to take the land.

Lieutenant Colonel George Custer led some of the soldiers. Two of the chiefs leading the Sioux were Sitting Bull and Crazy Horse. Custer attacked the Sioux and their Cheyenne allies at the Little Bighorn River. His soldiers were quickly surrounded by 2,500 Indians. In the battle that followed, Custer and all the soldiers he led into the battle were killed.

After the Battle of the Little Bighorn, the government sent more soldiers into the Black Hills. The Sioux were made to return to their reservation, which was now much smaller

Culture

Shared Humanity and Unique Identity Have students compare and contrast the attitude of the Plains Indians toward the buffalo with that of the settlers toward the buffalo.

Fighting Back

Key Content Summary

Conflict between the Sioux and the United States Army intensified after the Sioux refused to sell their reservation back to the United States government when gold was discovered on the land.

Civics and Government

Purposes of Government Remind students that one of the purposes of government is to resolve conflicts through the use of treaties. Have students analyze how and why the United States government broke its own treaty with the Sioux.

Visual Analysis

Learn from Maps Have students answer the question in the caption. Montana; at Wounded Knee in South Dakota

Meet Individual Needs

ADVANCED LEARNERS Have advanced learners read a biography, choosing from the following: Buffalo Bill Cody, Crazy Horse, Chief Red Cloud, Sitting Bull, George Custer, Chief Joseph, or Geronimo. Ask students to prepare presentations for the class from the first-person perspective.

Background

WOUNDED KNEE MASSACRE The battle at Wounded Knee occurred because the U.S. government feared that the Sioux's new Ghost Dance religion would inspire the Indians to rise up against the government. Among the beliefs of the Ghost Dance followers was that a tidal wave of new earth would cover the white people and renew the land. To prevent an uprising, officials sent troops to arrest the tribal leaders. Chief Sitting Bull was killed during this attempted arrest. A short time later the followers of Chief Big Foot were captured and brought to Wounded Knee. When the troops ordered the Sioux to disarm, a shot rang out and the troops opened fire. Among the Sioux killed at the Wounded Knee massacre were many women and children.

The Nez Perces

Key Content Summary

The government tried to force the Nez Perces to change their lives by moving them from Oregon to a reservation in Idaho. Led by Chief Joseph, the Nez Perces refused to move and tried to escape to Canada. After they were caught by U.S. troops, Chief Joseph advised his people to give up.

Geography

Movement Have students trace the route of the Nez Perces on a physical map of the United States. Discuss the difficult terrain and the climate of the region in relation to the attempted escape.

History

People and Events Across Time and Place Challenge students to analyze why the United States Army did not let the Nez Perces cross the border into Canada.

Visual Analysis

Learn from Maps Have students answer the questions in the caption. east to west; as the settlers moved from the East to the West, they took more and more land from the Indians.

PRIMARY SOURCE

Source: *Chief Joseph: The Biography of a Great Indian.* Chester Anders Fee. Wilson-Ericson, 1936.

than the one the government originally had promised.

In 1890 a terrible massacre took place at Wounded Knee Creek in South Dakota. About 300 Sioux were killed. It was the last battle between the Sioux and the United States Army.

REVIEW ***Why did Custer attack the Sioux?*** to try to take back Sioux reservation land

The Nez Perces

The United States government used force against other Indian tribes, including the Nez Perces (NES PER•suhz). The Nez Perces lived on the Columbia Plateau in Oregon. In 1877 the government told the tribe it had to move to a small reservation in Idaho. The Nez Perce leader, Chief Joseph, said no.

During the summer of 1877, Chief Joseph and 800 men, women, and children tried to escape to Canada. They traveled for 15 weeks through the present-day states of Idaho, Wyoming, and Montana. Less than 40 miles (64 km) from the Canadian border, the group was caught by United States soldiers. Telling his people to give up, Chief Joseph said,

> “I am tired of fighting. Our chiefs are killed. . . . It is cold and we have no blankets. Our little children are freezing to death. . . . My heart is sick and sad. From where the sun now stands, I will fight no more forever.”

REVIEW ***Why did Chief Joseph surrender?*** He was tired of fighting, and his people were dying.

Movement This map shows when Indian tribes lost their lands to the United States government. Some lands were bought through treaties. Others were taken. Some lands were never officially given up.

- *In what direction were lands lost over time? How does this relate to the movement of settlers?*

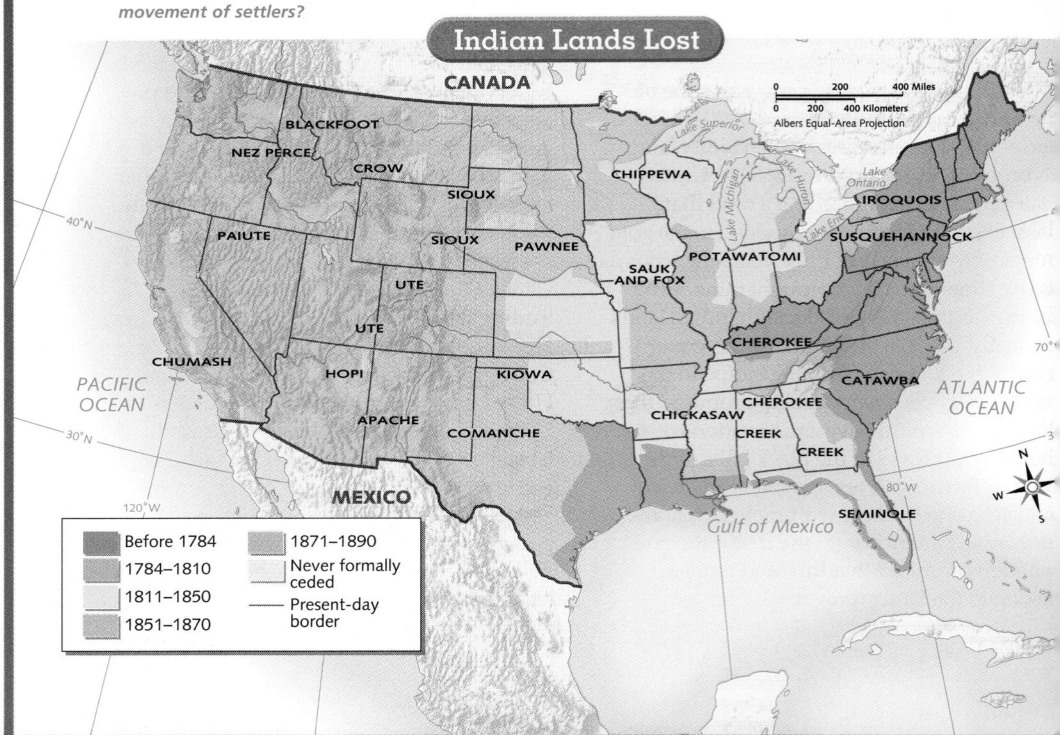

Activity Choices

Smithsonian Institution®

Go to the Internet site at *http://www.si.edu/harcourt/socialstudies* to examine a portrait of Chief Joseph in Native Americans at the National Portrait Gallery.

Link to Language Arts

WRITE TO EXPLAIN Have students reread the statement made by Geronimo as he surrendered to the soldiers. Ask them to write an interpretation of the statement and explain the feelings it seems to express. You may want to have student volunteers share their writings orally with the class.

Extend and Enrich

COOPERATIVE LEARNING

PAINT A SCENE Divide the class into three groups, and assign each group a tribe discussed in the lesson. Ask each group to plan a scene that represents the tragedy the assigned tribe experienced in losing its homelands. Provide large paper for a wall display, and have the groups sketch out their scenes in pencil and then paint them. Have the groups share and discuss the scenes they have created.

The Apaches

By 1880 almost all the Indians in the Jnited States had been made to move onto eservations. Among the last to give up were he Apaches (uh•PACH•eez), who were led by chief named Geronimo. The Apaches fought ne of the longest of the many wars between Native Americans and the United States.

The war began in the 1850s when miners nd settlers started moving onto the Apache ands of present-day New Mexico and Arizona. Fear and hate grew as each side ttacked the other. In 1877 the United States government made the Apaches move to the San Carlos Reservation in Arizona.

On the hot, dry reservation land, it was hard o grow food. Food that the government gave o the reservation was often spoiled. In 1881 he government found out that the Apaches planned to rebel. Soldiers were sent onto the eservation. Afraid that the army would attack, Geronimo and about 75 of his people went to he Sierra Madre of Mexico. From these mountains, they attacked Arizona settlers.

The Indians escaped capture for the next five ears. Then, in 1886, an Apache scout working or the United States Army led the soldiers to Geronimo's hiding place. Geronimo told the oldiers, "Once I moved about like the wind. Now I surrender to you and that is all."

Geronimo's surrender ended years of war between American Indians and the government. Although there was still some fighting, most Indians had been made to leave their ands and move onto reservations. Once the ndians were on reservations, the government tried to change the Indians' traditional ways of life. The Indians would not accept his. By the 1920s government officials realzed that their efforts to change the Indians were not working. In 1924 Congress granted citizenship to all American Indians and later gave control of reservation lands to the ndians that lived on them.

REVIEW *Why did the Apaches plan to rebel?*
Because it was hard to grow food on their reservation, and food from the government was often spoiled.

Geronimo's Apache name, Goyaale, means "the smart one." The Mexicans gave him the name Geronimo, which means "Jerome" in Spanish.

LESSON 4 REVIEW

Check Understanding

1. **Remember the Facts** What was the most important resource for the Plains Indians?
2. **Recall the Main Idea** How did Native Americans in the late 1800s work to keep their ways of life?

Think Critically

3. **Personally Speaking** How do you think you might feel if you were made to change your way of life?
4. **Think More About It** How could the government have ended the conflict with the Plains Indians peacefully? Explain your answer.

Show What You Know

Time Line Activity With a partner, draw and illustrate a time line for the major events in this lesson. Display your time line in the classroom.

The Apaches

Key Content Summary

A long-standing conflict between the Apaches in the Southwest and the United States government ended in 1886 when the skillful Apache leader, Geronimo, finally surrendered to the United States Army.

Geography

Human–Environment Interactions

Have students analyze how the environment of the San Carlos Reservation reinforced the Apaches' determination not to live on a reservation.

3. CLOSE

Have students consider again the Focus question on page 528.

In what ways do people today work to keep their traditions?

Have students use what they have learned in this lesson to compare the ways the Plains Indians worked to keep their traditions with the ways people today work to keep their traditions.

LESSON 4 REVIEW—Answers

Check Understanding

1. the buffalo
2. by fighting the government's efforts to move them off their lands and send them to reservations

Think Critically

3. Students will probably say that they would feel angry about such efforts and would resist them.
4. Suggestions might include honoring treaties with the Indians; creating reservations on the Indians' own traditional lands rather than moving them elsewhere; allowing them to follow their traditions; and keeping settlers off Indian territory.

Show What You Know

Performance Assessment Display the time lines on the bulletin board, and have students discuss the dates of the actions against Indian tribes from different regions.

What to Look For Look for evidence that students understand the sequence of events covered in the lesson.

Reteach the Main Idea

COOPERATIVE LEARNING

MAKE A CHART Divide the class into small groups, and ask each group to use the textbook as a resource to make a chart describing how the various Indian tribes worked to keep their traditions. The title of the chart could be *Preserving Traditions.* The column titles could be *Sioux, Nez Perces,* and *Apaches.* Use the charts as a basis for reviewing the main idea and for having students note the similarities among the tribes in their attempts to preserve their traditions.

ACTIVITY BOOK

Reinforce & Extend

Use ACTIVITY BOOK, p. 106.

Time Line

Ask students to share what they recall about each event shown on the time line.

Connect Main Ideas

Use the organizer to review the main ideas of the chapter. Have students use their textbooks to complete or check their work. Allow time for them to discuss and compare their responses.

ACTIVITY BOOK

Summarize the Chapter

A copy of the graphic organizer appears on ACTIVITY BOOK p. 107.

TRANSPARENCY

A copy of the graphic organizer appears on TRANSPARENCY 43.

Write More About It

Write an Advertisement

Responses will vary. Students' advertisements should focus on the attractive aspects of the Great Plains environment, such as the fertile soil and the vast expanses of land.

Write a Conversation

Accept all answers that reflect why the Nez Perces might have chosen to escape to Canada rather than be forced to resettle in Idaho.

TECHNOLOGY

Use THE AMAZING WRITING MACHINE™ to complete the writing activities.

TECHNOLOGY

Use TIMELINER™ DATA DISKS to complete and summarize the chapter.

CHAPTER 16 REVIEW

1840 — 1855

1849 • California gold rush begins

1862 • Homestead Act passed

Connect Main Ideas

Use this graphic organizer to show how the chapter's main ideas are connected. Write the main idea of each lesson. A copy of the organizer appears on page 107 of the Activity Book.

Possible answers to the graphic organizer appear on page 512C of this Teacher's Edition.

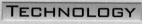

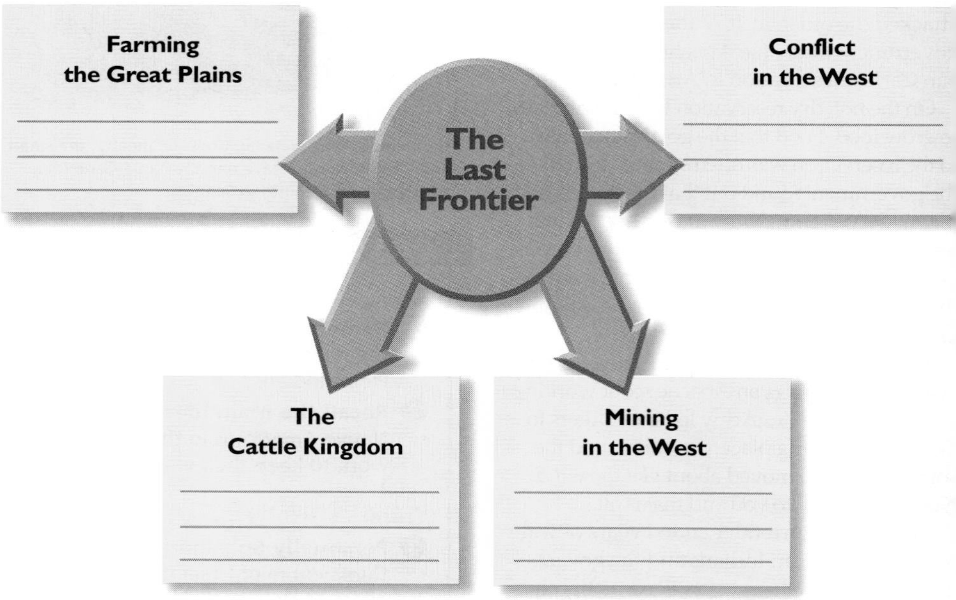

Write More About It

Write an Advertisement To attract easterners to the Great Plains, the railroads placed advertisements in newspapers, offering low-cost land to settlers. Write an advertisement describing the benefits of living in the Great Plains region that would encourage people to move there.

Write a Conversation Write a conversation that could have taken place between Chief Joseph and other leaders of the Nez Perces as they tried to escape to Canada in 1877. The conversation should describe the Indians' experiences as they fled from the United States Army soldiers.

532 • Chapter 16

Use Vocabulary

1. open range (p. 522)
2. prospector (p. 525)
3. homesteader (p. 513)
4. vigilance (p. 527)
5. reservation (p. 529)

Check Understanding

6. More settlers would bring them more business. (p. 513)
7. James Oliver (p. 515)
8. they provided a way for people to g their cattle to market (p. 520)
9. barbed wire (p. 524)
10. Vigilance Committees (p. 527)
11. the battle at Wounded Knee Cre (p. 530)
12. by making them move to new lan (pp. 529–530)

1885 • 1900 • 1915 • 1930

Late 1800s
• The Cattle Kingdom comes to an end

1924
• U.S. citizenship granted to all American Indians

CHAPTER 16

REVIEW

Use Vocabulary

Choose a term from this list to complete each of the sentences that follow.

homesteader **reservation**
open range **vigilance**
prospector

1. The government allowed ranchers on the Great Plains to use the land as _____.
2. A _____ searched for gold, silver, or other mineral resources.
3. A _____ was a person who settled government land.
4. _____ means watching over someone or something.
5. When gold was discovered on the Sioux _____, thousands of miners went there to look for gold.

Check Understanding

6. Why did railroad owners want people to settle on the Great Plains?
7. Who invented a stronger plow that helped farmers cut through the thick sod?
8. How were railroads important to early cow towns?
9. What new invention caused the range wars in the Plains?
10. Who brought law and order to mining towns?
11. What was the last battle between the Sioux and the United States Army?
12. How did the government try to change the way Indians lived?

Think Critically

13. **Past to Present** When the buffalo disappeared, the Plains Indians lost a resource that was very important to them. Name some natural resources that, if lost today, would greatly change the way we live.
14. **Personally Speaking** Would you have chosen to be a homesteader, a cowhand, or a prospector? Explain your answer.

Apply Skills

Understand a Climograph Use the climographs on page 519 to answer the questions.

15. Which city has about the same amount of precipitation every month?
16. Which city has a warmer average temperature in March?
17. What conclusion can be made about the average temperatures in June, July, and August for both cities?

Read More About It

Pioneer Girl by Andrea Warren. Morrow Junior Books. This book tells the true story of Grace McCance, a young pioneer who lived on a Nebraska homestead with her family.

Visit the Internet at **http://www.hbschool.com** for additional resources.

Chapter 16 • **533**

Read More About It

Additional books are listed in the Multimedia Resource Center on page 476D of this Teacher's Edition.

Unit Project Check-Up

Check to make sure that students have added to their lists of details for their conversations. Some events that might be on their lists include mining and mining communities.

ASSESSMENT PROGRAM

Use CHAPTER 16 TEST, pp. 131–134.

Think Critically

13. Answers will vary. Some students may discuss changes that might result from scarce oil, timber, or water resources. Accept all answers that show an understanding of the connection between key natural resources and lifestyle.
14. Responses will vary but should show an understanding of the life of a homesteader, cowhand, or prospector.

Apply Skills

Understand a Climograph

15. Philadelphia
16. Philadelphia
17. The temperatures for both cities are nearly the same, and this is the hottest time of the year for both cities.

Making Social Studies Relevant

See the Link

Personal Response

To help students understand the reasons people immigrate, have them discuss why they, their ancestors, or people they know came to the United States. You may wish to write students' responses on the board.

The Main Idea

Have students read the selection and analyze why people immigrate to the United States today.

Q. **Why did people come to the United States?** Many came to start new lives or to get away from hard times in their homelands.

Understand the Link

Culture

Thought and Expression Have students analyze the meaning of the quotation from Emma Lazarus's poem. Ask them to speculate on the reactions immigrants might have to the Statue of Liberty as they enter New York Bay today.

Visual Analysis

Interpret Pictures Ask students to conclude why the American flag and the Statue of Liberty were the pictures chosen for this feature.

Q. **What do you think these American symbols mean to immigrants?** freedom, hope, caring, opportunity for a better life

"Give me your tired, your poor, Your huddled masses yearning to breathe free..."

Coming to the United States Today

Since colonial times, people from all over the world have come to the Americas, many of them to the United States. Some chose to come to start new lives, sometimes because of hard times in their homelands.

In 1883 an American named Emma Lazarus wrote "The New Colossus," a poem that helped welcome the hundreds of thousands of people who were immigrating to the United States each year. The poem is written on the base of the Statue of Liberty, which stands in New York Bay. Part of it says

> "Give me your tired, your poor,
> Your huddled masses yearning to
> breathe free . . ."

The Statue of Liberty and Lazarus's words continue to welcome the large numbers of immigrants who come to the United States today. The United States still attracts people from all over the world who hope to find better lives and greater freedom. The Statue of Liberty has become a well-known symbol of this freedom.

534 • Unit 8

Activity Choices

Background

THE LARGE PICTURE Remind students that the stars on the flag represent the 50 states of the United States and that the stripes stand for the 13 original colonies. In 1782 Congress designated a meaning for each color on the flag: red for hardiness and courage; blue for vigilance, perseverance, and justice; white for purity and innocence.

The Statue of Liberty is one of the largest statues in the world. Lady Liberty, as it is sometimes called, holds in her left hand a tablet inscribed with the date of the Declaration of Independence. At her feet a broken shackle symbolizes the overthrow of tyranny.

Think and Apply

BUILDING CITIZENSHIP

Think about why people come to the United States today. Collect magazine and newspaper articles about present-day immigrants. Compare their reasons for moving with those of immigrants of the early twentieth century. Report your findings to the class.

HARCOURT BRACE — Visit the Internet at **http://www.hbschool.com** for additional resources.

CNN Turner Learning — Check your media center or classroom video library for the Making Social Studies Relevant videotape of this feature.

History

Connections Past to Present to Future On the board, draw an immigration chart with *Then* and *Now* columns. Have students recall earlier units and volunteer reasons why people came to the Americas in the past. Write their responses in the *Then* column. Ask students why people come to the United States today, and write their reasons in the *Now* column. Have students discuss the reasons for similarities and differences in the two columns.

Complete the Link

Summarize

After Europeans explored the Americas, people from all over the world were drawn there for a variety of reasons. Today many immigrants want to come to the United States, and some take great risks to gain the freedoms and economic opportunities the United States has to offer.

Think and Apply

Have students use their articles about present-day immigrants to create a bulletin board display on immigration. In addition, you may wish to have the class prepare and send a letter to a regional immigration center requesting current information about immigration.

Meet Individual Needs

ENGLISH LANGUAGE LEARNERS Ask volunteers to relate how they felt when they first came to the United States. Ask them to describe their experiences. Then invite volunteers to tell what the Statue of Liberty means to them.

Link to Reading

WRITE BOOK REPORTS Ask the school librarian to help students in locating books that tell an immigration story, such as *Immigrant Girl: Becky of Eldridge Street* by Harvey Brett; *Kiki: A Cuban Boy's Adventures in America* by Hilda Perera; *It's Only Goodbye* by Virginia T. Gross; *If Your Name Was Changed at Ellis Island* by Ellen Levin; or *The Long Way to a New Land* by Joan Sandin. Have students write book reports focusing on the immigration experiences of the main characters and their reasons for immigrating.

Technology

HARCOURT BRACE — Visit the Internet at **http://www.hbschool.com** for additional resources.

Video

CNN Turner Learning™ **Check your media center or classroom video library for the Making Social Studies Relevant videotape of this feature.**

Visual Summary

Take a Look

Remind students that a visual summary is a way to represent the main events in a story. Point out that this visual summary reviews some of the main events students read about in Unit 8.

Visual Analysis

Interpret Pictures Have students, individually or in small groups, examine this visual summary. Ask them to identify the images shown and explain what each image tells about United States history from 1865 to 1920.

Summarize the Main Ideas

Have students read the summary statements on pages 536–537. Lead a class discussion about each scene, and have students offer supporting details for each main idea illustrated.

UNIT 8 REVIEW

Visual Summary

Summarize the Main Ideas
Study the pictures and captions to help you review the events you read about in Unit 8.

Illustrate a Story
Make your own visual summary for one of the following: 1) the growth of hub cities, 2) the migration of African Americans to northern cities, 3) the building of skyscrapers, or 4) the working conditions for factory workers during the late 1800s.

1 After the Civil War, American industry grew and changed. Asian immigrants worked on the transcontinental railroad, which linked the Atlantic and Pacific coasts.

3 During the late 1800s and early 1900s, millions of immigrants came to the United States hoping to find better lives.

4 Offers of free and low-cost land brought many settlers to the Great Plains.

6 Mining towns developed, as prospectors movec to the West in the hope of finding gold.

536 • Unit 8

Activity Choices

Meet Individual Needs

ENGLISH LANGUAGE LEARNERS Provide key words to help students provide supporting details for each main idea illustrated. For beginning language learners you may wish to ask them to point to the area on the visual summary that relates to the events as they are being discussed.

UNIT POSTER

Use the UNIT 8 VISUAL SUMMARY POSTER to summarize the unit.

2 Inventions helped industry grow. A new process allowed steel to be produced more cheaply. The inventions of the lightbulb and the telephone changed everyday life.

5 Ranchers on the Great Plains raised cattle. Cowhands worked hard, especially on cattle drives and roundups.

7 Indians on the Great Plains fought for their homelands against United States soldiers. But by 1890, most Indians in the United States had been forced onto reservations.

Sharing the Activity

Provide time for students to complete the Illustrate a Story activity on page 536. Allow time for students to present their completed visual summaries to the rest of the class. Urge students to ask questions about images or details in the illustrations they find interesting or difficult to understand.

SUMMARIZE THE UNIT

Pair students and have them use the illustrations in the unit and in the visual summary to tell the unit's "story" to their partners. Or have the class play a game similar to Pictionary®, using the content of the unit as the basis for their picture clues.

TECHNOLOGY

HARCOURT BRACE

Use TIMELINER™ DATA DISKS to discuss and summarize the unit.

TECHNOLOGY

HARCOURT BRACE

Use THE AMAZING WRITING MACHINE™ RESOURCE PACKAGE to complete the writing activities.

Extend and Enrich

COOPERATIVE LEARNING

MAKE A DIORAMA Divide the class into small groups, and ask each group to plan and make a diorama of one of the important events in the unit. Have each group obtain a large box from a local grocery store, and help the groups brainstorm ideas for materials to be used in their dioramas. Ask each group to sketch out the plan for the diorama. All group members should contribute to the collection of materials for the dioramas and to their construction. Have groups share and explain their completed dioramas. Then you may wish to have students set up a hall display.

Use Vocabulary

1. refinery (p. 485)
2. monopoly (p. 486)
3. regulate (p. 494)
4. naturalization (p. 499)
5. vaquero (p. 522)
6. boom (p. 526)

Check Understanding

7. inland, close to the natural resources needed by mills and factories (p. 486)
8. by forming labor unions and going on strike (pp. 491–492)
9. Cattle sold for much more there than they did on the Plains. (p. 520)
10. Lieutenant Colonel George Custer; when gold was discovered the United States government wanted to take the land back from the Sioux (p. 529)

Think Critically

11. Student answers will vary. Accept all that are well-supported. Look for responses to include similarities such as the need to make a profit, conflict between workers and owners, and use of new technologies. One major difference is increased government regulation to reduce pollution and to ensure fair and equal treatment of workers.
12. Students should recognize that hearing a familiar language in a new place, cooking some of the same foods, and helping each other get adjusted are reasons immigrants might like to live in neighborhoods made up of people from the same country. Accept all reasonable responses.
13. Students' personal opinions will differ. Some might feel government leaders did not care about them and only cared about the rich; others might express agreement because they believe government noninterference is the only way that industry can grow.
14. Students should recognize that because of the work of the AFL, business leaders began to listen to workers' demands. Among these demands were higher wages, a shorter workday, better working conditions, accident insurance, and an end to child labor.

UNIT 8 REVIEW

Use Vocabulary

Write the term that correctly matches each definition below.

boom	**refinery**
monopoly	**regulate**
naturalization	**vaquero**

1. a factory where crude oil is made into usable products
2. almost complete control of an industry
3. to control by law
4. the process through which immigrants become citizens
5. a Mexican cowhand
6. a time of quick economic growth

Check Understanding

7. Where did new industrial cities develop in the late 1800s and early 1900s?
8. How did workers try to improve their working conditions in the late 1800s?
9. Why was it important for ranchers to get their cattle to northern cities?
10. Who led United States soldiers into the Battle of the Little Bighorn? What caused this battle?

Think Critically

11. **Past to Present** How are industries in the United States today like industries in the late 1800s? How are they different?
12. **Think More About It** Why do you think immigrants often moved to neighborhoods made up of other immigrants from the same country?
13. **Personally Speaking** Suppose you were a worker in the late 1800s. How might you feel about people who thought that government should leave factory owners and their businesses alone? Explain your answer.
14. **Cause and Effect** What effect did the American Federation of Labor have on the treatment of workers by business leaders?

Apply Skills

Use a Time Zone Map Suppose you live in Nevada and you have a friend who lives in Utah. Use the map below to answer the questions.

15. When you are getting ready for school at 7:00 A.M., what time is it in Utah?
16. When your friend gets home from school at 3:00 P.M. in Utah, what time is it in Nevada?

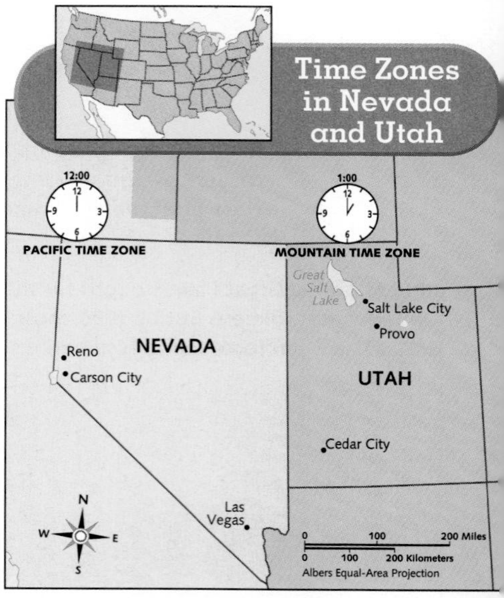

538 • Unit 8

Apply Skills

Use a Time Zone Map

15. 8:00 A.M.
16. 2:00 P.M.

ASSESSMENT PROGRAM

Use UNIT 8 TEST,
Standard Test, pp. 135–139.
Performance Tasks, pp. 140–141.

REMEMBER
- Share your ideas.
- Cooperate with others to plan your work.
- Take responsibility for your work.
- Help one another.
- Show your group's work to the class.
- Discuss what you learned by working together.

ACTIVITY

Make a **Diorama**

With some classmates, make a diorama that shows a ranch, a homestead, an Indian village, or a mining camp. Include a scene that shows how the people lived and the work they did. Display your diorama in the classroom.

ACTIVITY

Paint a **Mural**

Work with a group of classmates to paint a mural that shows how cities were changing in the late 1800s and early 1900s. Show both the problems that cities faced and the opportunities they offered. Display the mural in your classroom.

ACTIVITY

Hold a **Debate**

Hold a debate on the need for labor unions in the late 1800s and early 1900s. To prepare for the debate, work in groups. With the other members of your group, make a list of the issues that concern factory owners. Then make a list of the issues that concern workers. Your class should decide which groups will represent each side in the debate. During the debate, group members should take turns speaking.

Unit Project Wrap-Up

Perform a Simulation Work with two of your classmates to complete the Unit Project on page 477. Write a conversation that might have taken place among three immigrants from different countries. From your lists, you and your partners should decide on which details to include in your conversation. You should also decide which country each member of your group will represent. Write the conversation with your partners, and perform it for your classmates. While role-playing the conversation, each member of your group should hold the flag from the country he or she is representing.

539

Cooperative Learning Workshop

MAKE A DIORAMA

Performance Assessment Provide students with materials to make a diorama. Divide the class into groups based on the scene each student prefers to create. Skill levels will vary, so encourage students to choose which part of the diorama they would like to help with: cutting, designing, labeling, painting, or presenting.

What to Look For Make sure students work cooperatively. The dioramas should present accurate depictions of what life was like and the work the people had to perform in order to survive.

UNIT 8 REVIEW

PAINT A MURAL

Performance Assessment Provide students with drawing materials and a suitable surface on which they can draw their mural. Link this activity to the unit theme of conflict and cooperation by examining the completed mural with the class and having them point out examples of conflict and cooperation in their work together and in urban America.

What to Look For Look for an understanding of what changes were happening in the cities.

HOLD A DEBATE

Performance Assessment Assign each group a different concern to research: the right to strike, the right to form a union, working conditions, wages, hours, child labor, benefits, or job safety. Begin by having a group representing the factory owners present its opinion on an issue.

What to Look For Look for an understanding of the reasons why workers during this time period decided to join together to fight for workers' rights and why factory owners resisted unions.

Unit Project Wrap-Up

Performance Assessment
Students' conversations should show what life was like for immigrants. Link this activity to the theme of commonality and diversity by discussing the similarities and differences between immigrants. Also discuss hardships immigrants had to face. You may want to videotape the conversations.

What to Look For Conversations should show why immigrants came to the United States as well as the obstacles and prejudice they faced.

GAME TIME!

Use GAME TIME! to reinforce content.

Unit 9

pages 540–603

BECOMING A WORLD POWER

The major objectives in this unit are organized around the following themes:

UNIT THEMES

- ▶ CONFLICT & COOPERATION
- ▶ COMMONALITY & DIVERSITY
- ▶ INDIVIDUALISM & INTERDEPENDENCE
- ▶ CONTINUITY & CHANGE

Preview Unit Content

Unit 9 focuses on the expanding role of the United States as a world power in the first half of the twentieth century. Students learn about new U.S. territories, the country's influence overseas, domestic problems and Americans' efforts to solve them, and inventions that changed life in the United States forever. Students will also discover why the United States became involved in World War I and World War II.

You may wish to begin the unit with the Unit 9 Visual Summary Poster and activity. The illustration that appears on the poster also appears on pages 600–601 in the Pupil Book to help students summarize the unit.

UNIT POSTER

Use the UNIT 9 VISUAL SUMMARY POSTER to preview the unit.

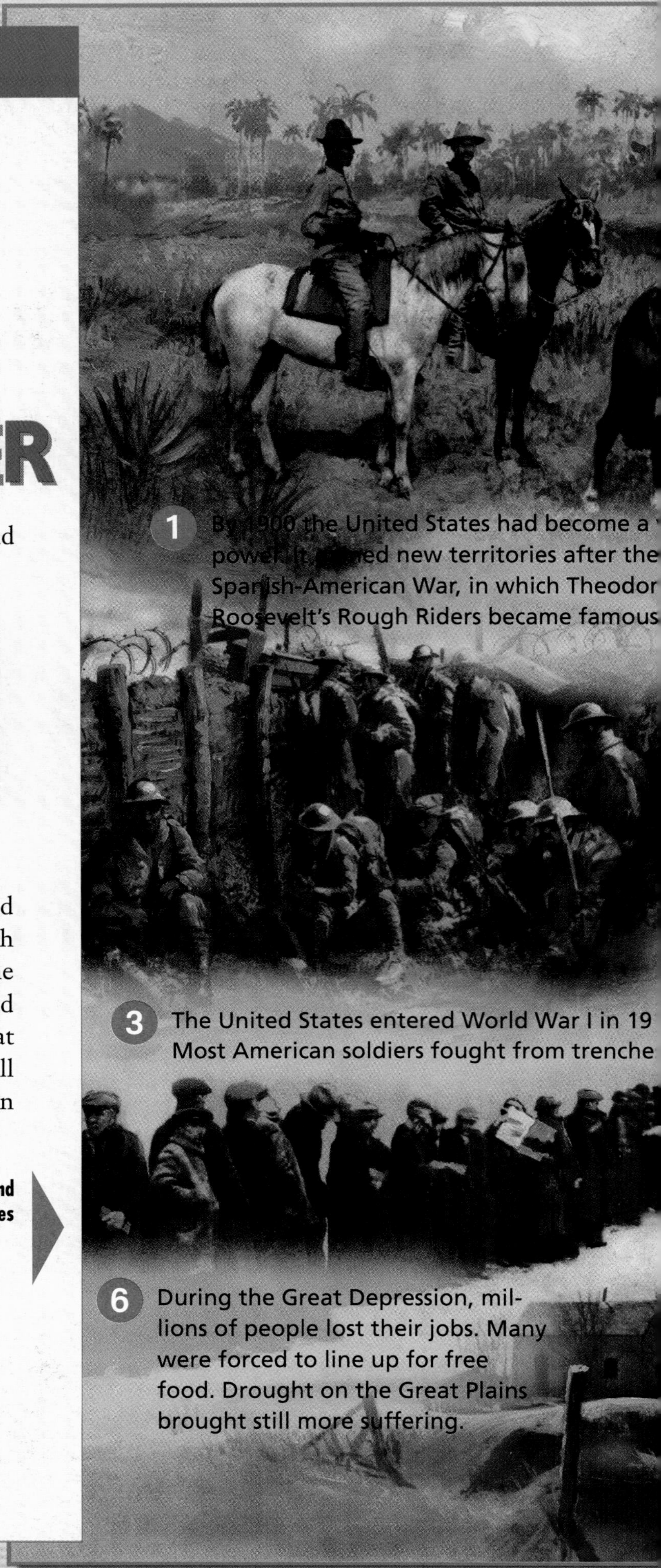

1 By 1900 the United States had become a power. It gained new territories after the Spanish-American War, in which Theodor Roosevelt's Rough Riders became famous

3 The United States entered World War I in 19 Most American soldiers fought from trenche

6 During the Great Depression, millions of people lost their jobs. Many were forced to line up for free food. Drought on the Great Plains brought still more suffering.

2 The Panama Canal opened in 1914. It linked the Atlantic and Pacific oceans.

WOMEN'S RIGHT
TO VOTE!

4 Women gained the right to vote in 1920, when the Nineteenth Amendment to the Constitution was ratified.

5 Automobiles became popular in the 1920s. During the Roaring Twenties, the United States economy boomed.

7 The United States entered World War II in 1941, when Pearl Harbor was attacked.

8 After World War II, The United Nations was formed to help keep world peace.

Unit 9 Planning Chart

	CONTENT AND SKILLS	RESOURCES INCLUDING ▶ TECHNOLOGY
UNIT INTRODUCTION **Becoming a World Power** pp. 540–545	Unit Opener and Unit Preview Set the Scene with Literature **This Man's War** by Charles F. Minder	Unit 9 Visual Summary Poster Unit 9 Home Letter Unit 9 Text on Tape Audiocassette Video Experiences: Social Studies ▶ TIMELINER
CHAPTER 17 **The United States and the World** pp. 546–567	LESSON 1: Building an Empire **SKILL:** Compare Map Projections LESSON 2: Progressives and Reform LESSON 3: The Great War **SKILL:** Recognize Propaganda Chapter Review	Activity Book, pp. 108–114 Music Audiocassette Transparencies 44A–44B Transparency 45 Transparency 46 Assessment Program Chapter 17 Test, pp. 143–146 ▶ MAPSKILLS ▶ THE AMAZING WRITING MACHINE ▶ TIMELINER ▶ INTERNET
CHAPTER 18 **Good Times and Bad** pp. 568–597	LESSON 1: The Roaring Twenties LESSON 2: The Great Depression and the New Deal LESSON 3: Learn History through Literature **Children of the Dust Bowl** by Jerry Stanley LESSON 4: World War II LESSON 5: The Allies Win the War **SKILL:** Read Parallel Time Lines Chapter Review	Activity Book, pp. 115–121 Transparency 47 Transparency 48 Assessment Program Chapter 18 Test, pp. 147–150 ▶ THE AMAZING WRITING MACHINE ▶ TIMELINER ▶ INTERNET
UNIT WRAP-UP pp. 598–603	Making Social Studies Relevant Unit 9 Visual Summary Unit Review	Making Social Studies Relevant Video Unit 9 Visual Summary Poster Game Time! Assessment Program Unit 9 Test, Standard Test, pp. 151–155 Performance Tasks, pp. 156–157 ▶ THE AMAZING WRITING MACHINE ▶ TIMELINER ▶ INTERNET

TIME MANAGEMENT

4 WEEKS

WEEK 1	WEEK 2	WEEK 3	WEEK 4
Unit Introduction / Chapter 17	Chapter 17	Chapter 18	Chapter 18 / Unit Wrap-Up

See pages 546A and 568A for Chapter Planning Charts with details by lesson.

Multimedia Resource Center

Books

Easy

Fritz, Jean. *You Want Women to Vote, Lizzie Stanton?* Putnam, 1995. The story of Elizabeth Cady Stanton, Susan B. Anthony, and the women's suffrage campaign.

Parker, Nancy Winslow. *Locks, Crocs, & Skeeters: The Story of the Panama Canal.* Greenwillow, 1996. A colorful look at the great feat of building the Panama Canal.

Average

Colman, Penny. *Rosie the Riveter: Women Working on the Home Front During World War II.* Crown, 1995. An examination of the way World War II changed women's lives and the impact of those changes on the United States.

Freedman, Russell. *Eleanor Roosevelt: A Life of Discovery.* Clarion, 1997. This award-winning book looks at the life and achievements of Eleanor Roosevelt.

Stanley, Jerry. *Children of the Dust Bowl: The True Story of the School at Weedpatch Camp.* Crown, 1992. Examines the lives of children of migrant workers living in a federal labor camp in the 1930s.

Van der Rol, Ruud, Rian Verhoeven, and Anna Quindlen. *Anne Frank: Beyond the Diary: A Photographic Remembrance.* Viking, 1993. Primary sources and historical essays detail the life of Anne Frank.

Challenging

Chamber, Veronica, and B. Marvis. *The Harlem Renaissance* (African American Achievers series). Chelsea House, 1997. A description of the vibrant cultural life in Harlem's African American community in the 1920s.

Stanley, Jerry. *I Am an American.* Crown, 1994. A true story of life in a Japanese American relocation camp in 1942.

Whitelaw, Nancy. *Theodore Roosevelt Takes Charge.* Albert Whitman, 1992. Highlights the life and accomplishments of the twenty-sixth President of the United States.

LIBRARY

See the SOCIAL STUDIES LIBRARY for additional resources.

Computer Software

CD-ROM

Timecity Flashback Atlas. Cambrix Publishing, 1995, URL *http://www.cambrix.com/index.htm,* (813) 993-4274. Macintosh/Windows dual format. An archive of aerial photos of major cities in the United States allows students to experience life in major cities throughout the United States in the 1930s and 1940s. Images of the same places today show the changes that have occurred over the years.

World War I Era. National Geographic Educational Services, 1998, URL *http://www.nationalgeographic.com,* (800) 368-2728. Students explore the causes and aftermath of World War I. The involvement of women and African Americans in the war is discussed.

Video

Videotape

The Great Depression and the New Deal. Schlessinger Media, 1996, URL *http://www.libraryvideo.com/sm/smhome.html,* (610) 645-4000. Introduces the causes of the Great Depression and the impact of the stock market crash. It also covers the New Deal and the Dust Bowl.

The Magic Decade: America in the 1920s. Thomas S. Klise, 1994, URL *http://www.klise.com,* (800) 937-0092. Students explore the changes in culture that took place in the United States following World War I, including flappers, flagpole sitters, ukuleles, and other pastimes.

FREE & INEXPENSIVE MATERIALS

Activity

For free resources and activities relating to key events that took place between 1915 and 1945, including European politics and the Great Depression, visit the Internet at: *http://www.bbc.co.uk/education/modern*

Lesson Plans

For a set of lesson plans titled *First Lady of the World: Eleanor Roosevelt at Val-Kill,* which examines the humanitarian efforts of Eleanor Roosevelt, write or phone:

Jackdaw Publications
P.O. Box 503
Armawalk, NY 10501
(800) 789-0022

For an order form and a list of 54 other classroom lesson plans, visit: *http://www.cr.nps.gov/nr/twhp/descrip.html*

TECHNOLOGY

Visit the Internet at **http://www.hbschool.com** for additional resources.

Note that information, while correct at time of publication, is subject to change.

Linking Social Studies

BULLETIN BOARD IDEA

Create a Family Tree Show President Franklin Delano Roosevelt's background by creating his family tree. Divide the class into three groups. Have one group outline a tree with many branches on the bulletin board and create an appropriate title for the display. Have the second group research Roosevelt's mother's side of the family and fill in the right side of the tree. Have them label this side with FDR's mother's name. Have students in the third group research Roosevelt's father's side of the family and fill in the left side of the tree. Have them label this side with FDR's father's name. (See below for an example of what the completed tree might look like, or see *American Heritage Illustrated History of the United States,* Volume 14, *The Roosevelt Era,* by Robert G. Athearn.) If there is time, challenge students to research President Theodore Roosevelt's relation to Franklin Roosevelt. Extend this activity by having students work at home with a family member to create their own family trees. Post volunteers' completed family trees around the outside of the bulletin board.

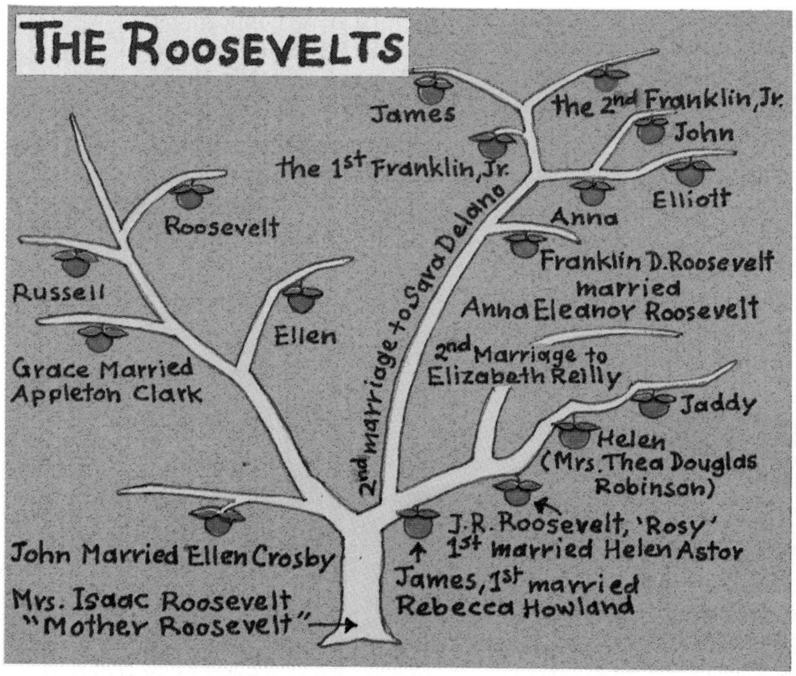

LANGUAGE ARTS

Write Japanese Senryu To help students understand the feelings of Japanese Americans during World War II, have the class write poems like the ones below that first-generation Japanese Americans wrote while imprisoned in relocation camps. Explain that some relocation camp prisoners wrote Japanese poetry called *senryu,* or three-line poems that compress intense emotion into a brief statement. Here are three examples of *senryu:*

Thirty years
in America
become a dream. *Sasabune*

As one
of the Japanese
I gather my belongings. *Keiho*

Enduring
and still enduring
the color of my skin. *Kikyo*

Divide the class into small groups and have them imagine what it would be like to live in a relocation camp. Have each group write five *senryu* poems about these feelings and read their completed poems to the class.

TECHNOLOGY

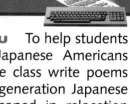

Visit the Internet at **http://www.hbschool.com** for additional resources.

Smithsonian Institution®

Harcourt Brace Social Studies helps to bring the Smithsonian Institution to your classroom. Visit the Internet site at *http://www.si.edu/harcourt/socialstudies* for a directory of virtual tours, on-line exhibits, and pictures of primary sources from the Smithsonian Institution.

Across the Curriculum

MUSIC

Sing About the Depression To expand students' comprehension of the effects of the Great Depression, play the song "Brother, Can You Spare a Dime?" by E. Y. Harburg and Jay Gorney. This song became the "anthem" of the Great Depression. Divide the class into small groups. Have each group write a song with at least two verses and a chorus that expresses life during the Depression. Have each group share the completed song with the rest of the class. Discuss the feelings portrayed in each song and the reasons the Depression raised these feelings.

READING

Create a Story Map To extend students' use of story maps, have them design a posterboard story map. Divide the class into four groups. Assign one of the following topics to each group: the Depression, the Dust Bowl, the Holocaust, and the bombing of Hiroshima. Have each group choose a book to read on the assigned topic. After all students have read their group's book, provide each group with markers, old magazines, scissors, and a large sheet of posterboard. Have each group use the markers and posterboard to create a story map of the book illustrated with drawings or magazine pictures. Display the completed posters.

SCIENCE

Make a Submarine To help students understand how a submarine works, have them make their own submarine. Divide the class into small groups. Provide the following supplies for each group: a plastic bottle with a lid (cut a small hole in the lid and in the bottom of the bottle), a large bowl of water, and a short length of plastic tubing. Have one student put a finger over the hole in the bottom of the bottle while another student fills the bottle with as much water as possible. Put the lid on the bottle. Push the tubing through the bottle-top opening and slide it into the bottle. Lower the bottle into the bowl of water and blow hard into the plastic tube. As the air goes inside the bottle, it will push out some of the water. The bottle will rise as more air is forced into it. This principle—buoyancy—allows the submarine to "float."

HOW TO INTEGRATE YOUR DAY

Use these topics to help you integrate social studies into your daily planning.

READING THEMES

- Life Stories
- Family
- Technology
- Music for a Purpose

ART

Make a Display, p. 562
Research Depression-Era Photographs, p. 575

INTEGRATED LANGUAGE ARTS

Write Japanese Senryu, p. 540E
Write Propaganda, p. 564
Read Poetry, p. 572
Write to Persuade, p. 585

MATHEMATICS

Compare Distance Accuracy, p. 555
Calculate the Value of the Dollar, p. 570

MUSIC

Sing About the Depression, p. 540F
Sing World War I Songs, p. 561

SCIENCE

Make a Submarine, p. 540F
Collect and Display Facts, p. 551
Demonstrate Aerodynamics, p. 571
Make a Diagram, p. 577
Report on Technology, p. 585
Draw a Diagram, p. 591

HEALTH AND PHYSICAL EDUCATION

Research Diseases and Cures, p. 551
Report on Polio, p. 576

READING

Create a Story Map, p. 540F
Read and Interpret Poems, p. 550
Read and Summarize a Biography, p. 560
Read and Discuss, p. 584

WORLD LANGUAGES

Research the Holocaust, p. 590

Unit 9

Assessment Options

The **Assessment Program** allows all learners many opportunities to show what they know and can do. It also provides ongoing information about each student's understanding of social studies.

FORMAL ASSESSMENT

- *Lesson Reviews* (**Pupil Book,** at end of lessons)
- *Chapter Reviews* (**Pupil Book,** at end of chapters)
- *Chapter Tests* (**Assessment Program,** pp. 143–150)
- *Unit Review* (**Pupil Book,** pp. 602–603)
- *Unit Assessment* (**Assessment Program:** *Standard Test,* pp. 151–155 *Individual Performance Task,* p. 156 *Group Performance Task,* p. 157)

STUDENT SELF-EVALUATION

- *Individual End-of-Project Summary* (**Assessment Program,** p. 6)
- *Group End-of-Project Checklist* (**Assessment Program,** p. 7)
- *Individual End-of-Unit Checklist* (**Assessment Program,** p. 8)

INFORMAL ASSESSMENT

- REVIEW *Questions* (**Pupil Book,** throughout lessons)
- *Think and Apply* (**Pupil Book,** at end of skill lessons)
- *Visual Summary* (**Pupil Book,** pp. 600–601)
- *Social Studies Skills Checklist* (**Assessment Program,** pp. 4–5)

PERFORMANCE ASSESSMENT

- *Show What You Know* (**Pupil Book,** at end of Lesson Reviews)
- *Cooperative Learning Workshop* (**Pupil Book,** at end of Unit Review)
- *Scoring Rubric for Individual Projects* (**Assessment Program,** p. 9)
- *Scoring Rubric for Group Projects* (**Assessment Program,** p. 10)
- *Scoring Rubric for Presentations* (**Assessment Program,** p. 11)

PORTFOLIO ASSESSMENT

Student-selected items may include:

- *Link to Language Arts—Write to Persuade* (**Teacher's Edition,** p. 585)
- *Practice and Apply* (**Activity Book,** pp. 109–110)
- *Home Involvement* (**Teacher's Edition,** p. 541)
- *A Guide to My Social Studies Portfolio* (**Assessment Program,** p. 12)

Teacher-selected items may include:

- *Unit Assessment* (**Assessment Program,** pp. 151–157)
- *Individual End-of-Unit Checklist* (**Assessment Program,** p. 8)
- *Social Studies Portfolio Summary* (**Assessment Program,** p. 13)
- *Portfolio Family Response* (**Assessment Program,** p. 14)

Objectives

Chapter 17

- ▶ Explain how the United States benefited from its acquisition of Alaska. (p. 547)
- ▶ Describe the conflict of interests over the acquisition of Hawaii. (p. 547)
- ▶ Analyze the causes and effects of the Spanish-American War. (p. 547)
- ▶ Evaluate the role of President Theodore Roosevelt in world affairs. (p. 547)
- ▶ Summarize the steps Roosevelt took to build the Panama Canal. (p. 547)
- ▶ Recognize two map projections. (p. 554)
- ▶ Identify advantages and disadvantages of different map projections. (p. 554)
- ▶ Summarize the Square Deal. (p. 556)
- ▶ Evaluate the reforms made in the Wisconsin state government. (p. 556)
- ▶ Explain how the NAACP and the NUL worked to make life better for African Americans. (p. 556)
- ▶ Analyze the consequences of the alliances of major European nations in 1914. (p. 559)
- ▶ Identify the reasons the United States entered the Great War. (p. 559)
- ▶ Describe the weapons introduced in World War I. (p. 559)
- ▶ Summarize the ways American women helped in wartime. (p. 559)
- ▶ Explain the purpose of the League of Nations. (p. 559)
- ▶ Recognize propaganda. (p. 564)
- ▶ Analyze and evaluate a propaganda statement. (p. 564)

Chapter 18

- ▶ Identify the boom economy that followed World War I. (p. 569)
- ▶ Analyze the impact of the assembly line on automobile production. (p. 569)
- ▶ Explain how Charles Lindbergh's solo flight affected travel. (p. 569)
- ▶ Identify popular forms of entertainment in the 1920s. (p. 569)
- ▶ Summarize African American achievements in the arts in the 1920s. (p. 569)
- ▶ Analyze why the good times of the 1920s ended. (p. 574)
- ▶ Describe the Great Depression. (p. 574)
- ▶ Summarize the goals of the New Deal. (p. 574)
- ▶ Identify and evaluate the major government programs of the New Deal. (p. 574)
- ▶ Explain the term "Dust Bowl." (p. 579)
- ▶ Explain how the dust storms affected people. (p. 579)
- ▶ Describe how people tried to protect themselves from the storms. (p. 579)
- ▶ Analyze reasons for the rise of dictators in the 1930s. (p. 583)
- ▶ Describe how dictators' aggressive actions led to World War II. (p. 583)
- ▶ Identify the events that caused the United States to enter World War II. (p. 583)
- ▶ Summarize the cooperation and sacrifices of Americans on the home front. (p. 583)
- ▶ Discuss the treatment of Japanese Americans during the war. (p. 583)
- ▶ Summarize the Allied battle plans that led to D day. (p. 589)
- ▶ Describe the Holocaust. (p. 589)
- ▶ Analyze how the Allies defeated Japan. (p. 589)
- ▶ Identify the causes of the Cold War. (p. 589)
- ▶ Compare two parallel time lines. (p. 595)
- ▶ Relate events in Europe to those in the Pacific in 1945. (p. 595)

STANDARD TEST

NAME ______________________ DATE __________

Unit 9 Test

Part One: Test Your Understanding *(4 points each)*

DIRECTIONS: ***Circle the letter of the best answer.***

1. Which of the following events led the United States into a war with Spain?
- **A.** the American attack on Manila
- **B.** the Spanish attack on Miami, Florida
- **(C.)** the sinking of the battleship *Maine*
- **D.** the firing on Fort Sumter

2. The Panama Canal is important to world trade because
- **A.** it links the Indian Ocean with the Caribbean Sea.
- **B.** it is the only body of water in the world large enough for cargo ships to travel on.
- **C.** it connects the Mississippi River to the Pacific Ocean.
- **(D.)** it provides a shortcut between the Atlantic and Pacific oceans.

3. President Theodore Roosevelt promoted the conservation of natural resources by
- **A.** making it illegal for hunters to shoot animals for sport.
- **B.** passing strong laws against pollution.
- **C.** forcing manufacturers to pay heavy fines for the use of raw materials.
- **(D.)** setting aside land for national parks and wilderness areas.

4. What was the purpose of Governor Robert La Follette's merit system?
- **A.** to give the government control over the meat industry
- **(B.)** to give government jobs only to people who were qualified
- **C.** to stop businesses from charging prices that were too high
- **D.** to stop strikes by workers' unions

5. What organization was formed in 1909 by W. E. B. Du Bois and other leaders to help African Americans?
- **A.** Interstate Commerce Commission
- **B.** Urban League
- **C.** Hull House
- **(D.)** National Association for the Advancement of Colored People

(continued)

UNIT 9 TEST   Assessment Program 151

STANDARD TEST

NAME ______________________ DATE ____________

6. During World War I, Russia, France, Italy, Britain, and the United States fought against the
   A. Allied Powers.
   (B.) Central Powers.
   C. Communist Powers.
   D. Axis Powers.

7. In World War I soldiers fought one another
   A. in tanks.
   B. in submarines.
   (C.) from ditches dug in the ground.
   D. with propaganda.

8. As a result of Charles Lindbergh's flight across the Atlantic Ocean,
   A. U.S. military leaders decided to use airplanes in World War I.
   (B.) people became more interested in air travel.
   C. the price of airplanes decreased.
   D. the Wright brothers decided to buy Lindbergh's airplane designs.

9. An important poet in the Harlem Renaissance was
   A. Carrie Chapman Catt.
   B. W. E. B. Du Bois.
   C. D. W. Griffith.
   (D.) Langston Hughes.

10. When the banks failed and Americans lost their money,
    (A.) people bought fewer goods and factory workers lost their jobs.
    B. people in France and Britain sent donations of food and money.
    C. only people who had invested in the stock market could pay for food.
    D. the government gave all homeless people free houses.

11. How did the New Deal affect the power and size of the federal government?
    (A.) The power and size of the federal government increased.
    B. The states gained more power than the federal government.
    C. Workers were able to take power away from the federal government by forming unions.
    D. The federal government became smaller but more powerful.

(continued)

STANDARD TEST

NAME ______________________ DATE ____________

12. After World War I, the countries of Germany, the Soviet Union, Spain, Italy, and Japan
    A. paid Britain and France for the costs of the war.
    (B.) were ruled by dictators.
    C. voted to become democratic countries.
    D. started the Cold War.

13. The United States entered World War II
    A. when Germany invaded Poland.
    B. when the United States started island-hopping.
    (C.) after Japan bombed Pearl Harbor.
    D. before the Philippines attacked Japan.

14. What caused Japan to surrender at the end of World War II?
    A. The Japanese army was trapped on Iwo Jima.
    B. Allied armies invaded the Japanese islands.
    (C.) The United States dropped two atomic bombs on Japan.
    D. Germany stopped giving the Japanese any aid.

(continued)

STANDARD TEST

NAME ______________________ DATE ____________

Part Two: Test Your Skills (24 points)

DIRECTIONS: Use the two maps below to answer the questions that follow.

MAP A

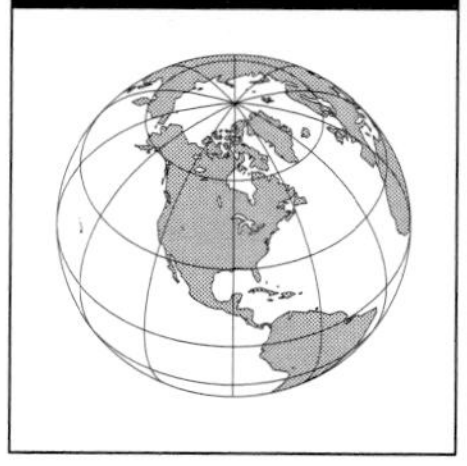

MAP B

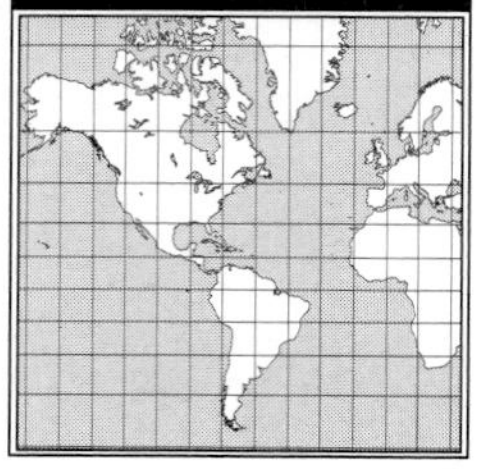

15. On which map are the meridians spaced equally? on Map B
16. On which map are the parallels spaced equally? on Map A
17. On which map do meridians get closer at the pole? on Map A
18. On which part of the maps do the land shapes appear the same?
    in the center of the maps
19. On which part of the maps are the land shapes the most different?
    near the North Pole
20. Which map shows direction more accurately?
    Map B

(continued)

STANDARD TEST

NAME ______________________ DATE ____________

Part Three: Apply What You Have Learned

DIRECTIONS: Complete each of the following activities.

21. ***Popular Entertainment*** (4 points)
    List two new forms of entertainment that became popular in the 1920s.
    Possible responses:
    listening to the radio
    going to the movies

22. ***Participants in World War II*** (6 points)
    During World War II, the Axis Powers fought against the Allies. List the countries that made up each side in the war.

Axis Powers	Allies
a. Germany	d. United States
b. Italy	e. Britain
c. Japan	f. Soviet Union

23. ***Essay*** (10 points)
    Theodore Roosevelt and Franklin D. Roosevelt both served as President of the United States. Write a one-paragraph essay describing the reforms made by these two Presidents while in office.
    Possible response:
    Both Presidents made reforms designed to make America a better place to live. Theodore Roosevelt's reforms included the Interstate Commerce Commission, the Pure Food and Drug Act, and the Meat Inspection Act. He also was involved in the conservation movement. Franklin Roosevelt's reforms included the Civilian Conservation Corps (CCC) and the Works Progress Administration (WPA). He also was involved in making unions legal, setting a minimum wage, establishing Social Security, and building hydroelectric dams.

PERFORMANCE TASK

NAME ______________________ DATE ____________

Individual Performance Task

Graph It!

In this activity you will use the facts at the right to make a line graph about unemployment in the United States. Then you will use your graph to answer some questions.

PERCENTAGE OF UNEMPLOYED WORKERS, 1929–1943

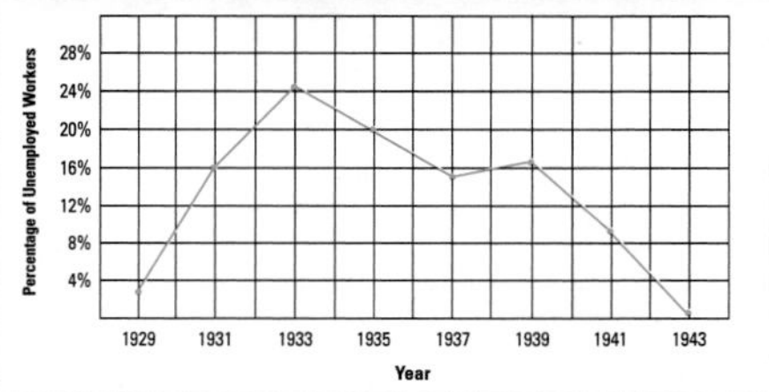

Year	Percentage
1929	3%
1931	16%
1933	25%
1935	20%
1937	14%
1939	17%
1941	10%
1943	2%

Source: U.S. Department of Commerce, Bureau of the Census, *Historical Statistics of the United States from Colonial Times to 1970*, Volume 1

1. What effect did the stock market crash have on unemployment in the United States?
   Possible response: It caused unemployment to rise.

2. What effect did the New Deal have on unemployment in the United States?
   Possible response: It caused unemployment to fall slightly.

3. What effect did World War II have on unemployment in the United States?
   Possible response: It caused unemployment to fall a lot.

PERFORMANCE TASK

NAME ______________________ DATE ____________

Group Performance Task

Billboard Advertising

A billboard along a highway or street is designed to advertise a product, a service, or a cause to the people passing by. Most people have only 10 to 15 seconds to read a billboard. In this task your group will design and make a mural-size billboard that might have been used in World War II.

Step 1 Each person in your group should do research on one of the following billboard ideas:

- a billboard to get men or women to join one branch of the military (The military branches in World War II were the Army, Army Air Corps, Navy, Marines, and Coast Guard. Each branch of the military had a special unit for women.)
- a billboard to support rationing
- a billboard encouraging security and secrecy
- a billboard on women in the workforce
- a billboard on buying bonds to finance the war

Step 2 As a group, select the topic you want to use for the billboard.

Step 3 As a group, decide what words and pictures will be on your billboard. Remember that you must get your message across in a very brief period of time. Look at billboards in your area to see how they use just a few words to get their messages across.

Step 4 Make a rough sketch of your mural-size billboard. Then use watercolors or markers to make a final copy. Display your billboard where others can see it.

Rubrics

SCORING RUBRICS The scoring rubrics for evaluating individual projects, group projects, and student presentations may be found in the **Assessment Program**, pages 9–11.

CRITERIA The criteria listed below may be used to measure students' understanding of social studies and their ability to think critically.

Individual Task

Graph It!

✓ Create line graphs using data supplied in tabular form.

✓ Use a line graph to interpret relationships between unemployment, the stock market crash, the New Deal, and World War II.

✓ Use a line graph to interpret the relationship between the New Deal and unemployment.

Group Task

Billboard Advertising

✓ Identify the essential elements of selected products, services, or causes from World War II.

✓ Create a billboard that portrays one or more of the essential elements of the selected product, service, or cause, and convinces the viewer to endorse or purchase the advertised product, service, or cause.

REMINDER

You may wish to preview the performance assessment activities in the COOPERATIVE LEARNING WORKSHOP on page 603. Students may complete these activities during the course of the unit.

Unit 1	Unit 2	Unit 3	Unit 4	Unit 5
The Ancient Americas	Explorations and Encounters	Our Colonial Heritage	The American Revolution	The New Nation

Introduce the Unit

Personal Response

Have students recall what they learned in the previous unit about events that took place in the United States during the late 1800s. Explain that while the United States was developing into a strong economic power, it was also becoming more involved in international affairs. Ask students to analyze possible connections between the new economic strength of the United States and the nation's interest in people and places outside its borders.

Link Prior Learning

Use the titles on the bar across the top of pages 540–541 to review the chronology of earlier units. Use the painting on these pages to lead a discussion concerning what students already know about U.S. involvement in international affairs from 1890 to 1945.

Q. **What appears to be the theme of this unit, according to the painting?** war

Becoming a World Power

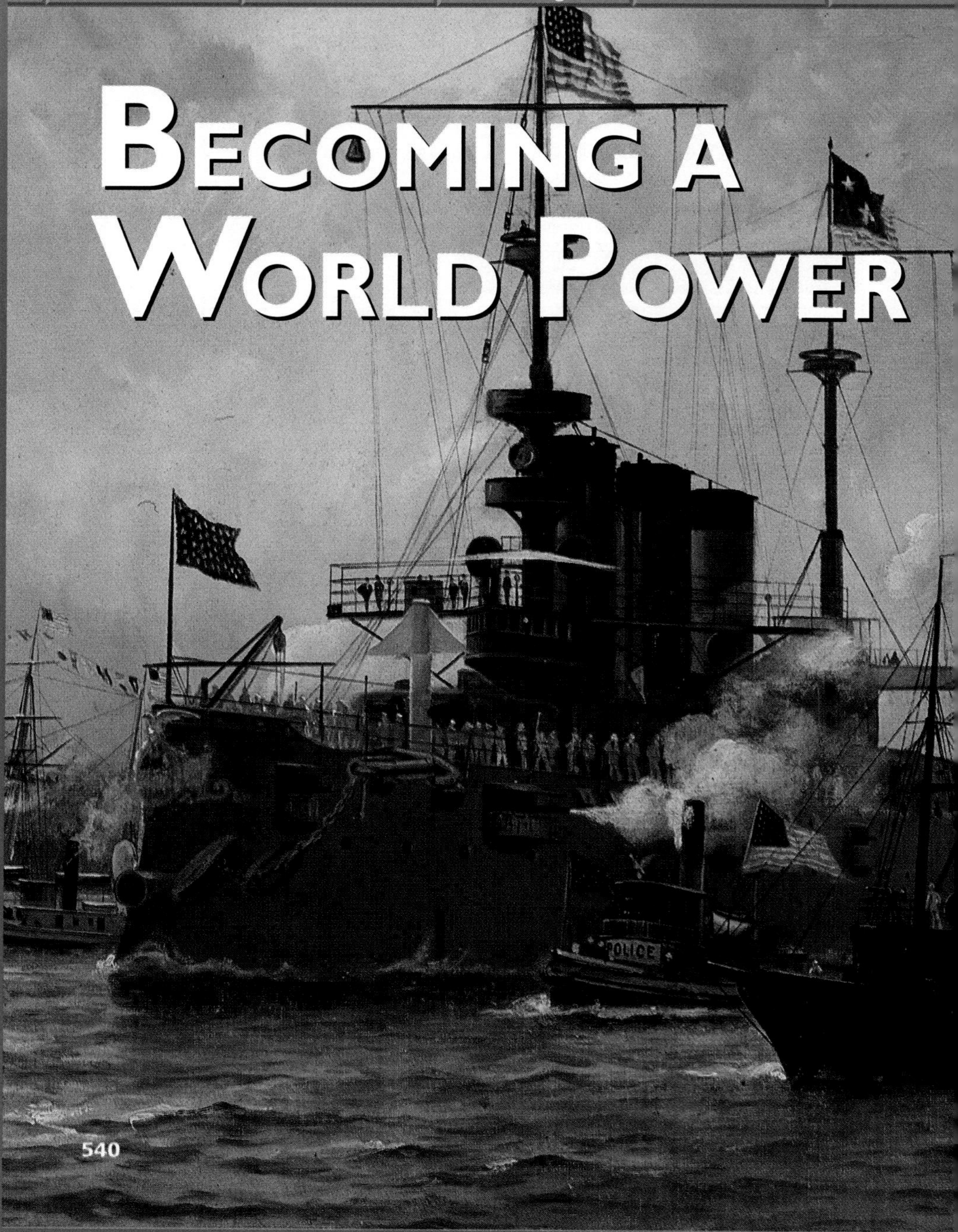

Activity Choices

Background

THE LARGE PICTURE After the 1862 Civil War battle of the ironclads *Monitor* and *Merrimack*, warships in the United States and Europe were built of steel. The guns on these new warships were mounted on revolving turrets, reducing the number of maneuvers a ship had to make during battles. Commodore George Dewey was in command of the navy's Asiatic Squadron when he received orders in 1898 to capture or destroy the Spanish fleet in Manila, Philippines. Dewey had four cruisers—the *Olympia*, *Baltimore*, *Boston*, and *Raleigh*—and two gunboats. In less than 24 hours, Dewey's fleet had destroyed Spain's ten cruisers and gunboats. Later, Admiral Dewey presided over the first General Board of the Navy Department, formed in 1900.

AUDIO

Use the UNIT 9 TEXT ON TAPE AUDIOCASSETTE for a reading of this unit.

Unit 9

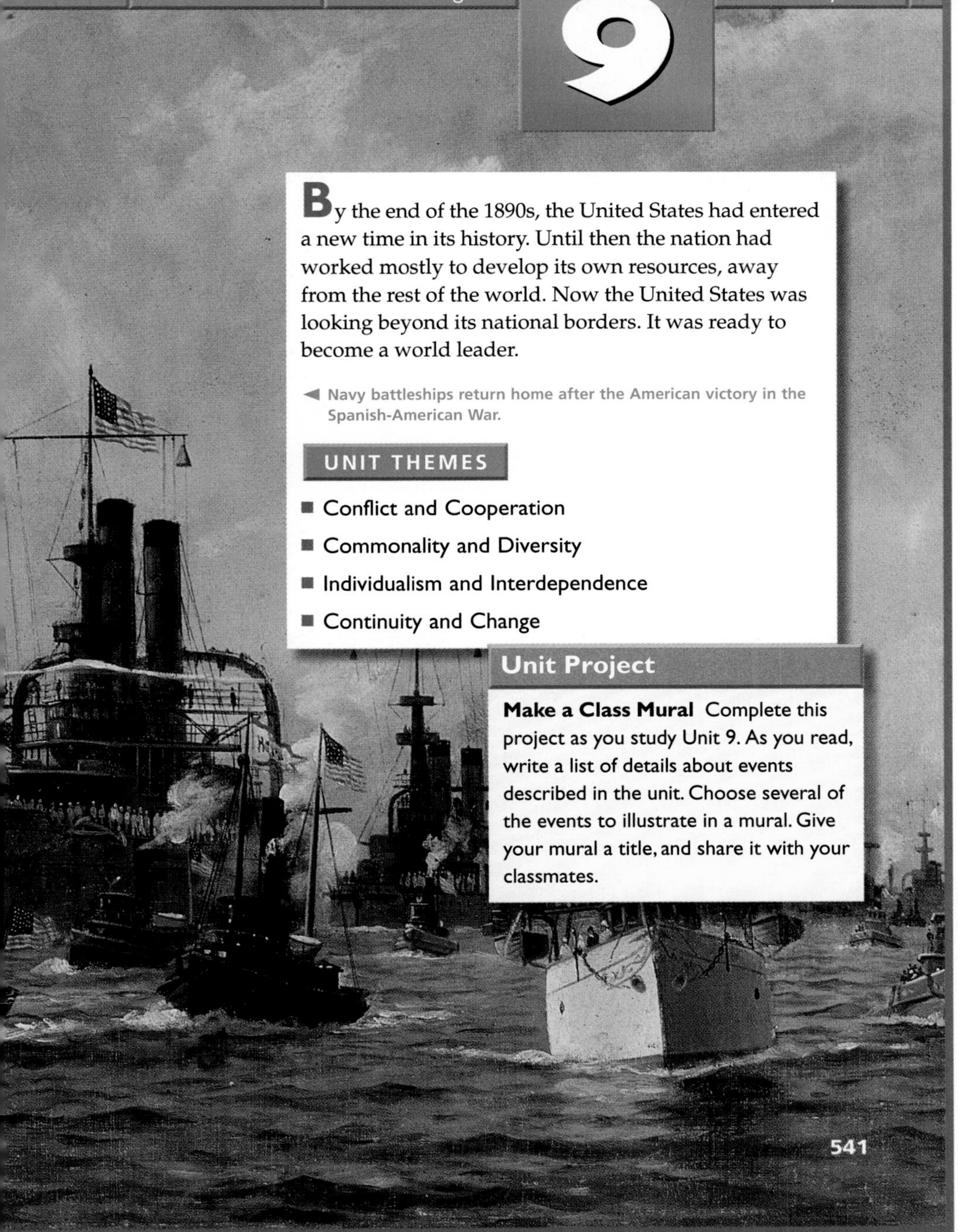

By the end of the 1890s, the United States had entered a new time in its history. Until then the nation had worked mostly to develop its own resources, away from the rest of the world. Now the United States was looking beyond its national borders. It was ready to become a world leader.

◀ Navy battleships return home after the American victory in the Spanish-American War.

UNIT THEMES

- Conflict and Cooperation
- Commonality and Diversity
- Individualism and Interdependence
- Continuity and Change

Unit Project

Make a Class Mural Complete this project as you study Unit 9. As you read, write a list of details about events described in the unit. Choose several of the events to illustrate in a mural. Give your mural a title, and share it with your classmates.

541

Options for Reading

Read Aloud Read each lesson aloud as students follow along in their books. Strategies for guiding students through the text and visuals are provided with each lesson.

Read Together Have pairs or small groups of students take turns reading each page or paragraph of the lesson aloud. Encourage students to use the new vocabulary words as they discuss what they read.

Read Alone Strong readers may wish to read the lessons independently before you read or discuss each lesson with the class.

Read the Introduction

Have students read the unit introduction on page 541.

Q. **What major change was taking place in the United States at the end of the 1890s?** The United States was becoming a world leader.

Why do you think this change was taking place? The United States had become a relatively wealthy nation and trade with other countries had grown.

Visual Analysis

Interpret Pictures Have students look at the painting on these pages and discuss how the country's naval power had changed since the Civil War.

Unit Themes

Discuss with students the Unit Themes. You may wish to post these themes on the board or classroom wall for easy reference and reinforcement after each lesson.

Unit Project Start-Up

Read the details of the Unit Project on page 541, and decide on student groups. To help students keep track of important events for the Unit Project, have them designate a notebook, index cards, or a sheet of paper as a place to record events for the class mural.

Home Involvement

Have students ask adult family members about experiences relatives may have had in World War II. Ask students to write short summaries of the experiences. Lead a class discussion in which volunteers share what they have learned.

HOME LETTER

Use UNIT 9 HOME LETTER. See Teacher's Edition, pp. HL 17–18.

PREVIEW THE UNIT

Link Prior Learning

Have students discuss what they already know about the first half of the 1900s. Tell them that this is the era of the boom-and-bust economy as well as of conflict in Europe and the Pacific. Have students look at the map and the time line to preview the other topics in Unit 9.

Understanding the Map

This map shows the nation's railroads and the most populated cities in 1890. Ask students to identify the major rivers and landforms that railroad lines had to cross.

Q. **Which states did not have a major railroad in 1890?** South Dakota, Kentucky, Connecticut, Vermont, Rhode Island

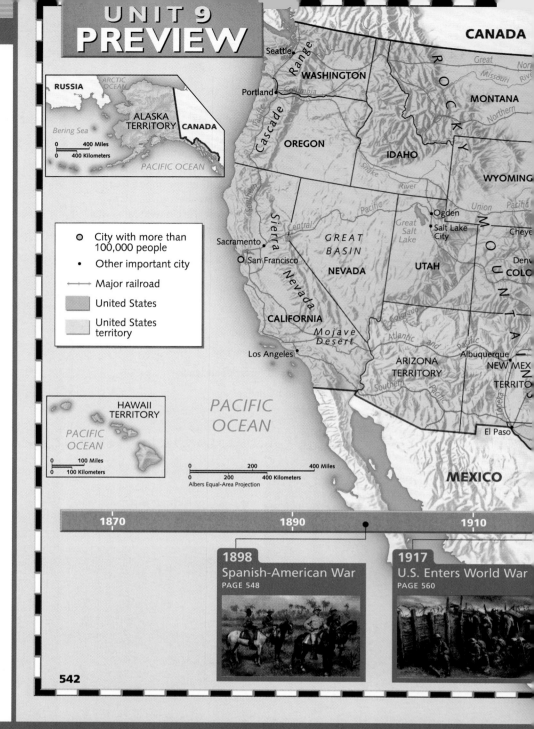

UNIT 9 PREVIEW

1870 — 1890 — 1910

1898 Spanish-American War
PAGE 548

1917 U.S. Enters World War
PAGE 560

542

ACTIVITY CHOICES

Meet Individual Needs

TACTILE LEARNERS Have students trace railroad routes that travelers could take to various parts of the country. Point out that in some areas travelers could choose among several routes, and ask students to find the shortest one. Have students trace routes from New York to San Francisco; from New Orleans to Los Angeles; from Chicago to Jacksonville; from Fargo to Augusta; from Columbia to Minneapolis; from Boston to Dallas; from Denver to Los Angeles; from Detroit to Kansas City; and from Washington, D.C., to Seattle. Then have the class make a list of cities to which they would recommend building extensions of existing railroad lines in the early 1900s. NOTE: Passengers were not permitted on all railroad lines, but for the sake of the activity, ask students to pretend that travelers could take any route.

VIDEO

VIDEO EXPERIENCES: SOCIAL STUDIES
Memories on the Homefront
See the video guide for additional enrichment material.

TECHNOLOGY

Use TIMELINER™ DATA DISKS to discuss and summarize the unit.

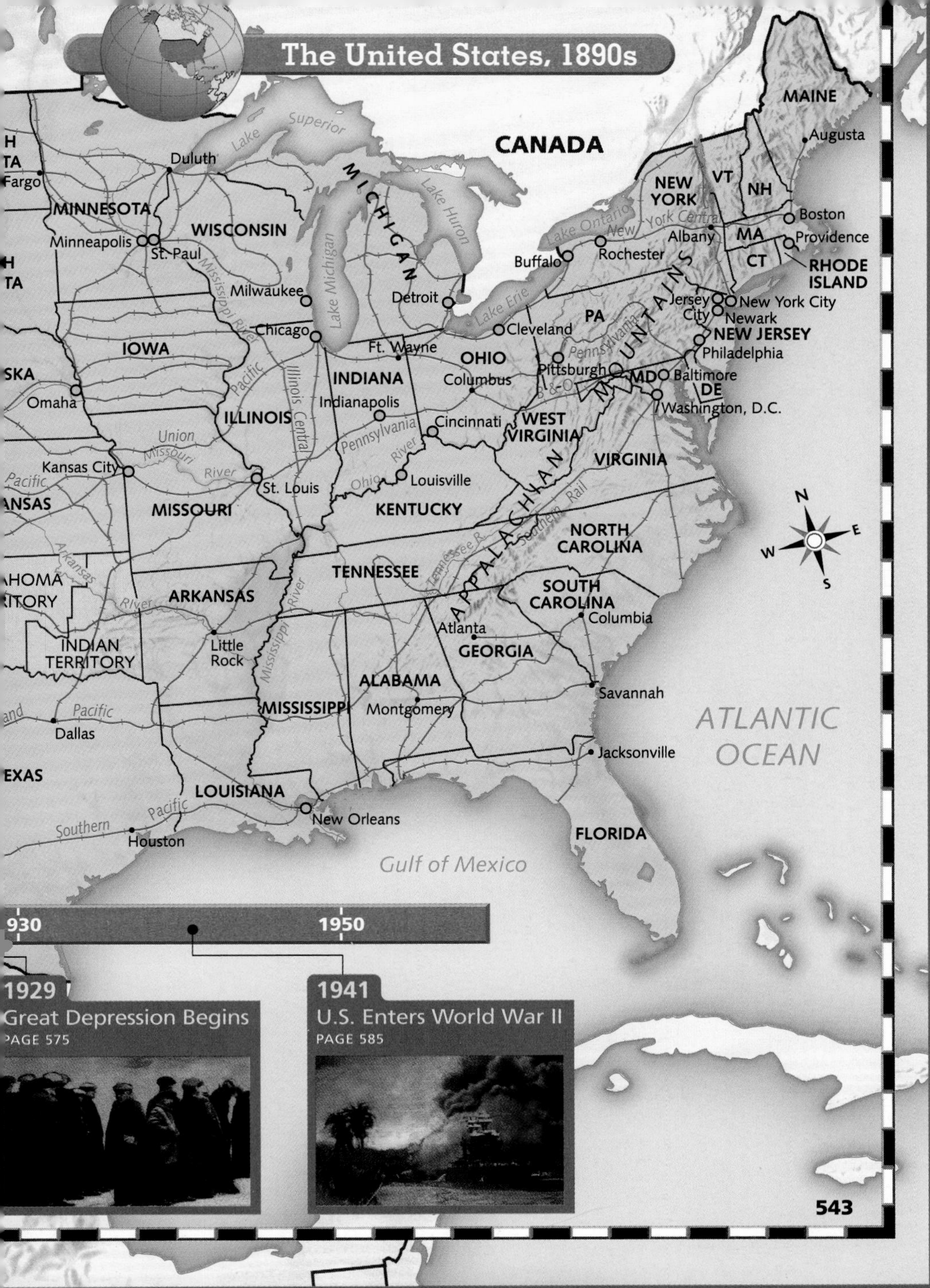

Understanding the Time Line

Explain to students that the scenes at the bottom of pages 542–543 show events that took place from the turn of the century to the middle of the 1900s.

Q. **What can you tell or infer about each event by looking at the scenes and the dates?** 1898—Soldiers fought on horseback in the Spanish-American War; 1917—Soldiers in World War I fought in trenches; 1929—People were poor during the Depression and stood in line for food; 1941—The U.S. entered World War II

Look Ahead to the Unit

To help students synthesize the information in the unit, lead a discussion on what it means to be a world power. Have volunteers list on the board the characteristics of a nation that is perceived by other nations to be a world power. Leave space below each characteristic. As students read the unit, have them write in actions and achievements that illustrate the characteristics.

Background

THE TIME LINE During the Spanish-American War, "Teddy" Roosevelt and his Rough Riders fought in the Battle of San Juan Hill and the siege of Santiago, Cuba.

New technology made fighting in World War I more treacherous.

In stark contrast to the boom economy of the Roaring Twenties, the Great Depression forced even wealthy Americans into soup lines.

When the Japanese attacked Pearl Harbor, the United States joined the Allied forces the same day.

These events are also shown in the Visual Summary on pages 600–601 in the Pupil Book.

UNIT POSTER

Use the UNIT 9 VISUAL SUMMARY POSTER to preview the unit.

Set the Scene with Literature

Prereading Strategies

Personal Response

Ask volunteers to describe how they might feel if they were soldiers facing enemy fire. Explain that they will read about a soldier who was frightened but remained determined as he faced German machine-gun fire in France during World War I.

Set the Purpose

The literature selection is from a book of letters written by a young soldier named Charles F. Minder, who served in France during World War I. In this letter to his mother, Minder tells of his company's encounter with German machine-gun fire in a French village.

Read & Respond

Auditory Learning

Listen for Detail Read the introduction aloud or have student volunteers do so. Ask the class to listen for the name of the person writing the letter, the person receiving the letter, and the circumstances under which the letter was written.

Understanding the Story

Select a student volunteer to read the first three paragraphs of the letter aloud. Ask the student to try to convey Minder's feelings as he or she reads, and ask listeners to picture in their minds Minder's situation. Discuss Minder's feelings and have students express how they would feel under similar circumstances.

Q. **How can you tell that Minder and his squad are in a difficult situation?** They were spotted by a German machine gunner; they were tired and hungry and had to hide behind a cement wall; day was coming.

SET THE SCENE with Literature

THIS MAN'S WAR

by CHARLES F. MINDER

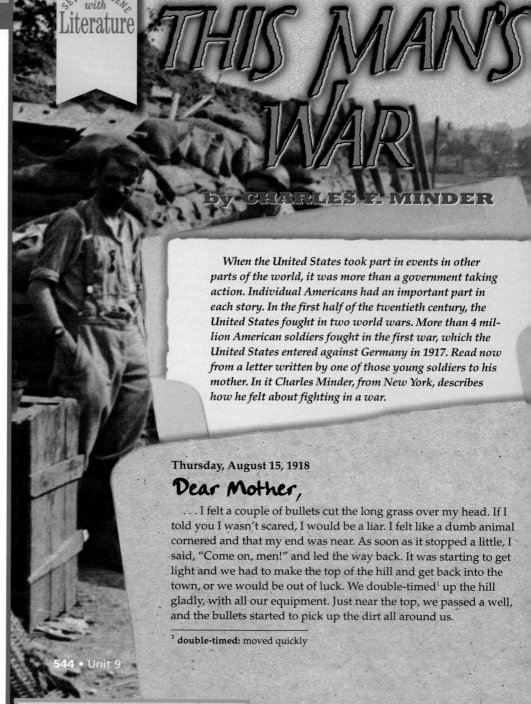

When the United States took part in events in other parts of the world, it was more than a government taking action. Individual Americans had an important part in each story. In the first half of the twentieth century, the United States fought in two world wars. More than 4 million American soldiers fought in the first war, which the United States entered against Germany in 1917. Read now from a letter written by one of those young soldiers to his mother. In it Charles Minder, from New York, describes how he felt about fighting in a war.

Thursday, August 15, 1918

Dear Mother,

. . . I felt a couple of bullets cut the long grass over my head. If I told you I wasn't scared, I would be a liar. I felt like a dumb animal cornered and that my end was near. As soon as it stopped a little, I said, "Come on, men!" and led the way back. It was starting to get light and we had to make the top of the hill and get back into the town, or we would be out of luck. We double-timed[1] up the hill gladly, with all our equipment. Just near the top, we passed a well, and the bullets started to pick up the dirt all around us.

[1] **double-timed:** moved quickly

544 • Unit 9

Activity Choices

Background

THE LITERATURE SELECTION AND THE AUTHOR Charles Frank Minder was 23 years old when he wrote this letter to his mother on August 15, 1918. During his tour of duty in France in World War I, Minder kept a personal narrative of his experiences in his letters to his mother. He wrote to her almost daily from April 12, 1918, until he was killed in October 1918. Minder, a pacifist, was not happy about serving in World War I. His letters indicate that he often felt overcome by the atrocities of war. Minder's letters were first published in 1931.

Some German machine gunner had •otted us. We all knelt on the other :le of the well and, one by one, managed crawl just a little farther, where we got •hind a cement wall. It was almost day- ;ht. . . . I looked at my watch and it was /e o'clock. We were all dead tired and fell leep and didn't wake up until nine this orning. We were hungry and opened up a •uple of cans of corned-beef and hardtack[2] ıd, with some water in our canteens, that as our breakfast.

We saw some signs showing we were in a wn called Fismes[3]. It sure had been recked by artillery[4] fire. I don't member seeing one house at wasn't hit, and all being :serted, it was a very mysterious oking town. Marching back ru the town, we saw hun- 'eds of dead Germans and nericans lying where ey fell. It was the most 'uesome sight I have en yet, and made me alize more than ever, ›w ridiculous and ınecessary this business war is.

I figured that the rest of e company must have turned to the next town ver, Villersavoye, where we arted out from yesterday ternoon. I was right, and when e got back there at noon today, ey were all surprised to see me ıd my squad. They thought that e had been killed last night.

Three of the men in my squad, who were with me last night, went to the hospital this afternoon, Purcell, Kujawa and Stadler. My squad is shot to pieces, yet we are going back again tonight, when it gets dark, to where we started for yesterday.

We could smell some very beautiful lilacs last night while we were on the way up and took deep whiffs of their perfume in the dark, thinking that there was a lilac bush near by. We found out today that the smell was gas. Our Captain and Lieutenant Krell were gassed, and a lot of men in the other two platoons. My throat is raw and my eyes have been watering all afternoon, but outside of that I am all right.

We just had a good meal at four o'clock, and everybody has been resting and cleaning up this afternoon, as we go up again tonight to relieve the other machine-gun company that is in the line. I found out this afternoon that the place where we were last night is called the "Valley of Death." It is such a terrible position, because the Germans are on top of the hill on the other side and can shoot down on top of us and across the valley into the town of Fismes. It is one hot spot. So it looks like we are in for a little excitement. As soon as it gets dark, we start, so will close, Mother Dear. I wish I was home now.

Charles

[2] ıardtack: biscuits baked ıard to last a long time

[3] Fismes: (FEEM)

[4] artillery: large guns on wheels

Culture

Thought and Expression Ask volunteers to discuss why Minder wrote "how ridiculous and unnecessary this business of war is." Then have students write their own opinions about the necessity of war. Collect the papers and hold them until the students have completed the unit. At the end of the unit, give the papers back and ask students to reread them. Then have students discuss what they would leave the same and what they would change, based on what they learned about the two world wars.

Understanding the Story

After students have read the last three paragraphs aloud, lead a class discussion on the idea of using poisonous gas as a weapon. Have students conclude why the Germans scented the chemical with lilac. Remind students that Charles and his squad had to return to the battleground that evening. Ask them why companies rotated during battle.

Summarize the Literature

Charles Minder's experience was similar to that of many soldiers in World War I who fought in foreign lands. Tell students that soldiers have always chronicled their war experiences in letters, stories, and poems and ask why these documents are important to future generations.

Link Literature

The books shown are other selections that may be used during the course of this unit with students of differing reading abilities. In addition to these titles, you may suggest some of the other books listed in the Multimedia Resource Center on page 540D of this Teacher's Edition.

EASY
Locks, Crocs, & Skeeters: The Story of the Panama Canal **by Nancy Winslow Parker. Greenwillow, 1996.**

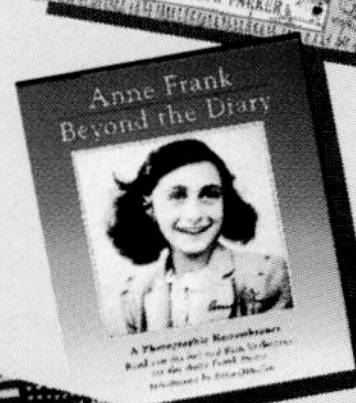

AVERAGE
Anne Frank: Beyond the Diary: A Photographic Remembrance **by Ruud van der Rol, Rian Verhoeven, and Anna Quindlen. Viking, 1993.**

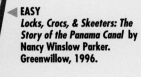

CHALLENGING
I Am an American **by Jerry Stanley. Crown, 1994.**

Planning Chart

	THEMES • Strands	VOCABULARY	MEET INDIVIDUAL NEEDS	RESOURCES INCLUDING ▶ TECHNOLOGY
LESSON 1 **Building an Empire** pp. 547–553	**COMMONALITY & DIVERSITY** • Geography • History • Economics • Civics and Government	imperialism armistice	Advanced Learners, p. 549 Tactile Learners, p. 552 Extend and Enrich, p. 552 Reteach the Main Idea, p. 553	Activity Book, p. 108
SKILL **Compare Map Projections** pp. 554–555	**BASIC STUDY SKILLS** • Map and Globe Skills	distortion projection	Advanced Learners, p. 554 Reteach the Skill, p. 555	Activity Book, pp. 109–110 Transparencies 44A–44B ▶ MAPSKILLS
LESSON 2 **Progressives and Reform** pp. 556–558	**INDIVIDUALISM & INTERDEPENDENCE** • Civics and Government	progressive commission conservation merit system political boss civil rights	Extend and Enrich, p. 557 Reteach the Main Idea, p. 558	Activity Book, p. 111
LESSON 3 **The Great War** pp. 559–563	**CONFLICT & COOPERATION** • History • Civics and Government • Geography • Culture	alliance military draft no-man's-land isolation	Auditory Learners, p. 560 English Language Learners, p. 561 Extend and Enrich, p. 562 Reteach the Main Idea, p. 563	Activity Book, p. 112 Music Audiocassette ▶ TIMELINER
SKILL **Recognize Propaganda** pp. 564–565	**BUILDING CITIZENSHIP** • Critical Thinking Skills	propaganda	Reteach the Skill, p. 565	Activity Book, p. 113 Transparency 45 ▶ THE AMAZING WRITING MACHINE
CHAPTER REVIEW pp. 566–567				Activity Book, p. 114 Transparency 46 Assessment Program Chapter 17 Test, pp. 143–146 ▶ THE AMAZING WRITING MACHINE ▶ TIMELINER ▶ INTERNET

7 DAYS

TIME MANAGEMENT

DAY 1	DAY 2	DAY 3	DAY 4	DAY 5	DAY 6	DAY 7
Lesson 1	Skill	Lesson 2	Lesson 3	Skill	Chapter Review	Chapter Test

Activity Book

LESSON 1
Interpret a Political Cartoon

NAME ______________________ DATE ____________

The Big-Stick Policy

Interpret a Political Cartoon

***DIRECTIONS:** Study the political cartoon. Then answer the questions that follow.*

THE BIG STICK IN THE CARIBBEAN SEA

1. The character shown is President Theodore Roosevelt. Describe his appearance.
Accept responses that describe his clothing, stature, stance, and expression.

2. What is Roosevelt doing? He is wading in the Caribbean Sea and pulling U.S. warships behind him.

3. What symbols of power are shown with Roosevelt? Accept responses that mention a big stick, a gun, a knife, and U.S. warships.

4. What do you think the artist was trying to say about Roosevelt?
Accept responses that indicate that he thought he could treat the Caribbean as a wading pool.

SKILL PRACTICE
Apply Map and Globe Skills

NAME ______________________ DATE ____________

HOW TO COMPARE MAP Projections

Only a globe can show exact shape, size, direction, and distance on the Earth. Cartographers try to show these four features of the Earth on a flat map as exactly as possible, but all map projections have distortions.

Apply Map and Globe Skills

***DIRECTIONS:** Study the map projections on this page and the following page. Then read each statement on the next page. Decide whether the statement applies to a Mercator projection, to a Mollweide projection, or to both projections. Place a check on the correct line or lines.*

MERCATOR PROJECTION

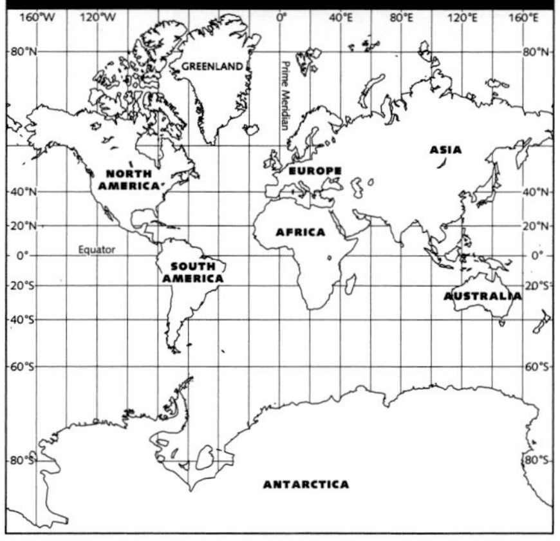

(continued)

SKILL PRACTICE
Apply Map and Globe Skills

NAME ______________________ DATE ____________

MOLLWEIDE (EQUAL-AREA) PROJECTION

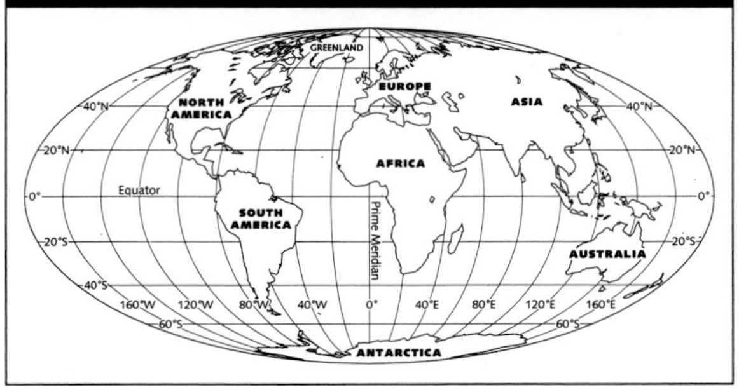

Mercator	Mollweide	
✓	✓	**1.** Shows the seven continents.
	✓	**2.** Shows the curved feature of the Earth.
✓		**3.** Uses straight lines for all lines of latitude and longitude.
✓		**4.** Shows all lines of latitude and longitude at right angles to each other.
✓	✓	**5.** Uses a straight line for the equator.
✓	✓	**6.** Uses a straight line for the prime meridian.
	✓	**7.** Shows meridians intersecting at the top and bottom of the map.
✓	✓	**8.** Shows parallels NOT intersecting.
✓	✓	**9.** Uses straight lines to show latitude.
	✓	**10.** Shows sizes of places true to scale.
✓		**11.** Shows Greenland as about the same size as Africa.
	✓	**12.** Uses curved lines to show longitude.

LESSON 2
Identify Progressives and Their Reforms

NAME ______________________ DATE ____________

Which Progressive SAID THAT?

Identify Progressives and Their Reforms

***DIRECTIONS:** The statements that follow express the ideas of Theodore Roosevelt, Robert La Follette, and W. E. B. Du Bois. Write TR next to statements that could have been made by Theodore Roosevelt, LF next to those that could have been made by La Follette, and DB next to those that could have been made by Du Bois.*

LF **1.** My reform program was called the Wisconsin Idea.

TR **2.** My reform program was called the Square Deal.

DB **3.** I helped start the National Association for the Advancement of Colored People (NAACP).

TR **4.** I encouraged Congress to pass the Pure Food and Drug Act and the Meat Inspection Act.

LF **5.** I set up the merit system to make sure people were qualified for government jobs.

DB **6.** I wanted African Americans to be proud of their heritage and culture.

LF **7.** With my help, my state legislature passed a law listing jobs for which children could not be hired.

DB **8.** I worked to change laws that did not give full civil rights to African Americans.

TR **9.** I had land in many parts of the country set aside for wilderness areas and national parks.

LF **10.** I encouraged the passage of a law limiting the workday to no more than ten hours.

LESSON 3
Understand Patriotic Songs

NAME ______________________ DATE __________

OVER THERE

Understand Patriotic Songs

***DIRECTIONS:** George M. Cohan's song "Over There" served as the American theme song for World War I. Study the song's words, and complete the activities that follow.*

Hear them calling you and me;
Ev'ry son of liberty.
Hurry right away, no delay, go today,
Make your daddy glad, to have had such a lad,
Tell your sweetheart not to pine,
To be proud her boy's in line.

CHORUS:
Over there, over there,
Send the word, send the word over there,
That the Yanks are coming,
The Yanks are coming,
The drums rum-tumming ev'ry where—
So prepare, say a pray'r,
Send the word, send the word to beware,
We'll be over, we're coming over,
And we won't come back till it's over over there.

Hoist the flag and let her fly,
Like true heroes, do or die.
Pack your little kit, show your grit, do your bit,
Soldiers to the ranks from the towns and the tanks,
Make your mother proud of you,
And to liberty be true.

1. Underline the people in the song whom the soldiers are going to make proud.
2. In the first line of the first verse, who does "them" refer to? U.S. armed forces
3. Reread the chorus. Who are the Yanks? Americans

   Who needs to beware of the Yanks? the enemy; Central Powers—Germany, Austria-Hungary, the Ottoman Empire, and Bulgaria
4. Explain what you think Cohan is saying in the chorus. U.S. troops are on the way to fight overseas and will stay until the war is over and won.

 Use after reading Chapter 17, Lesson 3, pages 559–563.

SKILL PRACTICE
Apply Critical Thinking Skills

NAME ______________________ DATE __________

HOW TO RECOGNIZE PROPAGANDA

TEAM WORK WINS!
Your work here makes their work over there possible
With your help they are invincible
Without it they are helpless

Apply Critical Thinking Skills

***DIRECTIONS:** Look at the illustration at the right. Then answer the questions that follow.*

1. To whom is this poster addressed?
   American workers
2. What points are being made by this poster?
   Factory workers and soldiers are on the same team in the effort to win the war. Both workers and soldiers are important.
3. What arguments are being used to make these points?
   Work done by people in the United States is necessary for soldiers to be able to fight. The United States will win the war because workers and soldiers are a team.
4. How does the poster illustration help make its point?
   It shows a factory worker making a machine gun and a soldier using the same kind of gun in the war.
5. What actions do those who created the poster hope people will take?
   that workers will work harder and will feel that they have an important part in the effort to win the war
6. How would this poster influence you, if you were a worker?
   Accept answers that reflect serious contemplation about the message of the poster.

Use after reading Chapter 17, Skill Lesson, pages 564–565.

CHAPTER 17 REVIEW
Connect Main Ideas

NAME ______________________ DATE __________

The United States and the World

Connect Main Ideas

***DIRECTIONS:** Use this organizer to show that you understand how the chapter's main ideas are connected. Write the main idea of each lesson.*

The United States and the World

Building an Empire	Progressives and Reforms	The Great War
At the end of the 1800s, the United States decided to add to its land and increase its power around the world in order to acquire new sources of raw materials and new markets for its products.	The progressives worked to make life better in the United States by enacting such reforms as changing unfair government and business practices, improving conditions for workers and children, ending prejudice, and extending democracy.	The leaders of the United States decided to enter World War I after German U-boats destroyed British and American ships and killed Americans.

 Use after reading Chapter 17, pages 546–567.

COMMUNITY RESOURCES

Ideas for using community resources, including speakers and field trips

Historical Societies and World War I Experts:

____
____
____
____
____

Museums and Historic Sites:

____
____
____
____
____

Chapter 17 Assessment

For ongoing **PERFORMANCE ASSESSMENT**, see Show What You Know, pp. 553, 558, 563.

CONTENT

NAME ______________________ DATE __________

Chapter Test 17

Part One: Test Your Understanding *(4 points each)*

DIRECTIONS: *Circle the letter of the best answer.*

1. Americans became interested in Alaska
   - A. as a good place to grow cotton.
   - (B.) after gold was discovered there.
   - C. until they realized that it had few natural resources.
   - D. because it was so close to Germany.
2. Which of these Americans gained control of the land and trade in Hawaii?
   - (A.) missionaries and sugar planters
   - B. tobacco planters and cotton planters
   - C. sea captains and merchants
   - D. owners of fishing and whaling ships
3. Which two areas gained by the United States in the Spanish-American War remain U.S. territories today?
   - A. Guam and Cuba
   - (B.) Puerto Rico and Guam
   - C. Puerto Rico and the Philippines
   - D. Cuba and the Philippines
4. President Theodore Roosevelt wanted the United States to use its power in the world because
   - A. most countries around the world considered the United States to be weak.
   - B. he wanted to fight in all the world's wars.
   - C. he wanted to force other countries to buy only American-made goods.
   - (D.) he believed that events in the rest of the world affected the United States.
5. Why did the United States want to build the Panama Canal?
   - A. to move the navy out of the Caribbean Sea into the Pacific
   - B. to fight in the Spanish-American War
   - (C.) to link American territories in the Atlantic and Pacific
   - D. to increase trade between Mexico and the United States
6. The main goals of the progressives were to
   - (A.) improve government and make life better.
   - B. end wars and make peace.
   - C. stop immigration and foreign trade.
   - D. help farmers learn new ways and grow new crops.

(continued)

CONTENT

NAME ______________________ DATE __________

7. Theodore Roosevelt called his program of progressive reforms the
   - (A.) Square Deal.
   - B. Promise to People Policy.
   - C. Government in Action Program.
   - D. United Way.
8. Governor Robert La Follette started a merit system in Wisconsin to
   - A. reduce the number of hours in a workday from 16 to 14.
   - B. make sure that children could be hired for any jobs they wanted.
   - (C.) make sure that people who got government jobs were qualified for them.
   - D. make sure that young people who graduated from high school could read and write.
9. The goal of the National Association for the Advancement of Colored People was to
   - A. help unions win the right to strike.
   - (B.) achieve full civil rights for African Americans.
   - C. stop the railroads from charging high fares.
   - D. stop immigrants from coming to the United States.
10. Why did the United States enter World War I?
    - A. Russia asked for its help.
    - B. France started killing American soldiers.
    - C. The Turkish navy sank the battleship *Maine.*
    - (D.) German submarines sank American ships.
11. The most feared of the new weapons used in World War I was
    - A. barbed wire.
    - (B.) poison gas.
    - C. the machine gun.
    - D. the handgun.
12. How did women contribute to the war effort in World War I?
    - A. They helped men fight in the trenches in France.
    - B. They were drafted into the army and navy.
    - C. They flew airplanes in battles over France.
    - (D.) They took over the jobs left by men going to war.
13. American women won the right to vote with the passage of the
    - A. Thirteenth Amendment.
    - (B.) Nineteenth Amendment.
    - C. Fourteenth Amendment.
    - D. Tenth Amendment.
14. The members of Congress voted **not** to join the League of Nations because
    - (A.) they wanted the United States to stay out of other countries' problems.
    - B. the League refused to elect an American to head the organization.
    - C. the League wanted the United States to pay for the organization.
    - D. they believed that wars were the only way to win new territories.

(continued)

SKILLS

NAME ______________________ DATE __________

Part Two: Test Your Skills *(24 points)*

DIRECTIONS: On May 7, 1915, a German U-boat sank the British passenger ship Lusitania. Americans were outraged, accusing the Germans of "piracy on the high seas." Germans defended the action, saying that the Lusitania was traveling in a war zone and that the ship was carrying weapons to help the British war effort. Leaders on both sides used propaganda to try to gain support for their cause. Read the quotation below by Germany's Baron von Schwarzenstein, and then read the statements that follow. Circle T if the statement is true and F if the statement is false.

> *In the case of the* Lusitania *the German Ambassador even further warned Americans through the great American newspapers against taking passage thereon. Does a pirate act thus? . . . Nobody regrets more sincerely than we Germans the hard necessity of sending to their deaths hundreds of men. Yet the sinking was a justifiable act of war. . . . The scene of war is no golf links, the ships of belligerent powers no pleasure places. . . . We have sympathy with the victims and their relatives, of course, but did we hear anything about sympathy . . . when England adopted her diabolical plan of starving a great nation?*

(T) F **15.** Baron von Schwarzenstein claimed that the sinking of the *Lusitania* was an act of war.

(T) F **16.** Both facts and opinions are presented in the baron's statement.

T (F) **17.** The statement was meant to convince people that Germany should not have attacked a passenger ship even though it was in a war zone.

T (F) **18.** The baron said that Germans had no sympathy for the victims or their relatives.

(T) F **19.** The baron accused Britain of trying to starve the people of Germany.

(T) F **20.** Baron von Schwarzenstein's statement is propaganda.

(continued)

APPLICATION/WRITING

NAME ______________________ DATE __________

Part Three: Apply What You Have Learned

DIRECTIONS: *Complete each of the following activities.*

21. Participants in World War I (10 points)
Identify the two sides that fought each other in World War I. Then list the countries that first made up each alliance.

a. Allied Powers	f. Central Powers
b. Russia	g. Germany
c. France	h. Austria-Hungary
d. Britain	i. the Ottoman Empire
e. Italy	j. Bulgaria

22. Essay (10 points)
Write a one-paragraph essay explaining how the progressives used the power of the federal government to make life better for Americans. Be sure to include the law or the name of the government agency involved.

Possible response:
The progressives used the power of the federal government to make life better for Americans. For example, they used this power to set rates on the railroads (Interstate Commerce Commission), to monitor the quality of food and drugs (Pure Food and Drug Act, Meat Inspection Act), and to conserve the nation's resources (national park system).

Introduce the Chapter

This chapter examines the expanding interests of the United States overseas. It explains how and why the United States acquired Alaska and Hawaii and analyzes the growing presence of the United States in the Caribbean and Pacific regions after the Spanish-American War. The chapter also explores President Theodore Roosevelt's influence in the international arena, especially his part in the building of the Panama Canal.

Personal Response

Have students review what they know about the expansion of the boundaries of the United States in continental North America. Remind them that economic opportunities and a growing population led to the rapid settlement of newly acquired territories. Challenge students to identify the two present-day states that were not included in the United States territory during the continental expansion.

Visual Analysis

Interpret Pictures Direct students to the photograph of Theodore Roosevelt, who became President of the United States after William McKinley was assassinated in 1901. Ask students what they think the photographer wanted this picture to show about Roosevelt.

Auditory Learning

Interpret Primary Sources Have a student read aloud the quotation from Theodore Roosevelt while the class listens carefully.

Q. **Why do you think Roosevelt liked the West African proverb?** because it fit his belief that he was more likely to achieve his political goals if he backed them up with power (monetary, military, or otherwise)

"PRIMARY SOURCE"

Source: *The Letters of Theodore Roosevelt, Vol. 2, The Years of Preparation, 1898–1900.* Elting E. Morison, ed. Harvard University Press, 1951.

CHAPTER 17

The United States and the World

"I have always been fond of the West African proverb: Speak softly and carry a big stick, you will go far."

Theodore Roosevelt, Governor of New York and later President of the United States, 1900

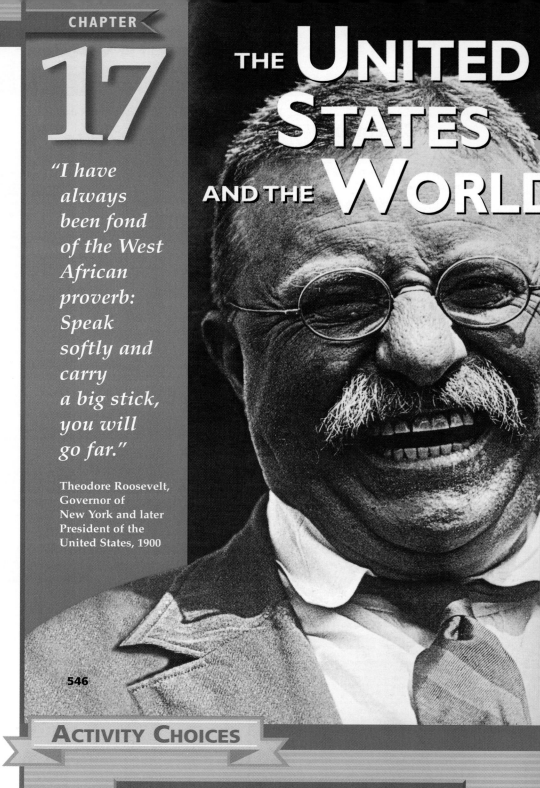

546

Activity Choices

Background

THEODORE ROOSEVELT Roosevelt believed strongly in the benefits of an active life and had seemingly inexhaustible energy and enthusiasm. Often ill as a child, Roosevelt followed a strict program of physical fitness to maintain his good health. He ran a ranch in the Dakotas, hunted wild animals in Africa, explored the Amazon jungles, and led a regiment in the Spanish-American War. He brought the same passion for action to his life in the White House, expanding the power of the presidency in both domestic and foreign affairs.

LESSON 1

Building an Empire

By the late 1800s, the United States led the world in ıdustry and agriculture. Like many European nations at that me, the United States wanted to stretch its borders and set p colonies. Now that the western frontier had been settled, ıany Americans were ready to find new frontiers. American aders also felt that new lands would bring new sources of ıw materials and new markets for the nation's goods. The me seemed right for the United States to become a world ower.

FOCUS

Why might a country today decide to take a more active part in what is going on in the world?

Main Idea As you read, find out why the United States decided at the end of the 1800s to add to its territory and power around the world.

Vocabulary

imperialism
armistice

Alaska

In 1867 the United States bought Alaska from Russia for 7.2 million—about two cents an acre. Most Americans knew ttle about Alaska or its peoples. Many thought it was foolish f the United States to buy a piece of land so far north. Some ılled it the "Polar Bear Garden."

Then, in 1896, prospectors found gold in the Klondike ·gion. The Klondike was in Canada's Yukon Territory, near s border with Alaska. The discovery started a gold rush like ıe one in California in 1849. From 1897 to 399 more than 100,000 people raced to laska hoping to get rich. Some did find old. But conditions were harsh, and ıousands died.

Alaska brought new wealth to the 'nited States. The land was full of natral resources, such as fish, timber, ɔal, and copper. Because buying laska turned out to be so profable, many Americans soon ıought the United States should y to get more new lands across ıe seas.

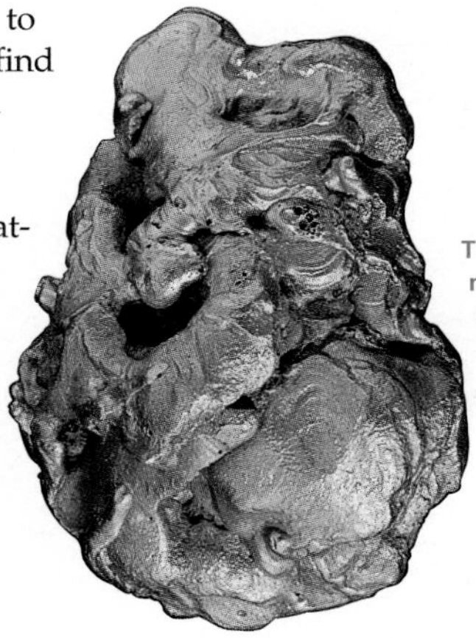

The discovery of gold brought many prospectors to Alaska with hopes of getting rich.

REVIEW ***What caused people to ecome interested in Alaska?***
iold was discovered there.

Reading Support

PREVIEW AND READ THE LESSON Provide students with the following visual framework.

The United States Expands Overseas	
Territory	Year Acquired
Alaska	1867
Hawaii	1898
Cuba, Puerto Rico, the Philippines, Guam	1898
Panama Canal Zone	1903

Objectives

1. Explain how the United States benefited from its acquisition of Alaska.
2. Describe the conflict of interests over the acquisition of Hawaii.
3. Analyze the causes and effects of the Spanish-American War.
4. Evaluate the role of President Theodore Roosevelt in world affairs.
5. Summarize the steps Roosevelt took to build the Panama Canal.

Vocabulary

imperialism (p. 548) armistice (p. 550)

1. ACCESS

The Focus Question

Ask students to provide recent examples of situations in which the United States took an active role in events occurring in other parts of the world. Have students discuss why the United States became involved.

The Main Idea

In this lesson students explore President Theodore Roosevelt's role in the expansion of the United States beyond its borders and the use of the growing power of the United States. After students have read the lesson, have them analyze the reasons for U.S. expansion overseas in the late 1800s and early 1900s.

2. BUILD

Alaska

Key Content Summary

In 1867 the United States bought Alaska from Russia for $7.2 million. The purchase proved to be more valuable than the price paid because Alaska was rich in natural resources, including gold.

The Hawaiian Islands

Key Content Summary

As American missionaries and businesspeople settled in Hawaii, they began to take economic control of the islands. In 1893 Americans took over the government of Hawaii from Queen Liliuokalani and set up a republic. Five years later Hawaii became a territory of the United States.

Geography

Place Ask a volunteer to locate the Hawaiian Islands on a classroom wall map or atlas. Have students compare and contrast the distance from Hawaii to the U.S. mainland with the distance from Alaska to the state of Washington. Then have them analyze why there was less protest about the acquisition of Hawaii than the acquisition of Alaska.

War with Spain

Key Content Summary

In 1898 conflict arose between the United States and Spain, which led to war. After defeating the Spanish forces in the Philippines and Cuba, the United States acquired new territories from Spain.

The Hawaiian Islands

The Hawaiian Islands are about 2,400 miles (3,862 km) southwest of California, in the Pacific Ocean. Polynesian people in the Pacific migrated to Hawaii by the eighth century, and the islands were ruled by Polynesian kings and queens. By the 1800s many Americans had settled there.

Among the first Americans to arrive in Hawaii were Christian missionaries. They began to settle in the islands about 1820. Soon after, American business people started cattle ranches and sugar plantations there. By the 1870s American missionaries and sugar planters controlled much of the land and trade in Hawaii.

In 1887 the Hawaiian king, Kalakaua (kah•lah•KAH•ooh•ah), tried to keep the Americans from taking over the islands. The Americans then decided to take away the king's authority. They wanted the United States to annex Hawaii. The Americans mad Kalakaua sign a new constitution that left th Hawaiian monarchy without authority.

In 1893 the new Hawaiian ruler, Queen Liliuokalani (lih•lee•uh•woh•kuh•LAH•nee) tried to bring back the monarchy's authority. Liliuokalani promised to make "Hawaii for Hawaiians" once again. But the Americans made her give up her throne. They took ove the government and set up a republic. In 189 Congress decided to annex Hawaii to the United States.

REVIEW ***How did Hawaii become a part the United States?*** Americans took over the government and set up a republic.

Lydia Liliuokalani became queen of Hawaii in 1891. Queen Lil', as she was called, wrote the well-known song "Aloha Oe," or "Farewell to Thee." The Hawaiian Islands (below) are beautiful volcanic lands.

War with Spain

After the United States took control of Alaska and Hawaii, some people accused th country's leaders of **imperialism**, or empire building. This brought the United States into conflict with European nations that had also spread beyond their borders—especially Spain.

By the end of the 1800s, Cuba and Puerto Rico were the only two colonies Spain had left in the Western Hemisphere. Many Cubans wanted their island to be independent from Spain. Twice, in 1868 and in 1895, they had rebelled against Spanish rule, but the rebellions failed.

Activity Choices

Smithsonian Institution®

Go to the Internet site at *http://www.si.edu/harcourt/socialstudies* to visit the virtual festival "Lu'au in Hawaii" in the Center for Folklife Programs and Cultural Studies.

Background

THE SANDWICH ISLANDS The first European known to set foot on the Hawaiian Islands was Captain James Cook, a British explorer who landed there in 1778. He named the islands the Sandwich Islands in honor of his patron, the Earl of Sandwich (the British noble who gave his name to the sandwich). Cook's discovery led the way for fur traders from the United States to come to the islands for supplies on their way to China.

Multicultural Link

Point out that the descendants of the native peoples of Alaska and Hawaii have tried to preserve their traditions. The Aleuts and other Indians of Alaska still fish and hunt in much the same way their ancestors did. The caribou are a major source of food, clothing, and tools. In Hawaii the descendants of the Polynesians are called Hawaiians. They have preserved their own language, including words such as *aloha* and *mahalo*, and traditions such as the luau, the hula, and Hawaiian music.

Nearly one-fourth of the United States soldiers who fought in Cuba were African Americans. The soldiers in this photograph served in the United States Cavalry. All soldiers who had fought in the war were given a medal like the one shown here.

Many Americans supported the Cubans' fight for independence, including Americans who had moved there to start businesses. Newspapers in the United States were full of stories about Spain's harsh rule of the island. As the fighting continued, President William McKinley ordered the battleship *Maine* to Havana, Cuba, to protect the lives and property of Americans living there. On February 15, 1898, the *Maine* exploded in Havana's harbor. More than 200 sailors were killed. It was not clear why the ship blew up. The United States, however, blamed Spain. "Remember the *Maine!*" Americans cried, calling for action. On April 25, the United States declared war on Spain.

The first battles of the Spanish-American War were not fought in Cuba. They were fought halfway around the world. Less

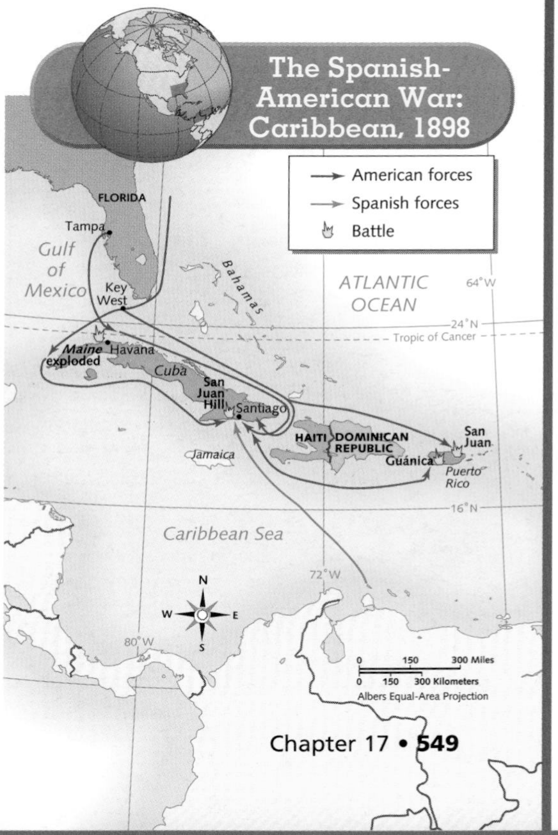

Movement This map shows the main movements of Spanish and American forces around Cuba.

■ *About how many miles from Tampa is the place where the Maine exploded?*

History

Origins, Spread, and Influence Have students discuss the concept of imperialism and give examples of British, French, and Spanish imperialism from previous units. Then have them analyze why the United States became imperialistic and how imperialism can lead to conflict.

Economics

Interdependence and Income Point out that the original source of conflict was between the Spanish and the Cubans. Have students explore the economic factors that drew the United States into the conflict.

Geography

Movement Refer students to the map on this page and have them locate Havana and Santiago. Ask students to analyze President McKinley's decision to send the *Maine* to Cuba and to discuss possible explanations for the explosion of the *Maine*.

Visual Analysis

Learn from Maps Have students answer the question in the caption. about 320 miles

Background

CUBA'S STRUGGLE FOR INDEPENDENCE Throughout the 1800s several people made attempts to free Cuba from Spain. In 1821 José Francisco Lemu led a revolutionary movement, but it failed after five years. In the 1820s Mexican leaders and Simón Bolívar, a South American general, organized an army to invade and free Cuba from Spanish rule. When the United States threatened to support Spain, Bolívar dropped the plan. The Ten Years' War began in 1868 when Carlos de Céspedes led a Cuban revolutionary movement demanding independence and the abolition of slavery. A treaty was signed in 1878 providing for political reforms and the gradual abolition of slavery. José Martí became a devoted leader of the revolutionary movement in 1895.

Meet Individual Needs

ADVANCED LEARNERS Have students write news reports on one of the following topics: the Alaskan Gold Rush, Queen Liliuokalani, President William McKinley, the story of the *Maine*, Commodore George Dewey, or the Battle of San Juan Hill. Have students use library or Internet resources to prepare their reports. Ask volunteers to present their news reports to the class.

Theodore Roosevelt

Key Content Summary

As President, Roosevelt believed the United States should use its power in the world. He intervened to bring about cooperation between warring Russia and Japan. He also sent the Great White Fleet around the world to show the strength of the American military.

Civics and Government

Political Institutions and Processes Discuss with students the assassination of President McKinley, and have them apply their knowledge of the Constitution to explain why Roosevelt became President. Explain to students that McKinley was shot by an anarchist named Leon F. Czolgosz. As the crowd started beating Czolgosz, the dying McKinley said, "Let no one hurt him."

History

Leaders and Achievers Have students discuss the qualities of leadership as they apply to Roosevelt. Then have students compare and contrast Roosevelt with other great leaders in the United States.

than two weeks after war was declared, the United States Navy was sent to the Philippine Islands. Led by Commodore George Dewey, the navy destroyed the Spanish fleet and captured Manila Bay.

In the United States, many thousands of Americans volunteered to fight in the war. The army grew from about 30,000 soldiers to more than 274,000. Among those who volunteered was Theodore Roosevelt, who had been assistant secretary of the navy. He had quit his job to form a fighting company made up mostly of cowhands and college athletes. In Cuba, the Rough Riders, as they were called, took part in the Battle of San Juan Hill and the siege of Santiago. The siege ended on July 17, 1898, and the Spanish in Santiago soon signed an armistice. An **armistice** is an agreement to stop fighting a war.

The Spanish-American War lasted less than four months. More than 5,000 American soldiers died, most from diseases such as malaria and yellow fever. But the war helped the United States become a stronger world power. Under the peace treaty, Spain agreed to give the United States control of Cuba, Puerto Rico, Guam, and the Philippine Islands. Cuba became an independent country in 1901. The Philippine Islands gained independence in 1946. Puerto Rico and Guam remain territories of the United States today.

REVIEW ***Why did the United States go to war with Spain?***

to protect lives and property of Americans living in Cuba; Americans believed that Spain was responsible for the explosion of the *Maine*

Theodore Roosevelt

Theodore Roosevelt returned from Cuba well known and well liked. He was soon elected governor of New York. Two years later he was Vice President, serving under President William McKinley. On September 6, 1901, President McKinley was shot in Buffalo, New York, by a person who was against the government. McKinley died eight days later, and Roosevelt became President.

Roosevelt was a man of action. He believed that the United States should actively use its power to shape events in the world. He believed that what happened in the rest of the world affected the United States.

When Russia and Japan were at war with one another in 1904 and 1905, President Roosevelt helped the two nations work out a peace agreement. Because of his work, Roosevelt became the first American to receive the Nobel Peace Prize. The Nobel Peace Prize is awarded each year to a person or an organization that helps bring peace to the world.

In 1907 President Roosevelt, the peacemaker, decided to remind other countries that he was also the leader of a powerful military force. He sent a fleet of warships, painted a dazzling white, on a world cruise. According to Roosevelt, the Great White Flee

BIOGRAPHY

José Martí
1853–1895

José Martí (mar•TEE), a leader of the Cuban revolution, is a national hero in Cuba today. He was a writer who spoke out against Spanish rule in the late 1800s. Many of Martí's poems, articles, and speeches were printed in newspapers in the United States. They helped tell the Cubans' story. Martí died three years before the Spanish-American War. Even so, many people feel he did more than any other Cuban leader to win Cuba's freedom from Spain.

Activity Choices

Link to Reading

READ AND INTERPRET POEMS Have student volunteers read aloud two or three poems about Cuba's struggle for independence from José Martí's *Ismaelillo* or *Simple Verses*. Explain that Martí was twice exiled from Cuba for his political activities. He was killed on the island in 1895 during a revolt against Spanish rule. Ask the class to interpret Martí's poems and speculate on why he was popular in Cuba.

Background

THE GREAT WHITE FLEET In sending the fleet with its 16 battleships around the world, Roosevelt aimed to impress not only other nations but also the United States Congress. Roosevelt wanted Congress to provide more money for the navy. The voyage was a great success, impressing every nation it visited. One unintended result of the cruise was that it so impressed Japanese admirals that they began to expand their own navy. This expansion would haunt the United States in years to come.

Smithsonian Institution®

Go to the Internet site at *http://www.si.edu/harcourt/socialstudies* to examine portraits of William McKinley and Theodore Roosevelt in the Hall of Presidents at the National Portrait Gallery.

United States Possessions, 1900

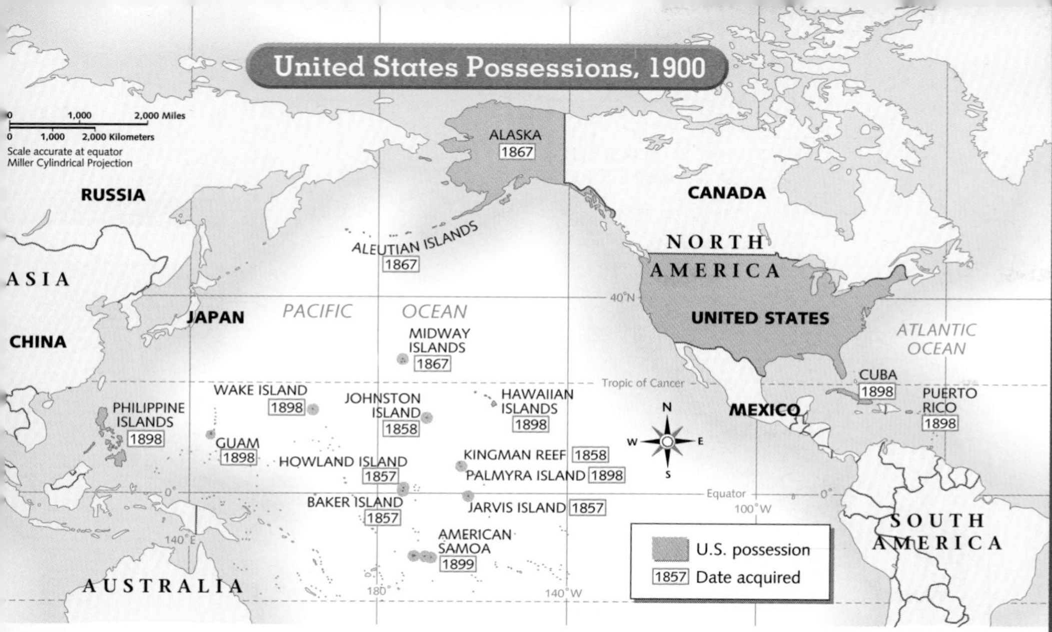

MAP THEME Location This map shows when the United States gained lands in different places around the world.

- *In what year did the United States acquire the lands that would become the state of Alaska? When did it acquire the lands that would become the state of Hawaii?*

showed the world that now "the Pacific was as much our home as the Atlantic."

REVIEW ***Why did Roosevelt believe the United States should use its power to shape events in the world?*** He believed that what happened in the rest of the world affected the United States.

The Panama Canal

One of President Roosevelt's goals was to build a canal in Panama, in Central America. The canal would link the Atlantic and Pacific oceans. This, in turn, would link American territories in the Atlantic with those in the Pacific. "I wish to see the United States the dominant power on the shores of the Pacific Ocean," Roosevelt said.

For years people had talked about building a canal in Panama. Such a canal would cut across the isthmus that joined North America and South America. A French company had tried to build such a canal in the 1880s but had given up because of the thick jungle and the diseases that killed many of the workers.

In 1902 Congress voted to build the canal. But the Isthmus of Panama did not belong to the United States. It belonged to Colombia, a South American country. The United States offered Colombia $10 million for the right to build the canal. But Colombia would not agree to sell.

Roosevelt then spread the word that he would welcome a revolution in Panama to end Colombian rule. He sent the United States Navy to protect the isthmus. If a revolution began, the navy was to keep Colombian troops from landing on shore.

History

Patterns and Relationships Have students discuss the cruise of the Great White Fleet.

Q. How do you think other nations reacted to the presence of the Great White Fleet in their waters? Most students will probably agree that these nations were impressed by the power of the United States. Other students may conclude that some nations resented the show of force by the United States.

Visual Analysis

Learn from Maps Have students answer the questions in the caption. 1867; 1898

The Panama Canal

Key Content Summary

President Roosevelt believed a canal across Panama was so important that, after a cooperative effort with Colombia failed, he encouraged Panamanians to revolt and end Colombian rule. Panama did, and gave the United States the right to build the canal.

History

Leaders and Achievers Have students analyze President Roosevelt's motivation for building the Panama Canal and the steps he took to reach that goal. Discuss the advantages a canal across the Isthmus of Panama would provide to the United States.

Link to Science

COLLECT AND DISPLAY FACTS (COOPERATIVE LEARNING) Have small groups of students collect facts about the environment of Panama and the technology used by the canal builders to overcome problems they encountered. Have students write the facts on strips of colored paper to use in a display. Have them draw a diagram of the Panama Canal that shows the locations of the locks, lake, and cuts for the center of the display. Yarn may be used to connect each fact to the area of the canal it describes.

Link to Health

RESEARCH DISEASES AND CURES
Select student volunteers to research the causes and symptoms of malaria and yellow fever and report their findings to the class. Select other student volunteers to research the steps that were involved in understanding and controlling malaria and yellow fever, including William Gorgas's role in freeing the Isthmus of Panama from those diseases. Have students present their findings to the class.

History

Cause and Effect Have students identify and diagram the cause-and-effect relationships that led to the revolution of Panama against Colombia. Ask students to express their views on the actions taken by Roosevelt to force the revolution.

Visual Analysis

Read Maps Have students use the inset map to locate the Panama Canal and the land area over which the United States gained control.

Q. **How do you think the people of Panama benefited from the building of the canal?** They earned money by working on the canal and by providing services to those who worked on the canal. After the canal opened, it provided new economic opportunities to the people of Panama.

Geography

Human–Environment Interactions Use the visuals and the text to identify the environmental obstacles the canal builders had to overcome. Have students discuss examples of cooperative effort that went into the successful construction and completion of the Panama Canal.

Visual Analysis

Learn from Maps Have students answer the question in the caption. by about 7,800 miles (12,553 km)

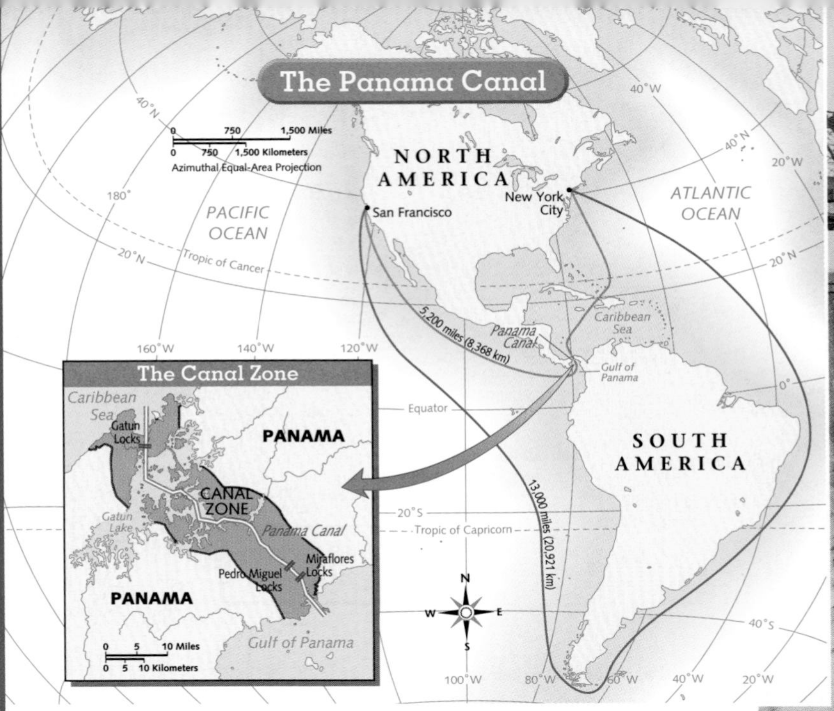

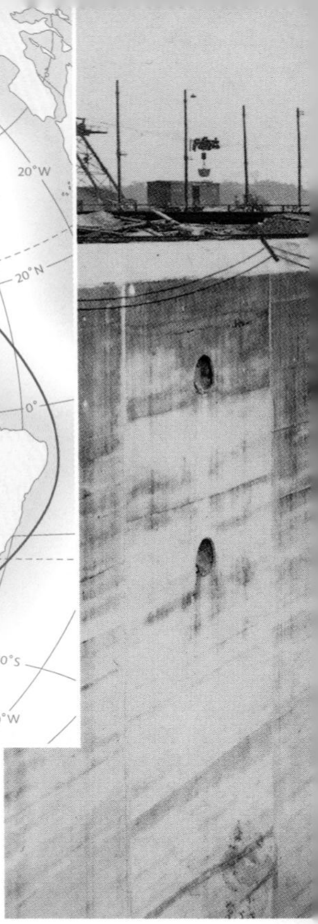

Movement After its construction, the Panama Canal (right) provided an important shortcut for voyages between the Atlantic and Pacific oceans.

■ *By how many miles did the canal shorten a voyage between New York City and San Francisco?*

Within three months such a revolution took place, and the people of Panama formed a new nation. Panama's new leaders then gave the United States the right to build the canal. The United States would control the canal and an area 5 miles (8 km) wide on each side of it.

Work on the canal began in 1904. Workers guided huge earth-moving machines to cut down the trees and thick growth of jungle. Engineers designed huge canal locks to help ships move through the waterway.

Unlike the French workers who had first tried to build the canal, American workers were able to stay healthy. Doctors now knew that malaria and yellow fever, the diseases that had stopped the French, were carried by mosquitoes. The Americans learned to control the mosquitoes by draining all of the swamps where the insects lived.

Building the canal took ten years and cost about $380 million. In 1906 Roosevelt visited the canal site. It was the first time a President had left the United States while in office. The first ship passed through the Panama Canal on August 15, 1914. Today the canal helps move people and goods around the world.

REVIEW ***Why did the United States want to build the Panama Canal?*** to link America territories in the Atlantic with those in the Pacific

Activity Choices

Meet Individual Needs

TACTILE LEARNERS Have students make time lines of events from this lesson. Guide them in setting up time lines that cover the years 1867 to 1914. Remind students that they may write the events both above and below the time line. You may wish to have a class discussion about the completed time lines.

Background

THE PANAMA CANAL TREATY After the Panama Canal opened in 1914, the United States established the Panama Canal Zone there. Many Panamanians, however, opposed United States control of the Panama Canal and the Canal Zone. They wanted Panamanians to control these areas. In 1977 the United States signed a treaty with Panama agreeing to transfer control of the Canal Zone to Panama in 1979. The treaty also provided for the transfer of the canal to Panama's control in 1999.

Extend and Enrich

COOPERATIVE LEARNING

MAKE A DIORAMA Divide the class into five groups, and assign each group one of the five subsections of the lesson as the topic for creating a group diorama. Suggest to students that they use cardboard boxes and a variety of materials for their dioramas. Challenge students to use library reference materials to aid them in planning their scenes. When the dioramas have been completed, have each group choose a spokesperson to present the group's diorama to the class.

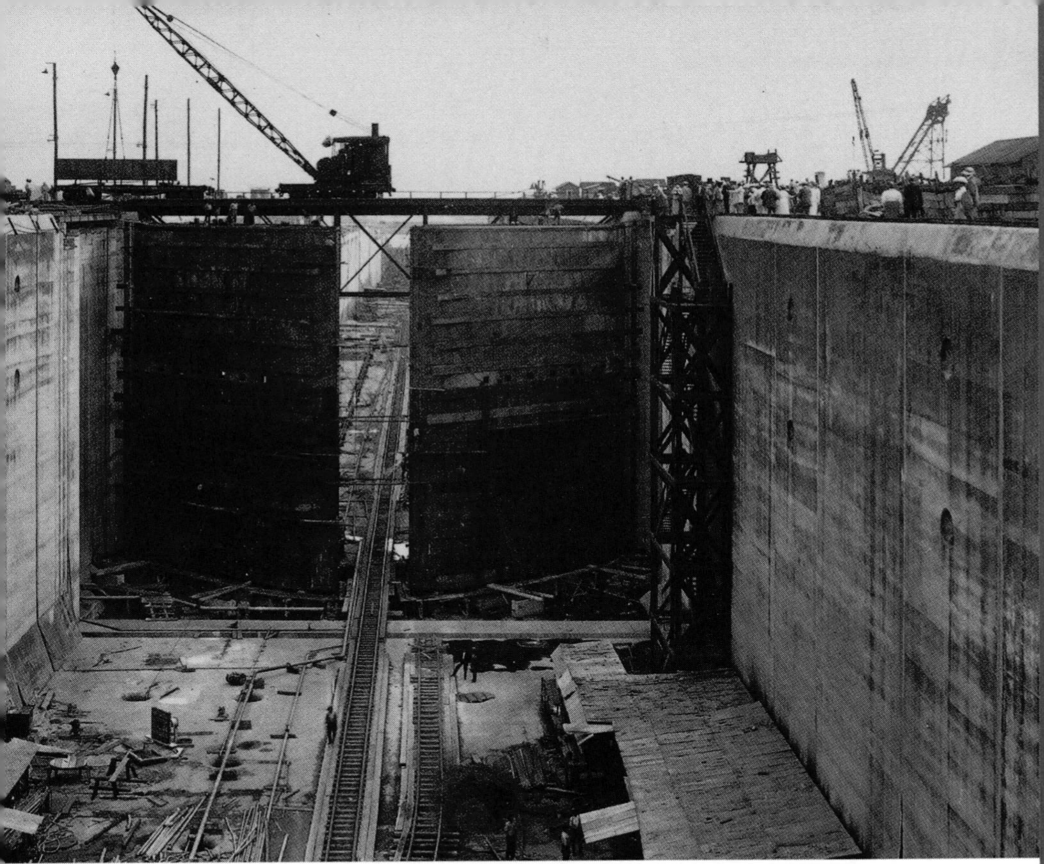

ESSON 1 REVIEW

Check Understanding

1. **Remember the Facts** What lands did the United States gain in the 1800s?
2. **Recall the Main Idea** Why did the United States decide at the end of the 1800s to add to its territory and power around the world?

Think Critically

3. **Explore Viewpoints** What do you think Queen Liliuokalani meant by the phrase, "Hawaii for Hawaiians"?
4. **Past to Present** Do you think the Panama Canal is as important today as it was when it opened? Why or why not?

Show What You Know

Globe Activity Work with a partner to trace water routes around the world. Use your finger to follow the routes a ship might follow from the east coast to the west coast of the United States before and after the opening of the Panama Canal.

Visual Analysis

Interpret Pictures Have students use the photograph on this page to speculate on why it took ten years to complete the Panama Canal project. Explain that the total length of the canal is 50.72 miles (81.7 km).

3. CLOSE

Have students consider again the Focus question on page 547.

> **Why might a country today decide to take a more active part in what is going on in the world?**

Have students use what they have learned about the overseas expansion of the United States between 1867 and 1914 to speculate on the reasons that a country today might decide to take a more active part in world events.

LESSON 1 REVIEW—Answers

Check Understanding

1. Alaska, the Hawaiian Islands, Cuba, Puerto Rico, the Philippines, and Guam
2. to acquire new sources of raw materials and new markets for its products

Think Critically

3. Hawaiians wanted to preserve their homeland and traditions and not have them taken over by the United States.
4. Possible response: Yes; it continues to be the safest and shortest water passage from the Atlantic Ocean to the Pacific Ocean for goods and people.

Show What You Know

Performance Assessment You may want to provide students with outline maps of the world on which they can trace the water routes.

What to Look For Look for evidence that students understand why the United States would want to build a canal.

Reteach the Main Idea

COOPERATIVE LEARNING

MAKE A CHART Divide the class into small groups. Challenge each group to use the textbook as a resource to make a chart that explains why the United States added to its territory and power around the world at the end of the 1800s. The chart could be titled *Expansion of the United States.* Column one could be titled *Land Acquired* and column two *Reasons for Acquisition.* Have the groups share and discuss their charts with the other groups.

ACTIVITY BOOK

Reinforce & Extend

Use ACTIVITY BOOK, p. 108.

Objectives

1. Recognize two map projections.
2. Identify advantages and disadvantages of different map projections.

Vocabulary

distortion (p. 554) projection (p. 554)

1. ACCESS

Draw a simple map of the world on an inflated, round balloon. Show your improvised globe to the students, puncture it, and use scissors to make one cut from top to bottom. Then attempt to stretch the map into a rectangle, pinning it with tacks to a bulletin board or other surface.

Introduce the term *distortion*, pointing out how areas of the Earth are distorted as you stretch the balloon-globe. Explain that the flat map you have created is a rough example of what is called a map *projection*. Discuss the meaning of that term.

2. BUILD

Have students locate the name of each projection written below the map scale on each map. Discuss the characteristics of the two projections, as described in Understand the Process. Have students compare the projections with a globe.

To discover the differences between the two projections, have students answer the questions. Remind them to consider advantages and disadvantages of each projection as they work.

Compare Map Projections

1. Why Learn This Skill?

Because the Earth is round and maps are flat, maps cannot represent the Earth's shape exactly. Only a globe, which is round, can do that. To show the round Earth on a flat piece of paper, cartographers must change the shape of the globe, splitting or stretching it to make it flat. As a result, every map has **distortions**, or areas that are not accurate.

Over the years, cartographers have found different ways of showing the Earth on flat paper. These different views are called **projections**. All map projections have distortions, but different kinds of projections have different kinds of distortions. Identifying areas on a map that are distorted will help you understand how different kinds of maps can best be used.

2. Understand the Process

Map A and Map B both show the same area of the Earth, but they are different projections. Map A is an equal-area projection. Equal-area projections show the sizes of regions in correct relation to one another, but they distort, or change, their shapes. There are many kinds of equal-area projections. The azimuthal (a•zuh•MUH•thuhl) equal-area projection on

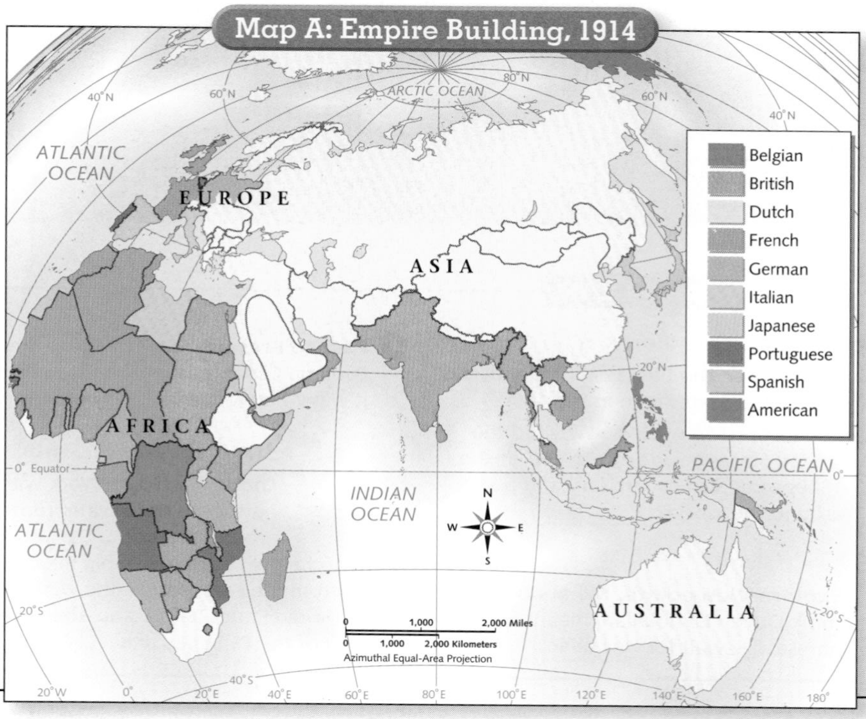

ACTIVITY CHOICES

Meet Individual Needs

ADVANCED LEARNERS Have advanced learners research and report on maps that use interrupted, equidistant, polyconic, or other map projections. Have them stress uses of the various projections and compare them with the ones in this lesson.

TECHNOLOGY

Use MAPSKILLS to complete this activity.

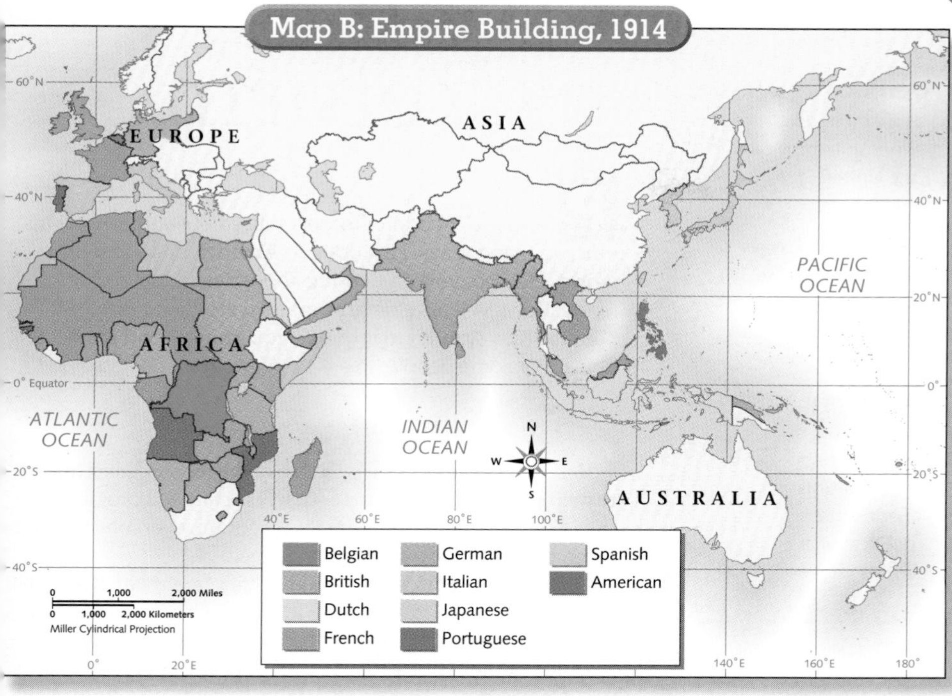

Map A is one kind. Another is the Albers equal-area projection.

Map B is a conformal projection. Notice that the meridians are all an equal distance apart. On a globe, however, these lines get closer together as they approach the poles. Notice also that the parallels closer to the poles are farther apart than those near the equator. On a globe the parallels are all equal distances apart. Conformal projections show directions correctly, but they distort sizes, especially of the places near the poles. The Miller cylindrical projection used on Map B is just one example of a conformal projection. Another is the orthographic (or•thuh•GRAF•ihk) projection.

Use Map A and Map B to answer the following questions.

1. On which parts of Maps A and B do the shapes of the land areas appear to be the same?
2. On which map does Africa appear to be larger? On which map is the size of Africa more accurate?
3. On which map do the meridians get closer together toward the poles?
4. On which map does the space between the parallels get greater toward the poles?

3. Think and Apply

Look at the maps in the Atlas on pages A2–A15 to see other map projections. Write a paragraph about the advantages and disadvantages of using equal-area and conformal projections.

1. the center of the maps: India, the Middle East, central Asia
2. Africa appears to be larger on Map A, the equal-area projection. Its size is more accurate on Map A.
3. The meridians get closer together toward the poles on Map A.
4. The space between the parallels gets larger toward the poles on Map B.

3. CLOSE

Have students complete the Think and Apply activity. Paragraphs will vary but should include some of the following information.

Conformal projections have the advantage of showing directions correctly. If you follow a parallel from left to right on a conformal projection, you will always be moving from west to east. Sailors have long used conformal projections to find compass directions on a map. Conformal projections have the disadvantage of distorting sizes and, therefore, are not suitable for comparing the sizes of continents or other areas.

Because they have the advantage of showing sizes accurately, equal-area projections are useful for comparing the sizes of land or sea areas. However, they are less convenient for determining directions, and they distort shapes in the polar regions.

Link to Mathematics

COMPARE DISTANCE ACCURACY Explain to students that a desirable feature of a map—in addition to true shape, equal area, and accurate direction—is equal distance. That is, the distance scale ideally should be the same for all parts of the map. Have students use the map scales in this lesson to compare conformal and equal-area projections in respect to equal distance. Have them compute and compare distances on the maps between two points at the equator and at a parallel close to one of the poles.

Reteach the Skill

COOPERATIVE LEARNING

RESEARCH MAP PROJECTIONS Have students work in small groups to find world maps in this textbook as well as in atlases and encyclopedias. Have students compare the maps they find with those in this lesson. How many equal-area and conformal maps did they find? For what purposes are these two types of map projections used in the textbook and in reference books?

ACTIVITY BOOK

Practice & Apply

Use ACTIVITY BOOK, pp. 109–110.

TRANSPARENCY

Use TRANSPARENCIES 44A and 44B.

Objectives

1. Summarize the Square Deal.
2. Evaluate the reforms made in the Wisconsin state government.
3. Explain how the NAACP and the NUL worked to make life better for African Americans.

Vocabulary

progressive (p. 556)
commission (p. 556)
conservation (p. 556)
merit system (p. 557)
political boss (p. 557)
civil rights (p. 558)

1. ACCESS

The Focus Question

Have students think about what improvements they would like to see in their neighborhood, town, or city. Ask volunteers how they would go about having these improvements made.

The Main Idea

In this lesson students learn about the progressives, people who worked to improve government and the quality of life in the United States in the early 1900s. After students have read the lesson, have them evaluate the work of the progressives.

2. BUILD

The Square Deal

Key Content Summary

President Theodore Roosevelt saw the need for changes in government to make sure people were treated fairly. His Square Deal program regulated businesses and railroads, set standards for foods and medicines, and conserved the nation's resources.

LESSON 2

FOCUS
How do people today work to improve life in the United States?

Main Idea As you read, look for ways people worked to improve life in the United States in the early 1900s.

Vocabulary
progressive
commission
conservation
merit system
political boss
civil rights

Progressives and Reform

President Theodore Roosevelt used the authority of his office in many ways. He added to American power in the world. He also worked to bring about needed reform at home. Roosevelt and his supporters were called **progressives** because they wanted to improve government and make life better. For some people, this is what progress meant.

The Square Deal

Roosevelt believed it was the job of the federal government to help citizens as much as possible. He started a program called the Square Deal. Under this program, everyone was to be given the same opportunities to succeed.

To make sure that people could get fair treatment, Roosevelt wanted the federal government to make rules for businesses. He set up or increased the authority of special committees called **commissions**. One of these was the Interstate Commerce Commission. Part of its job was to study railroad fares. When the commission decided fares were too high, it made railroad owners lower them.

The explorer and writer John Muir helped persuade Congress to establish Yosemite (yoh•SEH•muh•tee) National Park in 1890. Muir (right) met there with Theodore Roosevelt (left) in 1903.

Roosevelt asked Congress to give the government the authority to see that foods and medicines were safe. In 1906 Congress passed the Pure Food and Drug Act. The act said that all foods and medicines had to meet government safety standards. Congress also passed the Meat Inspection Act. This act said that inspectors would go to all plants that packaged meat to make sure the meat was handled safely.

Roosevelt also was interested in conservation. **Conservation** is a way to protect the environment by keeping natural resources from being wasted or destroyed. Roosevelt set aside millions of acres of land in different parts of the country as national parks. Among these were the Grand Canyon, Mesa Verde, and Glacier national parks.

REVIEW *What was the Square Deal?* Roosevelt's program to give all people the same opportunities to succeed

556 • Unit 9

ACTIVITY CHOICES

Reading Support

USE CONTEXT CLUES Write *progressive* and *conservation* on the board and have students figure out the root word for each. Ask students the meanings of the root words, and have them infer the meanings of *progressive* and *conservation* based on the root words. Provide the following sentences for the remaining vocabulary words, and ask students to use context clues to define them.

1. The Interstate Commerce **Commission** can order railroads to lower their fares if they are too high.
2. In a **merit system,** the person who gets the highest score on a test gets the job.
3. William Tweed was a **political boss** who robbed New York City taxpayers of millions of dollars.
4. African Americans worked to change laws that did not give them their full **civil rights.**

Ask students how each of the last four terms might relate to government.

State and City Reforms

Progressives also worked in state governments. In Wisconsin, Governor Robert La Follette did for his state what Roosevelt was doing for the nation. La Follette made so many reforms that Roosevelt called Wisconsin a "laboratory of democracy."

Elected officials in many states had been giving government jobs to people who did favors for them. To keep this from happening in Wisconsin, Robert La Follette started a **merit system** to make sure that people were qualified for their jobs. Each person applying for a government job was given a test. The person who got the highest score on the test got the job.

La Follette wanted to help workers. He asked the state legislature to pass a law saying that a workday must be no more than ten hours. A second law was passed listing jobs for which children could not be hired. A third law said that the state would pay workers who were hurt on their jobs. To provide the money to do this, factory owners had to make payments to the state.

People in other states called what La Follette was doing the Wisconsin Idea. Many states copied his changes. By 1918, 20 of the 48 states had passed progressive laws like those in Wisconsin.

Many progressive reforms affected city governments, which were often run by political bosses. Some city leaders—especially mayors—were called **political bosses** because they controlled the city government. Most of these bosses had dishonest people working for them. Some of these people gave money to voters so they would vote for the boss. Sometimes they cheated in elections by counting the votes of people who were not citizens or of people who had died. In this way, political bosses often were elected to office again and again.

Th: Nast
THE "BRAINS"
That achieved the Tammany Victory at the Rochester Democratic Convention.

This political cartoon by Thomas Nast suggests that money was used to influence political decision making in New York City. Nast's political cartoons helped bring an end to William Tweed's boss rule in the city.

One of the best-known political bosses was William Tweed. Boss Tweed, as he was called, ran New York City for years and robbed it of millions of dollars. He protected himself by controlling the city police department.

Progressives wanted to end boss rule. One way to do this was to change the form of city government. To keep one person—the mayor—from having all the authority, some city governments set up commissions made up of several people. Each commission member took care of one part of the government, such as the police department, the fire department, or water services. Before long, more than 400 cities had set up commission governments.

REVIEW *What reforms were made by states and cities?*

Civil Rights

Progressive leaders showed what governments could do to make life better for many of the nation's people. However, they did little about the problems of prejudice. So

The workday was shortened, child labor was reduced, and the state was required to pay workers hurt on the job. Boss rule ended.

Civics and Government

Purposes of Government Have students discuss what social problems in the United States encouraged people to start the progressive movement. Then have students analyze how Square Deal laws helped people then and still help people today.

State and City Reforms

Key Content Summary

Progressives worked to change state and city governments. Wisconsin introduced a merit system for government jobs and laws that helped workers. Many other states copied the Wisconsin Idea. To end boss rule in city government, progressives pushed for the commission form of government.

Civics and Government

Political Institutions and Processes Have students evaluate the effects of the progressive movement on state governments and explain why the term *laboratory of democracy* is a good description of La Follette's reforms in Wisconsin.

Civil Rights

Key Content Summary

African American leaders used progressive ideas to address prejudice and work for civil rights. They formed the National Association for the Advancement of Colored People and the National Urban League.

Background

THE NAACP The event that spurred the formation of the NAACP was a race riot in Springfield, Illinois, in which more than 70 people were killed. The riot shocked the nation and led to a meeting in May 1909 in New York City that was attended by nearly 300 African Americans and white liberals. Among the African Americans were W. E. B. Du Bois and Ida Wells-Barnett. Among the liberals were the grandson of William Lloyd Garrison, the abolitionist; Jane Addams; members of the clergy; and social workers. The meeting led to the founding of the NAACP. With Du Bois editing the organization's magazine, the NAACP soon became the most active and effective organization fighting for the rights of African Americans. Within two years it had more than 90,000 members.

Extend and Enrich

COOPERATIVE LEARNING

CONDUCT RESEARCH Divide the class into groups, and assign each group one of the following topics to research: Boss Tweed, Samuel "Golden Rule" Jones, national parks formed under Roosevelt's administration, muckrakers, W. E. B. Du Bois, Ida Wells-Barnett, Jane Addams, the 1902 anthracite coal strike in Pennsylvania, and the Food and Drug Administration today. Have the groups present the information they gather to the class.

Civics and Government

Rights and Responsibilities of Citizens Have students evaluate the work of the NAACP and the National Urban League. Ask them to analyze how the progressive movement helped African Americans directly and indirectly in the early 1900s.

Q. **How do people today work to end prejudice and achieve civil rights?** form organizations; hold marches and demonstrations; write letters and sign petitions; educate the public

3. CLOSE

Have students consider again the Focus question on page 556.

How do people today work to improve life in the United States?

Have students use what they have learned in this lesson to describe ways people today work to improve life in the United States.

LESSON 2 REVIEW—Answers

Check Understanding

1. Theodore Roosevelt, Robert La Follette, W. E. B. Du Bois
2. They worked to change unfair government and business practices and to end prejudice.

Think Critically

3. by working to change unfair laws or business practices; by forming organizations to protect civil rights
4. They improved government and helped to make life better.

Show What You Know

Performance Assessment Consider having students present their views in the form of a television round table.

What to Look For Students should show they understand what problems existed in the early 1900s and the progressives' views on those problems.

BIOGRAPHY

Booker T. Washington 1856–1915

Booker T. Washington was born into slavery. Freed after the Civil War, he worked his way through school as a janitor. After graduating he became a teacher. During Reconstruction, he had seen how hard it was for African American people to fight prejudice. He believed that African Americans could get fair treatment only by becoming skilled workers. Washington led an effort to provide African Americans with more opportunities for education and training. In 1881 he helped found Tuskegee Institute, a trade school for African Americans, in Alabama.

W. E. B. Du Bois 1868–1963

W. E. B. Du Bois strongly disagreed with Washington's point of view. He wanted African Americans to improve their situation by fighting for equal rights. Du Bois graduated from Fisk University and received a doctorate from Harvard. A gifted speaker, teacher, and writer, he devoted his career to improving life for African Americans. In the later years of his life, Du Bois believed that prejudice in the United States would never be broken down. He decided to leave the United States in 1961 and spent the rest of his life in the West African country of Ghana (GAH•nuh).

African American leaders used progressive ideas to try to solve the problem.

One important African American leader of this time was W. E. B. Du Bois (doo•BOYS). In 1909 Du Bois and other progressive leaders formed the National Association for the Advancement of Colored People (NAACP). Members of the NAACP worked to change state laws that did not give full civil rights to African Americans. **Civil rights** are the rights guaranteed to all citizens by the Constitution.

The National Urban League, founded in 1910, also worked for equal rights. It worked to find jobs and homes for African Americans living in cities.

REVIEW ***How did people try to fight prejudice in the early 1900s?*** They worked to change state laws that did not give full civil rights to African Americans.

LESSON 2 REVIEW

Check Understanding

1. **Remember the Facts** Who were the leading progressives in the United States in the early 1900s?
2. **Recall the Main Idea** How did people work to improve life in the United States in the early 1900s?

Think Critically

3. **Past to Present** How do people work for civil rights today?
4. **Think More About It** How were the reforms of the Wisconsin Idea examples of progressive thinking?

Show What You Know

Simulation Activity Imagine that you are a progressive reformer from the early 1900s. Think about one of the problems you read about in this lesson. State your view about the problem to the class.

ACTIVITY CHOICES

ACTIVITY BOOK

Reinforce & Extend

Use ACTIVITY BOOK, p. 111.

Reteach the Main Idea

COOPERATIVE LEARNING

MAKE POSTERS Divide the class into three groups. Assign each group one of the following topics: *national reforms, state reforms,* or *local reforms.* Have each group identify the important reforms in their category and make posters that illustrate the reforms. Ask a spokesperson from each group to share the group's posters with the class. Have students discuss how the reforms illustrated continue to be important today.

The Great War

T he United States entered the twentieth century as a trong nation. When conflict among the nations of Europe xploded into war in 1914, the United States hoped to stay out f the fighting. In time, however, the nation's leaders decided o enter what was then known as the Great War. Later it vould be called World War I.

Dangerous Alliances

On one side in the war were the Allied Powers, or Allies—ncluding Russia, France, Britain, and Italy. On the other side vere the Central Powers—Germany, Austria-Hungary, the)ttoman Empire, and Bulgaria.

The European countries had formed these **alliances**, or artnerships, to protect themselves. In each alliance the mem-ers promised to help one another if they were attacked by nother country. They hoped that this would prevent war. But : had the opposite effect.

Serbia, a country in southern Europe, bordered ustria-Hungary. Many Serbs lived in the southern part f Austria-Hungary and longed to be a part of their erbian homeland. On June 28, 1914, a Serb rebel shot nd killed two members of Austria-Hungary's royal amily in the city of Sarajevo (sar•uh•YAY•voh). ustria-Hungary soon declared war on Serbia. Because f their alliances, the European nations were drawn one y one into the conflict.

At first the United States did not join an alliance. resident Woodrow Wilson asked Americans to be impartial in thought as well as in action." He and nany other Americans wanted the country to be eutral in the war.

But Americans were soon drawn into the conflict. rowling the seas were German submarines, called *Interseeboots*, or U-boats. On May 7, 1915, a U-boat sank ne British passenger ship *Lusitania*. Almost 1,200 people vere killed. Among the dead were 128 Americans. People

LESSON 3

FOCUS
Why do people today sometimes decide to take part in other people's disagreements?

Main Idea As you read, find out why the leaders of the United States decided to enter World War I.

Vocabulary
- alliance
- military draft
- no-man's-land
- isolation

This 1917 poster of "Uncle Sam" was used to bring people into the United States Army.

Reading Support

ANTICIPATION GUIDE Before students read the lesson, ask them to predict which statements are true and which are probably false. Students may correct their predictions as they read.

1. World War I began when a German rebel killed a member of the British royal family. false
2. The United States entered World War I by sinking the German passenger ship *Lusitania*. false
3. The military draft was necessary for the United States to have enough soldiers. true
4. Women's contributions to the Great War helped them gain the right to vote. true
5. Without American soldiers and supplies, the Allies might have lost the Great War. true

Objectives

1. Analyze the consequences of the alliances of major European nations in 1914.
2. Identify the reasons the United States entered the Great War.
3. Describe the weapons introduced in World War I.
4. Summarize the ways American women helped in wartime.
5. Explain the purpose of the League of Nations.

Vocabulary

alliance (p. 559)	no-man's-land (p. 561)
military draft (p. 560)	isolation (p. 563)

1. ACCESS

The Focus Question

Have volunteers discuss occasions when they have taken sides in disputes between their friends. Ask whether their taking sides helped settle the disputes or served to make matters worse.

The Main Idea

In this lesson students explore the reasons for U.S. involvement in the Great War. After students have read the lesson, have them analyze how conflict and cooperation were involved in the events leading up to the war, in the war itself, and in the peace treaty ending the war.

2. BUILD

Dangerous Alliances

Key Content Summary

In World War I the major European nations formed two opposing alliances—the Allied Powers and the Central Powers. Although the United States tried to remain neutral, Americans became angry when the Germans sank the British ship *Lusitania*.

History

Cause and Effect Have students discuss why the European nations had formed alliances prior to the start of World War I. Ask students to identify the advantages and disadvantages of the European alliances.

Q. **What event tested the alliances of European nations?** the assassination in Sarajevo of two members of Austria-Hungary's royal family, which resulted in Austria-Hungary's declaration of war on Serbia

The United States Enters the War

Key Content Summary

The United States joined the conflict on April 2, 1917, after German U-boats had sunk American merchant ships. Congress agreed with President Wilson's request to declare war on Germany. The United States instituted a military draft.

Civics and Government

Purposes of Government Remind students that the U.S. government is supposed to promote order and security and manage conflict. Have students conclude why President Wilson found it necessary to change from a position of neutrality to one of war.

Q. **Why do you think President Wilson felt that democracy was threatened?** The Germans were taking away American trading rights and lives.

in the United States were angry at Germany. Some began to believe the United States should enter the war on the side of the Allies. But President Wilson still hoped to keep the United States neutral. In 1916 he was again elected President. His campaign slogan was "He kept us out of war."

REVIEW ***Which countries were the Allied Powers and which were the Central Powers?***

The United States Enters the War

In early 1917 German leaders said that U-boats would attack all ships in British waters. U-boats then sank three American merchant ships, killing many Americans aboard. President Wilson had finally had enough. On April 2, 1917, he asked the United States Congress to declare war on Germany, saying, "The world must be made safe for democracy." Four days later, the United States joined the Allied Powers.

The United States was not ready for war. Its army was small, and it did not have many weapons. To make the army larger, Congress passed the Selective Service Act. The new law provided for a **military draft**, a way of bringing people into the army. All men between the ages of 21 and 30 had to sign up with special committees called draft boards. Soldiers were then chosen from the list of names. A year later the draft age range was changed to include men between the ages of 18 and 45.

Many Americans thought the draft was a good idea since it would bring together soldiers of different backgrounds. However, many Native Americans, Mexican Americans, African Americans, and immigrants faced the same prejudices in the military as they did at home. They were kept in separate units and were not allowed to do certain jobs. Yet all American soldiers, no matter what their backgrounds, faced the same dangers.

REVIEW ***What was the purpose of the draft?*** to bring men into the army

The *Lusitania*, shown in port, was a passenger ship. Before the ship was attacked, a warning (right) was printed in newspapers. It said that the German government might destroy British ships and that passengers traveled at their own risk.

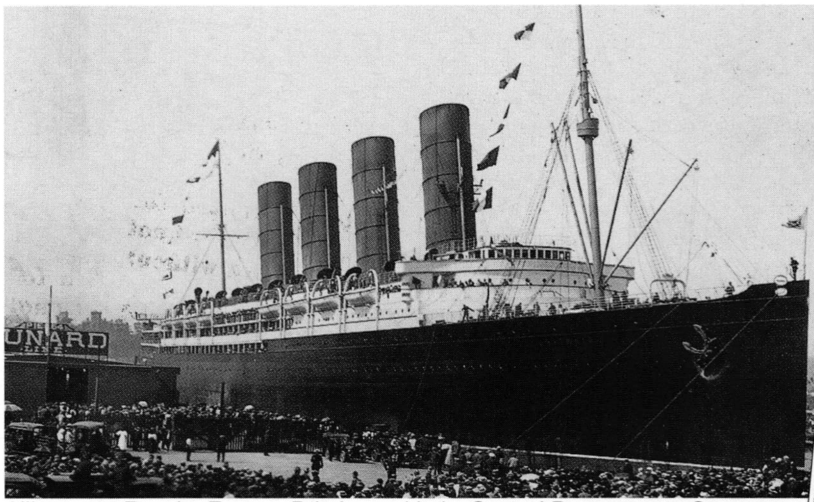

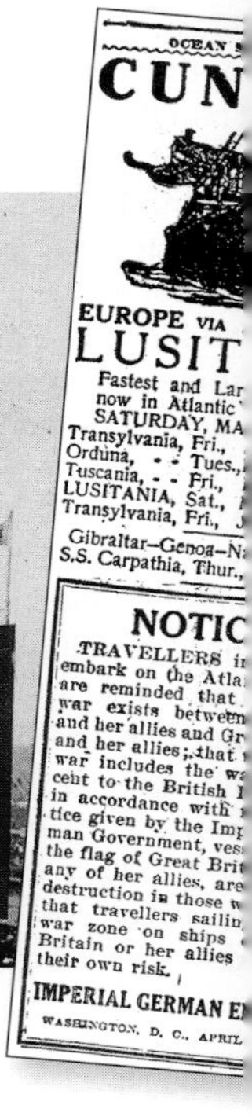

Allies were Russia, France, Britain, and Italy; Central Powers were Germany, Austria-Hungary, the Ottoman Empire, and Bulgaria.

ACTIVITY CHOICES

Background

THE LUSITANIA The sinking of the *Lusitania* has been a subject of dispute for many years. Recent evidence has revealed that the vessel was carrying ammunition for the Allies. Historians also have pointed out that the Germans sent out advertisements warning Americans not to sail on the *Lusitania* and that the Americans who did so must have been aware of the risk they were taking. The Germans wanted to show the world how strong their U-boats were, and they did not care about American public opinion.

Meet Individual Needs

COOPERATIVE LEARNING

AUDITORY LEARNERS Divide the class into two groups: one in favor of entering the Great War after the sinking of the *Lusitania*, the other opposed. Ask each group to use the textbook and library resources to prepare for a debate. Each group should select one moderator and four or five students to represent their views during the debate. After the debate, have the class discuss and evaluate the experience.

Link to Reading

READ AND SUMMARIZE A BIOGRAPHY Have students read a biography of a person who was important in World War I, such as General John J. Pershing, "Billy" Mitchell, Sergeant Alvin C. York, Captain Harry S. Truman, Rear Admiral William S. Sims, Edith Cavell, or Eddie Rickenbacker. Then have students write summary biographies that focus on the role of the person in World War I. Ask students to share their biographies by reading them aloud to the class.

Regions This map shows regions controlled by the Central Powers, the Allied Powers, and neutral countries in Europe during World War I.
■ *What problems do you think Germany had because of Allied Powers on both its eastern and western borders?*

New Weapons

When American soldiers arrived in Europe ɹring the summer of 1917, many were sent France, where most of the fighting took ace. In France, most soldiers fought one ıother from trenches, or ditches, dug in the ound. The trenches of the two opposing des were separated by a **no-man's-land**. ıis was land not held by either side but led with barbed wire and land mines, or ɔmbs buried in the ground.

Soldiers in the trenches faced terrible new eapons. The Germans had developed a achine gun that fired hundreds of bullets each minute. To fight against the machine gun, the British developed the tank. Tanks could cross the no-man's-land, crushing the barbed wire. Machine gun bullets could not go through the tank walls. Against the tank, the Germans used poison gas, the most feared of the new weapons. It killed soldiers—even those in tanks—by making them unable to breathe. While battles raged on the ground, dozens of airplane pilots fought overhead in air battles called dogfights.

During the summer of 1918, the war went on with neither side gaining much ground. The number of Americans in the trenches grew from 27,000 in early June to 500,000 by

History

Turning Points Discuss the fact that half the people who served in the U.S. armed forces during World War I were volunteers. Have students analyze why Americans would be willing to fight a war that was centered around conflicts in Europe.

Geography

Location Refer students to the map on this page and have them locate and identify the countries that supported the Allies and the Central Powers, as well as those that remained neutral.

Visual Analysis

Learn from Maps Have students answer the question in the caption. Germany had to split its army to protect both borders.

New Weapons

Key Content Summary

New weapons, such as machine guns, tanks, and poison gas, were introduced in World War I. This also was the first war in which airplanes played a role. More than 8 million people around the world died in the war.

History

People and Events Across Time and Place Have students discuss the advantages and disadvantages of trench warfare. Also have students compare and contrast the weapons used during World War I with those used during the Civil War.

Smithsonian Institution®

ɜo to the Internet site at *http://www.si.edu/ ·arcourt/socialstudies* to visit the exhibit "Great Var in the Air" at the National Air and Space Auseum.

Link to Music

SING WORLD WAR I SONGS The war inspired many songwriters to write about the war experience. The songs helped raise the spirits of the soldiers on the battlefield and of the families and friends waiting for them at home. Ask the music teacher to teach students to sing World War I songs, such as "Over There"; "Tipperary"; "Pack Up Your Troubles in Your Old Kit Bag and Smile, Smile, Smile"; and "Keep the Home Fires Burning." Have students analyze the meanings of the lyrics in the songs.

Meet Individual Needs

ENGLISH LANGUAGE LEARNERS Have students work in pairs and take turns reading paragraphs of the text aloud and asking one another questions about the content. Before moving on to the next paragraph, both students should summarize in their own words what they know about the subject.

Women in the War

Key Content Summary

Women contributed during the war by replacing men in factories and on farms. Others served as nurses, ambulance drivers, clerks, and telegraph operators for the Army and the Navy. Women's contributions helped them gain the right to vote after the war.

Culture

Social Organizations and Institutions Have students give examples of ways women contributed to the war effort and explain how the war changed women's traditional roles. Ask students to speculate on whether women would be able to continue in their new roles after the war.

Visual Analysis

Learn from Time Lines Direct students' attention to the time line and have them answer the caption question. 3 years

HISTORY

1917

While World War I was taking place in Europe, revolutions were taking place in other parts of the world. In 1910 Francisco Madero led a revolution in Mexico against President Porfirio Díaz, who ruled as a dictator. Several leaders fought for power in Mexico in the years that followed. In 1917 a new constitution was written. It is the basis of government in Mexico today.

A revolution also took place in Russia, where life for many was hard. In 1917 a group of revolutionaries led by Vladimir Illyich Lenin took control. Russia's monarch, Nicholas II, was killed. Life for the Russians became even worse when harsh new rulers came to power.

the end of August. Before the war ended, about 53,000 Americans were killed. Another 230,000 were wounded. More than 8 million people from countries around the world died in the war.

REVIEW ***What new weapons were used in the war?*** machine guns, tanks, poison gas

Women in the War

The United States government did not let women fight in the war. Instead, many women took over jobs left by men who had gone to fight in the war. Some women became mechanics or farm workers. Others became police officers. Some women worke in weapons factories. Some went to Europe as nurses or ambulance drivers. Thousands more joined the army and the navy as clerks and telegraph operators.

Katherine Stinson of San Antonio, Texas, wanted to become a fighter pilot in the war. Stinson and her mother opened a flying school in 1913. The army, however, would not let her fly in battle. So she flew across the United States, raising money for the Red Cross. Then she went to Europe and served as an ambulance driver.

Women's wartime work helped bring one very important change after the war. The Nineteenth Amendment to the Constitution was passed in 1920. This amendment gave women the right to vote. Carrie Chapman Catt, a women's suffrage leader, later called the Nineteenth Amendment "the greatest thing that came out of the war."

REVIEW ***How did women help in wartime*** They took over many jobs previously held b men, worked in weapons factories, and served as military nurses, ambulan drivers, clerks, and telegraph operators.

LEARNING FROM TIME LINES This time line shows some of the key events of World War I. During the war some American women served as ambulance drivers.

■ *For how many years after the beginning of World War I did the United States remain neutral?*

World War I

1913 — 1916 — 1919

- **1913** • Wilson becomes President
- **1914** • World War I begins
- **1915** • *Lusitania* is attacked
- **1917** • The United States enters World War I
- **1918** • World War I ends

Activity Choices

Link to Art

MAKE A DISPLAY Challenge student volunteers to prepare a visual display illustrating how traditions for women changed because of World War I. Students may illustrate changes in areas such as job opportunities, voting rights, clothing styles, and hairstyles. Have students locate books that have photographs of women before and during World War I to guide their drawings. Make sure students label their illustrations.

Extend and Enrich

COOPERATIVE LEARNING

MAKE MAPS, DIAGRAMS, CHARTS, AND TIME LINES Divide the class into small groups. Assign each group one of the following projects: a map of the western front, the eastern front, or the Italian-Austrian front; a diagram of the trenches, the howitzer, or World War I airplanes; a chart of jobs taken over by women; or a time line of major events in World War I. Have students use encyclopedias and other library resources to develop their assigned topics. Have each group share and discuss its completed project with the other groups.

Technology

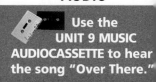

Use TIMELINER™ to complete this activity.

Audio

Use the UNIT 9 MUSIC AUDIOCASSETTE to hear the song "Over There."

This painting by John Christen Johansen shows Allied leaders at the signing of the Treaty of Versailles.

The War Ends

Americans made an important difference the Great War. Soldiers gave military help. ıiploads of American wheat, canned foods, ıd guns helped supply the Allied armies. orking together, the Allies began to push ıck the German army. Finally, on November , 1918, the Germans surrendered. On that ıy they signed an armistice that ended the ghting.

The Great War was over, and American ldiers came home. Leaders of the Allies thered to make peace terms. During these lks President Wilson described his idea for League of Nations, to which all nations could belong. Wilson hoped the organization would help find peaceful ways to solve problems among nations.

The Treaty of Versailles (ver•SY), which had ended the war, set up the League of Nations. But the United States did not join. The United States Senate must vote to approve treaties. It voted not to approve the Treaty of Versailles because many senators did not want the United States to belong to the League of Nations. They believed that the United States should stay out of other countries' problems. They felt that the nation should adopt a policy of **isolation**—remaining separate from other countries.

REVIEW *What was the League of Nations?*
an organization that would work for peaceful solutions to problems among nations

ESSON 3 REVIEW

Check Understanding

1. **Remember the Facts** Why did European countries form alliances in the early 1900s?
2. **Recall the Main Idea** Why did the leaders of the United States decide to enter World War I?

Think Critically

3. **Think More About It** Could the United States have avoided entering the war? Explain.
4. **Past to Present** How does the United States use its power to affect what happens in the world today?

Show What You Know

Journal-Writing Activity Imagine that you are a soldier in a trench in 1918. Write a journal entry that describes what you see and hear. Include a description of how you spend your days. Share your work with a family member.

The War Ends

Key Content Summary

The American soldiers helped turn the tide of war toward an Allied victory. The Treaty of Versailles ended the war and set up a League of Nations.

3. CLOSE

Have students consider again the Focus question on page 559.

Why do people today sometimes decide to take part in other people's disagreements?

Have students use what they have learned in this lesson about U.S. participation in World War I to describe situations in which people today might decide to take part in other people's disagreements.

LESSON 3 REVIEW—Answers

Check Understanding

1. to protect themselves and help one another if they were attacked by another country
2. because German U-boats had destroyed U.S. merchant ships and killed Americans

Think Critically

3. Accept reasonable responses that students can defend.
4. by sending troops and supplies into trouble spots, by joining with other members of the United Nations in trying to prevent armed conflicts, by sending financial aid to needy countries, and by forming alliances whose purpose is to defend member countries from possible attack

Show What You Know

Performance Assessment Consider presenting students' journal entries as part of a bulletin board display. Have students illustrate their journal entries for the display.

What to Look For Make sure students understand trench warfare and the difficult life of a soldier on the front lines.

Reteach the Main Idea

COOPERATIVE LEARNING

MAKE A TIME LINE Divide the class into small groups. Challenge each group to use the textbook as a resource to make a time line of events that led United States leaders to decide to enter World War I. Have the groups share and discuss their completed time lines.

ACTIVITY BOOK

Reinforce & Extend

Use ACTIVITY BOOK, p. 112.

TECHNOLOGY

Use TIMELINER™ to complete this activity.

MODEL & APPLY SKILLS

Objectives

1. Recognize propaganda.
2. Analyze and evaluate a propaganda statement.

Vocabulary

propaganda (p. 564)

1. ACCESS

On the board, write two brief opposing statements of propaganda about issues currently in the news, or use the following fictitious example:

1. The Freedom Force is a band of patriots who seek to protect the liberty of all New Landian people.
2. The so-called Freedom Force is a gang of thugs who endanger the New Landian way of life.

Introduce the term *propaganda*. Explain that both of the statements above are propaganda, one designed to help a cause and one designed to harm it. Point out the positive words—*freedom*, *band*, *patriots*, *liberty*—in the first example and the negative words—*so-called*, *gang*, *thugs*, *endanger*—in the second. Emphasize the importance of recognizing propaganda to being able to make wise decisions.

In Remember What You Have Read, have students review the descriptions of the entry of the United States into World War I and the wartime propaganda campaigns.

2. BUILD

Have students examine the posters and read the pamphlet for German American soldiers, as instructed in Understand the Process. Then have them answer the questions.

Critical Thinking Skills

Recognize Propaganda

1. Why Learn This Skill?

Propaganda is information or ideas designed to help or harm a cause. It is used by people to persuade others to share their views. Being able to recognize propaganda will help you make thoughtful and informed decisions.

2. Remember What You Have Read

Each side in a war often uses propaganda to help win support for its cause. Think about what you have read about World War I. The United States remained neutral during the early years of the war. Then, after German U-boats began to sink American ships, the United States joined the Allied Powers and declared war on Germany.

One week after war was declared, President Wilson set up the Committee on Public Information, headed by George Creel. Creel's job was to "sell the war to the Americ[a]n people." To do this, Creel hired artists and writers to wage a propaganda campaign in support of the war. The committee printed mi[l]lions of leaflets and posters praising America[n] soldiers for fighting for democracy. At the sa[me] time, they accused the German government o[f] carrying out terrible crimes in their effort to take over the world.

Posters, like those shown below, were designed to help gather support for United States troops during World War I. Poster A encouraged Americans to enlist in the army. Poster B encouraged Americans not to waste food, which was needed to support United States troops. The troops needed plenty of fo[od] to keep their strength in battle.

A

B

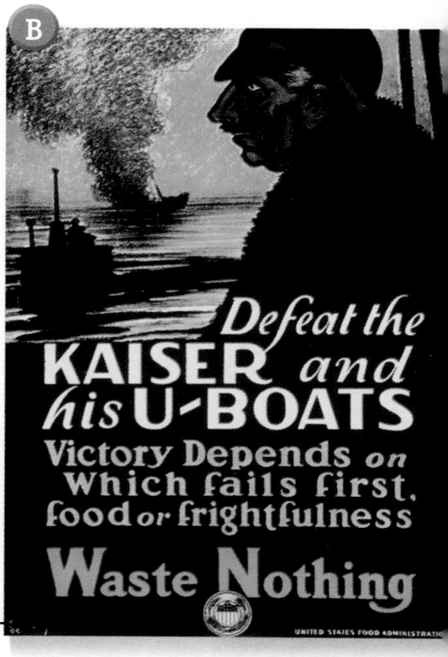

ACTIVITY CHOICES

Link to Language Arts

WRITE PROPAGANDA Choose an issue that interests the students. Have half of the students write paragraphs of propaganda in favor of the issue. Have the other half write paragraphs opposing the issue. Instruct students to use techniques learned in the lesson. Conduct a sharing session in which students analyze propaganda techniques their classmates have used.

TECHNOLOGY

Use THE AMAZING WRITING MACHINE™ to complete this writing activity.

To the American soldiers of German descent.

You say in your loose leaf that you serve in an honorable way in the U. S. Army. Do you think it honorable to fight the country that has given birth to your fathers or forefathers? . . . We are fighting for everything dear to us, for our homes, our very existence. What are you fighting for, why did you come over here, four thousand miles away from your own home? Did Germany do you any harm, did it ever threaten you? Your leaders are Misleaders, they have lied to you that we were slaves of a tyrant, and you are guilty of gross ignorance if you believe one word of it. . . . There is more freedom in Germany indeed than in the land of Dictator Wilson. We do not try to deceive you, we do not promise you a farm, but we assure you that every honest man willing to work has infinitely better chances in Germany where we do not suffer corrupt politicians, deceiving land speculators, nor cheating contractors. Lay down your gun, your innermost soul is not in this fight. Come to us, you will not regret it.

The German government waged a propa-
nda campaign of its own during the war.
erman soldiers dropped leaflets like the one
own above from airplanes or hot-air bal-
ons. The leaflets were dropped near where
merican troops were stationed. Some leaflets
ere packed in artillery shells and shot across
e trenches to the Americans.

. Understand the Process

Study the posters on page 564 and read the
aflet above. Then answer the following ques-
ons to help you learn about these primary-
urce documents.

1. To whom are the posters addressed? To whom is the leaflet addressed?
2. What points are being made on the posters? What points are being made in the leaflet?
3. Do you think the posters would persuade you to support the American troops?
4. What facts does the writer of the leaflet give? What opinions does the writer give?
5. If you were a German American soldier, do you think you would believe the arguments on the leaflet? Why or why not?

4. Think and Apply

Draw a poster that could have been used to call for support in the United States for the Allied Powers in World War I. Your poster should focus on the idea of "making the world safe for democracy."

1. Posters A and B are addressed to Americans; the leaflet is addressed to American soldiers of German descent.
2. It is important for Americans to enlist and not waste resources; German American soldiers should not fight Germany. They should defect to Germany.
3. Answers will vary, but encourage students to explain why or why not.
4. Answers will vary but should include the idea that the writer uses few facts and many opinions.
5. Answers will vary, but make sure that students explain their answers.

3. CLOSE

Have students complete the Think and Apply activity. As they share their posters, look for an understanding of the nature of propaganda. Stress the importance of recognizing propaganda to making sound decisions.

Community Involvement

Invite a communications teacher from a local university or from your own school system to speak to the students about propaganda. Ask the speaker to stress the techniques of propaganda as well as how to recognize it.

Reteach the Skill

ANALYZE CURRENT PROPAGANDA
Find and present to the students a pamphlet, article, editorial, or other piece of current propaganda. Have the students analyze the material, using questions like those in Understand the Process. Look for the ability to recognize propaganda.

ACTIVITY BOOK

Practice & Apply

Use ACTIVITY BOOK, p. 113.

TRANSPARENCY

Use TRANSPARENCY 45.

CHAPTER 17 REVIEW

Time Line

Ask students to share what they recall about each event shown on the time line.

Connect Main Ideas

Use the organizer to review the main ideas of the chapter. Have students use their textbooks to complete the organizer or check their work. Allow time for them to discuss and compare their responses.

ACTIVITY BOOK

Summarize the Chapter

A copy of the graphic organizer appears on ACTIVITY BOOK, p. 114.

TRANSPARENCY

A copy of the graphic organizer appears on TRANSPARENCY 46.

Write More About It

Write a Letter

Students should explain that some Hawaiians wanted Hawaii to be ruled by Hawaiians, while many Americans wanted to control government, resources, and trade of the islands. Students should include their own opinions in their letters.

Write a Newspaper Article

As newspaper reporters, students must state facts about the new kinds of weapons they observe. Students should describe how the new weapons are affecting the fighting.

TECHNOLOGY

Use THE AMAZING WRITING MACHINE™ to complete the writing activities.

TECHNOLOGY

Use TIMELINER™ DATA DISKS to discuss and summarize the chapter.

CHAPTER 17 REVIEW

1860 1870 1880

1867
• United States buys Alaska from Russia

CONNECT MAIN IDEAS

Use this graphic organizer to show how the chapter's main ideas are connected. Write the main idea of each lesson. A copy of the organizer appears on page 114 of the Activity Book.

Possible answers to the graphic organizer appea[r] on page 546C of this Teacher's Edition.

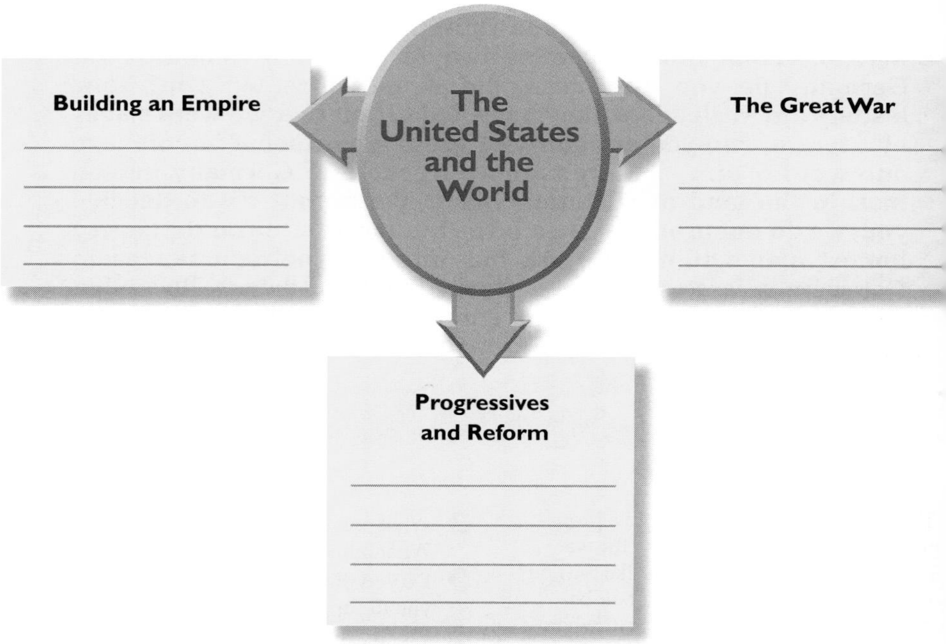

WRITE MORE ABOUT IT

Write a Letter Imagine that you are living in the Hawaiian Islands during the late nineteenth century. Write a letter to a friend explaining why some people want the United States to annex Hawaii and others do not. Be sure to tell your friend how you feel about the issue.

Write a Newspaper Article Imagine that you are a newspaper reporter covering the fighting in Europe during World War I. Write a short newspaper article describing what you have seen. Tell how tanks, machine guns, barbed wire, mines, and poison gas are affecting the fighting.

Use Vocabulary

1. imperialism (p. 548)
2. progressive (p. 556)
3. conservation (p. 556)
4. civil rights (p. 558)
5. alliance (p. 559)
6. isolation (p. 563)

Check Understanding

7. Cuba, Guam, the Philippine Islan[ds] and Puerto Rico (p. 550)
8. by welcoming a revolution to e[nd] Colombian rule (p. 551)
9. People had to take qualifying tests [to] get government jobs. (p. 557)
10. They worked to end prejudice a[nd] to gain equal rights for Afric[an] Americans. (p. 558)

1900 | 1910 | 1920 | 1930

…nish-American …r

1909
• NAACP founded

1917
• United States enters World War I

1920
• Women gain right to vote

…se Vocabulary

…Write the term that correctly matches each …finition. Then use the term in a sentence.

alliance	**imperialism**
civil rights	**isolation**
conservation	**progressive**

empire building

a person who wants to improve government and make life better

keeping natural resources from being wasted or destroyed

the rights guaranteed to all citizens by the Constitution

a partnership

remaining separate from other countries

…heck Understanding

What territories became part of the United States as a result of the Spanish-American War?

How was President Roosevelt able to get permission from Panama to build a canal in that country?

How did the merit system prevent officials from giving government jobs to people who did favors for them?

Why were the NAACP and the National Urban League important?

What alliance of countries won World War I? What alliance was defeated?

Why did Congress vote not to join the League of Nations?

Think Critically

13. **Cause and Effect** How did alliances help lead to World War I?
14. **Past to Present** What effect did the passage of the Nineteenth Amendment have on American women?

Apply Skills

Compare Map Projections One kind of map projection shows the sizes of regions in correct relationship to one another but distorts shapes. Another kind of projection correctly shows directions but distorts sizes of places. Which kind is a conformal projection, and which kind is an equal-area projection?

Recognize Propaganda Choose a cause that concerns you. Create a leaflet that uses propaganda to call for support from others for your cause. Share your leaflet with a classmate.

Read More About It

Theodore Roosevelt Takes Charge by Nancy Whitelaw. Albert Whitman & Company. This book describes the life and accomplishments of the twenty-sixth President of the United States.

Visit the Internet at **http://www.hbschool.com** for additional resources.

CHAPTER 17 REVIEW

Apply Skills

Compare Map Projections
conformal shows correct directions; equal-area shows correct sizes

Recognize Propaganda Students can work in groups to create the leaflets. Leaflets should present only one point of view and be persuasive in nature.

Read More About It

Additional books are listed in the Multimedia Resource Center on page 540D of this Teacher's Edition.

Unit Project Check-Up

Check to see that students have determined which events they are responsible for in the class mural. They should have completed a rough sketch of their part of the mural, including details that represent the event.

ASSESSMENT PROGRAM

Use CHAPTER 17 TEST, pp. 143–146.

Allied Powers; Central Powers (p. 563)

Congress felt that the nation should return to a policy of isolation. (p. 563)

Think Critically

13. Answers should demonstrate an understanding of how alliances brought countries into the conflict one by one.
14. Women gained the right to vote as a result of the Nineteenth Amendment, which furthered their efforts in gaining equal rights.

CHAPTER 18

Planning Chart

	THEMES • Strands	VOCABULARY	MEET INDIVIDUAL NEEDS	RESOURCES INCLUDING ▶ TECHNOLOGY
LESSON 1 **The Roaring Twenties** pp. 569–573	CONTINUITY & CHANGE • Economics • History • Culture	consumer good, installment buying, assembly line, aviation, commercial industry, jazz	Advanced Learners, p. 570 Extend and Enrich, p. 572 Reteach the Main Idea, p. 573	Activity Book, p. 115
LESSON 2 **The Great Depression and the New Deal** pp. 574–578	INDIVIDUALISM & INTERDEPENDENCE • Economics • History • Civics and Government	stock market, depression, bureaucracy, unemployment, minimum wage, hydroelectric dam	English Language Learners, p. 575 Extend and Enrich, p. 577 Reteach the Main Idea, p. 578	Activity Book, p. 116
LESSON 3 **Learn History through Literature** **Children of the Dust Bowl** by Jerry Stanley pp. 579–582	INDIVIDUALISM & INTERDEPENDENCE • Geography		Tactile Learners, p. 581 Extend and Enrich, p. 581 Reteach the Main Idea, p. 582	Activity Book, p. 117
LESSON 4 **World War II** pp. 583–588	CONFLICT & COOPERATION • History • Economics • Geography • Culture • Civics and Government	concentration camp, civilian, rationing, relocation camp	Auditory Learners, p. 584 Advanced Learners, p. 586 Extend and Enrich, p. 587 Reteach the Main Idea, p. 588	Activity Book, p. 118 ▶ THE AMAZING WRITING MACHINE
LESSON 5 **The Allies Win the War** pp. 589–594	CONFLICT & COOPERATION • Geography • History • Civics and Government	front, D day, Holocaust, island-hopping, communism, free world, cold war	Advanced Learners, p. 591 Extend and Enrich, p. 593 Reteach the Main Idea, p. 594	Activity Book, p. 119
SKILL **Read Parallel Time Lines** p. 595	BASIC STUDY SKILLS • Chart and Graph Skills		Reteach the Skill, p. 595	Activity Book, p. 120 Transparency 47 ▶ TIMELINER
CHAPTER REVIEW pp. 596–597				Activity Book, p. 121 Transparency 48 Assessment Program Chapter 18 Test, pp. 147–150 ▶ THE AMAZING WRITING MACHINE ▶ TIMELINER ▶ INTERNET

8 DAYS

TIME MANAGEMENT

DAY 1	DAY 2	DAY 3	DAY 4	DAY 5	DAY 6	DAY 7	DAY 8
Lesson 1	Lesson 2	Lesson 3	Lesson 4	Lesson 5	Skill	Chapter Review	Chapter Test

Activity Book

LESSON 1
Interpret a Chart

NAME ______________________ DATE __________

WHO'S DRIVING?

Interpret a Chart

DIRECTIONS: ***Study the chart below. Then complete the activities that follow.***

FAMOUS U.S. AUTO AND TRUCK MAKERS

NAME	YEARS LIVED	HERITAGE	VEHICLE NAME	INTERESTING FACTS
Louis Chevrolet	1879–1941 62	Swiss	Chevrolet	Drove a race car and worked as a car mechanic. Founded Chevrolet in 1911 with William Durant.
Henry Ford	1863–1947 84	Irish	Ford	Manufactured the Model T, a car that working people could afford. Started company with $28,000 of other people's money.
Augustus Mack	1873–1940 67	German	Mack Truck ★	Made truck used in WWI. Nicknamed Bulldog. Phrase *built like a Mack truck* coined from how well truck withstood use in war.
Ransom Eli Olds	1864–1950 86	English	Oldsmobile	Mass-produced Oldsmobiles four years before Ford sold first car. Known as *Father of the Popular-priced Car.*

1. Determine how long each person lived, and write your answers in the Years Lived column. Circle the dates of the person who lived the longest.
2. Underline the name of the person who was the first to mass-produce cars.
3. Put a star next to the vehicle that was used in World War I.
4. Use the information in the chart to decide how the early vehicle makers were similar. Then write the similarities on the blank lines below.
   - **a)** Years Lived: all born in mid- to late 1800s and died in the first half of the 1900s
   - **b)** Heritage: all of European heritage
   - **c)** Vehicle Names: all named with person's last name

DIRECTIONS: ***Choose one of the people mentioned in the chart. On a separate sheet of paper, write a paragraph about this person using the information from the chart.***
Students' paragraphs should be based on information contained in the chart.

LESSON 2
Interpret Information on a Map

NAME ______________________ DATE __________

Unemployment: 1934

Interpret Information on a Map

DIRECTIONS: ***The map below shows what percentage of each state's population was receiving unemployment relief in 1934. Study the map. Then complete the activities that follow.***

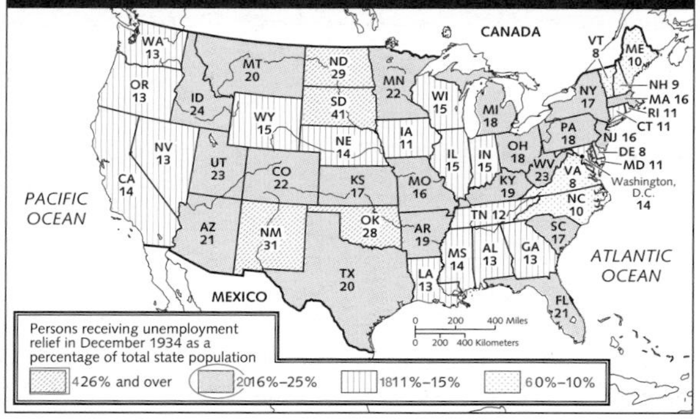

1. Select a color for each of the categories shown in the map key. Then, using the appropriate color, shade in the states that belong in each category.
2. Count the number of states for each category in the map key.
   - **a)** Write each total next to the appropriate key box for each category.
   - **b)** Draw a box around the key box of the category with the fewest states.
   - **c)** Circle the key box of the category with the most states.
3. Why do you think Alaska and Hawaii are not shown on this map?
   They were not yet states.

LESSON 3
Complete a Story Map

NAME ______________________ DATE __________

MAPPING LITERATURE

Complete a Story Map

DIRECTIONS: ***After reading*** **Children of the Dust Bowl** ***in your textbook, complete the following story map to help organize what you have read. You may wish to copy the story map onto a separate sheet of paper.***

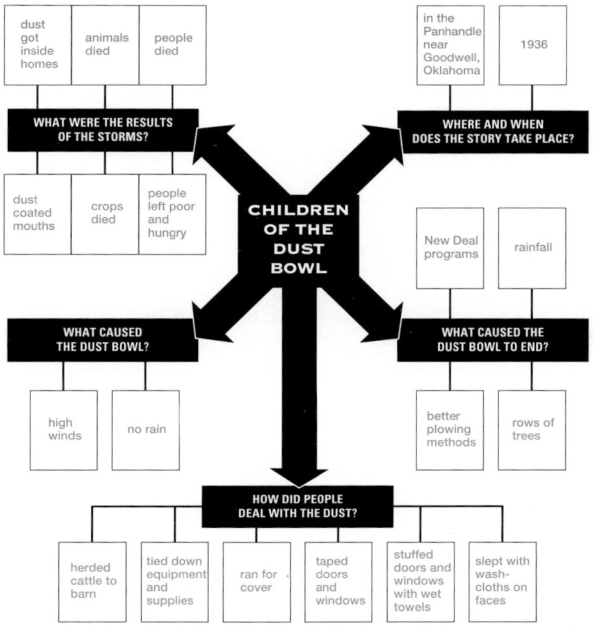

LESSON 4
Distinguish Between Fact and Opinion

NAME ______________________ DATE __________

Navajo Code Talkers

Distinguish Between Fact and Opinion

DIRECTIONS: ***Read the information below about Navajo code talkers. Then determine which of the statements that follow are based on facts and which are based on opinions. Write F next to the facts and O next to the opinions.***

Secret communication is important to winning wars. If the enemy breaks secret codes, there are no surprise attacks. During World War II, codes were broken quickly by using charts based on the number of times letters are used in a language. But when the United States used Navajo code talkers, the country had an unbreakable code.

The Navajo language is difficult to learn, especially for adults. By 1940 fewer than 30 people outside the tribe knew it! The Navajo language has no written form. Different syllables and tones have different meanings based on the Navajo worldview. Four tones of voice—low, high, rising, and falling—are part of the language's sounds. About 400 Navajo volunteers served as Marine Corps code talkers during World War II. Because the code was never broken, Navajo code talkers continued to help the United States in the Korean and Vietnam wars.

Navajo code talkers were very important to the war effort. Military experts believe that code talkers shortened the war in the Pacific by at least a year. Others believe that the United States might not have won without them.

O **1.** Secret communication is the most important key to winning a war.
F **2.** Frequency charts allowed codes other than the Navajo code to be broken.
F **3.** The Navajo language is difficult for many people, especially adults, to learn.
F **4.** The Navajo language is based on four tones of voice.
O **5.** World War II would have ended differently without the code talkers.
F **6.** There is no written form of Navajo.
O **7.** The code talkers made the most valuable contribution to the war effort.
F **8.** Navajo code talkers served in several wars.
F **9.** The Navajo language is based on the Navajo worldview.
O **10.** The code talkers shortened the war by a year.

LESSON 5
Outline News Stories

NAME ______________________ DATE __________

WORLD WAR II NEWS

Outline News Stories

DIRECTIONS: When newspaper reporters write nonfiction stories, they answer the questions: Who? What? When? Where? Why? and How? Before reporters write, they outline the answers to these six questions. Study the outlines below, and fill in the missing information.

WHO? Japanese fighter planes
WHAT? Surprise attack on Pearl Harbor naval base
WHEN? December 7, 1941
WHERE? Pearl Harbor, Hawaii
WHY? To damage U.S. Pacific fleet
HOW? Flying over the Pacific Ocean and attacking U.S. ships

WHO? Allied troops
WHAT? D day
WHEN? June 6, 1944
WHERE? Normandy, France
WHY? Invasion of Europe to recapture European lands from the Germans
HOW? Crossing the English Channel and landing on the beaches

WHO? Crew of the *Enola Gay*
WHAT? Dropping of atom bomb
WHEN? August 6, 1945
WHERE? Hiroshima, Japan
WHY? To force Japan to surrender
HOW? Flying over Hiroshima in the U.S. bomber *Enola Gay*

SKILL PRACTICE
Apply Chart and Graph Skills

NAME ______________________ DATE __________

HOW TO READ Parallel Time Lines

Apply Chart and Graph Skills

DIRECTIONS: Use Unit 9 of your textbook to find the year each of the following events took place. Write the year in the space provided. Then, if the event is not related to World War II, write the letter of the event on the appropriate date above the time line labeled Events Not Related to the War. Write the letters of all war-related events at the appropriate date above the time line labeled Events Related to the War.

1929 **A.** Stock market crash
1927 **B.** Babe Ruth hits his sixtieth home run
1945 **C.** Bombing of Hiroshima and Nagasaki
1920 **D.** First commercial radio station broadcast
1942 **E.** Japanese Americans relocated
1941 **F.** United States enters World War II
1903 **G.** First flight at Kitty Hawk
1933 **H.** Nazi party takes over German government
1941 **I.** Japanese attack Pearl Harbor
1945 **J.** V-E Day
1944 **K.** D day
1939 **L.** World War II begins

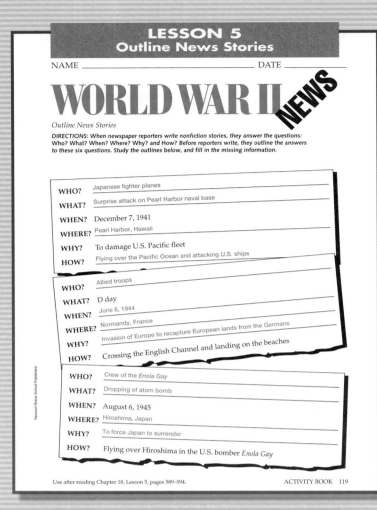

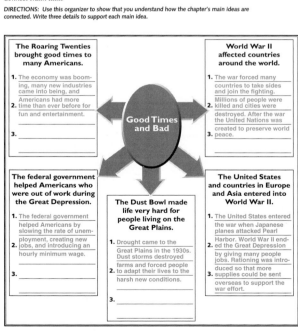

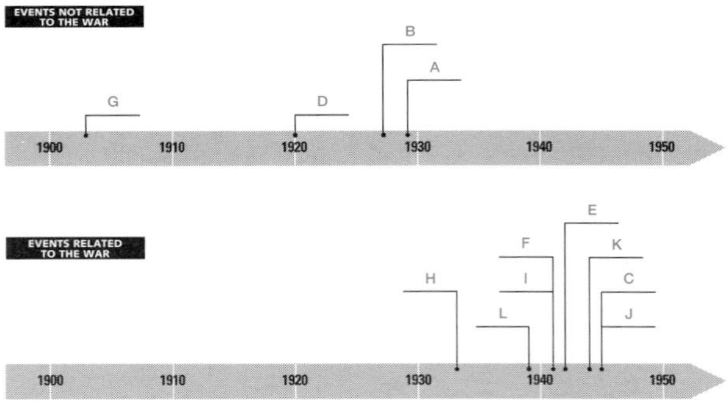

CHAPTER 18 REVIEW
Connect Main Ideas

NAME ______________________ DATE __________

Good Times and Bad

Connect Main Ideas

DIRECTIONS: Use this organizer to show that you understand how the chapter's main ideas are connected. Write three details to support each main idea.

Good Times and Bad

The Roaring Twenties brought good times to many Americans.
1. The economy was booming, many new industries came into being, and
2. Americans had more time than ever before for fun and entertainment.
3. ______

World War II affected countries around the world.
1. The war forced many countries to take sides and join the fighting.
2. Millions of people were killed and cities were destroyed. After the war the United Nations was
3. created to preserve world peace.

The federal government helped Americans who were out of work during the Great Depression.
1. The federal government helped Americans by slowing the rate of unemployment, creating new
2. jobs, and introducing an hourly minimum wage.
3. ______

The Dust Bowl made life very hard for people living on the Great Plains.
1. Drought came to the Great Plains in the 1930s. Dust storms destroyed farms and forced people
2. to adapt their lives to the harsh new conditions.
3. ______

The United States and countries in Europe and Asia entered into World War II.
1. The United States entered the war when Japanese planes attacked Pearl Harbor. World War II end-
2. ed the Great Depression by giving many people jobs. Rationing was introduced so that more
3. supplies could be sent overseas to support the war effort.

COMMUNITY RESOURCES

Ideas for using community resources, including speakers and field trips

Historical Societies and World War II Experts:

______
______
______
______
______

Museums and Historic Sites:

______
______
______
______
______

Chapter 18 Assessment

For ongoing PERFORMANCE ASSESSMENT, see Show What You Know, pp. 573, 578, 588, 594.

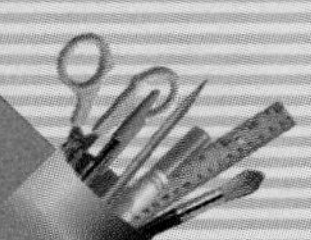

CONTENT

NAME ______________________ DATE __________

Chapter Test 18

Part One: Test Your Understanding *(4 points each)*

DIRECTIONS: ***Circle the letter of the best answer.***

1. Henry Ford found that he could produce cars less expensively by
- **A.** using plastic instead of steel for some car parts.
- **B.** hiring only immigrants to work in his factory.
- **(C.)** using a moving assembly line.
- **D.** using designs made in Japan.

2. Jazz developed from the musical heritage of
- **A.** Native Americans.
- **B.** rock and roll.
- **C.** German immigrants.
- **(D.)** African Americans.

3. What was the Harlem Renaissance?
- **A.** a system whereby people could pay a little money each month for consumer goods
- **B.** a program for rebuilding large areas of New York City after a fire
- **C.** the migration of African Americans from the North to the South during the 1920s
- **(D.)** a time of interest and activity in the arts among African American writers, musicians, and artists

4. The stock market crash of 1929 occurred because
- **A.** there were too many people without full-time jobs.
- **(B.)** more people wanted to sell stock than wanted to buy stock.
- **C.** farmers could not produce enough food for the country.
- **D.** World War I caused the economy to crash.

5. After the stock market crashed, many banks had to close because
- **A.** bankers had used bank money to invest in Roosevelt's Alphabet Soup.
- **(B.)** large numbers of people took their saved money out of banks in order to live.
- **C.** the government needed the banks' money to run its many programs.
- **D.** the government ordered them to do so.

6. How did the New Deal affect the federal government?
- **A.** The federal government lost power to the state governments.
- **B.** The New Deal let the President take the country to war.
- **(C.)** The federal government got more authority and more workers.
- **D.** The New Deal stopped government control over the railroads.

(continued)

CONTENT

NAME ______________________ DATE __________

7. The Works Progress Administration hired workers to
- **A.** take the place of union members who were on strike.
- **B.** invest government money in the stock market.
- **C.** take over the banks that had been closed.
- **(D.)** build roads, airports, and public buildings.

8. The building of hydroelectric dams helped economic development by
- **(A.)** allowing the government to sell electricity at low rates.
- **B.** allowing farmers to sell water at high rates.
- **C.** giving investors the opportunity to buy shares of stock in the dams.
- **D.** giving farmers more land on which to grow crops.

9. As the ruler of Germany, Adolf Hitler
- **A.** attacked United States naval bases in Hawaii.
- **B.** put only Jewish people into positions of leadership.
- **C.** caused the German stock market to crash.
- **(D.)** rebuilt Germany's economy by preparing for another war.

10. World War II began in Europe when
- **A.** Italy took over Ethiopia.
- **B.** Japan invaded Manchuria.
- **(C.)** Germany invaded Poland.
- **D.** Germany attacked France.

11. The United States entered World War II the day after
- **A.** Britain declared war on Germany.
- **B.** Russia invaded Britain.
- **(C.)** the Japanese bombed Pearl Harbor.
- **D.** the Germans attacked New York City.

12. How did the United States government make sure there were enough supplies to send to soldiers overseas?
- **A.** by closing many grocery stores
- **(B.)** by rationing
- **C.** by helping farmers
- **D.** by raising prices

13. During World War II, the United States government set up relocation camps for
- **A.** Native Americans.
- **B.** German Americans.
- **C.** African Americans.
- **(D.)** Japanese Americans.

14. What was the Holocaust?
- **A.** the German invasion and bombing of Poland
- **(B.)** Hitler's mass murder of European Jews
- **C.** German plans in World War II to invade eastern Europe
- **D.** the destruction of German cities by firebombs

(continued)

SKILLS

NAME ______________________ DATE __________

Part Two: Test Your Skills *(16 points)*

DIRECTIONS: ***Use the information in the time lines to answer the following questions.***

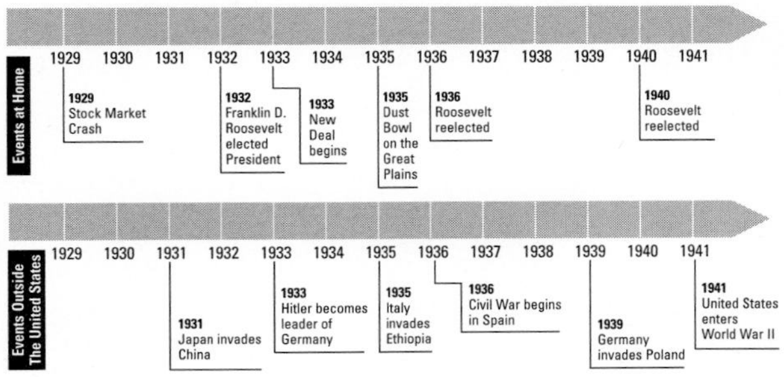
Events at Home
1929 1930 1931 1932 1933 1934 1935 1936 1937 1938 1939 1940 1941
1929 Stock Market Crash
1932 Franklin D. Roosevelt elected President
1933 New Deal begins
1935 Dust Bowl on the Great Plains
1936 Roosevelt reelected
1940 Roosevelt reelected
Events Outside The United States
1929 1930 1931 1932 1933 1934 1935 1936 1937 1938 1939 1940 1941
1931 Japan invades China
1933 Hitler becomes leader of Germany
1935 Italy invades Ethiopia
1936 Civil War begins in Spain
1939 Germany invades Poland
1941 United States enters World War II

15. What was happening outside the United States at the same time as the Dust Bowl on the Great Plains?

Italy was invading Ethiopia.

16. Did the United States enter World War II before or after the New Deal began?

after the New Deal began

17. Was Franklin Roosevelt elected to office before or after Japan invaded China?

after Japan invaded China

18. Which event took place first—the stock market crash or the invasion of Poland?

the stock market crash

(continued)

APPLICATION/WRITING

NAME ______________________ DATE __________

Part Three: Apply What You Have Learned

DIRECTIONS: ***Complete each of the following activities.***

19. ***Economic Relationships*** *(6 points)*
Explain the relationships among consumer goods, advertisements, and installment buying by defining the terms in the chart below.

CONSUMER GOODS	ADVERTISEMENTS	INSTALLMENT BUYING
Possible responses: Consumer goods are products for personal use.	Advertisements encourage people to buy consumer goods.	Installment buying allows people to buy consumer goods over time.

20. ***Which One Does Not Belong?*** *(12 points)*
In each of the groups of words below, there is one word or phrase that does not belong. Circle that word or phrase, and give a brief explanation as to why it does not belong with the others.

Possible responses:

a. front island-hopping (relocation camps)

Front and *island-hopping* are words that apply to the fighting overseas in World War II. Relocation camps were set up in the United States during the war.

b. (rationing) free world communism

The free world and communist countries were on opposite sides in the Cold War. Rationing was the way the government controlled goods during World War II.

c. Harlem Renaissance jazz (minimum wage)

Harlem Renaissance and jazz both relate to African American tradition. Minimum wage applies to all workers.

21. ***Essay*** *(10 points)*
Write a one-paragraph essay explaining why the Cold War developed.

Possible response: After World War II, the United States and its allies, known as the free world, worked to stop the spread of communism. The Cold War developed out of hostilities between the free world and the communist nations. This "war" did not involve armies and shooting, but rather money and propaganda.

INTRODUCE THE CHAPTER

This chapter explores the changes that took place in the United States in the years following World War I and the events that led to World War II. It covers the booming consumer economy, the growth of automobile and air travel, new forms of entertainment, and the burst of creativity in the arts during the Harlem Renaissance. The chapter also examines the events surrounding the Great Depression and how President Roosevelt worked to end the crisis. It concludes with America's involvement in World War II and the changes the war introduced.

Link Prior Learning

Have students review the important changes that took place in the United States after the Civil War. Explain that life in the United States also changed dramatically after World War I.

Visual Analysis

Interpret Pictures Have students carefully observe this picture of Zora Neale Hurston and read the caption.

Q. What conclusions might you draw about Zora Neale Hurston from this picture and the caption? Responses may include that she was an African American writer and anthropologist; she was successful, confident, and strong.

Auditory Learning

Interpret Primary Sources Ask a student volunteer to read aloud the quotation from Zora Neale Hurston's *Dust Tracks on a Road.*

Q. What does this quotation tell you about Zora Neale Hurston? She indicates that time and place—when she lived and where she lived—had a great deal of influence on her life.

"PRIMARY SOURCE"
Source: *Dust Tracks on a Road.* Zora Neale Hurston. HarperCollins, 1996.

CHAPTER 18

GOOD TIMES AND BAD

"Time and place have had their say. So you will have to know something about the time and place where I came from, in order that you may interpret the . . . directions of my life."

Zora Neale Hurston, writer and anthropologist, in her 1942 book *Dust Tracks on a Road*

ACTIVITY CHOICES

Background

ZORA NEALE HURSTON Zora Neale Hurston was born on January 7, 1903. She grew up in Eatonville, Florida, the first incorporated black township in the United States. Her father, a Baptist minister, served as Eatonville's mayor for three terms. Hurston was sent to a boarding school in Jacksonville, Florida, and later worked her way through high school at Morgan Academy in Baltimore, Maryland. Hurston attended Howard University and Barnard College, where she studied anthropology and African American folk traditions. During the Harlem Renaissance, she wrote for newspapers and journals and published plays, novels, and short stories. She also did anthropological work in Jamaica, Haiti, and the Bahamas. Her writings, such as *Mules and Men* (1935) and *Their Eyes Were Watching God* (1937), provide a vivid portrayal of African American life in the rural South.

The Roaring Twenties

LESSON 1

FOCUS
What words might be used to describe the present decade?

Main Idea As you read, find out why the 1920s were described as the Roaring Twenties.

Vocabulary
consumer good
installment buying
assembly line
aviation
commercial industry
jazz

After the serious days of World War I, the 1920s brought good times to many Americans. People were eager for change and wanted to enjoy themselves. For this reason, the 1920s are often called the Roaring Twenties.

The Boom Economy

When the United States entered World War I in 1917, the economy changed greatly. Factories began producing weapons and other war supplies. When the war was over, factories started to make new products. They made vacuum cleaners, washing machines, radios, and other appliances for the home. In the 1920s Americans bought more of these **consumer goods**—the name given to products made for personal use. Never before had there been such a variety of goods to choose from.

Americans learned about consumer goods through advertisements in newspapers and magazines and on the radio. Business owners used advertisements in the hopes of making people want to buy their goods.

It was hard for many people to pay for goods all at once, so installment buying became common. **Installment buying** allows a buyer to take home a product after paying only a part of the selling price. The buyer then makes an installment, or payment, each month until the full price of the product has been paid.

While business boomed, agriculture slumped. Farmers had produced large amounts of food during World War I, when food was badly needed overseas. But the end of the war meant the end of high wartime demand. Farmers now had too many crops and no one to buy them.

REVIEW *What led to a boom in the economy in the 1920s?* the making of consumer goods, advertisements, and installment buying

Nipper, the dog on RCA Victor's label, first appeared on phonographs and records in 1901.

Reading Support

ANTICIPATION GUIDE Before students read the lesson, ask them to predict which statements are true and which are false. Students may correct their predictions as they read.

1. Installment buying made it easier for people to buy goods. true
2. Farmers had great financial success during the Roaring Twenties. false
3. The assembly line increased the cost of making automobiles. false
4. After World War I there was not much need for the airplane. false
5. Most Americans did not want to buy radios in the 1920s. false
6. In the 1920s African Americans used the arts to express their feelings about living in the United States. true

Objectives

1. Identify the boom economy that followed World War I.
2. Analyze the impact of the assembly line on automobile production.
3. Explain how Charles Lindbergh's solo flight affected travel.
4. Identify popular forms of entertainment in the 1920s.
5. Summarize African American achievements in the arts in the 1920s.

Vocabulary

consumer good (p. 569)
installment buying (p. 569)
assembly line (p. 570)
aviation (p. 571)
commercial industry (p. 571)
jazz (p. 572)

1. ACCESS

The Focus Question

Explain that nations, like people, go through periods that can be characterized by a word or phrase. Give students some examples, such as the Civil War years or Reconstruction. Ask students what words or phrases they would use to describe the present decade.

The Main Idea

In this lesson students explore the 1920s, which were a time of change and enjoyment. The economy boomed, automobiles and airplanes became popular, and there were new forms of entertainment, including those created by African American artists.

2. BUILD

The Boom Economy

Key Content Summary

The close of World War I brought changes to the American economy. Former weapons and war-supplies factories now produced new household products. Farmers, however, suffered from losing their wartime markets.

Economics

Interdependence and Income Draw a simple diagram on the board to illustrate the debtor/creditor relationship involved in installment buying. Have students analyze the advantages and disadvantages of installment buying.

The Automobile

Key Content Summary

After Henry Ford developed the assembly line, the cost of cars decreased. Finally, millions of Americans could afford to buy cars.

Economics

Markets and Prices Focus on the low cost of automobiles produced on assembly lines.

Q. **Why did an assembly-line car cost less to manufacture?** Assembly line workers could produce cars in less time, cutting the cost of the labor required to make a car.

Visual Analysis

Learn from Graphs Have students answer the questions in the caption. 1920: about 2 million; 1929: about 4.5 million

LEARNING FROM GRAPHS As a young man Henry Ford (below) worked as a machine operator. His idea of producing cars on an assembly line (above) helped increase sales of automobiles.

■ *About how many cars were sold in 1920? in 1929?*

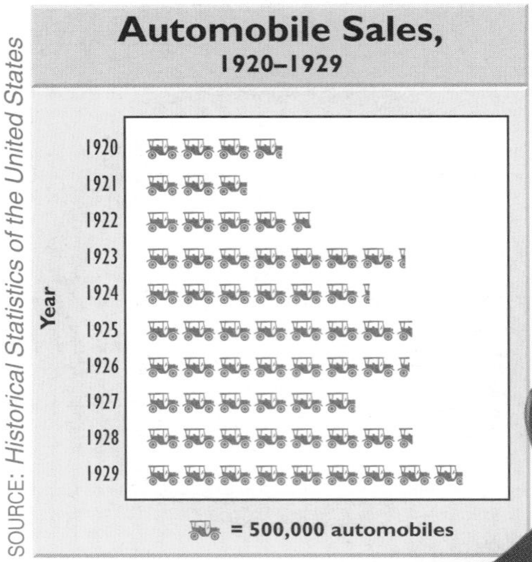

The Automobile

One reason for the boom of the 1920s was the growth of new industries. One of the most important of these was the automobile industry.

The first successful gasoline-powered automobile, or car, was built in the 1890s. By the time the United States entered World War I, automobile companies were producing about 1 million cars a year. By 1923 they were making more than 3 million a year.

Leading the American automobile industry was a man from Michigan named Henry Ford. Ford had found a way to produce automobiles less expensively. The Ford Motor Company's system of mass production used a moving **assembly line**. Instead of being built one at a time, Ford's cars were assembled, or put together, as they were moved past a line of workers. Each worker did only one task, such as putting in headlights or seats. The assembly line cut the amount of time it took to make a car from about 12 hours to less than 2 hours. Workers on the assembly line could now produce 6 cars in the time it once took to produce a single car. Ford passed on the savings to his customers. By 1925 a person could buy a new Ford car for about $260.

As more people bought automobiles the need for other new industries grew. The need for automobile tires led to the growth of the rubber industry. The need for gasoline as fuel led to the growth of the oil industry. Gas stations were built in cities and along roadsides, and hundreds of thousands of miles of roads were paved. The United States was becoming a nation on wheels.

REVIEW *How did Henry Ford change the automobile industry?* He used a moving assembly line to mass-produce cars.

Activity Choices

Link to Mathematics

CALCULATE THE VALUE OF THE DOLLAR Explain to the class that the value of the dollar has changed since the 1920s. The fact that in 1925 a car cost $260 illustrates this point. Have students discuss the cost of cars today. Tell them to assume a basic car costs $10,400, and have them calculate how much more a dollar might have bought in 1925 than today: 10,400 ÷ 260 = 40; a dollar in 1925 would have bought about 40 times as much as a dollar today.

Meet Individual Needs

ADVANCED LEARNERS Have students select an industry that uses assembly-line production, and ask them to draw diagrams or make models of the steps involved in the assembly lines. Set up an assembly-line display in the class, and allow time for the students to explain their diagrams and models.

Smithsonian Institution®

Go to the Internet site at *http://www.si.edu/harcourt/socialstudies* to examine "American Automobiles" on the Timeline at the National Museum of American History.

The Wright brothers' *Flyer* (above) takes off on the first piloted flight in 1903. Charles Lindbergh (right) stands next to the *Spirit of St. Louis*, the airplane that he flew across the Atlantic Ocean in 1927.

Aviation

Air transportation, or **aviation**, also became an important industry in the 1920s. Two brothers, Orville and Wilbur Wright, made the first flight in 1903 at Kitty Hawk, North Carolina. Over the years, the airplane was improved. It was used in World War I, but after the war not many people traveled by plane. By 1927 that began to change.

On May 20, 1927, Charles Lindbergh, an American airmail pilot, took off from New York in a small plane named the *Spirit of St. Louis*. His goal was to be the first person to fly alone across the Atlantic Ocean. If he did, he would win a $25,000 prize. Fighting off sleep, Lindbergh kept to his course over the open ocean. "My back is stiff; my shoulders ache; my eyes smart," he wrote in his journal.

It seemed impossible for Lindbergh to go on, but he did. He landed in Paris, France, about 34 hours after leaving New York. As news of his flight spread, Charles Lindbergh became a hero all over the world.

Lindbergh's flight helped make people more interested in air travel, and soon commercial airlines were making flights. A **commercial industry** is one that is run to make a profit. Between 1926 and 1930, the number of people traveling by plane grew from about 6,000 to about 400,000.

REVIEW ***Who was Charles Lindbergh?*** the first person to fly across the Atlantic Ocean alone

Entertainment

Many Americans heard the news of Lindbergh's flight on the radio. The first commercial radio stations began broadcasting in the 1920s. Detroit's WWJ and Pittsburgh's KDKA were two of the earliest commercial radio stations. By 1929 more than 800 stations were reaching about 10 million families.

Aviation

Key Content Summary

The use of airplanes as a means of transportation was spurred by Charles Lindbergh's historic transatlantic flight in 1927. The number of people traveling by plane grew from 6,000 in 1926 to about 400,000 in 1930.

History

Connections Past to Present to Future Have students analyze the significance of Lindbergh's flight and discuss how it has changed life in the United States.

Entertainment

Key Content Summary

The 1920s saw the introduction of new forms of entertainment. Millions of Americans listened to news, sports, and music on the radio and went to the movies.

History

Origins, Spread, and Influence Have students analyze how the introduction of radio and movies changed life in the United States. Ask them to discuss the advantages and disadvantages of these technological changes.

Q. **What recent technological advances have changed the way people communicate?** computers, fax machines, cellular telephones, communications satellites

Smithsonian Institution®

Go to the Internet site at *http://www.si.edu/harcourt/socialstudies* to examine pictures of the Wright 1903 Flyer in "Milestones of Flight" at the National Air and Space Museum.

Link to Science

COOPERATIVE LEARNING

DEMONSTRATE AERODYNAMICS Assign a group of students to research aerodynamics in an encyclopedia or other resource. Ask them to find and practice several simple experiments that they can present to the class that explain the principles of aerodynamics. Examples: the lift a hat receives when the wind blows it off a person's head, or the movement of a sheet of paper held by a person who is standing still compared with its movement when a person runs with it.

Background

THE ACADEMY AWARDS The Academy of Motion Picture Arts and Sciences was founded in May 1927. The academy was formed to recognize leading craftspeople in every phase of filmmaking. It also fosters cooperation, excellence, and progress in the filmmaking industry. The academy began presenting the annual awards for motion picture categories in 1927. *Wings* was the first motion picture to win an Academy Award for best picture. You may wish to show students a portion of *Wings* so that they can compare movies of the 1920s with movies today.

Culture

Thought and Expression Have students discuss how music and other areas of entertainment can help people of different cultural backgrounds learn more about each other.

Q. **Why are the 1920s also called the Jazz Age?** because jazz was very popular among both black and white Americans

Visual Analysis

Interpret Pictures Have students observe the picture of the dancers. Explain that the Charleston was one of many reasons the 1920s were called the Roaring Twenties.

“PRIMARY SOURCE”

Source: Writings of D. W. Griffith, film producer and director, 1929.

The Harlem Renaissance

Key Content Summary

In the 1920s New York City's Harlem neighborhood became the center of change, bursting with artistic energy that came to be known as the Harlem Renaissance. African Americans created poetry, paintings, and music that appealed to both black and white Americans.

Radio made possible an audience of millions of people at one time. Listening to the radio, Americans could follow sports around the country. In 1926, millions listened as Gene Tunney beat Jack Dempsey in a ten-round boxing match. Yankee fans cheered when Babe Ruth hit his sixtieth home run during the 1927 baseball season.

Over their radios Americans could also hear a new kind of music called jazz. **Jazz** grew out of the African American musical heritage. This heritage was made up of music brought from West Africa and spirituals sung by enslaved people in the United States. Jazz was so popular among both black and white Americans that some have called the 1920s the Jazz Age.

Movies were another new form of entertainment enjoyed by many people in the 1920s. The movie business, which was based in Hollywood, California, started with silent films. By 1927 many movies were being made with sound. D. W. Griffith, a film director, saw a bright future for what were known as talking pictures. Griffith predicted,

> “Talkies, squeakies, moanies, songies, squawkies . . . But whatever you call them, I'm absolutely serious in what I have to say about them. Just give them ten years to develop and you're going to see the greatest artistic medium the world has known.”

REVIEW *What new forms of entertainment were popular in the 1920s?* listening to sports news, and music on the radio and going to the movies

The Harlem Renaissance

In the 1920s the New York City neighborhood of Harlem became a center of artistic development for African Americans. So many writers, musicians, and artists lived in Harlem during the 1920s that this period is now known as the Harlem Renaissance. The French word *renaissance* (REH•nuh•sahns) means

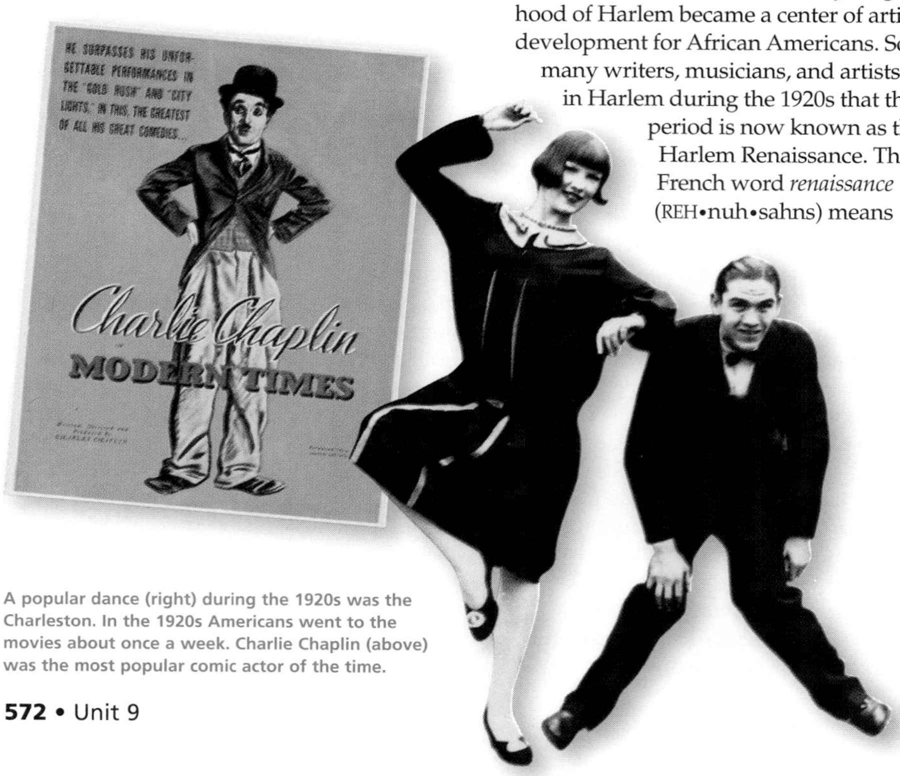

A popular dance (right) during the 1920s was the Charleston. In the 1920s Americans went to the movies about once a week. Charlie Chaplin (above) was the most popular comic actor of the time.

Activity Choices

Link to Language Arts

READ POETRY Ask student volunteers to use library resources or the Internet to find examples of poetry written during the Harlem Renaissance by poets such as Langston Hughes, Claude McKay, and Countee Cullen. Have the students read their selections to the class and discuss the meanings of the poems.

Extend and Enrich

COOPERATIVE LEARNING

RESEARCH AND PRESENT FACTS Divide the class into groups, and assign each group one of the following topics: the boom economy, the automobile, aviation, entertainment, or the Harlem Renaissance. Ask each group to find at least ten interesting facts about their topic that are not included in the lesson. Challenge students to find pictures in their resource materials that illustrate the interesting facts. Have each group share the facts and pictures with the other groups.

Smithsonian Institution®

Go to the Internet site at *http://www.si.edu/harcourt/socialstudies* to examine “A Centennial Salute to Cinema” at the National Museum of American History.

"rebirth." It is used to describe a time of new interest and activity in the arts.

Among the best-known of the Harlem writers was the poet Langston Hughes. He described Harlem during the 1920s as a magnet for African Americans from across the country. Young writers such as Claude McKay, Countee Cullen, and Zora Neale Hurston came to Harlem to share their work and encourage one another. Many of these artists and writers painted and wrote about what it was like to be African American in the United States.

Large audiences of both black and white Americans came to Harlem to hear trumpeter Louis Armstrong, singer Billie Holiday, and bandleader Duke Ellington. They also came to see actors such as Paul Robeson perform.

REVIEW *What was the Harlem Renaissance?*

During the Harlem Renaissance, Langston Hughes (left) wrote poems about African American life. The Savoy Ballroom (above) was a popular dance club in Harlem.

LESSON 1 REVIEW

Check Understanding

1. **Remember the Facts** What new industries helped the nation's economy grow in the 1920s?
2. **Recall the Main Idea** Why were the 1920s described as the Roaring Twenties?

Think Critically

3. **Personally Speaking** Charles Lindbergh set for himself the goal of being the first person to fly alone across the Atlantic Ocean. Why is it a good idea for people to set goals?
4. **Explore Viewpoints** How do you think the viewpoints of farmers in the 1920s differed from those of people living in cities in the 1920s?

Show What You Know

Poster Activity Review what you learned about consumer goods, advertisements, and installment buying. Choose a product that was popular during the 1920s. Make a poster to advertise the product that might make people want to buy it. Display your poster in the classroom.

a time of great interest and activity in the arts among African American writers, musicians, and artists

Reteach the Main Idea

COOPERATIVE LEARNING

DRAW A PICTURE Divide the class into small groups. Challenge each group to use the textbook as a resource to draw pictures showing the reasons that the 1920s were called the Roaring Twenties. Group members should plan and draw their pictures and then share and discuss the pictures with the other groups.

ACTIVITY BOOK

Reinforce & Extend

Use ACTIVITY BOOK, p. 115.

History

Origins, Spread, and Influence Explain that Harlem was one of the urban neighborhoods where migrating African Americans settled during World War I.

3. CLOSE

Have students consider again the Focus question on page 569.

What words might be used to describe the present decade?

Have students use what they have learned about the 1920s to identify the reasons a period in history may be described in a word or phrase. Ask them to reevaluate the words or phrases they created at the beginning of the lesson for the present decade.

LESSON 1 REVIEW—Answers

Check Understanding

1. automobiles, gasoline, roads, aviation, appliances, entertainment, communication, and advertising
2. the booming economy, easier travel, more time for fun and entertainment

Think Critically

3. Setting both short-term and long-term goals helps people organize their lives, build their self-esteem and sense of purpose, and give direction to their actions.
4. Farmers lost markets for their crops after the war. They may have viewed the 1920s as a time of lost income. People living in cities may have viewed the 1920s as a time of growth and excitement.

Show What You Know

Performance Assessment Consider taking class votes on whether each of the advertisements would make the students buy what is being advertised.

What to Look For Make sure students understand and can explain the goals of their advertising posters.

Objectives

1. Analyze why the good times of the 1920s ended.
2. Describe the Great Depression.
3. Summarize the goals of the New Deal.
4. Identify and evaluate the major government programs of the New Deal.

Vocabulary

stock market (p. 574)
depression (p. 575)
bureaucracy (p. 576)
unemployment (p. 577)
minimum wage (p. 577)
hydroelectric dam (p. 578)

1. ACCESS

The Focus Question

Ask students to describe ways that the federal government helps people who are out of work. Have students discuss the advantages and disadvantages of government help, such as unemployment insurance and Social Security.

The Main Idea

In this lesson students learn about the Great Depression of the 1930s and the efforts of the government to deal with that economic and social crisis. After students have read the lesson, have them evaluate the success of the New Deal programs.

2. BUILD

The Good Times End

Key Content Summary

On October 29, 1929, prices on the stock market plunged, ruining thousands of individual investors and bringing the good times of the 1920s to an abrupt end. Soon the country had fallen into what became known as the Great Depression.

LESSON 2

FOCUS How does the federal government today help people who are out of work?

Main Idea Read to learn how the federal government helped Americans who were out of work during the Great Depression.

Vocabulary
stock market
depression
bureaucracy
unemployment
minimum wage
hydroelectric dam

The Great Depression and the New Deal

Many Americans thought that the good times of the 1920s would go on forever. President Herbert Hoover, elected in 1928, shared that hope. He had gained fame for his efforts to help poor and hungry people in Europe after World War I. He saw a much happier picture in the United States in 1928. "We in America today are nearer to the final triumph over poverty than ever before in the history of any land," he said. Little did he know how quickly that would change.

The Good Times End

In the 1920s thousands of Americans pinned their hopes on a rich future by investing money in the stock market. The **stock market** is a place where people can buy and sell stocks. If more people want to buy than sell a certain stock, the price of shares goes up. If more people want to sell than buy, the price goes down.

During the 1920s the prices on one stock market, the New York Stock Exchange, kept going higher. By 1929 some stocks were being sold at prices three times higher than they were sold for in 1920. People began to borrow money to buy stocks. "How can you lose?" they asked. Before long they learned the answer.

Beginning in the fall of 1929, some people decided to take their money out of the stock market. This caused stock prices to fall. As prices fell, many investors got nervous and decided to sell, too. Soon panicked stockholders were trying to sell all of their stocks. On October 24, 1929, thousands of investors wanted to sell stocks instead of buy them. They all wanted to turn their stocks into cash. With many sellers and few buyers, prices fell fast. On October 29, 1929, stock prices could go no lower. The stock market crashed. Nearly everyone who owned stocks lost money.

During the Great Depression, some people without jobs sold apples on the street to make money.

574

ACTIVITY CHOICES

Reading Support

DEVELOP THE LESSON VOCABULARY Provide students with index cards, and ask them to write the term *Economy* on the front side of the card and the term *Government* on the back. Ask students to skim the lesson, locate the vocabulary words, and read their meanings. Have students write the vocabulary words that relate to the economy on the front side of the index cards. Have them write the vocabulary words that relate to the government on the back. Alert students to the fact that two of the vocabulary terms can be placed in both categories.

On the day of the stock market crash, people gathered on New York City's Wall Street, where stocks are traded. Stock certificates like this one (right) had lost much of their value.

The crash of the stock market ended the good times of the Roaring Twenties. It was the beginning of a long, difficult period known as the Great Depression. During a **depression** there is little money, little economic growth, and many people are out of work.

REVIEW ***What caused the stock market to crash in 1929?*** More investors sold stocks than bought them; stock prices fell and the stock market crashed.

The Great Depression

As people lost their jobs after the stock market crash, many needed to spend their savings in order to live. When large numbers of people tried to take money out of the banks, many banks had to close. People who had money in these banks lost all of their savings.

Because people had little money, they bought few goods. Manufacturers could not sell what they had made. Factory workers then lost their jobs because the factory owners could not pay their wages. When workers lost their jobs, they could not pay what they owed to banks or businesses. So more banks and businesses began to fail.

During the Great Depression, poverty and hardship affected almost every American. President Hoover tried to give everyone hope. "Prosperity," he said, "is just around the corner." But it was not. In fact, times got worse.

By 1932 thousands of businesses had closed. One of every four American workers was without a job. People were starving. Hungry people stood in line for bread or for free meals at soup kitchens. Because they could not pay their rent or house payments, many people lost their homes. Those who were homeless spent the night in public shelters or out on the streets. Entire families often had to live in shacks made of scraps of wood.

One woman, a teenager during the Great Depression, remembers being sent by her mother to wait in line for free soup.

> "If you happened to be one of the first ones in line, you didn't get anything but the water on top. So we'd ask the guy that was putting the soup into the buckets . . . to please dip down to get some meat and potatoes from the bottom of the kettle. But he wouldn't do it."

REVIEW ***What hardships did the Great Depression cause for many Americans?*** Businesses and banks failed; people lost jobs and savings; many people were hungry and homeless.

Economics

Markets and Prices Explore with students the concepts of stock ownership and stock prices. Provide students with examples from newspapers of stock-price fluctuations and explain the reasons for price changes, such as the health of the economy, the stability of individual companies, and price/earnings ratios.

Q. **Why was the stock market important to people in the 1920s?** It was a place where people could buy and sell stocks and expect to make money.

The Great Depression

Key Content Summary

Following the stock market crash, the economy took a sharp downturn. Because of the interdependent nature of the economy, banks failed, factories closed, and many people lost their jobs and homes. A sense of hopelessness spread throughout the nation.

Economics

Interdependence and Income Have students develop a web diagram that illustrates the interdependent nature of the economy and the domino effect that occurred in the early years of the Great Depression.

"PRIMARY SOURCE"

Source: *Hard Times: An Oral History of the Great Depression.* Studs Terkel. Pantheon Books, 1970.

Meet Individual Needs

ENGLISH LANGUAGE LEARNERS At the beginning of the lesson, have students write a sentence using each vocabulary term. As the students read the sections and learn more about the meaning and use of the terms, they may revise their sentences as needed.

Link to Art

COOPERATIVE LEARNING

RESEARCH DEPRESSION-ERA PHOTOGRAPHS Have a small group of students locate books in the library that contain dramatic photographs of life during the Great Depression. Ask the students to work together to select 10 to 15 photographs they would like to share with the class. Tell the students to make sure they can explain each photograph, answering *where*, *when*, *what*, and *why* questions.

Background

STOCK PRICES In the 1920s stock prices rose to staggering heights. Rather than looking at the real value of the stocks, investors believed stock prices would continue to rise. Between 1925 and 1929, the market value of stocks rose from $27 billion to $87 billion. By the late 1920s, however, the economy had begun to slow down. On October 29, 1929, stock prices started falling. Investors began to panic and sell off their stocks. By the end of the day, the average price of stocks had been cut in half.

Visual Analysis

Interpret Graphs Ask students to compare the graphs on this page showing business failures and unemployment. Then have students answer the questions in the caption. The trends are similar. When the number of business failures was high, fewer jobs were available and more people were out of work. When the number of business failures was low, more jobs were available and fewer people were out of work.

Q. **In what year were business failures the highest?** 1931
In what year was unemployment the highest? 1933

Franklin Roosevelt and the New Deal

Key Content Summary

President Roosevelt believed that the federal government had to take bold steps to end the depression. In his first 100 days in office, Roosevelt launched a series of programs known as the New Deal.

SOURCE: *Historical Statistics of the United States*

Business Failures, 1929–1945

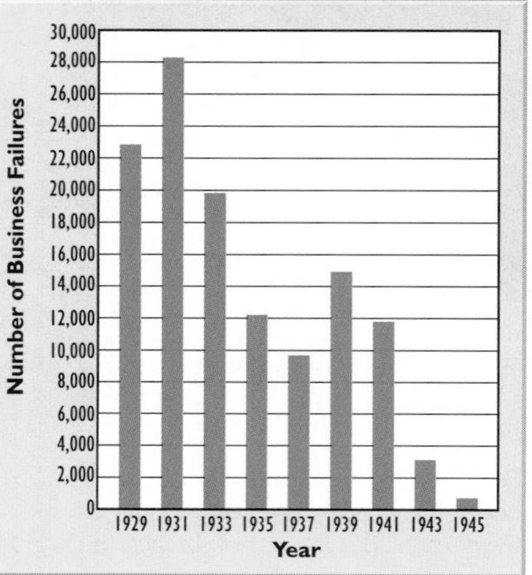

LEARNING FROM GRAPHS The bar graph shows the number of companies that went out of business from 1929 to 1945. The line graph shows the number of people who lost their jobs during the same period.
■ *Compare the trends shown on these graphs. Are the trends similar? Why or why not?*

Unemployment, 1929–1945

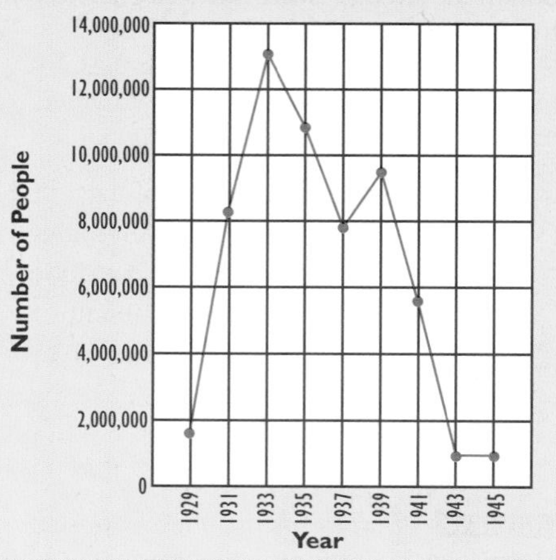

SOURCE: *Historical Statistics of the United States*

Franklin Roosevelt and the New Deal

In the summer of 1932, the Democratic party chose New York governor Franklin Delano Roosevelt as its presidential candidate. Roosevelt had served as the assistant secretary of the navy and had been his party's candidate for vice president in 1920. Roosevelt was a cheerful, likable person. Franklin Roosevelt told the Democrats, "I pledge you, I pledge myself to a new deal for the American people." The words became the name for his plan—the New Deal—to end the Great Depression. In November 1932 the American people elected Roosevelt to be President.

President Roosevelt believed that to end the Great Depression, the federal government needed to take bold, new action. On his inauguration day, Roosevelt told the American people,

> "The only thing we have to fear is fear itself."

He gave people hope that everything would be all right—that the government would do something to help. "This nation asks for action, and action now," he said.

In his speech Roosevelt called on Congress to act quickly. It did. Between March 9 and June 16, 1933, Congress passed many of Roosevelt's plans. During this time, later known as The 100 Days, more new laws were passed than at any other time since the founding of the nation.

The New Deal gave the federal government more authority. It also made it larger. The growing number of government workers formed a **bureaucracy**—the many workers and groups that are needed to run government programs.

REVIEW ***What was the name of Franklin Roosevelt's plan to end the Great Depression?*** the New Deal

Activity Choices

Multicultural Link

African Americans were among those hardest hit by the Great Depression. As factory workers, they were often the last to be hired and the first to be fired. Their unemployment rate was double the national average. African American tenant farmers were also victims of the Great Depression. Many were evicted from the farms they worked because the owners could not afford to keep the land in production. After the New Deal programs went into effect, however, African Americans did benefit from government aid. Eighteen percent of WPA workers were African American. Almost 200,000 African American young people were employed in the CCC. In addition, President Roosevelt was the first President to form what was called the "Black Cabinet" to keep communication open with the African American community.

Link to Health

REPORT ON POLIO Tell students that President Roosevelt was unable to walk because of polio. Ask several student volunteers to prepare an oral report on the causes and characteristics of polio, how polio is combatted today, and why President Roosevelt had a swimming pool installed at the White House.

Government Programs

The New Deal's goal was to get people ack to work. To provide jobs, it created a umber of programs that were nicknamed oosevelt's Alphabet Soup. The Civilian onservation Corps, or CCC, hired young eople to plant trees and take care of the iany national parks. The Works Progress dministration, or WPA, hired workers to uild roads, airports, and public buildings ıch as schools, libraries, and post offices. he WPA also hired writers and artists to ecord life during the Great Depression in ords, paintings, and photographs.

Even with these government programs, **nemployment**, or the number of workers ithout jobs, stayed high. But at least unemloyment did not get worse.

The government helped workers who ad jobs by supporting labor unions. There ad often been strikes and conflicts over ıe rights of workers to organize unions. Jew laws gave workers the right to form nions and the right to an hourly **minimum wage**, the lowest pay a worker can receive by law.

Workers were also helped by the Social Security Act. It was one of the most important programs of the New Deal. Social Security provides income for workers after

This photograph from 1930 shows people waiting in line for free bread at a mission in New York City. Without money to pay for food, many people went hungry.

BIOGRAPHY

Franklin Delano Roosevelt
1882–1945

In 1921, eleven years before he won election as President, Franklin Roosevelt became ill with polio. The disease left him unable to walk. Polio forced him to leave politics for a time. But through hard work and the encouragement of his family, he recovered and learned to walk with the help of leg braces. In 1928 Roosevelt was elected governor of New York. In 1932 he was elected President of the United States. Roosevelt was reelected three more times, making him the only President to have been elected to four terms in office.

History

Leaders and Achievers Have students recall the characteristics of other leaders and achievers in United States history, and ask the students to evaluate the qualities that made Franklin D. Roosevelt a popular leader.

Q. **How might Roosevelt's statement "The only thing we have to fear is fear itself" have helped Americans during the Great Depression?** It probably gave them encouragement that the new President was not afraid to take action.

History

Turning Points Remind students that the leaders at the Constitutional Convention wanted to give the national government enough power to be effective but didn't want it to have too much power. Ask students to analyze how Roosevelt's actions to end the depression might have concerned Washington, Madison, and Franklin.

Government Programs

Key Content Summary

Many of the New Deal programs were aimed at getting individuals back to work and protecting the rights of workers. Several huge public works projects, including the building of hydroelectric dams, opened the door for more employment opportunities.

Link to Science

COOPERATIVE LEARNING

MAKE A DIAGRAM Have a small group of students work together to research, draw, and label a diagram of a hydroelectric power plant. After the group has presented and explained the diagram to the class, lead a discussion analyzing why the federal government chose to build hydroelectric power plants during the New Deal.

Extend and Enrich

COOPERATIVE LEARNING

RESEARCH NEW DEAL PROJECTS Divide the class into groups, and have them find examples of the lasting legacy of New Deal work programs across the United States. Assign each group an area to focus on, such as Tennessee, North Carolina, California, South Dakota, Wyoming/Montana, or Washington/Oregon. In addition to conducting library research, each group may want to write to their assigned area's tourist department to gather more information. Have each group organize a presentation, including pictures or drawings of the public works projects. After all the presentations have been made, have a class discussion about how people today benefit from Roosevelt's New Deal programs.

Civics and Government

Purposes of Government Have students identify the programs of the New Deal and explain what each program tried to accomplish.

3. CLOSE

Have students consider again the Focus question on page 574.

> **How does the federal government today help people who are out of work?**

Have students use what they have learned about the New Deal programs to identify the government programs that are still in place today to help people who are out of work.

LESSON 2 REVIEW—Answers

Check Understanding

1. a series of government programs designed to help people get back to work during the Great Depression
2. It helped people by slowing the rate of unemployment and creating jobs through public works programs.

Think Critically

3. During the depression, so many people had financial problems for so long that they lost hope that things would ever get better. Without hope, they did not know where to begin to improve their lives.
4. The 1920s were a period of economic growth, prosperity, and hope, while the 1930s were a time of economic disaster when many people lost their jobs and homes and felt hopeless.

Show What You Know

Performance Assessment Consider asking students to make graphs showing the movement of selected stocks. Then ask them to calculate whether they would have lost or made money.

What to Look For Look for evidence that students understand how people would have lost or made money in the stock market before the Great Depression.

they have retired. In addition, it gives help to children of workers who have no means of support. Money for the program comes from taxes on workers' earnings.

The federal government also started huge building projects that put thousands of people back to work. Among these projects was the building of **hydroelectric dams**. These dams use the water they store to produce electricity. The government sold the electricity at low rates to users. The dams helped bring about growth in the regions where they were built.

In 1933 Congress created the Tennessee Valley Authority, or TVA. TVA workers built hydroelectric dams and locks on the Tennessee River. Also during the New Deal, workers built the Hoover Dam on the Colorado River. This dam supplied electricity to southern California and Arizona and helped these areas grow. The Grand Coulee and Bonneville dams on the Columbia River helped areas in eastern Washington and Oregon grow.

REVIEW ***What was Roosevelt's Alphabet Soup?*** the nickname for New Deal programs to get people back to work

During the Great Depression, artists like the ones this photograph were hired by the WPA to paint pictures of American life.

LESSON 2 REVIEW

Check Understanding

1. **Remember the Facts** What was the New Deal?
2. **Recall the Main Idea** How did the federal government help solve some of the problems of the Great Depression?

Think Critically

3. **Personally Speaking** Some people have said that the most valuable thing people lost during the Great Depression was hope. What do you think that means?
4. **Think More About It** How did the 1920s compare with the 1930s? Use the pictures in this chapter to help you.

Show What You Know

Newspaper Activity Have a family member help you look at the stock market report in the newspaper. Choose one stock and follow it for a week. Record the stock's closing price every day. With a classmate, figure out if you would have lost or made money by investing in the stock.

ACTIVITY CHOICES

ACTIVITY BOOK

Reinforce & Extend

Use ACTIVITY BOOK, p. 116.

Reteach the Main Idea

COOPERATIVE LEARNING

BROADCAST A FIRESIDE CHAT Explain to students that Roosevelt used the radio to win the confidence of Americans. On a regular basis, Roosevelt spoke to the nation by radio, explaining his goals and what action had been taken. These broadcasts came to be known as Roosevelt's fireside chats. Divide the class into small groups, and have each group prepare a fireside chat to explain one of the New Deal programs. Have each group present its fireside chat to the other groups.

CHILDREN OF THE DUST BOWL

LESSON 3
LEARN HISTORY *through* Literature

by Jerry Stanley

Farm families did not share in ıe good times of the 1920s. ˈrop and livestock prices ropped so low that farmers ɔuld not make a profit. When ırmers could not pay off loans ɔ the banks, they lost their ırms. By the time of the New eal, many farm families faced ıe same poverty and hardship s city families. The New Deal elped farmers by giving them loans so they would not lose their farms. But many farmers soon faced a new problem.

A drought came to the Great Plains early in the 1930s. Where healthy crops had grown, dry earth blew away in the strong winds. Dust storms turned day into night. The western Great Plains became known as the Dust Bowl. The Oklahoma Panhandle had the worst time. As you read the following account of life in the Dust Bowl, think about how the "Okies," the people of Oklahoma, learned to live in hard times.

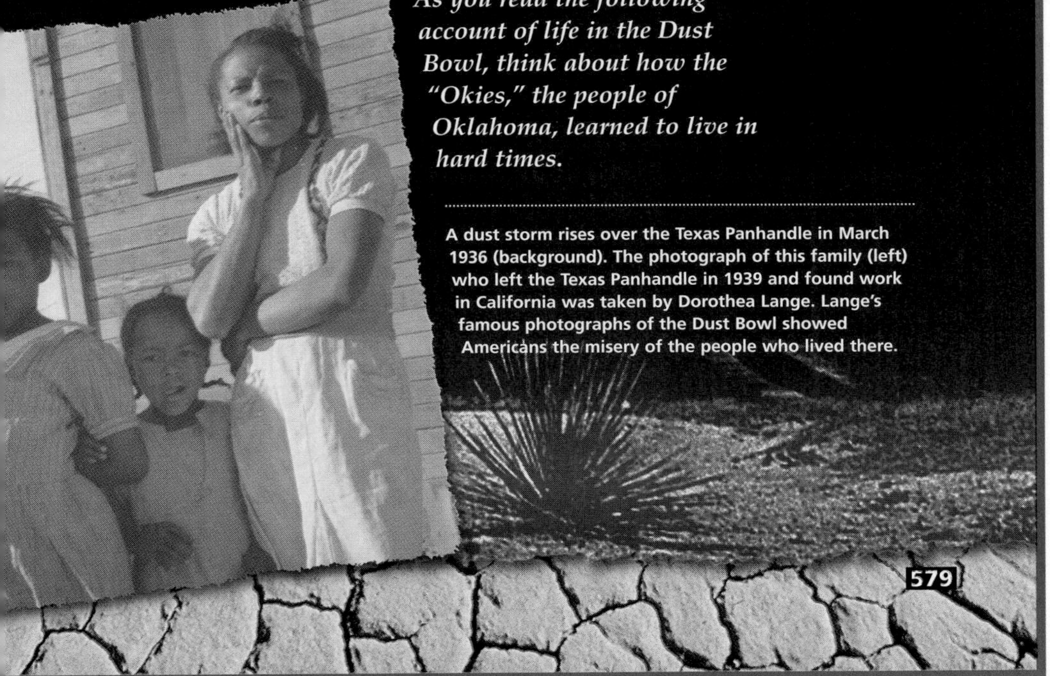

A dust storm rises over the Texas Panhandle in March 1936 (background). The photograph of this family (left) who left the Texas Panhandle in 1939 and found work in California was taken by Dorothea Lange. Lange's famous photographs of the Dust Bowl showed Americans the misery of the people who lived there.

579

Reading Support

PREVIEW AND READ THE LESSON Provide students with the following visual framework.

WINDS RISE; SKY TURNS DARK AND REDDISH-BROWN FROM BLOWING CLOUDS OF DUST.	Rabbits run.
	Thousands of birds race away.
	Herd cows into the barn.
	Tie down farm equipment.
	Rush into house or storm cellar.

Objectives

1. Explain the term "Dust Bowl."
2. Summarize how the dust storms affected people.
3. Describe how people tried to protect themselves from the storms.

1. ACCESS

Ask students to recall a time when they had to protect themselves against some act of nature, such as a blizzard, a severe thunderstorm, or a flood. Have them summarize the ways people cope with natural disasters.

The Main Idea

Students read about the dust storms that destroyed the farms of the Great Plains in the 1930s and the ways the "Okies" adapted their lives to the harsh conditions.

2. BUILD

Key Content Summary

The Oklahoma Panhandle was one of the most seriously affected areas of the Dust Bowl. As clouds of dust swept across the plains, the sun was blocked out, the crops were torn out of the ground, and many animals and people died.

Visual Analysis

Interpret Pictures The photographs on pages 579–582 show people who survived the dust storms. Have students describe how these people might have felt.

Auditory Learning

Express Ideas Orally Have one or two volunteers read aloud the introduction to the literature selection. Ask students to explain why farmers were in trouble.

Q. **Why did many farmers lose their farms?** Farmers who could not repay their bank loans lost their farms.

Understanding the Story

Before students read the paragraphs on this page, have them discuss the conditions farmers need to raise crops. After students have read this page, have them identify the problems that made it impossible for farmers in the Dust Bowl to grow crops.

Q. **Why did it seem as though nature was playing a cruel joke on the "Okies"?** The farmers had already suffered through a five-year drought when the wind started blowing the extremely dry soil away. The dust storms lasted for four more years.

Geography

Location Have students use a classroom wall map or an atlas to locate the area of the Dust Bowl, using the description in the textbook as a guide.

...every day it blew harder and harder, as if nature were playing a cruel joke...

Then when it seemed that things couldn't get any worse, they did. The year was 1936 It hadn't rained more than a few drops in the Panhandle for five straight years. One day the wind started to blow, and every day it blew harder and harder, as if nature were playing a cruel joke on the Okies. The wind blew the dry soil into the air, and every morning the sun rose only to disappear behind a sky of red dirt and dust. The wind knocked open doors, shattered windows, and leveled barns.

It became known as the Great Dust Bowl and it was centered in the Panhandle near Goodwell, Oklahoma. From there it stretched to the western half of Kansas, the eastern half of Colorado, the northeastern portion of New Mexico, and northern Texas. In these areas, and especially in the Panhandle, the dry winds howled for four long years, from 1936 to 1940. Frequently the wind blew more than fifty miles an hour, carrying away the topsoil and leaving

This abandoned farm (right) in Oklahoma was overcome by dust storms. To escape the Dust Bowl, many families left Oklahoma to start new lives in California. But life was hard there, too. Some people (below) who went to California lived in squatter camps made up of tents and shacks.

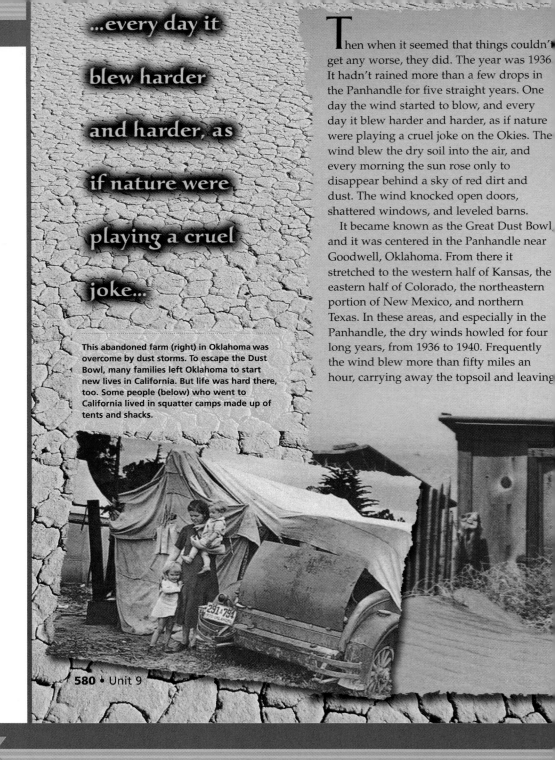

Activity Choices

Background

THE LITERATURE SELECTION In *Children of the Dust Bowl: The True Story of the School at Weedpatch Camp*, Jerry Stanley focuses on an educator named Leo Hart, who worked with the children at the camp. Hart believed in the children's ability and potential, even though many of them had never been educated. Through his love and determination, Hart found supplies and dedicated educators. The teachers and children built the school, which would later be considered the best in Kern County.

THE AUTHOR *Children of the Dust Bowl* is Jerry Stanley's first book. Stanley is a professor of history at California State University at Bakersfield, and he has written many articles for magazines and journals. As part of his research for the book, he interviewed people who had helped build Weedpatch Camp.

nly hard red clay, which made farming npossible.

In the flatlands of the Panhandle people ɔuld see the dust storms coming from venty to thirty miles away. The winds ıade the sky "boil red, blood red," said Iorace Ray Conley of Foss, Oklahoma. You could see the northers[1] coming," he ecalled. "It carried that old red dirt, and ıe whole sky would be red. They were ıean clouds, ugly clouds." As a child, Iorace walked to school backward to keep ıe dirt from scraping him in ıe face. He remembered he 'as often let out of school to o to the family storm cellar 'here he would be safe.

As the clouds rose and ɔiled[2] each day, thousands f birds and rabbits raced ı front of the approaching :orms. That was the signal to ıe Okies to hurry before it was too late. They had to herd their cows into the barn quickly, tie down farm equipment and whatever supplies they had outside, then run for cover. Cracks around windows and doors were taped or stuffed with wet towels, but it was impossible to escape the dust. At night families slept with wet washcloths or sponges over their faces to filter out the dust, but in the morning they would find their pillows and blankets caked with dirt, their tongues and teeth coated with grit.

Every morning the house had to be cleaned. Everett Buckland of Waynocka said, "If you didn't sweep the dust out right quick between storms, you'd end up scooping it out with a shovel." And every morning someone had to go check the animals. The fierce gales buried chickens, pigs, dogs, and occasionally cattle. Children were assigned the task of cleaning the nostrils of cows two or three times a day. . . .

orther: windstorm blowing from the ɔrth
oiled: stirred up

Chapter 18 • 581

Understanding the Story

Have students read pages 581–582 and ask them to describe in their own words what it must have been like to live in the Dust Bowl.

Q. **How did the farmers know when a storm was coming?** They would see thousands of birds and rabbits racing to avoid the storm.

How did the farmers try to protect their animals and themselves from the dust storms? They put their farm animals into the barns, stayed in their cabins or storm cellars, stuffed the cracks around doors and windows with tape or wet towels, and slept with wet washcloths or sponges over their faces.

Visual Analysis

Interpret Pictures Have students carefully observe the photographs on pages 581–583.

Q. **Why do you think these people stayed under such terrible conditions?** Responses may include that many people had everything they owned tied up in their farms. They did not know what to do besides try to keep farming, and they probably never expected the crisis to last as long as it did.

Geography

Movement Discuss with students the complex steps families must take when they move to another state.

Meet Individual Needs

TACTILE LEARNERS To help students better understand the dust storms, provide them with buckets of fine, bone-dry soil. Ask them to feel the soil with their hands and notice the residue on their hands afterward. Have them try to keep the soil from going through the cracks between their dry fingers. Then have them try to keep the soil from going between wet fingers and discuss the difference. Finally, ask students to release handfuls of the dry soil outside on a windy day and describe what happens to it.

Extend and Enrich

COOPERATIVE LEARNING

DRAW A SCENE Divide the class into groups and assign each group one or two of the remaining eight chapters from *Children of the Dust Bowl* to read aloud together. Have the members of each group decide how they want to visually represent the events in their chapter(s). Provide the groups with construction paper and have them draw one or more scenes. When the groups have finished, have them present their drawings to the rest of the class, following the order of the chapters in the book. After all the presentations have been made, allow students time to express their views on the Okies' experiences.

Understanding the Story

After students have finished reading the selection, have them discuss the Okies' seemingly hopeless situation. Ask students what they would have done if they had lived in Oklahoma during that time. Then have them evaluate the New Deal ideas for helping people in this situation.

***Q.* Why was the Dirty Thirties a good name for the 1930s in the Dust Bowl?** The farmers had to live with the ever-present dirt, and the times were "dirtied" because they were so difficult for the farmers.

3. CLOSE

Ask students the following question to focus on the way people learn to cope with natural disasters.

What must people do to learn to cope in hard times?

Have students use what they have learned about the Okies and the Dust Bowl to explain what people might have to do in a present-day flood, drought, or other condition that creates hard times.

LITERATURE REVIEW—Answers

1. They kept their animals in the barn, tied down their farm equipment, stayed in their homes or storm cellars, blocked out the dust with tape and wet towels, covered themselves at night, and swept the dust out of their homes every morning.
2. Students might express fear, disgust, frustration, fascination, or a desire to leave the Dust Bowl.
3. Students who role-play people who wish to stay may argue that they have lived here all their lives and do not want to leave the only home they have ever known. They may also express concern that everything they own is tied up in their farms. Students who play the part of people who wish to leave may argue that there is no future in Oklahoma and that the dust storms will never end and might mean death. They may say that they want to start new lives elsewhere.

The Dust Bowl killed people who stayed out too long without shelter. Roland Hoeme of Hooker almost lost his grandmother to one storm. "I remember my grandmother hanging on to a fence post," he said. "The wind was blowin' so hard she looked like a pennant in a breeze." However, more people died from "dust pneumonia"—when the dust caused severe damage to the lungs. Bessie Zentz of Goodwell summed up the nightmare experienced by the "Dust Bowlers," as they came to be called: "The dust storms scared us to pieces," Bessie said. "It was dark as the middle of the night, and it stayed that way all day."

The storms ended any hope of farming in the Panhandle. The Okies planted mulberry trees for windbreaks and plowed furrows deep in the ground to help keep the soil in place. But the wind blasted the seeds from the furrows and whipped the crops from the earth. . . .

The Okies were broke, they were without land, and they were hungry. And still the wind blew day and night, scraping all life from the earth. It's little wonder that Okies named this period in their lives the Dirty Thirties.

An Oklahoma farmer and his son raise the height of a fence to keep it from being buried by drifts of blowing soil.

To help end conditions in the Dust Bowl, President Franklin Roosevelt started a conservation program as part of the New Deal. Th goal was to stop the dust storms an save the land. An important part of the program was planting rows of large trees to stop the wind. These rows of trees are called windbreaks. In time, better plowing methods, mo rainfall, and the new windbreaks ended the terrible dust.

LITERATURE REVIEW

1. What did people do to make it through the Dust Bowl days in Oklahoma?
2. How do you think you would have felt about living in the Dust Bowl?
3. Many people left Oklahoma to escape the Dust Bowl, but many stayed through all the hardships. With a partner, role-play a conversation between a person who is staying and a person who is leaving. Make sure the conversation gives the reasons for each person's decision. Present your conversation to the class.

ACTIVITY CHOICES

ACTIVITY BOOK

Reinforce & Extend

Use ACTIVITY BOOK, p. 117.

Reteach the Main Idea

COOPERATIVE LEARNING

WRITE DISASTER GUIDELINES Divide the class into small groups and have students in each group imagine that they are members of a Dust Bowl disaster command center. Have students in each group write Dust Bowl disaster guidelines to help the farmers survive the changing conditions in Oklahoma in 1936. The guidelines should include what farmers must do to protect themselves and their property from the effects of the storms. Let the group members share and discuss their lists with one another and with other groups.

World War II

LESSON 4

FOCUS
What might cause conflict between countries today?

Main Idea As you read, look for the reasons that caused the United States and countries in Europe and Asia to go to war in the 1930s and 1940s.

Vocabulary
concentration camp
civilian
rationing
relocation camp

The United States was not the only country to suffer an
conomic depression in the 1930s. The depression was world-
vide. Many Europeans, still rebuilding their countries after
Vorld War I, had a hard time finding jobs to support their
amilies. In some places in Asia, countries were running out of
he resources needed to make their economies grow. Strong
eaders in both Europe and Asia promised to solve their coun-
ries' problems by force. Another war was on its way. This
econd world war, or World War II, would be even worse
han the first.

The Rise of Dictators

After World War I the Allied Powers expected Germany to
ay for the costs of the war. But Germany did not have the
noney to do so. Its economy had been destroyed by the war
nd the depression that followed the war.

During the 1920s a German leader named Adolf Hitler tried
o convince people that Germany had not been treated fairly
fter World War I. He believed that the Germans who had
lond hair and blue eyes were the "true Germans" and were
etter than all other Germans and other peoples of the world.
Hitler made life especially difficult for Germany's Jews,
vhom he blamed for many of Germany's problems.

Hitler became the leader of a political party in Germany
alled the National Socialists, or Nazis. The Nazi party grew
n power and set up an army. Its soldiers, who called them-
elves storm troopers, attacked Jewish people and others who
vere against Hitler. Soon the Nazis began to round up people
vho did not agree with them. They put some
f these people in terrible prisons called
oncentration camps.

In 1933 the Nazi party, led by Adolf Hitler (inset, right), took control of Germany. Hitler addressed a crowd of 50,000 (below) at Nuremberg, Germany, in 1937.

Chapter 18 • 583

Objectives

1. Analyze reasons for the rise of dictators in the 1930s.
2. Describe how dictators' aggressive actions led to World War II.
3. Identify the events that caused the United States to enter World War II.
4. Summarize the cooperation and sacrifices of Americans on the home front.
5. Discuss the treatment of Japanese Americans during the war.

Vocabulary

concentration camp (p. 583)
civilian (p. 585)
rationing (p. 587)
relocation camp (p. 588)

1. ACCESS

The Focus Question

Ask students to bring to class newspaper or newsmagazine articles about international conflicts. Lead a class discussion about the articles during which students identify similarities and differences in the reasons the conflicts are occurring.

The Main Idea

In this lesson students explore the reasons many nations in the world were drawn into World War II in the 1930s and 1940s. After students have read the lesson, ask them to identify the major warring nations and their reasons for entering the war.

2. BUILD

The Rise of Dictators

Key Content Summary

In the 1930s bad economic conditions led to the rise of dictators in a few European countries and in Japan. The dictators thought they could improve the economies in their own countries by invading and conquering other countries.

Reading Support

PREVIEW AND READ THE LESSON Provide students with the following visual framework.

A SECOND WORLD WAR

GERMANY	
1938	Invades Austria and Czechoslovakia
1939	Invades Poland
1940	Invades Netherlands, Belgium, Luxembourg, Denmark, Norway, and France

JAPAN	
1931	Invades Manchuria
1937	Starts war against China
1940	Invades French Indochina
1941	Attacks and destroys most of the United States fleet at Pearl Harbor

1941 The United States enters World War II

History

Origins, Spread, and Influence Have students identify the reasons for Adolf Hitler's rise to power in Germany and analyze his treatment of the Jewish people there.

Q. **How do you think the Germans felt about losing World War I?**
They were angry and resentful.

Economics

Economic Systems Have students identify the ways that dictators in Europe and Japan wanted to use their power to force a change in their nations' economies.

The War Begins

Key Content Summary

Dictators in Japan, Germany, and Italy invaded other countries between 1931 and 1938. The rest of the world watched until 1939 when Germany invaded Poland, causing Britain and France to declare war on Germany. The United States wanted to stay out of World War II, but began preparing for possible conflict.

Geography

Location Have students locate Italy, Germany, and Japan and the countries they conquered on a class wall map or atlas of the world. Then provide students with outline maps of Europe and have them color and label all the countries Germany conquered between 1938 and 1940.

The Nazis used force against Jews and other people whom they labeled as enemies.

In 1933 the Nazi party took control of the German government, and representative government in Germany came to an end. Hitler ruled as a dictator. He rebuilt Germany's economy by preparing for another war. Factories produced tanks, guns, and other war supplies. Hitler dreamed that Germany would one day rule the world.

Dictators came to power in other countries in Europe, too. Joseph Stalin ruled the Soviet Union, which had become a dictatorship—a country ruled by a dictator—after the Russian Revolution in 1917. Francisco Franco ruled Spain. In Italy Benito Mussolini (buh•NEE•toh moo•suh•LEE•nee) came to power in the 1920s. He wanted Italy to regain the power and glory it had in ancient times, when it was the center of the Roman Empire.

Dictators also ruled the Asian country of Japan. The emperor, Hirohito, had little authority after military officers took control of the government. Trade and industry were growing, but Japan did not have all the resources it needed. Japan's military leaders planned to get oil, rubber, and iron for their country by conquering other countries in Asia and the Pacific.

REVIEW ***In what countries did dictators rule after World War I?*** Germany, the Soviet Union, Spain, Italy, and Japan

The War Begins

In 1931 Japan invaded Manchuria, a part of China. In 1935 Italy took over the African country of Ethiopia. In 1937 Japan started a war against the rest of China. In 1938 Germany took over Austria and Czechoslovakia. Other countries, including the United States, did little to stop the fighting.

Then, on September 1, 1939, Germany invaded Poland. German forces attacked with tanks on land and planes in the air. The

ACTIVITY CHOICES

Link to Reading

READ AND DISCUSS Ask students to select a fiction or nonfiction book about the Jewish people during World War II, such as *The Night Crossing* by Karen Ackerman, *The Grey Striped Shirt: How Grandma and Grandpa Survived the Holocaust* by Jacqueline Jules, *Touch Wood: A Girlhood in Occupied France* by Renee Roth-Hano, *Daniel's Story* by Carol Matas, *The Shadow Children* by Steven Schnur, or *The Diary of Anne Frank.* When students have finished reading their books, have them form a large circle in the class and share what they have learned about the Holocaust, individualism, interdependence, and the human spirit under difficult conditions.

Meet Individual Needs

COOPERATIVE LEARNING

AUDITORY LEARNERS Divide the class into two groups. Assign one group to argue for democracy as the best form of government. Assign the other group to argue for a dictatorship as the best form of government. Allow each group time to do research, prepare for the debate, select representatives to sit on the debating panel, and practice for the debate. Select a student from each group to act as moderators during the debate. At the conclusion of the debate, lead a class discussion about the debate and have students decide which form of government they would prefer and why.

stroyed cities, roads, and communication
es. Leaders in Britain and France had
ally had enough. They declared war on
ermany on September 3, 1939. World War II
d begun.

The British and French armies were not
le to stop the Germans from taking over
ost of Europe. By 1940 German troops
d conquered the Netherlands, Belgium,
xembourg, Denmark, Norway, and most
France. German bombers attacked British
ies, but Britain fought on.

Many people in the United States felt that
eir country should stay out of the war.
esident Franklin Roosevelt had promised
keep the United States out of the war, but
wanted the country to be prepared in case
was attacked. The United States started
aking tanks, bombers, and other war sup-
ies. It also began to send equipment and
pplies to help Britain.

In 1940 Japanese troops invaded French
dochina, which is now made up of the
untries of Laos, Cambodia, and Vietnam. American leaders feared that Japan would soon threaten the Philippines and other places in the Pacific. They were right.

REVIEW ***When did World War II begin?*** September 3, 1939

The United States Enters the War

At 7:55 A.M. on Sunday, December 7, 1941, the roar of Japanese planes shattered the early morning calm over the Hawaiian Islands. The planes dropped bombs on American ships docked at Pearl Harbor. Pearl Harbor is an American naval base in the Hawaiian Islands. World War II had come to the United States.

In less than two hours, the attack was over. Much of the United States' Pacific fleet had sunk or lay burning in the harbor. At nearby Hickam Airfield, about 150 planes were destroyed. More than 2,000 sailors and soldiers and 68 civilians were killed. A **civilian** is a person who is not in the military.

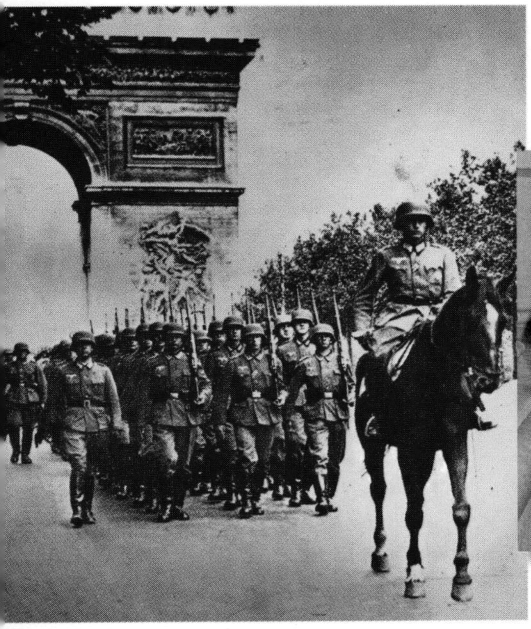

German soldiers invaded Poland in 1939 and marched through Paris in 1940 (left). What do you suppose Americans of that time were thinking when they read headlines about the war?

History

Patterns and Relationships Have students recall how the United States was reluctant to enter World War I and describe the significant contribution the United States made to the outcome of that war.

Q. **Why do you think the United States hesitated about entering World War II?** Europe was far away and most people, if given a choice, would have preferred to avoid war.

Visual Analysis

Learn from Pictures Have students answer the question in the caption. Americans probably were glad that they were far from Europe. They were concerned, but most wanted to stay out of the conflict.

The United States Enters the War

Key Content Summary

On December 7, 1941, the Japanese attacked the U.S. naval base at Pearl Harbor in the Hawaiian Islands. The next day the United States declared war on Japan. Americans were now embroiled in World War II, fighting alongside Britain and the Soviet Union.

History

Turning Points Have students recall the 1898 Treaty of Paris, which gave the United States control over the Philippines. Ask students to discuss why U.S. control of the Philippines might have motivated the Japanese to cripple the Pacific fleet.

Link to Science

COOPERATIVE LEARNING

REPORT ON TECHNOLOGY Have a small group of students research and prepare an oral report about the changes in warfare technology from World War I to World War II. Ask them to make illustrations to accompany their reports. The illustrations could show new military weapons, airplanes, submarines, ships, and land vehicles.

Link to Language Arts

WRITE TO PERSUADE Divide the class into two groups. Have students in one group write speeches to persuade the American people that the United States should not ignore the aggressive actions of Germany, Italy, and Japan. Have students in the other group write speeches to persuade the American people that the United States can provide war supplies to Britain and its allies, but must stay out of the war. Ask student volunteers to read their speeches to the class.

TECHNOLOGY

HARCOURT BRACE

Use THE AMAZING WRITING MACHINE™ to complete this writing activity.

Culture

Thought and Expression The attack on the U.S. Pacific fleet shocked the nation and temporarily prevented the navy from blocking Japanese aggression in the Pacific.

Q. **How do you think Americans reacted to the Japanese attack on Pearl Harbor?** They were united in their fury at the Japanese, and their opposition to Roosevelt's policies about war preparations evaporated.

Visual Analysis

Read Maps Refer students to the map on this page and have them locate Pearl Harbor. Also have students use the locator globe to find the United States and Japan in relation to Hawaii.

History

Origins, Spread, and Influence Have students review the reasons for alliances among nations.

Q. **Which countries formed the Axis Powers?** Germany, Italy, and Japan **The Allies?** Britain, the Soviet Union, and the United States

"PRIMARY SOURCE"

Source: President Franklin D. Roosevelt, in a speech to Congress, December 8, 1941.

GEOGRAPHY

Pearl Harbor

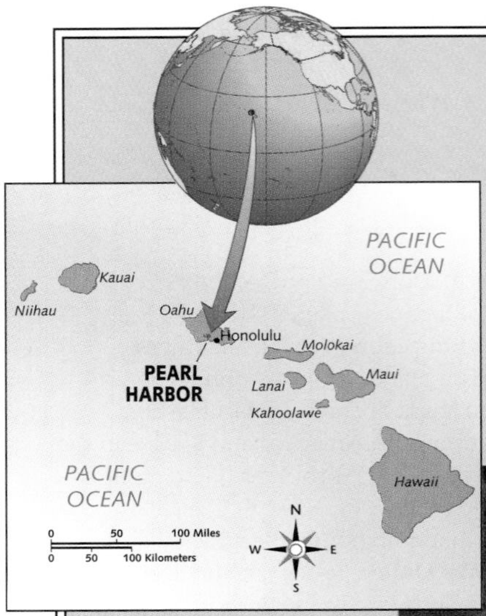

Pearl Harbor is one of the largest natural harbors in the world. It is located on the Hawaiian island of Oahu (oh•AH•hoo) and lies west of downtown Honolulu, the capital of Hawaii. The United States began using Pearl Harbor as a coal station for its steamships in 1887. The navy started using it as a base in 1902. The surprise attack on Pearl Harbor by Japanese forces led the United States to enter World War II. Today the USS *Arizona* Memorial stands above one of the ships sunk in the attack.

During the attack on Pearl Harbor, 19 American warships were sunk or disabled. Three others were damaged. The Japanese hoped that by the time the United States rebuilt its forces, Japan would have taken over more lands in Asia and the Pacific.

The day after the attack, President Roosevelt spoke to Congress:

> "Yesterday, December 7, 1941—a date which will live in infamy—the United States of America was suddenly and deliberately attacked by naval and air forces of the Empire of Japan. . . . I ask that the Congress declare that since the . . . attack by Japan . . . a state of war has existed between the United States and the Japanese Empire."

Congress declared war on Japan the same day. Three days later, when Japan's allies, Germany and Italy, declared war on the United States, Congress recognized a state of war with them, too. Germany, Italy, and Japan were known as the Axis Powers. The United States joined Britain and the Soviet Union. These three countries were known as the Allies.

REVIEW ***When did the Japanese attack the American ships docked at Pearl Harbor?*** December 7, 1941

ACTIVITY CHOICES

Background

DORIE MILLER There were fewer than 5,000 African Americans in the United States military at the beginning of World War II. They served in segregated units, and could not become members of the Army Air Corps or the Marine Corps. However, one of the first heroes of World War II was Dorie Miller, an African American naval mess attendant who worked in the kitchen of the battleship *West Virginia.* On December 7, 1941, Miller heard the exploding bombs. When he rushed up on deck, he saw Japanese aircraft dropping bombs and his captain lying wounded. After moving the captain to safety, Miller grabbed a machine gun and shot down four Japanese planes. He received the Navy Cross for his bravery.

Meet Individual Needs

ADVANCED LEARNERS Have students use library resources to compile a list of the names of all the ships destroyed at Pearl Harbor. Have them compile a second list of all the ships that were disabled. You may want to have students work together to draw a diagram of Pearl Harbor as it looked on December 7, 1941.

Americans at War

After the bombing at Pearl Harbor, the nited States began to produce more airlanes, tanks, and other war supplies. This ork gave many people jobs. Now instead f not enough jobs, there were not enough orkers. World War II ended the Great epression in the United States.

As they had in World War I, women took ver jobs in factories, fields, and offices. ther women served in the armed forces. hey made maps, drove ambulances, and orked as clerks or nurses. Some women ained as pilots and flew airplanes from ctories to airfields in Europe and the acific.

The demands of fighting a war led to furer growth in the federal government's uthority. To produce war supplies and feed ousands of soldiers, the government took ntrol of many businesses, setting prices nd wages.

The new government rules also called for **rationing**, or limiting, what Americans could purchase, so that more supplies could be sent overseas. Government coupons were needed for such goods as butter, sugar, meat, home-heating oil, and gasoline. Each citizen had a coupon book for each kind of item. Without the coupons, people could not buy the rationed goods.

REVIEW ***What did the government do to produce war supplies and feed its soldiers?*** set up controls on prices, wages, household supplies, and gasoline

Problems for Japanese Americans

War with Japan led to terrible problems for Japanese Americans. Some United States military officials believed that Japanese Americans would help Japan invade the United States.

In February 1942 President Roosevelt ordered the army to put about 110,000

EARNING FROM GRAPHS The graph shows how the number of women who orked outside the home increased between the years 1900 and 1950. Many omen, like the woman in the photograph (right), worked in airplane factories uring World War II.

By 1950, about how many American women were working outside the home?

OURCE: *Historical Statistics of the nited States*

587

Americans at War

Key Content Summary

World War II ended the Great Depression in the United States. Factories geared up to produce war supplies, men and women joined the armed forces, women took over jobs left behind by men, and the government rationed food, heating oil, and gasoline.

Visual Analysis

Learn from Graphs Have students answer the question in the caption. about 17 million

Civics and Government

Purposes of Government Have students discuss the reasons for the shortages of goods caused by the war.

Q. **How did the government control the rationing of food and other goods?** by issuing coupon books, which citizens had to use to buy the rationed items

Problems for Japanese Americans

Key Content Summary

Some U.S. military officials feared that Japanese Americans would help Japan invade the United States. Although President Roosevelt ordered about 110,000 Japanese Americans into relocation camps, 17,000 Japanese Americans served with distinction in the U.S. Army.

Multicultural Link

Until 1943, Japanese Americans were barred from serving in the United States armed forces. Then the ban was lifted, and the army actively sought volunteers among the Japanese Americans living in the relocation camps. One man who had volunteered later said, "We wanted to show the rest of America that we meant business. Even though my older brother was living in Japan, I told my parents that I was going to enlist because America was my country." The 442nd Regiment Combat Team, in which the Japanese Americans served, received more than 18,000 individual decorations for bravery. Known as the Purple Heart Battalion, it successfully liberated a town in France.

Extend and Enrich

COOPERATIVE LEARNING

MAKE A WALL DISPLAY

Divide the class into groups, and assign each group one of the following topics: Hitler, Germany, and the Nazis; the British Royal Air Force; Mussolini, Italy, and fascism; Japan and Admiral Isoroku Yamamoto; women in the United States military; or jobs created by the war. Have group members use library resources to help them decide what they would like to include in their section of a wall display about the early years of World War II. When the display is completed, ask group members to discuss their section with the other groups.

Culture

Thought and Expression Have students express their views about the U.S. treatment of Japanese Americans during the war. Point out that many of the Japanese Americans were United States citizens.

3. CLOSE

Have students consider again the Focus question on page 583.

What might cause conflict between countries today?

Have students use what they have learned in this lesson about World War II to consider whether the same kinds of conditions exist within or between any countries today.

LESSON 4 REVIEW—Answers

Check Understanding

1. Germany, Italy, Spain, the Soviet Union, and Japan
2. economic conditions, desire for natural resources in other countries, desire for glory, the perception of unfair treatment following World War I, attacks by other countries

Think Critically

3. Students may mention feelings of anger and resentment about being singled out for such treatment, or feelings of resignation to make the best of a bad situation.
4. Many men left their homes and jobs to serve in the military. Many women went to work in factories and offices and served in the armed forces. Food and other products were rationed.

Show What You Know

Performance Assessment Consider having students tape their interviews, play them for the class, and compare and contrast the responses.

What to Look For Look for evidence that students understand the impact of the Pearl Harbor attack well enough to ask appropriate questions of the interviewees.

These Japanese American soldiers arrived at Camp Shelby, Mississippi, in 1943. Like other United States citizens of Japanese origin, they fought bravely.

Japanese Americans in what were called **relocation camps**. These camps were like prisons. Barbed wire fenced people in. Soldiers with guns guarded the camps to keep people from leaving.

Even though most Japanese Americans were loyal United States citizens, they had to sell their homes, businesses, and belongings. They were moved to relocation camps in California, Arizona, Wyoming, Utah, Arkansas, and Idaho. Every Japanese American had to wear an identification tag.

"Our home was one room in a large army-style barracks, measuring 20 by 25 feet," remembers one woman. "The only furnishings were an iron pot-belly stove and cots." Another woman recalls, "Can you imagine the despair and utter desolation of all of us? Everybody was weeping, youngsters hanging onto parents, fear and terror all around."

While their families and friends were in the relocation camps, more than 17,000 Japanese Americans served in the army. Japanese Americans formed the 442nd Combat Team. This unit received more service awards than any other unit its size in World War II.

REVIEW ***Why did President Roosevelt order the army to put Japanese Americans in relocation camps?*** Some military officials believed Japanese Americans would help Japan invade the United States.

LESSON 4 REVIEW

Check Understanding

1. **Remember the Facts** What countries were ruled by dictators in the 1930s?
2. **Recall the Main Idea** What caused different countries to take part in World War II?

Think Critically

3. **Personally Speaking** How do you think you might feel as an American citizen if you were forced to live in a relocation camp?
4. **Think More About It** How did World War II change life for many Americans?

Show What You Know

Interviewing Activity Talk to people who are old enough to remember the Japanese attack on Pearl Harbor. Ask them to recall when they first heard the news about the attack and how they felt at the time. Write down your findings and report them to the class.

ACTIVITY CHOICES

ACTIVITY BOOK

Reinforce & Extend

Use ACTIVITY BOOK, p. 118.

Reteach the Main Idea

COOPERATIVE LEARNING

WRITE AN OUTLINE Divide the class into small groups. Have each group use the textbook as a resource to make an outline showing the reasons Japan, the United States, and many countries in Europe went to war in the 1930s and 1940s. Ask the groups to share and discuss their outlines, and use their ideas to compose a class outline on the board.

The Allies Win the War

World War II was a new kind of war. Soldiers did not fight from trenches, as they had in World War I. Instead, they moved quickly by tank, ship, and airplane. Bombs dropped in air raids destroyed factories, hospitals, and homes and killed hundreds of thousands of civilians. The war was fought over an area much larger than that of any other war—almost half the world. It was fought on two major **fronts**, or battle lines. The first was in Africa and Europe. The second was in the Pacific. Victory on both fronts would be needed to win the war.

LESSON 5

FOCUS
How do events that happened in the past affect today's world?

Main Idea As you read, learn how World War II affected countries around the world.

Vocabulary
front
D day
Holocaust
island-hopping
communism
free world
cold war

War in Africa and Europe

The first step in the Allies' battle plan in Europe was to gain control of the Mediterranean Sea. To do this, the Allies had to fight the Germans and Italians in North Africa and then invade Italy. The Allies won North Africa in May 1943 and then started pushing north through Italy. In September the Italian government surrendered. However, heavy fighting went on until June 1944, when the Americans captured the city of Rome.

While the Allies were fighting in Italy, they were planning another invasion of Europe. On June 6, 1944, the date known as **D day**, the Allies worked together in the largest water-to-land invasion in history.

American General Dwight D. Eisenhower led the invasion. On the morning of June 6, he told his troops,

> “You are about to embark upon the great crusade. . . . The hopes and prayers of liberty-loving people everywhere march with you.”

On D day American, British, and Canadian troops crossed the English Channel. They landed on the beaches of Normandy,

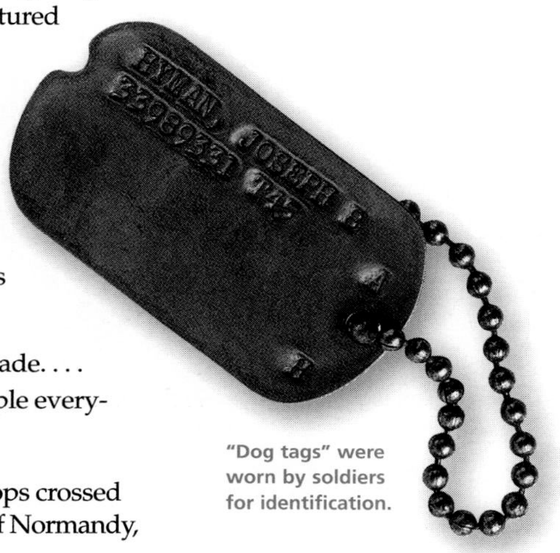

"Dog tags" were worn by soldiers for identification.

Objectives

1. Summarize Allied battle plans that led to D day.
2. Describe the Holocaust.
3. Analyze how the Allies defeated Japan.
4. Identify the causes of the Cold War.

Vocabulary

front (p. 589)
D day (p. 589)
Holocaust (p. 591)
island-hopping (p. 591)
communism (p. 593)
free world (p. 593)
cold war (p. 593)

1. ACCESS

The Focus Question

Ask students to recall events in United States history that have had a lasting effect. Write on the board a list of the events and their present-day impact. Then have students discuss whether the events have had positive or negative consequences on today's world.

The Main Idea

In this lesson students follow the major events of World War II from 1942 to 1945. After students have read the lesson, have them analyze the lasting effects of World War II on countries around the world.

2. BUILD

War in Africa and Europe

Key Content Summary

The Allies' strategy in the war focused on Germany. The United States and Britain pushed back the German army on the western front. At the same time Soviet troops advanced against the Germans on the eastern front. On May 8, 1945, the victorious Allies accepted Germany's surrender.

Reading Support

ANTICIPATION GUIDE Before students read the lesson, ask them which of the following statements they might associate with the war on the North African and European front and which they might associate with the war on the Pacific front. Students may correct their predictions as they read.

1. The Allies wanted to get control of the Mediterranean Sea. North African and European front
2. Allied leaders decided on a plan of island-hopping. Pacific front
3. On D day, U.S., British, and Canadian troops attacked the Germans on the beaches at Normandy. North African and European front
4. Many soldiers died at Iwo Jima and Okinawa. Pacific front
5. The new atomic bomb was used on Hiroshima to end the war quickly. Pacific front
6. From the east the Soviets pushed back the enemy and captured Berlin. North African and European front

Geography

Movement Refer students to the map on pages 592–593 and have them trace the Allied invasion strategy from North Africa into Italy, and across the English Channel to Normandy, France. Also have students trace the Soviet push to recapture Poland and other eastern European countries on their drive toward Berlin.

History

Turning Points Have students analyze why D day was a major turning point in the war against Germany.

Q. **Why do you think D day is remembered on June 6 every year by Britain, France, and the United States?** to remember the soldiers who sacrificed their lives and to celebrate the success of the invasion against Nazi oppression

PRIMARY SOURCE

Source: Letters of Sergeant Ralph G. Martin, June 6, 1944.

The Holocaust

Key Content Summary

Allied soldiers invading German-held Europe were horrified to find that millions of people had been killed in concentration camps. Most of them were Jews. The mass murder of the European Jews came to be known as the Holocaust.

in France, where the German forces met them with heavy gunfire. One soldier remembered:

> "Everything was confusion. . . . Shells were coming in all the time; boats burning; vehicles with nowhere to go bogging down, getting hit; supplies getting wet; boats trying to come in all the time, some hitting mines, exploding."

Many soldiers died on D day, but the invasion was successful. The Allies broke through the German lines and began moving inland from the west, pushing back the enemy. At the same time, the Soviets were pushing back the German armies from the east. In April 1945, Allied troops met near Berlin, the German capital. There they learned that Hitler had killed himself.

Berlin fell to the Soviets on May 2, 1945, and the German military leaders asked to surrender. On May 8, the Allies accepted the surrender. This day was called V-E Day, or Victory in Europe Day. It marked the end of the war in Europe.

REVIEW ***What happened on D day?*** The Allies invaded Normandy.

The Holocaust

Only when the war in Europe was over did people discover everything that Hitler and the Nazis had done. Allied soldiers found the Nazis' concentration camps. The Allies learned that more than 12 million men, women, and children had been murdered in these camps. One of the largest of the death camps was at Auschwitz (OWSH•vits), in Poland.

BIOGRAPHY

Dwight D. Eisenhower
1890–1969

Dwight David Eisenhower grew up in Abilene, Kansas. He attended West Point Military Academy and spent more than 40 years as a soldier. In 1939 the Army put Eisenhower in charge of war planning. He headed the Allied invasion of North Africa in 1942. In 1944 Eisenhower became commander of all Allied forces in Europe. After the war he served as president of Columbia University. In 1952 Dwight Eisenhower was elected President of the United States.

General Eisenhower talks with his troops (above right) before they leave for the D day invasion. On D day, 600 warships and 4,000 landing craft carried 176,000 soldiers across the English Channel (right).

ACTIVITY CHOICES

Background

D DAY The Allied invasion of Normandy involved the largest amphibious force in history, supported by 11,000 aircraft. In the months before the invasion, Allied aircraft had bombed the Normandy coast to keep the Germans from fortifying it. On D day, paratroopers were flown in first to blow up bridges, cut railroad lines, and take landing fields. During the next two months at least another 2 million troops were landed on the Normandy coast, along with 16 million tons of arms, supplies, and munitions. General Dwight D. Eisenhower's successes with the Allied invasion of North Africa in 1942 led to his appointment as supreme commander of Allied forces in Europe in December 1943. This Texas-born grandson of German and Swiss immigrants had graduated from West Point in 1915. Eisenhower spearheaded the 1944 invasion of Normandy.

Link to World Languages

RESEARCH THE HOLOCAUST The word *holocaust* comes from an ancient Greek word that means a burnt offering or a sacrifice. Historically, even before World War II, the term was applied to any great or widespread destruction. When the magnitude of Hitler's deeds became known to the general public, it seemed appropriate to apply the term *holocaust* to what is now generally recognized as one of the most heinous crimes in human history.

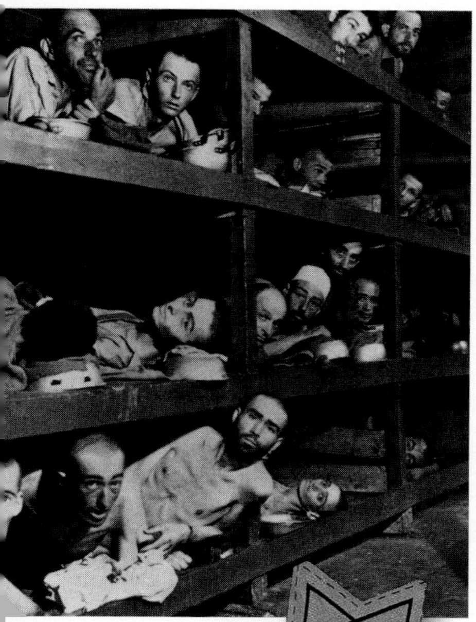

Prisoners in concentration camps suffered horribly. The Nazis forced Jews to wear a yellow Star of David to make them stand out.

The Nazis killed people for their religious and political beliefs. People who were ill or disabled and could not work were also killed. The largest group of victims were Jews, the people Hitler had blamed for Germany's problems.

During the war more than 6 million people were murdered on Hitler's orders because they were Jews. This terrible mass murder of European Jews came to be known as the **Holocaust** (HOH•luh•kawst). Hitler had called it the "final solution to the Jewish question." It was a deliberate attempt to destroy an entire people.

REVIEW *What was Hitler's "final solution"?* to destroy the Jewish people

War in the Pacific

In the Pacific, Allied leaders planned to defeat the Japanese by forcing them back from the lands and islands they had conquered. Allied leaders decided on a plan of **island-hopping**. This meant that Allied troops would take back the islands one at a time until they reached Tokyo. At the same time, the Allies would bomb Japan from the air.

Battles on the islands of Iwo Jima (EE•woh JEE•muh) and Okinawa (oh•kuh•NAH•wah) showed island-hopping to be a costly plan. At Iwo Jima, an island 750 miles (1,207 km) from Tokyo, Japan's capital, more than 4,000 American soldiers lost their lives. More than 20,000 Japanese soldiers died. At Okinawa, 350 miles (563 km) from Tokyo, 11,000 Americans died. The Japanese lost more than 100,000 people. As the Allies came closer to Tokyo, the losses grew.

By early April 1945 victory in the Pacific seemed near. But President Franklin Roosevelt did not live to see the end of the war. He died on April 12, 1945. Vice President Harry S. Truman became President.

After he became President, Truman learned that Roosevelt had agreed to the development of the most powerful bomb the world had ever known—the atom bomb. By the summer of 1945, this new weapon was ready. President Truman made the difficult decision to drop the atom bomb on Japan. He wanted to end the war quickly and save American lives.

On August 6, 1945, the American bomber *Enola Gay* flew over the industrial city of Hiroshima (hir•uh•SHEE•muh), Japan. A single bomb was dropped. There was a flash like an exploding sun. Then a mushroom-shaped cloud rose from the city. The bomb flattened a huge area of Hiroshima and killed more than 75,000 people, mostly civilians.

As terrible as the atom bomb was, Japan did not surrender. On August 9 the United States dropped a second bomb, this time on

Visual Analysis

Interpret Photographs Have students analyze what the faces of the men in the photograph indicate about life in a concentration camp.

War in the Pacific

Key Content Summary

The Allies adopted the policy of island-hopping in the Pacific war against Japan. There was a heavy loss of lives on both sides. In August 1945, President Harry S. Truman ordered military leaders to drop atom bombs on two Japanese cities. Japan surrendered soon after.

Geography

MAP THEME

Human–Environment Interactions Have students conclude why fighting to take back the islands one at a time might result in a heavy loss of lives.

Meet Individual Needs

ADVANCED LEARNERS Ask students to select one of the battles on the Pacific front, such as Iwo Jima, Bataan, Corregidor, or Okinawa. Have students research the strategy of the battle they select, from both the American and Japanese viewpoints. Also have them provide some facts about the battle and its outcome. Ask them to present the information to the class and to be prepared to answer questions.

Link to Science

COOPERATIVE LEARNING

DRAW A DIAGRAM Select a small group of student volunteers to research the technology that made aircraft carriers critical to the war in the Pacific. Ask the group to draw a large diagram of the World War II carrier U.S.S. *Yorktown* and explain aircraft carrier technology to the class. Have a second group of student volunteers research the technology of submarines and draw a large diagram of the World War II submarine U.S.S. *Barb.* Ask the group to explain submarine technology to the class.

Geography

Location Refer students to the map on pages 592–593 and have them conclude why the navy had a key role in U.S. war strategy against Japan. Also have students locate the Pacific islands mentioned in the textbook.

Q. **Why did both the United States and Japan consider the Pacific islands important?** There were such vast distances to cover in the Pacific Ocean that the islands provided critical bases of operations for aircraft, ship repairs, and supply depots.

Visual Analysis

Learn from Maps Have students answer the question in the caption. The United States was far enough away from both the Pacific and European fronts to be safe from invasion and bombing raids. Factories and military bases could continue operations.

A Changed World

Key Content Summary

Before the war ended, 50 countries had formed the United Nations to keep world peace. After the war, the Soviet Union set up communist governments in the eastern European countries it had invaded during the war. The spread of communism brought on the Cold War between the United States and the Soviet Union.

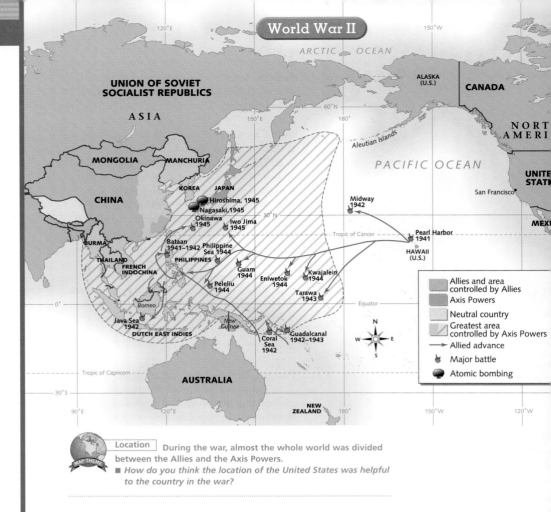

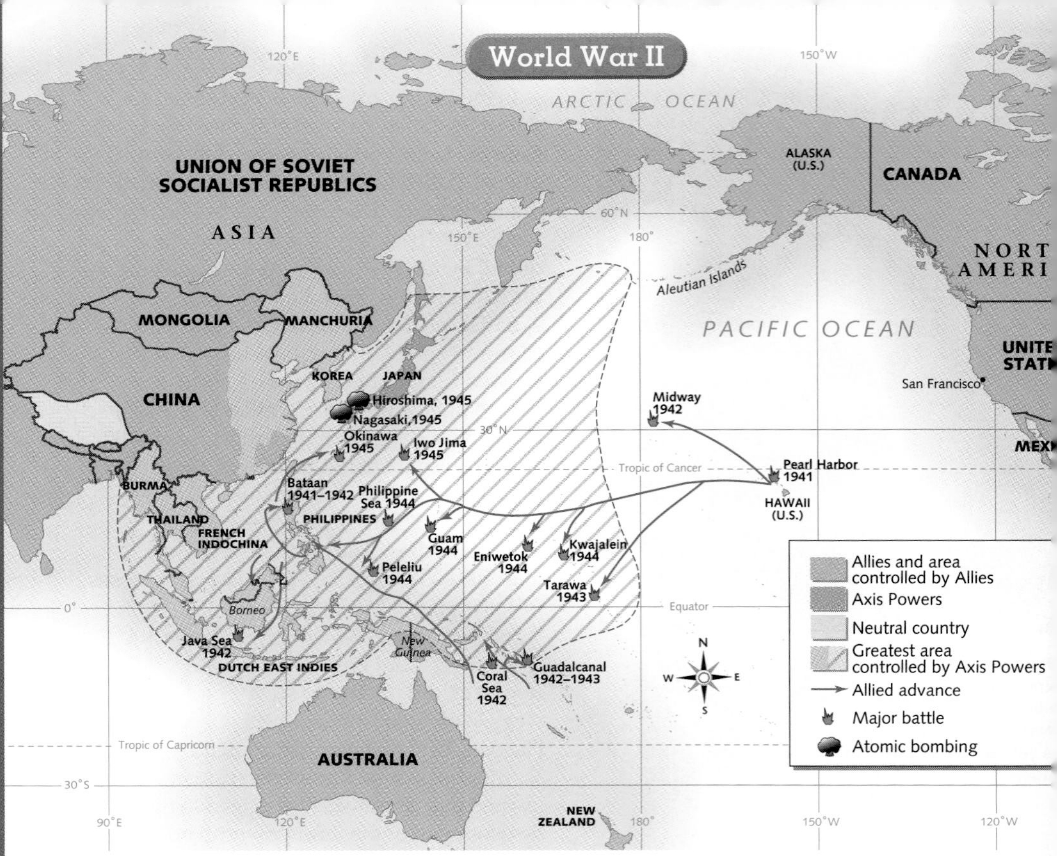

Location During the war, almost the whole world was divided between the Allies and the Axis Powers.

■ *How do you think the location of the United States was helpful to the country in the war?*

Nagasaki (nah•guh•SAH•kee). Only then did Japan agree to surrender. On August 15, Americans celebrated V-J Day, or Victory over Japan Day.

World War II was finally over. More than 300,000 American soldiers and close to 15 million soldiers from other countries had died in the fighting.

REVIEW ***Why did Japan surrender to the United States?*** because the United States had dropped atom bombs on Hiroshima and Nagasaki

A Changed World

Just as they had after World War I, world leaders after World War II turned to the idea of an organization of nations. This time the United States supported the idea. In April 1945, delegates from 50 countries met in San Francisco to form the United Nations, or UN. The purpose of the UN is to keep world peace and promote cooperation among nations.

592 • Unit 9

ACTIVITY CHOICES

Simulation Activity

COOPERATIVE LEARNING

DEBATE Explain to students that President Truman defended his decision to drop the atom bomb on the grounds that it saved the lives of many thousands of American soldiers who would have been killed in a land attack on Japan. Since then some Americans have criticized the use of the bomb on two grounds: it should never have been used against civilians, and it launched the postwar nuclear arms race. Divide the class into two groups to prepare for and conduct a debate. Have one group represent the argument for dropping the atom bomb on Japan and the other group represent the argument against dropping the atom bomb on Japan. At the conclusion of the debate, have the class discuss the validity of the arguments made.

Background

THE MARSHALL PLAN When the war ended, European countries were in desperate shape. There were shortages of food, fuel, and raw materials. Industries and transportation systems had been destroyed. The United States provided money through the Marshall Plan to help these countries rebuild. One of the reasons the United States did so was the fear that continued economic chaos would lead people in western European countries to elect communist governments.

The United States came out of World War II as the strongest nation in the world. Americans used this strength to help other nations rebuild. Yet even as the war was ending and plans for peace were being made, new conflicts were beginning.

The United States and the Soviet Union were allies during World War II. After the war this quickly changed. The Soviet Union set up communist governments in the eastern European countries it had invaded during the war. **Communism** is a social and economic system in which all land and industries are owned by the government. Individuals have few rights and little freedom.

The United States saw the spread of communism as a threat to freedom. It began to help countries fight communism by giving them military and economic help. In the fight against communism, the United States and its allies were known as the **free world**.

Hostility, or unfriendliness, developed between the free world and the communist nations. This hostility became known as the Cold War. A **cold war** is fought with propaganda and money rather than with soldiers and weapons. For much of the second half of the 1900s, the Cold War shaped world events.

REVIEW ***How did the United States help fight communism?*** by giving military and economic help to other countries to fight communism

History

People and Events Across Time and Place Have students recall the League of Nations and identify the similarities between the League of Nations and the United Nations.

Q. **Why do you think the United States joined the United Nations even though it had not joined the League of Nations?** United States leaders realized that it was not possible to be isolated from the rest of the world. After the war, the United States, as one of the strongest nations in the world, wanted to work for peace.

Civics and Government

Purposes and Types of Government Have students describe the communist form of government and conclude why the United States saw the spread of communism as a threat to democracy.

History

Cause and Effect Have students identify the cause-and-effect relationship between the rise of communism and the development of the Cold War. Have them compare Cold War tactics with armed conflict tactics.

Community Involvement

Have students write a class letter to the local Veterans of Foreign Wars organization and invite one or more members to speak to the class about their experiences in World War II. After the guest(s) has made the presentation, have students write a summary of the speaker(s)' war experiences. Also have students write a class thank-you letter to their guest(s). If a local veteran is not available, have the class write to the national Veterans of Foreign Wars Administration, the Defenders of Bataan and Corregidor, or other World War II organizations for videotaped interviews and other information.

Extend and Enrich

COOPERATIVE LEARNING

HOLD A "MEETING OF THE MINDS" Have students select biographies about some of the key figures of World War II, such as Franklin D. Roosevelt, Adolf Hitler, Benito Mussolini, Winston Churchill, Harry S. Truman, Joseph Stalin, Hermann Göring, Erwin Rommel, George Patton, Douglas MacArthur, Eleanor Roosevelt, Mildred McAfee, Oveta Culp Hobby, or Charity Adams. After students have read the biographies, have volunteers hold a "meeting of the minds" to discuss the war and its aftermath from the perspectives of their selected people.

Visual Analysis

Learn from Maps Have students answer the question in the caption. Germany lost some of its land and was divided into East Germany and West Germany.

3. CLOSE

Have students consider again the Focus question on page 589.

How do events that happened in the past affect today's world?

Have students use what they have learned in this lesson to identify events from World War II that continue to influence decisions made in the world today.

LESSON 5 REVIEW—Answers

Check Understanding

1. American, Canadian, and British troops under General Dwight D. Eisenhower; June 6, 1944
2. The war forced many countries to take sides and join the fighting. Millions of military people and civilians were killed, cities were destroyed, food and other goods were in short supply, and the United Nations was created to preserve world peace.

Think Critically

3. When it appeared that the Soviet Union was trying to spread communism in Europe, the United States began to give military and economic aid to countries there to try to preserve freedom among nations. The Cold War then developed between the two countries.
4. In World War I the United States was not directly attacked, although some American civilians on a British ship had been killed by the Germans. In World War II, the United States Navy was directly attacked by another nation.

Show What You Know

Performance Assessment Have volunteers share their letters with the rest of the class.

What to Look For Look for evidence that students understand the inhumanity of the concentration camps. Also check for good letter-writing form, correct grammar and punctuation, and well-organized thoughts.

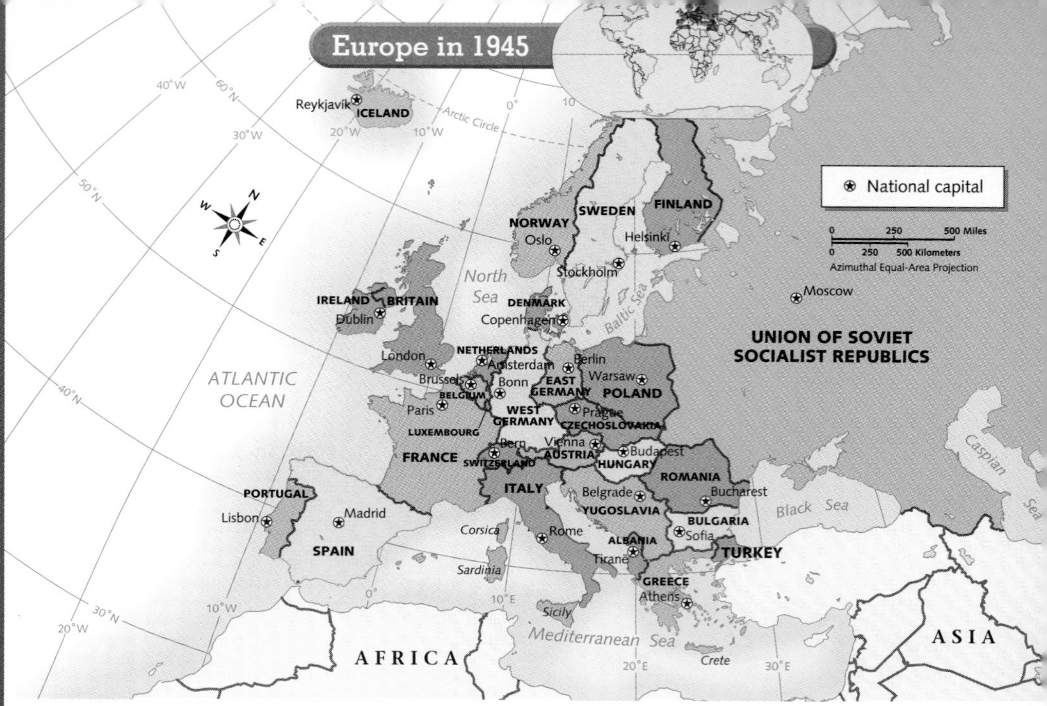

Place World War II changed Europe in ways that would affect the world for years to come.

■ *What does this map show about changes that took place in Germany after World War II?*

LESSON 5 REVIEW

Check Understanding

1. **Remember the Facts** Who led the D day invasion? When did the invasion take place?
2. **Recall the Main Idea** In what ways did World War II affect countries around the world?

Think Critically

3. **Cause and Effect** How did differences between the United States and the Soviet Union cause problems after World War II?
4. **Think More About It** How were the reasons for fighting in World War I different from the reasons for fighting in World War II?

Show What You Know

Writing Activity Imagine that you are an Allied soldier who has helped free the people from a Nazi concentration camp. Use the picture in this lesson to write a letter home that describes what you saw there. Share your letter with a family member.

ACTIVITY CHOICES

ACTIVITY BOOK

Reinforce & Extend

Use ACTIVITY BOOK, p. 119.

Reteach the Main Idea

COOPERATIVE LEARNING

MAKE A LIST Divide the class into small groups, and have each group use the lesson as a resource to list the countries mentioned and to explain how those countries were affected by World War II. Ask each group to share and discuss its list with the other groups. You may wish to compile a class list on the board.

Chart and Graph Skills

Read Parallel Time Lines

1. Why Learn This Skill?

When there are many events happening at about the same time, it can be difficult to put them in order. It even can be difficult to show them on one time line. Parallel time lines can help. Parallel time lines are two or more time lines that show the same period of time. Parallel time lines can also show events that happened in different places.

2. Understand the Process

The parallel time lines on this page show events that took place in 1945, the last year of World War II. Time Line A shows the important events that affected Europe. Time Line B shows the important events that affected the Pacific. You can use these parallel time lines to compare when different events happened.

1. Which event took place first, V-E Day or V-J Day?
2. Why do you think the label *Truman becomes President* is on both time lines?
3. Did the United States drop the atom bomb on Hiroshima before or after Soviet troops surrounded Berlin?
4. What was happening in Europe while the Battle of Iwo Jima was being fought?

3. Think and Apply

Create parallel time lines of events that have happened in your lifetime. Use one time line to show the important events in your life, beginning with the year you were born and ending with the present year. Use the other time line to show important events that have taken place in the United States during these same years.

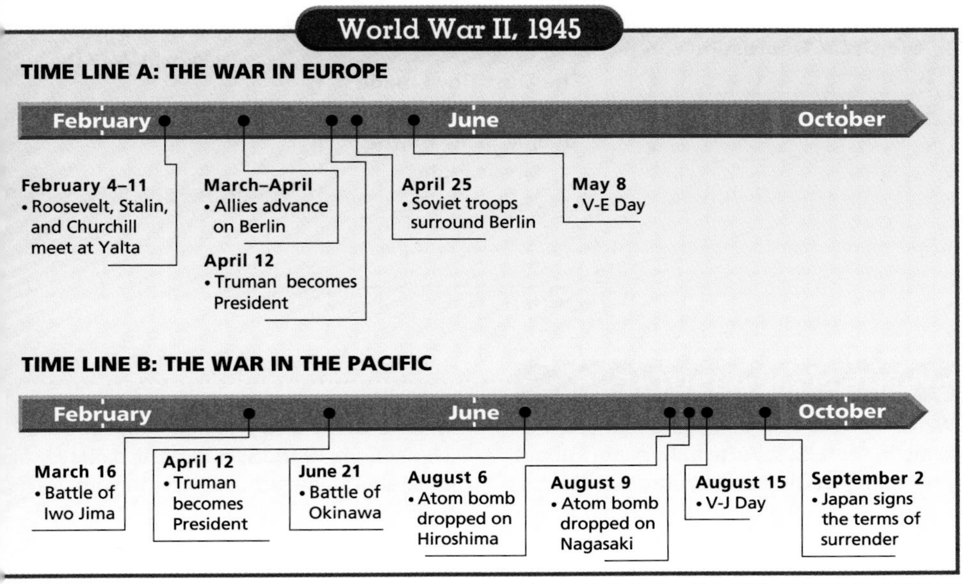

MODEL & APPLY SKILLS

Objectives

1. Compare two parallel time lines.
2. Relate events in Europe to those in the Pacific during 1945.

1. ACCESS

Remind the class that the final year of World War II was both a sad and a joyful time for Americans. People around the world were dying in the war, but major events were bringing the war closer to an end. Some of those events occurred in Europe; others in the Pacific. Parallel time lines can help students understand how battles in those two locations were related in time.

2. BUILD

Introduce the time lines. As students read Understand the Process, make sure they realize that the time lines cover the same period of time but different geographic areas. Have students answer the questions.

1. V-E Day
2. Possible answer: The event is important to other events in both areas.
3. after
4. The Allies were advancing on Berlin.

3. CLOSE

Have students complete the Think and Apply activity. Have them use encyclopedias and world histories to create their time lines. Suggest that they recruit family members to reconstruct the personal data. Look for an ability to relate two contemporaneous time lines.

ACTIVITY BOOK

Practice & Apply

Use ACTIVITY BOOK, p. 120.

Reteach the Skill

CREATE PARALLEL TIME LINES

Have students create two time lines, one for Europe and one for the Pacific. Time lines should show events leading up to World War II as well as the early events of the war itself. Have students use Lesson 4 as a source of dates. Stress the importance of having a world view in understanding history.

TRANSPARENCY

Use TRANSPARENCY 47.

TECHNOLOGY

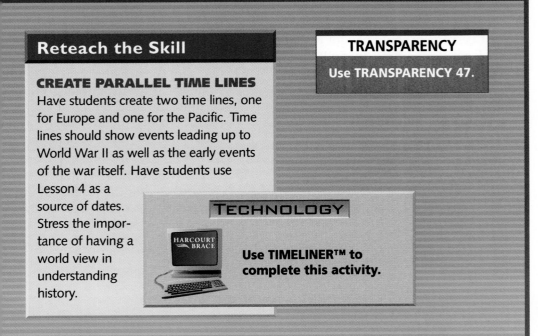

Use TIMELINER™ to complete this activity.

Time Line

Ask students to share what they recall about each event shown on the time line.

Connect Main Ideas

Use the organizer to review the main ideas of the chapter. Have students use their textbooks to complete the organizer. Allow time for them to discuss and compare their responses.

ACTIVITY BOOK

Summarize the Chapter

A copy of the graphic organizer appears on ACTIVITY BOOK, p. 121.

TRANSPARENCY

A copy of the graphic organizer appears on TRANSPARENCY 48.

Write More About It

Write a Short Story
Students may describe their first ride in the car as fun, or they may describe themselves as fearful of the car's speed and the sensation of movement.

Write a Diary Entry
Diary entries should mention the lack of certain items, the shortage of others, and the need to use ration coupons to buy some items. Effects on families might include male and female members serving in the armed forces and female members working in vital wartime jobs.

TECHNOLOGY

Use THE AMAZING WRITING MACHINE™ to complete the writing activities.

TECHNOLOGY

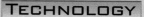

Use TIMELINER™ DATA DISKS to discuss and summarize the chapter.

CHAPTER 18

REVIEW

1900 — 1910

1903
• First airplane flight

Connect Main Ideas

Use this graphic organizer to show how the chapter's main ideas are connected. Write three details to support each main idea. A copy of the organizer appears on page 121 of the Activity Book.

Possible answers to the graphic organizer appear on page 568C of this Teacher's Edition.

Good Times and Bad

The Roaring Twenties brought good times to many Americans.
1. ______
2. ______
3. ______

World War II affected countries around the world.
1. ______
2. ______
3. ______

The federal government helped Americans who were out of work during the Great Depression.
1. ______
2. ______
3. ______

The Dust Bowl made life very hard for people living on the Great Plains.
1. ______
2. ______
3. ______

The United States and countries in Europe and Asia entered into World War II.
1. ______
2. ______
3. ______

Write More About It

Write a Short Story Imagine that you are living in the 1920s. Write a short story about your family getting its first automobile. In your story describe what it is like to ride in a car for the first time. Also tell how the car has changed your family's life.

Write a Diary Entry Imagine that you are living during World War II. Write a diary entry about going shopping with your family. Tell how the war has affected what you can buy. Also describe other ways the war has affected your family.

596 • Chapter 18

Use Vocabulary

1. Stores created *installment buying* so that customers could pay for *consumer goods* a little at a time. (p. 569)
2. When Henry Ford began to produce cars on an *assembly line*, automobile manufacturing grew as a *commercial industry*. (pp. 570, 571)
3. The crash of the *stock market* led to an economic *depression*, which caused *unemployment* for many people. (pp. 574, 575, 577)
4. While American soldiers fought i Europe and the Pacific, *civilians* fo lowed rules that called for *rationi* their supplies. (pp. 585, 587)
5. On the European *front*, the Allie strategy was to invade Germa occupied France on *D day*. On th Pacific front, their strategy again the Japanese was *island-hoppin* (pp. 589, 591)
6. The Soviet Union wanted to sprea *communism*, but the leaders of the *fr world* wanted to stop it. A *cold war* w the result. (p. 593)

1920 1930 1940 1950

- 1929 • Stock market crashes
- 1939 • World War II begins
- 1941 • U.S. enters World War II
- 1945 • Germany and Japan surrender, ending World War II

Use Vocabulary

For each group of terms, write a sentence or two explaining how the terms are related.

1. consumer good, installment buying
2. assembly line, commercial industry
3. stock market, depression, unemployment
4. civilian, rationing
5. front, D day, island-hopping
6. communism, free world, cold war

Check Understanding

7. What advantage did installment buying offer the consumer?
8. How was Henry Ford able to produce cars less expensively?
9. What event helped make air travel a commercial industry?
10. How did jazz develop?
11. Why did Harlem attract so many people in the 1920s?
12. Why did many banks close during the Great Depression?
13. How did New Deal programs help workers?
14. What event caused the United States to enter the fighting in World War II?
15. Who were the largest group of victims in the Holocaust?
16. What did the United States see as a threat to freedom following World War II?

Think Critically

17. **Personally Speaking** In the 1920s, movies and radio allowed Americans to learn about the world around them. How do you get information about the world?
18. **Cause and Effect** What effects did forced relocation have on the lives of Japanese Americans during World War II?

Apply Skills

Read Parallel Time Lines Use the parallel time lines on page 595 to answer the questions.

19. What happened on April 12, 1945?
20. Did the Battle of Okinawa happen before or after Soviet troops surrounded Berlin?
21. Which happened first, the Battle of Iwo Jima or V-E Day?

Read More About It

Rosie the Riveter by Penny Colman. Crown, 1995. This book uses primary sources to describe the American women who took over the jobs left behind by men during World War II.

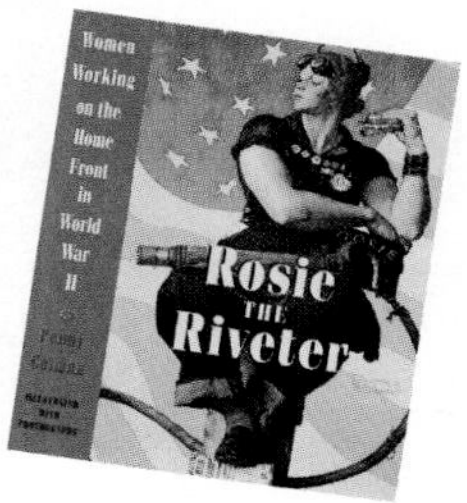

Visit the Internet at **http://www.hbschool.com** for additional resources.

Chapter 18 • **597**

Check Understanding

7. It allowed the consumer to take home a product after paying only a part of the price. (p. 569)
8. by reducing the amount of time needed to make each car and saving labor costs (p. 570)
9. Charles Lindbergh's flight (p. 571)
10. It grew out of the African American musical heritage. (p. 572)
11. It was a center of artistic development for African Americans. (p. 572)
12. People rushed to take their savings out, and other people couldn't repay their bank loans. (p. 575)
13. created jobs; made new laws about labor unions, the minimum wage, and Social Security (p. 577)
14. Japan's bombing of Pearl Harbor (p. 586)
15. Jews (p. 591)
16. communism (p. 593)

Think Critically

17. In addition to radio and movies, students will likely mention television and the Internet. Some students may also mention newspapers, magazines, and books.

Chapter 18 Review

18. Students' answers should focus on the loss of freedom and the confinement of these American citizens. Some students will recognize that businesses would be lost and that homes would be unprotected or would have to be sold.

Apply Skills

Read Parallel Time Lines

19. Truman becomes President
20. after
21. the Battle of Iwo Jima

Read More About It

Additional books are listed in the Multimedia Resource Center on page 540D of this Teacher's Edition.

Unit Project Check-Up

The students may begin the class mural after you have approved each student's sketches. Once the heavy paper is measured and ready, select two students to oversee the schedule for creating the mural. They should mark off each student's section of the paper based on the chronology of events and arrange the schedule so only a few students are working on the mural at a time.

ASSESSMENT PROGRAM

Use CHAPTER 18 TEST, pp. 147–150.

Making Social Studies Relevant

See the Link

Personal Response

To help students relate the growing influence of the United States to influences today, have them discuss products or ideas that come from other countries. Then ask volunteers to share examples with the rest of the class.

The Main Idea

Have students read the selection and examine the illustrations. Have them point out what is familiar in the photographs and what is not.

Q. **What parts of American culture have people in other countries accepted into their own culture?** fast food and beverage products, media, entertainment, clothing

Understand the Link

Visual Analysis

Interpret Pictures After students have looked at the pictures on these pages, have them list other products or ideas that may be known throughout the world.

Making Social Studies Relevant

American Ideas and Products

During the 1900s the United States became a world power. As a result, American culture has spread. Today people everywhere are familiar with American ideas and products.

Millions of people around the world go to see American movies. They also watch the news on CNN, the Atlanta-based cable news network, and tune into American television shows.

American products are also popular internationally. Hundreds of millions of people outside the United States drink Coca-Cola. In fact, 95 percent of Coca-Cola's sales come from outside the country. People from Moscow to Singapore line up at McDonald's, often wearing American jeans and athletic shoes.

598 • Unit 9

Activity Choices

Background

THE LARGE PICTURE The influence of American culture on other countries is evident in the worldwide demand for American products. The American products shown above are just a handful of those that are popular in other countries today. Families in many countries around the globe can enjoy shopping at Wal-Mart stores, drinking Coca-Cola, eating at McDonald's, driving Ford automobiles, and being entertained by Mickey Mouse.

Community Involvement

Ask a representative from a local McDonald's restaurant or a Coca-Cola distributor to visit the class to discuss how its company has fared in the global marketplace. The representative may be able to give students packets of information from the company's headquarters. Have students prepare questions for the visit, and have students write thank-you letters to the guest speaker after the visit.

Think and Apply

BUILDING CITIZENSHIP

With a partner, create a poster showing fifth graders in different countries using American products. Include American clothes, foods, and other products that you think children in other countries like. Share your poster with the class.

HARCOURT BRACE — Visit the Internet at **http://www.hbschool.com** for additional resources.

CNN Turner Le@rning — Check your media center or classroom video library for the Making Social Studies Relevant videotape of this feature.

History

Origins, Spread, and Influence Describe to students Coca-Cola's strong presence outside the United States during World War II. Tell them that after the war, U.S. soldiers were stationed for many years in Japan and in Germany. Their presence exposed local residents to American ways.

Complete the Link

Summarize

During the 1900s the United States' growing influence in world affairs exposed Europeans and Asians to American culture. Many ideas and products from the United States appealed to people in these areas, especially the young people. Today, American culture still has a strong influence on other cultures.

Think and Apply

Encourage students to look up distinctive symbols from the countries they select to use as background illustrations. You may want to suggest that they use American ideas and products other than those shown on pages 598–599.

Background

COCA-COLA Created in 1886, Coca-Cola's early advertising showed Americans in scenes from everyday life. During World War II, Coca-Cola promoted its soda to the armed forces as a morale booster. Coca-Cola's advertising became more and more patriotic during the war and in time, Coca-Cola established itself as a symbol of the United States at home and abroad.

Technology

HARCOURT BRACE — Visit the Internet at **http://www.hbschool.com** for additional resources.

Video

CNN Turner Le@rning™ **Check your media center or classroom video library for the Making Social Studies Relevant videotape of this feature.**

Visual Summary

Take a Look

Remind students that a visual summary is a way to represent the main events in a story. Explain that this visual summary reviews some of the main events students read about in Unit 9.

Visual Analysis

Interpret Pictures Have students examine this visual summary individually or in small groups. Ask them to identify the images and explain what each image says about the United States in the first half of the twentieth century.

Summarize the Main Ideas

Have students read each scene's caption and relate it to the elements of the scene. Lead a class discussion about each scene and have students offer supporting details for each of the main ideas illustrated. Challenge students to decide whether each event helped strengthen the nation's status as a world power.

UNIT 9
REVIEW

VISUAL SUMMARY

Summarize the Main Ideas
Study the pictures and captions to help you review the events you read about in Unit 9.

Write a Newspaper Article
Imagine that you are a newspaper reporter covering one of the events in this visual summary. Write an article describing the event.

1 By 1900 the United States had become a world power. It gained new territories after the Spanish-American War, in which Theodore Roosevelt's Rough Riders became famous.

3 The United States entered World War I in 1917. Most American soldiers fought from trenches.

6 During the Great Depression, millions of people lost their jobs. Many were forced to line up for free food. Drought on the Great Plains brought still more suffering.

600 • Unit 9

Activity Choices

Meet Individual Needs

COOPERATIVE LEARNING

AUDITORY LEARNERS Organize the students into eight groups and have each group write a verse to a song. Each stanza should summarize the key facts about one of the events in the visual summary. The verses should be set to a simple tune that is familiar to most students. When the verses are written, arrange them in chronological order and have each group practice singing its own stanza. Then the class should practice the entire song together. You may want students to type the lyrics, so that they may use them to prepare for the unit assessment.

UNIT POSTER

Use the UNIT 9 VISUAL SUMMARY POSTER to summarize the unit.

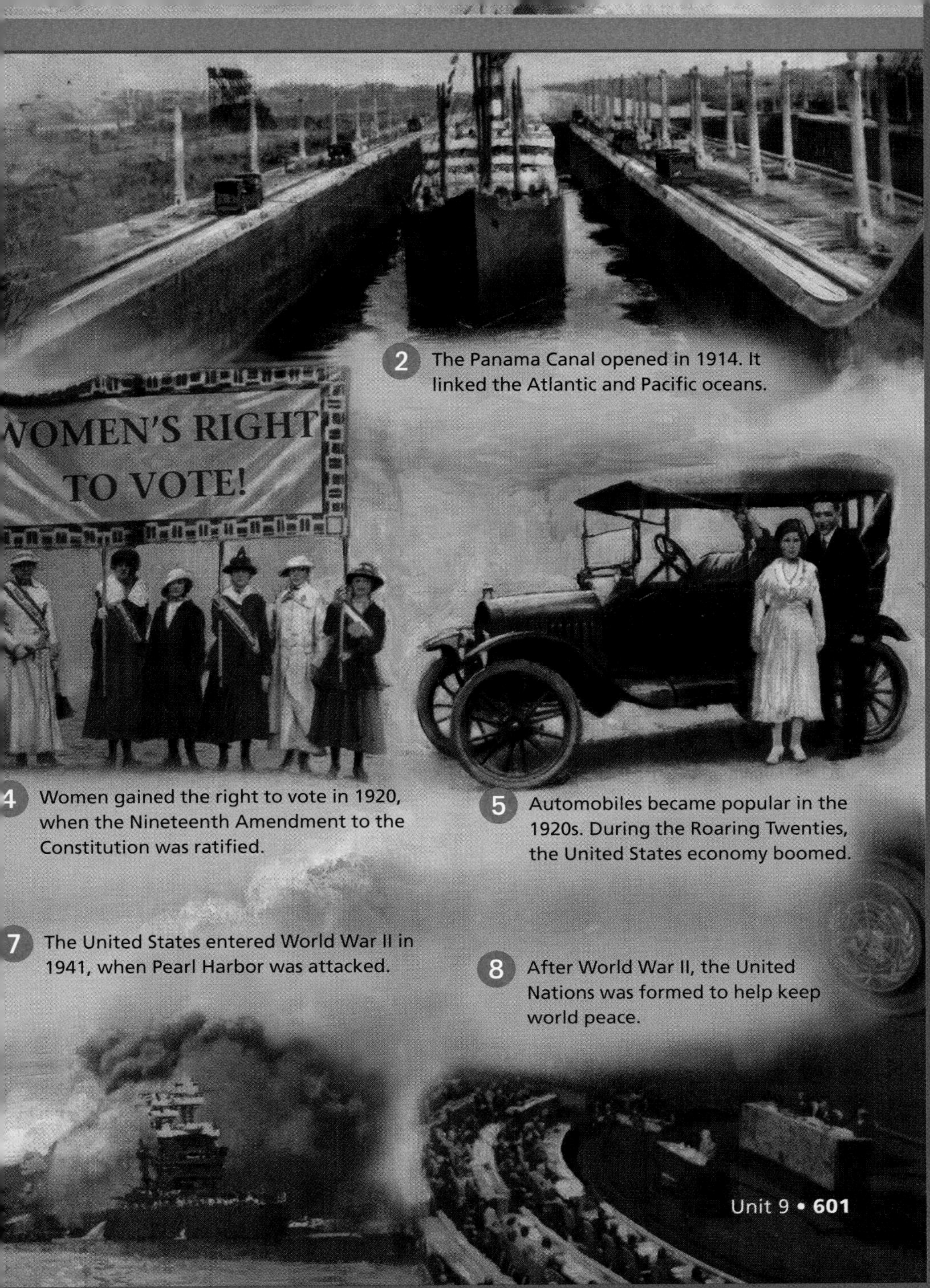

2 The Panama Canal opened in 1914. It linked the Atlantic and Pacific oceans.

4 Women gained the right to vote in 1920, when the Nineteenth Amendment to the Constitution was ratified.

5 Automobiles became popular in the 1920s. During the Roaring Twenties, the United States economy boomed.

7 The United States entered World War II in 1941, when Pearl Harbor was attacked.

8 After World War II, the United Nations was formed to help keep world peace.

Sharing the Activity

Provide time for students to complete the Write a Newspaper Article activity on page 600. You may wish to divide the eight events among students to make sure all the events are covered in the newspaper articles. Ask students to share their articles with the class.

SUMMARIZE THE UNIT

Have pairs of students use the illustrations in the unit and the visual summary to tell the unit's "story" to their partners. Or have the pairs play a game in which one student names the event and the other student offers three important facts about the event.

Extend and Enrich

WRITE A PERSONAL NARRATIVE Have each student select an event of particular interest that occurred during the period covered by the unit. Ask students to imagine that they experienced these events themselves. Then have them write a short narrative about the experience—for example, living in Hawaii at the time of the attack on Pearl Harbor, hearing jazz for the first time, joining the Army, listening to a radio broadcast, piloting a World War I reconnaissance mission, riding in the family's new car, or standing in a food line during the Great Depression.

TECHNOLOGY

Use THE AMAZING WRITING MACHINE™ RESOURCE PACKAGE to complete this writing activity.

TECHNOLOGY

Use TIMELINER™ DATA DISKS to discuss and summarize the unit.

Use Vocabulary

1. According to the *merit system*, a person must pass a test before he or she is hired for a government job. (p. 557)
2. The *military draft* required men between the ages of 21 and 30 to sign up with draft boards. (p. 560)
3. Charles Lindbergh's flight helped make *aviation* a commercial industry. (p. 571)
4. *Jazz* was a type of music that became popular during the Roaring Twenties. (p. 572)
5. A government's *bureaucracy* is made up of all the workers who run that government's programs. (p. 576)
6. If the *unemployment* rate is low, it means that most people have jobs. (p. 577)
7. Most people earn the *minimum wage* when they get their first job. (p. 577)
8. The Nazis took Jews and other people to *concentration camps* during World War II. (p. 583)

Check Understanding

9. The United States declared war on Spain because it blamed Spain for the destruction of the *Maine*. (p. 549)
10. It provides a way to move goods and people easily between the Atlantic and Pacific oceans. (pp. 551–552)
11. The automobile and aviation industries became important; radio stations and "talking" pictures were developed. (pp. 570–572)
12. People lost their savings, stocks, and jobs, and many became homeless and hungry. (p. 575)
13. The United States dropped atom bombs on the Japanese cities of Hiroshima and Nagasaki. (pp. 591–592)

Think Critically

14. Students may suggest the United Nations is an alliance that affects the world; other students may suggest that trade agreements and economic alliances have the greatest impact in the world today. Military alliances serve to protect member nations against aggression. Students should demonstrate an understanding of how the alliances they name affect the world.

UNIT 9 REVIEW

USE VOCABULARY

Use each term in a sentence that will help explain its meaning.

1. merit system
2. military draft
3. aviation
4. jazz
5. bureaucracy
6. unemployment
7. minimum wage
8. concentration camp

CHECK UNDERSTANDING

9. What part did the battleship *Maine* play in the Spanish-American War?
10. How is the Panama Canal important to world trade?
11. How did transportation and communications change in the 1920s?
12. How did the Great Depression affect Americans?
13. What ended World War II in the Pacific?

THINK CRITICALLY

14. **Past to Present** How do alliances among countries affect the world today?
15. **Cause and Effect** What caused hostility to develop between the United States and the Soviet Union following World War II?

APPLY SKILLS

Compare Map Projections Map A is an azimuthal equal-area projection. Map B is an orthographic projection. Use these maps to answer the questions.

16. On which map does the United States look larger?
17. On which map can you more clearly see the North Pole?
18. What are the advantages and disadvantages of each type of projection?

Map A: The Northern Hemisphere

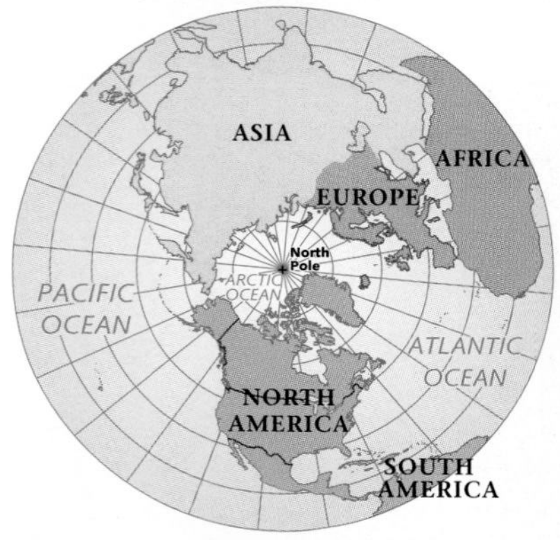

Map B: The Western Hemisphere

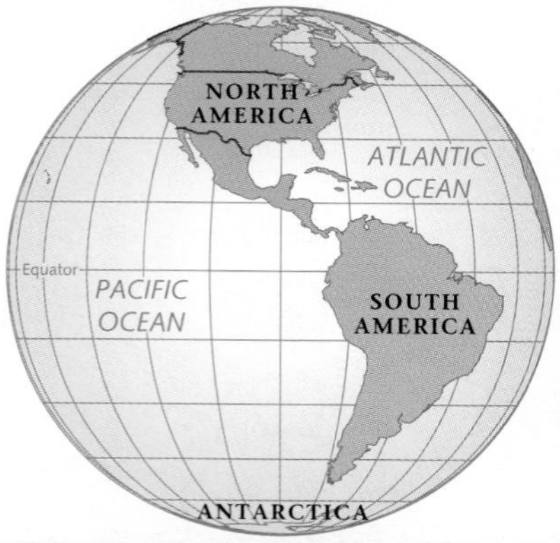

15. The Soviet Union promoted communism; the United States promoted democracy. This difference in ideologies caused hostility between the countries.

Apply Skills

Compare Map Projections

16. Map B
17. Map A
18. Students' answers will vary. Map A advantage: easier to see how land sizes are related; disadvantage: land shapes are distorted. Map B advantage: shows directions correctly; disadvantage: sizes are distorted.

ASSESSMENT PROGRAM

Use UNIT 9 TEST,
Standard Test, pp. 151–155.
Performance Tasks, pp. 156–157.

REMEMBER
- Share your ideas.
- Cooperate with others to plan your work.
- Take responsibility for your work.
- Help one another.
- Show your group's work to the class.
- Discuss what you learned by working together.

ACTIVITY

Give a Talk

Work in groups to research either the Roaring Twenties or the Great Depression. Find out how life in each decade was similar to and different from life today. When your research is complete, give a short talk to the class. If possible, play music from the 1920s or 1930s, and show pictures of people from the decade your group chose.

ACTIVITY

Invite Guest Speakers

Work in groups to invite several guest ›eakers to your class. With your teacher's elp, choose a date and time for them to ›me. Then write a letter to a seniors' group ı your community, inviting members to talk › your class about life during World War II.

Unit Project Wrap-Up

Make a Class Mural With your classmates, create a mural of American history from the 1890s through the 1940s. To complete this project, the class should divide into six groups, one for each decade. Members of each group should come up with scenes that illustrate important events that occurred during the decade. Be sure to think about the experiences of farmers, soldiers, industrial workers, women, and African Americans during your period. Group members should work together to paint or draw the scenes they have chosen.

UNIT 9
REVIEW

GIVE A TALK

Performance Assessment Ask the school librarian to meet with your class to provide help with research. If possible, show a movie set in the 1920s or 1930s. Have students make costumes for their talk. They need not be elaborate; long beads will do for girls and bow ties for boys. Have each member of the group give a portion of the talk.

What to Look For Look for an appreciation of the flair of the 1920s or an understanding of the despair of the Great Depression. Make sure students compare the decade to today's world.

Unit Project Wrap-Up

Performance Assessment Have students work in their groups to finish the scenes of the class mural. Reinforce the Unit Themes by discussing what theme each scene reflects. Discuss how well students cooperated with one another in creating visual images of this unit.

What to Look For Look for a fair representation of the many groups of Americans who lived, worked, and fought during this time period.

GAME TIME!

Use GAME TIME! to reinforce content.

›ooperative Learning Workshop

IVITE GUEST SPEAKERS

›rformance Assessment Students ay need help writing letters to invite e guest speakers. Before the speakers rive, discuss questions the students ay have about what life was like for e speakers during World War II. To inforce the theme of continuity and ıange, suggest that some questions nter on what was different on the ›me front during the war and what ayed the same. After the program, ake sure students write thank-you ›tes to the speakers.

What to Look For Students should listen attentively and ask appropriate questions. Look for an understanding of the ways war affects families.

Unit

10

pages 604–673

THE AMERICAS TODAY

The major objectives in this unit are organized around the following themes:

UNIT THEMES

- ▶ CONFLICT & COOPERATION
- ▶ COMMONALITY & DIVERSITY
- ▶ CONTINUITY & CHANGE
- ▶ INDIVIDUALISM & INTERDEPENDENCE

Preview Unit Content

Unit 10 describes the recent history of the United States from the end of World War II to the present. In the course of studying this unit, students will trace the events of the Cold War from its beginnings with the building of the Berlin Wall to its end when the wall was torn down. Students also will learn about the civil rights movement, the moon landing, the Vietnam War, the Watergate scandal, and current domestic and foreign issues, as well as the challenges facing the nations of the Western Hemisphere today.

You may wish to begin the unit with the Unit 10 Visual Summary Poster and activity. The illustration that appears on the poster also appears on pages 670–671 in the Pupil Book to help students summarize the unit.

UNIT POSTER

Use the UNIT 10 VISUAL SUMMARY POSTER to preview the unit.

1 The Cold War began after World War II. The Soviet Union cut off land routes to West Berlin in 1948, but an airlift brought in supplies.

3 In 1963 Martin Luther King, Jr., spoke for civil rights at a huge gathering in Washington, D.C.

2 War seemed near in 1962 when the Soviet Union sent missiles to Cuba. President Kennedy ordered a blockade of the island. Finally, Soviet leader Nikita Khrushchev agreed to remove the missiles.
United States
the first per-
on the moon
969.
5 Americans were divided over the Vietnam War. After many deaths, the war ended in 1975.
nges in the
iet Union
ught an end to
Cold War. In
9 the Berlin Wall
s torn down.
7 Today many of the countries in the Western Hemisphere face problems with their economies and governments. A major problem in South America is the clearing of rain forests.
8 Mexico, the United States, and Canada have signed the NAFTA agreement to remove tariffs on trade between these countries.

Unit

10 Planning Chart

	CONTENT AND SKILLS	RESOURCES INCLUDING ▶ TECHNOLOGY
UNIT INTRODUCTION **The Americas Today** pp. 604–609	Unit Opener and Unit Preview Set the Scene with Literature **On the Pulse of Morning** by Maya Angelou	Unit 10 Visual Summary Poster Unit 10 Home Letter Unit 10 Text on Tape Audiocassette Video Experiences: Social Studies ▶ TIMELINER
CHAPTER 19 **The Cold War Years** pp. 610–641	LESSON 1: The Cold War Begins LESSON 2: Learn History Through Literature **One Giant Leap** by Mary Ann Fraser LESSON 3: The Struggle for Equal Rights **SKILL:** Act as a Responsible Citizen LESSON 4: Vietnam War and Protests at Home COUNTERPOINTS: Hawk or Dove? LESSON 5: The Cold War Ends **SKILL:** Understand Political Symbols Chapter Review	Activity Book, pp. 122–130 Transparency 49 Transparency 50 Transparency 51 Music Audiocassette Assessment Program Chapter 19 Test, pp. 159–162 ▶ TIMELINER ▶ THE AMAZING WRITING MACHINE ▶ INTERNET
CHAPTER 20 **The Western Hemisphere Today** pp. 642–667	LESSON 1: Mexico Today LESSON 2: Learn Culture Through Literature **Save My Rainforest** by Monica Zak **SKILL:** Use Population Maps LESSON 3: Democracy in the Caribbean and in Central America LESSON 4: Challenges in South America LESSON 5: The Peoples of Canada Chapter Review	Activity Book, pp. 131–142 Transparencies 52A–52B, 53 Assessment Program Chapter 20 Test, pp. 163–166 ▶ TIMELINER ▶ IMAGINATION EXPRESS ▶ MAPSKILLS ▶ GRAPH LINKS ▶ THE AMAZING WRITING MACHINE ▶ INTERNET
UNIT WRAP-UP pp. 668–673	Making Social Studies Relevant Visual Summary Unit Review	Making Social Studies Relevant Video Unit 10 Visual Summary Poster Game Time! Assessment Program, Unit 10 Test, Standard Test, pp. 167–171 Performance Tasks, pp. 172–173 ▶ THE AMAZING WRITING MACHINE ▶ TIMELINER ▶ INTERNET

4 WEEKS

TIME MANAGEMENT

WEEK 1	WEEK 2	WEEK 3	WEEK 4
Unit Introduction; Chapter 19	Chapter 19	Chapter 20	Chapter 20; Unit Wrap-Up

See pages 610A and 642A for Chapter Planning Charts with details by lesson.

Multimedia Resource Center

Books

Easy

Hall, Diane and Joe Viesti. *Celebrate! In Central America.* Lothrop, Lee & Shepard, 1997. A look at the background and customs associated with some important festivals in Central America.

Levert, Susan. *Canada Facts and Figures.* Chelsea House, 1992. A look at the government, economy, people, and provinces of Canada.

Average

Burch, Joann. *Chico Mendes: Defender of the Rain Forest.* Millbrook, 1994. This book details one man's efforts to protect the Amazon rain forest.

Collins, Michael. *Flying to the Moon: An Astronaut's Story*. Farrar, Straus & Giroux, 1994. An astronaut relates his exciting experiences of space exploration.

Fraser, Mary Ann. *One Giant Leap.* Henry Holt, 1993. This book explores the first moon landing.

Italia, Bob. *Maya Lin: Honoring Our Forgotten Heroes.* A look at the life of the young architect who designed the Vietnam War Memorial.

Parks, Rosa and Gregory J. Reed. *Dear Mrs. Parks: A Dialogue with Today's Youth.* Lee and Low Books, 1997. Rosa Parks answers letters from children.

Parks, Rosa. *Rosa Parks: My Story.* Dial, 1992. This book chronicles the life of this pivotal figure of the Civil Rights movement.

Challenging

Curtis, Christopher Paul. *The Watsons Go to Birmingham: 1963.* Delacorte/BDD, 1995. This novel is about an African American family that travels south in 1963 and witnesses a tragic event during the Civil Rights movement.

Hopkins, Lee Bennett. *Hand in Hand: An American History Through Poetry.* Simon & Schuster, 1994. This collection of poems conveys the dynamic history of the United States.

Computer Software

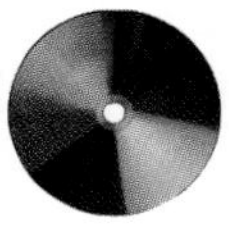

CD-ROM

Civil Rights. National Geographic Society, Educational Services, 1988, URL *http://www.nationalgeographic.com*, (800) 368-2728. Macintosh/Windows dual format. This package documents the struggle for racial equality in America and the impact of the Civil Rights Act of 1964.

The Complete National Geographic. National Geographic Society, Educational Services, 1997, URL *http://www.nationalgeographic.com*, (800) 368-2728. Macintosh/Windows dual format. Thirty-one CD-ROMs offer images and stories from National Geographic magazine 1888–1996. Annual updates are available.

Video

Videotape

Martin Luther King, Jr.: The Enduring Dream. Thomas S. Klise Company, 1993, URL *http://www.klise.com*, (800) 937-0092. This videotape provides insight into the contributions of Martin Luther King, Jr., and the period in which he lived.

Talking Peace with Jimmy Carter. Close Up Foundation, 1995, (800) 765-3131. In this videotape Jimmy Carter shares the building blocks of peace and the steps to successful mediation.

FREE & INEXPENSIVE MATERIALS

Magazine

For the January 1998 issue of *Faces* magazine, entitled *French-Speaking Canada*, which includes articles on Canadian lifeways, send $4.50/copy plus 10% shipping and handling to:

Cobblestone Publishing Company
30 Grove Street
Peterborough, NH 03458

(For 20 or more issues, send $3.95/copy plus 10% shipping and handling.)

On-Line Publication

For the United Nations' *ASAP: Atlas of Student Action for the Planet* detailing what 100 student programs in 25 countries are doing for the environment, visit: *http://www.un.org/Pubs/CyberSchoolBus/* or, for more information, e-mail *inquiries@un.org*

LIBRARY

See the SOCIAL STUDIES LIBRARY for additional resources.

TECHNOLOGY

Visit the Internet at **http://www.hbschool.com** for additional resources.

Note that information, while correct at time of publication, is subject to change.

Linking Social Studies

BULLETIN BOARD IDEA

Project outline maps of North and South America, and have students draw the outlines of the continents on the bulletin board. Then divide the class into six groups to create a cultural map of the two continents. Assign each group one of the following cultural topics: food, music, art, language, literature, and dance. Have students in each group research the assigned topic for any five places of their choice in North and South America. Have each group use five sheets of colored construction paper (one for each place) to record and illustrate (with cutouts of pictures or original drawings) the information about the topic that pertains to each place. Have students place the completed cultural sheets on the correct location on the outline map on the bulletin board. Label the bulletin board *The Many Cultures of North and South America.* Use the completed bulletin board to discuss the similarities and differences in cultures of the Americas.

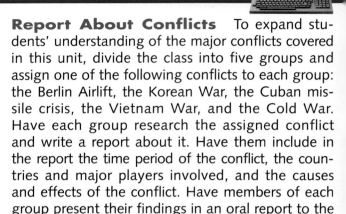

LANGUAGE ARTS

Report About Conflicts To expand students' understanding of the major conflicts covered in this unit, divide the class into five groups and assign one of the following conflicts to each group: the Berlin Airlift, the Korean War, the Cuban missile crisis, the Vietnam War, and the Cold War. Have each group research the assigned conflict and write a report about it. Have them include in the report the time period of the conflict, the countries and major players involved, and the causes and effects of the conflict. Have members of each group present their findings in an oral report to the class.

Give a Presidential Speech To expand students' understanding of the many Presidents covered in this unit, have students give State of the Union speeches. Divide the class into small groups. Assign a U.S. President covered in this unit to each group. Allow time for students in each group to research the assigned President and the important events that occurred during his term in office. Have students work together to compose a speech for their President to deliver to the American people, detailing the State of the Union and outlining goals for the following year. Then have each group select a representative to deliver the speech to the class. Have the other groups take turns trying to guess which President is being portrayed.

TECHNOLOGY

HARCOURT BRACE

Visit the Internet at **http://www.hbschool.com** for additional resources.

Smithsonian Institution®

Harcourt Brace Social Studies helps to bring the Smithsonian Institution to your classroom. Visit the Internet site at *http://www.si.edu/harcourt/socialstudies* for a directory of virtual tours, on-line exhibits, and pictures of primary sources from the Smithsonian Institution.

Across the Curriculum

MUSIC

Research Protest Songs To help students relate to the reasons for civil rights demonstrations and war protests, have them research protest songs that were popular during the 1960s. Divide the class into six groups and assign one of the following songs to each group: *Where Have All the Flowers Gone?* by Pete Seeger, *Blowin' in the Wind* by Bob Dylan, *If I Had a Hammer* by Lee Hays and Pete Seeger, *Last Night I Had the Strangest Dream* by Ed McCurdy, *Ballad of Birmingham* by Dudley Randall, and *Little Boxes* by Malvina Reynolds. Have students in each group find the lyrics and a recording of the assigned song to play to the class. Or, have these materials available for the class. Have each group listen to the words of the song, discuss what the songwriter was protesting, and brainstorm reasons for that protest. Have each group play the song to the class and report its findings. Then discuss with the whole class the impact these songs had on the Civil Rights movement and war protests.

ART

Design Folk Art Have students design a folk-art village scene. Discuss with the class what folk art is (art that reflects the general culture of a group of people), and explain that it is very popular in Cuba, Guatemala, and the Dominican Republic. Divide the class into small groups. Provide each group with the following materials: one piece of black poster board, scraps of bright colored felt and fabric, scissors, glue, straight pins, tracing paper, and pencils. Have each group draw on tracing paper designs of simple but bold houses, trees, animals, stars, clouds, or any other design to create a village scene. Then use the tracing-paper designs as patterns to pin onto the felt or material and cut out the desired shapes. The patterns can be used again with different colored materials. Then glue the designs on the black poster board to create a village scene with lots of bright colors and designs. Have each group present the folk-art poster to the class and discuss the parts of the culture it represents. Display completed posters on the walls of the classroom.

HOW TO INTEGRATE YOUR DAY

Use these topics to help you integrate social studies into your daily planning.

Reading Themes

- World Corners
- Growing and Changing
- Improving the World
- Folk Art
- Conflict Resolution

INTEGRATED LANGUAGE ARTS

- Report About Conflicts, p. 604E
- Give a Presidential Speech, p. 604E
- Write Possible Sentences, p. 606
- Write a Letter, p. 618
- Write a Biographical Sketch, p. 624
- Write a Letter, p. 635
- Write to Persuade, p. 650

HEALTH AND PHYSICAL EDUCATION

- Report on Astronaut Training, p. 620

SCIENCE

- Present Facts About the Moon, p. 619
- Research Conservation Groups, p. 649

ART

- Design Folk Art, p. 604F
- Analyze Photographs, p. 630
- Create Political Cartoons or Posters, p. 639
- Research Puerto Rican Art, p. 655
- Create Collages, p. 669

READING

- Read and Display News Articles, p. 604
- Read a Biography, p. 613

MATHEMATICS

- Make a Calculation, p. 636
- Calculate Devaluation, p. 644
- Make a Circle Graph, p. 663

MUSIC

- Research Protest Songs, p. 604F
- Listen to a Moon Song, p. 619
- Interpret Lyrics, p. 623

Unit 10

Assessment Options

The **Assessment Program** allows all learners many opportunities to show what they know and can do. It also provides teachers with ongoing information about each student's understanding of social studies.

Formal Assessment

- *Lesson Reviews* (**Pupil Book,** at end of lessons)
- *Chapter Review* (**Pupil Book,** at end of chapters)
- *Chapter Tests* (**Assessment Program,** pp. 159–166)
- *Unit Review* (**Pupil Book,** pp. 672–673)
- *Unit Assessment* (**Assessment Program:** *Standard Test,* pp. 167–171 *Individual Performance Task,* p. 172 *Group Performance Task,* p. 173)

Student Self-Evaluation

- *Individual End-of-Project Summary* (**Assessment Program,** p. 6)
- *Group End-of-Project Checklist* (**Assessment Program,** p. 7)
- *Individual End-of-Unit Checklist* (**Assessment Program,** p. 8)

Informal Assessment

- REVIEW *Questions* (**Pupil Book,** throughout lessons)
- *Think and Apply* (**Pupil Book,** at end of skill lessons)
- *Visual Summary* (**Pupil Book,** pp. 670–671)
- *Social Studies Skills Checklist* (**Assessment Program,** pp. 4–5)

Performance Assessment

- *Show What You Know* (**Pupil Book,** at end of Lesson Reviews)
- *Cooperative Learning Workshop* (**Pupil Book,** at end of Unit Review)
- *Scoring Rubric for Individual Projects* (**Assessment Program,** p. 9)
- *Scoring Rubric for Group Projects* (**Assessment Program,** p. 10)
- *Scoring Rubric for Presentations* (**Assessment Program,** p. 11)

Performance Assessment

Student-selected items may include:

- *Link to Language Arts—Write a Biographical Sketch* (**Teacher's Edition,** p. 624)
- *Practice and Apply* (**Activity Book,** p. 125)
- *Home Involvement* (**Teacher's Edition,** p. 652)
- *A Guide to My Social Studies Portfolio* (**Assessment Program,** p. 12)

Teacher-selected items may include:

- *Unit Assessment* (**Assessment Program,** pp. 167–173)
- *Individual End-of-Unit Checklist* (**Assessment Program,** p. 8)
- *Social Studies Portfolio Summary* (**Assessment Program,** p. 13)
- *Portfolio Family Response* (**Assessment Program,** p. 14)

Objectives

Chapter 19

- ▶ Evaluate the Allied solution to the Berlin crisis. (p. 611)
- ▶ Identify the causes and results of the Korean War. (p. 611)
- ▶ Describe Kennedy's actions during the Cuban missile crisis. (p. 611)
- ▶ Analyze the reasons for the arms race between the United States and the Soviet Union. (p. 611)
- ▶ Analyze the ways individual astronauts cooperated to achieve a moon landing. (p. 616)
- ▶ Evaluate the importance of the moon landing. (p. 616)
- ▶ Explain why the Supreme Court ordered an end to segregation in public schools. (p. 622)
- ▶ Analyze the Montgomery bus boycott. (p. 622)
- ▶ Summarize Martin Luther King, Jr.'s, role in promoting the passage of the Civil Rights Act of 1964. (p. 622)
- ▶ Compare and contrast the views of Malcolm X and Martin Luther King, Jr. (p. 622)
- ▶ Identify the ways American Indians and Mexican Americans worked for change. (p. 622)
- ▶ Discuss the rights women had gained by the 1970s. (p. 622)
- ▶ Analyze examples of responsible citizenship. (p. 627)
- ▶ Apply the steps for acting as a responsible citizen. (p. 627)
- ▶ Identify the causes and effects of inflation during Lyndon Johnson's presidency. (p. 628)
- ▶ Analyze why Americans were divided over the Vietnam War. (p. 628)
- ▶ Summarize the Watergate scandal and the resolution to the war in Vietnam. (p. 628)
- ▶ Describe hawks and doves. (p. 632)
- ▶ Explain the different viewpoints on the war in Vietnam. (p. 632)
- ▶ Summarize the causes for improved U.S. relations with China and the Soviet Union. (p. 634)
- ▶ Analyze why tensions increased between the U.S. and the Soviet Union and Iran. (p. 634)
- ▶ Analyze the end of the Cold War. (p. 634)
- ▶ Explain why President Bush hoped for a "new world order." (p. 634)
- ▶ Evaluate the consequences of a large budget deficit in the United States. (p. 634)
- ▶ Recognize political symbols. (p. 639)
- ▶ Practice interpreting political symbols. (p. 639)

Chapter 20

- ▶ Summarize the growth of Mexico as an industrial nation. (p. 643)
- ▶ Analyze the advantages and disadvantages of NAFTA for Mexico today. (p. 643)
- ▶ Summarize the sacrifices Omar and his father were willing to make to save the rain forest. (p. 647)
- ▶ Evaluate the importance and success of Omar's mission. (p. 647)
- ▶ Recognize three ways to show population on maps. (p. 652)
- ▶ Analyze population data. (p. 652)
- ▶ Analyze Puerto Rico's relationship with the United States. (p. 654)
- ▶ Describe the effect of political changes on the people of Cuba. (p. 654)
- ▶ Summarize Haiti's struggle against military rule. (p. 654)
- ▶ Compare and contrast the effects of politics in Nicaragua and in Costa Rica. (p. 654)
- ▶ Identify the political and economic problems faced by South American countries. (p. 659)
- ▶ Identify the new problems in South America that have an impact on many other parts of the world. (p. 659)
- ▶ Summarize the reasons Canada wrote a new constitution in 1982. (p. 662)
- ▶ Analyze the objections of the Québecois to the Constitution of 1982. (p. 662)
- ▶ Describe the gains in equal rights made by Canada's Indian groups. (p. 662)

STANDARD TEST

NAME ______________________ DATE ____________

Unit 10 Test

Part One: Test Your Understanding *(4 points each)*

DIRECTIONS: *Circle the letter of the best answer.*

1. Which of the following United States Presidents ordered a naval blockade of Cuba during the Cuban missile crisis?
- **A.** Richard Nixon
- **(B.)** John F. Kennedy
- **C.** Ronald Reagan
- **D.** Jimmy Carter

2. What was the main goal of both the United States and the Soviet Union in the arms race?
- **A.** to control the entire world
- **B.** to bring an end to the Berlin crisis
- **(C.)** to have the most powerful weapons
- **D.** to start a war in Asia

3. Neil Armstrong was
- **(A.)** the first person to set foot on the moon.
- **B.** a U.S. military leader during the Vietnam War.
- **C.** the lawyer who argued for the desegregation of public schools.
- **D.** the first U.S. President to visit communist China.

4. Martin Luther King, Jr., thought that the best way to work for civil rights was to
- **A.** have a complete separation between white people and black people.
- **(B.)** use nonviolent protest.
- **C.** use any means necessary.
- **D.** organize a strike.

5. César Chávez started an organization to
- **A.** bring an end to the Vietnam War.
- **(B.)** win better wages and improve working conditions for farmworkers.
- **C.** work for the right of Indian tribes to run their own businesses and health and education programs.
- **D.** make sure that all jobs were open to both men and women.

6. President Lyndon Johnson's program to make life better for all Americans was called the
- **(A.)** Great Society.
- **B.** New Horizon.
- **C.** Square Deal.
- **D.** New Deal.

(continued)

STANDARD TEST

NAME ______________________ DATE __________

7. Mikhail Gorbachev helped bring about change in the former Soviet Union through his policy of
- **A.** Québecois.
- **B.** Nunavut.
- **(C.)** *perestroika.*
- **D.** deforestation.

8. The fall of the Berlin Wall and the breakup of the Soviet Union led to
- **A.** the United States blockade of Cuba.
- **(B.)** the end of the Cold War.
- **C.** the growth of the middle class in Mexico.
- **D.** the resignation of President Jimmy Carter from office.

DIRECTIONS:* *Match the description on the left with the term or name on the right. Then write the correct letter in the space provided.

9. __E__ Canadian province that wants to secede from Canada to protect its French culture

10. __C__ free trade agreement between the United States, Canada, and Mexico

11. __F__ amounts that banks charge customers to borrow money

12. __A__ country in which Jean-Bertrand Aristide was elected president

13. __D__ cities and all the suburbs and other population areas around them

14. __B__ group that tries to settle problems between nations in the Western Hemisphere

- **A.** Haiti
- **B.** Organization of American States
- **C.** NAFTA
- **D.** metropolitan areas
- **E.** Quebec
- **F.** interest rates

(continued)

STANDARD TEST

NAME ______________________ DATE __________

Part Two: Test Your Skills (20 points)

DIRECTIONS:* *Below are four political symbols of American history and politics. Explain what each symbol is and what it represents.

Symbol / **Meaning**

15. 

Possible response: The Liberty Bell represents freedom and liberty in the United States. It also represents the rights of all citizens.

16. 

Possible response: George Washington was the leader in the Revolutionary War and the first President of the United States. He represents the ideals of leadership and patriotism.

17. 

Possible response: The Statue of Liberty represents freedom and the warm welcome that people immigrating to the United States receive.

18. 

Possible response: Abraham Lincoln, the sixteenth President of the United States, represents honesty and national unity.

(continued)

STANDARD TEST

NAME ______________________ DATE __________

Part Three: Apply What You Have Learned

DIRECTIONS:* *Complete each of the following activities.

19. ***Which One Does Not Belong?*** *(8 points)*
Listed below are groups of terms or names. Circle the one that does not belong in each group and explain why.

hawk (embargo) dove

Possible response: Hawks and doves are people for and against war. Embargo is the United States policy toward trade with Cuba.

commonwealth Puerto Rico (Brazil)

Possible response: Puerto Rico is a commonwealth of the United States. Brazil is an independent country.

AIM United Farm Workers (OAS)

Possible response: AIM and UFW are organizations that work for equal rights. The OAS is an international organization of countries in the Western Hemisphere.

(Fidel Castro) nonviolence Martin Luther King, Jr.

Possible response: Nonviolence was the basis of the policy of Martin Luther King, Jr. Fidel Castro is the dictator of Cuba.

(continued)

STANDARD TEST

NAME ______________________ DATE __________

20. **Action** *(6 points)*
Sometimes nations or peoples take strong action to achieve their goals. Listed below are three such actions. Explain the results of each.

Action	Results of the Action
a. Berlin blockade	Possible response: The Berlin blockade was the result of Soviet actions to prevent land travel to Berlin. The Allied powers responded by using an airlift to supply food and fuel to the city. The Allied action kept the city free.
b. American blockade of Cuba during the Cuban missile crisis	Possible response: When the Soviet Union put missiles in Cuba, the United States sent its navy to blockade the island. This action forced the Soviets to remove their missiles.
c. Mohawk Indians in Quebec, Canada, protested the building of a golf course on their land	Possible response: The Mohawks' protests succeeded in stopping the construction on their land.

21. **Essay** *(10 points)*
Write a one-paragraph essay explaining what caused the Korean War and what the outcome of the war was.

Possible response:
The Korean War was caused when North Korea, backed by the Soviet Union, invaded South Korea. The outcome of the war was that South Korea, with United States help, remained a free and independent country.

PERFORMANCE TASK

NAME ______________________ DATE __________

Individual Performance Task

Stamp It Out!

A postage stamp has a value stated in numbers, an illustration, and often the name of a country and a title or an explanation. In this task you will make a postage stamp (on an 8 1/2-inch-by-11-inch sheet of paper) that honors one of the following people or events:

- the Berlin Airlift
- the end of the Cold War
- the actions of Rosa Parks
- the end of the Vietnam War
- the passage of NAFTA

Step 1 Select one of the topics above for the subject of a postage stamp or, with your teacher's approval, select a topic from this unit. Use materials in the textbook or do research in your school library to learn more about your topic.

Step 2 Make a rough sketch of a postage stamp. Show it to a classmate and ask whether it is clear and understandable.

Step 3 Make improvements in the rough sketch. Then make a final copy.

Step 4 Display the final copy of the postage stamp where others can see it.

PERFORMANCE TASK

NAME ______________________ DATE __________

Group Performance Task

Eyewitness News

In a television news story one or more reporters will talk to one or more people who have taken part in some event. The news story usually has an introduction, an interview with a person or persons, and a conclusion. In this task your group will prepare a news story as though it were to be broadcast on a television news program.

Step 1 Select one of the following topics for a news story or, with the approval of your teacher, select your own topic. Decide which role each member of the group will take.

Topic	Roles
Berlin Airlift	a reporter, a citizen of Berlin, and an Air Force pilot
Vietnam War	a reporter, two hawks, and two doves
Canadian separatists	a reporter, a person opposed to the separatists, and a person in favor of the separatists
Puerto Rico's relationship to the United States	a reporter, a person who wants Puerto Rico to be a state, a person who wants Puerto Rico to remain a commonwealth, and a person who wants Puerto Rico to be an independent country
the struggle for equal rights	a reporter, a person from AIM, a person from the United Farm Workers, and a person from NOW

Step 2 Use the textbook and library resources to learn more about your topic. The members of the group should try to find information that is close to what they would say if they were on a television news program.

Step 3 As a group, make a rough outline of the questions the reporter will ask and the answers that the others will give. Each person in the group will have specific things to say.

Step 4 Practice the news story. Time the story with a watch to determine how long it will take to present to the class. All members of the group should memorize what they are going to say.

Step 5 Have at least one complete dress rehearsal of the news story presentation.

Step 6 Present the news story to the rest of the class. Act as though you were on a live television program.

Rubrics

SCORING RUBRICS The scoring rubrics for evaluating individual projects, group projects, and student presentations may be found in the **Assessment Program**, pages 9–11.

CRITERIA The criteria listed below may be used when looking for evidence of the students' understanding of social studies content and ability to think critically.

Individual Task

Stamp It Out!

- ✓ Identify a topic studied in this unit and gather background information on the topic.
- ✓ Create a graphic illustration that symbolizes the selected topic.

Group Task

Eyewitness News

- ✓ Ask questions that raise the key issues of the historical event.
- ✓ Portray the person's position accurately.
- ✓ Differentiate the positions among those interviewed.

REMINDER

You may wish to preview the performance assessment activities in the COOPERATIVE LEARNING WORKSHOP on page 673. Students may complete these activities during the course of the unit.

Introduce the Unit

Personal Response

Have students use what they have learned about United States history to analyze why the United States became a world leader and to explain the responsibilities they think go with being a world leader. Ask them to identify some of the challenges the United States faces today and to discuss the advantages and disadvantages of living in a country that is a world leader.

Link Prior Learning

Have students look at the titles on the bar across the top of pages 604–605 to review the chronology of earlier units. Then discuss the photograph.

Q. **What does the photograph tell you about the United States?** The United States explores space.

The Americas Today

Activity Choices

Background

THE LARGE PICTURE The space shuttle *Discovery* was developed by NASA to place communications satellites into orbit. The satellites receive radio, television, and other electronic signals from Earth and transmit those signals to any part of the world. In addition, *Discovery* is used to launch space probes, scientific research satellites, and military satellites into space. From those space probes and scientific research satellites, scientists are gathering detailed information about the other planets in our solar system.

Link to Reading

READ AND DISPLAY NEWS ARTICLES During the course of this unit, have students collect, share, and discuss news articles about Canada, Puerto Rico, Nicaragua, Cuba, Haiti, the space program, and the United States as a world power. Ask students to relate the articles to the content as they study the unit. You may wish to display the articles on a bulletin board.

Unit 10

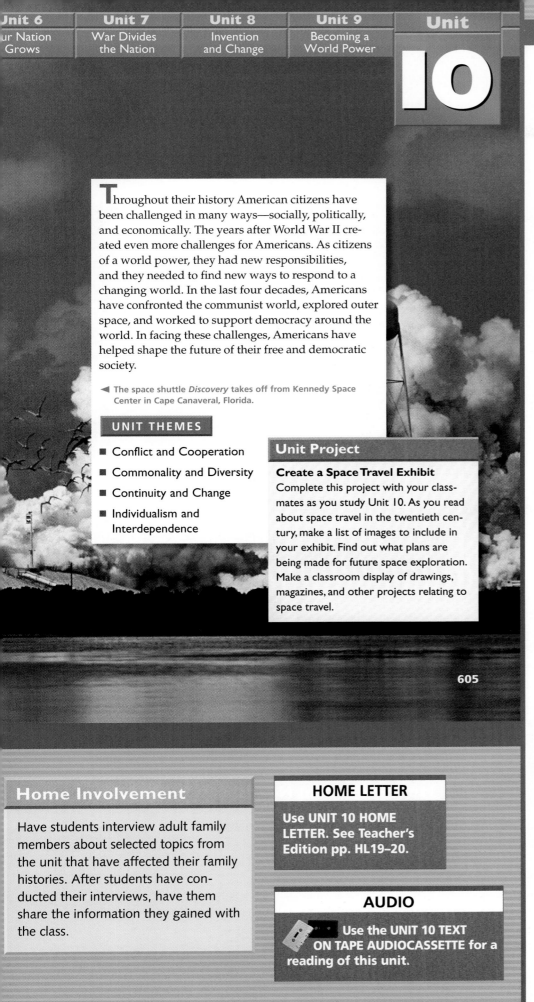

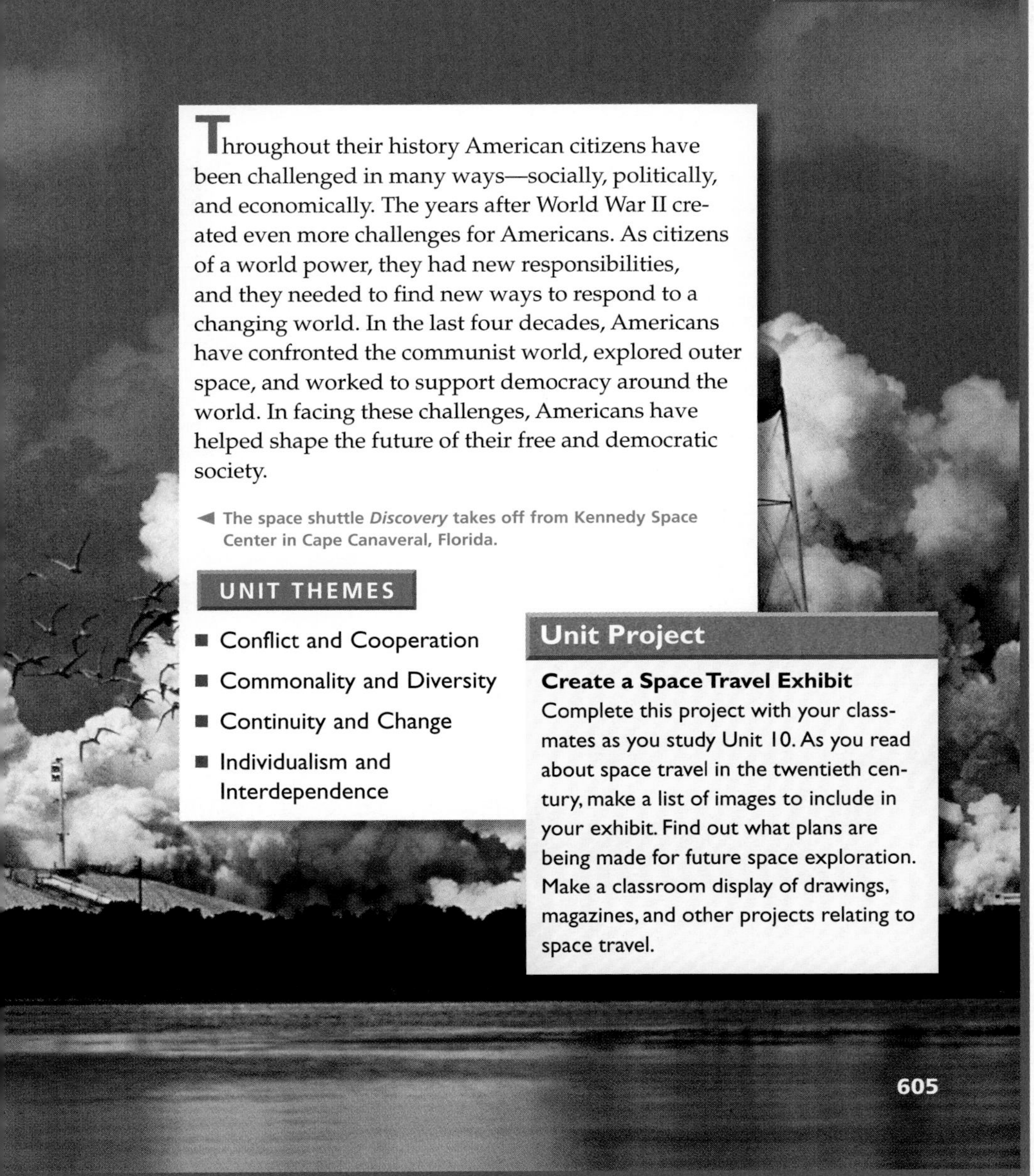

Throughout their history American citizens have been challenged in many ways—socially, politically, and economically. The years after World War II created even more challenges for Americans. As citizens of a world power, they had new responsibilities, and they needed to find new ways to respond to a changing world. In the last four decades, Americans have confronted the communist world, explored outer space, and worked to support democracy around the world. In facing these challenges, Americans have helped shape the future of their free and democratic society.

◄ The space shuttle *Discovery* takes off from Kennedy Space Center in Cape Canaveral, Florida.

UNIT THEMES

- Conflict and Cooperation
- Commonality and Diversity
- Continuity and Change
- Individualism and Interdependence

Unit Project

Create a Space Travel Exhibit
Complete this project with your classmates as you study Unit 10. As you read about space travel in the twentieth century, make a list of images to include in your exhibit. Find out what plans are being made for future space exploration. Make a classroom display of drawings, magazines, and other projects relating to space travel.

605

Home Involvement

Have students interview adult family members about selected topics from the unit that have affected their family histories. After students have conducted their interviews, have them share the information they gained with the class.

HOME LETTER

Use UNIT 10 HOME LETTER. See Teacher's Edition pp. HL19–20.

AUDIO

Use the UNIT 10 TEXT ON TAPE AUDIOCASSETTE for a reading of this unit.

Options for Reading

Read Aloud Read each lesson aloud as students follow along in their books. Strategies for guiding students through the text and visuals are provided with each lesson.

Read Together Have pairs or small groups of students take turns reading each page or paragraph aloud. Encourage students to use the new vocabulary words as they discuss what they read.

Read Alone Strong readers may wish to read the lessons independently before you read or discuss each lesson with the class.

Read the Introduction

Ask students to read the unit introduction on this page.

Q. **What do you think is the greatest challenge facing the United States today?** Student responses will vary but may include maintaining a strong economy, helping keep world peace, and caring for the environment.

Unit Themes

Discuss with students the Unit Themes. Throughout the study of this unit, ask for volunteers to identify the events, maps, illustrations, and photographs that represent each of these themes.

Unit Project Start-Up

Ask students to search through reference books you have collected. Then have the class brainstorm a list of specific topics about space exploration. Decide on a set of six topics and form groups to study them. Outline the parameters of the exhibit and the performance expectations for the groups. Schedule work periods and set a final deadline.

PREVIEW THE UNIT

Link Prior Learning

Have students discuss what they already know about the decades since World War II. Emphasize that since the 1950s, the United States has played an important role as world leader. Trade with other countries has become increasingly important to the American economy because of technological advances that make international travel and communication faster and easier. Reinforce the fact that the United States has become the world's only superpower, and is using its influence to help solve conflicts between other countries.

Understanding the Map

This map shows the nation's interstate and U.S. highway systems and cities with a population of 100,000 or more. Ask students why they think the eastern half of the United States has more people and more highways than the western half.

Q. **Which states have no large cities?**
Montana, Wyoming, North Dakota, Delaware, Maine, Vermont, and New Hampshire

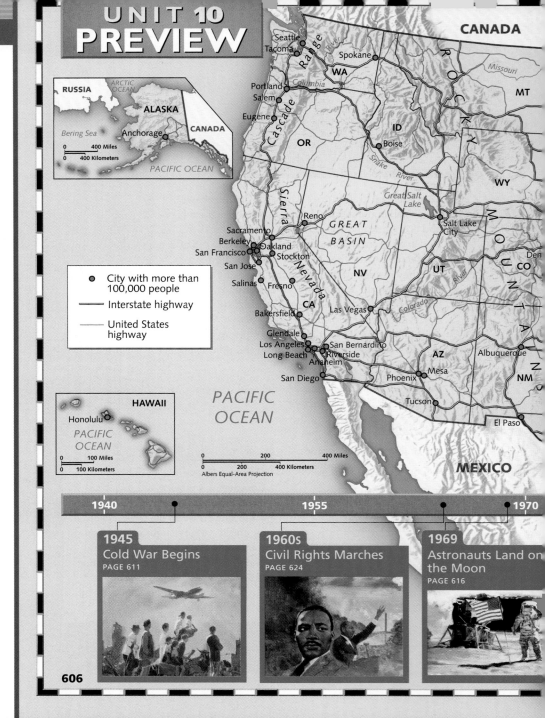

UNIT 10 PREVIEW

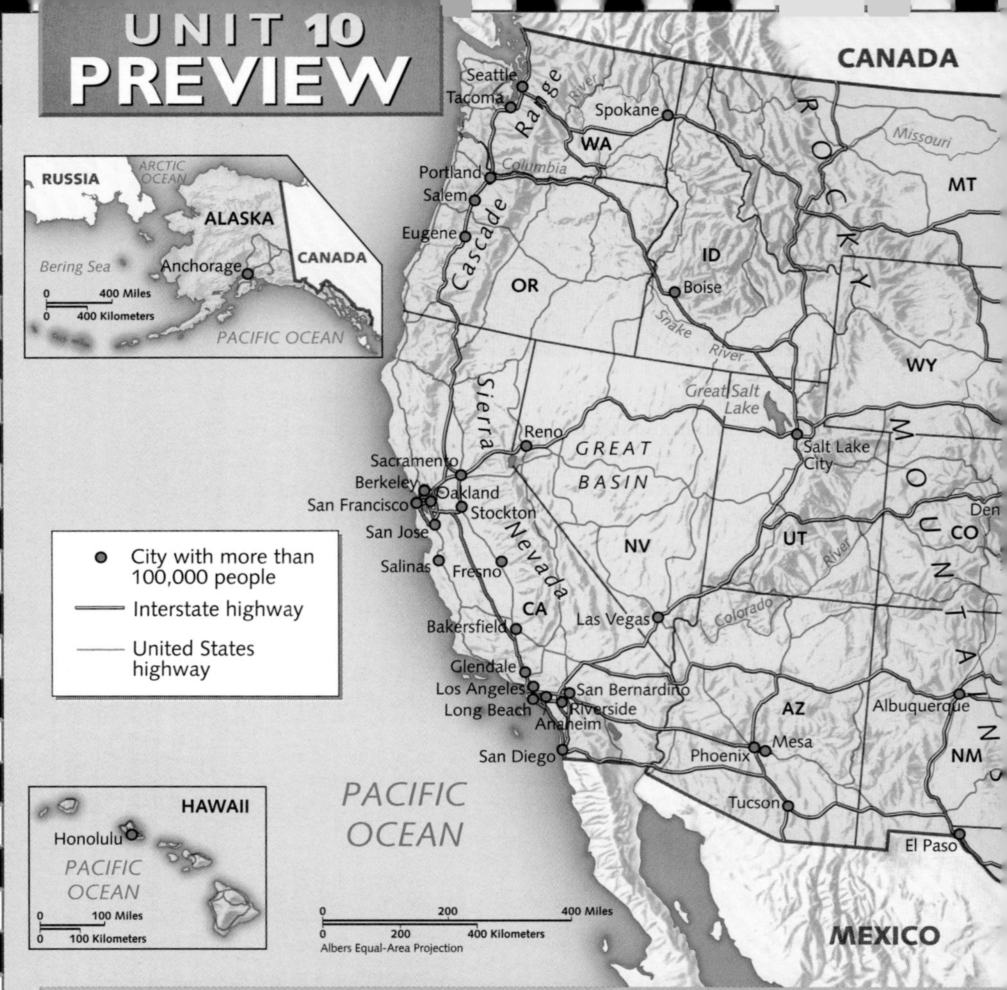

1940 — 1955 — 1970

1945
Cold War Begins
PAGE 611

1960s
Civil Rights Marches
PAGE 624

1969
Astronauts Land on the Moon
PAGE 616

ACTIVITY CHOICES

Link to Language Arts

WRITE POSSIBLE SENTENCES Write on the board the key events from the time line: the Cold War, the Civil Rights movement, the moon landing, the end of the Vietnam War, the end of the Cold War, and the NAFTA agreement. Ask students to write a complete sentence for each event that states what they already know or believe about it. Tell them that these are "possible" sentences they can change as they study the unit. Have students evaluate their sentences later in the unit and edit or rewrite them based on what they have come to understand about the events.

Meet Individual Needs

ENGLISH LANGUAGE LEARNERS Have students examine each of the pictures in the time line and give key words that describe the action in the picture. As you summarize each event for the class, use the English language learners' key words in your summaries.

VIDEO

VIDEO EXPERIENCES SOCIAL STUDIES
See the video guide for additional enrichment material.

1985 — 2000

1975
Vietnam War Ends
PAGE 630

1989
The Berlin Wall is Torn Down
PAGE 636

1994
NAFTA Agreement Goes into Effect
PAGE 645

Understanding the Time Line

Explain to students that the pictures illustrating the time line on pages 606–607 show pictures of events from the second half of the 1900s.

Q. **How long did the Cold War last?** from 1945 until 1989, or 44 years

What important recent event in the United States do you think should be added to the time line? Answers will vary.

Look Ahead to the Unit

Students may wish to preview the chapters, lessons, and illustrations in the unit to observe the events and people they will be studying.

Background

THE TIME LINE After World War II, a war without weapons developed between the Soviet Union and the United States.

At home, civil rights leaders such as Martin Luther King, Jr., helped African Americans gain federal protection against discrimination.

The Cold War was also fought in space. The Soviets launched satellites, and American astronauts walked on the moon.

America's involvement in the Vietnam War divided its citizens into "hawks" and "doves."

The symbol of Cold War communism, the Berlin Wall, came down as the Soviet Union changed its government and economy to improve its people's lives.

Canada, the United States, and Mexico signed the free-trade agreement known as NAFTA.

These events are also shown in the Visual Summary on pages 670–671 in the Pupil Book.

UNIT POSTER

Use the UNIT 10 VISUAL SUMMARY POSTER to preview the unit.

TECHNOLOGY

Use TIMELINER™ DATA DISKS to discuss and summarize the unit.

SET THE SCENE WITH LITERATURE

PREREADING STRATEGIES

Personal Response

Ask students to think about what topic or topics they would choose to write about if they were asked to write a poem for the President's inauguration. List their suggestions on the board. After students have read Maya Angelou's poem, compare its message with the students' suggestions.

Set the Purpose

Maya Angelou, a well-known African American poet, was asked by Bill Clinton to compose a poem for his inauguration. As students read Angelou's poem, have them analyze how it sends a message of hope to all Americans.

READ AND RESPOND

Auditory Learning

Read Dramatically Ask one or more student volunteers to read the poem aloud to the class. Ask the students to read the poem with feeling, as it might have been read before an audience of millions of people during President Clinton's inauguration.

Understanding the Poem

Ask students to identify the images projected by Angelou's words in the poem, and write a list of those images on the board.

Q. **What dream is Angelou referring to in the beginning of her poem?** Answers will vary, but may include the ideas of a dream of freedom, equality, or peace, or of the dream that Martin Luther King, Jr., spoke about in his famous "I Have a Dream" speech.

Have students analyze why Angelou writes:

Do not be wedded forever
To fear, yoked eternally
To brutishness.

SET THE SCENE with Literature

On the pulse of morning

by
MAYA ANGELOU

Maya Angelou (AN•juh•loh) wrote her poem "On the Pulse of Morning" for the inauguration of Bill Clinton as President of the United States. Clinton took the oath of office on January 20, 1993. In her poem Angelou wanted to show that she loves her country despite its problems. She also wanted to celebrate the past while speaking hopefully about the future. As you read the poem, think about the problems and hopes Americans had in the years after World War II.

608 • Unit 10

ACTIVITY CHOICES

Background

THE LITERATURE SELECTION AND THE AUTHOR "On the Pulse of Morning" was written by Maya Angelou—a poet, author, playwright, editor, actress, director, composer, and teacher. Angelou wrote the poem specifically at the request of Bill Clinton for his inauguration as President of the United States. Angelou was born in St. Louis, Missouri, in 1928. She is perhaps best known for her autobiography, *I Know Why the Caged Bird Sings*, in which she tells what it was like to be an African American girl growing up during the Great Depression. Her writing style is often described as exuberant and realistic. In addition to four books of poems, she also has written plays and screenplays and composed songs. Her works of poetry include *Just Give Me a Cool Drink of Water 'fore I Diiie* and *I Shall Not Be Moved*.

Lift up your eyes
Upon this day breaking for you.
Give birth again
To the dream.

Women, children, men,
Take it into the palms of your hands,
Mold it into the shape of your most
Private need. Sculpt it into
The image of your most public self.
Lift up your hearts.
Each new hour holds new chances
For a new beginning.
Do not be wedded forever
To fear, yoked eternally
To brutishness.

The horizon leans forward,
Offering you space
To place new steps of change.
Here, on the pulse of this fine day,
You may have the courage
To look up and out and upon me,
The Rock, the River, the Tree, your country.
No less to Midas than the mendicant [beggar].
No less to you now than the mastodon then.

Here, on the pulse of this new day,
You may have the grace to look up and out
And into your sister's eyes,
And into your brother's face,
    Your country,
    And say simply
    Very simply
    With hope—
    Good morning.

Make sure students understand the line "No less to Midas than the mendicant" by asking them to recall the story of King Midas and the Midas touch. Then have a volunteer read to the class the meaning of *mendicant* ("beggar") from a dictionary, and have students analyze the meaning of the line within the context of the poem.

Ask students to reread the poem silently and select favorite passages to read aloud to the class, explaining afterward why the passages are their favorites.

Culture

Thought and Expression Maya Angelou has carried on the tradition of creativity and energy in writing that students read about earlier in connection with the Harlem Renaissance.

Q. **Do you think Angelou believes it is possible for Americans to solve their problems?** Yes; she sees room for change in the expanding horizons provided by people who have the courage to look beyond the present.

Summarize the Literature

On the occasion of the inauguration of a new President, poet Maya Angelou asks Americans to renew their faith in the country by looking beyond the concerns of the present in order to build a new future with hope for everyone.

Link Literature

The following are selections that can be used during the course of this unit with students of differing reading abilities. In addition to these titles, you may wish to suggest some of the books listed in the Multimedia Resource Center on page 604D of this Teacher's Edition.

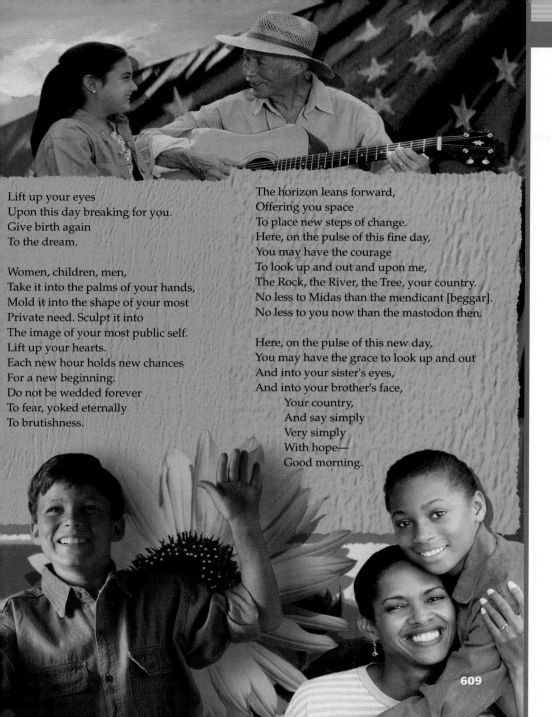

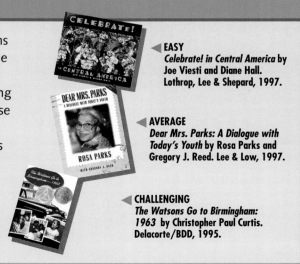

EASY
***Celebrate! in Central America* by Joe Viesti and Diane Hall. Lothrop, Lee & Shepard, 1997.**

AVERAGE
***Dear Mrs. Parks: A Dialogue with Today's Youth* by Rosa Parks and Gregory J. Reed. Lee & Low, 1997.**

CHALLENGING
***The Watsons Go to Birmingham: 1963* by Christopher Paul Curtis. Delacorte/BDD, 1995.**

CHAPTER 19

Planning Chart

	THEMES • Strands	VOCABULARY	MEET INDIVIDUAL NEEDS	RESOURCES INCLUDING ▶ TECHNOLOGY
LESSON 1 **The Cold War Begins** pp. 611–615	CONFLICT & COOPERATION • Geography • History • Civics/Government	superpower, arms race, airlift, cease-fire, missile	Advanced Learners, p. 612 Extend and Enrich, p. 614 Reteach, p. 615	Activity Book, p. 122 ▶ TIMELINER
LESSON 2 **Learn History Through Literature** One Giant Leap by Mary Ann Fraser pp. 616–621	INDIVIDUALISM & INTERDEPENDENCE • Culture • History • Geography		English Language Learners, p. 617 Extend and Enrich, p. 620 Reteach, p. 621	Activity Book, p. 123 ▶ THE AMAZING WRITING MACHINE
LESSON 3 **The Struggle for Equal Rights** pp. 622–626	CONTINUITY & CHANGE • Civics/Government • History • Economics	nonviolence, integration	Advanced Learners, p. 623 Auditory Learners, p. 624 Extend and Enrich, p. 625 Reteach, p. 626	Activity Book, p. 124
SKILL **Act as a Responsible Citizen** p. 627	BUILDING CITIZENSHIP • Participation Skills		Reteach the Skill, p. 627	Activity Book, p. 125 Transparency 49
LESSON 4 **Vietnam War and Protests at Home** pp. 628–631	CONTINUITY & CHANGE • History • Economics • Civics/Government • Geography	hawk, dove, scandal	Extend and Enrich, p. 630 Reteach, p. 631	Activity Book, p. 126
COUNTERPOINTS **Hawk or Dove?** pp. 632–633	BUILDING CITIZENSHIP • Participation Skills • Critical Thinking Skills		Reteach, p. 633	
LESSON 5 **The Cold War Ends** pp. 634–638	INDIVIDUALISM & INTERDEPENDENCE • Civics/Government • History/Economics • Culture	arms control, deficit, détente, terrorism, hostage	Visual Learners, p. 636 Extend and Enrich, p. 637 Reteach, p. 638	Activity Book, p. 127 Music Audiocassette ▶ THE AMAZING WRITING MACHINE
SKILL **Understand Political Symbols** p. 639	BUILDING CITIZENSHIP • Participation Skills		Reteach the Skill, p. 639	Activity Book, pp. 128–129 Transparency 50
CHAPTER REVIEW pp. 640–641				Activity Book, p. 130 Transparency 51 Assessment Program Chapter 19 Test, pp. 159–162 ▶ THE AMAZING WRITING MACHINE ▶ TIMELINER ▶ INTERNET

10 DAYS

TIME MANAGEMENT

DAY 1	DAY 2	DAY 3	DAY 4	DAY 5	DAY 6	DAY 7	DAY 8	DAY 9	DAY 10
Lesson 1	Lesson 2	Lesson 3	Skill	Lesson 4	Counterpoints	Lesson 5	Skill	Chapter Review	Chapter Test

Activity Book

LESSON 1
Apply Map and Globe Skills

NAME ________________ DATE ________

THE BERLIN WALL

Apply Map and Globe Skills

DIRECTIONS: Study the historical map of the Berlin Wall below. Then complete the activities that follow.

1. In which country was Berlin located? East Germany
2. The Berlin Wall divided Berlin into what two parts? East Berlin and West Berlin
3. Using two different colors, shade in East and West Berlin. Fill in the key to match the map.
4. Circle the Soviet War Memorial on the map. Why do you think it was located in this part of Berlin? Students' answers should reflect an understanding of the Soviet Union as part of the Allied forces in World War II.
5. Trace a route from Police Headquarters to the Reichstag. Would most people have been able to travel this route? Why? No; it would have been necessary to cross from East Berlin into West Berlin.

LESSON 2
Plot a Story

NAME ________________ DATE ________

The *FIRST* Moon *Landing*

Plot a Story

DIRECTIONS: Reread the selection One Giant Leap on pages 616–621 in your textbook. On the organizer below, fill in the beginning, middle, and ending of the story. Include any challenges faced and resolved by the characters.

One Giant Leap

Main Event

moon landing

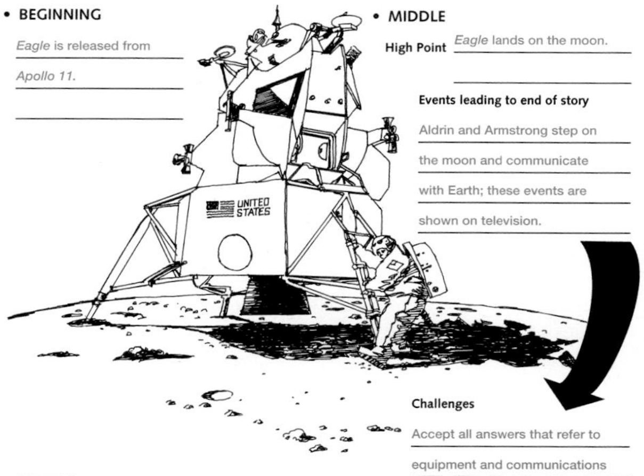

- **BEGINNING**
  Eagle is released from *Apollo 11.*
- **MIDDLE**
  High Point *Eagle* lands on the moon.
  Events leading to end of story Aldrin and Armstrong step on the moon and communicate with Earth; these events are shown on television.

Challenges Accept all answers that refer to equipment and communications failures, miscalculations, moon surface, or fuel.

- **ENDING**
  U.S. astronauts prove landing on the moon is possible.

LESSON 3
Link Music to History

NAME ________________ DATE ________

Sing About CIVIL RIGHTS

Link Music to History

DIRECTIONS: Read the words to the following civil rights song "If You Miss Me from the Back of the Bus." Then answer the questions and complete the activities that follow.

If you miss me from the back of the bus,
And you can't find me nowhere,
Come on up to the front of the bus,
I'll be riding up there,
I'll be riding up there,
I'll be riding up there,
Come on up to the front of the bus,
I'll be riding up there.

If you miss me from the front of the bus,
And you can't find me nowhere,
Come on up to the driver's seat,
I'll be drivin' up there.
I'll be drivin' up there,
I'll be drivin' up there,
Come on up to the driver's seat,
I'll be drivin' up there.

1. Who does "me" represent in the song? African Americans
2. Circle the words that describe the part of the bus where members of this group were first required to sit. Why did they sit there? Segregation laws required them to do so.
3. In the second verse of the song, who is in the driver's seat? an African American
4. What is the purpose of this protest song? Answers should include references to nonviolent means of achieving equal rights.
5. Describe in your own words what civil rights mean to you. Accept answers that reflect an understanding of equal rights and the rights guaranteed by Amendments 13, 14, 15, and 19 of the U.S. Constitution.

SKILL PRACTICE
Apply Participation Skills

NAME ________________ DATE ________

HOW TO ACT AS A RESPONSIBLE CITIZEN

Apply Participation Skills

DIRECTIONS: An effective way to be a responsible citizen is to write a letter to an elected official about an issue that concerns you. On a separate sheet of paper, write a letter using the format below. Accept letters that follow the format and are well reasoned.

Heading — Your return address and the date

423 Happy Trail
Nice Town, TX 77111
May 22, 2000

The President
The White House
Washington, D.C. 20500

Inside Address — Name and title of person being addressed and mailing address

Dear Mr. President:

Greeting — Make sure you properly address the person. Officials are addressed by specific titles such as "The Honorable," "Governor," or "Mayor." If you do not know the specific name and title of the person you are addressing, research it. Use a colon (:) for business letters and a comma (,) for personal letters.

Body — State your purpose in the first sentence. If you are writing for or against a certain cause, identify it and state your position at the beginning of the letter. Stick to one cause per letter. Keep it short and polite. If you write to a legislator other than your own, send a copy of your letter to your own representative. This is considered good manners and might persuade your representative to help.

Sincerely yours,
John Q. Public
John Q. Public

Closing — Show respect by using "Sincerely yours" or "Respectfully yours."

Signature — Type or print your name below your handwritten signature.

LESSON 4
Edit a Story

NAME ______________________ DATE __________

MAYA LIN

Edit a Story

***DIRECTIONS:** Read the following story about Maya Lin. The story has some mistakes in it. Use the proofreader's marks shown in the box below to edit, or make changes to, the story.*

PROOFREADER'S MARKS

MARK	MEANING	EXAMPLE
¶	make new paragraph	
℘	take out, or delete, something	they time is
^	add, or insert, something	We go class. (to)
/	make lowercase letter	my Mother
≡	capitalize, or make uppercase letter	mr. President
∿	transpose, or move, letters or words	Daed

Have you had a chance to visit the Vietnam Veterans Memorial in washington, D.C.? The memorial is a simple, black granite wall. It is covered with thousands of namess of Americans who lost their lives in the war. this memorial one is of Maya Lin's most well-known designs. Her entry, number 1,026 out of 1,420 entries, won the contest to design the Vietnam Veterans memorial. She was a 21-year-old student at Yale University when she won won!

¶ Later, as an Architect, Lin was asked to desing the Civil Rights Memorial in Montgomery, alabama. This memorial is also made of black granite, But appears to float in the air. It has water flowing evenly slowly across its surface. Beneath the water, the names and events that tell the history of the Civil Rights movement are etched in stone. lin captured the spirit of the Civil Rights Movement with this monument.

Lin believes that the vietnam Veterans Memorial and the Civil Rights memorial are special. They helped our country heal some histroical wounds. She says, "If you don't remember history accurately, how can you learn"

 Use after reading Chapter 19, Lesson 4, pages 628–631.

LESSON 5
Place Events in Historical Context

NAME ______________________ DATE __________

THE COLD WAR ERA

Place Events in Historical Context

***DIRECTIONS:** In the space provided, write the date of each of the following events. Then draw a line from the event to the name of the person who was President at the time the event took place. Use pages R16–R18 of the Almanac in your textbook to help you complete this activity.*

1950	1. The North Korean army invades South Korea.	Lyndon B. Johnson
1962	2. The Cuban missile crisis occurs.	Gerald Ford
1969	3. The *Eagle* lands on the moon.	Richard M. Nixon
1955	4. Rosa Parks is arrested for sitting in the wrong section of a bus.	Harry S. Truman
1984	5. Geraldine Ferraro is the first woman nominated for Vice President by a major political party.	Dwight D. Eisenhower
1975	6. South Vietnam surrenders to North Vietnam.	Ronald Reagan
1982	7. The Vietnam Veterans Memorial opens to visitors.	John F. Kennedy
1972	8. The President visits communist China.	Jimmy Carter
1979	9. The Soviet Union invades Afghanistan.	George Bush
1989	10. Germans tear down the Berlin Wall.	

Use after reading Chapter 19, Lesson 5, pages 634–638.

SKILL PRACTICE
Apply Participation Skills

NAME ______________________ DATE __________

Apply Participation Skills

***DIRECTIONS:** Study the cartoons on page 128. Then complete the following activities.*

1. One of the most widely used political symbols representing the United States is the eagle. The bear is a political symbol representing the Soviet Union. The cartoon titled "The Odd Couple" appeared in the newspaper in 1973. Why do you think the United States and the Soviet Union were called the "odd couple"?
   Answers should include reference to the fact that the United States and the Soviet Union were enemies during the Cold War.
2. Circle another political symbol on the cartoon that represents the United States. Circle one that represents the Soviet Union. circle flag crest on eagle's chest; circle star on bear's hat
3. "The Odd Couple" cartoon symbolizes détente between the United States and the Soviet Union. Using the cartoon and the information in your textbook, write your own definition of détente. Answers should reflect textbook definition, which is the easing of tensions between countries.
4. What does the dove in the baby carriage symbolize? peace
5. In February 1972, President Nixon made his historic visit to the People's Republic of China. In the cartoon titled "Marco Polo," circle the political symbol that shows that Nixon was a member of the Republican party. Put a box around the political symbol that shows that Nixon represented the United States. circle around elephant; box around U.S. flag
6. What does the cartoon show Nixon bringing into China, and what do these things represent? the flag, which stands for the U.S. government and U.S. ideals; bundles of goods labeled "trade," which symbolize free trade; and a dove, which symbolizes peace

***DIRECTIONS:** Choose a topic from this chapter. Then, on a separate sheet of paper, illustrate that topic by using political symbols.*
Accept reasonable illustrations that include political symbols.

Page 128 of the Activity Book does not appear here, but is included in the full-sized book. There are no answers on that page.

Use after reading Chapter 19, Skill Lesson, page 639.

CHAPTER 19 REVIEW
Connect Main Ideas

NAME ______________________ DATE __________

The Cold War Years

Connect Main Ideas

***DIRECTIONS:** Use this organizer to show that you understand how the chapter's main ideas are connected. Complete the organizer by writing the main idea of each lesson.*

The Cold War Years

The Cold War Begins
Tensions grew between the United States and the Soviet Union during the Cold War, resulting in an arms race.

One Giant Leap
The first moon landing was achieved by American astronauts from *Apollo 11* in 1969.

The Struggle for Equal Rights
Protesters such as Martin Luther King, Jr., fought to end segregation and gain civil rights through peaceful protests and marches.

Vietnam War and Protests at Home
The Vietnam War deeply divided Americans and their government leaders.

The Cold War Ends
Mikhail Gorbachev made many changes in the Soviet Union, easing Cold War tensions. The Berlin Wall was torn down in 1989. The end of the Cold War brought new challenges to the United States.

 Use after reading Chapter 19, pages 610–641.

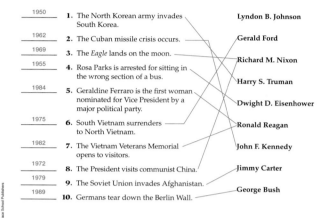

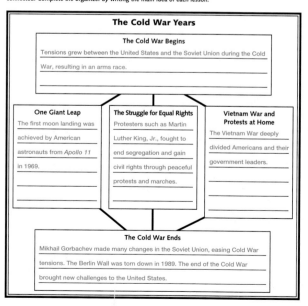

Chapter 19 Assessment

For ongoing **PERFORMANCE ASSESSMENT,** see Show What You Know, pp. 615, 626, 631, 638.

CONTENT

NAME ______________________ DATE __________

Chapter Test 19

***Part One: Test Your Understanding** (4 points each)*

DIRECTIONS: *Use the words or names from the box below to complete the sentences that follow.*

airlift	César Chávez	Cold War
hawks	inflation	integration
missiles	Richard M. Nixon	nonviolent
Rosa Parks	Ronald Reagan	segregation
South Vietnam	superpowers	

1. In the years after World War II, the United States and the Soviet Union became the world's ___superpowers___.

2. When the Soviet Union blocked supplies from getting to Berlin, the Allies used an ___airlift___ to take food and fuel to the city.

3. The United States blockaded Cuba when the Soviet Union placed ___missiles___ on the island.

4. In 1954 the Supreme Court ordered an end to ___segregation___ in public schools.

5. The Montgomery, Alabama, bus boycott was started when ___Rosa Parks___ refused to give up her seat on a bus to a white man.

6. Marches and boycotts are examples of ___nonviolent___ protest to bring about change.

(continued)

CONTENT

NAME ______________________ DATE __________

7. The bringing together of all races in education, jobs, and housing is called ___integration___.

8. ___César Chávez___ formed the United Farm Workers to win better wages and conditions for farm workers.

9. In the Vietnam War, the United States fought on the side of ___South Vietnam___.

10. The costs of the Vietnam War and the Great Society programs led to ___inflation___ in the U.S. economy.

11. ___Hawks___ were Americans who supported the Vietnam War at any cost.

12. ___Richard M. Nixon___ was the first United States President to resign from office.

13. In 1985 President ___Ronald Reagan___ met with Soviet leader Mikhail Gorbachev to discuss the "cause of world peace."

14. When President George Bush referred to "a new world order," he meant a world without the ___Cold War___.

(continued)

SKILLS

NAME ______________________ DATE __________

***Part Two: Test Your Skills** (24 points)*

DIRECTIONS: *It is the duty of all United States citizens to act responsibly. Complete the following activities on citizenship.*

15. What are four things a student can do to be a responsible citizen?

Possible responses: help keep the neighborhood clean; mow the lawn for an elderly person; recycle old newspapers and cans; collect food for the hungry; volunteer to work in a hospital; collect clothing and blankets for the homeless; visit with elderly people in a nursing home

16. Describe how civil rights leaders such as Dr. Martin Luther King, Jr. and Rosa Parks acted as responsible citizens to fight injustice.

Possible responses: Dr. King led peaceful protest marches and made speeches; Mrs. Parks refused to give up her seat on a bus.

(continued)

APPLICATION/WRITING

NAME ______________________ DATE __________

Part Three: Apply What You Have Learned

DIRECTIONS: *Complete each of the following activities.*

17. *Time Line* (10 points)
Match the letters on the time line with the events from the list below. Place the correct letter in the space provided.

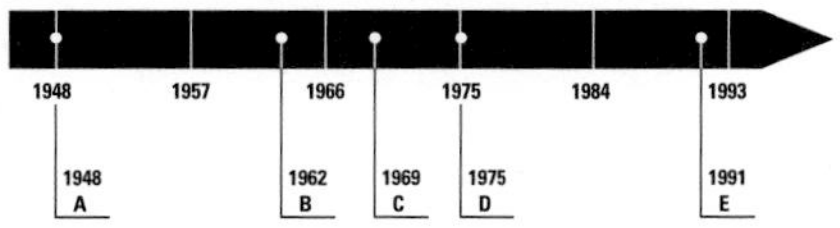

___E___ breakup of the Soviet Union
___A___ Berlin Airlift
___B___ Cuban missile crisis
___C___ *Apollo 11* mission to the moon
___D___ Vietnam War ends

18. *Essay* (10 points)
While he was President, Richard M. Nixon did much to ease Cold War tensions among the United States, China, and the Soviet Union. Write a one-paragraph essay explaining what President Nixon did to ease tensions.

Possible response:
President Nixon did much to ease Cold War tensions with China and the Soviet Union. For example, he visited both countries, he increased trade with both countries, he increased scientific and cultural cooperation with both countries, and he negotiated arms-control agreements with the Soviet Union.

INTRODUCE THE CHAPTER

This chapter tells the story of the United States from the end of World War II to the present. It covers the tense years of the Cold War and the events that led to the end of the Cold War. The chapter also looks at the years of turmoil in the United States over civil rights and the Vietnam War. In addition, the chapter tells the thrilling story of how American astronauts became the first people to land on the moon.

Link Prior Learning

Have students share what they already know about cooperation and conflict between the United States and the Soviet Union during and after World War II. Also have them recall the progress African Americans and women made toward equal rights.

Visual Analysis

Interpret Photographs Explain that this photograph shows Martin Luther King, Jr., a southern minister who took a leadership role in helping African Americans bring about civil rights changes through peaceful protest.

Q. **What do you think the photographer wanted you to know about Martin Luther King, Jr.?** Students may mention that the photographer wanted people to know that King was a strong and determined person.

Auditory Learning

Interpret Primary Sources Have a student volunteer read aloud the quotation. Explain that this quotation is part of King's speech given during the March on Washington, which was organized to protest racial injustice and to celebrate the 100th anniversary of the Emancipation Proclamation.

Q. **Why is it important to judge people by who they are, rather than by what they look like?** Looks can be deceiving. Actions give better clues to a person's character.

"PRIMARY SOURCE"

Source: *Lend Me Your Ears: Great Speeches in History.* William Safire. W. W. Norton, 1997.

CHAPTER

19

THE COLD WAR YEARS

"I have a dream that my four little children will one day live in a nation where they will not be judged by the color of their skin but by the content of their character."

Martin Luther King, Jr., Washington, D.C., August 28, 1963

ACTIVITY CHOICES

Background

MARTIN LUTHER KING, JR. Martin Luther King, Jr., was born in Atlanta, Georgia. His father and his maternal grandfather were Baptist ministers. His paternal grandfather was a sharecropper. King was ordained a minister in 1948. He attended Morehouse College, Crozer Theological Seminary, and Boston University. He helped establish the Southern Christian Leadership Conference in 1957 in response to the needs of civil rights groups. As the SCLC's first president, King worked against racial discrimination and for the voting rights of African Americans by means of peaceful demonstrations, boycotts, marches, and sit-ins. Since King's death, his wife, Coretta Scott King, and his children have continued to work toward his dream "that one day this nation will rise up and live out the true meaning of its creed: 'We hold these truths to be self-evident, that all men are created equal.'"

The Cold War Begins

In the years after World War II, the United States and the Soviet Union became the world's most powerful nations. They were called **superpowers** because of the important roles they played in world events. The two superpowers were very different from one another, and there were many conflicts between them. These conflicts were fought mostly with words and economic weapons. Even so, the threat of a real war was always present. These years, from 1945 to 1991, have become known as the Cold War years. They were a frightening time for many people.

LESSON 1

FOCUS
What can happen when powerful friends become enemies?

Main Idea Read to find out what happened when two World War II Allies—the United States and the Soviet Union—became enemies after the war.

Vocabulary
superpower
airlift
cease-fire
missile
arms race

The Berlin Crisis

At the end of World War II, the Allies divided Germany into four parts. Each of the major Allies took charge of one part. The United States, Britain, and France worked together to build a strong West Germany out of their parts. The Soviet Union held East Germany and formed a communist country there. Under this system, the government took over land and businesses. The people had little freedom to make decisions about how their country should be run.

Berlin, the capital of Germany, was in East Germany. It was divided into four parts, too. But the Soviet Union would not let the Western Allies send supplies to the area the Allies controlled, which made up the city of West Berlin. The Soviets blocked highway, rail, and water routes so that no food or fuel could get into the city. They hoped to drive the Western Allies out of West Berlin.

To get around the blockade, the Allies started the Berlin Airlift in 1948. An **airlift** is a system of bringing in supplies by

These children in West Berlin are cheering as a plane carrying supplies flies over their city.

Objectives

1. Evaluate the Allied solution to the Berlin crisis.
2. Identify the causes and results of the Korean War.
3. Describe Kennedy's actions during the Cuban missile crisis.
4. Analyze the reasons for the arms race between the United States and the Soviet Union.

Vocabulary

superpower (p. 611)
airlift (p. 611)
cease-fire (p. 613)
missile (p. 614)
arms race (p. 615)

1. ACCESS

The Focus Question

Ask students to imagine what might happen if two powerful nations that had once worked together came to disagree about many world issues.

The Main Idea

In this lesson students explore the antagonism that mushroomed between the United States and the Soviet Union from 1945 to the 1960s. After students have read the lesson, have them identify the reasons for the animosity.

2. BUILD

The Berlin Crisis

Key Content Summary

The first crisis between the United States and the Soviet Union concerned West Berlin. The Soviet Union tried to take control of the city by blocking all supply routes. The Allies countered the blockade by airlifting food and other supplies to West Berlin. The Soviet Union also built the Berlin Wall to keep East Germans from fleeing communist rule.

Reading Support

ANTICIPATION GUIDE Before students read the lesson, ask them to predict which of the following statements are true and which are false. Students may correct their predictions as they read.

1. The Soviet Union and the United States remained friends after World War II. false
2. The United States and the Soviet Union both built a wall between East Berlin and West Berlin. false
3. Only five years after the end of World War II, the United States was engaged in another war. true
4. During the Kennedy administration, the United States almost went to war over Puerto Rico. false
5. The United States and the Soviet Union both had atom bombs in the 1960s. true

Geography

Place Refer students to the map on this page and have them locate East Berlin and West Berlin. Then have students speculate on the problems faced by West Berliners because of their location in East German territory.

Visual Analysis

Learn from Maps Have students answer the question in the caption. East Germany, Poland, Czechoslovakia, Hungary, Romania, Yugoslavia, Albania, Bulgaria, Union of Soviet Socialist Republics

History

People and Events Across Time and Place Have students identify the reasons for conflict between the Western Allies and the Soviet Union in 1948.

Q. **Why were the Allies so concerned about protecting and helping West Berlin?** They did not want any more territory to fall into the hands of the communists.

Geography

Regions Have students conclude why Germans would want to escape from East Berlin and go to West Berlin.

Q. **What did the Berlin Wall symbolize?** the political division between the free world and the communist world

Regions Communist countries were said to be "behind the Iron Curtain." The Iron Curtain was a term used to express the idea that the people in communist countries were cut off from the rest of the world. This East German worker (right) is helping build the Berlin Wall.

■ *Which European countries were "behind the Iron Curtain?"*

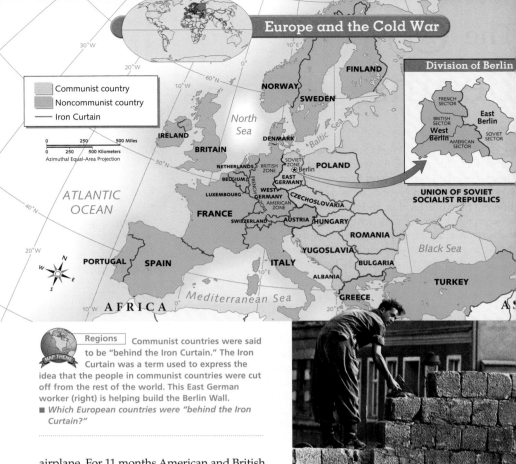

airplane. For 11 months American and British pilots made more than 272,000 flights over East Germany to West Berlin. They carried more than 2 million tons of food and supplies to the people of West Berlin. Finally, the Soviets backed down and allowed supplies to be delivered over land.

After the blockade ended, many people tried to leave East Berlin to escape from communist rule. In 1961 the East German government, with Soviet help, built a fence to keep people from leaving. Then East Germany took down the fence and put up a concrete wall with barbed wire on the top. The Berlin Wall, as it came to be known, was guarded by soldiers ready to shoot anyone who tried to cross it. The wall became one of the best-known symbols of the Cold War. It stood for the division between the free world and the communist countries.

REVIEW ***How did the Western Allies solve the problem of getting supplies to West Berlin?*** by starting an airlift

Activity Choices

Background

THE SOVIET VIEWPOINT To the Soviet Union, the existence of West Berlin in the heart of communist East Germany was, in Nikita Khrushchev's words, "a bone in the throat" of the USSR. To the Soviets, West Berlin was a symbol that Soviet domination of eastern Europe was not absolute. The communists continued the blockade for a year before they finally gave up the idea of taking over West Berlin.

Meet Individual Needs

ADVANCED LEARNERS Have a small group of students trace a large map of East Berlin and West Berlin that shows the water, road, and rail transportation routes used by West Berliners before and after the blockade. Also have them show the location of the Berlin Wall. Ask the students to use library resources about the Berlin Airlift to help them create a news report that explains how the airlift was planned and executed. Have them present their report and the map to the class.

Background

THE McCARTHY ERA During the 1950s, in what has come to be known as the "McCarthy era," Republican U.S. Senator Joseph McCarthy leveled charges of communist activity against many innocent people in the United States. The investigations that followed garnered national attention and publicity. Even after McCarthy was formally censured by the other senators for making such charges without proof, the stigma of communist allegiance followed many of the accused people for years to come.

The Korean War

Just as Germany was divided after World ar II, Korea was divided into two parts. viet troops occupied North Korea, and nerican troops occupied South Korea. 1948 North Korea formed a communist vernment, and South Korea formed a public.

In 1950 the North Korean army, which had en trained and equipped by the Soviet nion, invaded South Korea. North Korea anted to make all of Korea communist. orth Korea was also helped by China, hich had become communist in 1949.

United States President Harry S. Truman ickly sent more American soldiers to sup- ort South Korea. The United Nations also nt troops to stop the invasion. About 15 untries were now fighting a new war—the orean War.

So many American soldiers died in the ghting that the Korean War became a ajor issue in the 1952 election for President the United States. Dwight D. Eisenhower, e famous World War II general, promised at if he was elected, he would work to end e war. Soon after his election he kept his omise. By 1953 the North Korean troops d been pushed back into North Korea. A **ase-fire**, or an end to the shooting and mbing, was then declared, and an armistice as signed to stop the fighting. South Korea mained an independent country.

EVIEW *What were the results of the orean War?* North Korean troops were ushed back into North Korea. South Korea mained an independent country.

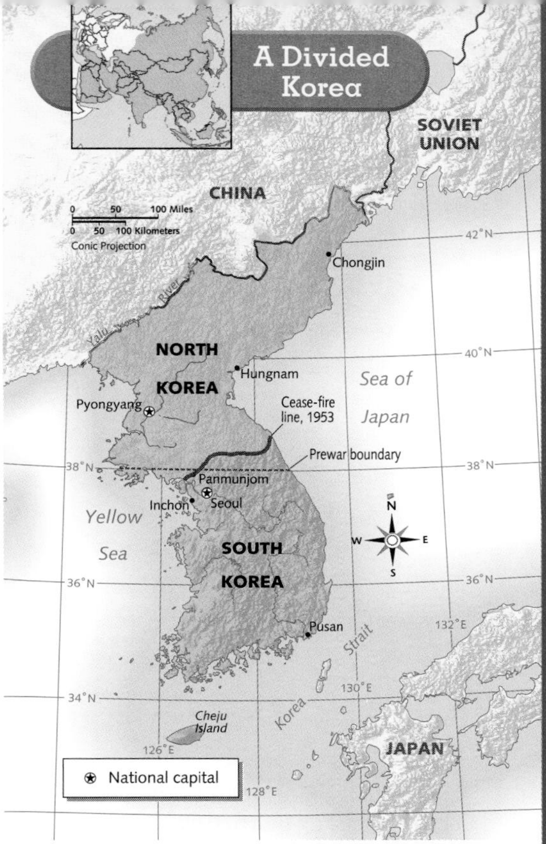

MAP THEME **Movement** At the end of World War II, Soviet troops in Korea were north of the 38th parallel, and American troops were south of it.

■ *How did the cease-fire line of 1953 change the northern boundary of South Korea?*

The Cuban Missile Crisis

In 1961 John F. Kennedy took the oath of fice as President of the United States. Only years old, Kennedy was the youngest erson ever elected President. At his inaugu- tion, the new President tried to inspire Americans to work for the good of their country. He said,

> "Ask not what your country can do for you; ask what you can do for your country."

His energy and his enthusiasm made him especially popular with young people. Soon

The Korean War

Key Content Summary

When communist North Korea invaded the republic of South Korea in 1950, the United States and the United Nations moved quickly to stop the invasion. By 1952 the casualty rate among American soldiers was so high that once elected, President Eisenhower worked out an armistice.

History

Origins, Spread, and Influence Have students analyze why the United States would get involved in another war thousands of miles from its shores.

Visual Analysis

Learn from Maps Have students answer the question in the caption. It gave South Korea territory north of the 38th parallel.

The Cuban Missile Crisis

Key Content Summary

When the Soviet Union began installing missiles in Cuba, just 90 miles from the United States, President John F. Kennedy ordered a blockade of the island. The missile crisis ended when the Soviet Union agreed to stop the shipment of missiles. A year later, President Kennedy was assassinated.

Community Involvement

Have students write a class letter to the local Veterans Administration or Veterans of Foreign Wars organization to request that a veteran of the Korean War come to speak to the class about that war experience. Ask students to learn more about the land and climate of Korea and to prepare a list of questions before the speaker arrives. Assign students to practice their letter-writing skills the day after the speech by writing thank-you letters to the speaker.

Multicultural Link

The Korean War marked the first time the armed forces of the United States were integrated. In late 1950, with the army in need of personnel to help stem communist advances, military units began to be integrated. By August 1951, 30 percent of the U.S. fighting force was integrated. Within a year after the end of the Korean War, integration of the entire U.S. military was complete.

Link to Reading

READ A BIOGRAPHY Have student volunteers read biographies about President John F. Kennedy or Fidel Castro and prepare oral reports to present to the class.

History

Origins, Spread, and Influence Ask students to summarize how the Cold War affected Kennedy's term in office. Have them infer how the United States learned that the Soviets had built launch sites in Cuba.

Visual Analysis

Learn from Maps Refer students to the map and have them locate Florida and Cuba. Help them understand that the Cuban missile crisis brought the Cold War to the doorstep of the United States. Then have students answer the question in the caption. to prevent Soviet ships from reaching Cuba

History

People and Events Across Time and Place Have students recall what they learned about the assassinations of President Lincoln and President McKinley and compare and contrast them with the assassination of President Kennedy. Then have students discuss the risks involved in being a national or world leader. Discuss what steps are taken today to protect U.S. Presidents.

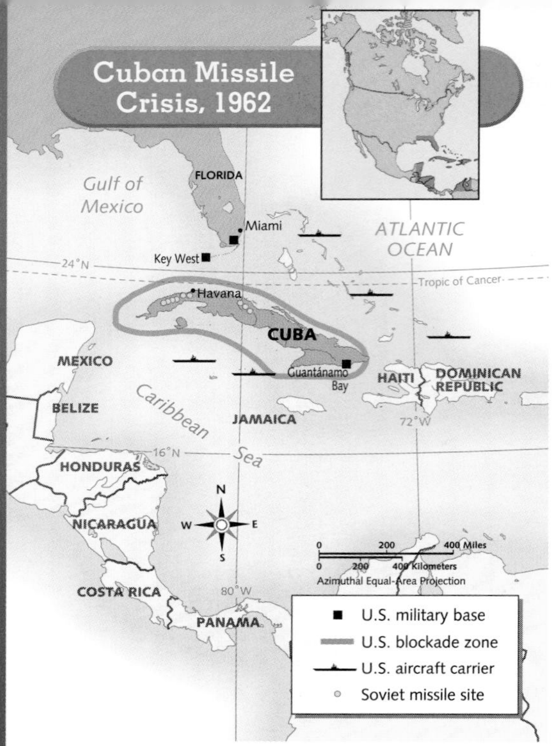

MAP THEME Human-Environment Interactions

President John F. Kennedy (above right) ordered a naval blockade of Cuba during the 1962 missile crisis. He often discussed problems with his brother Attorney General Robert F. Kennedy (above left).

■ *Why do you think U.S. aircraft carriers were placed where they were?*

after he took office, Cold War problems began to take up much of his time.

In October 1962 President Kennedy learned that the Soviet Union had built several launch sites for missiles in Cuba, just 90 miles (145 km) off the southern tip of Florida. A **missile** is a rocket that can carry a bomb over a long distance. Fidel Castro had taken control of Cuba in 1959. With the help of the Soviet Union, Castro had formed a communist government.

Worried that the Soviets would attack the United States from Cuba, Kennedy ordered a blockade of the island nation. The United States Navy would stop Soviet ships that were carrying missiles from reaching Cuba. Americans worried as they listened to the news on radio and television. What if the ships refused to stop? Would there be a war?

Finally, the Soviet Union agreed to stop sending missiles to Cuba and to remove all the missiles that were already there. The United States agreed to end the blockade.

Kennedy's success in handling the missile crisis increased his popularity. But he knew he would have to work hard to be elected President again. On November 22, 1963, the President and Jacqueline Kennedy, his wife, visited Dallas, Texas, to meet with supporters there. They were waving to the crowds as their car drove through the streets. Suddenly shots rang out. President Kennedy was killed. A few hours after the assassination, Vice President Lyndon Baines Johnson took the oath of office as the new President.

REVIEW ***Why did the United States take action when the Soviet Union set up missile bases in Cuba?*** Americans feared that the Soviets would attack the United States from Cuba.

ACTIVITY CHOICES

Extend and Enrich

COOPERATIVE LEARNING

MAKE A TIME LINE Divide the class into four groups, and assign a lesson subsection to each group. Select one student from each group to make a large wall time line that starts in 1945 and ends in 1963. Have the other students in each group write the dates and descriptions of historical events related to their section of the lesson on strips of colored paper to be posted on the time line. Challenge the groups to use library resources to find additional dates and events related to their topics. Have groups share and discuss what they learned from the activity.

TECHNOLOGY

Use TIMELINER™ to complete this activity.

In the early 1960s, Americans worried about being attacked by Soviet missiles. During drills like the one shown here, students were trained to prepare for a missile attack.

The Arms Race

The Cold War helped start an arms race tween the two superpowers. In an **ms race** one country builds weapons protect itself against another country. e other country then builds even more eapons to protect itself. Both the United ates and the Soviet Union believed that ving the most and the strongest weapons ould keep their people safe.

The arms race started with the atom bomb. e Soviet Union knew what atom bombs d done to the Japanese cities of Hiroshima d Nagasaki. It feared the power of the United States to destroy a whole city with one bomb. Soon the Soviet Union was building its own atom bombs.

After the Soviet Union had the atom bomb, however, the United States made an even more powerful bomb. Scientists said that the hydrogen bomb, or the H-bomb, was 1,000 times more powerful than the atom bombs dropped on Japan during World War II. Other atomic weapons were made, too. By the 1960s the superpowers had missiles that could carry bombs to targets halfway around the world.

Both the Americans and the Soviets lived in fear during the Cold War. Some Americans built special shelters below ground as protection in case of an attack. They stocked their shelters with flashlights, radios, first-aid kits, canned food, water, and other supplies. At schools across the country, "duck-and-cover" drills were held to teach children to get under their desks if a missile attack came.

REVIEW ***What was each side's goal in the arms race?*** to have the most and the strongest weapons

ESSON 1 REVIEW

Check Understanding

1. **Remember the Facts** What events contributed to Cold War conflicts?
2. **Recall the Main Idea** How did relations between the United States and the Soviet Union change after World War II?

Think Critically

3. **Think More About It** Why do you think the Soviet Union wanted to drive the Western Allies out of West Berlin?
4. **Personally Speaking** How do you think people in the United States and people in the Soviet Union felt about one another during the Cold War?

Show What You Know

Letter-Writing Activity Imagine that you are living during the Cold War. Write a letter to President Kennedy telling him how you feel about the arms race. Read the letter to your classmates.

The Arms Race

Key Content Summary

As the Cold War progressed, both the United States and the Soviet Union built up their stockpiles of powerful weapons. By the 1960s each side had enough nuclear power to destroy targets halfway around the world.

Civics and Government

Purposes of Government Ask students to evaluate the effectiveness of the arms race. Then ask them to conclude why both the United States and the countries that made up the former Soviet Union have reduced their nuclear arsenals.

3. CLOSE

Have students consider again the Focus question on page 611.

What can happen when powerful friends become enemies?

Have students use what they have learned to analyze the effects that political and social changes can have on relations between two nations.

LESSON 1 REVIEW—Answers

Check Understanding

1. the Soviets' attempt to make West Berlin communist through a blockade of Allied supplies, Soviet support of North Korea's invasion into South Korea, Soviet aid in establishing communism in Cuba and building missile sites there, and the arms race
2. The two former allies became enemies.

Think Critically

3. because the Soviet Union wanted control over all of Berlin since it was in East Germany
4. fearful and distrustful

Show What You Know

Performance Assessment Have students read their letters aloud and share their thoughts about the Cold War.

What to Look For Look for evidence that students understand the facts surrounding the Cold War and the seriousness of the arms-race threat.

Reteach the Main Idea

DRAW A POLITICAL CARTOON (COOPERATIVE LEARNING) Divide the class into small groups. Challenge each group to create political cartoons that represent what happened when the United States and the Soviet Union became enemies after World War II. Have the groups share and discuss their political cartoons before putting them on display.

ACTIVITY BOOK

Reinforce & Extend

Use ACTIVITY BOOK, p. 122.

Objectives

1. Analyze the ways individual astronauts cooperated to achieve a moon landing.
2. Evaluate the importance of the moon landing.

1. ACCESS

Have students share what they know about the U.S. space program and the National Aeronautics and Space Administration (NASA). Explain that the space program began in the United States in the late 1950s and accelerated throughout the 1960s. Have students describe recent space ventures and analyze why the space program is still important today.

The Main Idea

Students examine the events surrounding the first moon landing. They learn about the dangers of the moon flight, the way the mission was conducted, and the significance of the event.

2. BUILD

Key Content Summary

On July 20, 1969, *Apollo 11* was orbiting the moon. Neil Armstrong and Edwin E. "Buzz" Aldrin prepared themselves and the spacecraft *Eagle* for its descent to the moon's surface. With barely enough fuel left to complete the landing, Armstrong skillfully guided the *Eagle* to a safe landing. After making final preparations, Armstrong and Aldrin opened the hatch, climbed down the ladder, and became the first people to walk on the moon.

Auditory Learning

Express Ideas Orally Have one or two volunteers read aloud the introduction to the literature selection. Ask students to explain why President Kennedy set the goal of landing a person on the moon.

LESSON 2

LEARN HISTORY *through* Literature

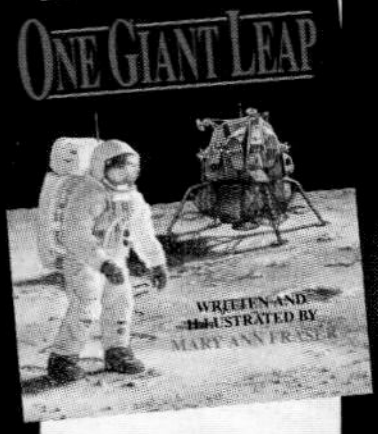

ONE GIANT LEAP

written by Mary Ann Fraser

The United States and the Soviet Union took the Cold War into space. In 1957 the Soviets surprised the United States by launching* Sputnik *(SPUT•nik).* Sputnik *was the world's first space satellite, an object sent by a rocket into an orbit around the Earth.

Because of* Sputnik*, the United States speeded up its own efforts to explore space. In 1958 Congress set up the National Aeronautics and Space Administration, or NASA, to develop the nation's space program. Then, in 1961, President John F. Kennedy set a goal for the United States. The goal was to put a person on the moon by the end of the 1960s.

In 1962 John Glenn became the first American astronaut to orbit the Earth. Then a series of explorations called the Apollo program prepared for a moon landing. In 1968 astronauts in* Apollo 8 *first circled the moon. By the next year NASA was ready to try a moon landing. On July 16, 1969,* Apollo 11 *blasted off from Cape Canaveral, Florida. On board were astronauts Neil Armstrong, Edwin "Buzz" Aldrin, Jr., and Michael Collins. NASA scientists at Mission Control in Houston, Texas, followed their flight closely. Now read the story of the first moon landing four days later.

The astronauts' view of Earth from the moon

616

ACTIVITY CHOICES

Reading Support

USE CONTEXT CLUES Before students read the literature selection, have them work in small groups to brainstorm words and ideas they believe they will come across in the selection. Have them list these words and ideas under headings, such as *Dangers of the Voyage* and *Walking on the Moon*. After they have read the selection, have them review their lists and add or delete terms as appropriate. Lists may include the following:

DANGERS OF THE VOYAGE	WALKING ON THE MOON
fuel supply	safety of the surface
achieving orbit	air supply
landing on the moon	ability to communicate
leaving the moon	inspecting the moon's surface

July 20, 1969

As the sun rose in Houston, Mission
ontrol gently woke the crew. "*Apollo 11,*
pollo 11—good morning from the Black
eam."

Michael Collins replied, "Good
orning, Houston . . . oh my, you guys
ake up early."

The astronauts may not have been ready
o wake up, but this was the day they had
aited and trained for: landing day. After
reakfast and a briefing from Mission
ontrol, Aldrin and Armstrong put on
heir liquid-cooling undergarments.
rabbing hold of the handrails, they
loated into *Eagle*. Collins remained
ehind so he could help his fellow
stronauts if anything went wrong.

On *Apollo 11*'s thirteenth orbit, Collins pushed the switch to release the final latches. Gently the modules drifted apart to become two independent vehicles.

Houston broke through the static as *Eagle* soared from behind the moon. "Roger. How does it look?"

Armstrong was now controlling *Eagle*. He answered, "*Eagle* has wings."

One-and-a-half hours later tension mounted again as *Eagle* followed *Columbia* toward the back side of the moon to begin its descent. In less than 11 minutes Armstrong and Aldrin had to cross 300 miles of the moon's surface in *Eagle*, dropping in a long curve from 50,000 feet to touchdown.

Any equipment failure or miscalculation would mean turning back or certain disaster. If a leg on the lunar module came to rest on a boulder or slope and the module toppled over, *Eagle* would not be able to take off. The men would be stranded. Some scientists thought that the moon's windless surface had a dangerously deep coating of dust. They worried that the module or men would sink into this loose lunar soil.

Apollo 11 blasts off.

617

Understanding the Story

As students read the selection, have them think about the character traits the members of the *Apollo 11* crew must have had. Ask students to analyze the important role of Mission Control.

Q. **What safeguards were put in place before astronauts Armstrong and Aldrin left the *Columbia*?** Mission Control reviewed their instructions, the astronauts put on special protective clothing, and Collins was assigned to stay with the *Columbia* in case he had to rescue Armstrong and Aldrin.

Visual Analysis

Interpret Pictures Have students look at the photographs on pages 616–617.

Q. **How do you think the astronauts felt waiting for takeoff?** nervous, cramped, excited, focused

How did they feel out in space? very excited, in awe, very small

Background

THE LITERATURE SELECTION *One Giant Leap* invites readers to experience the tension and excitement of the first moon landing. They blast into space with the astronauts—Lieutenant Colonel Michael Collins, Mission Commander Neil Armstrong, and Colonel Edwin E. "Buzz" Aldrin—and follow them through their historic mission. The author's illustrations, diagrams, and story, developed from the transcript of *Apollo 11*, bring alive this astonishing accomplishment of the United States space program.

THE AUTHOR Mary Ann Fraser is both author and illustrator of *One Giant Leap.* Fraser received her college degree from the University of California at Los Angeles and her advanced training in art at the Exeter College of Art and Design in England. Other books by Fraser include *Ten Mile Day* and *On Top of the World.*

Meet Individual Needs

ENGLISH LANGUAGE LEARNERS Ask the school or community librarian to locate a videotape of the first moon landing. Show scenes from the videotape in class to help students understand the content of the literature selection.

Understanding the Story

Ask students to identify the steps involved in bringing the *Eagle* to a safe landing, and write those steps on the board. Make sure students understand some of the technical procedures involved.

Q. **At what points during the landing did it seem as though there were problems?** when the astronauts lost direct contact with Mission Control; when the alarm went off and the guidance computer was overloaded with data; when the computer was taking them to a crater littered with ancient boulders, rock, and rubble; when Armstrong was frantically trying to find a safe landing site through the dust clouds; when the fuel was about to run out

Culture

Thought and Expression Have students discuss the reasons journalists packed the newsrooms and millions of people all over the world were glued to their radios or televisions on July 20, 1969. Ask them to identify the emotions people must have felt as they waited for the astronauts to land safely on the moon.

Visual Analysis

Interpret Pictures Have students examine the picture on pages 618–619 and draw conclusions about the surface of the moon.

Back on Earth, hundreds of journalists packed newsrooms while millions of TV viewers and radio listeners tuned in for word of the astronauts. The people of Mission Control waited for the static on their headsets to clear.

Eagle swung around from behind the moon, heading for the landing site on the Sea of Tranquility. Armstrong's voice finally came through. "The burn was on time."

"Current altitude about 46,000 feet, continuing to descend," reported the flight controller in Houston.

Just then ground control lost direct communication with *Eagle*. All commands had to be relayed through Mike Collins in *Columbia*. Armstrong adjusted *Eagle*'s position in flight, and Mission Control tried again to communicate directly. "*Eagle*, Houston. You are go. Take it all at four minutes. Roger, you are go—you are go to continue power descent."

"Roger." Aldrin had heard the message and commented, "And the earth right out our front window."

Suddenly an alarm went off in the cabin. "Twelve-o-two—twelve-o-two!" shouted Armstrong. "Give us the reading on the twelve-o-two program alarm."

The guidance computer was overloaded with data, but Mission Control decided *Eagle* should still proceed with landing. "Roger . . . we got—we're go on that alarm."

Armstrong peered through his small, triangular window. The computer was taking them to a stadium-size crater littered with ancient boulders, rock, and rubble. With the flip of a switch, Armstrong seized full manual control from the computer. Now he had to use all the flying skills he had learned as a pilot.

Activity Choices

Link to Language Arts

WRITE A LETTER Ask a small group of student volunteers to write letters to NASA at the John F. Kennedy Space Center at Cape Canaveral, Florida, and the Lyndon B. Johnson Space Center in Houston, Texas. Have the students request information about the history of the space program, current projects, the training program for astronauts, and the functions of the particular space center. Have the group share information they receive with the class.

COOPERATIVE LEARNING

Technology

Use THE AMAZING WRITING MACHINE™ to complete this writing activity.

Smithsonian Institution®

Go to the Internet site at *http://www.si.edu/harcourt/socialstudies* to visit the exhibit "Apollo to the Moon" at the National Air and Space Museum.

:z Aldrin poses
a photo next to
United States
on the moon.

He adjusted the spacecraft's hovering position while Aldrin guided him. "Lights on. Forward. Good. Forty feet, down two and a half. Picking up some dust. Thirty feet, two and a half down. Faint shadow. Four forward. Four forward, drifting to the right a little." The rocket's firing was creating dust clouds, making it difficult to see.

Armstrong frantically searched for a site. Mission Control interrupted, "30 SECONDS!" Only 30 seconds of fuel for landing remained. Armstrong had to land immediately.

Slowly he lowered the craft. The blue light in the cockpit flashed. "Contact light," reported Aldrin. One of the three probes, like a feeler on a giant insect, had touched ground. "Okay, engine stop." They had landed four miles west of their original target, but still within the planned area.

"Houston, Tranquility Base here. The *Eagle* has landed," said Armstrong.

"Roger, Tranquility, we copy you on the ground," replied Mission Control. "You've got a bunch of guys about to turn blue. We're breathing again. Thanks a lot."

Back on Earth people of all nationalities celebrated the moon landing. But while Americans Armstrong and Aldrin had been skillfully piloting their spacecraft toward the Sea of Tranquility, the [Soviet Union's unmanned] *Luna 15* had crashed into the moon's Sea of Crises at nearly 300 miles per hour.

For several seconds Aldrin and Armstrong, the first humans on the moon, waited for the dust to settle about their spacecraft. Slowly they got their first glimpse of an alien world that had not changed for millions of years.

Understanding the Story

Have students analyze the actions Armstrong and Aldrin took to manage the crises that occurred during the moon landing.

Q. **Why did Armstrong turn off the computer control and land the *Eagle* manually?** The computer could not process the data fast enough and was guiding the craft to a dangerous landing spot; Armstrong believed he could use his skills as a pilot to land the *Eagle*.

How did the astronauts work cooperatively to land safely? Armstrong handled the controls while Aldrin watched out the window to guide him to a safer area.

History

Leaders and Achievers Have students describe the characteristics that made Collins, Armstrong, and Aldrin right for the challenge of the moon-landing project.

Culture

Thought and Expression Have students think about the thoughts and emotions of the people at Mission Control in Houston.

Q. **What does Mission Control mean by the statement, "You've got a bunch of guys about to turn blue"?** The people on the ground were so anxious that they felt as though they could not breathe until they knew that the *Eagle* had landed safely.

.ink to Music

ISTEN TO A MOON SONG Have
udents listen to recordings of songs
at use the moon as a theme. Examples
clude "By the Light of the Silvery Moon,"
On Moonlight Bay," and "Moon
ver." You also may wish to have stu-
ents listen to Ludwig van Beethoven's
oonlight Sonata and Claude
ebussy's *Clair de Lune (Moonlight)*.
ave students speculate on why song-
riters and composers often use the
oon as a theme for their music.

Background

THE MOON IN HISTORY In ancient times the phases of the moon provided a way for people on Earth to measure time. The Romans had a moon goddess named Diana, who used the crescent moon for her bow and moonbeams for her arrows. The ancient Greeks, Egyptians, and Babylonians also had moon goddesses. Some Native Americans celebrated the sun and moon as brother and sister gods.

Link to Science

COOPERATIVE LEARNING

PRESENT FACTS ABOUT THE MOON Assign a small group of students to make a fact chart about the moon. Have them use encyclopedias and other library resources to find important and interesting facts about the moon. Provide them with poster board and ask them to list between 15 and 20 scientific facts about the moon. When group members present their chart to the class, you may wish to have them show some of NASA's photographs of the moon's surface that they find in source books.

Understanding the Story

As students read the last two pages of the selection, have them imagine how they would have felt if they had been Armstrong and Aldrin. Also have students imagine how people in the Soviet Union must have felt about the failure of the *Luna 15* and the success of the American moon mission.

Q. **What do you think was going on in the minds of Armstrong and Aldrin as they stepped off the lunar module?** Possible responses: Will the moon's surface be safe? Will my suit protect me? Will I be able to walk? Will I be able to get back to the lunar module?

Culture

Shared Humanity and Unique Identity
Have students analyze why people all over the world were interested in the moon landing.

Q. **Why was this an event that brought peoples of all cultures together?** No matter what the culture, people have always been curious about and possibly a little awed by the moon.

Geography

Human-Environment Interactions
Have students make inferences about the environment on the moon based on the equipment Armstrong and Aldrin wore.

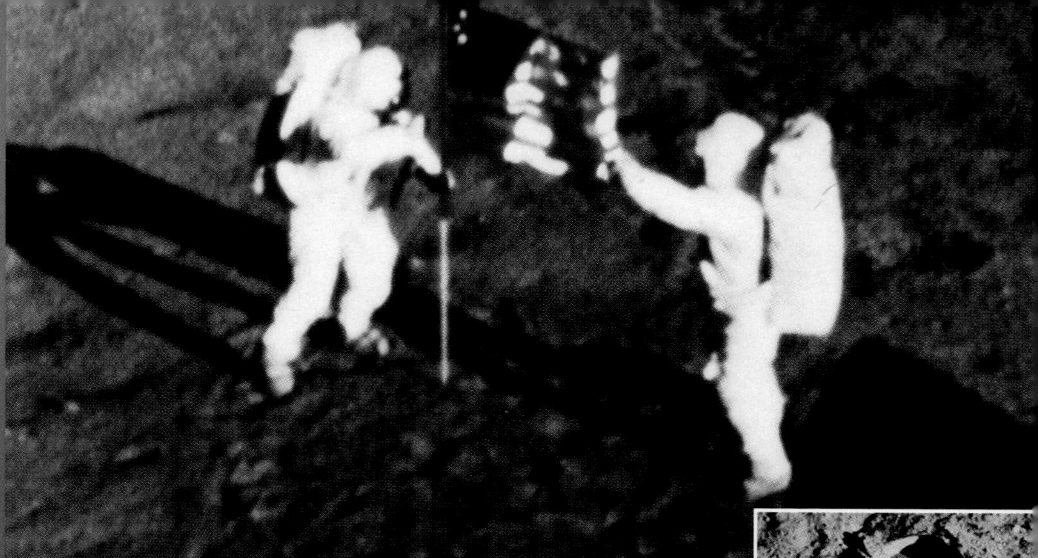

Armstrong (above left) and Aldrin (above right) are photographed on the moon's surface from a camera mounted in the lunar module. Neil Armstrong left his footprint (right) when he took the first step on the moon.

Meanwhile Collins in *Columbia* orbited to the back side of the moon, totally on his own for the first time.

A billion people from all over the world anxiously waited for the first steps onto the moon. Aldrin and Armstrong were no longer being viewed as Americans, but as representatives of all humanity.

With the last snap of their helmets in place, Armstrong and Aldrin could see but could no longer hear, taste, smell, or feel anything outside their space suits. The suits were their only protection against the moon's extreme temperatures, which ranged from –247 to 212 degrees Fahrenheit. Any tear in the suit could be fatal.

With Aldrin guiding him, Armstrong carefully stepped down the nine rungs o the ladder toward the moon's airless, waterless surface.

"I'm at the foot of the ladder. . . . The surface appears very, very fine grained a you get close to it." Armstrong could see that *Eagle*'s landing pads had barely sun into the lunar dust. The moon's surface seemed safe. "I'm going to step off the LM [lunar module] now."

Exactly 109 hours, 24 minutes and 15 seconds into the mission, Armstrong stepped off the landing pad and placed the first human footprint on the moon.

"That's one small step for man, one giant leap for mankind," he said.

620 • Unit 10

Activity Choices

Link to Physical Education

COOPERATIVE LEARNING

REPORT ON ASTRONAUT TRAINING Have a small group of students use library resources and information from NASA to write a report about astronaut training. Ask the group to include the kinds of physical fitness and health tests candidates must take even before they are admitted to the astronaut program. Then have students research the kinds of physical training and health tests astronauts must undergo after they have been accepted into the program. Have group members share what they have learned with the class and ask students to discuss any aspirations they may have to become astronauts.

Extend and Enrich

COOPERATIVE LEARNING

MAKE A DIORAMA Divide the class into groups. Have each group make a diorama of an accomplishment in either the Soviet space program or the U.S. space program after 1969. Possible scenarios include other lunar landings made during the Apollo program, the Soviet Union's orbiting space station, and probes sent to Mars, Venus, Jupiter, Saturn, Uranus, and Neptune. Have the members of each group conduct library research, develop a plan for the diorama, gather materials, and participate in putting the diorama together. Ask each group to assign a spokesperson to share and explain its diorama.

He had meant to say, "one small step for a man," t in his excitement and nervousness he left out e *a*. A few moments later Aldrin joined him. With those first prints in the lunar dust the ople of Earth proved they could reach beyond eir planet and touch the moon. Neil Armstrong, zz Aldrin, and Michael Collins, through skill, urage, and teamwork, had helped realize nturies of dreams. Other men and women uld now follow in their footsteps.

After a total of six moon landings, SA began new space explorations. manned spacecraft were launched into the solar system to learn re about other planets. Today ace shuttles and space stations bit the Earth, and astronauts nduct scientific experiments space.

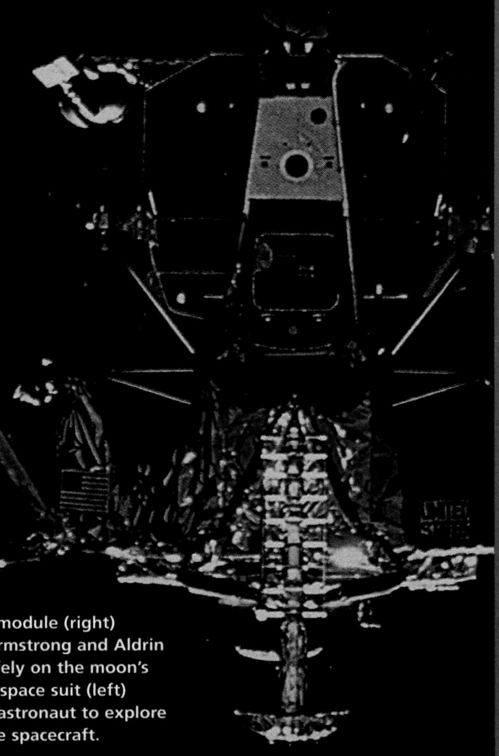

The lunar module (right) allowed Armstrong and Aldrin to land safely on the moon's surface. A space suit (left) allows an astronaut to explore outside the spacecraft.

LITERATURE REVIEW

1. When did the first astronauts land on the moon?
2. What kinds of problems do you think the scientists at NASA had to solve in building a spacecraft to carry people to the moon?
3. Draw pictures about the space program. You may want to draw the *Apollo 11* astronauts landing on the moon or the space shuttle taking off or landing. Write captions for your pictures and share them with your classmates.

Reteach the Main Idea

ROLE-PLAY AN INTERVIEW (COOPERATIVE LEARNING) Divide the class into several groups and ask each group to assign members to play the roles of news reporters, the President of the United States, and astronauts Armstrong, Aldrin, and Collins. Have each group prepare and practice role-playing a scene in which the reporters interview the President and the astronauts at a press conference held after the moon landing. Tell the news reporters to focus their questions on the reasons for the push to beat the Soviet Union into space, the value a moon landing has for the United States, how the astronauts felt about the experience, and why Armstrong thought the accomplishment was "one giant leap for mankind." After each group has presented its interview to the other groups, allow time for students to discuss the role-playing experience.

Understanding the Story

Have students analyze the impact of the moon landing. Explain to them that the statement Armstrong made when he first set foot on the moon's surface is now famous and is often quoted.

Q. **What do you think Armstrong meant by the statement he made when he stepped onto the moon's surface?** Although he himself was taking only a small step, his small step represented a great achievement for all people.

3. CLOSE

Ask the following question to focus students on what individuals working together can achieve.

What are some recent examples of important achievements generated by individuals working together toward a goal?

Have students use what they have learned about the knowledge, effort, and skill that went into the first moon landing to identify other great achievements today.

LITERATURE REVIEW—Answers

1. July 20, 1969
2. designing a smaller spacecraft that could leave the main spacecraft and travel independently to the moon, having enough fuel for the landing and return, producing a spacecraft and spacesuits that could withstand the environment of the moon's surface, creating a failure-proof communication system
3. Look for evidence that students comprehend the goals and accomplishments of the space program.

ACTIVITY BOOK

Reinforce & Extend

Use ACTIVITY BOOK, p. 123.

Objectives

1. Explain why the Supreme Court ordered an end to segregation in public schools.
2. Analyze the Montgomery bus boycott.
3. Summarize Martin Luther King, Jr.'s, role in promoting the passage of the Civil Rights Act of 1964.
4. Compare and contrast the views of Malcolm X and Martin Luther King, Jr.
5. Identify the ways American Indians and Mexican Americans worked for change.
6. Discuss the rights women had gained by the 1970s.

Vocabulary

nonviolence (p. 623) integration (p. 624)

1. ACCESS

The Focus Question

Ask students to give examples of how people in their community have worked together to improve their city or town.

The Main Idea

In this lesson students learn how people worked to change laws that would help to improve people's lives in the United States. After students have read the lesson, ask them to make a chart that lists the new laws.

2. BUILD

A Court Ruling

Key Content Summary

The NAACP supported a group of African American parents when they appealed to the Supreme Court for equal rights in their children's education. In 1954 the Court ordered an end to segregation in public schools.

LESSON 3

FOCUS
How do individuals today work to improve life in the United States?

Main Idea As you read, look for ways individuals worked to improve life in the United States in the twentieth century.

Vocabulary
nonviolence
integration

The Struggle fo Equal Rights

In the years after World War II, Americans hoped for peace. Instead, they were in a cold war and an arms race wi the Soviet Union. The struggle to bring peace to an uneasy world was not the only problem that Americans faced after World War II. People across the country continued to strugg for equal rights.

A Court Ruling

Seven-year-old Linda Brown of Topeka, Kansas, wanted t go to school with the other children in her neighborhood. Sh did not understand why state laws in Kansas said that African American children had to go to separate schools. Federal laws supported this segregation, or separation of th races, as long as the separate schools were equal. In most cases, however, they were not.

Thirteen African American families, among them Linda Brown's, decided to try to get these laws changed. The NAACP agreed to help them. One of its lawyers, Thurgood Marshall, presented the case before the United States Supreme Court. Marshall argued that separate schools did not provide equal education.

In 1954 the Supreme Court made a decision that supported what Thurgood Marshall had said. Chief Justice Earl Warren said, "In the field of education the doctrine [idea] o 'separate but equal' has no place." The Court ordered an end to segregation i public schools. However, many states were slow to obey that order. Their schools and other public places remained segregated.

REVIEW *What did the Supreme Court say about segregation in publi schools?* that it has no place in the field of education

These lawyers—(left to right) George Hayes, Thurgood Marshall, and James Nabrit—argued against school segregation. They are standing outside the Supreme Court Building just after the Court's decision to end segregation in public schools.

ACTIVITY CHOICES

Reading Support

PREVIEW AND READ THE LESSON Provide students with the following visual framework.

WORKING FOR EQUAL RIGHTS	
YEAR	ACTION
1954	Supreme Court orders an end to segregation in public schools
1955	African Americans boycott Montgomery buses
1964	Congress passes Civil Rights Act
1965	California grape pickers go on strike
1966	Activists form the National Organization for Women
1975	Congress passes the Indian Self-Determination Act

The Montgomery Bus Boycott

On December 1, 1955, Rosa Parks of
Iontgomery, Alabama, got on a city bus and
it in the middle section. Under Alabama law,
frican Americans had to sit in the back. They
ould sit in the middle section only if the seats
ere not needed for white passengers.

As the bus filled up, the bus driver told
osa Parks to give up her seat to a white man.
he refused. The bus driver called the police,
nd Parks was arrested and taken to jail.

Many African Americans were angry when
ey heard what had happened. They held a
eeting and decided to show the bus com-
any's owners how they felt. They knew the
ompany needed the money from African
mericans' bus fares. So they passed the
ord—"Don't take the bus on Monday." A
us boycott began.

One of the leaders of the protest was
Iartin Luther King, Jr., a young minister
Montgomery. For more than a year, King
nd other African Americans boycotted the buses. King said that by working together they could bring about change peacefully. At last the Supreme Court ruled that all public transportation companies had to end segregation.

King believed in using **nonviolence**, or peaceful ways, to bring about change. He said that nonviolence would change people's minds and hearts, while violence would only make matters worse. So, many African Americans protested segregation in other public places—lunch counters, bus stations, schools, and other public buildings—in non-violent ways.

The protesters often used songs to tell their goals. They sang,

> "We shall overcome,
> We shall overcome,
> We shall overcome someday.
> Oh, deep in my heart, I do believe,
> We shall overcome someday."

REVIEW ***What did the protesters hope the Montgomery bus boycott would do?*** They hoped it would end segregation on buses.

osa Parks (below) is fingerprinted after her arrest for
fusing to move to the back of the bus. During the
56 bus boycott in Montgomery, a bus (right) is
most empty.

Civics and Government

Rights and Responsibilities of Citizens Have students identify the way people against school segregation worked to win equal rights and analyze why the support of the NAACP was important.

The Montgomery Bus Boycott

Key Content Summary

When Rosa Parks was arrested after refusing to move to the rear of a Montgomery, Alabama, bus, Martin Luther King, Jr., was among the leaders who organized African Americans in a nonviolent bus boycott.

History

Contributors to Change Have students analyze why African Americans admired the courage displayed by Rosa Parks.

Economics

Economic Systems and Institutions Have students conclude why the bus boycott was an effective way for African Americans to get their message across.

"PRIMARY SOURCE"

Source: *Ebony Pictorial History of Black America.* Editors of Ebony. Johnson Publishing Company, 1971.

Smithsonian Institution®

Go to the Internet site at *http://www.si.edu/harcourt/socialstudies* to visit the exhibit "Sitting for Justice" on the Timeline at the National Museum of American History.

Link to Music

INTERPRET LYRICS Provide students with copies of the lyrics to "We Shall Overcome" and to the spiritual "Free at Last." Have students read and analyze the lyrics. Then have them discuss the reasons songs such as these helped give African Americans a sense of unity and the courage to continue their struggle for equal rights.

Meet Individual Needs

ADVANCED LEARNERS Have students use library resources to find out how African Americans traveled around Montgomery, Alabama, during the long bus boycott. Also have them find out how the boycott affected the bus company. Have students use the information they gather to prepare an in-depth news report to be presented to the class. The students might wish to conduct "interviews" of citizens and political leaders in Montgomery as part of their report.

Civil Rights Marches

Key Content Summary

Martin Luther King, Jr., quickly became the leader in the fight against segregation. In April 1963, he led marches in Birmingham, Alabama, and called for integration. Later, at a march in Washington, D.C., he delivered his famous "I Have a Dream" speech. In 1964 a new Civil Rights Act was passed.

History

Leaders and Achievers Have students analyze why the marches led by Martin Luther King, Jr., were effective in bringing about change. Have students reread the quotations from his "I Have a Dream" speech both on this page and at the beginning of the chapter.

"PRIMARY SOURCE"

Source: *Lend Me Your Ears: Great Speeches in History.* William Safire. W. W. Norton, 1997.

Working for Change

Key Content Summary

King's nonviolent methods were challenged by Malcolm X, who wanted change to happen faster. Even though both Malcolm X and King were assassinated, African Americans continued to work for change.

HERITAGE

Martin Luther King, Jr., Federal Holiday

Dr. Martin Luther King, Jr., was born on January 15, 1929, in Atlanta, Georgia. With the Montgomery bus boycott, he became a leader of the Civil Rights movement. He worked tirelessly for racial justice, despite many arrests and many threats on his life. On April 4, 1968, King was assassinated. Just four days later, people in Congress began working to make his birthday a federal holiday. But it was not until 1983 that a law was signed making the third Monday in January Martin Luther King, Jr., Day. The holiday was first observed on January 20, 1986. Today people celebrate the day with parades and other events. The special activities help them think about how they can keep alive King's dream of equality, justice, and peace.

Civil Rights Marches

Many African Americans looked to Martin Luther King, Jr., as their leader in the fight against segregation and for civil rights. In April 1963 King led marches in Birmingham, Alabama. The marchers wanted an end to all segregation. They called for **integration**, or the bringing together of people of all races in education, jobs, and housing.

For eight days there were marches. Many of the marchers were arrested, and King was one of those taken to jail. While King was held in jail, he wrote, "We know through painful experience that freedom is never voluntarily given. . . . It must be demanded."

Later that year 250,000 people from all di ferent backgrounds gathered for a march in Washington, D.C. The marchers were showing their support for a new civil rights law that President Kennedy had asked the United States Congress to pass. As the marchers assembled in front of the Lincoln Memorial, Martin Luther King, Jr., spoke to them of his hopes. He said,

> "I have a dream that one day on the red hills of Georgia the sons of former slaves and the sons of former slaveowners will be able to sit down together at the table of brotherhood. . . ."

In 1964 Congress passed the new civil rights law. The Civil Rights Act of 1964 mad segregation in public places illegal. It also said that people of all races should have equal job opportunities.

REVIEW ***What was the importance of the Civil Rights Act of 1964?***

It made segregation in public places illegal and said tha people of all races should have equal job opportunities.

Working for Change

In 1964 Martin Luther King, Jr., received the Nobel Peace Prize. He won the award fo his use of nonviolent ways to bring about change. Not all African American leaders shared King's belief in nonviolent protest, however. One of them, Malcolm X, wanted change to happen faster.

Malcolm X was named Malcolm Little when he was born. He changed his last nam to X to stand for the unknown African name his family had lost through slavery.

Malcolm X was a member of the Nation of Islam, or the Black Muslims. In his early speeches he called for a complete separation between white people and black people. Only in this way, he said, could African Americans truly be free. Malcolm X believe that freedom should be brought about "by

ACTIVITY CHOICES

Meet Individual Needs

AUDITORY LEARNERS Have the school librarian locate a copy of Martin Luther King, Jr.'s, "I Have a Dream" speech. Assign one or more students in the class to deliver the speech as they think King would have. Ask the remainder of the class to listen carefully and be prepared to identify and analyze the main points made by King in his speech. An alternative would be to play for the class a videotape of King making his speech.

Link to Language Arts

WRITE A BIOGRAPHICAL SKETCH Assign each student a leader or achiever who worked for equal rights. Examples include Rosa Parks, Martin Luther King, Jr., Thurgood Marshall, Chief Justice Earl Warren, President John Kennedy, President Lyndon Johnson, Malcolm X, César Chávez, Betty Friedan, Sandra Day O'Connor, Barbara Jordan, and Shirley Chisholm. Ask students to use library resources to write and illustrate a biographical sketch about the person, focusing on his or her contribution to the struggle for equal rights.

roud of his African heritage, Malcolm X visited Egypt in 1964.

ny means necessary." Later, after a trip to he Islamic holy city of Mecca in April 1964, e talked less about separation and more bout cooperation among groups.

Malcolm X had little time to act on his deas. In February 1965 he was assassinated. hen, in April 1968, Martin Luther King, Jr., lso was assassinated.

Even though they had lost two important eaders, African Americans continued to ork for change. Voting is one way that eople bring about change. Knowing this, ivil rights workers helped register African mericans to vote. By 1968 more than half of ll African Americans who were old enough o vote were registered voters.

REVIEW ***How did Malcolm X's views hange later in his life?*** He talked less about separation and more bout cooperation among groups.

Other Groups Claim Their Rights

Following the lead of the African merican Civil Rights movement, other roups of Americans began to organize for hange. They, too, wanted equal rights under he law.

American Indians formed groups to work or the rights that they had been guaranteed in earlier treaties with the federal government. Although the government had promised these rights, in many cases the treaties had not been honored. Groups such as the National Congress of American Indians, the National Tribal Chairman's Association, and the American Indian Movement (AIM) began to work for American Indian rights. In 1975 the Indian Self-Determination and Educational Assistance Act was signed into law. For the first time Indian tribes were allowed to run their own businesses and health and education programs.

In the 1960s César Chávez organized a group that would become the United Farm Workers. Its members were mostly Mexican Americans. Like Martin Luther King, Jr., Chávez called for nonviolent action. In 1965 he called a strike of California grape pickers and started a boycott of grapes across the country. His goal was to get better wages and to improve working conditions. In 1970 Chávez reached agreement with the growers and helped the workers gain more rights.

REVIEW ***What did groups such as the American Indian Movement and the United Farm Workers want to achieve?*** equal rights under the law

César Chávez (center) became a leader of labor organizations for farmworkers. Chávez was still working for the rights of farmworkers when he died in 1993.

625

History

Contributors to Change Ask students to compare and contrast the methods and beliefs of Malcolm X with those of Martin Luther King, Jr.

***Q.* Why do you think Malcolm X changed the emphasis of his efforts from separation to cooperation?** He may have realized that it is harder to bring about change when people become angry and do not try to work together.

Other Groups Claim Their Rights

Key Content Summary

Other groups of Americans learned from the African American experience and began to demand their rights. These groups included Mexican Americans and American Indians.

Civics and Government

Rights and Responsibilities Have students identify the rights denied American Indians and summarize the actions taken to gain their rights.

History

Origins, Spread, and Influence Have students speculate on why César Chávez copied the nonviolent methods of Martin Luther King, Jr., in helping the farmworkers gain more rights.

Background

CÉSAR CHÁVEZ Up to the age of 10, César Chávez enjoyed his family's farm in Yuma, Arizona. In 1937 his parents lost their farm because of the Great Depression. They moved to California and became migrant workers. During those years Chávez learned about the unfair treatment of migrant workers. As an adult, Chávez took on leadership positions in the community and in organizing the migrant workers. Although Chávez received numerous death threats as a union leader, he believed that the "truest act of courage, the strongest act of manliness, is to sacrifice ourselves for others in a totally nonviolent struggle for justice."

Extend and Enrich

MAKE BANNERS AND POSTERS Divide the class into several groups. Challenge each group to imagine that they are fighting for equal rights related to one of the issues in the lesson. Ask them to make banners and posters to carry in a demonstration for their rights. The banners and posters should detail the rights they are demanding. Have groups share and discuss their banners and posters.

The Women's Rights Movement

Key Content Summary
Groups such as the National Organization for Women formed to work for women's rights. By the 1970s new laws had given women more job opportunities.

Visual Analysis

Learn from Graphs Have students answer the questions in the caption. about 34 million; about 2.5 times as many

3. CLOSE

Have students consider again the Focus question on page 622.

How do individuals today work to improve life in the United States?

Have students compare the past efforts of various people to improve life with the efforts of people today.

LESSON 3 REVIEW—Answers

Check Understanding

1. Martin Luther King, Jr., Thurgood Marshall, Chief Justice Earl Warren, President John F. Kennedy, Malcolm X, César Chávez, and Betty Friedan
2. appealed to the Supreme Court, defied local segregation laws, confronted federal authorities, organized boycotts and marches, formed organizations, won political office

Think Critically

3. People feel better about themselves, work better, and are happier if they are treated equally. In addition, the principles of democracy are based on natural rights and the equal treatment of all people.
4. All people have the right to vote; people may not be discriminated against because of their race or gender and schools must not segregate students on the basis of race.

Show What You Know

Performance Assessment Have student volunteers role-play their conversations for the class.

What to Look For Look for evidence that students understand the significance of King's speech.

SOURCES: *Statistical Abstract of the United States; Historical Statistics of the United States*

Women in the Labor Force, 1960–1990

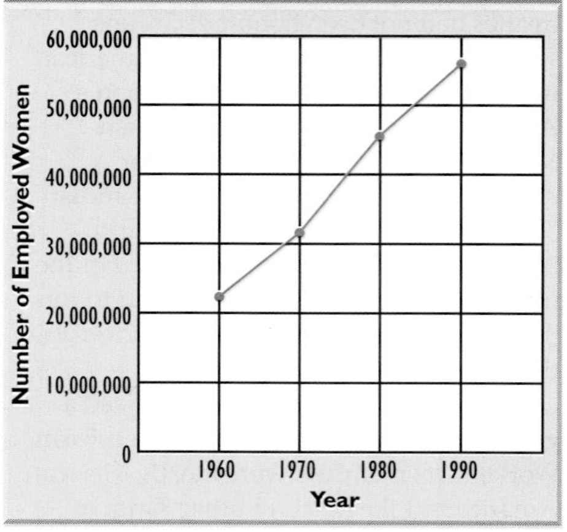

LEARNING FROM GRAPHS This graph shows how the number of women who worked outside the home increased from 1960 to 1990.

- *About how many more women were employed in 1990 than in 1960? About how many times as many were employed in 1990 than in 1960?*

The Women's Rights Movement

Although the Civil Rights Act of 1964 said that all people should have equal job opportunities, many jobs still were not open to women. When men and women did have the same kind of job, women were often paid less than men. As a result, in 1966 writer Betty Friedan and others started the National Organization for Women, or NOW.

NOW and other women's rights groups helped elect many women to public office. They believed that these women would be able to get unfair laws changed.

By the 1970s new laws had been passed saying that employers must treat men and women equally. No job could be open to men only or women only. As a result, more women began careers in law, medicine, and business. Some became astronauts, construction workers, and firefighters. Others won elections and became members of Congress, governors of states, or mayors of cities. In 1981 Sandra Day O'Connor became the first woman appointed to the United States Supreme Court. In 1984 Geraldine Ferraro became the first woman nominated for Vice President by a major political party. Today women hold many important positions in government and in private companies.

REVIEW *What rights had women gained by the 1970s?* the right to equal job opportunities and the right to be treated equally by employers

LESSON 3 REVIEW

Check Understanding

1. **Remember the Facts** Who were some of the main civil rights leaders in the United States in the twentieth century?
2. **Recall the Main Idea** How did individuals work to improve life in the United States in the twentieth century?

Think Critically

3. **Think More About It** Why is it important for everyone to be treated equally?
4. **Past to Present** What rights do people have today as a result of the many struggles in the 1950s and 1960s?

Show What You Know

Simulation Activity Imagine that it is 1963, and you are listening to Martin Luther King, Jr., speak at the march in Washington, D.C. With a partner, role-play a conversation between you and another marcher. Discuss how you feel about King's speech.

ACTIVITY CHOICES

ACTIVITY BOOK

Reinforce & Extend

Use ACTIVITY BOOK, p. 124.

Reteach the Main Idea

COOPERATIVE LEARNING

MAKE AN OUTLINE Divide the class into groups. Have each group create an outline that identifies the groups of people that worked for equal rights, details the methods they used, and describes the gains they made. Ask the groups to share their outlines. Use their ideas to create a class outline on the board.

Participation Skills

Skills

Act as a Responsible Citizen

1. Why Learn This Skill?

Democratic nations need responsible citizens. Citizens must know what is happening in their country, choose wise leaders, and take part in government. When a nation faces problems, its citizens may need to take action to solve those problems.

2. Remember What You Have Read

You have read about the struggle for civil rights in the United States during the 1950s and 1960s. Many citizens took part in the Civil Rights movement, which won important rights for African Americans. Martin Luther King, Jr., was a leader of this movement. The peaceful protests he led caught the attention of people around the world. King was not the only citizen to make a difference in the Civil Rights movement. Rosa Parks, who refused to give up her seat on a bus in Montgomery, Alabama, was one of hundreds of ordinary citizens to take part. Many risked their lives as they worked to gain civil rights for all.

Martin Luther King, Jr., used his skills as a public speaker to help the Civil Rights movement. Here he addresses a huge crowd during the March on Washington.

3. Understand the Process

Acting as a responsible citizen is not always as difficult as it was during the struggle for civil rights. It can be as simple as listening to the news or voting. It does, however, require both thought and action.

Civil rights workers followed these five steps to act as responsible citizens:

1. They learned about the problems of prejudice and injustice in their country.
2. They thought about what could be done to bring about change.
3. They decided how to bring about change in a way that would be good for the whole country.
4. Each person decided what contribution he or she could best make.
5. People worked as individuals or with others to bring about change.

4. Think and Apply

BUILDING CITIZENSHIP

Some acts of citizenship, such as voting, can be done only by adults. Others can be done by citizens of almost any age. The steps above can help anyone know how to act as a responsible citizen. Use the five steps as you decide on ways you and your classmates might act as responsible citizens of your community.

Community Involvement

Invite a representative of a community civic organization to talk with the students about responsible citizenship. Ask the visitor to discuss contributions that can be made by students.

TRANSPARENCY

Use TRANSPARENCY 49.

Reteach the Skill

IDENTIFY RESPONSIBLE CITIZENS Have students look through newspapers and magazines to find examples of responsible citizenship. Have them use the five steps to analyze the action taken by each responsible citizen. Do all of the steps apply? How was the action important to the community's or nation's well-being?

MODEL & APPLY SKILLS

Objectives

1. Analyze examples of responsible citizenship.
2. Apply the steps for acting as a responsible citizen.

1. ACCESS

Ask students to review the responsibilities of citizens that they learned about in Unit 5. Discuss with students why democratic nations cannot endure without responsible citizens.

Review the information about the Civil Rights movement from Lesson 3 and from Remember What You Have Read. Point out that many of the movement's members were ordinary citizens.

2. BUILD

Use examples from the Civil Rights movement to model on the board the steps in Understand the Process. For example:

1. African Americans in the South were often prevented from voting.
2. They considered violent and nonviolent methods of bringing about changes.
3. They chose nonviolent methods.
4. Some marched; others registered to vote or helped others register.
5. Many worked as parts of organizations.

3. CLOSE

Have students complete the activity in Think and Apply. Encourage them to follow up on their discussions with responsible action.

ACTIVITY BOOK

Practice & Apply

Use ACTIVITY BOOK, p. 125.

Objectives

1. Identify the causes and effects of inflation during Lyndon Johnson's presidency.
2. Analyze why Americans were divided over the Vietnam War.
3. Summarize the Watergate scandal and the resolution to the war in Vietnam.

Vocabulary

hawk (p. 629) scandal (p. 630)
dove (p. 629)

1. ACCESS

The Focus Question

Have students recall examples of how people's opinions have affected the actions of the United States government in the past. Ask students to cite examples of how people's opinions affect government action today.

The Main Idea

In this lesson students learn how the United States became involved in the war in Vietnam and how public opinion in the United States eventually pressured the government to bring United States troops home. After students have read the lesson, have them analyze the power of public opinion.

2. BUILD

The Vietnam War

Key Content Summary

In the late 1950s and early 1960s, the United States became involved in a conflict between North Vietnam and South Vietnam. At the same time millions of dollars were spent on Great Society programs to reduce poverty in the United States. The costs of the war and the Great Society programs led to inflation.

LESSON 4

FOCUS
How can people's opinions affect the actions of their government?

Main Idea As you read, think about how people's opinions brought about change during the 1960s and 1970s.

Vocabulary
hawk
dove
scandal

Vietnam War and Protests at Home

While many groups were trying to win better treatment and equal rights, President Lyndon Johnson was working on government programs to make life better for all Americans. These programs were part of Johnson's dream—what he called the Great Society. Johnson built on programs that President Franklin Roosevelt brought about during the New Deal. Johnson's Great Society programs included medical care for older people and help with education, housing, and jobs for those who needed it.

Between 1965 and 1968, President Johnson was able to get Congress to pass many new laws. In three years he got more programs started than any other President except Franklin Roosevelt. Like Roosevelt, however, Johnson led the country during a time of war—the Vietnam War. Many people thought the Vietnam War was unnecessary and wrong.

The Vietnam War

Like Korea, Vietnam was divided into two countries after World War II. North Vietnam became a communist country, and South Vietnam became a republic. In the late 1950s South Vietnamese communists, called the Vietcong, tried to take over the South Vietnamese government. They were helped by North

Many American soldiers reached Vietnam by ship. Soldiers' helmets (inset) were covered in different shades of green to help the soldiers blend in with the jungle.

628

ACTIVITY CHOICES

Reading Support

DEVELOP THE LESSON VOCABULARY Divide the class into small groups, and have each group of students write the following words and names on index cards.

Great Society Vietcong marches Gulf of Tonkin hawk dove draft cards Watergate scandal communism inflation protests

Ask each group to classify the words in categories such as *United States Programs, United States Issues,* and *The Vietnam War.* After students have read the lesson, have the groups check their classifications and change them as necessary.

ietnam. Between 1956 and 1962, the United :ates sent money, war supplies, and soldiers help South Vietnam fight the Vietcong.

By the time Johnson became President in 63, the Vietcong were winning the war. hen, in August 1964, it was reported that a orth Vietnamese gunboat attacked a United :ates Navy ship in the Gulf of Tonkin near ietnam. Johnson sent more soldiers to South ietnam to prevent another attack. The sol- iers also fought the Vietcong.

When United States and South Vietnamese oops failed to defeat the Vietcong quickly, e United States sent planes to bomb North ietnam. Johnson hoped the bombing would op the flow of supplies from North Vietnam the Vietcong. He also sent more troops to outh Vietnam. By 1968 more than 500,000 nited States soldiers were serving there.

The Vietnam War now was costing the nited States billions of dollars each year. t the same time, President Johnson was arting many of his Great Society programs. hnson said that the nation could afford oth. As it turned out, he was wrong. To pay r both the Vietnam War and the programs the Great Society, the government had to orrow a lot of money. This borrowing led inflation. When there is inflation, people n buy less with the money they earn. A ountry's economy suffers.

EVIEW ***How did the Vietnam War affect e economy of the United States?*** It caused flation.

SOURCE: *Statistical Abstract of the United States*

Rate of Inflation, 1960–1990

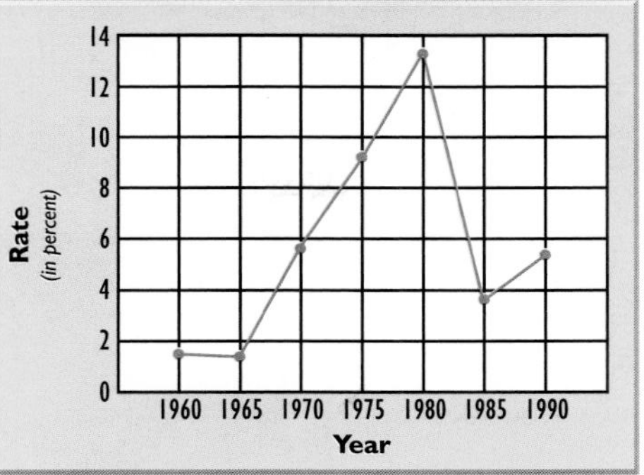

LEARNING FROM GRAPHS This graph shows how inflation increased during the 1960s and 1970s and then decreased during the 1980s.
■ *How was the rate of inflation related to the country's changing role in the war?*

Americans Are Divided

The Vietnam War divided merican public opinion. Some eople said the war was needed stop the spread of commu- ism. Others said it was a civil ar that should be settled by e Vietnamese without out- de help.

This division was also seen in the government. Most government leaders were either hawks or doves. **Hawks** were people who supported the war. **Doves** were those who wanted the war to end.

As the number of Americans killed in Vietnam climbed into the thousands, more and more people began to oppose the war. All over the United States, protests and

President Lyndon B. Johnson had much on his mind in 1968. Here he is shown preparing for a major speech on Vietnam.

629

History

Origins, Spread, and Influence Have students compare United States involvement in the Vietnam War with its involvement in the Korean War.

Q. **What was the main concern of U.S. government leaders in both wars?** to stop the spread of communism

Economics

Productivity and Economic Growth Write a list on the board as students volunteer examples of war costs. Write a second list that shows students examples of Great Society programs, such as Medicare, housing aid, aid for education, and aid to improve living standards for the poor.

Visual Analysis

Learn from Graphs Have students answer the question in the caption. As the United States became more involved in the war, the inflation rate increased.

Americans Are Divided

Key Content Summary

Public opinion about the war in Vietnam was divided. Antiwar protests and marches grew in number as the death toll of American soldiers rose. In 1968 Americans elected Richard M. Nixon to the presidency on the promise of "an honorable end to the war."

Background

ROBERT MCNAMARA During he Kennedy and Johnson presiden- :ies, Robert McNamara served as ecretary of defense. In 1995 he pub- ished a book entitled *In Retrospect: The Tragedy and Lessons of Vietnam.* n this book McNamara reports that Vietnamese officials have told him that he Gulf of Tonkin incident—in which a North Vietnamese gunboat was said o have attacked an American ship— never happened.

Multicultural Link

The Vietcong were the guerrilla and terrorist forces sent by communist North Vietnam into South Vietnam. The term *Vietcong* is a shortened form of the words *Viet Congsan,* meaning "Vietnamese communists." The Vietcong blew up roads and bridges, destroyed railroads, attacked farming villages, and killed local South Vietnamese leaders.

Background

VIETNAM The Vietnamese ruled Vietnam from the 1400s to the 1800s. In 1858 French troops began to attack southern Vietnam. France took control of all of Vietnam and ruled it until 1940 when the Japanese seized Indochina during World War II. In 1954 Vietnam was divided into two parts by international agreement. In South Vietnam the people elected a president. In North Vietnam the communists took over. In 1957 the Vietcong began raids on South Vietnam in an attempt to take over the country.

Civics and Government

Civic Values and Democratic Principles Have students relate freedom of speech and freedom of assembly to the strong expressions of public opinion about the war in Vietnam. Have them analyze the advantages and disadvantages of having those freedoms during wartime.

***Q.* How did public opinion about Vietnam affect the U.S. government?** Leaders were divided; Johnson decided not to run for reelection; people voted for a candidate who promised peace.

Geography

Location Refer students to a wall map of the world and have them locate Vietnam in relation to the United States.

Visual Analysis

Learn from Maps Have students answer the question in the caption. to bypass the South Vietnamese and U.S. troops

Nixon Resigns

Key Content Summary

The Watergate scandal marred President Nixon's second term and led to his resignation. Prior to his resignation, Nixon had worked to bring the Vietnam War to an end. In January 1973, Nixon agreed to a cease-fire.

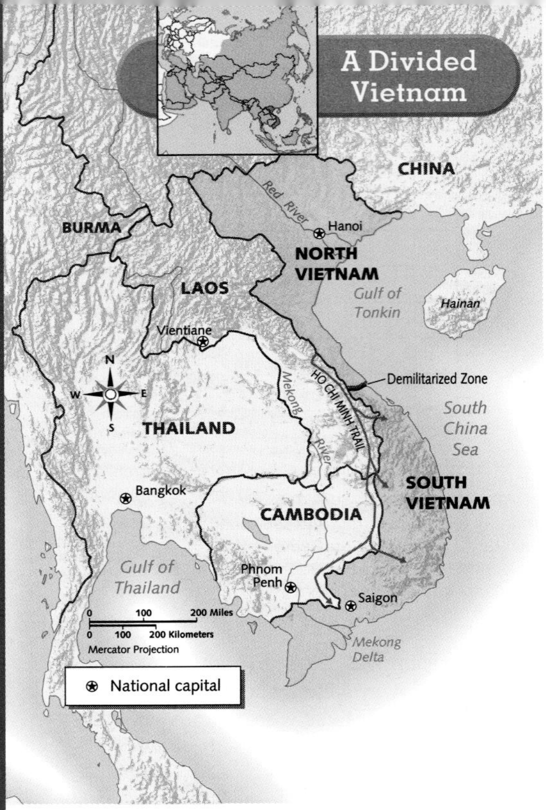

Movement The Ho Chi Minh Trail was a supply route from North Vietnam to South Vietnam. It was named for the communist leader of North Vietnam.

■ *Why do you think the trail went through other countries?*

marches against the war took place. Some young Americans resisted being drafted, or made to serve in the war. They burned their draft cards in protest. Some even moved out of the United States to avoid military service. Many of them went to Canada.

Because of the problems caused by the war President Johnson decided not to run for reelection. In 1968 the American people elected a new President—Richard M. Nixon. Nixon tried to end the war by bombing North Vietnam even more than before. He also sent American soldiers into Cambodia, a country bordering Vietnam. Nixon's goal was to "bring an honorable end to the war." But the war did not end, and the protests against the war grew.

REVIEW ***Why did some people protest the Vietnam War?***

Because they believed the war was wrong and unnecessary, and because the number of Americans killed in Vietnam climbed into the thousands.

Nixon Resigns

In 1972 President Nixon was reelected. In his second term, however, the Watergate scandal ended his presidency. A **scandal** is an action that brings disgrace. During the election campaign, some people working to help Nixon, who was a Republican, did some things that were against the law. One thing they did was to break into an office of the Democratic party in the Watergate Hotel. Many thought that President Nixon knew about this illegal act and tried to cover it up.

President Nixon and his family say farewell to White House staff members at the time of the President's resignation.

Activity Choices

Link to Art

ANALYZE PHOTOGRAPHS (Cooperative Learning) Have a small group of volunteers locate books that have photographs of U.S. soldiers in Vietnam and antiwar demonstrators in the United States. Ask the students to select between 10 and 15 photographs to show to the class. Have the class research the kind of fighting U.S. soldiers did in Vietnam and compare and contrast it with the kind of fighting U.S. soldiers did in World War II. Also have students link the protests and marches at home to the protests and marches for civil rights.

Extend and Enrich

MAKE A DIORAMA (Cooperative Learning) Divide the class into groups, and assign each group one of the Great Society programs, such as better living conditions in the Appalachian region, stronger safety measures for automobiles, education aid, housing aid, and Medicare. Ask each group to read library resources that describe their assigned Great Society program, and have them plan and make a Great Society diorama. When the dioramas are finished, have a spokesperson from each group present information to the class about his or her group's diorama.

HERITAGE

Veterans Day

To celebrate the signing of the armistice ending World War I, Armistice Day was first observed on November 11, 1919. In 1954 President Dwight D. Eisenhower changed the name of Armistice Day to Veterans Day. This day is dedicated to world peace and honors all veterans of the United States armed forces. Today Veterans Day is still observed on November 11. People celebrate with parades and speeches that honor the service that members of the military have given their country. Many European nations still celebrate Armistice Day.

A Vietnam veteran and his son search for people's names during a visit to the Vietnam Veterans Memorial.

Despite the scandal, President Nixon worked to end the Vietnam War. In 1969 he had begun to bring American troops home. But his plan to defeat the Vietcong by bombing North Vietnam harder failed. In January 1973 Nixon agreed to a cease-fire. He also agreed to bring the remaining American soldiers back from Vietnam.

The Watergate scandal, however, forced Nixon to step down. On August 9, 1974, he became the first President of the United States to resign. On that same day, Vice President Gerald Ford became President.

Without help from the United States, South Vietnamese soldiers could not win the war. On April 30, 1975, the government of South Vietnam surrendered. The government of North Vietnam gained control of the whole country. The unpopular war was finally over.

On Veterans Day in 1982, the Vietnam Veterans Memorial in Washington, D.C., was opened to visitors. Part of the memorial is a large wall of polished black stone. The wall lists the names of more than 58,000 American men and women who fought for their country and died or were reported missing during the Vietnam War.

REVIEW *How did the Vietnam War end?* American troops left Vietnam, and the government of South Vietnam surrendered.

LESSON 4 REVIEW

Check Understanding

1. **Remember the Facts** Why did President Nixon resign?
2. **Recall the Main Idea** How did people's opinions bring about change during the 1960s and 1970s?

Think Critically

3. **Think More About It** What might have happened if people had not protested against the Vietnam War?
4. **Past to Present** Why do you think many Americans today have painful memories of the Vietnam War?

Show What You Know

Art Activity Write down your ideas about what different groups thought about the Vietnam War. Then make a mural that shows what these groups did to express how they felt about the conflict. Present your mural to the class.

Reteach the Main Idea

COOPERATIVE LEARNING

CONDUCT A DEBATE Remind students that President Johnson was being pressured by people and groups with many different viewpoints about the Vietnam War. Divide the class into groups, and assign each group a viewpoint to represent. Have the groups research and prepare for a debate. Assign a student from each group to act as moderator. At the end of the debate, ask the class to vote on whether the United States should have been involved in the Vietnam War.

ACTIVITY BOOK

Reinforce & Extend

Use ACTIVITY BOOK, p. 126.

Civics and Government

Political Institutions and Processes Ask students to describe how the Constitution provides for the immediate replacement of the President if this becomes necessary.

Q. **Under what circumstances might it become necessary to replace a President?** death, resignation, impeachment conviction

3. CLOSE

Have students consider again the Focus question on page 628.

How can people's opinions affect the actions of their government?

Have students use what they have learned in this lesson to explain how public opinion can influence government actions.

LESSON 4 REVIEW—Answers

Check Understanding

1. because of the Watergate scandal
2. People's opinions and actions pressured Johnson and Nixon to find ways to end the war quickly.

Think Critically

3. The war might have continued, with growing numbers of casualties and no victory. The President might have come to the same conclusion that the war must be ended quickly. The President might have increased bombing raids and have kept troops in Vietnam long enough to win the war.
4. The war caused conflict and protest at home. It was the only major war the United States did not win. It is painful that lives were lost over a war that many did not support.

Show What You Know

Performance Assessment Have students look at and discuss pictures of soldiers in Vietnam and marchers and protesters during the late 1960s and early 1970s before planning their sections of the mural.

What to Look For Look for evidence that students understand the strong public opinions about the Vietnam War.

Objectives

1. Describe hawks and doves.
2. Explain the different viewpoints on the war in Vietnam.

1. ACCESS

Ask volunteers to try to identify situations in which they would support fighting in a war and situations in which they would oppose it. Remind students that the war in Vietnam caused strong feelings in the United States, both in support of the war and in opposition to it.

2. BUILD

Identify the Issue and the Speakers

Have students read pages 632–633, and lead a class discussion to build understanding of the issue and the speakers. Ask students to read the introduction and each speaker's opinion.

Q. **Who are the people taking a stand on the Vietnam issue?** President Lyndon B. Johnson and Senator J. William Fulbright

What was the difference between a hawk and a dove on this issue? A hawk was a person who wanted the war in Vietnam to continue until South Vietnam and the United States won. A dove was a person who wanted the Vietnam War to end immediately so that no more people would die.

Comparing Viewpoints

Hawk o

Like most wars in United States history, the Vietnam War had both supporters and nonsupporters. The hawks—named for the fierce bird of prey—wanted the war to continue until victory was achieved. They believed that communism would spread to other countries unless the United States helped South Vietnam win the conflict. The doves—named for the traditional symbol of peace—wanted the war to end immediately. They believed people were dying needlessly in a conflict that South Vietnam could not win. Each side strongly believed that it was right and the other side was wrong. There seemed to be no possible compromise.

Can you tell a hawk from a dove? Read the following quotations, and decide what each speaker believed about the Vietnam War.

President Lyndon B. Johnson

"Why are we in South Vietnam? We are there because we have a promise to keep. Since 1954 every American President has offered support to the people of South Vietnam. We have helped to build, and we have helped to defend. Thus, over many years, we made a national pledge to help South Vietnam defend its independence. . . . To dishonor that pledge, to abandon this small and brave nation to its enemies, and to the terror that must follow, would be an unforgivable wrong."

ACTIVITY CHOICES

Background

LYNDON BAINES JOHNSON Johnson, a Texas Democrat, started his political career as a secretary to Texas Representative Richard Kleberg in 1931. In 1937 he won his first election to the United States Congress. Johnson joined the navy during World War II, but a presidential directive sent him back to Congress. He became a powerful and influential leader in the House and in the Senate before becoming John F. Kennedy's running mate.

J. WILLIAM FULBRIGHT This Arkansas Democrat and Rhodes Scholar became a powerful and well-respected United States senator. He held his Senate seat from 1945 to 1974 and was chairperson of the Senate Foreign Relations Committee from 1959 to 1974. He became a leading critic of U.S. involvement in the war in Vietnam.

Dove?

In this photo from 1970, United States soldiers patrol an area southwest of Saigon, South Vietnam, near the Cambodian border.

Senator J. William Fulbright

"We are in a war to 'defend freedom' in South Vietnam. . . . When we talk about the freedom of South Vietnam, we may be thinking about how our pride would be injured if we settled for less than we set out to achieve; we may be thinking about our reputation as a great power, as though a compromise settlement would shame us before the world, marking us as a second-rate people with flagging [failing] courage and determination. Such fears are nonsensical. They are unworthy of the richest, most powerful, most productive, and best educated people in the world."

Compare Viewpoints

1. Was President Johnson a hawk or a dove? How do you know?
2. What viewpoint about the war did Senator Fulbright hold? How do you know?

Think and Apply

BUILDING CITIZENSHIP

Choose one of the wars you have studied in American history. Use encyclopedias and other references to identify some individuals or groups who were hawks and some who were doves during that war. Describe the point of view of each.

Compare Viewpoints

Use the Compare Viewpoints questions to guide a discussion of Johnson's and Fulbright's statements.

1. President Johnson was a hawk. He said the United States should not abandon South Vietnam to its enemies.
2. Senator Fulbright was a dove. He said the United States was more worried about its pride than about ending the war.

Explore with students how the speakers' ideas were different and why they think those differences existed.

3. CLOSE

Have students summarize the viewpoints that Johnson and Fulbright held on the war in Vietnam. Then use the Think and Apply activity to have students identify times in history when Americans differed on whether the United States should be involved in a war. Have students share their findings with the class.

"PRIMARY SOURCE"

Lyndon B. Johnson
Source: *The Nation in Turmoil: Civil Rights and the Vietnam War (1960–1973)*. Gene Brown. Twenty-first Century Books, 1993.

J. William Fulbright
Source: *The Arrogance of Power*. J. William Fulbright. Vintage Books, 1966.

Background

THE ISSUE The United States had helped South Vietnam for decades. President Truman provided military aid to the French when they were fighting the Vietminh in Vietnam. President Eisenhower sent economic and military aid to South Vietnam. President Kennedy sharply increased the number of military advisers in South Vietnam. President Johnson continued the aid. U.S. involvement in Vietnam escalated rapidly following the Gulf of Tonkin incident in 1964.

Reteach

COOPERATIVE LEARNING

DEBATE THE ISSUE You may wish to reinforce students' understanding of the arguments for and against the war in Vietnam by holding a debate. Divide the class into two groups: the hawks and the doves. Ask each group to plan and prepare its arguments and select its spokespersons. Remind students they must use facts to back up their arguments.

Objectives

1. Summarize the causes for improved U.S. relations with China and the Soviet Union.
2. Analyze why tensions increased between the U.S. and the Soviet Union and Iran.
3. Analyze the end of the Cold War.
4. Explain why President Bush hoped for a new world order.
5. Evaluate the consequences of a large budget deficit in the United States.

Vocabulary

arms control (p. 634)
détente (p. 635)
terrorism (p. 635)
hostage (p. 635)
deficit (p. 638)

1. ACCESS

The Focus Question

Have students recall strong individuals from the past who brought about change. Then ask students to identify people who are influencing the history of the world today.

The Main Idea

In this lesson students learn how powerful individuals in the United States, China, and the Soviet Union helped end the Cold War. After students have read the lesson, have them analyze the roles of the individual leaders.

2. BUILD

Nixon Visits China and the Soviet Union

Key Content Summary

In 1972 President Richard M. Nixon met with leaders from China and the Soviet Union to improve trade and cultural and scientific relations. An arms control agreement with the Soviet Union eased tensions and led to a period of détente.

LESSON 5

FOCUS
How do people help influence history?

Main Idea Read to learn how individuals helped bring the Cold War to an end.

Vocabulary
arms control
détente
terrorism
hostage
deficit

The Cold War Ends

Although he resigned in disgrace, President Nixon accomplished many important things while he was in office. His most important achievement may have been reducing tensions between the free world and the communist nations. Nixon became the first American President to visit both China and the Soviet Union. Later, Cold War tensions would rise and fall and then nearly disappear.

Nixon Visits China and the Soviet Union

The United States cut ties with China after the Asian nation became a communist country in 1949. Trade, travel, and communication between the two countries came to a complete end.

In 1972 President Nixon accepted an invitation from China's leader, Mao Zedong (MOW zeh•DOONG), to visit China. As a result of Nixon's visit, the two nations agreed to trade with each other and to allow visits from each other's scientific and cultural groups.

Standing on the Great Wall of China are (center) President Nixon and Patricia Nixon, his wife.

Three months after visiting China, Nixon flew to Moscow to meet with Soviet leader Leonid Brezhnev (BREZH•nef). Nixon told Brezhnev, "There must be room in the world for two great nations with different systems to live together and work together."

As a result of this meeting, the United States and the Soviet Union agreed to increase trade with each other and to work together on scientific and cultural projects. Most importantly, they agreed to **arms control**, or limiting the number of weapons that each

ACTIVITY CHOICES

Reading Support

PREVIEW AND READ THE LESSON Provide students with the following visual framework.

THE UNITED STATES AND INTERNATIONAL RELATIONS

PRESIDENTS	COUNTRIES
Richard M. Nixon →	China, Soviet Union
Jimmy Carter →	Soviet Union, Afghanistan, Iran
Ronald Reagan →	Soviet Union
George Bush →	Soviet Union, Iraq, former Yugoslavia
Bill Clinton →	Japan, South Korea, Taiwan

He visited both countries; made economic, scientific, and cultural agreements; and agreed to arms control.

nation may have. The agreement signed by Nixon and Brezhnev limited the number of nuclear, or atomic, missiles on each side. This agreement marked the beginning of a period of **détente** (day•TAHNT), or an easing of tensions, between the United States and the Soviet Union. But this period of détente did not last long.

REVIEW ***How did President Nixon ease tensions with China and the Soviet Union?***

Increased Tensions

Southwest Asia, or the Middle East, as Europeans and Americans have called the region, has long been a trouble spot. People there are divided by religious, cultural, and political differences. Some of the people have turned to **terrorism**, the use of violence to promote a cause. There have also been wars in the region. In 1948, 1956, 1967, and 1973, Israel fought wars with Egypt, Jordan, and Syria. In these wars the United States took the side of Israel. The Soviet Union took the side of the Arab nations. In taking sides, the United States and the Soviet Union increased Cold War tensions.

Then, in December 1979, Soviet troops invaded the country of Afghanistan (af•GAN•uh•stan) in Southwest Asia. The invasion moved Soviet troops much closer to the region's rich oil fields. President Jimmy Carter, who had been elected in 1976, called the invasion a threat to world peace.

President Carter insisted that the Soviets leave Afghanistan. When they did not, he cut back American trade with the Soviets and refused to agree to further arms control. He also said that American athletes would not take part in the 1980 Olympic games to be held in Moscow.

The fighting in Afghanistan continued for years. The Afghan rebels fought so fiercely that it was difficult for the Soviets to control the country. Finally, in 1988, the Soviet Union began to withdraw its troops from Afghanistan.

President Carter (center) earned worldwide praise for bringing about a peace agreement between two old enemies, Egypt and Israel. Carter is shown with President Sadat (suh•DAHT) of Egypt (left) and Prime Minister Begin (BAY•gin) of Israel (right). The peace treaty they signed was known as the Camp David Accords.

Another problem in Southwest Asia proved to be even more troubling for President Carter. In 1979 a revolution took place in Iran. The shah, the country's leader, fled. Leaders of the revolution were angry at Americans because the United States had supported the shah. To show their anger, the revolutionaries attacked the United States embassy in Tehran, Iran's capital. They captured 53 Americans and made them hostages. **Hostages** are people held as prisoners until their captors' demands are met. President Carter was unable to win the release of the hostages. Many Americans lost confidence in him. In 1980 Carter ran again for President but lost. On the day the new President, Ronald Reagan, took the oath of office, the Iranians finally released the hostages.

REVIEW ***What actions did Carter take when the Soviets invaded Afghanistan?***

He cut back trade with the Soviets, refused further arms control, and would not allow American athletes to take part in the Olympic games in Moscow.

Civics and Government

Purposes of Government Have students infer why it was important for President Nixon to accept Mao Zedong's invitation.

History

Patterns and Relationships Have students conclude how relations in trade, science, and culture might help two nations better understand each other.

Q. **How did the arms control agreement help international relations?** It encouraged trust and reduced tensions.

Increased Tensions

Key Content Summary

Tension and conflict between the United States and the Soviet Union continued in the 1970s and 1980s in Southwest Asia. The United States faced further challenges when 53 Americans became hostages of Iranian revolutionaries.

History

Patterns and Relationships Have students identify the cause-and-effect relationships that increased international tensions.

Link to Language Arts

WRITE A LETTER Ask students to imagine that they are living during President Carter's administration. Have students select one of two topics: the issue of not sending U.S. athletes to participate in the 1980 Olympic Games, or the problem of securing the release of the American hostages in Iran. Then have students research the topics they select and write letters to President Carter expressing their views. Ask volunteers to share their letters with the class.

TECHNOLOGY

Use THE AMAZING WRITING MACHINE™ to complete this writing activity.

Background

SOUTHWEST ASIA Conflicts between Jews and Muslims over land have led to war and terrorism in Southwest Asia since the nation of Israel was founded in 1948. Peace talks in the 1990s led to a series of agreements in which the Israelis gave up land in return for peace.

The Cold War Ends

Key Content Summary

Relations between the United States and the Soviet Union improved dramatically in 1985 when Mikhail Gorbachev, the new Soviet leader, gave the Soviet people more freedom and agreed to increase arms limitations. By the end of 1989, the Cold War was ending.

Culture

Shared Humanity and Unique Identity Have students analyze the significance of Nikita Khrushchev's conclusion about the use of hydrogen bombs.

History

Patterns and Relationships Have students conclude why President Ronald Reagan welcomed the chance to meet with Mikhail Gorbachev and agreed to more arms treaties.

Q. **Why did Americans feel more comfortable with the new Soviet policies?** The new policies encouraged greater freedom for the Soviet people, bringing them a little closer to democracy.

Soviet leader Gorbachev (right) and President Reagan (far right) shake hands at their first meeting. They met each year from 1985 through 1988.

The Cold War Ends

In 1956, when the Soviet leader Nikita Khrushchev (krush•CHAWF) first learned about the destruction that hydrogen bombs could cause, he was so upset that he tossed and turned for nights, unable to sleep. "Then I became convinced," he said, "that we could never possibly use these weapons, and when I realized that I was able to sleep again."

Neither the Soviets nor the Americans used nuclear weapons during the Cold War. But throughout this period, both countries built more and more of them.

"Peace through strength" was Ronald Reagan's motto as he increased defense spending. He called the Soviet Union "an evil empire" and said that the Cold War was a "struggle between right and wrong, good and evil." Soviet leaders did not soften their stand, either. They continued building more weapons and helping communist rebels all over the world.

Then a new leader took over the Soviet Union, and nothing was the same again. Mikhail Gorbachev (mee•kah•EEL gawr•buh•CHAWF) became leader of the Soviet Union in 1985. President Reagan said he would welcome the chance to meet the new Soviet leader in the "cause of world peace." In April 1985 Gorbachev agreed to a meeting. He said that better relations between the United States and the Soviet Union were "extremely necessary—and possible."

The first meeting between Reagan and Gorbachev in November 1985 marked the beginning of a real thaw in the Cold War. The President called it a "fresh start" in United States–Soviet relations. Soon the United States and the Soviet Union agreed to more treaties limiting nuclear missiles.

In the Soviet Union, Mikhail Gorbachev was already changing many of the old Soviet ways of doing things. He called for *perestroika* (pair•uh•STROY•kuh), or a "restructuring" of the Soviet government and economy. He also called for a new "openness," or *glasnost* (GLAZ•nohst). This would give the Soviet people more of the freedoms they wanted. Soviet citizens would be allowed to vote in free elections. They would be free to start and run their own businesses.

Reforms in the Soviet Union led to changes in many other communist nations. People in

Activity Choices

Meet Individual Needs

VISUAL LEARNERS Provide students with outline maps of eastern European countries and Russia before and after *perestroika.* Have students use atlases to help them in coloring and labeling the nations of this region. Make sure they use color to identify the nations that were part of the Soviet Union before gaining their independence. Have students infer how the people in eastern Europe might have felt about becoming independent of the Soviet Union.

Link to Mathematics

MAKE A CALCULATION In 1975 the federal government spent $86.5 billion on defense. By 1985 that figure had grown to $252.7 billion, contributing to the budget deficit. Have students calculate the actual difference in dollars spent on defense between 1975 and 1985 ($166.2 billion). Then have students calculate the percentage increase in dollars spent on defense between 1975 and 1985 (192% increase in dollars spent).

AUDIO

Use the UNIT 10 MUSIC AUDIOCASSETTE to hear the song "God Bless the U.S.A."

Poland, Czechoslovakia, and Hungary gained new freedoms. In communist East Germany, government leaders removed the armed guards from the Berlin Wall and opened its gates. In 1989 the German people tore down the Berlin Wall. The next year they reunited their country.

In 1989 the new President of the United States, George Bush, met with Mikhail Gorbachev on a ship near Malta, a rocky island in the middle of the Mediterranean Sea. As a storm raged outside, the two men faced each other across a table. Years of mistrust between their countries made the outcome of the meeting uncertain. Neither one knew what to expect.

The two leaders talked about the many changes taking place in Europe and the Soviet Union. At the end Gorbachev looked Bush in the eye. "I have heard you say that you want *perestroika* to succeed," he said, "but frankly I didn't know this. Now I know." The Cold War was finally ending.

REVIEW ***What changes did Gorbachev bring to the Soviet Union?*** a restructuring of the government and economy and a new openness

A man standing on the newly opened Berlin Wall makes a peace sign as East Germans flood into West Berlin.

A New World Order

Talking about the idea of a world without the Cold War, President George Bush said,

> "Now we can see . . . the very real prospect of a new world order. A world in which freedom and respect for human rights find a home among all nations."

By "a new world order," President Bush meant a world without the alliances and conflicts of the past. However, conflicts in the world have continued.

In 1990 the nation of Iraq, led by its ruler, Saddam Hussein (hoo•SAYN), invaded neighboring Kuwait (koo•WAYT), a major oil producer. When Iraq refused to withdraw, the allied forces of the United States, Britain, France, Egypt, and Saudi Arabia attacked. During Operation Desert Storm the Iraqis were pushed back, and Kuwait's rulers were returned to power.

In the meantime the end of communism in eastern Europe set off fighting in what was once the nation of Yugoslavia. The civil war there has taken hundreds of thousands of lives. In 1991 the Soviet Union itself broke up into independent countries. Many of these countries are fighting one another for power and the right to self-government.

REVIEW ***What did Bush mean by "a new world order"?*** a world without the alliances and conflicts of the past

New Challenges at Home

In 1993 Bill Clinton was elected President. In his 1995 State of the Union Address, Clinton said, "You know, tonight this is the first State of the Union Address ever delivered since the beginning of the Cold War when not a single Russian missile is pointed at the children of America."

Visual Analysis

Interpret Pictures Direct students' attention to the picture of the newly opened Berlin Wall.

A New World Order

Key Content Summary

The end of the Cold War brought hope for peace to the world. However, new conflicts arose in the former Yugoslavia and in countries that had been part of the Soviet Union. New conflicts also arose in Southwest Asia when Iraq invaded Kuwait.

History

Patterns and Relationships Have students discuss changes that might be a part of the "new world order" President Bush hoped might come to pass.

"PRIMARY SOURCE"

Source: "The War is Over," delivered to the Joint Session of Congress, March 6, 1991.

New Challenges at Home

Key Content Summary

Today the United States faces new challenges. These challenges include maintaining a balanced budget, reducing the nation's international trade deficit, fighting crime, caring for the environment, and achieving equality for all Americans.

Smithsonian Institution®

Go to the Internet site at *http://www.si.edu/harcourt/socialstudies* to examine portraits of Jimmy Carter, Ronald Reagan, George Bush, and William Clinton in the Hall of Presidents at the National Portrait Gallery.

Extend and Enrich

COOPERATIVE LEARNING

RESEARCH AND ROLE-PLAY Divide the class into groups, and assign each group one of the U.S. Presidents mentioned in the lesson: Richard M. Nixon, Jimmy Carter, Ronald Reagan, George Bush, and Bill Clinton. Have the groups use library resources or the Internet to learn more about the actions and accomplishments of their assigned President. Ask the groups to choose members to role-play the Presidents and other members to role-play interviewers. Have the groups write questions and answers to use when they role-play their interviews. After each group has presented its interview to the class, have the groups compare and contrast the accomplishments of these Presidents.

Economics

Interdependence and Income To help students understand the concept of income, budgets, and budget deficits, have the class work together to create a diagram on the board. The diagram should show taxes as income to the government, costs for government programs, and the deficit between income and spending. You may wish to make up dollar amounts for the students to use.

3. CLOSE

Have students consider again the Focus question on page 634.

How do people help influence history?

Have students recall the significant contributions of individual leaders in ending the Cold War. Ask students to discuss how current leaders might resolve conflicts and change the course of history.

LESSON 5 REVIEW—Answers

Check Understanding

1. China and the Soviet Union
2. Gorbachev gave the Soviet people more freedom and recognized the need for better relations with the United States. President Reagan met with Gorbachev, and the two leaders agreed on further arms control. President Bush met with Gorbachev and convinced him that the United States would support *perestroika*.

Think Critically

3. Mao may have wanted to improve China's economy by opening up trade with the United States. He also may have wanted to learn about the scientific advances the United States had made.
4. Reforms have sparked civil war in some nations. Reforms have also sparked fights for power and the right to self-government in other nations.

Show What You Know

Performance Assessment Have students bring in their magazines and newspapers and brainstorm ideas before they make their picture essays.

What to Look For Look for evidence that the students understand both the conflicts and the cooperation that occurred within and among nations because the Cold War ended.

After the Cold War ended, however, the United States faced many new challenges. Among the most important were to work for equality for all Americans, fight crime, and care for the environment.

Another important concern had to do with the economy. In the 1990s the United States remained a military superpower. But many Americans believed it was no longer the economic superpower it once was. It had the largest economy in the world, but it had economic problems. One reason was the government's budget **deficit**, or shortage. The government spent more money than it took in each year in taxes and other income. To help solve this problem, Congress passed a balanced-budget amendment to the Constitution in 1997. This amendment requires the government to spend no more money than it takes in each year.

By the end of the twentieth century, the economy of the United States had improved greatly. Under the leadership of President Clinton, the nation achieved a balanced budget. However, the United States is still challenged by an international trade deficit. It buys more goods from other countries than it sells. Inexpensive imports from countries such as Japan, South Korea, and Taiwan are snapped up by American consumers. As a result, American businesses producing similar goods have suffered.

President Clinton held televised "town meetings" to listen to people's concerns and hear their views about the government.

According to many economists, what is needed to be a world leader today is different from what was needed during the Cold War. World leadership, they say, is based more and more on economic strength. Many Americans believe that one of the most important challenges for the United States today is to continue to be an economic superpower.

REVIEW ***How can the United States remain a world leader?*** by continuing to be an economic superpower

LESSON 5 REVIEW

Check Understanding

1. **Remember the Facts** President Nixon's visits to what two countries led to a time of détente?
2. **Recall the Main Idea** How did individuals help bring an end to the Cold War?

Think Critically

3. **Think More About It** What could have been some of the reasons Mao Zedong invited President Nixon to China?
4. **Cause and Effect** How did the reforms of the Soviet Union in the 1980s affect other communist nations in eastern Europe?

Show What You Know

Picture-Essay Activity Use information and pictures from current newspapers and magazines to make a picture essay titled *The World After the Cold War.* Share your picture essay with a partner, and discuss what it shows.

ACTIVITY CHOICES

ACTIVITY BOOK

Reinforce & Extend

Use ACTIVITY BOOK, p. 127.

Reteach the Main Idea

COOPERATIVE LEARNING

MAKE A CHART Divide the class into small groups. Have each group make a chart titled *Leaders Who Brought the Cold War to an End.* Under the first column heading, *Leaders*, have the groups write the names of the leaders. Under the second column heading, *Actions*, have them summarize what each leader did to help bring the Cold War to an end. Have the groups share and discuss their charts. Ask students to conclude what they think was the single most important action that brought the Cold War to an end.

Participation Skills

Skills

Understand Political Symbols

1. Why Learn This Skill?

People often recognize sports teams, clubs, and other organizations by their symbols. The same is true for political parties, the President, Congress, the Supreme Court, and even voters. Being able to identify political symbols and what they stand for can help you better understand news reports, political cartoons, and other sources of information.

2. Recognizing Symbols

Two of the country's most famous political symbols are animals. The donkey represents the Democratic party. The elephant represents the Republican party. The donkey was probably first used to represent President Andrew Jackson, a Democrat, in the 1830s. Later the donkey became a symbol for the entire party. Cartoonist Thomas Nast introduced the elephant as a symbol of the Republican party in 1874. Both symbols are still used today.

One of the symbols for the national government is Uncle Sam—a white-haired man wearing a red, white, and blue hat and suit. The bald eagle and the Statue of Liberty are other symbols for our government. Buildings are often used as political symbols. The White House is a symbol for the President, and the United States Capitol is a symbol for Congress.

3. Understand the Process

When you see a political symbol, answer these questions to help you understand its meaning:

1. Do you recognize the symbol? Does it stand for the national government as a whole or only part of the national government? Does it stand for a person or a group that is involved in government, such as a political party?
2. Where did you see the symbol? If it appeared in a newspaper, did the writer give you any clues about its meaning?
3. Are there any captions or other words that help explain what the symbol means? A symbol labeled "The Halls of Justice," for example, might tell you that it stands for a court.

4. Think and Apply

BUILDING CITIZENSHIP

Look through current newsmagazines or the editorial pages of newspapers. Find an example of a political symbol. Cut out the example and paste it on a sheet of paper. Below the symbol, write a brief description of what it stands for.

The donkey is the symbol of the Democratic party.

The elephant is the symbol of the Republican party.

Link to Art

CREATE POLITICAL CARTOONS OR POSTERS Have students design and draw political cartoons or posters that include party symbols. They could use the symbols they have chosen in Reteach the Skill or those of the two national parties.

Reteach the Skill

COOPERATIVE LEARNING

CREATE PARTY SYMBOLS Divide the class into groups. Have the groups set up mock political parties and decide what issues their parties support. Have each group choose a symbol to represent its party. Remind them to keep the functions of such a symbol in mind as they work.

TRANSPARENCY

Use TRANSPARENCY 50.

MODEL & APPLY SKILLS

Objectives

1. Recognize political symbols.
2. Practice interpreting political symbols.

1. ACCESS

Invite students to discuss school and sports symbols. Perhaps one of your school teams has an animal symbol that connotes speed or power. Ask students how they feel when they see or wear the symbol. What does it mean to them? Explain that political symbols work in similar ways.

Review the functions of political symbols discussed in Why Learn This Skill? Ask students to share knowledge they may have concerning political symbols. Find and display examples of the other symbols described in the lesson.

2. BUILD

Have the students work through the questions listed in Understand the Process. Choose a symbol from a current publication and use it to model the questions.

3. CLOSE

Have students complete the activity in Think and Apply. Have students use the questions listed in Understand the Process to interpret the symbols they find. Look for the ability to interpret political symbols. Point out that an understanding of political symbols can help people become better informed.

ACTIVITY BOOK

Practice & Apply

Use ACTIVITY BOOK, pp. 128–129.

CHAPTER 19
REVIEW

Time Line
Ask students to share what they recall about each event shown on the time line.

Connect Main Ideas
Use the organizer to review the main ideas of the chapter. Have students use their textbooks to complete the organizer or check their work. Allow time for them to discuss and compare their responses.

ACTIVITY BOOK

Summarize the Chapter

A copy of the graphic organizer appears on ACTIVITY BOOK, p. 130.

TRANSPARENCY

A copy of the graphic organizer appears on TRANSPARENCY 51.

Write More About It
Write a Radio News Report
Students should demonstrate an understanding of the situation in Berlin during the airlift. Make sure they describe the airlift and accurately identify West Berlin as part of democratic West Germany and East Berlin as part of communist East Germany.

Write Your Opinion
Students' opinions should demonstrate an understanding of the importance of the voyage and the risks the crew faced.

TECHNOLOGY

Use THE AMAZING WRITING MACHINE™ to complete the writing activities.

TECHNOLOGY

Use TIMELINER™ DATA DISKS to discuss and summarize the chapter.

CHAPTER 19
REVIEW

1940 · 1950 · 196

1948 • Berlin Airlift

1962 • Cubar missil crisis

CONNECT MAIN IDEAS

Use this graphic organizer to show how the chapter's main ideas are connected. Write the main idea of each lesson. A copy of the organizer appears on page 130 of the Activity Book.

Possible answers to the graphic organizer appear on page 610C of this Teacher's Edition.

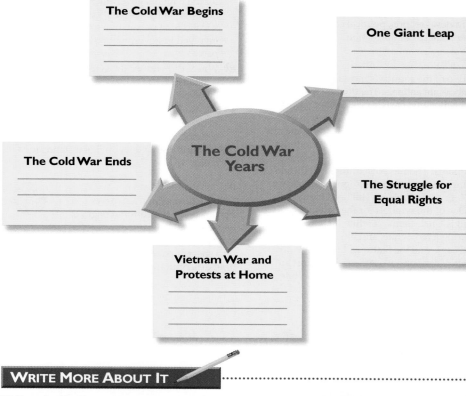

The Cold War Years

- **The Cold War Begins**
- **One Giant Leap**
- **The Struggle for Equal Rights**
- **Vietnam War and Protests at Home**
- **The Cold War Ends**

WRITE MORE ABOUT IT

Write a Radio News Report Imagine that you are living in West Berlin during the Berlin Airlift. The radio station you work for has asked you to report on the conflict. Write what you will say about how the Allies are getting supplies to Berlin.

Write Your Opinion The three astronauts aboard *Apollo 11* faced many dangers during their trip to the moon, but they also made history. Write a paragraph or two telling why you would or would not have wanted to be an astronaut on board that historic flight.

640 • Chapter 19

Use Vocabulary
1. superpower (p. 611)
2. nonviolence (p. 623)
3. integration (p. 624)
4. hawk (p. 629)
5. détente (p. 635)

Check Understanding
6. The blockade would stop Soviet ship from carrying missiles to Cuba. Th United States worried that the Soviet would attack from Cuba. (p. 614)
7. It ended segregation. (p. 622)
8. They led to inflation. (p. 629)
9. Richard Nixon; The United State agreed to trade and make cultural an scientific exchanges with China, an the United States agreed to arms con trol, to increase trade, and to work o scientific and cultural projects wit the Soviet Union. (p. 634)

1964 Civil Rights Act is passed

1969 • Astronauts land on the moon

1975 • Vietnam War ends

1985 • The Cold War begins to come to an end

1991 • Soviet Union splits into independent countries

1970 1980 1990 2000

USE VOCABULARY

Write a term from this list to complete each of the sentences that follow.

détente **nonviolence** **hawk** **superpower** **integration**

- The United States is a ____ because of the important role it plays in world events.
- Working for change using ____ was important to Martin Luther King, Jr.
- The bringing together of all races in education, jobs, and housing is called ____ .
- President Johnson was a ____ because he wanted the United States to continue fighting the war in Vietnam.
- In 1972 the United States and the Soviet Union began a period of ____ , the easing of military tensions between countries.

CHECK UNDERSTANDING

- Why did President Kennedy order a blockade of Cuba?
- How did a Supreme Court decision in 1954 change public schools?
- How did the costs of the Great Society programs and the Vietnam War affect the economy of the United States?
- Who was the first American President to visit both China and the Soviet Union? What was the important result of these visits?
- What happened in eastern Europe after Mikhail Gorbachev became leader of the Soviet Union?

THINK CRITICALLY

11. **Explore Viewpoints** How were the views of Malcolm X different from the views of Martin Luther King, Jr.?
12. **Think More About It** In what ways has the women's rights movement changed the United States?

APPLY SKILLS

Act as a Responsible Citizen
Identify a person who you think is a responsible citizen. Write a paragraph telling why you think that person is acting responsibly.

Understand Political Symbols
A donkey, an elephant, the Capitol, the White House, and Uncle Sam are all political symbols. What does each represent?

READ MORE ABOUT IT

Rosa Parks: My Story by Rosa Parks. Dial. This autobiography describes the life of Rosa Parks, a woman whose struggle for racial equality helped start the Civil Rights movement.

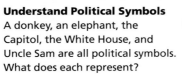

Visit the Internet at **http://www.hbschool.com** for additional resources.

CHAPTER 19 REVIEW

Read More About It

Additional books are listed in the Multimedia Resource Center on page 604D of this Teacher's Edition.

Unit Project Check-Up

Have students work in groups to decide on each person's assignment. Some may work on finding photographs in the collected reference books. Others may write about major events and major contributors. Others may wish to locate excerpts from videos that they can play during exhibit hours. Each group should submit a plan.

ASSESSMENT PROGRAM

Use CHAPTER 19 TEST, pp. 159–162.

People in eastern Europe gained new freedoms, the Berlin Wall was torn down, and East Germany and West Germany were reunited. (pp. 636–637)

Think Critically

Students should explain that at first Malcolm X wanted change by any means possible, and that Martin Luther King, Jr., wanted change through nonviolence.

Students should note that NOW and other women's groups have helped elect women to public office, pass laws that say employers must treat men and women equally, and open professions to women that had formerly been closed to them.

Apply Skills

Act as a Responsible Citizen
Students should identify a person who works for the community, for the nation, or for the world.

Understand Political Symbols
Democratic Party; Republican party; Congress; the President of the United States; the United States

Planning Chart

	THEMES • Strands	VOCABULARY	MEET INDIVIDUAL NEEDS	RESOURCES INCLUDING ▶ TECHNOLOGY
LESSON 1 **Mexico Today** pp. 643–646	CONFLICT & COOPERATION • Geography • Economics	metropolitan area middle class interest rate free-trade agreement	Extend and Enrich, p. 645 Reteach the Main Idea, p. 646	Activity Book, p. 131 ▶ TIMELINER
LESSON 2 **Learn Culture Through Literature** **Save My Rainforest** by Monica Zak, pp. 647–651	INDIVIDUALISM & INTERDEPENDENCE • Civics and Government • Economics • Geography		Extend and Enrich, p. 650 Reteach the Main Idea, p. 651	Activity Book, pp. 132–133 ▶ IMAGINATION EXPRESS
SKILL **Use Population Maps** pp. 652–653	BASIC STUDY SKILLS • Map and Globe Skills	cartogram population density	English Language Learners, p. 653 Reteach the Skill, p. 653	Activity Book, pp. 134–135 Transparencies 52A–52B ▶ MAPSKILLS
LESSON 3 **Democracy in the Caribbean and in Central America** pp. 654–658	INDIVIDUALISM & INTERDEPENDENCE • Civics and Government • Culture • History • Economics • Geography	commonwealth embargo free election	Advanced Learners, p. 656 Tactile Learners, p. 657 Extend and Enrich, p. 657 Reteach the Main Idea, p. 658	Activity Book, pp. 136–137 ▶ MAPSKILLS
LESSON 4 **Challenges in South America** pp. 659–661	INDIVIDUALISM & INTERDEPENDENCE • Civics and Government • Geography • Economics	liberate mestizo deforestation	Extend and Enrich, p. 660 Reteach the Main Idea, p. 661	Activity Book, pp. 138–139
LESSON 5 **The Peoples of Canada** pp. 662–665	COMMONALITY & DIVERSITY • Geography • Civics and Government • Culture • History	province separatist	Extend and Enrich, p. 664 Reteach the Main Idea, p. 665	Activity Book, pp. 140–141 ▶ GRAPH LINKS
CHAPTER REVIEW pp. 666–667				Activity Book, p. 142 Transparency 53 Assessment Program Chapter 20 Test, pp. 163–166 ▶ THE AMAZING WRITING MACHINE ▶ TIMELINER ▶ INTERNET

8 DAYS

TIME MANAGEMENT

DAY 1	DAY 2	DAY 3	DAY 4	DAY 5	DAY 6	DAY 7	DAY 8
Lesson 1	Lesson 2	Skill	Lesson 3	Lesson 4	Lesson 5	Chapter Review	Chapter Test

Activity Book

LESSON 1
Read a Table

NAME ______________________ DATE __________

Comparing NAFTA Countries

Read a Table

***DIRECTIONS:** Examine the table below to see how the NAFTA countries compare in various categories. Then answer the questions that follow.*

COMPARE COUNTRIES

	CANADA	UNITED STATES	MEXICO
Population	29,123,000	267,636,000	97,563,000
Population growth rate (1990–2000)	1.2%	1.0%	1.9%
Telephones per 100 people	59	56	8
Newspapers per 1,000 people	228	249	133
Televisions per 1,000 people	639	814	147

1. Which country has the largest population? United States
2. Which country's population is growing at the fastest rate? Mexico
3. Which categories shown in the table reflect means of communications?
   telephones, newspapers, and televisions
4. Which country has the most telephones per 100 people? Canada
5. How many telephones per 100 people are there in the United States?
   56
6. Which country has the fewest newspapers per 1,000 people?
   Mexico
7. Which country has the most newspapers per 1,000 people?
   the United States
8. How many more televisions per 1,000 people does the United States have than Mexico?
   814 − 147 = 667 more television sets per 1,000 people

LESSON 2
Link to the Environment

NAME ______________________ DATE __________

SAVE THE RAIN FOREST

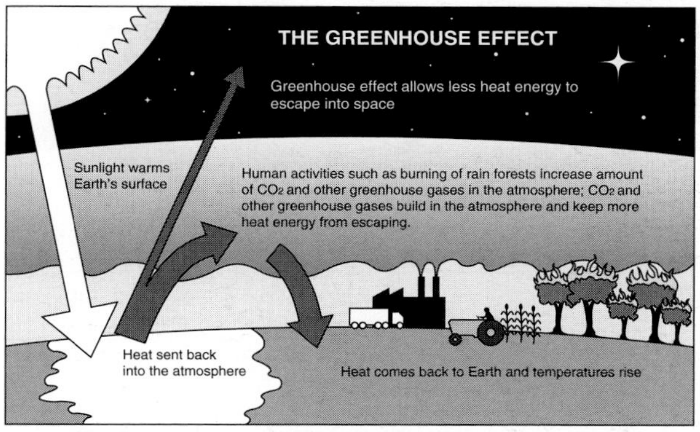
THE GREENHOUSE EFFECT
Greenhouse effect allows less heat energy to escape into space
Sunlight warms Earth's surface
Human activities such as burning of rain forests increase amount of CO2 and other greenhouse gases in the atmosphere; CO2 and other greenhouse gases build in the atmosphere and keep more heat energy from escaping.
Heat sent back into the atmosphere
Heat comes back to Earth and temperatures rise

GREENHOUSE GASES AND THEIR SOURCES

GREENHOUSE GAS	SOURCES	LIFE SPAN IN ATMOSPHERE
carbon dioxide (CO_2) ✓	fossil fuels, deforestation, soil destruction	500 years
chlorofluorocarbons (CFCs 11 and 12)	refrigeration, air conditioning, aerosols, foam blowing, solvents	65 to 110 years
methane (CH_4)	cattle, rice paddies, gas leaks, mining, termites	7 to 10 years
nitrous oxide (N_2O) ✓	fossil fuels, soil cultivation, deforestation	140 to 190 years
ozone and other trace gases	photochemical processes, gasoline-powered vehicles, power plants, solvents	hours to days

(continued)

LESSON 2
Link to the Environment

NAME ______________________ DATE __________

Link to the Environment

***DIRECTIONS:** Study the diagram on page 132. Then complete the activities that follow.*

1. Follow the arrow from the sun to the Earth's surface. What happens when the sunlight hits the Earth's surface? Heat is sent back into the atmosphere.
2. Follow the split arrow leaving the Earth's surface. What barrier does it hit?
   greenhouse gases in the atmosphere
3. Read the caption and study the illustrations in the diagram that show what causes this barrier. Describe what you think causes it. Accept answers that mention human activities such as burning of rain forests, clearing of farmland, and factory pollution.
4. Follow the split arrow to its two ends. List the results produced by the greenhouse effect.
   Less heat energy escapes into space; more heat energy comes back to Earth and temperatures rise.

***DIRECTIONS:** Study the chart on page 132. Then complete the activities that follow.*

5. Circle the names of the greenhouse gases that are produced by deforestation.
6. Put an **X** through the name of the greenhouse gas that takes the longest to disappear from the atmosphere.
7. Put a check mark next to the names of the two greenhouse gases that are produced by fossil fuels.
8. Underline the names of the greenhouse gases produced by gasoline-powered vehicles.
9. Study the diagram and the chart. Write a paragraph on a separate sheet of paper describing specific things that you can do to help stop the greenhouse effect.
   Accept paragraphs that describe reasonable suggestions.

SKILL PRACTICE
Apply Map and Globe Skills

NAME ______________________ DATE __________

HOW TO USE POPULATION MAPS

Apply Map and Globe Skills

***DIRECTIONS:** The size of each state shown on this map is based on the population of the state and not the area, or geographic size, of the state. Examine this map and compare it to the map of the United States on page A8 in your textbook. Then answer the questions on page 135.*

CARTOGRAM: POPULATION OF THE UNITED STATES

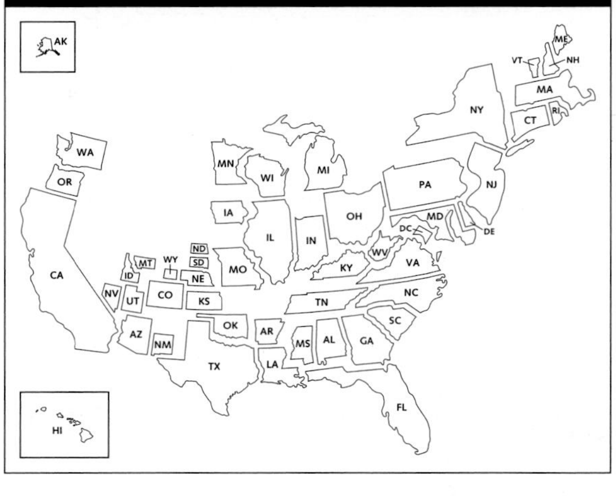
AK
ME
VT
NH
MA
RI
CT
NY
WA
OR
MN
WI
MI
PA
NJ
IA
OH
MD
DC
DE
IL
IN
WV
VA
ND
SD
MT
WY
ID
NE
MO
KY
CA
NV
UT
CO
KS
TN
NC
OK
AR
SC
AZ
NM
MS
AL
GA
TX
LA
FL
HI

(continued)

SKILL PRACTICE
Apply Map and Globe Skills

NAME ______________________ DATE __________

1. Look at the map on page A8 of your textbook. What is the largest state in the United States? Alaska
2. Why does the cartogram on page 134 show California as the largest state? because population, not area, is the feature used to show the comparative sizes of states
3. Can you tell from the cartogram which is the largest state in the United States in terms of geographic size? Why? No; the size of the states shown on the cartogram is based on population rather than on area.
4. What are the five most populated states in the United States? California, New York, Texas, Florida, and Pennsylvania
5. Which state has the larger population—New Jersey or Washington? New Jersey
6. The population of Ohio is about how many times greater than the population of the state of Washington? about two times greater
7. If the population of the state of Washington is about 5,500,000, about what is the population of Ohio? about 11,000,000
8. Of the following three states, which two are closest in population: Pennsylvania, Illinois, Indiana? Pennsylvania and Illinois
9. Give an example to illustrate that the cartogram shows relative populations of the states and not exact population numbers for them. Example—the cartogram shows that Illinois has a population about twice that of Indiana, but it does not provide the total population of either state.
10. Color in your state on the cartogram on page 134.

LESSON 3
Identify Regions

NAME ______________________ DATE __________

Card Catalog

Identify Regions in the Caribbean and in Central America

***DIRECTIONS:** Use the map on page 655 in your textbook and an almanac to help you complete the cards that follow. Color in the main parts of the flags as accurately as possible.*

Name: Haiti (flag: blue, white, red)
Capital: Port-au-Prince
Shares Borders with (Country Names): Dominican Republic
Fact: Shares island of Hispaniola with Dominican Republic

Name: Puerto Rico (flag: blue, red, white)
Capital: San Juan
Shares Borders with (Country Names): None; surrounded by Caribbean Sea and Atlantic Ocean
Fact: A commonwealth of the United States

Name: Nicaragua (flag: white, blue)
Capital: Managua
Shares Borders with (Country Names): Costa Rica and Honduras
Fact: Arnoldo Alemán elected president in 1996

(continued)

LESSON 3
Identify Countries

NAME ______________________ DATE __________

Country Name: Dominican Republic (flag: blue, white, red)
Capital: Santo Domingo
Shares Borders with (Country Names): Haiti
Country Fact: Located on eastern part of the island of Hispaniola

Country Name: Cuba (flag: red, blue, white)
Capital: Havana
Shares Borders with (Country Names): None; surrounded by Atlantic Ocean and Caribbean Sea
Country Fact: Fidel Castro rules as communist leader.

Country Name: Costa Rica (flag: white, blue, red)
Capital: San José
Shares Borders with (Country Names): Nicaragua and Panama
Country Fact: Has a democratic government

LESSON 4
Apply Map and Globe Skills

NAME ______________________ DATE __________

TROPICAL RAIN FORESTS

Apply Map and Globe Skills

***DIRECTIONS:** Study the map of tropical rain forests on this page. Then complete the activities that follow.*

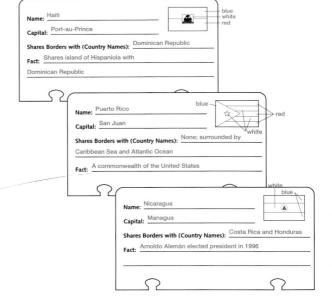

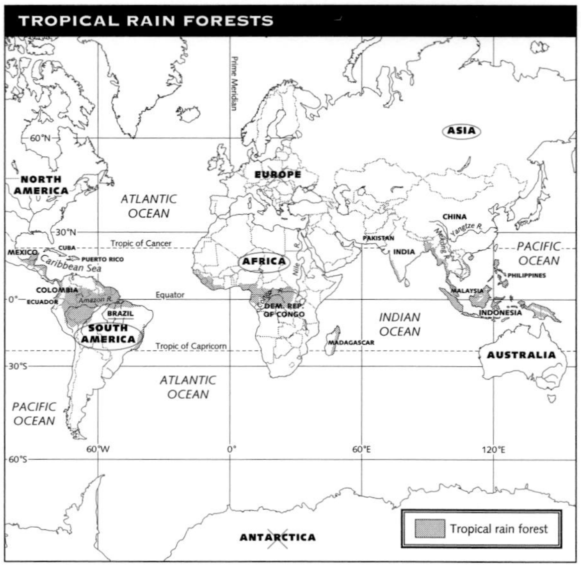

(continued)

LESSON 4
Apply Map and Globe Skills

NAME ______________________ DATE ____________

1. Draw an X through the names of the continents that have no tropical rain forests.
2. Draw a circle around the names of the three continents that have the most tropical rain forests.
3. Underline the name of the country in which deforestation has left many American Indians homeless.
4. List the reasons for deforestation of this country. clearing of forests for planting crops, raising cattle, and mining
5. Which two rivers flow through tropical rain forests? Amazon and Congo
6. Between which two special lines of latitude are most of the tropical rain forests located? Tropic of Cancer and Tropic of Capricorn
7. Why do you think most tropical rain forests lie between these two lines of latitude? Answers should address the tropical climate of the area.
8. What line of latitude passes through rain forests in Brazil, Democratic Republic of the Congo and Malaysia? the equator
9. Are there any tropical rain forests north of 60° N latitude? no
10. Are there any tropical rain forests north of 60° S latitude? yes
11. Are there any tropical rain forests shown in the continental United States? no

LESSON 5
Apply Map and Globe Skills

NAME ______________________ DATE ____________

Canada

Apply Map and Globe Skills

DIRECTIONS: ***Use the map on page 663 in your textbook to help you to label Canada's capital and the capital of each province and territory on the map below.***

DISTRIBUTION OF FRENCH CANADIANS

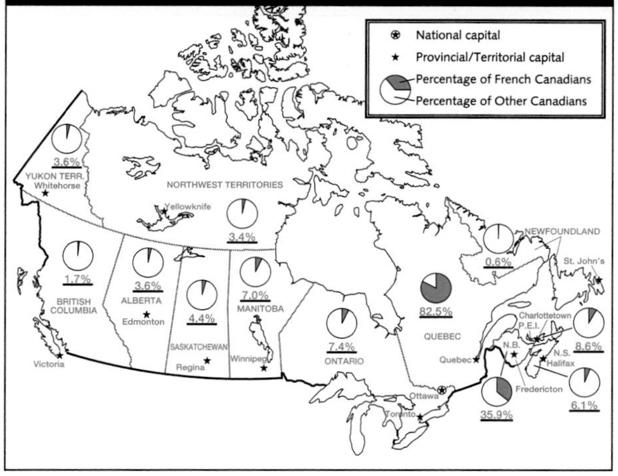

(continued)

LESSON 5
Apply Map and Globe Skills

NAME ______________________ DATE ____________

DIRECTIONS: ***Use the information in the table below to complete the activities that follow.***

CANADA

PROVINCE/TERRITORY	FRENCH CANADIANS (in percentages)	OTHERS (in percentages)
Newfoundland	0.6	99.4
Prince Edward Island	8.6	91.4
Nova Scotia	6.1	93.9
New Brunswick	35.9	64.1
Quebec	82.5	17.5
Ontario	7.4	92.6
Manitoba	7.0	93.0
Saskatchewan	4.4	95.6
Alberta	3.6	96.4
British Columbia	1.7	98.3
Northwest Territories	3.4	96.6
Yukon Territory	3.6	96.4

1. Write the percentage of French Canadians in each province and territory from the above table on the appropriate write-on lines on the map on page 140.
2. Color or shade each circle graph to show the percentage of French Canadians in each province and territory on the map on page 140. Fill in the key box to show the color you used to show the percentage of French Canadians.
3. Determine the percentage of other groups living in each province and territory. Write this percentage in the appropriate column in the above table.
4. On a separate sheet of paper, write a paragraph summarizing why Quebec would want to separate from Canada. Use the information on the map, in the table, and in your textbook to help you. Accept paragraphs that include data from the map, the table, or the textbook.

CHAPTER 20 REVIEW
Connect Main Ideas

NAME ______________________ DATE ____________

THE WESTERN HEMISPHERE *TODAY*

Connect Main Ideas

DIRECTIONS: ***Use this organizer to show that you understand how the chapter's main ideas are connected. Complete the organizer by writing the main idea of each lesson.***

The Western Hemisphere Today

Mexico Today
Although many people believe the free-trade agreement will help the Mexican economy by allowing manufacturers to sell their goods in the United States and Canada, it is opposed by people who fear it will hurt many farmers.

Democracy in the Caribbean and in Central America
Many citizens in this region reap the benefits of democracy, but many others still struggle to bring about political change.

The Peoples of Canada
The Canadian government's Charter of Rights and Freedoms was written to protect the rights and cultural differences of all Canadians, but not all citizens feel that the charter fully recognizes them.

Challenges in South America
South American countries face long-term problems of social and economic inequality, deforestation, and the production and sale of illegal drugs. Many of these problems affect the United States and other parts of the world.

COMMUNITY RESOURCES

Ideas for using community resources, including speakers and field trips

Historical Societies:

Academic Experts and Community Members:

Museums:

Historic Sites:

Chapter 20 Assessment

For ongoing PERFORMANCE ASSESSMENT, see Show What You Know, pp. 646, 658, 661, 665.

CONTENT

NAME ______________________ DATE ____________

Chapter Test 20

Part One: Test Your Understanding *(4 points each)*

DIRECTIONS: ***Circle the letter of the best answer.***

1. The devaluation of Mexico's money in 1994 made it difficult for Mexico's middle class to
   - A. vote in elections.
   - (B.) buy consumer goods.
   - C. communicate with people living outside Mexico.
   - D. stage peaceful protests against the government.

2. The purpose of NAFTA is to
   - (A.) increase trade among the United States, Canada, and Mexico.
   - B. protect the cultures of the American Indians living in North America.
   - C. place an embargo on imports into Canada.
   - D. bring democracy to the countries of Central and South America.

3. In 1993 the people of Puerto Rico voted to
   - A. declare independence from Britain.
   - B. become a state of the United States.
   - C. become a territory of Britain.
   - (D.) remain a commonwealth of the United States.

4. Fidel Castro is the communist dictator of
   - A. the Dominican Republic.
   - (B.) Cuba.
   - C. Jamaica.
   - D. Brazil.

5. What is the purpose of the United States embargo on Cuba?
   - (A.) It stops the United States from trading its goods with Cuba.
   - B. It keeps the Soviet Union from sending missiles to Cuba.
   - C. It prevents Cuba from holding free elections.
   - D. It allows free trade to develop between Cuba and North America.

6. The United States military helped Jean-Bertrand Aristide return to power in 1994 as president of
   - A. Bolivia.
   - B. Venezuela.
   - (C.) Haiti.
   - D. Chile.

(continued)

CONTENT

NAME ______________________ DATE ____________

7. Violeta Chamorro ended her country's communist government when she was elected president of
   - A. El Salvador.
   - (B.) Nicaragua.
   - C. Guatemala.
   - D. Mexico.

8. Deforestation is a major problem in
   - A. Canada.
   - B. Cuba.
   - (C.) Brazil.
   - D. Haiti.

9. The main purpose of the OAS is to settle disagreements
   - A. between the free world and communist nations.
   - (B.) among nations of the Western Hemisphere.
   - C. among nations that fought in World War II.
   - D. between the United States and Japan.

10. The Charter of Rights and Freedoms is
    - A. an agreement to end communism in all South American countries.
    - B. a bill of rights proposed by the Cuban people.
    - C. the document that broke up the Soviet Union.
    - (D.) a section that was added to Canada's Constitution of 1982.

11. What was the main effect of the Canadian Constitution of 1982?
    - A. It caused a civil war in Canada.
    - (B.) It divided the people of Canada.
    - C. It led to closer relations with the government of Britain.
    - D. It weakened the economy of Canada.

12. Which of the following Canadian provinces has objected most to the Constitution of 1982?
    - A. Alberta
    - B. New Brunswick
    - C. British Columbia
    - (D.) Quebec

13. Most people who live in Quebec, Canada, are
    - A. Mexican Canadians.
    - B. British Canadians.
    - (C.) French Canadians.
    - D. German Canadians.

14. People in Canada who are separatists want
    - A. British Columbia to become a state in the United States.
    - B. to end free trade between the United States and Canada.
    - C. to limit French language and culture.
    - (D.) Quebec to secede from Canada and become an independent nation.

(continued)

SKILLS

NAME ______________________ DATE ____________

Part Two: Test Your Skills *(15 points)*

DIRECTIONS: *Figure A below is a map showing the borders of countries in Central America. Figure B below is a cartogram showing the number of immigrants that came from each country to the United States. Use the information in the map and the cartogram to answer the questions that follow.*

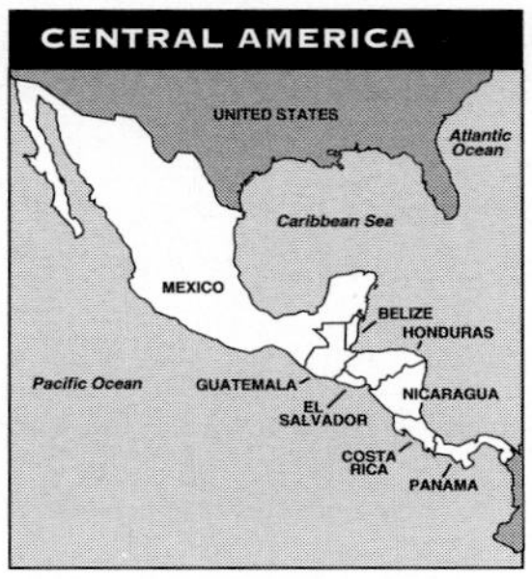

Figure A

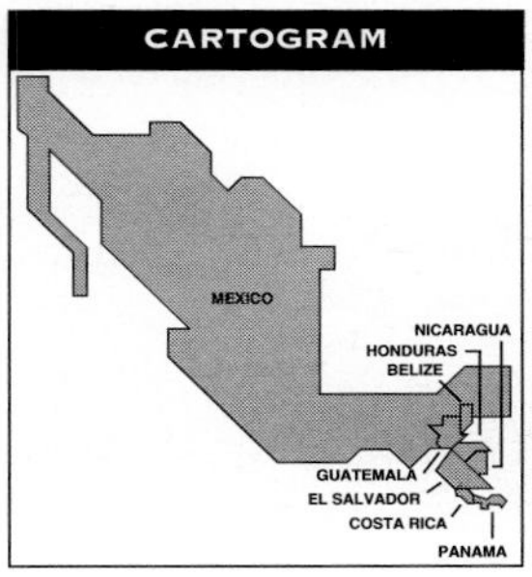

Figure B

15. Which country sent the largest number of immigrants to the United States?

    How can you tell? Mexico; it is the largest country on the cartogram.

16. Which country sent more immigrants to the United States—El Salvador or Belize?

    How can you tell? El Salvador; it is larger than Belize on the cartogram.

17. Which country sent the fewest immigrants to the United States? How can you tell?

    Costa Rica; it is the smallest country on the cartogram.

(continued)

APPLICATION/WRITING

NAME ______________________ DATE ____________

Part Three: Apply What You Have Learned

DIRECTIONS: ***Complete each of the following activities.***

18. ***Problems and Their Causes*** *(12 points)*
    Describe the cause of each of the problems listed below.

Problems of Nations in the Americas	Causes of Problems
the revolt of farmers in Chiapas, Mexico	Possible response: The farmers in Chiapas revolted because the government of Mexico would not protect their land or their culture from the consequences of the NAFTA agreement.
the conflict to restore democracy in Haiti	Possible response: Jean-Bertrand Aristide, the elected president, had been removed from office by the military in Haiti.
the desire of people in Quebec, Canada, to secede	Possible response: The separatists did not believe that the Constitution of 1982 recognized their special role in Canada. They wanted a veto over national decisions and the right to use the French language only.

19. ***Use Vocabulary*** *(7 points)*
    Match the term on the left with the correct description on the right. Write the correct number in the space provided.

a. 4 deforestation	1. a political region of Canada
b. 6 interest rate	2. a person of Indian and European background
c. 1 province	3. a kind of territory
d. 5 liberate	4. the widespread cutting down of forests
e. 7 metropolitan area	5. to set free
f. 3 commonwealth	6. what a bank charges to borrow money
g. 2 mestizo	7. a city and all the suburbs around it

20. ***Essay*** *(10 points)*
    Write a one-paragraph essay describing the special relationship between the United States and Puerto Rico.
    Possible response: Puerto Rico is a commonwealth of the United States. The people of Puerto Rico are United States citizens. They are self-governing and make their own decisions about their government, but they also have close political ties to the government of the United States.

INTRODUCE THE CHAPTER

This chapter examines the countries of the Western Hemisphere other than the United States, and looks at ways in which the history of these countries relates to the problems they face at the present time. The chapter details the lives of the diverse people who live in these countries and looks at how they are governed.

Link Prior Learning

Have students recall what they learned in Units 1 and 2 about the early civilizations of the Americas and the colonization of the region by European nations. Explain that almost all of the countries continued to be European colonies long after the United States had declared its independence in 1776.

Visual Analysis

Interpret Photographs Explain that this picture is of Cinthya Guzman, a 12-year-old Mexican American girl who now lives in California.

Q. **What do you think the photographer wanted you to know about Cinthya Guzman?** that she is happy with her life in the United States

Auditory Learning

Interpret Primary Sources Ask a student volunteer to read the quotation aloud. Have students discuss the challenges faced by immigrants whose native language is not English when they move to the United States.

Q. **Why do you think Cinthya Guzman dreams in both Spanish and English?** She is probably comfortable with both languages and speaks Spanish at home, but speaks English in school and with her friends.

"PRIMARY SOURCE"

Source: *The Other Side: How Kids Live in a California Latino Neighborhood.* Kathleen Krull. Lodestar Books, 1994.

CHAPTER

20 THE WESTERN HEMISPHERE TODAY

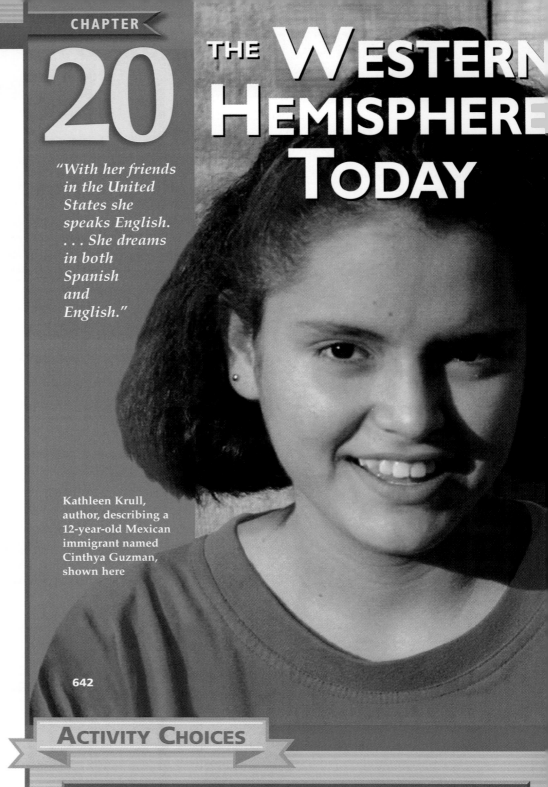

"With her friends in the United States she speaks English. . . . She dreams in both Spanish and English."

Kathleen Krull, author, describing a 12-year-old Mexican immigrant named Cinthya Guzman, shown here

642

ACTIVITY CHOICES

Background

CINTHYA GUZMAN When Cinthya Guzman first moved to the United States as a second grader, she was terrified. During her first month here, she cried every day before going to school. She started out in a Spanish-speaking class because she did not know English. Soon she was shifted to a bilingual class, and today she is a straight-A student in all English-speaking classes.

Guzman's family, like many other Mexican families, moved to the United States for better jobs, better pay, and a better life. Just a year after they moved to the United States, Guzman's father offered to move back to Mexico because he could see that his daughter was not happy. However, even at age 8, Guzman knew she would have a better future in the United States. She reassured her father that she would be all right. Today her family is urging her to plan for a college education, and she hopes someday to be a nurse, a veterinarian, or a lawyer.

LESSON

1

FOCUS

How might economic differences among people in a country cause problems?

Main Idea Read to learn how economic conditions have divided many of the people of Mexico.

Vocabulary

metropolitan area
middle class
interest rate
free-trade agreement

Mexico Today

The Republic of Mexico shares the North American con-
ıent with Canada and the United States. Mexico's lands are verse—including coastal plains, rain forests, and moun-ıins. These lands provide harvests of corn, wheat, and many her crops as well as natural resources such as silver, gold, ıd oil. All of these crops and resources have helped Mexico's onomy in the past. In recent years, however, Mexico's onomy has been troubled by many problems.

The Growth of Cities and the Middle Class

Seven out of every ten Mexicans live in urban areas. In the ountry's central and northern states, the urban population ıs boomed in recent years. Among the fastest-growing cities Mexico City, in the central region.

Mexico City, ringed by volcanic mountains, stands on the te of the Aztec capital of Tenochtitlán. When the Aztecs built eir capital in the 1300s, it was one of the world's largest ties. In the early 1500s, the Spanish conquered the Aztecs ıd destroyed Tenochtitlán. In its place they built Mexico City be the capital of the Spanish colony of New Spain.

Today Mexico City remains the nation's capital, or Federal istrict. Its population is the largest of all the cities in the orld. More than 8 million people live within Mexico City. lmost 21 million people live in the metropolitan area. A **etropolitan area** is a city and all the suburbs and other pop-ation areas around it. The largest metropolitan area in the nited States is New York City. New York City's metropolitan ea has about 20 million people.

Between 1940 and 1970 many factories were built in the orthern region of Mexico. Cities there grew quickly. Hoping find factory jobs, great numbers of people moved from ıral areas to Monterrey, Ciudad Juárez (SEE•u•dahd WAR•ays), Matamoros (mah•tah•MOH•rohs), and Tijuana ee•WAH•nah).

Mexico City, like all large cities, has crowded streets at rush hour.

Reading Support

ANTICIPATION GUIDE Before students read the lesson, ask them to predict which of the following statements are true and which are false. Students may correct their predictions as they read.

1. Most Mexicans live in rural areas. false
2. A metropolitan area is just the center city. false
3. Factories made the rich richer and kept the poor still poor. false
4. NAFTA is a free-trade agreement that helps Mexican business people. true
5. Farmers are afraid that NAFTA will hurt their farm trade. true

Objectives

1. Summarize the growth of Mexico as an industrial nation.
2. Analyze the advantages and disadvantages of NAFTA for Mexico today.

Vocabulary

metropolitan area (p. 643)
middle class (p. 644)
interest rate (p. 644)
free-trade agreement (p. 645)

1. ACCESS

The Focus Question

Lead students in a discussion of economic differences among peoples and have them identify the reasons for these economic differences. Ask students to speculate on how people would react if they thought they would not be able to meet their basic needs.

The Main Idea

In this lesson students explore the economic achievements of the people of Mexico and the economic uncertainties the country faces today. After students have read the lesson, ask them to analyze why economic conditions have divided many of the people of Mexico.

2. BUILD

The Growth of Cities and the Middle Class

Key Content Summary

As industries developed in cities of northern Mexico between 1940 and 1970, they attracted large numbers of people from rural areas and created a strong middle class. In 1994 an economic crisis caused concern among the people of Mexico.

Geography

Regions Refer students to the map of Mexico on page 645, and ask them to locate Mexico City and the cities in northern Mexico. Also have them locate the long border Mexico shares with the United States.

Q. Why do you think Mexico's manufacturing was concentrated in the northern region of the country? to be close to the United States market

Economics

Economic Systems and Institutions Explain to the class that World War II contributed significantly to Mexico's industrial growth. Mexico supplied raw materials, laborers, and war equipment to the United States.

Q. What led to the growth of a large middle class in Mexico? the growth of manufacturing

Economics

Productivity and Economic Growth Make sure students understand how and why money becomes devalued. Have students imagine that the dollar was devalued by 50 percent, and ask them to figure out how much more it would cost them to buy familiar items.

Q. Why would high interest rates on bank loans discourage people from buying houses and cars? The high rates would make these items much too expensive.

Some members of Mexico's middle-class families have jobs making computers and other products in factories built along the United States–Mexico border.

As in the United States, the growth of manufacturing in Mexico led to the growth of a large **middle class**, an economic level between the poor and the wealthy. Shopkeepers, factory managers, lawyers, and other workers and their families make up the middle class. By the 1990s Mexico's middle class was one of the largest in all the countries of the Americas.

For many years most middle-class families in Mexico had enough money to buy the many new products manufactured in their country. Then, in 1994, Mexico's money suddenly became devalued. That is, the value of Mexico's money suddenly dropped. This caused prices to rise sharply. Some prices doubled. Others tripled. **Interest rates**, or the amounts that banks charge customers to borrow money, rose as high as 80 percent. Middle-class families found it very difficult to buy houses, cars, and most consumer products. The Mexicans called this economi disaster "the devaluation of 1994." The deva uation was caused by inflation and the Mexican government's need to pay its debts

REVIEW ***How did the devaluation of 1994 affect Mexico's middle class?***

HERITAGE

Colorfully dressed dancers celebrate Cinco de Mayo in Austin, Texas.

Cinco de Mayo

Cinco de Mayo, also known as Battle of Puebla Day, is a national holiday in Mexico. *Cinco de Mayo* means "fifth of May" in Spanish. On May 5, 1862, the Mexican army fought the French army in the Mexican city of Puebla. The French were trying to take control of the Mexican government. Although the French army was much larger, the Mexican army was able to hold off the French Army. Today the Mexican people and many Mexican Americans celebrate Cinco de Mayo with parades and fireworks. The holiday is important as a day to celebrate Mexican independence and national pride.

Middle-class families found it difficult to buy houses, cars, and most consume products.

ACTIVITY CHOICES

Link to Mathematics

CALCULATE DEVALUATION Explain to the class that devaluation is usually an official act by a government to reduce the fixed rate at which it exchanges its own currency for foreign currency or for gold. A government often devalues its currency in order to stimulate exports and reduce imports. Have students work out this devaluation problem: Two weeks ago a blanket exported from the United States cost the equivalent of $20.00 in foreign currencies. Last week the United States devalued the dollar by 20 percent. Would the exported blanket now cost more or less in a foreign currency? less

Background

MAQUILADORAS Many of the factories in the Mexican cities along the United States border are owned by U.S. companies. They are called *maquiladoras.* Most Mexican workers are paid relatively low wages, allowing U.S. companies owning *maquiladoras* to cut costs. The manufacturing plants employ thousands of Mexican workers, who turn out everything from electronic equipment to children's toys. With the passage of the NAFTA agreement in 1994, U.S. companies set up many more *maquiladoras.*

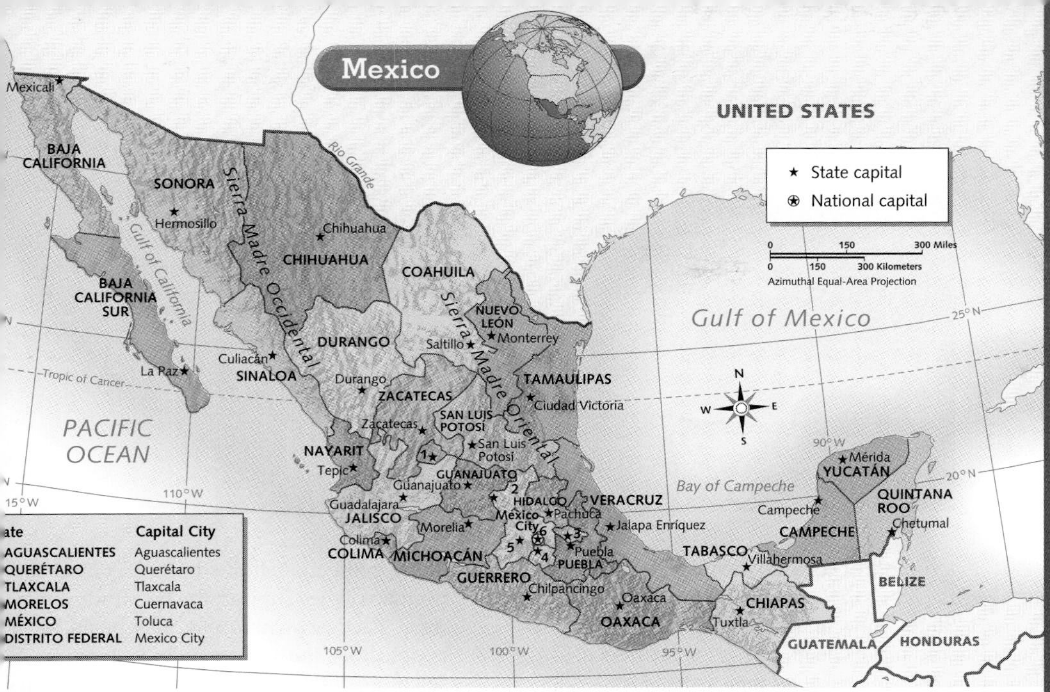

MAP THEME **Regions** Mexico is divided into 31 states.
■ *Which Mexican states border the United States?*

Reaction to NAFTA

Mexico's economy had caused problems for its people for many years. With the devaluation of 1994, the problems were made worse. People at all economic levels lost their jobs. Mexico's poor people, who make up 45 percent of the country's almost 98 million people, suffered the most. For them, even basic foods such as beans and eggs became luxuries.

Before the devaluation, the Mexican government had decided that one way the nation could make its economy stronger was to join the United States and Canada in signing the North American Free Trade Agreement, known as NAFTA. A **free-trade agreement** is a treaty in which countries agree to charge no tariffs on goods they buy from each other and sell to each other. Such an agreement gives businesses in these countries the chance to compete more fairly.

But the NAFTA agreement did not make everyone in Mexico happy. Among those who were angry that the Mexican government had signed the NAFTA agreement were many of the country's farmers. On January 1, 1994, the date NAFTA went into effect, about 2,000 poor farmers in the southern Mexican state of Chiapas (chee•AH•pahs) took control of several towns. Fighting between the farmers and Mexican soldiers soon broke out, and more than 100 people were killed.

Most of the farmers in Chiapas are of American Indian heritage. They make up half the population of the state. They were afraid that free trade would bring large

Reaction to NAFTA

Key Content Summary

Following the devaluation of 1994, Mexico's economic problems worsened, with poor people suffering most. Farmers in Chiapas rebelled, fearing the effects of NAFTA. People in Mexico's urban and industrial centers, however, believe NAFTA will benefit Mexico's economy.

Economics

Markets and Prices Have students explain the conditions of a free-trade agreement.

Q. **Why do you think the Mexican government wanted to join the United States and Canada in NAFTA?** Government officials hope that NAFTA will make the Mexican economy stronger.

Visual Analysis

Learn from Maps Have students answer the questions in the caption. Baja California, Sonora, Chihuahua, Coahuila, Nuevo León, Tamaulipas

Economics

Economic Systems and Institutions Have students compare and contrast the reactions of the farmers to NAFTA with the reactions of the factory owners and other business people, and ask them how NAFTA might change the Mexican economy.

Background

THE CHIAPAS REBELLION The rebels of Chiapas called themselves the Zapatista National Liberation Army, invoking the name of Emiliano Zapata, who led a rebellion against the government in the early 1900s. Zapata, like the Chiapas rebels, fought to give land to the people who worked it. The Chiapas rebels and the Mexican government reached a tentative agreement in 1995 to improve economic conditions in the region.

Extend and Enrich

COOPERATIVE LEARNING

MAKE A TIME LINE Divide the class into groups, and put each group in charge of researching one or two decades of Mexican history in the 1900s. Have each group use library resources to find and record the important events in Mexican history during their assigned time period. Ask each group to make a section of a class time line and insert the dates and events they chose. After the class time line is completed, have the groups share and discuss the events they chose.

Technology

Use TIMELINER™ to complete this activity.

3. CLOSE

Have students consider again the Focus question on page 643.

How might economic differences among people in a country cause problems?

Have students use what they have learned about the economy of Mexico to explain how economic differences among people in a country might cause problems.

LESSON 1 REVIEW—Answers

Check Understanding

1. Mexico City
2. The growth of industry in Mexico's northern cities led to the development of a middle class that hopes to benefit from trade with the United States and Canada. Mexico's farmers, many of whom are already poor, fear that the free-trade agreement will force them to lose their farm markets to the United States and Canada.

Think Critically

3. The devaluation of 1994 caused high prices, and it limited the ability of the middle class to buy houses, cars, and many consumer products. Mexico's poor could hardly afford to buy basic foods.
4. To farmers, NAFTA poses a threat to their livelihood. They fear that farm products from the United States and Canada will be sold more cheaply than the farmers of Chiapas could sell their products. Mexican business people hope that NAFTA will help them sell more of their goods in the United States and Canada.

Show What You Know

Performance Assessment Have students look at maps in encyclopedias and atlases and brainstorm ideas before drawing their maps. You may wish to have students work in pairs or in small groups to create the maps.

What to Look For Look for evidence that students have used references to accurately identify and place the cities, states, landforms, and products on the map.

This woman baking tortillas is from Oaxaca (wuh•HAH•kuh), a state in southern Mexico. Many people in southern Mexico depend on farming to make a living.

amounts of corn, soybeans, wheat, and other farm products to Mexico from the United States and Canada. These products could be sold more cheaply than the farmers of Chiapas could sell their crops. One leader of the farmers said, "The free-trade agreement is a death certificate for the Indian peoples of Mexico."

While many Mexicans living in the rural southern states are against NAFTA, those living in the more industrialized central and northern states support the free-trade agreement. Factory owners and other business people hope the agreement will help them sell more of their goods in the growing markets of the United States and Canada. They believe that this trade will create more jobs in Mexico and will strengthen the country's economy as a whole.

REVIEW *What is NAFTA?*

LESSON 1 REVIEW

Check Understanding

1. **Remember the Facts** Which city in Mexico has the largest population of all cities in the world?
2. **Recall the Main Idea** How have economic conditions divided many of the people of Mexico?

Think Critically

3. **Cause and Effect** What effects did the devaluation of 1994 have on Mexico's middle class? What effects did it have on Mexico's poor people?
4. **Explore Viewpoints** How did farmers in southern Mexico view the NAFTA agreement? How did Mexico's business people view the agreement?

Show What You Know

Map Activity Make a map that shows the states and major cities of Mexico. Add illustrations that show landforms and products. Discuss what you have learned about Mexico as you compare your map with those of your classmates.

the North American Free Trade Agreement, a treaty in which countries agree to charge no tariffs on goods they buy from each other and sell to each other

ACTIVITY CHOICES

ACTIVITY BOOK

Reinforce & Extend

Use ACTIVITY BOOK, p. 131.

Reteach the Main Idea

DRAW ILLUSTRATIONS Challenge students to use the textbook as a resource to draw illustrations that show some of the differences between Mexicans who live in the northern cities and the farmers of southern Mexico. Ask students to write captions to accompany their pictures. Have student volunteers read their captions to the class. You may wish to display the completed illustrations.

Save My Rainforest

LESSON 2

LEARN CULTURE *through* Literature

by Monica Zak
illustrations by Bengt-Arne Runnerström
English version by Nancy Schimmel

Omar Castillo lives in Mexico City, which is over an 800-mile (1,287 km) walk from the Selva Lacandona (SEL•vuh lah•kahn•DOH•nah), Mexico's last remaining rain forest. On the television news, Omar hears that the rain forest is in danger of being destroyed. He decides that he must try to do something to save the rain forest. With the help of his father, Omar sets out on foot to make a long, difficult journey that he will never forget.

Chapter 20 • 647

Reading Support

CAUSE AND EFFECT Provide students with the following visual framework. Then have students complete the cause and effect chart.

Rain Forest	
Cause Omar Castillo's reason for going to Chiapas __________ __________ __________	**Effect** results of Omar's trip __________ __________ __________

Objectives

1. Summarize the sacrifices Omar and his father were willing to make to save the rain forest.
2. Evaluate the importance and success of Omar's mission.

1. ACCESS

Have students recall some of the individuals they have read about in U.S. history who have undertaken projects against great odds. Ask them to evaluate the advantages and disadvantages of the challenges those individuals faced. Ask students to identify individuals today who are undertaking projects against great odds.

The Main Idea

In this lesson students read about young Omar Castillo, who, with his father, hikes more than 800 miles (1,287 km) to try to persuade the governor of Chiapas to save Mexico's last rain forest. After students have read Omar's story, ask whether they would have accompanied Omar on his journey and why.

2. BUILD

Auditory Learning

Express Ideas Orally Select a student to read aloud the introduction to Omar's story. Have students infer why a rain forest is important not only to the country in which it is located but to other countries as well.

Q. **Why do you think a boy from a city would be eager to save a rain forest?** He may have worried about the endangered animals and plants in the rain forest. Also, because he lived in a city, he may have a strong appreciation for open, natural spaces and clean air.

Key Content Summary

Omar and his father set out to walk to the governor's office in Tuxtla Gutiérrez in the state of Chiapas. After walking for a week in the mountains, they reach the plains but run out of money to pay for food. Nevertheless, they decide to continue their 870-mile journey.

Understanding the Story

Students may find it difficult to believe that anyone as young as Omar would be willing to make such a difficult journey for the sake of an ideal.

Q. **Is Omar ever inclined to give up the journey?** Early on, after his feet are blistered, he says he is too tired to proceed.

Why does Omar revive when the woman at the fruit stand asks about the banner? Her question reminds Omar of the reason for his journey, and he realizes that he does not want to quit.

Visual Analysis

Interpret Pictures Have students observe the picture and describe the land and climate where Omar and his father are walking.

Civics and Government

Purposes of Government Have students discuss why Omar decided that the best way to try to save the rain forest was to talk to the governor of Chiapas.

Early one morning Omar and his father start walking. At first Omar is smiling and singing. On the road at last! And tonight, for the first time in his life, he will sleep in a tent.

For hours and hours they walk on the hot pavement. Finally, they leave the dirty yellow air of the city for the clear, clean air of the countryside. But Omar is too tired to notice. Then his feet begin to hurt. He goes a good ways before he says anything. When he does, his father stops and takes Omar's shoes off.

"You have blisters. I'll put a bandage on . . . there. Now we can get started again."

"But Papa, I'm too tired. I can't go on."

"I'm tired too," says his father, "but try to go a little farther. I'll buy us a cool drink at the next store." They find a fruit stand where a woman with long braids sells them tall glasses of pineapple drink.

She looks at them curiously and finally asks, "What does your banner say? I can't read."

Omar revives at once. "This side says 'Let's protect the rainforest' and the other side says 'Walk—Mexico City—Tuxtla Gutiérrez.'[1] Tuxtla's a long way south of here, but that's where we decided to go, to see the governor of the state of Chiapas, where the rainforest is. He is responsible for taking care of it. We need to tell him to save the rainforest so there will still be a rainforest in Mexico for us children when we grow up."

"You must be sent from heaven!" she says.

Omar's father smiles. "No, he's just a regular kid. All kids have good ideas, but usually people don't listen to them. It

[1] **Tuxtla Gutiérrez:** (TOOST•lah goo•TYAIR•ehs)

648 • Unit 10

ACTIVITY CHOICES

Background

THE LITERATURE SELECTION The reading is from a book called *Save My Rainforest,* which is a true story of Omar Castillo's dedication to the Selva Lacandona rain forest. As an eight-year-old, Omar hopes that he will be able to visit the rain forest when he is an adult. But when he learns that the rain forest is about to be cut down by loggers, he embarks on a 39-day trek to save it. Although he is unsuccessful in this effort, he continues his fight to save rain forests by enlisting the help of Mexico's children.

THE AUTHOR *Save My Rainforest* was written by Monica Zak, a native of Germany. After she moved to Sweden during World War II, she became a newspaper reporter. She then moved to Latin America, where she began to write children's books in Spanish. The English translation of *Save My Rainforest* was named a Notable Trade Book in the Field of Social Studies.

never made any difference to me that they were destroying the rainforest and the animals, but when I thought about what my son said, I realized that he knew what he was talking about. That's why I decided to come with him."

Another day, the sun beats down through the thin mountain air. This time it is Omar's father who has blisters. He calls, "Must you walk so fast, Omar?"

After walking more than a week, they come down out of the mountains. They can see banana plantations now, and *mango* trees. They camp by the side of the road.

Omar lies in the tent and listens. The night before, he heard coyotes howling near the tent: ah-ooo, ah-ooo, ah-ooo. He was afraid. Now he listens to the murmuring leaves. *What if a snake should get into the tent? What if robbers attack us?* he thinks. An enormous truck rumbles past and shakes the tent. *What if the driver fell asleep and . . .*

"Omar, are you awake?" his father asks.

"Mm-hm," answers Omar. "I can't sleep."

"Well," says Omar's father, "we really had a tough day. Heat, no shade, and traffic. Now it's pleasant. We won't be cold tonight."

"No," says Omar, smiling. "Remember the first night in the tent? I thought it would be wonderful, camping, but then the rain started . . ."

"Yes," says his father, "and the water came in. At three in the morning! Remember how good that hot *pozole* tasted after we walked in the dark and cold?"

Understanding the Story

Have students discuss why it is important that they and their peers become aware of how the decisions people make today will affect their future.

Q. **Why did Omar's father decide to go with Omar to Chiapas?** He realized that Omar's ideas about the rain forest were important and that he should support his son in this worthy cause.

Economics

Interdependence and Income Have students analyze the economic sacrifices Omar's father is making for his son's mission. Make sure they understand that Omar's father has spent all the money he brought, and he has lost income while away from his job. Ask students to predict how Omar and his father might get food for the rest of the trip.

Link to Science

RESEARCH CONSERVATION GROUPS
Have student volunteers use library resources to find out the names of organizations and governments that are working to preserve the rain forests. Ask students to write to several of the organizations to gather information on the activities of these groups, and have students report their findings to the class. The class may wish to organize an activity of their own to help the effort to save the rain forest.

Background

RAIN FORESTS Most of the biological diversity of a rain forest is found in the canopy, which is why scientists find the rain forest difficult to study. In 1989 a group of French scientists used inflated rafts dropped onto the canopy from a dirigible to help them establish a place from which they could study that important ecosystem. Many scientists believe they are in a race against time to find out more about the rain forests before they are completely destroyed. They are hoping also that their discoveries will convince people that the rain forests hold the answers to improving food production and to discovering new cures for diseases. Scientists predict that if the logging and burning continue at their present rate, the rain forests could be gone in 20 years. They also fear the consequences of such a dramatic change in Earth's ecological balance.

Understanding the Story

Before students resume their reading of the story, ask them to predict whether Omar and his father will or will not reach Tuxtla.

Q. **What new experiences occurred that could have discouraged Omar and his father from continuing the trip?** Omar started missing his friends and toys; he got bored; they were told the shortcut was too dangerous; they heard that an earthquake had hit Mexico City, and they worried terribly about their family.

Geography

Human–Environment Interactions

Have students discuss the effects of earthquakes on people and their environment. Ask them why Omar and his father were crying when they saw the Mexico City hospital in a pile of rubble.

Visual Analysis

Read Maps Refer students to the map on this page and have them trace Omar's trek from Mexico City to Tuxtla Gutiérrez.

"Papa, how many more days do we have to walk?"

"I thought it would take fifteen or twenty days, but it will take much longer. I don't want to disappoint you, but I don't believe we can go on."

"But why?" asks Omar, astounded.

"We are running out of money."

They decide to keep going.

"We will have to beg for food," says Omar.

They go into a restaurant and Omar's father explains to the owner why they are walking. "We have no more money," Omar's father says, "and my son is awfully hungry." The owner turns them out without giving them even a glass of water. But then a woman sitting outside a little hut motions them in, makes a fresh pot of coffee, and serves them coffee and bread. It goes like that. Some days people give them food, but often they have to walk the whole day without eating anything. Those days are hard.

When Omar sees boys playing soccer, he stops and watches with envy, but they never ask him to play. Sometimes there are things to look at in the road: a huge scorpion or snakes run over by cars. But more often, walking is boring. Omar throws rocks at fenceposts, thinking *Why didn't I bring anything to play with?* Then somebody who hears he is going to the rainforest gives him a toy Tarzan. He passes the time pretending Tarzan is in the rainforest, swinging from vines.

People warn them not to take the shortest way to Tuxtla, the road that goes through poor villages. "They'll attack you and rob you. It's too dangerous!" But Omar and his father take that road anyway, because it is 125 miles shorter. At first they are a little afraid, but no one attacks them. In fact, women and children come out and give them oranges and *tortilla* chips. . . .

A few days later they stop in a little town to eat in a restaurant. An announcer

Activity Choices

Link to Language Arts

WRITE TO PERSUADE Have students imagine that they are friends of Omar Castillo. Ask them to write letters to the governor of Chiapas giving reasons why they support Omar in his efforts to save the Selva Lacandona.

Technology

Use IMAGINATION EXPRESS:™ DESTINATION RAINFOREST to complete this activity.

Extend and Enrich

COOPERATIVE LEARNING

CREATE A DISPLAY Divide the class into groups. Assign each group a topic about the rain forest, such as plants of the rain forest, animals of the rain forest, insects of the rain forest, locations of rain forests around the world, how scientists study the rain forest, and discoveries in the rain forest that help people. Have each group use library resources or the Internet to research the assigned topic and prepare a display to teach other students in the class about the topic. You may wish to have students present their information to other classes or display their work in the hall.

comes on television to say there has been a terrible earthquake in Mexico City. They see a picture of a big pile of rubble and hear that it is the hospital where Omar's grandmother works! Omar starts to cry. His father has tears in his eyes. No one can reach Mexico City by telephone because the lines are out. Then a ham radio operator in the town promises he will help them get news.

After four days of waiting, the radio operator says, "Your *abuela* is alive, Omar. She wasn't in the hospital when the earthquake came. Your mother is well. She sends you kisses and says your house wasn't hurt at all. She wishes you a safe journey."

And now they can continue.

After thirty-nine days of walking, Omar and his father come to Tuxtla Gutiérrez. They have travelled 870 miles and they are tired. They have to wait the whole day outside the governor's office, but finally the moment comes that Omar has been hoping for.

His heart beats loudly as he faces the governor and says, "Save my rainforest and stop the hunting of the rainforest animals for the next twenty years." The governor pats Omar on the head and says there is nothing to worry about.

Omar still worries. *He is treating me like a kid,* he thinks. *He won't do anything.*

But Omar does get to see a rainforest. When Tuxtla was built, a piece of the rainforest was left as a park. At first, Omar is disappointed in the rainforest, too. There aren't lots of strange animals running around in plain sight. Just gigantic trees and a clean wet smell.

Omar stands quietly for a long time in the deep green light amid the huge trunks, listening to all the birds singing high above in the canopy of leaves. Then he knows that being in a real rainforest at last is worth the trouble of walking 870 miles.

LITERATURE REVIEW

1. Why did Omar and his father walk from Mexico City to Tuxtla Gutiérrez?
2. For what reasons might you take an action like Omar's?
3. In the years after his long journey, Omar Castillo continued to work with other children to save the rain forest. With a partner, brainstorm other environmental problems in the world today. Make a list of the actions you might take to help solve one of these problems.

Understanding the Story

Have students decide whether they agree with Omar that his individual actions were worth the effort.

Q. **Why does Omar believe that the governor will not do anything to save the rain forest?** He can tell by the way the governor treats him.

Share with students the fact that Omar went on to organize children to help save the rain forest.

3. CLOSE

Ask students the following question to focus on individualism and interdependence.

Why did Omar and his father make great sacrifices to try to save the Selva Lacandona in Chiapas?

Have students use what they have learned about the efforts of Omar and his father to explain why it is sometimes important to take individual action. Also have students analyze how Omar's efforts might have been more successful if he had used interdependent action to save the rain forest.

LITERATURE REVIEW—Answers

1. to try to save the Selva Lacandona rain forest from being destroyed
2. to protest an action that students believe might damage their homes, neighborhoods, country, or future
3. Problems might include above-ground nuclear weapons testing, dumping harmful chemicals into streams or lakes, killing of endangered animals such as elephants or tigers, or causing other animals to become endangered. Lists of actions might include writing letters to newspapers, politicians, and polluters; joining organizations that work to solve environmental or other problems; and organizing groups among their peers to work on environmental problems in their own community.

Reteach the Main Idea

COOPERATIVE LEARNING

ROLE-PLAY AN INTERVIEW Divide the class into groups, and ask each group to imagine that they are television reporters assigned to interview Omar and his father in Tuxtla Gutiérrez. Have each group prepare a list of appropriate questions focusing on the reasons for the trip, the results of the trip, and Omar's and his father's hopes for the future. Ask each group to select one member to be Omar and another to be his father. Have each group role-play the interview in the form of a television news program.

ACTIVITY BOOK

Reinforce & Extend

Use ACTIVITY BOOK, pp. 132–133.

Objectives

1. Recognize three ways to show population on maps.
2. Analyze population data.

Vocabulary

cartogram (p. 652) | population density (p. 652)

1. ACCESS

Have students look at both of the maps in this lesson. Point out that, although the maps appear quite different, both provide population information. Emphasize that population maps provide information about where people live in a country as well as about how the populations of different countries compare.

2. BUILD

Have students use the information in Understand the Process to interpret the population density of Mexico. Have them compare the information in the map key with the map to interpret the population density of different parts of the country. Note the concentration of population around cities.

Call students' attention to the different-size dots that indicate the size of cities. Have students use the map key and the information in the lesson to interpret the size of cities. Guadalajara is larger than Mérida. Oaxaca has fewer people. Have students locate a city with a population larger than 10,000,000 Mexico City; from 1 to 10 million Guadalajara and Monterrey; from 500,000 to 1 million Mexicali and León; and under 500,000 possible responses include Durango and Mérida

Map and Globe Skills

Use Population Maps

1. Why Learn This Skill?

Like most other geographic information, population is shown on maps in many different ways. One way is with color. Another is with dots. A third way to show population is on a special kind of map called a cartogram. A **cartogram** is a map that shows information by changing the size of places. Knowing how to read different kinds of population maps can make it easier for you to find out the number of people who live in different areas.

2. Understand the Process

Look at the key on the population map of Mexico below. The key tells you that the colors on the map stand for different population densities. **Population density** is the number of people who live in 1 square mile or 1 square kilometer of land. On the map the color yellow stands for the least crowded areas. Red stands for the most crowded areas. Read the map key to find the areas in Mexico that have more than 250 people per square mile or more than 100 people per square kilometer. Is Mexico more populated in the central part of the country or in the northern part?

The population of cities is also given on the population map of Mexico. Different-sized dots stand for cities with different population sizes. The largest dot on the map stands for a city

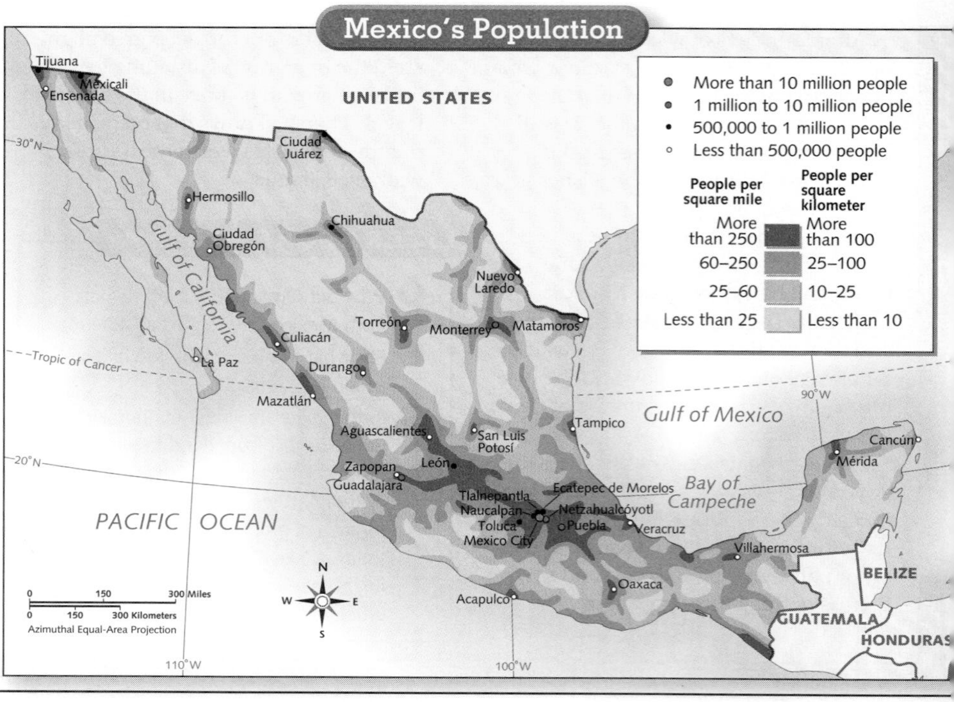

ACTIVITY CHOICES

Home Involvement

Have students invite their family members to help them look for road maps that use a dot system to indicate the size of cities. They should use the key on the road map to analyze the system. Then have them interpret the dots to determine the sizes of various cities on the map. Also have students note other ways road maps can indicate the size of cities.

TECHNOLOGY

Use MAPSKILLS to complete this activity.

with a population of more than 10 million people. The next-smaller dot stands for cities of 1 to 10 million people. These symbols do not give the exact populations of cities. But they do help you compare the population sizes of cities. Find the dots for the cities of Guadalajara and Mérida. Which city has more people? Which city has fewer people, Monterrey or Oaxaca?

Now look at the cartogram of the Western Hemisphere. This cartogram also shows information about population, but in a very different way. On most maps, the size of a country is based on its land area. On a population cartogram, however, the size of a country is based on its population instead of its land area.

A cartogram does not show the number of people who live in each country. But it does show how each country's population compares with that of another country. Countries with larger populations are larger on a cartogram. Countries with smaller populations are smaller on a cartogram.

Find Canada and Mexico on a globe or a map. You will notice that Canada has a larger land area than Mexico, so it is larger in size. Which of these two countries is larger on the cartogram below? What does the cartogram show about these countries?

3. Think and Apply

MAP SKILLS

Study the population information given on the map on page 652 and on the cartogram below. Then show some of the same information by using a chart, graph, or table. You might make a bar graph comparing the numbers of cities with different populations in Mexico or a table showing the five countries with the largest populations.

Cartogram: Population of the Western Hemisphere

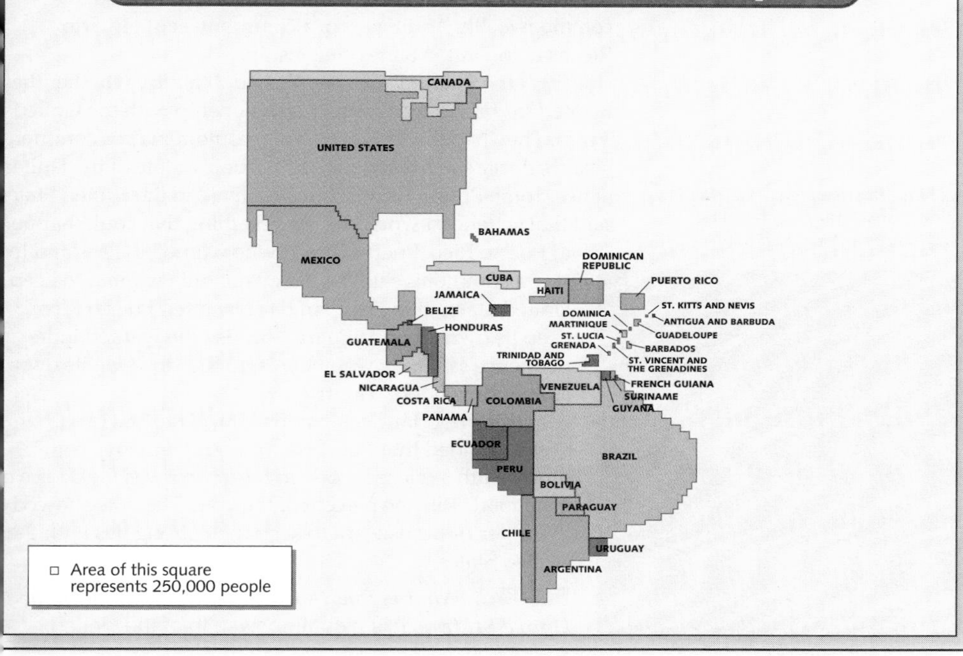

Now turn to the cartogram. Students will probably notice that it looks quite different from most maps of the Western Hemisphere they have seen. Emphasize that on a population cartogram the size of each country is based on its population rather than its land area.

Display a land-area map or globe of North America. Have students compare the sizes of Mexico and Canada on the land-area map with their sizes on the cartogram to answer the questions in the lesson. Mexico is larger on the cartogram. The cartogram shows that Mexico has a much denser population than Canada. You may want to point out that Canada's area is almost five times that of Mexico's, while Mexico's population is more than three times that of Canada's.

3. CLOSE

Have students complete the activity in Think and Apply. Review the form and function of bar graphs, charts, and tables and provide samples to which the students may refer. As students work, look for an understanding of how to extract information from different population maps.

Meet Individual Needs

ENGLISH LANGUAGE LEARNERS Have Spanish-speaking students help others learn to pronounce the names of Mexican cities. Also encourage them to share with the class any information they have about population density in Mexico and other Latin American countries. Suggest that they talk with people they know who have lived in Mexico and report their findings to the class.

Reteach the Skill

ANALYZE POPULATION DENSITY OF STATES Have students look in encyclopedias or atlases to find population density maps of various states. Have them use skills from Understand the Process to interpret the maps. Ask them to note how the maps are similar to and different from the one in this lesson.

ACTIVITY BOOK

Practice & Apply

Use ACTIVITY BOOK, pp. 134–135.

TRANSPARENCY

Use TRANSPARENCIES 52A–52B.

Objectives

1. Analyze Puerto Rico's relationship with the United States.
2. Describe the effect of political changes on the people of Cuba.
3. Summarize Haiti's struggle against military rule.
4. Compare and contrast the effects of politics in Nicaragua and in Costa Rica.

Vocabulary

commonwealth (p. 654)
embargo (p. 656)
free election (p. 657)

1. ACCESS

The Focus Question

Ask students to consider how much the election of government leaders such as the President affects the way people live in the United States. Then ask students to skim recent news magazines to find examples of political changes that affect the way people in other nations live today.

The Main Idea

In this lesson students explore the political instability of many countries in the Caribbean and in Central America and its impact on the people there. After students have read the lesson, have them synthesize the causes of political unrest in this region.

2. BUILD

Puerto Rico

Key Content Summary

In 1993 the Puerto Rican people voted on their island's political future. The largest number of Puerto Ricans chose to continue their status as a commonwealth of the United States rather than become an independent nation or a state of the United States.

LESSON 3

FOCUS How might political changes affect the way people live in a country?

Main Idea Read to find out how political changes have affected the way people live in the Caribbean and in Central America.

Vocabulary
commonwealth
embargo
free election

Democracy in the Caribbean and in Central America

Like the United States, many nations in the Caribbean and in Central America have a history of democracy. Costa Rica has a long democratic tradition. So does Puerto Rico, with its ties to the United States. In other places in the region, however, people continue to struggle for democracy.

Puerto Rico

In 1898, after the Spanish-American War, the United States took control of Puerto Rico from Spain. In 1952 Puerto Rico became a kind of territory of the United States called a **commonwealth**. As citizens of a commonwealth, Puerto Ricans hold United States citizenship.

In 1993 the Puerto Rican people had to decide whether they wanted to change their political relationship with the United States. They had three choices. They could remain a commonwealth, declare independence, or become a state of the United States. Some Puerto Ricans who had lived in the United States said that statehood would be the best thing that could happen to Puerto Rico. Puerto Ricans who wanted their island to stay a commonwealth said they not only wanted to keep United States citizenship but also wanted Puerto Rico to keep its own identity. Puerto Ricans who wanted independence said they wanted Puerto Rico to be on its own as an independent country.

In this important vote, more than 48 percent of the voters decided that Puerto Rico should remain a commonwealth. A close second in the voting was the choice of statehood, with 46 percent of the vote. The vote showed that Puerto Ricans want to keep their strong ties with the United States.

REVIEW ***What is Puerto Rico's relationship with the United States?*** It is a commonwealth of the United States.

Crowds of people wave Puerto Rican flags during a Puerto Rico Day parade in New York City.

ACTIVITY CHOICES

Reading Support

PREVIEW AND READ THE LESSON Provide students with the following visual framework.

GOVERNMENT IN THE CARIBBEAN AND IN CENTRAL AMERICA

COUNTRY	LOCATION	POLITICAL STATUS
Puerto Rico	Caribbean	Commonwealth of the United States
Cuba	Caribbean	Communist dictatorship
Haiti	Caribbean	Democratic government
Nicaragua	Central America	Democratic government
Costa Rica	Central America	Democratic government

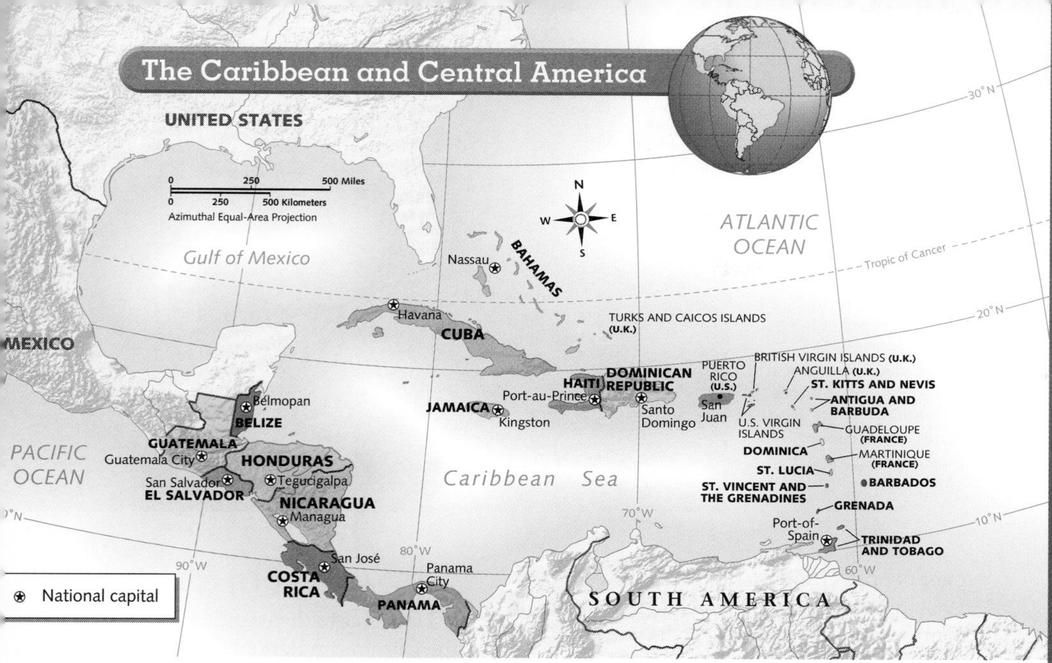

MAP THEME **Location** Caribbean countries are on islands, and Central American countries are on the mainland.

■ *Which island is made up of more than one country?*

Cuba

Like Puerto Rico, Cuba came under the control of the United States after the Spanish-American War. However, Cuba became independent soon after the war. Leaders of the newly independent Cuba wanted to build a strong economy. Political control soon fell into the hands of landowners and other wealthy Cubans.

Over the years, differences in the rights of the rich and the poor angered many of Cuba's farmers and workers. In 1959 a group of rebels led by Fidel Castro took over Cuba's government. They said their goal was to bring equal rights to all citizens and to solve many of Cuba's social and economic problems. To reach this goal, however, Castro made Cuba a communist nation. He has ruled Cuba as a dictator ever since.

Under communism, Cuba's government took

Cuba's leader, Fidel Castro

Civics and Government

Purposes and Types of Government Have students explore the nature of Puerto Rico's commonwealth status.

Q. **Why might it be advantageous for Puerto Ricans to keep their status as a commonwealth of the United States?** They are citizens of the United States and also retain their own identity as a country.

Visual Analysis

Learn from Maps Have students answer the question in the caption. Haiti and the Dominican Republic share an island.

Cuba

Key Content Summary

After Cuba became a communist country, the United States imposed an embargo against that island nation. Cuba became dependent on the Soviet Union for money and supplies, but lost Soviet aid after the Cold War ended. Today Cubans living in the United States are hoping for a change to democracy and a free-enterprise system in Cuba.

Culture

Human Relationships Have students analyze how unfair and unequal treatment of Cubans led to a communist government. Discuss why communism did not bring equal treatment.

Link to Art

RESEARCH PUERTO RICAN ART Ask two or three student volunteers to write to El Museo del Barrio in New York City to gather information about Puerto Rican art. This art museum shows the works of Puerto Rican artists and is part of an effort by the Puerto Rican community in the United States to preserve Puerto Rican culture.

Background

CUBAN AMERICANS More than one million Cuban Americans live in the United States today. They started fleeing to the United States soon after Fidel Castro came to power. In 1965 Castro allowed Cubans with relatives in the United States to leave Cuba. The United States supplied the planes to airlift about 4,000 Cubans each month. The Freedom Airlift, as it was called, continued well into the 1970s. About 600,000 Cubans have settled in Miami, Florida, and are an important economic force there. Union City, New Jersey, is another Cuban American center.

History

Patterns and Relationships Have students analyze why the former Soviet Union would be interested in Cuba.

Q. **Why do you think the Soviet Union supplied Cuba with money and essential goods?** The Soviet Union, as a communist power, wanted communist Cuba to succeed so that communism would spread to other Caribbean countries. The Soviet Union also understood the strategic location of Cuba in relation to the United States.

Economics

Interdependence and Income Help students understand why communism did not help Cuba become economically self-sufficient. Have students analyze why the United States continues to hesitate about lifting the embargo.

Haiti

Key Content Summary

For much of its history, poverty-stricken Haiti has been ruled by harsh dictators and military leaders. In 1991 thousands of Haitians fled to the United States after their elected president was overthrown and violence erupted. In 1994 the United States helped restore Haiti's president to power.

Economic conditions in Cuba have gotten worse since the end of the Cold War, and supplies have been scarce. These Cubans are waiting in line to receive potatoes according to a rationing system. The amount they receive is based on family size.

over people's property and businesses. In 1962 the United States, which feared having a communist nation so close to its borders, set up an embargo against Cuba. During an **embargo** one country refuses to trade its goods with another country.

Cut off from the United States, Cuba came to depend on the Soviet Union for money and supplies. When the Cold War ended, however, the former Soviet Union was no longer able to support Cuba. Life in Cuba became very difficult. Many factories closed, and people lost their jobs. "If you don't have work," said one unemployed worker, "you can't even eat an orange any more."

Today many Cubans believe that the best hope for their nation is for the United States to lift its embargo. Many Cubans now living in the United States want their homeland to return to the free-enterprise system. Free enterprise, they say, will encourage people to start businesses that will create jobs. For this to happen, Cuba will need a democratic government that will allow free enterprise.

REVIEW ***What changes do some Cubans living in the United States want for Cuba?*** They want Cuba to return to the free-enterprise system.

Haiti

Haiti shares the island of Hispaniola with the Dominican Republic. Haiti is the second-oldest republic in the Western Hemisphere, after the United States. During the Haitian Revolution, which began in 1791, the people of the island rebelled against their French rulers. Haiti became an independent country in 1804.

For much of its history, however, Haiti has been ruled by dictators.

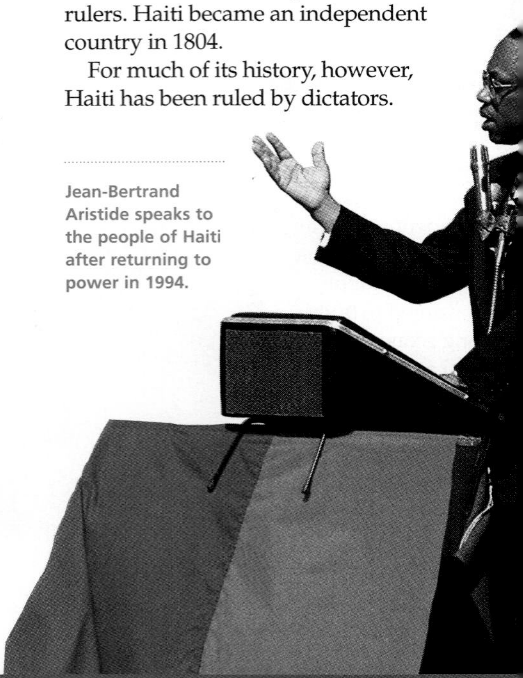

Jean-Bertrand Aristide speaks to the people of Haiti after returning to power in 1994.

656 • Unit 10

Activity Choices

Meet Individual Needs

ADVANCED LEARNERS Have students select one of the leaders from the lesson, such as Fidel Castro, Jean-Bertrand Aristide, or Violeta Barrios de Chamorro, or a present-day leader of one of the countries in the lesson. Ask students to prepare biographies on their selected leaders and present the biographies to the class.

Multicultural Link

Haiti is officially called the République D'Haiti (French for the Republic of Haiti) and French is the official language of the country. Although Hispaniola was originally claimed and settled by the Spanish, the French gained control of one-third of the island by 1697 and were successful in developing large coffee and spice plantations. The Spanish had treated the Indians so poorly, forcing them to farm and mine for gold, that most of the Indian population was gone by 1530. The Spanish started bringing in Africans as slaves to do the work. After the French took control, they also brought in Africans to work the large plantations. By 1788 the African population was eight times as large as the French population.

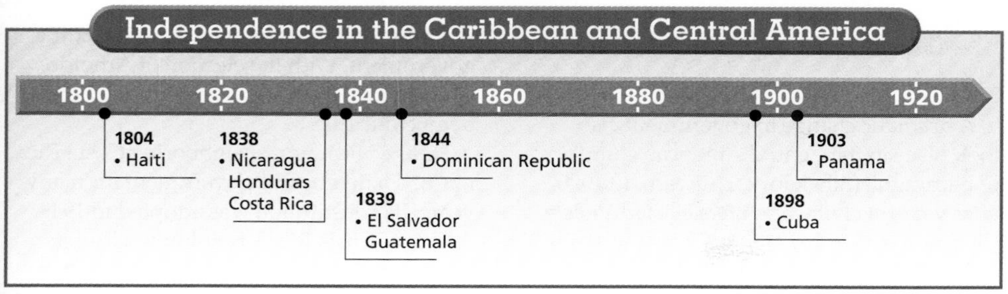

LEARNING FROM TIME LINES This time line shows when countries in the Caribbean and Central America became independent, after being controlled by other countries.
■ *In what year did Cuba become independent?*

In January 1988, Haitians chose new leaders by holding a **free election**—one in which there is a choice of candidates. It was the first free election held in Haiti in many years. But by June military leaders had overthrown the newly elected government and seized control of the country.

In 1990 a free election was held once again in Haiti. The people chose Jean-Bertrand Aristide (air•uh•STEED) as their president. But in 1991 his government, too, was overthrown by military leaders. He escaped to the United States.

The years of military rule in Haiti were harsh. Soldiers killed almost 4,000 of the country's 6 million people. Many Haitians wanted to go to the United States to escape the violence. Some risked death by traveling across the ocean in boats and on small rafts. When the Haitians arrived, however, the United States did not allow them to stay.

In 1994 the United States helped end military rule in Haiti by sending soldiers to Haiti. Soon President Aristide returned to office. He told his people,

> "Let us live in peace. All the guns must be silent."

In January 1996 the Haitian people held another free election. The people elected René Préval to be president. Although Préval replaced Aristide as President, the government continued as a democracy.

Haiti still faces hard times, however. Its people are among the poorest in the Western Hemisphere, and its economic problems have yet to be solved.

REVIEW ***What important events happened in Haiti in 1988?*** Haitians held a free election, but military leaders overthrew the new government.

An American soldier talks with students at the Saint Anne Elementary School, in Port-au-Prince, Haiti, in 1994. During Operation Restore Democracy, American troops helped end years of violent rule by the Haitian military in the island nation.

History

Patterns and Relationships Have students provide examples of other nations ruled by dictators, in both the past and the present. Then have students analyze why people are usually happier under a democracy than under a dictatorship.

Geography

MAP THEME

Movement Have students use the map on page 655 to trace the route across the ocean from Haiti to Florida.

Q. **About how far would a raft from Haiti have to travel to reach Florida?** about 600 miles (966 km)

Visual Analysis

Learn from Time Lines Have students answer the question in the caption. 1898

"PRIMARY SOURCE"

Source: Rother, Larry. "After the Homecoming, the Hard Part." *New York Times*, October 16, 1994.

Meet Individual Needs

TACTILE LEARNERS Have students create maps of Central America and the Caribbean. Provide them with a solid base, such as heavy cardboard or wood, for their maps. Also provide them with a copy of an outline map of Central America and the Caribbean and some colored sand. Have students cut out the outline map and glue it onto the base. Then have them use glue and colored sand to color the countries and bodies of water of the region. Finally, have students use markers or fine-tipped bottles of cloth paint to label the countries and the bodies of water.

Extend and Enrich

COOPERATIVE LEARNING

MAKE A MAP Divide the class into groups, and assign each group one of the countries discussed in the lesson. Ask each group to use encyclopedias and other library resources to make a large map of their assigned country. The map should show major rivers, mountains, and economic resources of the country, such as mining, agriculture, manufacturing, tourism, fishing, and port cities for trade. Have each group share its findings with the other groups before putting up the maps for display.

TECHNOLOGY

HARCOURT BRACE

Use MAPSKILLS to complete this activity.

Nicaragua and Costa Rica

Key Content Summary

After years of civil war, Nicaragua became a democracy in 1990. Neighboring Costa Rica has long been a democracy.

3. CLOSE

Have students consider again the Focus question on page 654.

> **How might political changes affect the way people live in a country?**

Have students use what they have learned about the effects of political change on peoples' lives to explain what kinds of political changes might benefit people and what kinds might harm them.

LESSON 3 REVIEW—Answers

Check Understanding

1. Some have fled to escape from communist leaders, dictators, or harsh military rule. Others want to escape poverty.
2. Under dictatorships and military rule, people have lost their political rights and have suffered from poverty. Without oppressive rulers, the people have chosen their leaders.

Think Critically

3. Some Puerto Ricans were in favor of joining the United States as a state. Other Puerto Ricans wanted to remain a commonwealth so they could have their United States citizenship and their identity as a country. A smaller number of Puerto Ricans wanted complete independence from the United States.
4. At the end of the Cold War, the Soviet Union was no longer able to supply Cuba with money and goods. Cuba's economy suffered, factories closed, and people lost their jobs.

Show What You Know

Performance Assessment Consider having students work in small groups. You may wish to have them use an overhead projector.

What to Look For Look for evidence that students know how to draw a time line.

Nicaragua and Costa Rica

A dramatic change in government also took place in the Central American country of Nicaragua (nih•kah•RAH•gwah). In 1990, after years of civil war, voters elected Violeta Chamorro (vee•oh•LAY•tah chah•MAWR•oh) as Nicaragua's democratic president. Leaders in the United States were happy about Chamorro's victory. For many years the United States had helped democratic groups who wanted to end rule by Nicaraguan rebels known as Sandinistas. The United States had even placed an embargo against Nicaragua, as it had done against Cuba.

Years of fighting and natural disasters had hurt Nicaragua's economy. "War, hurricane, earthquake, tidal wave—Nicaragua has suffered all of that," explains one Nicaraguan citizen. "Now there is real hunger." After the election of Chamorro, the United States lifted the embargo and sent aid to help Nicaragua's economy and to strengthen the democratic government. With the election of Arnoldo Alemán in 1996, Nicaragua continued under democratic rule.

Unlike Nicaragua, neighboring Costa Rica has had a democratic government for many years. Its constitution was adopted in 1949.

One of Costa Rica's best-known leaders is former president Oscar Arias Sánchez. President Arias won the 1987 Nobel Peace Prize for his leadership in creating a peace plan for Central America.

REVIEW ***In what year did rule by the Sandinistas in Nicaragua end?*** 1990

BIOGRAPHY

Violeta Barrios de Chamorro 1929–

Violeta Chamorro was born in the Nicaraguan town of Rivas. She spent her early adult years raising her family. Chamorro's husband was a respected politician and the editor of a major newspaper. In 1978 the Nicaraguan dictator, Anastasio Somoza, ordered her husband killed. After his death, Chamorro ran the newspaper. She also served for a short time in the Sandinista government. Until her election as president in 1990, Chamorro spoke openly against the Sandinistas. Many people think that her bravery helped her win the presidential election.

LESSON 3 REVIEW

Check Understanding

1. **Remember the Facts** Why have some people left countries in the Caribbean and in Central America to come to the United States?
2. **Recall the Main Idea** How have political changes affected the way people live in the Caribbean and in Central America?

Think Critically

3. **Explore Viewpoints** What different viewpoints did Puerto Ricans hold on the question of statehood?
4. **Cause and Effect** How did the end of the Cold War affect Cuba?

Show What You Know

Time Line Activity Gather news articles on how democratic reforms have affected a country in the Caribbean or in Central America. Use these articles and other resources to create a time line of political events in the country you chose. Share your time line with your classmates.

ACTIVITY CHOICES

ACTIVITY BOOK

Reinforce & Extend

Use ACTIVITY BOOK, pp. 136–137.

Reteach the Main Idea

COOPERATIVE LEARNING

MAKE A CHART Divide the class into small groups. Challenge each group to use the textbook as a resource to make a chart comparing and contrasting how political changes have affected the way people live in the Caribbean and in Central America. Have the groups share and discuss their charts with one another and use their information to make a class chart on the board.

Challenges in South America

LESSON 4

FOCUS
How can problems in countries that seem far away affect the United States?

Main Idea As you read, think about how the problems of South America affect other parts of the world.

Vocabulary
liberate
mestizo
deforestation

N ative peoples lived in South America for thousands of ears. Then, in the 1500s, Spain, Portugal, and other European ountries began to build colonies there. European countries oon ruled most of the continent. By the mid-1800s most arts of South America had been **liberated**, or set free, from uropean rulers. Leaders of the independence movements ncluded Simón Bolívar (see•MOHN boh•LEE•var) in Venezuela nd José de San Martín (san mar•TEEN) in Argentina. Inde- endence, however, did not solve all of the problems that any South American countries had faced as colonies.

New Countries with Old Problems

Disagreements based on social class and economic level ave long caused conflicts in South America. In many places, nall groups of wealthy European landowners wanted run South American countries after they became ndependent. But much larger groups wanted an qual say in the new governments. These roups were native peoples, enslaved fricans, and **mestizos** (meh•STEE•zohz), eople of mixed native and European ackgrounds.

New leaders promised to solve their ountries' problems. But almost all of these aders were military rulers supported by e European landowners. In the late 1800s nd early 1900s, dictators ruled many South merican countries. They did not solve the roblems of social and economic inequality at continue in many nations today.

EVIEW *What problems have many countries South America faced since becoming independent?* isagreements based on social class and conomic level that have caused conflicts

Simón Bolívar began leading revolutions for independence in Caracas, Venezuela, his place of birth. He helped Venezuela, Bolivia, Colombia, Ecuador, and Peru gain independence from Spain.

Reading Support

USE CONTEXT CLUES Have students scan the lesson to find the vocabulary terms and their accompanying definitions. Then have students write sentences of their own using the terms. Call on volunteers to read their sentences aloud, omitting the vocabulary terms. Invite other class members to guess the missing terms.

Objectives

1. Identify the political and economic problems faced by South American countries.
2. Identify the new problems in South America that have an impact on many other parts of the world.

Vocabulary

liberate (p. 659)
mestizo (p. 659)
deforestation (p. 660)

1. ACCESS

The Focus Question

Ask students to volunteer examples of items they own that were made in other countries. Lead students in a discussion focusing on the increasing interdependence among nations of the world today. Have students analyze how problems in other countries might affect the United States.

The Main Idea

In this lesson students explore the economies and political conditions of South American countries. After students have read the lesson, ask them to analyze how the problems of South American countries affect the United States and other countries of the world.

2. BUILD

New Countries with Old Problems

Key Content Summary

After South American countries achieved their independence, many of them continued to face political, social, and economic problems. Dictators who had promised to solve problems of inequality did not do so.

Civics and Government

Purposes and Types of Government Have students use what they have learned about dictatorships to analyze why so many South American countries are politically unstable.

Q. **What conclusions can you draw about the connection between dictatorships and problems in a nation?** Dictatorships often lead to political unrest, unhappiness, and lack of economic opportunity.

New Problems for All Countries

Key Content Summary

Deforestation and the production and sale of illegal drugs are two major problems in South America that affect many other nations of the world. The Organization of American States is working to improve understanding and trade among the many peoples of the Americas.

Geography

Human–Environment Interactions Have students summarize what happens when people destroy the natural rain forest environments of South America.

Visual Analysis

Learn from Maps Have students answer the question in the caption. Brazil

New Problems for All Countries

Perhaps the greatest problem South Americans face today is how best to use the continent's vast resources. Thousands of square miles of rain forest have been destroyed to clear the land for planting crops, raising cattle, and digging mines.

Clearing the forest land provides jobs for many people. But the burning has caused problems for the environment. Some scientists believe that it has led to a warming of the Earth. If average temperatures rise too high, the Earth's weather patterns could change. That might harm the plants and animals on which people everywhere depend.

In Brazil the widespread cutting down of the forests, or **deforestation**, has left many native peoples homeless. Most of Brazil's native peoples live in the thick rain forests o the country's Amazon River region. Becaus of deforestation many native peoples are struggling to keep their way of life. "We must hold on to our land and culture," says Pedro Inácio Pinheiro, a leader of the Tikun people. "We can never give these up." Toda the Brazilian government is working on wa to use the resources of the rain forest while also preserving it.

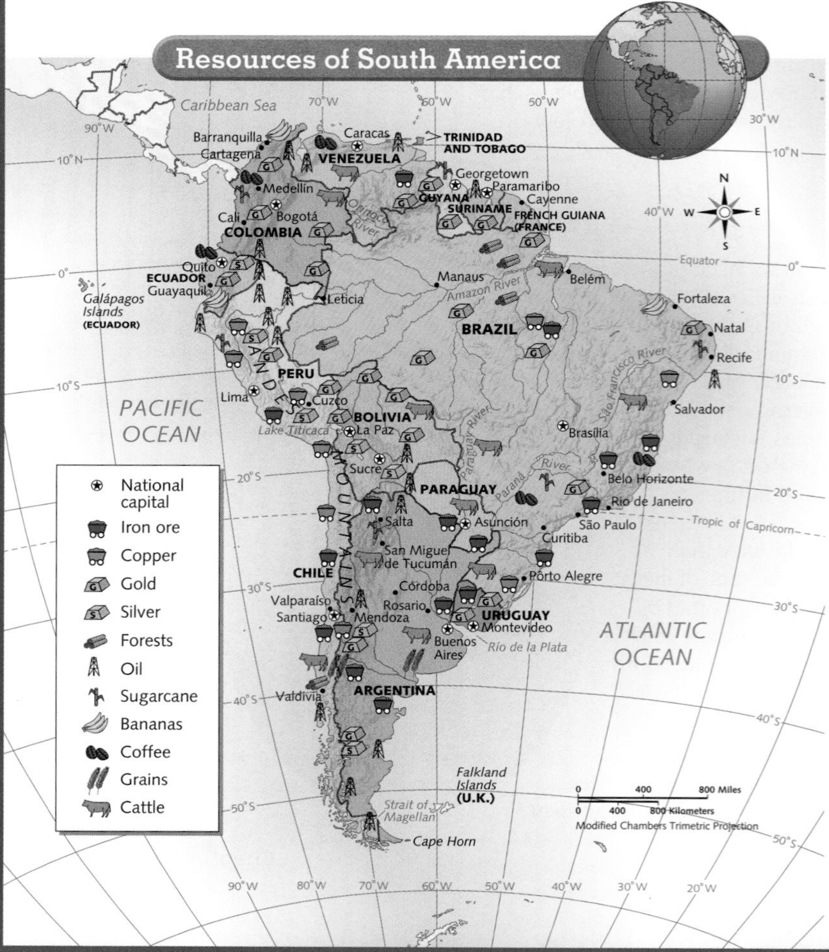

Regions South America is a huge continent wi many resources. Peopl in most South Americ countries speak Spanis In Brazil they speak Portuguese.

■ *Which country is the largest in South America?*

Activity Choices

Background

COLOMBIA Colombia has suffered from the effects of military dictatorships, terrorism, and drug cartels. Between 1948 and 1957, political violence resulted in the deaths of more than 250,000 people and in a military coup that brought a dictator to power. In 1990 three presidential candidates were assassinated. A new constitution went into effect in 1991 that stabilized the political situation. However, drug cartels continued to operate and violence occurred among rival drug cartels. Several government officials who tried to clean up the cartels were assassinated. At the same time, Colombia's economy, supported primarily by coffee exports, is one of the healthiest in South America.

Extend and Enrich

COOPERATIVE LEARNING

CREATE A DISPLAY Divide the class into groups, and assign each group a project that will become part of a bulletin board display about South America. Projects might include a large map of South America showing political boundaries, major rivers, lakes, deserts, islands, and major mountain ranges; a chart listing the names of the countries their capital cities, official languages, areas, and populations; a chart showing major plants and animals; and a chart showing miner als and food products. Hav students select a spokesper son from each group to present the projects to the class before displaying the on the bulletin board.

The powerful Iguazú (ee•gwah•ZOO) Falls form part of the Argentina-Brazil border. Both Argentina and Brazil have established national parks near the falls to protect the surrounding lands. Although deforestation remains a problem in South America, some efforts have been made to prevent the destruction of natural resources.

Another problem in South America that ffects other parts of the world is the produc-on and sale of illegal drugs. In some areas of outh America, especially in Bolivia and 'olombia, farmers can earn more money by rowing crops used to make harmful drugs ian by producing other crops. People can iake huge profits selling these illegal drugs ı Europe and the United States. Conflicts ave broken out between countries over topping the trade in illegal drugs.

To build greater cooperation among the countries of the Western Hemisphere, the Organization of American States, or OAS, was formed in 1948. Almost all the countries of South America, Central America, and the Caribbean, along with Mexico, Canada, and the United States, have joined. The OAS helps settle disagreements and works to improve trade and understanding among its member nations.

REVIEW *What is the OAS?*

ESSON 4 REVIEW

Check Understanding

1. **Remember the Facts** What kinds of disagreements have caused conflicts all over South America?
2. **Recall the Main Idea** How have the problems of South America affected the United States and other parts of the world?

Think Critically

3. **Personally Speaking** How do you think the history of South America is like the history of the United States? How do the histories seem different?
4. **Think More About It** In what ways is the Organization of American States similar to the United Nations?

Show What You Know

News-Writing Activity With a partner, choose one country in South America. Work with your partner to prepare an article for a newsmagazine. The article should describe life in that country today. Focus on the important issues facing the people there. Compare your article with those written by your classmates.

he Organization of American States, an organization formed to build greater cooperation mong countries of the Western Hemisphere

Reteach the Main Idea

CREATE A SKIT Divide the class into two groups. Challenge one group to create a skit showing how the deforestation of South America affects other parts of the world. Challenge the other group to create a skit showing how the cultivation and selling of harmful drugs in South America affects other parts of the world. Ask each group to include problem solving in their skits. Allow time after the presentation of the skits for the class to comment on the issues presented.

ACTIVITY BOOK

Reinforce & Extend

Use ACTIVITY BOOK, pp. 138–139.

Economics

Scarcity and Choice Have students analyze the motivations South American farmers have for growing harmful drug crops rather than other crops and suggest ways that the farmers might be persuaded to stop growing such crops.

3. CLOSE

Have students consider again the Focus question on page 659.

How can problems in countries that seem far away affect the United States?

Ask students to use what they have learned in this lesson to identify problems in other countries that affect the United States today. Have them analyze ways that the United States can help solve the problems or protect against their effects.

LESSON 4 REVIEW—Answers

Check Understanding

1. disagreements related to social class and land ownership, inequality of rights, sale of illegal drugs, and destruction of the way of life of native peoples and the rain forest
2. Deforestation is affecting world climate, and illegal drugs produced in South America have affected people's lives in many parts of the world.

Think Critically

3. Similarities include seeking independence from European control, ethnic diversity of the people, and destruction of Indian lands and ways of life. Differences include dictatorships, the difficulty of establishing democratic governments, slow economic development, and the ownership of much land by only a few people.
4. Like the United Nations, the OAS works to build cooperation among countries.

Show What You Know

Performance Assessment Have each pair of students read their articles to the class and answer questions that other students may have about the country.

What to Look For Look for evidence that students understand the important issues facing the people in their chosen country.

LESSON 5 PAGES 662–665

Objectives

1. Summarize the reasons Canada wrote a new constitution in 1982.
2. Analyze the objections of the Québecois to the Constitution of 1982.
3. Describe the gains in equal rights made by Canada's Indian groups.

Vocabulary

province (p. 662) separatist (p. 664)

1. ACCESS

The Focus Question

Have students use what they have learned about the history of the United States to decide what policies are most important for a nation to protect the rights of all of its citizens.

The Main Idea

In this lesson students explore the provisions of Canada's Constitution of 1982 and the reaction of Canadian citizens to it. After students have read the lesson, have them analyze why it is sometimes difficult for a nation that has a diverse population to protect the rights of all of its citizens.

2. BUILD

The Constitution of 1982

Key Content Summary

Canada did not become completely independent until 1982, when it wrote its own constitution. This constitution provides for the protection of Canada's multicultural heritage. However, the western and eastern provinces were divided over which region should have a greater say in the national government.

LESSON 5

FOCUS
How might a nation protect the rights of all its citizens?

Main Idea As you read, find out how Canada has worked to protect the rights of its diverse groups of citizens.

Vocabulary
province
separatist

The Peoples of Canada

Canada is the second-largest country in the world in area and covers almost half of North America. More than 29 million people live in this vast land. As in the United States, the first people in Canada were American Indians, who have lived there for thousands of years. In the 1500s the French arrived. In 1763, after Britain won the French and Indian War, Canada became a British colony. It remained a colony until 1867, when it was given limited independence. Not until 1982, when a new constitution was written, was Canada's independence complete.

The Constitution of 1982

The Constitution of 1982 is in many ways like the British constitution, which Canada had been using since 1867. But there is an important difference. Canada added a section called the Charter of Rights and Freedoms. This statement of rights is similar to the Bill of Rights in the United States Constitution.

The flag of Canada shows a maple leaf, a symbol of the country.

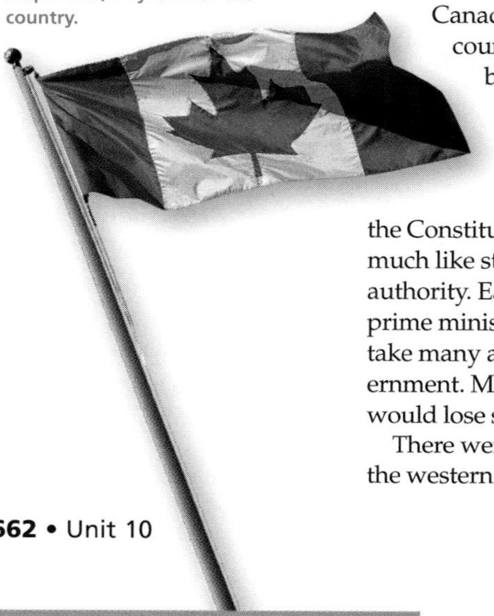

The Canadian charter recognizes the rights of Canada's diverse peoples and promises to protect the country's multicultural heritage. The charter allows both French and English to be used in public schools and in the courts. It also states that treaties with American Indians in Canada will be upheld.

But not all Canadians in the nation's ten provinces and two territories were happy with the Constitution of 1982. The **provinces** are political regions much like states in the United States, but they have more authority. Each province has its own government and its own prime minister, or leader of the government. A province can take many actions without the approval of the national government. Many leaders in the provinces worried that they would lose some of their authority under the new constitution.

There were also regional divisions in the country. People in the western provinces—Manitoba, Saskatchewan, Alberta,

ACTIVITY CHOICES

Reading Support

ANTICIPATION GUIDE Before students read the lesson, ask them if they agree (+) or disagree (–) with the following statements. After students have read the lesson, ask them if they have changed any of their opinions. Have them defend their changes by referring to the lesson.

1. Canada is a bigger country than the United States. (+)
2. The Québecois try to push their culture on all other Canadians. (–)
3. Many Québecois want Quebec to be a country independent of the rest of Canada. (+)
4. Canada's Charter of Rights and Freedoms addresses the rights and freedoms only of the people of British heritage. (–)

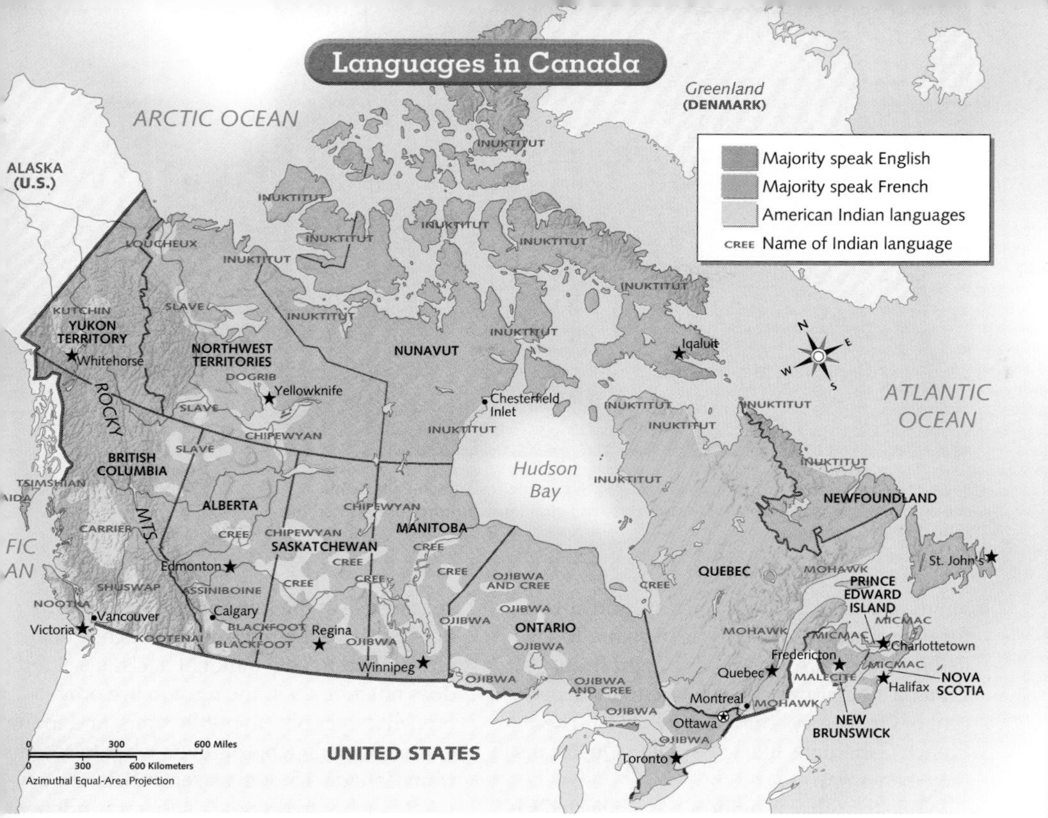

Places While most Canadians speak English, many other languages can be heard in different places. Notice that Quebec has many French speakers.

■ *What language do most people living in Winnipeg, Manitoba speak?*

and British Columbia—felt they should have a greater say in the national government because the western provinces contain most of the country's natural resources. People in the eastern provinces—Ontario, Quebec, New Brunswick, Newfoundland, Nova Scotia, and Prince Edward Island—felt they should have more control because they have more people than the western provinces do.

REVIEW ***Why were Canadian people divided over the country's Constitution of 1982?*** Leaders in many provinces worried that they would lose some of their authority. People in both the western and the eastern provinces wanted a greater say in the national government.

Quebec Opposes the Constitution

Of all the provinces, Quebec has objected most to the Constitution of 1982. The reason for this can be found in the province's history.

Quebec was the oldest and most important part of the colony of New France, which was founded in the early 1600s. Even after the British took control of New France in 1763, French culture remained strong in Quebec. French families there have kept alive their

Geography

Location Refer students to the map and have them locate and name Canada's ten provinces and two territories.

Q. **Why do you think Canada, which is much larger than the United States, is divided into only twelve political units?** Canada has a much smaller population than the United States, so it does not need as many political units. Also, much of northern Canada's land and climate is too harsh for development.

Civics and Government

Purposes and Types of Government Have students compare and contrast the government in Canada with the government in the United States.

Visual Analysis

Learn from Maps Have students answer the question in the caption. English

Quebec Opposes the Constitution

Key Content Summary

Quebec, with its heritage strongly rooted in French culture, has refused to accept the Constitution of 1982 because the document does not give the Québecois the rights they want. Some Québecois want Quebec to become a separate nation.

Link to Mathematics

MAKE A CIRCLE GRAPH Have students use the percentage of population figures in the Multicultural Link box to the right to draw a circle graph illustrating Canada's diverse population. Ask them to label and color their graphs. You may wish to display the graphs on the bulletin board.

TECHNOLOGY

Use GRAPHLINKS to complete this graphing activity.

Multicultural Link

Canada has the second most diverse population in the Western Hemisphere after the United States. The total population of Canada is about 28 million. Two groups, those of French origin and those of British origin, make up a large majority of the population. About 27 percent of the population are French Canadians, most of whom are concentrated in the province of Quebec. People of British origin account for about 40 percent of the total population. People of other northern, southern, and eastern European origins make up about 20 percent of the total population. American Indians account for 5 percent of the total. People of Asian origin constitute another 5 percent of the total, and those of Caribbean origin make up about 3 percent.

Culture

Shared Humanity and Unique Identity Have students recall the history of New France and analyze why the Québecois want to preserve their culture and traditions, which are different from the rest of Canada.

Q. **What are the advantages and disadvantages of making Quebec independent of Canada?** Advantages: The Québecois could run Quebec the way they want and not be answerable to the English-speaking provinces. Disadvantages: Quebec would be surrounded by a nation that the Québecois rejected, and it would lose the advantages of being part of a large nation that has more resources and services.

Visual Analysis

Learn from Time Lines Have students answer the questions in the caption. 1867; a dominion

History

Connections Past to Present to Future Have students speculate on how the people in the other provinces in Canada might feel about Quebec's constitutional demands and the idea that some Québecois want to have their own country. Tell students that the people of Quebec voted in 1995 on whether or not to become a separate nation. Although the vote was very close, the separatists lost.

ARRÊT
STOP

A visit to Quebec City (above) allows people to experience French-Canadian culture firsthand. Signs in Quebec, like this stop sign (above right), are printed in both French and English.

language, laws, Catholic religion, and cultural traditions for hundreds of years. Today its French culture sets Quebec apart from Canada's other provinces. More than 82 percent of Quebec's people speak French. These French Canadians like to be called Québecois (kay•beh•KWAH).

While the other provinces have objected to the Constitution of 1982, only Quebec has refused to accept it. Many Québecois feel that the constitution does not recognize their special role in the founding of Canada. It does not give them the authority they have always had to veto national decisions. And it does not give them the right to use only French in schools, on public signs, and in the courts. Some Québecois even want to secede from Canada. Known as **separatists**, they want Quebec to become a separate, independent nation.

REVIEW ***Why have French Canadians in Quebec refused to accept the constitution?***

LEARNING FROM TIME LINES An important event in Canada's history took place when the British Parliament passed the British North America Act, making Canada a self-governing nation partly under British control.

■ *When was this act passed? What type of nation was Canada called?*

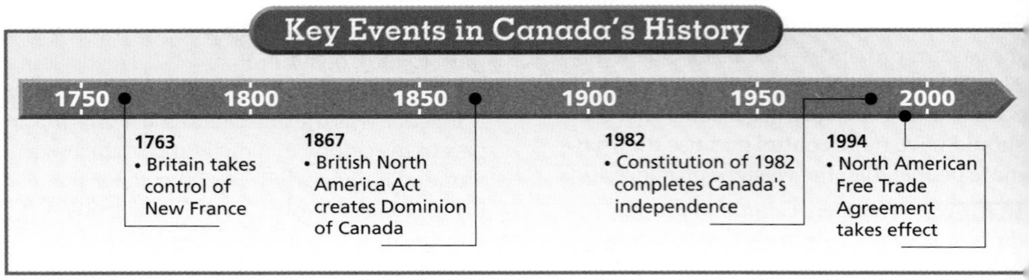
Key Events in Canada's History
1750
1800
1850
1900
1950
2000
1763
• Britain takes control of New France
1867
• British North America Act creates Dominion of Canada
1982
• Constitution of 1982 completes Canada's independence
1994
• North American Free Trade Agreement takes effect

Many feel that the constitution does not recognize their special role in Canada. It does not give them the authority to veto national decisions. It does not give them the right to use only French in schools, on public signs, and in the courts.

664 • Unit 10

Activity Choices

Background

THE LANGUAGE BATTLE Because of the efforts of the Québecois to make French the only acceptable public language in Quebec, thousands of English and English-based businesses moved to other areas of Canada. French is now, by law, the official language of Quebec. Public signs are in French. Signs in stores must be in French, or, if French and English are used, the French words must be larger than the English words. Forty percent of radio broadcasts must be in French. Immigrants must send their children to French schools to learn the language.

Extend and Enrich

COOPERATIVE LEARNING

MAKE COMPARISON CHARTS Divide the class into groups, and have each group make a chart comparing Canada and the United States. Ask each group to choose their headings, use encyclopedias and other library resources as necessary, and add illustrations to their charts as appropriate. When the groups have completed their charts, allow time for them to share and discuss their findings. You may wish to have students create a class chart that compiles the findings of the groups.

Standing Up for Native Rights

Like the Québecois, the native peoples of
anada want greater protection for their cul-
ıres and their rights. Even with the Charter
Rights and Freedoms, which clearly states
ıe rights of American Indians to keep their
wn land and to form their own govern-
ıents, some Indian groups feel these rights
ave been ignored.

In the summer of 1990, a violent conflict
oke out in the town of Oka, in Quebec.
ome people in Oka wanted to make a golf
ourse larger, using part of a Mohawk burial
round. Mohawk men, women, and children
ut up a barrier to keep the builders away.
hrough their protests the Mohawks suc-
eeded in stopping the construction on their
nd, but the deeper problem was not solved.
There is still great anger here," explains
lohawk artist Deborah Etienne. "The land is
ur identity, our life, and they wanted to take
away from us. . . . Our land claims are not
ttled. Nothing is resolved."

In other cases, native groups have per-
uaded the Canadian government to take

This Inuit family lives on Holman Island in the Northwest Territories. Native peoples make up a large part of the population in Canada's Arctic region.

action. In 1984 the Canadian government gave the Cree and Naskapi (NAS•kuh•pee) peoples greater self-government. In 1992 the Inuits of Canada's Northern Territories won the right to form their own self-governing region. The territory, which the Inuits call Nunavut, meaning "our land," split from the Northern Territories. By these and similar actions, the Canadian government supports cultures in the Americas that are thousands of years old.

REVIEW ***What document lists the rights of the native peoples of Canada?***
the Charter of Rights and Freedoms

ESSON 5 REVIEW

Check Understanding

1. **Remember the Facts** What are some of the diverse groups that live in Canada?
2. **Recall the Main Idea** How has Canada worked to protect the rights of its diverse groups of citizens?

Think Critically

3. **Personally Speaking** What might happen if Quebec decides to secede from Canada? What do you think might happen if a large state like California broke away from the United States?
4. **Cause and Effect** What caused the Indian groups to take action to protect their rights? What have been the effects of their actions?

Show What You Know

Writing Activity Study maps and other resource materials that give information about the geography of Canada. Find the province in Canada that is most like the state in which you live. Then write a paragraph comparing and contrasting the two places. Share your paragraph with a classmate.

Standing Up for Native Rights

Key Content Summary

Canada's Indian peoples have struggled, with some success, to persuade the government to abide by the provisions of the Constitution of 1982, which protects their rights and cultures.

3. CLOSE

Have students consider again the Focus question on page 662.

How might a nation protect the rights of all its citizens?

Have students use what they have learned about Canada's efforts to safeguard the rights of its various ethnic groups to explain how a nation might go about protecting the rights of its people.

LESSON 5 REVIEW—Answers

Check Understanding

1. American Indians, French, and people of British origin
2. The Constitution of 1982 has a Charter of Rights and Freedoms, which recognizes the rights of Canada's diverse peoples, allows French and English to be used in public schools and courts, and upholds treaties with Canada's native peoples.

Think Critically

3. In either case, civil war could occur or peaceful transitions could be worked out.
4. When the Mohawks realized other people were taking their land away, they protested and saved it. Other Indian groups persuaded the Canadian government to give them more self-government. The government agreed, and now the Inuits rule Nunavut.

Show What You Know

Performance Assessment Consider having students present the Canadian portion of their comparisons as travelogues or as television commercials.

What to Look For Look for evidence that students understand the geography of the Canadian province they have selected and that of their own state.

Reteach the Main Idea

ROLE-PLAY A MEETING

COOPERATIVE LEARNING

Divide the class into three groups, and assign each group to represent either the people of British origin, the Québecois, or the American Indians. Have students in each group plan and role-play a meeting of the three groups during which they discuss the protection of their rights as provided for in the Constitution of 1982. Allow group members the opportunity to negotiate for more protection of their rights as they see necessary. Have the groups summarize the conclusions and accomplishments of their meeting.

ACTIVITY BOOK

Reinforce & Extend

Use ACTIVITY BOOK, pp. 140–141.

CHAPTER 20
REVIEW

Connect Main Ideas

Use the organizer to review the main ideas of the chapter. Have students use their textbooks to complete or check their work. Allow time for them to compare and discuss their responses.

ACTIVITY BOOK

Summarize the Chapter
Use ACTIVITY BOOK, p. 142.

TRANSPARENCY

A copy of the graphic organizer appears on TRANSPARENCY 53.

Write More About It

Write a Poem
Poems will vary but should focus on saving forests or conserving the environment.

Write a Postcard
Students should describe Quebec as a French-speaking province and give examples of how that affects the province's culture.

TECHNOLOGY

Use THE AMAZING WRITING MACHINE™ to complete the writing activities.

TECHNOLOGY

Use TIMELINER™ DATA DISKS to discuss and summarize the chapter.

CHAPTER 20 REVIEW

1940 | 1950 | 1

1948 • The OAS is formed

1952 • Puerto Rico becomes a United States territory

1959 • Fidel Castro becomes the leader of Cuba

Connect Main Ideas

Use this organizer to show how the chapter's main ideas are connected. Complete the organizer by writing two or three sentences that summarize the main idea of each lesson. A copy of the organizer appears on page 142 of the Activity Book.

Possible answers to the graphic organizer appear on page 642D of this Teacher's Edition.

The Western Hemisphere Today

Mexico Today

____
____
____
____

Democracy in the Caribbean and in Central America

____
____
____

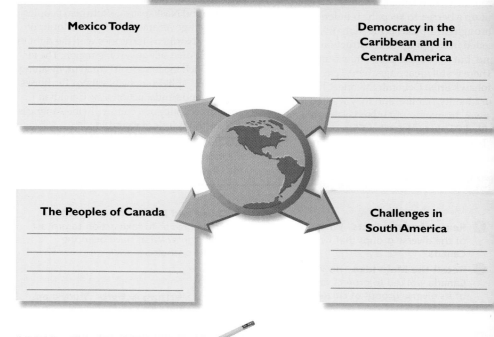

The Peoples of Canada

____
____
____
____

Challenges in South America

____
____
____

Write More About It

Write a Poem Omar and his father carried a banner that said, "Let's protect the rainforest." Write a poem about saving forests or conserving the environment.

Write a Postcard Suppose that you are traveling through Canada on vacation. Write a postcard to a friend. Explain how Quebec is different from Canada's other provinces.

Use Vocabulary

1. metropolitan area; The New York *metropolitan area* has about 20 million people living in it. (p. 643)
2. interest rate; The *interest rate* determines how much profit a bank makes when it loans money to people. (p. 644)
3. embargo; The *embargo* against Cuba hurt its economy. (p. 656)
4. liberate; Simón Bolívar helped *liberate* his country from foreign rulers. (p. 659)
5. deforestation; *Deforestation* is taking away the homes of American Indian peoples who live in the rain forest. (p. 660)
6. province; Quebec is a *province* in Canac (p. 662)

Check Understanding

7. The people found it difficult to b houses, cars, and most consum products. (p. 644)
8. a treaty in which countries agree charge no tariffs, or taxes, on goo they buy from each other and sell each other; Mexico, the United State and Canada (p. 645)
9. to remain a commonwealth (p. 654)
10. The former Soviet Union is no long able to support Cuba. (p. 656)

1970 1980 1990 2000

1982
• Canada's new constitution is written

1990
• Violeta Chamorro becomes president of Nicaragua

1994
• The NAFTA agreement goes into effect

Use Vocabulary

Write the term that correctly matches each definition. Then use each term in a complete sentence.

deforestation	**liberate**
embargo	**metropolitan area**
interest rate	**province**

1. a city and all the suburbs and other population areas around it
2. the amount that a bank charges customers to borrow money
3. the refusal of one country to trade its goods with another country
4. to set free
5. the widespread cutting down of forests
6. a political region that is much like a state

Check Understanding

7. How did the devaluation of 1994 affect Mexico's middle class?
8. What is a free-trade agreement? What three nations signed NAFTA?
9. What did the Puerto Rican people decide about their political relationship with the United States in the 1993 election?
10. Why has life in Cuba become very difficult since the end of the Cold War?
11. What is the chief purpose of the OAS?
12. What is the Charter of Rights and Freedoms?
13. What do the separatists in Canada want?

Think Critically

14. **Personally Speaking** Omar walked 870 miles to be in a real rain forest. Describe a time when you had to work hard to do something. How did working hard to accomplish something make you feel?
15. **Cause and Effect** What effect did the election of Violeta Chamorro as president have on Nicaragua?

Apply Skills

MAP SKILLS

Use Population Maps Use the population map on page 652 and the cartogram on page 653 to answer these questions.

16. Which city has more people, Monterrey or Tijuana?
17. In what part of Mexico is the population density the greatest?
18. Which country has more people, Costa Rica or Haiti?

Read More About It

Chico Mendes: Defender of the Rain Forest by Joann J. Burch. Millbrook. This book describes one man's efforts to protect the Amazon rain forest.

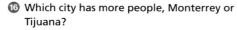

Visit the Internet at **http://www.hbschool.com** for additional resources.

- to settle disagreements among the member nations (p. 661)
- a statement of rights, which is part of Canada's Constitution of 1982 (p. 662)
- for Quebec to become a separate, independent nation (p. 664)

Think Critically

14. Personal stories and experiences will vary. Some will conclude that the hard work was worthwhile, others that the result was not worth all the hard work.
15. The election of Violeta Chamorro led the United States to lift the trade embargo and to send aid to help Nicaragua's economy.

CHAPTER 20 REVIEW

Apply Skills

Use Population Maps

16. Monterrey
17. the area around Mexico City
18. Haiti

Read More About It

Additional books are listed in the Multimedia Resource Center on page 604D of this Teacher's Edition.

Unit Project Check-Up

Give students time to review with their groups the images and documents they have collected for the exhibit. Then ask groups to plan how they are going to organize and present the exhibit.

ASSESSMENT PROGRAM

Use CHAPTER 20 TEST, pp. 163–166.

Making Social Studies Relevant

See the Link

Personal Response

Have students review what makes a government a democracy. Encourage students to look through their textbook for examples of ideas that led to a democratic form of government in the United States and the principles that make up a democracy.

The Main Idea

Have students read the selection and analyze why many countries in the Americas have democratic governments.

Q. **Why do you think many people prefer a democratic government over a dictatorship?** In a democracy people have more rights and freedoms.

Understand the Link

Geography

Location Use a classroom wall map or an atlas to have students identify the countries that make up the Western Hemisphere.

Visual Analysis

Learn from Photographs Ask students to examine the photographs on pages 668–669. Then have volunteers explain how each photo relates to democracy in the Americas.

Making Social Studies Relevant

DEMOCRACY in the Americas

Since colonial times, the ideas of freedom and democracy have been important to the people of the United States. These ideas are also important to people of other countries in the Americas. The United States has set an example of democracy for its neighboring countries in the Western Hemisphere.

Today every country in the Americas except Cuba has a democratic form of government. The United States and Canada have had democratic governments for a long time. Canada's constitution guarantees its people many of the same freedoms as those found in the United States Constitution.

During much of the twentieth century, many Latin American countries were ruled by military dictators. These dictatorships began to fall in the 1980s and 1990s. Many of those countries now have written constitutions like that of the United States. By following the example of the United States and other democratic nations, people in the Americas have achieved greater freedom than they ever had before.

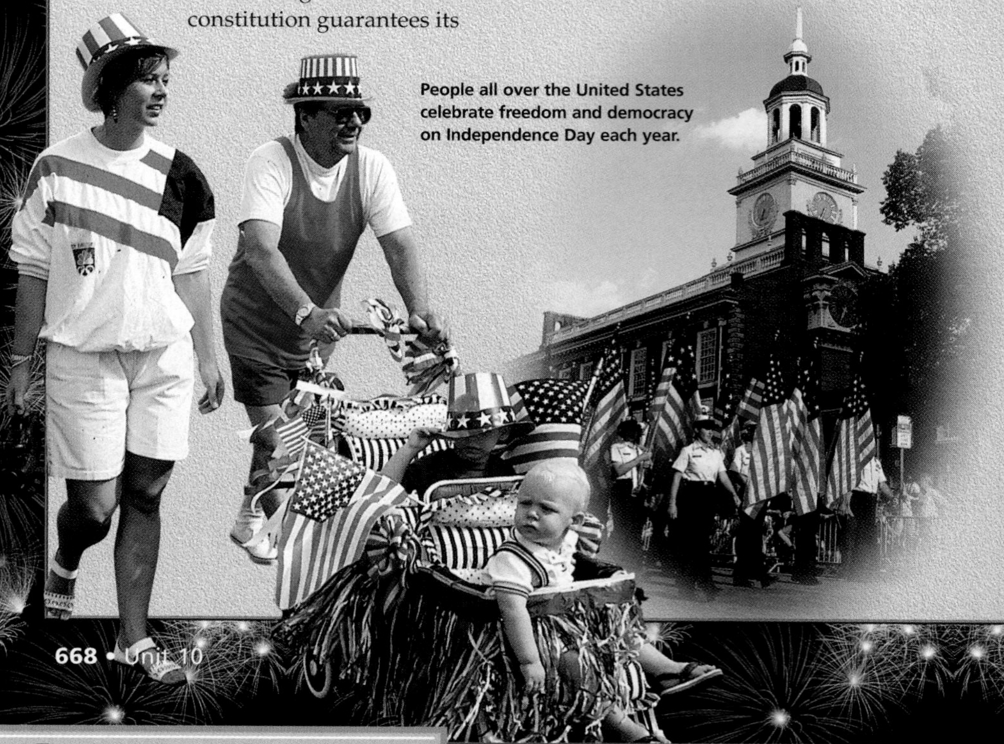

People all over the United States celebrate freedom and democracy on Independence Day each year.

668 • Unit 10

Activity Choices

Background

DEMOCRACY The idea of democracy began in ancient Greece in the city of Athens. The government of Athens encouraged citizens to take part in decisions that affected the community. This participation grew into a system of democracy. Unlike the democracy of the United States, the democracy of Athens was a direct democracy. Each citizen took a direct role in government decisions. Today most countries have too many people to have a direct democracy.

The United States and other countries in the Americas have representative democracies. In these democracies, large numbers of citizens elect other citizens as representatives to make governmental decisions for them.

Canadians (above) and many Latin Americans (below) also have special days to celebrate their independence and the freedoms they enjoy because of democracy. Today almost all countries in Latin America hold free elections (bottom right) in which people can vote for the candidates of their choice.

Think and Apply

BUILDING CITIZENSHIP

Choose a country in the Americas, other than the United States, that has a democratic government. Use the Internet, encyclopedias, and other resources to find out how the country's government is organized. Make a chart that shows the government's different parts and how they work together. Then write a paragraph that tells how the government of the country you researched is similar to and different from the government of the United States. Share your findings with the class.

HARCOURT BRACE Visit the Internet at **http://www.hbschool.com** for additional resources.

CNN Turner Le@rning Check your media center or classroom video library for the Making Social Studies Relevant videotape of this feature.

Complete the Link

Summarize

Democratic ideas are important to many people in the Americas. The United States and Canada have had democratic governments for a long time, which has helped set an example for neighboring countries in the Western Hemisphere. With the exception of Cuba, people throughout the Americas are experiencing more of the freedoms guaranteed by a democracy.

Think and Apply

Encourage students to include symbols from their chosen country on their charts or as a background illustration. Students may want to work with a partner to complete their charts.

Meet Individual Needs

ENGLISH LANGUAGE LEARNERS Ask volunteers to share information about their country of origin. They might enjoy explaining the form of government found there or pointing out the location of their country's capital on a map. Encourage students to explain what it was like to live in a place with a different system of government.

Link to Art

COOPERATIVE LEARNING

CREATE COLLAGES Have students work together to create a collage that illustrates what life is like in a democracy. Students may use old magazines or draw pictures to complete the collages. Encourage students to show examples of campaign posters or people voting. Have students share and explain their completed collages with the rest of the class.

Technology

HARCOURT BRACE Visit the Internet at **http://www.hbschool.com** for additional resources.

Video

CNN Turner Le@rning **Check your media center or classroom video library for the Making Social Studies Relevant videotape of this feature.**

Visual Summary

Take a Look

Remind students that a visual summary is a way to represent the main events in a story. Explain that this visual summary reviews some of the main events students read about in Unit 10.

Visual Analysis

Interpret Pictures Have pairs or small groups of students examine this visual summary. Ask them to take turns reading each caption, identifying the elements in each image, and explaining why each event shown was significant to the United States during the second half of the twentieth century. Ask them also to identify and explain the images that tell about other countries in the Western Hemisphere.

Summarize the Main Ideas

Lead a class discussion about each scene and have students add supporting details to the description in each caption. Have students decide whether the event had an impact only on Americans or on other countries as well.

UNIT 10 REVIEW

VISUAL SUMMARY

Summarize the Main Ideas
Study the pictures and captions to help you review the events you read about in Unit 10.

Choose an Event
From this visual summary, choose the event that you think will have the most important effect on the future. Write a paragraph to explain your choice.

1 The Cold War began after World War II. The Soviet Union cut off land routes to West Berlin in 1948, but an airlift brought in supplies.

3 In 1963 Martin Luther King, Jr., spoke for civil rights at a huge gathering in Washington, D.C.

4 The United States put the first person on the moon in 1969.

6 Changes in the Soviet Union brought an end to the Cold War. In 1989 the Berlin Wall was torn down.

670 • Unit 10

Activity Choices

Meet Individual Needs

ENGLISH LANGUAGE LEARNERS (COOPERATIVE LEARNING) Organize the class into eight groups. Ask students to write a script for a speech that may have been made by someone shown in the visual summary. The script should reveal the most important facts about the issue the scene represents. Students may want to outline the facts before they begin the script. Then have the groups select members to give the speech.

UNIT POSTER

Use the UNIT 10 VISUAL SUMMARY POSTER to summarize the unit.

2 War seemed near in 1962 when the Soviet Union sent missiles to Cuba. President Kennedy ordered a blockade of the island. Finally, Soviet leader Nikita Khrushchev agreed to remove the missiles.

5 Americans were divided over the Vietnam War. After many deaths, the war ended in 1975.

Today many of the countries in the Western Hemisphere face problems with their economies and governments. A major problem in South America is the clearing of rain forests.

8 Mexico, the United States, and Canada have signed the NAFTA agreement to remove tariffs on trade between these countries.

Sharing the Activity

Provide time for students to complete the Choose an Event activity on page 670. Before they begin writing, remind them to follow the steps of the writing process from first draft to final copy. Ask student volunteers to read their paragraphs aloud to the class, and allow time for students to react to the paragraphs. Lead a class discussion about other current events that may have a significant impact on the future.

Summarize the Unit

Have pairs of students test each other's knowledge. Have one student name an important event from a decade covered in the unit—late 1940s, 1950s, 1960s, 1970s, 1980s, 1990s. The other student must name another important event from the same decade. When students have finished with one decade, they should move on to another.

Technology

Use TIMELINER™ DATA DISKS to discuss and summarize the unit.

Technology

Use THE AMAZING WRITING MACHINE™ RESOURCE PACKAGE to complete the writing activities.

Extend and Enrich

COOPERATIVE LEARNING

WRITE AND PRESENT A NEWS REPORT Divide the class into small groups and assign each group a place covered in the visual summary, such as Berlin, Cuba, or Vietnam. Ask the groups to use library resources such as news magazines and current encyclopedias to find out about recent events in their assigned places, and have them write news reports to present to the class. After each group presents its news report, allow time for the class to ask questions and discuss the importance of the place in today's world.

UNIT 10 REVIEW

Use Vocabulary

1. The allies used an *airlift* to bring supplies to West Berlin. (p. 611)
2. After President Nixon agreed to a *cease-fire*, the United States stopped bombing North Vietnam. (p. 613)
3. When the Soviet Union and the United States agreed to *arms control*, the agreement limited the number of weapons each nation would have. (p. 634)
4. The *middle class* is the economic level between the poor and the wealthy. (p. 644)
5. Haitians chose their leader in a *free election*. (p. 657)
6. *Mestizos* are people who are of mixed native and European backgrounds. (p. 659)

Check Understanding

7. President Kennedy (p. 614)
8. Neil Armstrong (p. 620)
9. through nonviolent means (p. 623)
10. Gorbachev called for a restructuring of the Soviet government and free elections, and he decided that the people should be free to start their own businesses. (p. 636)
11. It led to the growth of a large middle class. (p. 644)
12. The Constitution of 1982 recognizes the rights of Canada's diverse peoples and promises to protect the country's multicultural heritage; allows both French and English to be used in public schools and in the courts; and states that treaties with Indians in Canada will be upheld. (p. 662)

Think Critically

13. Answers will vary, but students should note that with the changes Gorbachev was making in his country, he knew that the United States could help with information on business, free elections, and how people live together in a free society. Gorbachev also knew his country was having economic problems and the United States could provide economic aid.
14. Opinions will vary. Students should defend the choices they make.

UNIT 10 REVIEW

USE VOCABULARY

Use each term in a complete sentence that will help explain its meaning.

1. airlift
2. cease-fire
3. arms control
4. middle class
5. free election
6. mestizo

CHECK UNDERSTANDING

7. Which President ordered a naval blockade during the Cuban missile crisis?
8. Who was the first person to set foot on the moon?
9. How did Martin Luther King, Jr., work to bring about change?
10. How did Mikhail Gorbachev help change the Soviet Union?
11. How did the growth of manufacturing affect Mexico?
12. What are some important rights guaranteed by Canada's Charter of Rights and Freedoms?

THINK CRITICALLY

13. **Explore Viewpoints** Why do you think that Soviet leader Mikhail Gorbachev wanted to work toward better relations between the Soviet Union and the United States?
14. **Personally Speaking** Which United States President do you think made the greatest contributions to world peace? Explain your choice.

APPLY SKILLS

Use Population Maps Use the population map of South America below to answer the following questions.

15. Are there more areas of high population density in the coastal areas or in the central areas of South America?
16. Which country has the most areas of high population density?
17. Which countries have the least areas of high population density?
18. Which capital cities are surrounded by areas where there are only 2–25 people per square mile?

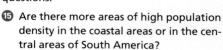

Apply Skills

Use Population Maps

15. coastal areas
16. Brazil
17. Guyana, Suriname, French Guiana
18. Georgetown, Guyana; Paramaribo, Suriname

ASSESSMENT PROGRAM

Use UNIT 10 TEST,
Standard Test, pp. 167–171.
Performance Tasks, pp. 172–173.

REMEMBER
Share your ideas.
Cooperate with others to plan your work.
Take responsibility for your work.
Help one another.
Show your group's work to the class.
Discuss what you learned by working together.

ACTIVITY
Create a
Hall of Fame

People from different
nnic groups and cultures
ve worked to bring about
ange in the United States
d in other countries in
e Americas. Your class
ould list 25 of these
ople to include in a
ll of Fame. They may
people that you read
out in this unit or ear-
units. The 25 names
the list should then
divided among small
ups. Each group
ould make a poster for
h person assigned to
group. The poster
uld include a drawing
d a short biography of
person. Display all
posters together on
assroom wall or in a
way.

ACTIVITY
Prepare a
Newscast

Work in a group to prepare a newscast that covers one of the following events: the Cuban missile crisis, the Montgomery bus boycott, the civil rights march in Washington, D.C., the Watergate scandal, Nixon's visit to China, or the 1985 Reagan and Gorbachev meeting. Each member of your group should have a job, such as researcher, writer, reporter, or set designer. When planning your newscast, include information that describes the changes that the event brought about. Present your newscast to your class.

Unit Project Wrap-Up

Create a Space Travel Exhibit
Continue working with your classmates on your exhibit about space travel. Make sure you find out what the United States and other countries are planning to do to explore space in the years to come. Among the items you may want to include are posters, drawings, books, magazines, photographs, and any other objects related to space exploration. When you are finished, invite another class to visit the exhibit.

673

UNIT 10 REVIEW

CREATE A HALL OF FAME

Performance Assessment Provide groups with markers, colored pencils, and poster board. Also provide old magazines that may have pictures of people students can use for their posters. Remind students that they are honoring the people for some change they have brought about in the United States and in other countries, and that this should be mentioned in the biographies. Discuss what other information should be in the biographies, such as birth date, death date if applicable, education, family, and profession.

What to Look For The posters should show an appreciation for the contributions made by the Hall of Fame members and should explain how they changed life in the United States and in other countries.

Unit Project Wrap-Up

Performance Assessment Have students arrange their exhibit. Then ask each group to add a title to their exhibit that points out the main idea.

What to Look For Look for factual information with a balance of visuals and written summaries.

GAME TIME!

Use GAME TIME! to reinforce content.

operative Learning Workshop

PARE A NEWSCAST

formance Assessment Discuss with
ents the tasks of each member of a
s team—researcher, reporter, direc-
anchor, cameraperson, and any other
s you want to assign. Have groups
ose different events. Explain to stu-
ts that the success of their newscasts
ends on teamwork. Remind them to
s their newscasts on how the event
cted history. For example, President
on's visit to China started a period of
nte between the two nations.

What to Look For Look for evidence of teamwork and an understanding by the group of how their event affected history.

For Your Reference

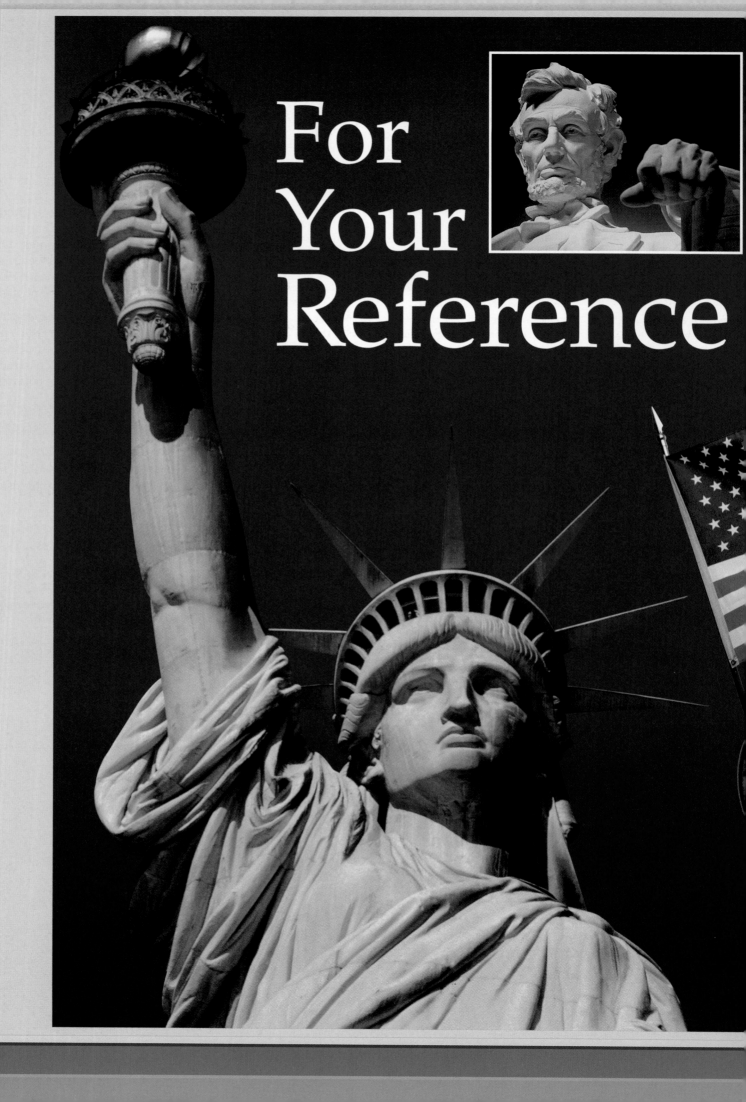

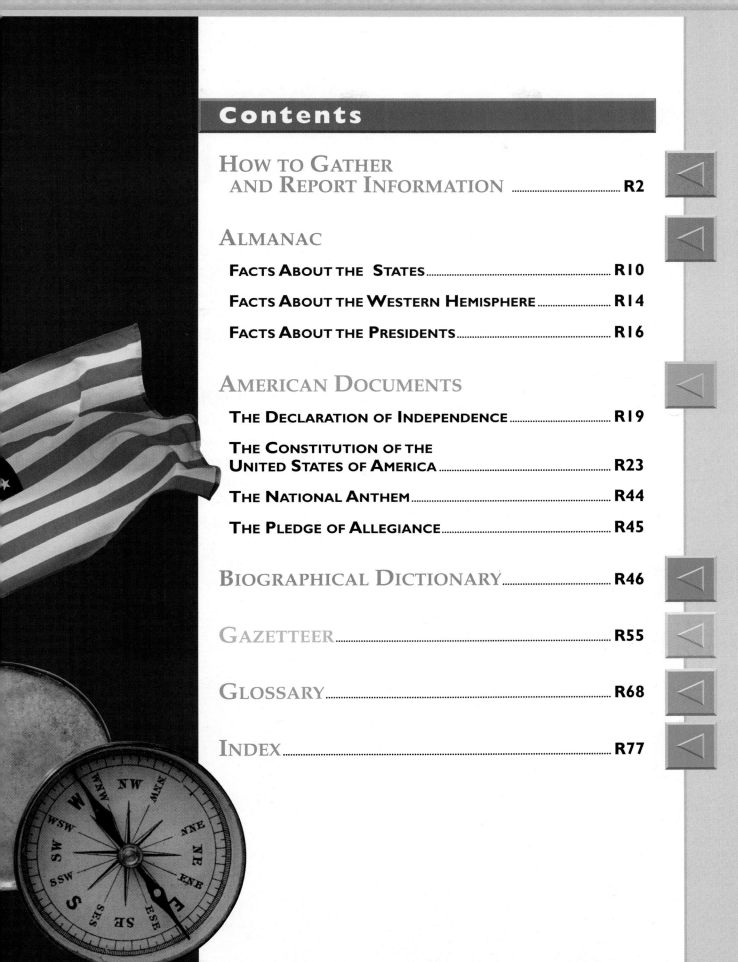

Contents

How to Gather and Report Information

To write a report, make a poster, or do many other social studies projects, you may need information that is not in your textbook. You would need to gather this information from reference books, electronic references, or community resources. The following guide can help you in gathering information from many sources and in reporting what you find.

How to Use Reference Tools

Reference works are collections of facts. They include books and electronic resources, such as almanacs, atlases, dictionaries, and encyclopedias. In a library a reference book has *R* or *REF*—for *reference*—on its spine with the call number. Most reference books are for use only in the library. Many libraries also have electronic references on CD-ROM and on the Internet.

R2

WHEN TO USE AN ENCYCLOPEDIA

An encyclopedia is a good place to begin to look for information. An encyclopedia has articles on nearly every subject. The articles are in alphabetical order. Each gives basic facts about people, places, and events. Some electronic encyclopedias allow you to hear music and speeches and see short movies.

WHEN TO USE A DICTIONARY

A dictionary can give you information about words. Dictionaries explain word meanings and show the pronunciations of words. A dictionary is a good place to check the spelling of a word. Some dictionaries also include the origins of words and lists of foreign words, abbreviations, well-known people, and place names.

WHEN TO USE AN ATLAS

You can find information about places in an atlas. An atlas is a book of maps. Some atlases have road maps. Others have maps of countries around the world. There are atlases with maps that show crops, population, products, and many other things. Ask a librarian to help you find the kind of atlas you need.

WHEN TO USE AN ALMANAC

An almanac is a book or electronic resource of facts and figures. It shows information in tables and charts. However, the subjects are not in alphabetical order. You will need to use the index, which does list the subjects in alphabetical order. Most almanacs are brought up to date every year. So an almanac can give you the latest information.

These students are researching information that they need to prepare a report on the American Revolution.

A card file can help you find the nonfiction book you want.

How to Find Nonfiction Books

Nonfiction books give facts about real people and things. In a library, all nonfiction books are numbered and placed in order on the shelves. To find the nonfiction book you want, you need to know its call number. You can find this number by using a card file or a computer catalog, but you will need to know the book's title, author, or subject. Here are some sample entries for a book on American Indians.

Subject Card

INDIANS OF NORTH AMERICA.

970.004 America's fascinating Indian heritage /
REA [editor, James A. Maxwell]. -- Pleasantville,
N.Y. : Reader's Digest Association, c1978.

416 p. : ill. ; 29 cm.

ISBN 0-89577-019-9

E77.A56

Author Card

Maxwell, James A., 1912-

970.004 America's fascinating Indian heritage /
REA [editor, James A. Maxwell]. -- Pleasantville,
N.Y. : Reader's Digest Association, c1978.

416 p. : ill. ; 29 cm.

ISBN 0-89577-019-9

E77.A56

Title Card

970.004 America's fascinating Indian heritage /
REA [editor, James A. Maxwell]. -- Pleasantville,
N.Y. : Reader's Digest Association, c1978.

416 p. : ill. ; 29 cm.

At head of title: Reader's Digest.
Includes index.
ISBN 0-89577-019-9

1. Indians of North America. I. Maxwell,
James A., 1912- II. Title: Reader's Digest.

E77.A56 970'.004
78-55614

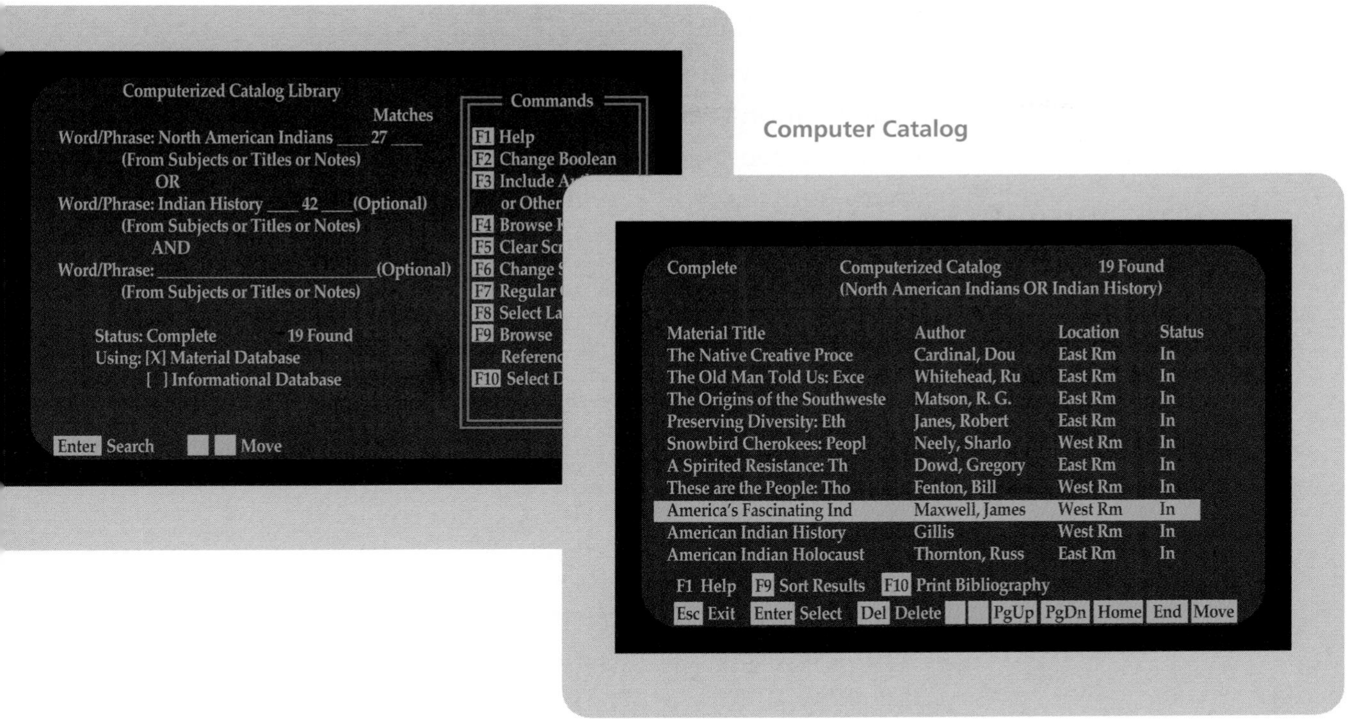

Computer Catalog

HOW TO FIND PERIODICALS

Libraries have special sections for periodicals—newspapers and magazines. Periodicals are good sources for the latest information and for topics not covered in books. New issues of periodicals are usually displayed on a rack. Older issues are stored away, sometimes on film. Most libraries have an index or guide that lists magazine articles by subject. The most widely used guides are the *Children's Magazine Guide* and the *Readers' Guide to Periodical Literature.*

The entries in these guides are usually in alphabetical order by subject, author, or title. Abbreviations may be used for many parts of an entry, such as the name of the magazine and the date of the issue. Here is a sample entry for an article on the Civil War.

Heading
The general topic you are researching
Title
The title of the article
CIVIL WAR
The End of Slavery in America, Newsweek 4 92: pp 58–70
Name
The name of the periodical
Date
The date of the periodical in which the article appears
Page Number(s)
The page(s) on which the article appears

How to Find Internet Resources

The World Wide Web, part of the Internet, is a rich resource for information. You can use the World Wide Web to read documents, see photographs and artworks, and examine other primary sources. You can also use it to listen to music, read electronic books, take a "tour" of a museum, or get the latest news.

Information on the World Wide Web changes all the time. What you find today may not be there tomorrow, and new information is always being added. Much of the information you find may be useful, but remember that some of it may not be accurate.

Plan Your Search

1. Make a list of your research questions.
2. Think about possible sources for finding your answers.
3. Identify key words to describe your research topic.
4. Consider synonyms and variations of those terms.
5. Decide exactly how you will go about finding what you need.

Search by Subject

To search for topics, or subjects, choose a search engine. You can get a list of available search engines by clicking the SEARCH or NET SEARCH button at the top of your screen.

If you want to find Web sites for baseball, for example, enter "baseball" in the search engine field. Then click SEARCH or GO on the screen. You will see a list of sites all over the World Wide Web having to do with baseball. Because not all search engines list the same sites, you may need to use more than one search engine.

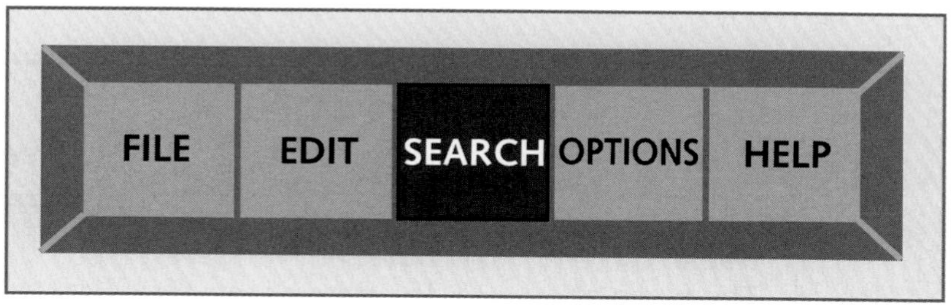

Search by Using Addresses

Each site on the World Wide Web has an address called a Uniform Resource Locator, or URL for short. A typical URL is shown in the box below.

To find URL listings, look in manuals, books, newspapers, magazines, and television and radio credits. To use a URL to go to a Web site, type the URL in the LOCATION/GO TO or NETSITE box in the upper left corner of the screen.

Go To http://www.hbschool.com

Bookmark Your Resources

Once you have found a site that you think will be helpful, you can bookmark it. Bookmarking makes a copy of a URL and keeps a record of it so you can easily go back to the site later.

While you are at the site you want to bookmark, click BOOKMARKS at the top of your screen and choose ADD BOOKMARK. Your list of bookmarks might look like this:

BOOKMARKS

- Harcourt Brace School Publishers: The Learning Site
- Library of Congress Home Page
- The Smithsonian Institution Home Page
- National Archives Online Exhibit Hall

Knowing how to use the Internet can help you find a wide range of information on a topic quickly and easily.

R7

Conducting an interview can be a good way to gather firsthand information about a topic.

How to Conduct an Interview

Conducting interviews, or asking people questions, is a good way to get facts and points of view.

Planning an Interview

1. Make a list of people to interview.
2. Call or write to each person to request an interview. When you contact the person, identify yourself and let the person know what you want to talk about.
3. Ask the person you will interview to set a time and place to meet.

Before the Interview

1. Read more about your topic, and, if possible, about the person. That way, you will be better able to talk with the person about your topic.
2. Make a list of questions to ask.

During the Interview

1. Listen carefully. Do not interrupt or argue with the person.
2. Take notes, and write down the person's exact words.
3. If you want to use a tape recorder, first ask the person if you may do so.

After the Interview

1. Before you leave, thank the person you interviewed.
2. Follow up by writing a thank-you note.

How to Conduct a Survey

A good way to get information about the views of people in your community is to conduct a survey.

1. Identify your topic, and make a list of questions. Write them so that they can be answered with "yes" or "no" or with "for" or "against." You may also want to give a "no opinion" or "not sure" choice.
2. Make a tally sheet for recording the responses.
3. Decide how many people you will ask and where you will conduct your survey.
4. During the survey, record the responses carefully on the tally sheet.
5. When you have finished your survey, count the responses and write a summary statement or conclusion that your survey supports.

How to Write for Information

People in places far away can also give you information. You can write a letter to ask for information about a certain topic. When you write, be sure to do these things:

- Write neatly or use a computer.
- Say who you are and why you are writing.
- Make your request specific and reasonable.
- Provide a self-addressed, stamped envelope for the answer.

How to Write a Report

You may be asked to write a report on the information you have gathered. Most reports are 300 to 500 words long.

Gather and Organize Your Information

Gather information about your topic from reference books, electronic references, or community resources. Then organize the information you have gathered.

- Take notes as you find information for your report.
- Review your notes to make sure that you have all the information you need.
- Outline your information.
- Make sure the information is in the right order.

Draft Your Report

- Review your information. Decide whether you need more.
- Remember that the purpose of your report is to share information about your topic.
- Write a draft of your report. Put all your ideas on paper.

Revise

- Check that you have followed the order of your outline. Move sentences that seem out of place.
- Add any information that seems needed.
- Add quotations that show people's exact words.
- Reword sentences if too many follow the same pattern.

Proofread and Publish

- Check for errors.
- Make sure nothing has been left out.
- Write a clean copy of your report, or use a computer.

A good report is well-organized and full of important information about a topic.

Almanac

Facts About the States

State Flag	State	Year of Statehood	Population*	Area (sq. mi.)	Capital	Origin of State Name
	**Alabama**	1819	4,319,000	51,609	Montgomery	Choctaw, *alba ayamule*, "one who clears land and gathers food from it"
	**Alaska**	1959	609,000	586,412	Juneau	Aleut, *alayeska*, "great land"
	**Arizona**	1912	4,555,000	113,909	Phoenix	Papago, *arizonac*, "place of the small spring"
	**Arkansas**	1836	2,523,000	53,104	Little Rock	Quapaw, "the downstream people"
	**California**	1850	32,268,000	158,693	Sacramento	Spanish, a fictional island
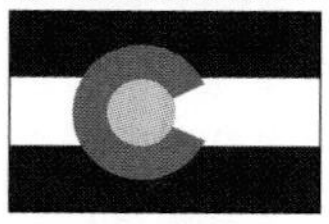	**Colorado**	1876	3,893,000	104,247	Denver	Spanish, "red land" or "red earth"
	**Connecticut**	1788	3,270,000	5,009	Hartford	Mohican, *quinnitukqut*, "at the long tidal river"
	**Delaware**	1787	732,000	2,057	Dover	Named for Lord de la Warr
	**Florida**	1845	14,654,000	58,560	Tallahassee	Spanish, "filled with flowers"
	**Georgia**	1788	7,486,000	58,876	Atlanta	Named for King George II of England
	**Hawaii**	1959	1,187,000	6,450	Honolulu	Polynesian, *hawaiki* or *owykee*, "homeland"
	**Idaho**	1890	1,210,000	83,557	Boise	Shoshone, "light on the mountains"

State Flag	State	Year of Statehood	Population*	Area (sq. mi.)	Capital	Origin of State Name
	**Illinois**	1818	11,896,000	56,400	Springfield	Algonquian, *iliniwek*, "men" or "warriors"
	**Indiana**	1816	5,864,000	36,291	Indianapolis	*Indian + a*, "land of the Indians"
	**Iowa**	1846	2,852,000	56,290	Des Moines	Dakota, *ayuba*, "beautiful land"
	**Kansas**	1861	2,595,000	82,264	Topeka	Sioux, "land of the south wind people"
	**Kentucky**	1792	3,908,000	40,395	Frankfort	Cherokee, *kentake*, "meadowland"
	**Louisiana**	1812	4,352,000	48,523	Baton Rouge	Named for King Louis XIV of France
	**Maine**	1820	1,242,000	33,215	Augusta	Named after a French province
	**Maryland**	1788	5,094,000	10,577	Annapolis	Named for Henrietta Maria, Queen Consort of Charles I of England
	**Massachusetts**	1788	6,118,000	8,257	Boston	Algonquian, "at the big hill" or "place of the big hill"
	**Michigan**	1837	9,774,000	58,216	Lansing	Chippewa, *mica gama*, "big water"
	**Minnesota**	1858	4,686,000	84,068	St. Paul	Dakota Sioux, "sky-blue water"
	**Mississippi**	1817	2,731,000	47,716	Jackson	Chippewa, *mici sibi*, "big river"
	**Missouri**	1821	5,402,000	69,686	Jefferson City	Algonquian, "muddy water"or "people of the big canoes"

*These population figures are from the most recent available statistics.

Facts About the States

State Flag	State	Year of Statehood	Population*	Area (sq. mi.)	Capital	Origin of State Name
	**Montana**	1889	879,000	147,138	Helena	Spanish, "mountainous"
	**Nebraska**	1867	1,657,000	77,227	Lincoln	Omaha, *ni-bthaska*, "river in the flatness"
	**Nevada**	1864	1,677,000	110,540	Carson City	Spanish, "snowy" or "snowed upon"
	**New Hampshire**	1788	1,173,000	9,304	Concord	Named for Hampshire County, England
	**New Jersey**	1787	8,053,000	7,836	Trenton	Named for the Isle of Jersey
	**New Mexico**	1912	1,730,000	121,666	Santa Fe	Named by Spanish explorers from Mexico
	**New York**	1788	18,137,000	49,576	Albany	Named after the Duke of York
	**North Carolina**	1789	7,425,000	52,586	Raleigh	Named after King Charles II of England
	**North Dakota**	1889	641,000	70,665	Bismarck	Sioux, *dakota*, "friend" or "ally"
	**Ohio**	1803	11,186,000	41,222	Columbus	Iroquois, *oheo*, "beautiful, beautiful water"
	**Oklahoma**	1907	3,317,000	69,919	Oklahoma City	Choctaw, "red people"
	**Oregon**	1859	3,243,000	96,981	Salem	Algonquian, *wauregan*, "beautiful water"
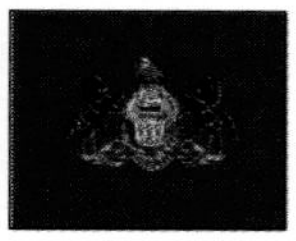	**Pennsylvania**	1787	12,020,000	45,333	Harrisburg	*Penn + sylvania*, meaning "Penn's woods"

State Flag	State	Year of Statehood	Population*	Area (sq. mi.)	Capital	Origin of State Name
	**Rhode Island**	1790	987,000	1,214	Providence	Dutch, "red-clay island"
	**South Carolina**	1788	3,760,000	31,055	Columbia	Named after King Charles II of England
	**South Dakota**	1889	738,000	77,047	Pierre	Sioux, *dakota,* "friend" or "ally"
	**Tennessee**	1796	5,368,000	42,244	Nashville	Name of a Cherokee village
	**Texas**	1845	19,439,000	267,338	Austin	Native American, *tejas,* "friend" or "ally"
	**Utah**	1896	2,059,000	84,916	Salt Lake City	Ute, "land of the Ute"
	**Vermont**	1791	589,000	9,609	Montpelier	French, *vert,* "green," and *mont,* "mountain"
	**Virginia**	1788	6,734,000	40,817	Richmond	Named after Queen Elizabeth I of England
	**Washington**	1889	5,610,000	68,192	Olympia	Named for George Washington
	**West Virginia**	1863	1,816,000	24,181	Charleston	From the English-named state of Virginia
	**Wisconsin**	1848	5,170,000	56,154	Madison	Possibly Algonquian, "grassy place" or "place of the beaver"
	**Wyoming**	1890	480,000	97,914	Cheyenne	Algonquian, *mache-weaming,* "at the big flats"
	District of Columbia		529,000	67		Named after Christopher Columbus

*These population figures are from the most recent available statistics.

Almanac

Facts About the Western Hemisphere

Country	Population*	Area (sq. mi.)	Capital	Origin of Country Name
North America				
Antigua and Barbuda	66,000	171	St. Johns	Named for the Church of Santa María la Antigua in Seville, Spain
Bahamas	262,000	5,382	Nassau	Spanish, *bajamar,* "shallow water"
Barbados	258,000	166	Bridgetown	Means "bearded"—probably referring to the beardlike vines early explorers found on its trees
Belize	225,000	8,867	Belmopan	Mayan, "muddy water"
Canada	29,123,000	3,849,674	Ottawa	Huron-Iroquois, *kanata,* "village" or "community"
Costa Rica	3,534,000	19,730	San José	Spanish, "rich coast"
Cuba	10,999,000	42,804	Havana	Origin unknown
Dominica	83,000	290	Roseau	Latin, *dies dominica,* "Day of the Lord"
Dominican Republic	8,228,000	18,704	Santo Domingo	Named after the capital city
El Salvador	5,662,000	8,124	San Salvador	Spanish, "the Savior"
Grenada	96,000	133	St. George's	Origin unknown
Guatemala	11,558,000	42,042	Guatemala City	Indian, "land of trees"
Haiti	6,611,000	10,695	Port-au-Prince	Indian, "land of mountains"
Honduras	5,751,000	43,277	Tegucigalpa	Spanish, "profundities"—probably referring to the depth of offshore waters
Jamaica	2,616,000	4,244	Kingston	Arawak, *xamayca,* "land of wood and water"
Mexico	97,563,000	756,066	Mexico City	Aztec, *mexliapan,* "lake of the moon"
Nicaragua	4,386,000	50,880	Managua	From *Nicarao,* the name of an Indian Chief
Panama	2,693,000	29,157	Panama City	From an Indian village's name

Almanac

Country	Population*	Area (sq. mi.)	Capital	Origin of Country Name
St. Kitts-Nevis	42,000	104	Basseterre	Named by Christopher Columbus—Kitts for St. Christopher, a Catholic saint; Nevis, for a cloud-topped peak that looked like las nieves, "the snows"
St. Lucia	160,000	238	Castries	Named by Christopher Columbus for a Catholic saint
St. Vincent and the Grenadines	119,000	150	Kingstown	May have been named by Christopher Columbus for a Catholic saint
Trinidad and Tobago	1,273,000	1,980	Port-of-Spain	Trinidad, from the Spanish word for "trinity"; Tobago, named for tobacco because the island has the shape of an Indian smoking pipe
United States of America	267,636,000	3,787,318	Washington, D.C.	Named after the explorer Amerigo Vespucci

South America

Argentina	35,798,000	1,073,518	Buenos Aires	Latin, *argentum,* "silver"
Bolivia	7,670,000	424,164	La Paz/Sucre	Named after Simón Bolívar, the famed liberator
Brazil	164,511,000	3,286,470	Brasília	Named after a native tree that the Portuguese called "bresel wood"
Chile	14,508,000	292,135	Santiago	Indian, *chilli,* "where the land ends"
Colombia	37,418,000	440,831	Bogotá	Named after Christopher Columbus
Ecuador	11,691,000	105,037	Quito	From the Spanish word for *equator,* referring to the country's location
Guyana	706,000	83,044	Georgetown	Indian, "land of waters"
Paraguay	5,652,000	157,048	Asunción	Named after the Paraguay River, which flows through it
Peru	24,950,000	496,255	Lima	Quechua, "land of abundance"
Suriname	443,000	63,251	Paramaribo	From an Indian word, *surinen*
Uruguay	3,262,000	68,037	Montevideo	Named after the Uruguay River, which flows through it
Venezuela	22,396,000	352,144	Caracas	Spanish, "Little Venice"

*These population figures are from the most recent available statistics.

R15

Almanac

FACTS ABOUT THE
Presidents

1 George Washington

Birthplace: *Westmoreland County, VA*
Home State: *VA*
Political Party: *None*
Age at Inauguration: *57*
Served: *1789–1797*
Vice President: *John Adams*
1732–1799

2 John Adams

Birthplace: *Braintree, MA*
Home State: *MA*
Political Party: *Federalist*
Age at Inauguration: *61*
Served: *1797–1801*
Vice President: *Thomas Jefferson*
1735–1826

3 Thomas Jefferson

Birthplace: *Albemarle County, VA*
Home State: *VA*
Political Party: *Democratic-Republican*
Age at Inauguration: *57*
Served: *1801–1809*
Vice Presidents: *Aaron Burr, George Clinton*
1743–1826

4 James Madison

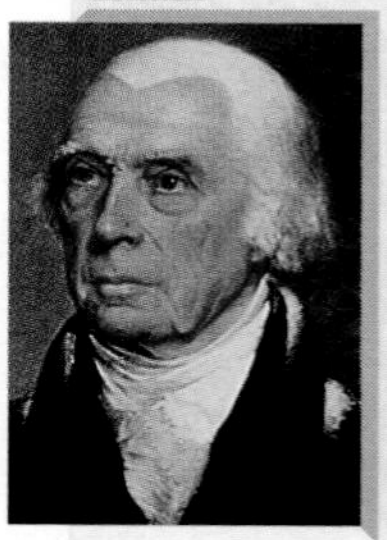

Birthplace: *Port Conway, VA*
Home State: *VA*
Political Party: *Democratic-Republican*
Age at Inauguration: *57*
Served: *1809–1817*
Vice Presidents: *George Clinton, Elbridge Gerry*
1751–1836

5 James Monroe

Birthplace: *Westmoreland County, VA*
Home State: *VA*
Political Party: *Democratic-Republican*
Age at Inauguration: *58*
Served: *1817–1825*
Vice President: *Daniel D. Tompkins*
1758–1831

6 John Quincy Adams

Birthplace: *Braintree, MA*
Home State: *MA*
Political Party: *Democratic-Republican*
Age at Inauguration: *57*
Served: *1825–1829*
Vice President: *John C. Calhoun*
1767–1848

7 Andrew Jackson

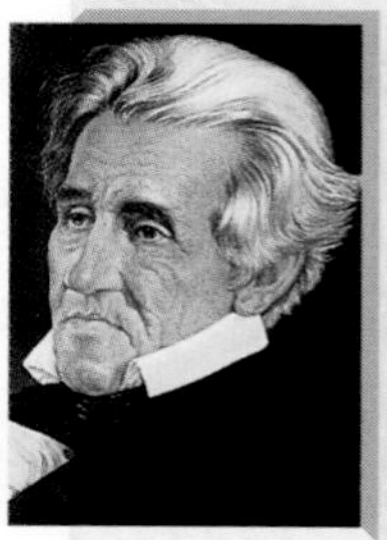

Birthplace: *Waxhaw settlement, SC*
Home State: *TN*
Political Party: *Democratic*
Age at Inauguration: *61*
Served: *1829–1837*
Vice Presidents: *John C. Calhoun, Martin Van Buren*
1767–1845

8 Martin Van Buren

Birthplace: *Kinderhook, NY*
Home State: *NY*
Political Party: *Democratic*
Age at Inauguration: *54*
Served: *1837–1841*
Vice President: *Richard M. Johnson*
1782–1862

9 William H. Harrison

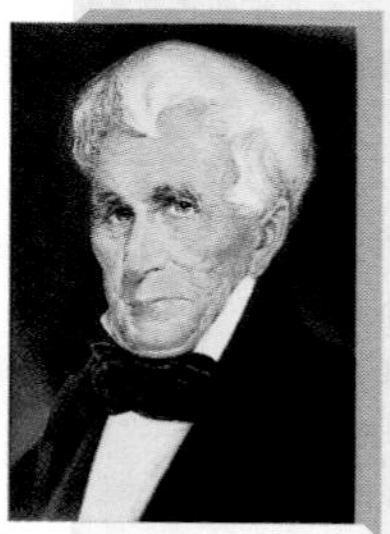

Birthplace: *Berkeley, VA*
Home State: *OH*
Political Party: *Whig*
Age at Inauguration: *68*
Served: *1841*
Vice President: *John Tyler*
1773–1841

10 John Tyler

Birthplace: *Greenway, VA*
Home State: *VA*
Political Party: *Whig*
Age at Inauguration: *51*
Served: *1841–1845*
Vice President: *none*
1790–1862

11 James K. Polk

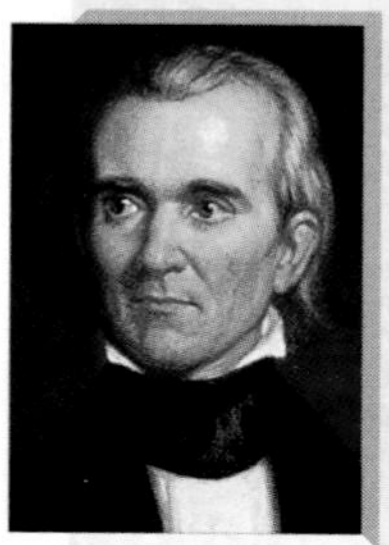

Birthplace: *near Pineville, NC*
Home State: *TN*
Political Party: *Democratic*
Age at Inauguration: *49*
Served: *1845–1849*
Vice President: *George M. Dallas*
1795–1849

12 Zachary Taylor

Birthplace: *Orange County, VA*
Home State: *LA*
Political Party: *Whig*
Age at Inauguration: *64*
Served: *1849–1850*
Vice President: *Millard Fillmore*
1784–1850

13 Millard Fillmore

Birthplace: *Locke, NY*
Home State: *NY*
Political Party: *Whig*
Age at Inauguration: *50*
Served: *1850–1853*
Vice President: *none*
1800–1874

Home state refers to the state of residence when elected.

14 Franklin Pierce

Birthplace: *Hillsboro, NH*
Home State: *NH*
Political Party: *Democratic*
Age at Inauguration: *48*
Served: *1853–1857*
Vice President: *William R. King*

1804–1869

15 James Buchanan

Birthplace: *near Mercersburg, PA*
Home State: *PA*
Political Party: *Democratic*
Age at Inauguration: *65*
Served: *1857–1861*
Vice President: *John C. Breckinridge*

1791–1868

16 Abraham Lincoln

Birthplace: *near Hodgenville, KY*
Home State: *IL*
Political Party: *Republican*
Age at Inauguration: *52*
Served: *1861–1865*
Vice Presidents: *Hannibal Hamlin, Andrew Johnson*

1809–1865

17 Andrew Johnson

Birthplace: *Raleigh, NC*
Home State: *TN*
Political Party: *National Union*
Age at Inauguration: *56*
Served: *1865–1869*
Vice President: *none*

1808–1875

18 Ulysses S. Grant

Birthplace: *Point Pleasant, OH*
Home State: *IL*
Political Party: *Republican*
Age at Inauguration: *46*
Served: *1869–1877*
Vice Presidents: *Schuyler Colfax, Henry Wilson*

1822–1885

19 Rutherford B. Hayes

Birthplace: *near Delaware, OH*
Home State: *OH*
Political Party: *Republican*
Age at Inauguration: *54*
Served: *1877–1881*
Vice President: *William A. Wheeler*

1822–1893

20 James A. Garfield

Birthplace: *Orange, OH*
Home State: *OH*
Political Party: *Republican*
Age at Inauguration: *49*
Served: *1881*
Vice President: *Chester A. Arthur*

1831–1881

21 Chester A. Arthur

Birthplace: *Fairfield, VT*
Home State: *NY*
Political Party: *Republican*
Age at Inauguration: *51*
Served: *1881–1885*
Vice President: *none*

1829–1886

22 Grover Cleveland

Birthplace: *Caldwell, NJ*
Home State: *NY*
Political Party: *Democratic*
Age at Inauguration: *47*
Served: *1885–1889*
Vice President: *Thomas A. Hendricks*

1837–1908

23 Benjamin Harrison

Birthplace: *North Bend, OH*
Home State: *IN*
Political Party: *Republican*
Age at Inauguration: *55*
Served: *1889–1893*
Vice President: *Levi P. Morton*

1833–1901

24 Grover Cleveland

Birthplace: *Caldwell, NJ*
Home State: *NY*
Political Party: *Democratic*
Age at Inauguration: *55*
Served: *1893–1897*
Vice President: *Adlai E. Stevenson*

1837–1908

25 William McKinley

Birthplace: *Niles, OH*
Home State: *OH*
Political Party: *Republican*
Age at Inauguration: *54*
Served: *1897–1901*
Vice Presidents: *Garret A. Hobart, Theodore Roosevelt*

1843–1901

26 Theodore Roosevelt

Birthplace: *New York, NY*
Home State: *NY*
Political Party: *Republican*
Age at Inauguration: *42*
Served: *1901–1909*
Vice President: *Charles W. Fairbanks*

1858–1919

27 William H. Taft

Birthplace: *Cincinnati, OH*
Home State: *OH*
Political Party: *Republican*
Age at Inauguration: *51*
Served: *1909–1913*
Vice President: *James S. Sherman*

1857–1930

28 Woodrow Wilson

Birthplace: *Staunton, VA*
Home State: *NJ*
Political Party: *Democratic*
Age at Inauguration: *56*
Served: *1913–1921*
Vice President: *Thomas R. Marshall*

1856–1924

29 Warren G. Harding

Birthplace: *near Blooming Grove, OH*
Home State: *OH*
Political Party: *Republican*
Age at Inauguration: *55*
Served: *1921–1923*
Vice President: *Calvin Coolidge*

1865–1923

30 Calvin Coolidge

Birthplace: *Plymouth Notch, VT*
Home State: *MA*
Political Party: *Republican*
Age at Inauguration: *51*
Served: *1923–1929*
Vice President: *Charles G. Dawes*

1872–1933

31 Herbert Hoover

Birthplace: *West Branch, IA*
Home State: *CA*
Political Party: *Republican*
Age at Inauguration: *54*
Served: *1929–1933*
Vice President: *Charles Curtis*

1874–1964

32 Franklin D. Roosevelt

Birthplace: *Hyde Park, NY*
Home State: *NY*
Political Party: *Democratic*
Age at Inauguration: *51*
Served: *1933–1945*
Vice Presidents: *John N. Garner, Henry A. Wallace, Harry S. Truman*

1882–1945

33 Harry S. Truman

Birthplace: *Lamar, MO*
Home State: *MO*
Political Party: *Democratic*
Age at Inauguration: *60*
Served: *1945–1953*
Vice President: *Alben W. Barkley*

1884–1972

34 Dwight D. Eisenhower

Birthplace: *Denison, TX*
Home State: *NY*
Political Party: *Republican*
Age at Inauguration: *62*
Served: *1953–1961*
Vice President: *Richard M. Nixon*

1890–1969

35 John F. Kennedy

Birthplace: Brookline, MA
Home State: *MA*
Political Party: *Democratic*
Age at Inauguration: *43*
Served: *1961–1963*
Vice President: *Lyndon B. Johnson*

1917–1963

36 Lyndon B. Johnson

Birthplace: *near Stonewall, TX*
Home State: *TX*
Political Party: *Democratic*
Age at Inauguration: *55*
Served: *1963–1969*
Vice President: *Hubert H. Humphrey*

1908–1973

37 Richard M. Nixon

Birthplace: *Yorba Linda, CA*
Home State: *NY*
Political Party: *Republican*
Age at Inauguration: *56*
Served: *1969–1974*
Vice Presidents: *Spiro T. Agnew, Gerald R. Ford*

1913–1994

38 Gerald R. Ford

Birthplace: *Omaha, NE*
Home State: *MI*
Political Party: *Republican*
Age at Inauguration: *61*
Served: *1974–1977*
Vice President: *Nelson A. Rockefeller*

1913–

39 Jimmy Carter

Birthplace: *Plains, GA*
Home State: *GA*
Political Party: *Democratic*
Age at Inauguration: *52*
Served: *1977–1981*
Vice President: *Walter F. Mondale*

1924–

40 Ronald W. Reagan

Birthplace: *Tampico, IL*
Home State: *CA*
Political Party: *Republican*
Age at Inauguration: *69*
Served: *1981–1989*
Vice President: *George H. W. Bush*

1911–

41 George H. W. Bush

Birthplace: *Milton, MA*
Home State: *TX*
Political Party: *Republican*
Age at Inauguration: *64*
Served: *1989–1993*
Vice President: *Dan Quayle*

1924–

42 William Clinton

Birthplace: *Hope, AR*
Home State: *AR*
Political Party: *Democratic*
Age at Inauguration: *46*
Served: *1993–2001*
Vice President: *Albert Gore*

1946–

43 George W. Bush

Birthplace: *New Haven, CT*
Political Party: *Republican*
Age at Inauguration: *54*
Served: *2001–*
Vice President: *Richard Cheney*

1946–

Home state refers to the state of residence when elected.

American Documents

The Declaration of Independence

In Congress, July 4, 1776.
The unanimous Declaration of the thirteen United States of America,

When in the Course of human events it becomes necessary for one people to dissolve the political bands which have connected them with another, and to assume among the powers of the earth, the separate and equal station to which the Laws of Nature and of Nature's God entitle them, a decent respect to the opinions of mankind requires that they should declare the causes which impel them to the separation.

Preamble
The Preamble tells why the Declaration was written. It states that the members of the Continental Congress believed the colonies had the right to break away from Britain and become a free nation.

We hold these truths to be self-evident, that all men are created equal, that they are endowed by their Creator with certain unalienable Rights, that among these are Life, Liberty and the pursuit of Happiness.
That to secure these rights, Governments are instituted among Men, deriving their just powers from the consent of the governed,
That whenever any Form of Government becomes destructive of these ends, it is the Right of the People to alter or to abolish it, and to institute new Government, laying its foundation on such principles and organizing its powers in such form, as to them shall seem most likely to effect their Safety and Happiness. Prudence, indeed, will dictate that Governments long established should not be changed for light and transient causes; and accordingly all experience hath shown, that mankind are more disposed to suffer, while evils are sufferable, than to right themselves by abolishing the forms to which they are accustomed. But when a long train of abuses and usurpations, pursuing invariably the same Object evinces a design to reduce them under absolute Despotism, it is their right, it is their duty, to throw off such Government, and to provide new Guards for their future security.

Statement of Rights
The opening part of the Declaration tells what rights the members of the Continental Congress believed that all people have. All people are equal and have the rights to life, liberty, and the pursuit of happiness. These rights cannot be taken away. When a government tries to take these rights away from the people, the people have the right to change the government or do away with it. The people can then form a new government that gives them these rights.

Such has been the patient sufferance of these Colonies; and such is now the necessity which constrains them to alter their former Systems of Government. The history of the present King of Great Britain is a history of repeated injuries and usurpations, all having in direct object the establishment of an absolute Tyranny over these States. To prove this, let Facts be submitted to a candid world.

Charges Against the King
The Declaration lists more than 25 charges against the king. He was mistreating the colonists, the Declaration says, in order to gain total control over the colonies.

He has refused his Assent to Laws, the most wholesome and necessary for the public good.

The king rejected many laws passed by colonial legislatures.

He has forbidden his Governors to pass Laws of immediate and pressing importance, unless suspended in their operation till his Assent should be obtained; and when so suspended, he has utterly neglected to attend to them.

He has refused to pass other Laws for the accommodation of large districts of people, unless those people would relinquish the right of Representation in the Legislature, a right inestimable to them and formidable to tyrants only.

The king made the colonial legislatures meet at unusual times and places.

He has called together legislative bodies at places unusual, uncomfortable, and distant from the depository of their public Records, for the sole purpose of fatiguing them into compliance with his measures.

The king and the king's governors often dissolved colonial legislatures for disobeying their orders.

He has dissolved Representative Houses repeatedly, for opposing with manly firmness his invasions on the rights of the people.

He has refused for a long time, after such dissolutions, to cause others to be elected; whereby the Legislative powers, incapable of Annihilation, have returned to the People at large for their exercise; the State remaining in the mean time exposed to all the dangers of invasion from without, and convulsions within.

The king stopped people from moving to the colonies and into the western lands.

He has endeavored to prevent the population of these States; for that purpose obstructing the Laws for Naturalization of Foreigners; refusing to pass others to encourage their migrations hither, and raising the conditions of new Appropriations of Lands.

The king prevented the colonists from choosing their own judges. The king chose the judges, and they served only as long as the king was satisfied with them.

He has obstructed the Administration of Justice, by refusing his Assent to Laws for establishing Judiciary powers.

He has made Judges dependent on his Will alone, for the tenure of their offices, and the amount and payment of their salaries.

The king hired people to help collect taxes in the colonies.

He has erected a multitude of New Offices, and sent hither swarms of Officers to harrass our people, and eat out their substance.

The king appointed General Thomas Gage, commander of Britain's military forces in the Americas, as governor of Massachusetts.

He has kept among us, in times of peace, Standing Armies without the Consent of our legislatures.

He has affected to render the Military independent of and superior to the Civil power.

He has combined with others to subject us to a jurisdiction foreign to our constitution, and unacknowledged by our laws; giving his Assent to their Acts of pretended Legislation:

The king expected the colonists to provide housing and supplies for the British soldiers in the colonies.

For quartering large bodies of armed troops among us:

For protecting them, by a mock Trial, from punishment for any Murders which they should commit on the Inhabitants of these States:

For cutting off our Trade with all parts of the world:

The king and Parliament demanded that colonists pay many taxes, even though the colonists did not agree to pay them.

For imposing Taxes on us without our Consent:

Colonists were tried by British naval courts, which had no juries.

For depriving us in many cases, of the benefits of Trial by Jury:

Colonists accused of treason were sent to Britain to be tried.

For transporting us beyond Seas to be tried for pretended offences:

For abolishing the free System of English Laws in a neighboring Province, establishing therein an Arbitrary government, and enlarging its Boundaries so as to render it at once an example and fit instrument for introducing the same absolute rule into these Colonies:

For taking away our Charters, abolishing our most valuable Laws, and altering fundamentally the Forms of our Governments:

For suspending our own Legislatures, and declaring themselves invested with power to legislate for us in all cases whatsoever.

He has abdicated Government here, by declaring us out of his Protection and waging War against us.

He has plundered our seas, ravaged our Coasts, burnt our towns, and destroyed the lives of our people.

The king allowed General Gage to take military action to enforce British laws in the colonies.

He is at this time transporting large Armies of foreign Mercenaries to complete the works of death, desolation and tyranny, already begun with circumstances of Cruelty & perfidy scarcely paralleled in the most barbarous ages, and totally unworthy the Head of a civilized nation.

He has constrained our fellow Citizens taken Captive on the high Seas to bear Arms against their Country, to become the executioners of their friends and Brethren, or to fall themselves by their Hands.

The king hired Hessian mercenaries and sent them to fight the colonists.

He has excited domestic insurrections amongst us, and has endeavored to bring on the inhabitants of our frontiers, the merciless Indian Savages, whose known rule of warfare, is an undistinguished destruction of all ages, sexes and conditions.

The king's governor in Virginia promised freedom to all enslaved people who joined the British forces. The British also planned to use Indians to fight the colonists.

In every stage of these Oppressions We have Petitioned for Redress in the most humble terms: Our repeated Petitions have been answered only by repeated injury. A Prince, whose character is thus marked by every act which may define a Tyrant, is unfit to be the ruler of a free people.

Nor have We been wanting in attentions to our British brethren. We have warned them from time to time of attempts by their legislature to extend an unwarrantable jurisdiction over us. We have reminded them of the circumstances of our emigration and settlement here. We have appealed to their native justice and magnanimity, and we have conjured them by the ties of our common kindred to disavow these usurpations, which, would inevitably interrupt our connections and correspondence. They too have been deaf to the voice of justice and of consanguinity. We must, therefore, acquiesce in the necessity, which denounces our Separation, and hold them, as we hold the rest of mankind, Enemies in War, in Peace Friends.

The Declaration explained the efforts of the colonists to avoid separation from Britain. But the colonists said that the king had ignored their protests. Because of the many charges against the king, the writers of the Declaration concluded that he was not fit to rule free people.

We, therefore, the Representatives of the united States of America, in General Congress, Assembled, appealing to the Supreme Judge of the world for the rectitude of our intentions, do, in the Name, and by Authority of the good People of these Colonies, solemnly publish and declare, That these United Colonies are, and of Right ought to be Free and Independent States; that they are Absolved from all Allegiance to the British Crown, and that all political connection between them and the State of Great Britain, is and ought to be totally dissolved; and that as Free and Independent States, they have full Power to levy War, conclude Peace, contract Alliances, establish Commerce, and to do all other Acts and Things which Independent States may of right do.

A Statement of Independence The writers declared that the colonies were now free and independent states. All ties with Britain were broken. As free and independent states, they had the right to make war and peace, to trade, and to do all the things free countries could do.

R21

To support the Declaration, the signers promised one another their lives, their fortunes, and their honor.

And for the support of this Declaration, with a firm reliance on the protection of divine Providence, we mutually pledge to each other our Lives, our Fortunes and our sacred Honor.

John Hancock

NEW HAMPSHIRE
Josiah Bartlett
William Whipple
Matthew Thornton

MASSACHUSETTS
John Adams
Samuel Adams
Robert Treat Paine
Elbridge Gerry

NEW YORK
William Floyd
Philip Livingston
Francis Lewis
Lewis Morris

RHODE ISLAND
Stephen Hopkins
William Ellery

NEW JERSEY
Richard Stockton
John Witherspoon
Francis Hopkinson
John Hart
Abraham Clark

PENNSYLVANIA
Robert Morris
Benjamin Rush
Benjamin Franklin
John Morton
George Clymer
James Smith
George Taylor
James Wilson
George Ross

DELAWARE
Caesar Rodney
George Read
Thomas McKean

MARYLAND
Samuel Chase
William Paca
Thomas Stone
Charles Carroll of Carrollton

NORTH CAROLINA
William Hopper
Joseph Hewes
John Penn

VIRGINIA
George Wythe
Richard Henry Lee
Thomas Jefferson
Benjamin Harrison
Thomas Nelson, Jr.
Francis Lightfoot Lee
Carter Braxton

SOUTH CAROLINA
Edward Rutledge
Thomas Heyward, Jr.
Thomas Lynch, Jr.
Arthur Middleton

CONNECTICUT
Roger Sherman
Samuel Huntington
William Williams
Oliver Wolcott

GEORGIA
Button Gwinnett
Lyman Hall
George Walton

Members of the Continental Congress stated that copies of the Declaration should be sent to all Committees of Correspondence and to commanders of the troops and that it should be read in every state.

Resolved, That copies of the Declaration be sent to the several assemblies, conventions, and committees, or councils of safety, and to the several commanding officers of the continental troops; that it be proclaimed in each of the United States, at the head of the army.

THE CONSTITUTION OF THE UNITED STATES OF AMERICA

Preamble*

We the people of the United States, in order to form a more perfect Union, establish justice, insure domestic tranquillity, provide for the common defense, promote the general welfare, and secure the blessings of liberty to ourselves and our posterity, do ordain and establish this Constitution for the United States of America.

PREAMBLE
The introduction to the Constitution states the purposes and principles for writing it. The writers wanted to set up a fairer form of government and to secure peace and freedom for themselves and for future generations.

ARTICLE I
THE LEGISLATIVE BRANCH

SECTION 1. CONGRESS

All legislative powers herein granted shall be vested in a Congress of the United States, which shall consist of a Senate and House of Representatives.

CONGRESS
Congress has the authority to make laws. Congress is made up of two groups of lawmakers: the Senate and the House of Representatives.

SECTION 2. THE HOUSE OF REPRESENTATIVES

(1) The House of Representatives shall be composed of members chosen every second year by the people of the several states, and the electors in each state shall have the qualifications requisite for electors of the most numerous branch of the state legislature.

(1) ELECTION AND TERM OF MEMBERS
Qualified voters are to elect members of the House of Representatives every two years. Each member of the House of Representatives must meet certain requirements.

(2) No person shall be a Representative who shall not have attained to the age of twenty-five years, and been seven years a citizen of the United States, and who shall not, when elected, be an inhabitant of that state in which he shall be chosen.

(2) QUALIFICATIONS
Members of the House of Representatives must be at least 25 years old. They must have been citizens of the United States for at least seven years. They must live in the state that they will represent.

(3) Representatives [*and direct taxes*]** shall be apportioned among the several states which may be included within this Union, according to their respective numbers [*which shall be determined by adding to the whole number of free persons, including those bound to service for a term of years, and excluding Indians not taxed, three-fifths of all other persons*]. The actual enumeration shall be made within three years after the first meeting of the Congress of the United States, and within every subsequent term of ten years, in such manner as they shall by law direct. The number of Representatives shall not exceed one for every 30,000, but each state shall have at least one Representative [*; and until such enumeration shall be made, the State of New Hampshire shall be entitled to choose three; Massachusetts eight; Rhode Island and Providence Plantations one; Connecticut five; New York six; New Jersey four; Pennsylvania eight; Delaware one; Maryland six; Virginia ten; North Carolina five; South Carolina five; and Georgia three*].

(3) DETERMINING APPORTIONMENT
The number of representatives a state may have depends on the number of people living in each state. Every ten years the federal government must take a census, or count, of the population in every state. Every state will have at least one representative.

*Titles have been added to make the Constitution easier to read. They did not appear in the original document.

**The parts of the Constitution that no longer apply are printed in italics within brackets [ ]. These portions have been changed or set aside by later amendments.

(4) FILLING VACANCIES
If there is a vacancy in representation in Congress, the governor of the state involved must call a special election to fill it.

(4) When vacancies happen in the representation from any state, the executive authority thereof shall issue writs of election to fill such vacancies.

(5) SPECIAL AUTHORITY
The House of Representatives chooses a Speaker as its presiding officer. It also chooses other officers as appropriate. The House is the only government branch that may impeach, or charge, an official in the executive branch or a judge of the federal courts for failing to carry out his or her duties. These cases are tried in the Senate.

(5) The House of Representatives shall choose their Speaker and other officers; and shall have the sole power of impeachment.

SECTION 3. THE SENATE

(1) NUMBER, TERM, AND SELECTION OF MEMBERS
Each state is represented by two senators. Until Amendment 17 was passed, state legislatures chose the senators for their states. Each senator serves a six-year term and has one vote in Congress.

(1) The Senate of the United States shall be composed of two Senators from each state [*chosen by the legislature thereof*], for six years, and each Senator shall have one vote.

(2) OVERLAPPING TERMS AND FILLING VACANCIES
One-third of the senators are elected every two years for a six-year term. This grouping allows at least two-thirds of the experienced senators to remain in the Senate after each election. Amendment 17 permits state governors to appoint a replacement to fill a vacancy until the next election is held.

(2) [*Immediately after they shall be assembled in consequence of the first election, they shall be divided as equally as may be into three classes. The seats of the Senators of the first class shall be vacated at the expiration of the second year, of the second class at the expiration of the fourth year, and of the third class at the expiration of the sixth year, so that one-third may be chosen every second year; and if vacancies happen by resignation, or otherwise, during the recess of the legislature of any state, the executive thereof may make temporary appointments until the next meeting of the legislature, which shall then fill such vacancies.*]

(3) QUALIFICATIONS
Senators must be at least 30 years old. They must have been citizens of the United States for at least nine years. They must live in the state that they will represent.

(3) No person shall be a Senator who shall not have attained to the age of thirty years, and been nine years a citizen of the United States, and who shall not, when elected, be an inhabitant of that state for which he shall be chosen.

(4) PRESIDENT OF THE SENATE
The Vice President acts as chief officer of the Senate but does not vote unless there is a tie.

(4) The Vice President of the United States shall be President of the Senate, but shall have no vote, unless they be equally divided.

(5) OTHER OFFICERS
The Senate chooses its other officers and a president pro tempore, who serves if the Vice President is not present or if the Vice President becomes President. *Pro tempore* is a Latin term meaning "for the time being."

(5) The Senate shall choose their other officers, and also a President *pro tempore*, in the absence of the Vice President, or when he shall exercise the office of the President of the United States.

(6) The Senate shall have the sole power to try all impeachments. When sitting for that purpose, they shall be on oath or affirmation. When the President of the United States is tried, the Chief Justice shall preside; and no person shall be convicted without the concurrence of two-thirds of the members present.

(6) Impeachment Trials
If the House of Representatives votes articles of impeachment, the Senate holds a trial. A two-thirds vote is required to convict a person who has been impeached.

(7) Judgment in cases of impeachment shall not extend further than to removal from office, and disqualification to hold and enjoy any office of honor, trust, or profit under the United States; but the party convicted shall nevertheless be liable and subject to indictment, trial, judgment and punishment, according to law.

(7) Penalty for Conviction
If convicted in an impeachment case, an official is removed from office and may never hold office in the United States government again. The convicted person may also be tried in a regular court of law for any crimes.

SECTION 4. ELECTIONS AND MEETINGS

(1) The times, places, and manner of holding elections for Senators and Representatives shall be prescribed in each state by the legislature thereof; but the Congress may at any time by law make or alter such regulations, [*except as to the places of choosing Senators*].

(1) Holding Elections
Each state makes its own rules about electing senators and representatives. However, Congress may change these rules at any time. Today congressional elections are held on the Tuesday after the first Monday in November, in even-numbered years.

(2) The Congress shall assemble at least once in every year, [*and such meeting shall be on the first Monday in December, unless they shall by law appoint a different day*].

(2) Meetings
The Constitution requires Congress to meet at least once a year. That day is the first Monday in December, unless Congress sets a different day. Amendment 20 changed this date to January 3.

SECTION 5. RULES OF PROCEDURE

(1) Each house shall be the judge of the elections, returns and qualifications of its own members, and a majority of each shall constitute a quorum to do business; but a smaller number may adjourn from day to day, and may be authorized to compel the attendance of absent members, in such manner and under such penalties as each house may provide.

(1) Organization
Each house of Congress may decide if its members have been elected fairly and are able to hold office. Each house may do business only when a quorum—a majority of its members—is present. By less than a majority vote, each house may compel absent members to attend.

(2) Each house may determine the rules of its proceedings, punish its members for disorderly behavior, and, with the concurrence of two-thirds, expel a member.

(2) Rules
Each house may decide its own rules for doing business, punish its members, and expel a member from office if two-thirds of the members agree.

(3) Each house shall keep a journal of its proceedings, and from time to time publish the same, excepting such parts as may in their judgment require secrecy; and the yeas and nays of the members of either house on any question shall, at the desire of one-fifth of those present, be entered on the journal.

(3) Journal
The Constitution requires each house to keep records of its activities and to publish these records from time to time. The House Journal and the Senate Journal are published at the end of each session. How each member voted must be recorded if one-fifth of the members ask for this to be done.

(4) Adjournment
When Congress is in session, neither house may take a recess for more than three days without the consent of the other.

(4) Neither house, during the session of Congress, shall, without the consent of the other, adjourn for more than three days, nor to any other place than that in which the two houses shall be sitting.

SECTION 6. PRIVILEGES AND RESTRICTIONS

(1) Pay and privileges
Members of Congress set their own salaries, which are to be paid by the federal government. Members cannot be arrested or sued for anything they say while Congress is in session. This privilege is called congressional immunity. Members of Congress may be arrested while Congress is in session only if they commit a crime.

(1) The Senators and Representatives shall receive a compensation for their services, to be ascertained by law and paid out of the Treasury of the United States. They shall in all cases, except treason, felony, and breach of the peace, be privileged from arrest during their attendance at the session of their respective houses, and in going to and returning from the same; and for any speech or debate in either house, they shall not be questioned in any other place.

(2) Restrictions
Members of Congress may not hold any other federal office while serving in Congress. A member may not resign from office and then take a government position created during that member's term of office or for which the pay has been increased during that member's term of office.

(2) No Senator or Representative shall, during the time for which he was elected, be appointed to any civil office under the authority of the United States, which shall have been created, or the emoluments whereof shall have been increased, during such time; and no person holding any office under the United States shall be a member of either house during his continuance in office.

SECTION 7. MAKING LAWS

(1) Money-Raising Bills
All money-raising bills must be introduced first in the House of Representatives, but the Senate may suggest changes.

(1) All bills for raising revenue shall originate in the House of Representatives; but the Senate may propose or concur with amendments as on other bills.

(2) How a Bill Becomes a Law
After a bill has been passed by both the House of Representatives and the Senate, it must be sent to the President. If the President approves and signs the bill, it becomes law. The President can also veto, or refuse to sign, the bill. Congress can override a veto by passing the bill again by a two-thirds majority. If the President does not act within ten days, two things may happen. If Congress is still in session, the bill becomes a law. If Congress ends its session within that same ten-day period, the bill does not become a law.

(2) Every bill which shall have passed the House of Representatives and the Senate shall, before it become a law, be presented to the President of the United States; if he approve, he shall sign it, but if not, he shall return it, with his objections, to that house in which it shall have originated, who shall enter the objections at large on their journal, and proceed to reconsider it. If after such reconsideration two-thirds of that house shall agree to pass the bill, it shall be sent, together with the objections, to the other house, by which it shall likewise be reconsidered, and, if approved by two-thirds of that house, it shall become a law. But in all such cases the votes of both houses shall be determined by yeas and nays, and the names of the persons voting for and against the bill shall be entered on the journal of each house respectively. If any bill shall not be returned by the President within ten days (Sundays excepted) after it shall have been presented to him, the same bill shall be a law, in like manner as if he had signed it, unless the Congress by their adjournment prevent its return, in which case it shall not be a law.

(3) Orders and Resolutions
Congress can pass orders and resolutions, some of which have the same effect as a law. Congress may decide on its own when to end the session. Other such acts must be signed or vetoed by the President.

(3) Every order, resolution, or vote to which the concurrence of the Senate and House of Representatives may be necessary (except on a question of adjournment) shall be presented to the President of the United States; and before the same shall take effect, shall be approved by him, or being disapproved by him, shall be repassed by two-thirds of the Senate and House of Representatives, according to the rules and limitations prescribed in the case of a bill.

SECTION 8. POWERS DELEGATED TO CONGRESS
The Congress shall have power

(1) To lay and collect taxes, duties, imposts and excises, to pay the debts and provide for the common defense and general welfare of the United States; but all duties, imposts and excises shall be uniform throughout the United States;

(1) TAXATION
Only Congress has the authority to raise money to pay debts, defend the United States, and provide services for its people by collecting taxes or tariffs on foreign goods. All taxes must be applied equally in all states.

(2) To borrow money on the credit of the United States;

(2) BORROWING MONEY
Congress may borrow money for national use. This is usually done by selling government bonds.

(3) To regulate commerce with foreign nations, and among the several states [*and with the Indian tribes*];

(3) COMMERCE
Congress can control trade with other countries and between states.

(4) To establish a uniform rule of naturalization, and uniform laws on the subject of bankruptcies throughout the United States;

(4) NATURALIZATION AND BANKRUPTCY
Congress decides what requirements people from other countries must meet to become United States citizens. Congress can also pass laws to protect people who are bankrupt, or cannot pay their debts.

(5) To coin money, regulate the value thereof, and of foreign coin, and fix the standard of weights and measures;

(5) COINS, WEIGHTS, AND MEASURES
Congress can print and coin money and decide its value. Congress also decides on the system of weights and measures to be used throughout the nation.

(6) To provide for the punishment of counterfeiting the securities and current coin of the United States;

(6) COUNTERFEITING
Congress may pass laws to punish people who make fake money, bonds, or stamps.

(7) To establish post offices and post roads;

(7) POSTAL SERVICE
Congress can build post offices and make rules about the postal system and the roads used for mail delivery.

(8) To promote the progress of science and useful arts by securing for limited times to authors and inventors the exclusive right to their respective writings and discoveries;

(8) COPYRIGHTS AND PATENTS
Congress can issue patents and copyrights to inventors and authors to protect the ownership of their works.

(9) To constitute tribunals inferior to the Supreme Court;

(9) FEDERAL COURTS
Congress can establish a system of federal courts under the Supreme Court.

(10) To define and punish piracies and felonies committed on the high seas and offenses against the law of nations;

(10) CRIMES AT SEA
Congress can pass laws to punish people for crimes committed at sea. Congress may also punish United States citizens for breaking international law.

(11) DECLARING WAR
Only Congress can declare war.

(11) To declare war, [*grant letters of marque and reprisal,*] and make rules concerning captures on land and water;

(12) THE ARMY
Congress can establish an army, but it cannot vote enough money to support it for more than two years. This part of the Constitution was written to keep the army under civilian control.

(12) To raise and support armies, but no appropriation of money to that use shall be for a longer term than two years;

(13) THE NAVY
Congress can establish a navy and vote enough money to support it for as long as necessary. No time limit was set because people thought the navy was less of a threat to people's liberty than the army was.

(13) To provide and maintain a navy;

(14) MILITARY REGULATIONS
Congress makes the rules that guide and govern all the armed forces.

(14) To make rules for the government and regulation of the land and naval forces;

(15) THE MILITIA
Each state has its own militia, now known as the National Guard. The National Guard can be called into federal service by the President, as authorized by Congress, to enforce laws, to stop uprisings against the government, or to protect the people in case of floods, earthquakes, and other disasters.

(15) To provide for calling forth the militia to execute the laws of the Union, suppress insurrections and repel invasions;

(16) CONTROL OF THE MILITIA
Congress helps each state support the National Guard. Each state may appoint its own officers and train its own guard according to rules set by Congress.

(16) To provide for organizing, arming, and disciplining the militia, and for governing such part of them as may be employed in the service of the United States, reserving to the states, respectively, the appointment of the officers, and the authority of training the militia according to the discipline prescribed by Congress;

(17) NATIONAL CAPITAL AND OTHER PROPERTY
Congress may pass laws to govern the nation's capital (Washington, D.C.) and any land owned by the government.

(17) To exercise exclusive legislation in all cases whatsoever, over such district (not exceeding ten miles square) as may, by cession of particular states, and the acceptance of Congress, become the seat of government of the United States, and to exercise like authority over all places purchased by the consent of the legislature of the state in which the same shall be, for the erection of forts, magazines, arsenals, dock-yards, and other needful buildings; —and

(18) OTHER NECESSARY LAWS
The Constitution allows Congress to make laws that are necessary to enforce the powers listed in Article I. This clause allows Congress to stretch its authority when new situations arise.

(18) To make all laws which shall be necessary and proper for carrying into execution the foregoing powers, and all other powers vested by this Constitution in the government of the United States, or in any department or officer thereof.

SECTION 9. POWERS DENIED TO CONGRESS

(1) [*The migration or importation of such persons as any of the states now existing shall think proper to admit shall not be prohibited by the Congress prior to the year 1808; but a tax or duty may be imposed on such importation, not exceeding 10 dollars for each person.*]

(1) SLAVE TRADE
Some authority is not given to Congress. Congress could not prevent the slave trade until 1808, but it could put a tax of ten dollars on each slave brought into the United States. After 1808, when a law was passed to stop slaves from being brought into the United States, this section no longer applied.

(2) The privilege of the writ of habeas corpus shall not be suspended, unless when in cases of rebellion or invasion the public safety may require it.

(2) HABEAS CORPUS
A writ of habeas corpus is a privilege that entitles a person to a hearing before a judge. The judge must then decide if there is good reason for that person to have been arrested. If not, that person must be released. The government is not allowed to take this privilege away except during a national emergency, such as an invasion or a rebellion.

(3) No bill of attainder or ex post facto law shall be passed.

(3) SPECIAL LAWS
Congress cannot pass laws that impose punishment on a named individual or group, except in cases of treason. Article III sets limits to punishments for treason. Congress also cannot pass laws that punish a person for an action that was legal when it was done.

(4) [*No capitation or other direct tax shall be laid, unless in proportion to the census or enumeration herein before directed to be taken.*]

(4) DIRECT TAXES
Congress cannot set a direct tax on people, unless it is in proportion to the total population. Amendment 16, which provides for the income tax, is an exception.

(5) No tax or duty shall be laid on articles exported from any state.

(5) EXPORT TAXES
Congress cannot tax goods sent from one state to another or from a state to another country.

(6) No preference shall be given by any regulation of commerce or revenue to the ports of one state over those of another; nor shall vessels bound to, or from, one state, be obliged to enter, clear, or pay duties in another.

(6) PORTS
When making trade laws, Congress cannot favor one state over another. Congress cannot require ships from one state to pay a duty to enter another state.

(7) No money shall be drawn from the Treasury, but in consequence of appropriations made by law; and a regular statement and account of the receipts and expenditures of all public money shall be published from time to time.

(7) PUBLIC MONEY
The government cannot spend money from the treasury unless Congress passes a law allowing it to do so. A written record must be kept of all money spent by the government.

(8) Titles of Nobility and Gifts
The United States government cannot grant titles of nobility. Government officials cannot accept gifts from other countries without the permission of Congress. This clause was intended to prevent government officials from being bribed by other nations.

(8) No title of nobility shall be granted by the United States; and no person holding any office of profit or trust under them, shall, without the consent of the Congress, accept of any present, emolument, office, or title, of any kind whatever, from any king, prince, or foreign state.

SECTION 10. POWERS DENIED TO THE STATES

(1) Complete Restrictions
The Constitution does not allow states to act as if they were individual countries. No state government may make a treaty with other countries. No state can print its own money.

(1) No state shall enter into any treaty, alliance, or confederation; grant letters of marque and reprisal; coin money; emit bills of credit; make anything but gold and silver coin a tender in payment of debts; pass any bill of attainder, ex post facto law, or law impairing the obligation of contracts, or grant any title of nobility.

(2) Partial Restrictions
No state government can tax imported goods or exported goods without the consent of Congress. States may charge a fee to inspect these goods, but profits must be given to the United States Treasury.

(2) No state shall, without the consent of the Congress, lay any imposts or duties on imports or exports, except what may be absolutely necessary for executing its inspection laws; and the net produce of all duties and imposts, laid by any state on imports or exports, shall be for the use of the Treasury of the United States; and all such laws shall be subject to the revision and control of the Congress.

(3) Other Restrictions
No state government may tax ships entering its ports unless Congress approves. No state may keep an army or navy during times of peace other than the National Guard. No state can enter into agreements called compacts with other states without the consent of Congress.

(3) No state shall, without the consent of Congress, lay any duty of tonnage, keep troops, or ships of war in time of peace, enter into any agreement or compact with another state, or with a foreign power, or engage in war, unless actually invaded, or in such imminent danger as will not admit of delay.

ARTICLE II
THE EXECUTIVE BRANCH

SECTION 1. PRESIDENT AND VICE PRESIDENT

(1) Term of Office
The President has the authority to carry out our nation's laws. The term of office for both the President and the Vice President is four years.

(1) The executive power shall be vested in a President of the United States of America. He shall hold his office during the term of four years, and together with the Vice President, chosen for the same term, be elected as follows:

(2) The Electoral College
This group of people is to be chosen by the voters of each state to elect the President and Vice President. The number of electors in each state is equal to the number of senators and representatives that state has in Congress.

(2) Each state shall appoint, in such manner as the legislature thereof may direct, a number of electors, equal to the whole number of Senators and Representatives to which the state may be entitled in the Congress; but no Senator or Representative, or person holding an office of trust or profit under the United States, shall be appointed an elector.

(3) Election Process
This clause describes in detail how the electors were to choose the President and Vice President. In 1804 Amendment 12 changed the process for electing the President and the Vice President.

(3) [*The electors shall meet in their respective states, and vote by ballot for two persons, of whom one at least shall not be an inhabitant of the same state with themselves. And they shall make a list of all the persons voted for, and of the number of votes for each; which list they shall sign and certify, and transmit sealed to the seat of the government of the United States, directed to the president of the Senate. The president of the Senate shall, in the presence of the Senate and House of Representatives, open all the certificates, and the votes shall then be counted. The person having the greatest number of votes shall be the President, if such number be a majority of the whole number of electors appointed; and if*

there be more than one who have such majority, and have an equal number of votes, then the House of Representatives shall immediately choose by ballot one of them for President; and if no person have a majority, then from the five highest on the list the said House shall in like manner choose the President. But in choosing the President the votes shall be taken by states, the representation from each state having one vote: A quorum for this purpose shall consist of a member or members from two-thirds of the states, and a majority of all the states shall be necessary to a choice. In every case, after the choice of the President, the person having the greatest number of votes of the electors shall be the Vice President. But if there should remain two or more who have equal votes, the Senate shall choose from them by ballot the Vice President.]

(4) The Congress may determine the time of choosing the electors, and the day on which they shall give their votes; which day shall be the same throughout the United States.

(4) Time of Elections
Congress decides the day the electors are to be elected and the day they are to vote.

(5) No person except a natural-born citizen [*or a citizen of the United States, at the time of the adoption of this Constitution,*] shall be eligible to the office of the President; neither shall any person be eligible to that office who shall not have attained to the age of thirty-five years, and been fourteen years a resident within the United States.

(5) Qualifications
The President must be at least 35 years old, be a citizen of the United States by birth, and have been living in the United States for 14 years or more.

(6) [*In case of the removal of the President from office, or of his death, resignation, or inability to discharge the powers and duties of the said office, the same shall devolve on the Vice President, and the Congress may by law provide for the case of removal, death, resignation or inability, both of the President and Vice President, declaring what officer shall then act as President, and such officer shall act accordingly, until the disability be removed, or a President shall be elected.*]

(6) Vacancies
If the President dies, resigns, or is removed from office, the Vice President becomes President.

(7) The President shall, at stated times, receive for his services, a compensation, which shall neither be increased nor diminished during the period for which he shall have been elected, and he shall not receive within that period any other emolument from the United States, or any of them.

(7) Salary
The President receives a salary that cannot be raised or lowered during a term of office. The President may not be paid any additional salary by the federal government or any state or local government. Today the President's salary is $200,000 a year, plus expenses for things such as housing, travel, and entertainment.

(8) Before he enter on the execution of his office, he shall take the following oath or affirmation:—"I do solemnly swear (or affirm) that I will faithfully execute the office of President of the United States, and will to the best of my ability, preserve, protect, and defend the Constitution of the United States."

(8) Oath of Office
Before taking office, the President must promise to perform the duties faithfully and to protect the country's form of government. Usually the Chief Justice of the Supreme Court administers the oath of office.

SECTION 2. POWERS OF THE PRESIDENT

(1) The President shall be Commander in Chief of the Army and Navy of the United States, and of the militia of the several states, when called into the actual service of the United States; he may require the opinion, in writing, of the principal officer in each of the executive departments, upon any subject relating to the duties of their respective offices, and he shall have power to grant reprieves and pardons for offenses against the United States, except in cases of impeachment.

(1) The President's Leadership
The President is the commander of the nation's armed forces and of the National Guard when it is in service of the nation. All government officials of the executive branch must report their actions to the President when asked. The President can excuse people from punishment for crimes committed.

(2) TREATIES AND APPOINTMENTS
The President has the authority to make treaties, but they must be approved by a two-thirds vote of the Senate. The President appoints justices to the Supreme Court, ambassadors to other countries, and other federal officials with the Senate's approval.

(3) FILLING VACANCIES
If a government official's position becomes vacant when Congress is not in session, the President can make a temporary appointment.

DUTIES
The President must report to Congress on the condition of the country. This report is now presented in the annual State of the Union message.

IMPEACHMENT
The President, the Vice President, or any government official will be removed from office if impeached, or accused, and then found guilty of treason, bribery, or other serious crimes. The Constitution protects government officials from being impeached for unimportant reasons.

FEDERAL COURTS
The authority to decide legal cases is granted to a Supreme Court and to a system of lower courts established by Congress. The Supreme Court is the highest court in the land. Justices and judges are in their offices for life, subject to good behavior.

(1) GENERAL AUTHORITY
Federal courts have the authority to decide cases that arise under the Constitution, laws, and treaties of the United States. They also have the authority to settle disagreements among states and among citizens of different states.

(2) SUPREME COURT
The Supreme Court can decide certain cases being tried for the first time. It can review cases that have already been tried in a lower court if the decision has been appealed, or questioned, by one side.

(2) He shall have power, by and with the advice and consent of the Senate, to make treaties, provided two-thirds of the senators present concur; and he shall nominate, and by and with the advice and consent of the Senate, shall appoint ambassadors, other public ministers and consuls, judges of the Supreme Court, and all other officers of the United States, whose appointments are not herein otherwise provided for, and which shall be established by law; but the Congress may by law vest the appointment of such inferior officers, as they think proper, in the President alone, in the courts of law, or in the heads of departments.

(3) The President shall have power to fill up all vacancies that may happen during the recess of the Senate, by granting commissions which shall expire at the end of their next session.

SECTION 3. DUTIES OF THE PRESIDENT

He shall from time to time give to the Congress information of the state of the Union, and recommend to their consideration such measures as he shall judge necessary and expedient; he may, on extraordinary occasions, convene both houses, or either of them, and in case of disagreement between them, with respect to the time of adjournment, he may adjourn them to such time as he shall think proper; he shall receive ambassadors and other public ministers; he shall take care that the laws be faithfully executed, and shall commission all the officers of the United States.

SECTION 4. IMPEACHMENT

The President, Vice President and all civil officers of the United States, shall be removed from office on impeachment for, and conviction of, treason, bribery, or other high crimes and misdemeanors.

ARTICLE III
THE JUDICIAL BRANCH

SECTION 1. FEDERAL COURTS

The judicial power of the United States shall be vested in one Supreme Court, and in such inferior courts as the Congress may from time to time ordain and establish. The judges, both of the supreme and inferior courts, shall hold their offices during good behavior, and shall, at stated times, receive for their services a compensation, which shall not be diminished during their continuance in office.

SECTION 2. AUTHORITY OF THE FEDERAL COURTS

(1) The judicial power shall extend to all cases, in law and equity, arising under this Constitution, the laws of the United States, and treaties made or which shall be made, under their authority; to all cases affecting ambassadors, other public ministers and consuls; to all cases of admiralty and maritime jurisdiction; to controversies to which the United States shall be a party; to controversies between two or more states; [*between a state and citizens of another state;*] between citizens of different states; —between citizens of the same state claiming lands under grants of different states, [*and between a state or the citizens thereof, and foreign states, citizens, or subjects.*]

(2) In all cases affecting ambassadors, other public ministers and consuls, and those in which a state shall be party, the Supreme Court shall have original jurisdiction. In all the other cases before mentioned, the Supreme Court shall have appellate jurisdiction, both as to law and fact, with such exceptions, and under such regulations as the Congress shall make.

(3) The trial of all crimes, except in cases of impeachment, shall be by jury; and such trial shall be held in the state where the said crimes shall have been committed; but when not committed within any state, the trial shall be at such place or places as the Congress may by law have directed.

(3) Trial by Jury
The Constitution guarantees a trial by jury for every person charged with a federal crime. Amendments 5, 6, and 7 extend and clarify a person's right to a trial by jury.

SECTION 3. TREASON

(1) Treason against the United States shall consist only in levying war against them, or in adhering to their enemies, giving them aid and comfort. No person shall be convicted of treason unless on the testimony of two witnesses to the same overt act, or on confession in open court.

(1) Definition of Treason
Acts that may be considered treason are making war against the United States or helping its enemies. A person cannot be convicted of attempting to overthrow the government unless there are two witnesses to the act or the person confesses in court to treason.

(2) The Congress shall have power to declare the punishment of treason, but no attainder of treason shall work corruption of blood, or forfeiture except during the life of the person attainted.

(2) Punishment for Treason
Congress can decide the punishment for treason, within certain limits.

ARTICLE IV
RELATIONS AMONG STATES

SECTION 1. OFFICIAL RECORDS

Full faith and credit shall be given in each state to the public acts, records, and judicial proceedings of every other state. And the Congress may by general laws prescribe the manner in which such acts, records, and proceedings shall be proved, and the effect thereof.

Official Records
Each state must honor the official records and judicial decisions of other states.

SECTION 2. PRIVILEGES OF THE CITIZENS

(1) The citizens of each state shall be entitled to all privileges and immunities of citizens in the several states.

(1) Privileges
A citizen moving from one state to another has the same rights as other citizens living in that person's new state of residence. In some cases, such as voting, people may be required to live in their new state for a certain length of time before obtaining the same privileges as citizens there.

(2) A person charged in any state with treason, felony, or other crime, who shall flee from justice, and be found in another state, shall on demand of the executive authority of the state from which he fled, be delivered up, to be removed to the state having jurisdiction of the crime.

(2) Extradition
At the governor's request, a person who is charged with a crime and who tries to escape justice by crossing into another state may be returned to the state in which the crime was committed.

(3) [*No person held to service or labor in one state, under the laws thereof, escaping into another, shall in consequence of any law or regulation therein, be discharged from such service or labor, but shall be delivered up on claim of the party to whom such service or labor may be due.*]

(3) Fugitive Slaves
The original Constitution required that runaway slaves be returned to their owners. Amendment 13 abolished slavery, eliminating the need for this clause.

(1) Admission of New States
Congress has the authority to admit new states to the Union. All new states have the same rights as existing states.

SECTION 3. NEW STATES AND TERRITORIES

(1) New states may be admitted by the Congress into this Union; but no new state shall be formed or erected within the jurisdiction of any other state; nor any state be formed by the junction of two or more states, or parts of states, without the consent of the legislatures of the states concerned as well as of the Congress.

(2) Federal Property
The Constitution allows Congress to make or change laws governing federal property. This applies to territories and federally owned land within states, such as national parks.

(2) The Congress shall have power to dispose of and make all needful rules and regulations respecting the territory or other property belonging to the United States; and nothing in this Constitution shall be so construed as to prejudice any claims of the United States, or of any particular state.

Guarantees to the States
The federal government guarantees that every state have a republican form of government. The United States must also protect the states against invasion and help the states deal with rebellion or local violence.

SECTION 4. GUARANTEES TO THE STATES

The United States shall guarantee to every state in this Union a republican form of government, and shall protect each of them against invasion; and on application of the legislature, or of the executive (when the legislature cannot be convened) against domestic violence.

Amending the Constitution
Changes to the Constitution may be proposed by a two-thirds vote of both the House of Representatives and the Senate or by a national convention called by Congress when asked by two-thirds of the states. For an amendment to become law, the legislatures or conventions in three-fourths of the states must approve it.

ARTICLE V
AMENDING THE CONSTITUTION

The Congress, whenever two-thirds of both houses shall deem it necessary, shall propose amendments to this Constitution, or, on the application of the legislatures of two-thirds of the several states, shall call a convention for proposing amendments, which, in either case, shall be valid to all intents and purposes, as part of this Constitution, when ratified by the legislatures of three-fourths of the several states, or by conventions in three-fourths thereof, as the one or the other mode of ratification may be proposed by the Congress; provided that [*no amendment which may be made prior to the year 1808 shall in any manner affect the first and fourth clauses in the Ninth Section of the First Article; and that*] no state, without its consent, shall be deprived of its equal suffrage in the Senate.

ARTICLE VI
GENERAL PROVISIONS

(1) Public Debt
Any debt owed by the United States before the Constitution went into effect was to be honored.

(1) All debts contracted and engagements entered into, before the adoption of this Constitution, shall be as valid against the United States under this Constitution, as under the Confederation.

(2) Federal Supremacy
This clause declares that the Constitution and federal laws are the highest in the nation. Whenever a state law and a federal law are found to disagree, the federal law must be obeyed so long as it is Constitutional.

(2) This Constitution, and the laws of the United States which shall be made in pursuance thereof, and all treaties made, or which shall be made, under the authority of the United States, shall be the supreme law of the land; and the judges in every state shall be bound thereby, anything in the Constitution or laws of any state to the contrary notwithstanding.

(3) Oaths of Office
All federal and state officials must promise to follow and enforce the Constitution. These officials, however, cannot be required to follow a particular religion or satisfy any religious test.

(3) The Senators and Representatives before mentioned, and the members of the several state legislatures, and all executive and judicial officers, both of the United States and of the several states, shall be bound by oath or affirmation, to support this Constitution; but no religious test shall ever be required as a qualification to any office or public trust under the United States.

ARTICLE VII
RATIFICATION

The ratification of the conventions of nine states, shall be sufficient for the establishment of this Constitution between the states so ratifying the same.

Done in convention by the unanimous consent of the states present the seventeenth day of September in the year of our Lord one thousand seven hundred and eighty seven and of the independence of the United States of America the Twelfth. In witness whereof we have hereunto subscribed our names.
George Washington—President and deputy from Virginia

DELAWARE
George Read
Gunning Bedford, Jr.
John Dickinson
Richard Bassett
Jacob Broom

MARYLAND
James McHenry
Daniel of St. Thomas Jenifer
Daniel Carroll

VIRGINIA
John Blair
James Madison, Jr.

NORTH CAROLINA
William Blount
Richard Dobbs Spaight
Hugh Williamson

SOUTH CAROLINA
John Rutledge
Charles Cotesworth Pinckney
Charles Pinckney
Pierce Butler

GEORGIA
William Few
Abraham Baldwin

NEW HAMPSHIRE
John Langdon
Nicholas Gilman

MASSACHUSETTS
Nathaniel Gorham
Rufus King

CONNECTICUT
William Samuel Johnson
Roger Sherman

NEW YORK
Alexander Hamilton

NEW JERSEY
William Livingston
David Brearley
William Paterson
Jonathan Dayton

PENNSYLVANIA
Benjamin Franklin
Thomas Mifflin
Robert Morris
George Clymer
Thomas FitzSimons
Jared Ingersoll
James Wilson
Gouverneur Morris

ATTEST: William Jackson, secretary

RATIFICATION
In order for the Constitution to become law, 9 of the 13 states had to approve it. Special conventions were held for this purpose. The process took 9 months to complete.

R35

Basic Freedoms
The Constitution guarantees our five basic freedoms of expression. It provides for the freedoms of religion, speech, the press, peaceable assembly, and petition for redress of grievances.

AMENDMENT 1 (1791)***
BASIC FREEDOMS

Congress shall make no law respecting an establishment of religion, or prohibiting the free exercise thereof; or abridging the freedom of speech, or of the press; or the right of the people peaceably to assemble, and to petition the government for a redress of grievances.

Weapons and the Militia
This amendment was included to prevent the federal government from taking away guns used by state militias.

AMENDMENT 2 (1791)
WEAPONS AND THE MILITIA

A well-regulated militia, being necessary to the security of a free state, the right of the people to keep and bear arms shall not be infringed.

Housing Soldiers
The federal government cannot force people to house soldiers in their homes during peacetime. However, Congress may pass laws allowing this during wartime.

AMENDMENT 3 (1791)
HOUSING SOLDIERS

No soldier shall, in time of peace, be quartered in any house, without the consent of the owner; nor in time of war, but in a manner to be prescribed by law.

Searches and Seizures
This amendment protects people's privacy and safety. Subject to certain exceptions, a law officer cannot search a person or a person's home and belongings unless a judge has issued a valid search warrant. There must be good reason for the search. The warrant must describe the place to be searched and the people or things to be seized, or taken.

AMENDMENT 4 (1791)
SEARCHES AND SEIZURES

The right of the people to be secure in their persons, houses, papers, and effects, against unreasonable searches and seizures, shall not be violated; and no warrants shall issue but upon probable cause, supported by oath or affirmation, and particularly describing the place to be searched, and the persons or things to be seized.

Rights of Accused Persons
If a person is accused of a crime that is punishable by death or of any other crime that is very serious, a grand jury must decide if there is enough evidence to hold a trial. People cannot be tried twice for the same crime, nor can they be forced to testify against themselves. No person shall be fined, jailed, or executed by the government unless the person has been given a fair trial. The government cannot take a person's property for public use unless fair payment is made.

AMENDMENT 5 (1791)
RIGHTS OF ACCUSED PERSONS

No person shall be held to answer for a capital, or otherwise infamous crime, unless on a presentment or indictment of a grand jury, except in cases arising in the land or naval forces, or in the militia, when in actual service in time of war or public danger; nor shall any person be subject for the same offense to be twice put in jeopardy of life or limb; nor shall be compelled in any criminal case to be a witness against himself; nor be deprived of life, liberty, or property, without due process of law; nor shall private property be taken for public use without just compensation.

*** The date beside each amendment is the year that the amendment was ratified and became part of the Constitution.

AMENDMENT 6 (1791)
RIGHT TO A FAIR TRIAL

In all criminal prosecutions, the accused shall enjoy the right to a speedy and public trial, by an impartial jury of the state and district wherein the crime shall have been committed, which district shall have been previously ascertained by law, and to be informed of the nature and cause of the accusation; to be confronted with the witnesses against him; to have compulsory process for obtaining witnesses in his favor, and to have the assistance of counsel for his defense.

RIGHT TO A FAIR TRIAL
A person accused of a crime has the right to a public trial by an impartial jury, locally chosen. The trial must be held within a reasonable amount of time. The accused person must be told of all charges and has the right to see, hear, and question any witnesses. The federal government must provide a lawyer free of charge to a person who is accused of a serious crime and who is unable to pay for legal services.

AMENDMENT 7 (1791)
JURY TRIAL IN CIVIL CASES

In suits at common law, where the value in controversy shall exceed 20 dollars, the right of trial by jury shall be preserved, and no fact tried by a jury shall be otherwise re-examined in any court of the United States, than according to the rules of the common law.

JURY TRIAL IN CIVIL CASES
In most federal civil cases involving more than 20 dollars, a jury trial is guaranteed. Civil cases are those disputes between two or more people over money, property, personal injury, or legal rights. Usually civil cases are not tried in federal courts unless much larger sums of money are involved or unless federal courts are given the authority to decide a certain type of case.

AMENDMENT 8 (1791)
BAIL AND PUNISHMENT

Excessive bail shall not be required, nor excessive fines imposed, nor cruel and unusual punishments inflicted.

BAIL AND PUNISHMENT
Courts cannot treat harshly people accused of crimes or punish them in unusual or cruel ways. Bail is money put up as a guarantee that an accused person will appear for trial. In certain cases bail can be denied altogether.

AMENDMENT 9 (1791)
RIGHTS OF THE PEOPLE

The enumeration in the Constitution, of certain rights, shall not be construed to deny or disparage others retained by the people.

RIGHTS OF THE PEOPLE
The federal government must respect all natural rights, whether or not they are listed in the Constitution.

AMENDMENT 10 (1791)
POWERS OF THE STATES AND THE PEOPLE

The powers not delegated to the United States by the Constitution, nor prohibited by it to the states, are reserved to the states respectively, or to the people.

POWERS OF THE STATES AND THE PEOPLE
Any rights not clearly given to the federal government or denied to the states belong to the states or to the people.

AMENDMENT 11 (1798)
SUITS AGAINST STATES

The judicial power of the United States shall not be construed to extend to any suit in law or equity, commenced or prosecuted against one of the United States or citizens of another state, or by citizens or subjects of any foreign state.

SUITS AGAINST STATES
A citizen of one state cannot sue another state in federal court.

ELECTION OF PRESIDENT AND VICE PRESIDENT
This amendment replaces the part of Article II, Section 1, that originally explained the process of electing the President and Vice President. Amendment 12 was an important step in the development of the two-party system. It allows a party to nominate its own candidates for both President and Vice President.

AMENDMENT 12 (1804)
ELECTION OF PRESIDENT AND VICE PRESIDENT

The electors shall meet in their respective states, and vote by ballot for President and Vice President, one of whom, at least, shall not be an inhabitant of the same state with themselves; they shall name in their ballots the person voted for as President, and in distinct ballots the person voted for as Vice President, and they shall make distinct lists of all persons voted for as President, and of all persons voted for as Vice President, and of the number of votes for each, which lists they shall sign and certify, and transmit, sealed, to the seat of government of the United States, directed to the President of the Senate; the President of the Senate shall, in the presence of the Senate and House of Representatives, open all the certificates, and the votes shall then be counted; the person having the greatest number of votes for President shall be the President, if such a number be a majority of the whole number of electors appointed; and if no person have such majority; then from the persons having the highest numbers not exceeding three on the list of those voted for as President, the House of Representatives shall choose immediately, by ballot, the President. But in choosing the President, the votes shall be taken by states, the representation from each state having one vote; a quorum for this purpose shall consist of a member or members from two thirds of the states, and a majority of all the states shall be necessary to a choice. [*And if the House of Representatives shall not choose a President whenever the right of choice shall devolve upon them, before the fourth day of March next following, then the Vice President shall act as President, as in the case of the death or other constitutional disability of the President.*] The person having the greatest number of votes as Vice President, shall be the Vice President, if such number be a majority of the whole number of electors appointed, and if no person have a majority, then, from the two highest numbers on the list the Senate shall choose the Vice President; a quorum for the purpose shall consist of two thirds of the whole number of Senators, and a majority of the whole number shall be necessary to a choice. But no person constitutionally ineligible to the office of President shall be eligible to that of Vice President of the United States.

END OF SLAVERY
People cannot be forced to work against their will unless they have been tried for and convicted of a crime for which this means of punishment is ordered. Congress may enforce this by law.

AMENDMENT 13 (1865)
END OF SLAVERY

SECTION 1. ABOLITION
Neither slavery nor involuntary servitude, except as a punishment for crime whereof the party shall have been duly convicted, shall exist within the United States, or any place subject to their jurisdiction.

SECTION 2. ENFORCEMENT
Congress shall have power to enforce this article by appropriate legislation.

CITIZENSHIP
All persons born or naturalized in the United States are citizens of the United States and of the state in which they live. State governments may not deny any citizen the full rights of citizenship. This amendment also guarantees due process of law. According to due process of law, no state may take away the rights of a citizen. All citizens must be protected equally under law.

AMENDMENT 14 (1868)
RIGHTS OF CITIZENS

SECTION 1. CITIZENSHIP
All persons born or naturalized in the United States and subject to the jurisdiction thereof, are citizens of the United States and of the state wherein they reside. No state shall make or enforce any law which shall abridge the privileges or immunities of citizens of the United States, nor shall any state deprive any person of life, liberty, or property, without due process of law; nor deny to any person within its jurisdiction the equal protection of the laws.

American Documents

SECTION 2. NUMBER OF REPRESENTATIVES

Representatives shall be apportioned among the several states according to their respective numbers, counting the whole number of persons in each state, [*excluding Indians not taxed*]. But when the right to vote at any election for the choice of electors for President and Vice President of the United States, representatives in Congress, the executive and judicial officers of a state, or the members of the legislature thereof, is denied to any of the [*male*] inhabitants of such state, being [*twenty-one years of age and*] citizens of the United States, or in any way abridged, except for participation in rebellion or other crime, the basis of representation therein shall be reduced in the proportion which the number of such [*male*] citizens shall bear to the whole number of [*male*] citizens [*twenty-one years of age*] in such state.

Number of Representatives
Each state's representation in Congress is based on its total population. Any state denying eligible citizens the right to vote will have its representation in Congress decreased. This clause abolished the Three-fifths Compromise in Article 1, Section 2. Later amendments granted women the right to vote and lowered the voting age to 18.

SECTION 3. PENALTY FOR REBELLION

No person shall be a Senator or Representative in Congress, or elector of President and Vice President, or hold any office, civil or military, under the United States, or under any state, who, having previously taken an oath, as a member of Congress, or as an officer of the United States, or as a member of any state legislature, or as an executive or judicial officer of any state, to support the Constitution of the United States, shall have engaged in insurrection or rebellion against the same, or given aid or comfort to the enemies thereof. But Congress may, by a vote of two thirds of each house, remove such disability.

Penalty for Rebellion
No person who has rebelled against the United States may hold federal office. This clause was originally added to punish the leaders of the Confederacy for failing to support the Constitution of the United States.

SECTION 4. GOVERNMENT DEBT

The validity of the public debt of the United States, authorized by law, including debts incurred for payment of pensions and bounties for services in suppressing insurrection or rebellion, shall not be questioned. But neither the United States nor any state shall assume or pay any debt or obligation incurred in aid of insurrection or rebellion against the United States, [*or any claim for the loss or emancipation of any slave;*] but all such debts, obligations, and claims shall be held illegal and void.

Government Debt
The federal government is responsible for all public debts. It is not responsible, however, for Confederate debts or for debts that result from any rebellion against the United States.

SECTION 5. ENFORCEMENT

The Congress shall have power to enforce, by appropriate legislation, the provisions of this article.

Enforcement
Congress may enforce these provisions by law.

AMENDMENT 15 (1870)
VOTING RIGHTS

SECTION 1. RIGHT TO VOTE

The right of citizens of the United States to vote shall not be denied or abridged by the United States or by any state on account of race, color, or previous condition of servitude.

SECTION 2. ENFORCEMENT

The Congress shall have power to enforce this article by appropriate legislation.

Right to Vote
No state may prevent a citizen from voting simply because of race or color or condition of previous servitude. This amendment was designed to extend voting rights to enforce this by law.

AMENDMENT 16 (1913)
INCOME TAX

The Congress shall have power to lay and collect taxes on incomes, from whatever source derived, without apportionment among the several states, and without regard to any census or enumeration.

Income Tax
Congress has the power to collect taxes on its citizens, based on their personal incomes rather than on the number of people living in a state.

American Documents

DIRECT ELECTION OF SENATORS
Originally, state legislatures elected senators. This amendment allows the people of each state to elect their own senators directly. The idea is to make senators more responsible to the people they represent.

AMENDMENT 17 (1913)
DIRECT ELECTION OF SENATORS

SECTION 1. METHOD OF ELECTION

The Senate of the United States shall be composed of two Senators from each state, elected by the people thereof, for six years; and each Senator shall have one vote. The electors in each state shall have the qualifications requisite for electors of the most numerous branch of the state legislatures.

SECTION 2. VACANCIES

When vacancies happen in the representation of any state in the Senate, the executive authority of such state shall issue writs of election to fill such vacancies: *Provided,* that the legislature of any state may empower the executive thereof to make temporary appointments until the people fill the vacancies by election as the legislature may direct.

SECTION 3. EXCEPTION

[*This amendment shall not be so construed as to affect the election or term of any Senator chosen before it becomes valid as part of the Constitution.*]

PROHIBITION
This amendment made it illegal to make, sell, or transport liquor within the United States or to transport it out of the United States or its territories. Amendment 18 was the first to include a time limit for approval. If not ratified within seven years, it would be repealed, or canceled. Many later amendments have included similar time limits.

AMENDMENT 18 (1919)
BAN ON ALCOHOLIC DRINKS

SECTION 1. PROHIBITION

[*After one year from the ratification of this article the manufacture, sale, or transportation of intoxicating liquors within, the importation thereof into, or the exportation thereof from the United States and all territory subject to the jurisdiction thereof for beverage purposes is hereby prohibited.*]

SECTION 2. ENFORCEMENT

[*The Congress and the several states shall have concurrent power to enforce this article by appropriate legislation.*]

SECTION 3. RATIFICATION

[*This article shall be inoperative unless it shall have been ratified as an amendment to the Constitution by the legislatures of the several states as provided in the Constitution, within seven years from the date of the submission hereof to the states by the Congress.*]

WOMEN'S VOTING RIGHTS
This amendment granted women the right to vote.

AMENDMENT 19 (1920)
WOMEN'S VOTING RIGHTS

SECTION 1. RIGHT TO VOTE

The right of citizens of the United States to vote shall not be denied or abridged by the United States or by any state on account of sex.

SECTION 2. ENFORCEMENT

Congress shall have power to enforce this article by appropriate legislation.

TERMS OF OFFICE
The terms of the President and the Vice President begin on January 20, in the year following their election. Members of Congress take office on January 3. Before this amendment newly elected members of Congress did not begin their terms until March 4. This meant that those who had run for reelection and been defeated remained in office for four months.

AMENDMENT 20 (1933)
TERMS OF OFFICE

SECTION 1. BEGINNING OF TERMS

The terms of the President and Vice President shall end at noon on the 20th day of January, and the terms of Senators and Representatives at noon on the 3rd day of January, of the years in which such terms would have ended if this article had not been ratified; and the terms of their successors shall then begin.

SECTION 2. SESSIONS OF CONGRESS

The Congress shall assemble at least once in every year, and such meeting shall begin at noon on the 3rd day of January, unless they shall by law appoint a different day.

SESSIONS OF CONGRESS
Congress meets at least once a year, beginning at noon on January 3. Congress had previously met at least once a year beginning on the first Monday of December.

SECTION 3. PRESIDENTIAL SUCCESSION

If, at the time fixed for the beginning of the term of the President, the President-elect shall have died, the Vice President-elect shall become President. If a President shall not have been chosen before the time fixed for the beginning of his term, or if the President-elect shall have failed to qualify, then the Vice President-elect shall act as President until a President shall have qualified; and the Congress may by law provide for the case wherein neither a President-elect nor a Vice President-elect shall have qualified, declaring who shall then act as President, or the manner in which one who is to act shall be selected and such person shall act accordingly until a President or Vice President shall be qualified.

PRESIDENTIAL SUCCESSION
If the newly elected President dies before January 20, the newly elected Vice President becomes President on that date. If a President has not been chosen by January 20 or does not meet the requirements for being President, the newly elected Vice President becomes President. If neither the newly elected President nor the newly elected Vice President meets the requirements for office, Congress decides who will serve as President until a qualified President or Vice President is chosen.

SECTION 4. ELECTIONS DECIDED BY CONGRESS

The Congress may by law provide for the case of the death of any of the persons from whom the House of Representatives may choose a President whenever the right of choice shall have devolved upon them, and for the case of the death of any of the persons from whom the Senate may choose a Vice President whenever the right of choice shall have devolved upon them.

SECTION 5. EFFECTIVE DATE

[Sections l and 2 shall take effect on the l5th day of October following the ratification of this article.]

SECTION 6. RATIFICATION

[This article shall be inoperative unless it shall have been ratified as an amendment to the Constitution by the legislatures of three fourths of the several states within seven years from the date of its submission.]

AMENDMENT 21 (1933)
END OF PROHIBITION

END OF PROHIBITION
This amendment repealed Amendment 18. This is the only amendment to be ratified by state conventions instead of by state legislatures. Congress felt that this would give people's opinions about prohibition a better chance to be heard.

SECTION 1. REPEAL OF AMENDMENT 18

The eighteenth article of amendment to the Constitution of the United States is hereby repealed.

SECTION 2. STATE LAWS

The transportation or importation into any state, territory, or possession of the United States for delivery or use therein of intoxicating liquors, in violation of the laws thereof, is hereby prohibited.

SECTION 3. RATIFICATION

[This article shall be inoperative unless it shall have been ratified as an amendment to the Constitution by conventions in the several states, as provided in the Constitution within seven years from the date of the submission hereof to the states by Congress.]

TWO-TERM LIMIT FOR PRESIDENTS
A President may not serve more than two full terms in office. Any President who serves less than two years of a previous President's term may be elected for two more terms.

AMENDMENT 22 (1951)
TWO-TERM LIMIT FOR PRESIDENTS

SECTION 1. TWO-TERM LIMIT

No person shall be elected to the office of the President more than twice, and no person who has held the office of President, or acted as President, for more than two years of a term to which some other person was elected President shall be elected to the office of the President more than once. [*But this article shall not apply to any person holding the office of President when this article was proposed by the Congress, and shall not prevent any person who may be holding the office of President, or acting as President, during the term within which this article becomes operative from holding the office of President, or acting as President, during the remainder of such term.*]

SECTION 2. RATIFICATION

[*This article shall be inoperative unless it shall have been ratified as an amendment to the Constitution by the legislatures of three-fourths of the several states within seven years from the date of its submission to the states by the Congress.*]

PRESIDENTIAL ELECTORS FOR DISTRICT OF COLUMBIA
This amendment grants three electoral votes to the national capital.

AMENDMENT 23 (1961)
PRESIDENTIAL ELECTORS FOR DISTRICT OF COLUMBIA

SECTION 1. NUMBER OF ELECTORS

The District constituting the seat of Government of the United States shall appoint in such manner as Congress may direct:

A number of electors of President and Vice President equal to the whole number of Senators and Representatives in Congress to which the District would be entitled if it were a state, but in no event more than the least populous state; they shall be in addition to those appointed by the states, but they shall be considered, for the purposes of the election of President and Vice President, to be electors appointed by a state, and they shall meet in the District and perform such duties as provided by the twelfth article of amendment.

SECTION 2. ENFORCEMENT

The Congress shall have power to enforce this article by appropriate legislation.

BAN ON POLL TAXES
No United States citizen may be prevented from voting in a federal election because of failing to pay a tax to vote. Poll taxes had been used in some states to prevent African Americans from voting.

AMENDMENT 24 (1964)
BAN ON POLL TAXES

SECTION 1. POLL TAX ILLEGAL

The right of citizens of the United States to vote in any primary or other election for President or Vice President, for electors for President or Vice President, or for Senator or Representative in Congress, shall not be denied or abridged by the United States or any state by reason of failure to pay any poll tax or other tax.

SECTION 2. ENFORCEMENT

The Congress shall have power to enforce this article by appropriate legislation.

PRESIDENTIAL VACANCY
If the President is removed from office or resigns from or dies while in office, the Vice President becomes President.

AMENDMENT 25 (1967)
PRESIDENTIAL SUCCESSION

SECTION 1. PRESIDENTIAL VACANCY

In case of the removal of the President from office or of his death or resignation, the Vice President shall become President.

SECTION 2. VICE PRESIDENTIAL VACANCY

Whenever there is a vacancy in the office of the Vice President, the President shall nominate a Vice President who shall take the office upon confirmation by a majority vote of both houses of Congress.

Vice Presidential Vacancy
If the office of the Vice President becomes open, the President names someone to assume that office and that person becomes Vice President if both houses of Congress approve by a majority vote.

SECTION 3. PRESIDENTIAL DISABILITY

Whenever the President transmits to the President pro tempore of the Senate and the Speaker of the House of Representatives his written declaration that he is unable to discharge the powers and duties of his office, and until he transmits to them a written declaration to the contrary, such powers and duties shall be discharged by the Vice President as Acting President.

Presidential Disability
This section explains in detail what happens if the President cannot continue in office because of sickness or any other reason. The Vice President takes over as acting President until the President is able to resume office.

SECTION 4. DETERMINING PRESIDENTIAL DISABILITY

Whenever the Vice President and a majority of either the principal officers of the executive departments or of such other body as Congress may by law provide, transmit to the President pro tempore of the Senate and the Speaker of the House of Representatives their written declaration that the President is unable to discharge the powers and duties of his office, the Vice President shall immediately assume the powers and duties of the office as Acting President.

Thereafter, when the President transmits to the President pro tempore of the Senate and the Speaker of the House of Representatives his written declaration that no inability exists, he shall resume the powers and duties of his office unless the Vice President and a majority of either the principal officers of the executive department or of such other body as Congress may by law provide, transmit within four days to the President pro tempore of the Senate and the Speaker of the House of Representatives their written declaration that the President is unable to discharge the powers and duties of his office. Thereupon Congress shall decide the issue, assembling within 48 hours for that purpose if not in session. If the Congress, within 21 days after receipt of the latter written declaration, or, if Congress is not in session, within 21 days after Congress is required to assemble, determines by two-thirds vote of both houses that the President is unable to discharge the powers and duties of his office, the Vice President shall continue to discharge the same as Acting President; otherwise the President shall resume the powers and duties of his office.

Determining Presidential Disability
If the Vice President and a majority of the Cabinet inform the Speaker of the House and the president pro tempore of the Senate that the President cannot carry out his or her duties, the Vice President then serves as acting President. To regain the office, the President has to inform the Speaker and the president pro tempore in writing that he or she is again able to serve. But, if the Vice President and a majority of the Cabinet disagree with the President and inform the Speaker and the president pro tempore that the President is still unable to serve, then Congress decides who will hold the office of President.

AMENDMENT 26 (1971)
VOTING AGE

SECTION 1. RIGHT TO VOTE

The right of citizens of the United States, who are 18 years of age or older, to vote shall not be denied or abridged by the United States or any state on account of age.

SECTION 2. ENFORCEMENT

The Congress shall have the power to enforce this article by appropriate legislation.

Voting Age
All citizens 18 years or older have the right to vote. Formerly, the voting age was 21.

AMENDMENT 27 (1992)
CONGRESSIONAL PAY

No law, varying the compensation for the services of the Senators and Representatives, shall take effect, until an election of Representatives shall have intervened.

Congressional Pay
A law raising or lowering the salaries for members of Congress cannot be passed for that session of Congress.

American Documents

"The Star-Spangled Banner" was written by Francis Scott Key in September 1814 and adopted as the national anthem in March 1931. The army and navy had recognized it as such long before Congress approved it.

During the War of 1812, Francis Scott Key spent a night aboard a British warship in the Chesapeake Bay while trying to arrange for the release of an American prisoner. The battle raged throughout the night, while the Americans were held on the ship. The next morning, when the smoke from the cannons finally cleared, Francis Scott Key was thrilled to see the American flag still waving proudly above Fort McHenry. It symbolized the victory of the Americans.

There are four verses to the national anthem. In these four verses, Key wrote about how he felt when he saw the flag still waving over Fort McHenry. He wrote that the flag was a symbol of the freedom for which the people had fought so hard. Key also told about the pride he had in his country and the great hopes he had for the future of the United States.

The National Anthem

The Star-Spangled Banner

(1)

Oh, say can you see by the dawn's early light
What so proudly we hail'd at the twilight's last gleaming,
Whose broad stripes and bright stars through the perilous fight
O'er the ramparts we watch'd were so gallantly streaming?
And the rockets' red glare, the bombs bursting in air,
Gave proof through the night that our flag was still there.
Oh, say does that star-spangled banner yet wave
O'er the land of the free and the home of the brave?

(2)

On the shore dimly seen through the mists of the deep,
Where the foe's haughty host in dread silence reposes,
What is that which the breeze, o'er the towering steep,
As it fitfully blows, half conceals, half discloses?
Now it catches the gleam of the morning's first beam,
In full glory reflected now shines in the stream.
'Tis the star-spangled banner, oh, long may it wave
O'er the land of the free and the home of the brave!

(3)

And where is that band who so vauntingly swore
That the havoc of war and the battle's confusion
A home and a country should leave us no more?
Their blood has wash'd out their foul footstep's pollution.
No refuge could save the hireling and slave
From the terror of flight or the gloom of the grave,
And the star-spangled banner in triumph doth wave
O'er the land of the free and the home of the brave.

(4)

Oh, thus be it ever when freemen shall stand
Between their lov'd home and the war's desolation!
Blest with vict'ry and peace may the heav'n-rescued land
Praise the power that hath made and preserv'd us a nation!
Then conquer we must, when our cause it is just,
And this be our motto, "In God is our Trust,"
And the star-spangled banner in triumph shall wave
O'er the land of the free and the home of the brave.

THE PLEDGE OF ALLEGIANCE

I pledge allegiance to the Flag
of the United States of America,
and to the Republic
for which it stands,
one Nation under God, indivisible,
with liberty and justice for all.

The flag is a symbol of the United States of America. The Pledge of Allegiance says that the people of the United States promise to stand up for the flag, their country, and the basic beliefs of freedom and fairness upon which the country was established.

Biographical Dictionary

The Biographical Dictionary lists many of the important people introduced in this book. The page number tells where the main discussion of each person starts. See the Index for other page references.

A

Adams, Abigail *1744–1818* Patriot who wrote about women's rights in letters to John Adams, her husband. p. 257, 284

Adams, John *1735–1826* 2nd U.S. President and one writer of the Declaration of Independence. p. 253

Adams, Samuel *1722–1803* American Revolutionary leader who set up a Committee of Correspondence in Boston and helped form the Sons of Liberty. p. 238

Addams, Jane *1860–1935* American reformer who brought the idea of settlement houses from Britain to the United States. With Ellen Gates Starr, she founded Hull House in Chicago. p. 506

Aldrin, Edwin, Jr. *1930–* American astronaut who was one of the first people to set foot on the moon. p. 616

Anderson, Robert *1805–1871* Union commander of Fort Sumter who was forced to surrender to the Confederacy. p. 432

Anthony, Susan B. *1820–1906* Women's suffrage leader who worked to enable women to have the same rights as men. pp. 395, 396

Aristide, Jean-Bertrand (air•uh•STEED, ZHAHN bair•TRAHN) *1953–* Freely elected president of Haiti who was overthrown in 1991 but was returned to office in 1994. p. 656

Armstrong, Louis *1901–1971* Noted jazz trumpeter who helped make jazz popular in the 1920s. p. 573

Armstrong, Neil *1930–* American astronaut who was the first person to set foot on the moon. p. 616

Arnold, Benedict *1741–1801* Continental army officer who became a traitor and worked for the British army. p. 267

Atahuallpa (ah•tah•WAHL•pah) *1502?–1533* Inca ruler who was killed in the Spanish conquest of the Incas. p. 137

Attucks, Crispus *1723?–1770* Patriot and former slave who was killed during the Boston Massacre. p. 237

Austin, Moses *1761–1821* American pioneer who wanted to start an American colony in Texas. p. 383

Austin, Stephen F. *1793–1836* Moses Austin's son. He carried out his father's dream of starting an American colony in Texas. p. 383

B

Balboa, Vasco Núñez de (bahl•BOH•ah, NOON•yes day) *1475–1519* Explorer who in 1513 became the first European to reach the western coast of the Americas—proving to Europeans that the Americas were separate from Asia. p. 128

Banneker, Benjamin *1731–1806* African who helped survey the land for the new capital of the United States. p. 329

Barker, Penelope *1700s* One of the first politically active women in the American colonies, she led the women of Edenton, North Carolina, in a "tea party" of their own to boycott British tea. p. 240

Barrett, Janie Porter *1865–1948* African American teacher who founded a settlement house in Hampton, Virginia. p. 506

Barton, Clara *1821–1912* Civil War nurse and founder of the American Red Cross. p. 445

Beauregard, Pierre Gustave (BOH•ruh•gard) *1818–1893* Confederate army officer. p. 411

Bee, Barnard Elliott *1824–1861* Confederate army officer. p. 412

Behaim, Martin (BAY•hym) *1436?–1507* German geographer who in 1492 made the first world globe in Europe. p. 113

Bessemer, Henry *1813–1898* British inventor of a way to produce steel more easily and cheaply than before. p. 484

Bienville, Jean Baptiste Le Moyne, Sieur de (byan•VEEL, ZHAHN ba•TEEST luh MWAHN) *1680–1747* French explorer who—with his brother, Pierre Le Moyne, Sieur d'Iberville—started an early settlement at the mouth of the Mississippi River. p. 181

Bolívar, Simón (boh•LEE•var, see•MOHN) *1783–1830* Leader of independence movements in Bolivia, Colombia, Ecuador, Peru, and Venezuela. p. 659

Bonaparte, Napoleon (BOH•nuh•part, nuh•POH•lee•uhn) *1769–1821* French leader who sold all of the Louisiana region to the United States. p. 353

Boone, Daniel *1734–1820* American who was one of the first pioneers to cross the Appalachians. p. 205, 349

Booth, John Wilkes *1838–1865* Actor who assassinated President Abraham Lincoln. p. 458

Bowie, James *1796–1836* American soldier killed at the Alamo. p. 384

Bradford, William *1590–1657* Governor of Plymouth Colony. p. 155

Breckinridge, John *1821–1875* Democrat from Kentucky who ran against Abraham Lincoln in the 1860 presidential election. p. 431

Brendan *485?–578* Irish monk who is said to have sailed to an unknown land between Europe and Asia. p. 111

Brezhnev, Leonid (BREZH•nef) *1906–1982* Leader of the Soviet Union from 1964 until his death in 1982. President Nixon's 1972 visit with him in the Soviet Union led to arms control and began a period of détente. p. 634

Brown, John *1800–1859* American abolitionist who seized a weapons storehouse to help slaves rebel. He was caught and hanged. p. 422

Brown, Linda *1943–* African American student whose family was among a group that challenged public-school segregation. p. 622

Brown, Moses *1738–1836* Textile pioneer who built the first textile mill in the United States, using Samuel Slater's plans. p. 373

Burgoyne, John (ber•GOYN) *1722–1792* British general who lost a battle to the Continental army on October 17, 1777, at Saratoga, New York. p. 266

Burnet, David G. *1788–1870* 1st president of the Republic of Texas, when it was formed in 1836. p. 385

Bush, George *1924–* 41st U.S. President. He was President at the end of the Cold War and during Operation Desert Storm. p. 637

Byrd, William, II *1674–1744* Early Virginia planter who kept a diary of his daily life. p. 202

C

Cabeza de Vaca, Álvar Núñez (kah•BAY•sah day VAH•kuh) *1490?–1560?* Spanish explorer who went to Mexico City and told stories of the Seven Cities of Gold. p. 140

Caboto, Giovanni *1450?–1499?* Italian explorer who in 1497 sailed from England and landed in what is now Newfoundland, though he thought he had landed in Asia. The English gave him the name John Cabot. p. 126

Calhoun, John C. *1782–1850* Vice President under John Quincy Adams and Andrew Jackson. He was a strong believer in states' rights. p. 380

Calvert, Cecilius *1605–1675* First proprietor of the Maryland colony. p. 184

Cameahwait (kah•MEE•ah•wayt) *1800s* Chief of the Shoshones during the Lewis and Clark expedition. He was Sacagawea's brother. p. 356

Carnegie, Andrew *1835–1919* Entrepreneur who helped the steel industry grow in the United States. p. 484

Carter, Jimmy *1924–* 39th U.S. President. He brought about a peace agreement between Israel and Egypt. p. 635

Cartier, Jacques (kar•TYAY, ZHAHK) *1491–1557* French explorer who sailed up the St. Lawrence River and began a fur-trading business with the Hurons. p. 147

Castro, Fidel *1926–* Leader who took over Cuba in 1959 and made it a communist nation. p. 614

Cavelier, René-Robert (ka•vuhl•YAY) *See* La Salle.

Chamorro, Violeta (chuh•MAWR•oh, vee•oh•LET•uh) *1929–* Nicaragua's democratic president, elected in 1990, after years of communist rule. p. 658

Champlain, Samuel de (sham•PLAYN) *1567?–1635* French explorer who founded the first settlement at Quebec. p. 148

Charles I *1500–1558* King of Spain. p. 144

Charles I *1600–1649* British king who chartered the colonies of Massachusetts and Maryland. p. 184

Charles II *1630–1685* British king who granted a charter for the Carolina colony. Son of Charles I and Henrietta Maria. p. 189

Chávez, César *1927–1993* Labor leader and organizer of the United Farm Workers. p. 625

Clark, William *1770–1838* American explorer who aided Meriwether Lewis in an expedition through the Louisiana Purchase. p. 355

Clay, Henry *1777–1852* Representative from Kentucky who worked for compromises on the slavery issue. p. 426

Clinton, George *1739–1812* American politician who helped form the Democratic-Republican party. p. 316

Clinton, William *1946–* 42nd U.S. President. p. 637

Cody, William (Buffalo Bill) *1846–1917* Cowhand known for shooting many buffalo. p. 528

Collins, Michael *1930–* American astronaut who remained in the lunar orbiter during the *Apollo 11* moon landing. p. 616

Columbus, Christopher *1451–1506* Italian-born Spanish explorer who in 1492 sailed west from Spain and thought he had reached Asia but had actually reached islands near the Americas, lands that were unknown to Europeans. p. 111

Cooper, Peter *1791–1883* American manufacturer who built *Tom Thumb*, one of the first locomotives made in the United States. p. 378

Cornish, Samuel *1795–1858* African who in 1827 helped John Russwurm found an abolitionist newspaper called *Freedom's Journal*. p. 393

Cornwallis, Charles *1738–1805* British general who surrendered at the Battle of Yorktown, resulting in victory for the Americans in the Revolutionary War. p. 267

Coronado, Francisco Vásquez de (kawr•oh•NAH•doh) *1510?–1554* Spanish explorer who led an expedition from Mexico City into what is now the southwestern United States in search of the Seven Cities of Gold. p. 140

Cortés, Hernando (kawr•TEZ) *1485–1547* Spanish conquistador who conquered the Aztec Empire. p. 135

Crazy Horse *1842?–1877* Sioux leader who fought against General George Custer. p. 529

Crockett, Davy *1786–1836* American pioneer who was killed at the Alamo. p. 384

Custer, George *1839–1876* U.S. army general who led an attack against Sioux and Cheyenne Indians. Custer and all of his men were killed in the battle. p. 529

D

da Gama, Vasco (dah GAH•muh) *1460?–1524* Portuguese navigator who sailed from Europe, around the southern tip of Africa, and on to Asia between 1497 and 1499. p. 119

Dare, Virginia *1587–?* First child born of English parents in America. She vanished with the other settlers of the Lost Colony. p. 152

Davis, Jefferson *1808–1889* United States senator from Mississippi who became president of the Confederacy. p. 432

Dawes, William *1745–1799* American who, along with Paul Revere, warned the Patriots that the British were marching toward Concord. p. 241

de Soto, Hernando (day SOH•toh) *1496?–1542* Spanish explorer who led an expedition into what is today the southeastern United States. p. 141

de Triana, Rodrigo Sailor on the *Pinta* during Columbus's first voyage; he was the first to sight land. p. 122

Dekanawida (deh•kahn•uh•WIH•duh) *1500s* Legendary Iroquois holy man who called for an end to the fighting among the Iroquois, a view that led to the formation of the Iroquois League. p. 86

Dewey, George *1837–1917* American naval commander who destroyed the Spanish fleet and captured Manila Bay in the Spanish-American War. p. 550

Dias, Bartholomeu (DEE•ahsh) *1450?–1500* Portuguese navigator who in 1488 became the first European to sail around the southern tip of Africa. p. 119

Dickinson, John *1732–1808* Member of the Continental Congress who wrote most of the Articles of Confederation, adopted in 1781. p. 285

Douglas, Stephen A. *1813–1861* American legislator who wrote the Kansas-Nebraska Act and debated Abraham Lincoln in a race for a Senate seat from Illinois. p. 429

Douglass, Frederick *1817–1895* Abolitionist speaker and writer who had escaped from slavery. p. 394

Drake, Francis *1543–1596* English explorer who sailed around the world. p. 151

Du Bois, W. E. B. (doo•BOYS) *1868–1963* African American teacher, writer, and leader who helped form the National Association for the Advancement of Colored People (NAACP). p. 558

E

Edison, Thomas *1847–1931* American who invented the phonograph and the electric lightbulb; he also built the first power station to supply electricity to New York City. p. 480

Eisenhower, Dwight D. *1890–1969* 34th U.S. President and, earlier, American general who led the D day invasion. pp. 589, 590

Elizabeth I *1533–1603* Queen of England during the middle to late 1500s. p. 151

Ellicott, Andrew *1754–1820* American surveyor who helped survey land for the new United States capital. p. 329

Ellington, Edward Kennedy (Duke) *1899–1974* Band leader who became well-known playing jazz during the 1920s. p. 573

Emerson, Ralph Waldo *1803–1882* American poet who wrote the "Concord Hymn." p. 242

Equiano, Olaudah (ek•wee•AHN•oh, OHL•uh•dah) *1750–1797* African who was kidnapped from his village and sold into slavery. He later wrote a book describing his experiences. p. 202

Eriksson, Leif (AIR•ik•suhn, LAYV) *?–1020?* Viking explorer who sailed from Greenland to North America in the A.D. 1000s. p. 112

Eriksson, Thorvald (AIR•ik•suhn, TUR•val) *1000s* Brother of Leif Eriksson. Thorvald Eriksson led one trip to Vinland. p. 112

Estéban (ehs•TAY•bahn) *1500–1539* African explorer who went with Cabeza de Vaca to Mexico City and told stories of the Seven Cities of Gold. Estéban was killed on a later expedition, the purpose of which was to find out whether the stories were true. p. 140

F

Farragut, Jorge (FAIR•uh•guht, HAWR•hay) *1755–1817* Spanish-born man who fought in the Continental army and the navy. p. 266

Ferdinand II *1452–1516* King of Spain who—with Queen Isabella, his wife—sent Christopher Columbus on his voyage to find a western route to Asia. p. 120

Ferraro, Geraldine *1935–* First woman to be nominated as a major party's candidate for Vice President of the United States. p. 626

Finley, John Fur trader who helped Daniel Boone find the way across the Appalachian Mountains to Kentucky. p. 349

Ford, Gerald *1913–* 38th U.S. President. The Vietnam War ended during his term. p. 631

Ford, Henry *1863–1947* American automobile manufacturer who mass-produced cars at low cost by using assembly lines. p. 570

Forten, James *1766–1842* Free African in Philadelphia who ran a busy sail factory and became wealthy. p. 425

Franklin, Benjamin *1706–1790* American leader who was sent to Britain to ask Parliament for representation. He was a writer of the Declaration of Independence, a delegate to the Constitutional Convention, and a respected scientist and business leader. p. 235

Frémont, John C. *1813–1890* Surveyor who led an early expedition to make maps of the West. His careful descriptions helped thousands of settlers. p. 386

Frick, Henry Clay *1849–1919* Manager of a steel mill in Homestead, Pennsylvania. His announcement of a pay cut led to a violent strike. p. 492

Friedan, Betty *1921–* Writer who helped set up the National Organization for Women to work for women's rights. p. 626

Frontenac, Louis de Buade, Count de (FRAHN•tuh•nak) *1622–1698* French leader who was appointed governor-general of New France. p. 178

G

Gage, Thomas *1721–1787* Head of the British army in North America and colonial governor. p. 239

Gálvez, Bernardo de (GAHL•ves) *1746–1786* Spanish governor of Louisiana who sent supplies to the Patriots in the Revolutionary War and led his own soldiers in taking a British fort in Florida. p. 266

Garrison, William Lloyd *1805–1879* American abolitionist who started a newspaper called *The Liberator*. p. 393

Gates, Horatio *1728–1806* American general who defeated the British in 1777, at Saratoga, New York. p. 266

George II *1683–1760* British king who chartered the Georgia colony. p. 189

George III *1738–1820* King of England during the Revolutionary War. p. 227

Geronimo *1829–1909* Apache chief who fought one of the longest wars between Native Americans and the United States government. p. 531

Gerry, Elbridge *1744–1814* Massachusetts delegate to the Constitutional Convention. p. 309

Glenn, John H., Jr. *1921–* American astronaut who was the first person to orbit the Earth. p. 616

Glidden, Joseph *1813–1906* Inventor of barbed wire. p. 523

Gompers, Samuel *1850–1924* Early labor union leader who formed the American Federation of Labor. p. 491

Gorbachev, Mikhail (gawr•buh•CHAWF, myik•uh•EEL) *1931–* Leader of the Soviet Union from 1985 to 1991. He improved relations with the United States and expanded freedom in the Soviet Union. p. 636

Gorham, Nathaniel *1738–1796* Massachusetts delegate to the Constitutional Convention. p. 310

Granger, Gordon Union general who read the order declaring all slaves in Texas to be free. p. 463

Grant, Ulysses S. *1822–1885* 18th U.S. President and, earlier, commander of the Union army in the Civil War. p. 453

Grenville, George *1712–1770* British prime minister who passed the Stamp Act in 1765. p. 231

H

Hallidie, Andrew S. *1836–1900* American inventor of the cable car. p. 508

Hamilton, Alexander *1755–1804* American leader in calling for the Constitutional Convention and winning support for it. He favored a strong national government. p. 291

Hammond, James Henry *1807–1864* Senator from South Carolina. p. 418

Hancock, John *1737–1793* Leader of the Sons of Liberty in the Massachusetts colony. p. 241

Harrison, William Henry *1773–1841* 9th U.S. President. Earlier he directed U.S. forces against the Indians at the Battle of Tippecanoe and was a commander in the War of 1812. p. 359

Hays, Mary Ludwig *1754?–1832* Known as Molly Pitcher, she carried water to American soldiers during the Battle of Monmouth; when her husband fell during the battle, she began firing his cannon. p. 257

Henrietta Maria *1609–1669* Queen of Charles I of England. The Maryland colony was named in her honor. p. 184

Henry *1394–1460* Henry the Navigator, prince of Portugal, who set up the first European school for training sailors in navigation. p. 118

Henry, Patrick *1736–1799* American colonist who spoke out in the Virginia legislature against paying British taxes. His views became widely known, and Loyalists accused him of treason. p. 233

Henry IV *1553–1610* King of France. p. 148

Hiawatha (hy•uh•WAH•thuh) *1500s* Onondaga chief who persuaded other Iroquois tribes to form the Iroquois League. p. 86

Hirohito *1901–1989* Emperor of Japan from 1926 until his death. p. 584

Hitler, Adolf *1889–1945* Nazi dictator of Germany. His actions led to World War II and the killing of millions of people. p. 583

Holiday, Billie *1915–1945* Jazz singer who sang in Harlem during the Harlem Renaissance. p. 573

Hooker, Thomas *1586?–1647* Minister who helped form the Connecticut colony. His democratic ideas were adopted in the Fundamental Orders. p. 185

Hoover, Herbert *1874–1964* 31st U.S. President. When the Depression began, he thought that the economy was healthy and conditions would improve. p. 574

Houston, Sam *1793–1863* President of the Republic of Texas and, later, governor of the state of Texas. p. 385

Huascar (WAHS•kar) Brother of Atahuallpa, who killed him to become the last Inca king of Peru. p. 137

Hudson, Henry *?–1611* Explorer who sailed up the Hudson River, giving the Dutch a claim to the area. p. 149

Hughes, Langston *1902–1967* Poet and one of the best-known Harlem writers. p. 573

Huishen *500s* Chinese Buddhist monk said to have sailed to an unknown land between Europe and Asia. p. 111

Hurston, Zora Neale *1903–1960* Novelist and one of the best-known Harlem writers. p. 573

Hutchinson, Anne Marbury *1591–1643* English-born woman who left Massachusetts because of her religious beliefs. She settled near Providence, which joined with other settlements to form the Rhode Island colony. p. 186

I

Iberville, Pierre Le Moyne, Sieur d' (ee•ber•VEEL) *1661–1706* French explorer who—with his brother, Jean Baptiste Le Moyne, Sieur de Bienville—started an early settlement at the mouth of the Mississippi River. p. 181

Idrisi, al- (uhl•ih•DREE•see) *1100–1165* Arab geographer and cartographer. p. 113

Isabella I *1451–1504* Queen of Spain who—with King Ferdinand, her husband—sent Columbus on his voyage to find a western route to Asia. p. 120

J

Jackson, Andrew *1767–1845* 7th U.S. President and, earlier, commander who won the final battle in the War of 1812. As President he favored a strong Union and ordered the removal of Native Americans from their lands. p. 361, 379

Jackson, Thomas (Stonewall) *1824–1863* Confederate general. p. 410

James I *1566–1625* King of England in the early 1600s. The James River and Jamestown were named after him. p. 153

Jay, John *1745–1829* American leader who wrote letters to newspapers, defending the Constitution. He became the first chief justice of the Supreme Court. p. 318

Jefferson, Thomas *1743–1826* 3rd U.S. President and the main writer of the Declaration of Independence. p. 253

Jenney, William *1832–1907* American engineer who developed the use of steel frames to build tall buildings. p. 507

John I *1357–1433* King of Portugal during a time of great exploration. Father of Prince Henry, who set up a school of navigation. p. 118

Johnson, Andrew *1808–1875* 17th U.S. President. Differences with Congress about Reconstruction led to his being impeached, though he was found not guilty. p. 465

Johnson, Lyndon B. *1908–1973* 36th U.S. President. He started Great Society programs and expanded the Vietnam War. p. 614

Joliet, Louis (zhohl•YAY, loo•EE) *1645–1700* French fur trader who explored lakes and rivers for France, with Marquette and five others. p. 179

Jones, Jehu Free African who owned one of South Carolina's best hotels before the Civil War. p. 425

Joseph *1840–1904* Nez Perce chief who tried to lead his people to Canada after they were told to move onto a reservation. p. 530

K

Kalakaua (kah•lah•KAH•ooh•ah) *1836–1891* Hawaiian king who tried but failed to keep Americans from taking over the Hawaiian Islands. p. 548

Kalb, Johann, Baron de *1721–1780* German soldier who helped the Patriots in the Revolutionary War. p. 264

Kennedy, John F. *1917–1963* 35th U.S. President. He helped pass the Civil Rights Act of 1964. p. 613

Key, Francis Scott *1779–1843* American lawyer and poet who wrote the words to "The Star-Spangled Banner." p. 365

King, Martin Luther, Jr. *1929–1968* African American civil rights leader who worked for integration in nonviolent ways. King won the Nobel Peace Prize in 1964. pp. 470, 624

King, Richard *1825–1885* Rancher in South Texas who founded the country's largest ranch. p. 522

King, Rufus *1755–1827* Massachusetts delegate to the Constitutional Convention. p. 310

Knox, Henry *1750–1806* Secretary of war in the first government under the Constitution. p. 326

Kosciuszko, Thaddeus (kawsh•CHUSH•koh) *1746–1817* Polish officer who helped the Patriots in the Revolutionary War. He later returned to Poland and led a revolution there. p. 264

Kublai Khan (KOO•bluh KAHN) *1215–1294* Ruler of China who was visited by Marco Polo. p. 115

L

La Follette, Robert *1855–1925* Wisconsin governor who began many reforms in his state, including a merit system for government jobs. p. 557

La Salle, René-Robert Cavelier, Sieur de (luh•SAL) *1643–1687* French explorer who found the mouth of the Mississippi River and claimed the whole Mississippi Valley for France. p. 180

Lafayette, Marquis de (lah•fee•ET) *1757–1834* French noble who fought alongside the Americans in the Revolutionary War. p. 264

Lafon, Thomy *1810–1893* Free African who made a fortune from businesses in New Orleans. p. 425

Las Casas, Bartolomé de (lahs KAH•sahs, bar•toh•luh•MAY day) *1474–1566* Spanish missionary who spent much of his life trying to help Native Americans. p. 144

Law, John *1671–1729* Scottish banker who was appointed proprietor of the Louisiana region in 1717. p. 181

Lazarus, Emma *1849–1887* Poet who wrote, in 1883, the poem now on the base of the Statue of Liberty. p. 534

Le Moyne, Jean-Baptiste (luh•MWAHN, ZHAHN ba•TEEST) *See* Bienville.

Le Moyne, Pierre *See* Iberville.

Lee, Charles *1731–1782* American officer during the Revolutionary War. p. 247

Lee, Richard Henry *1732–1794* American Revolutionary leader who said to the Continental Congress that the colonies should become independent from Britain. p. 252

Lee, Robert E. *1807–1870* United States army colonel who gave up his post and became commander of the Confederate army in the Civil War. p. 443

L'Enfant, Pierre Charles *1754–1825* French-born American engineer who planned the buildings and streets of the new capital of the United States. p. 329

Lewis, Meriwether *1774–1809* American explorer chosen by Thomas Jefferson to be a pathfinder in the territory of the Louisiana Purchase. p. 355

Liliuokalani, Lydia (li•lee•uh•woh•kuh•LAH•nee) *1838–1917* Hawaiian queen who tried but failed to bring back the Hawaiian monarchy's authority. p. 548

Lincoln, Abraham *1809–1865* 16th U.S. President, leader of the Union in the Civil War, and signer of the Emancipation Proclamation. pp. 429, 431, 435, 445, 446

Lincoln, Benjamin *1733–1810* Continental army general. p. 267

Lincoln, Mary Todd *1818–1882* Wife of Abraham Lincoln. p. 443

Lindbergh, Charles *1902–1974* Airplane pilot who was the first to fly solo between the United States and Europe. p. 571

Livingston, Robert R. *1746–1813* One of the writers of the Declaration of Independence. p. 253

Louis XIV *1638–1715* King of France. p. 178

Lowell, Francis Cabot *1775–1817* Textile pioneer who set up an American mill in which several processes were completed under one roof. p. 374

Lucas, Eliza *1722?–1793* South Carolina settler who experimented with indigo plants. She gave away seeds, and indigo then became an important cash crop in the colonies. p. 189

M

Madison, Dolley *1768–1849* James Madison's wife and First Lady during the War of 1812. p. 361

Madison, James *1751–1836* 4th U.S. President. He was a leader in calling for the Constitutional Convention, writing the Constitution, and winning support for it. p. 290

Magellan, Ferdinand (muh•JEH•luhn) *1480?–1521* Portuguese explorer who in 1519 led a fleet of ships from Spain westward to Asia. He died on the voyage, but one of the ships made it back to Spain, completing the first trip around the world. p. 129

Malcolm X *1925–1965* African American leader who disagreed with the views of Martin Luther King, Jr., on nonviolence and integration. p. 624

Malintzin (mah•LINT•suhn) *1501?–1550* Aztec princess who interpreted for Hernando Cortés and helped him in other ways to conquer Mexico. p. 136

Mann, Horace *1796–1859* American school reformer in the first half of the 1800s. p. 392

Mao Zedong (MOW zeh•DOONG) *1893–1976* Leader of China from 1949 until his death. President Nixon's 1972 visit with him in China led to trade and cultural exchange with the United States. p. 634

Marion, Francis *1732?–1795* Known as the Swamp Fox, he led Continental soldiers through the swamps of South Carolina on daring raids against the British. p. 259

Marquette, Jacques (mar•KET, ZHAHK) *1637–1675* Catholic missionary who knew several American Indian languages. With Joliet, he explored lakes and rivers for France. p. 179

Marshall, James *1810–1885* Carpenter who found gold at John Sutter's sawmill near Sacramento, California, leading to the California gold rush of 1849. p. 389

Marshall, John *1755–1835* Chief Justice of the Supreme Court in 1832; Marshall ruled that the United States should protect the Cherokees and their lands in Georgia. p. 382

Marshall, Thurgood *1908–1993* NAACP lawyer who argued the school segregation case that the Supreme Court ruled on in 1954 and, later, was the first African American to serve on the Supreme Court. p. 622

Martí, José (mar•TEE) *1853–1895* Cuban leader who did much to win Cuban independence from Spain. p. 550

Mason, George *1725–1792* Virginia delegate to the Constitutional Convention who argued for an end to the slave trade. p. 300

Massasoit (ma•suh•SOYT) *?–1661* Chief of the Wampanoags, who lived in peace with the Pilgrims. p. 156

McCormick, Cyrus *1809–1884* Inventor of a reaping machine for harvesting wheat. p. 517

McCoy, Joseph *1837–1915* Cattle trader who arranged to move large herds by using stockyards near railroad tracks. p. 520

McKinley, William *1843–1901* 25th U.S. President. The Spanish-American War was fought during his term. p. 549

Menéndez de Avilés, Pedro (meh•NEN•des day ah•vee•LAYS) *1519–1574* Spanish leader of settlers in St. Augustine, Florida, the first permanent European settlement in what is now the United States. p. 173

Mongoulacha (mahn•goo•LAY•chah) *1700s* Indian leader who helped Bienville and Iberville. p. 181

Monroe, James *1758–1831* 5th U.S. President. He established the Monroe Doctrine, which said that the United States would stop any European nation from expanding its American empire. p. 362

Morris, Gouverneur (guh•vuh•NIR) *1752–1816* American leader who was in charge of the final wording of the United States Constitution. p. 293

Morse, Samuel F. B. *1791–1872* American who developed the telegraph and invented Morse code. p. 484

Motecuhzoma (maw•tay•kwah•SOH•mah) *1466–1520* Emperor of the Aztecs when they were conquered by the Spanish. He is also known as Montezuma. p. 135

Mott, Lucretia *1793–1880* American reformer who, with Elizabeth Cady Stanton, organized the first convention for women's rights. p. 395

Muhlenberg, Peter *1746–1807* Young minister, son of the colonies' Lutheran leader, who became a Patriot militia officer. p. 256

Murray, John *1732–1809* Royal governor of Virginia during the Revolutionary War. He promised enslaved Africans their freedom if they would fight for the British government. p. 259

Mussolini, Benito (moo•suh•LEE•nee, buh•NEE•toh) *1883–1945* Dictator of Italy from 1925 until 1943. p. 584

N

Nixon, Richard M. *1913–1994* 37th President. He tried to end the Vietnam War, he reduced tensions with communist nations, and he resigned the presidency because of the Watergate scandal. pp. 630, 634

Niza, Marcos de (day NEE•sah) *1495–1558* Spanish priest who was sent with Estéban to confirm stories of the Seven Cities of Gold. When he returned to Mexico City, he said he had seen a golden city. p. 140

O

O'Connor, Sandra Day *1930–* First woman to be appointed to the United States Supreme Court. p. 626

Oglethorpe, James *1696–1785* English settler who was given a charter to settle Georgia. He wanted to bring in debtors from England to help settle it. p. 189

Osceola *1804–1838* Leader of the Seminoles in Florida. p. 381

Oswald, Richard *1705–1784* British merchant who met with Benjamin Franklin to negotiate terms between America and Britain at the end of the Revolutionary War. p. 268

Otis, James *1725–1783* Massachusetts colonist who spoke out against British taxes and called for "no taxation without representation." p. 232

P

Paine, Thomas *1737–1809* Author of a widely read pamphlet called *Common Sense,* in which he attacked King George III and called for a revolution to make the colonies independent. p. 252

Parks, Rosa *1913–* African American woman whose refusal to give up her seat on a Montgomery, Alabama, bus started a year-long bus boycott. p. 623

Paterson, William *1745–1806* Constitutional delegate from New Jersey who submitted the New Jersey Plan, under which each state would have one vote, regardless of population. p. 297

Penn, William *1644–1718* Proprietor of Pennsylvania under a charter from King Charles II of Britain. Penn was a Quaker who made Pennsylvania a refuge for settlers who wanted religious freedom. p. 187

Perry, Oliver Hazard *1785–1819* American naval commander who won an important battle in the War of 1812. p. 361

Pickett, Bill *1870–1932* Cowhand who was the first African American elected to the National Cowboy Hall of Fame and Western Heritage Center. p. 522

Pike, Zebulon *1779–1813* American who led an expedition down the Arkansas River to explore the southwestern part of the Louisiana Purchase. p. 357

Pinzón, Martín Captain of the *Pinta*. Brother of Vincente Pinzón. p. 122

Pinzón, Vincente Captain of the *Niña*. Brother of Martín Pinzón. p. 122

Pizarro, Francisco (pee•ZAR•oh) *1475?–1541* Spanish conquistador who conquered the Inca Empire. p. 137

Pocahontas (poh•kuh•HAHN•tuhs) *1595–1617* Indian chief Powhatan's daughter. p. 153

Polk, James K. *1795–1849* 11th U.S. President. He gained land for the United States by setting a northern boundary in 1846 and winning a war with Mexico in 1848. p. 386

Polo, Maffeo Trader from Venice; uncle of Marco Polo. p. 115

Polo, Marco *1254–1324* Explorer from Venice who spent many years in Asia in the late 1200s. He wrote a book about his travels that gave Europeans information about Asia. p. 115

Polo, Niccolò Trader from Venice; father of Marco Polo. p. 115

Ponce de León, Juan (PAHN•say day lay•OHN) *1460–1521* Spanish explorer who landed on the North American mainland in 1513, near what is now St. Augustine, Florida. p. 139

Powhatan (pow•uh•TAN) *1550?–1618* Chief of a federation of Indian tribes that lived in the Virginia territory. Pocahontas was his daughter. p. 153

Ptolemy, Claudius (TAH•luh•mee) *100s* Astronomer in ancient Egypt. p. 127

Pulaski, Casimir (puh•LAS•kee) *1747–1779* Polish noble who came to the British colonies to help the Patriots in the Revolutionary War. p. 264

R

Raleigh, Sir Walter (RAH•lee) *1554–1618* English explorer who used his own money to set up England's first colony in North America, on Roanoke Island near North Carolina. p. 151

Randolph, Edmund *1753–1813* Virginia delegate to the Constitutional Convention who wrote the Virginia Plan, which stated that the number of representatives a state would have in Congress should be based on the population of the state. p. 297

Read, George *1733–1798* Delaware delegate to the Constitutional Convention who thought the states should be done away with in favor of a strong national government. p. 296

Reagan, Ronald *1911–* 40th U.S. President. His meetings with Soviet leader Mikhail Gorbachev led to a thaw in the Cold War, including advances in arms control. p. 635

Red Cloud *1822–1909* Sioux chief who led his people on a three-year fight to keep miners and army troops off a road that ran through Sioux land. p. 529

Revere, Paul *1735–1818* American who warned the Patriots that the British were marching toward Concord, where Patriot weapons were stored. pp. 241, 242

Riis, Jacob (REES) *1849–1914* Reformer and writer who described the living conditions of the poor in New York City. p. 505

Robeson, Paul *1898–1976* African American actor and singer who performed in Harlem and outside the United States. p. 573

Rockefeller, John D. *1839–1937* American oil entrepreneur who joined many refineries into one business, called the Standard Oil Company. p. 485

Roosevelt, Franklin Delano *1882–1945* 32nd U.S. President. He began New Deal programs to help the nation out of the Depression, and he was the nation's leader during World War II. pp. 576, 577

Roosevelt, Theodore *1858–1919* 26th U.S. President. He showed the world America's strength, made it possible to build the Panama Canal, and worked for progressive reforms and conservation. pp. 550, 556

Ross, John *1790–1866* Chief of the Cherokee nation. He fought in United States courts to prevent the loss of the Cherokees' lands in Georgia. Though he won the legal battle, he still had to lead his people along the Trail of Tears to what is now Oklahoma. p. 381

Ruffin, Edmund *1794–1865* Agriculturist from Virginia. He fired the first shot on Fort Sumter. p. 436

Russwurm, John *1799–1851* Helped Samuel Cornish found an abolitionist newspaper called *Freedom's Journal* in 1827. p. 393

Rutledge, John *1739–1800* Delegate to the Constitutional Convention, South Carolina governor, and Supreme Court Justice. p. 300

S

Sacagawea (sak•uh•juh•WEE•uh) *1786?–1812?* Shoshone woman who acted as an interpreter for the Lewis and Clark expedition. pp. 355, 356

Salem, Peter *1750?–1816* African who fought with the Minutemen at Concord and at the Battle of Bunker Hill. p. 258

Samoset *1590?–1653?* Native American chief who spoke English and who helped the settlers at Plymouth. p. 155

San Martín, José de (san mar•TEEN) *1778–1850* Leader of an independence movement in Argentina. p. 659

Santa Anna, Antonio López de *1794–1876* Dictator of Mexico; defeated Texans at the Alamo. p. 384

Scott, Dred *1795?–1858* Enslaved African who took his case for freedom to the Supreme Court and lost. p. 428

Scott, Winfield *1786–1866* American general in the war with Mexico. p. 388

Biographical Dictionary

Seguín, Juan (say•GEEN) Defender of the Alamo, where he was killed. p. 384

Sequoyah (sih•KWOY•uh) *1765?–1843* Cherokee leader who in 1921 created a writing system for the Cherokee language. p. 381

Serra, Junípero *1713–1784* Spanish missionary who helped build a string of missions in California. p. 175

Seward, William H. *1801–1872* Secretary of state in the cabinet of Abraham Lincoln. p. 450

Shays, Daniel *1747?–1825* Leader of Shays's Rebellion, which showed the weakness of the government under the Articles of Confederation. p. 287

Shen Tong Student from Beijing University in China who compared the Tiananmen Square massacre with the Boston Massacre. p. 272

Sherman, Roger *1721–1793* One of the writers of the Declaration of Independence. Connecticut delegate to the Constitutional Convention who worked out the compromise in which Congress would have two houses—one based on state population and one with two members from each state. pp. 253, 301

Sherman, William Tecumseh *1820–1891* Union general who, after defeating Confederate forces in Atlanta, led the March to the Sea, on which his troops caused great destruction. p. 456

Sitting Bull *1831–1890* Sioux leader who fought against General George Custer. p. 529

Slater, Samuel *1768–1835* Textile pioneer who helped bring the Industrial Revolution to the United States by providing plans for a new spinning machine. p. 373

Slocumb, Mary *1700s* North Carolina colonist who fought in the Revolutionary War. p. 257

Smith, John *1580–1631* English explorer who, as leader of the Jamestown settlement, saved its people from starvation. p. 153

Smith, Joseph *1805–1844* Mormon leader who settled his people in Illinois and was killed there. p. 387

Spalding, Eliza *1807–1851* American missionary and pioneer in the Oregon country. p. 386

Spalding, Henry *1801–1874* American missionary and pioneer in the Oregon country. p. 386

Sprague, Frank *1857–1934* American inventor who built the trolley car, an electric streetcar. p. 508

Squanto *See* Tisquantum.

Stalin, Joseph *1879–1953* Dictator of the Soviet Union from 1929 until his death. p. 584

Stanton, Elizabeth Cady *1815–1902* American reformer who, with Lucretia Mott, organized the first convention for women's rights. p. 395

Starr, Ellen Gates *1860–1940* Reformer who, with Jane Addams, founded Hull House in Chicago. p. 506

Steuben, Friedrich, Baron von (vahn SHTOY•buhn) *1730–1794* German soldier who helped train Patriot troops in the Revolutionary War. p. 264

Stinson, Katherine *1891–1977* American pilot who wanted to become a fighter pilot in World War I but was not allowed to fly in battle. p. 562

Stowe, Harriet Beecher *1811–1896* American abolitionist who in 1852 wrote the book *Uncle Tom's Cabin*. p. 393

Stuyvesant, Peter (STY•vuh•suhnt) *1610?–1672* Last governor of the Dutch colony of New Netherland. p. 187

Sutter, John *1803–1880* American pioneer who owned the sawmill where gold was discovered, leading to the California gold rush. p. 389

T

Taney, Roger B. (TAW•nee) *1777–1864* Supreme Court Chief Justice who wrote the ruling against Dred Scott. p. 428

Tascalusa (tuhs•kah•LOO•sah) *1500s* Leader of the Mobile people when they battled with Spanish troops led by Hernando de Soto. p. 141

Tecumseh (tuh•KUHM•suh) *1768–1813* Shawnee leader of Indians in the Northwest Territory. He wanted to form a strong Indian confederation. p. 358

Tenskwatawa (ten•SKWAHT•uh•wah) *1768–1834* Shawnee leader known as the Prophet. He worked with his brother Tecumseh and led the Indians at the Battle of Tippecanoe in 1811. p. 358

Tisquantum *1585?–1622* Native American who spoke English and who helped the Plymouth colony. p. 156

Tompkins, Sally *1833–1916* Civil War nurse who eventually ran her own private hospital in Richmond, Virginia. She was a captain in the Confederate army, the only woman to achieve such an honor. p. 444

Tonti, Henri de (TOHN•tee, ahn•REE duh) *1650–1704* French explorer with La Salle. p. 181

Toussaint-Louverture, Pierre (TOO•san LOO•ver•tur) *1743–1803* Haitian revolutionary and general who took over the government of St. Domingue from France and became the ruler of Haiti. p. 354

Travis, William B. *1809–1836* Commander of the Texas force at the Alamo, where he was killed. p. 384

Truman, Harry S. *1884–1972* 33rd U.S. President. He sent American soldiers to support South Korea in 1950. p. 591

Truth, Sojourner *1797?–1883* Abolitionist and former slave who became a leading preacher against slavery. p. 394

Tubman, Harriet *1820–1913* Abolitionist and former slave who became a conductor on the Underground Railroad. She led about 300 slaves to freedom. p. 424

Turner, Nat *1800–1831* Enslaved African who led a rebellion against slavery. More than 100 slaves were killed, and Turner was caught and hanged. p. 422

Tweed, William (Boss) *1823–1878* New York City political boss who robbed the city of millions of dollars. p. 557

V

Vanderbilt, Cornelius *1843–1899* American railroad owner during the railroad boom of the late 1800s. p. 484

Vespucci, Amerigo (veh•SPOO•chee, uh•MAIR•ih•goh) *1454–1512* Italian explorer who made several voyages from Europe to what many people thought was Asia. He determined that he had landed on another continent, which was later called America in his honor. p. 126

Biographical Dictionary

W

Wald, Lillian *1867–1940* Reformer who started the Henry Street Settlement in New York City. p. 506

Waldseemüller, Martin (VAHLT•zay•mool•er) *1470–1518?* German cartographer who published a map in 1507 that first showed a continent named America. p. 127

Ward, Artemas *1727–1800* American commander during the Revolutionary War. p. 247

Warren, Earl *1891–1974* Chief Justice of the Supreme Court who wrote the 1954 decision against school segregation. p. 622

Warren, Mercy Otis *1728–1814* Massachusetts colonist who spoke out against new British taxes on goods. p. 232

Washington, Booker T. *1856–1915* African American who founded Tuskegee Institute in Alabama. p. 558

Washington, George *1732–1799* 1st U.S. President, leader of the Continental army during the Revolutionary War, and president of the Constitutional Convention. pp. 247, 325

Westinghouse, George *1846–1914* American inventor who designed an air brake for stopping trains. p. 483

Wheatley, John *1700s* Boston slave owner who bought a young African girl to be maidservant to his wife; the family educated the girl and freed her. She became one of the earliest American poets, Phillis Wheatley. p. 258

Wheatley, Phillis *1753?–1784* American poet who wrote poems that praised the Revolution. pp. 257, 258

White, John *?–1593?* English painter and cartographer who led the second group that settled on Roanoke Island. p. 152

Whitman, Marcus *1802–1847* American missionary and pioneer in the Oregon Country. p. 386

Whitman, Narcissa *1808–1847* American missionary and pioneer in the Oregon Country. p. 386

Whitney, Eli *1765–1825* American inventor who was most famous for his invention of the cotton gin and his idea of interchangeable parts, which made mass production possible. pp. 374, 417

Williams, Roger *1603?–1683* Founder of Providence in what is now Rhode Island. He had been forced to leave Massachusetts because of his views. p. 186

Wilson, James *1742–1798* Pennsylvania delegate to the Constitutional Convention who argued for a single chief executive elected by an electoral college. p. 303

Wilson, Woodrow *1856–1924* 28th U.S. President. He brought the country into World War I after trying to stay neutral. He favored the League of Nations, but the Senate rejected U.S. membership in the league. p. 559

Woods, Granville T. *1856–1910* African American who improved the air brake and developed a telegraph system for trains. p. 483

Wright, Orville *1871–1948* Pioneer in American aviation who—with his brother, Wilbur—made and flew the first successful airplane, at Kitty Hawk, North Carolina. p. 571

Wright, Wilbur *1867–1912* Pioneer in American aviation who—with his brother, Orville—made and flew the first successful airplane, at Kitty Hawk, North Carolina. p. 571

Y

York *1800s* Enslaved African whose hunting and fishing skills contributed to the Lewis and Clark expedition. p. 355

Young, Brigham *1801–1877* Mormon leader who came after Joseph Smith. He moved his people west to the Great Salt Lake valley. p. 387

Gazetteer

The Gazetteer is a geographical dictionary that will help you locate places discussed in this book. The page number tells where each place appears on a map.

A

Abilene A city in central Kansas on the Smoky Hill River; a major railroad town. (39°N, 97°W) p. 514

Acadia Original name of Nova Scotia, Canada; once a part of New France. p. 169

Adena (uh•DEE•nuh) An ancient settlement of the Mound Builders; located in southern Ohio. (40°N, 81°W) p. 64

Adirondack Mountains (a•duh•RAHN•dak) A mountain range in northeastern New York. p. 86

Alamo A mission in San Antonio, Texas; located in the southeastern part of the state; used as a fort during the Texas Revolution. (29°N, 98°W) p. 385

Alaska Range A mountain range in central Alaska. p. 40

Albany The capital of New York; located in the eastern part of the state, on the Hudson River. (43°N, 74°W) p. 188

Albemarle Sound (AL•buh•marl) An inlet of the Atlantic Ocean; located in northeastern North Carolina. p. 152

Alcatraz Island (AL•kuh•traz) A rocky island in San Francisco Bay, California; formerly a U.S. penitentiary, closed in 1963. (38°N, 123°W) p. 498

Aleutian Islands (uh•LOO•shuhn) A chain of volcanic islands; located between the North Pacific and the Bering Sea, extending west from the Alaska Peninsula. (52°N, 177°W) p. 40

Allegheny River (a•luh•GAY•nee) A river in the northeastern United States; flows southwest to join the Monongahela River in Pennsylvania, forming the Ohio River. p. 86

Altamaha River (AWL•tuh•muh•haw) A river that begins in southeastern Georgia and flows into the Atlantic Ocean. p. 189

Amazon River The longest river in South America, flowing from the Andes Mountains across Brazil and into the Atlantic Ocean. p. 137

American Samoa (suh•MOH•uh) A United States territory in the Pacific Ocean. p. 551

Anastasia Island (an•uh•STAY•zhuh) An island in northeastern Florida; located south of St. Augustine, off the coast of St. Johns County. (30°N, 81°W) p. 174

Andes Mountains (AN•deez) The longest chain of mountains in the world; located along the entire western coast of South America. p. 137

Angel Island An island in San Francisco Bay, California. (38°N, 123°W) p. 498

Annapolis (uh•NA•puh•luhs) The capital of Maryland; located on Chesapeake Bay; home of the United States Naval Academy. (39°N, 76°W) p. 189

Antietam (an•TEE•tuhm) A creek near Sharpsburg in north central Maryland; site of a Civil War battle in 1862. (39°N, 78°W) p. 457

Antigua An island in the eastern part of the Leeward Islands, in the eastern West Indies. p. 655

Appalachian Mountains (a•puh•LAY•chuhn) A mountain system of eastern North America; extends from southeastern Quebec, Canada, to central Alabama. p. 40

Appomattox (a•puh•MA•tuhks) A village in central Virginia; site of the battle that ended the Civil War in 1865; once known as Appomattox Courthouse. (37°N, 79°W) p. 409

Arkansas River A tributary of the Mississippi River, beginning in central Colorado and ending in southeastern Arkansas. p. 40

Asunción A city in South America, located on the eastern bank of the Paraguay river where the Paraguay and Pilcomayo rivers join. (25°S, 57°W) p. 660

Athabasca River A southern tributary of the Mackenzie River in Alberta, west central Canada; flows northeast and then north into Lake Athabasca. p. 168

Atlanta Georgia's capital and largest city; located in the northwest central part of the state; site of a Civil War battle in 1864. (33°N, 84°W) p. 34

Augusta A city in eastern Georgia; located on the Savannah River. (33°N, 82°W) p. 189

B

Baffin Bay A large inlet of the Atlantic Ocean between western Greenland and the Northwest Territories, Canada. p. 41

Baffin Island The largest and easternmost island in the Canadian Arctic Islands; once known as Helluland. p. 41

Bahamas An island group in the North Atlantic; located southeast of Florida and north of Cuba. p. 40

Baja California A peninsula in northwestern Mexico extending south-southeast between the Pacific Ocean and the Gulf of California. (32°N, 115°W) p. 40

Baltimore A major seaport in Maryland; located on the upper end of Chesapeake Bay. (39°N, 77°W) p. 169

Barbados An island in the Lesser Antilles, West Indies; located east of the central Windward Islands. p. 655

Barbuda A flat coral island in the eastern West Indies. p. 655

Baxter Springs A city in the southeastern corner of Kansas. (37°N, 94°W) p. 521

Beaufort Sea (BOH•fert) That part of the Arctic Ocean between northeastern Alaska and the Canadian Arctic Islands. p. 40

Beijing (BAY•JING) The capital of China; located on a large plain in northeastern China; once known as Khanbalik. (40°N, 116°E) p. 272

Belém A seaport city in northern Brazil, on the Pará River. (1°S, 48°W) p. 660

Belmopan A town in Central America; capital of Belize. (17°N, 88°W) p. 655

Belo Horizonte A city in eastern Brazil. (20°S, 44°W) p. 660

Benin (buh•NEEN) A former kingdom in West Africa; located along the Gulf of Guinea; present-day southern Nigeria. p. 145

Bennington A town in the southwestern corner of Vermont; site of a major Revolutionary War battle in 1777. (43°N, 73°W) p. 265

Bering Strait A narrow strip of water; separates Asia from North America. p. 48

Beringia (buh•RIN•gee•uh) An ancient land bridge that once connected Asia and North America. p. 48

Big Hole A national battlefield in southwestern Montana; site of the battle on August 9, 1877, between U.S. troops and Nez Perce Indians under Chief Joseph. p. 529

Birmingham A city in north central Alabama. (34°N, 87°W) p. 343

Black Hills A group of mountains in South Dakota; its highest peak, more than 7,000 feet (2,134 m), is the highest point in the Plains states p. 527

Black Sea A large inland sea between Europe and Asia. p. 116

Bogotá A city in South America located on the plateau of the Andes; capital of Colombia. (4°N, 74°W) p. 660

Boise (BOY•zee) Idaho's capital and largest city; located in the southwestern part of the state. (44°N, 116°W) p. 527

Bonampak An ancient settlement of the Mayan civilization; located in present-day southeastern Mexico. (16°N, 91°W) p. 92

Boone's Trail Daniel Boone's trail that began in North Carolina and ended in Tennessee. p. 350

Boonesborough (BOONZ•buhr•oh) A village in east central Kentucky; site of a fort founded by Daniel Boone; now called Boonesboro. (38°N, 84°W) p. 350

Boston The capital and largest city of Massachusetts; a port city located on Massachusetts Bay. (42°N, 71°W) p. 169

Boston Harbor The western section of Massachusetts Bay; located in eastern Massachusetts; the city of Boston is located at its western end. p. 241

Brainerd A town in southeastern Tennessee; once part of the Cherokee Nation. (35°N, 85°W) p. 381

Brandywine A battlefield on Brandywine Creek in southeastern Pennsylvania; site of a major Revolutionary War battle in 1777. (40°N, 76°W) p. 265

Brasília A city in South America on the Paraná River; capital of Brazil. (15°S, 48°W) p. 660

Brazos River (BRAH•zuhs) A river in central Texas; flows southeast into the Gulf of Mexico. p. 140

British Columbia One of Canada's ten provinces; located on the west coast of Canada and bordered by the Yukon Territory, the Northwest Territories, Alberta, the United States, and the Pacific Ocean. p. 663

Brookline A town in eastern Massachusetts; west-southwest of Boston. (42°N, 71°W) p. 241

Brooklyn A borough of New York City, New York; located on the western end of Long Island. (41°N, 74°W) p. 498

Brooks Island An island off the coast of California, in San Francisco Bay. (39°N, 122°W) p. 498

Brooks Range A mountain range crossing northern Alaska; forms the northwestern end of the Rocky Mountains. p. 40

Buenos Aires The capital of Argentina. (34°S, 58°W) p. 660

Buffalo A city in western New York; located on the northeastern point of Lake Erie. (43°N, 79°W) p. 343

Bull Run A stream in northeastern Virginia; flows toward the Potomac River; site of a Civil War battle in 1861 and in 1862. p. 457

Butte (BYOOT) A city in southwestern Montana; located on the plateau of the Rocky Mountains. (46°N, 112°W) p. 527

C

Cahokia (kuh•HOH•kee•uh) A village in southwestern Illinois; site of an ancient settlement of the Mound Builders. (39°N, 90°W) p. 64

Cajamarca (kah•hah•MAR•kah) A town in northern Peru; located on the Cajamarca River, northwest of Lima. (7°S, 79°W) p. 137

Calgary A city in southern Alberta, Canada; located on the Bow River. (51°N, 114°W) p. 663

Calicut (KA•lih•kuht) A city in southwestern India; located on the Malabar Coast. (11°N, 76°E) p. 107

Cambridge A city in northeastern Massachusetts; located near Boston. (42°N, 71°W) p. 241

Camden A city in north central South Carolina, near the Wateree River; site of a major Revolutionary War battle in 1780. (34°N, 81°W) p. 265

Canal Zone A strip of territory in Panama. p. 552

Canary Islands An island group in the Atlantic Ocean off the northwest coast of Africa. (28°N, 16°W) p. 125

Canton A port city in southeastern China; located on the Canton River; known in China as Guangzhou. (23°N, 113°E) p. 107

Cape Cod A peninsula of southeastern Massachusetts, extending into the Atlantic Ocean and enclosing Cape Cod Bay. (42°N, 70°W) p. 186

Cape Fear A cape at the southern end of Smith Island; located off the coast of North Carolina, at the mouth of the Cape Fear River. (34°N, 78°W) p. 189

Cape Fear River A river in central and southeastern North Carolina; formed by the Deep and Haw rivers; flows southeast into the Atlantic Ocean. p. 189

Cape Hatteras (HA•tuh•ruhs) A cape on southeastern Hatteras Island; located off the coast of North Carolina. (35°N, 75°W) p. 189

Cape Horn A cape on the southern tip of South America, on Horn Island; named by Dutch explorers. p. 660

Cape of Good Hope A cape located on the southernmost tip of Africa. (34°S, 18°E) p. 119

Cape Verde Islands (VERD) A group of volcanic islands off the western coast of Africa. (16°N, 24°W) p. 119

Caracas A city in northern Venezuela; capital of Venezuela. (10°N, 67°W) p. 660

Caribbean Sea A part of the Atlantic Ocean between the West Indies and Central and South America. p. 41

Carson City The capital of Nevada; located in the western part of the state, near the Carson River. (39°N, 120°W) p. 538

Cartagena (kahr•tah•HAY•nah) A seaport on the northwestern coast of Colombia. (10°N, 75°W) p. 660

Cascade Range A mountain range in the western United States; a continuation of the Sierra Nevada; extends north from California to Washington. p. 40

Cayenne A city on the northwestern coast of Cayenne Island, in northern South America; capital of French Guiana. (5°N, 52°W) p. 660

Cemetery Hill A hill where much of the fighting of the first two days of the Battle of Gettysburg took place; located in Gettysburg, Pennsylvania, at the end of Cemetery Ridge. p. 460

Chachapoyas (chah•chah•POH•yahs) A town in northern Peru. (6°S, 78°W) p. 137

Chaco Canyon (CHAH•koh) An ancient settlement of the Anasazi; located in present-day northwestern New Mexico. (37°N, 108°W) p. 64

Chancellorsville (CHAN•suh•lerz•vil) A location in northeastern Virginia, just west of Fredericksburg; site of a Civil War battle in 1863. (38°N, 78°W) p. 457

Chapultepec (chah•POOL•teh•pek) An ancient settlement of the Aztec civilization; located in present-day south central Mexico. (32°N, 116°W) p. 92

Charles River A river in eastern Massachusetts; separates Boston from Cambridge; flows into Boston Bay. p. 241

Charleston A city in southeastern South Carolina; a major port on the Atlantic Ocean; once known as Charles Towne. (33°N, 80°W) p. 169

Charleston Harbor An inlet of the Atlantic Ocean in eastern South Carolina; located near Charleston. (33°N, 80°W) p. 433

Charlestown A city in Massachusetts; located on Boston Harbor between the mouths of the Charles and Mystic rivers. p. 241

Charlotte The largest city in North Carolina; located in the south central part of the state. (35°N, 81°W) p. 265

Charlottetown The capital of Prince Edward Island, Canada; located in the central part of the island, on Hillsborough Bay. (46°N, 63°W) p. 663

Chattanooga (cha•tuh•NOO•guh) A city in southeastern Tennessee; located on the Tennessee River; site of a Civil War battle in 1863. (35°N, 85°W) p. 457

Chattooga Village A town in northwestern Georgia; once part of the Cherokee Nation. (35°N, 85°W) p. 381

Cherokee Nation (CHAIR•uh•kee) A Native American nation located in present-day northern Georgia, eastern Alabama, southern Tennessee, and western North Carolina. p. 381

Chesapeake Bay An inlet of the Atlantic Ocean; surrounded by Virginia and Maryland. p. 156

Cheyenne (shy•AN) The capital of Wyoming; located in the southeastern part of the state. (41°N, 105°W) p. 521

Chicago A city in Illinois; located on Lake Michigan; the third-largest city in the United States. (42°N, 88°W) p. 343

Chickamauga (chik•uh•MAW•guh) A city in northwestern Georgia; site of a Civil War battle in 1863. (35°N, 85°W) p. 457

Chihuahua A city in northern Mexico. (28°N, 85°W) p. 645

Cholula (choh•LOO•lah) An ancient settlement of the Aztec civilization, located in present-day south central Mexico. (19°N, 98°W) p. 92

Cincinnati (sin•suh•NA•tee) A large city in southwestern Ohio; located on the Ohio River. (39°N, 84°W) p. 409

Cleveland The largest city in Ohio; located in the northern part of the state, at the mouth of the Cuyahoga River on Lake Erie. (41°N, 82°W) p. 343

Coast Mountains A mountain range in western British Columbia and southern Alaska; a continuation of the Cascade Range. p. 40

Coast Ranges Mountains along the Pacific coast of North America, extending from Alaska to Baja California. p. 40

Cold Harbor A location in east central Virginia, north of the Chickahominy River; site of a Civil War battle in 1862 and in 1864. (38°N, 77°W) p. 457

Colorado River A river in the southwestern United States; its basin extends from the Rocky Mountains to the Sierra Nevada; flows into the Gulf of California. p. 40

Columbia River A river that begins in the Rocky Mountains in southwestern Canada, forms the Washington–Oregon border, and empties into the Pacific Ocean below Portland; supplies much of that area's hydroelectricity. p. 40

Columbus The capital of Ohio; located in the central part of the state, on the Scioto River. (40°N, 83°W) p. 543

Compostela (kahm•poh•STEH•lah) A city in west central Mexico. (21°N, 105°W) p. 140

Comstock Lode A mining area near Virginia City, Nevada, that once supplied half the silver output of the United States. p. 527

Concord A town in northeastern Massachusetts, near Boston; site of a major Revolutionary War battle in 1775. (42°N, 71°W) p. 186

Concord River A river in northeastern Massachusetts; formed by the junction of the Sudbury and Assabet rivers; flows north into the Merrimack River at Lowell. p. 241

Connecticut River The longest river in New England; begins in New Hampshire, flows south, and empties into Long Island Sound in New York. p. 186

Constantinople (kahn•stant•uhn•OH•puhl) A port city in northwestern Turkey. (41°N, 29°E) p. 107

Copán (koh•PAHN) An ancient settlement of the Mayan civilization; located in present-day Honduras, in northern Central America. (15°N, 89°W) p. 92

Cowpens A town in northwestern South Carolina; located near the site of a major Revolutionary War battle in 1781. (35°N, 82°W) p. 265

Coxcatlán (kohs•kaht•LAHN) An ancient settlement of the Aztec civilization; located in present-day south central Mexico. p. 92

Cozumel (koh•soo•MEL) An island in the Caribbean Sea; located east of the Yucatán Peninsula; part of present-day Mexico. (21°N, 87°W) p. 92

Crab Orchard An ancient settlement of the Mound Builders; located in present-day southern Illinois. (38°N, 89°W) p. 64

Cuba An island country in the Caribbean; the largest island of the West Indies. (22°N, 79°W) p. 41

Gazetteer

Culp's Hill A hill in Pennsylvania where much of the fighting of the first two days of the Battle of Gettysburg took place; located at the end of Cemetery Ridge. p. 460

Cumberland Gap A pass through the Appalachian Mountains; located in northeastern Tennessee. p. 350

Cumberland River A river in southern Kentucky and northern Tennessee; flows west to the Ohio River. p. 265

Cuzco (KOOS•koh) The ancient capital of the Inca empire; a city located in present-day Peru, in western South America. (14°S, 72°W) p. 106

D

Dahlonega (duh•LAHN•uh•guh) A city in northern Georgia; once part of the Cherokee Nation. (35°N, 85°W) p. 381

Dallas A city in northeastern Texas; located on the Trinity River. (33°N, 97°W) p. 343

Dawson A city in the Yukon Territory, Canada; located on the right bank of the Yukon River, near the joining of the Yukon and Klondike rivers. (64°N, 139°W) p. 527

Deadwood A city in western South Dakota; located in Deadwood Gulch in the northern Black Hills. (44°N, 106°W) p. 527

Deerfield A town in northwestern Massachusetts. (43°N, 73°W) p. 186

Delaware Bay An inlet of the Atlantic Ocean; located between southern New Jersey and Delaware. p. 188

Delaware River A river in the northeastern United States; begins in southern New York and flows into the Atlantic Ocean at Delaware Bay. p. 86

Denver Colorado's capital and largest city. (40°N, 105°W) p. 514

Des Moines (dih•MOYN) Iowa's capital and largest city. (42°N, 94°W) p. 181

Detroit The largest city in Michigan; located in the southeastern part of the state, on the Detroit River. (42°N, 83°W) p. 169

Dickson An ancient settlement of the Mound Builders; located in present-day central Illinois. p. 64

Dodge City A city in southern Kansas; located on the Arkansas River; once a major railroad center on the Santa Fe Trail. (38°N, 100°W) p. 521

Dominica An island and a republic in the West Indies; located in the center of the Lesser Antilles between Guadeloupe and Martinique; used to be a self-governing state in association with Britain. p. 655

Dominican Republic A country in the West Indies, occupying the eastern part of Hispaniola. p. 549

Dover (DE) The capital of Delaware; located in the central part of the state. (39°N, 76°W) p. 188

Dover (NH) A city in southeastern New Hampshire. (43°N, 71°W) p. 186

Durango A city in northwestern central Mexico. (24°N, 104°W) p. 645

E

East River A strait located in New York; connects Long Island Sound and New York Bay. p. 498

Edenton (EE•duhn•tuhn) A town in northeastern North Carolina; located on Albemarle Sound, near the mouth of the Chowan River. (36°N, 77°W) p. 189

Edmonton The capital of Alberta, Canada; located in the south central part of the province on both banks of the north Saskatchewan River. (53°N, 113°W) p. 663

El Paso A city at the western tip of Texas; located on the Rio Grande. (32°N, 106°W) p. 342

Ellesmere Island (ELZ•mir) An island located in the northeastern part of the Northwest Territories; the northernmost point of Canada. p. 40

Ellis Island An island in Upper New York Bay; located southwest of Manhattan. (40°N, 74°W) p. 498

Ellsworth A city in central Kansas. p. 521

Emerald Mound An ancient settlement of the Mound Builders; located in present-day southwestern Mississippi. (32°N, 91°W) p. 64

Erie Canal The longest canal in the world; located in New York; connects Buffalo (on Lake Erie) with Troy (on the Hudson River). p. 377

F

Fairbanks A city in central Alaska. (65°N, 148°W) p. 527

Falkland Islands A British colony in the Atlantic Ocean; located east of the Strait of Magellan p. 660

Falmouth (FAL•muhth) A town in southwestern Maine. (44°N, 70°W) p. 186

Fort Atkinson A fort in southern Kansas; located on the Sante Fe Trail. (43°N, 89°W) p. 390

Fort Boise (BOY•zee) A fort in eastern Oregon; located on the Snake River and on the Oregon Trail. p. 390

Fort Bridger A present-day village in southwestern Wyoming; once an important station on the Oregon Trail. (41°N, 110°W) p. 390

Fort Crevecoeur (KREEV•KER) A fort in central Illinois; located on the Illinois River; built by La Salle in 1680. (41°N, 90°W) p. 180

Fort Crown Point A French fort; located in northeastern New York, on the shore of Lake Champlain. p. 227

Fort Cumberland A British fort located in northeastern West Virginia, on its border with Maryland. p. 227

Fort Dearborn A fort in northeastern Illinois; built in 1803; eventually became part of Chicago; site of a major battle in the War of 1812. (42°N, 88°W) p. 360

Fort Donelson A fort located in northwestern Tennessee; site of a major Civil War battle in 1862. p. 457

Fort Duquesne (doo•KAYN) A French fort in present-day Pittsburgh, southwestern Pennsylvania; captured and renamed Fort Pitt in 1758. (40°N, 80°W) p. 227

Fort Edward A British fort in eastern New York, on the Hudson River; a present-day village. (43°N, 74°W) p. 227

Fort Frontenac (FRAHNT•uhn•ak) A French fort once located on the site of present-day Kingston, Ontario, in southeastern Canada; destroyed by the British in 1758. (44°N, 76°W) p. 180

Fort Gibson A fort in eastern Oklahoma; end of the Trail of Tears. (36°N, 95°W) p. 404

Fort Hall A fort in southeastern Idaho; located on the Snake River, at a junction on the Oregon Trail. p. 390

Fort Laramie A fort in southeastern Wyoming; located on the Oregon Trail. (42°N, 105°W) p. 390

Fort Ligonier (lig•uh•NIR) A British fort; located in southern Pennsylvania near the Ohio River. p. 227

Fort Louisbourg (LOO•is•berg) A French fort; located in eastern Canada on the coast of the Atlantic Ocean. (46°N, 60°W) p. 227

Fort Mackinac (MA•kuh•naw) A fort located on the tip of present-day northern Michigan; site of a major battle in the War of 1812. (46°N, 85°W) p. 360

Fort Mandan A fort in present-day central North Dakota, on the Missouri River; site of a winter camp for the Lewis and Clark Expedition. (48°N, 104°W) p. 354

Fort McHenry A fort in central Maryland; located on the harbor in Baltimore; site of a major battle in the War of 1812. (39°N, 77°W) p. 360

Fort Miamis A French fort located on the southern shore of Lake Michigan, in present-day southwestern Michigan. p. 180

Fort Necessity A British fort located in southwestern Pennsylvania; located in present-day Great Meadows. (38°N, 80°W) p. 227

Fort Niagara A fort located in western New York, at the mouth of the Niagara River. (43°N, 79°W) p. 227

Fort Oswego A British fort; located in western New York, on the coast of Lake Ontario. (43°N, 77°W) p. 227

Fort Sumter A fort on a human-made island, off the coast of South Carolina, in Charleston Harbor; site of the first Civil War battle in 1861. (33°N, 80°W) p. 433

Fort Ticonderoga (ty•kahn•der•OH•gah) A historic British fort on Lake Champlain, in northeastern New York. (44°N, 73°W) p. 227

Fort Vancouver A fort in southwestern Washington, on the Columbia River; the western end of the Oregon Trail; present-day Vancouver. (45°N, 123°W) p. 390

Fort Walla Walla A fort in southeastern Washington; located on the Oregon Trail. (46°N, 118°W) p. 390

Fort William Henry A British fort located in eastern New York. (43°N, 74°W) p. 227

Fort Worth A city in northern Texas; located on the Trinity River. (33°N, 97°W) p. 521

Fortaleza A port in northern Brazil. (3°S, 38°W) p. 660

Fox River Located in southeast central Wisconsin; flows southwest toward the Wisconsin River, and then flows northeast and empties into Green Bay. p. 180

Franklin (MO) A city in central Missouri, on the Missouri River. (39°N, 93°W) p. 377

Franklin (TN) A city in central Tennessee; site of a major Civil War battle in 1864. (36°N, 87°W) p. 525

Fredericksburg A city in northeastern Virginia; located on the Rappahannock River; site of a Civil War battle in 1862. (38°N, 77°W) p. 189

Fredericton The capital of New Brunswick, Canada; located in the southwestern part of the province. (46°N, 66°W) p. 663

Frenchtown A town in present-day eastern Michigan; site of a major battle in the War of 1812. (42°N, 83°W) p. 360

G

Gatun Lake (gah•TOON) A lake in Panama; part of the Panama Canal system. p. 552

Georgetown A city in South America located at the mouth of the Demerara River; capital of Guyana. (6°N, 58°W) p. 660

Germantown A residential section of present-day Philadelphia, on Wissahickon Creek, in southeastern Pennsylvania; site of a major Revolutionary War battle in 1777. (40°N, 75°W) p. 265

Gettysburg A town in southern Pennsylvania; site of a Civil War battle in 1863. (40°N, 77°W) p. 409

Golconda (gahl•KAHN•duh) A city in the southeastern corner of Illinois; a point on the Trail of Tears. (37°N, 88°W) p. 404

Gonzales (gohn•ZAH•lays) A city in south central Texas; site of the first battle of the Texas Revolution. (30°N, 97°W) p. 385

Governors Island An island in New York Bay; located near the mouth of the East River. (41°N, 74°W) p. 498

Great Basin One of the driest parts of the United States; located in Nevada, Utah, California, Idaho, Wyoming, and Oregon; includes the Great Salt Lake Desert, the Mojave Desert, and Death Valley. p. 40

Great Bear Lake A lake located in northwest central Mackenzie district, Northwest Territories, Canada. p. 40

Great Lakes A chain of five lakes; located in central North America; the largest group of freshwater lakes in the world. p. 64

Great Plains A continental slope in western North America; borders the eastern base of the Rocky Mountains from Canada to New Mexico and Texas. p. 40

Great Salt Lake The largest lake in the Great Basin; located in northwestern Utah. p. 40

Great Slave Lake A lake in the south central mainland part of the Northwest Territories, Canada. p. 40

Greenland The largest island on Earth; located in the northern Atlantic Ocean, east of Canada. p. 41

Grenada (grah•NAY•duh) An island in the West Indies; the southernmost of the Windward Islands. p. 655

Groton (GRAH•tuhn) A town in southeastern Connecticut; located on Long Island Sound at the mouth of the Thames River. (41°N, 72°W) p. 186

Guadalajara A city in western central Mexico; capital of Jalisco state. (20°N, 103°W) p. 645

Guam (GWAHM) U.S. territory in the Pacific Ocean; largest of the Mariana Islands. p. 551

Guánica (GWAHN•ih•kah) A town in southwestern Puerto Rico; located on the Guánica Harbor. (18°N, 67°W) p. 549

Guantánamo Bay (gwahn•TAH•nah•moh) A bay in eastern Cuba; located on the southeastern coast of Oriente province. p. 614

Guatemala City A city in Central America; capital of Guatemala (the republic); largest city in Central America. (14°N, 90°W) p. 655

Guayaquil (gwy•ah•KEEL) A seaport in southwestern Ecuador; capital of Guayas province. (2°S, 80°W) p. 660

Guilford Courthouse (GIL•ferd) A location in north central North Carolina, near Greensboro; site of a major Revolutionary War battle in 1781. (36°N, 80°W) p. 265

Gulf of Alaska A northern inlet of the Pacific Ocean; located between the Alaska Peninsula and the southwestern coast of Canada. p. 40

Gulf of California An inlet of the Pacific Ocean located between Baja California and the northwestern coast of Mexico. p. 40

Gulf of Mexico An inlet of the Atlantic Ocean; located on the southeastern coast of North America; surrounded by the United States, Cuba, and Mexico. p. 40

Gulf of Panama A large inlet of the Pacific Ocean; located on the southern coast of Panama. p. 552

Gulf of St. Lawrence A deep gulf of the Atlantic Ocean, located on the eastern coast of Canada, between Newfoundland and the Canadian mainland. p. 148

Gunter's Landing A town in northeastern Alabama on the Tennessee River. (34°N, 86°W) p. 381

H

Haiti A country in the West Indies, occupying the western part of the island of Hispaniola. p. 549

Halifax The capital of the province of Nova Scotia, Canada; a major port on the Atlantic Ocean; remains free of ice all year. (44°N, 63°W) p. 663

Hampton Roads A channel in southeastern Virginia that flows into Chesapeake Bay; site of a Civil War naval battle in 1862 between two iron-clad ships, the *Monitor* and the *Merrimack*. p. 457

Harrodsburg A city in central Kentucky; located at an end of the Wilderness Road. (38°N, 85°W) p. 350

Hartford The capital of Connecticut. (42°N, 73°W) p. 186

Havana The capital of Cuba; located on the northwestern coast of the country. (23°N, 82°W) p. 140

Hawaiian Islands A chain of volcanic and coral islands; located in the north central Pacific Ocean. p. 551

Hawikuh (hah•wee•KOO) A former village in southwestern North America; located on the route of the Spanish explorer Coronado in present-day northwestern New Mexico. p. 140

Helena The capital of Montana (47°N, 112°W) p. 527

Hispaniola (ees•pah•NYOH•lah) An island in the West Indies made up of Haiti and the Dominican Republic; located in the Caribbean Sea between Cuba and Puerto Rico. p. 41

Honolulu (hahn•nuhl•OO•loo) Hawaii's capital and largest city. (21°N, 158°W) p. 586

Hopewell An ancient settlement of the Mound Builders; located in present-day southern Ohio. (39°N, 83°W) p. 64

Horseshoe Bend A location in eastern Alabama; site of a battle in the War of 1812; a present-day national military park. p. 360

Houston A city in southeastern Texas; third-largest port in the United States; leading industrial center in Texas. (30°N, 95°W) p. 343

Hudson Bay An inland sea in east central Canada surrounded by the Northwest Territories, Manitoba, Ontario, and Quebec. p. 41

Hudson River A river in the northeastern United States beginning in upper New York and flowing into the Atlantic Ocean; named for the explorer Henry Hudson. p. 86

I

Iceland An island country in the northern Atlantic Ocean, between Greenland and Norway. p. 593

Illinois River A river in western and central Illinois; flows southwest into the Mississippi River. p. 180

Independence A city in western Missouri; the starting point of the Oregon Trail. (39°N, 94°W) p. 390

Indianapolis Indiana's capital and largest city. (39°N, 86°W) p. 343

Isthmus of Panama (IHS•muhs) A narrow strip of land that connects North America and South America. p. 129

J

Jacksonville A city in northeastern Florida; located near the mouth of the St. Johns River. (30°N, 82°W) p. 343

Jamaica (juh•MAY•kuh) An island country in the West Indies, south of Cuba. p. 125

James River A river in central Virginia; begins where the Jackson and Cowpasture rivers join; flows east into Chesapeake Bay. p. 156

Jamestown The first permanent English settlement in the Americas; located in eastern Virginia, on the shore of the James River. (37°N, 76°W) p. 156

Jerusalem The capital of Israel; located in the central part of the country. (32°N, 35°E) p. 107

Juneau (JOO•noh) The capital of Alaska; located in the southeastern part of the state. (58°N, 134°W) p. 527

K

Kahoolawe (kah•hoh•uh•LAY•vay) One of the eight main islands of Hawaii; located west of Maui. p. 586

Kansas City The largest city in Missouri; located in the west central part of the state, on the Missouri River. (39°N, 95°W) p. 487

Kaskaskia (ka•SKAS•kee•uh) A village in southwestern Illinois; site of a major Revolutionary War battle in 1778. (38°N, 90°W) p. 265

Kauai (KOW•eye) The fourth-largest of the eight main islands of Hawaii. p. 586

Kennebec River (KEN•uh•bek) A river in west central and southern Maine; flows south from Moosehead Lake to the Atlantic Ocean. p. 186

Kennesaw Mountain (KEN•uh•saw) An isolated peak in northwestern Georgia, near Atlanta; site of a Civil War battle in 1864. p. 457

Kentucky River A river in north central Kentucky; flows northwest into the Ohio River. p. 350

Key West A city in southwestern Florida, on Key West Island. (25°N, 82°W) p. 549

Kings Mountain A ridge in northern South Carolina and southern North Carolina; site of a Revolutionary War battle in 1780. p. 265

Kingston A commercial seaport in the West Indies; capital of Jamaica. (18°N, 76°W) p. 655

Klondike An area in the Yukon Territory, Canada; gold was discovered there in 1896. p. 527

L

La Paz A city in South America; capital of Bolivia. (16°S, 68°W) p. 660

La Venta An ancient settlement of the Olmecs; located in present-day southern Mexico, on an island near the Tonalá River. (18°N, 94°W) p. 64

Labrador A peninsula in northeastern North America; once known as Markland. p. 41

Labrador Sea Located south of Greenland and northeast of North America. p. 41

Lake Champlain (sham•PLAYN) A lake between New York and Vermont. p. 86

Lake Erie The fourth-largest of the Great Lakes; borders Canada and the United States. p. 41

Lake Huron The second-largest of the Great Lakes; borders Canada and the United States. p. 41

Lake Michigan The third-largest of the Great Lakes; borders Michigan, Illinois, Indiana, and Wisconsin. p. 41

Lake Ontario The smallest of the Great Lakes; borders Canada and the United States. p. 41

Lake Superior The largest of the Great Lakes; borders Canada and the United States. p. 41

Lake Texcoco (tes•KOH•koh) A dry lake in present-day Mexico City; site of the ancient Aztec capital city of Tenochtitlán. p. 95

Lake Titicaca (tih•tih•KAH•kah) The highest navigable lake in the world; located on the border between Peru and Bolivia. p. 137

Lake Winnipeg A lake located in south central Manitoba, Canada. p. 41

Lanai (luh•NY) An island in central Hawaii; a major pineapple-producing area. p. 586

Lancaster A city in southeastern Pennsylvania. (40°N, 76°W) p. 188

Las Vegas (lahs VAY•guhs) A city in the southeastern corner of Nevada. (36°N, 115°W) p. 538

Lava Beds A national monument located in northern California; made of lava and ice caves; battleground of the Modoc Wars in 1873. p. 529

Leadville (LED•vil) A town in Colorado. (39°N, 106°W) p. 527

Leticia A town in southeastern Colombia, on the Amazon River. (4°S, 70°W) p. 660

Lexington A town in northeastern Massachusetts; site of the first battle of the Revolutionary War in 1775. (42°N, 71°W) p. 241

Liberty Island A small island in Upper New York Bay; the Statue of Liberty is located there; once known as Bedloe's Island. p. 498

Lima (LEE•mah) The capital of Peru; located on the Rimac River (12°S, 77°W) p. 660

Lisbon The capital of Portugal; a port city located in the western part of the country. (39°N, 9°W) p. 107

Little Bighorn A location near the Little Bighorn River in southern Montana; site of a fierce battle between Sioux and Cheyenne Indians and U.S. Army soldiers led by General George Armstrong Custer. p. 529

London A city located in the southern part of England; capital of present-day Britain. (52°N, 0°) p. 107

Long Island An island located east of New York City and south of Connecticut; lies between Long Island Sound and the Atlantic Ocean. p. 188

Los Adaes Site of a mission of New Spain; located in present-day eastern Texas. p. 175

Los Angeles The largest city in California; second-largest city in the United States; located in the southern part of the state. (34°N, 118°W) p. 280

Louisiana Purchase A territory in the west central United States; it doubled the size of the nation when it was purchased from France in 1803; extended from the Mississippi River to the Rocky Mountains, and from the Gulf of Mexico to Canada. p. 354

Louisville (LOO•ih•vil) The largest city in Kentucky; located in the north central part of the state, on the Ohio River. (38°N, 86°W) p. 343

M

Machu Picchu (mah•choo PEEK•choo) The site of an ancient Inca city on a mountain in the Andes, northwest of Cuzco, Peru. (13°S, 73°W) p. 137

Mackenzie River A river located in western Mackenzie district, Northwest Territories, Canada; flows north-northwest into Mackenzie Bay; second-longest river in North America. p. 40

Macon (MAY•kuhn) A city in central Georgia; located on the Ocmulgee River. (33°N, 84°W) p. 377

Madeira (mah•DAIR•uh) An island group in the eastern Atlantic Ocean, off the coast of Morocco. p. 125

Managua A city in Central America; capital of Nicaragua; located on the south shore of Lake Managua. (12°N, 86°W) p. 655

Manaus (mah•NOWS) A city located in western Brazil on the left bank of Rio Negro. (3°S, 60°W) p. 660

Manhattan An island in southeastern New York; located at the mouth of the Hudson River. (41°N, 74°W) p. 498

Manitoba (ma•nuh•TOH•buh) A province in central Canada; bordered by Hudson Bay, Ontario, the United States, and Saskatchewan; located on the Interior Plains of Canada. p. 663

Massachusetts Bay An inlet of the Atlantic Ocean on the eastern coast of Massachusetts; extends from Cape Ann to Cape Cod. p. 186

Matamoros (mah•tah•MOH•rohs) A town in Coahuila state, northeastern Mexico. (26°N, 97°W) p. 652

Maui (MOW•ee) The second-largest island in Hawaii. p. 586

Maumee River (maw•MEE) A river located in Indiana and Ohio; flows east and then northeast into Lake Erie. p. 265

Meadowcroft The site of an archaeological dig in southwestern Pennsylvania. p. 53

Medford A city in northeastern Massachusetts, north of Boston. (42°N, 71°W) p. 241

Mediterranean Sea (meh•duh•tuh•RAY•nee•uhn) An inland sea, enclosed by Europe on the west and north, Asia on the east, and Africa on the south. p. 116

Memphis A city in the southwestern corner of Tennessee; located on the Mississippi River. (35°N, 90°W) p. 409

Mendoza A city located southeast of Aconcagua in Argentina. (33°S, 69°W) p. 660

Menotomy Located in northeastern Massachusetts. p. 241

Mérida A city in southeastern Mexico; capital of Yucatán state. (21°N, 89°W) p. 645

Merrimack River A river in southern New Hampshire and northeastern Massachusetts; formed by the junction of the Pemigewasset and Winnipesaukee rivers; empties into the Atlantic. p. 186

Mesa Verde (MAY•suh VAIR•day) An ancient settlement of the Anasazi; located in present-day southwestern Colorado. (37°N, 108°W) p. 64

Mexico City A city on the southern edge of the Central Plateau; the present-day capital of Mexico. (19°N, 99°W) p. 168

Miami A city in southeastern Florida; located on Biscayne Bay. (26°N, 80°W) p. 614

Midway Islands A United States territory in the Pacific Ocean. p. 551

Milwaukee (mil•WAW•kee) The largest city in Wisconsin; located in the southeast part of the state, on Lake Michigan. (43°N, 88°W) p. 343

Minneapolis The largest city in Minnesota; located in the southeast central part of the state, on the Mississippi River; twin city with St. Paul. (45°N, 93°W) p. 487

Mississippi River The longest river in the United States; located centrally, its source is Lake Itasca in Minnesota; flows south into the Gulf of Mexico. p. 40

Missouri River A tributary of the Mississippi River; located centrally, it begins in Montana and ends at St. Louis, Missouri. p. 40

Mobile (moh•BEEL) The only seaport city in southern Alabama; located at the mouth of the Mobile River. (31°N, 88°W) p. 409

Mobile Bay An inlet of the Gulf of Mexico; located off the coast of southern Alabama; the site of a Civil War naval battle in 1864. p. 457

Mohawk River A river in central New York that flows east to the Hudson River. p. 86

Molokai (mah•luh•KY) An island in Hawaii. p. 586

Monte Albán (MAHN•tay ahl•BAHN) An ancient settlement of the Aztec civilization; located in present-day south central Mexico. (17°N, 97°W) p. 92

Monterrey A city in northeastern Mexico; capital of Nuevo León state. (25°N, 100°W) p. 645

Montevideo A seaport city located in the southern part of the north shore of La Plata estuary; capital of Uruguay. (35°S, 56°W) p. 660

Montgomery The capital of Alabama; located in the southeast central part of the state. (32°N, 86°W) p. 409

Montreal The largest city in present-day Canada; located in southern Quebec, on Montreal Island at the north bank of the St. Lawrence River. (46°N, 73°W) p. 148

Morristown A town in northern New Jersey, located west-northwest of Newark. (41°N, 74°W) p. 188

Moscow The capital and largest city of Russia; located in the western part of the country. (56°N, 38°E) p. 107

Moundville An ancient settlement of the Mound Builders; located in present-day central Alabama. (33°N, 88°W) p. 64

Mount Vernon The home and burial place of George Washington; located in Fairfax County, Virginia, on the Potomac River, below Washington, D.C. (39°N, 77°W) p. 329

Murfreesboro A city in central Tennessee; located on the west fork of the Stones River; a site on the Trail of Tears. (36°N, 86°W) p. 404

Mystic River A short river rising in the Mystic Lakes; located in northeastern Massachusetts; flows southeast into Boston Harbor north of Charlestown. p. 241

N

Narragansett Bay An inlet of the Atlantic Ocean in southeastern Rhode Island. (41°N, 71°W) p. 186

Nashville The capital of Tennessee. (36°N, 87°W) p. 343

Nassau A city on the northeastern coast of New Providence Island; capital of the Bahamas. (25°N, 77°W) p. 655

Natal A seaport city in northeastern Brazil. (5°S, 35°W) p. 660

Natchez A city in southwestern Mississippi; located on the Mississippi River. (32°N, 91°W) p. 281

Natchitoches (NAH•kuh•tahsh) The first settlement in present-day Louisiana; located in the northwest central part of the state. (32°N, 93°W) p. 354

Nauvoo (naw•VOO) A city in western Illinois; located on the Mississippi River; beginning of the Mormon Trail. (41°N, 91°W) p. 390

Nazca (NAHS•kah) Site of an Indian civilization; located on the west central coast of Peru. (15°S, 75°W) p. 137

New Amsterdam A Dutch city on Manhattan Island that later became New York City. (41°N, 74°W) p. 156

New Bern A city and port in southeastern North Carolina. (35°N, 77°W) p. 189

New Brunswick One of Canada's ten provinces; bordered by Quebec, the Gulf of St. Lawrence, Northumberland Strait, the Bay of Fundy, the United States, and Nova Scotia. p. 663

New Echota (ih•KOHT•uh) A Native American town in northwestern Georgia; chosen as the capital of the Cherokee Nation in 1819. (34°N, 85°W) p. 381

New France The possessions of France in North America from 1534 to 1763; included Canada, the Great Lakes region, and Louisiana. p. 169

New Guinea (GIH•nee) An island of the eastern Malay Archipelago; located in the western Pacific Ocean, north of Australia. p. 592

New Haven A city in southern Connecticut; located on New Haven Harbor. (41°N, 73°W) p. 186

New London A city in southeastern Connecticut; located on Long Island Sound at the mouth of the Thames River. (41°N, 72°W) p. 208

New Orleans The largest city in Louisiana; a major port located between the Mississippi River and Lake Pontchartrain. (30°N, 90°W) p. 169

New River A river in southwestern Virginia and southern West Virginia; flows north across Virginia and into south central West Virginia. p. 350

New Spain The former Spanish possessions from 1535 to 1821; included the southwestern United States, Mexico, Central America north of Panama, the West Indies, and the Philippines. p. 168

New York City The largest city in the United States; located in southeastern New York at the mouth of the Hudson River. (41°N, 74°W) p. 169

Newark A port in northeastern New Jersey; located on the Passaic River and Newark Bay. (41°N, 74°W) p. 188

Newfoundland (NOO•fuhn•luhnd) One of Canada's ten provinces; among the earliest Viking settlements in North America; once known as Vinland. p. 41

Newport A city on the southern end of Rhode Island; located at the mouth of Narragansett Bay. (41°N, 71°W) p. 186

Newton A city in south-central Kansas. (38°N, 97°W) p. 521

Niihau (NEE•how) An island in northwestern Hawaii. p. 586

Nome A city on the southern side of the Seward Peninsula; located in western Alaska. (65°N, 165°W) p. 527

Norfolk (NAWR•fawk) A city in southeastern Virginia; located on the Elizabeth River. (37°N, 76°W) p. 189

North Pole The northernmost point on the Earth. p. 124

Northwest Territories One of Canada's two territories; located in northern Canada. p. 663

Norwich A city located in east central Vermont. p. 294

Nova Scotia (NOH•vuh•SKOH•shuh) A province of Canada; located in the eastern part of the country, on a peninsula. p. 148

Nueces River (noo•AY•says) A river in southern Texas; flows into Nueces Bay, which is at the head of Corpus Christi Bay. p. 385

O

Oahu (oh•AH•hoo) The third-largest of eight main islands of Hawaii; Honolulu is located there. p. 586

Oakland A city in western California; located on the eastern side of San Francisco Bay. (38°N, 122°W) p. 498

Oaxaca (wuh•HAH•kuh) A city and state in southern Mexico. (17°N, 96°W) p. 645

Ocmulgee (ohk•MUHL•gee) An ancient settlement of the Mound Builders; located in present-day central Georgia. p. 64

Ocmulgee River (ohk•MUHL•gee) A river in central Georgia; formed by the junction of the Yellow and South rivers; flows south to join the Altamaha River. p. 189

Ogallala (oh•guh•LAHL•uh) A city in western Nebraska on the South Platte River. (41°N, 102°W) p. 521

Ohio River A tributary of the Mississippi River, beginning in Pittsburgh, Pennsylvania, and ending at Cairo, Illinois. p. 41

Omaha (OH•muh•hah) The largest city in Nebraska; located in the eastern part of the state, on the Missouri River. (41°N, 96°W) p. 390

Ontario (ahn•TAIR•ee•oh) One of Canada's ten provinces; located between Quebec and Manitoba. p. 663

Oregon Country A former region in western North America; located between the Pacific coast and the Rocky Mountains, from the northern border of California to Alaska. p. 269

Oregon Trail A former route to the Oregon Country; extending from the Missouri River northwest to the Columbia River in Oregon. p. 391

Orinoco River A river in Venezuela; flows west then north forming a section of the Colombia–Venezuela boundary, then turns east in central Venezuela and empties through a wide delta into the Atlantic Ocean. p. 660

Ottawa (AH•tuh•wuh) The capital of Canada; located in Ontario on the St. Lawrence Lowlands. (45°N, 75°W) p. 663

Outer Banks A chain of narrow peninsulas and islands off the coast of North Carolina. p. 152

P

Palenque (pah•LENG•kay) An ancient settlement of the Mayan civilization; located in present-day Chiapas, in southern Mexico. (18°N, 92°W) p. 92

Palmyra Island (pal•MY•ruh) One of the northernmost of the Line Islands; located in the central Pacific Ocean. p. 551

Palo Duro Canyon A canyon on the Red River; located in northwestern Texas; contains a state park. p. 529

Panama Canal A canal across the Isthmus of Panama; extends from the Caribbean Sea to the Gulf of Panama. p. 552

Panama City The capital of Panama; located in Central America. (9°N, 80°W) p. 655

Paraguay River A river in south central South America; empties into the Paraná at the southwestern corner of Paraguay. p. 660

Paramaribo A seaport city located on the Suriname River; capital of Suriname. (5°N, 55°W) p. 660

Paraná River A river in southeast central South America; formed by the joining of the Rio Grande and the Paranaíba River in south central Brazil. p. 660

Pearl Harbor An inlet on the southern coast of Oahu, Hawaii; the Japanese attacked an American naval base there on December 7, 1941. p. 586

Pecos River (PAY•kohs) A river in eastern New Mexico and western Texas; empties into the Rio Grande. p. 521

Pee Dee River A river in North Carolina and South Carolina; forms where the Yadkin and Uharie rivers meet; empties into Winyah Bay. p. 189

Perryville A city in east central Kentucky; site of a major Civil War battle in 1862. (38°N, 90°W) p. 409

Perth Amboy A port city in central New Jersey; located on Raritan Bay. (40°N, 74°W) p. 188

Petersburg A port city in southeastern Virginia; located on the Appomattox River; site of a series of Civil War battles from 1864 to 1865. (37°N, 77°W) p. 457

Philadelphia A city in southeastern Pennsylvania, on the Delaware River; a major United States port. (40°N, 75°W) p. 169

Philippine Islands A group of more than 7,000 islands off the coast of southeastern Asia, making up the country of the Philippines. p. 129

Pikes Peak A mountain in east central Colorado; part of the Rocky Mountains. p. 354

Pittsburgh The second-largest city in Pennsylvania; located in the southwestern part of the state, on the Ohio River. (40°N, 80°W) p. 281

Platte River (PLAT) A river in central Nebraska; flows east into the Missouri River below Omaha. p. 168

Plattsburg A city in northeastern New York; located on the western shore of Lake Champlain; site of a major battle in the War of 1812. (45°N, 73°W) p. 360

Plymouth A town in southeastern Massachusetts, on Plymouth Bay; site of the first settlement built by the Pilgrims, who sailed on the *Mayflower*. (42°N, 71°W) p. 156

Port Royal A town in western Nova Scotia, Canada; name changed to Annapolis Royal in honor of Queen Anne; capital city until 1749. (45°N, 66°W) p. 148

Port-au-Prince A seaport located on Hispaniola Island, in the West Indies, on the southeastern shore of the Gulf of Gonave; capital of Haiti. (18°N, 72°W) p. 655

Portland (ME) A port city in southwestern Maine; located on the Casco Bay. (44°N, 70°W) p. 294

Portland (OR) Oregon's largest city and principal port; located in the northwestern part of the state on the Willamette River. (46°N, 123°W) p. 514

Pôrto Alegre A seaport city in southern Brazil; located on an inlet at the northern end of Lagoa dos Patos. p. 660

Port-of-Spain A seaport in the northwestern part of the island of Trinidad on the Gulf of Paria; capital of Trinidad and Tobago. (10°N, 61°W) p. 655

Portsmouth (NH) (PAWRT•smuhth) A port city in southeastern New Hampshire; located at the mouth of the Picataqua River. (43°N, 71°W) p. 186

Portsmouth (RI) A town in southeastern Rhode Island; located on the Sakonnet River. (42°N, 71°W) p. 186

Potomac River (puh•TOH•muhk) A river on the Coastal Plain of the United States; begins in West Virginia and flows into Chesapeake Bay; Washington, D.C., is located on this river. p. 189

Potosí (poh•toh•SEE) One of the highest cities in the world; located in present-day south central Bolivia. (20°S, 66°W) p. 137

Prince Edward Island One of Canada's ten provinces; located in the Gulf of St. Lawrence. p. 663

Princeton A borough in west central New Jersey; site of a major Revolutionary War battle. (40°N, 75°W) p. 265

Providence Rhode Island's capital and largest city; located in the northern part of the state, at the head of the Providence River. (42°N, 71°W) p. 169

Puebla A city in southeastern central Mexico. (19°N, 98°W) p. 645

Pueblo (PWEH•bloh) A city in Colorado. p. 521

Pueblo Bonito (pweh•bloh boh•nee•toh) Largest of the prehistoric pueblo ruins; located in Chaco Canyon National Monument, New Mexico. p. 102

Puerto Rico An island of the West Indies; located southeast of Florida; a commonwealth of the United States. p. 41

Put-in-Bay A bay on South Bass Island, north of Ohio in Lake Erie; site of a major battle in the War of 1812. (42°N, 83°W) p. 360

Q

Quebec (kwih•BEK) The capital of the province of Quebec, Canada; located on the northern side of the St. Lawrence River; the first successful French settlement in the Americas; established in 1608. (47°N, 71°W) p. 148

Queens A borough of New York City; located on the western end of Long Island. (41°N, 74°W) p. 498

Quito (KEE•toh) A city in northwestern South America; located near the equator; present-day capital of Ecuador. (0°, 79°W) p. 137

R

Raleigh (RAW•lee) The capital of North Carolina; located in the east central part of the state. (36°N, 79°W) p. 34

Recife (rih•SEE•fee) A seaport located in eastern Brazil at the mouth of the Capibaribe River, near Point Plata. (8°S, 35°W) p. 660

Red Clay A town located in southeastern Tennessee; once part of the Cherokee Nation. p. 381

Red River A tributary of the Mississippi River; rises in eastern New Mexico, flows across Louisiana and into the Mississippi River; forms much of the Texas–Oklahoma border. p. 354

Regina (rih•JY•nuh) The capital of Saskatchewan, Canada; located in the southern part of the province. (50°N, 104°W) p. 663

Richmond The capital of Virginia; a port city located in the east central part of the state, on the James River. (38°N, 77°W) p. 189

Rio Balsas (BAHL•sahs) A river in southern Mexico. p. 40

Rio de Janeiro A commercial seaport in southeastern Brazil on the southwestern shore of Guanabara Bay. (23°S, 43°W) p. 660

Rio de la Plata A river on the southeastern coast of South America. p. 660

Rio Grande A river in southwestern North America; it begins in Colorado and flows into the Gulf of Mexico; forms the border between Texas and Mexico. p. 40

Rio Usumacinta (oo•sooh•mah•SIN•tah) A river located in southern Mexico; forms part of the border between Mexico and Guatemala. p. 92

Roanoke Island (ROH•uh•nohk) An island near the coast of North Carolina; the site of the lost colony. (36°N, 76°W) p. 152

Roanoke River A river in southern Virginia and northeastern North Carolina; flows east and southeast across the North Carolina border and into Albemarle Sound. p. 189

Rochester (RAH•chuh•stər) A port city located in western New York. (43°N, 78°W) p. 395

Rocky Mountains A range of mountains in the western United States and Canada, extending from Alaska to New Mexico; these mountains divide rivers that flow east from those that flow west. p. 40

Roxbury A residential district in southern Boston, Massachusetts; formerly a city, but became part of Boston in 1868; founded in 1630. (42°N, 71°W) p. 241

S

Sabine River (suh•BEEN) A river in eastern Texas and western Louisiana; flows southeast to the Gulf of Mexico. p. 385

Sacramento The capital of California; located in the north central part of the state, on the Sacramento River. (39°N, 121°W) p. 342
Sacramento River A river in northwestern California; rises near Mt. Shasta and flows south into Suisun Bay. p. 390
Salem A city on the northeastern coast of Massachusetts. (43°N, 71°W) p. 186
Salisbury (SAWLZ•bair•ee) A city in central North Carolina; the beginning of Boone's Trail. (36°N, 80°W) p. 294
Salt Lake City Utah's capital and largest city; located in the northern part of the state, on the Jordan River. (41°N, 112°W) p. 390
Salvador A seaport city in eastern Brazil, located on All Saints Bay. (13°S, 38°W) p. 660
San Antonio A city in south central Texas; located on the San Antonio River; site of the Alamo. (29°N, 98°W) p. 280
San Antonio River A river in southern Texas; flows southeast and empties into San Antonio Bay. p. 385
San Diego A large port city in southern California; located on San Diego Bay. (33°N, 117°W) p. 175
San Francisco The second-largest city in California; located in the northern part of the state, on San Francisco Bay. (38°N, 123°W) p. 175
San Francisco Bay An inlet of the Pacific Ocean, located in west central California. p. 498
San Jacinto (jah•SIN•toh) A location in southeastern Texas; site of a battle in the Texas Revolution in 1836. (31°N, 95°W) p. 385
San José A city in Central America; capital of Costa Rica. (10°N, 84°W) p. 655
San Jose A city in western California; located southeast of San Francisco Bay. (37°N, 122°W) p. 606
San Juan (san•WAHN) Puerto Rico's capital and largest city. (18°N, 66°W) p. 549
San Juan Hill (san•WAHN) A hill in eastern Cuba; captured by Cuban and American troops during the Spanish-American War in 1898. p. 549
San Juan River (san•WAHN) A river in Colorado, New Mexico, and Utah; flows southwest across the Colorado–New Mexico border, bends west and then northwest across southwestern Colorado, flows into Utah, and then empties into the Colorado River. p. 102
San Lorenzo An ancient settlement of the Olmecs; located in present-day southern Mexico. (29°N, 113°W) p. 64
San Salvador One of the islands in the southern Bahamas; Christopher Columbus landed there in 1492. p. 125
Santa Fe (SAN•tah FAY) The capital of New Mexico; located in the north central part of the state. (36°N, 106°W) p. 168
Santa Fe Trail A former commercial route to the western United States; extended from western Missouri to Santa Fe, in central New Mexico. p. 390
Santee River A river in southeast central South Carolina; formed by the junction of the Congaree and Wateree rivers; flows southeast into the Atlantic Ocean. p. 189
Santiago (san•tee•AH•goh) A seaport on the southern coast of Cuba; second-largest city in Cuba. (20°N, 75°W) p. 549
Santo Domingo The capital city of the Dominican Republic. (18°N, 70°W) p. 655
São Francisco River A river in eastern Brazil; flows north, northeast, and east into the Atlantic Ocean south of Maceió. p. 660
São Paulo A city in southeastern Brazil; capital of São Paulo state. p. 660
Saratoga A village on the western bank of the Hudson River in eastern New York; site of a major Revolutionary War battle in 1777; present-day Schuylerville. (43°N, 74°W) p. 265
Saskatchewan (suh•SKA•chuh•wahn) One of Canada's ten provinces; located between Alberta and Manitoba. p. 663
Savannah The oldest city and a principal seaport in Georgia; located in the southeastern part of the state, at the mouth of the Savannah River. (32°N, 81°W) p. 169
Savannah River A river that forms the border between Georgia and South Carolina; flows into the Atlantic Ocean at Savannah, Georgia. p. 189
Schenectady (skuh•NEK•tuh•dee) A city in eastern New York; located on the Mohawk River. (43°N, 74°W) p. 188
Seattle The largest city in Washington; a port city located in the west central part of the state, on Puget Sound. (48°N, 122°W) p. 514
Sedalia (suh•DAYL•yuh) A city in west central Missouri. (39°N, 93°W) p. 521
Seneca Falls (SEN•uh•kuh) A town located in west central New York on the Seneca River. (43°N, 77°W) p. 395
Serpent Mound An ancient settlement of the Mound Builders; located in present-day southern Ohio. (39°N, 83°W) p. 64
Shiloh (SHY•loh) A location in southwestern Tennessee; site of a major Civil War battle in 1862; also known as Pittsburg Landing. (35°N, 88°W) p. 457
Siberia A region in north central Asia, mostly in Russia. p. 48
Sierra Madre Occidental (see•AIR•ah MAH•dray ahk•sih•den•TAHL) A mountain range in western Mexico, running parallel to the Pacific coast. p. 40
Sierra Madre Oriental (awr•ee•en•TAHL) A mountain range in eastern Mexico, running parallel to the coast along the Gulf of Mexico. p. 40
Sierra Nevada A mountain range in eastern California that runs parallel to the Coast Ranges. p. 40
Silver City A town in southwestern New Mexico. (33°N, 108°W) p. 527
Snake River A river that begins in the Rocky Mountains and flows west into the Pacific Ocean; part of the Oregon Trail ran along this river. p. 168
Sonoran Desert An arid region in western North America; includes southwestern Arizona and southeastern California; in Mexico includes western Sonora and northern Baja California. p. 40
South Pass A pass in southwestern Wyoming; crosses the Continental Divide; part of the Oregon Trail. p. 390
South Pole The southernmost point on the Earth. p. 124
Spiro An ancient settlement of the Mound Builders; located in eastern Oklahoma. (35°N, 95°W) p. 64
Spokane (spoh•KAN) A city in eastern Washington on the falls of the Spokane River. (48°N, 117°W) p. 527
Spring Place A town in northwestern Georgia; once part of the Cherokee Nation. (35°N, 85°W) p. 381

Springfield (MA) A city in southwestern Massachusetts; located on the Connecticut River. (42°N, 73°W) p. 186

Springfield (MO) A city in southwestern Missouri. (37°N, 93°W) p. 404

St. Augustine (AW•guh•steen) A city on the coast of northeastern Florida; the oldest city founded by Europeans in the United States. (30°N, 81°W) p. 140

St. Croix (KROY) A city in Maine; located west of Port Royal. (45°N, 67°W) p. 148

St. Ignace (IG•nuhs) A city in Michigan; located on the southeastern side of Michigan's upper peninsula. (46°N, 85°W) p. 180

St. John's A city on the southeastern coast of Canada, on the Atlantic Ocean; the capital of Newfoundland. (47°N, 52°W) p. 663

St. Joseph A city in northwestern Missouri on the Missouri River. (40°N, 95°W) p. 521

St. Lawrence River A river in northeastern North America; begins at Lake Ontario and flows into the Atlantic Ocean; forms part of the border between the United States and Canada. p. 41

St. Louis A major port city in east central Missouri; known as the Gateway to the West. (38°N, 90°W) p. 181

St. Lucia An island and an independent state of the Windward Islands; located in the eastern West Indies, south of Martinique and north of St. Vincent. p. 655

St. Marys A village in southern Maryland; the capital until 1694; present-day St. Marys City. (38°N, 76°W) p. 189

St. Paul The capital of Minnesota; located in the eastern part of the state, on the Mississippi River. (45°N, 93°W) p. 487

Strait of Magellan (muh•JEH•luhn) The narrow waterway between the southern tip of South America and Tierra del Fuego; links the Atlantic Ocean with the Pacific Ocean. p. 129

Sucre A city in Bolivia, South America. (19°S, 65°W) p. 660

Sudbury River A river in western Massachusetts; connects with the Concord River. p. 241

Suriname A country in north-central South America. p. 660

Susquehanna River (suhs•kwuh•HA•nuh) A river in Maryland, Pennsylvania, and central New York; rises in Otsego Lake, New York, and empties into northern Chesapeake Bay. p. 86

T

Tampa A city in western Florida; located on the northeastern end of Tampa Bay. (28°N, 82°W) p. 549

Tegucigalpa A city in Central America; capital of Honduras. (14°N, 87°W) p. 655

Tennessee River A tributary of the Mississippi River; begins in eastern Tennessee and flows into the Ohio River in Kentucky. p. 181

Tenochtitlán (tay•nohch•teet•LAHN) The ancient capital of the Aztec Empire, on the islands of Lake Texcoco; located in present-day Mexico City, in southern Mexico. (19°N, 99°W) p. 92

Tiahuanaco (tee•ah•wah•NAH•koh) A site of prehistoric ruins, located in western South America, in present-day Bolivia. (17°S, 69°W) p. 137

Tikal (tih•KAHL) An ancient settlement of the Mayan civilization; located in present-day southern Central America. (17°N, 89°W) p. 92

Timbuktu A town in Mali; located in western Africa, near the Niger River. (17°N, 3°W) p. 107

Toledo (tuh•LEE•doh) A port city located in northwestern Ohio, at the southwestern corner of Lake Erie. (42°N, 84°W) p. 487

Tombstone A city in the southeastern corner of Arizona; formerly a mining center widely known for its rich silver mines. (32°N, 110°W) p. 527

Toronto The capital of the province of Ontario, in Canada; located near the northwestern end of Lake Ontario; third-largest city in Canada. (43°N, 79°W) p. 663

Trail of Tears A trail that was the result of the Indian Removal Act of 1830; extended from the Cherokee Nation to Fort Gibson, in the Indian Territory. p. 404

Treasure Island An artificial island in San Francisco Bay, California; present-day naval base. (38°N, 122°W) p. 498

Trenton The capital of New Jersey; located in the west central part of the state; site of a major Revolutionary War battle in 1776. (40°N, 75°W) p. 265

Tres Zapotes (TRAYS sah•POH•tays) An ancient settlement of the Olmecs; located in southern Mexico. (18°N, 95°W) p. 64

Trinidad and Tobago An independent state made up of the islands of Trinidad and Tobago; located in the Atlantic Ocean off the northeastern coast of Venezuela. p. 655

Troy A city in eastern New York; located on the eastern bank of the Hudson River and on the Erie Canal. (43°N, 74°W) p. 343

Tucson (TOO•sahn) A city in southern Arizona; located on the Santa Cruz River. (32°N, 111°W) p. 168

Tula An ancient settlement of the Aztec civilization; located in present-day central Mexico, north of Tenochtitlán. (23°N, 100°W) p. 92

Tumbes (TOOM•bays) A town in northwestern Peru; located on the Tumbes River, near the Peru-Ecuador border. (4°S, 80°W) p. 137

Turkey Town A town in eastern Alabama; once part of the Cherokee Nation. (34°N, 86°W) p. 381

Turtle Mound An ancient settlement of the Mound Builders; located on the present-day east central coast of Florida. (29°N, 81°W) p. 64

U

Uxmal (oosh•MAHL) An ancient settlement of the Mayan civilization; located in the northern Yucatán Peninsula. (20°N, 90°W) p. 92

V

Valdivia A city located in the Los Lagos region in south central Chile, on the Valdivia River. (39°S, 73°W) p. 660

Valley Forge A location in southeastern Pennsylvania, on the Schuylkill River; site of General George Washington's winter headquarters during the Revolutionary War. (40°N, 77°W) p. 265

Valparaíso A seaport located in Chile, west-northwest of Santiago on the Bay of Valparaíso; capital of Valparaíso. (33°S, 71°W) p. 660

Vancouver Canada's eighth-largest city; located where the northern arm of the Fraser River empties into the Pacific Ocean. (49°N, 123°W) p. 663

Vancouver Island An island off the southwestern coast of British Columbia, Canada. p. 40

Vandalia (van•DAYL•yuh) A city in south central Illinois. (39°N, 89°W) p. 377

Venice A port city in northeastern Italy; located on 118 islands in the Lagoon of Venice. (45°N, 12°E) p. 107

Veracruz (veh•rah•KROOZ) A seaport in Veracruz, Mexico; located in the eastern part of the country, on the Gulf of Mexico. (19°N, 96°W) p. 136

Vicksburg A city in western Mississippi; located on the Mississippi River; site of a major Civil War battle in 1863. (32°N, 91°W) p. 409

Victoria The capital of British Columbia, Canada; located on Vancouver Island. (48°N, 123°W) p. 663

Victoria Island The third-largest of Canada's Arctic Islands; located north of the central mainland part of the Northwest Territories. p. 40

Vincennes (vihn•SENZ) A town in southwestern Indiana; oldest town in Indiana. (39°N, 88°W) p. 169

Virginia City A village in western Nevada. (39°N, 119°W) p. 527

W

Wabash River (WAW•bash) A river in western Ohio and Indiana; flows west and south to the Ohio River, to form part of the Indiana–Illinois border. p. 265

Wake Island A United States territory in the Pacific Ocean. p. 551

Warrior's Path A Native American path that began in North Carolina and crossed the Appalachian Mountains to Kentucky and Ohio. p. 350

Washington, D.C. The capital of the United States; located between Maryland and Virginia, on the Potomac River in a special district that is not part of any state. (39°N, 77°W) p. 281

West Indies The islands stretching from Florida in North America to Venezuela in South America. p. 198

West Point A United States military post since the Revolutionary War; located in southeastern New York on the western bank of the Hudson River p. 265

Whitehorse The capital of the Yukon Territory, Canada; located on the southern bank of the Yukon River. (60°N, 135°W) p. 663

Whitman Mission Site of a Native American mission, established in 1836 by Marcus Whitman and his wife; located in present-day southeastern Washington. p. 390

Wilderness Road A pioneer road that began in Tennessee and crossed the Appalachian Mountains into Kentucky. p. 350

Williamsburg A city in southeastern Virginia; located on a peninsula between the James and York rivers. (37°N, 77°W) p. 169

Wilmington A city in northern Delaware; located where the Delaware and Christina rivers meet Brandywine Creek. (40°N, 76°W) p. 169

Winchester A city in northern Virginia; located in the Shenandoah Valley. (39°N, 78°W) p. 294

Winnipeg The capital of the province of Manitoba, in Canada; located on the Red River; fourth-largest city in Canada. (50°N, 97°W) p. 663

Wisconsin River A river located in central Wisconsin that flows south and southeast to the Mississippi River. p. 180

Y

Yadkin River The upper course of the Pee Dee River; flows south across North Carolina. p. 350

Yagul An ancient settlement of the Aztec civilization; located in present-day southern Mexico. p. 92

Yellowknife A town in southern Mackenzie district, Canada; located on the northwestern shore of Great Slave Lake at the mouth of the Yellowknife River; capital of the Northwest Territories. (62°N, 114°W) p. 663

Yellowstone River A river in northwestern Wyoming, southeastern Montana, and northwestern North Dakota; flows northwest to the Missouri River. p. 354

Yorktown A small town in southeastern Virginia; located on Chesapeake Bay; site of the last major Revolutionary War battle in 1781. (37°N, 76°W) p. 265

Yucatán Peninsula (yoo•kah•TAN) A peninsula in southeastern Mexico and northeastern Central America; separated from Cuba by the Yucatán Channel. p. 41

Yukon River A river that begins in the southwestern part of the Yukon Territory, Canada; flows through Alaska, and empties into the Bering Sea. p. 40

Yukon Territory One of Canada's two territories; bordered by the Arctic Ocean, the Northwest Territories, British Columbia, and Alaska. p. 663

Glossary

The Glossary contains important social studies words and their definitions. Each word is respelled as it would be in a dictionary. When you see this mark (´) after a syllable, pronounce that syllable with more force than the other syllables. The page number at the end of the definition tells where to find the word in your book.

add, **ā**ce, **câ**re, **pä**lm; **e**nd, **ē**qual; **i**t, **ī**ce; **o**dd, **ō**pen, **ô**rder; t**o͝o**k, p**o͞o**l; **u**p, b**û**rn; y**o͞o** as *u* in *fuse*; **oi**l; p**ou**t; **ə** as *a* in *above*, *e* in *sicken*, *i* in *possible*, *o* in *melon*, *u* in *circus*; **ch**eck; ri**ng**; **th**in; **th**is; **zh** as in *vision*

A

abolish (ə•bä′lish) To end. p. 393

abolitionist (a•bə•li′shən•ist) A person who wants to abolish slavery. p. 393

absolute location (ab′sə•lo͞ot lō•kā′shən) Exact location on the Earth. p. 31

adobe (ä•dō′bā) A mixture of sand and straw that is dried into bricks. p. 66

agent (ā′jənt) A person who does business for other people. p. 149

agriculture (a′grə•kul•chər) Farming. p. 59

airlift (âr′lift) A system of delivering supplies by airplane. p. 611

allegiance (ə•lē′jənts) Loyalty. p. 252

alliance (ə•lī′əns) Partnership. p. 559

ally (al′ī) A friend, especially in time of war. p. 226

ambassador (am•ba′sə•dər) A representative from one country to another. p. 286

amendment (ə•mend′mənt) An addition or change to the Constitution. p. 322

analyze (a′nəl•īz) To break something into its parts and look closely at how those parts connect with one another. p. 29

annex (ə•neks′) To add on. p. 362

Anti-Federalist (an′tī•fe′də•rə•list) A citizen who was against ratification of the Constitution. p. 318

apprentice (ə•pren′təs) A person who learns a trade by living with the family of a skilled worker and working for several years. p. 198

archaeologist (är•kē•o′lə•jist) A scientist who studies the cultures from people from long ago. p. 49

arid (âr′əd) Very dry. p. 76

armada (är•mä′dä) A fleet of warships. p. 152

armistice (är′mə•stis) An agreement to stop fighting. p. 550

arms control (ärmz kən•trōl′) A limit to the number of weapons nations can have. p. 634

arms race (ärmz rās) Competition between countries for the most bombs and the most powerful weapons. p. 615

artifact (är′tə•fakt) An object that early people had made. p. 49

assassination (ə•sa•sən•ā′shən) The murder of a political leader such as a President. p. 458

assembly line (ə•sem′blē līn) A system of mass production in which parts of a product, such as a car, are put together as they move past a line of workers. p. 570

auction (ôk′shən) A public sale. p. 202

authority (ə•thär′ə•tē) Control over someone or something. p. 228

aviation (ā•vē•ā′shən) Air transportation. p. 571

B

backcountry (bak′kən•trē) An area beyond settled lands. p. 204

band (band) A small group of people who work together to do activities. p. 48

barbed wire (bärbd wīr) A wire with sharp points or barbs along it used to make fences. p. 523

barrio (bär′ē•ō) A neighborhood of Spanish-speaking people. p. 497

barter (bär′tər) To exchange goods with other people. p. 74

bill (bil) An idea for a new law. p. 298

Bill of Rights (bil uv rīts) A list of freedoms that was added to the Constitution as the first ten amendments. p. 322

blockade (blä•kād′) To use warships to prevent other ships from entering or leaving a harbor. p. 239

bonanza farm (bə•nan′zə färm) A large farm on the Great Plains in which people from the East invested money. p. 515

boom (bo͞om) A time of quick economic growth. p. 526

border state (bôr′dər stāt) During the Civil War, a state between the North and the South that allowed slavery but did not secede from the Union. p. 441

borderlands (bôr′dər•landz) Areas of land on or near the borders of two adjoining countries, colonies, or regions. p. 173

boycott (boi′kät) A refusal to buy goods or services. p. 234

broker (brō′kər) A person who is paid to buy and sell for someone else. p. 201

buffer (bu′fər) An area of land that serves as a barrier. p. 173

bureaucracy (byo͝o•rok'rə•sē) The many workers and groups needed to run government programs. p. 576
bust (bust) A time of quick economic decline. p. 526

C

Cabinet (kab'nit) The group of the President's most important advisers. p. 326
campaign (kam•pān') A race for office. p. 329
canal (kə•nal') A human-made waterway. p. 375
capital resource (kap'ə•təl rē'sôrs) Money to run a business. p. 484
cardinal direction (kär'də•nəl də•rek'shən) One of the main directions: north, south, east, or west. p. 35
carpetbagger (kär'pət•ba•gər) A Northerner who went to the South after the Civil War to try to help with Reconstruction or to make money buying land or opening a business. p. 467
cartogram (kär'tə•gram) A map that shows information by changing the sizes of places. p. 652
cartographer (kär•tä'grə•fər) A person who makes maps. p. 113
cash crop (kash krop) A crop that people raise to sell rather than to use themselves. p. 183
cause (coz) Any action that makes something happen. p. 29
cease-fire (sēs•fīr') An end to shooting and bombing. p. 613
census (sen'səs) A population count. p. 302
century (sen'chə•rē) A period of 100 years. p. 61
ceremony (ser'ə•mō•nē) A service performed for a special purpose, such as for a religion. p. 77
charter (chär'tər) A document giving a person or group official approval to take a certain action. p. 183
checks and balances (cheks and ba'lən•səz) A system that gives each branch of government different powers so that each branch can check the authority of the others. p. 305
chronology (krə•nä'lə•jē) Time order. p. 29
citizen (si'tə•zən) A member of a town, state, or country. p. 19
city-state (si'tē•stāt) A city that has its own ruler and government. p. 90
civil rights (si'vəl rīts) The rights guaranteed to all citizens by the Constitution. p. 558
civil war (si'vəl wôr) A war between people of the same country. p. 137
civilian (sə•vil'yən) A person who is not in the military. p. 586
civilization (si•və•lə•zā'shən) A culture that has developed forms of government, religion, and learning. p. 62
claim (klām) To declare that you or your country owns something. p. 141
clan (klan) A group of families that are related to one another. p. 73
class (klas) A group of people treated with the amount of respect that is given to the group's place in society. p. 90
classify (kla'sə•fī) To sort. p. 191
climograph (klī'mə•graf) A graph that shows the average monthly temperature and the average monthly precipitation for a place. p. 518
cold war (kōld wôr) A war fought with propaganda and money rather than with soldiers and weapons. p. 593
colonist (kä'lə•nist) A person who lives in a colony. p. 143
colony (kä'lə•nē) A settlement ruled by another country. p. 143
commercial industry (kə•mûr'shəl in'dəs•trē) An industry run to make a profit. p. 571
commission (kə•mi'shən) A special committee. p. 556
Committee of Correspondence (kə•mi'tē uv kôr•ə•spän'dəns) A group set up in each of the colonies to quickly share information about taxes and other issues by writing letters to groups in the other colonies. p. 238
common (kä'mən) An open area where sheep and cattle grazed. p. 195
commonwealth (kom'ən•welth) An area whose people have the rights of citizens of the mother country but that functions mostly independently. p. 654
communism (kom'yə•niz•əm) A social and economic system in which all industries, land, and businesses are owned by a government. p. 593
compact (käm'pakt) An agreement. p. 155
compass (kəm'pəs) An instrument used to find direction. It has a needle that always points north. p. 117
compass rose (kəm'pəs rōz) A direction marker on a map. p. 35
compromise (käm'prə•mīz) To give up some of what you want in order to reach an agreement. p. 296
concentration camp (kon•sən•trā'shən kamp) A guarded camp where prisoners are held. p. 583
conclusion (kən•klo͞o'zhən) A decision or an idea reached by thoughtful study. p. 127
Conestoga (kä•nə•stō'gə) A large covered wagon used by farmers to carry their produce to market towns. p. 196
Confederacy (kən•fe'də•rə•sē) The Confederate States of America, a new country that was formed by Southern states that seceded from the Union after Abraham Lincoln was elected President in 1860. p. 432
confederation (kən•fe•də•rā'shən) A loosely united group of governments. p. 86
congress (kän'grəs) A meeting of representatives who have the authority to make decisions. p. 236
conquistador (kän•kēs'tə•dôr) Any of the Spanish conquerors in the Americas during the early 1500s. p. 136

R69

consequence (kän′sə•kwens) The result of an action. p. 239
conservation (kon•sər•vā′shən) Keeping resources and the environment from being wasted or destroyed. p. 556
consolidate (kən•sä′lə•dāt) To join one business with another. p. 485
constitution (kän•stə•tōō′shən) A plan of government. p. 285
consumer good (kən•sōō′mər good) A product made for personal use. p. 569
Continental (kän•tən•en′təl) A soldier in the first colonial army, which was headed by George Washington. p. 249
Continental Congress (kän•tən•en′təl kän′grəs) A meeting of representatives of the British colonies. p. 240
convention (kən•ven′shən) An important meeting. p. 291
corporation (kôr•pə•rā′shən) A business that sells shares of stock to investors. p. 484
cotton gin (kä′tən jin) A machine that removes the seeds from cotton fibers. p. 417
council (koun′səl) A group that makes laws. p. 86
county (koun′tē) A large part of a colony. Today, it is a part of a state. A county has its own local government. p. 197
county seat (koun′tē sēt) The main town for a large part of a colony. Today, it is the city where a county government is located. p. 197
coureur de bois (kōō•rûr′də bwä) A French word meaning "runner of the woods." This was a person who traded with American Indians for furs. p. 207
cultural diffusion (kul′chə•rəl di•fyōō′zhən) The spread of a culture from one place to another. p. 63
cultural region (kul′chə•rəl rē′jən) An area where peoples share some ways of life. p. 71
culture (kul′chər) A people's way of life. pp. 21, 49

D

D day (dē dā) June 6, 1944, the day the World War II Allies worked together in the largest water-to-land invasion in history. p. 589
debate (di•bāt′) To argue opposite sides of an issue. p. 298
debtor (de′tər) A person who had been in prison for owing money. p. 189
decade (de′kād) A period of ten years. p. 61
declaration (de•klə•rā′shən) An official statement. p. 253
deficit (def′ə•sit) A budget shortage caused by spending more money than is earned. p. 638
deforestation (dē•fôr•ə•stā′shən) The widespread cutting down of forests. p. 660
delegate (de′li•gət) A representative. p. 291
democracy (di•mä′krə•sē) A government in which the people take part. p. 225
depression (di•presh′ən) A period during which there is little money and little economic growth, and many people are out of work. p. 575
desertion (di•zûr′shən) Running away from duties, such as military service. p. 142
détente (dā•tänt′) The easing of military tensions between countries. p. 635
dictator (dik′tā•tər) A leader who has total authority. p. 384
distortion (di•stôr′shən) An area that is not accurate on a map. p. 554
diversity (də•vûr′sə•tē) Differences, such as those among different peoples. p. 71
doctrine (däk′trən) A government plan of action. p. 362
dove (duv) A person who supports an end to the fighting of a war. p. 629
drought (drout) A long dry spell. p. 67
due process of law (dōō prä′ses uv lä) A process that guarantees the right to a fair public trial. p. 322
dugout (dug′out) A boat made from a large, hollowed-out log. p. 73

E

earthwork (ərth′wərk) A mound, or hill of earth, that people have built. p. 63
economy (i•kä′nə•mē) The way people use resources to meet their needs. p. 37
effect (i•fekt′) What happens because of an action. p. 29
electoral college (i•lek′tə•rəl kä′lij) A group of electors chosen by citizens to vote for the President. p. 303
elevation (e•lə•vā′shən) The height of land. p. 391
Emancipation Proclamation (i•man•sə•pā′shən prä•klə•mā′shən) The presidential order of 1863 that freed enslaved people in the Confederate states. p. 445
embargo (im bär′gō) A refusal by one country to trade its goods with another country. p. 656
emperor (em′pər•ər) The ruler of an empire. p. 93
empire (em′pīr) A conquered land of many peoples and places governed by one ruler. p. 93
encounter (in•koun′tər) A meeting, such as one between peoples who have never met before. p. 112
encroach (in•krōch′) To move onto without asking permission. p. 258
enlist (in•list′) To join. p. 250
entrepreneur (än•trə•prə•nûr′) A person who sets up a new business, taking a chance on making or losing money. p. 484
equality (i•kwä′lə•tē) The same rights for all people. p. 393
evidence (e′və•dəns) Proof. p. 50

executive branch (ig•ze′kyə•tiv branch) The branch of government that carries out the laws. p. 302
expedition (ek•spə•di′shən) A journey made for a special reason. p. 129
exploration (ek•splə•rā′shən) Searching the unknown. p. 113
export (ek′spôrt) A good sent from one country to another to be sold. p. 197
extinct (ik•stingkt′) No longer living, like a kind of animal that has died out. p. 58

F

fact (fakt) A statement that can be proved true. p. 131
fall line (fôl līn) A location where the land drops sharply, causing the rivers to form waterfalls. p. 204
farm produce (färm prō′do͞os) Grains, fruits, and vegetables that farmers can trade for goods and services or sell for money. p. 196
federal system (fe′də•rəl sis′təm) A governing system in which the states share authority with the national government. p. 296
Federalist (fe′də•rə•list) A citizen who was in favor of ratifying the Constitution. p. 318
federation (fe•də•rā′shən) An organization made up of many related groups. p. 492
forty-niner (fôr•tē•nī′nər) A gold seeker who arrived in California in the year 1849. p. 389
free election (frē i•lek′shən) An election in which there is a choice of candidates. p. 657
free enterprise (frē en′tər•prīz) An economic system in which people are able to start and run their own businesses with little control by the government. p. 483
free state (frē stāt) A state that did not allow slavery. p. 426
free world (frē wûrld) The United States and its allies who worked together to fight communism. p. 593
free-trade agreement (frē•trād ə•grē′mənt) A treaty in which countries agree to charge no tariffs, or taxes, on goods they buy from and sell to each other. p. 645
front (frunt) A battle line. p. 589
Fundamental Orders (fən•də•men′təl ôr′dərz) The first written system of government in North America. It was adopted in Connecticut. p. 186

G

generalization (jen•rə•lə•zā′shən) A statement that summarizes facts and shows how they are related. p. 208
geographer (jē•ä′grə•fər) A person whose work is to study geography. p. 31
Gettysburg Address (ge′tēz•bûrg ə•dres′) A short speech given by Abraham Lincoln in 1863 at the dedication of a cemetery at Gettysburg. p. 455
glacier (glā′shər) A huge sheet of ice. p. 48
grant (grant) A gift of money to be used for a special purpose. p. 139
grid (grid) On a map, the north-south and east-west lines that cross each other to form a pattern of squares. p. 36
grievance (grē′vəns) A complaint. p. 254

H

hacienda (ä•sē•en′dä) A large estate. p. 174
hatch lines (hach līnz) A pattern of lines often used on historical maps to indicate land that was claimed by two or more countries. p. 229
hawk (hôk) A person who supports the fighting of a war. p. 629
heritage (her′ə•tij) Culture that has come from the past and continues today. p. 37
historical empathy (hi•stôr′i•kəl em′pə•thē) Understanding the actions and feelings of people from other times and other places. p. 28
hogan (hō′gän) A cone-shaped house built by covering a log frame with mud or grass. p. 79
Holocaust (hol′ə•kôst) The murder of more than six million people in concentration camps during World War II. p. 591
homesteader (hōm′sted•ər) A person who settled government land between 1862 and 1900. p. 513
hostage (hos′tij) A person held as a prisoner by a captor until demands are met. p. 635
hub (hub) A city where many trains make stops on their way to different destinations. p. 487
human features (hyo͞o′mən fē′chərz) The buildings, bridges, farms, roads, and people themselves that are found in a place. p. 32
human resource (hyo͞o′mən rē′sôrs) A person who is a worker. p. 490
human rights (hyo͞o′mən rīts) Freedoms that all people should have. p. 323
hydroelectric dam (hī•drō•i•lek′trik dam) A dam that uses stored water to generate electricity. p. 578

I

immigrant (i′mi•grənt) A person who comes to live in a country from his or her home country. p. 188
impeach (im•pēch′) To accuse a government official, such as the President, of wrongdoing. p. 304
imperialism (im•pir′ē•ə•liz•əm) Empire building. p. 548
import (im′pôrt) A good brought into one country from another, to be sold. p. 196
impressment (im•pres′mənt) Forcing people into military service. p. 360

indentured servant (in•den′shərd sər′vənt) A person who agrees to work for another person without pay for a certain length of time in return for travel expenses. p. 201
independence (in•də•pen′dəns) Freedom to govern on one's own. p. 252
indigo (in′di•gō) A plant from which blue dye is made. p. 189
Industrial Revolution (in•dus′trē•əl re•və•lo͞o′shən) A time during the late 1700s and early 1800s when new inventions changed the way people lived, worked, and traveled. p. 373
inflation (in•flā′shən) An economic condition in which it takes more and more money to buy the same goods. p. 287
inset map (in′set map) A small map within a larger map. p. 36
installment buying (in•stôl′mənt bī′ing) Paying a small part of the purchase price for an item, taking it home, and paying the remaining cost on a schedule. p. 569
integration (in•tə•grā′shən) The bringing together of people of all races in education, jobs, and housing. p. 624
interchangeable parts (in•tər•chān′jə•bəl pärts) Identical copies of parts made by machines so that if one part breaks, an identical one can be installed. p. 374
interest rate (in′tə•rəst rāt) The amount that a bank charges customers to borrow money. p. 644
intermediate direction (in•tər•mē′dē•it də•rek′shən) One of the in-between directions: northeast, northwest, southeast, or southwest. p. 35
interpreter (in•tûr′prə•tər) A person who translates from one language to another. p. 156
invest (in•vest′) To buy a share of a business in the hope of making a profit. p. 484
Iroquois League (ir′ə•kwoi lēg) A group of Iroquois tribes that worked together for peace. p. 86
island-hopping (ī′lənd•hä′ping) The process of the Allies capturing island after island as they advanced toward Japan. p. 591
isolation (ī•sə•lā′shən) Remaining separate from other countries. p. 563
isthmus (is′məs) A narrow strip of land that connects two larger land areas. p. 128

J

jazz (jaz) A kind of music that grew out of the African American musical heritage. p. 572
judicial branch (jo͞o•di′shəl branch) The branch of government that settles differences about the meaning of the laws. p. 302
jury (jûr′ē) A group of citizens who decide a case in court. p. 323
justice (jus′təs) A judge who serves on the Supreme Court. p. 304

K

kachina (kə•chē′nə) One of the spirits that are important in the religion of the Hopis and other Pueblo peoples. p. 77
kiva (kē′və) A special underground room where the Anasazi held religious services. p. 67
knoll (nōl) A small, round hill. p. 112

L

labor union (lā′bər yo͞on′yən) A group of workers who take action to improve their working conditions. p. 491
legend (le′jənd) A story handed down over time, often to explain the past. p. 86
legislative branch (le′jəs•lā•tiv branch) The branch of government that makes the laws. p. 302
legislature (le′jəs•lā•chər) The lawmaking branch of a colony, a state government, or the national government. p. 226
liberate (li′bə•rāt) To set free. p. 659
liberty (lib′ər•tē) Freedom. p. 234
lines of latitude (līnz uv la′tə•to͞od) East-west lines on a map or globe that are always the same distance apart. Also called parallels. p. 36
lines of longitude (līnz uv lon′jə•to͞od) North-south lines on a map or globe that run from pole to pole. Also called meridians. p. 36
locator (lō′kā•tər) A small map or picture of a globe. It shows where the area shown on the main map is located in a state, in a country, on a continent, or in the world. p. 35
locomotive (lō•kə•mō′tiv) A railroad engine. p. 378
lodge (läj) A circular house built over a shallow pit and covered with sod. p. 81
loft (loft) The part of a house between the ceiling and the roof. p. 205
long drive (long drīv) A cattle drive in which Texas ranchers drove herds of cattle north to be sold in northern markets. p. 521
longhouse (long′hous) A long wooden building in which several Indian families lived together. p. 86
Loyalist (loi′ə•list) A colonist who supported the British monarch and laws. p. 232

M

mainland (mān′land) The main part of a continent, rather than an island near the continent. p. 139
maize (māz) Corn. p. 60
majority (mə•jôr′ə•tē) The greater part of a whole. p. 302

Manifest Destiny (ma′nə•fest des′tə•nē) The belief shared by many Americans that it was the certain future of the United States to stretch from the Atlantic Ocean to the Pacific Ocean. p. 383

map key (map kē) A part of a map that explains what the symbols on the map stand for. Also called a legend. p. 35

map scale (map skāl) A part of a map that compares a distance on the map to a distance in the real world. p. 35

map title (map tī′təl) Words on a map that describe the subject of the map. p. 35

mass production (mas prə•duk′shən) A way of manufacturing that produces large amounts of goods at one time. p. 374

massacre (ma′si•kər) The killing of people who cannot defend themselves. p. 237

Mayflower Compact (mā′flou•ər käm′pakt) An agreement by those on the *Mayflower* to make and obey laws for their colony. This was the first example of self-rule by American colonists. p. 155

mercenary (mer′sən•âr•ē) A hired soldier. p. 249

meridians (mə•ri′dē•ənz) North-south lines on a map or globe that run from pole to pole. Also called lines of longitude. p. 124

merit system (mer′ət sis′təm) A way of making sure that the most qualified people get government jobs. p. 557

mesa (mā′sä) A high, flat-topped hill. p. 66

mestizo (me•stē′zō) A person of mixed Native American and European background. p. 659

metropolitan area (met•rə•pol′ə•tən âr′ē•ə) A city and all the suburbs and other population areas around it. p. 643

middle class (mid′əl klas) An economic level between the poor and the wealthy. p. 644

migration (mī•grā′shən) A movement of people from one place to another. p. 47

military draft (mil′ə•ter•ē draft) A way of bringing people into the military. p. 560

militia (mə•li′shə) A volunteer army. p. 195

millennium (mə•le′nē•əm) A period of 1,000 years. p. 61

minimum wage (min′ə•məm wāj) The lowest pay a worker can receive by law. p. 577

Minuteman (mi′nət•man) A member of the Massachusetts colony militia who could quickly be ready to fight the British. p. 241

missile (mi′səl) A rocket that can carry a bomb thousands of miles. p. 614

mission (mi′shən) A small religious community. p. 175

missionary (mi′shə•ner•ē) A person who teaches his or her religion to others. p. 143

monarch (mä′närk) A king or queen. p. 117

monopoly (mə•nop′ə•lē) To have almost complete control. p. 486

movement (mo͞ov′mənt) An effort by many people. p. 257

N

nationalism (na′shə•nəl•i•zəm) Pride in a country. p.362

naturalization (na•chə•rə•lə•zā′shən) The process of becoming an American citizen by living in the country for five years and then passing a test. p. 499

navigation (na•və•gā′shən) The study or act of planning and controlling the course of a ship. p. 118

negotiate (ni•gō′shē•āt) To talk with one another to work out an agreement. p. 269

neutral (no͞o′trəl) Not taking a side in a conflict. p. 256

noble (nō′bəl) A person from an important family. p. 91

nomad (nō′mad) A wanderer who has no settled home. p. 48

no-man's-land (nō′manz•land) In a war, land that is not held by either side but is filled with obstacles such as barbed wire and land mines. p. 561

nonviolence (nän•vī′ə•ləns) The use of peaceful ways to bring about change. p. 623

Northwest Passage (nôrth•west′ pa′sij) A water route that explorers wanted to find so that traders could cut through North America to Asia. p. 147

O

olive branch (ä′liv branch) A symbol of peace. p. 247

open range (ō′pən rānj) The huge unfenced grassland area of the Great Plains where cattle were allowed to roam and graze. p. 522

opinion (ə•pin′yən) A statement that tells what a person believes. p. 131

opportunity cost (ä•pər•to͞o′nə•tē kost) The cost of giving up one thing to get another. p. 243

oral history (ôr′əl his′tə•rē) Accounts that tell the experiences of people who did not have a written language or who did not write down what happened. p. 27

ordinance (ôr′də•nəns) A law or a set of laws. p. 289

origin story (ôr′ə•jən stōr′ē) A story that tells of a people's beliefs about the world and their place in it. p. 50

override (ō′və•rīd) A vote to cancel. p. 305

overseer (ō′vər•sē•ər) A person who was hired to watch slaves to see that they did their work. p. 421

P

pacifist (pa′sə•fist) A believer in a peaceful settlement of differences. p. 257

parallels (pâr′ə•lelz) East-west lines on a map or globe that are always the same distance apart. Also called lines of latitude. p. 124

Parliament (pär'lə•mənt) The part of the British government in which members make laws for the British people. p. 225

pathfinder (path'fīn•dər) Someone who finds a way through an unknown region. p. 355

Patriot (pā'trē•ət) A colonist who was against British rule. p. 241

patriotism (pā'trē•ə•ti•zəm) Love of one's country. p. 324

permanent (pər'mə•nənt) Long-lasting. p. 173

perspective (pər•spek'tiv) Point of view. p. 28

petition (pə•ti'shən) A request for action signed by many people. p. 234

physical features (fi'zi•kəl fē'chərz) The landforms, bodies of water, climate, soil, plant and animal life, and other natural resources that a place has. p. 32

pilgrim (pil'grəm) A person who makes a journey for a religious reason. p. 154

pioneer (pī•ə•nir') A person who first settles a new place. p. 349

pit house (pit hous) A house built partly over a hole dug in the earth so that some of its rooms are under the ground. p. 73

plantation (plan•tā'shən) A huge farm. p. 143

political boss (pə•li'ti•kəl bôs) An elected official—especially a mayor—who has many dishonest employees and who is able to control the government. p. 557

political cartoon (pə•li'ti•kəl kär•to͞on') A cartoon that expresses opinions about politics or about government. p. 251

political party (pə•li'ti•kəl pär'tē) A group of people involved in government who try to get others to agree with their ideas and who choose leaders who share the group's points of view. p. 327

population density (pop•yə•lā'shən den'sə•tē) The number of people who live in 1 square mile or 1 square kilometer of land. p. 652

portage (pôr'tij) The carrying of canoes and supplies around waterfalls and rapids or overland between rivers. p. 179

potlatch (pät'lach) A special Native American gathering at which the hosts give away valuable gifts. p. 74

Preamble (prē'am•bəl) The introduction to the Constitution. p. 293

prediction (pri•dik'shən) A telling beforehand of what will most likely happen next, based on what has happened before. p. 363

prejudice (pre'jə•dəs) A negative feeling some people have against others because of their race or culture. p. 495

presidio (prā•sē'dē•ō) A fort. p. 173

primary source (prī'mer•ē sôrs) A record made by people who saw or took part in an event. p. 26

prime meridian (prīm mə•ri'dē•ən) The meridian marked 0°. It runs north and south through Greenwich, England. p. 124

profit (prä'fət) In a business, money left over after everything has been paid for. p. 153

progressive (prə•gre'siv) A person who wants to improve government and make life better. p. 556

projection (prə•jek'•shən) One of many different views showing the round Earth on flat paper. p. 554

propaganda (prä•pə•gan'də) Information or ideas designed to help or harm a cause. p. 564

proprietary colony (prə•prī'ə•ter•ē kä'lə•nē) A colony that was owned and ruled by one person who was chosen by a king or queen. p. 181

proprietor (prə•prī'ə•tər) An owner. p. 181

prospector (prä'spek•tər) A person who searches for gold, silver, and other mineral resources. p. 525

province (prov'ins) A political region in Canada, much like an American state. p. 662

public opinion (pu'blik ə•pin'yən) What the people of a community think. p. 234

public school (pu'blik sko͞ol) A school paid for by taxes and open to all children. p. 392

pueblo (pwe'blō) A group of adobe houses that the Anasazi and other Pueblo peoples lived in. p. 66

purchase (pûr'chəs) To buy. p. 354

Puritan (pyûr'ə•tən) A member of the Church of England who settled in North America in order to follow Christian beliefs in a more "pure" way. p. 185

pyramid (pir'ə•mid) A building with three or more triangle-shaped sides that slant toward a point at the top. p. 62

Q

quarter (kwôr'tər) To provide or pay for housing. p. 239

R

range war (rānj wôr) A fight between farmers and ranchers during the late 1800s. p. 524

ratify (ra'tə•fī) To agree to something and so make it a law. p. 315

rationing (rash'ə•ning) Limiting what people can buy. p. 587

Reconstruction (rē•kən•struk'shən) A time of rebuilding the country after the Civil War. p. 465

refinery (ri•fī'nə•rē) A factory where crude, or raw, oil is made into usable products. p. 485

reform (ri•fôrm') A change for the better. p. 392

refuge (re'fyo͞oj) A safe place. p. 184

regiment (re'jə•mənt) A troop of soldiers. p. 259

region (rē'jən) An area on the Earth with features that make it different from other areas. p. 33

regulate (reg′yə•lāt) To control by the use of laws. p. 494
relative location (re′lə•tiv lō•kā′shən) The location of a place in relation to what it is near. p. 31
relief (ri•lēf′) Differences in height of an area of land. p. 390
religion (ri•li′jən) Beliefs about God or gods. p. 60
relocation camp (re•lō•kā′shən kamp) Prisonlike camps in which Japanese Americans were held after the bombing of Pearl Harbor. p. 588
repeal (ri•pēl′) To undo a law or tax. p. 236
representation (re•pri•zen•tā′shən) Acting or speaking on behalf of someone or something. p. 233
republic (ri•pu′blik) A form of government in which people elect representatives to run a country. p. 286
reservation (rez•ər•vā′shən) An area of land set aside by the government for American Indians. p. 529
resist (ri•zist′) To act against. p. 422
revolution (re•və•lo͞o′shən) A sudden, complete change of government. p. 252
right (rīt) A freedom. p. 241
royal colony (roi′əl kä′lə•nē) A colony controlled by a king or queen. p. 178
ruling (ro͞o′ling) A decision. p. 382
rumor (ro͞o′mər) A story that has been told but has not been proved. p. 140

S

saga (sä′gə) An adventure story about brave deeds of people long ago. p. 111
scalawag (ska′li•wag) A person who supports something for his or her own gain. p. 467
scandal (skan′dəl) An action that brings disgrace. p. 630
scarce (skers) Not plentiful. p. 174
scurvy (skûr′vē) A sickness caused by not getting enough vitamin C, which is found in fruit and vegetables. p. 130
secede (si•sēd′) To leave the Union. p. 380
secondary source (se′kən•dâr•ē sôrs) A record of an event, written by someone who was not there at the time. p. 27
sectionalism (sek′shə•nəl•i•zəm) Regional loyalty. p. 380
segregation (se•gri•gā′shən) Separation. p. 467
self-government (self•gu′vərn•mənt) A system of government in which people make their own laws. p. 225
self-sufficient (self•sə•fish′ənt) Self-supporting. p. 175
separation of powers (se•pə•rā′shən əv pou′erz) The division of the national government into three branches instead of having one all-powerful branch. p. 302
separatist (se′pə•rə•tist) A person who wants to become or remain separate from a government or group. p. 664
settlement house (se′təl•mənt hous) A community center where people can learn new skills. p. 506
shaman (shä′mən) A religious leader and healer. p. 80
sharecropping (sher′krä•ping) A system of working the land, in which the worker was paid with a share of the crop. p. 464
siege (sēj) A long-lasting attack. p. 266
skyscraper (skī′skrā•pər) A tall steel-frame building. p. 507
slave code (slāv kōd) A group of laws that shaped the day-to-day lives of enslaved people. p. 421
slave state (slāv stāt) A state that allowed slavery. p. 426
slavery (slā′və•rē) The practice of holding people against their will and making them carry out orders. p. 91
society (sə•sī′ə•tē) A human group. p. 37
sod (sod) Earth cut into blocks or mats that are held together by grass and its roots. p. 81
specialize (spesh′əl•īz) To work mostly on one job that could be done well. p. 60
spiritual (spir′i•chə•wəl) A religious song based on Bible stories. p. 422
states' rights (stāts rīts) The idea that individual states have final authority over the national government. p. 380
stock (stok) A share in a company or business. p. 484
stock market (stok mär′kit) A place where people can buy and sell stocks, or shares in businesses. p. 574
strike (strīk) To stop work in protest of working conditions. p. 491
suffrage (su′frij) The right to vote. p. 395
superpower (so͞o′pər•pou•ər) A very powerful nation with an important role in world events. p. 611
surplus (sûr′pləs) More than is needed. p. 60

T

tariff (târ′əf) A tax on goods brought into a country. p. 232
tax (taks) Money that is paid by people to run the country. p. 227
technology (tek•nä′lə•jē) The use of scientific knowledge or tools to make or do something. p. 58
temple (tem′pəl) A place of worship. p. 62
tenement (te′nə•mənt) A poorly built apartment house. p. 498
tepee (tē′pē) A cone-shaped tent made of poles covered with animal skins. p. 83
territory (ter′ə•tôr•ē) Land that belongs to a national government but is not a state. p. 289
terrorism (ter′ə•riz•əm) The use of violence to promote a cause. p. 635
textile mill (tek′stīl mil) A factory where fibers such as cotton and wool are woven into cloth. p. 373
theory (thē′ə•rē) A possible explanation for something. p. 49

time line (tīm līn) A diagram that shows the events that took place during a certain period of time. p. 61
time zone (tīm zōn) A region in which a single time is used. p. 488
totem pole (tō′təm pōl) A wooden post that is carved with shapes of people and animals to show a family's history. p. 75
town meeting (toun mē′ting) An assembly in the New England colonies in which male landowners could take part in government. p. 195
township (toun′ship) A square of land in the Northwest Territory that measured 6 miles per side. p. 289
trade network (trād net′wərk) A system in which trade takes place between certain groups of people. p. 149
trade-off (trād′of) What you have to give up buying or doing in order to buy or do something else. p. 243
transcontinental railroad (trans•kän•tən•en′təl rāl′rōd) A railroad that crosses a continent, such as one that links the Atlantic and Pacific coasts of the United States. p. 483
transport (trans•pōrt′) To carry. p. 375
travois (trə•voi′) A kind of carrier that is made up of two poles fastened to the harness of an animal. p. 84
treason (trē′zən) Working against one's own government. p. 233
treaty (trē′tē) An agreement between countries. p. 268
trend (trend) A pattern of change over time. p. 420
triangular trade route (trī•ang′gyə•lər trād rōōt) A shipping route that included Britain, the British colonies, and Africa. p. 197
tribe (trīb) A group made up of many bands of people with a shared culture and land. p. 60
tributary (tri′byə•ter•ē) A river or stream that feeds a larger river. p. 180
tribute (tri′byōōt) Payments a ruler demands from his or her people. p. 93

U

unconstitutional (ən•kän•stə•tōō′shə•nəl) Going against the Constitution. p. 305
Underground Railroad (un′dər•ground rāl′rōd) A system of escape routes for enslaved people, leading to a free state or territory. p. 424
unemployment (un•im•ploi′mənt) The number of workers without jobs. p. 577
Union (yōōn′yən) The United States of America. p. 300

V

vaquero (bä•kā′rō) A Mexican cowhand. p. 522
veto (vē′tō) A power the President has to reject a bill passed by Congress. p. 304
vigilance (vi′jə•ləns) Watching over something or someone. p. 527

Glossary

Index

Page references for illustrations are set in italic type. An italic *m* indicates a map. Page references set in boldface type indicate the pages on which vocabulary terms are defined.

A

B

C

Index

D

E

Index

J

N

O

P

U

V

For permission to reprint copyrighted material, grateful acknowledgment is made to the following sources:

Caroline House, Boyds Mills Press, Inc.: Cover photograph from *Erie Canal: Canoeing America's Great Waterway* by Peter Lourie. Copyright © 1997 by Peter Lourie.

Children's Book Press: From *The People Shall Continue* by Simon Ortiz. Text © 1977 by Children's Book Press; revised edition text © 1988 by Children's Book Press.

Childrens Press, Inc.: Cover illustration by Steven Gaston Dobson from *The World's Great Explorers: Jacques Marquette and Louis Jolliet* by Zachary Kent. Copyright © 1994 by Childrens Press®, Inc.

Clarion Books, a Houghton Mifflin Company imprint: Cover illustration by Jean Day Zallinger from *The Earliest Americans* by Helen Roney Sattler. Illustration copyright © 1993 by Jean Day Zallinger.

Crown Publishers, Inc.: From *Children of the Dust Bowl: The True Story of the School at Weedpatch Camp* by Jerry Stanley, cover photograph by Russell Lee. Text copyright © 1992 by Jerry Stanley. Cover photograph courtesy of the Library of Congress.

Dial Books for Young Readers, a division of Penguin Putnam Inc.: Cover photograph from *Rosa Parks: My Story* by Rosa Parks, with Jim Haskins. Copyright © 1992 by Rosa Parks.

Farrar, Straus & Giroux, Inc.: "Prayer" and "House Blessing"from *In the Trail of the Wind*, edited by John Bierhorst. Published by Farrar, Straus & Giroux, Inc., 1971.

Jane Feder, on behalf of Julie Downing: Cover illustration by Julie Downing from *If You Were There In 1776* by Barbara Brenner. Illustration copyright © 1994 by Julie Downing. Cover illustration by Julie Downing from *If You Were There In 1492* by Barbara Brenner.

Harcourt Brace & Company: From *1787* by Joan Anderson. Text copyright © 1987 by Joan Anderson. Cover illustration by Stephen Alcorn from *Lincoln: In His Own Words*, edited by Milton Meltzer. Illustration copyright © 1993 by Stephen Alcorn. From *Guns for General Washington: A Story of the American Revolution* by Seymour Reit, cover illustration by Dan Andreasen. Text and cover illustration copyright © 1990 by Seymour Reit.

HarperCollins Publishers: Cover illustration from *Stranded at Plimoth Plantation 1626* by Gary Bowen. Illustration copyright © 1994 by Gary Bowen. *The Great Migration* by Jacob Lawrence. Text copyright © 1993 by The Museum of Modern Art, New York, and The Phillips Collection.

Holiday House, Inc.: From *Cassie's Journey: Going West in the 1860s* by Brett Harvey. Text copyright © 1988 by Brett Harvey. Cover photograph by Lawrence Migdale from *Potlatch: A Tsimshian Celebration* by Diane Hoyt-Goldsmith. Photograph copyright © 1997 by Lawrence Migdale.

Henry Holt and Company: From *One Giant Leap* by Mary Ann Fraser. Text copyright © 1993 by Mary Ann Fraser. "The Americas in 1492" from *The World in 1492* by Jean Fritz, Katherine Paterson, Patricia and Fredrick McKissack, Margaret Mahy and Jamake Highwater. Text copyright © 1992 by The Native Land Foundation.

Houghton Mifflin Company: Cover illustration by Heather Collins from *A Pioneer Sampler: The Daily Life of A Pioneer Family in 1840* by Barbara Greenwood. Illustration copyright © 1994 by Heather Collins/Glyphics. From *The Pueblo* by Charlotte and David Yue. Text copyright © 1986 by Charlotte and David Yue.

Lincoln Cathedral Library, Lincoln, England: From the 1630 handbill *Proportion of Provisions.*

Lothrop, Lee & Shepard Books, a division of William Morrow & Company, Inc.: Cover illustration by Giulio Maestro from *A More Perfect Union: The Story of Our Constitution* by Betsy and Giulio Maestro. Illustration copyright © 1987 by Giulio Maestro.

The McGraw-Hill Companies: From book #60660 *The Log of Christopher Columbus* by Robert Fuson. Text copyright 1987 by Robert H. Fuson. Original English language edition published by International Marine Publishing Company, Camden, ME.

The Millbrook Press, Inc.: Cover photograph from *Chico Mendes* by Joann J. Burch. Photograph courtesy of Paulo Jares/Abril Imagens. Cover illustration from *Colonial Places* by Sarah Howarth. Copyright © 1994 by Sarah Howarth. Cover illustration from *The Boston Tea Party* by Laurie A. O'Neill. Copyright © 1996 by Laurie A. O'Neill

Glenn Morris: From "Breaking the Bering Strait Barrier" by Glenn Morris. Originally published in *Indian Country Today*, October 27, 1993.

Morrow Junior Books, a division of William Morrow & Company, Inc.: Cover illustration from *Pioneer Girl: Growing Up On the Prairie* by Andrea Warren. Copyright © 1998 by Andrea Warren.

The Newborn Group: Cover illustrations by Teresa Fasolino from *1787* by Joan Anderson.

Pantheon Books, a division of Random House, Inc.: From *Hard Times: An Oral History of the Great Depression* by Studs Terkel. Text copyright © 1970 by Studs Terkel.

G. P. Putnam's Sons: From *Shh! We're Writing the Constitution* by Jean Fritz, illustrated by Tomie dePaola. Text copyright © 1987 by Jean Fritz; illustrations copyright © 1987 by Tomie dePaola. From *Stonewall* by Jean Fritz. Text copyright © 1979 by Jean Fritz. Cover illustration from *The Great Little Madison* by Jean Fritz. Copyright © 1989 by Jean Fritz.

Random House, Inc.: From "On the Pulse of Morning" in *On the Pulse of Morning* by Maya Angelou. Text and cover copyright © 1993 by Maya Angelou. From *The Story of Thomas Alva Edison* by Margaret Cousins, cover illustration by Dominick D'Andrea. Text copyright © 1965 by Margaret Cousins; text copyright renewed 1993 by Margaret Cousins and Random House, Inc.; cover illustration copyright © 1981 by Dominick D'Andrea.

Norman Rockwell Family Trust: Cover illustration by Norman Rockwell from *Rosie the Riveter* by Penny Colman. Illustration copyright © 1999 by the Norman Rockwell Family Trust.

Scholastic Inc.: Cover from *A House Divided: The Lives of Ulysses S. Grant and Robert E. Lee* by Jules Archer. Copyright © 1995 by Jules Archer. From *By the Dawn's Early Light* by Steven Kroll, illustrated by Dan Andreasen. Text copyright © 1994 by Steven Kroll; illustrations copyright © 1994 by Dan Andreasen.

Simon & Schuster Books for Young Readers, an imprint of Simon & Schuster: From "The Wilderness Is Tamed" in *Away Goes Sally* by Elizabeth Coatsworth. Text copyright 1934 by Macmillan Publishing Company; text copyright renewed © 1962 by Elizabeth Coatsworth Beston.

Volcano Press, Inc.: From *Save My Rainforest* by Monica Zak, illustrated by Bengt-Arne Runnerström, English version by Nancy Schimmel. Text © 1987 by Monica Zak; English language text © 1992 by Volcano Press, Inc. Originally published in Sweden under the title *Rädda Min Djungel* by Bokförlaget Opal, 1989.

Walker and Company, 435 Hudson St., New York, NY 10014: Cover illustration by Peter E. Hanson from *I, Columbus: My Journal 1492-1493*, edited by Peter and Connie Roop. Illustration copyright © 1990 by Peter E. Hanson.

Albert Whitman & Company: From *Samuel's Choice* by Richard Berleth. Text copyright © 1990 by Richard J. Berleth. Cover photograph from *Theodore Roosevelt Takes Charge* by Nancy Whitelaw. © 1992 by Nancy Whitelaw.

ILLUSTRATION CREDITS:
Dan Andreasen, pp. 364–369; Paul Bachem, pp. 222–223; Luigi Galante, pp. 73, 87, 351; Ben Garvie, p. 58; Jim Griffin, pp. 600–601; Dave Henderson, pp. 100–101, 274–275, 472–473, 668–671; Mark Hess, pp. 196, 201, 206; Uldis Klavins, pp. 162–163, 402–403; Mike Lamble, pp. 78–79, 176–177; Albert Lorenz, p. 330; Dennis Lyall, pp. 75, 266–267; Ed Martinez, pp. 344–347; Bill Maughan, pp. 208–209, 260–263, 336–337; Angus McBride, pp. 56–57; Ed Parker, pp. 298–299; Richard Schlecht, pp. 117, 128, 376–377, 507, 536–537; Steven Snider, pp. 418–419; John Suh, pp. 108–109.

COVER CREDITS:
Design Studio: Miriello Grafico Inc.;
Photography: Ken West Photography.

All maps by GeoSystems

PHOTO CREDITS:
PAGE PLACEMENT KEY: (t)-top, (c)-center, (b)-bottom, (l)-left, (r)-right, (bg)-background.

COVER PHOTO CREDITS (by object)**:**
Flag, Rafael Macia/Photo Researchers; Statue of Liberty, Kelly-mooney Photography/Corbis; all others, Ken West Photography/Miriello Grafico, Inc.

TABLE OF CONTENTS

HARCOURT BRACE & COMPANY iii (b) Harcourt Brace & Company/P & F Communications.
OTHER iv (tl) Werner Forman/Art Resouces; iv (bl) Michael Heron/Woodfin Camp and Associates; v (tl) Scala/Art Resource; v (bl) E. T. Archive; vi (tl) The Santa Barbara Mission; vi (bl) Founders Society Purchase, Gibbs-Williams Fund, The Detroit Institute of the Arts; vii (tl) Library of the Boston Athenaeum; vii (bl) Bequest of Winslow Warren/courtesy, Museum of Fine Arts, Boston; viii (tl) New York Historical Association, Cooperstown, Photo by Richard Walker; viii (bl) Corcoran Gallery of Art/Corbis Media; ix (tl) Colorado Historical Society; ix (bl) Archives Division-Texas State Library; x (tl) National Portrait Gallery, Smithsonian Institution/Art Resource, NY; x (bl) Library of Congress; xi (tl) Isiah West Tabor Photo; xi (bl) The Denver Public Library, Western History Department; xii (tl) Theodore Roosevelt Collection/Harvard College Library; xii (bl) Print Courtesy Stetson Kennedy; xiii (tl) Corbis-Bettmann; xiii (bl) David Hautzig; xiv (bl) Hartman-Dewit/Comstock.

INTRODUCTION

HARCOURT BRACE & COMPANY 18, 19 (br) Weronica Ankarorn/Harcourt Brace & Company; 21 (br) Victoria Bowen; 24 (b) Weronica Ankarorn; 26 (tr) (br) Victoria Bowen; 27 (br) Harcourt Brace & Company; 28 Weronica Ankarorn; 29 Terry Sinclair; 30 Terry Sinclair; 31 Victoria Bowen; 37 (tr) Victoria Bowen.
OTHER A-1 David Wagner/Phototake; 27 (tr) Archive Photos; 32 (tr) Superstock; 32 (c) Tony Stone Images; 32 (br) Joe Towers/The Stock Market; 37 (c) Chip Henderson/Tony Stone Images; 37 (br) Bob Daemmrich.

UNIT 1

HARCOURT BRACE & COMPANY: 42 (tl) Victoria Bowen; 97(b) Victoria Bowen; 103 Sheri O'Neal.
OTHER 38-39 Courtesy of Abell-Hanger Foundation and Permian Basin Petroleum Museum, Midland, Texas, where painting is on display. (c) 1973, Abell-Hanger Foundation; 42 (c) Courtesy: Richard Howard Collection/Jerry Jacka Photography; 42-43 (bg) Pete Saloutos/The Stock Market; 43 (bl) #3837(4) Courtesy of Library Services, American Museum of Natural History; 43 (tr) America Hurrah Archive; 44-45 (bg) David Muench/David Muench Photography; (b) Rota/American Museum of Natural History; 45 (tr) Lee Boltin; 46 Werner Forman/Art Resource, NY; 48 Mark Newman/Alaska Stock Images; 49 J.M. Adovasio/Mercyhurst Archaeological Institute; 50 (t) Dr. Thomas D. Dillehay, Department of Anthropology, The University of Kentucky; 50 (b) Mercyhurst Archaeological Institute; 51 (l) Amerind Foundation, Inc., Dragoon, Arizona; 51 (r) National Museum of American Art, Washington, DC; 54 John Maier, Jr./JB Pictures; 55 Tom Wolff/St. Remy Press; 57 Aiuppy Photographs; 59 Courtesy of the National Museum of the American Indian, Smithsonian Institution (slide #S3242); 50 (t) Vera Lentz; 62 Michael Zebe; 63 Felipe Davalos/National Geographic Image Collection; 65 (insert) Photograph (c) The Detroit Institute of Arts; 65 (tr) Tony Linck; 66-67 (bg) Jerry Jacka Photography; 67 (insert-l) Amerind Foundation, Dragoon, Arizona-Robin Starcliff Inc.; 67 (insert-r) Object from the Smithsonian National Museum of Natural History, photo by Mark Gulezian; 70 Michal Heron /Woodfin Camp & Associates; 71 Lynn Johnson Photographer; 73 Corbis Images; 74 #1 4075(2), Courtesy Department of Library Services, American Museum of Natural History; 76 John Doyle; 77 John Cancalosi/Stock Boston; 79 Colorado Historical Society; 80 Jerry Jacka; 81 Courtesy of The National Museum of the American Indian, Smithsonian Institution (#S3771); 82 (l) National Museum of American Art/Art Resource, NY; 82 (r) Courtesy of The National Museum of the American Indian, Smithsonian Institution (slide #S2600); 83 (tr) R. Webber/The Bata Shoe Museum; 83 (b) Detail of The Pecos Pueblo about 1500, By Tom Lovel, Artist. Courtesy of Abell-Hanger Foundation and Permian Basin Petroleum Museum, Midland, Texas, where painting is on display. (c) 1973, Abell-Hanger; 85 (bl) "Iroquois Bone Comb," Herbert Bigford, Sr. Collection, Longyear Museum of Anthropology/ Colgate University; 87 (tl) "Photo used courtesy of Pathways Productions, Inc. All rights reserved. Copyright 1994."; 88 (tl) Peabody Museum-Harvard University, photograph by Hillel Burger; 88 (tr) Rare Books & Manuscripts Division, The New York Public Library, Astor, Lenox, and Tilden Foundations; 90 Michael Zebe; 91 Peter Menzel/Stock, Boston; 92 (r) Justin Kerr; 93 (bl) Michael Zebe; 93 (br) Eric A. Weissman/Stock, Boston; 94-95 Detail of The Great City of Tenochtitlan, by Diego Rivera, 1945. Mural, 4.92 x 9.71 m. Patio Corridor, National Palace, Mexico City, D.F., Mexico. Schalkwijk/Art Resource; 98 (bc) First Light; 98 (br) Paul Grebliunas/Tony Stone Images; 98 (tc) Steve Dunwell/The Image Bank; 99 (cl) David Young Wolff/Tony Stone Images; 99 (bl) Harald Sund/The Image Bank; 99 (bc) Peter Hendrie Photo/The Image Bank; 99(c) Art Brewer/Tony Stone Images; 99 (tr) First Light.

UNIT 2

HARCOURT BRACE & COMPANY 108 (tl) Victoria Bowen; 120 Harcourt Brace & Company; 159 Victoria Bowen; 160-161 Harcourt Brace & Company; 165 Harcourt Brace & Company.
OTHER 104-105 Rijksmuseum Amsterdam; 110 Scala/Art Resource, NY; 111 Werner Forman/Art Resource, NY; 112 Werner Forman/Art Resource, NY; 113 The Granger Collection; 114 (tl) Giraudon/Art Resource, NY; 114 (tc) The New York Public Library Map Division, Astor, Lenox, & Tilden Foundations; 115 Giraudon/Art Resource, NY; 116 (tl) Collection of the National Palace Museum, Taipei, Taiwan, Republic of China; 117 (bc) Michael Holford; 117 (br) National Maritime Museum Picture Library; 118 (bl) Bibliotheque Nationale, Paris; 118 (br) Bibliotheque Nationale, Paris; 121 Rebecca E. Marvil/Light Sources Stock; 122 National Graphics, Inc.; 123 Scala/Art Resource, NY; 126 ZIN41924 Selection of Arab and European Astrolabes from the 14th to 16th century, copper, Museum of the History of Science, Oxford/Bridgeman Art Library, London; 127 The New York Public Library, Map Division; 130 AKG London; 131 The Bettman Archive; 134 E. T. Archive; 135 Scala/Art Resource; 136 American Museum of Natural History; 137 Werner Forman Archive, Museum fur Volkerkunde, Berlin/Art Resource; 138 Detail, Collection of the J. Paul Getty Museum, Malibu, California; 139 Courtesy of the Oakland Museum of California; 143 (c) Mel Fisher/Maritime Heritage Society, Key West, FL. Photo by Scott Nierling; 144 (tl) Courtesy of The Hispanic Society of America, New York; 144 (tr) Archivo Fotographico Sevillo; 145 Werner Forman, Art Resource, New York; 146 The Granger Collection, New York; 147 The Granger Collection, New York; 149 (l) "The Surveyor: Portrait of Captain John Henry Lefroy," Paul Kane, Glenbow Collection, Calgary, Alberta, Canada; 149 (r) From the Collection of the Minnesota Historical Society; 150 (l) The Minnesota Historical Society, #67.230.177; 150 (r) The Granger Collection, New York; 151 BAL1648 Elizabeth I, Armada portrait by Anonymous. Private Collection/Bridgeman Art Library, London; 152 (tl) the British Museum; 153 (l) The Library of Virginia; 153 (r) A.H. Robins, photo by Don Eiler; 155 Courtesy of The Pilgrim Society, Plymouth, Massachusetts.

UNIT 3

HARCOURT BRACE & COMPANY 193 (br) Victoria Bowen; 211 (br) Victoria Bowen; 217 Weronica Ankerorn.
OTHER 166-167 Print Collection, Miriam and Ira Wallach Division of Art, Prints, and Photographs, The New York Public Library, Astor, Lenox, and Tilden Foundations; 170 (tl) Rare Books & Manuscripts Division, The New York Public Library, Astor, Lenox, & Tilden Foundation; 170 (bl) Courtesy of The Pilgrim Society, Plymouth, Massachusetts; 171 (t) Courtesy of The Pilgrim Society, Plymouth, Massachusetts; 171 (r) Walter Meayers Edwards/National Geographic Image Collection; 171 (lr) The Pilgrim Society; 171 (bl) Courtesy of The Pilgrim Society, Plymouth, Massachusetts; 172 The Santa Barbara Mission; 173 Florida Museum of Natural History; 174 (tc) St. Augustine National Park Service; 177 George H.H. Huey; 178 Corbis-Bettmann; 179 (t) Courtesy of The Adirondack Museum, Photo by James Swedberg; 179 (b) Kevin Magee/Tom Stack & Associates; 182 The Historic New Orleans Collection, Accession No. 1991.60; 183 Science and Technology Section, Science, Industry & Business Library. The New York Public Library, Astor, Lenox, and Tilden Foundation; 184 Courtesy of the Jamestown-Yorktown Educational Trust; 185 (t) Worcester Art Museum, Worcester, Massachusetts. Gift of Mr. and Mrs. Albert Rice; 185 (b) Courtesy of The Pilgrim Society, Plymouth, Massachusetts; 186 (b) The Bettmann Archive; 187 (t) Culver Pictures, Inc.; 187 (b) Collection of the Albany Institute of History and Art, Bequest of Ledyard Cogswell, Jr.; 188 (bl) Giraudon/Art Resource, NY; 188 (c) The Historical Society of Pennsylvania; 194 Founders Society Purchase, Gibbs-Willams Fund, The Detroit Institute of the Arts; 195 New York Public Library Picture Collection; 197 Colonial Williamsburg Foundation; 200 Arthur C. Smith, III/Grant Heilman Photography; 202 (c) Courtesy, American Antiquarian Society; 202 (r) EX 17082 Negro Portrait: Olaudah Equiano by English School (18th Century). Royal Albert Memorial Museum, Exeter/Bridgeman Art Library, London; 203 The Metropolitan Museum, Gift of Edgar William and Bernice Chrysler Garbisch, 1963 (63.201.3). Photograph (c) 1984 The Metropolitan Museum of Art; 204 National Geographic Image Collection; 207 "American Beaver," by J.J. Audubon (detail). Taken from Plate XLVI Vivb., Quadrupeds of North America. Missouri Historical Society, St. Louis; 212-213 (bg) Chip Henderson/Tony Stone Images; 250 (bl) Mark E. Gibson; 251 (bl) Louis Grandadam/Tony Stone Images; 251 (br) Henley & Savage/The Stock Market.

UNIT 4

HARCOURT BRACE & COMPANY 222 (tl) Victoria Bowen; 225 Weronica Ankarorn; 238 Weronica Ankarorn; 245 Victoria Bowen; 260 (tl) Victoria Bowen; 271 Victoria Bowen; 277 Harcourt Brace & Company.
OTHER 218-219 Historical Society of Pennsylvania; 224 Library of Boston Athanaeum; 226 (bc) Library of Congress; 228 Dan McCoy/Rainbow; 230 The Granger Collection, New York; 231 By courtesy of the National Portrait Gallery, London; 232 Peabody Essex Museum, Salem, MA. Photo by Mark Sexton; 233 (c) Fraunces Tavern Museum, New York; 233 (bl) Massachusetts Historical Society; 233 (lc) Massachusetts Historical Society; 233 (cr) Corbis Media; 234 Virginia Historical Society; 235 Christie's Images; 236 (cr) Ed Eckstein for The Franklin Institute Science Museum; 236 (bl) Historical Society of Pennsylvania; 237 (tl) The Granger Collection, New York; 237 (tc) Stock Montage, Inc.; 237 (cr) Library Company of Philadelphia; 239 (tl) Deposited by the City of

Boston. Courtesy, Museum of Fine Arts, Boston; 239 (bc) Daughters of the American Revolution Museum, Washington, DC; 240 The Bridgeman Art Library International Ltd.; 241 (bc) Courtesy of the Concord Museum, Concord, Massachusetts, photograph by Chip Fanelli; 242 Gift of Joseph W. Revere, William B. Revere and Edward H.R. Revere. Courtesy, Museum of Fine Arts, Boston; 243 Archive Photos; 246 Bequest of Winslow Warren/Courtesy, Museum of Fine Arts, Boston; 247 The New York Public Library/Harcourt Brace and Company; 248 (tl) Historical Society of Pennsylvania; 249 (bl) Library of Congress; 249 (br) Yale University Art Gallery, Gift of the Associates; in Fine Arts and Mrs. Henry B. Loomis in Memory of Henry Bradford Loomis, B.A. 1875; 250 Delaware Art Museum, Howard Pyle Collection; 251 The Granger Collection, New York; 252 (portrait) Detail, Thomas Paine, John Wesley Jarvis, Gift of Marian B. Maurice (c) Board of Trustees, National Gallery of Art, Washington, DC; 253 (tl) Corbis-Bettmann; 253 (tr) Smithsonian Institution; 254 Yale University Art Gallery, Trumbull Collection; 255 Sisse Brimberg/Woodfin Camp & Associates; 256 Ted Spiegel; 257 (tr) Fraunces Tavern Museum, New York City; 258 (br) The Granger Collection, New York; 259 Amon Carter Museum, Fort Worth, Texas; 264 Ted Spiegel/National Geographic Society; 267 (inset) A detail, John Trumbull, "The Surrender of Lord Cornwallis At Yorktown, 19 October 1871," Yale University Art Gallery, Trumbull Collection; 272-273 Reuters/Bettmann.

UNIT 5

HARCOURT BRACE & COMPANY 282 Victoria Bowen; 292 (c) Harcourt Brace & Company; 301 Harcourt Brace & Company; 306 Victoria Bowen; 313 Victoria Bowen; 319 Weronica Ankarorn; 333 Victoria Bowen; 339 Weronica Ankarorn.
OTHER 278-279 Architect of the Capital/National Graphics Center; 284 New York Historical Association, Cooperstown, Photo by Richard Walker; 285 Historical Society of Pennsylvania; 286 Cranbrook Institute of Science; 287 (tl) Corbis-Bettmann; 287 (tr) Courtesy, American Antiquarian Society; 289 Smithsonian Institution, Division of Political History, Neg. #81-5397; 290 Courtesy Commonwealth of Massachusetts. Photo by Douglas Christian; 292 (b) Independence National Historical Park; 293 North Wind Picture Archives; 296 (tl) Courtesy of The National Archives; 296 (bl) The Granger Collection, New York; 297 (tc) The Library of Virginia; 297 (tr) Emmet Collection, Rare Books and Manuscripts Division, The New York Public Library, Astor, Lenox and Tilden Foundations; 298 (tl) New York Public Library; 298 (tc) Princeton University, Bequest of William Paterson, grandson of the subject, in 1899; 299 "Residences and Slave Quarters of Mulbery Plantation," by Thomas Coram, The Gibbes Museum of Art, Charleston, SC; 301 Ralph Earl Roger Sherman (1721-1793), M.A. (Hon.) 1786. Yale University Art Gallery, Gift of Roger Sherman White, B.A. 1899, L.L.B. 1902; 302 U.S. Senate Collection; 304 Wally McNamee/Woodfin Camp; 308 Michael Bryant/Woodfin Camp; 309 National Portrait Gallery, Smithsonian Institution/Art Resource, NY; 310 Metropolitan Museum of Art, New York City/Superstock; 311 Tom McHugh/Photo Researchers; 314 Corcoran Gallery of Art/Corbis; 315 Independence National Historical Park; 316 (tl) Michael Bryant/Woodfin Camp; 316 (tr) Michael Bryant/Woodfin Camp; 316 (b) The Granger Collection, New York; 318 (bl) The Granger Collection, New York; 318 (br) Collection of The New York Historical Society; 320 (cl) Archive Photos; 320 (cr) Archive Photos; 320 (tl) Colonial Williamsburg Foundation; 320 (tr) The White House Historical Association; 322 The Smithsonian Institution, National Numismatic Collection; 323 The New York Historical Society; 324 Dover Publications; 325 Smithsonian Institution; 326 Mr. & Mrs. John Harney; 327 Sally Anderson-Bruce; 328 (tc) Independence National Historical Park Collection; 328 (tr) Independence National Historical Park Collection; 329 (bl) Maryland Historical Society; 331 American Numismatic Association; 334-335 Museum of Political Life, University of Hartford.

UNIT 6

HARCOURT BRACE & COMPANY 344 Victoria Bowen; 364 Victoria Bowen; 371 Victoria Bowen; 399 Victoria Bowen; 405 Harcourt Brace & Company.
OTHER 340-341 The National Cowboy Hall of Fame and Western Heritage Center, Oklahoma City, Oklahoma; 348 South Dakota State Archives; 349 Hulton Getty Picture Collection/Tony Stone Images; 350 (tl) George Caleb Bingham, Daniel Boone Escorting Settlers through the Cumberland Gap, 1851-52, detail. Oil on canvas, 36 1/2 x 50 1/4." Washington University Gallery of Art, St. Louis; 351 Reynolda House, Museum of American Art, Photography by Jackson Smith; 353 Collection of the New York Historical Society; 354 The Bettmann Archive; 355 (bl) Amon Carter Museum; 355 (br) North Wind Picture Archives; 356 Courtesy of The Montana Historical Society; 357 (l) Courtesy, Independence National Historical Park; 357 (r) Bob Thomason/Tony Stone Images; 358 National Portrait Gallery, Smithsonian Institution/Art Resource, NY; 359 (tl) The Field Museum Neg # A93851c; 359 (tr) Prophetstown used courtesy of Pathway Productions, Inc. All rights reserved. Copyright 1994; 361 (bl) The Granger Collection; 361 (br) Collection of the New York Historical Society; 362 The Bettmann Archive; 363 (bl) "Westward the Course of Empire Takes Its Way," ca. 1861, Oil on canvas, 0126.1615, from the Collection of Gilcrease Museum, Tulsa; 369 (bl) Library of Congress; 372 Archives Division-Texas State Library; 373 North Wind Picture Archives; 374 (l) Smithsonian Institution; 374 (r) Smithsonian Institution, Division of Engineering, Neg. #86-9625; 375 (bl) Progress for Cotton - No. 4 Carding, detail, Yale University Art Gallery, Mabel Brady Garvin Collection; 375 (br) Museum of American Textile History; 378 B&O Railroad Museum; 379 The Granger Collection; 381 (bc) National Portrait Gallery, Smithsonian Institution/Art Resource, NY; 382 Craig Smith/Philbrook Museum of Art, Tulsa, OK; 383 Archives Division-Texas State Library; 384 Friends of the Governor's Mansion, Austin, TX; 386 (t) National Portrait Gallery; 386 (bc) San Joaquin County Historical Society; 387 David W. Hawkinson/Brigham Young University Museum of Art; 389 California State Library; 391 (tl) The Kansas State Historical Society, Topeka, KS; 392 The Bettmann Archive; 393 State Archives of Michigan; 394 (r) State Archives of Michigan; 394 (l) Harriet Beecher Stowe Center, Hartford, CT; 395 (bl) The Bettmann Archives; 396 The Bettmann Archive; 400 (bl) Picture Perfect; (br) Charles Nicklin/Al Giddings' Images, Inc.; 401 (tl) Ron Church/Photo Researchers, Inc.; 401 (bl) Photo Researchers, Inc.; 401 (br) World Perspectives/Tony Stone Images; 401 (tc) World Perspectives/Tony Stone Images.

UNIT 7

HARCOURT BRACE & COMPANY (bg) 406-407 High Impact Photography; 410 (tl) Victoria Bowen; 475 Weronica Ankarorn.
OTHER 410-411 (bg) Peter Gridley/FPG International; 410 (c) Brown Brothers; 411 Peter Gridley/FPG International; 412-413 (bg) Ellis-Sawyer/FPG International; 412 (bl) Valentine Museum, Richmond, VA; 412 (br) The Bettmann Archive; 413 (tc) Anne S.K. Brown Military Collection, Brown University Library; 413 (tr) Eleanor S. Brockenbrough Library/The Museum of the Confederacy, Richmond, Virginia, photograph by Katherine Wetzel; 414 National Portrait Gallery, Smithsonian Institution/Art Resource, NY; 415 James H. Karales/Peter Arnold, Inc.; 416 (t) Superstock; 416 (c) The Library of Congress; 417 (br) The Granger Collection, New York; 421 Courtesy of The Charleston Museum, Charleston, South Carolina; 422 "Last Sale of Slaves on the Courthouse Steps" by Thomas Satterwhite Noble, 1860. Oil on canvas. Missouri Historical Society, St. Louis, MO #1939.003.0001; 423 (bl) The Brooklyn Museum; 423 (br) The Bettmann Archive; 424 (br) The Bettmann Archive; 426 The Metropolitan Museum of Art, Gift of I.N. Phelps Stokes, Edward S. Hawes, Alice Mary Hawes, Marion Augusta Hawes, 1937; 428 (tl) Missouri Historical Society, St. Louis; 428 (tr) Library of Congress; 429 Courtesy of the Illinois State Historical Library; 430 Sophia Smith Collection, Smith College, Northampton, MA; 431 Museum of Political Life; 432 (bl) Stock Montage; 432 (bc) Museum of American Political Life, University of Hartford, West Hartford, CT; 433 (bc) Library of Congress; 435 (bl) The Granger Collection; 435 (br) National Portrait Gallery, Washington, DC/Art Resource, NY; 440 Library of Congress; 441 (t) NMAH, Smithsonian, TLB 2717. From Echoes of Glory: Arms and Equipment of the Union. (c) 1991 Time-Life Books, Inc.; 441 (b) The Museum of the Confederacy, Richmond, VA. Photo by Larry Sherer. TLB 2713. From Echoes of Glory: Arms and Equipment of the Confederacy. (c) 1991 Time-Life Books, Inc.; 443 (t) Library of Congress #LC-US2623794; 443 (c) High Impact Photography; 445 National Archives; 446-447 The Granger Collection, NY; 449 The Bettmann Archive; 450 (t) National Portrait Gallery, Smithsonian Institution, Washington, DC; 450-451 (c) The Library of Congress; 452, Peter Newark; 453 Chicago Historical Society; 454 (tl) Corbis-Bettmann; 454 (c) Salamander Books; 456 The National Archives/Corbis; 458 Tom Lovell (c) National Geographic Society; 459 Jeffrey Sylvester/FPG International; 462 In the Collection of The Corcoran Gallery of Art, Museum Purchase, Gallery Fund; 464 Cook Collection, Valentine Museum; 465 The Metropolitan Museum of Art, Morris K. Jesup Fund, 1940; 466 (bl) The Library of Congress; 466 (br) The Library of Congress; 467 The Granger Collection; 470-471 (bg) UPI/Bettmann.

UNIT 8

HARCOURT BRACE & COMPANY 480 (tl) Mark Switzer; 492 Victoria Bowen; 500 (tl) Victoria Bowen; 533 (br) Mark Switzer; 539 Weronica Ankarorn/Harcourt Brace and Company.
OTHER 476-477 Library of Congress; 481

Michael Freeman; 482 Isiah West Tabor Photo/California History Section, California State Library; 483 Stanford University Museum of Art/AAA Gift of David Hewes; 484 Smithsonian Institution, Division of Electricity, Neg. #27-979; 485 (l) The Bettmann Archive; 485 (r) Corbis-Bettmann; 486 The Granger Collection, New York; 488 (bl) Culver Pictures; 488 (br) The Granger Collection, New York; 490 Brown Brothers; 491 The Bettmann Archive; 492 The George Meany Memorial Archives; 493 Brown Brothers; 494 Library of Congress/Corbis; 495 National Archives, Washington, DC/Jonathan Wallen Photography; 496 The Institute of Texan Cultures, San Antonio, Texas; 497 Brown Brothers; 499 Calumet Regional Archives, Indiana University Northwest; 500 The Phillips Collection, Washington, DC; 501 (t) "The migrants arrived in great numbers." Panel No. 40 from The Great Migration Series by Jacob Lawrence (1940-41: text and title revised by the artist, 1993). Tempera on gesso on composition board, 12 x 18" (30.5 x 45.7 cm). The Museum of Modern Art, New York. Gift of Mrs. David M. Levy. Photograph (c) 1999 The Museum of Modern Art; 501 (b) "They also worked on the railroads." Panel No. 38 from The Great Migration Series by Jacob Lawrence (1940-41: text and title revised by the artist, 1993). Tempera on gesso on composition board, 12 x 18" (30.5 x 45.7 cm). The Museum of Modern Art, New York. Gift of Mrs. David M. Levy. Photograph (c) 1999 The Museum of Modern Art; 502 "The migration gained in momentum." Panel No. 18 from The Great Migration Series by Jacob Lawrence (1940-41: text and title revised by the artist, 1993). Tempera on gesso on composition board, 12 x 18" (30.5 x 45.7 cm). The Museum of Modern Art, New York. Gift of Mrs. David M. Levy. Photograph (c) 1999 The Museum of Modern Art; 503 (tl) "But living conditions were better in the North." Panel No. 44 from The Great Migration Series by Jacob Lawrence (1940-41: text and title revised by the artist, 1993). Tempera on gesso on composition board, 12 x 18" (30.5 x 45.7 cm). The Museum of Modern Art, New York. Gift of Mrs. David M. Levy. Photograph (c) 1999 The Museum of Modern Art; 503 (br) The Phillips Collection, Washington, DC; 504 "In the North the African American had more educational opportunities." Panel No. 58 from The Great Migration Series by Jacob Lawrence (1940-41: text and title revised by the artist, 1993). Tempera on gesso on composition board, 12 x 18" (30.5 x 45.7 cm). The Museum of Modern Art, New York. Gift of Mrs. David M. Levy. Photograph (c) 1999 The Museum of Modern Art; 505 The Library of Congress/Corbis; 506 The Jacob A. Riis Collection, Museum of the City of New York; 508 Detail, "Trolley Car, Brooklyn Trolley Car Strike, 1899," The Museum of the City of New York, The Byron Collection; 509 (bl) Stock Montage; 509 (br) University of Illinois at Chicago/The University Library/Jane Addams Memorial Collection; 511 Penguin Books; 512 The Denver Public Library, Western History Department; 513 (c) Corbis/Bettmann; 513 (b) H. Abernathy/H. Armstrong Roberts; 515 Nebraska State Historical Society; 517 The Bettmann Archive; 518 Grant Heilman Photography; 520-521 David Stoecklein/Adstock Photos; 522 (br) UPI/Bettmann; 523 Corbis/Bettmann; 524 (l) Scott Berner/Phototri; 524 (r) Smithsonian Institution, Division of Political History, Neg. #94-186; 525 FPG International; 526 (bl) California State Library Neg. #912; 526 (r) Michael Friedman; 528 North Wind Picture Archive; 531 Culver Pictures; 534-535 (bg) Ken Biggs/Tony Stone Images; 535 (c) Joseph Pobereskin/Tony Stone Images; 535 (r) Jon Ortner/Tony Stone Images.

UNIT 9

HARCOURT BRACE & COMPANY 567 (br) Mark Switzer; 579 (tl) Mark Switzer; 597 (br) Mark Switzer; 351 (br) Harcourt Brace & Company.

OTHER 540-541 Fred Pansing/Image Bank; 544 FPG International; 545 Corbis/Bettmann; 546 Theodore Roosevelt Collection/Harvard College Library; 547 Gill C. Kenny, The Image Bank; 548 (t) Corbis-Bettmann; 548 (b) Jason Hailey/FPG International; 549 Ted Spiegel; 550 Brown Brothers; 553 The Bettmann Archive/Corbis-Bettmann; 556 Culver Pictures; 557 The Granger Collection; 558 (l) Corbis-Bettmann; 558 (r) Corbis-Bettmann; 559 Wood River Gallery, Mill Valley, CA; 560 (l) Culver Pictures; 560 (r) Culver Pictures; 562 Archive Photos; 563 National Portrait Gallery, Smithsonian Institute/Art Resource; 564 (l) James M. Flagg/The Granger Collection; 564 (r) Corbis; 565 Courtesy of The Library of Congress; 567 Mark Switzer; 568 Print Courtesy Stetson Kennedy; 569 Blank Archives/Archive Photos; 570 (t) From the Collections of the Henry Ford Museum & Greenfield Village; 570 (b) Culver Pictures; 571 (l) The Granger Collection; 571 (r) The Bettmann Archive/Corbis-Bettmann/; 572 (l) Archive Photos; 572 (r) Missouri State Historical Society; 573 (tr) Archive Photos; 573 (c) The Bettmann Archive/Corbis-Bettmann; 574 Archive Photos; 575 (l) New York Stock Exchange Archives; 575 (r) New York Stock Exchange Archives; 577 (bl) UPI/Bettmann; 577 (tr) The Bettmann Archive; 578 San Francisco History Room, San Francisco Public Library; 579-580 (bg) The Granger Collection; 579 (bl) The Library of Congress/Corbis; 580 (br) Dorothea Lange/Library of Congress; 581 (bg) Library of Congress/Corbis; 582 (bg) Library of Congress/Corbis; 582 (b) Arthur Rothstein/Library of Congress; 583 (b) UPI/Corbis-Bettmann; 583 (c) UPI/Corbis-Bettmann; 584 UPI/Bettmann Newsphotos; 585 (bl) UPI/Corbis-Bettmann; 585 (br) Culver Pictures; 586 (tl) UPI/Bettmann; 587 (br) Courtesy of The Library of Congress; 588 UPI/Corbis-Bettmann; 589 Private Collection; 590 (b) The Bettmann Archive; 590 (inset) UPI/Bettmann; 591 (l) Culver Pictures; 591 (r) Yellow Star, Germany, 1930s. Printed cotton. Gift of Moriah Artcraft Judaica. Photograph by Greg Staley, Courtesy of B'nai B'rith Klutznick National Jewish Museum; 598-599 Mark Richards/PhotoEdit; 599 (tl) Peter Morgan/Matrix International; 599 (tr) Tom Wagner/SABA; 599 (b) F. Hoffmann/The Image Works.

UNIT 10

HARCOURT BRACE & COMPANY 639 (l) Mark Switzer; 639 (r) Mark Switzer; 641 Harcourt Brace & Company; 673 Harcourt Brace & Company.

OTHER 604-605 Roger Ressmeyer/Corbis; 608 (t) Zane Williams/Tony Stone Images; 608 (l) Jim Stratford/Black Star; 609 (t) Jose L. Pelaez/Stock Market; 609 (bl) PhotoDisc; 609 (br) Ariel Skelley/Stock Market; 610 Corbis-Bettmann; 611 UPI/Corbis-Bettmann; 612 UPI/Bettmann; 614 Arthur Rickerby/Black Star; 615 (t) UPI/Bettmann/Corbis-Bettmann; 615 (tr) UPI/Corbis-Bettmann; 616-617 (bg) NASA Media Services; 617 NASA Media Services; 618-619 (bg) NASA Media Services; 620 (inset) Digital Vision; 620 (t) NASA Media Services; 621 (tr) NASA Media Services; 621 (bl) Digital Vision; 622 UPI/Bettmann; 623 (tl) AP/Wide World Photos; 623 (tr) Dan Weiner, Courtesy of Sandra Weiner; 624 (l) UPI/Corbis-Bettmann; 624 (br) John Lounois/Black Star; 625 Bob Fitch/Black Star; 627 UPI/Bettmann; 628 (bl) AP/Wide World Photos; 628 (br) UPI/Corbis-Bettmann; 629 UPI/Bettmann Newsphotos; 630 UPI/Corbis/Bettmann; 631 UPI/Bettmann Newsphotos; 632-633 (tc) UPI/Bettmann/Corbis-Bettmann; 632 (b) Dennis Brack/Black Star; 633 (b) UPI/Bettmann/Corbis-Bettmann; 634 UPI/Bettmann; 635 Dennis Brack/Black Star; 636 UPI/Bettmann; 637 AP/Wide World Photos; 638 AP/Wide World Photos; 642 David Hautzig; 643 Anthony Suau/Gamma Liaison; 644 (t) UPI/Bettmann; 644 (b) Bob Daemmerich; 646 Florence Parker/Archive Photos; 654 Comstock; 655 (bc) Tom Haley/Sipa Press; 656 (t) Cindy Karp/Black Star; 656 (b) Chantal Regnault/Gamma Liaison; 657 Alon Reininger/Contact Press; 658 Bill Gentile/Sipa Press; 659 Giraudon/Art Resource; 661 Will & Deni McIntyre/Photo Researchers; 662 John Brooks/Gamma Liaison; 664 (tl) Ron Watts/First Light; 664 (br) Paula Bronstein/TSW; 665 First Light; 668 (bl) B. Daemmrich/The Image Works; 668 (br) Joseph Nettis/Photo Researchers; 669 (t) Christopher Morris/SABA; 669 (c) Dante Busquets-Sordo/Gamma-Liaison; 669 (bl) S. Dooley/Liaison International; 669 (br) Paula Allen/Matrix International.

REFERENCE

Facing R1 Dennis Hallinan/FPG International; R1 (tl) Comstock; R1 (bl) Hartman-Dewit/Comstock; R2-R3 (b) Harcourt Brace & Company; R4 (t) Michael Heron/Woodfin Camp & Associates; R7 (br) Weronica Ankarorn; R9 (br) Harcourt Brace & Company; R16 Row 1 (tr) National Portrait Gallery; Row 2 (l) National Portrait Gallery; (c) Bettman; (r) National Portrait Gallery; Row 3 (l) National Portrait Gallery; (c) National Portrait Gallery; (r) The Granger Collection, New York; Row 4 (l) National Portrait Gallery; (c) National Portrait Gallery; (r) National Portrait Gallery; Row 5 (l) National Portrait Gallery; (c) The Granger Collection, New York; (r) The Granger Collection; R17 Row 1 (l) Bettmann; (c) National Portrait Gallery (r) The New York Historical Society; Row 2 (l) The Granger Collection; (c) The Granger Collection; (r) National Portrait Gallery; Row 3 (l) National Portrait Gallery; (c) National Portrait Gallery; (r) Harcourt Brace & Company; Row 4 (l) Harcourt Brace & Company; (c) Harcourt Brace & Company; (r) National Portrait Gallery; Row 5 (l) The Granger Collection; (c) Bettmann; (r) National Portrait Gallery; R18 Row 1 (l) National Portrait Gallery; (c) The Granger Collection; (r) The Granger Collection; Row 2 (l) The Granger Collection; (c) National Portrait Gallery; (r) Eisenhower Library; Row 3 (l) The Granger Collection, New York; (c) Wide World Photos; (r) The Granger Collection; Row 4 (l) National Portrait Gallery; (c) White House Historical Association; (r) Wide World Photos; Row 5 (l) David Valdez/The White House; (c) The White House.

Thinking Organizers

Many methods may be used to organize ideas and concepts. The contents of these pages are intended to act as guides for that organization. These copying masters may be used to help students organize the concepts in the lessons and chapters they have read. They can also be used to help students draw conclusions and make inferences about the material they are studying.

Contents

THE POWERFUL IDEAS

THEMES AND STRANDS OF SOCIAL STUDIES

THE FIVE THEMES OF GEOGRAPHY

Location

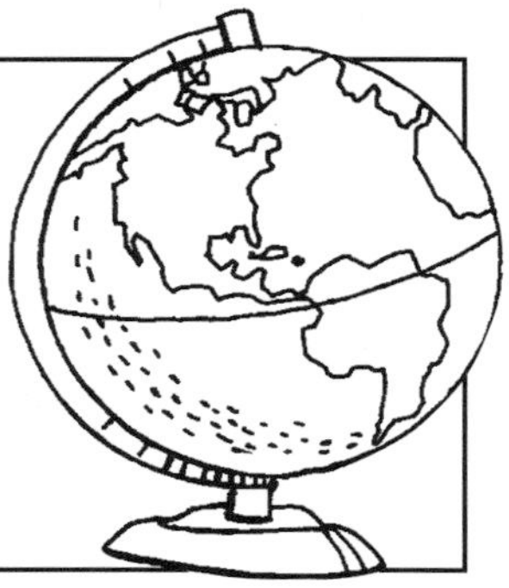

★ Where is a place located?
★ What is it near?
★ What direction is it from another place?
★ Why are certain features or places located where they are?

Place

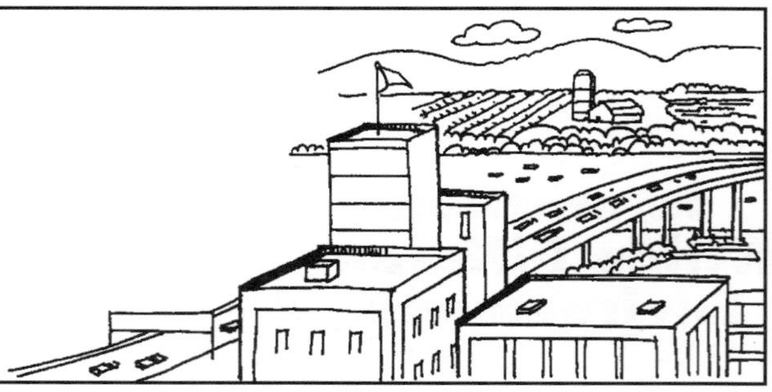

★ What is it like there?
★ What physical and human features does it have?

Human–Environment Interactions

★ How are people's lives shaped by the place?
★ How has the place been shaped by people?

Movement

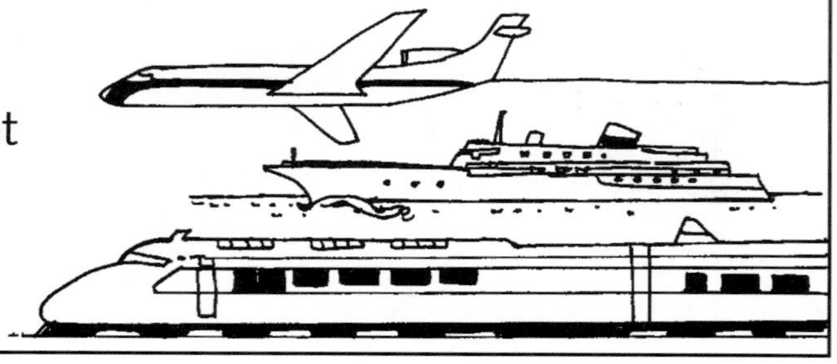

★ How did people, products, and ideas get from one place to another?
★ Why do they make these movements?

Regions

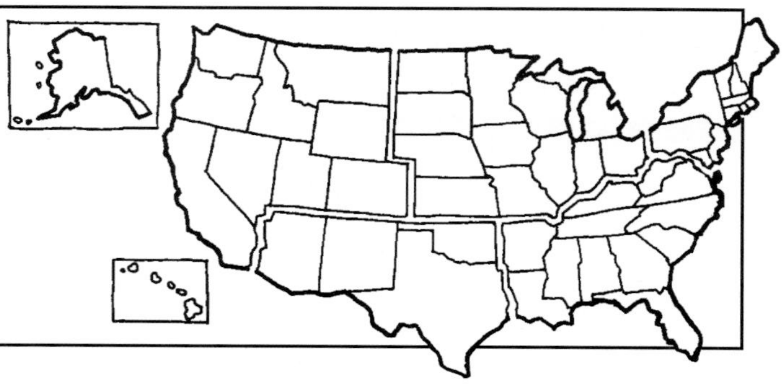

★ How is this place like other places?
★ What features set this place apart from other places?

ASK YOURSELF SOME HISTORY QUESTIONS

CURRENT EVENTS

Summary of an Important Event:

Who:

What:

When:

Where:

How:

Where did this take place?
Draw a map.

Why?

What was the cause?

What was the effect?

Comparison

This event is similar to...

Prediction

What do I think will happen next?

Personal Reaction

My reaction to the event:

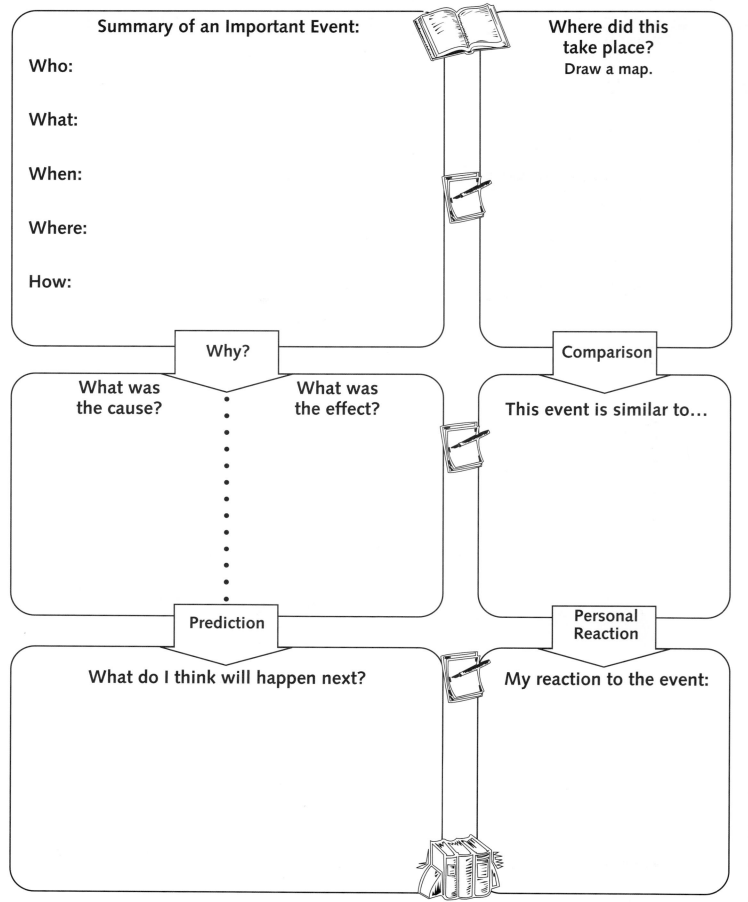

My Social Studies Journal

The single most important thing I learned was...

Something that confused me or that I did not understand was...

What surprised me the most was...

I would like to know more about...

Sources I can use to find answers to my questions...

The part that made the greatest impact on me was...

READING GUIDE

Questions I Have Before Reading				New Questions I Have After Reading
Question ❶	Question ❷	Question ❸	Question ❹	Question: Question:

Summary of What I Learned After Reading That Answers My Questions				Other Interesting Information I Learned While Reading
Question ❶	Question ❷	Question ❸	Question ❹	
General Summary:				My Reaction to What I Read:

UNDERSTAND THE MAIN IDEA

MAIN IDEA

SUPPORTING DETAIL

SUPPORTING DETAIL

SUPPORTING DETAIL

SUPPORTING DETAIL

TELL FACT FROM OPINION

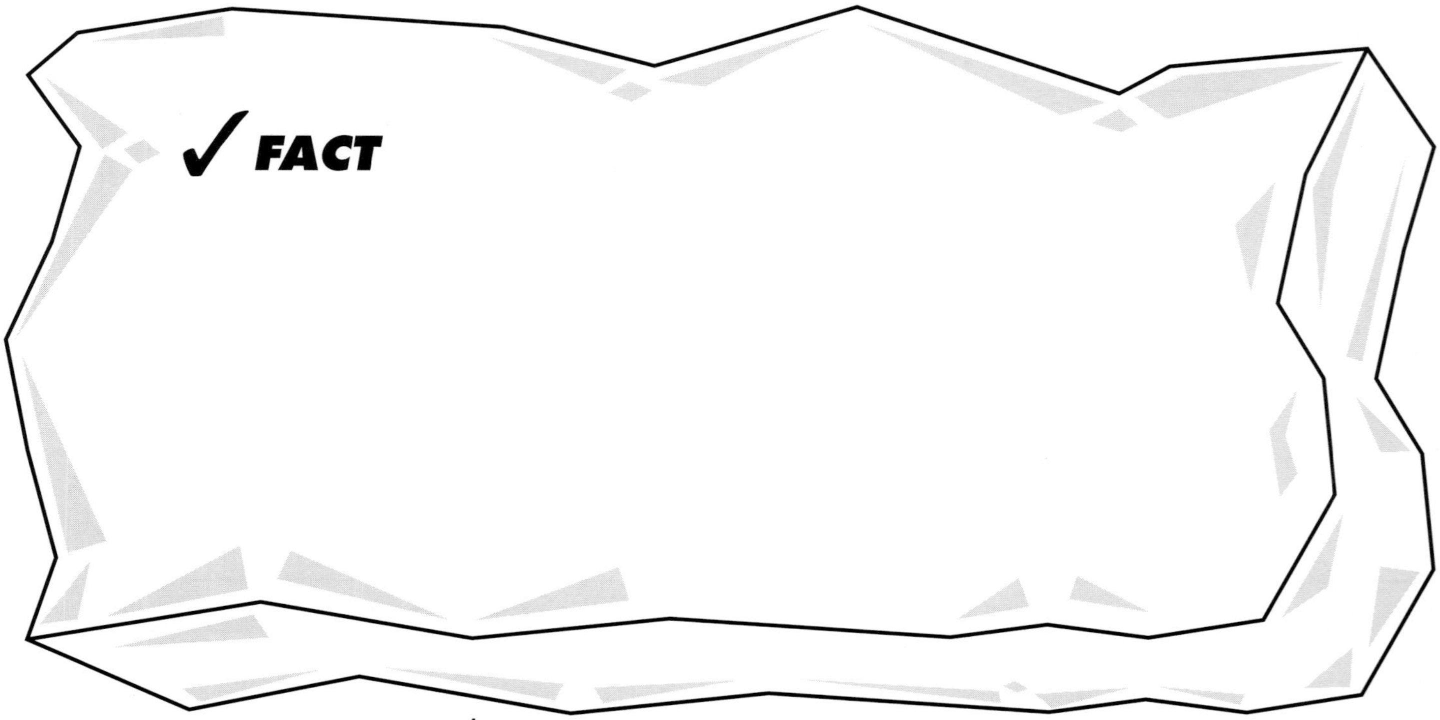

VISUAL ANALYSIS

Describe the artwork.	**Explain what is happening in the artwork.**
Explain what the artist is trying to show you.	**Explain the mood of the artwork.**

Multiple Causes and Effects

CAUSE

CAUSE

EFFECT

CAUSE

EFFECT

CAUSE

EFFECT

EFFECT

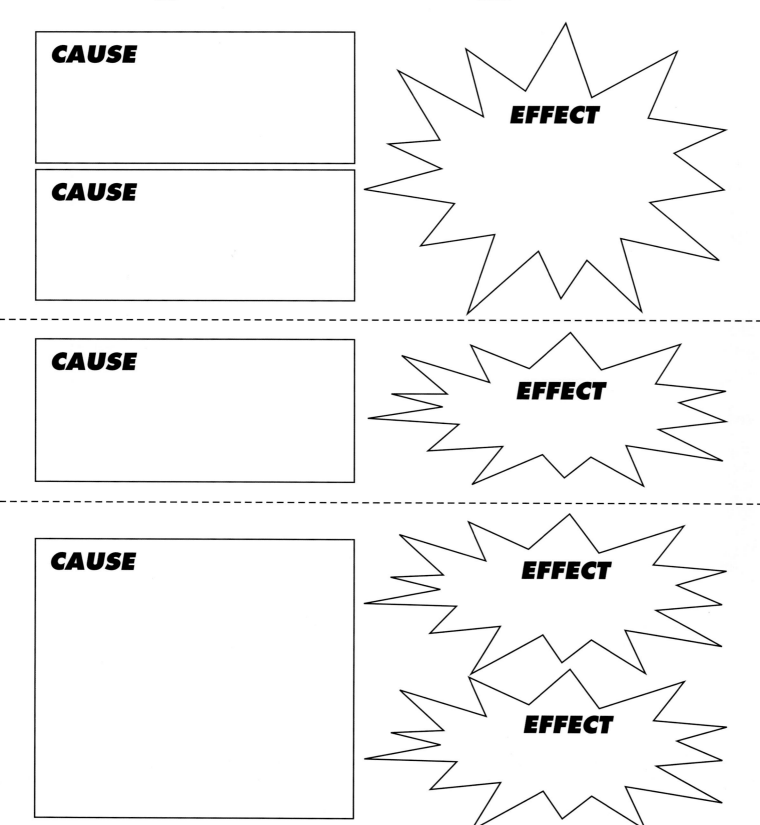

COMPARE AND CONTRAST

Information About "A"

Information About "B"

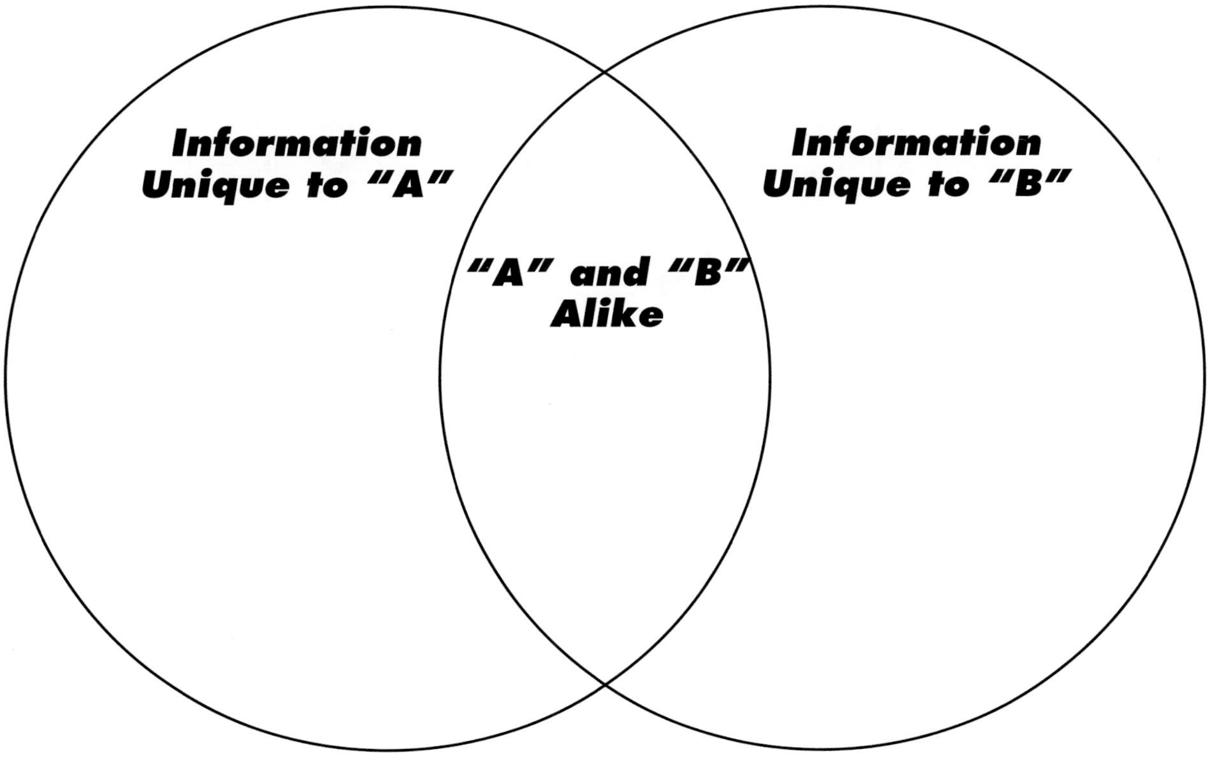

MAKE INFERENCES

Facts on the page

ON THE PAGE +

Background information and opinions in your head

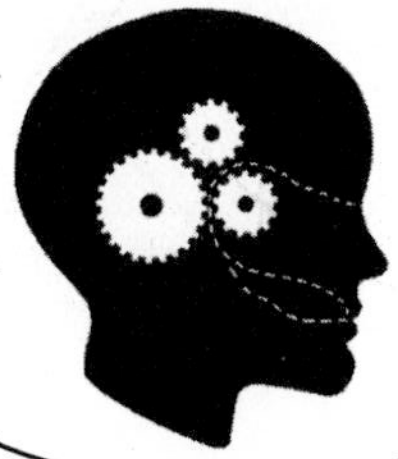

IN YOUR HEAD =

Inference

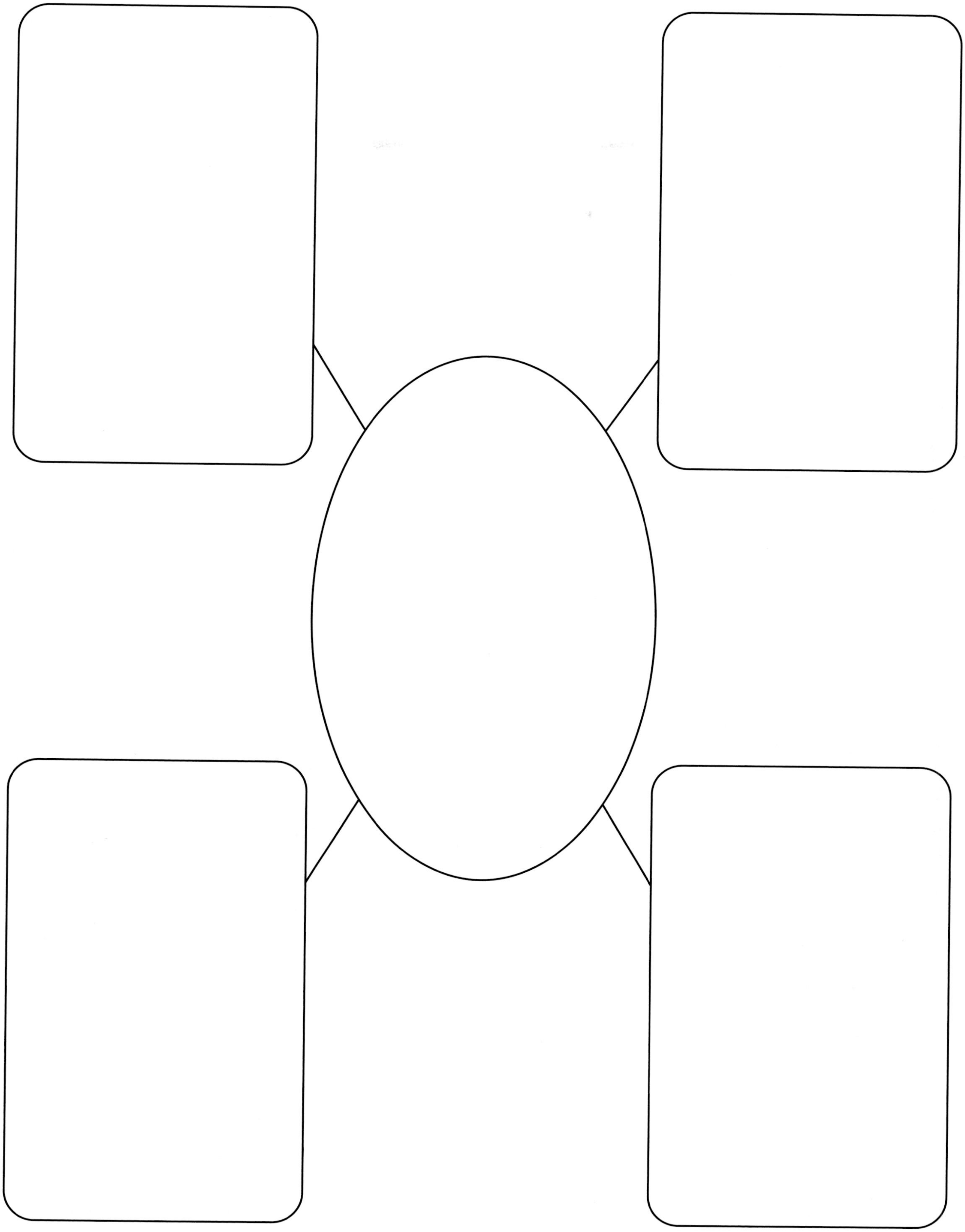

THE UNITED STATES

NORTH AMERICA

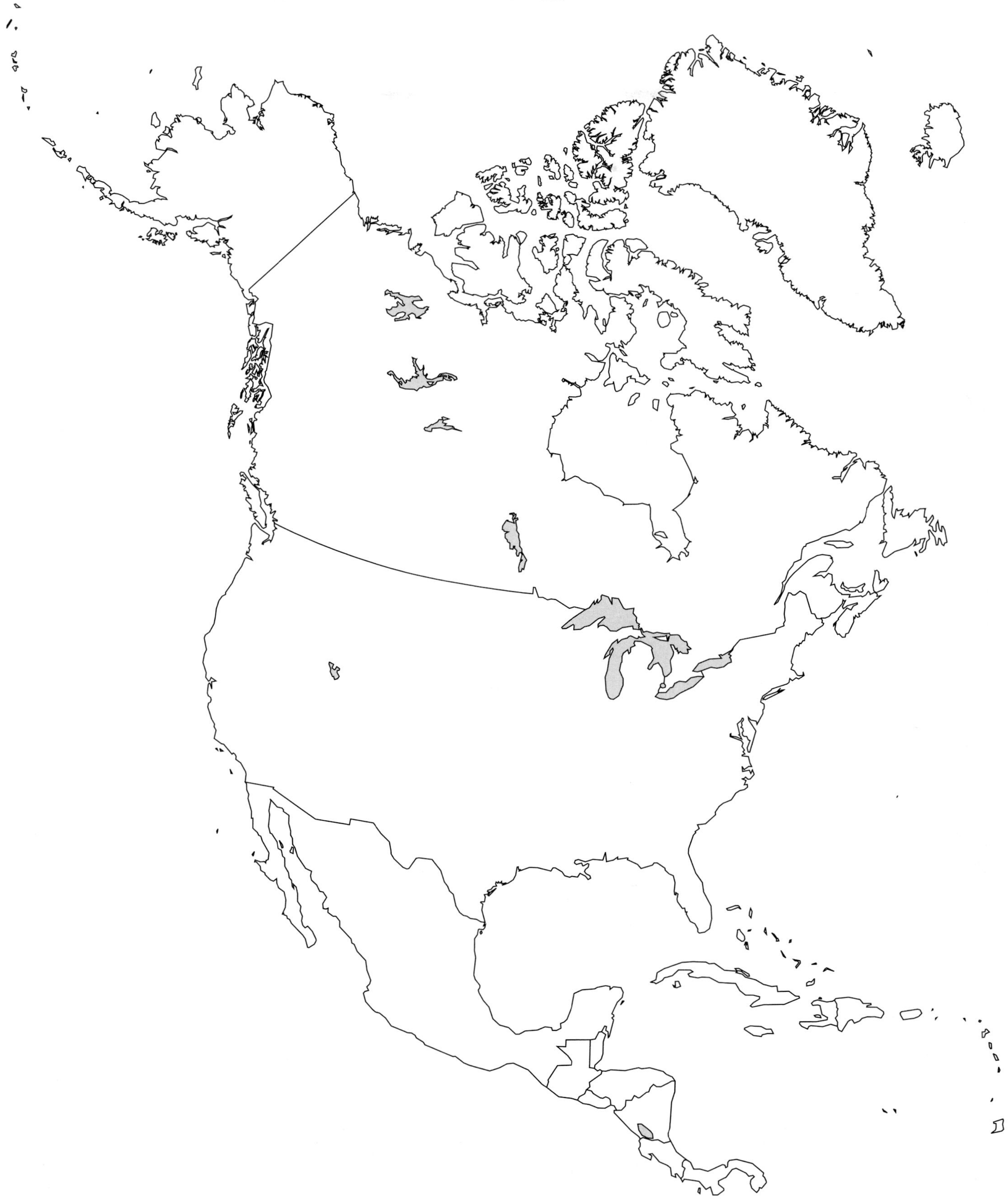

THE WORLD

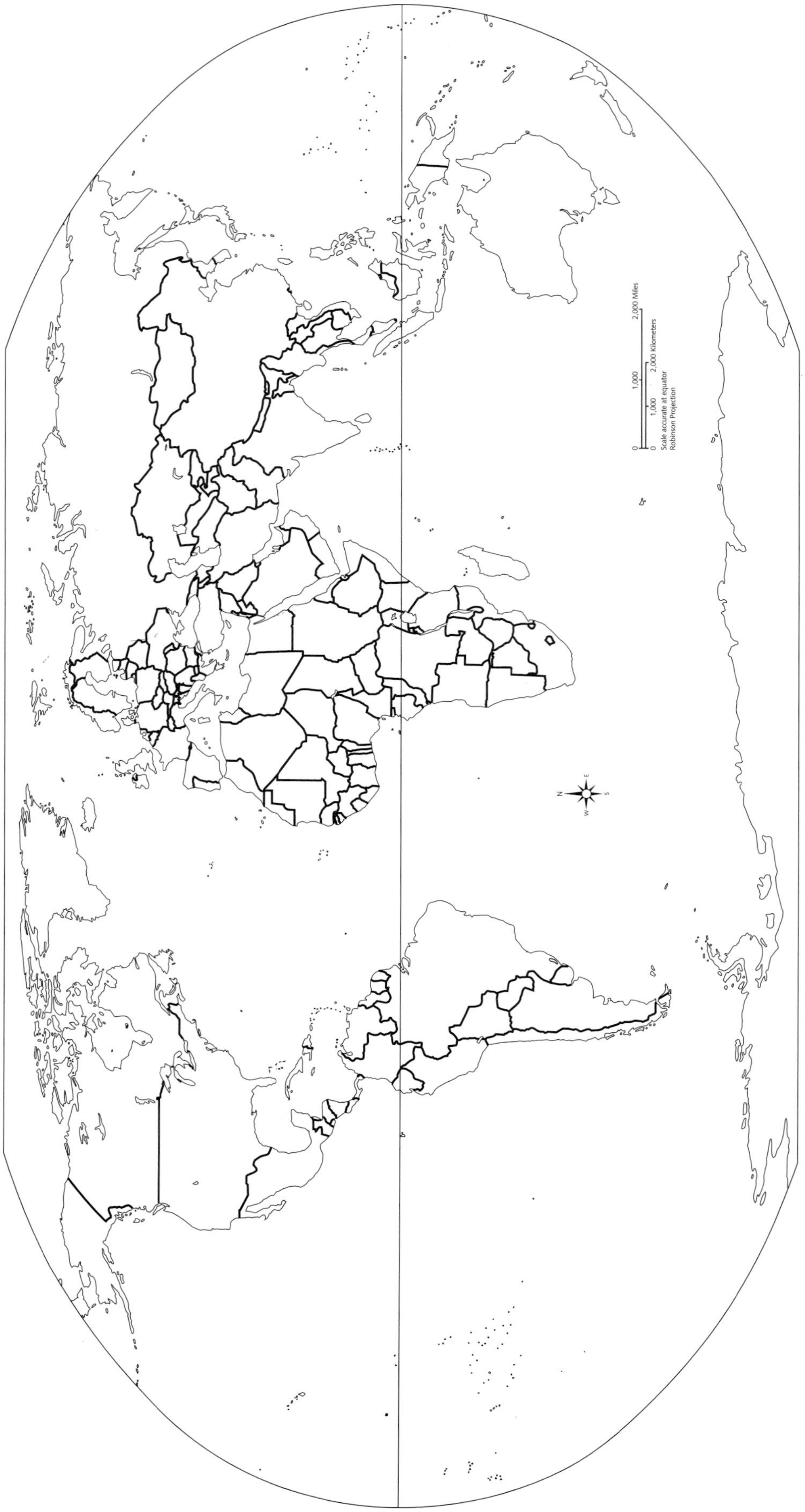
0
1,000
2,000 Miles
0
1,000
2,000 Kilometers
Scale accurate at equator
Robinson Projection
N
E
S
W

WESTERN HEMISPHERE

EASTERN HEMISPHERE

SOUTHERN HEMISPHERE

NORTHERN HEMISPHERE

Vocabulary Blacklines

This reproducible section will help you create word cards for the vocabulary found at the beginning of each lesson in your Teacher's Edition. The word cards may be used to preview the unit, to build vocabulary notebooks, to assist students with language difficulty or English language learners, and to review vocabulary at the end of each chapter. Use blank cards to add vocabulary to meet the special needs of your class.

Contents

pioneer Lesson 1	purchase Lesson 2
pathfinder Lesson 2	impressment Lesson 3
nationalism Lesson 3	annex Lesson 3
doctrine Lesson 3	prediction Skill Lesson

Industrial Revolution Lesson 1	textile mill Lesson 1
mass production Lesson 1	interchangeable part Lesson 1
transport Lesson 1	canal Lesson 1
locomotive Lesson 1	sectionalism Lesson 2
states' rights Lesson 2	secede Lesson 2
ruling Lesson 2	Manifest Destiny Lesson 3

dictator Lesson 3	forty-niner Lesson 3
relief Skill Lesson	elevation Skill Lesson
reform Lesson 4	public school Lesson 4
abolish Lesson 4	abolitionist Lesson 4
equality Lesson 4	suffrage Lesson 4

cotton gin	trend
Lesson 1	Skill Lesson
slave code	overseer
Lesson 2	Lesson 2
spiritual	resist
Lesson 2	Lesson 2
Underground Railroad	free state
Lesson 2	Lesson 3
slave state	Confederacy
Lesson 3	Lesson 4

Harcourt Brace School Publishers

border state Lesson 1	Emancipation Proclamation Lesson 1
Gettysburg Address Lesson 3	assassination Lesson 3
sharecropping Lesson 4	Reconstruction Lesson 4
scalawag Lesson 4	carpetbagger Lesson 4
segregation Lesson 4	

free enterprise Lesson 1	transcontinental railroad Lesson 1
capital resource Lesson 1	invest Lesson 1
stock Lesson 1	corporation Lesson 1
entrepreneur Lesson 1	consolidate Lesson 1
refinery Lesson 1	monopoly Lesson 1
hub Lesson 1	time zone Skill Lesson

human resource Lesson 2	strike Lesson 2
labor union Lesson 2	federation Lesson 2
regulate Lesson 2	prejudice Lesson 3
barrio Lesson 3	tenement Lesson 3
naturalization Lesson 3	settlement house Lesson 5
skyscraper Lesson 5	

homesteader Lesson 1	bonanza farm Lesson 1
climograph Skill Lesson	long drive Lesson 2
open range Lesson 2	vaquero Lesson 2
barbed wire Lesson 2	range war Lesson 2
prospector Lesson 3	boom Lesson 3
bust Lesson 3	vigilance Lesson 3

reservation

Lesson 4

imperialism	armistice
Lesson 1	*Lesson 1*
distortion	projection
Skill Lesson	*Skill Lesson*
progressive	commission
Lesson 2	*Lesson 2*
conservation	merit system
Lesson 2	*Lesson 2*
political boss	civil rights
Lesson 2	*Lesson 2*
alliance	military draft
Lesson 3	*Lesson 3*

Harcourt Brace School Publishers

no-man's-land Lesson 3	isolation Lesson 3
propaganda Skill Lesson	

consumer good Lesson 1	installment buying Lesson 1
assembly line Lesson 1	aviation Lesson 1
commercial industry Lesson 1	jazz Lesson 1
stock market Lesson 2	depression Lesson 2
bureaucracy Lesson 2	unemployment Lesson 2
minimum wage Lesson 2	hydroelectric dam Lesson 2

concentration camp Lesson 4	civilian Lesson 4
rationing Lesson 4	relocation camp Lesson 4
front Lesson 5	D day Lesson 5
Holocaust Lesson 5	island-hopping Lesson 5
communism Lesson 5	free world Lesson 5
cold war Lesson 5	

superpower	airlift
Lesson 1	*Lesson 1*
cease-fire	missile
Lesson 1	*Lesson 1*
arms race	nonviolence
Lesson 1	*Lesson 3*
integration	hawk
Lesson 3	*Lesson 4*
dove	scandal
Lesson 4	*Lesson 4*
arms control	détente
Lesson 5	*Lesson 5*

Harcourt Brace School Publishers

terrorism Lesson 5	hostage Lesson 5
deficit Lesson 5	

metropolitan area Lesson 1	middle class Lesson 1
interest rate Lesson 1	free-trade agreement Lesson 1
cartogram Skill Lesson	population density Skill Lesson
common-wealth Lesson 3	embargo Lesson 3
free election Lesson 3	liberate Lesson 4
mestizo Lesson 4	deforestation Lesson 4

province Lesson 5	separatist Lesson 5

Home Letters

These home letters offer a way of linking the student's study of social studies to the student's family members. There is one letter, available in both English and Spanish, for each unit. The focus for each letter is an activity or activities that students and family members can share.

Contents

Dear Family Members,

Our class is beginning a new social studies unit, called "Our Nation Grows." For the next few weeks, we will study the pioneers, who pushed west looking for land and opportunity. Students will learn how canals, steamboats, and railroads encouraged both travel and industrial growth. You can help your child get ready for this unit by doing the following activity. As you talk together, help your child make notes to share with the class.

Family Activity

With your child, make up a travel folder from the early to middle 1800s about a trip people could take in the United States. Tell where the trip will go, how people will get there, how much it will cost, and why people should make the trip. Add maps and pictures of the ways people traveled back then.

____

____

____

____

Family Reading

Visit your library for books to share about this time of growth in the United States. Your family might enjoy *Bridging the Continent: A Sourcebook on the American West* edited by Carter Smith. After you read, talk about what you remember most.

____

____

____

Thank you for supporting our social studies program.

Sincerely,

Queridos familiares,

Nuestra clase está comenzando una nueva unidad de estudios sociales que se llama "Nuestra nación crece". Durante las próximas semanas, estudiaremos a los pioneros que avanzaron hacia el oeste en busca de tierras y oportunidades. Los alumnos aprenderán cómo los canales, los barcos de vapor y los ferrocarriles estimularon tanto el desplazamiento de personas como el desarrollo industrial. Ustedes pueden ayudar a su hijo a prepararse para esta unidad haciendo las siguientes actividades. Mientras hablen, ayuden a su hijo a tomar apuntes que pueda compartir con la clase.

Actividad familiar

Con su hijo, hagan un folleto turístico sobre un viaje que los habitantes de Estados Unidos pudieron haber hecho al principio y durante la mitad del siglo XIX. Expliquen la ruta del viaje, el modo de transportación, cuánto costaría y las razones por las cuales las personas deberían hacer este viaje. Agreguen mapas e ilustraciones de las maneras en que las personas pudieron haber viajado en ese entonces.

Lectura familiar

Visiten la biblioteca para buscar libros sobre esta época de expansión en la historia de Estados Unidos. Puede ser que su familia disfrute *Bridging the Continent: A Sourcebook on the American West,* editado por Carter Smith. Después de la lectura, hablen sobre lo que mejor recuerden,

Agradecemos su apoyo a nuestro programa de estudios sociales.

Sinceramente,

Dear Family Members,

Our class is beginning a new social studies unit, called "War Divides the Nation." For the next few weeks, we will study the Civil War, one of the saddest events in our nation's history. We will look at its causes and at its effects on the nation. Students will learn about leaders from both sides, such as Abraham Lincoln and Robert E. Lee, and about the decisions they made. You can help your child get ready for this unit by doing the following activity. As you talk together, help your child make notes to share with the class.

Family Activity

Try to find out what was happening in your state during the Civil War and what your ancestors were doing. Did your ancestors or people from your state take part in the war? You might wish to visit a history museum and talk with the people there. If there are Civil War memorials, such as statues, in your town, you might find out about them.

___

___

___

___

Family Reading

Visit your library for books to share about the time of the Civil War. Your family might enjoy *The Civil War: An Illustrated History* by Geoffrey C. Ward with Ric Burns and Ken Burns. After you read, talk about what you remember most.

___

___

___

___

Thank you for supporting our social studies program.

Sincerely,

Queridos familiares,

Nuestra clase está comenzando una nueva unidad de estudios sociales que se llama "La guerra divide la nación". Durante las próximas semanas, estudiaremos la guerra civil, uno de los eventos más tristes de la historia de nuestra nación. Examinaremos sus causas y sus efectos en la nación. Los alumnos aprenderán sobre los líderes de ambos lados, como Abraham Lincoln y Robert E. Lee, y sobre las decisiones que tomaron. Ustedes pueden ayudar a su hijo a prepararse para esta unidad haciendo las siguientes actividades. Mientras hablen, ayuden a su hijo a tomar apuntes que pueda compartir con la clase.

Actividad familiar

Traten de determinar lo que pasó en su estado y lo que su familia hizo durante la guerra civil. ¿Participaron sus familiares u otras personas de su estado en la guerra? Posiblemente les gustaría visitar un museo de historia y hablar con las personas que trabajan allí. Algunos pueblos han levantado estatuas de personas que lucharon en la guerra civil.

Lectura familiar

Visiten la biblioteca para buscar libros sobre la época de la guerra civil. Quizás a su familia le gustaría leer *The Civil War: An Illustrated History* por Geoffrey C. Ward con Ric Burns y Ken Burns. Después de la lectura, hablen sobre lo que mejor recuerden.

Agradecemos su apoyo a nuestro programa de estudios sociales.

Sinceramente,

Dear Family Members:

Our class is beginning a new social studies unit called "Invention and Change." For the next few weeks, we will study how new inventions changed people's lives during the Gilded Age—the late 1800s and early 1900s—and how industry boomed as a result. Students will learn about immigration and the growth of big business. They will discover cowhands, miners, homesteaders, and Indian wars as they learn why and how the Great Plains were settled.

You can help your child get ready for this unit by doing the following activity at home. As you talk together, help your child make notes to share with the class.

Family Activity

An important idea of this unit is how the many inventions of the early 1900s changed the ways people lived, played, and worked. Talk with your child about ways in which recent inventions are changing our lives today. You may wish to contrast these ways with ways your ancestors handled the same tasks.

Family Reading

Visit your library for books to share about the turn of the century's age of invention. Your family might enjoy *Toilets, Toasters and Telephones: The How and Why of Everyday Objects* by Susan Goldman Rubin, Linda Zuckerman, and Ellen Warnick. After you read, talk about what you and your child remember most.

Thank you for supporting our social studies program.

Sincerely,

Queridos familiares:

Nuestra clase comienza una nueva unidad de estudios sociales que se llama "La invención y el cambio". Durante las próximas semanas, estudiaremos cómo los nuevos inventos cambiaron las vidas de la gente durante la Edad Dorada—a fines del siglo diecinueve y a principios del siglo veinte—y cómo creció la industria como resultado. Los estudiantes estudiarán la inmigración y el crecimiento de grandes negocios. Descubrirán a vaqueros, mineros, estancieros, y las guerras con los indios, mientras aprenden por qué y cómo fueron colonizadas las Grandes Llanuras.

Ustedes pueden ayudar a su hijo a prepararse para esta unidad haciendo la siguiente actividad en su casa. Mientras hablen, ayuden a su hijo a tomar apuntes para compartir con la clase.

Actividad familiar

Una idea importante de esta unidad es cómo las muchas invenciones que aparecieron a principios del siglo veinte cambiaron las formas en que la gente vivía, jugaba, y trabajaba. Hablen con su hijo de las maneras en que las invenciones más recientes cambian nuestras vidas hoy. Es posible que quieran contrastar la forma en que pueden hacer esta tarea hoy con la forma en que la hacían sus ancestros.

____

____

____

____

Lectura familiar

Visiten la biblioteca para buscar libros sobre la era de invención al final del siglo pasado y al comienzo de este siglo. Quizás disfrute su familia del libro *Toilets, Toasters and Telephones: The How and Why of Everyday Objects* por Susan Goldman Rubin, Linda Zuckerman, and Ellen Warnick. Después de la lectura, hablen de lo que mejor recuerden ustedes y su hijo.

____

____

____

____

Les agradezco su apoyo a nuestro programa de estudios sociales.

Sinceramente,

Dear Family Members:

Our class is beginning a new social studies unit called "Becoming a World Power." For the next few weeks, we will study the expanding role of the United States as a world power during the first half of the twentieth century. Students will learn about U.S. territorial expansion, its growing influence overseas, and the actions Theodore Roosevelt took toward this goal. Students also discover why the United States became involved in World War I and World War II.

You can help your child get ready for this unit by doing the following activity at home. As you talk together, help your child make notes to share with the class.

Family Activity

Watch the national news on television and have your child point out which stories describe conflict between two or more groups. Point out connections between current events and events in the first part of the 1900s.

___

___

___

___

Family Reading

Visit your library for books to share about the United States' growth. Your family might enjoy *World War Two: The Best of American Heritage* by Stephen W. Sears or *Sadako and the Thousand Paper Cranes* by Eleanor Coerr. After you read, talk about what you and your child remember most.

___

___

___

___

Thank you for supporting our social studies program.

Sincerely,

Queridos familiares:

Nuestra clase comienza una nueva unidad de estudios sociales que se llama "La nación se hace una potencia mundial". Durante las próximas semanas, estudiaremos cómo se amplió el papel del poder mundial logrado por los Estados Unidos durante la primera mitad del siglo veinte. Los estudiantes estudiarán la expansión territorial de los Estados Unidos, su influencia creciente en el extranjero, y las acciones tomadas por Theodore Roosevelt para alcanzar su meta. Los estudiantes descubrirán también por qué los Estados Unidos tomó parte en la Primera Guerra Mundial y en la Segunda Guerra Mundial.

Ustedes pueden ayudar a su hijo a prepararse para esta unidad haciendo la siguiente actividad en su casa. Mientras hablen, ayuden a su hijo a tomar apuntes para compartir con la clase.

Actividad familiar

Miren las noticias nacionales en la televisión y hagan que su hijo señale cuáles segmentos describen un conflicto entre dos o más grupos. Señalen ustedes las conexiones entre los acontecimientos actuales y los acontecimientos a principios del siglo veinte.

____

____

____

____

Lectura familiar

Visiten la biblioteca para buscar libros que traten sobre el crecimiento de Estados Unidos. Quizás disfrute su familia del libro *World War Two: The Best of American Heritage* por Stephen W. Sears y *Sadako and the Thousand Paper Cranes* por Eleanor Coerr. Después de la lectura, hablen de lo que mejor recuerden ustedes y su hijo.

____

____

____

____

Les agradezco su apoyo a nuestro programa de estudios sociales.

Sinceramente,

Dear Family Members,

Our class is beginning a new social studies unit, called "The Americas Today." For the next few weeks, we will study events in United States history since World War II. Students will also learn about some of our country's neighbors in the Western Hemisphere. You can help your child get ready for this unit by doing the following activity. As you talk together, help your child make notes to share with the class.

Family Activity

Sharing your memories of important events and of the leaders you remember will help make history come alive for your child. Talk about what it was like growing up during the Cold War. Tell what you recall about the Vietnam War and the Civil Rights movement. If you have lived in or visited Mexico, the Caribbean, Central America, or South America, be sure to share your memories with your child.

Family Reading

Visit your library for books about the United States, Canada, and Latin America in the past few years. Your family might enjoy *Canada* by David Marshall and Margot Richardson and *Mayeros: A Yucatec Maya Family* by George Ancona. After you read, discuss what you remember most.

Thank you for supporting our social studies program.

Sincerely,

Queridos familiares,

Nuestra clase está comenzando una nueva unidad de estudios sociales que se llama "Las Américas en la actualidad". Durante las próximas semanas, estudiaremos eventos en la historia de Estados Unidos después de la Segunda Guerra Mundial. Los alumnos también aprenderán sobre algunos de nuestros países vecinos en el hemisferio occidental. Ustedes pueden ayudar a su hijo a prepararse para esta unidad haciendo las siguientes actividades. Mientras hablen, ayuden a su hijo a tomar apuntes que pueda compartir con la clase.

Actividad familiar

El compartir sus memorias de eventos importantes y de los líderes que ustedes han conocido hará que la historia cobre vida para su hijo. Hablen de sus experiencias durante la guerra fría. Cuenten lo que recuerden sobre la guerra en Vietnam y el movimiento para los derechos civiles. Si han vivido o han visitado México, el Caribe, América Central o América del Sur, no dejen de compartir sus memorias con su hijo.

Lectura familiar

Visiten la biblioteca para buscar libros sobre Estados Unidos, Canadá y América Latina durante los últimos años. Quizás su familia disfrute *Canada* por David Marshall y Margot Richardson y *Mayeros: A Yucatec Maya Family* por George Ancona. Después de la lectura, hablen de lo que mejor recuerden.

Agradecemos su apoyo a nuestro programa de estudios sociales.

Sinceramente,

Scope and Sequence

Scope and Sequence

Harcourt Brace Social Studies builds consistent and cumulative learning from Kindergarten through Grade 6. The program allows students at each level to build on major understandings and skills already acquired and to prepare for learning yet to come. The powerful ideas in *Harcourt Brace Social Studies* provide the principal contexts within which students can integrate major understandings, skills, and their own experiences. These powerful ideas have been selected to help students organize their thinking and develop the competencies they will need as citizens in a diverse, changing, and interdependent world.

THE POWERFUL IDEAS
THEMES AND STRANDS OF SOCIAL STUDIES

Major Understandings

	K	1	2	3	4	5	6
Geography							
understanding location	•	•	•	•	•	•	•
relative and absolute (exact) location		•	•	•	•	•	•
factors influencing location		•	•	•	•	•	•
understanding place	•	•	•	•	•	•	•
physical features (landforms, bodies of water, vegetation)	•	•	•	•	•	•	•
human or cultural features		•	•	•	•	•	•
understanding human-environment interactions	•	•	•	•	•	•	•
seasons and climate	•	•	•	•	•	•	•
land use and natural resources	•	•	•	•	•	•	•
conservation and pollution	•	•	•	•	•	•	•
population density				•	•	•	•
understanding movement	•	•	•	•	•	•	•
people (immigration, colonization, settlement patterns)		•	•	•	•	•	•
products (trade)	•	•	•	•	•	•	•
ideas (cultural borrowing and cultural diffusion)		•	•	•	•	•	•
understanding regions		•	•	•	•	•	•
physical regions		•	•	•	•	•	•
cultural regions		•	•	•	•	•	•
political regions			•	•	•	•	•
economic regions			•	•	•	•	•
functional regions					•	•	•
time zones					•	•	•
History							
understanding time patterns and relationships among events	•	•	•	•	•	•	•
sequence of events (indefinite time order)	•	•	•	•	•	•	•
chronology (definite time order)		•	•	•	•	•	•
cause and effect		•	•	•	•	•	•
identifying and using historical evidence	•	•	•	•	•	•	•
types of evidence		•	•	•	•	•	•
quality of evidence		•	•	•	•	•	•
understanding the importance of individuals and groups across time and place	•	•	•	•	•	•	•
leaders and achievers	•	•	•	•	•	•	•
all people make a difference	•	•	•	•	•	•	•
founders and first persons		•	•	•	•	•	•
contributors to change	•	•	•	•	•	•	•
understanding the importance of events across time and place	•	•	•	•	•	•	•
innovations and inventions		•	•	•	•	•	•
impacts and turning points				•	•	•	•
revolutions and transformations				•	•	•	•
debates and controversies				•	•	•	•
understanding the times in which people lived	•	•	•	•	•	•	•
historical empathy		•	•	•	•	•	•
understanding origins, spread, and influence	•	•	•	•	•	•	•
growth and expansion			•	•	•	•	•

• A bullet indicates levels at which understandings are introduced, taught, applied, reinforced, or extended.
For more detailed information, refer to the index for each level.

	K	1	2	3	4	5	6
development of ideas					•	•	•
connecting past with present	•	•	•	•	•	•	•
comparing past with present	•	•	•	•	•	•	•

Civics and Government

	K	1	2	3	4	5	6
understanding patriotic identity	•	•	•	•	•	•	•
flags, symbols, anthems, mottoes, and pledges	•	•	•	•	•	•	•
patriotic customs, celebrations, and traditions	•	•	•	•	•	•	•
understanding civic values	•	•	•	•	•	•	•
recognizing and respecting authority figures	•	•	•	•	•	•	•
accepting and respecting others	•	•	•	•	•	•	•
working for the common good	•	•	•	•	•	•	•
understanding democratic principles	•	•	•	•	•	•	•
citizens as the source of government's authority			•	•	•	•	•
due process and equal protection under the law				•	•	•	•
majority rule and minority rights				•	•	•	•
government by law		•	•	•	•	•	•
understanding rights and freedoms of citizens	•	•	•	•	•	•	•
voting rights, property rights, civil rights, human rights		•	•	•	•	•	•
freedom of expression, worship, assembly, movement		•	•	•	•	•	•
understanding the responsibilities of citizens		•	•	•	•	•	•
voluntary responsibilities (voting, keeping informed)		•	•	•	•	•	•
responsibilities under the law (obeying laws, paying taxes)		•	•	•	•	•	•
understanding purposes of government	•	•	•	•	•	•	•
promoting order and security	•	•	•	•	•	•	•
promoting well-being and common good	•	•	•	•	•	•	•
providing for distribution of benefits and burdens of society	•	•	•	•	•	•	•
providing means of peaceful conflict resolution		•	•	•	•	•	•
protecting rights and freedoms of individuals			•	•	•	•	•
understanding types of government (democracy, monarchy, dictatorship)					•	•	•
understanding democratic institutions	•	•	•	•	•	•	•
levels of government (local, state, national)		•	•	•	•	•	•
branches of government (executive, legislative, judicial)			•	•	•	•	•
government bodies (councils, boards, legislatures)			•	•	•	•	•
government services and activities			•	•	•	•	•
government documents (Constitution, Bill of Rights, etc.)			•	•	•	•	•
political parties						•	•
understanding democratic processes		•	•	•	•	•	•
making, amending, and removing rules and laws		•	•	•	•	•	•
enforcing laws		•	•	•	•	•	•
voting and elections		•	•	•	•	•	•
becoming a citizen					•	•	•

Economics

	K	1	2	3	4	5	6
understanding scarcity and economic choice	•	•	•	•	•	•	•
wants and basic needs	•	•	•	•	•	•	•
goods and services		•	•	•	•	•	•
production and consumption		•	•	•	•	•	•
trade-offs and opportunity cost		•	•	•	•	•	•

A bullet indicates levels at which understandings are introduced, taught, applied, reinforced, or extended.
r more detailed information, refer to the index for each level.

	K	1	2	3	4	5	6
economic resources		•	•	•	•	•	•
spending and saving		•	•	•	•	•	•
conservation	•	•	•	•	•	•	•
understanding interdependence and income	•	•	•	•	•	•	•
transportation and communication links	•	•	•	•	•	•	•
mediums of exchange (barter and use of money)		•	•	•	•	•	•
trade		•	•	•	•	•	•
imports and exports (international trade)		•	•	•	•	•	•
understanding markets and prices		•	•	•	•	•	•
supply and demand			•	•	•	•	•
competition				•	•	•	•
understanding productivity and economic growth	•	•	•	•	•	•	•
kinds of work (jobs)	•	•	•	•	•	•	•
division of labor and specialization		•	•	•	•	•	•
production process		•	•	•	•	•	•
factors of production				•	•	•	•
effects of technology		•	•	•	•	•	•
understanding economic systems and institutions	•	•	•	•	•	•	•
public and private property	•	•	•	•	•	•	•
taxes			•	•	•	•	•
free enterprise and entrepreneurship		•	•	•	•	•	•
command, traditional, and market systems							•
Culture							
understanding ideas of shared humanity and unique identity	•	•	•	•	•	•	•
culture and cultural identity	•	•	•	•	•	•	•
customs and traditions (one's own and others)		•	•	•	•	•	•
cultural diversity and pluralism		•	•	•	•	•	•
multicultural societies		•	•	•	•	•	•
understanding social organizations and institutions	•	•	•	•	•	•	•
belonging to groups	•	•	•	•	•	•	•
family and community	•	•	•	•	•	•	•
social class structures	•	•	•	•	•	•	•
roles (gender, age, occupation)	•	•	•	•	•	•	•
religion and beliefs		•	•	•	•	•	•
education		•	•	•	•	•	•
understanding means of thought and expression	•	•	•	•	•	•	•
art, literature, music, dance, and architecture	•	•	•	•	•	•	•
language and communication	•	•	•	•	•	•	•
recreation	•	•	•	•	•	•	•
food preparation				•	•	•	•
understanding human relationships	•	•	•	•	•	•	•
between and among individuals	•	•	•	•	•	•	•
within a culture or society		•	•	•	•	•	•
between and among cultures or societies			•	•	•	•	•
philosophy and ethics	•	•	•	•	•	•	•
ideas and standards of behavior	•	•	•	•	•	•	•
resolving ethical issues	•	•	•	•	•	•	•
effects of belief on behavior				•	•	•	•

• A bullet indicates levels at which understandings are introduced, taught, applied, reinforced, or extended.
For more detailed information, refer to the index for each level.

Skills

	K	1	2	3	4	5	6
BASIC STUDY SKILLS							
Map and Globe Skills							
understanding globes	•	•	•	•	•	•	•
North and South Poles		•	•	•	•	•	•
equator			•	•	•	•	•
hemispheres			•	•	•	•	•
prime meridian					•	•	•
Tropics of Cancer and Capricorn					•	•	•
Arctic and Antarctic Circles					•	•	•
understanding the purpose and use of maps	•	•	•	•	•	•	•
map title		•	•	•	•	•	•
map key (legend)		•	•	•	•	•	•
compass rose (direction indicator)		•	•	•	•	•	•
map scale				•	•	•	•
grid system			•	•	•	•	•
comparing maps with globes	•	•	•	•	•	•	•
comparing maps with photographs		•	•	•	•	•	•
understanding map symbols	•	•	•	•	•	•	•
land and water	•	•	•	•	•	•	•
colors, tints, and patterns		•	•	•	•	•	•
object and picture symbols		•	•	•	•	•	•
lines and borders			•	•	•	•	•
roads, routes, and arrows		•	•	•	•	•	•
location symbols			•	•	•	•	•
relief and elevation					•	•	•
understanding directional terms and finding direction	•	•	•	•	•	•	•
cardinal directions		•	•	•	•	•	•
intermediate directions				•	•	•	•
understanding and measuring distance				•	•	•	•
miles and kilometers				•	•	•	•
insets				•	•	•	•
understanding and finding location		•	•	•	•	•	•
number and letter grids			•	•	•		
lines of latitude and longitude (parallels and meridians)					•	•	•
measurements in degrees					•	•	•
understanding map projections and distortions						•	•
understanding cartograms							•
Chart and Graph Skills							
understanding and using pictographs	•	•	•	•	•	•	•
understanding and using charts and diagrams	•	•	•	•	•	•	•

bullet indicates levels at which skills are introduced, taught, applied, reinforced, or extended.
more detailed information, refer to the index for each level.

	K	1	2	3	4	5	6
understanding and using bar graphs	•	•	•	•	•	•	•
understanding and using calendars and time lines	•	•	•	•	•	•	•
understanding and using tables and schedules		•	•	•	•	•	•
understanding and using line graphs					•	•	•
understanding and using circle (pie) graphs						•	•
understanding and using climographs						•	•
Reading and Research Skills							
understanding photographs and other picture illustrations	•	•	•	•	•	•	•
understanding artifacts and documents	•	•	•	•	•	•	•
understanding fine art		•	•	•	•	•	•
understanding safety and information symbols	•	•	•	•	•	•	•
understanding political cartoons						•	•
using context clues to understand vocabulary	•	•	•	•	•	•	•
using illustrations or objects to understand vocabulary	•	•	•	•	•	•	•
grouping and categorizing words (semantic maps)	•	•	•	•	•	•	•
understanding multiple meanings of words		•	•	•	•	•	•
understanding literal and implied meanings of words				•	•	•	•
understanding root words, prefixes, and suffixes				•	•	•	•
identifying abbreviations and acronyms				•	•	•	•
understanding facts and main ideas	•	•	•	•	•	•	•
identifying stated main ideas		•	•	•	•	•	•
generating unstated main ideas		•	•	•	•	•	•
recalling facts and details that support a generalization		•	•	•	•	•	•
using headings and prereading strategies to identify main ideas	•	•	•	•	•	•	•
identifying and understanding various types of text	•	•	•	•	•	•	•
informational and expository	•	•	•	•	•	•	•
narrative	•	•	•	•	•	•	•
fiction and historical fiction	•	•	•	•	•	•	•
biography and autobiography		•	•	•	•	•	•
journal, diary, and log		•	•	•	•	•	•
essay		•	•	•	•	•	•
letter		•	•	•	•	•	•
speech		•	•	•	•	•	•
legend, myth, and folklore		•	•	•	•	•	•
locating and gathering information		•	•	•	•	•	•
almanac			•	•	•	•	•
atlas and gazetteer		•	•	•	•	•	•
dictionary and glossary		•	•	•	•	•	•
encyclopedia		•	•	•	•	•	•
current news sources (television, radio, newspapers)		•	•	•	•	•	•
library and community		•	•	•	•	•	•
electronic resources (databases, CD-ROMs, Internet)		•	•	•	•	•	•
writing and dictating	•	•	•	•	•	•	•
expressing ideas in various ways (to inform, explain, persuade, describe)	•	•	•	•	•	•	•

• A bullet indicates levels at which skills are introduced, taught, applied, reinforced, or extended.
For more detailed information, refer to the index for each level.

	K	1	2	3	4	5	6
speaking and listening	•	•	•	•	•	•	•
expressing a point of view or opinion	•	•	•	•	•	•	•
dramatizing and role-playing simulations	•	•	•	•	•	•	•
making observations	•	•	•	•	•	•	•
asking questions	•	•	•	•	•	•	•
listing and ordering	•	•	•	•	•	•	•
constructing and creating	•	•	•	•	•	•	•
displaying, charting, and drawing	•	•	•	•	•	•	•
distinguishing primary from secondary sources					•	•	•
distinguishing fact from nonfact (fantasy, fiction, or opinion)			•	•	•	•	•
BUILDING CITIZENSHIP							
Critical Thinking Skills							
identifying cause-and-effect relationships	•	•	•	•	•	•	•
following sequence and chronology	•	•	•	•	•	•	•
classifying and grouping information	•	•	•	•	•	•	•
summarizing		•	•	•	•	•	•
synthesizing				•	•	•	•
making inferences and generalizations				•	•	•	•
forming logical conclusions	•	•	•	•	•	•	•
understanding and evaluating point of view and perspective		•	•	•	•	•	•
evaluating and making judgments	•	•	•	•	•	•	•
detecting bias or stereotypes						•	•
predicting likely outcomes		•	•	•	•	•	•
making thoughtful choices and decisions	•	•	•	•	•	•	•
solving problems	•	•	•	•	•	•	•
Participation Skills							
working with others	•	•	•	•	•	•	•
resolving conflict	•	•	•	•	•	•	•
acting responsibly	•	•	•	•	•	•	•
identifying the consequences of a person's behavior	•	•	•	•	•	•	•
keeping informed	•	•	•	•	•	•	•
respecting rules and laws	•	•	•	•	•	•	•
participating in a group or community	•	•	•	•	•	•	•
respecting people with differing points of view	•	•	•	•	•	•	•
assuming leadership and being willing to follow		•	•	•	•	•	•
identifying traits of a leader and a follower			•	•	•	•	•
making decisions and solving problems in a group setting		•	•	•	•	•	•
understanding patriotic and cultural symbols		•	•	•	•	•	•

A bullet indicates levels at which skills are introduced, taught, applied, reinforced, or extended.
r more detailed information, refer to the index for each level.

Test Preparation

Contents

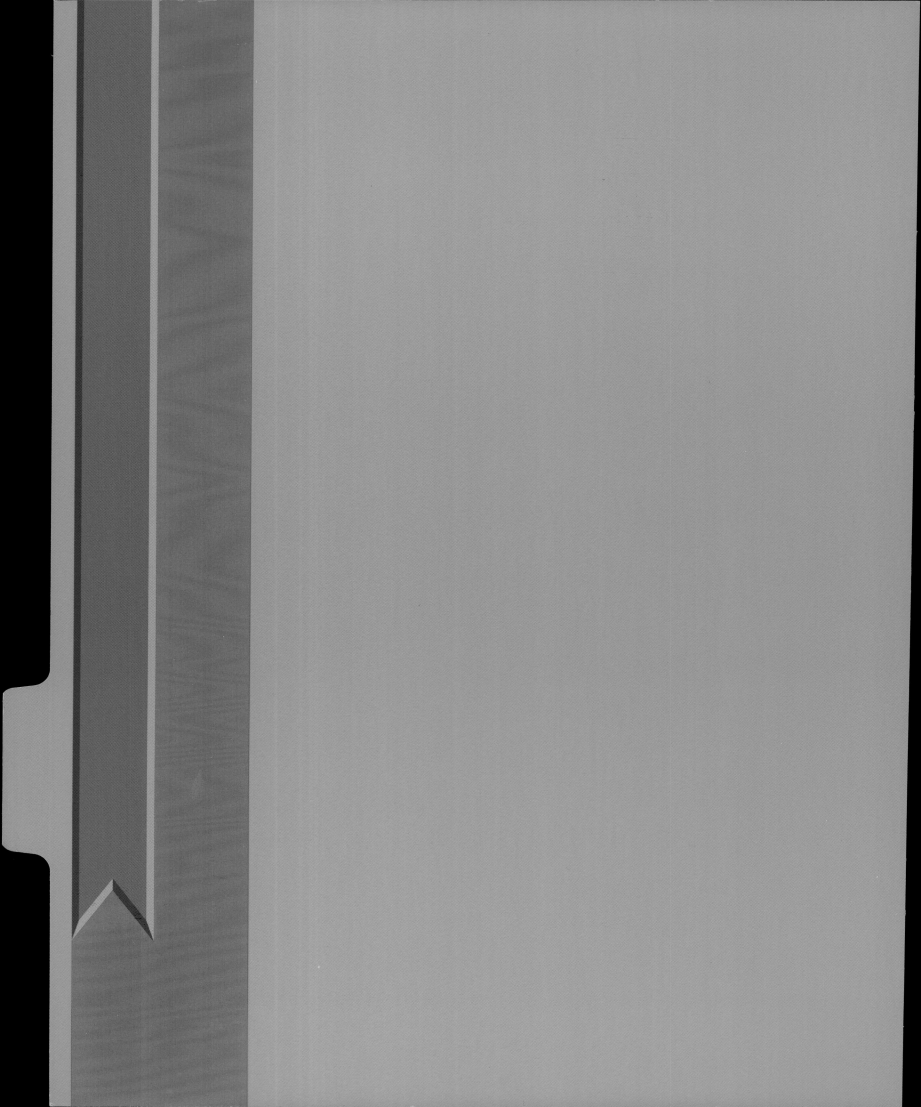

The lessons in this section have been designed to provide

- additional, motivating reading experiences for your students.
- content related to units in *United States.*
- opportunities to build background and reinforce reading skills.
- practice opportunities for standardized tests.
- reading strategy activities to help students organize information.

Conversion Chart for Scoring

After students complete the article and answer the questions, you can use the following chart to identify a grade.

Correct Number of Responses	Percentage Score
8	100%
7	88%
6	75%
5	63%
4	50%
3	38%
2	25%
1	13%

UNIT 6
Gold Fever

A•B•C LESSON PLANNER

1. Access

- **READING STRATEGY:** Use the Anticipation Guide on page TP24 before having small groups of students read the article. Write the statements on the board, or use the sheet as a copying master. Invite students to tell whether they agree or disagree with each statement. They can write their responses in their journals or learning logs. Do not expect students to know the answers. This activity is designed to help build interest, activate prior knowledge, and set purposes for reading.

2. Build

- Have students read the article, or read it aloud to them.
- As students read or after they finish reading the article, they may change their opinions about the statements. If they do, have them discuss why they revised their opinions, and have them state what they learned from their reading that allowed them to confirm or revise their opinions.

3. Close

- Have students complete the standardized-test-format questions after they read the article. (An item analysis that identifies the test objectives covered by each question, as well as an answer key, can be found on page TP AK.)
- **MATHEMATICS ACTIVITY:** Have students research the price of an ounce of gold today. Invite students to compare today's price with the price of an ounce during the gold rush. Encourage students to create word problems about gold and its prices.

Name____

Gold Fever

Anticipation Guide

Check One

	Agree	Disagree
1. James Marshall discovered gold at Sutter's Mill.		
2. By 1849 the rush for gold was over.		
3. A boat trip from Massachusetts to California could cost as much as $1,000.		
4. San Francisco was the port closest to the goldfields.		
5. Searching for gold was easy, enjoyable work.		

Name____

GOLD FEVER

When James Marshall thought he saw a small lump of gold in the river near Sutter's Mill, he could not believe his eyes. He reached down and picked the nugget up. "It made my heart thump," Marshall later recalled, "for I was certain it was gold." Although he wanted to keep his discovery a secret, Marshall could not resist bragging to his friends. Soon newspapers were spreading the word that there was gold to be found in California. By 1849 there were many more gold seekers on the Oregon Trail than *pioneers* who were traveling west to settle new places.

Travel by sea was much easier than travel by land, but it was also much more expensive. A boat trip from Massachusetts to California, for example, could cost as much as $1,000. Yet many people were willing to pay that. In fact, so many people signed up that shipbuilding companies on the East Coast had to build more ships to keep up with the demand.

When the ships reached California, they docked in San Francisco, the port closest to the goldfields. By the late 1850s, when "gold fever" reached its peak, about 500 ships lay empty in the harbor. Their crews had left and gone off to search for gold. Like most of the forty-niners, they found hard work and disappointment instead.

Searching for gold was boring, backbreaking work. A miner would bend over a stream and scoop up water and dirt in a pan. Then the miner would tilt the pan to separate any pieces of gold from the water and dirt. This process, called *panning,* went on for many hours from morning until night. On a good day a miner might find a few tiny nuggets of gold. That was not much, especially since an ounce of gold was worth only about $16 in today's money.

Few of the gold seekers ever got rich. Most were lucky if they did not end up in debt. Prices were so high in the mining camps that the miners had trouble just paying for supplies. A single egg could cost up to $3, a pair of boots about $100, and a barrel of flour as much as $400. There was money to be made in California after all. It was made by the merchants who sold supplies to the miners.

Name____

Gold Fever

Choose the best answer and mark the letter of your choice.

1. What is this article mostly about?
- **A.** the state of California
- **B.** Sutter's Mill
- **C.** trails to the west
- **D.** the gold rush

2. The article gives you enough information to conclude that James Marshall's friends
- **F.** told other people that he had discovered gold.
- **G.** discovered gold with the help of others.
- **H.** worked as employees at Sutter's Mill.
- **J.** lived on the East Coast.

3. In this article, the word *pioneers* means
- **A.** people who are looking for gold.
- **B.** merchants who sell goods to miners.
- **C.** people who first settle a new place.
- **D.** travelers on trips for pleasure.

4. According to the article, when did "gold fever" reach its peak?
- **F.** when gold was worth $16 an ounce
- **G.** by the late 1850s
- **H.** when the miners were panning for gold
- **J.** in 1849

5. Ships lay empty in San Francisco harbor because
- **A.** passengers left them to search for gold.
- **B.** crews left them to search for gold.
- **C.** it was expensive to travel by sea.
- **D.** they had reached California.

6. In this article, the word *panning* means
- **F.** a method of searching for gold.
- **G.** a method of selling gold.
- **H.** a way to sell supplies.
- **J.** a form of travel.

7. Which of these is a fact presented in the article?
- **A.** The forty-niners were lucky to get to California.
- **B.** Miners were lucky that they already knew how to pan for gold.
- **C.** Merchants who sold supplies to the miners made money.
- **D.** Many merchants panned for gold.

8. The article gives you enough information to conclude that
- **F.** searching for gold was a profitable activity.
- **G.** miners worked very hard for little gold.
- **H.** miners had enough money to pay for supplies.
- **J.** there was a lot of gold in California.

UNIT 7
Balloons in Battle

A·B·C LESSON PLANNER

1. Access

- **READING STRATEGY:** Use the Word Splash on page TP28 to help students make predictions about the article. Write the words on the board, or use the sheet as a copying master. Invite students to predict how each word, phrase, or date relates to the flag of the United States. Students can write their predictions in their journals or learning logs. Do not expect students to know the answers. This activity is designed to help build interest, activate prior knowledge, and set purposes for reading.

2. Build

- Have students read the article, or read it aloud to them.
- As students read or after they finish reading the article, they may change their Word Splash predictions. Have them identify the predictions that were correct, and have them state what they have learned from reading the article.

3. Close

- Have students complete the standardized-test-format questions after they read the article. (An item analysis that identifies the test objectives covered by each question, as well as an answer key, can be found on page TP AK.)
- **SCIENCE ACTIVITY:** Have small groups conduct research to find out how gas-filled balloons fly. Then have them find out about helium balloons and uses for balloons. Students can share their findings with other groups.

Name____

Balloons in Battle

Word Splash

the Union

military aircraft

gas-filled balloons

Civil War

Thaddeus Lowe

farseeing eyes for the soldiers

the Confederacy

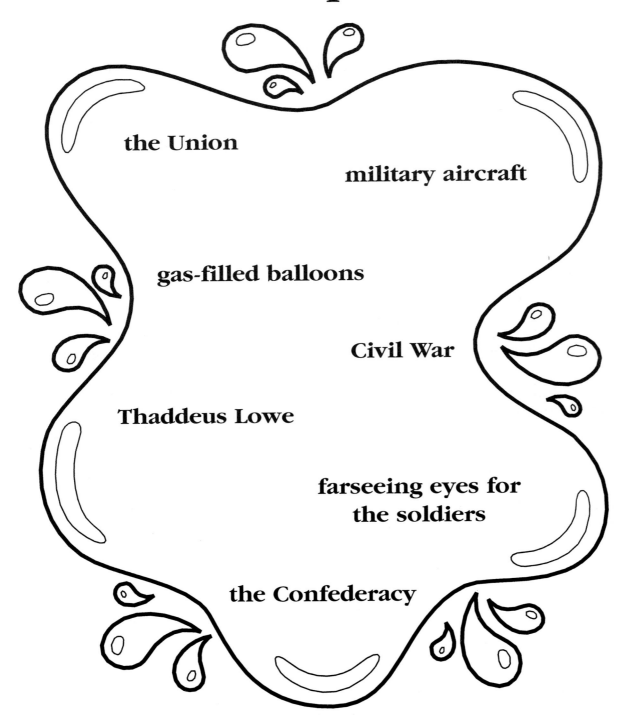

Name____

Balloons in Battle

Military aircraft were used for the first time in United States history during the Civil War. However, airplanes were not invented until 50 years after the war. What did the Civil War pilots fly? They flew huge gas-filled balloons. Pilots and their equipment rode in baskets attached to the bottom of each balloon.

Both the Union and the Confederacy tried using balloons in battle, but the Confederates had little success. They did not have the materials or people needed to build and keep up an air force.

The Union Army did have a well-trained Balloon Corps. It was commanded by a professional balloonist named Thaddeus Lowe.

Like many Northerners, Lowe did not take the war seriously at first. He was sure that the South's *rebellion* would end quickly and peacefully. The Confederates' revolt, Lowe believed, would not last. Lowe changed his mind, however, when he was taken prisoner by Confederate soldiers after a test flight to South Carolina.

Lowe was able to talk his way out of trouble, and he returned to the North. Then he set out to convince Union leaders that balloons would be of great value to their army.

To Lowe, the advantages, or good points, of using balloons were clear. Balloonists could see enemy soldiers and watch their movements. The balloonists could then signal their findings to soldiers on the ground. For the first time, officers would know everything that was happening on the battlefield.

Lowe's arguments were good, but it took a presidential order to get the Union Army to go along with the idea. Yet Lowe had set up seven balloon camps by early 1862. Where the *troops* went, the balloonists followed, acting as farseeing eyes for the soldiers.

Lowe himself seemed to be everywhere, whenever he was needed. After an important battle at Fair Oaks, General A.W. Greely wrote: "It may be safely claimed that the Union Army was saved from destruction . . . by the frequent and accurate reports of Lowe."

One of Lowe's greatest compliments came from Confederate General E. P. Alexander, who wrote this about the Balloon Corps: "Even if the observers never saw anything, they [the Balloon Corps] would have been worth all they cost for the annoyance and delay they caused us in trying to keep our movements out of their sight."

Name____

Balloons in Battle

Choose the best answer and mark the letter of your choice.

1. What is this article mostly about?
   - **A.** types of balloons
   - **B.** battles during the Civil War
   - **C.** Thaddeus Lowe's capture during the Civil War
   - **D.** balloons during the Civil War

2. Airplanes were invented
   - **F.** after the Civil War.
   - **G.** during the first year of the Civil War.
   - **H.** before the Civil War.
   - **J.** during the last year of the Civil War.

3. The Confederates had little success in using balloons because
   - **A.** they thought balloons were useless.
   - **B.** they did not know how to fly them.
   - **C.** they did not have the necessary materials or people.
   - **D.** they did not know how to make them.

4. In this article, the word *rebellion* means
   - **F.** battles.
   - **G.** revolt.
   - **H.** agreement.
   - **J.** secession.

5. Which of these is a fact presented in the article?
   - **A.** The Civil War was not serious at first.
   - **B.** Many Northerners did not take the war seriously at first.
   - **C.** Many Southerners did not take the war seriously at first.
   - **D.** From the start, Thaddeus Lowe thought the war was serious.

6. In this article, the word *troops* means
   - **F.** balloonists.
   - **G.** enemies.
   - **H.** officials.
   - **J.** soldiers.

7. The article gives you enough information to conclude that
   - **A.** balloons were never used after the Civil War.
   - **B.** balloons were useful to the Confederate Army.
   - **C.** balloons were useful to the Union Army.
   - **D.** balloons were not useful to either side.

8. The article gives you enough information to conclude that Thaddeus Lowe
   - **F.** was with the Union Army at the Battle of Fair Oaks.
   - **G.** never traveled with the troops.
   - **H.** was a friend of Union General A. W. Greely.
   - **J.** admired Confederate General E. P. Alexander.

UNIT 8
Edison's Talking Machine

A•B•C *L*ESSON *P*LANNER

1. *A*ccess

- **Reading Strategy:** Use the Anticipation Guide on page TP32 before having small groups of students read the article. Write the statements on the board, or use the sheet as a copying master. Invite students to tell whether they agree or disagree with each statement. They can write their responses in their journals or learning logs. Do not expect students to know the answers. This activity is designed to help build interest, activate prior knowledge, and set purposes for reading.

2. *B*uild

- Have students read the article, or read it aloud to them.
- As students read or after they finish reading the article, they may change their opinions about the statements. If they do, have them discuss why they revised their opinions, and have them state what they learned from their reading that allowed them to confirm or revise their opinions.

3. *C*lose

- Have students complete the standardized-test-format questions after they read the article. (An item analysis that identifies the test objectives covered by each question, as well as an answer key, can be found on page TP AK.)
- **Science Activity:** Have students research other inventions made by Thomas Edison. Invite students to find five facts about each invention. Students can then create an invention guessing game based on the facts.

Name____

Edison's Talking Machine

Anticipation Guide

Check One

	Agree	Disagree
1. Thomas Edison's favorite invention was the lightbulb.		
2. The first phonograph recording was a verse from a nursery rhyme.		
3. The phonograph made Edison famous throughout the world.		
4. Edison was trying to improve the telegraph when he got the idea for the phonograph.		
5. Edison thought of many different uses for the phonograph.		

Name____

Edison's Talking Machine

In a period of 60 years, Thomas Alva Edison worked on more than 1,000 inventions. Which was his favorite? The phonograph was the one. "This is my baby," he once told a reporter, "and I expect it to grow up and . . . support me in my old age."

Edison did not set out to invent the phonograph. He was trying to improve the telephone when he came up with an idea for a machine that could record voices. He worked on the machine for a year. Then, on December 6, 1877, he was ready to test it. He recited this familiar nursery rhyme for the test:

Mary had a little lamb,
Its fleece was white as snow,
And everywhere that Mary went
The lamb was sure to go.

When he finished speaking, Edison played the recording. It repeated his every word. Edison was amazed. He had hoped the machine would work, but he had not expected it to work so well! "I was never so taken aback in all my life," he said later. "I was always afraid of things that worked the first time."

People came from all over to try the phonograph, or "talking machine," as it was called in its early days. It made Edison famous throughout the world, and he became known as the Wizard of Menlo Park.

Menlo Park, New Jersey, was where Thomas Edison had his research *laboratory.* Today many large corporations have research laboratories. Edison's lab was the first of its kind in the United States. It was so impressive that many people who saw it decided to *invest* in Edison's inventions. Buying shares of his businesses seemed like a sure way to make a profit.

It was at Menlo Park that Edison developed the electric lightbulb. That project, and several others, took about ten years of his time. But by 1886, he was back at work on his favorite invention, the phonograph.

Thomas Edison made many improvements to the phonograph. He came up with many new ways to use it. He thought the phonograph could be used in advertisements, in toys, and even in talking books for the blind. He also predicted other ways it could be used. Edison was not really a wizard, but when it came to the phonograph, every prediction he made came true.

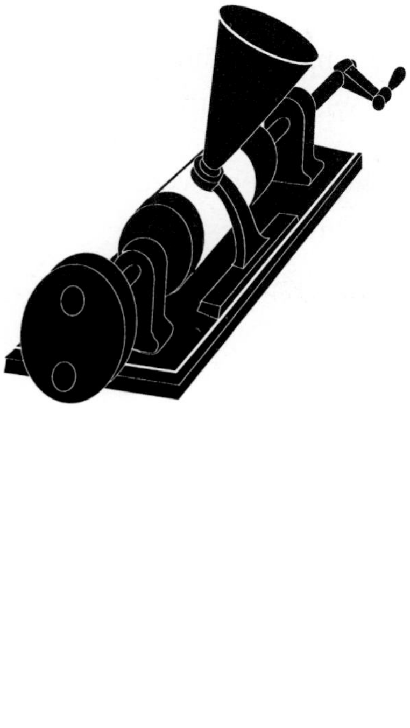

Name____

Edison's Talking Machine

Choose the best answer and mark the letter of your choice.

1. What is this article mostly about?

A. Thomas Alva Edison and the electric lightbulb

B. phonographs today

C. Edison's research laboratory

D. Thomas Alva Edison and the phonograph

2. When Edison said that he expected the phonograph to support him in his old age, he meant that he expected

F. to earn a lot of money from the phonograph.

G. the phonograph to be his last invention.

H. the phonograph to be his only invention.

J. to sell the phonograph to a corporation.

3. In this article, the word *laboratory* means

A. a secret room in an office.

B. a laundry area in a home.

C. a place where research goes on.

D. a room where meetings are held.

4. The first phonographs were called

F. Edison's machines.

G. recording machines.

H. voice machines.

J. talking machines.

5. Edison became known as the Wizard of Menlo Park because he

A. tried to improve the telephone.

B. invented the phonograph.

C. built the first research laboratory.

D. got people to invest in his inventions.

6. In this article, the word *invest* means

F. make a profit from a famous invention.

G. sell an invention to a large group of people who will resell it.

H. buy shares of a business in the hope of making a profit.

J. buy a company that makes something that people want in the hope of making a profit.

7. Thomas Edison is also known for his invention of

A. the telephone.

B. the electric lightbulb.

C. the telegraph.

D. electricity.

8. What is the main idea of the last paragraph?

F. The phonograph has many uses.

G. The phonograph needs to be improved.

H. Edison could predict the future.

J. It took ten years to develop the phonograph.

UNIT 9
The Model T

A·B·C *L*ESSON *P*LANNER

1. *A*ccess

- **Reading Strategy:** Use the Anticipation Guide on page TP36 before having small groups of students read the article. Write the statements on the board, or use the sheet as a copying master. Invite students to tell whether they agree or disagree with each statement. They can write their responses in their journals or learning logs. Do not expect students to know the answers. This activity is designed to help build interest, activate prior knowledge, and set purposes for reading.

2. *B*uild

- Have students read the article, or read it aloud to them.
- As students read or after they finish reading the article, they may change their opinions about the statements. If they do, have them discuss why they revised their opinions, and have them state what they learned from their reading that allowed them to confirm or revise their opinions.

3. *C*lose

- Have students complete the standardized-test-format questions after they read the article. (An item analysis that identifies the test objectives covered by each question, as well as an answer key, can be found on page TP AK.)
- **Art Activity:** Have students create a drawing of their dream car. Students who do not wish to draw may clip pictures of cars that appeal to them from magazines or newspapers. Invite students to describe what they like about the cars they have chosen or drawn.

Name ____________________

The Model T

Anticipation Guide

Check One

	Agree	Disagree
1. The first cars were very expensive and not very practical.		
2. The assembly line was not an efficient way to make cars.		
3. By 1920 half the cars in the United States were Model Ts.		
4. To improve the Model T, Henry Ford changed it often.		
5. New Model Ts were no longer sold after 1927.		

Name____________________

The MODEL T

In the early 1900s cars broke down often. They were expensive to repair. They were hard to drive on rough country roads. They also cost so much that few people could afford to buy them.

Henry Ford wanted to change that. He wanted to make cars that people could drive anywhere. He also wanted to sell cars at prices everyone could afford. Ford spent five years trying to make a better car. Finally, in 1908, he created his dream car, the Model T.

The Model T was a car that people could depend on. They could drive it on dirt roads, up hills, and over holes. They could drive it in rain, wind, ice, and snow. The Model T rarely broke down. When it did, it was easy to fix with simple tools.

Americans loved the Model T. Ford had so many orders, he could not fill them, but he still was not satisfied. In 1908 the Model T cost around $850. That was still too expensive for many people. Ford set out to find a way to lower the price. He succeeded, and by 1913 the price of a Model T was lower than $500.

How could Ford sell his cars at such a low price? He did it by using a moving *assembly line,* one which brought the car parts to the workers, who put them together. With this system of mass production, Ford made more cars in less time. The result was lower prices, which brought more customers.

By 1920 the Model T was very popular. People gave it the nickname *Tin Lizzie.* People wrote to Ford, praising his car and giving him advice. Many people asked him to make the Model T in different colors, not just black. "Anyone who wants a color other than black can just paint it himself," Ford replied.

Ford did not want to change the Model T at all. If he changed the car, he would have to change the assembly line. He did not want to do that because it would be expensive. However, his refusal to make changes was the beginning of the end for the Model T.

By 1925 the car was hopelessly old-fashioned. People made fun of it. One joke went like this: "Why is a Ford like a bathtub? Because nobody wants to be seen in one."

Sales dropped steadily during the next two years. The days of the Model T were at an end. On May 25, 1927, Ford announced that the car would no longer be made. The next day, he drove the last Model T off the assembly line. It was the 15 millionth.

While Henry Ford stopped making the Model T, he did not stop making cars. The Ford Motor Company is one of the leading car manufacturers today.

Name____

The Model T

Choose the best answer and mark the letter of your choice.

1. What is this article mostly about?
- **A.** Henry Ford
- **B.** cars in the early 1900s
- **C.** Henry Ford and the Model T
- **D.** cars in the 1920s

2. Americans loved the Model T because it was
- **F.** a car they could depend on.
- **G.** beautiful looking and impressive.
- **H.** faster than any other car.
- **J.** popular with young people.

3. In this article, the term *assembly line* means
- **A.** a system of mass production conducted by teams of robots that are controlled by computers.
- **B.** a system of mass production in which a product is put together as the parts move past a line of workers.
- **C.** a system of mass production in which machines put together cars.
- **D.** a system of mass production in which each worker puts together an entire product.

4. Henry Ford developed his company's moving assembly line
- **F.** before he invented the Model T.
- **G.** while he was building the first Model T.
- **H.** after he created his last car.
- **J.** after he invented the Model T.

5. *Tin Lizzie* was a nickname for
- **A.** the Ford Company.
- **B.** the first car ever made.
- **C.** a racing car.
- **D.** the Model T.

6. Which of these is a fact presented in the article?
- **F.** By 1925 the Model T looked like a bathtub.
- **G.** By 1925 everyone wanted a Model T.
- **H.** By 1925 people were making fun of the Model T.
- **J.** By 1925 the Model T was not made as well as it used to be.

7. Why was Ford unwilling to change the Model T?
- **A.** He liked the car the way it was.
- **B.** He did not want to change the assembly line.
- **C.** He thought all cars should be black.
- **D.** He was afraid no one would buy it.

8. The article gives you enough information to conclude that Ford might have been able to keep selling the Model T if he had
- **F.** been willing to make changes in it.
- **G.** lowered the price.
- **H.** spent less money making it.
- **J.** spent money on advertising.

UNIT 10
Food for Flight

A•B•C LESSON PLANNER

1. Access

- **READING STRATEGY:** Use the Anticipation Guide on page TP40 before having small groups of students read the article. Write the statements on the board, or use the sheet as a copying master. Invite students to tell whether they agree or disagree with each statement. They can write their responses in their journals or learning logs. Do not expect students to know the answers. This activity is designed to help build interest, activate prior knowledge, and set purposes for reading.

2. Build

- Have students read the article, or read it aloud to them.
- As students read or after they finish reading the article, they may change their opinions about the statements. If they do, have them discuss why they revised their opinions, and have them state what they learned from their reading that allowed them to confirm or revise their opinions.

3. Close

- Have students complete the standardized-test-format questions after they read the article. (An item analysis that identifies the test objectives covered by each question, as well as an answer key, can be found on page TP AK.)
- **HEALTH ACTIVITY:** Have students plan a balanced meal for astronauts on a space shuttle. Encourage students to include foods from each part of the Food Pyramid as they plan their menus.

Name____

Food for Flight

Anticipation Guide

Check One

	Agree	Disagree
1. During the early years of space travel, the astronauts complained about being cramped in tiny cabins.		
2. Early "space food" tasted terrible.		
3. Today astronauts can choose what they eat.		
4. Some of the foods that are eaten in space are sold in grocery stores on Earth.		
5. Snacks are not included in astronauts' diets.		

Name____

FOOD for FLIGHT

The year 1957 was not just the beginning of the space age. It was also the beginning of a race between two *superpowers*—the United States and the Soviet Union. Each of these powerful nations played an important role in world events. Each wanted to send humans into space. By 1961 each superpower had done so.

The early years of space travel were difficult and dangerous. They were also very uncomfortable. The astronauts were crammed into tiny cabins with barely enough room to stretch, but they did not complain. After all, the flights were short, and the astronauts had more important things to worry about. There was one thing, though, that they always complained about—the food!

Early "space food" came in different forms, including bite-sized cubes and freeze-dried powders. Some foods were packed in aluminum tubes, which had to be squeezed like toothpaste. All the foods were fast and easy to eat. But they all tasted terrible.

NASA officials listened to the complaints and began working on the problem. As space flights became longer, it was more important than ever to improve the food. As *spacecraft* became larger, there was also more room for food storage and preparation.

Today food research and development is an important part of NASA's work at the Johnson Space Center in Houston, Texas. Food scientists plan meals that are enjoyable as well as healthful. The result is food that is much like what we eat on Earth. In fact, some "space foods" are familiar items on grocery store shelves, such as "space" ice cream and powdered orange drinks.

Space shuttle crews are giving their meals good reviews. One reason is that they can plan their own menus before the flight begins. After the meals are chosen, they are packaged and stored on board the shuttle. A colored dot on each package identifies the owner.

A typical space shuttle menu might look like this: Breakfast—dried peaches, cornflakes, orange juice, cocoa; Lunch—ham and cheese on a tortilla, pineapple, nuts, strawberry drink; Dinner—chicken or turkey, cauliflower with cheese, brownie, grape drink.

What about snacks? There are many on board, including cookies, nuts, and dried fruits. Astronauts eat snacks when they are hungry, and, like many people on Earth, they also snack when they are bored.

Name____

Food for Flight

Choose the best answer and mark the letter of your choice.

1. What is this article mostly about?
- **A.** the space race
- **B.** the space shuttle
- **C.** food in space
- **D.** NASA

2. In this article, the word *superpowers* means
- **F.** powerful nations with important roles in world events.
- **G.** countries with more than 5 million people.
- **H.** large countries, like China, that were not interested in space exploration.
- **J.** nations that are members of the United Nations.

3. During the early years of space travel, astronauts complained about the
- **A.** short flights.
- **B.** tiny cabins.
- **C.** danger.
- **D.** food.

4. According to the article, a *spacecraft* is a
- **F.** vehicle that can travel in space.
- **G.** space shuttle crew.
- **H.** cabin on a spaceship.
- **J.** flight in space.

5. As a result of the work done by food scientists, food eaten in space became
- **A.** better than food eaten on Earth.
- **B.** much like food eaten on Earth.
- **C.** less healthful for the astronauts.
- **D.** less enjoyable to eat.

6. The article gives you enough information to conclude that NASA
- **F.** was not interested in what the astronauts had to say about their experiences in space.
- **G.** was not interested in improving conditions for the astronauts.
- **H.** listened to what the astronauts had to say about their experiences in space.
- **J.** let the astronauts plan the space missions.

7. Space shuttle crews are pleased with their meals now because
- **A.** the meals are cooked on board the shuttle.
- **B.** crew members plan their own menus before flight.
- **C.** the meals are packaged in aluminum tubes.
- **D.** crew members can eat snacks whenever they are bored.

8. In the future, "space food" will probably
- **F.** take more time to prepare.
- **G.** be less expensive.
- **H.** take less time to prepare.
- **J.** continue to get better.

Item Analyses and Answer Keys

Unit 6

Gold Fever

Item Analysis: 1. Identify the best summary; 2. Draw conclusions; 3. Use context clues; 4. Recall supporting facts and details; 5. Identify cause and effect; 6. Identify specialized/technical terms; 7. Distinguish between fact and nonfact; 8. Draw conclusions.

Answers: 1. D; 2. F; 3. C; 4. G; 5. B; 6. F; 7. C; 8. G

Unit 7

Balloons in Battle

Item Analysis: 1. Identify the best summary; 2. Identify sequence; 3. Identify cause and effect; 4. Use context clues; 5. Distinguish between fact and nonfact; 6. Identify specialized/technical terms; 7. Draw conclusions; 8. Draw conclusions.

Answers: 1. D; 2. F; 3. C; 4. G; 5. B; 6. J; 7. C; 8. F

Unit 8

Edison's Talking Machine

Item Analysis: 1. Identify the best summary; 2. Draw conclusions; 3. Identify specialized/technical terms; 4. Recall supporting facts and details; 5. Identify cause and effect; 6. Use context clues; 7. Recall supporting facts and details; 8. Identify the main idea.

Answers: 1. D; 2. F; 3. C; 4. J; 5. B; 6. H; 7. B; 8. F

Unit 9

The Model T

Item Analysis: 1. Identify the best summary; 2. Identify cause and effect; 3. Use context clues; 4. Identify sequence; 5. Recall supporting facts and details; 6. Distinguish between fact and nonfact; 7. Recall supporting facts and details; 8. Draw conclusions.

Answers: 1. C; 2. F; 3. B; 4. J; 5. D; 6. H; 7. B; 8. F

Unit 10

Food for Flight

Item Analysis: 1. Identify the best summary; 2. Use context clues; 3. Recall supporting facts and details; 4. Identify compound words; 5. Identify cause and effect; 6. Draw conclusions; 7. Identify cause and effect; 8. Predict probable future outcomes.

Answers: 1. C; 2. F; 3. D; 4. F; 5. B; 6. H; 7. B; 8. J

Index

Index

C

E